Politics **UK**

We work with leading authors to develop the strongest educational materials in Politics, bringing cutting edge thinking and best learning practice to a global market.

Under a range of well-known imprints, including Longman, we craft high quality print and electronic publications which help readers to understand and apply their content, whether studying or at work.

To find out about the complete range of our publishing please visit us on the World Wide Web at: www.pearsoneduc.com

Bill Jones (Editor)
Dennis Kavanagh
Michael Moran
Philip Norton

Edition 4

Politics UK

With additional material by

Barrie Axford, Simon Bulmer, Peter Byrd, Colin Copus, Andrew Flynn, Robert Pyper, Jonathan Tonge

and Concluding Comments by

Simon Heffer, Peter Kemp, David Piachaud, Peter Riddell and Tony Wright

An imprint of Pearson Education

Harlow, England · London · New York · Reading, Massachusetts · San Francisco
Toronto · Don Mills, Ontario · Sydney · Tokyo · Singapore · Hong Kong · Seoul
Taipei · Cape Town · Madrid · Mexico City · Amsterdam · Munich · Paris · Milan

Pearson Education Limited
Edinburgh Gate
Harlow
Essex CM20 2JE
England

and Associated Companies throughout the world

Visit us on the World Wide Web at:
www.pearsoneduc.com

ISBN 0-582-42333-3

British Library Cataloguing-in-Publication Data
A catalogue record for this book can be obtained from the British Library

Library of Congress Cataloging-in-Publication Data
A catalog record for this book can be obtained from the Library of Congress

10 9 8 7 6 5 4 3 2
05 04 03 02 01

Politics UK / Bill Jones editor . . . [et al.] – 4th ed.
p. cm.
Includes bibliographical references and index.
ISBN 0-582-42333-3 (alk. paper)
1. Great Britain – Politics and government – 1945– I. Jones, Bill, 1946–

JN231 .P69 2000
320.941 – dc21

00-022359

Typeset by 35 in 10/12pt ITC Century Light
Printed by Ashford Colour Press Ltd., Gosport

Contents

A Companion Web Site accompanies *Politics UK*, 4/e by Jones *et al.*

Visit the ***Politics UK*** Companion Web Site at *www.booksites.net/jones* to find valuable teaching and learning material including:

For Students:
- Study material designed to help you improve your results
- Comprehensive learning objectives detailing what you need to know
- Revision notes containing lots of valuable information that will help you digest the essence of the topics covered within the chapters and aid your revision
- Web links to sites relevant to the chapters

For Lecturers:
- A secure, password protected site with teaching material
- A downloadable version of the full Instructor's Manual, including teaching hints, sample lecture outlines and suggestions for discussion
- A syllabus manager that will build and host your very own course web page
- At least once a year, the authors will provide thorough updates on a range of key topics designed to keep your teaching up-to-date

Also: This regularly maintained site will also have a search functions, and email results functions.

Authors

Bill Jones joined the Extra-Mural Department at Manchester University as Staff Tutor in Politics and was Director of the Department from 1987 to 1992. His books include *The Russia Complex* (1978), *British Politics Today* (with Dennis Kavanagh, 6th edn, 1996) and *Political Issues in Britain Today* (5th edn, 1999). He undertakes regular consultancy work for publishers, radio and television and also writes books and articles on political education and continuing education. He was Chairman of the Politics Association from 1983 to 1985 and became a Vice-President in 1993. In 1992 he retired from full-time work on medical grounds but still maintains his undergraduate and adult student university teaching as well as his writing and consultancy interests. He is currently a Research Fellow in the Department of Government, University of Manchester.

Dennis Kavanagh has been Professor of Politics at the University of Liverpool since 1996. Before that he was Professor at Nottingham University. He is the author of numerous books, including *British Politics: Continuities and Change* (4th edn, 1996), *Thatcherism and British Politics: The End of Consensus* (2nd edn, 1990), *Election Campaigning: The Marketing of Politics* (1995), *The British General Election of 1997* (with David Butler, 1997) and *The Reordering of British Politics* (1997). His latest book is *The Powers behind the Prime Minister* (1999).

Michael Moran is Professor of Government in the Department of Government at the University of Manchester. He has written widely on British politics and comparative public policy. His publications include *The Politics of Banking* (1986), *Politics and Society in Britain* (1989), *The Politics of the Financial Services Revolution* (1990), *States, Regulation and the Medical Profession* (with Bruce Wood, 1993) and *Governing the Health Care State* (1999). He lectures on the main introductory government course at Manchester University and frequently lectures on British politics to sixth-form conferences. He was editor of *Political Studies* from 1993 to 1999 and from 2000 became joint editor of *Government and Opposition*.

Philip Norton (Lord Norton of Louth) was appointed Professor of Government at the University of Hull in 1986 (at the age of 35, making him the youngest professor of politics in the country). Since 1992 he has been Director of the Centre for Legislative Studies. His publications include *Back from Westminster* (1993), *Does Parliament Matter?* (1993), *The Conservative Party* (1996), *Parliaments and Governments in Western Europe* (1998) and *The British Polity* (4th edn, 2000). He is President of the Politics Association (since 1993) and Vice-President of the Political Studies Association (since 1999). In 1998 he was elevated to the House of Lords as a Conservative peer, Lord Norton of Louth. In 1999 he was appointed by the Conservative Party to Chair the Party's Commission to Strengthen Parliament and also serves as a member of Sub-Committee E, dealing with Law and Institutions, of the European Union Committee of the House of Lords. He is currently involved in a major research project, as part of the ESRC's Whitehall programme, on the role of senior ministers in British Government.

Additional material has been supplied by the following:

Barrie Axford is Professor of Politics at Oxford Brookes University. His publications include *The Global System: Economics, Politics and Culture* (1995), *Politics: An Introduction* (joint author, 1997) *Unity and Diversity in the New Europe* (joint editor, 2000) and *New Media – New Politics* (joint editor, 2000).

Simon Bulmer is Professor of Government in the Department of Government at the University of Manchester. His most recent book, *Germany's European Diplomacy: Shaping the Regional Milieu* (with Charlie Jeffrey and William Paterson) is due for publication in 2000. He was joint editor of *Journal of Common Market Studies* from 1991 to 1998.

Peter Byrd has been Director of Part-time Degrees in the Department of Continuing Education at the University of Warwick since 1987. His publications include *British Foreign Policy under Thatcher* (1998) and *British Defence Policy: Thatcher and Beyond* (1991).

Colin Copus is Lecturer in Local Government Political Management in the School of Public Policy at the University of Birmingham. He has written widely about the politics of local government, having spent ten years working for a number of London Boroughs and having served for sixteen years as a local councillor, sitting on four different local authorities.

Andrew Flynn is Senior Lecturer in Environmental Policy and Planning at the University of Wales, Cardiff. He has worked on a number of projects funded by the ESRC and European Regional Development Fund and his recent publications include *Consuming Interests* (joint author, 1999).

Simon Heffer started his career as political correspondent with the *Daily Telegraph* in 1987 and went on to become Deputy Editor of *The Spectator* between 1991 and 1994. He is currently a political commentator for the *Daily Mail*. In addition to his many pieces and articles he has also written a biography of Enoch Powell, entitled *Like the Roman*.

Sir Peter Kemp joined the Civil Service as a direct entry principal in 1967. He moved to the Treasury in 1972, and the Cabinet Office in 1988 as Second Permanent Secretary, working on the Next Steps project of civil service reform. He left the service in 1992. He is the author of a number of publications including *A Better Machine: Government for the 21st Century* (with David Walker, 1996), and a great many articles and pieces.

David Piachaud has taught at the London School of Economics since 1970 and has been Professor of Social Policy since 1988. Between 1974 and 1979 he was Social Policy Adviser in the Downing Street Policy Unit. He has written many books and articles on poverty, social security and economic inequality.

Robert Pyper is Reader in Public Administration at Glasgow Caledonian University. His publications include *The British Civil Service* (1995) and *Governing the UK in the 1990s* (with Lynton Robins, 1995). From June 2000 he will be editor of *Public Policy and Administration*.

Peter Riddell is political columnist and assistant editor (politics) of *The Times*. His publications include *The Thatcher Government* (1983), *The Thatcher Decade* (1989), *Honest Opportunism: The Rise of the Career Politician* (1993) and *Parliament Under Pressure* (1997).

Jonathan Tonge is Senior Lecturer in the Department of Politics and Contemporary History at the University of Salford. He is a regular writer and broadcaster on Northern Ireland and his books include *Northern Ireland: Conflict and Change* (1998) and *The New Civil Service* (1999).

Tony Wright (MP) is Honorary Professor of Politics at the University of Birmingham and has been the Labour Member of Parliament for Cannock Chase from 1992. He is the author of many books including *Citizens and Subjects* (1994), *Socialisms: Old and New* (1996) and *The British Political Process* (editor, 2000) and is editor of *The Political Quarterly*.

Preface

Politics is an exciting subject. We, the authors, are naturally biased in thinking it offers students very special attractions. It is a subject you digest with your breakfast each morning, its complex canvas unfolds with the daily papers, the *Today* programme, and the broadcast news; by the evening new details have been painted in and the picture subtly, sometimes dramatically, changed. Politics is unpredictable, dynamic, it affects us, it is about us. In one sense the canvas *is* us; a projection of ourselves and our aspirations, a measure of our ability to live together. Politics, despite the dismal image of its practitioners, is arguably the most important focus there is in the study of the human condition. We hope that this volume on the politics of the United Kingdom does the subject justice.

This book is designed to provide a comprehensive introduction to British politics both for the general reader and for the examination candidate. With the latter group in mind, we fashioned a text, which was, originally, unusual by British standards. When we studied A level politics all those years ago the transition from O level to A level was quite difficult. This was hardly surprising, because many of the A level texts were the same as those we went on to study at university, partly because of shared assumptions about A level and university students. It was believed that we should be treated as mature intellects (good), but also that it was up to us to extract meaning from the texts which – in the name of standards – made few concessions to our possible unfamiliarity with the subject (not so good). In these circumstances it is hardly surprising that so many aspirant university students gave up before the intrinsic interest of the subject could capture them.

Things have improved since then – in the field of textbooks remarkably so. Syllabuses have become much wider and now embrace stimulating new areas such as political sociology and current political issues. This has helped authors produce more interesting work but a revolution has also taken place on the production side. *Politics UK*, when it came out in 1990, was arguably the first to embrace the American approach of providing a comprehensive course textbook with a plethora of new features such as photographs, diagrams and many tables and illustrative figures. Since then most of our rival textbooks on British politics have adopted similar styles and, if imitation is the highest form of flattery, then we are accordingly, much flattered. The book has moved through three successful editions and this is the fourth. The key features of this edition are:

- it has been comprehensively 'Europeanised' in that each chapter has been looked at and amended to take account of the EU impact and influence;
- new chapters on devolution, globalisation and the record of the Blair government have been added;

- many of the chapters have been completely rewritten;
- all chapters not rewritten have been comprehensively updated up to early 2000;
- it embodies coverage and assessment of New Labour and Tony Blair's first three years in power;
- contains a new alphabetically sorted glossary defining those key terms emboldened in the text;
- contains the best guide available to useful web sites via the book's Companion Web Site as well as many other additional features, including a specially written set of Revision Notes for each chapter;
- presentation has been augmented by the use of some excellent cartoons (see below) and other visual images;
- The concluding comments at the end of each major section have been written, as before, by distinguished guest writers. This time they include:
    - Simon Heffer and Peter Riddell from the senior ranks of journalism;
    - David Piachaud, the leading researcher on poverty and income distribution;
    - Sir Peter Kemp, former Second Permanent Secretary and pilot of the Next Steps reforms of the civil service
    - Tony Wright, the admired academic and Labour MP.

The original line-up of principal authors has diminished from six to four – we are sorry to lose Anthony Seldon and Andrew Gray both through pressure of work. Simon Bulmer, Andrew Flynn and Jonathan Tonge continue to author their guest chapters and have been joined by other guest authors: Barrie Axford, Peter Byrd, Colin Copus and Robert Pyper.

The chapters on parliament in this book have always been authoritative and up to date; now they are even more so since Philip Norton became a member of the House of Lords himself in 1998. Thanks are due to all the contributors and to the staff at Pearson Education who have proved remarkably helpful and professional, especially Geraldine Lyons and David Harrison who piloted the book through its latter stages. We have to thank Chris Riddell for his brilliant cartoons, borrowed from his collection, *Tribal Politics*, Palmano Bennett, London 1999. A substantial debt of thanks is also owed to Graham Thomas for his invaluable and meticulous advice and to various anonymous reviewers whose comments proved to be extemely valuable. Not forgetting either to thank Simon Bulmer, for his specially written report, persuading us all to reflect EU influence in our chapters. Finally the biggest vote of thanks must go to Emma Mitchell, the commissioning editor at Pearson Education, whose professionalism – promptness, eye for detail, not to mention diplomacy – was central to keeping the whole show on the road long enough to produce the present volume. Lecturers and teachers are reminded that if they adopt the book they will receive, free of charge, the *Instructor's Manual*, written by Bill Jones and Graham Thomas. We hope readers find the book as useful and stimulating as previous editions.

Bill Jones
Michael Moran
Philip Norton
Dennis Kavanagh

January 2000

Acknowledgements

The publishers wish to thank the following for permission to reproduce the material below:

Figures 3.1–5, 10.1, 26.1, 26.3, 31.4–5 and Tables 14.3, 14.8–12, 31.4–5, 31.7: 6 charts from All power to Strasbourg from Survey of Britain, © The Economist, London (20 February 1993), 9 charts from Three million down, more to go, © The Economist, London (20 June, 1992), Number of employees, © The Economist, London (11 December 1993), A revolution fizzles. Share ownership, © The Economist, London (18 May 1996), Press depressed, © The Economist, London (17 July 1999), The Michael effect, © The Economist, London (15 May 1999), The voice of the regions, © The Economist, London (27 March 1999), Capital gains, © The Economist, London (27 March 1999), The growth conundrum, © The Economist, London (25 May 1996), Lagging Behind © The Economist, London (15 June 1996)

Figures 2.1, 17.3, 18.1–2, Tables 21.1–2 and Boxes 21.1–2, 21.4–6: The following Crown copyright is reproduced with the permission of the Controller of Her Majesty's Stationery Office:
Figure: Membership of International Defence Organisations (MOD website, 1997), The Scale of Next Steps by Autumn 1998 from Cabinet Office Next Steps Briefing Note, September 1998, Table: Next Steps Agencies Executive Agencies from Next Steps Team, 1998, Agency Chief Executive Appointments from Cabinet Office Next Steps Briefing Note, September 1998, Table: Former Next Steps Agencies from Next Steps Team, 1998, PFI in Practice – Docklands Light Railway Extension (HM Treasury), Service First: Principles & The Six Whitehall Standards (Cabinet Office), Tony Blair's Seven Challenges for the Civil Service (Cabinet Office). The following Parliamentary copyright is reproduced with the permission of the Controller of Her Majesty's Stationery Office on behalf of Parliament:
Early Day Motions, 696, 862, 892, Figure from House of Lords Annual Report and Accounts 1997–8, House of Lords 'Notices and Order Paper', 20 July

Figures 3.4a–b, 26.2 and Tables 3.1–2, 3.4, 13.5: Table: Regional inequality in Britain from Regional Trends 1995, Office for National Statistics © Crown Copyright 1995, Table: Distribution of marketable wealth in Britain from Social Trends 1999, p. 100, Office for National Statistics © Crown Copyright 1999, Table: Changing balance of main economic sectors, 1974–96 from Social Trends 1998, p. 16, Office for National Statistics © Crown Copyright 1998, Table 11.4 from Social Trends 1994, Office for National Statistics © Crown Copyright 1994, Figure 8.3: Expenditure on social protection benefits per head: EU comparison, 1996 from Social Trends 1999, Office for National Statistics © Crown Copyright 1999

Figures 3.2–a, 27.2–4 and Table 14.7: General Government Receipts 1997/98 (%), General Government Receipts 1997/98 (bn), General Government Expenditure (f) 1997–98, GDP per head 1985–1995 ($), Full-time, part-time & economically inactive, Reasons for economic inactivity (%), Workforce in employment and total unemployment [1951–1997], Males and females in employment, 1983–1997 (m) from Jamieson, *An Illustrated Guide to the British Economy* (1998) by permission of Gerald Duckworth & Co. Ltd

Figures 11.1–2, 30.1 and Tables 3.3, 9.5: Table 2 from Layton-Henry, Immigration and Contemporary British Politics, Politics Review 5.3, Philip Allan Publishers (1996), Table from Crewe, The Changing Basis of Party Choice, 1979–92, Politics Review 2.3, Philip Allan Publishers (1993), Figure 1 from Grant, Pressure Groups and the Policy Process, Social Studies Review 3.4, Philip Allan Publishers (1988), Figure 1 from Grant, Insider and Outsider Pressure Groups, Social Studies Review 1.1, Philip Allan Publishers (1985), Figure 1 from McCullagh and O'Dowd, Northern Ireland: The Search for a Solution, Social Studies Review 1.4, Philip Allan Publishers (1986)

Figure 14.3 and Tables 10.1, 16.1, 17.9, 17.11: Table: Changes in support for party by daily newspapers' readers, MORI, Figure: The strength of people's regional identification, MORI, Table: Question – Would you favour Britain becoming a republic or remaining a monarchy? from British Public Opinion, XXII (6), MORI, August 1999, Table: Question – Overall, how well or badly do you think Parliament works? From, British Public Opinion, XX1 (6), MORI, August 1998, Table: Statement – Parliament does not have sufficient control over what the government does from State of the Nation Poll, 1995)

Figures 22.1, 24.1, 24.3 and Table 14.1: Table: The 1997 Scottish Referendum Results from Mitchell, J., 'Devolution' from Political Issues in Britain Today, Manchester University Press, 1999, Figure: The structure of local government in England and Wales after 1974 adapted from Gray, A.G., Local Government in England and Wales, Jones W.D.A., and Kavanagh, D. (eds), British Politics Today, Manchester University Press, 1974, Figure: The Policy Making Process from Burch, M., Kavanagh, D., British Politics Today, Manchester University Press, 1978, Figure: Policy Networks from Baggott, R., Pressure Groups Today, p. 24, Manchester University Press, 1995

Figure 9.1 and Table 13.4: Table V 48 (2000) from Stoker *et al.*, Social capital and Urban governance, Political Studies, © Political Studies Association, Blackwell Publishers, 2000–04–13

Tables 13.2, 17.1: Table: Selected Characteristics of Labour and Conservative Members of Parliament, 1997 General Election from Butler and Kavanagh, The British General Election of 1997, Macmillan, Press, 1997, Table: University Education of candidates from Criddle 'MPs and Candidates', Butler and Kavanagh (eds), The British General Election of 1997, Macmillan Press, 1997

Table 10.3, 13.3, 26.1: Table: Impact of television on voters: response to question 'Has television coverage helped you in deciding who to vote for in the election?' (%) from Negrine, R., Politics and the Mass Media, 2nd Edition, p. 192, Routledge, 1995, Table: Ratio of expenditure per person in top fifth to that per person in bottom fifth from Goodin and Legrand, Not only the Poor: The Middle Classes and the Welfare State, p. 92, Allen and Unwin, 1987

Figure 2.2: Figure: London's position as a global financial centre from the Bank of England's 'Practical issues arising from the introduction of the Euro' publication, 11 June 1998

Figure 2.4: Figure: Euroland on 1 January 1999, © European Communities, 1995–2000

Table 10.2: Table: Newspapers' political allegiances and circulations 1997, Audit Bureau of Circulations – January–June 1992 and January–June 1997

Table 10.5: Table page 68: Dominance and Pluralism Models Compared from McQuail, Mass Communication Theory, Sage Publications, 1983

Box 11.1: Figure: Road Traffic Reduction Campaign logo, Friends of the Earth

Figure 11.4: Figure: The issue attention cycle from McCulloch, A., Politics and the Environment, Talking Politics, The Politics Association, 1988

Table 13.1: Table: % 'Yes'/at least once from Parry, Moyser and Day, Political Participation and Democracy in Britain, p. 44, Cambridge University Press, 1992

Figure 14.1: Map of Wales, The Daily Telegraph, 20 September 1997, © Telegraph Group Limited 1997

Table 17.2: Table: New MPs 1997: characteristics of MPs elected for the first time in the 1997 general election, expressed as a percentage of the new intake of each party from The Financial Times, 3 May 1997

Table 17.4: Table: Average length of legislative service, 1994 from Somit and Roemmele, The victorious legislative incumbent as a threat to democracy, Legislative Studies Newsletter, Vol. 18, No. 2, July 1995

Table 17.10: Table: Perceptions of MPs from Coleman, Electronic Media, Parliament and the Media, p. 20, Hansard Society, 1999

Figure 25.2: Figure from Violent Crime falling for the first time in years by Richard Ford, © Times Newspapers Limited, 13 October 1999

Though every effort has been made to trace the owners of copyright material, in a few cases this has proved impossible and we take this opportunity to apologise to any copyright holders whose rights may have been unwittingly infringed.

Part 1 Context

Chapter 1 Introduction: explaining politics

Bill Jones and Michael Moran

Learning objectives

- To explain and illustrate the concept of what politics is.
- To discuss why politicians become involved in their profession.
- To explain the essence of decision making in political situations.
- To discuss the kind of questions political science addresses and the variety of approaches that exist.
- To introduce some of the main political relationships between the state and the individual.
- To look at the rationales for studying politics together with some of the major themes and issues in the study of British politics.

Introduction

This opening chapter is devoted to a definition of 'politics' and the way in which its study can be approached. In the first section, we discuss decision making and identify what exactly is involved in the phrase 'political activity'. In the second section we examine the critical political questions. We then go on to describe how the more general activity called 'politics' can be distinguished from the workings of 'the state'. In the fourth section, we describe some of the most important approaches used in the study of politics and examine the chief reasons for its study in schools and colleges. We conclude by sketching in some of the themes raised in the study of British politics.

There has never been a perfect government, because men have passions; and if they did not have passions, there would be no need for government.

Voltaire, *Politique et legislation*

The love of power is the love of ourselves

Willian Hazlitt

Definitions and decision making

Is politics necessary?

'A good politician', wrote the American writer H.L. Mencken, 'is quite as unthinkable as an honest burglar'. Cynical views of politics and politicians are legion. Any statement or action by a politician is seldom taken at face value but is scrutinised for ulterior personal motives. Thus, when Bob Hawke, the Australian Prime Minister, broke down in tears on television in March 1989, many journalists dismissed the possibility that he was genuinely moved by the topic under discussion. Instead they concluded that he was currying favour with the Australian electorate – who allegedly warm to such manly shows of emotion – with a possible general election in mind.

Given such attitudes it seems reasonable to ask why people go into politics in the first place. The job is insecure: in Britain elections may be called at any time, and scores of MPs in marginal seats can lose their parliamentary salaries. The apprenticeship for ministerial office can be long, hard, arguably demeaning and, for many, ultimately unsuccessful. Even if successful, a minister has to work cripplingly long days, survive constant criticism – both well and ill informed – and know that a poor debating performance, a chance word or phrase out of place can earn a one-way ticket to the back benches. To gamble your whole life on the chance that the roulette wheel of politics will stop on your number seems to be less than wholly rational behaviour. Why, then, do politicians put themselves into the fray and fight so desperately for such dubious preferment?

In some political cultures, especially the undemocratic ones, it seems clear that politicians are struggling to achieve and exercise **power**, power for its own sake: to be able to live in the best possible way; to exercise the power of life and death over people, to be in fact the nearest thing to a god it is possible for a human being to be. We see that some early rulers were actually deified; turned into gods either in their lifetimes or soon after their deaths.

The Serbian leader Slobodan Milosevic fought hard to retain control of Serbia during the cruel civil war which racked the country from 1989 onwards. Someone who knows him well explained: 'I do not think he believes in anything, only in his own power. It is even possible he could be a peacemaker if he thinks that is what he has to do to hold on to power' (*Sunday Times*, 4 July 1993). George Orwell suggested in his famous novel, *Nineteen Eighty-Four*, that the state had potentially similar objectives (see quotations).

George Orwell suggested that for the totalitarian **state**, power was potentially an end in itself. Towards the end of his famous *Nineteen Eighty-Four*, the dissident Winston Smith is being interrogated under torture by O'Brien, a senior official of 'The Party'. O'Brien asks why the Party seeks power, explaining:

BOX 1.1 MINI BIOGRAPHY

George Orwell (1903–50)

Political writer. Born India and served in Burmese Imperial Police 1922–7 but moved back to Britain to try and become a successful writer. He eventually succeeded with *Down and Out in Paris and London* (1933) though not before a stint fighting in the Spanish Civil War. After this experience he found his true métier in political writing – novels and journalism. *The Road to Wigan Pier* (1937) was the first, *Homage to Catalonia* (1938 and based on his Spanish experiences) the second. His best-known books appeared after the Second World War: *Animal Farm* (1945), a biting satire on the USSR; and *Nineteen Eighty-Four* (1949), an attack on totalitarian tendencies in the post-War world. He died of tuberculosis, perhaps before his full promise had been revealed.

George Orwell and the abuse of power

Now I will tell you the answer to my question. It is this. The Party seeks power entirely for its own sake. We are not interested in the good of others; we are interested solely in power. Not wealth or luxury, or long life or happiness: only power, pure power. What pure power means you will understand presently. We are different from all oligarchies of the past, in that we

know what we are doing. All the others, even those who resembled ourselves, were cowards and hypocrites. The German Nazis and the Russian Communists came very close to us in their methods, but they never had the courage to recognize their own motives. They pretended, perhaps they even believed, that they had seized power unwillingly and for a limited time, and that just round the corner there lay a paradise where human beings would be free and equal. We are not like that. We know that no one ever seizes power with the intention of relinquishing it. Power is not a means, it is an end. One does not establish a dictatorship in order to safeguard revolution; one makes the revolution in order to establish the dictatorship. The object of persecution is persecution. The object of torture is torture. The object of power is power.

Later on he offers a chilling vision of the future under the Party:

There will be no loyalty, except loyalty towards the Party. There will be no love, except love of Big Brother. There will be no laughter, except the laugh of triumph over a defeated enemy. There will be no art, no literature, no science. When we are omnipotent we shall have no more need of science. There will be no distinction between beauty and ugliness. There will be no curiosity, no enjoyment of the process of life. All competing pleasures will be destroyed. But always – do not forget this, Winston – there will be the intoxication of power, constantly increasing and constantly growing subtler. Always, at every moment, there will be the thrill of victory, the sensation of trampling on an enemy who is helpless. If you want a picture of the future, imagine a boot stamping on a human face – for ever.

Orwell, 1955, pp. 211–15. From *Nineteen Eighty-Four* by George Orwell (Copyright © George Orwell, 1949) reproduced by permission of A M Heath & Co. Ltd. on behalf of Bill Hamilton as the Literary Executor of the Estate of the late Sonia Brownell Orwell and Martin Secker & Warburg Ltd.

In developed **democratic** countries the answer is more complex, although one, somewhat cynical, school of thought insists that naked power is still the chief underlying motivation (see below: ambition and the career politician). These countries have realised the dangers of allowing politicians too much power. Checks and balances, failsafe **constitutional** devices and an aware public opinion ensure that politicians, however much they may yearn for unlimited power, are unable realistically to expect or enjoy it. We have instead to look for more subtle motivations.

Biographies and interviews reveal an admixture of reasons: genuine commitment to a set of beliefs, the desire to be seen and heard a great deal, the trappings of office such as the official cars, important-looking red boxes containing ministerial papers and solicitous armies of civil servants. Senator Eugene McCarthy suggested politicians were like football coaches: 'smart enough to understand the game and dumb enough to think it's important'. A witty remark, but true in the sense that politics is an activity which closely resembles a game and which similarly exercises an addictive or obsessive hold on those who play it. Tony Benn cheerfully admits to being consumed with politics and I remember once asking an exhausted Labour ex-minister, David Ennals, why he continued to work so hard. 'Ah, politics', he replied, 'is just so fascinating you see'. But is the game worth playing? Words like 'betrayal', 'opportunism', 'exploitation', 'distortion' and 'fudge' are just some of the pejorative terms frequently used in describing the process. Would we not be better off without politics at all?

In his classic study *In Defence of Politics* (1982), Bernard Crick disagrees strongly. For him

BOX 1.2 MINI BIOGRAPHY

Bernard Crick (1929–)
Educated at London, Harvard and McGill Universities. Lectured at LSE, professor at Sheffield. Founded Politics Association, 1969. Biographer of Orwell (1980); wrote classic book on nature of politics: *In Defence of Politics* (1962). Chairman Labour government's Working Party on Citizenship 1997–8.

politics is 'essential to genuine freedom – something to be valued as a pearl beyond price in the history of the human condition'. He reminds us of Aristotle's view that politics is 'only one possible solution to the problem of order. It is by no means the most usual. **Tyranny** is the most obvious alternative, **oligarchy** the next'. Crick understands 'politics' as the means whereby differing groups of people with different, often conflicting, **interests** are enabled to live together in relative harmony. For him 'politics' describes the working of a **pluralist** political system 'in advanced and complex societies' which seeks to maximise the freedom and the power of all social groups. The system may be far from perfect but it is less imperfect than the various authoritarian alternatives.

This line of thinking provides an antidote to overly cynical analyses of politics. The compromises inherent in the process tend to discredit it: few will ever be wholly satisfied and many will feel hard done by. Similarly politicians as the imperfect practitioners of an imperfect system receive much of the blame. But without politicians to represent and articulate demands and to pursue them within an agreed framework we would be much the poorer. Whether Crick is right in reminding us to count our democratic blessings is a question which the reader must decide, and we hope that this book will provide some of the material necessary for the making of such a judgement.

Andrew Rawnsley in the *Observer*, 5 December 1999, expressed a very Crickian view of the then recently announced Northern Ireland settlement. First he quoted the British Social Attitudes Survey which revealed that 91 per cent of the public cynically expect a politician to 'lie in a tight corner'. Then he moved on to review the settlement acknowledging the brave role played by Mo Mowlam, when Secretary of State, in visiting the prisoners in the Maze Prison in December 1997. Next

BOX 1.1 **IDEAS AND PERSPECTIVES** 

What does government do?

If politics is largely about government then what are the things which governments do? Anthony Giddens, in his *The Third Way*, provides the following analysis:

- provide means for the representation of diverse interests;
- offer a forum for reconciling the competing claims of those interests;
- create and protect an open public sphere, in which unconstrained debate about policy issues can be carried on;
- provide a diversity of public goods, including forms of collective security and welfare;
- regulate markets in the public interest and foster market competition where monopoly threatens;
- foster social peace through the provision of policing;
- promote the active development of human capital through its core role in the education system;
- sustain an effective system of law;
- have a directly economic role, as a prime employer, in macro and micro intervention, plus the provision of infrastructure;
- more controversially, have a civilising aim – government reflects the widely held norms and values, but can also help shape them, in the educational system and elsewhere;
- foster regional and transnational alliances and pursue global goals.

Source: A. Giddens, The Third Way, 1998, pp. 47–8

he expressed admiration that David Trimble, the hardline leader of the Ulster Unionists, had 'displayed the special courage to change himself and then persuade others to follow'. He went on to say that 'The final victory of politics in Northern Ireland will be when it has become too mundane for the rest of the world to be bothered with', and concludes, memorably, with the words 'In the toughest of crucibles, politics has demonstrated that it does not have to be the art of the futile. It can even be a calling with a claim to nobility'.

Ambition and the career politician

'Politics is a spectator sport', writes Julian Critchley (1995, p. 80). An enduring question which exercises us spectators is 'Why are they doing it?' Dr Johnson, in his typically blunt fashion, said politics was 'nothing more nor less than a means of rising in the world'. But we know somehow this is not the whole truth. Peter Riddell of *The Times* in his wonderfully perceptive book, *Honest Opportunism* (1993), looks at this topic in some detail. He quotes Disraeli, who perhaps offers us a more rounded and believable account of his interest in politics to his Shrewsbury constituents: 'There is no doubt, gentlemen, that all men who offer themselves as candidates for public favour have motives of some sort. I candidly acknowledge that I have and I will tell you what they are: I love fame; I love public reputation; I love to live in the eye of the country'.

Riddell also quotes F.E. Smith, who candidly gloried in the 'endless adventure of governing men'. For those who think these statements were merely expressions of nineteenth-century romanticism, Riddell offers the example of Richard Crossman's comment that politics is a 'never ending adventure – with its routs and discomfitures, rushes and sallies', its 'fights for the fearless and goals for the eager'. He also includes Michael Heseltine whom he heard asking irritatedly at one of Jeffrey Archer's parties in 1986: 'Why shouldn't I be Prime Minister then?' The tendency of politicians to explain their taste for politics in terms of concern for 'the people' is seldom sincere. In the view of Henry Fairlie this is nothing more than 'humbug'. William Waldegrave agrees: 'Any politician who tells you he isn't ambitious is only telling you he isn't for some tactical reason; or more bluntly, telling a lie – I certainly wouldn't deny that I wanted ministerial office; yes, I'm ambitious'. As if more proof were needed, David Owen once said on television – and 'he should know', one is tempted to say – that 'Ambition drives politics like money drives the international economy'. Riddell goes on in his book to analyse how the ambitious political animal has slowly transformed British politics. He follows up and develops Anthony King's concept of the 'career politician', observing that a decreasing number of MPs had backgrounds in professions, or 'proper jobs' in the Westminster parlance, compared with those who centred their whole lives on politics and whose 'jobs' were of secondary importance, merely supporting the Westminster career. In 1951 the figure was 11 per cent; by 1992 it was 31 per cent. By contrast, the proportion of new MPs with 'proper jobs' fell from 80 per cent to 41 per cent. Many of this new breed begin life as researchers for an MP or

BOX 1.3 MINI BIOGRAPHY

Michael Ray Dibdin Heseltine (1933–)
Conservative politician. Born Swansea and educated at Shrewsbury School and Oxford. Made money from property before becoming an MP in 1966, ending up in the safe seat of Henley in 1974. Served as junior minister under Heath, where his energy was noted. He was originally somewhat too liberal for Mrs Thatcher but served her in Defence and Environment before resigning over the Westland dispute in 1986. Encouraged by Geoffrey Howe's resignation speech in November 1990, he stood against Thatcher for the leadership. He brought her down but failed to win, though winning office under John Major and becoming Deputy Prime Minister in 1995. His enthusiasm for things European won him enemies in the europsceptical Conservative Party in the mid-1990s but it was heart problems which prevented him from contesting the leadership in 1997.

Some silly quotations by politicians

I would have made a good Pope.

Richard Nixon

OK we've won. What do we do now?

Brian Mulroney on being re-elected Prime Minister of Canada

Outside the killings we have one of the lowest crime rates in the country

Marion Barry, former Mayor of Washington, DC

I have opinions of my own – strong opinions – but I don't always agree with them

George Bush

I didn't go down there with any plan for the Americas or anything. I went down to find out from them and learn their views. You'd be surprised. They're all individual countries.

Ronald Reagan on how his Latin American trip had changed his views

The real question for 1988 is whether we're going forward to tomorrow or past to the – back!

Dan Quayle

What a waste to lose one's mind – or not to have a mind. How true that is.

Dan Quayle

And finally (though there are many more): I stand by all the mis-statements. Dan Quayle

Oliver, 1992

in a party's research department, then proceed to seek selection as a candidate and from there into parliament and from then on ever onwards and upwards. The kind of MP who enters politics in later life is in steep decline; the new breed of driven young professionals has tended to dominate the field, proving firmer of purpose and more skilled in execution than those for whom politics is a later or learned vocation. The kind of businessman who achieves distinction in his field and then goes into politics is now a rarity rather than the familiar figure of the nineteenth century or the earlier years of the twentieth.

Politicians pride themselves on being fluent and always in control, but however powerful and mighty they might be, they can say some seriously stupid things as the examples below illustrate.

Defining politics

Politics is difficult to define yet easy to recognise. To some extent with the word 'politics' we can consider current usage and decide our own meaning, making our own definition wide or narrow according to our taste or purposes. From the discussion so far politics is obviously a universal activity; it is concerned with the governance of states, and (Crick's special concern) involves a conciliation or harmonisation process. Yet we talk of politics on a micro as well as a macro scale: small groups such as families or parent/teacher associations also have a political dimension. What is it that unites these two levels? The answer is: the conflict of different interests. People or groups of people who want different things – be it power, money, liberty, etc. – face the potential or reality of conflict when such things are in short supply. Politics begins when their interests clash. At the micro level we use a variety of techniques to get our own way: persuasion, rational argument, irrational strategies, threats, entreaties, bribes, manipulation – anything we think will work. At the macro level, democratic states establish complex procedures for the management of such conflicts, often – although famously not in Britain's case – codified in the form of written constitutions. Representatives of the adult population are elected to a **legislature** or parliament tasked with the job of discussing and agreeing changes in the law as well as exercising control over the **executive**: those given responsibility for day-to-day decisions in the running of the country.

Is the political process essentially peaceful? Usually, but not exclusively. If violence is involved on a widespread scale, e.g. war between states, it would be fair to say that politics has been abandoned for other means. But it must be recognised that:

1 Political order within a state is ensured through the implicit threat of force which a state's control of the police and army provides. As John Adams (nineteenth-century US President) pointed out, 'Fear is the foundation of most government'. Occasionally passions run high and the state's power is explicitly exercised – as in the 1984–5 miners' strike.

2 There are many situations in the world, for example in Northern Ireland or the Lebanon, where violence is regularly used to provide both a context for and an alternative to peaceful political processes.

So, while political activity is peaceful for most of the time in most countries, the threat of violence or its reality are both integral parts of the political process.

We should now be able to move towards a definition:

Politics is essentially a process which seeks to manage or resolve conflicts of interest between people, usually in a peaceful fashion. In its general sense it can describe the interactions of any group of individuals but in its specific sense it refers to the many and complex relationships which exist between state institutions and the rest of society.

Peaceful political processes, then, are the alternative, the antidote to brute force. As the practitioners of this invaluable art politicians deserve our gratitude. It was interesting to note that in July 1989 when Ali Akbar Rafsanjani emerged as the successor to the Iranian extremist religious leader, Ayatollah Khomeini, several Iranians were quoted in the press approving him as 'a political man': someone who would be likely to steer the country away from the internal violence which religious conflicts threatened at the time.

Does this mean that cynical attitudes towards politicians should be discouraged? Not exactly, in our view. It is wrong that they should be widely undervalued and often unfairly blamed, but experience suggests that it is better to doubt politicians rather than trust them unquestioningly. After all, politicians are like salesmen and in their enthusiasm to sell their messages they often exaggerate or otherwise distort the truth. They also seek power and **authority** over us and this is not a privilege we should relinquish lightly. Lord Acton noted that 'all power tends to corrupt' and history can summon any number of tyrants in support of this proposition. We are right to doubt politicians, but, as John Donne advised, we should 'doubt wisely'.

Decision making

Much political activity culminates in the taking of decisions and all decisions involve choice. Politicians are presented with alternative courses of action – or inaction – and once a choice has been made they have to try to make sure their decisions are accepted. Two examples follow which illustrate the micro and macro senses of politics and which also introduce some important related terminology.

Decision making I: micro-politics

When the outgoing school captain of chess goes to university a struggle ensues between three candidates for his position: John is a little short of things to cite as 'other activities' on his application forms to university, especially as he is not very good at more traditional sports; David is something of a 'chess prodigy' and wants to convince his father he can go on to become a Grand Master and earn his living from the game; Graham is already captain of soccer but enjoys the status of being in charge and thinks the addition of this more cerebral title might clinch the position of Head Boy for himself.

On the face of it, this commonplace situation has little to do with politics – yet it is an example of politics with a small 'p' or 'micro-politics', and political science terms can fruitfully be used to analyse the situation.

Interests in politics are defined as those things which people want or care about: usually financial resources but other things too such as status, power, justice, liberty or the avoidance of unwanted outcomes. In this example one boy (Graham) is interested mainly in the prestige and status of the office and the possible knock-on effect it may provide for an even more sought-after goal, whilst the other two are interested for future educational and career reasons.

Political actors in this instance include the three boys, the headmaster and Mr Stonehouse, the master with responsibility for chess in the school. Other actors, however, might easily be drawn into the political process as it develops.

Power in politics is the ability to get others to act in a particular way. Typically this is achieved through the exercise of threats and rewards but also through the exercise of *authority*: the acceptance of someone's right to be obeyed (see below for fuller explanation).

The *power relationship* in this case might be seen in the following terms. The boys are bereft of any real power: all the cards are held by the master in charge who has been given authority by the head to choose the boy for the job. Conceivably the two disappointed candidates might exercise a threat of disruptive behaviour if their claims are overlooked, but this threat, if it existed, would lack any real credibility and would be unlikely to affect the outcome. All three boys, moreover, accept the authority of Mr Stonehouse to make the decision and are likely to accept his verdict. The outcome of this conflict of interests will depend on a number of factors:

1. *Political will*: How prepared are any of the boys to advance their cause? John, for example, arranges to play a public simultaneous game against a visiting Nigel Short to give his candidature some extra weight – but such a strategy could backfire, if he loses badly, for example.
2. *Influence*: How open are either actors to rational argument, appeals to loyalty and so forth? Mr Stonehouse, for example, was once employed by David's father to give him extra chess lessons. Will this former contact create a sense of loyalty which will tip the balance in David's favour?
3. *Manipulation*: How effectively can the candidates involve the other actors? Graham's mother is a close friend of Mr Stonehouse and his father is a school governor. Could ambitious parents be mobilised to pull these possible levers of influence?

The *political process* would take place largely through face-to-face contacts, nods and winks in the case of Graham's father, for example (lobbying for his son could scarcely be done openly: such **influence** is not after all thought to be 'proper'). John, however, could advance his claim through a good performance against a Grandmaster. The whole political process could therefore take place virtually unseen by anyone except the actors themselves as they make their moves. Open discussion of their claims is unlikely to occur between candidates and Mr Stonehouse (not thought to be good form either). How did it pan out? (This is only a hypothetical situation but the reader may have become interested by now so I'll conclude the mini-drama.)

Well, John did well against Nigel Short and was the last to be beaten after an ingenious defensive strategy which actually put Short in difficulty after he lost a rook. David's ambitious father made an excuse to ring up Mr Stonehouse and at the end of the conversation just 'happened' to raise the subject of his son's chess prowess and his great commitment to the school team. Despite his efforts, however, the approach was a little unsubtle and Mr Stonehouse was unimpressed. Graham's father (the school governor, remember), however, had heavier guns to fire. He met Mr Stonehouse at a parents' evening and contrived to meet him afterwards in the pub for a quiet drink. There he was able to suggest in oblique but unmistakable terms that he would support Mr Stonehouse's interest in becoming head of his subject in exchange for Graham becoming head of chess. I would like to say that Mr Stonehouse was above such petty manoeuvring but he too was ambitious and was being urged by his wife to be more so. After some wrestling with his conscience, he ignored David and (arguably the most deserving) John, and appointed Graham. Moral: justice is seldom meted out by the political process and human frailties often intervene to ensure this is so.

Decision making II: macro-politics

A major national newspaper breaks a story that Kevin Broadstairs, a Cabinet minister, has been having an affair with an actress. The PM issues a statement in support of his colleague and old friend from university days. However, more embarrassing details hit the front pages of the tabloids, including the fact that the same actress has been also carrying on with a senior member of the Opposition. The 1922 Committee meet and influential voices call for a resignation.

This somewhat familiar situation is quintessentially political.

Interests: The PM needs to appear above suspicion of 'favouritism' but also needs to show that he is loyal and not a hostage to either groups of back-benchers or the press. Broadstairs obviously has an interest in keeping his job, retaining respect within his party and saving his rocky marriage. The governing party needs to sustain its reputation as the defender of family values. The press wishes to sell more newspapers.

Actors: In this situation are potentially numerous: the PM, Broadstairs, the actress, her former lovers, back-bench MPs, editors, television producers, the Opposition, Mrs Broadstairs and (unfortunately) her children, the church, feminists and anyone else willing to enter the fray.

Power: The power relationship in these circumstances is naturally influenced by the ability of each side to enforce threats. The PM has the power of political life or death over the minister but would like to show his strength by resisting resignation calls, Broadstairs effectively has no power in this situation and is largely dependent on the PM's goodwill and possible press revelations.

Authority: No one questions the PM's right to sack Broadstairs. The press's right to force resignations, however, is very much resisted by politicians. The ultimate authority of the governing party to call for the minister's head is also not questioned.

Political process: Will Broadstairs survive? Sir Bernard Ingham used to say that if no new developments in a story occurred after nine days it was effectively dead. Our minister in this situation is a hostage to the discretion of his mistress and other people either involved or perceiving an interest in the affair. The outcome will depend on the following:

1. *Political will*: How prepared are the PM and Broadstairs to stand firm against resignation calls? How long could he hold out once the 1922 Committee has given the thumbs down? How long would this Committee stay silent as it saw the issue eroding voter support? How effective also would Broadstairs' enemies in his own party be in hastening his downfall?
2. *Influence*: How much influence does the PM have in Fleet Street? The evidence suggests political sympathies of a paper count for nothing when a really juicy scandal is involved. Does Broadstairs have a body of support on the back benches or is he a 'loner'?
3. *Manipulation*: How good is the minister at coping with the situation? Can he make a clean breast of it like Paddy Ashdown regarding his extra-marital affair in January 1992 and survive with reputation arguably enhanced? Can he handle hostile press conferences and media interviews (as David Mellor did with aplomb)? Can the minister call up old favours on the back benches?

Let's suppose things quieten down for a few days, the PM defends his friend at Question Time and the wife says she'll stand by her man. If this was all there was to it, Broadstairs would survive and live to fight again, albeit with his reputation and prospects damaged. We saw that in the somewhat similar David Mellor case the revelations kept on coming (much to public amusement and his embarrassment) but the crucial revelations concerned acceptance of undeclared favours by the minister. After this, back-bench calls for a resignation and an excited press ensured that Mellor had to go.

The political process in this case is a little haphazard and depends to some extent on each day's tabloid headlines. It will also depend on the PM's judgement as to when the problem has ceased to be an individual one and has escalated to the point when his own judgement and the political standing of his party are in question. Once that point has been reached it is only a matter of time before the minister's career is over. There was much in ex-Prime Minister Harold Wilson's tongue-in-cheek comment that 'much of politics is presentation, and what isn't is timing'.

The critical political questions

Because politics studies the making and carrying out of decisions, the student of politics learns to ask a number of important immediate questions about the political life of any institution:

1. Who is included and who is excluded from the process of decision making? It is rare indeed for all the members of a community or organization to be allowed a part in the decision making process. Mapping the divide between those taking part and those not taking part is an important initial task of political inquiry.
2. What matters are actually dealt with by the political process? This is sometimes called 'identifying the political agenda'. Every community or body has such an agenda – a list of issues which are accepted as matters over which choices can be made. In a school the agenda may include the budget and the curriculum; in a church, the religious doctrine of the institution; within the government of a country such as Britain the balance of spending between defence and education. But the range of subjects 'on the political agenda' will vary greatly at different times and in different places. In modern Britain, for instance, the terms on which education is provided by the state is a major item of political argument. But before 1870, when compulsory education was first introduced, this was a matter which did not concern decision makers.
3. What do the various individuals or groups involved in the political process achieve? What are their interests and how clearly can they be identified?
4. What means and resources do decision makers have at their disposal to assist them in getting their way? When a decision is made, one set of preferences is chosen over another. In practice this means that one person or group compels or persuades others to give way. Compulsion or persuasion is only possible through the use of some resources. These are highly varied. We may get our way in a decision through the use of force, or money, or charm, or the intellectual weight of our argument. Studying politics involves examining the range of political resources and how they are employed.

Politics, government and the state

Every human being has some experience of politics, either as the maker of decisions or as the subject of decisions, because politics is part and parcel of social organisation. An institution which did not have some means of making decisions would simply cease to be an institution. But this book is not long enough to deal with the totality of political life in Britain; it concentrates on politics inside government and the organisations which are close to government.

The best way of understanding the special nature of macro-politics or politics with a capital 'P' is to begin by appreciating the difference between the state and other institutions in society. In a community like Britain there are thousands of organisations in which political activity takes place. By far the most significant of these is that body called 'the state', which can be defined as follows:

That institution in a society which exercises supreme power over a defined territory.

Three features of the state should be noted:

1. *The 'state' is more than the 'government'*: The state should not be equated with 'government', let alone with a particular government. When we speak of 'a Conservative government' we are referring to the occupancy of the leading positions in

government – such as the office of Prime Minister – by elected politicians drawn from a particular party. This in turn should be distinguished from 'government' in a more general sense, by which is meant a set of institutions, notably departments of state such as the Treasury and the Home Office, concerned with the conduct of policies, and everyday administration. The state certainly encompasses these departments of state, but it also embraces a wider range of institutions. Most important, it includes the agencies whose role it is to ensure that in the last instance the will of the state is actually enforced: these include the police, the courts and the armed forces (for a view of the functions of the state see Box 1.1).

2 *Territory is a key feature of the state*: What distinguishes the state from other kinds of institutions in which politics takes place is that it is the supreme decision maker in a defined territory. Other institutions in Britain take decisions which their members obey; but power in a family, a school or a firm is ultimately regulated by the will of the state. In Britain, this idea is expressed in the notion of **sovereignty**. The sovereign power of the state consists in the ability to prescribe the extent and limits of the powers which can be exercised by any other organisation in British society.

It follows that this sovereignty is limited territorially. The British state lives in a world of other states, and the extent of its rule is defined by its physical boundaries – which inevitably abut onto the boundaries of other states.

Disputes about the physical boundaries of state sovereignty are among the most serious in political life. It might be thought that an 'island state', which is how Britain is conventionally pictured, would have no difficulty in establishing its boundaries. In practice, identification is complicated and often leads to fierce disputes with other states over claims to territory. In 1982 a rival sovereign state, Argentina, had to be expelled by force when it occupied territory (which Britain claims for its own) in the Falkland Islands of the South Atlantic. Another source of dispute arises from the fact that the boundaries of a state are not identical with its land mass: states like Britain also claim jurisdiction over the air space above that land mass and over territorial waters surrounding the land. In recent decades, for instance, Britain has extended its 'territorial limits' – the area of sea over which it claims sovereignty – from three miles to two hundred miles beyond the shoreline, in order to possess the fishing and mineral exploration rights of those waters. This extension has often caused disputes between rival claimants.

The fact that there exists on earth only a finite amount of land, sea and air space means that the sovereignty of a particular state over territory is always subject to potential challenge from outside. Occasionally the ferocity of this challenge may actually lead to the destruction of a state: in 1945, for instance, the defeat of Germany at the end of the Second World War led to the destruction of the German state and the occupation of all German territory by its victorious opponents.

A state's sovereignty is, however, not only subject to external challenge; it can also be disputed internally. In 1916, for instance, the boundaries of the British state encompassed the whole island of Ireland. Between 1916 and 1921 there occurred a military uprising against British rule which ended in agreement to redraw territorial boundaries, creating an independent Irish state covering most of what had hitherto been British sovereign territory.

3 *State power depends on legitimacy*: As the example of the Falklands, the destruction of the German state after 1945 and the creation of an independent state in Ireland all show, control of the means of coercion is an important guarantor of sovereignty. But the sovereign power of a state depends not only on its capacity to coerce; it also rests on the recognition by citizens that the state has the authority or right to exercise power

over those who live in its territory. This is commonly called **legitimacy**. It would be extremely difficult for a state to survive if it did not command this legitimacy. Britain, like most other large communities with sophisticated and advanced economies, is far too complex a society to be governed chiefly by force. This is why the state in Britain, as in other advanced industrial nations, claims not only to be the supreme power in a territory, but also to be the supreme legitimate power.

This right to obedience is asserted on different grounds by different states at different times. The German social theorist Max Weber offered a famous distinction between three types of legitimacy: *traditional*, *charismatic* and *rational–legal*. The first of these rests on custom and appeals to continuity with the past. It is the principal ground, for instance, by which rule through a hereditary monarchy is justified. The second appeals to the divine-like, 'anointed' quality of leadership: in our century many of the greatest dictators, such as Adolf Hitler, have commanded obedience through their charismatic qualities. Rational–legal legitimacy rests on the ground that in making decisions agreed rules and agreed purposes are observed.

Although in any state elements of all three sorts of legitimacy can be identified, they will be emphasised in different ways. In Britain, charisma is relatively unimportant. Although some politicians are occasionally described as '**charismatic**' personalities, this is no more than a journalistic way of saying 'exciting' or 'appealing'. Political leadership in Britain does not rest on a claim that governors are 'anointed' with divine-like qualities. Tradition in Britain, by contrast, does have some importance. The crown is the symbol of political authority and the Queen's right to that crown of course rests on inheritance – she was born to the succession, like the monarch who preceded her and the one who will follow her. However, the legitimacy of the state in Britain rests only in part on tradition; for the main part it is rational–legal in character: its actions are taken in accordance with agreed procedures, in particular laws passed by Parliament. It is an absolute principle of the exercise of state authority that the state cannot legitimately command the obedience of citizens if its demands do not carry the backing of legislation, or the force of law (see also Chapter 5 on concepts).

Also central to the study of politics as well as the concept of 'the state' are the concepts of 'power' and 'authority'.

Power is one of the founding organising concepts in political science. We talk of a government being in 'power', of Thatcher being a 'powerful' Prime Minister. We talk of people with the 'power to make decisions'. In essence the concept means a quality, the ability of someone or some group to get others to do what they otherwise would not have done. In crude terms this can be achieved by coercion: a man with a gun can induce compliance through the fear which people naturally have of the consequences.

In real-life politics this rarely happens outside brutal tyrannies like Iraq, but the notion of compulsion in the face of threats lies somewhere close to the heart of political power; after all, when the chips are down, states go to war either to impose their will on other states or to prevent this happening to them. Normally, though, power is exercised by recognised politicians acting within an established system making important decisions on behalf of communities or nations.

Bachrach and Baratz (1981) argued that decisions *not* made by politicians were just as important as those actually made. If a matter can be marginalised or ignored completely through the ability of someone to exclude it, that person can be said to exercise power. For example, it could be argued that cars have been choking our cities for decades, that this problem has been recognised but that remedial action has been postponed for so long because the motor industry is so important to the economy and voters themselves have a potent love/hate relationship with their cars.

It can also be argued that power can be exercised through the ability of some groups to induce people to accept certain decisions without complaint. Marx believed that the ruling class was able to permeate the institutions of the state with its values so that the exploitation of capitalism was fully accepted and approved and consequently perceived as simultaneously natural, unavoidable and 'common sense'. With the advent of the modern media other theorists such as Antonio Gramsci argued that the exploited masses had been induced through a ruling class permeated culture to 'love their servitude'.

Authority is closely associated with power but is crucially different from the crude version of, say, a man with a gun. When our politicians announce new laws we accept them and obey them even if, say, we disagree with them, because we accept the right of politicians to discuss and pass legislation through a popularly elected chamber. In other words MPs have 'authority' to pass laws on our behalf. Something similar occurs when a traffic warden gives us a ticket: we may be furious but we pay up as we respect his/her authority, backed up as it is by statute law.

I think the critial difference between a dictatorship and a democracy is that in a dictatorship there are only two people out of every hundred who take a personal interest in politics; in a democracy there are three.

Healey, 1990, p. 156

Approaching the study of politics

We now have some idea of the nature of politics as an activity and some familiarity with the central ideas of state, power and authority. Politics, then, is the process by which conflicting interests are managed and authoritative choices made in social institutions as different as the family, the school and the firm. The most important set of political institutions are conventionally called 'the state', and it is the state which is the main focus of the discipline called 'political science'.

Political science is now a large and well-established academic discipline in both Europe and North America. For instance, the American Political Science Association has 12,000 members and in Britain the Political Studies Association and the Politics Association have over 1,000 members each. However, this is a relatively recent development. The emergence of political science as a separate discipline organised on a large scale in universities and colleges first developed in the United States in the early decades of this century. Even now, the overwhelming majority of people called 'political scientists' are American. Before the emergence of political science the subject was divided between specialists in different disciplines (see Figure 1.1). Constitutional lawyers studied the legal forms taken by states. Historians studied the relations between, and the organisation of, states in the past. Philosophers discussed the moral foundations, if any, of state authority. In large part, the modern discipline is the heir to these earlier approaches. It is important to be aware of the main approaches, because the approach employed in any particular study influences the kind of questions it asks, the evidence it considers relevant and the conclusions it draws.

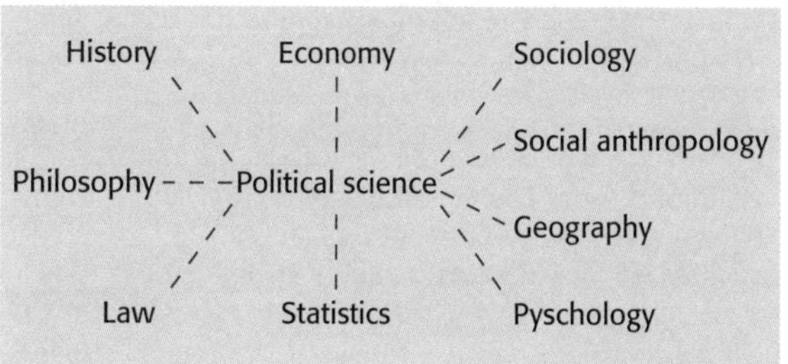

Figure 1.1 Some of the disciplines contributing to political science

Three important approaches are now sketched here: the *institutional*, the *policy cycle* and the *socio-political* (see Table 1.1 for summary). These, it should be emphasised, are not mutually exclusive. They are indeed complementary approaches; and just as we usually gain an appreciation of a physical object like a work of art if we look at it from a variety of angles, so we understand a system of government better if we examine it in a similarly varied way.

The *institutional* or *constitutional approach* to the study of politics was until recently dominant in the study of government in Britain. It has three distinctive features: its focus, its assumptions and

Table 1.1 Summary of important approaches to the study of politics

Approach	Focus	Main assumptions	Examples of characteristic evidence examined
Institutional	Formal machinery of government	Formal structures and legal rules are supreme	Structure of parliaments, cabinets, civil services
Policy cycle	Choices made by government	Government action shaped by mix of demands and resources; policy affects wider society	Kinds of resources (money, etc.); patterns of policy making and implementation
Socio-political	Social context, links between government and society	Structure and production of government shaped by wider society	Economic and class structure; organisation of interest groups

its choice of evidence. The focus of the institutional approach is on the formal institutions of government. In Britain this means a concentration on the bodies at the heart of what is sometimes called 'central government' in London: the two Houses of Parliament, the Cabinet, the individual ministries and ministers and the permanent civil servants in those ministries. The working assumption of this approach is that the legal structure of government and the formal organisations in which government activities happen have an importance in their own right. In other words, they are not just the reflections of other social influences; on the contrary, they are assumed to exercise an independent influence over the life of the community. In practical terms this means that the approach is dominated by an examination of the legal rules and the working conventions which govern the operation of these formal institutions.

It is sometimes objected that this approach is static, that it has a tendency to stress the character of government at one fixed moment, and to neglect the fact that political life is characterised by constant cycles of activity.

The *policy cycle approach* tries to capture this cyclical quality. Government is examined as a series of 'policy cycles'. It is pictured as a system of inputs and outputs, as shown in Figure 1.2. Political activity is pictured as a series of stages in the making and execution of decisions about policy. At the stage of policy initiation there exist both demands and resources. At any one moment in a community there will be a wide range of views about what government should do, which will manifest themselves as demands of various

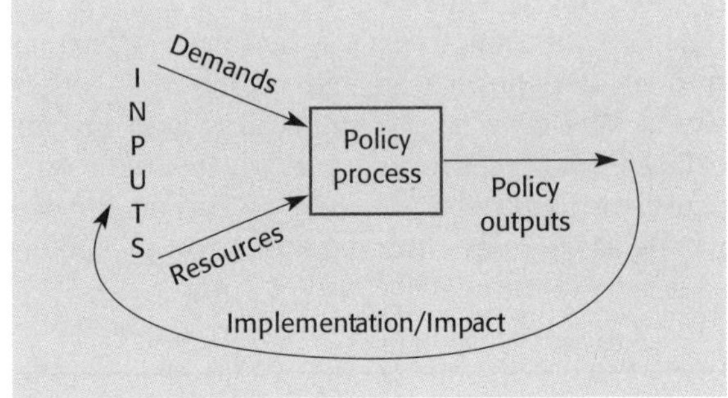

Figure 1.2 The policy cycle

kinds: that, for instance, government should provide particular services, such as free education for all under a certain age; that it should decide the appropriate balance of resources allocated to different services; or that it should decide the exact range of social activity which is appropriate for government, rather than for other social institutions, to regulate. Making and implementing policy choices in response to these demands requires resources. These are the second major input into government and include: people, like the administrators and experts necessary to make policy choices and to implement them; and money, which is needed to pay government personnel. These resources can be raised in a wide variety of ways: for example, revenue can be raised by taxation, by borrowing or by charging for the services that governments provide.

After examining the initial stages of resource raising and allocation, the policy cycle approach describes the processing of inputs; in other words, how the balance of different demands and the balance between demands and resources is allocated to produce policy choices. Finally, the process of what is sometimes called policy implementation and policy impact (see Figure 1.2) studies how government policies are put into effect and what consequences they may have for the subsequent balance of demands and resources. It is this emphasis on the linked nature of all stages in the policy process which leads us to speak of the policy cycle approach (see also Chapter 25). This approach is also distinguished by its particular focus, assumptions and choice of evidence. Although it resembles the institutional approach in concentrating attention on the institutions of government its focus is primarily on what these institutions do, rather than on how they are organised, because the most important assumption here is that what is interesting about government is that it makes choices – in response to demands and in the light of the scarce resources at its command. In turn this affects the sort of evidence on which the 'policy cycle' approach concentrates. Although much of this evidence concerns practical functioning and organisation of government, it also involves the wider environment of government institutions. This is necessarily so because the demands made on government and the resources which it can raise all come from that wider society. In this concern with the wider social context of government institutions the policy approach shares some of the concerns of the socio-political approach.

The *socio-political approach* has two particularly important concerns: the social foundations of the government order; and the links connecting government to the wider organisation of society. Close attention is paid to the wider social structure and to the kinds of political behaviour which spring from it. It is a working assumption of this approach that government is indeed part of a wider social fabric, and that its workings can only be understood through an appreciation of the texture of that wider fabric. Some versions make even stronger assumptions. For instance, most Marxist scholars believe that the workings of government in a community are at the most fundamental level determined by the kind of economic organisation prevailing in that community. The focus and assumptions of the socio-political approach in turn shape the kind of evidence on which it focuses. This includes information not only about the social structure, but also about the social influences which shape important political acts, such as voting and the kinds of economic and social interests (like business and workers) who influence the decisions taken in government.

Themes and issues in British politics

Britain's system of government is one of the most intensively examined in the world; not surprisingly, therefore, there is no shortage of issues and themes. We conclude this introductory chapter by selecting four which are of special importance and which recur in different ways in the chapters following. These themes are: democracy and **responsibility**; efficiency and effectiveness; the size and scope of government; and the impact of government on the wider society.

Democracy and responsibility

British government is intended to be democratic and responsible: it is meant to be guided by the choices of citizens, to act within the law and to give an account of its actions to society's elected representatives. The issue of how far democracy and responsibility do indeed characterise the political system is central to the debates about the nature of British government. Defenders of the system point to a variety of features. Democratic practices include the provision for election – at least once every five years – of the membership of the House of Commons by an electorate comprising 43 million from Britain's 57 million inhabitants. The membership of the Commons in turn effectively decides which party will control government during the duration of a Parliament's life, while all legislation requires a majority vote in the Commons. In addition to these formal practices, a number of other provisions support democratic political life. Freedoms of speech, assembly and publication allow the presentation of a wide variety of opinions, thus offering the electorate a choice when they express a democratic preference. The existence of competing political parties similarly means that there are clear and realistic choices facing voters when they go to the polls in elections.

Democracy means that the people can decide the government and exercise influence over the decisions governments take. *Responsibility* means that government is subject to the rule of law and can be held to account for its actions. Those who think British government is responsible in this way point to a variety of institutions and practices, some of which are formal in nature. They include the right to challenge the activities of government in the courts and to have the actions of ministers and civil servants overturned if it transpires that they are done without lawful sanction. They also include the possibility of questioning and scrutinising – for instance in the House of Commons – government ministers over their actions and omissions. In addition to these formal provisions responsibility rests on wider social restraints which are intended to hold government in check. The mass media report on and scrutinise the activities of politicians and civil servants while a wide range of associations and institutions, such as trade unions and professional bodies, act as counterweights in cases where government threatens to act in an unrestrained way.

Against these views a variety of grounds have been produced for scepticism about the reality of responsible democratic government in Britain. Some observers are sceptical of the adequacy of democratic institutions and practices. Is it possible, for instance, to practise democracy when the main opportunity offered to the population to make a choice only occurs in a general election held once every four or five years? It is also commonly observed that the links between the choices made in general elections and the selection of a government are far from identical. The workings of the British electoral system (see Chapter 8) mean that it is almost unheard of for the 'winning' party in a general election to attract the support of a majority of those voting.

Even greater scepticism has been expressed about the notion that government in Britain is 'responsible'. Many observers argue that the formal mechanisms for restraining ministers and civil servants are weak. Widespread doubt, for instance, has been expressed of the notion that the House of Commons can effectively call ministers and civil servants to account. Indeed, some experienced observers and participants have spoken of the existence of an 'elective dictatorship' in Britain: in other words, of a system where government, although it requires the support of voters every four or five years, is able in the intervening period to act in an unrestrained way. There have also been sceptical examinations of the wider mechanisms intended to ensure restraint and accountability. Some insist that the mass media, for instance, are far from being independent observers of the doings of government; that, on the contrary, they are systematically biased in favour of the powerful and against the weak in Britain. Similar claims have been made by observers of the judiciary – a key group since, according to the theory of responsible government, judges are vital in deciding when government has acted in a way which is not sanctioned by law. Finally, some radical observers go further and argue not merely that 'democratic responsibility' is defective, but that there is a 'secret state' in Britain; in other words, a system of unchecked power which operates outside the scrutiny of public institutions and which is able to act systematically outside the law.

Efficiency and effectiveness

Arguments about democracy and responsibility touch on the moral worth of the system of government in Britain, but government is not only to be evaluated by its moral credentials. It also is commonly judged by its working effectiveness – and justifiably so, for the worth of a system of government is obviously in part a function of its capacity to carry out in an effective way the tasks which the community decides are its responsibility.

Until comparatively recently it was widely believed that British government was indeed efficient and effective in this sense. Britain was one of the first countries in the world, for instance, to develop a civil service selected and promoted according to ability rather than to political and social connections. In the last quarter-century, however, the efficiency and effectiveness of British government have been widely questioned. Critics focus on three issues: the skills of public servants, the evidence of the general capabilities of successive British governments and the evidence of particular policy failures.

The most important and powerful public servants in Britain are acknowledged to be 'senior civil servants' – a small group of senior administrators, mostly based in London, who give advice about policy options to ministers. This senior civil service is largely staffed by what are usually called 'generalists' – individuals chosen and promoted for their general intelligence and capabilities rather than because they possess a particular managerial or technical skill. However, critics of the efficiency of British government have argued that the nature of large-scale modern government demands administrators who are more than generally intellectually capable; it demands individuals trained in a wide range of specialised skills (see Chapter 20).

The absence of such a group, drawn from disciplines such as engineering and accountancy, at the top of British government is often held to explain the second facet of poor effectiveness – the general inability of British government to manage its most important tasks effectively. In recent decades the chief task of government in Britain has been to manage the economy. That task has, measured by the standards of Britain's major competitors, been done with conspicuous lack of success. In the 1950s Britain was one of the richest nations in Western Europe; by the 1980s she was one of the poorest.

The debate about the general competence of British government has been heightened by a series of more particular instances of policy failure in recent decades. One observer, surveying the history of British policy initiatives, concluded that there existed only one instance of a major policy success (the introduction of 'clean air' legislation in the 1950s). On the other hand, every observer can produce numerous instances of policy disasters: the Concorde aeroplane, which should have assured the country a first place in modern aircraft manufacture, and which turned out to be an expensive commercial failure; a series of financial and technical disasters in the field of weapons development; and a comprehensive disaster in the building, during the 1950s and 1960s, of uninhabitable high-rise tower blocks in the effort to solve the country's housing problems.

The belief that the efficiency and effectiveness of British government have been defective has dominated debates about the organisation of the system in the last thirty years and has produced numerous proposals for reform in the machinery. A few of these have even been implemented. Local government, for instance, was reorganised in the early 1970s into larger units which, it was believed, would deliver services more efficiently. Within the last decade, however, a new argument has entered the debate. The belief that the problems of efficiency and effectiveness were due to a lack of particular skills, or lack of an appropriate organisational structure, has been increasingly displaced by a more radical notion: that the failings of the system were intrinsic to government, and that more efficient and effective institutions could only come when government itself was reduced to a more manageable size and scope. In other words, there is a link between the debates about efficiency and effectiveness and our third theme – the size and scope of government.

Size and scope of government

British government is big government. Major public services – the provision of transport, health care, education – are performed wholly or largely by public institutions. Many of the institutions are, by any standards, very large indeed, for example the National Health Service. As we will see in Chapter 3, Britain has a 'mixed' economy. In other words, goods and services are produced by a combination of private enterprise and public institutions. Nevertheless, an astonishing variety of goods and services are provided by what is commonly called 'the public sector'. What is more, until very recently this sector was steadily growing at the expense of the private sector.

The growth of government to gigantic proportions has prompted two main debates, about its efficiency as a deliverer of goods and services; and about the impact of a growing public sector on the wider economy. The efficiency debate we have already in part encountered. In the last decade, however, many free-market economists have argued that government failures are due to more than the failings of particular people and structures. They are, it is argued, built into the very nature of government. According to this view, the public sector lacks many of the most important disciplines and spurs to effectiveness under which private firms have to work. In particular, say its critics, the public sector rarely has to provide services in competition with others. Because the taxpayer always stands behind a public enterprise the discipline exercised by the possibility of losses and bankruptcy, which guides private firms, is absent in the case of government. Thus government has an inherent tendency towards wastefulness and inefficiency. Defenders of the public sector, on the other hand, while not denying the possibility of waste and inefficiency, argue that failures also happen in the private sector; and that, indeed, one of the most important reasons for the growth of government is the failure of private enterprise to provide vital goods and services on terms acceptable to consumers.

A more general argument about the problems of having a large-scale public sector concerns the resources which are needed to maintain this sector. In the 1970s perhaps the most influential explanation of the failings of the British economy rested on the claim that Britain had 'too few producers'. It was argued that non-productive services had grown excessively at the expense of the sector of the economy producing manufactured goods for the home market and for export. A large proportion of the excessive expansion of the 'service' sector consisted in the growth of public services such as welfare, health and education. These were in effect 'crowding out' more productive activities. Against this view, it has been argued that the growth of 'services' is more a consequence than a cause of the contraction of manufacturing in Britain, and that in any case 'non-productive' services, such as education, are actually vital to sustaining a productive manufacturing sector.

Whatever the rights and wrongs of these arguments we will see in succeeding chapters that critics of 'big government' have, in the 1980s and 1990s, enjoyed much influence over policy. Many activities once thought 'natural' to the public sector – such as the provision of services such as a clean water supply and energy for the home – have been, or are being, transferred to private ownership. Arguments about 'privatisation', as these transfers are usually called, have also cropped up in the final major theme we sketch here – the impact of government.

The impact of government

We already know from our description of the 'policy cycle' approach that government has powerful effects on the wider society. Modern government takes in society's resources – money, people, raw materials – and 'converts' them into policies. In turn, these policies plainly have a great effect on the lives of us all. On this there is general agreement, but there is great disagreement about the precise impact of government. This disagreement has crystallised into a long-standing argument about the extent to which the effects of government activity are socially progressive or regressive – in simpler terms, whether the rich or poor get most out of the policy process.

The most important way government raises resources in a country like Britain is through taxation. The taxation system in Britain is guided by the principle of 'progression': in other words, the wealthier the individual or institution, the greater the liability to pay tax. On the other hand, the services provided by government are consumed collectively (e.g. national defence), are consumed individually but are freely available to all (e.g. free art galleries) or are designed for the poor (e.g. supplementary welfare payments). By contrast, it is difficult to think of a public service which is designed to be consumed only by the rich. These considerations should ensure that the impact of government is redistributive between rich and poor. At the extremes of poverty, for instance, the poor should contribute nothing to taxation but nevertheless be eligible for a wide range of benefits paid for from the general taxes paid by everyone else in the community.

Critics of the view that the impact of government is redistributive in this way rest their case on several arguments. Firstly, some services of government, while not designed for the benefit of the better-off, may nevertheless be worth more to the rich than to the poor. An efficient police service, for instance, which deters theft, is correspondingly desirable according to the amount of property one stands to lose to thieves. Secondly, some services, while again designed to be universally enjoyed, may in practice be almost totally consumed by the better-off. In the arts, for example, opera attracts large public subsidies but is rarely patronised by the poor and is highly fashionable among the rich. Thirdly, some services, while designed actually to ensure equality of treatment for all, or even preferential treatment for the deprived, may nevertheless in practice be more widely used by the better-off than by the poor. It is widely alleged, for instance, that the National Health Service in Britain actually disproportionately devotes its resources to caring for the better-off. This is partly because the poorest in the community are least knowledgeable about the services available and least willing to make demands for these services; and partly because the actual distribution of resources inside the Health Service is alleged to be biased towards the more vocal and better-off groups in society.

Most of the argument about the redistributive effects of government focus on where the services provided by the public sector actually end up, but some observers also question how far the formally 'progressive' character of the taxation system is realised in practice. It is commonly argued that the very richest are also the most sophisticated at minimising their taxation obligations by the use of skilled advisers like accountants and tax lawyers, whose speciality is to arrange the financial affairs of a company or an individual so as to minimise the amount of tax which must legally be paid.

This opening chapter has discussed the meaning of politics, the characteristics of the state, approaches to the study of politics, reasons for studying the subject and some important themes and issues in British politics. The rest of the book, organised in seven parts, follows directly from the definition we adopted on p. 9.

Politics is about conflicting interests: Part I provides the historical, social and economic contexts from which such conflicts emerge in Britain. Part II, on ideology, examines the intellectual basis of such conflicts.

Politics is also centrally concerned with how state institutions manage or resolve conflicts within society: Parts III and IV deal respectively with the representative, legislative, and executive processes whereby such management takes place or is attempted. Finally, Part VI examines how these institutions handle the major policy areas.

Chapter summary

This introductory chapter has explained that politics is about the management and resolution of conflicts by what people want to do and achieve. The study of the subject focuses on how this process is performed, especially the way individuals relate to the state. Three approaches – institutional, policy cycle and socio-political – are outlined and it is suggested we study politics for understanding and improved citizenship. Major themes include the control citizens have over their government, the efficiency of the system and the extent of its intervention in everyday lives.

Discussion points

- Why do you think people go into politics and make it their life's work?
- Think of a typically political scenario and analyse it in the way demonstrated in the chapter.
- Which approach to politics, from the ones outlined, seem to be the most interesting and helpful to you in explaining political phenomena?

Further reading

Crick's classic work (1982) is essential reading as is Duverger (1966). Leftwich (1984) is worth reading as an easy-to-understand initiation and Laver (1983) repays study too. Renwick and Swinburn (1989) is useful on concepts though Heywood (1994) is by any standards a brilliant textbook. Axford *et al.* is also well worth looking into. Riddell (1993) is both highly perceptive and very entertaining – a must for anyone wondering if the subject is for them. O'Rourke (1992) is a humorous but insightful book. Oliver (1992) is a hilarious collection of silly quotations by politicians. A shorter introduction to British politics is Jones and Kavanagh (1998).

References

Axford, B., Browning, G.K., Huggins, R., Rosamand, B., Turner, J. (1997) *Politics: an Introduction* (Routledge).

Bachrach, P. and Baratz, M. (1981) 'The two faces of power', in F.G. Castles, D.J. Murray and D.C. Potter (eds), *Decision, Organisations and Society* (Penguin).

Crick, B. (1982) *In Defence of Politics*, 2nd edn (Penguin).

Critchley, J. (1995) *A Bag of Boiled Sweets* (Faber and Faber).

Duverger, M. (1966) *The Idea of Politics* (Methuen).

Healey, D. (1990) *The Time of My Life* (Penguin).

Heywood, A. (1994) *Political Ideas and Concepts* (Macmillan).

Jones, B. and Kavanagh, D. (1998) *British Politics Today*, 6th edn (Manchester University Press).

Laver, M. (1983) *Invitation to Politics* (Martin Robertson).

Leftwich, A. (1984) *What is Politics? The Activity and its Study* (Blackwell).

Oliver, D. (1992) *Political Babble* (Wiley).

O'Rourke, R.J. (1992) *Parliament of Whores* (Picador).

Orwell, G. (1955) *Nineteen Eighty-Four* (Penguin).

Renwick, A. and Swinburn, I. (1989) *Basic Political Categories*, 2nd edn (Hutchinson).

Riddell, P. (1993) *Honest Opportunism* (Hamish Hamilton).

Chapter 2

The historical context: globalisation

Barrie Axford

Learning objectives

- To describe the nature of **globalisation** as an historical process affecting the UK and identify some recent key trends that are shaping British politics and society.
- To illustrate the particular sensitivity and vulnerability of the UK to globalising and regionalising forces by looking at two areas of public policy increasingly subject to global and European constraints.
- To explore the ways in which internal political debates and national political agendas condition UK responses to both globalisation and Europeanisation.
- To assess the extent to which globalisation and Europeanisation may be out of control or beyond national political direction.

Introduction

For part of the eighteenth and much of the nineteenth century Britain was a global power. Indeed by the middle of the nineteenth century it was the dominant power on the world stage, and its 'Great Power' status remained a given for national policy makers until after the Second World War. In recent decades Britain has ceased to be an economic and a military giant in a world that is more and more interconnected and in which there have been seismic changes in the balance of economic and strategic might. In the period of intense globalisation since the early 1950s, weak or fluctuating economic performance, loss of empire and world role and a chronic ambivalence on European integration have all made the UK especially sensitive to global forces and trends. In line with other nation-states, successive British governments have adopted a variety of strategies to manage globalisation, and these reveal the ways in which domestic factors are affected by and in turn qualify the impact of global forces and trends.

What is globalisation? Why is it important?

Globalisation is a convenient shorthand for a process that is making the world more interconnected and interdependent. More fundamentally, globalisation challenges the borders around both territorial jurisdictions and identities. It is only in recent years that the concept has captured the attention of politicians, businesses and political activists across the world, despite the fact that globalisation is not a new phenomenon. Among such constituencies globalisation generates feelings of disquiet and enthusiasm in almost equal measure. On the one hand there is a feeling that the current phase of globalisation is wreaking a profound transformation in the nature of states and societies, cultures and economies around the world. Speaking in Washington, DC, in February 1998, Mr Tony Blair said 'We on the centre-left must try to put ourselves at the forefront of those who are trying to manage change in the global economy'. On the other hand, and contra Mr Blair, some sceptics believe that there is little new in the current phase of globalisation and that nation-states remain, or can remain, in charge of their destinies. To some extent being sceptical about the power of globalisation or enthusiastic about its promise misses the point, or reduces the argument to a polemic about good and bad effects. More interesting for an analysis of contemporary British politics is the manner in which such a complex process is mediated and possibly shaped by the agency of states and other sub-global actors.

At its most visible globalisation is a process that makes for greater depth, extent and diversity in cross-border connections and processes. Money, goods, technologies, images, communications and people are moving across national frontiers at an accelerating rate. Distance is no longer an obstacle to interaction, and many social relationships have been 'stretched' across time and space. In a world made up of independent nation-states, the most obvious impact of all these movements and connections is to make national borders less coincident with the organisation of economic life and, increasingly, with the conduct of **governance**. For many observers and not a few practising politicians, the growing integration of markets and the homogenising effects of cultural commodities signal the demise of the independent authority of the nation-state and the erosion of separate national cultures and identities. In the United Kingdom, the intensifying debate about the scale of national commitment to the European Union reflects these concerns, especially over ambitious projects such as monetary union, and thus prefigure what may be seminal changes in domestic policy and politics.

Globalisation is often discussed as just an economic phenomenon, seen in the spread of the ideology and practices of the market, in the increased extent and intensity of trade as practised by multinational corporations and in the power of global financial institutions. But globalisation is a multi-dimensional process, and, even where the driving force is economic, the consequences are often felt most in other areas of life. For example, the easy availability of what might be called 'global products', such as McDonald's and Sony PlayStation, have transformed the eating and leisure habits of young people the world over. In addition, the huge growth in relatively cheap inter-continental air travel exposes most parts of the world to the mixed blessings of the tourist gaze. Tying the United Kingdom into a single European currency would involve surrendering control over monetary policy (for example, setting interest rates) to European institutions, notably the European Central Bank. For some Britons such a departure would at least compromise the ability of British governments to act in the national interest, while others express fears about the possibility of extending democratic accountability to extra-national bodies. Still others lament the potential loss of sterling as a symbol of national pride and identity.

These are matters of current concern, but of course globalisation is not a new phenomenon, even if its scope and intensity have varied over the centuries. In the eighteenth century, the world was a patchwork of empires, some of them 'global' in reach or ambition (the British, Dutch, Spanish, French and Portuguese) others largely regional (the Japanese, Chinese and Russian). Indeed, the expansion of European empires from the middle of the nineteenth century was one of the primary mechanisms of globalisation during this period. With possessions that eventually covered almost one-quarter of the world's land surface, Britain was the pace-setter in this respect, with British advocates of *laissez-faire* deeply committed to the **liberalisation** of world trade.

This period is also remarkable for the growth in the number of inter-governmental organisations charged with regulating trading and commercial activities, and notable too for some major breakthroughs in communications technologies, whose effect was to 'compress the world' still further. For instance, from the 1840s, advances in telegraphy began to remove distance as an impediment to easy communication across borders and between continents. Between 1865 and 1910 thirty-three world organisations were established, including the Universal Postal Union (1874), the International Bureau on Weights and Measures (1875), the International Labour Office (1901) and the International Court of Justice (1907). In 1930, when opening the London Naval Conference, King George V made what amounts to the first global radio broadcast, when his message was relayed simultaneously to 242 stations across six continents. Since the end of the Second World War, in addition to the United Nations and its agencies, which claim a universal competence, there have been a rash of regional organisations. These included superpower-led mililtary alliances (such as NATO and the now defunct Warsaw Pact), anti-colonial groupings aimed at fostering national independence (the Organisation for African Unity) and a variety of sub-regional frameworks for collective security (the Gulf Co-operation Council and the Association of Southeast Asian Nations). As well as regional attempts at collective security, whose main purpose was to protect state sovereignty from external threat, there emerged in Western Europe a different sort of regional body, the European Economic Community (1957), with no strict security function, but whose institutions possessed or claimed jurisdiction over member states. The extent to which nation-states are now part of a dense fabric of world, regional and sub-regional groupings is conveyed in Figure 2.1 which shows the numbers and overlapping memberships of defence and collective security organisations.

In the last four decades or so it is evident that the pace and scope of globalisation and regionalisation have increased dramatically, along with a growing awareness on the part of politicians, activists, businesses and some citizens of the threats and opportunities thus posed. This period of more intensive globalisation is characterised by seven major trends.

The closer integration of the world economy

Flows of capital, goods, communications and to a much lesser extent labour across borders are on the increase. About $1.3 trillion (US) flows through the world's foreign exchange markets on a daily basis, an amount that is hugely in excess of the combined foreign exchange reserves of all the world's richest nations. In this world of 'footloose' capital, as it is sometimes called, the City of London occupies a key position as the world's largest foreign exchange market and 'knowledge centre' for the banking industry (Figure 2.2), a status it has reclaimed after several decades of decline earlier in the century. This resurgence suggests that globalisation may not always work against the interests of individual nation-states, as some commentators argue. Another area of significant growth is international tourism. In 1997 there were in excess of 500 million tourists compared with only 70 million in 1960. Some 95 per cent of the world's nations are part of the global trading system, although 80 per cent of trade in finished goods takes place between the countries of the Western-dominated Organisation for Economic Co-operation and Development (OECD). At the heart of the world economy are the multi-national corporations (MNCs), such as Nissan, Nestlé and IBM, whose allegiance to any one country may be tenuous. MNCs account for about one-third of world output and 80 per cent of international investment. Until the early 1970s the USA enjoyed economic dominance, but since then the global economy has become much more pluralistic and regionalised, with powerful trading blocs operating in Western Europe, the Americas and on the Pacific Rim.

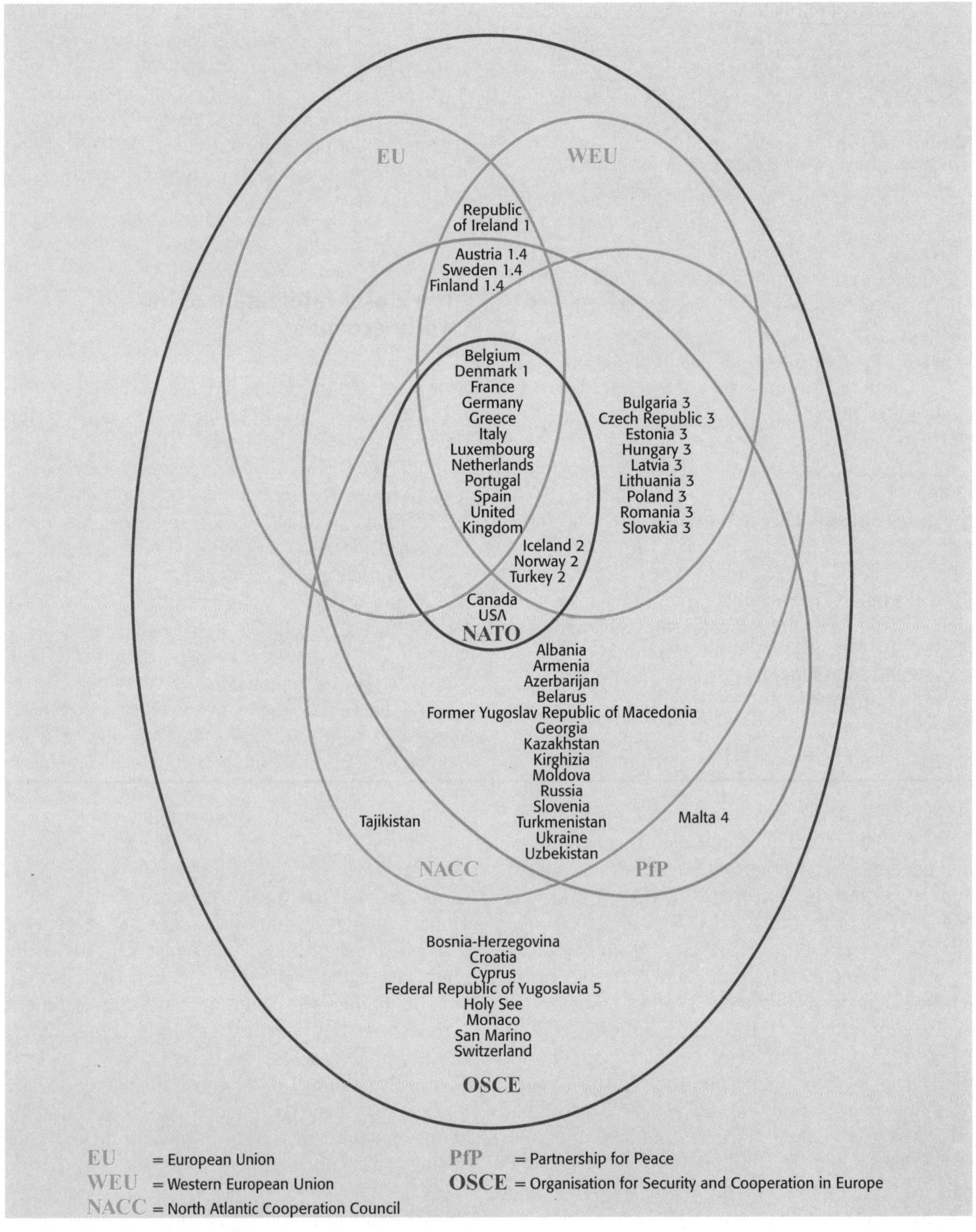

Figure 2.1 Membership of international organisations as at 1 April 1996: 1, observer in the WEU; 2, associate member of the WEU; 3, associate partner in the WEU; 4, members of PfP may attend NACC meeting as observers; 5, membership suspended

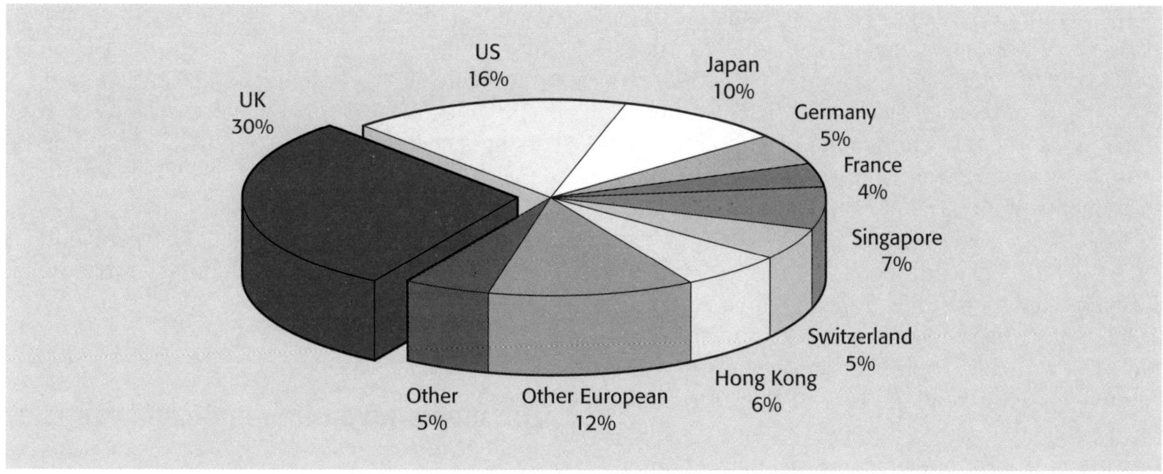

Figure 2.2 London's position as a global finance centre: foreign exchange trading

The dominance of market forces

Since the middle 1970s **neo-liberalism** has become the global economic ideology. Many countries, including Britain, have restructured their economies in line with neo-liberal dogmas. These include deregulating most aspects of economic activity, privatising public enterprises and trying to cut back on state expenditures. In the middle decades of the twentieth century, many of the richer member states of the OECD followed a 'welfare nationalist' policy, by which they aimed to promote full employment and a large measure of social protection through welfare. Following the oil crises of the early and mid-1970s and a series of recessions in the 1980s, these countries introduced cut-backs in welfare provision and invoked the disciplines of the market to make national economies more prosperous and competitive in the global marketplace. In some cases this discipline has imposed a harsh period of adjustment on individual states, but we should not overestimate the extent to which the power of market forces and the mobility of capital has diminished the authority of nation-states, or their capacity to make policy. A quick glance at patterns of government spending across some of the major economies in the past thirty years reveals modest increases in the amount of gross domestic product (GDP) taken up by public expenditures in many countries, rather than the opposite (Table 2.1). While the overall tendency in these figures is to increase spending, there is still evidence of substantial national variation. Even in the global age, there is still room for national diversity.

Table 2.1 Government spending as % of gross domestic product

	1960	1980	1998
Australia	21.2	31.4	32.9
Britain	*32.2*	*43.0*	*40.2*
Canada	28.6	38.8	42.1
France	34.6	46.1	54.3
Germany	32.4 (FRG)	47.9 (FRG)	46.9 (all)
Italy	30.1	42.1	49.1
Japan	17.5	32.0	36.9
Sweden	31.0	60.1	60.8
USA	26.8	31.4	32.8

Source: OECD, 1999

The transformation of production systems and labour markets

In general the effects of globalisation on the organisation of industrial production have been to introduce smaller and more flexible production systems, where flexibility means rapid production cycles; computer-based design systems and new patterns of working, including part-time contracts, multi-skilling and de-unionisation of the workforce. While some of these changes are driven by innovations in information and communications technology, they are also the fruit of massive and rapid movements of investment capital around the world as foreign direct investment (FDI). Since the passage of the Single European Act in 1986 and the formal completion of a European Single Market in 1992, Britain has been the major European recipient of inward FDI from both Japan and the USA. Companies with headquarters in those countries have been anxious to take advantage of UK membership in the European 'domestic' market and of the fact that the UK workforce is relatively highly skilled and relatively low paid. The attractiveness of Britain as a location for inward investment was enhanced under the Thatcher governments by far-reaching legislation that severely proscribed the power of trade unions and the incentives for workers to join them. Under 'New' Labour much of this legislation remains intact, witness to the Blair adminstration's commitment to keeping Britain open to continued high levels of inward investment. The rhetoric of free trade and open markets has been central to British economic policy for the past twenty years, the latest iteration of what is a much longer engagement with the global political economy and the doctrine of free trade.

The speed of technological change

In the last couple of decades there have been significant innovations in information and communications technologies (ICTs). The rapid spread in usage of personal computers, mobile phones and 'smart' diaries, along with the appeal of the internet as a medium of information and communication, linking the personal and the global, are key aspects of this technological 'revolution'. The internet has caught on faster than any technology in history, passing 50 million users world-wide in just four years. By comparison, personal computer use took thirteen years to reach the 50 million mark, television sixteen years, and radio thirty-eight years. Such changes are treated as seminal by some observers, heralding a new type of 'informational' or 'knowledge-based' economy, quite unlike the economy based on the mass production of goods that marked earlier periods of capitalism. With the zeal of the convert, New Labour is completely wedded to this version of the global future. At the very least, developments in ICTs intensify the trends noted above, as well as challenging the ability of national governments to police their cultural and, of course, their digital borders.

The media revolution and consumerism

Global media in the form of multi-media giants such as Time-Warner/Aol and the News International Group now produce and market products for world consumption, tailoring their output for local and niche audiences. Digital and satellite television reduces the cultural distances between countries and the ready availability of luxury and other exotic goods in local supermarkets and stores has revolutionised the eating habits of substantial sections of national populations. The evidence on whether consumers discriminate between goods with different national origins or whether they identify 'national' products at all is mixed. It is also very hard to say what effects media outputs have on traditional values and cultures, but probably too simplistic to argue that these are simply being eroded. Again, the key point is likely to be the degree to which a national culture is vulnerable to global forces and how far these same forces are used by locals to change the material conditions of their lives, but which may not affect their allegiances.

The spread of democracy

Globalisation has facilitated the spread of democratic values and practices around the world. Global ideologies stressing human rights and the necessity for regimes and societies to democratise have been important features of world politics in the last forty years. The fall of state socialism after 1989 provides the most dramatic evidence of this process, but there are other important features.

Figure 2.3 Tony Blair in Chicago

Major Western European powers such as the UK and France have de-colonised and international migration challenges the concept of citizenship as a purely national status. Humanitarian interventions in the world's trouble spots by regional and global organisations are treated as a much more legitimate feature of the world order after the fall of state socialism. In a speech to the Chicago Economic Club in April 1999, Tony Blair (Figure 2.3) unveiled his 'Doctrine of the International Community', which outlined the circumstances in which intervention in the affairs of independent states is legitimate. At the same time, demands for self-government or local autonomy can also receive a filip from globalisation or **regionalisation**, for example where Scottish and Welsh nationalists see the institutions of the European Union as a way of by-passing what they see as restrictions from Westminster.

National involvement in regional and international regimes

These days most, if not all, nation-states operate in a dense weave of regional, international and global regimes and authorities, such as the UN, the EU and the Council of Europe. After the end of the Second World War, the division of the world into two ideological blocs each dominated by a superpower decisively shaped the contours of the world order, and **bi-polarity**, as it was known, restricted a state's capacity to conduct independent foreign and defence policies. The ending of the **Cold War** has increased the involvement of states in a wide variety of security, humanitarian and economic organisations and groupings, reflecting the growing complexity of what are now **multi-polar** world politics. The proliferation of regional and international bodies follows from an awareness of the need for collective solutions to problems of world order and the uncertainty many states feel in a world where their scope for independent action has been limited.

Most states are concerned to maintain effective control of public policy by national governments, but in the case of Britain and the EU the issues seem to run much deeper. The increasing significance of the EU's role as a trading bloc, the economic and political implications of Economic and Monetary Union (EMU), and the post-Maastricht engagement with foreign policy and security matters, as well as social issues, all press on the decisional freedoms of national government. These issues have also provided the main context for domestic party politics for the past twenty years. They are likely to come to a head in the first term of office of the 'New' Labour government. Meanwhile, the Conservative Party, riven by doubts over Europe throughout the Thatcher and Major terms of office, may implode over the issue of the single currency. Membership of the EMU touches deep questions of identity for many Conservatives. In a speech to the Conservative Party annual conference in October 1999, the party leader, William Hague, offered a strong line on the virtues of things British when set against the shortcomings of Europe and Europeans.

These trends are all contemporary, but it is necessary to recognise that globalisation and the discourses through which it is mediated are historical phenomena. By turns, British political and business elites have embraced the world, or sought protection from its wiles.

Britain in the world

All the trends identified above raise serious questions about the ways in which and the extent to which the United Kingdom is addressing the current phase of globalisation. Some observers have argued that New Labour accepts the view that in the global age there is no alternative to the full acceptance of neo-liberal canons, to welfare cutbacks and to a pro-business stance in industrial relations. As a means of coming to terms with what Mr Blair has called 'the way of the world' these shifts in the policy agenda of national government appear quite radical, a deliberate attempt to undo history and ideology as a way of managing the present. But the relationships between global forces and domestic policy and politics are very complex. Having to come to terms with globalisation is not and never has been just a matter of dispensing with the legacies of the past or with the constraints of national culture and the domestic political agenda, however much policy makers might like to do this. In this section we will examine some of the key features of the international and global environment as these have emerged in the past 150 years or so, and discuss how Britain has been affected by, and, in turn, has affected such changes. Over the period as a whole the motif is one of relative decline in terms of Britain's standing in the world. From being an imperial power and a manufacturing giant towards the end of the nineteenth century, by the 1990s Britain has followed a path which leaves it increasingly bound to Europe, but still ambivalent about this tie. Its world role now depends on the actions of multilateral bodies such as the United Nations (UN) and the North Atlantic Treaty Organisation (NATO) and on the vitality of the City of London as a financial centre.

Shifting global balances in the nineteenth century: Britain as hegemon

In 1750, the UK accounted for 1.9 per cent of world manufacturing output. By 1880, this proportion had risen to 22.9 per cent, with its nearest single rival, the United States, a long way back on 14.7 per cent. It is worth underlining the depth of this comparative advantage. In 1860, Britain produced 53 per cent of the world's iron and 50 per cent of its coal. Britain's success as the first industrial nation only served to consolidate its already dominant position as a maritime, commercial power and world centre for financial credit. In the 1860s, it was responsible for two-fifths of world trade in manufactured goods and fully one-third of the world's merchant marine flew under the British flag, a proportion that continued to rise for some decades. In other words, the Victorian age saw Britain at the centre of the world's manufacturing and trading economy, and Victorians, eminent or otherwise, usually rejoiced in this position of dominance.

The interesting thing about Britain's economic dominance during these years is that it was not matched by its military capacity. Naval power remained an article of faith for Victorians, but expenditure on military hardware and the maintenance of large standing armies were deemed by many politicians and statesmen as costly and unproductive. This perception was due to the success of the ideology of *laissez-faire* political economy, first propounded by Adam Smith in 1776, which championed the cause of low government expenditure and the reduction of state control over both individuals and the economy as a whole. For proponents of this doctrine, peace was a necessary condition for prosperity, and war a means of last resort to prevent any violation of national territory and to secure the conditions of trade. Of course, both in Parliament and outside, *laissez-faire* was always a contested doctrine. But its appeal to the political and business classes can be measured by the steady dismantling of those **mercantilist** dogmas and institutions that had characterised much of the eighteenth-century trading economy, and which were based on the principle that national security and national wealth were inextricably linked. Tariffs which protected domestic producers were abolished, bans on the export of high-tech machinery lifted and a variety of imperial 'preferences' on designated goods were outlawed.

The upshot was that, by the middle decades of the century, Britain was a very reluctant player in international, and especially European, conflicts where engagements went beyond diplomatic interventions and the judicious appearance of a naval squadron. Direct involvement in the Crimea in the mid-1850s under the premiership of Palmerston was considered a costly disaster, and Britain sat out other important European conflicts, such as the defeat of Austria by Prussia in 1866 and the Franco-Prussian war of 1870. Even in the non-European empire, Britain was miserly in its deployment of British regiments and government personnel, including to the Indian sub-continent, the jewel in Britain's imperial crown.

Apart from its industrial capacity and commercial clout, the factors that underpinned British hegemony in the century following the Napoleonic Wars were three-fold:

- *Naval power*: No other country, no other maritime power came near to matching British strength.
- *An expanding colonial empire*: With no serious threats from other European powers, and only the beginnings of American rivalry in the western hemisphere, the British empire grew without much hindrance. Anti-imperial and protectionist sentiments flourished occasionally at home, but did little to check the expansion of the land empire. Apart from the economic benefits that accrued to Britain, the sheer scale of British possessions guaranteed that British influence and the British way of life were spread across the globe.
- *Financial power*: Vast sums of British investment capital were exported during the mid-to-late nineteenth century. Between 1870 and 1875, an average of £75 million was invested abroad annually, remarkable sums when translated into current numbers. Much of the lavish return on this investment was promptly re-invested, so contributing to a virtuous spiral whereby national wealth creation in turn contributed to the growth in world trade and communications infrastructures.

But the strengths of the British empire and trading economy during the nineteenth century were also potential weaknesses. For one thing, the law of comparative advantage eventually worked against British dominance, as competitor nations narrowed the technology gap and became thoroughly industrialised. In this regard the wealth-producing efforts of British inventors and investors overseas contributed in no small measure to the developments in American, Russian and central European manufacturing capacity. For another, the British economy was heavily reliant on international trade and finance. *Laissez-faire* liberals argued that the more Britain and other countries became integrated with the burgeoning world economy, the less likely that wars would ensue. However, in the event of a war between the great powers British export markets would be disrupted, the flow of imports restricted and financial markets damaged. Whether a mature economy like Britain's could survive such an upheaval, let alone retain its dominance, was open to doubt. Doubt was not a commodity in plentiful supply in Britain at the close of the nineteenth century.

Post-hegemony, 1900–45

In Queen Victoria's Diamond Jubilee year of 1897, Joseph Chamberlain, the British Minister for the Colonies, could still tell a conference that 'the tendency of the time is to throw all power into the hands of the greater empires, and the minor kingdoms – those which are non-progressive – fall into a secondary and subordinate place'. The next fifty years proved Chamberlain to be wrong, as the old empires fell apart and would-be new ones arose. A pacific world, so central to *laissez-faire* models of prosperity also went up in flames, as a more realist and bloody order took Europe and some other parts of the world into desolation and ruin.

In 1900 Britain still possessed the largest empire the world had ever seen along with a mighty navy and huge industrial strength. But there were strong challenges to British interests, and these were most pronounced in the Caribbean and Latin America (from the USA), in the Near East and Persian Gulf (Russia) and in China, where Great Power interest in carving up the Celestial Empire threatened Britain's domination of China's foreign trade. Such challenges were not new, but by the end of the century were being posed by countries that were stronger and less inclined to accord Britain the privileges of rank. The British economy was also less competitive than in the recent past, with a decline in the share of world production in key commodities such as coal, textiles and iron goods. For two decades up to 1894, industrial production grew at no more than 1.5 per cent annually, far below the growth of its keenest rivals. Increasingly Britain's open home market was flooded by lower-cost foreign manufactures, while British exports were subject to high tariff barriers in protected markets in North America and industrialised Europe. In 1880, the UK had 23.2 per cent of world trade; by 1914 this proportion was down to 14.1 per cent. During this critical period, when Britain was under sustained challenge from its economic rivals, the doctrine of free trade began to give way to the ideas of **Social Imperialism** and national protectionism, especially in the Conservative Party. These doctrines advocated the enlargement of the British empire as a way of holding on to Britain's status in the world economy.

Of course, decline was relative, and on other indicators the UK remained an economic giant. The ship-building industry, on which Britain's trade and defence depended, was still producing 60 per cent of the world's merchant tonnage in 1914, and 33 per cent of its warships. Britain still marshalled 43 per cent of the world's foreign investments, with $19.5 billion (US) invested overseas. On the eve of the First World War in 1914, Britain was hardly in a parlous state, but had lost out industrially to both the USA and Germany and was subject to growing pressure in commercial and maritime affairs, as well as over its imperial interests. For all this, in the pre-war international order Britain remained the major player.

The post-war world order that emerged was quite different from its predecessor. In many respects it was still a Eurocentric world, but some of the main protagonists of the old order, notably Britain, France and Germany, had been badly hurt, materially and pyschologically, by the war, while Russia had undergone a social revolution. In other respects the war simply accelerated trends that were already visible. Perhaps the most significant of these was the fact that the USA overtook Europe in terms of total industrial output by 1919, confirming its position as the new economic hegemon. The fragility of the post-war security settlement, based on the Versailles Treaty and the League of Nations, was soon apparent, along with the precariousness of the new commercial and financial order which led to the Wall Street crash of 1929 and the Great Depression of the early 1930s. By the mid-1930s, the **cosmopolitan** world order envisaged in the Versailles settlement had all but splintered into rival currency blocs – sterling, dollar, yen and gold – and into forms of national protectionism.

Dreams of world peace and internationalism, built around the League of Nations and on the horror of total war, also began to fragment in the late 1920s and early 1930s, giving way to a politics based on national security and spheres of influence. In Germany, the ravages of the Depression fanned the discontent left by the draconian peace settlement and contributed to the appeal of those who counselled national reconstruction through martial action and imposed order. Other fascist movements in Europe and the brand of militaristic nationalism that dominated Japanese politics echoed these sentiments. The 'revisionist' states of Germany, Italy and Japan were antagonistic not only towards the Western democracies who had brokered the peace in 1919, although Italy was a victor nation then, but also towards the Bolshevik Soviet Union, keeper of a new truth. In other respects the world was becoming much less Eurocentric. For Britain perhaps the most obvious and far-reaching example of this trend was the growing opposition to British rule in India, centred on Gandhi, which intimated imperial demise.

The slide into another European and then world war in 1939 stemmed from the failure to solve the German question after 1919. The 'twenty-year truce' between 1919 and 1939 saw Germany relinquish its tenuous grip on democracy under the Weimar Republic and embrace National Socialism. Throughout this period the USA remained outside the League of Nations and wedded to its doctrine of hemispheric isolation. Britain and France could not agree on the proper role for the League and so it never really developed teeth as a means of collective security. In 1939, the Western democracies were not well equipped to face the aggressive territorial ambitions of Hitler's new Reich. Of course, Britain was still a substantial power in the 1930s, but not one ready, in any sense of the word, to halt the German challenge. In many ways the policy of appeasement under Neville Chamberlain was a recognition of Britain's weakness and a mechanism for preserving what remained of British power. Rises in defence expenditure (from 5.5 per cent of GNP in 1937 to 12.5 per cent in 1939) placed severe pressure on industries already depleted by lack of investment and skills shortages. As a result government had to purchase arms from overseas, thereby eroding foreign currency reserves and threatening balance of payments difficulties. The decision to shore up Britain's 'continental commitment' and give the Mediterranean theatre priority over Singapore, in the way of naval resources, weakened the British military presence in the Far East, soon to be faced by Japanese expansionism. Over-stretched and under-resourced, Britain made the decision in 1939 to abandon appeasement of Hitler and his territorial ambitions and go to war.

Stable bi-polarity and unstable multi-polarity, 1945–89

The 'proper application of overwhelming force', made possible by US entry into the war in 1942, sealed the long-term fate of the Axis powers (Germany and Japan). It also set the seal on the old balance of power and of the key role played in it by the European Great Powers. The bi-polar world now emerging owed everything to the geo-military strength of the two superpowers and to the unrivalled economic clout of the Americans. In the 'free world' American influence was everywhere and a whole new world economic and strategic order was constructed in the image of American capitalism and commitment to Western democratic values. All the international economic institutions which grew out of the Second World War, the International Monetary Fund (IMF), the International Bank for Reconstruction and Development and the General Agreement on Tariffs and Trade (GATT), were apologists for a liberal world order based on open competition and the free convertibility of currencies. Countries wishing to reconstruct their economies (and this included most European states) were obliged to sing from the same hymn sheet as the Americans. The Soviet Union, at first invited to be a participant in this American-brokered renaissance, backed off when it became apparent that the price was to surrender socialist controls on economic activity. The USSR went its own way, constructing a defensive wall in east-central Europe to rival the North Atlantic Treaty Organisation (NATO) of 1949 and a socialist version of the economic co-operation that began to develop in western Europe in the early 1950s and was called the Council for Mutual Economic Co-operation (COMECON). In the style of many previous empires, it also began to build a military capacity that was well beyond its economic means, and which swallowed a massively disproportionate amount of GDP.

Britain emerged from the war intact, but with its status as a global power depleted. Of course it was still an imperial power and, through its seat as one of the Permanent Members of the United Nations Security Council, ostensibly still in the front rank of world powers. When possession of nuclear weapons became a potent symbol of national virility and a means of retaining some trace of Great Power independence in the early 1950s, Britain was anxious to be a member of the nuclear club. On the surface, as well as in the minds of many British people and politicians, the UK was still at the centre of the world politically and holding its own in economic affairs. The reality was rather less flattering and destined to get worse. For one thing, Britain's long-term industrial decline had been accelerated by the war and it no longer enjoyed primacy in the areas of financial services and invisible exports. The empire and Commonwealth were increasingly important to Britain in economic terms, but also burdensome because of the demands for overseas bases and the pressures of various anti-colonial movements. Europe and European reconstruction figured much less prominently in the world views of British policy makers than did the empire and British Commonwealth, the Atlantic relationship with the USA and the exigencies of economic decline. Early on in the Second World War, Churchill had spoken of the three 'circles' that defined British policy and interests: the empire, the 'special relationship' with the United States and, on the outer rim, Europe.

Empire and Commonwealth

The British Commonwealth was renamed the Commonwealth in the light of post-war de-colonisation. De-colonisation was begun in 1947 with the withdrawal from India and Burma, and in the next twenty-five years led to the dismantling of all but the residual outposts of empire. Nationalist pressure, American opposition and cost were the primary factors behind the withdrawal from empire, rather than any hint of drawing closer to Europe. The Suez fiasco of 1956 demonstrated Britain's inability to act independently of the USA and speeded up the process of decolonisation. Britain, France and Israel were forced by American and world pressure to withdraw their 'protective' military force from the Suez Canal Zone, where it was trying to wrest control of the strategic waterway from President Nasser's Egypt. Years later, during the Falklands crisis of 1982 the militarily audacious expedition to reclaim the islands from Argentine forces also relied on American diplomatic goodwill and satellite intelligence.

In the wake of empire, Britain turned to the Commonwealth to preserve its waning influence in former colonies and around the world. But the burgeoning Commonwealth was not in any sense a power bloc in world politics, still less a vehicle for British influence. Where Britain was America's firm partner in the conduct of the Cold War, many Commonwealth states declared themselves to be 'non-aligned'. Britain also lost markets in the Commonwealth to more aggressive European and Far Eastern rivals, and some Commonwealth members had to redirect their patterns of trade when Britain's entry to the EC in 1973 cut off or severely curtailed Commonwealth preference agreements for many agricultural products. At meetings of Commonwealth Heads of State and government, Britain often found itself in a minority, accused of bolstering racist regimes in South Africa and Southern Rhodesia, or failing to broker conflicts between Commonwealth states.

Relationship with the United States

By the early 1940s the UK recognised that it was incapable of holding onto its empire and its world role without help – or more to the point, without American help. Only the USA could oversee the conditions necessary to recreate a liberal world order and had the muscle to protect Europe by kick-starting its economic recovery. Relations with the USA had been poor during the pre-war years, but wartime co-operation improved them, giving the British, at any rate, a false sense of their importance to Washington. Britain now set out to support the American version of the new world order, a stance which has scarcely varied across successive governments. Over the years, Washington has been both cavalier and solicitous by turns in its dealings with Britain. In 1946 the US peremptorily cut off collaboration with the British in nuclear research, and the Suez affair demonstrated that, if there was a 'special relationship', it was not between equals. At the same time, the US has been willing to supply nuclear arms only to Britain and has benefited from the willingness of the British governments to legitimise and subvent its actions as a global policeman. When the new Labour government in the person of Prime Minister Harold Wilson refused to commit British troops to support the US sponsored government of SouthVietnam in 1964, the Americans were not

BOX 2.1 MINI BIOGRAPHY

Harold Wilson (1916–95)
Labour Prime Minister. Born in Huddersfield, educated Oxford (PPE); worked as civil servant during Second World War. Entered politics in 1945 for Ormskirk. Ability, and some good fortune, led him to be a Cabinet Minister by 1947. Resigned in 1951 over cuts in the health service and seen as leftwing in 1950s. Stood for leadership when Gaitskell died, becoming Prime Minister in 1964, increasing his majority in 1966. His administration was not marked by any great achievments but he presided over a great liberalisation of British society and was unlucky to lose to Heath in 1970. Led minority administration after 1974, winning a slim majority in October of same year. Gave up premiership in 1976. Has been rehabilitated to some extent by historians subsequently.

BOX 2.2 MINI BIOGRAPHY

Hugh Gaitskell (1906–63)
Labour leader in 1950s. Educated Oxford and associated with 'revisionist' wing of centre/right Labour intellectuals. Chancellor in 1951. Leader in 1955 when faced opposition from Nye Bevan but sought to move Labour away from fundamentalist positions, with limited success. Died before he could inherit his deserved occupancy of Number Ten.

only outraged, but baffled by British reluctance to get involved.

The more routine response of British governments has been to play the good neighbour. During the Thatcher–Reagan years, between 1980 and 1988, the leaderships of both countries shared a goal to liberalise world economies, and a fundamentally realist and aggressive stance on confronting the enemies of the West. In 1983 the UK offered full diplomatic support for the US invasion of Grenada, to oust its Marxist regime, and in 1986 the US made use of British air bases to launch its bombing raid on Libya in reprisal for Colonel Gadafi's support for international terrorism. During the Iran–Iraq war of the late 1980s British and American warships patrolled Gulf shipping lanes endangered by the conflict.

These excursions were taken by some in the British foreign policy community as evidence of the ability of the UK to play an effective world role, and to 'punch above its weight' in conflict situations. More critical responses questioned the value of such commitments to Britain and expressed unease at the over-stretching of British military resources and defence budgets to suit American interests. These fears have been exacerbated by more lavish, and potentially long-term, interventions in the 1990s. The ending of the Cold War between 1989 and 1991, when the Soviet Union collapsed, left the USA as the only superpower worth the name, but still in need of a little help from its friends in a world that was, if anything, more dangerous and volatile.

As part of the Gulf War coalition against Iraqi aggression in Kuwait in 1990, Britain contributed the second largest contingent to the **multilateral** force and has been a mainstay of UN and NATO interventions in parts of the former Yugoslavia. In 1999, under New Labour, Tony Blair was outspoken in his calls for NATO military action to reverse the forced expulsion of ethnic Albanians from Kosovo. The USA was seen as laggard in its commitment to intervention on humanitarian grounds, allowing Britain to take the moral high ground and Blair's leadership and hawkish position on the issue were no doubt principled. They were also a calculated play to demonstrate his credentials as an international statesman by reinforcing claims that New Labour was determined to be 'at the heart of Europe', if not in the first tranche of states to join a single currency, then in matters of defence and foreign policy. An apparent commitment to entanglements in one key area of policy and continued ambivalence about another is characteristic of Britain's demeanour over Europe, but looks increasingly uncomfortable as the stakes get bigger.

Over the years the perception of British subservience to the United States and its relative aloofness from developments on the mainland of Europe have made it difficult for governments to appear anything like sold on European integration. Britain's first two attempts to join the then European Economic Community (EEC) in1961–3 and 1967–8, foundered, in part, on the fears of France that Britain would be a 'Trojan horse' for American influence, as much as on the antipathy of the British for supra-national institutions. During these years, a grudging recognition that the fledgling EEC was becoming increasingly important to Britain's trading economy gradually overcame the reluctance to join a Western European economic order, but never extinguished the sense that almost any movement towards partnership would compromise British sovereignty. Britain finally joined the renamed European Community on 1 January 1973.

Britain and Europe

In many ways, the image of Britain as a reluctant European rings true, but many states in post-war Europe were also ambivalent about surrendering decision-making autonomy and abandoning national identity. As states recovered from their wartime travails, they became more selective in their commitment to co-operation. From the early 1950s, economic co-operation prospered through such bodies as the European Coal and Steel Community (ECSC) in 1952. At Messina in 1955, the six members of the ECSC took the decision to extend 'functional co-operation' to a much wider range of economic activity. The result was the EEC (1957). No such agreement existed over defence matters, and the European Defence Community, bruited as one of the three strands of a European Political Community (EPC) in 1952, proved abortive. The plans to amalgamate the ECSC, the EDC and the Council of Europe (the latter body first proposed by Churchill in 1945) were far too ambitious in what was still a quite fragile climate of co-operation. Although Britain was founder member of the Council of Europe, it remained just an interested spectator as the momentum for greater economic collaboration built up in the 1950s. Following rebuffs in the 1960s, Britain secured membership of the EC in 1973 under the Heath government, only to have the new Labour administration under Harold Wilson promise the electorate that it would renegotiate more favourable terms of entry. This promise was directed at internal party divisions over Europe as much as anything else. In 1975, the British people endorsed membership in a referendum, but largely on the premise that it would be inconvenient to undo what had been done, rather than because of any great enthusiasm for the European venture.

During the Thatcher years, between 1979 and 1990, a more pronounced and systematic '**Euroscepticism**' came to dominate British policy towards the EC. During this period, the prime minister was committed to Atlanticism, especially to the role of the USA as guarantor of Western security. In language increasingly reminiscent of the older liberal discourse, free trade and freer markets became the economic orthodoxy, along with the need to adapt domestic policies and practices to meet global competition. Until 1987, the Labour Party's alternative economic strategy was unreconstructed national protectionism, consisting of withdrawal from Europe, controls on capital and imports and a greater degree of national self-sufficiency. If this stance was consistently anti-European and anti-global, the Conservative position was more nuanced, almost paradoxical, despite the abrasive rhetoric often used (for example in 1984, when Mrs Thatcher argued successfully for a reduction in the UK contribution to the EC budget and in her landmark speech to the College of Europe in Bruges in 1988). Thatcher herself was a supporter of an open world economy, and this is still an article of faith for many Conservatives who are either strongly pro- or anti-Europe. Belief in the virtues of the open market goes some way to explain Mrs Thatcher's support for the Single European Act of 1985. This was a measure that opened the way for an internal market in goods, services, capital and people in the EC by 1992, but which also curtailed the veto power of national governments through the introduction of qualified majority voting in some areas of Community policy. For Thatcher, the EC was a barrier to the sort of globalisation she advocated because it was (or was seen as) protectionist, bureaucratic and willing to countenance profligate levels of public spending. As an economic venture, it was acceptable only if it embraced the shock of competition and the discipline of market forces. At the same time, the SEA and the internal market promised a type of regionalism which would function as an integral and dynamic part of the open global economy, rather than as a hedge against it.

But the re-launch of European integration through the SEA was not just an acknowledgement of the need to be competitive in global markets. It was also the signal for a renewed commitment to economic and monetary union and political integration in Europe. Negotiations over the Maastricht Treaty on European Union in 1991–2 intensified British ambivalence over the shape of Europe and the UK's role in it. The treaty created a European Union, although in deference to British sensitivities the word 'federal' was deleted. This sop apart, the treaty once again threw into bold relief the tensions between a Europe based on the concept of ever closer union, requiring the 'deepening' of institutions and practices, and the preferred British model in which the EU would develop as an association of states, growing in number to accommodate entrants from the 'new' Europe to the east.

The compromise solution was to allow Britain (and Denmark) to 'opt out' of certain treaty provisions and postpone decisions on others. Thatcher's successor, John Major, did not share her antipathy to Europe *per se*, but was sensitive to divisions within his own party and pressured by sections of British business. At Maastricht he negotiated a separate protocol to the treaty that dealt with social affairs and labour relations (the Social Chapter) and exempted Britain from its very general conditions. In the other key area of agreeing a timetable for the final stages of monetary union, Britain was allowed to choose whether and when it wanted to join the single currency. In the event, the UK did not join the third stage of EMU on 1 January 1999, preferring to wait until the 'proper' conditions for entry are available.

BOX 2.3 MINI BIOGRAPHY

John Major (1943–)
British Conservative Prime Minister. Born London from humble beginnings, he progressed via grammar school to a post in banking and from thence to a place on Lambeth council. Elected to Commons for Huntingdon 1979 and rose quickly to be Foreign Secretary in 1989 and then Chancellor in 1990. When Thatcher fell he was seen as the man to inherit her mantle and he was premier for seven years although this period was marred by party disputes over Europe; criticisms of his conciliatory style as 'weakness' and the outbreak of 'sleaze' among his back-benchers from 1995 onwards. Finally he lost the 1997 election heavily and suffered the ignominy of being 'airbrushed' out of party history at the 1999 party conference.

Since 1987, the Labour Party has gone through a long and bitter process of re-invention, not least in terms of where it stands on Europe. Under Tony Blair, it has endorsed almost all the changes enacted by the Thatcher government, notably on the need to make British labour relations and working practices fit for the rigours of a global economy. The post-Maastricht agenda for economic and monetary union and for greater co-operation in foreign and security policy is still being played out in Britain and in other EU member states. The impact on the domestic politics of each state is likely to be considerable, not least on domestic political cleavages and on the ideological framework of party politics. As we shall see, Tony Blair has travelled some way beyond the Thatcherite belief in the open global economy and a 'flexible' domestic economy, while the Conservatives seem bent on revitalising the discourse of national sovereignty in the guise of anti-Europeanism.

Sensitivity to globalisation

The EU dimension of British policy is itself part of the trans-nationalising of domestic politics and policy linked to the processes of globalisation. These days no state in the mainstream of world politics and economics is immune from these processes. At the same time, states are more or less sensitive and vulnerable to global forces. In part this variability is explained by material factors such as economic strength or military capacity, but it is also affected by the secureness of national institutions and practices, by all manner of cultural legacies and by the vagaries of the domestic political agenda. In other words, the processes of globalisation do not simply write on states and societies as if they are blank pages. We can illustrate the complexities of the interaction between the local and the global by reference to two key areas of policy.

Erosion of the welfare state?

The welfare states built after the Second World War were intended to protect some aspects of economic life and some categories of people from the impact of market forces. For the most part this meant shielding the poor and other vulnerable groups in the population by providing benefits of various sorts, including security of income. It also meant pursuing full employment and investing in programmes of public health. Mainstream thinking on industrial policy allowed the business cycle to be regulated, encouraged cushioning of strategic industries and national champions from the harsher climates of competition, and advocated co-operative arrangements between employers and organised labour to promote wage stability. There was, of course, significant national variation in the ways in which these policies were applied, although the existence of a generic 'European social model' is acknowledged. The broad aims of the post-war systems of welfare capitalism were to remove obstacles to the efficient functioning of markets but, crucially, to guard against and compensate for market failures.

In the UK before 1979 there was a large public sector and a great deal of state investment in major UK-based manufacturing enterprises, such as Rolls-Royce and Ferranti (an electronics arms manufacturer). Governments of both left and right periodically sought to control prices and incomes, and trade unions enjoyed important rights to immunity from civil damages in many trade disputes. However, the social and political conditions in which welfare states and managed economies were established have changed since the 1970s. International recessions early in the decade and later, in the 1980s, forced the Western industrial nations (then other parts of the world) to reassess some of the basic tenets of welfare nationalism. Indeed it became routine to blame the social model for at least some of the economic difficulties besetting countries like the UK. Labour market regulation was blamed for restricting the efficient use of labour, the high social charges of social protection were blamed for making businesses uncompetitive and stifling the entrepreneurial spirit and high public spending was charged with precipitating fiscal crises and fuelling inflation. To make matters worse the 1970s were years of 'stagflation', that is the phenomenon of economic stagnation and rising unemployment, coupled with rising inflation. Previously, **Keynesian** thinking had it that serious inflation was something that only happened to immature economies and that judicious state intervention could promote both growth and social justice.

Keynesian economic policies that accorded priority to growth and full employment were now seen as profligate and likely to lose the confidence of financial markets, leading to a massive exodus of capital. In 1976, a crisis produced by government spending promises and a slide in the value of sterling on the money markets saw the IMF impose a deal on the Labour government of Harold Wilson. A promise of cuts in government spending signalled a shift in the direction of national policy, from investment in public and social services and full employment to tighter controls on public expenditure and inflation. While 'crises' with a remarkably similar script were not uncommon, 1976 was symbolic of the shift to an era when it was becoming unacceptable for British governments to increase spending if this unbalanced the budget. Raising taxes as a way of achieving balance also became suspect, as this caused capital to flee the country and unsettled the financial markets.

In an attempt to make the economy competitive, since the late 1970s UK governments have adopted strategies that are much more market led. These include the reduction of taxation as a goal of public policy, greater flexibility in labour markets, the removal, through deregulation, of various obstacles to competition and a commitment to reducing the size of the public sector. Government has also placed great weight on the need for the acquisition of skills and training relevant to an enterprise culture in a global economy. In this sea-change, the Conservative Party under Margaret Thatcher was the driving force, embracing the disciplines of the market, where the Labour governments of Wilson and Callaghan had been reluctant converts to limiting government spending and controlling the money supply.

Under Thatcher, the rhetoric of the global marketplace flourished and became a canon of economic policy. In the midst of these changes, basic welfare provisions remained or were subject to only limited 'roll-back'. At the same time, data for the 1980s show that all of the countries that adopted neo-liberal formulas experienced deepening inequality and rising poverty. In the UK, between 1980 and 1990, earnings in the lowest decile of the workforce lost ground relative to the median, by some 14 per cent. There was also a substantial rise in what has become known as 'child poverty', because of the low earning capacity of many single mothers and the limited, but real, decline in some state benefits. The Labour Party adopted its radical *alternative economic strategy*, but remained unelected, and, on some accounts, unelectable. In its guise as New Labour, the party in government after 1997 has sought a notional 'third way', a means of 'combining economic dynamism with social justice in the modern world', as Mr Blair said at a dinner in The Hague in 1998. New Labour is as committed to an open economy as were the Conservatives. Its preferred methods – fighting inflation, controlling the money supply and relaxing controls on financial markets and the movement of capital – are classic neo-liberal tenets. It is also attempting to address what are known as 'supply-side' weaknesses in the UK economy through skills training, education reform, technology developments and reviews of the transport infrastructure. In the broadest sense of the term, Mr Blair is keen to make Britons employable in what he now sees as a global economy. At the same time, the government has been engaged in a modest re-investment in social protection – the restoration of some rights for trade unionists, the establishment of a national minimum wage and the adoption of the European Social Chapter. The impact of these measures is hard to gauge in the short term, but for some observers they pit New Labour policies against the received global wisdom from bodies like the IMF, whose recipe for good governance is profoundly neo-liberal. Instead of the Thatcherite mantra that macroeconomic parsimony will produce 'trickle down' social benefits, New Labour's stance intimates a renewed flirtation with state-sponsored capitalism, or perhaps a form of 'globalisation with a human face'. However, in Mr Blair's own words, such measures still leave the UK 'the most lightly regulated labour market of any leading economy in the world'.

Global finance

From the end of the Second World War up to the early 1970s the economic system of the Western world had been based on the Bretton Woods agreement. In July 1944, as the war was drawing to a close, the world's leading politicians – mostly from Northern countries – met in conference to reorganise the world economy. The Conference opted for a system based on the free movement of capital and goods with the US dollar as the international currency. By the late 1960s, the Bretton Woods dream of a stable monetary system of fixed exchange rates with the US dollar as the only international currency was collapsing under the strain of US trade and budgetary deficits. In the early 1970s, British governments of both main parties jumped on board the roller-coaster of floating exchange rates, borrowing heavily to finance expenditure on the welfare state, letting sterling fall in value to stimulate exports and pegging interest rates as low as possible. Such moves only served to mask the UK's deterioration in the world economy. Eventually, rising inflation, and loss of foreign reserves pushed the government into the arms of the IMF in 1976.

The increased openness and vulnerability of the British economy to the global economy after 1976 required national government to exercise fiscal prudence and to control inflation, as earnest of their neo-liberal credentials. In October 1979, the new Conservative government abolished exchange controls, just as the USA had done. The boost to inward investment encouraged Mrs Thatcher to support the Single European Act in 1985 in the expectation that this trend would continue. Once exchange controls had been abandoned in 1979, government efforts were directed at encouraging both inward and outward investment and accepting (at least in principle) the policy constraints imposed by the financial markets. In practice, in the mid-to-late 1980s, the Conservatives pushed ahead with expansion of the economy and cuts in income tax, showing a blithe disregard for the ways in which the markets would react. The upshot was a growing balance of payments deficit and high inflation. By the autumn of 1990 the government was presiding over an over-heated economy moving into recession, an exchange rate that was unsustainably high and a loss of confidence in sterling.

To counteract these debilitating factors and to ease pressure from the markets by stabilising sterling, Mrs Thatcher took Britain into the Exchange Rate Mechanism (ERM) a device which linked the exchange rates of the currencies of all participating member states in the EC to each other and to the European Currency Unit (ECU). The ERM was a mechanism of the European Monetary System (EMS), which was set up in 1979 as the basis on which to build monetary co-operation and eventual monetary union in the EC. The UK (along with Spain and later Portugal) was allowed a margin of fluctuation of up to 6 per cent above or below the central rate. The underlying rationale of the ERM was that, if currencies reached their tolerances, the Central banks of other member states would intervene to support them. By 1992, under the premiership of John Major, the bankruptcy of this policy and the fragility of British membership was exposed owing to massive instabilities in the currency markets and heavy speculative activity against some of the weaker currencies. On 'Black Wednesday', 16 September 1992, the UK suspended its membership of the ERM and allowed sterling to float. Italy followed suit on 17 September. In response to all these movements of 'hot money', members of the ERM had already agreed on 2 August 1992 to widen the bands within which currencies could float, to plus or minus 15 per cent.

Since then, governments in the UK have pursued policies intended to please the markets. These involve tight control over inflation, with a preference for monetary policy (manipulating interest rates and money supply) rather than fiscal policy (taxation) as the means to achieve this end. In this respect the Major and Blair governments have been at one, although both have increased the overall burden of taxation. In fact the success of these measures in removing the sobriquet 'sick man of Europe' from the UK has been contingent on factors beyond the direct control of the government. Chief among these have been the strength of the US dollar since 1995 and Britain's more favourable position in the economic cycle relative to rivals Germany and Japan. In addition, under Tony Blair and his Chancellor of the Exchequer, Gordon Brown, a minor revolution has taken place, which goes beyond the Thatcherite mission to roll back the state. Early in the new administration, the Bank of England was given operational freedom to set interest rates, a clear sign to global markets that the government is sticking to the anti-inflationary core of its economic policy. For some commentators, this change is a clear indication that Britain is willing to join European monetary union sooner rather than later.

Britain and the EMU

The decision to join or not to join the process of Economic and Monetary Union (EMU) in Europe once again reveals the tensions in UK–EU relationships, because monetary powers are seen as central to a state's independence and authority. It also highlights some of the ways in which global trends in finance are influencing national policy-making arrangements. Finally, the process offers pointers to the repositioning of the main political parties and other actors in what it is increasingly hard to call domestic politics.

In ratifying the Maastricht Treaty on European Union during 1992–3, most member states of the EU committed themselves to the 'irrevocable' locking together of their currencies from 1 January 1999. Britain, Denmark, Sweden and Greece were not among the first tranche of countries to create what has become known in the UK as 'Euroland' (Figure 2.4), but only the UK and Denmark have not committed themselves to joining as soon as possible. The Maastricht Treaty provides the legal underpinning for EMU and identifies three main stages through which that goal can be achieved. The first, already in train when member states met at Maastricht in December 1991, concerned the free movement of capital; the second, starting on 1 January 1994, dealt with preparations for the single currency, including the creation of a European Monetary Institute, to be dissolved in the third stage, and certain convergence criteria against which potential members could be judged. The third stage, beginning on 1 January 1999, establishes an independent European Central Bank and formally introduces the single currency (the Euro). 'Euro' banknotes and coins are scheduled for introduction in 2001, when they will replace the national variety.

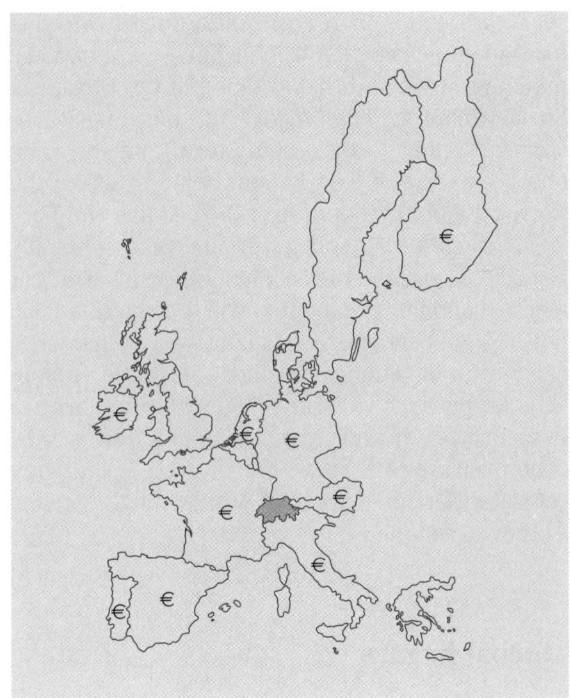

Figure 2.4 Euroland on 1 January 1999

The policy of the Blair government is to prepare to join the EMU, subject to five economic tests announced in October 1997. These tests are intended to judge membership in relation to whether it is good for jobs, trade, investment and industry in Britain. In a speech delivered on 14 October 1999 at the launch of the pro-Euro 'Britain in Europe' campaign, the Prime Minister reiterated his European sympathies, but, with an eye on public opinion, stated only that he 'would not rule out' British membership of EMU. The government sees some possible economic obstacles to membership, and some political hurdles to overcome, but no constitutional barrier to participating. It is committed, or apparently so, to holding a referendum on the subject of entry. In reality, British public opinion is deeply divided about the merits of a single currency. In opposition, the Conservative Party, fractured by feuds over Europe, opposes a decision to join EMU on both economic and constitutional grounds, either in the current parliament or the next. After that, in the familiar language, a decision to join is not ruled out.

Control of money has always been closely linked with national sovereignty, but, as we have suggested above, sovereignty over monetary policy is quite limited in an era of global finance. Indeed, one of the underlying justifications for EMU is that in recent years it has become less possible to exercise national power over monetary policy. That said, political debate within the UK still rehearses familiar arguments about looking for some more 'natural' grouping through which to manage currency issues, such the G7 group of leading industrial and trading nations. The arguments for joining EMU turn on the extent to which the UK would be marginalised in EU decision making if it stayed out and pushed into the second rank of European states. At the same time, it may be that the UK is still a big enough economy in world terms to chance its arm and stay outside. But for many people in the UK, the biggest question about the Euro is not economic gain or loss, but whether it will lead to fiscal union and then full political union. A single European currency will probably encourage a European economy that is at least as integrated as national economies are now, but there remains a large element of uncertainty about whether it will be successful. The prospects for the Euro being no more than a 'soft' currency in world terms, and subject to the same sorts of speculation it was designed to inhibit, are still a possibility.

Of course, it is not clear how far monetary union will necessitate closer integration in other matters deemed critical to national autonomy and sovereignty. When the UK government passed the Bank of England Act 1998, which gave the Bank independent powers to set interest rates, this was widely interpreted as paving the way for EMU. But in a world of deregulated currency markets and global financial flows, both governments and central banks have relatively little influence, although they can affect the climate in which changes take place. The creation of independent central banks is symptomatic of this era of global finance, because they are seen usually as the guardians of financial probity and committed to low inflation. For the financial markets, banks are more likely to preach the disciplines of the market than are politicians. While the Bank of England Act looks like a prelude to membership of EMU, the independence of central banks is really a function of globalisation.

In the midst of very technical discussions about EMU, other issues contribute to a richer politics of monetary union and Europeanisation. These issues include whether there are the means for holding the European Central Bank accountable, the fight to avoid relegating key items on the national political agenda, such as social protection, to the status of mere 'technical' data, and the impact of shared sovereignty on the decision-making autonomy and political culture of the UK. In the absence of British membership of EMU it is wrong to speculate too much on future constellations of politics in the UK. However, strains within political parties over EMU may result in new cross-party groupings, and in a fully integrated European economy there may well be transnational political parties. The neo-liberal agenda which has dominated UK politics and policy for two decades continues as a major constraint on policy makers. It is reflected too in the EU's 'Stability and Growth Pact' which acts as a benchmark for potential members of EMU. Regionalisation and globalisation now inform the very core of British political life.

Conclusion

For much of the past 200 years the United Kingdom has been involved in global matters, principally because of economic factors, but also through its status as a colonial power and key player in global geo-politics. Even during those periods when certain anti-global or protectionist sentiments characterised domestic politics, for example between 1914 and the late 1970s, Britain never ceased to be deeply involved in the global economy and embroiled in regional and global conflicts. Over this period the language or discourse of globalisation has informed much of national policy and been the context for a good deal of domestic politics. This includes both the 'high' politics of international diplomacy and the 'low' politics constituted by party conflict, organised interests and, occasionally, public opinion. It is accurate to say that, over the whole period, Britain has declined as a global power, so that at the close of the millennium it is largely shorn of the trappings of greatness. This is not to say that the UK is a clear-cut example of a modal phenomenon – the demise of the nation-state. Nation-states have been weakened by the forces of globalisation and some forms of regionalisation, but they are far from demise. Rather, there is a long-term transformation of the political architecture of world politics, in which states continue as important actors in a rich weave of formal and informal organisations, local, national, international and trans-national. It follows from what we have said above that an awareness of and accommodation to global constraints has been an enduring feature of UK politics over the years, and that while these constraints seem to be intensifying, their impact remains inchoate.

Chapter summary

- The UK was a global power for much of the last 200 years.
- Globalisation has been a major feature of British policy and political debate for all of this period, and in the last thirty years its significance has been on the increase.
- Britain's engagement with the global political economy can be conveniently periodised into that of hegemonic stability; post-hegemonic instability; bi-polar stability and multi-polar flux.
- Periods of *laissez-faire* liberalism and global neo-liberalism have been separated by interludes of national protectionism, but openness to the world economy has been an underlying theme.
- After the Second World War, Britain, a much diminished power, still clung to a global role through empire and was firmly Atlanticist rather than European.
- Grudging engagement with European integration has introduced an important regional dimension to British politics, the parameters of which are still emerging.
- Global and regional constraints have had impacts on welfare policy and on financial policy.
- The EMU process exemplifies many of the issues about national autonomy and sovereignty that lie at the heart of debate on globalisation.

Discussion points

- Is globalisation a process that affects you? For example, could you name any global factors which influence the way you, or people like you, live?
- Thinking about the impact of globalisation upon the UK, what sort of advantages and disadvantages are apparent? How would you weigh the balance?
- Do you think that Britain made the right choice in the early post-war years in giving European integration a low priority?
- Will global pressures push the UK into membership of EMU, or is there still room for manoeuvre?
- In what ways do you see British domestic politics changing because of European and global pressures?

Further reading

Hirst (1999): an iconoclastic account of the misuse of the concept of globalisation, in which the authors contend that nation-states remain key actors in global politics and economics.

Kennedy (1988): an account of the factors contributing to the rise and fall of the Great Powers since 1500. A book which had a great impact in academic and governmental circles on both sides of the Atlantic.

Krieger (1999): a case for the renewal of social democracy in an age of intense globalisation.

References

Axford, B. (1997) 'The processes of globalisation', in B. Axford, G.K. Browning, R. Huggins, B. Rosamond, J. Turner (eds), *Politics: an Introduction* (Routledge), pp. 475–511.

Calvocoressi, P. (1996) *World Politics Since 1945*, 7th edn (Longman).

Coates, D. (1994) *The Question of UK Decline* (Harvester Wheatsheaf).

Held, D., McGrew, A., Goldblatt, D. and Perraton, J. (1999) *Global Transformations: Politics, Economics and Culture* (Polity).

Hirst, P. and Thompson, G. (1999) *Globalization in Question*, 2nd edn (Polity).

Hutton, W. (1995) *The State We're In* (Cape).

Kennedy, P. (1988) *The Rise and Fall of the Great Powers: Economic Change and Military Conflict, 1500–2000* (Fontana).

Krieger, J. (1999) *British Politics in the Global Age: Can Social Democracy Survive?* (Polity).

Chapter 3

The social and economic contexts

Michael Moran

Learning objectives

- To sketch the social and economic settings of British politics.
- To explain how the national setting is part of a wider global and European system.
- To identify the main patterns of change in the social and economic contexts.
- To show how the wider global and European setting is continuing to reshape British politics and society.

Introduction

No political system operates in a vacuum. Everything that happens in politics is affected by the social and economic context within which institutions have to operate. Part of that context is internal to Britain, and consists of the social hierarchies and economic structures of British society. Part is external to Britain, and consists of the wider global economy and the developing European economy and political system of which Britain is a part. The chapter introduces both the internal and the external aspects of the social and economic settings.

Britain in a global setting

The best way to start is with the geography of the United Kingdom, because this is both the most basic aspect of the social and economic setting and the most obvious way to appreciate the significance of Britain's location in a wider world. Viewed in this way several features of the UK become clear:

1. It is small: only 244.1 thousand square kilometres.
2. It is densely populated: the number of persons per square kilometre in 1993 was just over 240, against an average for the fifteen members of the European Union of 115.
3. It is industrial: only 2 per cent of employed men work on the land.
4. It is rich: we live in one of a small number of rich countries in a largely poor world. Viewed internationally, the arguments about the allocation of resources in Britain are arguments between comparatively well off groups of people. Figure 3.1(a) illustrates Britain's long-term position in the 'league table' of world wealth. Despite long-term decline we remain in the 'premier league' of wealth as Figure 3.1(b) illustrates. That is reflected in the life chances of the British people compared with those of other inhabitants of the globe: life expectancy in the United Kingdom is seventy-five for men and eighty for women; in Africa the comparable figures are fifty-two and fifty-five.
5. It is capitalist: '**capitalism**' here is a neutral description; it describes a system where property is privately owned, and where goods and services are traded for a price by free exchange in markets.

Viewed from the 'outside', therefore, British society can look uniform. But when we examine it more closely, variety appears.

One of the most striking sources of variation is geography. Britain is a 'multi-national state': that is, it is a political unit ruled by a single sovereign authority but composed of territories which historically were different nations, and whose populations still retain distinct national identities.

There are at least five different national groupings in the United Kingdom: the English, Welsh, Scottish, Irish and those (mostly Protestants in Northern Ireland) who identify with 'Ulster'. Identity has been further complicated by another feature which reflects the fact that Britain is part of a wider global system: immigration. The United Kingdom has periodically received waves of immigrants

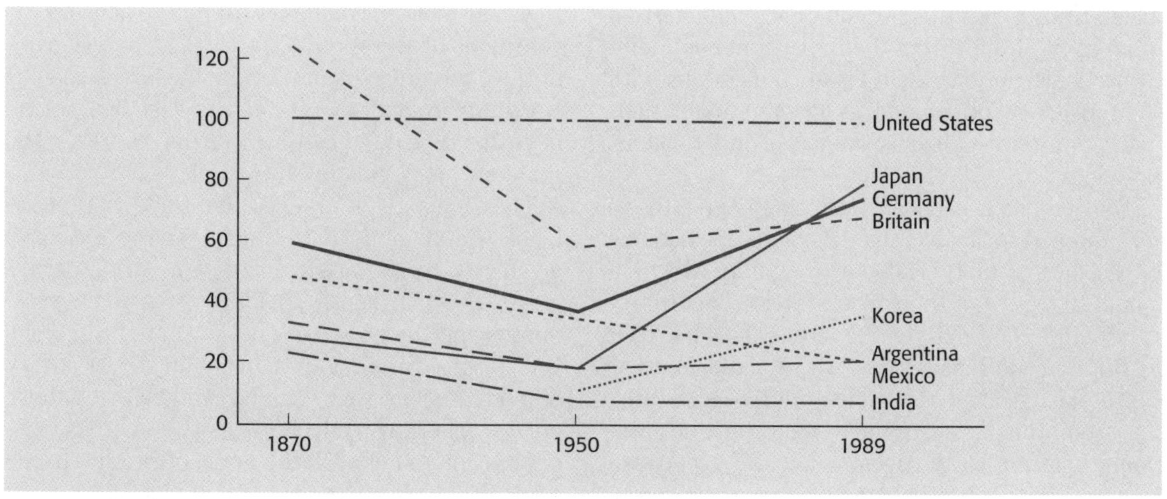

Figure 3.1(a) The wealth of Britain, compared over time with other countries
Source: The Economist, 20 June 1992, p. 155

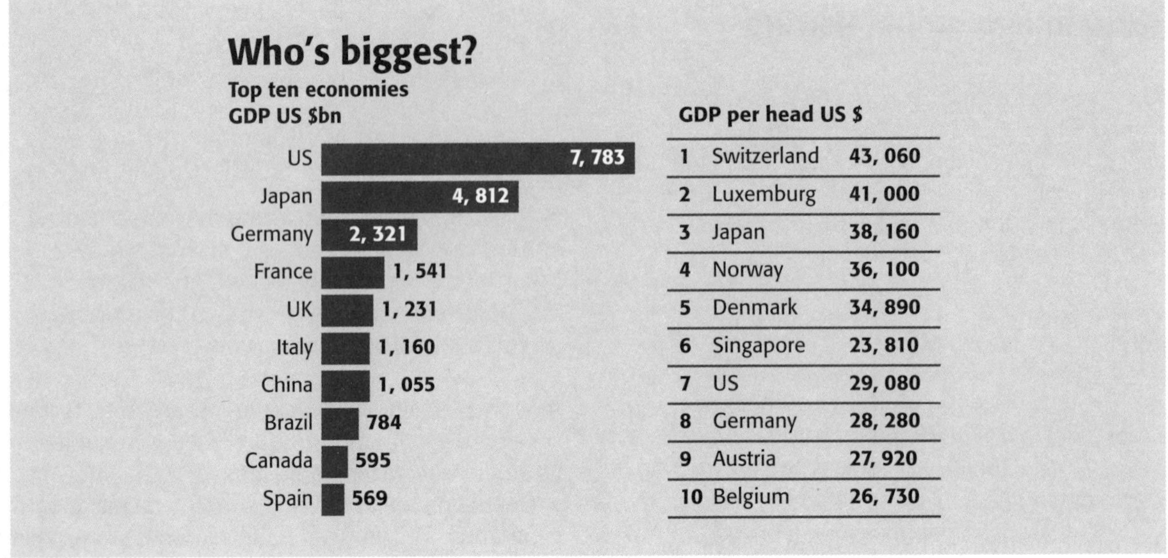

Figure 3.1(b) GDP per capita
Source: The Guardian, 9 September 1999

from abroad and in the 1950s and 1960s received particularly large numbers from what is conventionally called the 'new Commonwealth' – notably from our former colonial possessions in the West Indies and the Indian sub-continent. These immigrants and their children are for the most part permanently settled in Britain and are citizens of the community. They are conventionally called 'black Britons' but this oversimplifies the question of identity. Groups from the Indian sub-continent, in particular, often retain close connections with their place of origin and in Britain retain their own distinctive cultures, language and religious practices.

The question of national identity in Britain is therefore more complicated than the simple existence of a political unity called the United Kingdom would suggest. But there is a further aspect to territorial differences. Even the most casual traveller in Britain soon realizes that within national areas there exist striking variations – differences ranging from the most profound cultural and economic matters to the most mundane aspects of everyday life. Even inside the biggest nation in the United Kingdom, England, there also exist striking regional differences.

Although the actual figures change with time, for several decades real income in the south-east of England, and accompanying measures of well-being such as employment, have been more favourable than in any other part of the United Kingdom. The south-east is the powerhouse of the United Kingdom economy and – another sign of the impact of the wider global setting – in many ways has more in common with rich regions on the continent of Europe than with the poorest parts of the United Kingdom. Conversely, areas such as Northern Ireland and the north-west of England have for decades been among the poorest. The scale of this is illustrated in Table 3.1.

The regional differences identified here have been widely noticed in recent years and have given rise to the argument that in Britain there exists a 'north–south' divide between the prosperous and the poor parts of the United Kingdom. But despite the undoubted gaps in the wealth of different regions, such characterizations are, at best, only a part of the truth. There exist numerous prosperous communities in the north of Britain. In the heart of the prosperous south, in parts of London for instance, there are by contrast greatly impoverished communities. Part of the reason for this is

Table 3.1 Regional inequality in Britain, 1995

	South-east	West Midlands	East Anglia	South-west	East Midlands	Wales	North-west	Yorkshire and Humberside	North	Scotland	Northern Ireland
% of working age with a degree	17.1	10.6	12.1	11.6	10.6	11.5	12.1	11.4	9.9	12.7	11.0
Gross average weekly earnings per head (£)	437.5	346.3	341.2	349.6	338.2	331.4	354.2	337.1	331.7	350.7	330.9
Unemployed rate (%)	7.9	8.4	6.2	7.0	7.7	8.5	8.8	8.8	10.6	8.2	11.4
Perinatal mortality rate 1984–6[a]	5.5	5.3	5.2	5.3	6.9	6.2	6.2	7.7	6.3	6.2	6.1
% of households with one car or more (1994)	71	69	69	65	69	67	69	67	59	62	65

[a] Births and deaths under one week of age per 1,000 live and still births
Source: Regional Trends, 1995

that overlaying any divisions between regions are important differences between various parts of urban areas in Britain. See Figure 3.2 as evidence supporting the view that the north–south divide is less important than the differences within each region.

Urban problems and the city

It is common to speak of the 'urban problem' in Britain or, in the same breath, of 'the problems of the inner city'. But there is actually a wide array of social features summed up in a single phrase like the 'urban problem'. Similarly, although the 'inner city' has become a byword for poverty and misery, many areas of inner cities (witness parts of London) are the homes of the rich and fashionable, while in outer suburbs and even in rural areas there are, especially on public housing estates, areas of deep poverty. Nevertheless, a number of long-term social changes have combined to alter the character of the giant cities which were the characteristic creation of Britain's industrial revolution. Two should be noted.

Firstly, long-term shifts in population have changed both the numbers living in many inner city areas and the social balance of the remaining population. The figures of movement tell the story. Between 1981 and 1994, for instance, the population of Cheshire rose by 4.6 per cent, while that of Greater Manchester fell by 1.6 per cent. In the 'booming' south-east the population of Greenwich fell by 1.0 per cent, while the population of Buckinghamshire rose by 15.4 per cent.

This shift of population out of established areas of cities to suburbs and small towns reflects a second change: population decline is commonly a reflection of economic decline and social crisis. Often the white middle classes leave and the poor plus new immigrants tend to remain. The cities of the industrial revolution have seen their economic foundations decay as the traditional industries have decayed, with important consequences for prosperity and financial stability. In the biggest cities, especially London, 'averages' conceal huge inequalities in wealth, health and life chances.

Work and unemployment

Work is a central part of each individual's life – whether the worker is the unrewarded housewife

Divided Britain

1 Scotland
Significant variations in economic activity. Unemployment ranges from 2% in Shetland to 9.7% in West Dumbarton.

2 Northern Ireland
Economy performing relatively strongly. But long-term unemployment much higher than in rest of UK.

3 North-west
Merseyside has 'one of the most serious concentrations of unemployment' in Europe yet neighbouring Cheshire is one of England's most prosperous areas.

4 North-east
Lowest average house prices in Britain includes some of the most severely deprived communities in the contry.

5 Yorkshire and Humberside
Clusters of new knowledge-based businesses, But worrying gap – 'more important than north–south divide' – between rich and poor in two-speed cities, such as Leeds.

6 East Midlands
Considerable growth in information technology and insurance. Unemployment below average. But significant problems of deprivation.

7 West Midlands
Most heavily dependent on manufacturing. Unemployment gap with south-east begining to widen.

8 Wales
Successful in attracting overseas investment. High levels of permanent sickness affecting one in six of population.

9 South-west
Higher proportion of self-employed than any other region. Rural poverty and isolation; marked inequalities between accessible and remote areas.

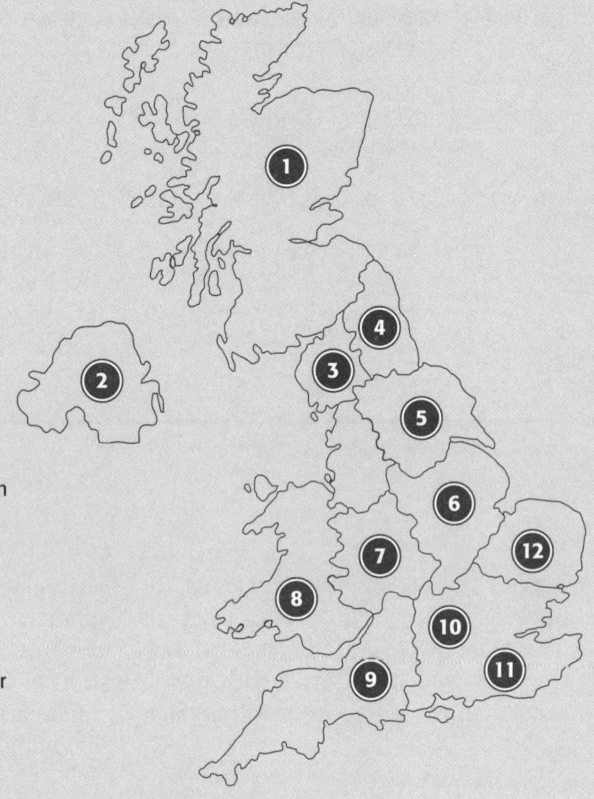

10 South-east
Described as advanced, high-cost and high-income. Good roads, with growing congestion. Deprived areas in Kent and along south coast. Jobless rate varies from 0.8% to 8.6%.

11 London
Accounts for 15% of UK GDP and 4m jobs UK wide. But prosperity disguises problems of severe poverty. Cost of living highest in UK.

12 Eastern England
Low unemployment and higher GDP per head than most regions. Significant concentration of R&D businesses, bio-technology and communications businesses arround Cambridge.

Figure 3.2 Regional differences in the UK
Source: The Guardian, 7 December 1999

or company chief executive earning £500,000 a year. But the nature of work is also important for wider social reasons. Occupation is the single most important influence on the social structure. The kind of work done is a key determinant of the material rewards and the status an individual enjoys. Indeed the class structure in Britain closely corresponds to the occupational structure. Definitions of class commonly mean **occupational class**: 'working class', for instance, usually refers to those people – and their families – who earn a living from 'manual' jobs. The central place of occupation in the political life of the country is well illustrated by the case of voting and elections, where occupational class has been, and remains, a key influence on the way people vote. Work is central to the life of the individual, but it is also central to the economic structure. Four aspects of this centrality are notable.

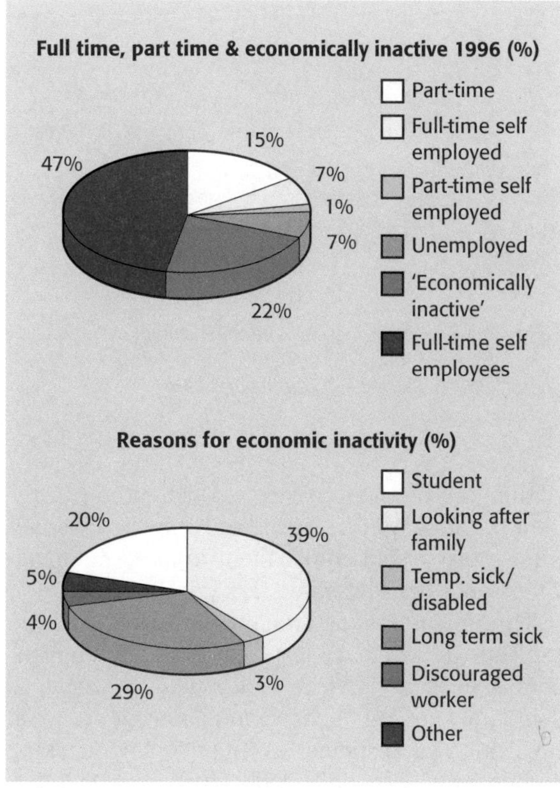

Figure 3.3
(a) Full time, part time and economically inactive, 1996
(b) Reasons for economic inactivity
Source: Jamieson, B. (1999) Illustrated Guide to the British Economy (Duckworth), p. 227

Most people in Britain live by selling their labour

Britain is a market economy in which the only significant tradeable resource controlled by the majority of the population is labour. There are indeed exceptions: a small minority of the wealthy control sufficient productive property to be able to live on the returns of that property; a larger group – such as pensioners, unemployed, some students – live off state-provided benefits. But most individuals either live by selling their labour to others, or – as in the case of children – are dependent on 'breadwinners'. Figure 3.3(a), gives the proportions of full- to part-time workers while Figure 3.3(b) provides the reasons for economic inactivity.

Most people sell their labour to private firms

Because Britain is a capitalist society only a minority of the workforce is employed in the public sector. Until the beginning of the 1980s there had occurred a long-term increase in the size of this minority – so marked that some observers argued that excessive growth of public sector employment was a main cause of Britain's economic difficulties. This trend has been reversed. A combination of cuts in numbers employed in public services and the **privatization** of many important industries means that the dominance of private firms as employers has been reinforced in recent years.

Women are becoming important in the work-force

Women have always worked but they have not always been paid for working. For example, until the beginning of this century 'domestic service' was a major source of paid employment for women. Social change has since almost eliminated domestic servants and their jobs are now done for

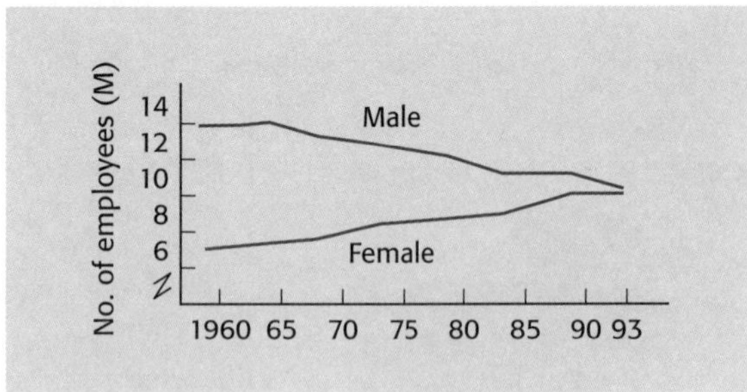

Figure 3.4 Trends in male and female employment in Britain
Source: The Economist, 11 December 1993

nothing by mothers, wives and daughters. In recent decades women – especially married women – have taken paid employment in large numbers. The trends are illustrated in Figure 3.4.

Three features of women's work should be noticed. Firstly, it is disproportionately concentrated in the 'service' sector and in what is sometimes called 'light manufacturing' – work involving, for instance, assembling and packing components. Secondly, while just over half the population are women, far more than half of working women are in jobs with low pay and status and far less than half are in high-status jobs: a disproportionately high proportion of women are cleaners in universities, and a disproportionately low number are teachers in them. Thirdly, women occupy a disproportionate number of casual and part-time jobs in the workforce. This observation links to the final feature of work and employment on which we focus.

Unemployment and part-time work have become more common

There has always been unemployment in Britain. For over three decades after 1940, however, it was conventional to speak of the existence of 'full employment'. Only a small proportion of the workforce was out of a job: in 1975, for instance, there were only 838,000 (3 per cent) registered unemployed. Unemployment, moreover, was largely accounted for by individuals who were unemployable (for instance through ill health) and by relatively high levels of joblessness in a few depressed parts of the country (for example, communities over-reliant on a single declining industry).

This era of full employment has gone. For over two decades now, large-scale unemployment has been the norm: the figure for registered unemployed topped one million by 1976, two million by 1981, three million by 1984; it only finally fell below two million again in the late 1990s. Even more significantly, unemployment has ceased to be a transient experience because the numbers of long-term unemployed have grown greatly. The unemployed are disproportionately concentrated among predictable groups: those with few or no formal educational qualifications; those who live in areas where the local economy is depressed; and those who come from some ethnic minorities (see Figure 3.5).

It is often pointed out that even in an era of mass unemployment the overwhelming majority of adults are nevertheless in work and that while jobs are lost in some industries they are being created in others. This is correct, but simple measures of job numbers fail to reveal important changes which are occurring in the structure of the workforce. Full-time jobs in manufacturing have been lost and have been disproportionately replaced by temporary or part-time jobs in the service sector. This hints at a division in the population which may in time become as significant as the divide between the employed and the unemployed. To an increasing degree large employers are dividing their workforce into a 'core' and a 'periphery'. The 'core' consists of workers in secure, long-term employment. There is also a tendency for these to be the better qualified and to enjoy the best pay and fringe benefits. The 'periphery' consists of a shifting group of temporary employees who can be taken on, and laid off, according to demand. There is a corresponding tendency for these workers to be disproportionately women, to be doing less-skilled jobs and to be comparatively poorly rewarded. The 'dual' labour market, as it is sometimes called, offers considerable advantages to employers. Temporary and casual labour is comparatively cheap, most of them are poorly

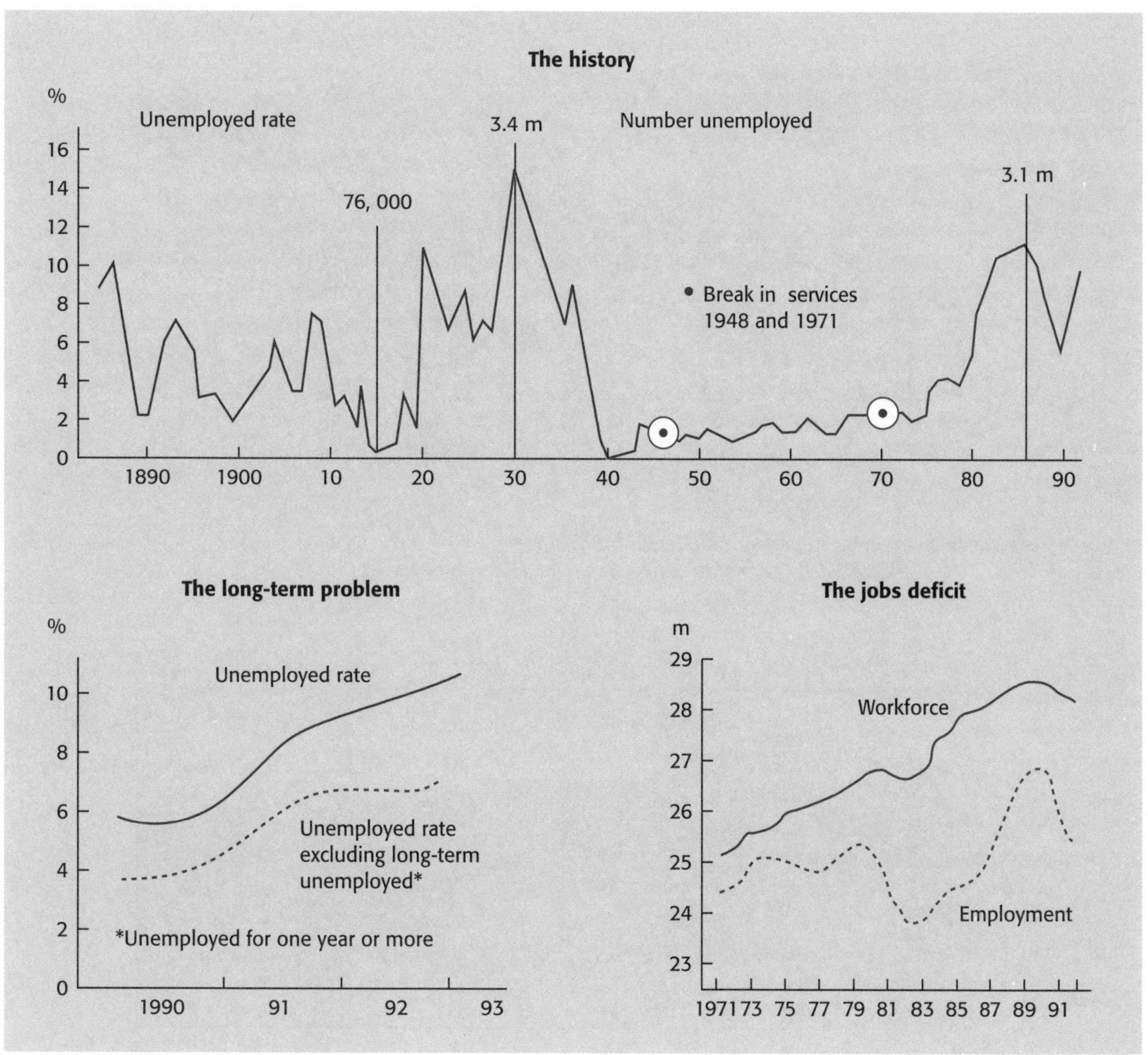

Figure 3.5(a) Anatomy of unemployment
Source: The Economist, 20 February 1993

organised in unions and legal protection against such eventualities as dismissal is more limited than in the case of the permanent workforce. Thus employers can use their 'peripheral' workforce in a highly flexible way to respond to changing market conditions.

For most people in Britain, their labour amounts to the only serious economic asset at their disposal. But for a minority economic resources come in the form of a considerable stock of wealth. This is examined next.

Wealth, property and the social structure

Only one thing can be said with certainty about the distribution of wealth in Britain: it has long been, in statistical terms, highly unequal. But the meaning and even the accuracy of the bald statistics are perhaps more uncertain here than in any other area of British society. Beyond the general proposition that a statistically small

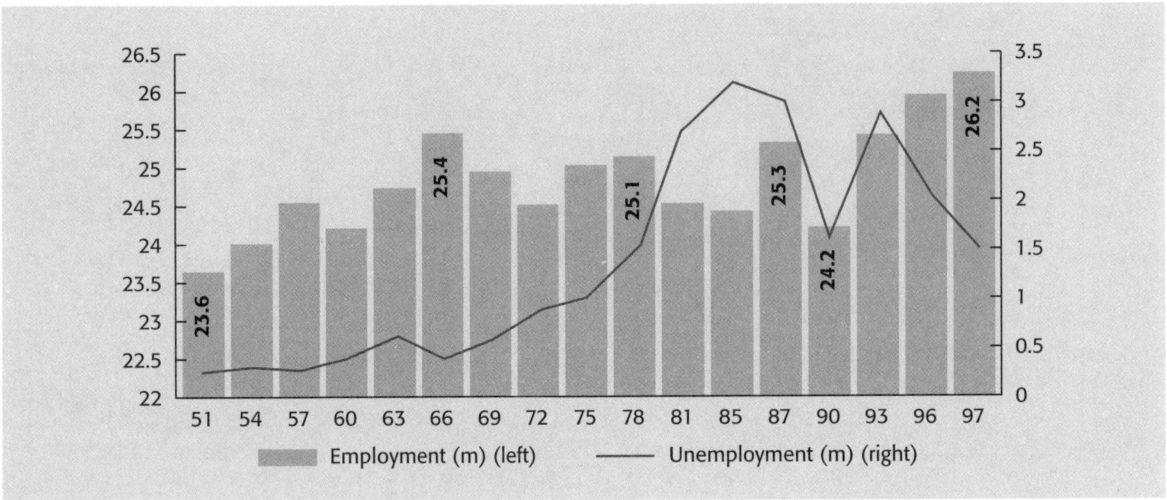

Figure 3.5(b) Workforce in employment and total unemployment
Source: Jamieson, B. (1999) Illustrated Guide to the British Economy (Duckworth), p. 221

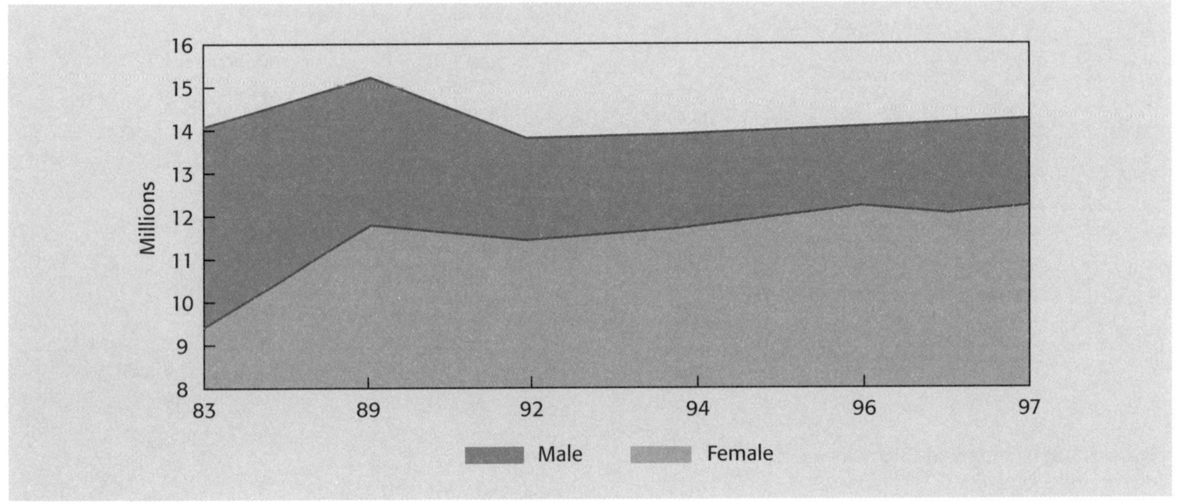

Figure 3.5(c) Rise in women at work
Source: Jamieson, B. (1999) Illustrated Guide to the British Economy (Duckworth), p. 221

group owns an arithmetically large amount of the nation's wealth, there exists little agreement.

Debate starts with the very significance of inequality. For some, the existence of a minority of very wealthy people in Britain is a good thing and any diminution of the wealth of the few a bad thing. According to this argument, great wealth is desirable because it shows the ability of the market system to reward the enterprising with great incentives, thus encouraging innovation and risk taking in the economy. In addition, the wealthy are a socially important group, because although a minority they are still, in absolute terms, large in number. This means that they support social diversity by, for example, sponsoring a variety of political causes, charities and artistic activities.

BOX 3.1

fact

Labour as an economic resource

The vast majority of employees in Britain are united by one single important feature: their labour power is their only significant economic resource. But otherwise employees in Britain are fragmented into numerous groups:

1. public-sector and private-sector workers;
2. manual and non-manual workers;
3. workers in service and manufacturing sectors;
4. part-timers and full-timers.

Without the wealthy, according to this view, society would be dull, uniform and dominated by the state. On the other hand, critics of the social order in Britain maintain that control of great wealth by a minority is illegitimate. It appropriates what is properly the wealth of the community for a few and contradicts the aim of democracy by lodging wealth – and thus power – in the hands of a minority.

These arguments are, in the long run, inconclusive because they involve competing notions of what a just social order should look like. But they have also proved inconclusive for a more mundane reason: nobody can agree on how definitively to measure wealth and its distribution. Most of us think we could recognise the existence of great wealth – but we would soon disagree about what exactly to include as a measure of wealth, and how to value what is actually included. We could probably agree, for instance, that the great landed estates still owned by some aristocrats are a form of wealth and should be counted as such. But should this also be said of even the most humble property, such as the family terraced house? In an age where domestic houses often fetch high prices, and where over 60 per cent of dwellings are owner occupied, this decision can make a big difference to estimates of the distribution of wealth. Similarly, there would probably be general agreement that ownership of shares in a large business corporation is a form of wealth. But should this also be said of more indirect stakes in ownership? In many of the largest corporations in Britain a substantial proportion of shares are owned by '**financial institutions**' – organisations such as insurance companies and pension funds, which invest the proceeds of the contributions of individual policy-holders or those paying into pension schemes. Since an individual making such contributions is entitled to a return on the investments, just as certainly as the direct shareholder is entitled to a dividend, it may be thought that participants in insurance schemes and pension funds should be counted as owning some of the wealth of the economy. If this is indeed so, it suggests not only that wealth is quite widely distributed but that it has become more equally distributed in recent decades, because the beneficiaries of life insurance and pension schemes have grown greatly in number. (For instance, in 1953 only 28 per cent of workers were in a pension scheme; thirty years later the figure was 52 per cent.) Table 3.2 shows how sensitive the figures can be to the definition of wealth, by comparing the results when we include or exclude the value of dwellings.

An additional complication is introduced by the difficulty of actually valuing wealth, even when

Table 3.2 Distribution of marketable wealth in Britain, Inland Revenue estimates

	1976	1995
Marketable wealth: percentage of wealth owned by		
Most wealthy 1%	21	19
Most wealthy 5%	38	38
Most wealthy 10%	50	50
Most wealthy 25%	71	73
Most wealthy 50%	92	92
Marketable wealth less value of dwellings: percentage owned by		
Most wealthy 1%	29	27
Most wealthy 5%	47	51
Most wealthy 10%	57	64
Most wealthy 25%	73	81
Most wealthy 50%	88	93

Source: Social Trends, 1999, p. 100

BOX 3.2 **IDEAS AND PERSPECTIVES**

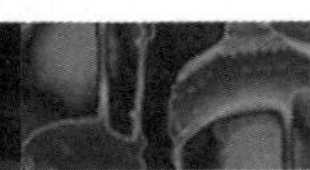

The British 'underclass'

According to the American sociologist Charles Murray, 'the concept of the "underclass" does not refer to a degree of poverty but a type of poverty'. He makes a distinction between the hardworking and worthy poor and the dishonest undeserving or 'feckless' poor who have an aversion to work, are spendthrift, are poor parents, keep their houses in dismal repair and often have a drink problem. He perceives a huge increase in the latter variety of poor during the 1960s and 1970s when poor communities began to fall apart in consequence of crime, drugs and the fear of casual violence. Murray came over to Britain in the late 1980s and diagnosed a similar problem. He blamed illegitimacy as 'the best predictor of an underclass in the making'. Murray found that the British rate had rocketed during the 1980s – to 26 per cent of all new births – and were concentrated in the poorest parts of the UK. He argues that illegitimacy is a catastrophe because 'communities need families. Commuities need fathers'. Children need strong role models to help them socialize effectively; without them children can grow up 'running wild' and develop into anti-social adults prone to crime and providing their children with a similar negative role model. Marriage and work constitute a potent civilising process for young men who otherwise can easily be seduced into thinking that deviant lifestyles are both more attractive and profitable. Murray foresaw a situation in which society would polarize into the 'New Victorians' – educated professionals living in middle-class 'ghettos' – and the 'New Rabble' – low-skilled working class, single parents, welfare dependent with high levels of criminality, impervious to remedial social action and living in their own 'ghettos' such as the sink council estates. Inevitably such an analysis is attractive to the right and has been seized on by some to demonise single-parent families and the unemployed working class. In Murray's booklet on the subject (Murray, 1990) his ideas are roundly criticised by Professors Deakin and Walker as a rehash of disapproving Victorian views that the poor were poor because they somehow deserved to be. They pointed out, moreover, that studies had shown that 'at least half of those born into a disadvantaged home do not repeat the pattern of disadvantage in the next generation' and that half of the so-called 'illegitimate' children are born to couples in a stable relationship (in Scandinavia the percentage was much higher).

All this is not to say that class does not matter. Adonis and Pollard point out that male manual workers have premature death rates nearly half as high as non-manual workers – 'People in unskilled professions are twice as likely to die prematurely as professionals' and 'children in the lowest social category class five are four times more likely to suffer accidental death than those in class one' (Adonis and Pollard, 1996, p. 171). Finally, Professor Ralf Dahrendorf has called the problems caused by the underclass 'the greatest challenge to civilised existence in Britain'.

we agree on what is to be included in a definition. The values of shares in companies, for instance, are decided on the open market. Falls in share prices can thus drastically reduce estimates of the riches of the (mostly wealthy) groups of large shareholders.

It is important to bear these cautionary remarks in mind when discussing arguments about wealth distribution and in interpreting the figures presented in Table 3.2. Nevertheless, three observations seem beyond reasonable doubt. Firstly, there is indeed a minority which owns a statistically disproportionate amount of the community's total wealth. Secondly, there is a very large group at the other end of the social scale which is virtually propertyless. Thirdly, there is occurring over time some redistribution of wealth away from the very richest, but the trickle of resources down the social scale is slow and uneven.

The social environment: continuity and change

In a famous introduction to the social fabric of British politics, published nearly forty years ago, Jean Blondel summarised Britain as a homogeneous society. By this he did not mean that social divisions were absent, but that Britain, when compared with the United States or with other important European nations, was marked by comparatively few important lines of divisions. Whereas religion, race, territory, were important lines of division elsewhere, the social context of British politics could be pretty fully understood by reference to class divisions alone: the most important 'blocks' in British society were classes, identified by their occupation. The key division was between manual and 'white-collar' workers.

That line of division remains important, and more generally the divisions between the rich and poor remain significant in British society. But two developments have combined to make this line of division less crucial.

First, the unity of the two big class 'blocks' has declined. This is most obvious in the case of the manual working class: the numbers of manual workers have declined; they have been internally divided between those in permanent, full-time jobs and those in temporary and/or part-time work; and there has been a growth in unemployment among those who would formerly have done manual work. Conversely, there has been a big increase in the numbers of white-collar workers, but this increase has also brought more internal variety: a wider span of jobs, and important divisions between those in fairly secure permanent work, and those on short-term and temporary contracts.

Second, there has been a rise in new kinds of social identification and a strengthening of old ones. Of the first of these, perhaps the most important has been the rise of different ethnic identities. The most important cause of this development is the large-scale migration, especially from the West Indies and the Indian sub-continent, which took place into Britain, especially in the 1950s and 1960s. These groups had very distinctive racial identities; many also brought a very strong sense of religious identity to a society where religion had been, for most of the population, a comparatively unimportant matter. The diversity and the complexity of the ethnic 'mix' in different parts of the UK are illustrated by Table 3.3.

At the same time, there has been a revival of traditional identities, notably those based on the

Table 3.3 The ethnic composition of Great Britain at the last (1991) census

Ethnic group	Great Britain (%)	England (%)	Wales (%)	Scotland (%)
White	94.5	93.8	98.5	98.7
Ethnic minorities	5.5	6.3	1.4	1.4
Black	1.6	1.9	0.3	0.1
Caribbean	0.9	1.1	0.1	0.0
African	0.4	0.4	0.1	0.0
Other	0.3	0.4	0.1	0.0
South Asian	2.7	3.0	0.6	0.6
Indian	1.5	1.8	0.2	0.2
Pakistani	0.9	1.0	0.2	0.4
Bangladeshi	0.3	0.3	0.1	0.0
Chinese and other	1.2	1.3	0.6	0.5
Chinese	0.3	0.3	0.2	0.2
Other Asian	0.4	0.4	0.1	0.1
Other	0.5	0.6	0.3	0.2
Total Population (000s)	**54,860**	**47,026**	**2,835**	**4,998**

Source: Layton-Henry, 1996

different nations that make up the 'United Kingdom'. This is especially noticeable in the case of Scotland, culminating in the establishment in 1999 of a separate Scottish Parliament in which there now sits a substantial minority from the Scottish National Party, a party committed, at least formally, to achieving full independence for Scotland.

A second very important source of identity beyond ethnicity is that based on gender. There is a close connection between changes in the job market and change in both perceptions of women and perceptions by women. The rise of the (paid) working woman has had important consequences even beyond the labour market itself. It undoubtedly lies at the root of a new sense of self-confidence and self-consciousness among many women reflected in, for instance, a heightened sense of dissatisfaction with long-established inequalities within and outside the workplace between men and women. It has greatly affected the culture and the structure of family life. In many groups – notably in traditional working-class communities – the spread of paid employment among women has accompanied a decline in the very occupations where manual workers were traditionally employed. The result is that the historic role of 'breadwinner' now lies with women rather than men in many instances, inevitably enforcing changes in power and authority within the family.

The economic structure: the public and the private

The United Kingdom, as we have seen, is a capitalist country: private ownership of property dominates; most people rely on the sale of their labour to make a living. But this capitalist country, like most others, also has a large **public sector**: the state is important in economic life. State involvement in economics is often thought of as meaning 'public ownership'; in fact that is only one way among many by which the state shapes economic structures, and these ways are summarised below.

The government as owner

Public ownership is the most visible form of state participation in the economic structure. Government has long been a major owner of productive property: for instance, the crown was already a great property holder when land was the main source of wealth in the community. In the nineteenth century government established a public monopoly in a major new industry of the time, posts and telecommunications. In modern Britain government is still a major owner of society's natural resources, such as coal, oil and gas. (The right to exploit these is only given by licence to private firms.) However, the best-known instances of public ownership are the result of what is usually called **nationalisation**. The nationalised industries are the product of conscious political choices. For most of the century until the start of the 1980s the nationalised sector grew, with successive governments of different political outlooks adding to the range. In the years between the two world wars, for instance, industries as different as broadcasting and electricity supply were nationalised (by the creation of, respectively, the British Broadcasting Corporation and the Central Electricity Generating Board). The years immediately after the Second World War saw a substantial increase in public ownership: coal, steel and railways were all taken into the state sector. The main reason for the post-war growth of public ownership was the belief that the enterprises, if left in private hands, would be run inefficiently or would even fail. This motivation also explains many of the important pieces of nationalisation accomplished in the 1960s and 1970s. These included shipbuilding and important sections of the aircraft and motor vehicle production industries.

Until the mid-1970s it seemed that the continued expansion of public ownership was an irreversible trend in Britain. However, Mrs Thatcher's Conservative administrations of the 1980s destroyed this assumption. Through a programme of 'privatisation' they sold into private hands about 40 per cent of what was in public ownership at the start of the decade. The 'privatised' concerns include many once thought 'natural' to the public sector, such as the gas supply and telecommunications industries. Privatisation marks a radical shift in the balance between the state and the market in Britain. However, the retreat of state ownership does not necessarily mean that total public participation in the economy is in decline. On the contrary, in most of the other five cases which we will consider the importance of government is apparently growing.

The government as partner

The state can act as a partner of private enterprise in numerous ways. Publicly controlled institutions in the financial sector commonly provide investment capital to allow private enterprises to set up or to expand. The major area of growth in partnership in recent years, however, has been at the local level. Faced with the need to redevelop declining and derelict areas of the cities, local authorities and local development corporations have embarked on numerous joint developments with private firms. Some of the best known examples of policy initiatives at the local level – such as the redevelopment of London's docklands – are the result of precisely such partnerships. The significance of the 'partnership' model has been magnified by the development of the Private Finance Initiative, an innovation of the Conservatives which was retained by the Labour Government after 1999. The Private Finance Initiative involves a partnership between private firms and public bodies (such as hospitals) to share the investment costs of major projects such as building construction.

The government as regulator

Although most debate about public intervention in the economy concerns ownership, it is arguably the case that the structure of the market economy in Britain is less influenced by ownership than by public regulation – in other words by sets of rules either contained in law or otherwise prescribed by government. Public regulation is of three kinds. First, the state sets a general framework for the conduct of life, including economic life. Criminal and civil law defines and enforces commercial contracts, identifies what constitutes honesty and dishonesty and provides a means for detecting and preventing fraud. Without this general framework of enforced rules the market economy could not operate.

A second category of regulation is directed at particular industries or sectors of the economy, governing the conduct of affairs inside individual enterprises. For instance, there now exists a large body of law governing relations in the workplace. Industrial relations law places obligations on both employers and trade unions in industrial bargaining. Health and safety legislation prescribes rules safeguarding the life and health of employees.

Finally, there is regulation governing the relations between firms in the private sector and the rest of society. The importance of this kind of regulation has grown greatly in recent years. Two of the most important instances concern pollution control and consumer protection. Pollution regulations govern the nature of industrial processes and restrict the emissions which firms can allow into the atmosphere. Consumer protection regulates the content of many products (in the interests of safety), how they can be advertised (in the interests of honesty and accuracy) and the terms of competition between firms (in the interests of ensuring fair prices).

One important form of regulation is sometimes called 'self-regulation'. Under this system an industry or occupation determines its own regulations and establishes its own institutions for policing and enforcement. Some important professions (such as the law) and major industries (such as advertising) are organised in this way. But most self-regulation should more accurately be called regulation under public licence, because what happens is that the state licenses a group to regulate itself – thereby saving the difficulty and expense of doing the job directly. This links to our next instance of public participation in the market economy.

The government as licensee

When government does not wish directly to engage in a particular economic activity, but nevertheless wants to retain control over that activity, it has the option of licensing a private firm to provide goods and services under prescribed conditions. This method is historically ancient: in the seventeenth and eighteenth centuries, for instance, government often granted monopolies to private corporations to trade in particular products or in particular areas. In the modern economy licensing is used extensively. The exploitation of oil reserves in the North Sea has largely been accomplished by selling licences to explore for oil to privately owned companies. The service of providing commercial radio and commercial television is handled in a similar way: thus the licence or 'franchise' to provide a commercial television service for the north-west of England has been held by a private firm, Granada TV, since the foundation of commercial television.

One of the most common ways of allocating licences is through a system of competitive bidding; the government, of course, can also use the competitive system by going to the private sector as a customer for goods and services.

The government as customer

We saw in the opening chapter that government can use a variety of means, including coercion, to raise goods and services. But government in Britain in fact normally uses the market. In other words, it employs the state's revenues (from such sources as taxation) to buy the goods and services it needs. A glance around any classroom or lecture theatre will show the importance of the public sector as a customer. The room itself will almost certainly have been built as the result of a contract with private firms of builders and architects. The teacher at the front of the room is a private citizen hired on the labour market. Virtually every piece of equipment in the room will also have been bought from private firms. This simple example is illustrated on a wider scale throughout government. Take the example of national defence. Although we usually think of government as providing the defence of the country, it actually buys most of the means of defence in the marketplace: soldiers, sailors and airmen have to be recruited from the labour market in competition with other recruiters of labour, such as private firms; most defence equipment is bought under contract from the private sector; and the everyday necessities of the forces – from the food eaten in the regimental mess to the fuel used by a regimental staff car – are bought in the marketplace.

The government is a customer in the market economy, but it is a very special kind of customer. Because government is the biggest institution in British society it is also the biggest customer. In some important areas it is to all intents and purposes the only customer. To take the example given above, in the supply of most important defence equipment – rockets, military aircraft, warships – the public sector is the sole purchaser. Here the 'producer–customer' relationship is obviously a very special one. Firms producing defence equipment, while nominally in private ownership, operate in such close contact with government agencies that they are in practical terms often indistinguishable from public bodies.

That the state is a customer of the private sector is well recognised; but in understanding the country's economic structure it is as important to emphasise the role of the public sector as a supplier of goods and services.

The government as supplier

Until recently government had a major role as a direct supplier of goods and services in Britain. Housing (council dwellings); transport (bus and rail services); energy (coal, gas, electricity); health care (NHS hospitals); education (schools and universities): these were just some of the important goods and services that were provided directly by central or local government, or by nationalised corporations. Perhaps the biggest change in the role of government produced by Conservative governments after 1979 was to shrink its importance as the direct supplier of goods and services. Even where the state has retained some responsibility in this area it has become a 'contract state', contracting out the delivery of services to private agencies. Nevertheless, the state retains a residual importance in this area, notably in the fields of education and health care.

The list in Box 3.3 is significant both because it shows how important is the state and because it shows how far the issues that are argued about in

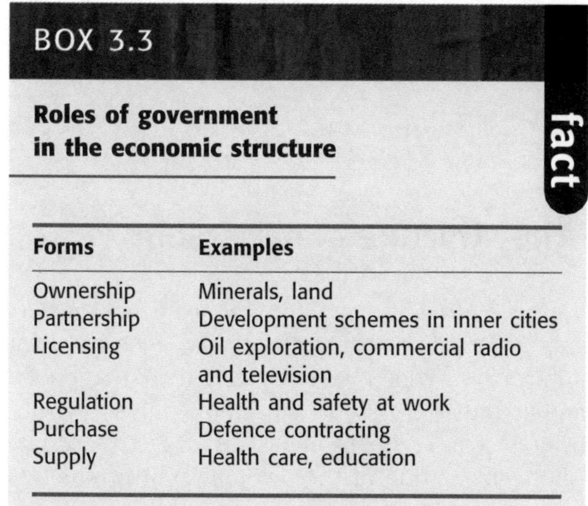

BOX 3.3

fact

Roles of government in the economic structure

Forms	Examples
Ownership	Minerals, land
Partnership	Development schemes in inner cities
Licensing	Oil exploration, commercial radio and television
Regulation	Health and safety at work
Purchase	Defence contracting
Supply	Health care, education

British politics concern the balance between its various roles. Take the single example of ownership. In the 1980s government 'privatised' many enterprises such as gas supply and the telephone service. At the same time it set up public bodies to regulate the newly privatised concerns: to fix prices and other conditions under which services are supplied to customers. Arguments between supporters and opponents of privatisation are not, therefore, arguments about whether or not government should be present in the economic structure; they turn on differences about whether, in particular cases, it is better for the state to be an owner or a regulator.

Economic structure: the balance of sectors

The role of public institutions is obviously a key aspect of a country's economic structure, but just as important is the balance between what are sometimes called 'sectors'. We often speak of Britain as an 'industrial' economy, but the industries dominant in the economy have changed greatly in the recent past and continue to change. These alterations have momentous wider consequences: they affect the social structure, noticeably the class structure, and thus feed through to politics. For instance, the declining proportion of manual workers in the economy has been a cause of declining votes for the Labour party, once the party of most manual workers.

It is conventional to make a distinction between '**primary**', '**secondary**' and '**tertiary**' (or 'service') **sectors**. The 'primary' sector extracts the basic raw material of production from nature: obvious examples include mining, forestry and agriculture. The 'secondary' sector is most closely identified with manufacturing – in other words, with turning raw materials into finished goods, be they cars, refrigerators or aeroplanes. The 'tertiary' (or 'service') sector refers to activities designed neither to extract and process materials, nor to manufacture goods, but to deliver services; hence the alternative, commonly used name. We saw in the last chapter that many important services – such as health and education – are provided by public institutions; but others, ranging from catering and tourism to financial services, are provided by privately owned firms operating in the market.

The three categories of sector are extremely broad, but their changing importance illuminates aspects of the developing economic structure. The decisive historical event in the evolution of the British economy was the Industrial Revolution. It began in the latter half of the eighteenth century and within a hundred years transformed the country. This revolution involved a shift in the balance between sectors. The key change was the decline in agriculture as a source of wealth and as a source of jobs. At the same time the economy began to depend increasingly on the production and sale of finished goods – at first cotton, then a wide range of manufactures based on the iron and steel industries. Thus the Industrial Revolution coincided with the rise of the 'secondary' or manufacturing industries. But in recent decades there has occurred a further stage in structural change: the decline of manufacturing and the rise of service industries in the 'tertiary' sector. In part this change is not specific to Britain. It reflects the characteristic development of most industrial economies. The reasons for the expansion of service industries are various. Technical advance has made the activities of extraction and manufacture much more efficient than in the past: in agriculture, for instance, a workforce which is the tiniest in Britain's history produces more food than ever

BOX 3.4

fact

Phases of economic development

Before the industrial revolution most economic activity involved agriculture

After the industrial revolution manufacturing was supreme

In recent decades service industries have become increasingly important

This is changing the class structure from one dominated by manual to one dominated by non-manual workers

Table 3.4 Changing balance of main economic sectors, 1974–96 (% of total employees)

	1974	1976
Services	55%	70%
Production	42%	27%
Agriculture	5%	2%

Note: Percentages do not sum to 100
Source: Social Trends, 1998, p. 16

before because of the use of advanced technology on the farm. At the same time, growing prosperity has created an increased demand for services of all kinds, ranging from education to catering and tourism. Britain, because it is a classic example of an advanced industrial economy, has shared in this common experience of economic change.

In Britain 'sectoral' change has been especially marked. The great industries on which Britain's nineteenth-century industrial might were built have almost universally declined – both in world markets and as components of the British economy. Coal, shipbuilding, steel and iron – all once major centres of economic power and employment – have become much less significant. This decline can be traced back over a century in the case of many industries, but in recent decades it has accelerated: the scale of recent change is summarised in Table 3.4.

The important changes in the balance between the sectors are also reflected in another important feature of the economy – the structure of ownership.

The structure of ownership

We have already examined one aspect of ownership in Britain's economy – the balance between enterprises owned and controlled in the public and private sectors. But the simple phrase 'private ownership' is complex, and deserves close scrutiny. The legal vesting of the ownership of productive property – factories, equipment and so on – in private hands is an important feature of the British economy. The changing structure of that ownership has implications for the functioning of the whole social system and for the kinds of policies which governments can pursue.

In the early stages of the industrial revolution Britain, like many other capitalist economies, was marked by what is sometimes called *the unity of ownership and control*: firms were for the most part small by modern standards; they were controlled by families or by partnerships; and the legal owners were usually those who took the main part in daily management. Like much else in Britain, this pattern has changed in modern times.

Three developments are important: the separation of the managerial function from the role of ownership; the changing structure of legal ownership in the most important enterprises; and the changing size and scope of firms' activities.

The development of a division of functions between those responsible for the daily control of firms and those vested with legal ownership actually began in the nineteenth century; it is now predominant among larger firms in the economy. It has been prompted by the growing complexity of the task of running a large business enterprise which has resulted in the emergence of a wide range of specialised managerial jobs covering finance, production, personnel, sales and so on. No one seriously disputes that there now exists in most large corporations a separation between, on one hand, individuals responsible for the daily running

BOX 3.5

fact

Changing structure of firms

The structure of private enterprise in recent decades has been marked by three great changes:

1. the rise of a specialised group of salaried managers responsible for the main functions inside firms;
2. the concentration of share ownership in the hands of institutional investors such as insurance companies;
3. the domination of many sectors by giant multinationals organising their markets on a world scale.

of the enterprise and, on the other, groups vested with legal ownership. There is, however, a serious argument about the implications – including the political implications – of this shift. Some argue that Britain is only one of a range of advanced capitalist nations where there has occurred a 'separation of ownership from control'. In other words real power in firms is no longer exercised by owners, but by salaried managers. The consequence is that one of the traditional characteristics of the capitalist system – the concentration of economic resources in the hands of private individuals motivated largely by the desire for profit – has been modified. Salaried managers, it is argued, have a wider set of motivations than pure profit and are responsive to the needs and wishes of the community. Others argue that, by contrast, the rise of the manager has only allocated traditional tasks in a new way. Managers, it is claimed, run firms in the traditional interests of owners – with profits in mind above all. They do this because many managers are also in part owners; because owners who are not managers still retain the power to dismiss managers who ignore the pursuit of profits; and because in any case most managers accept the philosophy that the point of a firm is to make profit.

The original notion that owners were no longer powerful in big firms arose because of changes in the legal nature of firms. Most big enterprises in Britain are no longer family-owned firms or partnerships. They are 'joint stock' companies – which means that ownership is vested jointly in a multiplicity of individuals who own the stock, or shares, in the firm. Where the owners are many and scattered, and managers are few and concentrated, it is natural that the latter should more effectively control decisions inside the company.

This connects to the second main development identified at the beginning of this section – the changing form of legal ownership. The largest and most important firms in the economy are typically owned jointly by many people scattered around the country – and in some cases around the world. Since important decisions – such as contests for membership of the board of directors – are decided by majority votes, with shareholders allotted votes in proportion to the number of shares owned, it is virtually impossible for numerous small shareholders to combine together in sufficient number to control decisions.

In recent years, however, changes in the nature of share ownership have altered this state of affairs. Although the number of individuals owning shares in Britain grew in the 1980s – principally because of widespread buying of the stock of newly privatised concerns such as British Telecom and British Gas – the proportion of total shares owned by private individuals has shown a long-term fall over recent decades. The facts are illustrated in Figure 3.6. In place of the private shareholder, ownership is increasingly in the hands of what are conventionally called 'institutions', notably insurance companies and pension funds.

This change has an important implication for the debate about the separation of ownership from control. The institutions' shareholdings are concentrated in the biggest and most important firms. Hence, the argument that managers have the power to wield influence over a dispersed mass of owners no longer holds. Indeed, there have been striking cases in recent years where the institutions have wielded their numerical resources to control and discipline managements of individual firms.

The rise of the giant firm is the third important feature of the structure of ownership in the

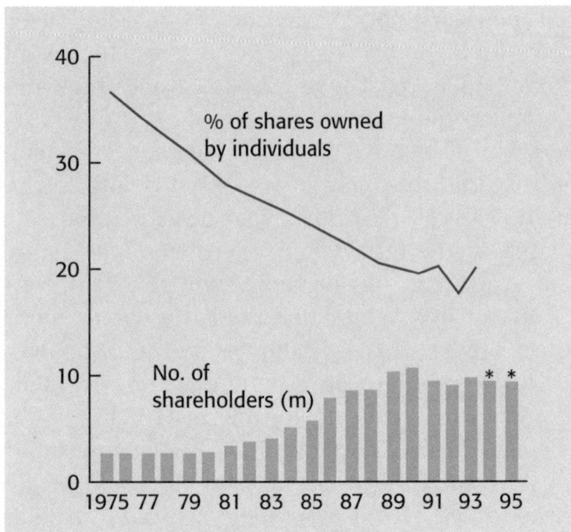

Figure 3.6 Patterns of share ownership
Source: The Economist, 18 May 1996

private sector. Most firms in Britain are tiny, but a small number of giant enterprises nevertheless dominate the economy. This is the result of a long-term trend: the domination of big firms has increased greatly in the twentieth century, a change mirrored in other advanced industrial economies. The giant firms dominant in the economy are also usually **multi-national** in scope. A multi-national is a firm which produces its goods in different nations and sells them in different national markets. The most sophisticated firms have an international 'division of labour': it is common, for instance, for different components of a motor car to be produced in factories in a variety of countries, and then to be assembled in yet another country. In the years since the Second World War the significance of multi-national companies has grown greatly. Many of the biggest British concerns have taken on a multi-national character. British markets have also themselves been deeply penetrated by foreign multi-nationals. Britain is one of the most popular locations for American firms expanding abroad, and even when firms are not located in Britain there are whole markets – for instance in motor cycles, electrical goods and automobiles – where the products of foreign multi-nationals either dominate or are a substantial part of the supply.

These observations connect to what is the most important theme of this chapter: the way the social and economic context of the political system is itself part of a wider context – of Britain as a global and European society.

Britain in context

That British society exists within a wider global and European context is obvious. But what implications does this have for the society, particularly insofar as the social context helps shape the kind of political system we have?

The answer lies in two 'contextual' developments – in other words, developments not special to the United Kingdom but those providing a wider setting for British politics and society:

- **Globalisation**: an ever more closely enmeshed global system is being developed. Although many of the features of the modern global economy can be found in the past, what is unique in the last generation is the combination of factors that all intensify global connections: greater ease of international human transportation; rapidly developing telecommunications and electronic communication; growing world trade, especially between the rich countries of the world, of whom Britain is one; the growing global organisation of markets for the production and sale of goods and services.
- **Europeanisation**: the development of the European Union, since its original foundation as a 'common market' uniting only six countries in the late 1950s has transformed, and continues to transform, European economy and society. This transformation takes many forms, most of which are examined in later pages of this book. In the realm of government, for example, European political institutions must now be considered an integral part of the decision-making system in Britain – they are not just important 'external' institutions. Socially and economically, Britain has become a much more obviously 'European' society in recent decades. Economically, the United Kingdom is now increasingly integrated with the economy

of the rest of the European Union – an integration reflected in trade, tourism and a host of other forms of communication. For instance, while in 1971 only 29 per cent of United Kingdom exports went to other EU member states, the figure had risen to 57 per cent in 1996.

These two forces – globalisation and Europeanisation – are bound together. The development of a more integrated European economy has been connected to the development of a more integrated global economy: European multinationals have penetrated beyond Europe, and American and Japanese multinationals established an often dominating presence in Europe. What have these two powerful contextual features to do with British politics? Much of that question is properly answered in the chapters that follow, but it is sensible to alert ourselves to the momentous consequences. Among the more important are the following:

- Thatcherite economic reforms, which dominated politics throughout the 1980s, were a sustained response to globalisation – and in part, also, one of the forces that helped accelerate the globalisation revolution. Thatcherism was an attempt to cope with the fact that, in a world of increasing global production and competition, the British economy as traditionally organised could not perform as effectively as the economies of some other leading industrial nations. Without globalisation we would not have Thatcherism; and without Thatcherism, in turn, globalisation would have been that much less pronounced.
- The way the response to globalisation was organised in the 1980s has had long-term consequences for the distribution of power and resources in the society and the political system. Some groups suffered badly. The most obvious case is the miners. In the 1970s the miners were a great political and economic power, partly responsible for the fall of the Conservative Government of Mr Heath in 1974. By the 1990s, after a comprehensive defeat in a landmark strike in the 1980s, privatisation of their industry and a programme of pit closures, they had all but disappeared as an occupation, and had completely disappeared as a political force. By contrast, the response to globalisation greatly enriched some groups who worked in financial markets, and made the markets themselves important arbiters of the economic policy of governments.
- Britain's experience as a member of the European Union was an important contributory factor to one of the most significant institutional innovations of the 1990s: the introduction in 1999 of devolved government, together with elected assemblies, in Scotland and Wales, for the notion that the two Celtic nations could operate successfully through the EU institutions to secure resources has undoubtedly been an important impetus behind the pressure for devolved government.
- More directly still, membership of the Union has had profound effects on the system of interest representation in the United Kingdom. A quarter of a century ago all important pressure groups directed their main activities to central government in Whitehall. Now, there is not a single important group which does not devote a large amount of its time and money to lobbying European institutions, especially the policy makers in the European Commission in Brussels. Many have their own offices in Brussels and belong to Europe-wide interest groups. In short, the growing salience of Britain as a European society has been matched by the 'Europeanisation' of the system of interest representation (see Chapter 11).
- Finally, the European dimension is clear in its impact on political parties and political debate. In the new millennium, attitudes to Europe – for instance, on the issue of how much deeper should be the integration of Britain into the Union – are a key line of division, both between the political parties and within them.

We can thus see the twin impacts of globalisation and Europeanisation at four levels of the political system: at the highest level of changes in the constitution; at the level of government policy-making, as in the integration of government decision making in Whitehall with the European system; at the level of the representation of interests; and at the level of debates conducted within and between the political parties.

Chapter summary

This chapter has described the context of British politics in several ways.

It has described how Britain looks from a global context; has described a range of domestic social hierarchies, relating to occupation, gender and wealth; has described the economic structure, stressing the role of government in that structure; and has described how the global and European setting of British society has helped shape politics.

Discussion points

- Who do you think have been the main winners and losers in the decline of manufacturing industry?
- What political problems have been caused by the impact of globalisation on British politics?
- Why has government become less important as an owner, and more important as a regulator, in recent years?

Further reading

A very good standard introduction to British society is Abercrombie and Warde (1994). Esping-Andersen (1990, 1999), while rather advanced for the beginning student, are excellent in 'setting' Britain into an international picture. Halsey (1986) remains one of the best introductions to the social structure. Perkin (1989), not easy going, is invaluable in describing historical evolution. Atkinson (1974) is still invaluable in describing the problems of estimating the distribution of wealth. Halsey (1988) brings together long term surveys of change in structure. Blondel (1963), while now dated, nevertheless remains one of the the most successful attempt to summarise the social fabric of British politics. Adonis and Pollard (1997) provides a more up-to-date analysis and repays close reading handsomely. Murray's (1990) thesis of the underclass is worth reading for its provocative conclusions and the criticisms provided in the IEA booklet.

The two most invaluable sources of up-to-date information on society and economy are published annually by Her Majesty's Stationery Office for the Office for National Statistics: *Regional Trends* and *Social Trends*. Rose (1971, 1982) are classics on the nature of national identity in the United Kingdom. Introductions to the history and changing structure of the economy include Cairncross (1992), Curwen (1990) and Pollard (1992). The impact of the Thatcher 'revolution' is discussed in Edgell and Duke (1991) and in Marsh (1992). The best overall introduction to the 'ownership and control' debate remains Nichols (1970).

References

Abercrombie, N. and Warde, A. (1994) *Contemporary Britain: a New Introduction to Sociology* (Polity).

Adonis, A. and Pollard, A. (1997) *A Class Act* (Hamish Hamilton).

Atkinson, A.B. (1974) *Unequal Shares* (Penguin).

Blondel, J. (1963) *Voters, Parties and Leaders* (Penguin).

Cairncross, A. (1992) *The British Economy Since 1945* (Blackwell).

Curwen, P. (ed.) (1990) *Understanding the UK Economy* (Macmillan).

Dahrendorf, R. (1987) 'The erosion of citizenship and the consequences for us all', *New Statesman*, 12 June.

Edgell, S. and Duke, V. (1991) *A Measure of Thatcherism: a Sociology of Britain* (Harper Collins).

Esping-Andersen, G. (1990) *The Three Worlds of Welfare Capitalism* (Polity).

Esping-Andersen, G. (1999) *Social Foundations of Industrial Economies* (Oxford University Press).

Halsey, A.H. (1986) *Change in British Society* (Macmillan).

Halsey, A.H. (1987) 'Social trends since World War II', in Central Statistical Office, *Social Trends*.

Halsey, A.H. (ed.) (1988) *British Social Trends Since 1900* (Macmillan).

Layton-Henry, Z. (1996) 'Immigration and contemporary British politics', *Politics Review*, February, pp. 21–4.

Marsh, D. (ed.) (1992) *Implementing Thatcherite Policies: Audit of an Era* (Open University Press).

Murray, C. (1990) *The Emerging British Underclass* (IEA Health and Welfare Unit).

Nichols, T. (1970) *Ownership, Control and Ideology* (Allen and Unwin).

Perkin, H. (1989) *The Rise of Professional Society: England Since 1888* (Routledge).

Office for National Statistics (1995) *Regional Trends 1995* (Her Majesty's Stationery Office).

Office for National Statistics (1998) *Social Trends 28* (Her Majesty's Stationery Office).

Office for National Statistics (1999) *Social Trends 29* (Her Majesty's Stationery Office).

Pollard, S. (1992) *The Development of the British Economy* (Edward Arnold).

Rose, R. (1971) *Governing Without Consensus: an Irish Perspective* (Faber).

Rose, R. (1982) *Understanding the United Kingdom* (Longman).

Concluding comment

Progress on poverty

Will Blair deliver on eliminating child poverty?

David Piachaud

For the first time in a generation Britain has a government that accepts the reality of poverty and the damage it causes and is committed to tackling it. The Prime Minister has said: 'Our historic aim will be for ours to be the first generation to end child poverty . . . It is a 20-year mission'. The Chancellor has gone further: 'It is not enough to tackle absolute poverty and simply prevent destitution. We should do more. It is not fair that children should be disadvantaged from the start of their lives because of who their parents are, what school they go to and where they live'.

That poverty should be a key concern cannot be doubted. Between 1979 and 1997 the number of individuals in poverty – defined here as below half average income level (adjusted for family size, after housing costs) – rose from five to fourteen million or one-quarter of the population. As Table 1 shows, poverty among adults was more common for women than for men; children were even more likely to be in a poor household. Unemployed households were the most likely to be poor, followed by lone parent families; the greatest number of the poor continued to be elderly. The aggregate amount by which the incomes of all those in poverty fell below the poverty level – the poverty gap – is about ten billion pounds, or $2\frac{1}{2}$ per cent of total disposable income; in families with children it is about four billion pounds.

Another indicator of the extent of poverty is the number on income support, the state's means-tested minimum income. In February 1999, 3.8 million claimants received income support; including

Table 1 Poverty by personal, economic and family status 1996–7

	Total number	Proportion poor	Number poor
Elderly	9.8m	31%	3.0m
Lone-parent family	4.6m	63%	2.9m
Unemployed	2.9m	78%	2.3m
Adult men	21.1m	20%	4.2m
Adult women	22.2m	24%	5.3m
Children	13.0m	35%	4.5m
All	56.3m	25%	14.1m

Poverty is defined as below 50 per cent of average income after housing costs
Source: Households Below Average Income 1979 to 1996–7

partners and dependents, 6.7 million; another 1.3 million were receiving Job Seekers Allowance. Thus eight million depended on the state's minimum.

What then has been done to tackle poverty and what impact is Government policy likely to have?

The first year of the new Labour Government was not promising. There was a commitment to Conservative spending plans at the Treasury, discord between Harman and Field at the Department of Social Security and dissent in the Commons over the abolition of the One Parent Benefit. On the basis of statements that social security benefit levels would be only price indexed, and would not therefore keep up with incomes generally, the prospect for poverty was a substantial increase by 2002 (see *New Economy*, March 1998).

In the last year much has changed and the prospects for poverty have improved. Yet the real progress is not without its paradoxes and potential problems.

Table 2 Income support levels

	Level of income support (£ per week)		
	April 1997	**April 1999**	**Real increase**
Single adult (25+)	49.15	51.40	+0.1%
Couple (one or both 18+)	77.15	80.65	0%
Couple with two children under 11	121.75	134.95	+6.1%
Lone parent with one child under 11	81.80	87.35	+2.2%
Single pensioner (aged 60–75, non-disabled)	68.80	75.00	+4.3%
Pensioner couple (aged 60–70, non-disabled)	106.80	116.60	+3.9%

Table 3 Income support numbers

	Number of claimants (thousands)		
	Feb 1997	**Feb 1999**	**Change**
Aged 60 or over	1,724	1,620	−6.0%
Lone parents	1,020	940	−7.8%
Disabled	809	914	+13.0%
All on income support	*3,954*	*3,815*	*−3.5%*
Job Seekers Allowance	*1,763*	*1,323*	*−25.0%*

Progress

To consider the impact of changes on poverty over the five-year period up to 2002, it is assumed that the appropriate poverty level is that which the Chancellor has used in discussing child poverty, namely a level of half average income. Based on Treasury figures and forecasts, average real incomes will rise by about 12 per cent from 1997 to 2002.

Most of those in poverty are dependent on income support. Over the last two years the level of income support has been substantially increased in real terms for families with children; this has been most marked for young children for whom the weekly allowance will have increased from £16.90 in 1997 to £24.90 by October 1999. The level for pensioners has also risen, but, as shown in Table 2, income support for others has been effectively frozen in real terms; the same is true of Job Seekers Allowance.

The numbers on income support and Job Seekers Allowance have in total fallen a little over the Labour Government's first two years, as shown in Table 3. The main fall has been due to the decline in unemployment but the number in lone parent families has also declined; only the number classified as disabled has continued to grow.

The decline in unemployment has been unequivocally good in terms of reducing poverty. The total claimant count fell from 1.7 million in April 1997 to 1.3 million in April 1999. Over this period the number of young claimants (18–24 years) unemployed over six months fell by three-fifths from 178,000 to 71,000 and the number of long-term unemployed (over twelve months) claimants nearly halved from 617,000 to 330,000. Most of this improvement can be attributed to ongoing economic recovery rather than welfare to work measures, but these can only have helped. This fall in unemployment has reduced the number of individuals in poverty by about 500,000.

The national minimum wage introduced in April 1999 should reduce the extent of low pay. The effect of this on poverty is complex since many low earners are in two-earner households and higher pay may be offset by lower means-tested benefits. Overall, the minimum wage may reduce the number in poverty by about 300,000.

An estimate of the impact of Budget changes on the extent of poverty can be made by using the analysis carried out by the University of Cambridge Microsimulation Unit. On average, households gained from the three Labour Budgets by about 5 per cent but those in the bottom and second deciles gained by 9.2 and 7 per cent respectively. Applying these estimates to the most recent income distribution data for 1997–8 based on the Family Expenditure Survey suggests that if all the Budget measures were applied at one time the number in poverty would be reduced by about two million. However, matters are not so simple.

It is convenient to consider separately families with children, non-retired households without children and retired households.

The main focus of the government's attack on poverty has been on low-income working families with increases in universal child benefit, the introduction of the Working Families Tax Credit in place of Family Credit and a new Children's Tax Credit that will be available to all except higher-rate tax payers. In addition, as already noted, children's allowances for income support have been increased.

These measures announced in the 1998 and 1999 Budgets are shown in Table 4. The Cambridge Microsimulation Unit found that the gains are substantially higher in families with children, with gains of 16 and 14 per cent in the lowest two deciles. Not all gain, however: 15 per cent of the households with children, many in lone-parent families, lost from the policy changes. But the overall effect of the Labour Budgets has been to concentrate gains particularly on poorer households with children. In combination the Budget measures direct over four billion pounds to families with children over and above price indexation, of which about two-fifths will go to those in poverty.

Table 4 Families with children: main budget changes, 1998 and 1999

Increases in income support	
Children's allowances	£550m
Working Families Tax Credit	£2,050m
Child Benefit increases	£255m
Children's Tax Credit	£1,400m
Total	£4,255m
Of which to poor families	£1,800m
Cost of increasing cash benefits to poor families in line with average incomes 1997–2002	£1,200m

Table 5 Main changes in poverty, 1997–2002

Reduction in unemployment	–500,000
Effect of national minimum wage	–300,000
Budget measures to reduce child poverty	
Children	–800,000
Parents	–550,000
Relative decline in social security benefits to non-retired households without children	+300,000
Retired households	little change
Overall change	*–1.85 million*

This, however, is not the whole story. If poverty in families with children is not to increase, benefits to poor families must keep up with the rise in average incomes; the cost of this will take up most of the apparent Budget gain. But there remains a relative improvement that will meet about one-sixth of the poverty gap in these families.

The Treasury has estimated that poverty measures taken so far should by the end of the Parliament reduce the number of children in poverty by around 800,000, with about 550,000 parents also raised out of poverty. This corresponds with the estimates presented in Table 5.

Turning to non-retired households without children, the poorest tenth of these are mostly out of employment and receive three-fifths of their gross income from social security benefits. Some of these may escape poverty as a result of welfare to work policies, which are considered later. For those who remain on social security, the present policy of freezing these benefits in real terms will mean this group will fall further behind and their poverty will increase. The effect of this over five years is estimated to be an increase in poverty of 200,000 households containing about 300,000 people. These households have not been a focus of policy although some form of earned income tax credit might be extended to them in the future. For the present, many of them are not able to keep up with the general growth in incomes.

The third group to consider is retired households, not least because the elderly still make up the largest group in poverty. As was seen in Table 2, so far income support for pensioners has broadly kept up with average incomes and the Winter Fuel Allowance, currently worth £100, has been equivalent to about 1 per cent more. The Green Paper on pensions makes clear that, while the basic state pension is only to be increased in line with prices, the intention in the long run is to increase the 'minimum income guarantee' (a new name for income support) in line with earnings 'as resources allow'. Assuming the latter is achieved, poverty in old age will remain broadly constant.

Overall, changes in policy should result in substantially less poverty after five years of Labour Government than would otherwise have occurred. The main changes are set out in Table 5. A reduction in poverty of the order of two million – from fourteen to twelve million – seems likely.

There are of course many uncertainties. Most substantial is the impact of measures being taken to tackle the causes of poverty. Some of these, such as steps to improve basic education or reduce teenage pregnancies, are unlikely to have any significant impact in the short term. The impact of the promotion of movement from welfare to work depends on what is happening in the labour market and, since the incidence of poverty is highest among the unemployed, what happens to unemployment is the greatest uncertainty when considering the prospects for poverty.

The Treasury's planning assumptions seem to imply that unemployment needs to rise to its supposed 'natural' rate of 5.5 per cent or 1.6 million by 2002; if this occurred it would result in an extra 250,000 people being in poverty in unemployed families. The benefits of the welfare to work programme could be nullified if unemployment was allowed or even encouraged to rise. On the other hand if welfare to work and other measures enable unemployment to fall to the average levels of the 1970s or even 1960s then poverty will be much reduced. The assumption made here is that it will remain at its current level. Other uncertainties exist where policy is yet to be determined and announced: probably the most significant for poverty is the future of Housing Benefit.

Appraisal

A reduction in poverty by about two million would be a significant achievement. But to put it in perspective, poverty would remain more than twice what it was in 1979. Child poverty will have been reduced over five years by some 800,000 or about just under one-fifth. This represents a most significant step on the Prime Minister's twenty-year mission to end child poverty. Yet to achieve the goal would require an acceleration in progress in the future. If the current rate of progress were maintained – a very big 'if' – only about two-thirds of child poverty would be abolished in twenty years, and its extent would be no lower than it was in 1979.

Most of the likely reduction in poverty is the result of old-style redistribution, even if some of it is achieved with new-style tax credits. This is ironic – although no less welcome – since 'redistribution' is a term now rarely used by members of the Government. Thus far most of the redistribution that has occurred has been achieved by stealth. Most of the redistribution to families with children is paid for by abolishing the married couple's tax allowance, which cannot be repeated.

This redistribution is being pursued with an increasing role for meanstesting. This may appear attractive in the short term as a means of concentrating available resources on those in greatest need. But in the long term it reduces incentives to work and to save. The Working Families Tax Credit will greatly increase the number of low-income families facing effective marginal tax rates of over 65 per cent (although numbers facing much higher rates will fall because of the reduction in the rate of taper, compared with Family Credit). Higher net incomes for low-paid workers may make work more attractive but the linking of tax credits to pay packets may create problems for irregular workers.

The withholding of the Children's Tax Credit from higher-rate tax payers will boost the marginal tax rate of many of those at the lower end of the higher tax rate band from 40 to 47 per cent; these are the very people who were considered untouchable in pre-election discussions on whether the higher rate of income tax should be raised as part of a more general redistribution and a partial reversal of the previous government's hand-outs to the better off.

Redistribution by stealth involves more means testing and reduced incentives, particularly at lower income levels. Thus, paradoxically and potentially problematically, while wishing to encourage independence and self-help, the effect of policy is in many ways to create disincentives that discourage, not encourage those close to the poverty level. For the future the scope for further redistribution by stealth will be limited. Further redistribution is needed if the momentum of reducing poverty is to be maintained. It is hard to see how that could be achieved without further increases in taxation.

In essence the Government has done what it said it would, promoting work for those who can work and security for those who cannot. The incomes of low-paid workers with children are being substantially improved. Yet, despite the Working Families Tax Credit, many on the minimum wage could still find themselves below the poverty level. Work is still no guarantee that poverty will be avoided.

Most of those now relying on the social security system will continue to do so. Welfare to work is not relevant for most pensioners and disabled people. For most of those in poverty what is critical is the level of income support. Levels of income support are compared with the poverty level in Table 6. The minimum income provided for most of those who do not have employment is far below the poverty level. For pensioners the deficit is not great. For families with children it is being reduced. For others it is increasing. The reduction of poverty, and, in the Prime Minister's words, the achievement of security for those who cannot work, depends on reducing these deficits. This can only be done by further redistribution.

Table 6 Income support and poverty levels 1999

	Income support £	**Poverty level £**	**Income support as % of poverty level**
Single adult (25+)	51.40	80.85	63.6%
Couple (one or both 18+)	80.65	147.00	54.9%
Couple with two children under 11	134.95	207.27	65.1%
Lone parent with one child under 11	87.35	114.66	76.2%
Single pensioner (aged 60–75, non-disabled)	75.00	80.85	92.8%
Pensioner couple (aged 60–75, non-disabled)	116.60	147.00	79.3%

Poverty is defined as 50 per cent of average income after housing costs
Poverty level for 1999 is based on poverty level for 1996–7 adjusted for actual and forecast rises in Real Household Disposable Income and Retail Price Index set out in *HM Treasury, The Pre-Budget Report*, November 1998 and *HM Treasury Economic and Fiscal Strategy Report and Financial Statement and Budget Report*, March 1999

A different issue arises over the measures to tackle the causes of poverty. That the government is taking such measures is to be welcomed. What is problematic is the limited extent of these measures. To take one example, resources are to be devoted to an innovative Sure Start programme to promote the pre-school development of the most disadvantaged children. At a cost of £180 million a year in 2001–2 this should help 200,000 children or 5 per cent of underfours. Yet the resources per child for Sure Start are less than one-quarter of those devoted to each student in higher education – the least educationally disadvantaged. The total resources for Sure Start amount to only one-third of the extra resources being directed to higher education over the next three years.

The Labour Government has, within tight overall expenditure limits, initiated many programmes aimed at tackling the causes of poverty. But either total public expenditure must grow substantially or existing programmes must be cut back if these new developments are to have a significant impact.

A final concern for the future is the Chancellor's approach to poverty. A transformation has occurred with the Treasury taking charge of policy on poverty and at every opportunity the Chancellor seems keen to integrate taxation and social security. This has advantages: the Teasury may be judged by its success in reducing poverty; arbitrary but limiting accounting distinctions between benefits and tax credits may be swept away.

But Treasury dominance has dangers. First, the Treasury has little experience of delivering services; those in or close to poverty often live from day to day, let alone from week to week. While one can only hope it does not occur, there is a risk of administrative problems with the Working Families Tax Credit that would dwarf those of the Child Support Agency or Passport Office. Second, the focus on in-work benefits may tend to residualise benefits for those who are not and cannot be in paid work.

Third, the erosion of social insurance, to which the Treasury seems indifferent, threatens long-run political support of the social security system; Britain risks being the only major OECD country without a secure social insurance foundation to tackle poverty. Further weakening of social insurance would hardly contribute to social cohesion or solidarity, which must be of concern to a government trying to reduce social exclusion.

Fourth, it is not outside the bounds of possibility that one day there will be a Chancellor less concerned about poverty than Gordon Brown, who will then have all the power and levers. Past Chancellors, even Labour ones, have usually regarded limiting public expenditure and taxation as more important than worrying about the poor. The Department of Social Security has been a key countervailing force within government defending the interests of the millions dependent on benefits. Time will tell whether having the Treasury in charge of tackling poverty is wise.

Conclusion

The measures and changes described will result in about two million fewer people being in poverty at the end of the Labour Government's first term. The Prime Minister's test – that if poverty were not reduced the government would not deserve to be re-elected – should be comfortably passed. Yet there will still be about 12 million remaining in poverty, more than twice as many as in 1979. This shows the scale of the Government's task, a product of the enormous growth in inequality that has occurred in Britain. If poverty is to be brought down to the level of 1979, and certainly if progress towards abolishing child poverty is to be maintained, two things will need to happen.

First, there will have to be much more redistribution. Most of those who remain in poverty will be those who cannot work; if they are to keep up, let alone catch up, with the rest of society then redistribution – whether it is through social security benefits or tax credits – will have to increase. There is little scope for further redistribution by stealth. Making the social security system more means tested and targeted will limit expenditure and may seem superficially attractive but it is fundamentally and inescapably at odds with the goal of encouraging self-help and independence.

Second, there will have to be much greater efforts to tackle the long-term causes of poverty. Further reductions in unemployment and tackling the causes of low pay are needed. To tackle some of the causes of poverty either public expenditure will have to increase in total or there will have to be far more significant restructuring of pubic expenditure than has so far occurred to give priority in policy to poverty reduction.

The Prime Minister has argued that the welfare state cannot be effective if it lacks popular support. In seeking to re-popularise it he has given pre-eminence to the need to tackle child poverty and improve life chances. This is a strategy that makes excellent sense in terms of equity and efficiency, as well as in political terms. A start has been made in pursuing this strategy – but only a start. Maintaining momentum and facing up to difficult choices which cannot please everyone are essential if there is to be any real prospect of abolishing child poverty in a generation.

Source: reprinted from New Economy, © 1999 IPPR.

Part 2

Defining the political world

Chapter 4

Ideology and the liberal tradition

Bill Jones

Learning objectives

- To clarify the concept of ideology.
- To trace the transition of new ideas from their 'revolutionary' inception to accepted othodoxy.
- To show how Classical Liberalism developed into New Liberalism, the creed which set the social agenda for the next century.

Introduction

This chapter begins by discussing what we mean by the term 'ideology'. It goes on to explain how 'liberal' ideas entered the political culture as heresies in the seventeenth and eighteenth centuries but went on to become the orthodoxies of the present age. Classical Liberalism in the mid-nineteenth century is examined together with the birth of modern Liberalism in the early twentieth century.

What is ideology?

For up to two decades after 1945 it seemed as if ideology as a factor in British politics was on the wane. The coalition comradeship of the war had drawn some of the sting from the sharp doctrinal conflicts between the two major political parties and in its wake the Conservatives had conceded – without too much ill grace – that Labour would expand welfare services and nationalise a significant sector of the economy. Once in power after 1951 the Conservatives presided over their socialist inheritance of a mixed economy and a welfare state. Both parties seemed to have converged towards a general consensus on political values and institutions: there was more to unite than to divide them. By the end of the 1950s some commentators – notably the American political scientist Daniel Bell – were pronouncing 'the end of ideology' (see Bell, 1960) in Western societies.

The faltering of the British economy in the 1960s, however, exacerbated in the early 1970s by the rise in oil prices, industrial unrest and raging inflation, re-opened the ideological debate with a vengeance. A revived Labour left hurled contumely at their right-wing Cabinet colleagues for allegedly betraying socialist principles. Margaret Thatcher, meanwhile, leader of the opposition after 1975, began to elaborate a position far to the right of her predecessor Edward Heath (Prime Minister 1970–4). The industrial paralysis of the 1978–9 'winter of discontent' provided a shabby end for Jim Callaghan's Labour government and a perfect backcloth against which Thatcher's confident assertions could be projected. From 1979 to 1990 ideology in the form of Thatcherism or the New Right triumphed over what has subsequently been labelled the 'post-war consensus'.

Ideology as a concept is not easy to define. It is to some extent analogous to philosophy but is not as open ended or as disinterested. It shares some of the moral commitment of religion but is essentially secular and rooted in this world rather than the next. On the other hand, it is more fundamental and less specific than mere policy. Perhaps it is helpful to regard ideology as applied philosophy. It links philosophical ideas to the contemporary world; it provides a comprehensive and systematic perspective whereby human society can be understood; and it provides a framework of principles from which policies can be developed.

Individuals support ideologies for a variety of reasons: moral commitment – often genuine, whatever cynics might say – as well as self-interest. Clearly, ideology will mean more to political theorists active within political parties, elected representatives or the relative minority who are seriously interested in political ideas. It has to be recognised that most people are ill informed on political matters and not especially interested in them. It is quite possible for large numbers of people to subscribe to contradictory propositions – for example that welfare services should be improved while taxes should be cut – or to vote for a party out of sentiment while disagreeing with its major policies. But the broad mass of the population is not completely inert. During election campaigns they receive a crash course in political education, and leaving aside the more crass appeals to emotion and unreason, most voters are influenced to some extent by the ideological debate. The party with the clearest message which seems most relevant to the times can win elections, as Labour discovered in 1945, the Conservatives in 1979 and Labour again in 1997.

BOX 4.1 **MINI BIOGRAPHY**

Edward Heath (1916–)

Conservative Prime Minister. Educated Oxford in the 1930s when he was concerned deeply about unemployment and the threat of fascism. He fought with distinction in the war and entered politics in its wake. Became leader of Conservatives a year after the defeat of 1964. Became Prime Minister in 1970 on a right-wing ticket but in power his greatest achievement was taking the country into Europe. Was replaced by Margaret Thatcher as leader in 1975 and could not hide his resentment at her disloyalty or her extreme right-wing policies. He remained a bitter critical figure, defending his record and Europe until the end of his career.

Classifying ideologies

This is a difficult and imperfect science but the following two approaches should help clarify it.

The horizontal left–right continuum

Left	Centre	Right

This is the most familiar classification used and abused in the press and in everyday conversations. It arose from the seating arrangements adopted in the French Estates General in 1789 where the aristocracy sat to the right of the King and the popular movements to his left. Subsequently the terms have come to represent adherence to particular groups of principles. Right-wingers stress freedom or the right of individuals to do as they please and develop their own personalities without interference, especially from governments, which history teaches are potentially tyrannical. Left-wingers believe that this kind of freedom is only won by the strong at the expense of the weak. They see equality as the more important value and stress the collective interest of the community above that of the individual. Those occupying the centre ground usually represent various kinds of compromise between these two positions.

The implications of these principles for economic policy are obviously of key importance. Right-wingers champion free enterprise, or capitalism: the rights of individuals to set up their own businesses, to provide goods and services and reap what reward they can. Left-wingers disagree. Capitalism, they argue, creates poverty amidst plenty – much better to move towards collective ownership so that workers can receive the full benefit of their labour. Politicians in the centre dismiss both these positions as extreme and damaging to the harmony of national life. They tend to argue for various combinations of left and right principles or compromises between them: in practice a mixed economy plus efficient welfare services. The left–right continuum therefore relates in practice principally to economic and social policy.

Left	Centre	Right
Equality	Less inequality	Freedom
Collectivism	Some collectivism	Individualism
Collective ownership	Mixed economy	Free enterprise

The vertical axis or continuum

The inadequacies of the left–right continuum are obvious. It is both crude and inaccurate in that many people can subscribe to ideas drawn from its whole width and consequently defy classification. H.J. Eysenck suggested in the early 1950s that if a 'tough' and 'tender' axis could bisect the left–right continuum, ideas could be more accurately plotted on two dimensions. In this way ideological objectives could be separated from political methodology – so tough left-wingers, e.g. communists, would occupy the top left-hand quarter, tough right-wingers, e.g. fascists, the top right-hand quarter, and so on. The diagram below illustrates the point.

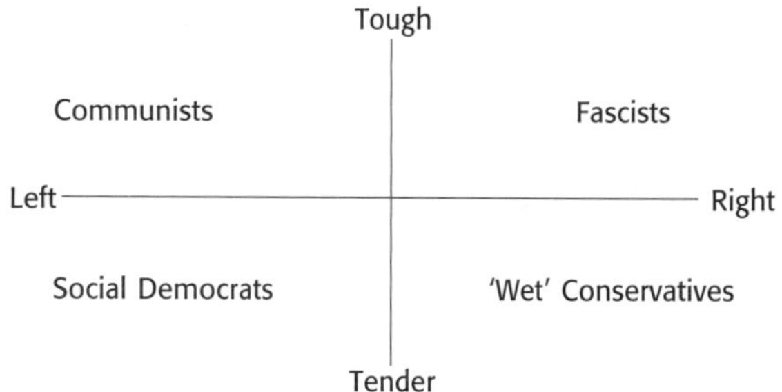

The vertical axis can also be used to plot other features:

1 An authoritarian–democratic axis is perhaps a more precise variation on the tough and tender theme.

2 A status quo–revolutionary axis is also useful. The Conservative Party has traditionally been characterised as defending the established order. Margaret Thatcher, however, was a committed radical who wanted to engineer major and irreversible changes. It was Labour and the Conservative 'wets' who defended the status quo in the 1980s. This approach produces some interesting placements on our two-dimensional diagram.

Status quo

Labour right

Conservative 'wets'

Left — Right

Bennite left

Thatcherite right

Socialist Workers' Party

Revolutionary

National Front

Political parties and the left–right continuum

Despite its inadequacies the left–right continuum is useful because it is commonly understood (however, see Box 4.1) It will be used as a guide to the following sections, but first a word on the way in which political parties relate to the political spectrum.

For most of the post-war period the major ideological divisions have not occurred between the two big parties, but within them. The Labour Party has covered a very wide spectrum from the revolutionary left to cautious social democrat right. Similarly, two major Conservative schools of thought developed in the late 1970s: traditional ('wet') Conservatism and the New Right or Thatcherite Conservatism. The centre ground for many years

BOX 4.1 **IDEAS AND PERSPECTIVES**

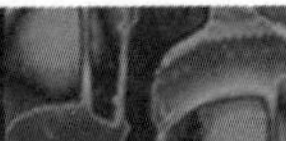

Left and right discussed

In his *The Third Way* (1998) Anthony Giddens suggests left and right are less than adequate terms. He points out that what was once left can now be right – such as nineteenth-century free market views. He quotes the Italian writer Bobbio who argues politics is adversarial and that 'left and right' encapsulates the familiar idea of bodily opposites, i.e. the left and right arms. He goes on to say that when ideas are evenly balanced most people accept the dichotomy but when one ideology seems 'the only game in town' neither side finds the terms suitable. The strong ideology seeks to claim it is the 'only' alternative while the weaker tries to strengthen its position by absorbing some elements of the stronger side and offering them as its own, producing a 'synthesis of opposing positions with the intentions in practice of saving whaever can be saved of one's own position by drawing in the opposing position and thus neutralising it'. Both sides then present their views as beyond the old left/right distinction and as something totally new and exciting. Giddens comments that 'the claim that Tony Blair has taken over most of the views of Thatcherism and recycled them as something new is readily comprehensible from such a standpoint'. Giddens insists that the 'left' is not just the opposite of 'right': the core of the former is concerned with social justice or 'emancipatory' politics while the right has shifted to anti-global and even racist positions.

He goes on to accept that socialism is no longer valid as a 'theory of economic management' and that in consequence the right/left distinction has lost relevance. Now people face 'life politics' decisions such as those connected to nuclear energy, work, global warming, devolution, the future of the EU, none of which fits easily into the old dichotomy. By talking of the 'radical centre' Giddens suggests that 'major gains' can be derived as it 'permits exchange across political fences which were much higher'. So to look at welfare reform, it is not merely an argument about high or low spending but comprises 'common issues facing all welfare reformers. The question of how to deal with an ageing population isn't just a matter of setting pension levels. It requires more radical rethinking in relation to the changing nature of ageing'.

Source: Giddens, 1998, pp. 37–46

was dominated by the Liberal Party, but during the 1980s it was first augmented by the Social Democratic Party (which split off from the Labour Party in 1981) and then was fragmented when the merger initiative following the 1987 election resulted in the awkward progeny of the Social and Liberal Democrats plus the rump Social Democratic Party led defiantly by David Owen until May 1990 when the party formally folded.

Ideas and values in politics

In politics, ideas and values cannot exist in isolation. They need a vehicle by which they can be transformed from abstract ideology into practical legislative effect. The vehicle is the political party . . .

It is more than nostalgia that justifies the party system. It is essentially the belief that some of the 'ideas and values' of politicians have a permanent importance. The policies by which those ideas and values are implemented may change with time and circumstance but the ideology abides.

Roy Hattersley, The Guardian, 30 September 1989

The liberal tradition

Since then, like so many other political labels coined as forms of abuse ('tory' was once a name given to Irish outlaws), the word has lost its derogatory connotations and fully traversed the ground between vice and virtue. Now liberalism denotes opinions and qualities which are generally applauded. Most people would like to think they are liberal in the sense of being open minded, tolerant, generous or rational. This is partly because the ideas of the English liberal philosophers from the mid-seventeenth to mid-nineteenth centuries became accepted as the dominant elements in our political culture. These were the ideas which helped create our liberal democratic political system in the late nineteenth century and since then have provided its philosophical underpinning.

Interestingly, in the USA the term came to assume a pejorative meaning in the early 1980s when the Republicans successfully linked it to being 'soft on communism' and therefore anti-American (see Box 4.2).

An important distinction clearly has to be made between liberal with a small 'l' and the Liberalism

BOX 4.2 **IDEAS AND PERSPECTIVES**

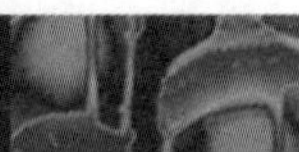

The demonising of the word 'liberal' in US politics

Guardian columnist John Sutherland meditated on Tony Blair's attacks on the 'forces of conservatism' at the 1999 Bournemouth conference. He wondered whether Blair was not trying to do for the 'c' word what had been done to the 'l' word in the USA.

Up to the mid eighties, 'liberal' was one of the blue chips of American political discourse. There was a negative side to liberalism. But it was the endearing quality of being so openminded – so small 'l' liberal – as to be 'wishy washy' . . . Some behind the scenes mastermind set up his masters to demonise the term. Liberals were not henceforth to be portrayed as weak kneed, well intentioned guys. They were powerful, cunning, and ruthlesss Machiavels. They had a sinister agenda and long term anti American goals. As Secretary for Education William Bennett's mantra was that 'liberalism has brought America to its present crisis' . . . The demonisation of the word 'liberal' was a triumph for the right. On talk shows Rush Limbaugh nowadays spits out the word as venomously and repetitively as McCarthy did 'reds'. And it always hits the mark. Democrats became terrified of the term of which they had been the proud possessors. Clinton's presidency has been one long lame duck and weave against any charge of liberalism. The L word now frightens the hell out of the liberals.

Source: Guardian, 25 October 1999

associated with the party of the same name until the 1987 merger. The Liberal Party always claimed a particular continuity with liberal philosophical ideas; but so deeply ingrained have these views become that most political parties also owe them substantial unacknowledged philosophical debts. For their part liberals have made contributions to political, social and economic thinking which have been hugely influential and have been plundered shamelessly by other parties. It makes sense, therefore, to begin with some consideration of the liberal tradition of both the philosophical 'l' and party political 'L' variety.

Philosophical liberalism

Bertrand Russell attributes the birth of English liberal thought in part to the French philosopher, René Descartes (1596–1650). His famous proposition 'I think, therefore I am' made 'the basis of knowledge different for each person since for each the starting point was his own existence not that of other individuals or the community' (Russell, 1965, p. 579). To us such propositions seem unexceptional; but in the mid-seventeenth century they were potentially revolutionary because they questioned the very basis of feudal society. This relied on unquestioning acceptance of the monarch's divine right to rule, the aristocracy's hereditary privileges and the church's explanation of the world together with its moral leadership. Feudal society was in any case reeling from the impact of the Civil War (1642–9), the repercussions of which produced a limited constitutional monarchy and the embryo of modern parliamentary government. Descartes had inaugurated a new style of thinking.

> **BOX 4.2 MINI BIOGRAPHY**
>
> **Bertrand Russell (1872–1970)**
> British philosopher and mathematician. *Principia Mathematica* was his most influential philosophical work but he wrote many popular books as well including his *History of Western Philosophy* (1946). A radical member of the Liberal party, he opposed the new creed of communism and after the Second World War he threw himself into opposing nuclear weapons as a passionate pacifist.

Rationality

John Locke (1632–1704) did much to set the style of liberal thinking as rational and undogmatic. He accepted some certainties such as his own existence, God and mathematical logic, but he respected an area of doubt in relation to most propositions. He was inclined to accept differences of opinion as the natural consequences of free individual development. Liberal philosophers tended to give greater credence to facts established by scientific enquiry – the systematic testing of theories against reality – rather than to assertions accepted as fact purely on the basis of tradition.

Toleration

This lack of dogmatism was closely connected with a liberal prejudice in favour of toleration and compromise. Conflicts between crown and Parliament, Catholicism and Protestantism had divided the country for too long, they felt: it was time to recognise that religious belief was a matter of personal conscience, not a concern of government.

Natural rights and the consent of the governed

This idea emerged out of the 'contract' theorists of the seventeenth and eighteenth centuries. These thinkers believed that each individual had made a kind of agreement to obey the government in exchange for the services of the state, principally protection from wrong-doing. The logical extension of this mode of thought was that if a contract of this sort had been somehow agreed, then the citizen had a right to reject a government which did not provide services up to the requisite standard. It was not suggested that anything had actually been signed; the idea was more of an application of the legal concept of rights to the philosophical realm. It was all a far cry from Sir

Robert Filmer's doctrine that the divine authority of monarchs to receive absolute obedience could be traced back to Adam and Eve from whom all monarchs were originally descended (see also Chapter 5 on the concept of rights).

Individual liberty

The idea of natural rights was closely allied to the concept of individual liberty which had already been established by the eighteenth century:

> These liberties included the freedom from arbitrary arrest, arbitrary search and arbitrary taxation; equality before the law, the right to trial by jury; a degree of freedom of thought, speech and religious belief; and freedom to buy and sell. (Gamble, 1981, p. 67; see also Chapter 5 on the concept of freedom)

Such liberties in practice were protected by constitutional checks and balances, limited government and representation.

Constitutional checks and balances

Locke argued that to ensure that executive power was not exercised arbitrarily by the King, the law-making or legislative arm of government should be separate, independent and removable by the community. This doctrine of the 'separation of powers' informed liberal enthusiasm for written constitutions (although ironically Britain has never had a written constitution nor, indeed, an effective separation of powers).

Limited government

Instead of the absolute power which Filmer argued the monarch was free to exercise, liberal philosophers, mindful of past abuses, sought to restrict the legitimacy of government to a protection of civil liberties. It was held to be especially important that government did not interfere with the right to property or the exercise of economic activity.

Representation

It followed that if the legislature was to be removable then it needed to be representative. Many liberal Whigs in the eighteenth century believed that Parliament was generally representative of the nation even though the franchise was small and usually based on a highly restrictive property qualification. Such positions were destined to be eroded, however, by the inherent logic of natural rights: if everyone had equal rights then surely they should have an equal say in removing a government not of their liking?

The influence of the liberal philosophers perhaps seems greater in retrospect that it was because they were often seeking to justify and accelerate political trends which were already well under way. Nevertheless, they were of key importance and provide ideas still used as touchstones in the present day.

Some commentators, such as Eccleshall and Gamble, see liberalism as providing the philosophical rationale for modern capitalist society. Certainly the idea of individual freedom, property rights and limited government suited the emergent entrepreneurial middle classes destined to come of political age in the next century. Liberal views on government, however, have enjoyed a general acceptance not just in Britain but in the USA, Western Europe and elsewhere. They have provided the commonly accepted ground rules of democratic behaviour, the 'procedural values' of toleration, fair play and free speech which Bernard Crick argues should be positively reinforced in our classrooms (see Chapter 1). They have provided in one sense an 'enabling' ideology which all major parties have accepted. Indeed, it is in some ways surprising that a creed originating in an agrarian, largely non-industrialised country should have provided a political framework which has survived so tenaciously and indeed triumphantly into the present day.

Classical Liberalism

The American and French Revolutions applied liberal principles in a way which shocked many of their more moderate adherents. The Napoleonic interlude caused a period of reaction but during the mid- to late nineteenth century Classical Liberalism took shape. Claiming continuity with the early liberals, this new school was based on the

BOX 4.3 MINI BIOGRAPHY

John Stuart Mill (1806–73)
British philosopher. Influenced by his father, James, he became a leading advocate of representative government. Sat as an MP in the 1860s and supported votes for women. Wrote *On Liberty* (1859) and *Utilitarianism* (1963).

economic ideas of Adam Smith and the radical philosophers Jeremy Bentham, James Mill and his son John Stuart Mill. Liberalism with a capital 'L' then took the stage in the form of the Liberal Party, a grouping based on the Whigs, disaffected Tories and the Manchester Radicals led by Richard Cobden and John Bright. Classical Liberalism was characterised by:

An acceptance of the liberal conception of the independent, rational and self-governing citizen as the basic unit of society.

For Liberals this concept now represented a goal or vision to be worked for. Liberals hoped that through the erosion of aristocratic privilege and the moral transformation of the working class, social differences would give way to a new society of equals.

Human nature

The liberal view of human nature was fairly optimistic. John Stuart Mill, for example, doubted whether working for the common good would induce citizens to produce goods as efficiently as when self-interest was involved. His awareness of human selfishness perhaps underlay his advice against too rapid a rate of social progress. At the heart of Liberal philosophy, however, was a belief in the potential of human nature to change into Locke's civilised reasonable human being, capable of being educated into responsible citizenship. Many Liberals felt such an education would take a great many years but that it was possible, especially through direct involvement of citizens in the economy and the political system.

Freedom

Classical Liberalism retained the emphasis on freedom. In his essay *On Liberty*, for example, Mill felt: 'It was imperative that human beings should be free to form opinions and to express their opinions without reserve'. The only constraint should be that in the exercise of his freedom, an individual should not impinge upon the freedom of others (again see Chapter 5).

Utilitarianism

Jeremy Bentham (1748–1832) took the rationality of liberal philosophy to new levels with his science of utilitarianism. His approach was based on what now seems an extraordinarily simplistic view of human psychology. He argued that human beings were disposed to seek pleasure and avoid pain. While they sought what was best for themselves they frequently made mistakes. The role of government therefore was to assist individuals in making the correct choices, in enabling the achievement of the greatest happiness for the greatest number. While Bentham embraced the *laissez-faire* economic system as highly utilitarian, he believed that most laws and administrative arrangements reflected aristocratic privilege and therefore were in need of reform. His ideas were criticised as simplistic and his Panopticon – his model prison based on his philosophy – was generally seen as risible, but he had a pervasive influence on Liberal legislators in the nineteenth century.

Minimal government

Bentham's influence paradoxically led to far-reaching legal and administrative reforms; for example, the regulatory framework for mines and factories. Other liberals, however, were strongly opposed to such regulation both as a violation of *laissez-faire* principles and as an interference in the moral education of the poor. Liberals such as Herbert Spencer (1820–1903) argued that welfare provision was wrong in that it sheltered the poor from the consequences of their behaviour. 'Is it not manifest', he argued, 'that there must exist in our midst an immense amount of misery which is a normal result of misconduct and ought not to be dissociated from it?' State support for the poor was therefore a dangerous narcotic likely to prevent the right lessons being learnt. The stern lesson Classical Liberals wished to teach was that the poorer classes would face the penalties of poverty unless they adopted the values and lifestyles of their economic superiors: thrift, hard work, moderate indulgence and self-improving pastimes.

Representative government

Bentham and James Mill (1773–1836) introduced arguments in favour of representative government. Bentham dismissed the natural rights argument as 'nonsense on stilts'. His own utilitarian reasoning was that such a form of government was the most effective safeguard for citizens against possibly rapacious rulers or powerful 'sinister interests'. As both men believed individuals to be the best judge of where their own interests lay they favoured universal franchise (although Mill sought to restrict it to men over 40). His son, J.S. Mill (1806–73), is probably the best known advocate of representative government. He urged adult male and female suffrage but to guard against a 'capricious and impulsive' House of Commons he advised a literacy qualification for voting and a system of plural voting whereby educated professional people would be able to cast more votes than ill-educated workers. Mill also believed that a participatory **democracy** and the sense of responsibility it would imbue would contribute towards the moral education of society: 'Democracy creates a morally better person because it forces people to develop their potentialities'.

Laissez-faire *economics*

Laissez-faire economics was predicated on the tenet of individual freedom: it asserted that the ability to act freely within the marketplace – to buy and sell property, employ workers and take profit – was central to any free society. Adam Smith's (1723–90) broadsides against the trade protection of the eighteenth-century mercantilist system provided the clearest possible statement of the case for economic activity free from political restrictions. According to Smith, producers should be allowed to supply products at the price consumers are willing to pay. Provided that competition was fair the 'hidden hand' of the market would ensure that goods were produced at the lowest possible price commensurate with the quality consumers required. Producers would be motivated by selfish pursuit of profit but would also provide social 'goods', through providing employment, creating wealth and distributing it in accordance with the energy and ability of people active in the economic system. Smith believed government intervention and regulation would impede this potentially perfect self-adjusting system. Liberals were not especially worried by the inequalities thrown up by *laissez-faire* economics, nor did they waste any sleep over the socialists' claim that the wage labour system enabled the middle-class property owners to exploit their workers. Classical Liberals were opposed to inherited financial advantages but not so concerned with the differences created by different performances in relation to the market. They favoured the meritocracy of the market: they were the high priests of capitalism.

Peace through trade

Liberals, especially the so-called Manchester Radicals, also applied their free trade principles to foreign affairs. Richard Cobden, for example, regarded diplomacy and war as the dangerous pastimes of the aristocracy. His answer to these perennial problems was: 'to make diplomacy open and subject to parliamentary control'; eliminate trade barriers; and encourage free trade worldwide. Commerce, he argued, was peaceful, beneficial and encouraged co-operation and contact between nations. If the world were a completely open market, national economies would become more integrated and interdependent and governments would be less likely to engage in conflicts or war.

The New Liberalism

The emphasis of Classical Liberalism was on *laissez-faire*, wealth production, toleration of inequality, minimal welfare, individual responsibility and moral education. Towards the end of the nineteenth century, however, Liberals themselves began to move away from their own ascetic economic doctrines. John Stuart Mill had argued that government was only justified in intervening in society in order to prevent injury to the life, property or freedom of others. To some Liberals it appeared that capitalist society had become so complex and repressive that the freedom of poor people to develop their potential was being restricted: even if they were inclined to emulate their middle-class betters their capacity to do so was held back by poverty, poor health and education, squalid living and working conditions. Liberal thinkers began to shift their emphasis away from 'negative' freedom – freedom from oppression – towards providing 'positive' freedom – the capacity of people to make real choices regarding education, employment, leisure, and so on.

State responsibility for welfare

T.H. Green (1836–82) helped initiate this movement for positive action to assist the poor by calling for a tax on inherited wealth. Alfred Marshall (1842–1924) believed capitalism now provided such material plenty that it had the capacity to redistribute some of its largesse to the disadvantaged so that they would be able genuinely to help themselves to become self-reliant. But it was L.T. Hobhouse (1864–1929) who perhaps marked the key shift of Liberals towards paternalism:

> The state as over-parent is quite as truly liberal as socialistic. It is the basis of the rights of the child, of his protection against parental neglect, of the equality of opportunity which he may claim as a 'future citizen'.

Hobhouse insisted that his version of paternalism should not be oppressively imposed; he favoured a basic minimum standard of living which would provide 'equal opportunities of self development'. He followed Green in proposing taxation to finance such welfare innovations as health insurance and pensions. The great Liberal victory of 1906 enabled the government to implement many of these new measures. Thereafter Liberals became firm advocates of **welfarism**; in 1942 the Liberal William Beveridge produced his famous blueprint for the post-war welfare state.

The mixed economy: Hobsonian and Keynesian economics

Government intervention of a different kind was proposed by J.A. Hobson (1858–1940). He was the first major Liberal economist (he later became a socialist) to argue that capitalism was fatally flawed. Its tendency to produce a rich minority who accumulated unspent profits and luxury goods meant that the full value of goods produced was not consumed by society. This created slumps and, indirectly, the phenomenon of economic imperialism. Capitalists were forced by such underconsumption to export their savings abroad, thus creating overseas interests with political and colonial consequences. Hobson argued that the state could solve this crisis with one Olympian move: redirect wealth from the minority to the poor via progressive taxation. The section of society most in need would then be able to unblock the mechanism which caused overproduction and unemployment, thus making moral as well as economic sense.

J.M. Keynes (1883–1946) completed this revolution in Liberal economic thought by arguing that demand could be stimulated not by redistribution of wealth to the poor but by government-directed investment into new economic activity. Confronted by a world recession and massive unemployment, he concentrated on a different part of the economic cycle. He agreed that the retention of wealth by capitalists under a *laissez-faire* economic system lay at the heart of the problem, but believed the key to be increased investment, not increased consumption. Instead of saving in a crisis governments should encourage businessmen to invest in new economic activity. Through the creation of new economic enterprises wealth would be generated, consumption increased, other economic activities stimulated and unemployment reduced. He envisaged a mixed economy in which the state would intervene with a whole range of economic controls to achieve full employment and planned economic growth. Keynes was not just concerned with the cold science of economics: his view of the mixed economy would serve social ends in the form of alleviated hardship and the extension of opportunity. But while Keynes was unhappy with capitalism in the 1930s he did not propose to replace

BOX 4.3 **BIOGRAPHY** 

JOHN MAYNARD KEYNES (1883–1946) **(picture: © Hulton-Deutsch Collection/Corbis)**

Born in Cambridge, Keynes was the son of an academic. He was educated at Eton and King's College, Cambridge, where he mixed in avant-garde intellectual circles, such as the 'Bloomsbury group', and taught sporadically. He served in the India Office (1906–8) and later wrote his first book on this subject. In the First World War he advised the Treasury and represented it at the Versailles Treaty negotiations but resigned at the terms proposed. His essay *The Economic Consequences of the Peace* (1919) brought his powerful radical intellect to the notice of the country's ruling elite. He attacked Churchill's restoration of the gold standard in 1925 and the unemployment caused by the Depression inspired his most famous work, *General Theory of Employment, Interest and Money* (1936). His views won support on the left and in the centre as well as helping to inspire the New Deal policies of Roosevelt in the USA.

Keynes married a Soviet ballerina and with her father founded the Vic-Wells ballet. In 1943 he established the Arts Theatre in Cambridge. In the same year he played a leading role in the Bretton Woods agreement, which set up a new international economic order, the establishment of the International Monetary Fund and negotiations following the ending of lend-lease (a financial agreement whereby aid was channelled to the UK during the war) after the war to secure a major loan to help Britain survive the rigours of the immediate post-war world. Most people achieve only a fraction in their lifetimes of what Keynes managed to do. He was one of the truly great figures of the century and his influence lives on today.

it – merely to modify it. He was no egalitarian, unlike socialist economists, and disagreed with Hobsonian calls for wealth redistribution which he felt would adversely affect the incentives to achieve which human nature required: 'for my own part I believe there is social and psychological justification for significant inequalities of income and wealth' (Keynes, 1985, p. 374).

Internationalism

Radical Liberals such as J.A. Hobson, Norman Angel, E.D. Moorel, C.R. Buxton, H.N. Brailsford, Lowes Dickinson and Charles Trevelyan produced an influential critique of the international system, arguing that the practice of secret diplomacy, imperialist competition for markets, haphazard balance of power policies and the sinister role of arms manufacturers made war between nations tragically inevitable. The First World War appeared to vindicate their analysis and encouraged them to develop the idea of an overarching international authority: the League of Nations. The idea was picked up by political parties and world leaders including the US President, Woodrow Wilson, and through the catalyst of war was translated into the League of Nations by the Versailles Treaty. Most of the Radical Liberals joined the Labour Party during and after the war but the Liberal Party subsequently remained staunchly internationalist and in favour of disarmament proposals throughout the interwar period.

Further development of democratic government

The New Liberals were no less interested than their predecessors in the development of representative democracy through extension of the franchise and the strengthening of the House of Commons. Lloyd George's device of including welfare proposals in his 1909 Budget – a measure which the House of Lords had traditionally passed 'on the nod' – precipitated a conflict between the two chambers which resulted in the House of Lords' power being reduced from one of absolute veto over legislation to one of delay only. In the early 1920s Liberals gave way to Labour as the chief opposition party, returning 159 MPs in 1923, 59 in 1929 and only 21 in 1935. The dramatic decline in the party's fortunes coincided with its support for a change in the electoral system from the 'first-past-the-post' system, which favoured big parties, to alternatives which would provide fairer representation to smaller parties, such as the Liberals, with thinly spread national support.

This chapter has sought to emphasise the centrality of the liberal (note small l) tradition in the evolution of modern British political thought. In the eighteenth century it helped establish reason, toleration, liberty, natural rights and the consent of the governed in place of religious dogma, feudal allegiance and the divine right of monarchs to rule. In the nineteenth century it added representative, democratic government with power shared between various elements. Having provided key guidelines for our modern system of government, Classical Liberalism argued for minimal government intervention in social policy and an economy run essentially in harmony with market forces.

The New Liberals, however, engineered a new intellectual revolution. They argued for government intervention to control an increasingly complex economy which distributed great rewards and terrible penalties with near-random unfairness. They also saw commerce not as the healing balm for international conflicts but as the source of the conflicts themselves. The irony is that the Liberals Keynes and Beveridge proved to be the chief architects of the post-war consensus between Labour and Conservatives while, as we shall see, Margaret Thatcher wrought her revolution not through application of traditional Conservatism but through a rediscovery of Classical Liberalism.

Postscript: Fukuyama and the end of history

No account of the development of the liberal tradition in politics can end without some reference to Francis Fukuyama, the formerly obscure official in the US State Department who argued in articles and a book that the liberal tradition had developed to the extent that, allied to free enterprise economics, it had eclipsed all its rivals on the left and right – communism, fascism, socialism – thus producing the 'universalisation of Western Liberal democracy as the final form of human government'.

He founded his reasoning on the Hegelian notion that civilisations successively develop, resolve internal conflicts and change for the better. The 'end of history' is when a point is reached whereby conflict is eradicated and the form of society best suited to human nature has evolved.

The importance of the article lay partly in its timing. The British Empire took a couple of decades to expire but Stalin's went up in a few years at the end of the 1980s. The intellectual world was deafened by the crashing of rotten regimes and astonished by the apparent vibrancy of their democratic successors. Moreover, after decades of defending liberal values against a grey and predatory communist bloc, the Western intelligentsia responded warmly to a thesis which appeared to say 'We've won'. Fukuyama's bold thesis fitted the facts and suited the mood of the times. Even in Britain the triumph of Thatcher in three successive elections between 1979 and 1987 seemed to reflect the thrust of the argument and her stated resolve to destroy socialism in her country. However, Fukuyama's thesis seems to ignore the exponential forces for change which are changing society at breakneck speed: computer technology and the information revolution; the huge pressure on finite world resources; the spread of nuclear weapons; the increasing concentration of wealth in a few hands; the huge and growing gap between rich and poor. Who is to say these forces will not undermine the liberal consensus and possibly usher in a new authoritarianism?

To assume the liberal underpinnings of many world political systems will survive can be seen as at best naive and at worst complacent.

Chapter summary

Ideology is a kind of applied philosophy. It can be classified on the right–left continuum, a flawed but still much used form. The liberal tradition, based on rights, freedom and representation, developed from the seventeenth century and set the ground rules for political activity during the nineteenth and twentieth. Classical Liberalism elevated the market economy but the New Liberalism, which was concerned to protect society from its excesses, still provides the rationales for the welfare state and the mixed economy.

Discussion points

- Are there better ways of classifying ideology than the left–right continuum?
- What are the grounds for thinking all human beings have rights?
- Should government resist interfering in the economy?
- Have the Liberals been exploited/robbed in ideological terms by the other two big parties?
- Defend the Fukuyama thesis that the evolution of political systems has reached its end point in liberal democratic free enterprise.

Further reading

Two excellent books have recently become available which introduce politics students to ideology. Adams (1999) is well written and subtly argued. Heywood (1998) is also essential reading. Useful in general terms are Eccleshall (1984) and Gamble (1981). Plant (1991) is more difficult but no less rewarding. On Liberalism, the texts by J.S. Mill in the References (1975, 1985a, 1985b) are as good a starting point for understanding liberalism as any. Eccleshall (1986) lays some claim to be the definitive text but Arblaster (1984) and Manning (1976) address wider readerships. Fukuyama (1992) elaborates the 'end of history' theory.

References

Adams, I. (1999) *Political Ideology Today*, 2nd edn (Manchester University Press).

Arblaster, A. (1984) *The Rise and Fall of Western Liberalism* (Blackwell).

Bell, D. (1960) *The End of Ideology* (Free Press).

Eccleshall, R. (1984) *Political Ideologies* (Hutchinson).

Eccleshall, R. (1986) *British Liberalism* (Longman).

Fukuyama, F. (1992) *The End of History and the Last Man* (Hamish Hamilton).

Gamble, A. (1981) *An Introduction to Modern Social and Political Thought* (Macmillan).

Giddens, A. (1998) *The Third Way* (Polity).

Heywood, A. (1998) *Political Ideologies: an Introduction*, 2nd edn (Macmillan).

Keynes, J.M. (1985) *A General Theory of Employment, Interest and Money*, Vol. VII of his *Collected Works* (Macmillan; first published 1936).

Manning, D.J. (1976) *Liberalism* (St Martin's Press).

Mill, J.S. (1975) *Representative Government* (Oxford University Press; first published 1861).

Mill, J.S. (1985a) *On Liberty* (Penguin; first published 1859).

Mill, J.S. (1985b) *Principles of Political Economy* (Penguin; first published 1848).

Plant, R. (1991) *Modern Political Thought* (Blackwell).

Russell, B. (1965) *The History of Western Philosophy* (Unwin).

Chapter 5

Political ideas: key concepts

Bill Jones

Learning objectives

- To introduce the conceptual approach to understanding political ideas as an alternative to the ideology-centred perspective traditionally employed.
- To explain the essence of some key concepts in the study of political science.
- To explain how these concepts are employed in the real world of politics.

Introduction

Chapter 4 touched on some key concepts; this one takes the examination further. It examines the field of political ideas through the perspective of concepts and it goes on to discuss some of the most familiar and most used ones, relating them to broader questions concerning political ideas. The most obvious starting point is with the notion of a concept itself.

What is a concept?

A concept is usually expressed by a single word or occasionally by a phrase. Concepts are frequently general in nature, representing a specific function or category of objects. For example the word 'table' usually refers to an individual human artefact, but it also embodies the whole idea of a table, which we might understand as a flat platform usually supported by legs designed to have objects rested upon it. Without this definition a table would be a meaningless object; it is the concept which gives it purpose and function. As Andrew Heywood (1994, p. 4) explains:

a concept is more than a proper noun or the name of a thing. There is a difference between talking about a chair, a particular and unique chair, and holding the concept of a 'chair', the idea of a chair. The concept of a chair is an abstract notion, composed of the various features which give a chair its distinctive character – in this case, for instance, the capacity to be sat upon.

It follows, therefore, that the concept of a 'parliament' refers not to a specific parliament in a given country but to the generality of them; the abstract idea underlying them. By the same token, as we grow up, we come to attribute meaning and function to everyday objects through learning the appropriate concepts – plates, cups, windows, doors, and so forth. Without these concepts we would be totally confused, surrounded by a mass of meaningless phenomena. In one sense concepts are the meaning we place on the world, impose on it, to enable us to deal with it. Similarly we come to understand the political world through concepts which we learn from our reading, the media and our teachers. Over the years we come to extend them and refine them in order to achieve a sophisticated understanding, to become 'politically literate'. To use a slightly different analogy, concepts are like the different lenses opticians place in front of us when attempting to find the one which enables us to see more effectively; without them we cannot bring a blurred world into focus – with them we achieve clarity and sharpness.

Some political concepts are merely descriptive, for example 'elections', but others embody a 'normative' quality – they contain an 'ought'. 'Representation' is both descriptive, in that it describes why MPs sit in legislatures, and normative, in that it carries the message that states ought to base their political system on some kind of electoral principle.

Ideologies are composites of complex concepts and we can understand them by focusing on these constituent elements. This chapter will proceed to examine briefly eight key concepts in political science: human nature, freedom, democracy, equality, social justice, rights, markets and planning.

Human nature

It is appropriate to refer again to the quotation by Voltaire which opens Chapter 1: 'There has never been a perfect government, because men have passions; and if they did not have passions, there would be no need for government'. Voltaire sums up the concern of the political scientist and philosopher with the vexed subject of human nature. Many other thinkers have been concerned with our relationships, individually and collectively, with political institutions and it is understandable they should focus on the nature of what is being organised and governed: ourselves. Many seek to identify something which explains what 'mankind is all about', a central core to our natures. Martin Hollis (cited in Plant, 1991, p. 28) writes:

All political and social theorists . . . depend on some model of man in explaining what moves people and accounts for institutions. Such models are sometimes hidden but never absent. There is no more central or persuasive topic in the study of politics.

Often these models will be the template of the related philosophy. Thomas Hobbes, for example, believed man outside society, in a 'natural' state, was disposed towards pleasure and against pain but in each case would be impelled to make individual choices. This would mean that agreement on what was desirable or undesirable would be lacking, resulting in a kind of perpetual state of war;

life, in his famous description would consequently be 'solitary, poor, nasty, brutish and short'. There would be no security of property 'no thine and mine distinct; but only that to be everyman's, that he can get; and for so long as he can keep it'.

He points out, to those who may doubt his pessimistic analysis, that a man already arms himself when taking a journey, locking doors and chests at night, even when he knows there are officers whose job it is to protect him. 'Does he not . . . as much accuse all mankind by his actions?' Hobbes goes on to argue the need for a sovereign power, a Leviathan, to impose order on society, to quell the inherent civil war of 'all against all'. Rousseau similarly predicated a state of nature in his philosophy based on man's nature in which the 'savage' was uncivilised although basically kindly. It was only the effects of organised modern society which made him bad. Already in this discussion it is possible to discern a pessimistic view of human nature, like that of Hobbes, and a more optimistic one, as in Rousseau and Locke (see Boxes 5.1 and 5.2).

In the nineteenth century the same tendencies can be seen. Marx was an optimist, believing mankind was much better than it appeared because of the corrupting effects of the harsh economic system of privately owned capital. Marx believed that human nature was a rogue product of a sick society: 'Environment determines consciousness'. It followed that to change the social environment for the better would be to improve human nature too. However, experience has tended to disappoint Marxist expectations. The Soviet Union was established after the 1917 revolution as a new experiment in political organisation. Progressive intellectuals and the working class the world over rallied to its cause, confidently expecting it to transform human nature, as, according to Marxist reasoning, the underlying capitalist economic system had been abolished. Right-wing politicians opposed it and sought to expose it as a harsh police-supported tyranny disguised by stirring rhetoric and naive left-wing support.

The debate continues but it is hard to deny that the pessimists were proved right. Through skilful manoeuvring and ruthless opportunism Joseph Stalin moved himself into a position of total power and exercised a bloody hegemony over a huge state for over two decades. Far from transforming human nature, the Soviet Union

BOX 5.1 **BIOGRAPHY**

JOHN LOCKE (1632–1704) (picture: © Bettman/Corbis)

Locke was one of the founding fathers of the English empirical approach and of liberal democracy. Born in Somerset and educated in Oxford, he was fascinated by medicine and science and became the personal physician of Lord Shaftesbury. After a spell in government service he retired to France (1675–9) where he made contact with the country's leading intellectual figures. When his patron fell from power he fled to Holland, where he supported, presciently enough, William of Orange, who was invited to take the English crown in 1688. Locke's *Two Treatises of Government* (1690, see Locke, 1956) were intended as a riposte to the divine right ideas of Robert Filmer and the 'total sovereignty' of Hobbes. Locke's works are characterised by tolerance and moderation and a less pessimistic view of human nature; sentiments often perceived as typically English.

BOX 5.2 **BIOGRAPHY** 

JEAN-JACQUES ROUSSEAU (1712–78) **(picture: © Bettman/Corbis)**

Rousseau's mother died giving birth in Geneva and he had little family life nor any formal education. In 1728 he ran away to Italy and became the lover of a baroness before moving to Paris in 1741, where he made a living from secretarial work and copying music. He established a lifelong relationship with an illiterate servant girl, Thérèse le Vasseur. He had four children by her and despite his expressed concern for children delivered them all to orphanages. He was a friend of famous intellectuals like Voltaire and Diderot, writing music and contributing articles to the latter's *Encyclopédie*, but his first famous work was his prize-winning essay on arts and sciences which argued that civilisation was corrupting man's natural goodness. He developed these ideas in a further essay on inequality in which he attacked private property. In 1762 he published his classic *Du Contrat social* (see Rousseau, 1913), which begins with the famous line: 'Man is born free but everywhere he is in chains'. This work, plus his slogan 'Liberty, Equality, Fraternity', became the founding text of the French Revolution.

merely demonstrated that in Herzen's phrase 'we are not the doctors, we are the disease'.

In the late nineteenth century, Charles Darwin formulated his theory of evolution, which argued that all species did not replicate themselves perfectly on all occasions; they sometimes developed exceptions or mutations in their bodily form. Those mutations which suited the environment survived and thrived and went on to establish a new strain which carried the banner for the species while the remaining strains faded away into extinction. This notion of the 'survival of the fittest' was used by a number of classical liberal thinkers – such as Herbert Spencer – to justify capitalism as the way in which the species was developing itself and to argue against government interference with the 'natural order' of things.

Despite their differences, these philosophies were united in assuming the basic rationality of man, that humans make rational decisions about their lives and act in accordance with reason for most of the time. The later part of the century, however, saw the emergence of a revolutionary new approach which had widespread repercussions for many kinds of thinking: the ideas of Sigmund Freud:

English philosopher. Was teacher, journalist and engineer before becoming a full-time writer. Usually seen as the author of 'Social Darwinism'; that there is a natural process in human society whereby only the fittest survive.

To live any kind of ordered life excludes the continuance of the pleasure principle, so drives are repressed and sublimated into socially useful activities like work and achievement:

> Sublimation of instinct is an essentially conspicuous feature of cultural development: it is what makes it possible for the higher psychical activities, in [the] scientific, artistic or ideological, to play such an important part in civilised life. (Freud, 1963, p. 34)

But whereas Freud applauds the constructive consequences of repression, others, such as Fromm and Marcuse, believed it to be harmful. Fromm argued that it created an alienated person who was in one sense mentally ill. To achieve 'mental health' he called for a number of reforms, many of them socialist in form. Critics such as Thomas Szasz pointed out shrewdly that 'mental health and illness are new ways of describing moral values'.

Marcuse agreed with Freud that some degree of repression – he called it 'basic repression' – is necessary for a society to function acceptably, but he believed that in Western society the degree of what he called 'surplus repression' based on class domination was unjustifiable and a revolution was necessary to correct the imbalance. Another variety of idea is based on a biological approach. Racialists, for example, posit different characteristics for different races. Nazis believed the Aryans to be the 'master race' and others to be inferior; others argue that some races are genetically inferior in terms of intelligence. Radical feminists also perceive huge irreconcilable 'essential' differences between the sexes, based on the male sex's disposition to dominate through rape or the fear of rape and violence (Brownmiller, 1975).

Freedom

> **The sense of liberty is a message read between the lines of constraint. Real liberty is as transparent, as odourless and tasteless as water.**
>
> Michael Frayn, *Constructions*, 1974

Freedom, as the above quote suggests, is not easy to define or describe, partly because it is so emotive: most politicians declare commitment to it or its synonym, 'liberty', and it is generally held to be a 'good thing'. To explore some of the intricacies and difficulties of this concept, consider the five cases listed below:

1. A man is locked in a cell for twenty-four hours a day; his fellow prisoners are beaten when they break the rules of the prison.
2. A man is left on a desert island where he can walk around but not escape.
3. A man lives in Toxteth on social security, unable to support his children or fulfil his ambition of becoming a professional musician.
4. A man is held up by a mugger and told to hand over his money or be attacked with a knife.
5. A man lives in a comfortable house in East Grinstead and fulfils his dream of becoming a successful novelist.

If the question is put 'are these men free?' then what can we conclude? Clearly the first man is not free in any sense; his movements are wholly restricted and he is prevented from leaving his cell by the locked door – he is the archetype of the person denied freedom. The second man is free to walk around but not beyond this to leave the restricted space of the island; he is effectively exiled or imprisoned. The third is free to walk wherever he wishes and in theory to do anything he pleases, but in practice he is prevented by lack of money/resources and is unable to fulfil his desire or life goal. The fourth man faces a dilemma: he can refuse to hand over his money but if he does he will face the prospect of being badly wounded, even killed, raising the question of whether he has any kind of choice. The final man is the archetypal successful man: he has the ability to move freely according to his choice; he can holiday abroad and has the resources to do so; he has fulfilled his ambitions regarding his career. It seems fair to conclude there are degrees of freedom with the first example the least free, the last, most so.

The cases discussed above reveal the range of debate about this elusive concept. The first and fourth men face physical coercion: if they refuse to obey what they are told, force will be used against them. They are classic victims of loss of freedom. Marginally close behind them is the occupant of the desert island: he is free from physical fear but he is not free to leave his restricted space. The argument gets difficult with the third man who lives in poverty. He is free from coercion but the problem is this: can he be said to be free if he has no resources to leave his less than salubrious living area, is uneducated and unable to become the person he wants to be?

These cases demonstrate the difference between 'freedom from' and 'freedom to': 'negative' and 'positive' freedom. Philosophers might say that men in cases one, two and possibly four were unfree in the negative sense: they are the victims of coercion, they are oppressed in one way or the other. The third man is free, although in the negative sense, free to improve himself, 'get on his bike' and look for a job. This sort of freedom is seen by certain thinkers, including nineteenth-century Classical Liberals, and politicians as the real core or 'essential' definition. Poverty, they argue, is not necessarily restrictive; it might even be the spur to prosperity and hence the route to more viable choices. Such thinkers defended the *laissez-faire* economic system and opposing regulatory government intervention as unjustifiable incursions into the freedoms of factory owners and other employers, not to mention the best interests of the individuals concerned.

It was the liberal philosopher T.H. Green (1988[1911]) who first argued, in modern times, for 'positive freedom'. He believed that anyone prevented from realising his/her full potential was in a real sense unfree. He defined freedom as the ability of people to 'make the best and most of themselves'. If they were not able to do this then they were not free. This definition, so attractive to socialists, opened up in theory the whole field of government intervention, especially via welfare services. Such a formulation of the concept also carries with it the clear implication that wealth should be redistributed to give more chances to more people.

Opponents of this approach, echoing Classical Liberals, claim that it is self-defeating: the government takes away the individual's freedom to improve his/her lot; it takes away the freedom of employers to employ workers at rates the market requires; it is part, in fact, of a subtle, incremental tyranny. In the twentieth century Friedrich Hayek and the economist Milton Friedman argued this case passionately, insisting that such a position was the 'road to servitude'. Sir Keith Joseph, a disciple of both thinkers, stated flatly 'Poverty is not unfreedom'.

Defenders insist that unless the individuals are empowered to realise their personal potential, then they are not truly free. They also argue that the kind of freedom right-wingers and classical liberals want is the freedom of the strong to dominate the weak, or, as R.H. Tawney (1969) vividly put it, 'the freedom of the pike is death to the minnows'.

Some dictatorial regimes claim to be 'free' when they are not. Fascist regimes, for example, claimed that the only 'true' freedom occurred when people were obeying the will of the national leader, i.e. total subjugation, not freedom as we in Western European countries would understand it. We in these countries tend to believe we are not free from government oppression unless it can be removed via unfettered elections.

Anarchists argue for a much wider kind of freedom; in fact they believe there is no need for any kind of authority and advocate complete freedom. This is generally not thought to be desirable, for it would give licence to murderers, child molesters, robbers and the like. J.S. Mill tried to solve this problem by advocating that people

BOX 5.2 MINI BIOGRAPHY

R.H. Tawney (1880–1962)
Socialist economist and philosopher. Educated Oxford where he became a fellow and author of many works on economic history. Active in the Workers' Educational Association; as a christian and a passionate advocate of equality. Professor at LSE 1931–49. His major works were *The Acquisitive Society* (1926); *Religion and the Rise of Capitalism* (1926); and *Equality* (1931).

should be allowed all freedoms except those which were harmful to others; the 'harm principle'. According to this approach, personal harm – like suicide or addictive drugs – would be acceptable as others would not be involved. Modern libertarians use similar arguments to urge the legalisation of harmful drugs such as heroin and cocaine.

Democracy

There are no wise few. Every aristocracy that has ever existed has behaved, in all essential points, exactly like a small mob.

G.K. Chesterton, *Heretics*, 1905

As with freedom/liberty, democracy is a universally regarded 'good thing' with many oppressive regimes claiming the title for propaganda purposes.

Rousseau's conception of democracy was based on his unusual idea of what constituted freedom; for him it had to be small scale and 'direct'. Citizens had to contribute personally to the formation of a 'general will' of the community by participating constantly in its governance. They could only be truly 'free' when they obeyed the imperatives which they themselves had helped create. It followed that those who failed to obey this general will were not obeying their 'true' natures and should be impelled to conform or be 'forced to be free'. Bertrand Russell believed this doctrine to be pernicious and the thin end of what eventually became the totalitarian wedge. Rousseau's idea of direct democracy hearkened back to the Greeks, but it must be clear to most enthusiasts for democracy that such a form of governance is not possible in the context of large nation-states. Even small groups find it hard to agree on simple things so it is stretching credence to the limits to believe that large groups can agree on big issues.

To maximise direct democracy, one of the aims of the left, some advocate the introduction of more and more referendums, but such devices would surely introduce unacceptable delays into government when decisions often have to be made quickly and emphatically. Some point out that today computer technology enables government to be carried out in theory on an 'interactive' basis, and some experiments along these lines have been tried in the USA and elsewhere. From one point of view our existing system is superior to any direct method, whether using ballot boxes or new technology, as many popular attitudes are authoritarian and illiberal. For example on penal policy (see Chapter 25) the public tend to favour harsh sentences for criminals and the death penalty for murderers. They can also be nationalistic and xenophobic. At least our existing system allows these extremes to be filtered out in favour of views which are the result of rational debate and intensive research. Still others accept the difficulties of scale and number and advocate instead the devolution of decision making down to the lowest level compatible with efficiency.

As a result of the inadequacies of direct democracy, an indirect form of it has been developed, called 'representative democracy', whereby people are elected to serve the community for a space of years; they become more or less full-time professional politicians, experienced in understanding the complexities both of public affairs and of interpreting the public mood. Most importantly they are also accountable to the public at election times and hence removable if they are deemed ineffective or unsuitable. This has also been called liberal democracy, the triumph of which some have discerned with the demise of communism in the late 1980s (see section on Fukuyama in Chapter 4, p. 86). Churchill famously said that this was the worst kind of government except for all the rest; but this should not blind us to its manifest imperfections.

On democracy

No one pretends that democracy is perfect or all wise. Indeed, it has been said that democracy is the worst form of government, except for all the others that have been tried from time to time.

Winston Churchill

The task of parliament is not to run the country but to hold to account those who do.

William Ewart Gladstone

1 Most people are bored by politics and functionally politically illiterate. This makes them a prey to unscrupulous politicians who can use the freedom of the system to abuse its fundamentals – Hitler subverted the Weimar Republic to seize power in the early 1930s.

2 Politicians, as already suggested, cannot be trusted to be wholly disinterested servants of the community. Dr Johnson once declared that politics was 'nothing more nor less than a means of rising in the world'; and the Nolan Committee's investigations have revealed that the cupidity of politicians remains a danger to the independence and honesty of our elected representatives.

3 Voting is an occasional ritual whereby the citizen briefly has the chance to change the government; as Rousseau dismissively pointed out, the electorate in Britain have power only on election days; once they have voted their power is vested in a body which is essentially able to do what it likes. He was right to the extent that majority voting is a fine principle but majorities can be as tyrannical as minorities; for example, the Protestant voters in Northern Ireland who used their position to disadvantage the Catholic minority over a number of decades. Lord Hailsham in the mid-1970s declared the British system of government had become an 'elective dictatorship' for the five years parties were allowed to govern before the next election (although, ever the politician, he seemed to lose his indignation when his party came to power in 1979).

4 As the German sociologist Robert Michels (1949) argued, there is a tendency for any democracy to be subverted by small elite groups: his so-called 'iron law of oligarchy'. Interestingly, Sir Anthony Eden supported this theory in the British case when he told the House of Commons in 1928 that 'We do not have democratic government today . . . What we have done in all the progress of reform and evolution is to broaden the basis of oligarchy.' Marxists tend to agree with Michels and argue further that the liberal democratic system is merely a decoration; behind the façade of elections and democratic process, the richest groups in society take all the major decisions in their own interests and against those of the masses.

5 In the modern era issues are increasingly complex, for example the arguments over the desirability of a unified European currency. This has meant that the natural reluctance of voters to involve themselves in political issues has been accentuated through an inability to absorb their complexities.

6 The political process is now dominated by the media – elections are essentially media events – and the politicians have been able to use their skills in manipulating the media, via the infamous 'spin doctors' and others, to disguise and obfuscate the real issues. Often issues are abandoned altogether in favour of 'negative campaigning'; a good example is the ploy of character assassination, as in the case of Neil Kinnock in the 1992 election who was the object of a highly personal campaign by the Murdoch-owned *Sun* newspaper.

Equality

What makes equality such a difficult business is that we only want it with our superiors.

Henri Becque, Querelles *Littéraires*, 1890

Equality is yet another hotly disputed concept. There is 'equality of opportunity' and 'equality of outcome'. The left prefer the latter, the right the former. Equality of opportunity is agreed now by all shades of opinion as a desirable thing; the liberal view has prevailed. Even South African supporters of the National Party now claim to have renounced their old apartheid attitudes which caused so much suffering and injustice. (Whether they have or not, of course, is hard to tell, but at least they no longer claim their racist views are correct, fair and God given.)

The problems arise when the equality of outcome argument is considered. For many on the left any inequality is deemed to be bad and remediable through government action. If the analogy of a race is employed, then everyone stands on the same starting line when embarking on their lives. The right-winger tends to say that how far and fast individuals progress in the race of life is a function of their ability, their energy and their will to succeed: 'winners' will strive and achieve and be admired; 'losers' will fall behind, be looked down on and make excuses. While the consensus after the war in Britain was that inequality was something to be deplored and reduced, Margaret Thatcher asserted the right of people to be 'unequal', to excel, to be better. In March 1995 John Major was asked in the House of Commons if he believed inequality should be reduced; perhaps surprisingly, he replied 'Yes'. Nevertheless, Major would not accept the left-wing argument regarding the requirement to help those who fall behind in life's race. He would be likely to argue that some differences in outcome were the consequence of 'natural inequalities', which are likely to affect anyone: some can run faster, others have exceptional memories, musical gifts, and so on. To interfere with 'nature' in this way is harmful, say right-wing theorists, likely to distort the internal dynamics of society.

The left-winger tends to interpret the 'equal start in life' argument as an illusion: most people carry handicaps; for some it might be a broken home, resulting in emotional turmoil and underachievement in school; for others it might be lack of resources, poverty, lack of adequate role models, and so forth. To maintain everyone has an equal chance in present society is to say, according to the left, that the fleet of foot have a clear opportunity to excel without any impediment over others less gifted or blessed by birth.

So the left tend to argue for a system which helps the slower to catch up, for their poverty to be alleviated, their special needs met; in some cases for special 'affirmative action', whereby those groups regularly excluded from success, such as racial minorities and women, are given some preference, perhaps in the form of 'quota' allocations for university entrance, as in the USA.

The right claim that, to work effectively, people need to be given an incentive. If wages are equalised, for example, then the lazy will have no incentive to work and will be idle while the industrious are exploited and denied proper reward for their effort. They claim this is fundamental for the effective functioning of the economy which is fuelled by incentives; when a role needs performing in society the market puts a price on filling it; when it is a freely available skill, like sweeping the streets, the rate is low but when the skills are rare and dependent on years of study plus high intellectual ability – as in the case of running a major company – the rates are high and rightly so. This argument was also employed by the Conservatives in the 1980s when they cut taxes for high earners. A corollary of this argument is that a hierarchy of reward stimulates effort: if someone desires advancement in the form of riches or status they are prepared to work for it and strain every effort. In the USA this is part of the so-called 'American Dream' whereby immigrants often arrived with nothing except their clothes yet within a generation or two had accumulated large fortunes or won senior places in society. Similarly Sir Keith Joseph was making the same point when he stated the apparent paradox that for 'the poor to become richer, we have to make society more unequal'.

Finally, right-wing polemicists claim that remedial intervention by the state is implicitly tyrannical as it involves taking away from the able – sometimes through the law, backed up by force – some of their just rewards. They also point to the former communist regimes where 'equality' was imposed on society through the agency of an oppressive regime complete with police powers, work camps and punitive prison sentences.

Social justice

Justice is the right of the weakest.

Joseph Joubert, *Pensées*, 1842

Who should get what in society? The left tend to favour an approach based on 'needs' and the right one based on 'rights' or 'desert'. In his book, *Modern Political Thought* (1991), Raymond Plant investigates this by positing the problem of the just distribution of one hundred oranges in a society of one hundred people. The obviously fair approach, especially if all members have been involved in the production process, is to give one orange to each person. However, if some people have a particular physical need for vitamin C, then the question arises whether their needs justify an unequal distribution. Maybe these special needs people need two each? Or three or even more? This is the kind of debate social justice discussions stimulate and it obviously has wider implications for the way in which income and wealth are distributed together with other material goods like welfare benefits, taxation, housing, and so forth.

Karl Marx declared that in a communist society the principle of material distribution would be: 'From each according to his ability, to each according his needs!' A charming fictional version of what life might be like in a truly socialist society is found in William Morris's novel *News from Nowhere* (1891; see Morris, 1993), in which the main character finds himself in a future socialist England in which money has been abolished, people work happily for the community and take what they need for basic consumption and leisure purposes. In reality this utopian vision would probably remain a mere vision, but some vestige of its moral force still informs current thinking on the left.

At the heart of this notion of social justice is that large accumulations of wealth, juxtaposed by poverty and ill health, are not justifiable. It follows, according to this approach, that wealth should be redistributed in society and, indeed, between nations. On the other hand, even left-wing theorists agree that some economic inequality is necessary to make the economic system work, so the real debate is how much redistribution is needed to achieve justice?

One influential thinker on the left has been John Rawls, whose book *A Theory of Justice* (1971) has occasioned much debate. He asked us to consider what distribution of goods we would endorse if we were rational people planning a society but, crucially, were unaware of our own capacities. In this way it would be possible to prevent people from favouring their own talents and strengths, for example preventing a clever person from advocating a meritocracy or a physically strong person a free-for-all society. This ensures that any decisions reached would be neutral. Rawls argues that all would agree on the greatest possible degree of liberty in which people would be able to develop their talents and life plans. In addition, however, Rawls posits the 'difference principle' whereby he maintains that social and economic inequalities – differences in wealth, income and status – are only just if they work to the advantage of most disadvantaged members of society and only if they can be competed for fairly by all. Rawls argues that in such a situation rational people would choose, through a sense of insecurity, a society in which the position of the worst-off is best protected; this would be a market economy in which wealth is redistributed through tax and welfare systems up to the point when it becomes a disincentive to the economic activity.

Right-wing theorists tend to ignore this notion of needs; indeed the very notion of social justice is denied by some (e.g. Friedrich Hayek). The right tend to favour 'rights'-based approaches, for example the fact that someone has made an artefact endows a property right upon the craftsman/woman. Similarly, if a person has bought something, the same right is presumed to be in place as money can be seen as a symbolic exchange for labour. Work, or the exercise of talent, is held to establish a right to material reward: 'Well, he's earned it' is often said about wealthy hard-working people. Alternatively, if someone is rich through unusual talent, as a writer maybe or an exceptional entertainer, the usual response is that 'he's worth it'. Robert Nozick (1974) has been an influential theorist on the right, arguing that wealth is justifiable if it is justly acquired in the first place – for example has not been stolen – and has been justly transferred from one person to another. He goes on to argue that if these conditions have not been met the injustice should be rectified. Nozick rejects the notion of 'social justice' or the idea that inequality is somehow morally wrong. If transfers of wealth take place between one group in society and another, it should be on the basis of private charity, made on the basis of personal choice. But Nozick's views do not necessarily bolster right-wing views on property as the rectification principle could imply the redistribution of much wealth, especially when it is considered that so much of the wealth of the West has been won at the expense of plunder and slavery in Third World countries.

Right-wing thinkers are also attracted by Social Darwinism. Herbert Spencer (see Spencer, 1982) argued that material circumstances were merely the reflection of differing innate abilities and talents: people are rich because they are more able than others and therefore deserving of reward. In his view this reflected the 'natural' order of things and as such should not be disturbed. He also believed it was wrong to intervene to assist people who had fallen on hard times: 'If we protect people from the consequences of their own folly we will people the world with fools'.

Rights

Rights that do not flow from duties well performed are not worth having.

Mohandas K. Ghandi, *Non-Violence in Peace and War*, 1948

Human 'rights' embodies the idea that every human has certain basic entitlements, and gives rise to a number of questions:

1 What is the basis of these rights? Are they legal?

Some are embodied in the law but others are not.

2 Are they related to religious ideas?

To some extent but not necessarily.

3 What are the sources of human rights?

Their origins lie more in moral than political philosophy. They were implicit in the notion of the social contract, popular in the seventeenth century and revived in a singular form by Rawls in the 1970s, as mentioned above. Before the seventeenth century political ideas were dominated by God and feudalism. All authority was vested in the monarch, sanctioned by God via the 'divine right of kings' theory. There were no thoughts of individuals having any rights beyond those invested by the law. Hobbes' theory was so unorthodox as it rested on the notion of a contract between individuals and the state whereby allegiance was given in exchange for protection from the anarchic disorder of an ungoverned society. However, if the state failed in its duty of providing protection then the obligation of citizens would 'last as long, and no longer, than the power by which he is able to protect them'. In other words, according to Hobbes, citizens retain a right of independence even under an all-powerful ruler. This notion of a social contract and fundamental rights was revolutionary in his time; it gathered strength during the century and in the thought of John Locke became a means whereby 'equal and independent people' in a state of nature could decide whether or not 'by their own consent to make themselves part of some political society'. It followed that everyone had rights independent of the state; and the authority of the government depended on the consent of the governed. Nearly a century later – 1776 – these ideas were neatly and wonderfully summarised in the American Declaration of Independence:

> We hold these truths to the self-evident, that all men are created equal, that they are endowed by their creator with certain unalienable rights, that among these are Life, Liberty and the pursuit of Happiness. That to secure these rights, Governments are instituted among men, deriving their just powers from the consent of the governed.

There is a clear distinction to be made between moral and legal rights. Legal or 'positive' rights are included in the law and can be enforced in the courts. Such rights can be a right to do something should one choose – such as walk on the highway – or a right not to be treated in a certain way –

such as not be the victim of violence – or they can be the empowering right to vote in an election. In Britain basic rights such as freedom of speech and worship are not enshrined in law; but instead they are not excluded – so are therefore allowed. In contrast, in the USA such rights are included in the constitution and are more easily defended (although similar legal safeguards in despotic regimes, such as the former USSR, have not protected human rights). Internationally human rights are held to exist as the basic conditions for a tolerable human existence. The United Nations issued its Universal Declaration of Human Rights, which 'set a common standard of achievement for all peoples and all nations'. Similar declarations exist in relation to economic, social and cultural rights. The European Union has its own set of declarations along very similar lines. Interestingly the European Convention has been the source of rulings made by virtue of British membership of the EU, which have over-ruled domestic law, as in the case of corporal punishment in schools. These international organisations have been very important in advancing the cause of human rights as they have brought them to the attention of transgressing and law-abiding nations alike.

As in the case of freedom and justice, there is a familiar left–right dichotomy over rights which relate to the operation of the economy. The right tend to stress 'negative' rights: the right to be left alone, not to be imprisoned or attacked by the state. The left stress 'positive rights', such as the UN's 'right to work' (Article 23) and 'right to education' (Article 26). Such rights are denied by the right; this conflict can also be seen in the Labour Party's adherence to the Social Chapter of the Maastricht Treaty and the Conservatives' opposition to it.

Some thinkers champion animal rights. Logically, if humans have rights by virtue of being alive, then other forms of life must have rights too. This makes vegetarianism a difficult philosophy to refute. True, animals cannot think and express themselves, but their very helplessness offers a reason why humans should protect and not exploit them through killing and eating them. The Animal Liberation Front feels especially strongly about experiments inflicted on animals for medical or, much worse, cosmetic research.

The market

You can't buck the markets.

Margaret Thatcher

At first sight this concept, central to how an unfettered economic system works, might seem closer to economics than politics and, while this may be true, anything which determines, as the market does, how shares of scarce resources are allocated must be highly political. At the heart of the 'free-market' model is the idea of a public market in which goods are offered for sale by a variety of producers who seek to sell their products or produce to consumers. Using the model we can see how such an economy works. Producers create their goods, whether manufactured or grown, and seek to make a profit on their sale. Within the market a subtle kind of communication occurs. People wishing to buy, for example, cotton shirts, will probably survey what is available, making judgements about quality and tempering them with calculations of price. Those stalls offering good quality at low price will find trade brisk while those offering poor quality at high prices will find it slow to non-existent. The favoured stalls will soon become well known and shirt purchasers will tell friends, who also wish to buy such products about the key options available in the market. The result will be, over time, that the recommended stalls will prosper while the others will face failure unless they change their mode of operation. They will need to rethink their production techniques, cutting down on costs wherever possible, introducing new equipment perhaps and experimenting with new styles. With this done satisfactorily, they can re-enter the market and, provided that the word gets around, will trade again but this time with success.

Adam Smith, already mentioned in Chapter 4, was the first influential theorist on the working of the market. He pointed out that the dynamic of the market is provided by the consumers who wish to buy and the providers who wish to sell: 'supply and demand'. Smith believed that any regulation of these complex processes, for example by government, would hinder their efficient working as they worked best when left alone. Edmund

> **BOX 5.3 MINI BIOGRAPHY**
>
> **Adam Smith (1723–90)**
> Scottish economist. His *Wealth of Nations* (1776) explained, analysed and advocated the system of modern capitalism, unhindered by government intervention. He perceived that division of labour was at the heart of economic efficiency and became the prophet of Classical Liberalism during both the nineteenth and the twentieth centuries.

Burke too declared 'The moment that government appears at market, all the principles of the market will be subverted'. The French term '*laissez-faire*' – to let be – is used to describe this approach to economics.

There is therefore, according to *laissez-faire* advocates, a 'natural' or 'magic' quality to the market which, if left to its own devices, works perfectly. Enoch Powell, a great advocate of unfettered markets, wrote of 'this wonderful silent automatic system – this computer' and 'the subtlest and most efficient system mankind has yet devised for setting effort and resources to their economic use'. The role of government should be strictly contextual or supportive according to free marketeers. It should sustain an inflation free currency; maintain frontiers from external attack; provide a peaceful and safe environment in which business can flourish; together with a framework of law in which business transactions can be legally validated and pursued in the courts if violated. The beauty of the market to its supporters is that:

1. It does not depend on qualities which 'ought' to be present in mankind but accepts what qualities there are and makes the best of them. So by pursuing his profits and becoming rich the business man provides employment for his workforce who also become consumers whose money helps to keep other businesses and thence the whole of society prosperous.
2. It provides the possibility of personal development for employers and workers alike: they can become the people they wish to be through hard work, savings and creating opportunities for themselves.
3. It enables individuals to influence via their purchases the future of the market or the economy. Purchases are likened to voting; if enough people 'vote' for a particular product it becomes established as a part of social life; if they reject them the product disppears. So electrical goods have become standard, computers are becoming so too; and it is all the product of thousands of individual choices freely made.
4. The market is wholly egalitarian. It cares nothing for the sex, religion or race of the producer or retailer; the only qualities which count are hard work, dedication and the talent to provide society with what it requires and wants.

However critics of the market point out that it is far from perfect.

1. The national and international markets can undergo rapid periods of growth which are then followed by slumps in which millions can be made unemployed and consigned to destitution.
2. The ability of those who supply or control the market to make large profits creates huge disparities of wealth and hence chronic inequality in which the producers of wealth, the workers, receive scant reward for their efforts. This inequality can also produce social unrest and political instability.
3. The emphasis on individual effort can encourage selfishness and a callous attitude towards those who fail to succeed in the market.
4. Unregulated markets produce fallouts which can harm society for example environmental pollution.
5. Markets do not provide for all the requirements of a successful society. For example governments have to step in to provide mechanisms to dispose of garbage or sewage or, the example cited by Heywood (1994, p. 280), provide lighthouses.

6 The existence of so many producers creates wasteful duplication of effort by workers and management alike.

7 The market is dependent on demand and may find it is merely serving those with money, producing luxury goods and neglecting the needs of society as a whole.

The dependence of successful business on individuals and entrepreneurs has tended to concentrate its support in the ranks of those who have benefited from the system. Accordingly opponents have tended to spring from those who have not benefited or those who have chosen to champion the cause of those who have not benefited.

Planning

Make no small plans: they have no power to stir the hearts of men.

Daniel H. Burnham, motto of city planners

Planning is to an extent, say the opponents of *laissez-faire*, its antidote. It is lack of regulation which creates the unjust excesses of capitalism and planning offers a means of distributing scarce or even plentiful resources on a more equitable and efficient basis. Planning is a rational means of achieving economic goals; it presupposes a defined goal and route to its achievement. However, planning as a concept has suffered from the close relationship it has in the popular imagination with the economic and political system of the former USSR. Here an ancient system was overthrown and replaced by one which aimed to change the basis of human nature itself. Initially, however, it had to compromise with reality as it existed in the early twenties. Lenin's New Economic Policy in 1921 allowed the activity of free enterprise in certain areas but soon ideological imperatives took over once Stalin tightened his grip over the embryonic new state. He set up a complex system of ministries which served Gosplan, the State Planning Committee, which itself took its orders from the highest political authority, the Politburo. Planning sometimes resembled that employed successfully in capitalistic enterprises – the techniques of mass production for example and the time and motion studies of the American management guru, F.W. Taylor. For a while such planning was applauded in the West and tribes of observers, of left and right, trailed around the Soviet Union seeing very much what the communist party wished them to see. Certainly planning laid the foundations of heavy industry in the country and established the strength which helped to see off Hitler and his armies. For a while it seemed after the war that maybe Stalin did represent the wave of the future and the *laissez-faire* economics had been superceded by a superior system. The launch of the orbiting Soviet Sputnik in the 1950s seemed to confirm Soviet ascendency but it probably marked a high tide from which it subsequently retreated. By the 1980s it became clear that the Soviet economy was imploding with net GDP actually shrinking in the early part of the decade. Once its economy ceased to function the USSR had to opt out of the arms race and when Gorbachev abandoned the Soviet economic and political system its days as a superpower were over; without economic efficiency no country can stay powerful politically for long. But this unhappy experience of planning should not blind us to its successes and advantages.

1 During the Second World War Britian introduced a centrally planned economic system which proved highy efficient and was arguably superior to the German equivalent.

2 Since the war Britain has introduced planning into policies affecting the environment with some success. Here the policy is not imposed from the centre but is open to scrutiny and democratic debate (although some claim what is available is insufficient).

3 Other countries such as The Netherlands, Germany and the Scandinavian countries, especially Sweden, have embraced a substantial degree of economic planning with results which are reflected in their high standards of living.

4 The activities of the EU are founded on the notion of careful planning in all policy areas, the aim being to encourage a Europe which is prosperous without its many existing areas of low economic performance. The EU has generally been judged a success in its economic and environmental policies.

5 The above successes prove that political authoritarianism is not the inevitable concomitant of planning.

6 Planning is a way of maintaining the dynamism of the free enterprise system while guarding against its unacceptable side-effects. Planning is accountable not to businessmen or shareholders but to elected politicians who can be called to account in the public interest.

7 Planned economic activity is more likely to be democratic, reflecting values of justice and fairness; its advocates claim such unselfish social policies and institutions inspire loyalty and greater effort by those involved.

One of the first attempts to develop a critique of planning was undertaken by Friedrich Hayek in The Road to Serfdom (1944). In an analysis elaborated in later writings, Hayek suggested that planning was inherently inefficient because planners were confronted by a range and complexity of information that was simply beyond their capacity to handle. Central planning means making 'output' decisions which allocate resources to them. However, given that there were well over 12 million products in the Soviet economy, some of which came in hundreds, if not thousands of varieties, the volume of information within the planning system was – according to economists – exceeding the number of atoms in the entire universe.

Andrew Heywood, Political Ideas and Concepts, p. 272

While planning can boast some successes it is obvious it has its downsides:

1 It is almost impossible to plan an economy efficiently for a whole nation. To do this planners must know exactly what consumer demand is, how much of each product will be required and when. The amount of data required for such planning is impossible to collect let alone compute (see quotation above). Consequently planners make educated guesses and frequently make mistakes creating shortages and queues. The Soviet Union was so beset by queues that some people used to make a living out of hiring themselves out to stand in queues for scarce products. Even when people earned reasonable salaries it was of little benefit to them as there was little to buy in the shops.

2 Some goods were completely unavailable in the Soviet Union and consequently could only be bought on the huge black market.

3 Because goods were in short supply shop assistants became key people in communist countries as they exerted some control over the flow of goods; rather as they did in Britain during the war when rationing was in place.

4 Planned economies tend to be sluggish and deter innovation. They may provide full employment but there is no incentive to work hard, to get ahead as in capitalist countries. Workers tended to serve their time in communist economies. Moreover, managers tried to keep planning targets low and once achieved to relax.

5 The idea that planning can inspire workers to work harder for the 'community' or the nation is not borne out in practice. Nationalised industries in the UK after the war were famous for being overmanned, inefficient and staffed by workers who resented their managers every bit as much as they had former private employers. Furthermore, such workers were more than willing to hold the country to ransom in the 1970s for more pay, even if the whole nation suffered as a result.

6 In planned economies a class of bureaucrat emerges in charge of the process. They tend

to fix things so that they benefit from the system, creating in the words of Yugoslav communist dissident Milovan Djilas, a New Class, privileged and able to exploit advantages rather like the upper middle classes in capitalist countries.

7 Political opponents such as Hayek argued that planning was the thin end of a wedge which could become totalitarian in character; when people objected to being planned – as Soviet farmers made it clear they did not wish to be collectivised in the 1930s – they were imprisoned and executed.

Chapter summary

A concept is like a lens placed in front of one's perception of the world and can be descriptive and normative. Many key concepts are interpreted differently according to the political perspective (see Figure 5.1 for summary of left and right versions of key concepts). Power is a crucial organising concept used in analysing why people do the bidding of politicians, and authority is essentially power plus legitimacy.

Left		Right
Optimistic	Human nature	Pessimistic
Positive	Freedom	Negative
Direct	Democracy	Indirect
Equality of outcome	Equality	Equality of opportunity
Needs	Social justice	Deserts
Positive	Rights	Negative
Interventionist	State	Minimal

Figure 5.1 Concepts and ideology

Discussion points

- In what ways does the study of concepts tell us more about political ideas than approaches based on looking at different ideologies?
- Of the nine concepts studied in this chapter, which three are the most central to the study of politics?
- Is the left-wing interpretation of concepts more defensible than that of the right?

Further reading

The best book on political concepts is Andrew Heywood's simply excellent *Political Ideas and Concepts* (1994). Also very useful are Plant (1991), Russell (1965) and Plamenatz (1963).

References

Brownmiller, S. (1975) *Against Our Will: Men, Women and Rape* (Simon and Schuster).

Freud, S. (1963) *Civilisation and its Discontents* (Hogarth Press; first published 1930).

Green, T.H. (1988) *Works*, ed. R. Nettleship (Oxford University Press; first published 1911).

Hayek, F. (1979) *The Road to Serfdom* (Routledge; first published 1944).

Heywood, A. (1994) *Political Ideas and Concepts* (Macmillan).

Locke, J. (1956) *The Second Treatise on Government*, ed. J. Gough (Blackwell; first published 1690).

Michels, R. (1949) *Political Parties* (Free Press).

Morris, W. (1993) *News from Nowhere* (Penguin; first published 1891).

Norton, P. and Aughey, A. (1981) *Conservatives and Conservatism* (Temple Smith).

Nozick, R. (1974) *Anarchy, State and Utopia* (Blackwell).

Plamenatz, J. (1963) *Man and Society* (Longmans).

Plant, R. (1991) *Modern Political Thought* (Blackwell).

Rawls, J. (1971) *A Theory of Justice* (Harvard University Press).

Rousseau, J.-J. (1913) *The Social Contract and Discourses* (Dutton; first published 1762).

Russell, B. (1965) *History of Western Philosophy*, (Unwin).

Spencer, H. (1982) *The Principles of Ethics*, ed. T. Machan (Liberty Classics; first published 1887).

Tawney, R.H. (1969) *Equality* (Allen and Unwin).

Chapter 6

Political ideas: the major parties

Bill Jones

Learning objectives

- To explain the provenance of Conservatism and the ideology of capitalist free enterprise; the difference between 'one nation' and neo-liberal Conservatism; and to assess the impact of Margaret Thatcher on her party's ideas.
- To trace the origins of Labour thinking to the rejection of nineteenth-century **capitalism**; its maturing into corporate **socialism** and revisionism plus the left-wing dissenters in the 1970s and 1980s; to analyse the impact of Labour's rapid move into the centre and the apparent embrace of neo-Thatcherite and communitarian ideas by Tony Blair.
- To sum up the message of the Liberal Party over the years including its alliance with the SDP and its evolution into the Liberal Democrats.

Introduction

In the aftermath of the Second World War some commentators felt that the two major political parties in Britain were 'converging' ideologically. Daniel Bell, the American sociologist, wrote of 'the end of ideology' and in the 1970s a post-war 'consensus' was discerned between the two parties on the desirability of a welfare state and a mixed economy. Britain's relative economic decline inclined both parties to adopt more radical remedies which drew on their ideological roots. Margaret Thatcher swung the Conservatives violently to the right while Labour went radically to the left in the early 1980s. Once Thatcher had gone, Major adopted a less overtly ideological stance, while Labour, following the failed experiment of Foot as leader, successively under Kinnock, Smith and Blair moved rapidly into the centre. This chapter analyses the evolution of the ideas of the major parties and brings up to date their most recent changes.

Eve-of-election quotes by party leaders, 1997

The language of politics is now a Conservative language. . . . It is we who have changed the whole thrust of politics and moved it in our direction.

John Major, Conservative

We live in a world of dramatic change and the old ideologies that have dominated the last century do not provide the answers.

Tony Blair, Labour

We are beginning to see the break-up of the two great monoliths that dominate British politics.

Paddy Ashdown, Liberal Democrat

The Conservative Party

Key elements

Conservatism has a long history stretching back before its formal emergence in the 1830s. Critics have doubted whether the party has ever possessed a coherent philosophy, and indeed Lord Hailsham (1959) has described it as not so much a philosophy as an attitude. However, it is possible to discern a number of key tenets on which this attitude and Conservative policies have been based:

1. *The purpose of politics is social and political harmony*: Conservatives have traditionally believed that politics is about enabling people to become what they are or what they wish to be. They believe in a balance, a harmony in society. They have avoided too much ideological baggage in favour of measured **pragmatism** which has always kept options open. Like Edmund Burke, they have tended to believe that 'all government . . . is founded on compromise'.
2. *Human nature is imperfect and corruptible*: This notion of 'original sin' lies at the heart of Conservatism, leading its supporters to doubt the altruism of humankind beyond close family; perceive most people as more interested in taking rather than giving; and see them as fairly easy to corrupt without the external discipline of strong government.
3. *The **rule of law** is the basis of all freedom*: Law restricts freedom yet without it there would be no freedom at all, but instead – given humanity's selfish, aggressive nature – anarchic chaos. Accepting the authority of the law is therefore the precondition of all liberty.
4. *Social institutions create a sense of society and nation*: Social and political institutions help to bind together imperfect human beings in a thing called society. Living together constructively and happily is an art and this has to be learnt. At the heart of the learning process lies the family, and the institution of marriage. The royal family provides an idealised and unifying 'micro-model'. At the macro level is the idea of the 'nation', ultimately a cause worth dying for.
5. *Foreign relations is the pursuit of state interests in an anarchic world*: States exhibit all the dangerous characteristics of individuals plus a few more even more unpleasant ones of their own. A judicious defence of national interests is the best guide for any country in the jungle of international relations.
6. *Liberty is the highest political end*: Individuals need freedom to develop their own personalities and pursue their destinies. Conservatives agree with Mill that it should entail freedom from oppression and be allowed to extend until it encroaches upon the freedom of others. It should not embrace the 'levelling' of wealth, as advocated by socialists, as this redistribution would be imposed upon a reluctant population by the state (see also Chapters 4 and 5).
7. *Government through checks and balances*: 'Political liberty', says Lord Hailsham, 'is nothing else than the diffusion of power'. This means in practice institutions which

divide power between them and all have a measure of independence and thus prevent any single arm of government from being over-mighty. Hailsham also argues that political factions should balance or alternate with each other, each taking a turn at government rather than allowing it to be the preserve of one party alone.

8 *Property*: Conservatives, like David Hume, believe that the right to property is the 'first principle of justice' on which the 'peace and security of human society entirely depend'. Norton and Aughey (1981) take this further, arguing that it is an 'education. It enlightens the citizens in the value of stability and shows that the security of small property depends upon the security of all property' (p. 34). The Conservative policy of selling council houses was in line with this belief in that it was assumed, probably rightly in this case, that people would cherish their houses more once they enjoyed personal ownership.

9 ***Equality of opportunity*** *but not of result*: Conservatives believe everyone should have the same opportunity to better themselves. Some will be more able or more motivated and will achieve more and accumulate more property. Thus an unequal distribution of wealth reflects a naturally unequal distribution of ability. Norton and Aughey maintain the party is fundamentally concerned with justifying inequality in a way which 'conserves a hierarchy of wealth and power and make[s] it intelligible to democracy' (p. 47). To do this, Conservatives argue that inequality is necessary to maintain incentives and make the economy work; equality of reward would reward the lazy as much as the industrious (see also Chapter 5).

10 *One nation*: Benjamin Disraeli, the famous nineteenth-century Conservative prime minister, added a new element to his party's philosophy by criticising the 'two nations' in Britain, the rich and the poor. He advocated an alliance between the aristocracy and the lower orders to create one nation. His advice was controversial and remains so.

11 *Rule by elite*: Conservatives believe the art of government is not given to all; it is distributed unevenly, like all abilities, and is carefully developed in families and outside it most commonly in good schools, universities and the armed forces.

12 *Political change*: Conservatives are suspicious of political change as society develops organically as an infinitely complex and subtle entity; precipitate change could damage irreparably things of great value. Therefore they distrust the system builders such as Marx, the root-and-branch reformers such as Tony Benn. But they do not deny the need for all change; rather they tend to agree with the Duke of Cambridge that the best time for it is 'when it can be no longer resisted', or with Enoch Powell that the 'supreme function of a politician is to judge the correct moment for reform'.

Impact of Thatcherism

This collection of pragmatic guides to belief and action was able to accommodate the post-war Labour landslide which brought nationalisation, the managed Keynesian economy, close co-operation with the trade unions and the welfare state. The role of Harold Macmillan was crucial here. In the 1930s he wrote *The Middle Way*, a plea for a regulated *laissez-faire* economy which would minimise unemployment and introduce forward planning into the economy. He was able to accept many of the reforms introduced by Labour and re-interpret them for his own party.

The post-war consensus continued with little difference over domestic policy between Macmillan and Gaitskell, Wilson and Heath. But when the economy began to fail in relation to competitors in the late 1960s and early 1970s a hurricane of dissent began to blow up on the right of the Conservative Party – and the name of the hurricane was Margaret Thatcher. She had no quarrel with traditional positions on law, property and liberty, but she was passionately convinced of a limited role for government (although not necessarily a weak one); she wanted to 'roll back' the socialist frontiers of the state. She was uninterested in checks and balances but wanted to maximise her power to achieve the things she wanted. She was opposed to equality and favoured the inequalities caused by a dynamic economy. She had scant respect for the aristocracy as she admired only ability and energy; qualities she owned in abundance. She was not in favour of gradual change but wanted radical alterations now, in her lifetime. She was a revolutionary within her own party and it has still not stopped reverberating from her impact.

Thatcherite economics

1 Margaret Thatcher was strongly influenced by Keith Joseph who was in turn influenced by the American economist Milton Friedman. He urged that to control inflation it was merely necessary to control the supply of money and credit circulating in the economy.

2 Joseph was also a disciple of Friedrich von Hayek, who believed that freedom to buy, sell and employ, i.e. economic freedom, was the foundation of all freedom. Like Hayek, he saw the drift to collectivism as a bad thing: socialists promised the 'road to freedom' but delivered instead the 'high road to servitude'.

3 Hayek and Friedman agreed with Adam Smith and the classical liberals, that, if left to themselves, market forces – businessmen using their energy and ingenuity to meet the needs of customers – would create prosperity. To call this 'exploitation' of the working man, as socialists did, was nonsense as businessmen were the philanthropists of society, creating employment, paying wages, endowing charities. When markets were allowed to work properly they benefited all classes: everyone benefited, even the poor.

4 Thatcher believed strongly that state intervention destroys freedom and efficiency through taking power from the consumer – the communist 'command' economies were inefficient and corrupt; protecting employment through temporary and harmful palliatives; controlling so much of the economy that the wealth-producing sector becomes unacceptably squeezed.

5 Trade unions were one of Thatcher's *bêtes noires*. She saw them as undemocratic, reactionary vested interests which regularly held the country to ransom in the 1970s. She was determined to confront and defeat them.

6 She believed state welfare to be expensive; morally weakening in that it eroded the self-reliance she so prized; and in addition monopolistic, choice denying as well as being less efficient than private provision.

7 Her defence of national interests was founded in a passionate patriotism which sustained her support for the armed forces and the alliance with the USA. During the Falklands War she showed great composure and courage in taking risks and ultimately triumphing. The reverse side of this was her preference for the US link over the European Union, which she suspected of being a Trojan horse for German plans to dominate the whole continent.

Margaret Thatcher therefore drove a battering ram through traditional Conservatism but it was in effect a return to the Classical Liberalism of the early/mid-nineteenth century (see Chapter 4). Andrew Heywood (see Further Reading) discerns another thread in Thatcherism, that of Neo-Conservatism, a pre-Disraelian emphasis on duty, responsibility, discipline and authority; although in her it was a reaction to the permissiveness of the 1960s, the defining decade of post-war socialistic culture. Many claimed to have been converted to her ideas but the 1980s witnessed a tough internal battle, which the Prime Minister finally won, between her and the so-called 'wet' wing of the party, which still hearkened back to the 'one nation' strand of the party's thinking.

The Major years

When John Major succeeded her following the virtual 'coup' in November 1990, many thought he would be the best hope of stern and unbending

Thatcherism, but he seemed much more conciliatory, more concerned with achieving unity even at the cost of compromise, a very un-Thatcherite course of action. As the years passed by, however, it became apparent that this initial analysis is far away from what happened. Major's government was almost wholly circumscribed by the ideas of his predecessor. As Andrew Heywood has pointed out, the Major government accepted her ideas; there was no conflict with 'wets' and even Heseltine, Clarke and Patten accepted the supremacy of markets by the mid-1990s. But he took her ideas further even than she dared in her day, privatising British Rail and introducing the market principle into many hitherto forbidden areas of the welfare state.

Heywood points out that the changes have been in style rather than substance. In the 1980s Thatcherism adopted a 'heroic' mode, smashing socialism and the power of the trade unions; it was like a continuous war or revolution as the Prime Minister tried to change 'the hearts and minds of the nation'.

Major replaced that style with a 'managerial' version. However, he also added another element: a return to Neo-Conservatism with a renewed emphasis on morality (the 'back to basics' campaign), obligation and citizenship. Conservatives have long been worried by the downside of market forces: growing inequality, the emergence of an underclass, insecurity at work and the loss of the 'feelgood factor', or the sense of the nation 'being at ease with itself' to use Major's phrase. There was a feeling in the mid-1990s that the nation's social fabric was in dire need of repair. Added to this market individualism plus Neo-Conservatism has been a shift towards a 'Little Englandism'. Most commentators did not believe Major was this kind of politician by instinct but he was forced to adjust his position on Europe quite drastically by the determined Euro-sceptic minority, elevated in the early 1990s, through the disappearance of the Conservatives' overall majority, into a position of great influence and potential power.

Major was criticised for being too weak on ideology and a poor leader. The *Sun* editorials attacked him as showing 'poor judgement and weak leadership'. Lord Rees-Mogg, a pillar of the right-wing establishment, wrote: 'He is not a natural leader, he cannot speak, he has no sense of strategy or direction'. Kenneth Clarke frankly stated that when he was first mooted as leader he thought him 'a nice bloke but not up to the job'. Norman Lamont applied the cruellest cut when he said the government gave the 'impression of being in office but not in power'. Major's predecessor wrote in her memoirs that he was prone to compromise and to 'drifting with the intellectual tide'.

Hague's new start

As soon as the Conservatives lost the 1997 election so calamitously Major resigned and a contest was held for a new leader. Kenneth Clarke, genial and successful former Chancellor, was the popular choice both in the country and the party but the Conservative Party in Parliament, trusted with choosing the new leader, had shifted decisively to the right; Clarke's pro-Europeanism just would not do. In the end the MPs chose the relatively unknown and untested William Hague, known to most politics watchers as the precocious sixteen year old who had impressed Thatcher with a right-wing speech at a 1970s party conference. He was at least, for those who regretted the demise of Thatcher, firm on the subject of Europe: he would have very little of it and would not join the emergent European single currency for at least a parliamentary term, if ever. Those who mocked this narrow, Little England perspective were checked when his party won the Euro elections handsomely in June 1999. At the party conference in

BOX 6.1 MINI BIOGRAPHY

William Hague (1961–)
English Conservative politician. Made his debut with a precocious speech at the 1977 conference. After Oxford, worked as management consultant and then became MP for Richmond in his native Yorkshire. Was seen as suitably opposed to Europe in 1997 and was preferred to Kenneth Clarke as leader. His early years were difficult with successes inside the Commons but rarely in the country.

BOX 6.2 MINI BIOGRAPHY

Michael Portillo (1953–)
Conservative politician. Educated Cambridge. Worked for Conservative Research Department, 1976–9, and as junior minister in various departments until he became a Cabinet minister in the early 1990s. Was defeated in 1997 election and missed his chance to lead the party then. Worked hard at being an advocate of 'Caring Conservatism' before becoming adopted as a candidate in the safe seat of Kensington. Made Shadow Chancellor in late 1999.

October 1997 many of the deposed party leaders spoke contritely of how the party had been guilty of arrogance and indifference to the needs of the disadvantaged; a 'Compassionate Conservatism' – although ill-defined – was the result. Subsequently Michael Portillo, the right-winger many felt would have won the leadership had he not astonishingly lost his huge majority to a novice Labour candidate, re-invented himself as the quintessence of such a notion. This flirtation with a softer image, however, did not last for the party as a whole. In October 1999 Hague unveiled his 'Commonsense Revolution', a bundle of right-wing measures focussing on five 'guarantees': to cut taxes as a share of the national income; to keep out of the single currency until at least the end of the next parliamentary session and to demand opt-outs on measures not in the national interest; a 'parents guarantee' whereby inefficient heads could be dismissed; a 'patients guarantee' setting maximum times for treatment; and a get tough guarantee on work dodgers who would lose all benefit if refusing work after eight weeks. In fact the conference represented a surprising swing back towards Thatcherism. The Lady herself appeared and was cheered to the echo as well as praised in speeches which pointedly ignored the contributions made by the Premier of seven years, John Major. Most of the right-wing press applauded the party's rediscovery of its identity – being right wing and Eurosceptic and proud of it. But others were not so sure. That shrewd commentator Peter Riddell wrote that 'The more William Hague roused his party faithful in Blackpool, the more he led them away from power . . . [his] main achievement . . . may have been to deepen the divisions within his own party and to reduce still further its chances of winning the next election' (*Times*, 12 October 1999).

Losing Conservative themes

The truth is that the European debate will not subside. It is at the heart of our economic and constitutional traditions. It will proceed into the next parliament with a vitality that challenges loyalties.

John Biffen, The Guardian, 17 February 1996

We are unpopular, above all, because the middle classes – and all those who aspire to join the middle classes – feel that they no longer have the incentives and opportunities they expect from a Conservative government.

Margaret Thatcher's attack on 'one nation' Conservatism, 11 January 1996

The Labour Party and socialism

Socialism

Socialism developed as a critique and alternative to capitalism and its political expression, Conservatism. It focused on economics as the key activity, but the full sweep of its message provided guidance on virtually all aspects of living. Perhaps the clearest statement of the idea is still provided in Robert Tressell's *Ragged Trousered Philanthropists* (1965), when the hero, Owen, addresses his scornful workmates on the subject by drawing an oblong in the dust with a charred stick to represent the adult population of the country: 'all those who help consume the things produced by labour'. He then divides the oblong up into five to represent five classes of people (Figure 6.1):

1 All those who do nothing, e.g. tramps, beggars and the aristocracy.

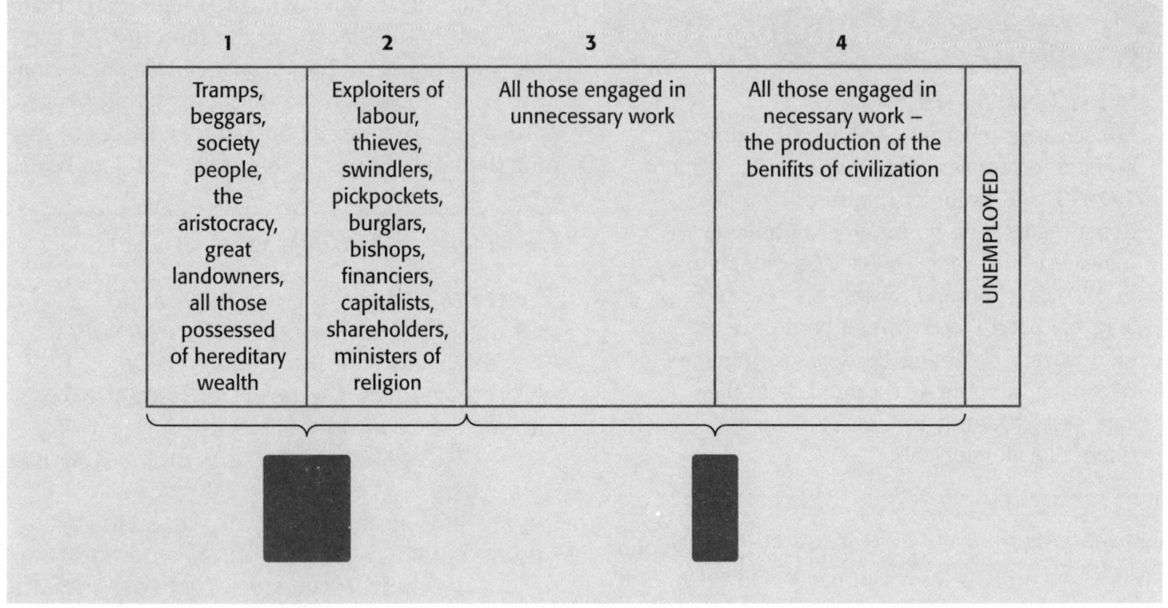

Figure 6.1 How the things produced by people in division 4 are 'shared out' among the different classes of the population
Source: Tressell, 1965 [1914]

2 All those engaged in mental work which benefits themselves and harms others, e.g. employers, thieves, bishops, capitalists.

3 All those engaged in unnecessary work 'producing or doing things which cannot be described as the necessaries of of life or the benefits of civilisation'. This is the biggest section of all, e.g. shop assistants, advertising people, commercial travellers.

4 All those engaged in necessary work producing the 'necessaries, refinements and comforts of life'.

5 The unemployed.

Underneath the oblong he then draws a small square which, he explains, is to represent all the goods produced by the producing class: group four. The crucial part comes next: how are all these goods shared out under the 'present imbecile system'?

As the people in divisions one and two are universally considered to be the most worthy and deserving we give them – two-thirds of the whole. The remainder we give to be 'Shared out' amongst the people represented by divisions three and four. (Tressell, 1965 [1914], p. 272)

Owen then proceeds to point out that it is groups three and four which battle most ferociously for their third while 'most of the people who do nothing get the best of everything. More than three quarters of the time of the working class is spent making things used by the wealthy'.

Despite his eloquence, Owen's workmates are reluctant to listen, so, as playwright Alan Sillitoe observes in his introduction to the 1965 edition, he calls them:

philanthropists, benefactors in ragged trousers who willingly hand over the results of their labour to the employers and the rich. They think it the natural order of things that the rich should exploit them, that 'gentlemen' are the only people with the right to govern. (Tressell, 1965 [1914], p. ii)

Towards the end of the book another character, Barrington, orates his vision of a socialist society: nationalisation of land, railways and most forms of production and distribution; the establishment of community culture and leisure facilities; the ending of unemployment; the abolition of the now redundant police force; equal pay; good homes for all; automation of industry and consequent reduction of the working day to four or five hours; free education to twenty-one and retirement at full pay at forty-five; and the ending of military conflict worldwide.

This classic account of socialism issues from a fundamental set of assumptions; provides a critique of capitalism and its related ideology; and offers a superior form of society as an achievable objective.

Critique of capitalism

Socialism asserted that capitalism 'exploited' the working masses by selling the fruits of their labour, taking the lion's share of the revenue and paying only subsistence wages. This produced huge disparities in income and disparities between the suburban-living rich and the urban-based poor. Because the ruling capitalists dominate all the institutions of the state they subtly intrude their values into all walks of life and a complex web of mystifications produce a 'false consciousness' in which the working class believe wrongly their best interests are served by supporting capitalist values. Capitalist championing of 'individualism' and 'freedom' are mere cloaks for the exploitation of the weak by the strong. The ruthlessness of the system induces a similar quality in society. Wage labour merely relieved employers of any residual obligations they might have felt towards their workers. By living in large urban settlements working men were alienated from each other while the automating of industry denied workers their creative satisfaction. A final criticism is that capitalism with its booms and slumps is inevitably inefficient and inferior to a planned economy.

Socialists argued that two large antagonistic classes emerge in capitalist societies: a small wealthy ruling class and a large impoverished proletariat living in the city.

Underlying principles of socialism

Socialism developed out of this critique of nineteenth-century capitalism. The principles underlying the new creed included the following:

1. *Human nature is basically good*: it is only the selfish competitive economic system of capitalism which distorts it.
2. '*Environment creates consciousness*': It followed from this Marxist axiom that a superior environment will create a superior kind of person.
3. *Workers create the wealth*: They are entitled to receive the full fruits of their efforts and not the small fraction which the rich bourgeois factory owners paid them.
4. *Equality*: Everyone has the right to start off in life with the same chances as anyone else; the strong should not exploit their advantage and impose themselves on the weak.
5. *Freedom*: The poor need more resources for the playing field of life to be level and thus be truly free.
6. *Collectivism*: Social solidarity should take the place of selfish individualism.

The Labour Party

Labour in power: Corporate Socialism

Labour held power briefly in the 1920s and began to formulate a more pragmatic and less emotional and incoherent version of socialism. During the 1930s and the war years socialist thinkers such as Hugh Dalton (1887–1962) and Herbert Morrison (1888–1965) developed what has since been called 'corporate socialism' comprising:

1. *Keynesian economics*: Management of the economy, using investment to cure slumps and squeeze out unemployment.
2. *Centralised planning of the economy*: this was the corollary of the Keynesian approach; it had worked brilliantly during the war and would do the same for the peace, promised Labour.
3. *Nationalisation*: Morrison devised this approach based on bringing an industry out of private and into public control via a board

accountable to Parliament. Once in power Labour nationalised 20 per cent of the economy, including the major utilities.

4 *Welfare state*. Labour established the National Health Service and expanded universal social services into a virtual 'welfare state' in which the state had obligations to citizens 'from the cradle to the grave'.

5 *Mixed economy*: The extent of nationalisation was not defined but, unlike the Soviet command economies, it was intended to maintain a private sector, albeit one subordinate to the public.

6 *Socialist foreign policy*: The trauma of two world wars convinced Labour that a new approach was needed based on disarmament and international collective security. The USSR proved resistant to fraternal overtures from a fellow left-wing government and ultimately Labour's combative Foreign Secretary, Ernest Bevin (1881–1952), was forced to attract the USA into the NATO alliance.

Revisionism

Some Labour intellectuals – such as Hugh Gaitskell (1906–63), Hugh Dalton, Roy Jenkins (1920–), Denis Healey (1917–) and, most importantly, Anthony Crosland (1918–77) – were not content, like Morrison, to declare that 'socialism is what the Labour government does'; they looked for a new direction after the huge achievements of Clement Attlee (1883–1967) and his government. Crosland's book, *The Future of Socialism* (1956), asserted that Marx's predictions of capitalist societies polarising before revolutions established left-wing government had been proved hopelessly wrong; the working class had ignored revolutions and had been strengthened by full employment. The business class had not fought the advance of socialism but had been tamed by it. Crosland argued that the ownership of the economy was no longer relevant as salaried managers were now the key players. He attacked another sacred cow by maintaining that nationalisation was not necessarily the most effective road to socialism and that other forms of collective ownership were more effective. He concluded that Labour should now concentrate its efforts on reducing inequality through progressive taxation and redistributive benefits and reducing class differences through an end of selection in education.

In practice revisionism was Labour's policy for the next thirty years, but when in government in the 1970s its fatal flaw was exposed: it was dependent on an expanding economy, and when this fell into decline cuts in public expenditure became inevitable. With the cuts came the end of socialist advances, dependent as they were on the availability of resources.

The left wing of the party never accepted revisionism and first Aneurin (Nye) Bevan, then Michael Foot, opposed the new drift towards a diluted ideology. In the 1960s Wilson defied the left in the parliamentary party, but when it teamed up with the trade unions trouble was in store for the 1970s administrations under both Wilson and Callaghan. Led by Tony Benn, the left now offered an alternative economic strategy based on workers' control; extended state control of the economy; **participatory democracy** at all levels of national life; fresh injections of funds into the welfare state; encouragement of extra-parliamentary activity; and unilateral abandonment of nuclear weapons. The revisionist leadership tried to ignore the left but when the 1979 election was lost to a new and militantly ideological leader, Margaret Thatcher, the left insisted that a similar return to the roots of socialist ideology was necessary. With the revisionist leadership defeated and discredited, the left made its move, managing to impose its candidate, Michael Foot, as leader in 1980, plus a radically left-wing set of policies on the party which resulted in the 1983 manifesto being dubbed by Gerald Kaufman 'the longest suicide note in history'. More significantly the left's ascendancy led to the defection of an important wing of the party to form the Social Democratic Party which split the anti-Tory vote and helped keep Thatcher in power for a decade.

Neil Kinnock, elected as Foot's successor, was a child of the left but soon recanted, dismissing its prescriptions as 'Disneyland thinking'. He assiduously began to nudge his party towards the centre ground via a series of policy reviews which

BOX 6.1 EXAMPLE

The brief, eventful life of the Social Democratic Party

On 1 August 1980, Shirley Williams, David Owen and William Rodgers published an open letter to the Labour Party in *The Guardian*: the famous 'Gang of Three' statement. It followed in the wake of Roy Jenkins' Dimbleby Lecture, in which he had suggested a new party might 'break the mould' of British politics. Members of the 'gang' had opposed previous proposals on the grounds that a centre party would 'lack roots and a coherent philosophy'; they warned, however, that if Labour's drift to the left continued, they would have to reconsider their position.

After the Wembley Conference in January 1981, which pushed through measures strengthening the control of left-wing party activists over the election of the leadership and the reselection of MPs, the three ex-Cabinet ministers joined Jenkins in creating the Social Democratic Party (SDP). Over the ensuing months some twenty to thirty centre-right Labour MPs made the journey over to the new party, plus a fair number of peers and other figures, not forgetting the solitary Conservative MP.

The Guardian article had called for a 'radical alternative to Tory policies . . . rejecting class war, accepting the mixed economy and the need to manage it efficiently'. The SDP fought the 1983 election in tandem with the Liberals, gaining 26 per cent of the vote, but their high hopes were dashed in 1987 when they only mustered 22 per cent. The resultant merger negotiations split the SDP into 'Owenite' and 'mergerite' camps and appeared to disperse finally the heady optimism which had attended its birth.

During its brief life, did the SDP truly offer a 'radical alternative'? Certainly SDP members elaborated on *The Guardian* manifesto in a spate of articles and books. Shirley Williams in *Politics is for People* drew heavily on the ideas of Robert Owen and Tawney, while Owen's *Face the Future* drew on Mill, William Morris and G.D.H. Cole. Both authors acknowledged their debts to the Fabians and Anthony Crosland.

The SDP was formed in a blaze of publicity and 'breaking the mould' rhetoric, but a genuine alternative was probably not on offer. In one sense its message represented an amalgam of policies picked up across the political spectrum. Decentralisation was close to the Liberal, Bennite and Green position; SDP views on the market economy and trade unions were close to Margaret Thatcher's position – she actually praised Owen for being 'sound' on both; and on social policy and defence the SDP was close to the position of the Callaghan government to which the SDP leaders had once belonged. This is not to say the SDP lacked a carefully worked out and detailed programme; merely that it lacked a distinctive alternative or even radical quality. History will judge the SDP as a party of protest with a limited appeal outside the middle classes.

When its twelve-point plan was announced in March 1981, *The Times* concluded that this 'new beginning' was no more than a modern version of '**Butskellism**' which was 'seeking essentially to bring that consensus up to date'. In other words, the SDP was merely developing Labour revisionist policies free of the political and rhetorical restrictions caused through working within the Labour Party. In Samuel Beer's (1982) view: 'What had happened was quite simple: the Labour Party had been a socialist party . . . [and] many of its adherents ceased to believe in socialism'.

In August 1980 the Gang of Three had written that a 'Centre Party . . . would lack roots and a coherent philosophy'. The final irony of the SDP is that its leaders succeeded in writing its obituary before its birth had even taken place.

essentially accepted the 'efficiency and realism' of the market as the best model of economic organisation. It was implicit in this new analysis – although hotly denied – that socialism was no longer relevant, and even the word disappeared from policy documents and manifestos. When he lost the crucial 1992 election, he resigned and John Smith continued this 'desocialising' work. When Smith died tragically of a heart attack in May 1994, Tony Blair was elected leader and soon placed his stamp on a party denied power for nearly fifteen years.

Views by Labour leaders past and present

As for Tony Blair, I still think, as I thought when I first met him, we're lucky to have him – both the Labour Party and the nation. He might have gone off and joined the Social Democrats and no-one would have heard of him again.

Michael Foot, The Observer, 6 September 1996

My view of Christian values has led me to oppose what I perceived to be a narrow view of self-interest that Conservatism – particularly in its modern, more right-wing form – represents.

Tony Blair, September, 1995

Having already abandoned its former policies of opposition to the European Community/Union, unilateral nuclear disarmament and nationalisation, Blair shifted the party even further to the right by attacking the power of trade unions in the party. He waged a spectacularly successful war against the 'collective ownership' Clause Four in the party's constitution; it was replaced in April 1995 by a massive majority at a special conference.

Clause Four rewritten

Philip Gould records the meeting in Blair's bedroom in March 1995 when the new Clause Four was drafted:

> In the end Blair wrote it himself . . . I liked the last draft and said so. The main sentence is long but has power. 'The Labour Party is a democratic socialist party. It believes that by the strength of our common endeavour we achieve more than we achieve alone, so as to create for each of us the means to realise our true potential and for all of us a community in which power, wealth and opportunity are in the hands of the many and not the few, where the rights we enjoy reflect the duties we owe, and where we live together freely, in a spirit of solidarity, tolerance and respect.' This is the essence of what Tony Blair has always believed: individuals should be advanced by strong communities, in which rights and responsibility are balanced. (Gould, 1998, p. 229)

The clause went on to endorse a 'dynamic economy, serving the public interest'; a 'just society which judges its strength by the condition of the weak as much as the strong'; 'an open democracy, in which government is held to account by the people'; and where 'decisions are taken as far as practicable by the communities they affect'.

Not content with this he nudged the party away from the social democratic heartland of full employment and welfare spending. This was for two reasons. Firstly it was deemed that the requisite high taxation would never be endorsed by middle-class voters – remember Labour was caught out badly by the Conservatives over tax in 1992. Secondly it was believed that the world's economy had changed. With modern technology the economy has become globalised so that flows of capital can break companies and even currencies in minutes. To maintain policies of high taxation risks massive withdrawals of capital by speculators and investors from any economy contemplating such socialistic measures.

'New Labour' has effectively embraced the economic side of Thatcherism: tax cuts, low inflation, a market economy plus encouragement of entrepreneurial activity. Tony Blair has even felt able to praise aspects of Thatcher's legacy and to endorse some of them as worth keeping. He has tried to strike out, however, and devise some distinctive policies for his party. He eschewed a major 'big' idea but came up with some middling-sized ones instead, a 'stakeholder society'. This is the idea associated with the economist John Kay and Will Hutton, a columnist of *The Guardian* and

BOX 6.2 **IDEAS AND PERSPECTIVES**

Blair's project

We worked our way towards our new political project. Slowly Blair gave substance to his ideas, fleshing them out. By the end of it, he would have priorities for government based upon his analysis of the problems facing Britain: lack of a first class education system for the majority of children; community disintegration leading to crime and pressure on families; the poor performance of the economy, and the unstable relationship between government and business; a centralised and secretive political system; and isolation and lack of influence overseas.

Source: Gould, 1998, p. 244

then editor of *The Observer,* who had been aiming his thoughts at the Labour leadership for a number of years. The basic thinking here is that everyone, individuals and groups, should have some investment in society, everyone should feel part of their community at all levels, economic, cultural and social. To the same end Blair wishes to encourage parental responsibility and social solidarity. The other biggish idea supported by Blair has been constitutional reform; Labour has embraced devolved assemblies for both Scotland and Wales plus reform of the House of Lords and a referendum on the electoral system. However, the changes are pitted with flaws, none more so than the unresolved so-called 'West Lothian question', whereby Scottish MPs would have the ability to vote on English issues but English MPs would not have the ability to reciprocate as the internally elected assembly would assume this role (see Chapter 14).

It is often said that Blair has moved Labour so far to the centre he is now even to the right of the 'one nation' Tories. Certainly his approach bears comparison with this strain of Conservatism and it must be significant that he happily uses the phrase 'one nation' socialism. The tactical purpose of the term is evident in that it implies the party which once claimed it as its own is arguably now the party of a narrow, nationalistic and divided collection of people.

The massive endorsement of New Labour in the election of 1 May 1997 was fulfilment of the strategy conceived and implemented by Tony Blair and his close collaborator Peter Mandelson to move the Labour Party into a position where it embraced the market economy and removed the fear of old-style socialism felt by the middle-class occupants of 'Middle England'. 'Blairism' is vaguely expressed and lends itself to wide interpretation but sceptical commentators wonder whether he has a framework of belief strong enough to survive the vicissitudes of several years in office and to resist the atavistic influences of the union-based old Labour ideology. Others disagree and claim Blairism can boast a coherent philosphical framework and a well worked out 'project'. Socially it is based on the idea of communitarianism. This derives from Blair's studies at university where he was very interested in the ideas of John McMurray, a Scottish philosopher with prescient ideas. He took issue with the modish idea of 'individualism', that the individual has choices and freedoms and is an autonomous unit. McMurray argued on the contrary that, as Adams puts it, 'People do not exist in a vacuum; in fact, they only exist in relation to others. The completely autonomous self of liberal theory is a myth. Peoples' personalities are created in their relationships with others, in the family and the wider community. By pursuing the interests of society as a whole we benefit individuals including ourselves' (pp. 148–9). Blair believes people should build communities based on the idea of responsibility, a sense of duty towards others maybe less fortunate; a recognition that one's actions have repercussions and may require reparation. Old Labour tended to see poor people as 'victims of the system'; to

Peter Mandelson directs New Labour's election campaign (13 August 1995)

speak of them having responsibilities is to borrow from another right-wing lexicon. Blair also subscribes to the idea of a Third Way. Apart from being an alternative to socialism and pro-capitalist ideology it is not clearly defined. This has not stopped Blair using the term frequently and participating in high-level seminars both in Europe and America. Another participant has been the eminent sociologist Anthony Giddens who is highly regarded by Blair and who has written a book, *The Third Way: The Renewal of Social Democracy*. This argues that the old definitions of left and right are obsolete (see Chapter 4) and that in the world of globalisation a new approach is required. He defines the overall aim of Third Way politics as helping citizens to 'pilot their way through the major revolutions of our time: globalisation, transformations in personal life and our relationship to nature . . . One might suggest as a prime motto for the new politics, "No rights without responsibilities"' (Giddens, pp. 64–5 – see also Box 6.3 and pp. 137–40 below).

The Liberal Democrats

After the war the Liberal Party continued to decline politically but still offered an alternative to voters in the centre of political ideas. At heart the party still adhered to the ideas of 'New Liberalism' covered in Chapter 4, with emphases on individual liberty, equality, a mixed economy, a developed welfare state and a reformed democratised system of government. Under the skilful leadership of Jo Grimond, Jeremy Thorpe and David Steel, the party survived the post-war decades but hardly prospered. And then in 1981 it joined forces with the breakaway SDP to form the 'Alliance'. It was not difficult to unite on policies, which were very close; rather it was personalities who caused the foundering of this short-lived collaboration. In 1987 the two elements of the alliance formally merged and fought the 1992 election as the Liberal Democrats. Its manifesto, *Changing Britain for Good*, called

BOX 6.3 **IDEAS AND PERSPECTIVES**

The Third Way

Richard Kelly summarises the Blairite Third Way usefully in *Politics Review*, September 1999, under five headings:

- *Class*: The Third Way fears a progressive fragmentation of society and the aim is to 'create a cohesive, mutually respectful community of disparate individuals (Tucker, 1998). The concepts of "citizenship" and "civic obligation" are thus considered vital and play a key part in the third way's reworking of the state'.
- *State intervention (macroeconomics)*: 'The trick, third wayers argue, is for macroeconomic policy to be carried out at European level, national sovereignty having been "pooled" to vital effect (Hutton,1998). The British economy, it is contested, is more affected than ever by supranational forces. It therefore needs a supranational form of government to control them'.
- *State intervention (welfare)*: Third wayers accept that welfare must change to reflect a society which has transformed since Beveridge in 1942. 'The government's "workfare" proposals give some indication of what this might involve, combining the provision of state welfare with much greater emphasis on individual initiative and responsibility . . . the third way acknowledges that the existing cost of welfare is unacceptable. It also recognises a high incidence of corruption and fraud and makes their elimination a priority' (Field, 1995).
- *State intervention (general)*: Third wayers accept that nationalisation is dead and that privatisation is here to stay. They see a state which has been 'decentralised and democratised, ensuring that state action is more accountable and more sensitive to consumer needs. Constitutional reform is thus essential. Having created their "democratic state" third wayers believe it will increase levels of public participation in politics which, in turn, will help achieve a heightened sense of community and citizenship'.
- *The nation*: Third wayers reject the Conservative celebration of the state but still believe a strong awareness of it should be nurtured, albeit in a 'modern' manner. Accordingly there have been Third Way attempts to rebrand the nation, reworking the British identity in a way that downgrades militarism and tradition while giving more emphases to Britain's cosmopolitan, multi-racial society and the 'artistic creativity' it spawns – a project encapsulated by the term Cool Britannia and developed in Heritage Secretary Chris Smith's book, *Creative Britain* (1998).

for a shift of power to the consumer and ordinary citizen, the development of worker shareholding and a market economy in which the market is the 'servant and not the master'. In addition the party repeated the traditional call for reform of the voting system and **devolution** of power to the regions. Following the 1992 election its new leader, Paddy Ashdown (elected 1988), made steady progress, and thc Liberal Democrats' policy of 'equidistance' between the two big parties was replaced by one of open co-operation. Iain McWhirter, writing in *The Observer* (17 April 1995), suggested, interestingly, that if indeed the Lib Dems come to support a Labour government, they can find a role to the left of Labour, acting as its conscience on constitutional reform and the welfare state. In 1996 a joint Labour/Lib Dem committee was set up to liaise on constitutional reform, a notoriously time-consuming set of proposals over which Labour felt it wise to maximise agreement in case votes from the smaller party were needed.

BOX 6.3 MINI BIOGRAPHY

Paddy Ashdown (1941–)

Former leader of Liberal Democrats. Formerly Captain in Marines, he saw active service in the Borneo. He also learnt to speak Chinese as part of the diplomatic corps 1971–6. Won Yeovil in 1983 as a Liberal and became leader of merged party 1989. He worked hard to build a close relationship with Labour. Lib Dems won forty-six seats in the 1997 election after which Ashdown retired as leader. Charles Kennedy took over in 1999.

The strong showing by the Liberal Democrats in the 1997 general election buttressed the claim of that party to be the *de facto* left-of-centre conscience of the new Blair order regarding constitutional reform and the nurturing of the welfare state, especially the educational system. The Lib Dems joined a Cabinet Committee tasked with studying the future of constitutional reform; a tempting whiff of power perhaps for a party starved of it since the Lib–Lab pact of 1977–9. In 1999 Paddy Ashdown stood down after a distinguished period as leader of Britain's third party. His successor was the amiable Charles Kennedy, popular on quiz shows and a witty clubbable man. He faced a problem, however: how could he put

Paddy Ashdown foresees the end of 'Tribal Politics' as the Liberal Democrats co-operate more closely with New Labour (15 November 1998)

his stamp on the party in a way different to his predecessor? In the event he chose not to. He rejected suggestions to take up a left of Labour stance as the kind of 'cul de sac' which had ruined Labour in the early 1980s. Instead he chose a 'business as usual' policy of 'constructive opposition' with Tony Blair. *The Guardian* commented (24 September 1999) that Kennedy's speech was a 'thin bowl of porridge' and that he had too little new or exciting to say, especially compared with Ashdown's inspiring valedictory address. Some commentators warned that his party stands on a knife edge; a swing of 2 per cent to the Conservatives at the next election would rob the Lib Dems of ten of their thirty-four seats in England; a 4.5 per cent swing would lose them seventeen. Some of the party's middle-class (some three-quarters), middle-aged (average fifty-eight) members still do not trust Labour and fear a backlash will hurt them at local and national levels if things go wrong for the government party. However, Blair does see an important role for the Lib Dems in his project. He wants to make the new century one dominated by the centre-left and not the centre-right like the last one. To achieve this he needs the co-operation of the third party to lock the Conservatives out indefinitely as well as building and sustaining a pro-European consensus against the sceptical alliances the Conservatives will try to construct.

Chapter summary

Conservatism is more than mere pragmatism in the ruling interest but includes a concern for unity, harmony and balance in a society based on property, equal opportunity, elite rule and gradual change. Margaret Thatcher gave major prominence to the neo-liberal strand in Conservatism which stressed the primacy of markets in economics. Major returned to the rhetoric of 'one nation' Conservatism but contained the practice of Thatcherism. Labour began as a socialist party dedicated to the replacement of capitalism by a collectively owned economy, but in government translated this into nationalisation, a policy of doubtful success. In opposition during the 1980s it gradually shed its socialist clothes and donned those of the free market and restricted public spending: in effect a compromise with Thatcherism. Liberal Democrats inherited the New Liberal ideas to which they have added a disposition to work with the Labour party in office.

Postscript

In response to an interview in the US magazine *Talk* in which Tony Blair had said his biggest mistake in May 1997 had been not to ask Paddy Ashdown to join his Cabinet, Charles Kennedy said the Lib Dems had no intention of merging their identity with the bigger party as they could exert more influence by being independent (*Guardian*, April 2000). In his interview with novelist Robert Harris, Blair said both parties were 'driven by the same value systems' and suggested he still harboured hopes of uniting the non Conservative left to make the new century a 'progressive' rather than a conservative one like the twentieth century had been.

Harris records that Blair believes his Ashdown ommission to be his greatest mistake in office. However Blair points out that with such a massive majority it was politically impossible to deny a post to his own party in favour of the Lib-Dem leader. Some commentators speculated in the press that the interview reveals Blair has never abandoned his vision of a Labour-Lib-Dem alliance to dominate the twenty-first century.

Discussion points

- To what extent was Margaret Thatcher a Conservative?
- Did John Major contribute anything distinctive to Conservative thinking?
- Did Labour sell out its principles during the 1980s?
- Is there room for a distinctive third set of political ideas in Britain, and do the Lib Dems offer them?

Further reading

I am grateful to Andrew Heywood for his lecture to the Politics Association Revision Week (April 1996) for some of the points included in this chapter. His book on *Political Ideologies* (1998) was also a valuable source, as was the similar book by Ian Adams (1998). The Giddens book, *The Third Way*, has been criticised as too vague but it is chock full of interesting ideas and more than repays a careful reading. Michael Foley's *Ideas that Shape Politics* (1994) is a useful collection of essays.

References

Adams, I. (1998) *Ideology and Politics in Britain Today* (Manchester University Press).

Crosland, C.A.R. (1956) *The Future of Socialism* (Cape).

Driver, S. and Mantell, L. (1998) *New Labour: Politics after Thatcherism* (Pluto).

Field, F. (1995) *Making Welfare Work* (Institute of Community Studies).

Foley, M. (1994) *Ideas that Shape Politics* (Manchester University Press).

Giddens, A. (1998) *The Third Way* (Polity).

Gould, P. (1998) *The Unfinished Revolution* (Little, Brown).

Heywood, A. (1998) *Political Ideologies*, 2nd edn (Macmillan).

Hutton, W. (1998) *The Stakeholding* (Polity).

Kelly, R. (1999) 'The Third Way', *Politics Review*, September.

Norton, P. and Aughey, A. (1981) *Conservatives and Conservatism* (Temple Smith).

Smith, C. (1998) *Creative Britain* (Faber and Faber).

Tressell, R. (1965) *The Ragged Trousered Philanthropists* (Panther; first published 1914).

Tucker, K. (1998) *Anthony Giddens and Modern Social Theory* (Sage).

Chapter 7

Political ideas: themes and fringes

Bill Jones

Learning objectives

- To explain and put into context the themes of:
  - feminism;
  - nationalism;
  - environmentalism.
- To identify, analyse and elucidate the political fringe on the far left and far right.
- To explain the intellectual source of ideas characterising the political fringe.

Introduction

The first three chapters in this section looked at ideology, political concepts, and party political ideas. This fourth chapter addresses three major themes – **feminism**, **nationalism** and **environmentalism** – followed by the rarefied world of the political fringe. This colourful assemblage of small parties are not always easy to identify; they may be seen selling their newspapers on the street or taking part in street demonstrations or even contesting national elections. However, their intellectual roots are often connected to major philosophical themes and are therefore of interest. Besides, the Labour Party was just such a fringe party at the turn of the century before the changing social reality enabled them to become a party of government within half a century.

Feminism

In 1980 a United Nations report stated:

While women represent 50 per cent of the world's population, they perform nearly two-thirds of all working hours, receive one-tenth of world income and own less than 1 per cent of world property.

Despite the existence of a worldwide feminist movement, the position of women has improved very slightly, if at all, since the dawn of feminism in the late eighteenth century. The rights of women were implicit in the recognition of the rights of 'men', but thinkers such as Locke did not include women in their scheme of things. Rousseau did, however, and in 1792 Mary Wollstonecraft's *Vindication of the Rights of Women* (see Wollstonecraft, 1967) articulated their rights explicitly (see Box 7.1) just as the French Revolution was asserting the rights of oppressed people everywhere. Whether women were 'oppressed' or not was a moot point. Most men assumed that women existed to perform domestic roles: producing and rearing children and caring for their husbands as well as all the household chores. Probably most women would have agreed had they ever been thought important enough to be consulted. They had no possibility of pursuing careers, voting or participating in public life. Their consolation was the power they exercised through this domestic role, influencing their menfolk and maybe even dominating them behind the scenes. But the legal position of women at this time was dire: they had no right to divorce (unlike their husbands); no right to marital property, and their husbands could beat them quite legally – even rape them should they wish. Moreover, men regularly used prostitutes while preaching fidelity for their wives and divorcing them when this failed to be upheld. In 'exchange' women were praised for their femininity, sensitivity and were idealised by the notion of romantic love. An unequal relationship indeed.

Emergent socialist ideas supported the position of women. Engels argued in his *Origin of the Family, Private Property and the State* (1884) that the pre-historical position of women had been usurped by men so that property now was passed on through the male line instead of the female because men wished to pass on property to their

BOX 7.1 **BIOGRAPHY** 

MARY WOLLSTONECRAFT (1757–97) (picture: © Corbis)

Mary Wollstonecraft was an Anglo-Irish writer and is often cited as the first modern feminist. At the age of twenty-eight she wrote a semi-autobiographical novel, *Maria*. She moved to London to become the 'first of a new genus' of women, a full-time professional writer and editor specialising in women and children. She was closely associated with the group of radical reforming writers called the English Jacobins, where she met her future husband, the philosopher William Godwin. In her *Vindication of the Rights of Women* (1792) she argued for equal rights for women in society, especially regarding educational opportunities. Her daughter with Godwin was Mary Shelley, the author of *Frankenstein*.

sons. The exploitative relationship between the propertied class and the proletariat was mirrored within the family by the relationship between men and women. A socialist revolution would sweep away private property and remove the economic basis of the exploitative monogamous marriage.

During the nineteenth century the women's movement, such as it was, concentrated on gaining the vote, the belief being that, once this citadel had fallen, the other injustices regarding the imbalance of political and legal rights compared with men would soon be remedied.

To an extent these early feminists were operating with the grain of history as the franchise for men was being progressively extended at this time. Nevertheless it took a bitter and militant struggle for the 'suffragettes', led by Emmeline and Christabel Pankhurst, to win through: in 1918 women received the vote but only if they fulfilled certain educational and property qualifications and were, bizarrely it now seems, over the age of thirty. In 1928 they finally achieved equal political rights, but this did not automatically transform their position. The women's movement subsided for a number of decades but the impact of two world wars, where women played leading roles on the home front, advanced their claims for better treatment. Their purpose was to put an end to the discrimination in a male-dominated world resulting from the widespread male belief that women should look after the home and leave the important jobs to the men. Simone de Beauvoir's *The Second Sex* (1952) attacked the asymmetry whereby men were defined as free independent beings and women merely in terms of their relationships with men.

But the so-called 'second wave' of feminism began with Betty Friedan's *The Feminine Mystique* (1963). This major work rejected the myth that women were different and were happy being the domestic adjuncts of their men. Having nominally equal rights did not deliver real equality in a world controlled by men and discriminating against women. In the late 1960s and 1970s, the work of Germaine Greer (*The Female Eunuch*, 1971) and Kate Millett (*Sexual Politics*, 1969) moved the focus of debate from the wider world of career and public life to the micro-worlds which we all inhabit. Greer developed some of the ideas of Herbert Marcuse (1964, 1969a, 1969b), who argued that Western society was sexually repressed. She suggested that women had absorbed the male idea of their sexuality as soft and yielding – a kind of sex image stereotype – while their true and possibly quite different nature was not allowed to be fulfilled. Concomitant with this went an assertion of lesbianism as a socially demonised activity. Instead of living out expected roles, Greer was insisting that people could be true to themselves, being 'male' or 'female' according to their own natures. Millett's emphasis was on how women are brainwashed into accepting a given image of themselves regarding their role and even their appearance. This image, according to her, was a reflection of 'patriarchy'; constructed by men with their interests in mind. What was attributed to gender roles was in fact no more than a socially constructed role which women were induced to accept from birth via a battery of socialising agencies, including family, tradition, law, the media and popular culture. Women were forced to accept a role of being gentle caring mother figures, whose job was to tend their men. Alternatively they were seen as whores and temptresses, equally subservient but this time more dangerous. Millett also directed attention at the family and home, pointing out that here was the most important arena in which the male controlled the key sexual relationship, dominating the female; it followed from this, in that key feminist phrase, that 'the personal is the political'.

In the 1970s it was observed that liberal feminists, who believed that reform and a high degree of equality were possible in society as it is, coexisted with socialist feminists, who believed that

BOX 7.1 MINI BIOGRAPHY

Germaine Greer (1939–)
Australian feminist, author and journalist. Lectured at Warwick University but best known for her *Female Eunuch* (1971) which attacked the institution of marriage. Modified her militant position in later life.

the main inequality was still between classes and not the sexes. They believed that major changes to the economy and society were necessary before women could be truly free. A third group soon emerged, the radical feminists. For them the problem lies not in society or the economy but in human nature, more precisely, male human nature. The problem with women, in other words, is men. In *The Dialectic of Sex* (1980, originally published 1971), Shulamith Firestone perceived a fundamental oppression of women by men as a result of their biological role. Sexual domination therefore both precedes and exceeds economic exploitation. What she advocates is a 'sexual revolution much larger than – inclusive of – a socialist one' to 'eradicate the tapeworm of exploitation'. She argues for a restructuring of society through science, whereby children would be produced artificially and looked after communally so that women's physical and psychological burdens would be removed and they would be free for the first time in history.

Susan Brownmiller – *Against our Will* (1975) – shifts the focus to the violence which men use to threaten women; the fear of rape is used to maintain male dominance and rapists act for all men in demonstrating the consquences of non-compliance. Other feminist writers, such as Andrea Dworkin and Dale Spender – often called 'supremacists' – assert female moral superiority and argue that the world would be better if women were in control. Often this type of feminist will be separatist in relation to men; their lesbianism consequently has a political quality to it. For them men are not necessary for women and women who live with men are 'man identified' instead of being 'woman identified'.

It is often said that since the 1970s the women's movement has lost momentum. Certainly the tone has become milder; Greer (1985) and Friedan (1982) have both disappointed radicals by writing approvingly of domesticity and child-rearing. The New Right in the USA and UK, moreover, have reinforced 'traditional values' of women's roles and the desirability of marriage (and by implication the subversive effects of one-parent families) to hold society together. In their book *Contemporary Feminist Politics* (1993), Lovenduski and Randall applaud the progress made by the women's movement in permeating institutions and professions and in disseminating feminist values so effectively that they have become widely accepted as orthodoxies. However, they lament the failure to replace activists when they bow out of activity, and the internecine squabbling and fragmentation which have weakened the movement. A report covered by *The Observer* (7 November 1999) questioned whether women have made much progress at all. The American Psychological Association's study concluded that

BOX 7.2 **IDEAS AND PERSPECTIVES** 

Sexual inequality at work

- The total number of women on the boards of major companies is 3.72 per cent.
- Women make up just 2.8 per cent of senior managers and 9.8 per cent of managers.
- The average female worker earns nearly 40 per cent less than the average male earner.
- Women managers earn 16 per cent less than their male counterparts.
- Between 1960 and 1990 the number of women working rose 34 per cent while the number of working men fell by 20 per cent.
- In 1960 women made up 35.5 per cent of the total workforce. By 1993 this was 49.5 per cent – many, however, in part-time jobs.

Source: The Guardian, 6 March 1995

'even though the fight for equal rights widened opportunities for many, it failed to give women control over their lives'. Experts cited in the article suggested the same could be said of the UK too; two-thirds of the 1,300 receiving electroconvulsive therapy each week for depressive illnesses are women. The strong showing of women candidates in the 1997 election – women MPs virtually doubled from sixty-two to 120, most of them Labour – cheered campaigners for more female representation and those who defended the special Labour measures to favour women candidates in winnable seats. However, some feminists have criticised 'Blair's babes' as they have been dubbed as performing a decorative but non-feminist role in the governing party.

Nationalism

Nationalism derives from the view that the world is divided naturally into national communities, all of which have the right to independence and the right to govern themselves. Nations often, although not necessarily, coincide with state frontiers; the notion of 'national territory' is potent, often stimulating countries to resort to war in its defence or re-acquisition. Argentina's military rulers attempted to win popularity by invading the 'Malvinas Islands', as they called the Falklands, in 1982, but were resisted and defeated by Britain, which defended the islands not essentially because they were part of the British state, but more for a mixture of national pride, principle and political expedience.

States usually contain a dominant ethnic type, but most have minorities living within their borders too, either indigenous or immigrant. Well-established countries usually have a sense of 'community', a combination of shared history, language and culture. In these circumstances it is normal for citizens to share a patriotic love of their country, to feel a sense of duty towards it and, ultimately, a willingness to die for it.

This was not always the case. It was not unusual for people to feel strong attachments to their country, as far back as the Ancient Greeks and Romans. In Shakespeare's time patriotism was acknowledged in, for example, Henry V's stirring address at Harfleur ('Cry God for Harry, England and Saint George!'). But it was quite possible for royal houses to be 'borrowed' from other countries or imported by invitation, as in the case of George I in 1714.

Modern nationalism, the notion that nations have the right to be in charge of their own destiny, was a product of the French Revolution. Here the liberal idea of natural rights, with its accompanying right of citizens to reject governments, was allied with Rousseau's idea of the General Will, that nations had a sense of what they wanted which could be interpreted and which endowed both freedom and 'sovereign' power: the first appearance of the idea that the will of the people was superior to any other, including the head of state and ruling class.

So the French, always patriotic and intensely proud of their country, acquired an additional mission: to carry the idea of national self-determination into the wider world. A further element was added through the Romantic movement in the late eighteenth century, which idealised national myths and heroes. In Germany Gottfried von Herder (1744–1803) attacked the tendency of the German ruling class to ape French customs and culture in an attempt to appear sophisticated. He believed a nation's language was the repository of its spirit, that it should be nurtured and artists working within it revered.

During the nineteenth century nationalism grew in two ways: firstly, through nations developing the will to unite, as in the cases of Germany and Italy, and, secondly, within the large multinational empires of Austria–Hungary and Turkey. In 1848 a number of revolutions erupted based on emergent nationalism.

Towards the end of the century the major European powers embarked on a kind of 'super'-nationalism – **imperialism** – whereby they colonised huge tracts of Africa and Asia, extracting wealth and brutally denying the native populations the rights to self-determination they insisted on for European peoples. Nationalism in Europe took on an ugly complexion, combining authoritarianism with ideas of racial superiority.

The emergent doctrine of socialism appeared initially to be the antithesis of nationalism when the Second International at Stuttgart in 1906 passed a resolution committing the working classes in the event of war to intervene to 'bring it promptly to an end'. And yet in the summer of 1914 the military machines of Europe proved firmer of purpose, more swift in motion than the ponderous political armies of socialism. One by one the major socialist parties accepted the *fait accompli* of the war and rallied to their respective national causes. On Saturday, 2 August, over 100,000 British socialists demonstrated against the war, but on 15 October a Labour Party manifesto duplicated the Liberal view of the war as a struggle between democracy and military despotism. Shortly afterwards, Labour took its place in the wartime coalition government. Socialism had briefly stood up to nationalism but the result had been a pushover.

At Versailles in 1918 a number of states were invented (Czechoslovakia) or re-invented (Poland) as the notion of self-determination reached its high-water mark. But by this time the colonial possessions of the imperial powers had begun to imbibe some of the ideas of their masters and apply them to their own cases. In India and Africa independence movements began to emerge and gained much impetus when Europe was weakened by the Second World War, itself initiated by the murderously aggressive nationalism of Nazi Germany, supported by that of Italy as well as Japan. In its wake India gained its freedom (1947) and during the 1950s and 1960s the map of the British Empire was effectively rolled up as the anticolonial 'wind of change' gathered storm force.

The establishment of the United Nations in 1945, followed by many other international organisations such as the North Atlantic Treaty Organisation (NATO) and the Organisation of Petroleum Exporting Countries (OPEC), marked the advance of internationalism at the expense of nationalism. This was especially true of the European Economic Community, set up in the 1950s and rapidly perceived as spectacularly successful. However, nationalism is still very much a motivating force in world politics, and in places such as the former Yugoslavia, Russia, the Middle East and the Indian sub-continent is capable of a sustained and virulent expression.

English people like to portray themselves as not especially nationalistic – theirs is a longstanding and confident arrangement – but occasions like the Euro '96 soccer championships and other sporting events reveal the English to be as fervently supportive of their country as any other. As Chapter 14 on devolution shows, Britain as such does not receive as much identification as its constituent national entities: within British politics nationalism also has an important role to play.

Ireland

Ireland was joined to the United Kingdom by the Act of Union in 1800 but the marriage was far from happy given the background of exploitation and savage suppression of revolts by the British.

In 1922 Ireland won its independence, but the six counties in the north-east of the island remained part of the UK, dominated by the Protestant majority, which discriminated against the Catholic minority, many of whom supported a united Ireland and are often referred to as the 'Nationalists'. Negative feelings were reciprocated; the BBC correspondent Fergal Keene described in a radio broadcast (Radio 4, November 1996) how, as a Catholic child, he regarded Protestants as being as weird as any 'Martian'.

After decades of misrule the province exploded into violence in the late 1960s and has been a tragic source of conflict ever since. The 'peace process' (initiated in 1994) promised to provide a negotiated solution between the Nationalists under Gerry Adams and the Unionist representatives of the Protestants but violence broke out again in the summer of 1996. With the IRA still insisting on its policy of violence, its political wing, Sinn Fein, performed surprisingly well in the 1997 election, winning two seats. In 1998 Tony Blair brokered the Good Friday Agreement which set up an assembly and a power-sharing executive provided that the parties to it could agree. Despite huge efforts by Blair, his Northern Ireland minister Mo Mowlam and Senator George Mitchell, the failure of the Unionists to accept the failure of the Nationalists to give up their arms proved the rock on which the negotiations foundered.

On Friday 3 December 1999 the deadlock was broken. All parties to the dispute agreed to proceed and the devolved powers were formally transferred to the new executive on Wednesday 1 December with new Cabinet ministers installed, including the controversial Martin McGuinness as Minister of Education. However, the failure of decommissioning to take place by February 2000 led to the reimposition of direct rule from London.

Scotland

In 1707 Scotland merged with England and Wales, but before then was an independent nation-state and even when part of Britain retained its own legal and educational systems plus a proud sense of national identity. In 1934 John McCormick founded the Scottish National Party (SNP) as a response to alleged English indifference to Scottish economic needs. It has always sought independence from Westminster with continued membership of the Commonwealth. To maximise support it has tended to be no more than mildly left of centre and has concentrated on economic issues such as demanding the alleged 'share' of North Sea oil to which Scotland was entitled.

Throughout the 1970s the SNP increased its electoral support and in 1992 it had three MPs (down from the seven it achieved in 1974, when it gained its highest share of the vote). In 1978 the referendum on devolution returned a majority in favour but not by the 40 per cent majority on which its parliamentary opponents had insisted. The SNP vote benefited from the widspread collapse of the Conservative vote in Scotland in May 1997, harvesting three new seats, making six in all. Labour's promise of a separate assembly for Scotland may well steal the thunder of the SNP as the Blair administration continues (see also Chapter 14).

Wales

Welsh nationalism is more of the romantic cultural variety, concentrating on the health of the language as a major theme. Plaid Cymru draws it greatest support, unsurprisingly, from the Welsh-speaking parts of Wales: the rural areas of the north and the centre. Politically the movement is anti-Conservative and mildly to the left; less so now than when the party was overtly socialist but probably more so than Labour in 1997. The chief objective of the party is a national assembly for Wales, but it is interesting that when a referendum was held on this issue in 1978 the proposal was soundly defeated. At the 1997 election, Plaid Cymru's vote held up well and it retained its four MPs (see also Chapter 14).

England

While Welshmen and Scots and those from Northern Ireland have their own distinctive identity, most of them also feel themselves to be 'British', although – with the exception of Ulster Unionists – this is seldom an important issue. The key issue in the 1990s regarding English nationalism has been that of the European Union. When Margaret Thatcher was deposed in 1990, the issue which sparked off her fall from power was the EU and its alleged aim of increasing integration to the point where national identities would be threatened. A band of loyal followers kept alive her passionate opposition within the governing party and indeed forced Major to trim his position in their favour between 1994 and 1997. The Conservative Party has always sought to present itself as the 'patriotic' party and to outflank his Euro-sceptical critics Major adeptly shrouded himself in the Union Jack throughout 1996.

The split in the Conservative Cabinet in the run-up to the 1997 election ran deep with Portillo, Lilley and Howard highly sceptical and others such as Dorrell and Rifkind seeking to position themselves in relation to the Euro-sceptics for possible post-election leadership reasons. During the election campaign over 200 Conservative candidates declared publicly that they were opposed to the single currency, in violation of the official 'wait and see' policy. The wipe-out result for the Conservatives in the May election removed Portillo and other leading sceptics but left the parliamentary party still deeply split between supporters and opponents of closer European integration. Some wish the UK to withdraw completely; others wish it to pursue a more independent line, advancing national interests more aggressively; while still others fear the possible domination of Europe by its most powerful economy, Germany.

Labour also has dissenters to its basically pro-EU stance, but they are quieter and less numerous than the Conservatives. In November 1996, Labour, partly for tactical political reasons, announced that it would hold a referendum before taking the country into a single currency. Despite the sound and fury of an expensive campaign the Referendum Party – Sir James Goldsmith's personal creation calling for a referendum on the nation's membership of the EU – polled only 800,000 votes, yet this did not stop it claiming to have assisted the demise of a number of leading Europhiles including its arch enemy David Mellor in Putney.

It should not be forgotten, however, that some people subscribe to a kind of 'anti-nationalism' or internationalism. Early in the twentieth century the Liberal Party campaigned strongly for an international organisation to manage relations between states but neither the League of Nations, emerging after the 1914–18 war, or the United Nations, which followed the 1939–45 one, proved able to do more than ameliorate some of the dealings between nation-states. A more successful approach was the economic integration one taken by such pioneers as Schumann and Jean Monnet, founders of the European Movement. They hoped that economic contacts would engender political unity and openly advocated an intensification of both. In Britain such supranationalism in relation to Europe included the Liberal Party and later the Lib Dems but in the major parties it has been a minority taste, restricted to such figures as Roy Jenkins and Shirley Williams in the Labour Party – Edward Heath and Michael Heseltine in the Conservatives.

In a chapter of the *13th British Social Attitudes Survey*, Dowds and Young (1996) distinguish four sub-sets of attitudes on nationalism:

1. *Supranationalists* (20 per cent of respondents): This group wishes to include foreign influences ('inclusive') and is not high on 'national' sentiment such as pride in national culture and heritage; likely to be educated, female, *Guardian* reading, Labour supporter.
2. *Patriots* (20 per cent): High on national sentiment but not so as to wish to exclude foreign influences ('exclusive'); likely to be well educated, attached to locality, likely to be *Daily Telegraph* readers and Conservative voters.
3. *John Bulls* (24 per cent): High on exclusion and national sentiment; attached to locality; *Mail* reading and Conservative voting.
4. *Belligerents* (17 per cent): High on exclusion; low on national sentiment; more likely to be male, authoritarian, not well educated, *Sun* reading.

According to the study, all four groups are more or less equally sized. The first two believe that membership of the EU is beneficial but only the supranationalists favour full integration, and of them only 28 per cent supported a single currency. The authors conclude that, taken overall, the 'moderate line' on the EU, favoured by both major parties, of a 'pragmatic pursuit of national interests within the sturdy framework of national sovereignty, is the position of a beleaguered minority' (*The Guardian*, 21 November 1996).

So nationalism in Britain is still a powerful force, although it operates in very different ways. In Ireland it threatens the peace; in Wales it takes a cultural/language-based form; in Scotland it is more economic and concerned with identity. In England, forgetting Mebyon Kernow, which wants independence for Cornwall, and similar rumblings from Yorkshire, nationalism is more inward-looking, defending the status quo and offering various degrees of hostility to Germany, fear of federalism and bureaucracy and old-fashioned suspicion of foreigners. Yet this English form of nationalism is no less powerful than that of the Celtic fringe; it reaches to the very heart of government, for years being responsible for a gaping chasm in the governing party. It still defines deep fault lines in both Labour and the Conservatives.

Green thinking

The ecological perspective rejects philosophies of the right, left and centre as more similar than dissimilar. Jonathan Porritt characterises them collectively as '**industrialism**'. This 'super-ideology', which is 'conditioned to thrive on the ruthless exploitation of both people and planet, is itself the greatest threat we face'. Conservatives, socialists and centre politicians argue about rival economic approaches – individualism versus collectivism and how the cake of national income should be sliced up and distributed – but they all agree that the size of the cake should be increased through vigorous economic growth. This is the central proposition which the Greens most emphatically reject. 'Industrialism', they say, is predicated on the continuous expansion of the goods and services and on the promotion of even more consumption through advertising and the discovery of an increasing range of 'needs'. It creates great inequalities whereby a rich and envied minority set the pace in lavish and unnecessary consumption while a substantial number – in many countries a majority – are either unemployed or live in relative, perhaps dire poverty. The Conservatives have presided over an increase in income differentials but have offered economic growth as a panacea: more for the rich and more for the poor. Porritt observes:

> If the system works, i.e. we achieve full employment, we basically destroy the planet; if it doesn't, i.e. we end up with mass unemployment, we destroy the lives of millions of people . . . From an industrial point of view it is rational to . . . promote wasteful consumption, to discount social costs, to destroy the environment. From the Green point of view it is totally irrational, simply because we hold true to the most important political reality of all: that all wealth ultimately derives from the finite resources of our planet. (Porritt, 1984, pp. 46–7)

The Green view goes on to adduce a number of basic principles:

1. *A world approach*: All human activity should reflect appreciation of the world's finite resources and easily damaged ecology.
2. *Respect the rights of our descendants*: Our children have the right to inherit a beautiful and bountiful planet rather than an exhausted and polluted one.
3. *Sufficiency*: We should be satisfied with 'enough' rather than constantly seeking 'more'.
4. *A conserver economy*: We must conserve what we have rather than squander it through pursuit of high-growth strategies.
5. *Care and share*: Given that resources are limited, we must shift our energies to sharing what we have and looking after all sections of society properly.
6. *Self-reliance*: We should learn to provide for ourselves rather than surrendering responsibility to specialised agencies.
7. *Decentralise and democratise*: We must form smaller units of production, encourage co-operative enterprises and give people local power over their own affairs. At the same time international integration must move forward rapidly.

Porritt maintains that this amounts to a wholly alternative view of rationality and mankind's existence. He contrasts the two world views of industrialism and ecology in Table 7.1.

Inevitably the other major parties have done all they can to climb aboard the Green bandwagon, cloaking their policies in light green clothes and shamelessly stealing the rhetoric of the environmentalists.

As it currently stands the Greens' political programme is unlikely to fall within the 'art of the possible'. But as Malcolm Muggeridge once pointed out 'utopias flourish in chaos', and if environmental chaos does arrive, it may well be the Greens who inherit what is left of the earth, if it is not already too late by then.

Table 7.1 Two worlds: industrialism versus ecology

Industrialism	**Ecology**
The environment	
Domination over nature	Harmony with nature
Environment managed as a resource	Resources regarded as strictly finite
High energy, high consumption	Low energy, low consumption
Nuclear power	Renewable sources of energy
Values	
An ethos of aggressive individualism	Co-operatively based communitarian society with emphasis on personal autonomy
Pursuit of material goods	Move towards spiritual non-material values
Rationality and packaged knowledge	Intuition and understanding
Patriarchal values, hierarchical structure	Post-patriarchal feminist values, non-hierarchical structure
Unquestioning acceptance of technology	Discriminating use and development of science and technology
The economy	
Economic growth and demand stimulation	Sustainability, quality of life and simplicity
Production for exchange and profit	Production for use
High income differentials	Low income differentials
A free-market economy	Local production for local need
Ever-expanding world trade	Self-reliance
Employment as a means to an end	Work as an end in itself
Capital-intensive production	Labour-intensive production
Political organisation	
Centralisation, economies of scale	Decentralisation, human scale
Representative democracy	Direct democracy, participative involvement
Sovereignty of nation-state	Internationalism and global solidarity
Institutionalised violence	Non-violence

Source: Adapted from Porritt, 1984, pp. 216–17

Giddens on the German Greens

The importance of ecological politics goes far beyond whatever influence green social movements might muster, or the proportion of the vote green parties might achieve. In concrete politics the influence of ecological groups has already been considerable, especially in Germany – it isn't surprising that the notion of 'subpolitics' originated there. In their work *The German Left*, Andrei Markowitz and Philip Gorski observe 'throughout the 1980s the greens developed into the German left's socializing agent in the sense that all its new ideas, political innovations, strategic formulations, lifestyle, originated from the greens and their milieu. Chancellor Willy Brandt was fond of saying the greens were the "lost children of the SPD"'

Giddens, 1998, p. 54.

The political fringe

The political fringe is the name given to those small factions and groups which often do their political work outside the conference halls of the main parties rather than within them. Those who belong are often determined ideologues, given to regular argument in groups prone to splits and factions. They do have some intrinsic interest, however, as microcosms of political ideas and conflicts. It must also be remembered that in the early part of this century the Labour Party was just such a small faction, snapping around the heels of the Liberal Party – yet within a couple of decades it was actually in power and destined to be there as the new millennium started.

Left and right extremes

We recognise only two classes in society . . . Our problems are the result of a rotten capitalist system.

Arthur Scargill, Socialist Labour Party

But what I am saying is that the prospect of the collapse of everything that is opposed to us is greater than at any time in 20th century Britain.

John Tyndall, British National Party

Far left

Marx, Lenin and Stalin

Most far left groups owe their intellectual debts to Karl Marx. He argued that under a capitalist economy rich property owners would so drive down wages in pursuit of profits and a competitive edge that a vast army of impoverished workers would eventually rise up and sweep away the whole corrupt system. Once private property had been abolished, working people would begin to live new and better lives in an economy in which people would work willingly for each other and not reluctantly for an employer. It did not quite work out that way.

After the Marxist takeover of power in Russia in 1917, a period of great hardship and economic instability followed. Lenin established a political system based on centralised control supported by a network of secret police. He believed in the need for a 'vanguard party' of professional revolutionaries to lead the masses when the time came. There had to be rigid discipline and acceptance of the vanguard party's 'dictatorship of the proletariat' while it implemented socialism. Communists claimed this was the transitional stage the USSR was in by the early 1920s when Lenin died.

Trotsky – advocate of 'worldwide revolution' – was the heir apparent but the dogged and unintellectual Joseph Stalin, Secretary of the Party, was cleverer than his brilliant colleague. He urged 'socialism in one country' rather than an international conflagration; he outmanoeuvred his rivals and plotted ruthlessly, succeeding in presenting Trotsky as a traitor to the revolution. He

BOX 7.3 **BIOGRAPHY**

LEON TROTSKY (1879–1940) **(picture: © Corbis)**

Leon Trotsky was a Russian Jewish revolutionary politician born in the Ukraine. He was arrested for being a Marxist at the age of nineteen but escaped from Siberia in 1902. After teaming up with Lenin, he became President of the first Soviet in St Petersburg after the abortive 1905 revolution. He escaped to the West but returned to Russia in March 1917 to assist Lenin in organising the Bolshevik Revolution in November of the same year. He conducted peace negotiations with Germans and led the Red Army of five million men in the ensuing civil war. An inspiring and charismatic leader as well as brilliant intellectually, Trotsky should have succeeded Lenin in 1924, but his theories of permanent world revolution were less well suited to the times than Stalin's pragmatic 'socialism in one country'. Moreover, Stalin was too devious and ruthless for him and he was eventually exiled in 1929, being assassinated in Mexico with an ice pick in 1940 by Ramon del Rio, an agent of Moscow. His ideas live on, but mostly on the radical intellectual fringe in developed countries.

BOX 7.2 MINI BIOGRAPHY

Joseph Stalin (1859–1953)

Soviet dictator. Trained as priest before becoming a revolutionary in Georgia, Russia. Was secretary to Lenin's Communist Party and after his death deviously manipulated his enemies out of power while placing his own supporters in key positions. Became unchallenged dictator in 1930s and tried to neutralise Hitler by doing a deal with him but Hitler broke the agreement and attacked USSR in 1941. After initial reverses the Soviets fought back and defeated Hitler. Despite his brutal behaviour Stalin won friends on the left in Western countries who persisted in believing his propaganda and seeing him as a force for progress.

eventually drove him into exile in Mexico, where his agents succeeded in assassinating him in 1940.

Stalin, by then, had become a brutal dictator, both paranoid and obsessed with power, claiming to be implementing communism but in reality imposing industrialisation, collective farming and his own tyrannical rule on a reluctant and starving peasantry. Anyone less than obsequiously worshipful of their leader was imprisoned, exiled or shot. Overseas communist parties were employed essentially to assist the development of the 'home of socialism' and any deviation from the party line was punished by expulsion or worse.

This is the legacy inherited by extreme left-wing parties in Britain. The Communist Party of Great Britain (CPGB) was founded in 1920 and became the willing tool of Moscow's message in this country, interpreting all the shifts in the official line and condemning anyone perceived as an enemy of the USSR. Members managed to survive the astonishing *volte-face* when Stalin ceased to oppose Hitler as first priority and signed a deal with him in 1939 to partition Poland. Once Hitler invaded Soviet Russia in 1941, British communists breathed a sigh of relief; they were at last able to luxuriate in a vast amphitheatre of approving views as the whole country applauded the heroic Soviet effort. After the war, Stalin's expansion into Eastern Europe, his blockade of Berlin in 1948 and the crushing, by his machine, of the Hungarian rising in 1956 quickly disillusioned communists and Moscow 'fellow travellers' alike. The Cold War effectively ruined the chances of communist parties of achieving power anywhere in Europe and they began to wither and atrophy.

In the 1970s and 1980s opposition to communism in Eastern Europe intensified and the accession to power of the liberal Gorbachev in Moscow was the signal for the bloodless revolutions throughout the former communist bloc, with only Cuba and China being spared. The CPGB split into a hardline pro-Moscow rump and a liberal 'Eurocommunist' wing, with the latter seizing control. It tried to transform itself into 'an open, democratic party of the new pluralistic and radical left'. In 1991 it ceased to be the CPGB and renamed itself the Democratic Left.

Trotskyism

A number of Trotskyite bodies sprang up during and after Trotsky's lifetime calling for worldwide revolution. Ted Grant, a South African, was involved with some of them such as the Militant Labour League in the 1930s. With Peter Taafe, Grant set up the *Militant* newspaper and adopted the tactic of 'entryism', the idea being to infiltrate members of a 'Militant Tendency' (notice only a 'tendency', and not a separate party, which would have breached Labour rules) into the decaying structure of the 1960s Labour Party and seize leadership at the grassroots level of that party and, in theory, the country once the time for revolution arrived. The Tendency virtually controlled Liverpool City Council in the 1980s and two members, Dave Nellist and Terry Fields, were elected MPs. They advocated a number of radical measures, including nationalisation of the top two hundred companies; extension of state control over the whole economy; workers' control in state-owned industries; nationalisation of the media; a slashing of defence spending; withdrawal from the EC; and abolition of the House of Lords. In 1992 the Tendency gave way to Militant Labour, still attempting to 'enter' the Labour Party, but most of the prominent members had faded away and the

Figure 7.1 The ghost of old Labour
Source: The Guardian, 29 January 1996

MPs not only lost their seats but were expelled from the party.

The Socialist Labour Party

This was formed in 1996 by miners' leader Arthur Scargill, following his failure to prevent the rewriting of Clause Four at Labour's conference in 1995 (Figure 7.1). 'We recognise only two classes in society, both of which are recognised by their relationship to the means of production', he explained. 'Our problems are the result of a rotten capitalist system'. Accordingly, his party favours common ownership of the economy, full employment, a four-day week, a ban on non-essential overtime, retirement at fifty-six, restoration of union rights, abolition of the monarchy, House of Lords and public schools, and withdrawal from the EU. Only 500 attended the launch in May 1996.

The Workers' Revolutionary Party

Gerry Healy, expelled from Labour for his Trotskyite views, put his energies into a new party to express and promote the views of his hero. The idea of the party is to build up battle-hardened cadres to seize power when capitalism collapses, as it must, in its view. Membership was never high but celebrity members such as Vanessa Redgrave and her brother Corin gave the party a high media profile.

The Socialist Workers' Party

Tony Cliff, who founded this organisation, was also expelled from Labour for being a Trotskyite. His party has concentrated on international revolution and international links are stressed. Paul Foot, nephew of Michael and a national columnist, is a high-profile and persuasive member.

The Socialist League

Ken Coates was the guru of this party, once known as the International Marxist Group; Tariq Ali, the British-educated Pakistani, was also a 1960s luminary and helped to win headlines when the International Marxist Group were seeking to emulate in Britain the exploits of 'Danny the Red' (Daniel Cohn-Bendit) and others in Paris, the home of left-wing activism in that decade. The SL wished to 'transform consciousness' and achieve liberation through ending 'alienation'.

Far right

Fascism

This set of ideas developed by Benito Mussolini in the 1920s and supplemented by Adolf Hitler in the 1930s was founded on xenophobic nationalism and total submission to the state. Democracy was scorned as the language of weakness and mediocrity; a one-party totalitarian state led by a charismatic leader was the preferred alternative. The leader and his team were seen as the result of an evolving process whereby the best people and ideas won through. It followed that the same thing happened when nations fought; war was the means whereby nations grew and developed. Hitler added a racial twist: the Aryans were the founding race of Europe, a race of conquerors and the Germans were their finest exemplars; all other races were inferior, and the Jews in particular were lower than vermin and should therefore be destroyed. In the stressful inter-war years, racked by economic depression and unemployment, these unwholesome ideas seemed attractive and full of hope to many who faced despair as their only alternative. It is emotionally satisfying perhaps to blame one's troubles on a single group in society, especially one which is quite easily recognisable physically and very successful economically and culturally.

In Britain Sir Oswald Mosley founded a party which evolved into the British Union of Fascists, offering himself as the strong charismatic national leader who would end the party bickering and lead the country into new successes. Mosley proposed that employers and workers should combine in the national interest and work in harmony; strikes and lock-outs should be banned; all major elements in the productive process should work together to plan the economy (corporatism). Moreover, he argued that the Empire would provide all the things the country needed and imports which could be made in Britain would be banned. Parliament and the old parties would be reformed and MPs would be elected according to occupational groups. Once elected, Parliament would pass on power to the leader to introduce the 'corporate state'. Parties and parliament would be ended; everyone and everything would be 'subordinated to the national purpose'. Mosley's anti-semitism was disguised in Britain but his coded references to 'alien influences' were clear enough to most Britons; he favoured sending all the Jews in the world to a barren reservation. When it was revealed that Hitler's remedy to his self-invented 'Jewish problem' had been genocide of the most horrifying kind, a revulsion set in against fascist ideas. But they have proved unnervingly resilient and still appear in the present time in a different form.

In 1967 the National Front (NF) was formed. Its central message is a racist one, warning against dilution of the British race via intermarriage with 'backward and primitive races', producing an 'inferior mongrel breed and a regressive and degenerate culture of tropical squalor'. Repatriation of black Britons is the answer offered. At the level of theory, however, the Jews are offered as the main threats, being characterised as an

BOX 7.3 MINI BIOGRAPHY

Adolf Hitler (1889–1945)

German dictator. Was originally Austrian who tried to make a living as an artist. Fought in the First World War and set up racist, expansionist Nazi movement in 1920s. Came to power in early 1930s and set about dominating Europe via threats, invasions and finally all-out war. In 1942 he dominated the continent but his decision to invade Russia plus declare war on the USA eventually proved his downfall.

international conspiracy to subvert the Western economies and introduce communism before setting up a world government based in Israel. This side of the NF and its utter contempt for democracy is disguised in public expressions, but it exercised considerable appeal to young men with a taste for violence and racial hatred. In 1983 the 'New' NF – later the British National Party – was born; this is dedicated to infiltration and is more secretive, having many contacts with neo-Nazi groups abroad and many terrorist groups too. Football supporters are often infiltrated by NF members and in 1994 a friendly football match between Ireland and England was ended by thuggish violence instigated by the NF. A related body called Combat 18 (the number in the name relates to the order in the alphabet of Hitler's initials: AH) openly supports Nazi ideas and embraces violence as a political method.

1997 election

As previously the general election of May 1997 saw the usual multi-coloured rainbow of fringe joke candidates, but for the far left and far right as well as the pranksters the result was widespread loss of deposits; voters may flirt with the fringe from time to time but when the election arrives they revert, perhaps fortunately, to 'sensible voting'.

Chapter summary

Feminism is concerned with the unequal position of women in society and falls into liberal, socialist and radical categories. Nationalism emerged in the nineteenth century, and, while it is now contested by internationalism, still retains much of its destructive force. Green thinking applies environmentalism to politics, calling for a revolutionary change in the way developed societies live. Far left fringe groups tend to draw on the ideas of Marx and Trotsky; their relevance has declined since the anti-communist revolutions but many followers still keep up the struggle. Far right groups tend to be neo-fascist and racialist; their support is small but their influence subversive.

Discussion points

- Has feminism achieved any major victories and if so what are they?
- Is nationalism more dangerous than terrorism?
- What chance is there of the Greens ever winning power in the UK?
- Why do you think people join fringe political groups?

Further reading

Lovenduski and Randall (1993) is a thorough review of feminism in Britain; the political ideas books by Adams (1993) and Heywood (1992) have good sections on nationalism; and Dobson (1990) and Porritt (1984) are good on ecology. An excellent study of totalitarianism is Arendt (1951). On fascism, also recommended is Cheles *et al.* (1991); Thurlow (1986) is a history of British fascism to the present day.

References

Adams, I. (1993) *Political Ideology Today* (Manchester University Press).

Adams, I. (1998) *Ideology and Politics in Britain Today* (Manchester University Press).

Arendt, H. (1951) *The Origins of Totalitarianism* (Allen and Unwin).

Brownmiller, S. (1975) *Against our Will: Men, Women and Rape* (Simon and Schuster).

Cheles, L., Ferguson, M. and Wright, P. (1991) *Neo-Fascism in Europe* (Longman).

de Beauvoir, S. (1968) *The Second Sex* (Bantam; first published 1952).

Dobson, A. (1990) *Green Political Thought* (Unwin Hyman).

Dowds, M. and Young, J. (1996) *13th British Social Attitudes Survey* (SPCR).

Firestone, S. (1980) *The Dialectic of Sex* (Women's Press).

Friedan, B. (1963) *The Feminine Mystique* (Norton).

Friedan, B. (1982) *The Second Stage* (Norton).

Giddens, A. (1998) *The Third Way* (Polity).

Greer, G. (1971) *The Female Eunuch* (Granada).

Greer, G. (1985) *Sex and Destiny* (Harper and Row).

Heywood, A. (1992) *Political Ideologies* (Macmillan).

Lovenduski, J. and Randall, V. (1993) *Contemporary Feminist Politics* (Oxford University Press).

Marcuse, H. (1964) *One Dimensional Man* (Beacon).

Marcuse, H. (1969a) *An Essay on Liberation* (Penguin).

Marcuse, H. (1969b) *Eros and Civilisation* (Sphere).

Millett, K. (1969) *Sexual Politics* (Granada).

Porritt, J. (1984) *Seeing Green* (Blackwell).

Thurlow, R. (1986) *Fascism in Britain* (Blackwell).

Wollstonecraft, M.A. (1967) *A Vindication of the Rights of Women* (Norton; originally published 1792).

Concluding comment

Finding the Third Way

Tony Wright

Politicians are constantly trying to find words and phrases that encapsulate messages in vivid and memorable terms. There is nothing reprehensible about this. Politics has communication at its centre and this involves finding effective means to convey philosophies, programmes and policies. Tony Blair believes that describing what New Labour is doing in terms of a 'Third Way' best expresses its approach (just as the Conservatives are trying to counter with their 'common sense revolution'). The real question is what lies behind such phrases. So what is this 'Third Way' that defines Blairism and New Labourism? It seems to me that it has a number of key ingredients:

1 *It is an argument about change and the need to respond to change*. Proponents of the Third Way emphasise the dramatic changes taking place in the world, such as globalisation and new technology, and argue that a dynamic and inventive kind of politics is required in response. This means rethinking traditional policies and old assumptions. While there is an affirmation of the continued validity of certain values, this is accompanied by an assertion of the necessity of applying such values in new and different ways. For example, the need for welfare reform is argued for as a necessary response to the social and economic changes that have taken place since the welfare state was constructed after the Second World War; and the introduction of tuition fees is viewed as an inevitable part of the rapid transition from elite to mass higher education. Third Wayers are congenital 'newists'. The newness of New Labour is only one expression of a more general attitude to change. It is not to be feared, but embraced. Thus Tony Blair embraces globalisation with almost evangelical zeal, as opportunity rather than threat. The task is to equip people to meet the challenge of change, especially through education and training. The battle cry of Third Wayers is 'modernisation'. This means being radical, but not in traditional ways.

2 *Old ideological positions are rejected and a new synthesis of positions is embraced.* It is claimed that a traditional left ideology of state collectivism is no longer satisfactory or appropriate; but neither is the right-wing alternative of market liberalism. It is in this key sense that the Third Way claims to be neither Old Left nor New Right. These represent the first and second ways of modern British politics – one dominating the 1970s, the other commanding the 1980s – while the Third Way is a route that cuts

through and confounds these competing ideological traditions. It takes its values of social justice and social inclusion from the left, while rejecting some of the left's traditional ways of implementing them. It takes from the right an understanding of the need for a competitive and dynamic market economy, while rejecting the right's identification of a market economy with a market society. More broadly, it blends into a new synthesis approaches that have conventionally been seen as antagonistic, replacing 'or' with 'and' on a range of fronts (for example, state and market, community and individual, rights and duties, enterprise and justice). This is why it is a mistake to see the Third Way as merely a soggy compromise between alternative and familiar positions, instead of a radically different approach to issues that opens up once the old ideological tram lines are departed from. It does represent a new kind of political consensus, but not one that comes from merely splitting the difference between ideological traditions. It is a distinctive political blend, with radical and innovative policy implications.

3 *What matters is what works.* This has become a Third Way slogan; but it does capture its approach to policy making. The emphasis is not on the ideological soundness of policies, but on their ability to deliver results. Delivery is all, rather than the identity of the deliverers. It does not matter who delivers public services, but whether they are delivered well. There is a constant search for policies and programmes, drawing on the widest range of sources, that can contribute to the achievement of policy goals. In this sense the Third Way does become a kind of pragmatic and technocratic managerialism, but only because its ability to deliver is the test of the synthesis of ideas upon which it is founded. It knows it has to live up to its promise. The idea of public–private partnerships is one characteristic example of its pragmatism: while the post-war 'mixed economy' thought in terms of separate ownership spheres between the state and the market, the emphasis now is on making state and market work together to deliver policy objectives. Across the whole policy field, from pathways into work to routes out of poverty, there is relentless policy energy and innovation. The Third Way represents an open house to all those with promising policy ideas, irrespective of where they come from, and will set them to work.

4 *There is not less, but more, for the state to do – although it will do it in new ways.* Far from representing a retreat on the part of the state, the Third Way demands a clever and busy state. It represents a reaffirmation of the ability of the state to deliver positive policy outcomes (something denied by its New Right predecessors), although not in traditional statist ways. It deliberately operates in a complex policy environment, and this requires an intelligent state that is able to develop new policy instruments for the tasks that have to be performed. For example, partnerships between the public and private sectors – whether to build hospitals or arrange pensions – demand more complex regulation to make them work than when state and market inhabited different spheres. Similarly, if modern electorates are reluctant to fund services through higher levels of direct income taxation (as they seem to be) then alternative routes have to be found, just as redistribution has to be crafted in new ways. The state may provide less and regulate more, but this means that it has an even more complex and demanding role. The issue is not whether the state should be bigger (Old Left) or smaller (New Right), but whether it performs its role well. Thus the Third Way emphatically requires a clever and energetic state.

5 *Both markets and the state must work in the public interest.* If one of the insights of the Third Way is that it is possible to combine social justice with economic efficiency in a market economy (denied by both Old Left and New Right), the further

claim is that both markets and the state can and should be disciplined by a public interest test. If market behaviour is anti-competitive, or if it cheats consumers or denies basic rights to workers, then it should be subjected to legislative correction. Similarly, if state services are inefficient, or serve the interests of the producer groups who work in them rather than of the people who use them, then they should be reformed to ensure that they perform better. On one side, therefore, the Blair Government has introduced a minimum wage and strengthened worker protection, notwithstanding its commitment to business and enterprise. On the other side, it has taken radical steps to improve the performance of public services (for example, by its action on schools), notwithstanding its general commitment to the idea of public service. The political right has traditionally proclaimed the virtues of markets and the vices of the state. The political left has traditionally proclaimed the vices of markets and the virtues of the state. The Third Way recognises the virtues and vices of both markets and the state – and the need to ensure that they serve the public interest. In terms of British politics, this insight comes as a revelation, although it should not.

6 *Social inclusion means ensuring decent life chances for all.* The idea of social inclusion is central to Third Way thinking, with a direct application to several policy areas. It belongs to a cluster of ideas – such as community, social solidarity and citizenship – which define the social purpose of politics as ensuring that everyone has access to the requirements of civilised life (in terms of income, work, education, health, etc.). This means providing a basic security for all those who need it, while also providing pathways of opportunity for individuals to improve their own lives. It differs from a right-wing approach which repudiates social solidarity and trumpets the virtues of individualism, but it also differs from the kind of left-wing approach which is concerned with equality of outcome or condition. The former is not committed to getting everyone on board the ship, believing that those who miss out have only themselves to blame; while the latter not only want to see everyone on board but also to give them the same berths. By contrast, the Third Way idea of social inclusion accepts the obligation to get everyone on board, but combines an insistence on good basic standards with an ample supply of ladders of further opportunity.

7 *There are mutual obligations between citizens, and between the state and its citizens.* As against those (on the right) who concentrate on the duties of citizens and those (on the left) who concentrate on their rights, the Third Way insists on the mutuality of rights and duties. Moreover, this extends to the relationship between state and citizens, where an implied contract exists in which each side has mutual obligations. For example, the state has a duty to ensure that there are opportunities to work, but citizens have a duty to take these opportunities; and the welfare system involves a duty by the state to ensure that people are not better off on benefit than in work and a duty on the part of people to take advantage of routes out of benefit dependency. In all of this – and it extends to areas such as schooling or crime – there is a bargain in which the state performs its side and citizens perform theirs. Neither simply imposes duties on the other, or extracts rights; both sides are locked into a relationship of mutual obligation. This has implications for the behaviour of citizens, but also for the behaviour of the state.

8 *There is a political strategy here, as well as a political theory.* The Third Way is about building a new progressive consensus in British politics. This is an explicit political strategy, central to Tony Blair's modernisation of the Labour Party. The long domination of government by the Conservative party during the twentieth century is seen as a consequence of the failure of the centre-left to equip itself with the ideas and policies capable of exerting a dominance of their own. The Third Way represents the attempt

> to supply this equipment. As such, it is necessary to see it not merely as a set of ideas but also, and essentially, as a political and electoral strategy that is designed to reshape British politics. This does not diminish its significance, but enhances it.

These, then, are some of the key ingredients of the Third Way. Although it finds its home in Britain, and Tony Blair is its leading advocate, it has to be seen in the context of the wider changes happening in the world. In some respects it is an ideology for the age that has buried ideology. Its hybrid, pick'n'mix kind of politics is a politics for the times. This is why it finds expression in different countries (as in the 'new middle' in Germany) and why it forms part of a new social democracy that is currently being forged. Rejecting old positions on left and right, it identifies the task as combining a market economy with a decent society in the context of a rapidly changing environment. It defines this as the new consensus – and wants to preside over it.

Part 3 The representative process

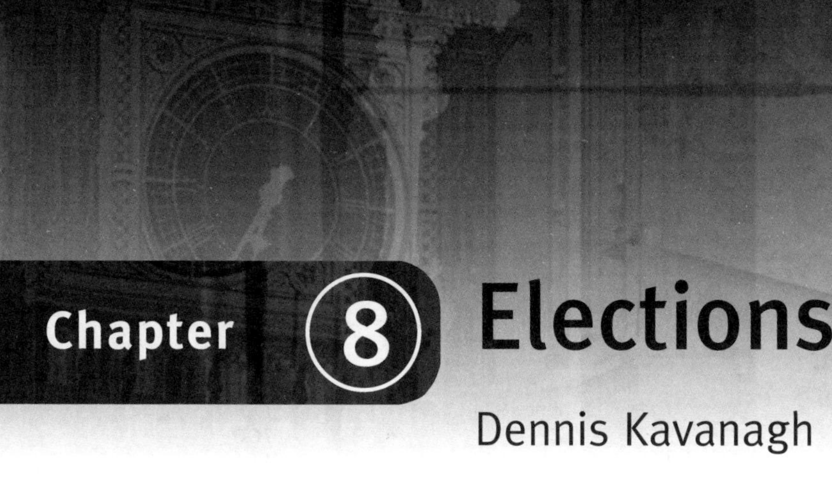

Chapter 8 Elections

Dennis Kavanagh

Learning objectives

- To understand the purpose of elections.
- To evaluate the electoral system and its strengths and shortcomings.
- To study changes in campaigns.

Introduction

This chapter begins by discussing the framework in which elections are held. It then considers who is entitled to vote, the rules of the electoral system, the nomination of candidates, expenditure and the role of election campaigns.

Competitive elections to choose governments lie at the heart of the democratic process; a crucial difference between democratic and non-democratic states is to be found in whether or not they hold competitive elections. The best indicator of such competition is the existence of a number of political parties at elections. In addition to choice there must also be widespread electoral participation. In Britain the entire adult population has the right to vote at least once every five years for candidates of different parties in the House of Commons.

Elections in Britain matter for other reasons. They are the most general form of political participation; at general elections since 1945 an average of over 75 per cent of adults on the **electoral register** turns out to vote (Table 8.1). Secondly, these votes are important, for they determine the composition of the House of Commons and therefore which party forms the government. Thirdly, elections are a peaceful way of resolving questions which in some other countries are settled by force; above all the question 'who is to rule?' They are also important in giving legitimacy to government and therefore oblige the public to obey the laws passed by Parliament. Voting in general elections is how we decide who is to govern us.

Table 8.1 Election turnouts 1945–97

Date	%
1945	73.3
1950	84.0
1951	82.5
1955	76.8
1959	78.7
1964	77.1
1966	75.8
1970	72.0
February 1974	78.1
October 1974	72.8
1979	76.0
1983	72.7
1987	75.4
1992	77.8
1997	71.3

Table 8.2 Extension of the suffrage

Date	Adult population with the vote (%)
1832	5
1867	13
1884	25
1919	75
1928	99
1969	99

What are elections?

Elections are a mechanism of social choice, a device by which people choose representatives to hold office and carry out particular functions. In a direct democracy, usually in small societies, people may of course do the tasks themselves or take turns (rotation) to carry them out. In large-scale societies, however, the election of representatives is necessary.

Election is not the only method by which rulers are chosen. Leaders may emerge, for example, through heredity (e.g. monarchy) or force (e.g. the military). Indeed, appointments in many walks of life are made without elections: in the civil service and in many professions appointment is on merit (demonstrated, for example, by passing competitive examinations, serving an apprenticeship or gaining degrees, diplomas or other marks of competence). But today competitive elections are widely regarded as the symbol of legitimate and representative democracy.

In Britain competitive elections were well established in the eighteenth and nineteenth centuries, even though only small numbers of males had the vote. The **suffrage**, or right to vote, was steadily broadened during the nineteenth century. Britain effectively had mass suffrage by 1928, when the vote was extended to virtually all men and women over the age of twenty-one (see Table 8.2).

General elections for the House of Commons are called under either of two circumstances: when the Parliament has run its full five years (until 1911 the permissible life span of a Parliament was seven years) or when it is dissolved by the monarch on the advice of the Prime Minister of the day. In the exceptional conditions of war the elections due to be held by 1916 and by 1940 were delayed until the cessation of hostilities in 1918 and 1945, respectively. The USA has calendar elections prescribed by the constitution; even in wartime elections for the Congress and Presidency went ahead.

Purpose of elections

What are elections for? As a first answer, most people would probably reply along the lines of: 'To express the democratic will of the electorate.' That answer, however, simply raises more questions. Are national elections about choosing effective executives or selecting competent legislatures? Should they provide each voter with a local MP, or each party with its fair share of MPs? In an ideal society one might like an election system which achieved both objectives. However, except in very rare circumstances, that is impossible. We have to decide priorities and strike compromises.

Peter Kellner, The Observer, 24 March 1996

Some commentators have argued that the advent of opinion polls and the power to time economic booms for the run-up to an election give the incumbent too great an advantage (Hailsham, 1979). While the Thatcher victories of 1983 and 1987 may support this thesis, Major's in 1992 does not. Indeed, the 1992 election turned some of the conventional wisdom on its head. John Major had delayed calling an election until late in the Parliament – hoping that signs of economic recovery would be more visible and that the opinion polls would move decisively in his favour. Neither had occurred when he had to call the election for April 1992. It is likely that the polls underestimated the Conservative share of the vote – and that the party was leading before and during the campaign – but Major was not to know that. The poor performance of the opinion polls increased the politicians' scepticism about their forecasting ability (see Box 8.1).

The government is expected to resign and recommend a dissolution if it is defeated on a major issue or it loses a vote of censure in the Commons. To date the only post-war case of a forced dissolution was in 1979, when the Labour government lost a vote of confidence following the failure of its Scottish and Welsh devolution plans to be carried by the necessary majorities in **referendum** in those two nations. This was unusual and arose because the government was in a minority in the Commons.

The other opportunity which British voters have for a nation-wide election of representatives is for members of the European Parliament every five years. A significant feature is that the **turnout**, usually around a third of the electorate (down to less than a quarter in 1999), has regularly been the lowest or second lowest, in any EU member state.

One might also note the introduction of referendums on constitutional issues – over British membership of the European Community in 1975, and in Scotland and Wales over devolution in 1979. Supporters of a referendum claim that when there is a single issue, particularly one which raises constitutional questions, and on which the parties are broadly agreed (so reducing the role of a general election in providing a choice for voters) a referendum is appropriate.

Who votes?

To be entitled to vote a person must have his or her name on the electoral register of the constituency in which he or she resides. The register is a list compiled each year by the local Registration Officer. For inclusion on the register the person must be resident in the constituency on the given date, be over 18 years of age and be a British citizen, or a citizen of a Commonwealth country and resident in Britain. Persons lacking a fixed address cannot be registered. One apparent anomaly is that citizens of the Irish Republic are also entitled to vote if they have had three months' continuous residence in the United Kingdom before the qualifying dates. Peers and aliens are not allowed to vote and traditionally, inmates of mental home were not either. However, in the Queen's Speech November 1999 it was proposed in The Representation of the People Bill that the 200,000 voluntary patients in mental hospitals will be given the vote for the first time. However, patients with criminal records will still be unable

BOX 8.1 **IDEAS AND PERSPECTIVES** 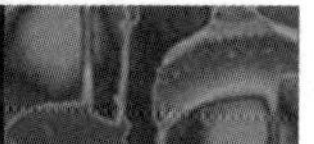

Opinion polls

Opinion polls are increasingly used to report on the state of public opinion. These are surveys of the views of a sample of between one and two thousand voters drawn randomly from the electorate. Sampling is done either by quota or probability methods. A quota sample is obtained by allowing the interviewer to find respondents who together match the known age, sex, class and other characteristics of the population. A probability sample is drawn by choosing every *n*th name on the electoral register. Today most polls rely on quotas. At elections the polls attract an enormous amount of attention for their prediction of which party will win. They claim to be able to predict parties' share of the votes to within 3 per cent in 95 per cent of cases.

The 1992 general election was the most exhaustively polled ever and the newspapers and television broadcasts often led with the latest results of the opinion poll. The polls do have a good record of predicting winners, although they came unstuck in the 'upset' elections of 1970, February 1974 and 1992. In the 1992 election the eve of poll predictions by the main polling organisations overestimated the Labour final share of the vote by 4 per cent, underestimated the Conservatives' by 4 per cent and overestimated the Alliance by 1 per cent. The average forecast of the four major polls published on polling day was for a Labour lead of 0.9 per cent. In the event the Conservatives won by 7.6 per cent – an 8.5 per cent error, the largest ever.

After 1992, the idea took hold that a number of Conservatives were more reluctant than supporters of other parties to admit their allegiance. Some pollsters therefore 'adjusted' their figures for voting intentions to follow for a so-called 'spiral of silence'.

Pollsters were quick to claim that the 1997 election was a vindication of their craft. All the polls correctly predicted a Labour victory, and a big one at that, and most came within a 3 per cent margin of error in their forecasts for each party's share of the vote. Yet self-congratulations were overdone. As can be seen in Table 8.3, there was a 12 per cent range in the polling organisations' final figures for Labour's lead, and four out of five overstated the Labour's share of the vote and its lead. Ivor Crewe (1997) points out that the mean error of 2.0 per cent in the final polls was the third largest since 1945. Had the election been close, the polls could have just as easily got it wrong again.

Table 8.3 Final opinion polls, 1997

	Conservative %	Labour %	Liberal Democrats %	Other %	Labour lead %
NOP	28	50	14	8	22
MORI	29	47	19	5	18
Harris	31	48	15	6	17
Gallup	33	47	14	6	14
ICM	33	43	18	6	10
Average	31	47	16	6	16
Actual result	31	43	17	9	13

It is unfortunate that there is so much concentration devoted to polls for election forecasting. However, they still remain the best guide to the state of public opinion and are quite superior to hunch, canvass returns, activists' perceptions of mood at public meetings and the views of the media. Polls also contain much useful information about the voters' perceptions of leaders, party images and policy preferences and, over time, they can register shifts in public opinion.

to vote. Homeless people will be allowed onto the electoral register if they provide a 'declaration of locality'. The Bill will also make it possible for voters to prevent their names being accessed from the register by commmercial firms. There will also be experiments with polling booths in supermarkets and weekend voting.

It remains true that the great majority of people confine their political activity to voting at elections, particularly general elections. But now a growing number of people pass up even that opportunity; in May 1997 turnout was 71.4 per cent, the lowest general election figure since 1935. This was in spite of fine weather on polling day, an increase in the number of parties and candidates, an up-to-date register and the opportunity to end eighteen years of one-party rule. The Blair landslide was supported by only 30.9 per cent of the eligible electorate, only just ahead of the number of non-voters. Concern increased further with the 24 per cent turnout in the European elections in May 1999 and a record low poll of 19.6 per cent in the by-election at Leeds Central in the same month. Leeds was a safe Labour seat and elections for the European Parliament did not stimulate much interest. But these have long been factors which depress voting. What one has to explain is the decline in the 1990s.

Voting apathy appears to be part of a broader problem, including a decline in party membership in Britain as well as other Western states. Voting participation is related to socio-economic factors such as social class, education and age; with the middle class, the well educated and the middle aged having above-average rates of participation. It is also higher among those who have more of an interest in politics, identification with a party and a sense of political efficacy, or a belief that one can influence a political system. It is also related to campaign factors such as the competitiveness of the general election and the constituency, and political stimuli such as being canvassed or receiving leaflets from the candidates. But it is difficult to believe that all of the above have turned adversely in recent years. Indeed, one would expect trends in social class and education to have increased voting. Some have also argued that the outcome in 1997 was foregone – but that was also true in 1987 – and that voters in the 1999 Euro-elections did not turn out because they were content with the Blair government. The last claim tends to be confined to Blair supporters.

What might be done to reverse the decline in electoral participation? Reformers advocate such devices as holding elections on a Sunday or a public holiday, installing ballot boxes in shopping precincts, or introducing **proportional representation** for Westminster in local elections, so that fewer people will feel that their votes are 'wasted'. Political leaders have often justified their rule on the good democratic grounds that they have a mandate expressed in an election. Low turnouts undermine the validity of the claim.

Constituency boundaries

The division of the country into constituencies is in the hands of permanent electoral Boundary Commissions. There is a separate Commission for each of the four nations of the United Kingdom and each has the task of establishing an approximately equal size of constituency electorate. The Commissions periodically (between ten and fifteen years) review and make recommendations about the size of the constituency electorates. They arrive at a notional **electoral quota** for each nation by dividing the total electorate by the available number of seats.

Notwithstanding the Commission's efforts, once allowances are made for such features as respecting the existing boundaries of counties and London boroughs, sparsely populated constituencies and the sense of 'community' in an existing seat, there are many inequalities in the size of the constituency electorates. In 1983, for example, the average electorate per constituency was around 65,000, yet a third of seats varied from this figure by some 15,000. Recent boundary reviews have had to take account of the more rapid growth of electorates in the south of Britain and the suburbs compared with the north and cities, and award relatively more seats to the former. Over time the recommendations have been helping the Conservative Party at the expense of Labour. It was largely for this reason that the Labour government avoided implementing the recommendations of the 1969 Boundary Review, which was calculated to be worth between five and twenty extra seats to the Conservative Party. Scotland and Wales have long been given more seats in the House of Commons than the size of their populations strictly justifies, because both were guaranteed a minimum number of seats by the 1944 Redistribution of Seats Act. At present their 'bonus' is nineteen seats; this helps Labour, which in the 1997 election won thirty-four of the forty Welsh seats and fifty-six of the seventy-two Scottish seats.

The electoral system

An electoral system is a set of rules governing the conduct of elections. Electoral systems aim to produce a legislature that is broadly representative of the political wishes of the voters, to produce a government that is representative of the majority of voters and to produce strong and stable government. These aims are not necessarily compatible with one another. A key feature prescribes how popular votes are translated into seats in the legislature. There are, broadly speaking, two types of electoral systems (Urwin, 1982). In proportional systems there is an attempt to establish a close relationship between the distributions of votes between parties and the allocation of seats in the legislature. How close depends on the type of system used. Proportional systems may be subdivided into party list and transferable vote systems (see Box 8.2). Setting a relatively high threshold (e.g. 5 per cent of votes in Germany) for a party to gain a seat can limit the number of parties represented. A low one (e.g. 0.67 per cent in the Netherlands) encourages fragmentation. In **first-past-the-post** systems the candidate who achieves a **plurality** of votes wins the seat. Proportional systems are found largely in Western European states and first-past-the-post systems are found in

BOX 8.2 **IDEAS AND PERSPECTIVES**

How proportional systems work

There are different systems of PR, more of which achieves perfect proportionality.

The additional member system (AMS) as used in Germany elects two types of MPs. A proportion are elected in single-member constituencies on a plurality basis, as in Britain. Others are elected by a second vote from party lists which are produced regionally. This allocation is used to achieve some proportionality between the totals of votes and MPs, although the degree depends on the balance struck between the two types of MP. This is the system used to elect members of the Scottish Parliament.

The single transferable vote (STV) is used in Ireland for large constituencies with several members. It is also used to elect MPs in Northern Ireland and will be used for the new Northern Ireland Assembly election. Each elector ranks the candidates in order of preference 1, 2, 3, etc. A quota is calculated from the formula: number of votes divided by number of seats plus one. Surplus votes for a candidate who has achieved the quota are transferred to other candidates according to the voters' second and lower preferences. Votes for candidates at the bottom are also redistributed as they are eliminated. This process continues until all the requisite number of candidates with votes above the quota are elected.

The list systems are also applied to large constituencies. The order of candidates is decided by the party machine and there is no direct link between member and constituency. Lists systems are widely used in Europe and operate in large constituencies. Under the closed party list system the party decides the ranking order of the candidates and voters choose a party list and have no choice of candidate. A number of other countries, including Denmark and Italy, allow a wider choice of candidate and the voter may choose candidates from more than one party list.

Anglo-American societies (the UK, Canada, and the USA).

The two systems also broadly correspond to multi-party versus predominantly two-party systems, respectively. But this list of countries has changed somewhat. In a referendum in 1993 Italians voted by a large majority to abandon PR and adopt a largely first-past-the-post system, tempered by proportionality, and New Zealanders by a large majority voted for the German additional member system. Desire for a change to the electoral rules is often a symptom of broader dissatisfaction with the political system. The Italians have become disillusioned with their political system – its weak coalitions, the lack of effective choice at elections, which means that the same parties and personalities are usually always in government, the lack of political responsibility and the corruption – and regard the PR electoral system as a major cause of the weaknesses. But when the 1995 New Zealand election failed to produce a party with a majority and increased the power of small parties, it prompted demands for the abandonment of PR.

The different types of electoral systems do seem to reflect national outlooks about government and politics. Proportional systems are often adopted in divided societies – to provide a form of reassurance to minorities and emphasise the importance of the legislature being broadly representative of society. Plurality systems are defended on the grounds that they help to provide a more stable government and, where there is one party in government, allow the voters to hold the government responsible for its record at the next election. Their disproportionality also means that a party often has a majority of seats for a minority of the vote. In October 1974 Labour won a majority of seats with only 39.2 per cent of the vote and in 1983 the Conservatives amassed 61 per cent of seats for 42 per cent of the vote.

Until recently the British public and much of the elite assumed that the electoral system was satisfactory. Undoubtedly it enjoyed the virtues of familiarity and clarity; in the post-war period, only in February 1974 has one party failed to gain an overall majority of seats. This assumption also accompanied the belief that the British system of government was superior to that of many Western European states. For the first half of the twentieth century Britain was an economic and industrial power of the first rank. Its record in resisting Hitler, avoiding political extremism (of both the left- and right-wing varieties) and maintaining political stability was superior to that of many West European states which had various forms of proportional representation. General elections were occasions when voters chose a party to form a government. The system had the advantage of allowing the voter to hold the government accountable at the next election, something not possible with a coalition. Of course all this depended on there being two dominant political parties, so that the voter was given an effective choice between alternative teams bidding to form a government. Above all, however, the two main parties were reluctant to introduce PR, even for direct elections to the European Parliament – which are not about choosing a government – because they would both lose seats.

In recent years, however, that complacency and, for Labour, political calculation have changed. Demand for reform or 'modernisation' of the constitution has grown, and this has included the electoral system. Critics of the adversarial two-party system have blamed, in part, the electoral system for poor policies.

It is not clear, however, how much responsibility for the country's poor economic performance rests with the political system in general, with the electoral and party systems in particular, or with other factors. A study of the economic performance of twenty-one advanced industrial countries shows that in the past three decades the rates of economic growth and unemployment were virtually identical in countries electing MPs by PR or on first past the post. But on both economic indicators Britain performed worse than the great majority of countries in either type of system (Rose, 1992).

Northern Ireland illustrates the shortcomings of the British electoral system when it operates in a bitterly divided society. The use of the first-past-the-post system meant that, as long as religion dictated voting, the Catholics were in a permanent minority and this was hardly calculated to build consent. Elections in Northern Ireland for its three seats to the European Parliament were using PR before its introduction to the rest of Britain in 1999.

Among the criticisms of Britain's first past the post are the following:

1 The system does not invariably produce secure majorities for one party. In at least three of the last nine general elections (1964, February 1974 and October 1974) the winning party did not have a majority sufficient to last for a full Parliament. Many commentators felt that in the era of three-party politics in the 1980s the chances of an indecisive outcome were greatly increased (Butler, 1983).

2 Because some three-quarters of seats are safe for the incumbent party, many voters for losing candidates are denied an effective choice in most seats. It produces a House of Commons and government which do not fairly represent the party support across the nation.

3 As the Liberal and Social Democratic Alliance parties gained significant support (over 20 per cent) in the 1980s, so the disproportional effects of the electoral system became more glaring (Table 8.4). It can be argued that when the Liberals were gaining less than 10 per cent of the vote this disproportionality was not too objectionable; but when a party gains a quarter of the vote and gets only 3.5 per cent of the seats (as in 1983 and 1987) the distortion is less acceptable. It is worth noting that the British system does not discriminate against all minor political parties. Where a party can consolidate its votes in a region, e.g. the Unionists in Northern Ireland, then it can collect a proportional number of seats. However, the system does penalise those parties which spread their votes widely, like the Liberals and now Liberal Democrats.

4 Critics of the adversarial party system (in which the opposition routinely attacks what the government does and promises to do) complain that the all-or-nothing nature of the British system encourages abrupt discontinuity in policy when one party replaces the other in government. Frequent reversals in policy in such fields as education, regional policy, housing, finance, incomes restraints and the economy may be highly damaging. Coalitions (a probable consequence of PR elections) would, it is claimed, provide for more consistency.

5 As the two main parties have become more regionally based between the north and south and between urban and suburban/rural areas, so they may become less national in their representation. Until 1992 the south of Britain and the Midlands cumulatively became more Conservative, while the north and Scotland became more solidly Labour. Only in 1997 did a good number of Labour MPs sit for the affluent and growing population in the south-east of Britain; Conservatives are hardly represented in the major cities and have no representation at all in Liverpool, Manchester, Glasgow, Bradford, Stoke, Newcastle upon Tyne, Leicester etc.

Table 8.4 Third party seats in House of Commons

Date	Number of seats
1945	34
1950	11
1951	9
1955	8
1959	7
1964	9
1966	14
1970	12
February 1974	37
October 1974	39
1979	27
1983	44
1987	44
1992	44
1997	75
Average	29

The 1992 election saw a reversal of the north–south division which had operated in all elections since 1959, and particularly during the 1980s. Labour actually gained some ground in the south and Midlands, while the Conservatives increased their share of the vote in Scotland and held their own or increased slightly in the north.

John Major declares he is confident of victory in the next general election despite his government's unpopularity (28 April 1996)

The 1997 election saw Labour greatly extend its support in the south and Midlands, and the Conservatives fall back in the north.

The 1997 general election produced an extremely disproportionate outcome, exaggerating Labour's 44 per cent share of the vote into a 65 per cent share of seats. The main reasons were tactical voting by Labour and Liberal supporters to oust a sitting Conservative and the low turnout in safe Labour compared with Conservative seats. Labour's vote is now distributed more efficiently across the country than the Conservative's. There were also regional disproportionalities: with 53 per cent of the vote in Scotland, Wales and the north of England, Labour gained 84 per cent of the seats, an 'extra' eighty-four seats compared with what it would have had under a proportional system.

The electoral system is now heavily biased against the Conservatives. John Curtice and Michael Steed (1997) show that on a uniform swing at the next (2001 or 2002) general election, Labour could still win an overall majority of seats even if it trailed the Conservatives in the popular vote; in the event of the two parties having equal shares of the votes, Labour would have seventy-nine seats more than the Conservatives.

One may point to shortcomings in most schemes of proportional representation and the coalitions that usually ensue. For example, it is difficult for the voters to assign responsibility to any one party for a government's record if there are coalition or minority governments. If a coalition government is formed then its programme will very likely be a result of post-election bargaining between the party leaders. Under the present British system disillusioned voters can turn a government out, but under PR some members of the ousted coalition would be members of the new one.

Critics also argue that, apart from wartime – when the over-riding goal is national survival – coalitions are likely to be unstable and lack coherence.

It is also likely that if a party list system is used (as in many West European states) and the party headquarters draws up the list of candidates in multi-member seats, then the direct link between an MP and his or her constituents will be weakened. Another form of PR – the additional member system in West Germany – also retains the link between constitency and MP. Finally, if a party is short of a working majority by a few seats in the House of Commons the bargaining power of a small party will be greatly increased. In West Germany the small Free Democrat party was, until 1998, almost 'perpetual' partners in coalition governments with Christian Democrats or Social Democrats. The crucial party may not necessarily be a centrist one. It could be the Ulster Unionists or a nationalist party.

BOX 8.1 **MINI BIOGRAPHY**

Lord Plant (1945–)
British Labour academic. Wrote philosophical books before becoming a life peer in 1989 and chairing Labour's commission on reforming the voting system.

Prospects for electoral reform

The public does not regard proportional representation as an important issue, certainly in comparison with the attention given by political scientists, commentators and politicians. Slight differences in question wording elicit different responses about attitudes to changing the voting system. In 1997 an ICM poll found that 55 per cent agreed that a new system should be introduced which would give parties seats in proportion to their votes, and 27 per cent disagreed. Thirty-five per cent also thought we should retain the present system because it was more likely to produce a single party government. Forty-three per cent disagreed.

Since 1987 there has been growing interest in electoral reform. In the past, supporters complained about the way in which the present system discriminated against the large Liberal vote and in the late 1970s it was argued that coalitions would provide more continuity and consensus on policy. The significant new factor is that many Labour politicians have come to support reform. Having by 1987 lost three successive elections to the Conservatives, who were able to gain landslide victories with only 42 per cent of the vote, and aware that a large number of Labour voters were virtually unrepresented in the south of England, some Labour leaders had second thoughts. The odd spell of Labour government seemed to be a poor return from the first-past-the-post system. Charter '88, a cross-party group, but drawn mainly from the Liberal and Labour parties, advocated constitutional reform, including proportional representation.

A decisive step for Labour was when Neil Kinnock agreed to set up a working party under Professor Raymond Plant to look at the electoral systems for a reformed second chamber and regional assemblies. Neil Kinnock agreed to the appointment of a committee as a way of promoting discussion, educating the public and party, appealing to the Liberal Democrats and also avoiding a party split on the issue before the 1992 election. At the 1991 party conference delegates successfully pressed for the committee also to review electoral arrangements for the House of Commons. Supporters of reform felt vindicated by the 1992 result. The Conservatives again won a majority of seats on 42 per cent of the vote. Labour support for reform would, it was argued, improve relations with the Liberal Democrats and mobilise the anti-Conservative vote. It also fitted in with Labour's programme of constitutional modernisation.

In 1993 the Plant Committee made a majority recommendation for a switch to the supplementary vote, only a minimal change from the present system. But John Smith rejected it, agreeing that a referendum could be held on the issue in the next Parliament, and Tony Blair endorsed the position. In 1997, in advance of the general election, a joint Lab–Lib commission agreed to support a referendum on retaining the present system or switching to PR.

BOX 8.3 **IDEAS AND PERSPECTIVES**

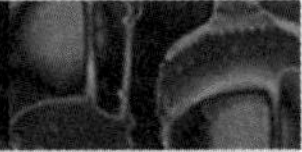

Jenkins. What next?

Some twelve months after it was submitted, it is still not clear what will happen to the Jenkins report. So far Tony Blair and other leading Labour figures have been non-committal. Jenkins regards Blair's support as crucial if the recommendation is to succeed. It is well known that John Prescott and Jack Straw are opposed but Robin Cook, Mo Mowlam and Peter Mandelson support the idea. It is still not decided whether the Labour party will impose a whip on its MPs on such a vote. After all, some Labour MPs will knowingly be voting themselves out of their seats. If the vote was carried when would a referendum be held? Supporters had hoped that it would be before the next general election. But if some Labour MPs campaigned against it and ministers sat on their hands, a referendum defeat would be a poor build up to the next general election. It is therefore more likely to be held, and be successful, following a Labour victory at a general election in 2001 or 2002.

If the referendum were successful then it would take some time (a) to pass a bill through parliament and (b) to draw up new constituencies for the new voting system. So, if a PR referendum were successful, say in 2002, it could be 2007 before the new system operated for Westminster elections. Over that time, public opinion, the views of politicians and the fortunes of the political parties could change. The prospects for reform are better than they have been for over eighty years, but there is still a long way to go.

In October 1997 Lord (Roy) Jenkins, a good friend of Blair, was appointed to chair an Independent Commission on the Voting System. Its terms of reference required it to balance the following objectives:

- proportionality
- stable government
- preserving the link between an MP and the constituencies

Jenkins reported in October 1998 and advocated a system of AVPLUS. This is a mixed form of AV, which would be used to elect 80 to 85 per cent of MPs, and a top up of 15 to 20 per cent of additional members distributed between the parties to achieve greater proportionality. Voters would cast two ballots, one for 530–560 constituency MPs, the other for a 'top up' of a hundred or so MPs. All constituency MPs would require the support of at least 50 per cent of those voting. The top-up MPs would be chosen from an open list, so that the elector could vote for a party or candidate on that list. The country would be divided up into eighty 'top-up' areas and MPs would be allocated so that the House of Commons would have a more proportional membership than had been achieved under the constituency ballot. Obviously, the larger the number of 'top-up' MPs the greater the possibility of achieving more proportionality. A political party would have to be registered, in order for the allocation of 'top-up' candidates to be made.

Supporters of the recommendation say that it achieved its objectives, achieving more although still incomplete proportionality. It seeks to combine the constituency link of the present system with fairness to minorities. Had the system been in operation in 1997, Labour would have had fewer seats, but would still be in a clear majority. AV on its own would have damaged the Conservative party, although the 'top up' system would have compensated.

The House of Commons debate on the report in the House of Commons revealed predictable Conservative opposition and Liberal Democrat support, Labour unease and the lack of enthusiasm on the part of the Home Secretary Jack Straw over the proposals. Some part of the reluctance is explained by the fact that as many as 100 Labour MP seats would not have been elected in the 1997 general election had the system been in operation. The Labour government will decide on the timing and wording of the referendum; the party conference in October 2000 is expect to decide the party's position.

In the meantime, the Labour government has taken significant steps in the direction of PR. For the European elections it introduced a regional party list. For the Scottish and Welsh elections nearly 60 per cent of constituency members are elected under FPTP and over 40 per cent are top-up members, drawn from a party list. In Scotland it was interesting to observe that in the 1999 elections to the parliament a large minority of Labour voters used their second vote to elect 'other' candidates, including Greens and an independent Labour member, Dennis Canavan.

The outcomes of PR elections in 1999 for the European Parliament, the Scottish Parliament and the Welsh Assembly have been seized on by critics of PR. The first did not prevent a sharp decline in turnout and the second produced a Lab–Lib Dem coalition in Scotland, and a minority administration in Wales. The bargaining between the Scottish Labour party and the Scottish Liberal Democrats have also been used by critics to show that PR produces political uncertainty. Such criticisms, however, are irrelevant for advocates of PR because it usually leads to coalition and bargaining between parties. A different electoral system produces a different style of Politics.

It would be understandable if the Conservatives now favoured PR, not least to gain seats in Scotland and Wales. But no PR system which takes account of a voter's second as well as their first preference is likely to help the party achieve at least proportionality, as long as most Liberal Democrats prefer Labour to Conservatives as their second choice. The Conservatives also suffered in 1997 because their vote was spread over the country and fairly low.

Different PR electoral systems will have different outcomes. A form of the additional member system (in which half MPs are elected in constituencies under the first-past-the-post system and half are chosen from a regional list to bring each party's share of seats into line with the share of votes in the region) would have produced a much more proportional outcome in 1997, and a minority government. The single transferable vote would not have achieved proportionality because Labour would have benefited from Liberal Democrat second preferences and probably gained an overall majority.

Unless and until the Labour Party comes out for proportional representation, electoral reform is unlikely to be a major political issue. Supporters of change face formidable opposition in the party, notably from John Prescott and Jack Straw, and the many Labour MPs who would lose their seats. It is also reported that Blair was not impressed with the lack of authority shown by leaders of coalition governments in the EU during the Kosovo conflict and the bargaining between Labour and Liberal Democrat leaders in the new Scottish Parliament. But if there were a series of deadlocked Parliaments and it seemed that minority governments were here to stay, then a coalition – which involved at least two parties – might seem the only way of ensuring stable government. In that case PR would be a logical development. The introduction of coalitions and/or a proportional representation system would be likely to alter radically the conduct of British government and politics.

Because the choice of electoral system influences a party's prospects of political power, questions of party tactics and advantage inevitably loom large. Interestingly, in Scotland, William Millar has observed that the political parties favour schemes which do not operate to their advantage. Thus:

- Conservatives favour FPTP, although they gained no seats in the 1997 general election under the system.
- Labour is considering PR even through it received a great bonus under FPTP.
- Liberal Democrats favour PR but, like Labour, did much better under FPTP in the 1997 general election than they would have done under PR.

A change in voting system may lead to more coalitions (as it has in the Scottish Parliament), more bargaining between parties and a less adversarial system. Critics warn of the disproportionate power of a small party whose support may enable a large party to form a government with a majority. In Germany, Free Democrats who have usually been supported by less than 10 per cent of the vote have often been in government. But the same criticism can be made of a minority in a government party which has a small overall majority; it can effectively veto measures which it dislikes. This was the fate of Jim Callaghan's minority Labour government in the late 1970s and, at times, of John Major's government. Critics also object that under some PR systems many of Thatcher's radical (and subsequently applauded) reforms would not have been carried out.

At present, British elections are fought under a maze of different systems. The Northern Ireland Assembly is elected by STV; the European elections have Regional Party lists; elections to the Scottish Parliament and Welsh Assemblies have FPTP and a 'top up' and there are proposals for PR in local government elections; Westminster still has FPTP.

The prospects for PR have certainly taken a large step forward at the end of the 1990s but the achievement is still far from certain at Westminster. If a referendum were to give a negative verdict, the prospects would be set back for a generation or so. Note that there were some twenty years between the first referendum on devolution for Scotland and Wales and its eventual implementation.

The electoral process

Nomination

For election to the House of Commons it is virtually necessary to be nominated as a candidate by a *major* political party. Each constituency party nominates a candidate and, if approved by the party headquarters, he or she becomes the constituency's prospective parliamentary candidate. Each major party maintains a list of approved candidates from which local parties may select. If a candidate is not already on the party list, then he or she has to be approved by party headquarters.

This power has been important in the Labour Party. In the 1950s the party's National Executive Committee (NEC) turned down a number of left-wing nominations by constituencies. In the early 1980s the NEC came under left-wing control and this power was not exercised. Indeed reforms at this time (see below) gave more power to constituency activists, who were usually more left-wing than MPs. But under Neil Kinnock the NEC, as part of its drive against Militant, became more interventionist in candidate selection at by-elections and this has continued since. In the 1992 Parliament it insisted, against some constituency opposition, on a number of all-women short-lists in safe Labour seats as part of the campaign to boost the number of women MPs. These were subsequently ruled illegal and abandoned, although not before a large number of women had been adopted. In the absence of such a steer from the centre, the Conservative and Liberal Democrat parties still have an overwhelmingly male list of MPs, but Conservative Central Office has become more influential in compiling a short-list at by-elections.

To be nominated, a parliamentary candidate must him- or herself be eligible to vote, be nominated by ten local voters and pay a deposit of £500 to the returning officer, which is forfeited if he or she fails to gain 5 per cent of the vote. Traditionally few people participate in the selection process; the numbers ranged from a few dozen in some Labour general management committees to a few hundred in some Conservative associations. The introduction of a system of allowing all members to vote in the selection of candidates has made the process more open.

For many years nomination was assured for virtually all MPs. In the late 1970s, however, Labour left-wingers, as part of their campaign to extend democracy in the party, changed the party rules so that all Labour MPs were subject to mandatory reselection in the lifetime of Parliament. This was widely regarded as a device to make MPs more beholden to left-wing activists in the constituencies than to the party whips in Westminster. Some (ten) Labour MPs were de-selected for the 1983 election, and some of the MPs who departed for the Social Democratic Party would probably not have been reselected by their local parties. For the 1987 election six were de-selected. The rule change did not prove to be the major force once expected for the advance of the left in the party. On the contrary, left-wingers have sometimes been threatened with de-selection and a number of constituency parties confine themselves to renominating the sitting MP. By 1990, mandatory

BOX 8.2 MINI BIOGRAPHY

Sir Anthony Meyer (1920–)
Conservative politician. Educated at Eton and Oxford. MP Eton and Slough and then West Flint before retiring as MP for Clwyd NW. Sole claim to fame was standing against Thatcher in 1989 in the leadership contest. He felt strongly about Europe and was politically a 'liberal' Tory. He was well beaten by Thatcher but his gesture paved the way for a successful assault on her power only one year later.

resolution was effectively overturned when Conference agreed that contests would take place only if a ballot of local members demanded one.

Conservative activists have usually been a force for loyalty. Sir Anthony Meyer, who challenged Margaret Thatcher for the party leadership in 1989, was shortly afterwards de-selected by his Clwyd North West association, and supporters of Michael Heseltine's challenge to her in 1990 also came under pressure. In 1996 the anti-Major MP Sir George Gardiner encountered strong opposition in his local Reigate party and was eventually de-selected in January 1997.

Expenditure

Elections cost money. In 1997 the cost to the government – more accurately, its Consolidated Fund – was over £52 million. In addition, the annual cost of maintaining the electoral register is £50 million.

British constituency elections are cheap in comparison with those in many other Western states, largely because expenditure by local candidates is strictly limited by law. Each candidate is required to appoint an election agent who is responsible for seeing that the limits on expenses are not broken. The legal limits are usually raised before each election in line with inflation. The maximum permitted in constituencies ranged between £6,000 and £7,000 in 1992. On average candidates for the main three parties spend under £6,000 each, with Conservatives usually spending the most. In 1997 Conservative and Labour candidates spent an average of £5,600 and Liberals £3,200. For all parties the victors were more likely to spend near to the maximum permitted. The bulk of this spending goes on printing a candidate's election leaflets and addresses. Local candidates also have free postage for their election leaflets and free hire of school halls for meetings. The limit on spending means that local candidates can legally do little or no opinion polling, telephone canvassing or media advertising.

In contrast, there has been no legal limit on the spending by national party organisations and no legal obligation on them to publish their election budgets. Most national spending goes on advertising, opinion polling, the party leader's tours and meetings, and grants to constituency parties. Increasingly, political parties have been caught in an expenditure 'arms race', particularly on advertising. In 1997 the Conservatives paid over £13 million to the M and C Saatchi agency, and Labour over £7 million to the BMP agency. Labour was also helped by the large press advertising campaigns run by public sector unions appealing for support for the public services.

Heavy spending has made the parties dependent on business or wealthy individuals and has led to inevitable suspicions that cash is traded, however indirectly, for influence. Financing political parties has long been a problem in the developed democracies. The chief concern is that influence may be bought by certain groups in society and their interests advantaged at the expense of others. It costs some £30 million per year to run the Conservative Party and not much less to run Labour.

As Garner and Kelly indicate (1998, pp. 201–17) there are three reasons why finance has become such a critical issue:

1 The electorate has ceased to feel so closely identified with the parties (see Chapter 9) and are less likely to want to join and pay subscriptions. Membership of both major parties has shrunk from over a million each in the 1950s to around a third of a million in the 1990s. This 'dealignment', ironically, has itself increased the need for funding through

the need for more vigorous and regular campaigning.

2 The enthronement of media exposure as the route to power, not to mention all the various hi-tech equipment required to communicate with the public, has added huge additional expenditure costs.

3 Now parties are forced to campaign almost non-stop for the plethora of elections from local to European which modern democratic government requires.

Conservatives used to derive most of their funding from business – in 1994 Hanson, P and O, Forte and Glaxo Welcome were the biggest donors – but the dog days of the Major government caused these wells to dry up. They also relied excessively on donations from overseas, in some cases from suspect sources for example the £450,000 it accepted from Asil Nadir, the businessman accused of fraud who fled the country in 1987. Other names including the Greek millionaire John Latsis and the Hong Kong banker Li Ka Shing attracted criticism which inevitably attached itself to the receiving party.

Labour used to receive most of its funds from the unions and similarly left itself open to the accusation that it exchanged influence for party funds cash. Labour faced its own allegations of sleaze in October 1997 when Bernie Ecclestone, the millionaire owner of Formula One racing, seemed to influence the exemption of his sport from the ban on tobacco advertising which Labour had promised in its manifesto. When it transpired that the diminutive tycoon had donated a million pounds to Labour, the critical voices became strident and the donation was handed back. Both parties also were accused of handing out honours to rich donors, thus further lowering the status of democratic politics. So there was some justification for the popular assumption in the public mind that Conservatives were in the pocket of business and Labour the unions. Such an assumption was strengthened by the practice of both parties of altering the law when in office to favour themselves and disadvantage the other.

Unsurprisingly, of the two, the Conservatives were the richer requiring, and getting, nearly £40 million a year while Labour's income was closer to half that sum. Journalist Martin Linton also argued in 1992 that the support given to the Conservatives by the press added another effective £37 million to Conservative income.

Liberal Democrats have no institutional links and few big business connections so have been the poor cousin in modern democratic politics. According to Thomas (1998, p. 317) the party raised £3.3 million in the two years before 1997 with most of the cash coming from members.

Remedies

The Houghton Report in 1976 suggested state funding of parties but no action had been taken on it before Labour fell from power in 1979. The Hansard Society report in 1981 suggested 'matching funding' for funds raised by the parties. The Commons Home Affairs Select Committee reported in 1994 but could not agree; the Conservative majority favoured the status quo while the Labour minority wanted state funding. The Conservatives argued that state funding in a democracy is harmful in that it substitutes a government input for what should be a voluntary one drawing on all sections of democratic society. The fact that such an argument is self-serving should not be seen as disqualifying it. However, many European countries fund their parties while the US and Canada provide tax relief on donations.

In October 1997 Lord Neill announced that his Committee on Standards in Public Life would look into the vexed area of party finance. His report a year later proposed to ban foreign donations and cap campaign budgets at £20 million (see Box 8.4).

In the Queen's Speech of November 1999, the promised Political Parties and Referendum Bill promised to implement Neill's recommendations: ban foreign donations; force parties to reveal the name of donors above £5000; limit general election spending to £20 million per party (both main parties spent over £25 million in 1997); and impose controls over spending on referendum campaigns. An Electoral Commission will also be set up responsible for registering political parties and checking on their finances. One important difference between election campaigns in Britain and the USA is that British parties are precluded

BOX 8.4 **IDEAS AND PERSPECTIVES** 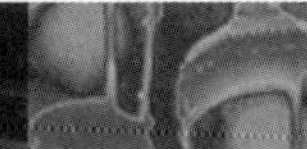

Neill Committee proposals on election spending

1. Donations over £5,000 nationally and £1,000 locally to be publicly declared. The figure includes payments in kind. Foreign donations banned. Company share holders to be balloted over corporate donations. End to 'blind trusts', or arrangements for providing funding by donors who are not known to the beneficiaries.
2. Tax relief for donations up to £500. Policy Development Fund to be provided with funds up to £1 million for policy work. Increase in money for opposition parties.
3. Limit general election spending to £20 million.
4. Provision for unregistered third parties to spend up to £25,000 and for those who are registered to spend up to £1 million in general election campaigns.
5. Electoral Commission to oversee the implementation of the votes. In the interest of greater transparency, parties are required to submit audited accounts to the Committee on Standards in Public Life.

Source: The Funding of Political Parties in the United Kingdom, October 1998

from purchasing time on the broadcasting media, although they can buy advertising in the press. In the USA there is little doubt that the opportunities for advertising have made elections very expensive and heightened the importance of personalities and the wealth of candidates. Over $100 million was spent by candidates in the 1996 US presidential compaign on television commercials alone. The time made available by television companies for election broadcasts is a considerable subsidy to the British parties.

Campaigns

There is a ritual element to British election campaigns. This is particularly so at the constituency level, with candidates and helpers pursuing their time-worn techniques of canvassing, addressing meetings and delivering election leaflets to electors' homes. At the national level the party leaders address public meetings in the major cities, attend morning press conferences and prepare for national election broadcasts. Elections today are effectively fought on a national scale through the mass media, particularly television. The activities of the party leaders – visiting party committee rooms, factories and old people's homes, speaking at evening rallies and making statements at morning press conferences – are conducted with an eye to gaining such coverage. If activities are not covered by peak-time television they are largely wasted as a means of communicating with the public. One of the most famous images of the 1979 election was Margaret Thatcher on a Norfolk farm, cuddling a new-born calf. This had little to do with discussion of political issues but the bonus for the Conservatives was that photographs of the event were carried prominently in almost every national newspaper and on the television screens. There is some Americanisation of campaigning in Britain; local face-to-face meetings have declined in importance, while the national parties employ their own opinion pollsters and advertising agencies and make use of computers, direct mail and other modern devices to 'market' themselves and appeal to target voters in key seats (Kavanagh, 1995).

It is difficult to prove that election campaigns make much difference to the final result. One party's good campaign in a constituency may fail to show a marked improvement because the opposi-

Voters endure a six-week general election campaign (27 April 1997)

tion parties have also made strenuous efforts in the seat. There is some evidence that an active new MP, perhaps using local radio and television over the lifetime of a Parliament, can gain up to 700 'personal' votes at the following general election. For many voters, however, the choice of whom to support on polling day is a product of a lifetime of influences, rather than the four weeks of an election campaign. In 1987 many observers were critical of the Conservatives' campaign but on polling day they had preserved the eleven-point lead over Labour enjoyed at the outset of the campaign. Compared with the disaster of 1983, Labour's campaign was admired for its smooth organisation and professionalism. But for all this, and Neil Kinnock's campaigning superiority to Michael Foot, Labour added just 3 per cent to its 1983 record low vote. In 1992 once more, communicators and, according to the polls, voters, judged that Labour and Neil Kinnock had campaigned better than the Conservatives and John Major. Even Conservative supporters were critical of their party's campaign. Yet Labour added only 3.6 per cent to its 1987 vote and the Conservative margin of victory in votes was greater than that achieved by any party in elections between 1950 and 1979. Packaging and presentation can only do so much.

In 1997 there was widespread admiration for the smoothness of the Labour campaign. Commentators talked about a 'Mandelson effect', named after the party's campaign director, Peter Mandelson. Its disciplined media operation, unit for rapid rebuttal (of opposition attacks), concentration of resources on its key 100 constituencies (those Conservative seats needed to be won for a Labour majority) and advertising all outscored the Conservative party. And throughout the five week campaign, the Conservatives were dogged by events – internal divisions over Europe, and damage from sleaze and sex scandals. Yet it is chastening to remember that the average Labour lead in the opinion polls actually fell from 22 per cent in the first week to 13 per cent on polling day; and that Labour's share of the vote in its target seats rose by fractionally less than it did in the non-targeted areas.

Referendums

Referendums have, quite suddenly, become an accepted part of the political scene. For a long time British politicians would have nothing to do with them. After all, referendums were difficult to square with the sovereignty of parliament, disciplined and programmatic political parties, and ideas of strong government. All of these features were part of a 'top down' view of government. The *Economist* (23 November 1996) quoted the Constitutional Unit's judgement: 'Across the world, politicians tend to dislike referendums. They take the decisions out of established hands and elected leaders can never take control'. Critics also complained that they were associated with dictatorships. When the first nation-wide British referendum was called by Labour Prime Minister Harold Wilson in 1975 to decide on Britain's continuing membership of the European Community, the decision was controversial. Wilson had earlier opposed the idea and Roy Jenkins resigned as deputy leader of the party in protest at the change of mind. Wilson claimed that it was a unique constitutional occasion, but most people knew that he called a referendum because his party was bitterly divided over British membership and, once the precedent has been set, others would follow.

Since then, and particularly since the election of a Labour government in 1997, referendums have proliferated; indeed, in 1999 some commentators wondered whether they might be inducing voter fatigue. They have been held in Scotland and Wales to approve the devolution plans in May 1998, in London over an elected Mayor and in September 1998 over the Good Friday Agreement in Northern Ireland. In addition, the main parties have promised to call a referendum before Britain joins the single European currency, and Labour has also promised to hold one on the reform of the electoral systems proposed by the Jenkins Commission (see above). Both of these are unlikely to take place before the next election.

Why have referendums flourished recently? Firstly, politicians will not have missed the fact that a large majority of voters say in polls that they like referendums if the issue is sufficiently important. Secondly, the authority of elected politicians has declined along with their reputations, and this device invokes the authority of the people in a very direct way. Both sides of a major issue can favour a referendum – as over the single currency issue – when both feel they could win the resultant vote. Interestingly, in the 1997 general election the late Sir James Goldsmith ran candidates with the banner of the Referendum Party, which sought a ballot on Britain's future relations with the EU. Thirdly, they can be useful when there is a difficult problem on which delay is thought advisable, such as devolution; and technically referendums are only advisory not binding (although it is hard to believe a government would totally ignore an emphatic result). Fourthly, they can be a useful uniting factor when a party cannot agree, as over membership of the EEC for Labour in 1975; in effect the party says to the country: 'We cannot decide so why don't you?'. John Major's Conservative party was divided over British membership of the single European currency and this was a factor which led it to embrace a referendum. Similarly Labour is divided over electoral reform – one group favours no change and another favours proportional representation; the referendum, it is fondly hoped, will square the circle, although it may merely make matters more complex as most voters are baffled by the respective arguments for and against. This also raises the question of whether referendums are a cop-out for politicians, a way of evading their responsibilities. How can voters decide on the arcane arguments over the single currency? Isn't it likely that the debate will be dominated by those who simplify and employ emotive slogans? Don't politicians get elected to make such decisions and use their judgement on behalf of the country? This question can be added to the discussion points below.

What most of the referendums, achieved and planned, have in common is that they deal with constitutional questions. It is now probable that any constitutional change will be preceded by approval in a referendum. So far politicians have resisted calling them on other issues, for example, capital punishment. Now that a referendum is clearly part of the constitutional framework there is a need to develop clear rules – for example about minimum turnout and funding, and the creation of an impartial body to regulate them. In 1998 the Neill Committee on Standards in Public Life proposed that the government should not use tax-payers' money to campaign for one side in a referendum. It also proposed a ceiling on spending during a referendum which could have an impact on business support for a 'yes' vote in a ballot on Britain joining a single currency. In summer 1999, it appeared that the government accepted the idea of a limit.

Chapter summary

The British electoral system has for a long time been admired for its simplicity and its effects in producing stable government. It is a quality much less admired today and reform is on the agenda. Reform is stimulated by changes in the party system, membership of the European Union and calculation of political advantage. Less is decided by elections than politicians claim, largely because of the limits on the autonomy of the British government.

Discussion points

There are a number of questions to ask about the working of the electoral system under the role of elections in Britain today:

- *Campaign funding*. How might party funding be improved? What might be the consequence for parties and campaigns of an effective limit on national spending or state provision of funding?
- *Electoral reform*. What considerations lead the Labour and Liberal Democrat Parties to be more sympathetic to electoral reform than the Conservative Party?
- *Scottish devolution*. What consequences might the creation of a Scottish parliament have on the electoral system and style of campaigning?
- *The importance of elections*. 'Elections have their limitations in deciding public policy'. Discuss.

Further reading

On the traditional and contemporary working of the British electoral system see Butler (1963 and 1983, respectively). On the consequences of different systems see Rose (1992) and Urwin (1982).

References

Butler, D. (1963) *The British Electoral System Since 1918*, 2nd edn (Oxford University Press).

Butler, D. (1983) *Governing Without a Majority* (Collins).

Crewe, I. (1997) 'The opinion polls: confidence restored?', *Parliamentary Affairs*, Vol. 50, No. 4, October.

Curtice, J. and Steed, M. (1997) 'The results analysed', in Butler, D. and Kavanagh, D., *The British General Election of 1997* (Macmillan).

Dunleavy, P. and Margetts, H. (1992) 'The electoral system', *Parliamentary Affairs*, Vol. 50, No. 4, October.

Garner, R. and Kelly, R. (1998) *British Political Parties Today* (Manchester University Press).

Hailsham, Lord (1979) *Dilemma of Democracy* (Collins).

Kavanagh, D. (1995) *Election Campaigning: The New Marketing of Politics* (Blackwell).

Rose, R. (1992) *What Are the Economic Consequences of PR?* (Electoral Reform Society).

Thomas, G. (1998) 'Party finance', in Jones (ed.), *Political Issues in Britain Today* (Manchester University Press), pp. 307–33.

Urwin, D. (1982) 'The mechanics and effects of various political systems', *Social Studies Review*, March.

Chapter 9 Voting behaviour

Dennis Kavanagh

Learning objectives

- To explain how voters are influenced.
- To understand electoral changes and the impact on them of society and class.
- To analyse and explain the outcome of the 1997 general election.

Introduction

It discusses the factors which shape voting behaviour, particularly those which have produced changes in party support in recent years. It also assesses the likely impact of these changes on the working of the political system. Finally it analyses the significance of the 1997 general election.

Explanations of voting behaviour

For the first half of the post-war period (1945–70) it was comparatively easy to provide broad explanations of voting behaviour in Britain. Three guidelines simplified analysis. The first was that people were regarded as being either middle or working class on the basis of their occupations. Although there were divisions within these groupings, notably between the skilled and unskilled working class, there was a strong correlation between class and vote: the majority of the working class voted Labour and most of the middle class voted Tory. Secondly, an average of about 90 per cent of voters supported either Labour or Conservative in general elections. Finally, most (over 80 per cent) of voters were partisans or **identifiers** with one or other of the above parties. Surveys indicated that for most people party allegiance hardened over time so that they were unlikely to turn to a new party. Identifiers were and are also more likely than other voters to agree with their party's policies and leaders.

During the 1960s it was generally believed by psephologists that most British people usually voted according to traditional associations of class and party. By the 1980s, however, such loyalties had waned, allowing issues to become more important. In an era of '**partisan dealignment**' (Sarlvik and Crewe, 1983) citizens no longer vote blindly for the party of their parents or workmates but, in the true spirit of pluralist democracy, listen to what the parties have to say on issues and react accordingly – sometimes in a volatile fashion. Sarlvik and Crewe distinguish between 'salience', the extent to which people are aware of an issue, and 'party preferred' in terms of policies on that issue. They believe the Conservative emphasis on taxes, law and order and trade union reform helped to win the 1979 election for them.

In 1987 and 1992, however, Labour led the Conservatives on three of the most salient issues – unemployment, health and education – yet easily lost both elections. Surveys showed that voters expected a Labour government to increase taxes and that most people were prepared to pay higher taxes to fund extra spending on public services.

Perhaps they were. But, crucially, a post-election Gallup poll found that 30 per cent said they would be better off and 48 per cent worse off under Labour's tax and budget proposals. Despite their identification of key issues and their preferences for Labour prescriptions, voters reacted to a personal consideration when it came to the crunch. They chose to vote for the party which they thought would deliver the highest degree of personal prosperity. This behaviour calls into question (a) the value of survey responses on issue questions and/or (b) the significance of **issue voting** – at least on this type of question.

A problem with research on issue voting is that one can never prove whether it is the party loyalty or vote which influences the issue preference, or vice versa (which is necessary for issue voting). And such questions are tied up with the broader image of the perceived 'competence' or trustworthiness of the party and the party leader (where Conservatives for long outscored Labour). At present political scientists are more impressed with the 'competence' and 'trust' factors as influences on the voter.

For most of the post-war period, therefore, social class and partisanship (and, as noted earlier, the electoral system) interacted to buttress the Labour/Conservative party system. There were relatively small margins of change in the parties' share of the vote from one general election to another. Between 1950 and 1970, for example, the Conservative share of the vote ranged from 49.7 per cent (1959) to 41.9 per cent (1945) and

BOX 9.1 **MINI BIOGRAPHY**

Ivor Crewe (1945–)

Political scientist. Educated Manchester Grammar School and Lancaster. Professor of Government at Essex University until made Vice Chancellor in 1995. Recognised as the leading psephologist and much used on television during election campaigns.

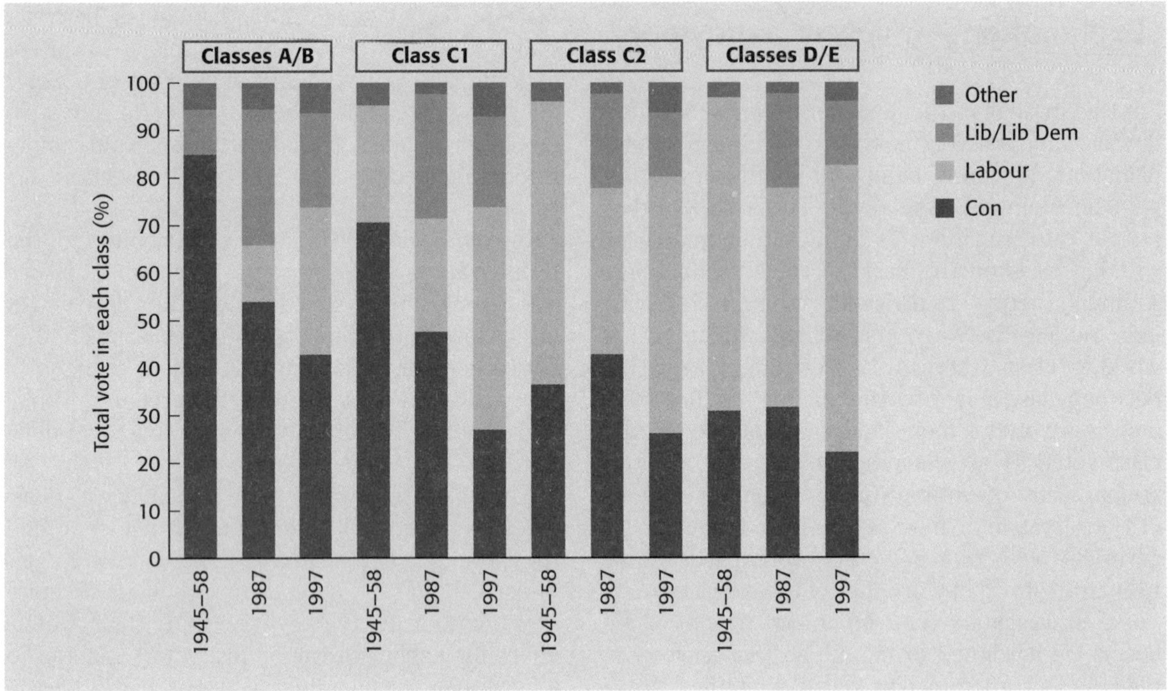

Figure 9.1 Partisan dealignment: class voting from 1945–58 to 1997
Source: Curtice, 1997

Labour's from 48.8 per cent (1951) to 43.8 per cent (1959). Stability was the order of the day and it was difficult to envisage a change in the party system.

The above description always needed some qualification. The most important is that between a quarter and a third of the working class usually voted Conservative. Without this '**deviant**' vote there would not have been a competitive two-party system and the Conservatives would hardly have been the 'normal' party of government in the twentieth century. Another is that class distribution was gradually changing as the proportion of the workforce engaged in manufacturing fell and the proportion employed in service and white-collar occupations grew. This trend has accelerated in the past two decades. This phenomenon has been labelled 'partisan dealignment'. This is the tendency of voters not to support the party which represents their cause: see Figure 9.1.

Yet for twenty-five years that old two-party, two-class model explains a diminishing part of British election behaviour. Firstly, consider partisanship: between 1964 and 1987 the proportion of the electorate identifying with the Labour and Conservative parties fell from 81 per cent to 70 per cent and strong identifiers from 38 per cent to 25 per cent over the same period, declining to 16 per cent by 1997. As an increasing number of voters have become less tied to parties, more votes are 'up for grabs' at elections.

Secondly, consider social class. The relationship between class and voting was fairly strong until the mid-1970s. Yet even in the 1960s surveys suggested that class loyalty was weakening in its intensity for many voters (Butler and Stokes, 1970, 1974). In general elections between 1970 and 1992, Labour's normal two-thirds share of the working-class vote fell to less than a half (and as low as 37 per cent in 1983). Over the same period the Conservatives' normal four-fifths share of the middle-class vote fell to just over half (Table 9.5). Within the middle class, Labour and Liberal support has been stronger among the public sector,

BOX 9.2 MINI BIOGRAPHY

David Butler (1924–)

Founding British psephologist. At Oxford he made election systems his subject of study. Moved on to electoral behaviour and became the recognised expert on elections in the 1970s and 1980s. His Nuffield studies of general elections since 1945 have become the recognised authoritative accounts of those events.

particularly among the teaching, nursing and local government professions. Quite separate from these trends has been the shift in the balance between the classes in the electorate. From a rough 40–60 split between the middle class and working class, the distribution today is the reverse, as a result of changing patterns of employment. In other words, Labour was gaining a diminishing share of a smaller working-class constituency.

Moreover, social changes, promoted in some degree by Thatcher reforms, have weakened the old class bases of the party system. Over 66 per cent of homes are now privately owned; since 1979 the proportion of council-rented properties fell from 45 per cent to 25 per cent of the housing stock. As a proportion of the workforce trade unionists fell from 53 per cent in 1979 to less than 40 per cent in the 1990s. Although many people are now in 'mixed' social class groups, e.g. working-class home-owners, Britain is increasingly becoming a middle-class society.

Finally, consider the level of support for the two main parties. The Labour and Conservative parties' combined share of 90 per cent of the vote in general elections between 1945 and 1970 has fallen to around 75 per cent in the elections since then. Electoral stability has been replaced by fluidity and the two-party, two-class model by three-party, less-class-based voting since 1983. As the moorings of class and partisanship have declined, so that election campaigns and the build-up to them (and the personalities, issues and events associated with them) may have more influence.

All the above factors make for a more unstable or volatile electorate. In the early months of 1982, Labour, Conservatives and the new Alliance parties were pretty level according to opinion polls and some Conservatives were even talking of the need to replace Margaret Thatcher as party leader. Yet after the Falklands victory in April the government shot into an overwhelming lead and gained a landslide victory – in terms of seats rather than votes – in the general election a year later. In September 1986 Labour had a clear lead in the opinion polls but by March 1987 it was twelve points adrift of the Conservatives who again won a clear election victory. For the six months following the Conservative general election victory in April 1992, Conservative and Labour were level pegging in the opinion polls. The humiliating exit of Britain from the exchange rate mechanism (ERM) on 'Black Wednesday' in September 1992 produced a sharp and enduring shift in attitudes to the parties. Tory support plummeted and Labour moved into a 20 per cent lead, a margin which it actually increased over the next four years, and in the 1997 general election had a lead of 13 per cent. Cautionary voices warn that Labour's 1997 coalition of voters (one-third of whom did not vote Labour in 1992) might just as easily disappear.

British voting behaviour has become less predictable and volatile for the following reasons:

1 *Partisanship*: Strong identifiers with parties have declined.

2 *Social class*: Class loyalties have weakened and the working class is diminishing in size.

3 *Social changes*: Housing and occupational patterns have changed, so that Britain is more property owning and middle class.

4 *Level of support for the two parties*: This reduced from 90 per cent in 1945 to 1970 to around 75 per cent since.

It is against this background that we should take account of the 1997 election result. For the first time ever, Labour gained as much middle-class support as did the Conservatives, and nearly two million 1992 Conservatives switched to Labour in 1997. So much for the strength of social class and party loyalty.

Social class

There are several different approaches to defining social class and different definitions and measurements have excited debates (Crewe, 1986; Heath *et al.*, 1985). Most researchers have long relied on the six-category scheme of the British Market Research Society (BMRS). This scheme relies on occupation combined with lifestyle and incomes as the basis for differentiating classes and splits the population 40–60 per cent between the middle and working class: see Table 9.1.

Another approach focusses more on the conditions in which incomes are earned and a person's degree of autonomy and authority at work. *How Britain Votes* (Heath *et al.*, 1985) uses this approach. Its middle class broadly corresponds to that of the BMRS and the proportion is pretty similar. The most dramatic change in this scheme is the reduction in the size of the working class of rank and file manual workers to one-third of the workforce. The study also creates other non-manual groups, including the intermediate class of clerical and sales workers and foremen (24 per cent) and the salariat of managers, executives and professionals (27 per cent). In addition they have a petite bourgeoisie of employers and self-employed which the BMRS allocate to the skilled working class.

Table 9.1 Different definitions of social class

Social class categories (Heath *et al.*) (%)	
Salariat	27
Routine non-manuals	24
Petite bourgeoisie	8
Foremen, technicians	7
Working class	34
Social class categories (Dunleavy and Husbands) (%)	
Manual workers	45
Non-manual	25
Controllers of labour	22
Employees/petite bourgeoisie	8
Social class categories (British Market Research Society) (%)	
A Upper middle	2
B Middle	13
C1 Lower middle	24
C2 Skilled workers	31
D Semi-skilled and unskilled workers	18
E Poor	2

There has been controversy over the changing relationships between social class and voting.

According to Crewe (1986), not only had the working class shrunk in size, but Labour's share of its electoral support also fell in the 1980s. For the first half of the post-war period, Labour and Conservative used to gain two-thirds of the class vote, i.e. Labour working class and Conservative middle class, but in the 1970s and 1980s the figure fell to less than half. In other words, there had been a class **dealignment**. According to another measure of class (Heath *et al.*, 1985), however, class voting had not declined, once we omit – and this is a large assumption – the large centre party vote from the calculation.

Party support

Conservative

The Conservatives have clearly been the dominant party in Britain in the twentieth century. Indeed some would argue that Britain has had a dominant-party system rather than a two-party one (King, 1993). Before the 1997 general election they were in office, alone or in coalition, for over two-thirds of the century and two-thirds of the period since 1945. Indeed, in this century the only four occasions in which the non-Conservative parties have had clear parliamentary majorities have been the 1906–10 Liberal government; the 1945–50 Labour government; the 1966–70 Labour government; and the 1997 Labour government. In recent years a significant part of the Conservative dominance in Parliament has been due to the effects of the first-past-the-post electoral system and the divided opposition. In 1979, 1983 and 1987, for example, 42 per cent of the vote was enough to produce Conservative majorities, including landslides in the House of Commons in 1983 and 1987 as the Alliance or Liberal and the Labour and other parties divided the non-Conservative vote between them. The Conservatives have also been the historical beneficiary of Labour's internal divisions, and until 1997 enjoyed strong support from the press and such powerful groups as the City, business and the farming sector. Labour supporters have felt particularly sensitive about the partisanship of the tabloids in 1992, and Neil Kinnock blamed Labour's defeat on their 'bias'. In 1992 most Labour and working-class voters, because they read a tabloid, were exposed to pro-Conservative papers.

Yet in the 1980s (as in the 1950s) the Conservative Party also identified itself firmly with economic prosperity. In spite of presiding over a return to mass unemployment and increasing levels of homelessness and inequality, Margaret Thatcher's party managed to fashion a constituency which had an interest in the continuation of Conservative rule. Among those who did well in the 1980s were many who lived in the affluent south and suburbs, home-owners, share-owners (who expanded from 7 per cent in 1979 to over 20 per cent) and most of those in work. In spite of the return of high levels of unemployment, the longest economic recession for over fifty years, the collapse of business confidence and a sharp decline in house prices, particularly in the Tory heartland of the south-east, the Conservatives still managed to outscore Labour when voters were asked to rate the parties' competence on economic management. This appears to have been a crucial influence on the vote in 1992. In view of the modest Conservative economic record, however, it was more of an emphatic thumbs down to Labour. Either in prosperity or in recession, most voters were not willing to trust it. As Ivor Crewe states, given the Conservative disadvantages, the key question about 1992 was 'why did Labour lose yet again?' (1992). In the 1992 Parliament, however, the Conservatives lost their reputation for economic competence and much press support and the party faces a major task to restore its position (see p. 174).

Table 9.2 How the nation voted

	May 1997	April 1992	June 1987	June 1983
Conservative	31.7	41.9	42.2	42.3
Labour	43.2	34.4	30.8	27.6
Alliance/Lib Dems	16.8	17.8	22.6	25.4
Others	9.3	5.8	3.4	4.7

Labour

As partisanship and class weakened in the 1970s and 1980s, so Labour's long-term future as a party of government became less secure. Its share of the vote fell below 40 per cent in all general elections between 1970 and 1992. Its 1983 share of 27.6 per cent was its lowest since 1918 (when Labour was still a new party and fighting its first nation-wide election). In 1987 and 1992, the party made a modest recovery, but only to 34.4 per cent, over 7 per cent behind the Conservative vote. This was close to the party's 'normal' or expected vote (Table 9.3). Increasingly, it seemed that Labour would require a remarkable combination of favourable circumstances to win outright victory at a general election (Table 9.4).

Optimists could claim that Labour lost general elections because of the special circumstances associated with each election. It did badly in 1979 largely because of the public's hostile reaction to the trade unions and Labour government after the 'winter of discontent'. Before the 1983 election, there were bitter internal party rows, changes in the party's constitution (see p. 245), the breakaway of the Social Democrats, the weakness of Michael

Table 9.3 Government parliamentary majorities, 1945–97

	Overall majority
1945	Labour 147
1950	Labour 6
1951	Conservative 16
1955	Conservative 59
1959	Conservative 99
1964	Labour 5
1966	Labour 97
1970	Conservative 31
1974 (February)	None
1974 (October)	Labour 4
1979	Conservative 44
1983	Conservative 144
1987	Conservative 102
1992	Conservative 21
1997	Labour 179

Table 9.4 Calculation of the normal vote 1974–92 (%) and comparisons with 1997

	Conservative	Labour	Liberal	Other
Mean, 1945–70	45.2	46.1	7.1	1.6
Mean, February 1974–92	40.7	34.4	19.5	5.5
Range, February 1974–92	39.8±4.1	33.4±5.8	19.6±5.8	5.5±?
Actual result 1997	30.7	43.2	16.8	9.3

Source: Rose, 1992, p. 453

Table 9.5 Social class and vote, 1979–92 (%)

	1979		1983		1987		1992	
	Non-manual	Manual	Non-manual	Manual	Non-manual	Manual	Non-manual	Manual
Conservative	55	36	51	35	49	37	49	35
Liberal/Alliance/LibDem	19	17	31	28	31	23	25	20
Labour	26	46	18	37	20	40	26	45
Non-manual Conservative + manual Labour as % of total vote	51		45		44		47	

Source: Harris/ITN exit polls, 3 May 1979, 9 June 1983, 11 June 1987, 9 April 1992; Crewe, 1993, p. 33

Foot as Labour leader and the bitter policy divisions. The 1987 election was held against a background of rising living standards; the platform of low inflation and falling unemployment would have made any government unbeatable.

It was difficult, however, to find a convincing alibi for 1992. Given the mismanagement of the economy, a Tory campaign that was widely regarded as lacklustre and a government that had been in office for thirteen years, the odds were against the Conservatives. If Labour could not capture 40 per cent of the vote in 1992, let alone win, then when could it? Clearly, fundamental changes have been at work, making the party into an electoral minority. Some political scientists asked whether 1992 was, or the following election would be, 'Labour's last chance' (Heath *et al.*, 1994). The changes are worthy of note. They are:

1 *Demographic*: The faster growth of population in the south compared with the north, spread of home ownership and decline of council tenancy, contraction of the public sector (through privatisation) and heavy manufacturing jobs and growth of employment in service industries, and fall in membership of unions have all weakened the traditional social sources of support for Labour. The old working class – members of trade unions, engaged in heavy industrial work, renting property from a council and employed in the public sector – is a steadily diminishing electoral minority. The 'new working class', as Crewe (1987) describes it, is increasingly home owning, living in south Britain, car owning, not in a union and employed in the private sector – and before 1997 less than half voted Labour (Table 9.5).

2 *Attitudinal*: Post-election research conducted for the party among wavering Conservatives showed the lack of enthusiasm for voting Labour. These target voters wanted to 'get on' or to consolidate the material gains which they had made under the Thatcher years. Although they liked Labour's social policies, they regarded the party as a threat to their hopes of material advancement; the party was associated with 'equalising down' and 'holding back'. When he became Labour

leader in 1994 Tony Blair was determined to win these people over to the party. The party had no future as a party of the working class but had to appeal to the middle class also. The 1997 election reflected his success.

Third party voting

The growth of a third vote – or decline of aggregate support for the two main parties – may have different meanings. In four elections (1983–92) less than 75 per cent of votes were for Labour and Conservative. In the House of Commons, however, nearly 95 per cent of seats have been Labour and Conservative. The disproportional effects of the first-past-the-post electoral system 'wasted' much Alliance and Liberal Democratic electoral support. Tactical voting and concentration of resources helped the Liberal Democrats to gain more seats in 1997, and the Labour–Conservative share of seats fell to 88 per cent for the 75 per cent share of the vote.

In the House of Commons now the third force is particularly heterogeneous. Apart from the Liberal Democrats it also includes Welsh and Scottish nationalists and the various Northern Ireland parties. Much of the popular support to date for 'other' parties outside Northern Ireland has not been translated into a sufficient number of seats to threaten the two main parties. In the 1974 elections the growth in Liberal support (to 19 per cent of the vote in the February election) and the rise of the nationalists in Scotland (to 30 per cent of the Scottish vote in October 1974) represented a potential threat. But these advances were not consolidated and both parties lost seats and votes in 1979. By 1997 nationalist support had recovered to 22 per cent in Scotland and climbed to 10 per cent in Wales.

Elections in Britain were pretty competitive over the 1945–79 period, as the Labour and Conservative parties were evenly matched in total votes and time in office. Between 1979 and 1992, as in the interwar years, we may say that electoral competition has been imbalanced, with the Conservatives clearly the dominant party. 1997 has not corrected the imbalance, although Labour is now dominant.

Table 9.4 provides a computation of each main party's normal vote, or the share it should gain in normal circumstances. It is derived from each party's average vote share over the 1974–92 elections. Special factors – e.g. a dynamic leader, the Falklands War or the winter of discontent, or an outstanding or a disastrous record – can produce a variation in the figure. It is seen that the Conservatives had a substantial advantage over Labour. Yet speculation about Conservative hegemony was rudely disrupted in the 1992 Parliament. Since the exit from the ERM, no government has fallen so low in public esteem since opinion polling began over fifty years ago (Crewe, 1994). The exit, tax increases and party divisions provided the circumstances which massively reduced the normal vote for the Conservatives. The 1997 election confirmed the collapse of Conservative support.

But, occasionally, there is also a realigning election, or series of elections, when a new party breaks through or there is durable shift in party strength. The most formidable threat yet to the dominance of the Labour–Conservative party system developed in 1981. Following the breakaway of a number of leading right-wingers from Labour to form the Social Democratic Party, its alliance with the Liberals enabled the new force to gain greatly from the unpopularity of the two major parties. Between March 1981 and March 1982 the Alliance was regularly first or second in the opinion polls and had a remarkable string of by-election successes. It failed to maintain its support and was disappointed in the 1983 election with its 25 per cent share of the vote and twenty-one seats.

The 1997 general election

The main voting study of the 1992 election had warned that social trends would continue on balance to erode Labour's traditional vote and that the party would need a post-war record **swing** to win an overall majority at the next election. Labour had not achieved such a swing in 1992, and the next election was likely to be fought in more adverse circumstances. The study concluded that the party's best hope was a hung Parliament. In turn, that would require co-operation with the Liberal Democrats and, probably, some measure of electoral reform, a step that would almost certainly end any party's chances of winning an overall majority. The authors warned: 'So while Labour may indeed be able to stop the Conservatives from winning office for the fifth time in succession, this will not necessarily herald the restoration of Britain's two-party system. Rather it could be its death knell' (Heath *et al.*, 1994, p. 295).

For the period 1993–97, however, Labour enjoyed record leads in the opinion polls and the Conservatives sank to a record low level of support. The 1997 election produced a devastating outcome for the Conservative Party. It lost a quarter of its 1992 vote, and its number of MPs has been reduced to its lowest since 1906. The 13 per cent gap by which it trailed Labour in vote share was comparable with its 15 per cent lead over Labour in the 1983 general election. Scotland and Wales became Conservative-free nations, suffering less because of the nationalists than the rise in Labour support. Yet Scotland and Wales hold a total of 112 seats.

Although the scale of the disaster came as a surprise to many, it was in line with the by-election and local election results and opinion polls for much of the parliament. Hitherto Conservative strongholds such as Hove and Wimbledon were lost. The party has virtually disappeared from the major cities and is more than ever a party of the English shires and suburbs.

The setback was remarkable for a party which has been the normal party of government and long admired for its tactical flexibility and the prowess of its election machine. In fact neither of these qualities has been much in evidence since 1992. The party's bitter divisions over Europe and the loss of membership and declining level of activity at grass roots level proved fatal. Electorally and organisationally the Conservative Party was in a state of crisis at the end of the twentieth century (see p. 236).

The scale of change in 1997 actually exceeds the previous landslides. Labour's majority of 179 dwarfs the Liberal one of 130 in 1906, Labour's 146 in 1945 and the Conservative's 142 in 1983. Labour's number of MPs (419) is greater than in 1945 (393). The 10 per cent swing from Conservative to Labour is the largest in any general election since 1945.

Most parties, except for the Conservatives, could find some consolation in the 1997 election. Indeed, they all fed on Conservative misfortune. Apart from Labour, the nationalists doubled their share of seats in Scotland and the Liberals gained their largest number of seats (46) in over 60 years.

The 1997 election campaign will be much analysed but it is difficult to believe that it made much difference to the outcome. The standing of the parties on election day was almost identical to that in the opinion polls when Britain was ejected from the ERM in September 1992. The 1997 election outcome was a verdict on the five years of the Major government or perhaps the eighteen years of Conservative government. Since 1992 the exit from the ERM, tax increases, sleaze, mishandling of the BSE crisis, divisions over Europe and the defection of traditionally Tory supporting newspapers all sapped the authority of the government. The above factors contributed to a powerful mood for change and the Conservatives had been in office for such a long time. Party divisions diminished the authority of John Major as a national and even as a party leader. There was an economic recovery, with record low levels of inflation, interest rates and mortgage rates, and falling unemployment, but voters were not in the mood to give the government any credit.

On the other hand, Labour had changed greatly since 1992. Under Tony Blair it made a hard-headed analysis of what had gone wrong in 1992 and what was required to win the next election. It was determined to abandon its tax and spend image. It accepted much of the Thatcherite agenda – privatisation, existing income tax rates for the next parliament, aggregate public spending figures for the next two years, trade union reforms and a 'wait and see' attitude to British membership of the single currency. It also had a leader who made a point of being seen to lead his party, and to lead it in a new direction.

During the campaign, John Major was forced to deal with the issue that was tearing his party apart. The government line on the single currency was to wait and see, or as Major expressed it to 'negotiate and decide' whether it would be in Britain's interest to join in the first wave planned

Scenes from an election no. 3 (27 April 1997)

for 1999. He believed in the wisdom of this stance and thought, in addition, that it offered the only hope of keeping the sceptics and the Europhiles together. However, nearly half of Conservative candidates broke ranks and declared in their election addresses that they were opposed to membership in principle. The focus on Europe distracted Conservatives from running on their economic record and advertised their disunity. Major also warned that Labour would lead Britain into a federal Europe and that its plans for devolution in Scotland would lead to the break up of the Union.

Labour made pledges to lower class sizes, not increase standard and top rates of income tax, cut hospital waiting lists and impose a windfall tax on the excess profits of utilities to help to get 250,000 young unemployed into work. Two features which had hampered Labour since 1979 were overturned. Thatcher and Major had always led Labour leaders, when voters were asked to rate party leaders as potential prime ministers. In 1997, however, Blair decisively outscored Major as the best prime minister; according to MORI, 40 per cent of voters thought that Blair would be the most capable prime minister compared with 23 per cent for John Major. In 1992 John Major led Neil Kinnock by 38–27 per cent. And on taxation, although most voters expected taxes to go up in the new parliament, Labour led the Conservatives when voters were asked which party they trusted most on handling taxation. Above all, Labour candidates showed an iron discipline during the campaign. No disagreements broke through, compared with the spectacular splits among Conservatives.

During the 1980s, and particularly during the 1992 election campaign, the Conservative-supporting tabloid newspapers had been relentlessly hostile to Labour. The tabloids helped to convey negative messages, some of them distorted, about Labour's tax plans in 1992. The Conservative party was assured of getting its message across. The reiterated propaganda message that 'You can't trust Labour' struck home. Newspapers such as the *Express*, *Mail*, *Sun* and *Telegraph* faithfully echoed Conservative Central Office anti-Labour claims and smears. Labour could only rely on the *Mirror* and *Guardian* for support. The tabloids, particularly the *Sun*, also had a large Labour-supporting working-class readership. That paper's virulent anti-Labour and anti-Kinnock campaign may have had some effect in producing a late swing to the Conservative party among its readers.

By 1997 the position was much changed. Many Conservative papers had been hostile to John Major personally and to his line on Europe throughout the 1992 Parliament. The failure of British participation in the ERM gave them a chance to break free and all but one of the Tory-supporting newspapers backed John Redwood when he challenged John Major for the party leadership in 1995. They had much material for negative coverage throughout the parliament, including tax rises, sleaze, internal divisions and sex scandals. Although some of the papers returned to the fold by 1997 they did so without the old enthusiasm. *The Times* bolted the Conservative stable door and, crucially, the largest-circulation daily, the *Sun*, and the Sunday *News of the World* endorsed the New Labour Party of Tony Blair. Before one assumes that the endorsement of these newspapers won the election for Labour, one should realise that they were only following their readers. Their editors could read the opinion polls as well as anybody else; the Conservatives were massively unpopular.

Was 1997 a critical election?

Not all general elections are of equal significance, when viewed in the long term. Some American political scientists (e.g. Key, 1955) have distinguished between elections which are:

- Maintaining, in which voters reassert party loyalties and vote along traditional social lines. We would expect the outcomes to resemble the 'normal' pattern of voting as in Table 9.3.
- Deviating, in which the traditional minority party wins, but the change proves to be short lived.
- Critical, in which new issues and events trigger a **realignment** in the shape of new bases of support for a political party, or the rise of a new party or a new balance between the political parties. Such a change (or changes) lasts for a number of elections.

The 1945 general election was clearly critical in the sense that, for the first time, Labour gained a clear majority of seats and was at last competitive with the Conservative party. The four elections between 1979 and 1992 might also be considered a critical era, because the Conservatives moved into an average 10 per cent lead in the share of the popular vote over Labour. Labour's large lead in the 1997 election was clearly a break with what had occurred before (see Table 9.3). Other symptoms of change included Labour's substantial increase in support in the south-east and among the middle class (Norris, 1997). But before we call 1997 critical we need to remember that Labour's previous election landslides in 1945 and 1966 proved short lived. Only the outcomes of later general elections will decide whether 1997 is a turning point.

Analysis of the significance of the 1997 election might take account of the following:

1. The convergence in policy between Labour and Conservative means that in large part the policy battles of the 1980s have been settled, for the present at least. Tony Blair has moved Labour to the new centre – largely Conservative defined – ground. There were some differences between the parties, notably over devolution and constitutional reforms and entry to the European Social Chapter. But Labour had

Tony Blair takes to the road to consult the people (18 January 1998)

substantially accepted the principles of a market economy, low levels of direct taxation and flexible labour markets. These are historic breaches with the party's traditions. The large number of 1992 Tories who switched to Labour in 1997 was as much a reflection of disillusion with the former as a feeling of security with the latter.

2 The election was as presidential as any preceding one, as all leaders dominated their party's media coverage. Tony Blair ran ahead of the party in the opinion polls and his appeal for trust was largely for himself. John Major also detached himself from his divided and unpopular party.

3 Third party support was as strong as ever. If we add the forty-six Liberal Democrat MPs to the twenty-nine 'other' MPs then the total of seventy-five is the highest in any post-war parliament.

4 The 1997 election campaign represented a new level of professionalism – spin doctoring and media management to shape public opinion, targeting of floating voters and key constituencies via computerised data banks, direct mail and telephone canvassing, and disciplined adherence by party spokespersons to messages or themes of the day. Much of this professionalism was more evident on the Labour rather than on the Conservative side. The new technologies have probably lessened the personal contact between candidates and voters. Anti-Conservative tactical voting was encouraged and Labour may have gained as many as an extra twenty-one seats and the Liberals an extra fourteen seats as a result.

5 In recent years much interest has developed in economic explanations of voting behaviour. The main proponent of such an analysis is Professor David Saunders of Essex University. He argues that the performance of the economy influences the economic expectations and optimism of people and this in turn shapes voting behaviour. The elections in 1983, 1987 and 1992 all coincided with a revival of economic optimism and the Conservative government was the beneficiary. Interestingly, the Conservative government presided over a much better set of economic indicators in 1997 than in 1992; inflation was lower, unemployment was falling and interest rates were lower than they had been for many years. Economic optimism was also returning as more voters recognised the recovery of the economy.

But, crucially, voters refused to give the Conservative Party credit for the economic recovery or to vote for it. What was more important in 1997 was the Conservatives' negative image and this was more powerful than economic factors (Hilton, 1999; Finkelstein, 1999). Voters no longer trusted the party because of its broken promises over tax, association with sleaze, and they no longer regarded it as economically competent because of the ERM exit and continuing divisions over Europe. Labour, on the other hand, had removed many of the negatives which plagued it through the 1980s and even through 1992. Blair's leadership and shifts in policies convinced many voters than Labour had indeed changed. 1997 is a good example of a general election in which macro-economic improvements or even improvements in personal circumstances do not automatically translate into expected voting behaviour.

6 It has already been argued that events pre-dating the campaign shaped the outcome. But the events of the campaign – the defection of many traditional Conservative newspapers to Labour, new sleaze allegations against Conservative MPs and continuing divisions over Europe – all harmed the Conservative party. They reinforced the mood that the party was untrustworthy and that it was time for change.

7 In all the understandable triumphalism of Labour, and to a lesser extent of Liberal Democrats, it was easy to overlook one damning feature of the election: the turnout of 71.4 per cent was the lowest since 1935.

8 The voting returns show that Labour made impressive gains across the country and among all groups (Table 9.6). Among the C1s, or lower-middle class, there was a massive swing to Labour. All regions moved to Labour but the swing was more modest in the north, where Labour was already strong. Labour has long trailed the Conservatives among women but in

Table 9.6 New Labour's conquest of middle Britain

	1997 vote, % (change on 1992 in parentheses)		
	Conservative	**Labour**	**Lib Dem**
All Great Britain voters	31 (–12)	44 (+9)	17 (–1)
Men	31 (–8)	44 (+6)	17 (–1)
Women	32 (–11)	44 (+10)	17 (–1)
AB voters	41 (–11)	31 (+9)	21 (0)
C1	26 (–22)	47 (+19)	19 (–1)
C2	25 (–15)	54 (+15)	14 (–4)
DE	21 (–8)	61 (+9)	13 (0)
First-time voters	19 (–16)	57 (+17)	18 (–3)
All 18–29	22 (–18)	57 (+19)	17 (0)
30–44	26 (–11)	49 (+12)	17 (–3)
45–64	33 (–9)	43 (+9)	18 (–2)
65+	44 (–3)	34 (–2)	16 (+2)
Home owners	35 (–12)	41 (+11)	17 (–3)
Council tenants	13 (–6)	65 (+1)	15 (+5)
Trades union members	18 (–9)	57 (+7)	20 (+2)

Source: 1992 data ITN/Harris exit poll; 1997 data BBC/NOP exit poll

1997 women were as likely as men to vote Labour. It also made large gains among the first-time voters (leading the Conservatives by a 3–1 margin), but still trailed among the over-sixty-fives, among whom there was only a 2.5 per cent swing to Labour.

9 For at least the past three decades two political nations have been emerging – a Labour north and a Conservative south. The Conservatives are still largely a party of the south-east as well as the shires and the suburbs in England. However, Labour now has a more national presence because of its gains in the south. It also profited greatly from the electoral system. It gained two-thirds of the seats (64 per cent) for only 44 per cent of the vote. The Conservative party gained only a quarter of the seats for 31 per cent of the vote and in Scotland for 17.5 per cent of the vote no seats. By contrast, the Liberals with only 12.5 per cent of the votes in Scotland got ten seats.

10 It is too early to talk of the long-term collapse of the Conservative Party or the hegemony of Labour. Only time will allow the 1997 election to be placed in a broader context, and to assess whether it is a turning point. In the short term, it clearly breaks with the Conservative dominance of post-1970. Labour's share of the vote is below the level which it reached in the 1960s and only slightly more than the Conservative share in 1992, although it was its highest vote share for over thirty years. If the vote was for change, it is difficult to argue that it was a mandate for radically different policies. After all, Labour had come to accept much of the Thatcher–Major agenda. It needs restating that the landslide in seats is largely a product of the electoral system and Lib–Lab tactical voting. Clearly, if proportional representation were brought about and Labour and Liberal Democrats worked together, it would be difficult for the Conservatives to get back into office.

Elections are largely decided by the performance of parties in government. But opposition parties still have to be electable. Labour was not electable in 1992, it was in 1997. The Conservatives have to resolve their position on the single European currency and European integration. At present the party in parliament and in the constituencies seems Eurosceptical, but is this strong enough to win a general election? Although the party ended the twentieth century in disarray, the twentieth century had still been a Conservative century.

The Liberal Democrat dilemma

Until the 1987 election there was talk of realignment (or change) in the British party system, largely based on the rise of the Alliance, a centre grouping of Social Democrats and Liberals. It then seemed possible that the Alliance might overtake Labour as the second largest party, perhaps replacing that party, or establishing itself as one of three major national parties.

The successor Liberal Democrat Party was formed in 1988 and has never approached the voting strength of the Alliance. As noted in Chapter 12, the transformation of Labour under Tony Blair has squeezed the centre ground for the Liberal Democrats. The logical response has been to seek co-operation with Labour, in return for a commission and a referendum on electoral reform.

Liberals have traditionally done better under Conservative governments, not least by attracting disillusioned Tory voters. Yet of the hundred seats which were most likely to fall to the Liberal Democrats in 1992 and 1997 the great majority were Conservative held. In 1997 a Liberal Democrat breakthrough came at the expense of Conservatives. In 1997 Liberals adopted some positions to the left of Labour, e.g. on taxation and redistribution. As a party of the metaphorical 'centre' the Liberals can gain from other parties but they may also get 'squeezed' in a close contest or lose support if they become too closely identified with Labour.

If there were to be a series of deadlocked Parliaments and coalition or minority governments ensued, and there was continued large support for a third party, pressure would almost certainly increase for a new set of rules of the electoral game. There is little historical evidence about how voters might react to such political and constitutional uncertainties. Multi-party politics provides voters with the opportunity to vote tactically – possibly against the party they most dislike.

Chapter summary

For much of the post-war period voting was fairly predictable. The dominance of the Conservatives in the 1980s produced new interpretations. There seemed to be a move to one-party government and Labour to long-term decline but this was reversed by Labour's landslide in 1997. The shift in voting behaviour has coincided with changes in party system and perhaps in the political system.

Discussion points

- Compare the impact of issues in the 1992 and 1997 general elections.
- What is the significance of party leaders in election campaigning?
- Are class factors still important in shaping voting behaviour?

Further reading

On recent electoral behaviour see Crewe (1993) and Norris (1997). On the 1997 election campaign Butler and Kavanagh (1997), Norris *et al.* (1999) and Norris and Galvin (1997) are useful. Denver (1994) is a still a very useful and clear introduction although it needs to be updated.

References

Butler, D. and Kavanagh, D. (1997) *The British General Election of 1997* (Macmillan).

Butler, D. and Stokes, D. (1970, 1974) *Political Change in Britain* (Macmillan).

Crewe, I. (1986) 'On death and resurrection of class voting', *Political Studies.*

Crewe, I. (1987) 'Why Mrs Thatcher was returned with a landslide', *Social Studies Review*, September.

Crewe, I. (1992) 'Why did Labour lose (yet again)?', *Politics Review*, September.

Crewe, I. (1993) 'The changing basis of party choice, 1979–1992', *Politics Review.*

Crewe, I. (1994) 'Electoral behaviour', in D. Kavanagh and A. Seldon (eds), *The Major Effect* (Macmillan).

Denver, D. (1994) *Elections and Voting Behaviour in Britain*, 2nd edn (Philip Allan).

Finkelstein, D. (1999) 'Why the Conservatives lost', in I. Crewe, B. Gosschalk and J. Bartle (eds), *Why Labour Won the General Election in 1997* (Frank Cass).

Heath, A., Jowell, R. and Curtice, J. (1985) *How Britain Votes* (Pergamon).

Heath, A., Jowell, R. and Curtice, J. (1994) *Labour's Last Chance?* (Dartmouth).

Hilton, S. (1999) 'The Conservative Advertising Strategy', in I. Crewe, B. Gosschalk and J. Bartle (eds), *Why Labour Won the General Election in 1997* (Frank Cass).

Key, V.O. (1955) 'A Theory of Critical Election', *Journal of Politics*, Vol. 17, No. 1, pp. 3–18.

King, A. (1993) *Britain at the Polls 1992* (Chatham House).

Norris, P. (1997) *Electoral Change since 1945* (Blackwell).

Norris, P. and Galvin, N. (1997) 'Britain Votes 1997', Special issue of *Parliamentary Affairs,* Vol. 50, 4 October.

Norris, P., Curtie, J., Saunders, O., Scammell, M., and Semetko, H. (1999) *On Message* (Sage).

Sarlvik, B. and Crewe, I. (1983) *Decade of Dealignment* (Cambridge University Press).

Chapter 10 The mass media and political communication

Bill Jones

Learning objectives

- To explain the workings of the media: press and broadcasting.
- To encourage an understanding of how the media interact and influence voting, elections and the rest of the political system.
- To discuss how the pluralist and Marxist dominance theories help explain how the media operate and influence society.

Introduction

Without newspapers, radio and pre-eminently television, the present political system could not work. The media are so omnipresent and all-pervasive that we are often unaware of the addictive hold they exert over our attentions and the messages they implant in our consciousness on a whole range of matters . . . including politics. This chapter assesses the impact of the mass media upon the working of our political system and different theories about how they work.

At the end of the pulsating European Cup Final in May 1999, the cameras roamed around the stadium, alighting briefly on delirious United fans waving scarves and chanting ecstatically. Then it moved to the other side of the stadium where the Bayern Munich fans stood dejectedly, heads bowed in defeat, some in tears. Then they suddenly saw their images on the big screen and, forgetting their gloom, erupted into delight when they realised their images were being broadcast to millions of people. This episode helps illustrate the point made by Canadian writer Marshall McLuhan that the principal means of communication in modern society, television, has become more important than the messages it carries; to some extent 'the medium' has become 'the message'. The impact of the mass **media** on society has been so recent and so profound that it is difficult as yet for us to gauge its impact with any precision. But it is important to try and perhaps some cautious conclusions can be drawn from careful study.

The term 'mass media' embraces books, pamphlets and film but is usually understood to refer to newspapers, radio and television; since the 1950s television has eclipsed newspapers and radio as the key medium. Surveys indicate that three-quarters of people identify television as the most important single source of information about politics. On average British people now watch over twenty hours of television per week and given that 20 per cent of television output covers news and current affairs, a fair political content is being imbibed. Indeed, the audience for the evening news bulletins regularly exceeds 20 million. Surveys also show that over 70 per cent of viewers trust television news as fair and accurate whilst only one-third trust newspapers.

Television is now such a dominant medium it is easy to forget its provenance has been so recent. During the seventeenth and early eighteenth centuries political communication was mainly verbal: between members of the relatively small political elite, within a broader public at election times, within political groups such as the seventeenth-century Diggers and Levellers, and occasionally from the pulpit. Given their expense and scarcity, books and **broadsheets** had a limited, although important, role to play.

The agricultural and industrial revolutions in the eighteenth century revolutionised work and settlement patterns. Agricultural village workers gave way to vast conglomerations of urban industrial workers who proved responsive to the libertarian and democratic values propagated by the American and French political revolutions. Orator Henry Hunt was able to address meetings of up to 100,000 people (the famous Peterloo meeting has been estimated at 150,000) which he did purely (and in retrospect, astonishingly) through the power of his own lungs. Later in the nineteenth century the Chartists and the Anti-Corn Law League employed teams of speakers supplementing their efforts with pamphlets – which could now be disseminated via the postal system.

By the end of the nineteenth century newspaper editorials and articles had become increasingly important: *The Times* and weekly journals for the political elite and the popular press – the *Mail*, *Mirror* and *Express* – for the newly enfranchised masses. **Press barons** such as Northcliffe, Rothermere and Beaverbrook became major national political figures, wooed and feared by politicians for the power which the press had delivered to them within a democratic political system. Britain currently has nine Sundays and ten daily newspapers; some three-quarters of the adult population read one. The **tabloid** *Daily Mirror* and the *Sun* have circulations of three million and nearly four million respectively. There is a smaller but slowly growing aggregate circulation for the 'qualities' such as *The Guardian*, *The Times*, *The Independent* and the *Daily Telegraph*. The tabloids have a predominantly working-class circulation, the 'qualities' a more middle-class and well-educated readership. The *Daily Express* and the *Daily Mail* are more up-market tabloids and have a socially more representative readership.

By tradition the British press has been pro-Conservative (see Table 10.1). In 1945 6.7 million readers of Conservative supporting papers outnumbered the 4.4 million who read Labour papers. During the 1970s the tabloid *Sun* increased the imbalance to the right and by the 1992 election the Labour-supporting press numbered only *The Guardian* and the *Daily Mirror*, with the vast

Table 10.1 Changes in support for party by daily newspapers' readers, 1992–7 (in percentages)

	Conservative			Labour			Liberal Democrat		
Newspaper	**General election 1992**	**January–March 1997**	**Change**	**General election 1992**	**January–March 1997**	**Change**	**General election 1992**	**January–March 1997**	**Change**
Daily Express	67	52	−15	15	32	+17	14	12	−2
Daily Mail	65	48	−17	15	34	+19	18	13	−5
Daily Mirror	20	12	−8	64	79	+15	14	7	−7
Daily Star	31	19	−12	54	67	+13	12	11	−1
Daily Telegraph	72	57	−15	11	27	+16	16	11	−5
Financial Times	65	43	−22	17	45	+28	16	9	−7
Guardian	15	6	−9	55	75	+20	24	14	−10
Independent	25	15	−10	37	67	+30	34	16	−18
Sun	45	27	−18	36	59	+23	14	8	−6
The Times	64	41	−23	16	38	+22	19	16	−3

Source: MORI

majority of dailies and Sundays supporting the government party: 9.7 to 3.3 millions. However, Major's administration witnessed an astonishing shift of allegiance. It had been anticipated by press irritation with Thatcher's imperious style, continued with the criticism Major received for being allegedly weak as a leader and insufficiently robust in relation to European issues; and intensified after the disastrous Black Wednesday in September 1992 when Britain was forced out of the Exchange Rate Mechanism. Stalwart Tory supporters such as the *Mail*, *Times* and *Telegraph* aimed their critical shafts at the government and did not desist after July 1995 when Major challenged his opponents to stand against him as party leader and won a none too convincing victory. In addition to these factors Labour had become New Labour, led by the charismatic Tony Blair and shorn of its unpopular policies on unions, taxes and high spending. As the election was announced the *Sun* caused a sensation by emphatically backing Blair. Its Murdoch-owned stablemate, the Sunday *News of the World*, followed suit later on in the campaign. It should be noted that by this time a large proportion of the reading public had decided to change sides and it could be argued editors were merely making a commercial judgement in changing sides too (see Table 10.2). As in 1992, the *Financial Times* backed Labour also and the *Express*, now owned by Labour peer Lord Hollick, wobbled temporarily a bit leftwards from its usual true blue course. No such doubts for the *Mail*, however, or the *Telegraph*, despite its determined scepticism over Europe. *The Times* refused to back any party in 1997 but urged its readers to vote for the Eurosceptic cause. Forced by its owner, Murdoch, to support the man he thought would be Prime Minister, the *Sun* found it difficult to avoid snarling over Blair's commitments to 'getting closer to the EU and giving more recognition to trade unions'. Moreover the *Sun* ran more stories in

BOX 10.1 **MINI BIOGRAPHY**

Rupert Murdoch (1931–)
Australian media magnate. Educated Oxford where briefly a Marxist. Learnt newspaper business in Australia but soon acquired papers in Britain, most famously *The Sun*, *The Times* and the *Sunday Times*. His company News International also owns Sky TV and he owns broadcasting outlets all over the world including China. Blair and Murdoch seem to get on well and he regularly calls to see the man he helped elect in 1997.

Table 10.2 Newspapers' political allegiances and circulations (figures in millions)

Newspaper	1997	
Dailies		
Sun	Labour	(3.84)
Mirror/Record	Labour	(3.08)
Daily Star	Labour	(0.73)
Daily Mail	Conservative	(2.15)
Express	Conservative	(1.22)
Daily Telegraph	Conservative	(1.13)
Guardian	Labour	(0.40)
The Times	Euro-Sceptic	(0.72)
Independent	Labour	(0.25)
Financial Times	Labour	(0.31)
Sundays		
News of the World	Labour	(4.37)
Sunday Mirror	Labour	(2.24)
People	Labour	(1.98)
Mail on Sunday	Conservative	(2.11)
Express on Sunday	Conservative	(1.16)
Sunday Times	Conservative	(1.31)
Sunday Telegraph	Conservative	(0.91)
Observer	Labour	(0.45)
Independent on Sunday	Labour	(0.28)

Source: Audit Bureau of Circulation

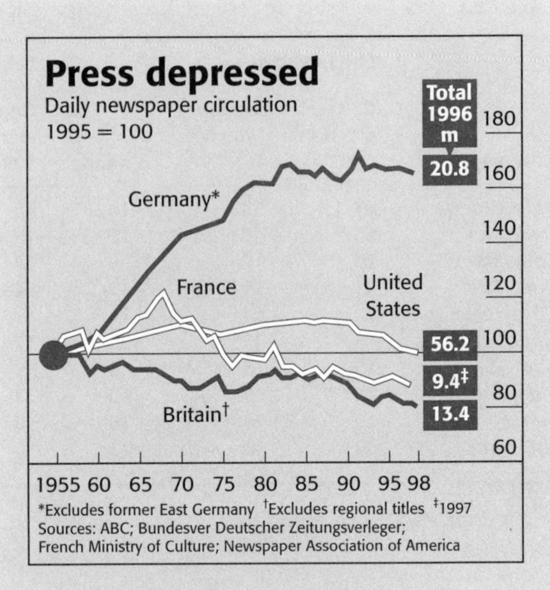

Figure 10.1 Newspaper readership
Source: The Economist, 17 July 1999, p. 21

favour of the Conservatives than Labour during the campaign, according to researchers at Loughborough University (Norris in King, 1997, p. 119). And in October 1999 it found itself praising the much derided Conservative leader William Hague, for promising to resist British entry into the single currency.

Tabloids

Many dismiss the tabloids as light on news and seriousness. It is true that the 'red-tops' have changed the angle of their coverage in recent years but the reason has been connected with the general decline in newspaper readership in the Western world (see Figure 10.1).

Sunday paper sales have declined from 17 million to 15 million 1990–8 while dailies have declined from 15 to 13 million. Tabloids, less likely to attract loyal readerships, have tried every possible trick to win readers from 'bimbos to bingo'. Marketing expert Winston Fletcher, writing in *The Guardian* (30 January 1998) pinpointed the formula, deplored by liberal opinion and politicians alike, which won readers: 'Publishers and editors know what is selling their newspapers with greater precision than ever before. And the figures show it is scandals, misfortunes and disasters'. In other words, 'sleaze sells'. But there is more to tabloids than lightweight stories; they sell by the million and even if a vote is bought through blackening a politician's name, it counts as much as any other vote on election day. Media experts working for parties read the tabloids very carefully and react accordingly. In recent elections a close correlation was noted between issues run by the Conservatives and lead stories in the tabloids; it was known certain tabloid editors had close links with Conservative Central Office. Blair's Press Secretary explains below why the tabloids are taken seriously by political parties.

The Sunday Times serialises Andrew Morton's book on Princess Diana. Sister paper *The Sun* publishes pictures of a weeping princess (13 June 1992)

Tabloids and Tony's spin doctor

I'm just saying that the weight of newspapers in setting a political agenda is significant. If at the time of an election, the Tory instinct is driving news agendas, then it will affect the way the broadcasters cover it. That's why we focus on the tabloids. They don't like us to acknowledge that the papers that really matter are the tabloids. I think one of the reasons Tony wanted me to work for him, and why I wanted to work for Tony, was that we both acknowledge the significance to the political debate of the tabloids.

Alastair Campbell, Tony Blair's Press Secretary, The Guardian, 17 February 1997

BOX 10.2 MINI BIOGRAPHY

Alastair Campbell (1957–)
Tony Blair's press secretary. Educated Cambridge, had career in tabloid journalism before joining Blair's personal staff. Often referred to as the 'Deputy Prime Minister', he has constant access to his boss and his words are held to carry the authority of the PM. He is well known to journalists and he will use charm and threats to get his own way. Some Labour voices believe he is too powerful but his appearance before a Commons Select Committee revealed he can defend himself with gusto and effectiveness.

Broadcasting

Adolf Hitler was the first politician fully to exploit the potential of radio for overtly propaganda purposes; Franklin Roosevelt with his fireside chats and Stanley Baldwin with his similar, relaxed, confidential style introduced the medium more gently to US and British political cultures. Some politicians such as Neville Chamberlain were quite skilled at addressing cinema audiences via Pathé News films, but others such as the fascist leader Oswald Mosley – a fiery platform speaker – proved (surprisingly) to be wooden and ineffective. During the war radio became the major and much-used medium for political opinion – Churchill's broadcasts were crucial – and news, while film drama was used extensively to reinforce values such as patriotism and resistance.

It was in 1952, however, that the television revolution began in earnest with Richard Nixon's embattled 'Checkers' broadcast, made to clear his name of financial wrongdoing. Offering himself as a hard-working honest person of humble origins, he finished his talk by telling viewers how his daughter had received a puppy as a present: he did not care what 'they say about it, we're gonna keep it!' (see quotation). This blatant appeal to sentiment proved spectacularly successful and confirmed Nixon's vice-presidential place on the Eisenhower ticket. Later on, television ironically contributed to Nixon's undoing through the famous televised debates with Kennedy during the 1960 presidential election contest. Despite an assured verbal performance – those listening on the radio thought he had bested Kennedy – Nixon, the favourite, looked shifty with his five o'clock shadow and crumpled appearance. Kennedy's good looks and strong profile gave him the edge. Politicians the world over looked, listened and learned that how you appear on television counts for as much as what you say (see below on 'image').

Richard Nixon – the 'Checkers' speech

I should say this: Pat doesn't have a mink coat, but she does have a respectable Republican cloth coat. One other thing I should probably tell you, because if I don't they'll be saying this about me too. We did get something, a gift, after the election . . . a little cocker spaniel in a crate all the way from Texas . . . And our little girl, Trisha, the six-year-old, named it Checkers. And you know, the kids love that dog, and I just want to say this right now, that regardless of what they say about it, we're gonna keep it!

Richard Nixon, US Vice-President, in the 'Checkers speech', after he had been accused of using campaign funds for his personal gain, 1952 (cited in Green, 1982)

What they say about the papers

The gallery where the reporters sit has become the fourth estate of the realm.

Lord Macaulay, 1828

The business of the New York journalist is to destroy the truth . . . We are the tools and vassals of rich men behind the scenes . . . We are intellectual prostitutes.

John Swinton, US journalist, 1880

As a journalist who became a politician . . . I formed rather a different view about the relations between government and the press. What shocked me when I was in government was the easy way in which information was leaked.

Norman Fowler, Memoirs, 1991

I am absolved of responsibility. We journalists don't have to step on roaches. All we have to do is turn on the light and watch the critters scuttle.

P.J. O'Rourke on the duties of journalists in relation to politics (Parliament of Whores, 1992, p. xix)

The British Broadcasting Corporation (BBC) was established as a public corporation in 1926, a monopoly that was defended on the grounds that it provided a public service. At first, under the influence of John (later Lord) Reith it struck a high moral and 'socially responsible' note. The BBC set an example and a standard which influenced emergent broadcasting systems all over the world. Commercial television (ITV) broke the BBC monopoly and began broadcasting in 1955; commercial radio in 1973. The BBC was granted a second television channel (BBC2) in 1964; a second ITV channel (Channel 4) began broadcasting in 1982 and Channel 5 in 1997. In February 1989 Rupert Murdoch's Sky Television began broadcasting using satellite technology. After a quiet start the new technology took hold and was operating at a profit by 1993. Many of the channels offer old films and popular programme repeats from the USA, but Sky News has established itself in the eyes of the public and politicians as a respectable and competent twenty-four-hour news channel.

Although the Prime Minister appoints the chairman of the BBC and its board of governors and the government of the day reviews and renews the BBC's charter, its governors are supposed to act in an independent fashion. The creation of the independent television network under the IBA in 1954 ended the BBC's monopoly in television broadcasting. Independent Television's chairman, like the BBC's, is appointed by the government. However, since ITV is financed out of advertising revenues it enjoys more financial independence from the government.

Broadcasting – especially television – has had a transforming impact on political processes.

Media organisations and the political process

Television has influenced the form of political communication

Two minutes of exposure at peak-time television enables politicians to reach more people than they could meet in a lifetime of canvassing, hand-wringing or addressing public meetings. Alternatively, speaking on BBC Radio 4's early morning *Today* programme gains access to an 'up-market' audience of over one million opinion formers and decision makers (Margaret Thatcher always listened to it and once rang in unsolicited to comment). In consequence, broadcasting organisations have become potent players in the political game: the regularity and nature of access to television and radio has become a key political issue; interviewers such as John Humphrys, David Dimbleby and Jeremy Paxman have become important national figures; and investigative current affairs programmes have occasionally become the source of bitter political controversy.

Veteran US broadcaster's views on television news

For all those who either cannot or will not read, television lifts the floor of knowledge and understanding of the world around them. But for the others, through its limited exploration of the difficult issues, it lowers the ceiling of knowledge.

The sheer volume of television news is ridiculously small. The number of words spoken in a half-hour broadcast barely equals the number of words on two-thirds of a standard newspaper page. That is not enough to cover the whole day's major events. Compression of facts, foreshortened arguments, the elimination of extenuating explanation – all are dictated by TV's restrictive time frame and all distort, to some degree, the news on television. The TV correspondent as well as his or her subjects is a victim of this compression. With inadequate time to present a coherent report, the correspondent seeks to craft a final summary sentence that might make some sense of the preceding gibberish. This is hard to do without coming to a single point of view – and a one line editorial is born. The greatest victim in all this is our political process and in my view this is one of the greatest blots on the recent record of television news. **Soundbite** journalism simply isn't good enough to serve the people in our national elections. Studies have shown that in 1988 the average block of uninterrupted speech by a presidential candidate on the news networks was 9.8 seconds. The networks faithfully promised to do better in 1992. The average soundbite that year was 8.2 seconds. The networks promised to do better in 1996. Further, figures compiled by Harvard researcher Dr Kiku Adatto showed that in 1988 there was not a single instance in which a candidate was given as much as one minute of uninterrupted time on an evening's broadcast.

Compare these figures with those of the newscasts in 1968. Then the average soundbite was 42.3 seconds . . . and 21 per cent of soundbites by presidential candidates ran at least a minute.

Walter Cronkite, A Reporter's Life, Knopf, 1997, extracted from The Guardian, 27 January 1997

In the nineteenth century it was commonplace for political meetings to entail formal addresses from great orators, such as Gladstone or Lloyd George, lasting an hour or more. Television has transformed this process. To command attention in our living-rooms politicians have to be relaxed, friendly, confidential – they have to talk to us as individuals rather than as members of a crowd. Long speeches are out. Orators are obsolete. Political messages have to be compressed into spaces of two to three minutes – often less. Slogans and key phrases have become so important that speech writers are employed to think them up. The playwright Ronald Millar was thus employed and helped produce Margaret Thatcher's memorable 'The lady's not for turning' speech at the 1981 Conservative Party conference.

Television and the image

Since the arrival of television appearances have been crucial. Bruce (1992) quotes a study which suggested 'the impact we make on others depends on . . . how we look and behave – 55 per cent; how we speak – 38 per cent and what we say only 7 per cent. Content and form must therefore synchronise for, if they don't, form will usually dominate or undermine content' (p. 41). So we saw Harold Wilson smoking a pipe to pre-empt what his adviser Marcia Williams felt was an overly aggressive habit of shaking his fist to emphasise a point. Margaret Thatcher was the first leading politician to take image building totally professionally under the tutelage of her media guru, Gordon Reece. Peter Mandelson, Labour's premier spin doctor of the 1980s and 1990s, commented that by the mid-1980s: 'every part of her had been transformed: her hair, her teeth, her nose I suspect, her eyebrows. Not a part of Mrs Thatcher was left unaltered'. Every politician now has a career reason to be vain; Granada television's *World in Action* in 1989 wickedly caught David Owen personally adding the final touch to his coiffure from his own can of hair-spray just before going on air.

Some politicians are arguably barred from the highest office on account of their looks. Some say Kinnock's red hair (such as it was) and abundant freckles turned people off. Labour's Robin Cook's red hair and gnome-like appearance are said by some experts to disqualify him from the party's leadership despite his brilliant forensic skills and being the foremost parliamentarian of his day. American political scientists also conjecture that, were he living today, Lincoln would never have been president with his jutting jaw and sunken eyes; similarly Herbert Hoover's obesity would have meant failure at the nomination stage. The perfect candidate was held by some to be Gary Hart, candidate for the presidency in 1988: very good-looking, charismatic, a good speaker, overloaded with charm and extremely intelligent. It was his excessive liking for pretty young women, and being found out, which proved his undoing with an American public which can insist on unreasonably high moral standards in its presidential hopefuls – although the success of the far from perfect Clinton in 1992 and 1996, not to mention his survival of an impeachment process over his affair with Monica Lewinsky, suggests the nation has become both more realistic and more tolerant.

Broadcasters have usurped the role of certain political institutions

Local party organisation is less important now that television can gain access to people's homes so easily and effectively. The message, however, is a more centralised national one, concentrating on the party leadership rather than local issues and local people. The phenomenon of the SDP has shown that a national party can now be created through media coverage without any substantial branch network. But it has also revealed how quickly such parties can decline once media interest wanes. However, local members are important; the work of Seyd and Whiteley (1992) has proved that high local party membership and activity rates still have a positive effect on voting behaviour and correlate positively with higher poll results.

The House of Commons has lost some of its informing and educative function to the media. Ministers often prefer to give statements to the media rather than to Parliament – often on College Green just outside the House – and interviewers gain much more exclusive access to politicians than the House of Commons can ever hope for. Even public discussion and debate are now purveyed via radio and television programmes such as the BBC's *Today*, *Newsnight* and *Question Time*. Some hoped that televising the House of Commons would win back some of these lost functions but others worried that the 'cure' would have damaging side-effects on the seriousness and efficacy of parliamentary procedures.

Peter Mandelson, MP, 'spinner' extraordinaire © AFP/Corbis

The appointment of party leaders

In 1951 Attlee was asked by a Pathé News reporter how the general election campaign was going. 'Very well', he replied. When it became obvious that the Prime Minister was not prepared to elaborate the interviewer asked him whether he wished to say anything else. 'No' was the reply. Such behaviour did not survive the 1960s. Sir Alec Douglas-Home's lack of televisual skills was believed to have helped Labour win the 1964 election: he was smartly replaced by Edward Heath – himself not much better as it turned out. The success of Wilson and to a lesser extent Callaghan as television communicators made media skills an essential element of any aspiring premier's curriculum vitae. This is what made the choice of Michael Foot as Labour's leader in 1981 such a mistake. A powerful public speaker, Foot was ill at ease on television, tending to address the camera like a public meeting and to give long rambling replies. Worse, he tended to appear with ill-chosen clothes and on one occasion with spectacles held together with sticking plaster. These shortcomings may seem trivial; but they are important on television; research shows that viewers make up their minds about people on television within seconds. And, as we saw above, manner and appearance are crucial in determining whether the reaction is positive or negative. It could be argued that Neil Kinnock was elected substantially as the televisual antidote to Foot; he was an improvement but still tended to give over-elaborate answers.

Personnel

Unsurprisingly, the media and politics have become more closely interrelated with media professionals such as David Steel, Tony Benn, Bryan Gould and Austin Mitchell going into politics, and Robert Kilroy-Silk, Brian Walden and Mathew Parris moving out of politics and into the media. The apotheosis of this tendency was represented by former US president, Ronald Reagan, who used his actor's ability to speak lines to the camera to compensate for other political inadequacies. His astonishing political success is testimony to the prime importance of media skills in the current age. Professional help has become commonplace, with many ambitious politicians attending television training courses.

Spin doctors

These fearsome-sounding new actors on the political stage focus their energies on ensuring that the media give the desired interpretation to events or statements. Their provenance is usually thought to have been the Dole–Mondale 1972 presidential debate when Republican advisers wanted to jump in first with their favourable verdicts on Dole's performance. Since then the popular idea is of somewhat shadowy figures moving around press

New Labour is criticised for an over reliance on spin doctors (17 January 1999)

conferences explaining what the party leader 'really' meant in his speech or on the phone to television executives cajoling and bullying to get their way. Kenneth Baker, when Chairman of the Conservative Party and therefore a *de facto* senior 'spinner', pulled off one of the great coups of the art in 1991 over the local government elections when Labour won 500 seats and the Conservatives lost 900. However, Baker had assiduously targeted the two 'flagship' boroughs of Wandsworth and Westminster – both setting very low poll tax – and when their majorities actually increased a wholly false impression of victory was conveyed to the press and reflected therein (although having a sympathetic press must have helped).

Peter Mandelson

The doyen of spin doctors, however, and the one most commonly associated with their black arts in recent years, is Peter Mandelson, initially in the Cabinet as Trade and Industry Secretary and then for Northern Ireland after October 1999. His ability to persuade and charm and to exert telling pressure was legendary but he was also highly instrumental in using his concern for presentation to influence Labour's swift move to the right after the débâcle of 1987. He fully acknowledges his affinity with his grandfather, Herbert Morrison, who 'rebuilt the Labour Party from the ashes of the thirties'. Mandelson was out of favour when John Smith was leader 1992–4 but he ran Blair's leadership campaign in 1994, although on a clandestine basis as Mandelson's subtle skills had made many enemies within his own party. The latter were jubilant when the arch manipulator slipped up astonishingly in 1998 when it transpired he had informed neither his senior officials nor Blair about the £373,000 loan he had received from fellow minister, the millionaire, Geoffrey Robinson. What damned the minister for the DTI was not the loan, but the fact that his ministry was currently investigating Robinson's finances.

Alastair Campbell

Another media guru even closer to Blair is Alastair Campbell who emerged as the most powerful person in the media after a hard-drinking and somewhat up and down career in tabloid journalism. Campbell is as fierce a protagonist of his boss as was Sir Bernard Ingham, the ex-*Guardian* journalist who became a devoted acolyte of Mrs Thatcher. Campbell has provided Blair with phrases to suit the occasion on innumerable occasions, including, famously, 'The People's Princess' slotted into his apparently spontaneous reaction to the death of Princess Diana in 1998 (see below for Blair and the media in office). Soon after the election Campbell was summoned before the Public Adminstration Select Committee to answer criticisms that he had become too powerful. The *Economist* commented on Campbell's tour de force performance in which he routed his critics as a 'class act' (3 July 1998).

Mr Campbell lives and breathes for Tony Blair. He is the tough aggressive half of Tony Blair, the side of Tony Blair you never see in public. He writes most of what Tony Blair says. He writes almost everything that appears under Tony Blair's name. So sometimes, when Mr Blair is answering questions in the Commons, I like to watch Mr Campbell as he sits above his boss in the gallery. You sense his face is reflecting what the Prime Minister is thinking but cannot possibly reveal to MPs. When he comes up with a good line, and the loyal sychophants behind him applaud, Mr Campbell beams happily.

Alastair Campbell, Blair's press secretary © Popperfoto

Sometimes he rolls his head in pleasure at his own jokes. When Mr Blair is worsted, as happens quite a lot these days, Mr Campbell has two expressions. One is merely glum; the other a contemptuous grimace, which implies only a moron could imagine that Mr Hague had scored any kind of point.

Simon Hoggart, The Guardian, 11 November 1999

Charlie Whelan and the 'briefing wars'

One characteristic of spin doctors and other political aides would appear to be their excessive loyalty to their masters. Their political ambitions may not be to star in the limelight but perhaps some of their own ambition is sublimated into zeal on behalf of their bosses. Campbell for example is famously loyal to his bosses; on one occasion, when working for the *Mirror*, he punched a fellow journalist for making a poor taste joke about the manner of *Mirror* owner Robert Maxwell's demise. Charlie Whelan also was famed for supporting his boss and it was not unusual in the two years after the election for 'briefing wars' to occur between the media minders. For example when a biography of Brown appeared to suggest he was still interested in becoming Prime Minister it was alleged Campbell was the source of the comment that Brown had 'psychological flaws'. On another occasion it was rumoured that Whelan, who blamed Mandelson for Blair's preferment over Brown, was the source of the loan story which led to the former's resignation. However, the Public Accounts Committee investigation concluded no rules had been broken.

The government uses the media more extensively to convey its messages

On 31 January 1989 Kenneth Clarke and other sundry ministers participated in a £1.25 million nationwide television link-up to sell the government's White Paper *Working for Patients*. The Conservative government in the 1980s embraced the media as the key vehicle for favourable presentations of its policies and programmes to the public. In the autumn of 1989 it was revealed that spending on government advertising had risen from £35 million to £200 million between 1979 and 1989. This made the government one of the country's ten biggest advertisers. Critics pointed out that a government which had passed legislation to prevent Labour local authorities using ratepayers' money to advance partisan policies seemed to be doing precisely the same at a national level – but on a vastly increased scale.

Public relations hype had been used extensively to sell early privatisations but, allegedly at the instigation of Lord Young (former Trade Secretary), had subsequently been used for party political purposes. This is clearly a grey area in that any government has to spend money to explain new laws and regulations to the public at large, and it is inevitable that such publicity will often reflect party political values. But clear Cabinet rules do exist on this topic: in using advertising governments should exercise restraint, should not disseminate party policy and, most importantly, should not advertise programmes which have not yet been enacted into law. On 4 September 1989 BBC's *Panorama* revealed that over £20 million had already been spent by the water boards to advertise their imminent privatisation. Michael Howard claimed this campaign was not advertising but 'part of an awareness raising campaign'. The same programme looked at the Action for Jobs campaign run just before the 1987 election, which seemed to be aiming reassuring messages at people in work in marginal constituencies in the south-east.

The televising of Parliament

When the proposal that the proceedings of Parliament be televised was first formally proposed in 1966, it was heavily defeated. While other legislative chambers, including the House of Lords, introduced the cameras with no discernible ill effects, the House of Commons resolutely refused, chiefly on the grounds that such an intrusion would rob the House of its distinctive intimate atmosphere: its 'mystique'. By the late 1970s, however, the majorities in favour of exclusion were wafer thin and the case would have been lost in the 1980s but for the stance of Margaret Thatcher. In November 1985 it had been rumoured she had changed her mind but at the last minute she decided to vote true to form and a number of Conservative MPs – known for their loyalty, or obsequiousness, depending on your viewpoint – about to vote for the televising of the House instead rushed to join their leader in the 'No' lobby.

Even after the vote in favour of a limited experiment the introduction of the cameras was substantially delayed, and the Select Committee on Procedure introduced severe restrictions on what the cameras could show: for example, only the head and shoulders of speakers could be featured, reaction shots of previous speakers were not allowed and in the event of a disturbance the cameras were to focus immediately on the dignified person of the Speaker. Finally, however, on 21 November 1989 the House appeared on television, debating the Queen's Speech. Margaret Thatcher reflected on the experience as follows:

> I was really glad when it was over because it is ordeal enough when you are speaking in the Commons or for Question Time without television, but when you have got television there, if you are not careful, you freeze – you just do . . . It is going to be a different House of Commons, but that is that. (*The Times*, 24 November 1989)

In January 1990 the broadcasting restrictions were relaxed: reaction shots of an MP clearly being referred to were allowed together with 'medium-range' shots of the chamber some four rows behind the MP speaking or from the benches opposite. By the summer of 1990 it was obvious even to critical MPs that civilisation as we know it had not come to an end. On 19 July the Commons voted 131–32 to make televising of the chamber permanent. David Amess MP opined that the cameras had managed to 'trivialise our proceedings and we have spoilt that very special atmosphere we had here'. His was a lone voice, although in December 1993 Michael Portillo surprisingly joined him, regretting his own vote in favour.

Television has transformed the electoral process

Since the 1950s television has become the most important media element in general elections. Unlike the USA, political advertising is not allowed on British television but party political broadcasts are allocated on the basis of party voting strength. These have become important during elections, have become increasingly sophisticated and some – like the famous Hugh-Hudson-produced party political broadcast on Neil Kinnock in 1987 – can have a substantial impact on voter perceptions. More important, however, is the extensive news and current affairs coverage, and here US practice is increasingly being followed:

1 Professional media managers – such as Labour's Peter Mandelson – have become increasingly important. Brendan Bruce, Conservative Director of Communications 1989–91, comments: 'The survival of entire governments and companies now depends on the effectiveness of these advisers yet few outside the inner circles of power even know these mercenaries exist or what their true functions are' (Bruce, 1992, p. 128). The Conservatives employ professional public relations agencies, the most famous of which was Saatchi and Saatchi. Labour could not afford such expensive help in the 1980s so a group of volunteers from the advertising world was set up known as the Shadow Communications Agency. Later Labour did employ a specialist PR company and Philip Gould, a former advertising executive, became one of Blair's closest advisers.

2 Political meetings have declined. Political leaders now follow their US counterparts in planning their activities in the light of likely media coverage. The hustings – open meetings in which debates and heckling occur – have given way to stage-managed rallies to which only party members have access. Entries, exits and ecstatic applause are all carefully planned with the audience as willing and vocal accomplices. Critics argue that this development has helped to reduce the amount of free public debate during elections and has shifted the emphasis from key issues to marketing hype. Defenders of the media answer that its discussion programmes provide plenty of debate; from 1974 Granada TV ran a television version of the hustings – *The Granada 500* – whereby a representative five hundred people from the north-west regularly questioned panels of politicians and experts on the important issues.

3 Given television's requirements for short, easily packaged messages, political leaders insert pithy, memorable passages into their daily election utterances – the so-called soundbite – in the knowledge that this is what television wants and will show in their news broadcasts and summaries throughout the day (see quote from Cronkite above).

Media and pressure groups

Just as individual politicians influence the media and seek their platforms to convey their messages, so do pressure groups as part of their function of influencing government policy. Pressure group campaigners such as Peter Tatchell of Outrage! and Lord Melchett of Friends of the Earth are expert in knowing about and massaging the form in which press and television like to receive stories. Because they have been so successful, much pressure group activity now concerns using the media. Anti-blood-sports campaigners use yellow smoke when trying to disrupt hunting events as they know television responds well to it. Greenpeace campaigners occupied the French ship in the Pacific during the nuclear tests in 1995 and kept in touch with the world's press right up to the moment they were forcibly ejected and able to adopt martyrs' clothes on behalf of their organisation. A similar approach was used by Friends of the Earth during the 1995 campaign to prevent Shell's oil platform, Brent Spar, from being disposed of by sinking it in the ocean. On a more limited but no less effective level, the Snowdrop campaign to achieve a total ban on handguns following the Dunblane massacre of schoolchildren by a crazed gunman in 1996 was able to win the nation's attention through a huge petition and high-profile appearances by its leaders at the 1996 Labour Party conference and on countless news bulletins on both television and radio. These examples merely underline the axiom that to a large extent in modern, developed societies politics is conducted via the media.

The mass media and voting behaviour

Jay Blumler *et al.* wrote in 1978 that 'modern election campaigns have to a considerable extent become fully and truly television campaigns'. But what impact do the mass media have on the way in which citizens cast their votes? Does the form which different media give to political messages make any major difference? Substantial research on this topic has been undertaken, although with little definite outcome. One school of thought favours the view that the media do very little to influence voting directly but merely reinforce existing preferences.

Blumler and McQuail (1967) argued that people do not blandly receive and react to political media messages but apply a filter effect. Denver (1992, p. 99) summarises this effect under the headings of selective exposure, perception and retention.

1. *Selective exposure*: Many people avoid politics altogether when on television or in the press, while those who are interested favour those newspapers or television programmes which support rather than challenge their views.
2. *Selective perception*: The views and values which people have serve to 'edit' incoming information so that they tend to accept what they want to believe and ignore what they do not.
3. *Selective retention*: The same editing process is applied to what people choose to remember of what they have read or viewed.

This mechanism is most likely to be at work when people read newspapers. Most people read a newspaper which coincides with their own political allegiances. Harrop's studies produce the verdict that newspapers exert 'at most a small direct influence on changes in voting behaviour among their readers' (quoted in Negrine, 1995, p. 208 – see Table 10.4 for differences between press and television influences).

Election results in 1983 and 1987 have given support to the reinforcement-via-filter-effect argument. In a thorough empirical study of these elections Newton (1992) found a result which was 'statistically and substantively significant'. The impact seemed to vary from election to election and to be greatest when the result was closest. It would also seem that the Labour press was more important for the Labour vote than the Conservative press for the Conservative vote (Newton, 1992, p. 68). Both these media-dominated election campaigns, moreover, had little apparent impact on the result. Over 80 per cent questioned in one poll claimed they had voted in accordance with preferences established before the campaign began and the parties' eventual share of the vote accorded quite closely with pre-campaign poll ratings. In 1983 the Conservatives kicked off with a 15.8 per cent lead over Labour and finished with a 15.2 per cent advantage. Some weeks before the election in 1987 the average of five major polls gave Conservatives 42 per cent, Labour 30.5 per cent and the Alliance 25.5 per cent; the final figures were 43, 32 and 23 per cent respectively – and this despite a Labour television campaign which was widely described as brilliant and admired even by their opponents. Perhaps people had 'turned off' in the face of excessive media coverage? Certainly, viewing figures declined and polls reflected a big majority who felt coverage had been either 'too much' or 'far too much'.

The filter-reinforcement thesis, however, seems to accord too minor a role to such an all-pervasive element. It does not seem to make 'common' sense. In an age when party preferences have weakened and people are voting much more instrumentally, according to issues (as we saw in Chapter 9), then surely the more objective television coverage has a role to play in switching votes? Is it reasonable to suppose the filter effect negates all information which challenges or conflicts with established positions? If so, then why do parties persist in spending large sums on party political broadcasts? Some empirical data support a direct-influence thesis, especially in respect of television:

Table 10.3 Impact of television on voters: response to question 'Has television coverage helped you in deciding who to vote for in the election?' (per cent)

	Stability of vote Same as 1979	Different from 1979	'New' voters
Yes	13	25	31
No	85	73	63
Don't know	1	2	6

Source: Negrine, 1995, p. 192

1 Professor Ivor Crewe maintains that during election campaigns up to 30 per cent of voters switch their votes, so despite the surface calm in 1983 and 1987 there was considerable 'churning' beneath the surface. These two elections may have been unusual in any case: the before and after campaign variations were much larger in 1979, 1974 and 1970 although not in the landslide 1997 election.

2 Many studies reveal that the four weeks of an election campaign provide too short a time over which to judge the impact of the media. Major shifts in voting preference take place between elections and it is quite possible that media coverage plays a significant role.

3 Crewe's research also suggests that the Alliance's television broadcasts did have a significant impact in 1983 and to a lesser extent in 1987 in influencing late deciders.

4 Following the Hugh-Hudson-produced party political broadcast in 1987 Neil Kinnock's personal rating leapt sixteen points in polls taken shortly afterwards. It could also be that without their professional television campaign Labour might have fared much worse.

5 Other research suggests that the impact of television messages will vary according to the group which is receiving them. This may help explain the pro-Alliance switchers and the responses recorded in Table 10.3. Here the question posed in 1983 was: 'Has television coverage helped you in deciding about who to vote for in the election?' The table shows that people who voted for the same party as in 1979 were less likely to answer 'yes' than those who voted for a different party. It also shows that young people, voting for the first time, were much more likely to attribute a decisive influence to television.

6 In the wake of their 1992 victory the former Conservative Party treasurer, Lord McAlpine, congratulated the tabloid press for effectively winning the election. The *Sun* responded with the headline (12 April) 'It's the *Sun* wot won it'. Neil Kinnock agreed. In November 1995 Martin Linton of *The Guardian* reported on a twelve-month study which supported the view that the *Sun* and other tabloids had made a crucial difference to the election result. Labour's post-mortem inquiry calculated that 400,000 votes were swung by the tabloids in the crucial last week of the campaign; MORI's research, based on 22,000 voters, reinforced this claim and the proposition that the tabloids could have made the difference between who won and lost.

Judging the effect of the media on voting behaviour is very difficult, because it is so hard to disentangle it from myriad factors such as family, work, region, class, and so forth, which play a determining role. It seems fair to say, however, that:

1 The media do reinforce political attitudes: This is important when the degree of commitment to a party can prove crucial when events between elections, as they always do, put loyalties to the test.

2 The media help to set the agenda of debate: During election campaigns party press conferences attempt to achieve this but the media do not always conform and between elections the media play a much more important agenda-setting role.

3 It is clear that media reportage has some direct impact on persuading voters to change sides, but research has not yet made clear whether this effect is major or marginal.

1997 election campaign

This campaign was dominated as usual by television and soundbites. However, there is some evidence that the long six-week campaign turned the public off (Norris in King, 1997, pp. 140–1). Viewing figures for the extended BBC *Nine o'Clock News* bulletins fell from an average of 5.5 million viewers at the outset to 3.3 million at the end of the campaign. Considerable heat was generated by Major's challenge to debate Blair on television. Incumbent candidates usually refuse to give opponents the dignity of such an opportunity and Major's challenge was widely interpreted as a sign of weakness from the 'losing' candidate. In the event negotiations broke down with both sides blaming the other. If the Deputy Prime Ministerial debate involving Prescott, Heseltine and Beith is any indication of how the 'big match' would have played, then the level would not have risen above that of a crude slanging match. The Tory belief that a long campaign would precipitate Blair's collapse into inexperienced gaffes proved well wide of the mark. With remarkable resilience the Labour leader maintained his punishing schedule to the very last day and seemed nerveless in all televised situations, despite an early attempt to shake him by Michael Heseltine, who accused him of being unable to cope, sweating before speeches and on the verge of a breakdown (ironically it was Heseltine's health which broke down shortly after the election). An unusual involvement by television journalism in the election was via the contest for Tatton, where the MP accused of taking cash for asking parliamentary questions, Neil Hamilton, was opposed by the BBC's Martin Bell, standing as an anti-corruption candidate unopposed by Labour or the Lib Dems. Throughout the bitterly fought campaign Hamilton accused Bell of libel as well as, astonishingly, corruption but on the vital day the voters chose to believe Bell who romped home with an unbelievable 11,000 majority.

Labour's disciplined election machine reacted sharply to neutralise any attempt to link the party with nationalisation, high taxation or a subservient union link. The documentary maker Molly Dineen made an interesting film for a party political broadcast (PPB) about Blair filmed mainly in his own Islington kitchen. The British National Party's PPB, featuring overtly racist comments, was shown on television but only in the face of substantial criticism. Finally, the results service on television was much watched and admired for its superb coverage, the often parodied Peter Snow in particular driving his excellent graphics presentations throughout a fascinating watershed night in British politics.

Focus groups

Much has been written about New Labour and focus groups and a great deal of it has been uncomplimentary. They have been cited as evidence of Labour's concern with the superficial, with adapting policy on the basis of marketing expediency and not principle – in other words, as the thin end of the Thatcherite wedge which Old Labour critics argue has robbed the party of its moral purpose and integrity. This point of view is hotly refuted by the chief enthusiast for the technique in the Blairite party: Philip Gould, former advertising expert who has written a fascinating book on the evolution of the 'new' party and its march to power (1999). In the following quotation he explains the technique and his own reasons for having faith in it.

I nearly always conduct focus groups in unassuming front rooms in Watford, or Edgware or Milton Keynes or Huddersfield, in a typical family room stacked with the normal knick-knacks and photos. The eight or so members of the group will have been

recruited by a research company according to a formal specification: who they voted for in the last election, their age, their occupation . . . I do not just sit there and listen. I challenge, I argue back, I force them to confront issues. I confront issues myself. I like to use the group to develop and test ideas.

I nearly always learn something new and surprising. People do not think in predictable ways or conform to conventional prejudice. In a group it is possible to test out the strength and depth of feeling around an issue, which can be more difficult, although not impossible with a conventional poll.

I do not see focus groups and market research as campaigning tools; increasingly I see them as an important part of the democratic process: part of a necessary dialogue between politicians and the people, part of a new approach to politics.

Gould, 1999, pp. 327–8

The Blair government and the media

One student of the media quoted a senior Labour spinner as saying: 'Communications is not an afterthought of our policy. It's central to the whole mission of New Labour.' (Ivor Gabor, 1998). Bob Franklin (1998) writes of how Campbell relishes the fact that now he is in power the boot is on the other foot from when the Tories froze him out. However, such power also attracts criticism. Both Campbell and Brown's spinner, Charlie Whelan, were criticised in December 1997 for 'arrogant rudeness' to foreign correspondents prompting the correspondent of *Die Zeit* to say 'They've started to think they own Europe as well'. Criticism also came from a lofty source in the heart of Westminster. Speaker Betty Boothroyd implied that Labour was using the skills it had developed during eighteen years of opposition to excessive lengths: 'There are too many of what I call government apparatchiks who are working in government departments . . . who have to be harnessed a little more.' (*Guardian*, 14 August 1998).

Those who thought naively that Labour would not be so paranoid about the BBC's alleged bias (see Box 10.1) were disappointed when Dave Hill, a senior Labour 'spinner', followed up a tough *Today* programme interview with Harriet Harman with a letter to the BBC saying that 'The John Humphrys problem has assumed new proportions. This can't go on'. The clear implication was that unless the interviews were softer ministers would be banned from appearing on *Today* and the programme denied a source of its lifeblood. Labour, on the other hand, did try to make the **lobby** system more transparent, allowing Campbell to be identified as an offical spokesman. But Franklin has no doubt that New Labour has maintained in government the tightness of discipline originating from opposition days. A Strategic Communications Unit has been set up comprising six civil servants under Campbell with a brief of co-ordinating communication across the full gamut of government. Now any minister wishing to make a speech has to clear it first with Campbell's office. The Government Information Service now has a thousand staff who are supposed to be impartial conduits for govenment information. However, Campbell has urged them fulsomely to be pro-active in featuring pro-Labour messages and government success stories. Franklin also points out that the political appointees have been given precedence over career civil servants. In a television documentary about Gordon Brown Jill Rutter from the Treasury complained that Charlie Whelan had 'taken over threequarters of my job'. A number of government information officers resigned soon after May 1997. Peter Riddell in *The Times* (31 December 1997) commented that 'The job of civil servants is to ensure that the government is successful, not that Labour is re-elected'. Mandelson was unabashed and said fears about the 'politicisation of the information service are groundless'. Labour's long spell in opposition has arguably made them obsessed with winning another term of government and more beyond that. Its mastery of the media enabled it to topple the Tories and is now being used to keep itself in power. The record high opinion poll ratings won by New Labour, sustained right into its third year of government – some twenty-five points ahead of the Conservatives – are just one indication of the party's ruthlessly effective media management.

The political impact of the media: the process

Given the ubiquity of media influence, Seymour-Ure is more than justified in judging that 'the mass media are so deeply embedded in the [political] system that without them political activity in its contemporary form could hardly carry on at all' (Seymour-Ure, 1974, p. 62; see also Table 10.4). He directs attention to the factors which determine the political effects of media messages and which will naturally have a bearing upon the way in which politicians attempt to manipulate them.

The timing of a news item 'can make all the difference to its significance' (p. 28). For example, Sir Alan Walters, Margaret Thatcher's part-time economic adviser, wrote an article in 1988 in which he described the European monetary system which Chancellor Nigel Lawson wanted Britain to join as 'half-baked'. Had it appeared immediately it might have caused some temporary embarrassment, but coming out as it did eighteen months later, in the middle of a highly publicised row over this very issue between Margaret Thatcher and her Chancellor, it contributed importantly to Nigel Lawson's eventual resignation on 26 October 1989.

The frequency with which items are featured in the mass media will influence their impact. The unfolding nature of the Westland revelations (when Michael Heseltine resigned over a dispute involving Westland Engineering), for example, kept Margaret Thatcher's political style on top of the political agenda for several damaging weeks in January and February 1986.

The intensity with which media messages are communicated is also a key element. The Westland crisis was so damaging to Margaret Thatcher because every daily and Sunday newspaper – serious and tabloid – and every radio and television news editor found these crises irresistible. The Lawson resignation story made the front page for over a week while two successive Brian Walden interviews with Margaret Thatcher and Lawson (29 October and 5 November 1990, respectively) were themselves widely reported news events.

Table 10.4 The press, television and political influence

Television	Press
Balanced	Partisan
Trusted	Not trusted
Mass audience	Segmented audience
'Passive' audience politically	'Active' audience
Most important source of information	Secondary source

Source: Lecture by David Denver, September 1996

The mass media and the theory of pluralist democracy

If the mass media have such a transforming impact on politics then how have they affected the fabric of British democracy? It all depends on what we mean by democracy. The popular and indeed 'official' view is that our elected legislature exerts watchdog control over the executive and allows a large degree of citizen participation in the process of government. This pluralist system provides a free market of ideas and a shifting, open competition for power between political parties, pressure groups and various other groups in society. Supporters of the present system claim that not only is how the system ought to work (a normative theory of government) but is, to a large extent, also descriptive: this is how it works in practice. According to this view the media play a vital political role:

1. They report and represent popular views to those invested with decision-making powers.
2. They inform society about the actions of government, educating voters in the issues of the day. The range of newspapers available provides a variety of interpretations and advice.
3. They act as a watchdog of the public interest, defending the ordinary person against a possibly overmighty government through their powers of exposure, investigation and interrogation. To fulfil this neutral, disinterested role it follows that the media need to be given extensive freedom to question and publish.

This pluralist view of the media's role, once again both normative and descriptive, has been criticised along the following lines.

Ownership and control influence media messages

Excluding the BBC, the media organisations are substantially part of the business world and embrace profit making as a central objective. This argument has more force since, following Murdoch's smashing of the union stranglehold over the press through his 'Wapping' revolution, newspapers now make substantial profits. This fact alone severely prejudices media claims to objectivity in reporting the news and reflecting popular feeling. In recent years ownership has concentrated markedly. About 80 per cent of newspaper circulation is in the hands of four conglomerates, Associated Newspapers owned by the Rothermere family and controlling the *Daily Mail* and the *Mail on Sunday*; Mirror Newspaper Group, owning the *Mirror*, *Sunday Mirror* and *Sunday People*; United Newspapers owning the *Express*, the *Sunday Express*, the *Star* and the *Standard*; and News International owning *The Times*, *Sunday Times*, *News of the World* and *The Sun*. These latter-day press barons and media groups also own rafts of the regional press and have strong television interests: Murdoch, of course, owns Sky Television.

Newspaper and television ownership is closely interlinked and has become part of vast conglomerates with worldwide interests. Does it seem likely that such organisations will fairly represent and give a fair hearing to political viewpoints hostile to the capitalist system of which they are such an important part?

True, Maxwell's newspapers supported the Labour Party, but they did not exhibit anything which could be called a coherent socialist ideology. Maxwell was certainly interested, however, in dictating editorial policy, using his papers as a personal memo pad for projecting messages to world leaders (there is little or no evidence that they ever listened). Murdoch's newspapers used to support the Tories loudly, although disenchantment with Major's leadership led a cooling off from about 1994 onwards until the election in 1997 precipitated a 'conversion' to Blair's campaign. In the case of *The Observer* and *The Guardian* it can be argued that ownership is separate from control. However, Tiny Rowlands when he owned the former used it shamelessly to advance his feud with Mohamed Al Fayed. Murdoch too exerts strong personal editorial control usually in support of his business interests; he decided to drop the BBC from his far-eastern satellite broadcasting operation for example, because the Chinese government objected to the criticism of human rights' suppression which the BBC included in its reports.

Nor is the press especially accountable: the Press Council used to be a powerful and respected watchdog on newspaper editors but in recent years it has meekly acquiesced in the concentration of ownership on the grounds that the danger of monopoly control is less unacceptable than the bankruptcy of familiar national titles. Moreover, since the *Sun* has regularly flouted its rulings, the Council has lost even more respect and has been unable, for example, to prevent the private lives of public figures being invaded by tabloid journalists to an alarming degree.

Television evinces a much clearer distinction between ownership and control and fits more easily into the pluralist model. The BBC, of course, is government owned and in theory at least its board of governors exercises independent control. Independent television is privately owned and this ownership is becoming more concentrated – five of the companies serve three-quarters of the national audience – but the Independent Broadcasting Authority (IBA) uses its considerable legal powers under the 1981 Broadcasting Act to ensure 'balance' and 'due accuracy and impartiality' on sensitive political issues. This is not to say that television can be acquitted of the charge of bias – as we shall see below – but merely that television controllers are forbidden by law to display open partisanship and that those people who own their companies cannot insist on particular editorial lines.

News values are at odds with the requirements of a pluralist system

In order to create profits media organisations compete for their audiences with the consequent pursuit of the lowest common denominator in public taste. In the case of the tabloids this means the relegation of hard news to inside pages and the promotion to the front page of trivial stories such as sex scandals, royal family gossip and the comings and goings of soap opera stars. On television the same tendency has been apparent with the reduction of current affairs programmes, their demotion from peak viewing times and the dilution of news programmes with more 'human interest' stories. As a result of this tendency it can be argued that the media's educative role in a pluralist democracy is being diminished. Some would go further, however, and maintain that the dominant news values adopted by the media are in any case inappropriate for this role. The experience of successful newspapers has helped to create a set of criteria for judging newsworthiness which news editors in all branches of the media automatically accept and apply more or less intuitively. The themes to which the public are believed to respond include:

1 *Personalities*: People quickly become bored with statistics and carefully marshalled arguments and relate to stories which involve disagreement, personality conflicts or interesting personal details. Westland and the Lawson resignation demonstrated this tendency in action when the clashes between Thatcher and her Cabinet colleagues were given prominence over the important European questions which underlay them.

2 *Revelations*: Journalist Nicholas Tomalin once defined news as the making public of something someone wished to keep secret. Leaked documents, financial malpractice and sexual peccadilloes are assiduously reported and eagerly read.

3 *Disasters*: The public has both a natural and a somewhat morbid interest in such matters.

4 *Visual back-up*: Stories which can be supported by good photographs or film footage will often take precedence over those which cannot be so supported.

It is commonly believed that newspapers which ignore these ground rules will fail commercially and that current affairs television which tries too hard to be serious will be largely ignored and described, fatally, as 'boring'. There is much evidence to suggest these news values are based on fact: these are the themes to which we most readily respond. It does mean, however, that the vast media industry is engaged in providing a distorted view of the world via its concentration on limited and relatively unimportant aspects of social reality.

Dumbing down televison

Steven Barrett and Emily Serymour's [study shows] that in the drama and current affairs departments television has become immeasurably more foolish. By comparing the time given to serious subjects in 1978 and 1998, they find that foreign coverage has all but disppeared from ITV and is increasingly confined to BBC2. There is less peak-time current affairs on ITV than ever before and on all channels crime documentaries are what the controllers want. (Crime is cheap. The police provide free help if you show them as the thin blue line fighting monstrous evil.)

Nick Cohen, The Observer, 24 October 1999

The lobby system favours the government of the day

The pluralist model requires that the media report news in a truthful and neutral way. We have already seen that ownership heavily influences the partisanship of the press, but other critics argue that the lobby system of political reporting introduces a distortion of a different kind. Some 150 political journalists at Westminster are known collectively as 'the lobby'. In effect they belong to a club with strict rules whereby they receive special briefings from government spokesmen in exchange for keeping quiet about their sources. Supporters claim this is an important means of obtaining information which the public would not otherwise receive, but critics disagree. Anthony Howard, the veteran political commentator, has written that lobby correspondents, rather like prostitutes, become 'clients' or otherwise 'instruments for a politician's gratification' (Hennessy, 1985, p. 9). The charge is that journalists become lazy, uncritical and incurious, preferring to derive their copy from bland government briefings – often delivered at dictation speed. Peter Hennessy believes that this system 'comes nowhere near to providing the daily intelligence system a mature democracy has the right to expect . . . as it enables Downing Street to dominate the agenda of mainstream political discussion week by week' (1985, pp. 10–11). *The Guardian* and *The Independent* were so opposed to the system that for a while they withdrew from it.

BOX 10.1 **IDEAS AND PERSPECTIVES**

Bias, broadcasting and the political parties

Harold Wilson was notoriously paranoid about the media and believed that not only the press but also the BBC was 'ineradicably' biased against him, full of 'card carrying Tories', in the words of Michael Cockerell. Perhaps it is being in government which explains it as in the 1980s it was Margaret Thatcher and her 'enforcer' Norman Tebbit who seemed paranoid. He launched ferocious attacks on the corporation calling it 'the insufferable, smug, sanctimonious, naive, guilt-ridden, wet, pink, orthodoxy of that sunset home of that third rate decade, the sixties'. Conservatives complained bitterly again when their campaign, supported by *The Sun*, in favour of stopping Greg Dyke being made Director General of the BBC failed in 1999; they claimed it was a disgrace that the job had gone to a man who donated £50,000 to the Labour party before the 1997 election.

BOX 10.3 **MINI BIOGRAPHY**

Greg Dyke (1947–)
Director-General BBC. Faced opposition from Murdoch and William Hague as a result of his £50,000 donation to the Labour party before the 1997 election before being appointed. However, he was widely seen as the most innovative and energetic candidate to run the world's largest and most prestigious broadcasting organisation with a £2 billion pa budget and 23,000 employees.

Answering questions in the House can be stressful amidst all the noise but ultimately the barbs can be ignored and the questions avoided easily. But on radio or television well briefed interviewers can put politicians on the spot. This is why ministers have complained so vehemently. Jonathan Aitken (then Chief Secretary to the Treasury) in March 1995 won ecstatic applause from Conservatives when he delivered a No.-10-cleared speech attacking the 'Blair Broadcasting Corporation'. In the firing line on this occasion were *Today* presenter John Humphrys (who had given him a bad time on the *Today* programme) and *Newsnight*'s Jeremy Paxman (the *bête noire* of all ministers), accused of 'ego trip interviewing'. Unfortunately for them the Director-General of the BBC, John Birt, had earlier made a speech in Dublin criticising 'sneering and overbearing' interviewers, although he took the trouble to write to both men denying he was attacking them (although it is hard to think to whom else he could have been referring). Cockerell explains that Humphrys is not a 'politically motivated questioner; his aim is to strip away the public relations gloss and to use his own sharp teeth to counter pre-rehearsed soundbites'. He continues, 'Aitken was really objecting to the BBC doing its job: it is one that the politicians of both parties have wanted to do since the earliest days' (*The Guardian*, 28 May 1996).

This probably gets to the heart of the perennial conflict between politicians and the media. Politicians in power ideally would like to control the media – Mrs Thatcher once said she did not like short interviews but would like instead to have four hours of airtime on her own – and resent the criticism which they receive from journalists and interviewers. In a pluralist democracy it is indeed the job of the media to make government more accountable to the public and perhaps it is when politicians do not like it that the media are doing their jobs most effectively.

Television companies are vulnerable to political pressure

Ever since the broadcasting media became an integral part of the political process during the 1950s governments of all complexions have had uneasy relationships with the BBC, an organisation with a worldwide reputation for excellence and for accurate, objective current affairs coverage. Margaret Thatcher, however, took government hostility to new lengths, indeed 'abhorrence of the BBC appeared for a while to be a litmus test for the Conservativeness of MPs' (Negrine, 1995, p. 125). Governments seek to influence the BBC in three major ways. Firstly, they have the power of appointment to the corporation's board of governors. The post of chairman is especially important; Marmaduke Hussey's appointment in 1986 was believed to be a response to perceived left-wing tendencies (according to one report he was ordered by Norman Tebbit's office to 'get in there and sort it out – in days and not months'). Secondly, governments can threaten to alter the licence system (although former Home Secretary, Willie Whitelaw, knew of no occasion when this threat had been used): Margaret Thatcher was known to favour the introduction of advertising to finance the BBC but the Peacock Commission on the financing of television refused to endorse this approach. Thirdly, governments attempt to exert pressure in relation to particular programmes – often citing security reasons. The range of disputes between the Thatcher governments and the BBC is unparalleled in recent history. In part this was a consequence of a dominant, long-established and relatively unchallenged Prime Minister as well as Thatcher's determination to challenge the old consensus – she long suspected that it resided tenaciously within the top echelons of the BBC. During the Falklands War, some Conservative MPs actually accused BBC reports of being 'treasonable' because they questioned government accounts of the progress of the war. On such occasions, they claimed, the media should support the national effort. In 1986 a monitoring unit was set up in Conservative Central Office and in the summer a highly critical report on the BBC's coverage of the US bombing of Libya was submitted together with a fusillade of accusations from Party Chairman, Norman Tebbit. The BBC rejected the accusations and complained of 'political intimidation' in the run-up to a general election. The pressure almost certainly had some effect on the BBC's subsequent news and current affairs presentation – supporting those who claim that the pluralist analysis of the media's role is inappropriate.

Television news coverage tends to reinforce the status quo

The argument here is that television news cannot accurately reflect events in the real world because it is, to use Richard Hoggart's phrase, 'artificially shaped' (Glasgow University Media Group, 1976, p. ix). ITN's editor, David Nicholas, says that '90 per cent of the time we are trying to tell people what we think they will want to know' (Tyne Tees TV, April 1986). It is what he and his colleagues think people want to know which attracts the fire of media critics. Faced with an infinitely multifaceted social reality television news editors apply the selectivity of news values, serving up reports under severe time constraints in a particular abbreviated form. According to this critical line of argument, television news reports can never be objective but are merely versions of reality constructed by news staff.

Reports will be formulated, furthermore, within the context of thousands of assumptions regarding how news personnel think the public already perceive the world. Inevitably they will refer to widely shared consensus values and perceptions and will reflect these in their reports, thus reinforcing them and marginalising minority or radical alternatives. So television, for example, tends to present the parliamentary system as the only legitimate means of reaching decisions and tends to present society as basically unified without fundamental class conflicts and cleavages. Because alternative analyses are squeezed out and made to seem odd or alien, television – so it is argued – tends to reinforce status quo values and institutions and hence protect the interests of those groups in society which are powerful or dominant. The Greens offer an interesting case study in that for many years they fell outside the consensus. Towards the end of the 1980s, however, it suddenly became apparent even to the main party leaders that the Green arguments had earned a place for themselves within rather than outside the mainstream of political culture.

The Glasgow University Media Group took this argument further. On the basis of their extensive programme analyses they suggest that television coverage of economic news tends to place the 'blame for society's industrial and economic problems at the door of the workforce. This is done in the face of contradictory evidence, which when it appears is either ignored [or] smothered' (1976, pp. 267–8). Reports on industrial relations were 'clearly skewed against the interests of the working class and organised labour . . . in favour of the managers of industry'. The Glasgow research provoked a storm of criticism. David Nicholas dismissed it as a set of conclusions supported by selective evidence (Tyne Tees TV, April 1986). In 1985 an academic counterblast was provided by Martin Harrison (1985) which criticised the slender basis of the Glasgow research and adduced new evidence which contradicted its conclusions.

Marxist theories of class dominance

The Glasgow research is often cited in support of more general theories on how the media reinforce, protect and advance dominant class interests in society. Variations on the theme were produced by Gramsci, in the 1930s by the Frankfurt School of social theorists and in the 1970s by the social–cultural approach of Professor Stuart Hall (for detailed analysis see McQuail, 1983, pp. 57–70; Watts, 1997), but the essence of their case is summed up in Marx's proposition that 'the ideas of the ruling class are in every epoch the ruling ideas'. He argued that those people who own and control the economic means of production – the ruling class – will seek to persuade everyone else that preserving status quo values and institutions is in the interests of society as a whole.

The means employed are infinitely subtle and indirect, via religious ideas, support for the institution of the family, the monarchy and much else. Inevitably the role of the mass media, according to this analysis, is crucial. Marxists totally reject the pluralist model of the media as independent and neutral, as the servant rather than the master of society. They see it merely as the instrument of class domination, owned by the ruling class and carrying their messages into every home in the land. It is in moments of crisis, Marxists would claim, that the fundamental bias of state institutions is made clear. In 1926, during the general strike, Lord Reith, the first Director-General of the BBC, provided some evidence for this view when he confided to his diary, 'they want us to be able to say they did not commandeer us, but they know they can trust us not to be really impartial'. Marxists believe the media obscures the fact of economic exploitation by ignoring radical critiques and disseminating entertainments and new interpretations which subtly reinforce the status quo and help to sustain a 'false consciousness' of the world based on ruling-class values. For Marxists, therefore, the media provide a crucial role in persuading the working classes to accept their servitude and to support the system which causes it. Table 10.5 usefully contrasts the pluralist with the class dominance model.

Which of the two models best describes the role of the media in British society? From the discussion so far the pluralist model would appear

Table 10.5 Dominance and pluralism models compared

	Dominance	**Pluralism**
Societal source	Ruling class or dominant elite	Competing political social, cultural interests and groups
Media	Under concentrated ownership and of uniform type	Many and independent of each other
Production	Standardised, routinised, controlled	Creative, free, original
Content and world view	Selective and coherent: decided from 'above'	Diverse and competing views responsive to audience demand
Audience	Dependent, passive, organised on large scale	Fragmented, selective, reactive and active
Effects	Strong and confirmative of established social order	Numerous, without consistency or predictability of direction, but often 'no effect'

Source: McQuail, 1983, p. 68

inadequate in a number of respects. Its ability to act as a fair and accurate channel of communication between government and society is distorted by the political bias of the press, the lobby system, news values and the tendency of television to reflect consensual values. The media, moreover, are far from being truly independent: the press is largely owned by capitalist enterprises and television is vulnerable to government pressures of various kinds. Does this mean that the dominance model is closer to the truth? Not really.

While the dominance model quite accurately describes a number of media systems operating under oppressive regimes, it greatly exaggerates government control of the media in Britain.

1 As David Nicholas observes (Tyne Tees TV, April 1986), 'trying to manipulate the news is as natural an instinct to a politician as breathing oxygen', but because politicians try does not mean that they always succeed. People who work in the media jealously guard their freedom and vigorously resist government interference. The *This Week* 'Death on the Rock' programme on the SAS killings in Gibraltar was after all shown in 1988 despite Sir Geoffrey Howe's attempts to pressure the IBA. And Lord Windlesham's subsequent inquiry further embarrassed the government by completely exonerating the Thames TV programme.

2 The media may tend to reflect consensual views but this does not prevent radical messages regularly breaking into the news – sometimes because they accord with news values themselves. Television also features drama productions which challenge and criticise the status quo: for example, at the humorous level in the form of *Spitting Image* and at the serious level in the form of BBC's 1988 legal series *Blind Justice*. Even soap operas such as *EastEnders* often challenge and criticise the status quo.

3 Programmes such as *Rough Justice* and *First Tuesday* have shown that persistent and highly professional research can shame a reluctant establishment into action to reverse injustices – as in the case of the Guildford Four, released in 1989 after fifteen years of wrongful imprisonment. Consumer programmes such as the radio series *Face the Facts* do champion the individual, as do regular newspaper campaigns.

4 News values do not invariably serve ruling-class interests, otherwise governments would not try so hard to manipulate them. Margaret Thatcher, for example, cannot have welcomed the explosion of critical publicity which surrounded Westland, her July 1989 reshuffle or the Lawson resignation. And it was Rupert Murdoch's *Times* which look

Table 10.6 Summary table to show 'democrativeness' of media elements

Democratic Criteria	Broadsheets	Tabloids	Radio	BBC	Commercial TV
Easily accessible (for target audience)	+	+	+	+	+
Varied and plentiful	+	+	+	+	+
Concentration of ownership	–	–	–	+	–
Reliable factually	+	–	+	+	+
High-value political content	+	–	0	–	+
Accountability 1	+	–	+	–	+
Accountability 2	–	–	–	–	–
Low bias	0	–	+	+	+

Accountability 1 = the tendency for the medium element to facilitate democracy
Accountability 2 = degree of accountability of medium to public
+ = high tendency to encourage democracy
– = low tendency to encourage democracy
0 = neutral effect (i.e. '0' is given for BBC radio as most of its five channels are music based and '0' for the bias of broadsheets as they tend to take give space to alternative opinions to their editorials)
Source: Jones, 2000

the lead in breaking the story about Cecil Parkinson's affair with his secretary, Sarah Keays, in 1983.

Each model, then, contains elements of the truth but neither comes near the whole truth. Which is the nearer? The reader must decide; but despite all its inadequacies and distortions the pluralist model probably offers the better framework for understanding how the mass media affects the British political system. Table 10.6 reveals the complexity of the argument: some elements fit neatly into a supporting role whilst others do not.

Language and politics

All this modern emphasis on technology can obscure the fact that in politics language is still of crucial importance. Taking the example of Northern Ireland, we have seen how the precise meaning of words has provided a passionate bone of contention. When the IRA announced its ceasefire in 1994, its opponents insisted it should be a 'permanent' one. The paramilitary organisation, however, did not wish to abandon its ability to use the threat of violence as a negotiating counter and refused to comply, insisting that its term 'complete' ceasefire was as good as the British government needed or would in any case get. Gerry Adams, President of the political wing of the IRA, Sinn Fein, had a similar problem over his attitude towards bombings. His close contact with the bombers made it impossible for him to condemn the bombing of Manchester in June 1996 so he used other less committing words like 'regret' or 'unfortunate'. Another aspect is tone of voice, which can bestow whole varieties of meaning to a statement or a speech. Sir Patrick Mayhew, for example, John Major's Northern Ireland Secretary, specialises in being 'calm'. After the reopening of violence in the summer of 1996 he had much need for this, enunciating his words slowly and with great care, as if attempting to soothe the wounded feelings of the antagonists and reassure the rest of the country that, contrary to appearances, everything was all right. A more absurd example is Margaret Thatcher's opposition to the wording on a proposed anti-AIDS poster; according to *The Guardian* (18 July 1996), she felt the clearly worded warnings about anal sex were too shocking to be used.

Another example of language being of crucial importance occurred in November 1996 when whip David Willetts was accused of interfering with the deliberations of the Commons Standards and Privileges Committee regarding the investigation of Neil Hamilton's alleged receiving of cash for parliamentary activities on behalf of Mohamed Al Fayed. According to Willetts' own notes of his meeting with the chairman of the committee, Sir Geoffrey Johnson-Smith, he 'wants' advice. On the face of it this seemed as if the government was interfering with the quasi-judicial procedures of the House. In explanation to the committee the whip said he meant the word in the biblical sense of 'needs'. Most commentators were unimpressed. Writing in *The Observer*, 24 October 1999, Andrew Marr noted the increase in vituperation characterising British politics: *The Times* running a cartoon on 'The Lying King'; *The Telegraph* reporting 'The New Labour Lie Machine' and Blair's 'repulsive political calculus'. On the other hand 'Labour attack dogs snarl at Hague – the cruel rejoicing at Thatcher's alleged "Wee Willie" remark, the jeering about his looks and voice. Galloping abuse inflation is everywhere . . . You would think from the violence of the language that our society was undergoing a nervous breakdown'. Marr concludes that journalists are 'using abuse too casually to secure our meal tickets in a difficult market.'

I went to the CBI conference in Birmingham to hear the Prime Minister speak, and there on a giant TV screen . . . was our very own Big Brother. This Big Brother smiles a lot in a self deprecating kind of way. He uses 'um' and 'well' as a rhetorical device, to convince us he's not reading out a prepared text, but needs to pause to work out exactly what he means. There is a prepared text of course but he adds to it phrases such as 'I really think' and 'you know I really have to tell you' and 'in my view'. This is the new oratory. The old politicians told us they were right, and that there was no room for doubt,

the new politician is not telling us truths, but selling us himself . . . His message is that you shouold take him on trust; you should believe him because you love him.

Simon Hoggart, The Guardian, 3 November 1999

The media and politics: future developments

The structure of television underwent an upheaval in the early 1990s at the hands of the 'deregulators' led by Thatcher. She had dearly wished to end the licence fee which funds the BBC but the lukewarm response of the Peacock Commission set up to look at this problem headed off this possibility for the time being at least (until 2007). In October 1991 franchises were sold off for independent television regions. Critics complain that these new developments will dilute still further the standards in broadcasting established by the BBC's famous former head, the high-minded Lord Reith. The inception of satellite broadcasting in 1982 via the Murdoch-owned Sky Television has opened up the possibility of a very large number of channels, all aimed at the same markets and all tending to move the locus of their messages down market. Sky News, a twenty-four-hour news service has allayed some fears by developing, after a shaky start, into a competent and well-respected service. With over 130 satellite channels in Europe and cable companies making a huge investment in access for their service, the expansion of choice is set to be exponential over the next decade or more. The inception of digital television, which entails the conversion of the broadcast signal into a computerised message, will revolutionise a sector virtually in permanent revolution anyway. This system requires the use of a set-top decoder and can receive signals from satellite or terrestrial stations. Some critics fear that Rupert Murdoch will be able to control access to this new technology by being the first in the field to provide the decoders – the argument being that consumers will happily buy one but not any more so that the company in first will effectively be the gatekeeper. Media companies hope that Murdoch will be forced by government regulation to make his technology available to other broadcasters, but the Australian multimillionaire is as much interested in power as in money and is unlikely to relinquish his option for more of both easily, if at all.

Some critics claim the new profusion of television channels will mark the end of quality. They point to the USA, where there is a very wide diversity yet an unremitting mediocrity, and predict that the UK will go the same way.

Meanwhile the press faces an immediate threat from the electronic flank. Xerox announced in October 1999 that it had signed a deal to produce electronic paper on an industrial scale. As Andrew Marr wrote wonderingly in the *Observer* – 17 October 1999 – 'It can be "bound" and loaded with a "wand", bringing whole books on to it at incredible speed. You can carry it in your pocket, and fold it, treat it as a newspaper or magazine updated every few minutes – so abolishing the daily deadline and the entire traditional process'.

For politics the technology with the most potential might well prove to be the internet, for which one needs a telephone line, a modem, some software and a computer. Currently 50 million are logged on worldwide but the service is expanding and has all kinds of implications:

1. *Information*: It is now possible to download immense amounts of up-to-date information about political issues via the net.
2. *Email*: It is possible to communicate with politicians and the politically active all over the world, extending enormously the scope of political action.
3. *Interactive democracy*: By being hooked up to the net it might be possible for politicians or government in democracies to seek endorsement for policies directly from the people. This would have all kinds of drawbacks, e.g. it could slow down the political process even more than at present in developed countries; it could give a platform to unsavoury messages like racism and power-seeking ideologues; it might enthrone the majority with a power it chooses to abuse. But these opportunities exist and it is virtually certain they will be experimented with if not adopted in the near future.

Chapter summary

The spoken voice was the main form of political communication until the spread of newspapers in the nineteenth century. Broadcasting introduced a revolution into the way politics is conducted as its spread is instant and its influence so great. New political actors have emerged specialising in the media and politicians have learnt to master its techniques. Press news values tend to influence television also, but the latter is more vulnerable to political pressure than the already politicised press. Class dominance theories suggest the media is no more than an instrument of the ruling class but there is reason to believe it exercises considerable independence and is not incompatible with democracy.

Postscript

In April 2000 the Labour Party announced it had contracted the advertising agency TBWA GGT Simons Palmer to handle its account. Some saw the irony – or maybe the ultimate cynicism of politics – of the fact the agency beat off a strong challenge from Saatchi and Saatchi, the agency demonised on the left for its destructive campaigns against Labour in behalf of the Conservatives in the eighties.

The creative director of the company entrusted with burnishing Labour's image in the run-up to the next election is tousle haired Trevor Beattie, the man responsible for the controversial 1994 'Hello Boys' Wonderbra ad featuring model Eva Herzigova. Even more controversial was his 'fcuk' ad for French Connection UK commercials. Beattie, a lifelong socialist whose company helped Nelson Mandela with his presidential campaign, says his philosophy is summed up in just two words: 'Get noticed. Nothing else matters'.

Discussion points

- Should British political parties be allowed to buy political advertising on television?
- Has televising Parliament enhanced or detracted from the efficacy of Parliament?
- Does television substantially affect voting behaviour?
- Do the media reinforce the political status quo or challenge it?
- Should interviewers risk appearing rude when confronting politicians?

Further reading

The best available study of the media and British politics is Watts (1997). Also useful is Negrine (1995). Budge *et al.* (1998) provide two excellent chapters (13 and 14) on the media and democracy; this topic is also dealt with by Jones (1993). The two most readable studies of leadership, the media and politics are both by Michael Cockerell (Cockerell, 1988; Cockerell *et al.*, 1984). Bruce (1992) is excellent on the behaviour of politicians in relation to the media. Blumler and Gurevitch (1995) is an essay on the crisis of communication for citizenship and as such is an interesting source of ideas. See Jones (1993) on the television interview. The most brilliant and funny book about the press is Chippendale and Orrie's history of the *Sun* (1992).

References

Bilton, A., Bennett, K., Jones, P., Skinner, D., Stanworth, M., Webster, A. (1996) *Introductory Sociology*, 3rd edn (Macmillan).

Blumler, J.G. and Gurevich, M. (1995) *The Crisis of Public Communication* (Routledge).

Blumler, J.G. and McQuail, D. (1967) *Television in Politics* (Faber and Faber).

Blumler, J.G., Gurevitch, M. and Ives, J. (1978) *The Challenge of Election Broadcasting* (Leeds University Press).

Bruce, B. (1992) *Images of Power* (Kogan Page).

Budge, I., Crewe, I., McKay, D., Newton, K. (1998) *The New British Politics* (Longmans).

Chippendale, P. and Orrie, C. (1992) *Stick it Up Your Punter* (Mandarin).

Cockerell, M. (1988) *Live from Number Ten* (Faber and Faber).

Cockerell, M., Walker, D. and Hennessy, P. (1984) *Sources Close to the Prime Minister* (Macmillan).

Denver, D. (1992) *Elections and Voting Behaviour*, 2nd edn (Harvester Wheatsheaf).
Donovan, P. (1998) *All Our Todays: Forty Years of the Today Programme* (Arrow).
Geddes, A. and Tonge, J. (1997) *Labour's Landslide* (Manchester University Press).
Glasgow University Media Group (1976) *Bad News* (Routledge and Kegan Paul).
Gould, P. (1999) *The Unfinished Revolution* (Abacus).
Green, J. (1982) *Book of Political Quotes* (Angus and Robertson).
Harrison, M. (1985) *TV News: Whose Bias* (Hermitage, Policy Journals).
Hennessy, P. (1985) *What the Papers Never Said* (Political Education Press).
Jones, B. (1993) '"The pitiless probing eye": politicians and the broadcast political interview', *Parliamentary Affairs*, January.
Jones, B. (2000) 'Media and Government', in R. Pyper and L. Robins, *Governance in the United Kingdom* (Macmillan).
King, A. (ed.) (1997) *New Labour Triumphs: Britain at the Polls* (Chatham House).
Marr. A. (1999) 'And the news is . . . electric', *Observer*, 17 October.
McQuail, D. (1983) *Mass Communication Theory: an Introduction* (Sage).
Negrine, R. (1995) *Politics and the Mass Media*, 2nd edn (Routledge).
Newton, K. (1992) 'Do voters believe everything they read in the papers?', in I. Crewe, P. Norris, D. Denver and D. Broughton (eds), *British Elections and Parties Yearbook* (Harvester Wheatsheaf).
O'Rourke, P.J. (1992) *Parliament of Whores* (Picador).
Sevaldsen, J. and Vardmand, O. (1993) *Contemporary British Society*, 4th edn (Academic Press).
Seyd, P. and Whiteley, P. (1992) *Labour's Grass Roots* (Clarendon Press).
Seymore-Ure, C. (1974) *The Political Impact of the Mass Media* (Constable).
Watts, D. (1997) *Political Communication Today* (Manchester University Press).
Whale, J. (1977) *The Politics of the Media* (Fontana).

Chapter 11 Pressure groups

Bill Jones

Learning objectives

- To explain that formal democratic government structures conceal the myriad hidden contacts between government and organised interests.
- To analyse and explain the way in which groups are organised and operate.
- To introduce some familiarity with theories regarding this area of government–public interaction.
- To provide some specific examples of pressure group activity.

Introduction

The Norwegian political scientist Stein Rokkan, writing about his country's system, said 'the crucial decisions on economic policy are rarely taken in the parties or in Parliament'. He judged 'the central area' to be 'the bargaining table' where the government authorities meet directly with the trade union leaders and other group leaders. 'These yearly rounds of negotiations mean more in the lives of rank and file citizens than formal elections'.

British politics is not as consensually well organised or co-operative as the Norwegian model, but there is a central core of similarity in respect of pressure group influence. Accordingly this chapter examines the way in which organised groups play their part in the government of the country. Democratic government is supposed to be government of the people, and politicians often claim to be speaking on behalf of public opinion. But how do rulers learn about what people want? Elections provide a significant but infrequent opportunity for people to participate in politics. These are held every four years or so, but pressure groups provide continuous opportunities for such involvement.

Definitions

'Interest' or '**pressure**' **groups** are formed by people to protect or advance a shared interest. Like political parties, groups may be mass campaigning bodies, but whereas parties have policies for many issues and, usually, wish to form a government, groups are sectional and wish to influence government only on specific policies.

The term pressure group is relatively recent; but organised groups tried to influence government long before the age of representative democracy. The Society for Effecting the Abolition of the Slave Trade was founded in 1787 and under the leadership of William Wilberforce and Thomas Clarkson succeeded in abolishing the slave trade in 1807. In 1839 the Anti-Corn Law League was established, providing a model for how a pressure group can influence government. It successfully mobilised popular and elite opinion against legislation which benefited landowners at the expense of the rest of society and in 1846 achieved its objective after converting to its cause the Prime Minister of the day, Sir Robert Peel. It proved wrong the cynical dictum that the rich and powerful will always triumph over the poor and weak. In the twentieth century the scope of government has grown immensely and impinges on the lives of many different groups. After 1945 the development of the mixed economy and the welfare state drew even more people into the orbit of governmental activity. Groups developed to defend and promote interests likely to be affected by particular government policies. For its own part government came to see pressure groups as valuable sources of information and potential support. The variety of modern pressure groups therefore reflects the infinite diversity of interests in society. A distinction is usually drawn between the following:

1 **Sectional or interest groups**, most of which are motivated by the particular economic interests of their members. Classic examples of these are trade unions, professional bodies (e.g. the British Medical Association) and employers' organisations.

2 **Cause groups**, which exist to promote an idea not directly related to the personal interests of its members. The Society for Effecting the Abolition of the Slave Trade was such a group and in modern times the Campaign for Nuclear Disarmament (CND), Child Poverty Action Group (CPAG) or the Society for the Protection of the Unborn Child (SPUC) can be identified. Of the environmental groups, the Ramblers Association, Greenpeace and Friends of the Earth are perhaps the best examples.

Other varieties of pressure group include:

- Peak associations: these are umbrella organisations which represent broad bands of similar groups such as employers – the Confederation of British Industry (CBI) – and workers – the Trades Union Congress (TUC).
- Fire brigade groups: so called because they form in reaction to a specific problem and disband if and when it has been solved. They are often 'single issue' groups; The Anti-Corn Law League could be regarded as one such and the coalition of environmental groups supporting the Road Traffic Reduction Campaign (see Box 11.1).
- Episodic groups: these are usually non-political but occasionally throw themselves into campaigning when their interests are affected, for example, sports clubs campaigning for more school playing fields and local hunts fearing the Blair government would ban foxhunting.

Membership of sectional groups is limited to those who are part of the specific interest group, for example coal miners or doctors. In contrast, support for a cause such as nuclear disarmament or anti-smoking can potentially embrace all adults. The two types of groups are not, however, mutually exclusive. Some trade unions take a stand on many political causes, for example on (in the past) apartheid in South Africa, poverty or sexual equality, and some members of cause groups may have a material interest in promoting the cause, for example teachers in the Campaign for the Advancement for State Education or teacher members of the Politics Association which campaigns for improved political literacy. It should be noted that pressure groups regularly seek to influence each other to maximise impact and often find themselves in direct conflict over certain

BOX 11.1 EXAMPLE

The Road Traffic Reduction Campaign

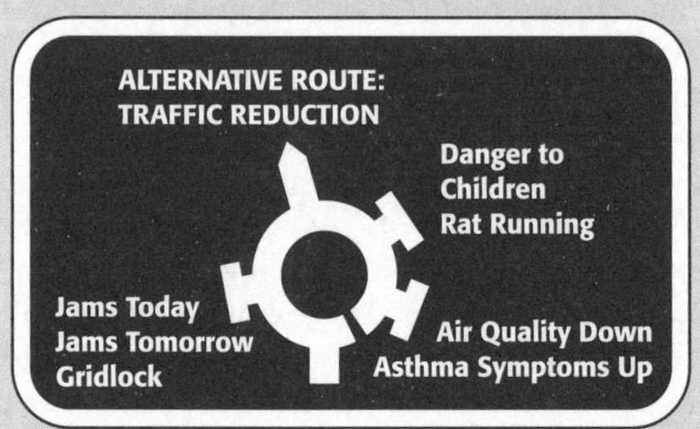

This campaign is a collaborative venture by groups perceiving a shared interest in reducing traffic congestion. If the campaign proves successful it could be regarded as a 'fire brigade' grouping. Members of the Campaign Steering Group include the Friends of the Earth, The National Asthma Campaign, the Civic Trust, the cycling group, Sustrans and the Green Party among many others.

In June 1999 they circulated an 'update' article to supporters which recorded their activities and noted their successes. Glenda Jackson, the Transport minister, was congratulated for saying (7 May 1999) 'We will set national traffic reduction targets before the end of this parliament' and Michael Meacher, Environment Minister, for saying that 'overall traffic reduction remains a commitment'. Such plaudits are disingenuous in that their main purpose is to repeat stated commitments important to the movement so that the politicians involved will find it more difficult to ignore them. On the reverse side of the article transcripts of the ministerial statements are revealed as the result of sharp questioining at public meetings by campaign members. Indeed a cynical reader of these transcripts might conclude the commitments were extracted from somewhat reluctant politicians. Whatever the truth about the politicians' commitment, the result is effective pressure group action. Campaign supporters were enjoined to undertake actions such as writing to congratulate the ministers on their statements; asking Labour groups on local councils to pass supporting resolutions; and to ask councillors to propose similar motions for the council to send.

Source: Road Traffic Reduction Campaign, 26–28 Underwood St, London N1 7JQ

issues. Baggott (1988) has shown how pressure groups lined up over the issue of longer drinking hours with brewers, the Campaign for Real Ale and the British Tourists Authority pro and the BMA, alcoholics' organisations and the Campaign against Drink Driving anti.

Civil society and groups

Civil society has a long provenance in political thought, being related to the seventeenth-century notion of a 'state of nature' which humans in theory inhabited before entering the protective confines of the state. The idea of such an independent social entity enabled the likes of Hobbes and Locke to argue that citizens had the right to overthrow a corrupt or failing government. Civil society was held to be the non-political relationships in society; those of family, business, church and, especially according to the modern sense of the term, voluntary organisations. These relationships help people to live together, co-operating, compromising; accepting both leadership and responsibility; providing the very basis of democratic activity. Some commentators have argued that, while citizen protest led to the overthrow of communist governments, the absence of a strong or 'thick' civil society in Eastern European countries has hindered their transition from totalitarian to democratic society. The ability to form organisations independent of the state is one of the hallmarks and, indeed, preconditions of a democratic society. A study by Ashford and Timms (1992) revealed substantial membership of groups in the UK including 16 per cent in church or religious organisations; 14 per cent in trade unions, 17 per cent in sporting organisations and 5 per cent in environmental or ecological groups.

An interesting change in the attitudes of the public has occurred over recent decades in most developed western societies: people are increasingly preferring to invest energy into groups – cause, single issue, protective – rather than in political parties. Indeed membership of political parties or groups mustered only 4.9 per cent in the Ashford and Timms' survey cited above. The increased membership of 'new social movements', especially those concerned with environmental concerns, has provided an inverse mirror of faith in the political system. In 1981 an opinion poll taken in eleven West European countries and repeated in 1991 registered a fall in confidence in government competence in six countries, no change in four and an increase in only one: Denmark (Nye, 1997). The same survey, however, perhaps explaining the appeal of the new social movements, revealed a 90 per cent endorsement of 'a democratic form of government' and of the suggestion that 'we should look for ways to develop democracy further'. Ulrick Beck writes of the emergence of 'sub politics': popular movements such as Greenpeace and Oxfam as well as single issue ones, that have gravitated downwards away from the legislature.

We were somewhat slow in understanding that these groups were tending to acquire authority. We underestimated the extent of these changes – we failed to engage in a serious dialogue with these new groups . . . simply put, the institutions of global society are being reinvented as technology redefines relationships between individuals and organisations.

World Chairman of Shell following its climbdown over the disposal of the Brent Spar oil rig in the face of widespread protest led by Greenpeace

Pressure groups and government

The relationship between interest groups and government is not always or even usually **adversarial**. Groups may be useful to government. Ministers and civil servants often lack the information or expertise necessary to make wise policies, or indeed the authority to ensure that they are implemented effectively. They frequently turn to the relevant representative organisations to find out defects in an existing line of policy and seek suggestions as to how things might be improved. They sound out groups' leaders about probable resistance to a new line of policy. Moreover, an interest group's support, or at least acceptance, for a policy can help to 'legitimise' it and thus maximise its chances of successful implementation. The accession to power of Labour in May 1997 raised the spectre of union influence once again dominating policy, as in the 1970s. Blair has been emphatic that unions, like any other group seeking influence, will receive 'fairness but no favours'. Indeed, Blair seems more concerned to woo business groups than the electorally unpopular unions.

In the several stages of the policy process groups have opportunities to play an important role (see Chapter 24). At the initial stage they may put an issue on the policy agenda (e.g. environmental groups have promoted awareness of the dangers to the ozone layer caused by many products and have forced government to act). When governments issue Green Papers (setting out policy options for discussion) and White Papers (proposals for legislation), groups may **lobby** back-benchers or civil servants. In Parliament groups may influence the final form of legislation. As we can see from Figure 11.1 groups are involved at virtually every stage of the policy process.

Insider–outsider groups

Groups are usually most concerned to gain access to ministers and civil servants – the key policy makers. Pressure group techniques are usually a means to that end. When government departments are formulating policies there are certain

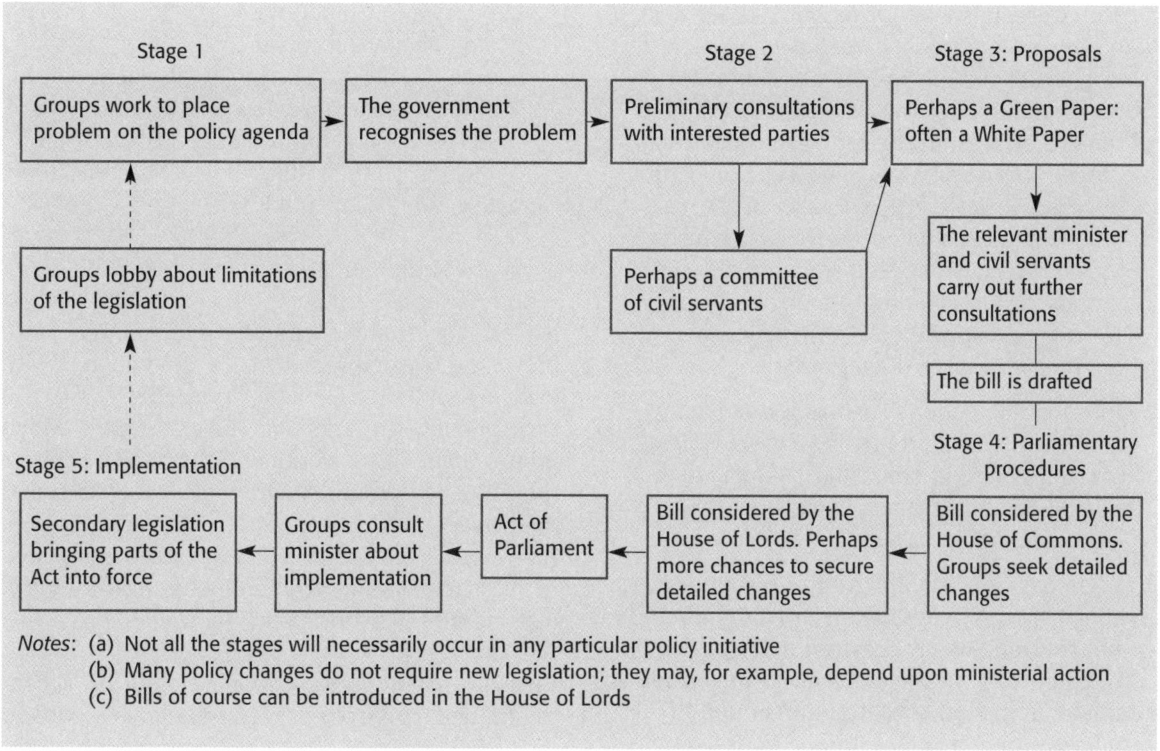

Stage 1
Stage 2
Stage 3: Proposals
Groups work to place problem on the policy agenda
The government recognises the problem
Preliminary consultations with interested parties
Perhaps a Green Paper: often a White Paper
Groups lobby about limitations of the legislation
Perhaps a committee of civil servants
The relevant minister and civil servants carry out further consultations
The bill is drafted
Stage 4: Parliamentary procedures
Stage 5: Implementation
Secondary legislation bringing parts of the Act into force
Groups consult minister about implementation
Act of Parliament
Bill considered by the House of Lords. Perhaps more chances to secure detailed changes
Bill considered by the House of Commons. Groups seek detailed changes
Notes: (a) Not all the stages will necessarily occur in any particular policy initiative
(b) Many policy changes do not require new legislation; they may, for example, depend upon ministerial action
(c) Bills of course can be introduced in the House of Lords

Figure 11.1 Pressure groups and the policy process
Source: Grant, 1988

groups which they consult. The Ministry of Agriculture, Fisheries and Food is in continuous and close contact with the Farmers' Union. Indeed in 1989, in the wake of the salmonella food poisoning scandal, it was alleged by some that the ministry neglected the interests of consumers compared with those of the producers. Wyn Grant (1985) has described groups which are regularly consulted as insider groups; in the study of pressure groups this has become possibly the important distinction.

On the other hand, the Campaign for Nuclear Disarmament, for example, mounts public campaigns largely because it has no access to Whitehall; in Grant's language it is an outsider. Not only does it lack specialist knowledge on foreign policy or defence systems, but the policies it advocates are flatly opposed to those followed by every post-war British government. Grant's classification of groups is summarised in Figure 11.2.

'High-profile' insiders
'Low-profile' insiders
'Prisoner' groups
Insider groups
Potential insider
Outsider groups by necessity
Ideological outsider groups
Outsider groups

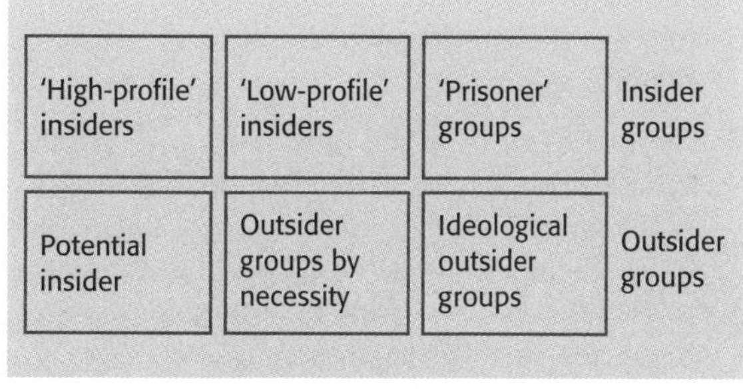

Figure 11.2 Grant's typology of pressure groups
Source: Grant, 1985

To gain access to the inner sanctums of decision making, groups usually have to demonstrate that they possess at least some of the following features:

1 Authority, which may be demonstrated in the group's ability to organise virtually all its potential members. The National Union of

Mineworkers spoke for nearly 100 per cent of miners for many years, but its authority was weakened not just by the fall-off in membership after the disastrous 1983–4 miners' strike but also by the formation in 1985 of the breakaway Union of Democratic Miners. Similarly, the authority of the teachers' unions has been weakened because of the divisions between so many different groups. Overwhelming support by members for their group leadership's policies is another guarantor of authority.

2 Information: Groups such as the British Medical Association or the Howard League for Penal Reform command an audience among decision makers because of their expertise and information.

3 The compatibility of a group's objectives with those of the government: For example, trade unions traditionally received a more friendly hearing when pressing for favourable trade union legislation or state intervention in industry from a Labour than a Conservative government. The TUC always received short shrift from Margaret Thatcher who made no effort to disguise her hostility or even contempt. It follows that even when likely to receive a friendly hearing, groups seeking access to the policy process should not put forward demands which the government regards as unreasonable.

4 Compatibility of group objectives with public sympathies: A group out of sympathy with public views – for example advocating the housing of convicted paedophiles in residential areas – is unlikely to gain inner access to decision making.

5 Reliable track record for sensible advice in the past and the ability, through knowledge of Whitehall to fit in with its procedures and confidential ethos

6 Possession of powerful sanctions: Some groups of workers are able to disrupt society through the withdrawal of their services. The bargaining power of coal miners, for example, was very strong in the mid-1970s when Middle East oil was in short supply and expensive but much weaker a decade later, when cheaper oil was more available as a source of energy. The ability of electricians to inflict injury on society was greater even than the miners' but after the privatisation of electricity their ability to 'close down' the nation was fragmented.

But becoming and remaining an insider group requires the acceptance of constraints. Group leaders, for example, should respect confidences, be willing to compromise, back up demands with evidence and avoid threats (Grant, 1989, 1990). All this amounts to a kind of Faustian pact which groups sign with government; if it fails to deliver the influence group leaders expect they can find themselves in trouble with their membership. Alternatively they can become so closely associated with a particular government policy that they can lose credibility if that policy fails.

Pressure group methods can be seen on a continuum running from peaceful methods to violent ones (see Figure 11.3). Anyone working for a pressure group, especially if it is a local one focusing on, say, a planning issue, will find themselves working hard at routine chores such as stuffing envelopes, ringing up supporters, delivering publicity and collecting signatures on petitions. However, other groups use different techniques. Trade unions use or threaten to use the 'denial of function' approach; in practice this means going on strike, a kind of holding to ransom those who benefit from their labour. In some cases, however, such methods encounter moral restraints; for example, should nurses refuse to look after patients in support of a pay dispute? Other groups are concerned to test the law. The Ramblers Association for example are quite happy to ignore notices from landowners denying them access if the notices are not legal; in such circumstances their members are happy to assert their legal rights and to clear any obstructions which may have been put in place. Other groups still are prepared to go even further. Some anarchist groups deliberately break the law as part of a strategy of undermining law and order and existing civil society.

Such groups and sentiments are still rare. Most groups concentrate their efforts at the peaceful end

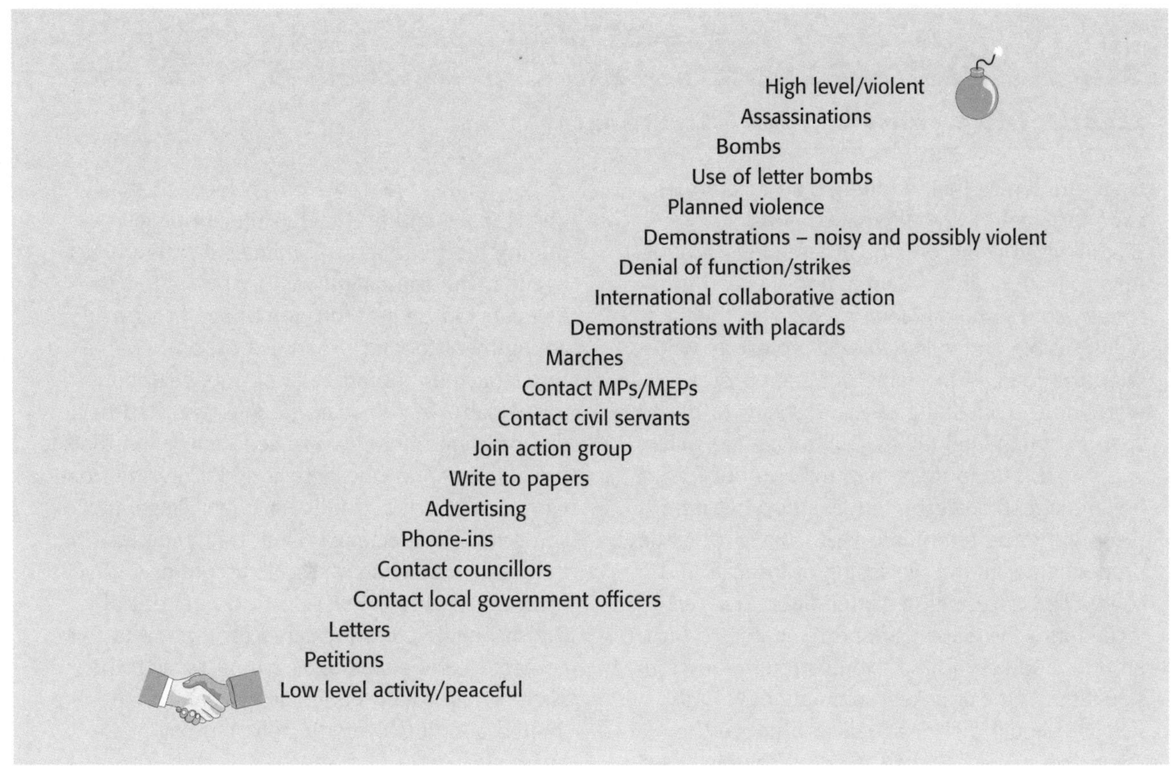

Figure 11.3 Pressure group methods continuum

of the spectrum but a change in the political culture, however, is discernible over the last decade.

The growth (and increasing respectability) of direct action

Some groups are either so passionate or have become so impatient with the slow moving wheels of government that they have deliberately used high profile and illegal tactics. The best known have been the protestors against the Newbury bypass and later the new runway at Manchester airport. These protestors have broken new ground in pressure group techniques by using their own bodies as shields. They have, for example, sought to implant themselves in places which would halt further work on the project concerned. These have included the building of tree houses which security guards have been obliged to scale in order to winkle out the intrepid protestors and the building of a network of tunnels within which some protestors have padlocked themselves to blocks of concrete. Some of the right-wing newspapers began by demonising these dirty illegal protests but the young people involved often turned out to be the children of middle-class professionals, articulate and attractive people not at all like the right-wing stereotype of Marxist ideologues. In consequence the protestors were often not criticised but lauded and turned into minor folk-heroes. Daniel Hooper, who under his activist name of 'Swampy' featured in many protests, became a frequent guest of chat shows and was given a newspaper column.

One of the the key reasons why such methods did not occasion the opprobrium usual for the excesses of youth was that the causes involved were often supported by middle-class people. The comfortable denizens of Wilmslow and surrounding areas were hotly opposed to the runway project and, while they might balk at some of the

BOX 11.2 **EXAMPLE**

Export of live animals, 1997, Brightlingsea

Once the ferries banned the export of animals, exporters had to find alternative ports. Brightlingsea could only be accessed via a three-mile road through residential housing and the movement of animal laden lorries was therefore highly visible and vulnerable to protestors who lined the road. Prime target for such protests were lorries containing calves destined to become veal on continental tables. Bull calves are much less valuable to farmers than milk producing heifers and so are exported to Europe at one week old to be tuned into veal. This is a heartless process entailing the enclosing of the calf in a solid sided crate with a slatted floor. They are locked into this darkened space, unable to turn around, and kept for six months until ready for slaughter. The calf is kept without straw and fed on a liquid diet designed to produce the distinctive white coloured meat. In January 1995 the animal welfare group, CIWF, issued a video of how calves were treated en route to their destinations and it attracted much publicity, putting the treatment of animals on the political agenda. The campaign was not presented as a vegetarian one – 'You don't have to stop eating meat to care – ban live exports' – and this attracted a broad base of public support. Respectable middle-class people who had never demonstrated before were seen lining the road to Brightlingsea, on one occasion blocking the road with sand. Such activities have lent illegal tactics some new 'respectability' but it all depends on the issue concerned. After all, according to McLeod's survey (1998) over 70 per cent of British people currently cared for a pet and this contact clearly encourages sympathy with the plight of agricultural animals who are often treated abominably by 'factory' farming techniques.

Source: adapted from Simpson, 1999

methods used, were certainly willing to offer moral support to the mud-covered martyrs. Perhaps the endorsement of 'respectable' middle-class opinion is crucial in terms of how the media cover such stories. The Greenham Common Women, who camped outside US cruise missile bases in the UK during the 1980s, were generally given negative coverage, especially by the right-wing press. Environmental protests, however, were in a different category as were those against the export of live animals (see Box 11.2). The *Observer* (6 June 1999) featured comments by six women supporting Gentetix Snowball 'leading the fight against GM crops'. The six women were all middle class, educated and committed to the cause. 'Do I look like an anarchist weirdo?' asked one. Another says 'Direct action is about ordinary people doing something, a problem for everybody to be involved in. If the government isn't going to get involved, then it's up to us. For me that's imperative'. Yet another points out: 'We may be a little dull. I don't have dreadlocks. I go climbing and walking around the Peak District. An awful lot of people think they are powerless. When you do something you realise the power you have'. Perhaps this new militancy is part of a growing awareness of political power amongst ordinary citizens.

When he [Bertrand Russell, venerable philosopher and CND stalwart] attempted, Luther like, to hammer a petition to the very door of the Ministry it opened before him, only to reveal an official armed with Sellotape. The police watched with scarcely veiled amusement. (Jonathan Green, *All Dressed Up: the Sixties and the Counter Culture*, 1999)

Terror tactics

The use of terroristic methods in Western societies has usually been strongly opposed by the general public but they have been used and not just by extremist political groups like the Bader Meinhof group in Germany. In the USA anti-abortion campaigners have shot doctors who undertake abortion work but closer to home the Animal Liberation Front has regularly held hostile and sometimes violent demonstrations outside laboratories conducting experiments on animals. In some cases the group has also planted bombs.

On 18 June 1999 the group Reclaim the Streets and an alliance of environmental groups took over the City of London in an action which involved violence. In the *Observer* 31 October 1999 entitled 'The New Revolutionaries', Jo Hamilton an anti-GM campaigner is quoted as saying: 'What some people would consider "criminal" action is appropriate in some cases, including criminal damage. You have to look at the action in a broader perspective. It is not a black and white area. I think there is real violence when there is enough food to eat but people are starving because of the economic system'.

Such sentiments reveal that some groups begin with limited aims focusing on one policy area then widen their focus to take in wider targets for change. Another activist for RTS is quoted as saying: 'We tried all the tree hugging at the Newbury bypass. It did get some great publicity, but the road still got built. We lost. There are a lot of us who now recognise we can't pick individual battles; we have to take on the whole system'.

The article also pointed out that some protest action has become international with co-ordination made easier through the internet.

Pressure groups seek to influence the political system at the most acessible and cost-effective power points. The obvious target areas include:

1 The public at large – groups seek to raise money, train staff, attract and mobilise membership, to assist in group activities and to apply pressure on their behalf.
2 Other pressure group members – groups with similar objectives will often duplicate membership, e.g. FOE members may also join Greenpeace. Moreover, such groups can combine forces over particular campaigns such as the traffic reduction one (see Box 11.1) or the Countryside Alliance which co-ordinates a heterogenous collection of groups against Labour's threatened ban on fox hunting.
3 Political parties – groups will seek to influence the party which seems most sympathetic to its views. Inevitably trade unions – the historical crucible of the labour movement – look to Labour and business groups tend to concentrate on the Conservatives (see below). Constitutional reform groups such as Charter 88 initially looked to the Liberal Democrats but, as such support was already solid, it embarked on a successful campaign to convert the Labour Party. Interestingly the Campaign for Nuclear Disarmament achieved a similar conversion back in the 1960s and in the early 1980s but never achieved its objective as Labour decided to abandon such a policy during the later part of the decade.
4 Parliament – especially the House of Commons, but in recent years increasingly the House of Lords. The Commons is more attractive to groups as this is where the important debates on legislation occur. As Box 11.1 shows groups often draft amendments for friendly MPs – often asked to hold voluntary office – to submit. MPs also are sought – and this may be their most important function for some groups – for their ability to provide access to even more important people, such as the increasingly important Selet Committees and (especially) regular meetings with ministers and civil servants (see Box 11.1 again). This ability to provide access – sometimes at a price – has been at the centre of the rows over sleaze which dogged Major's government and has also affected Blair's administration. The academic Study of Parliament Group surveyed a number of groups, discovering that over three-quarters were in regular contact with MPs; some 60 per cent said the same of members of the Lords.
5 Ministers and civil servants – clearly ministers and their civil servants are natural targets for groups. Regular access provides 'insider' status and potentially composition of

the policy-making 'triangle' comprising also minsters and civil servants (see Chapter 24). Baggott's research shows that 12 per cent of insider groups will see Cabinet ministers weekly, 45 per cent monthly; the figure for junior ministers were 14 and 67 respectively; for senior civil servants 25 and 49; for junior civil servants 55 and 76.

Groups anxiously seek membership of key bodies which include:

(i) Over 300 executive bodies with 4000 members with the power to disburse financial resources.
(ii) Nearly a thousand advisory committees with some 10,000 members.
(iii) Committees of Inquiry into a myriad of topics (Labour have especially favoured such task forces since coming to power).
(iv) Royal Commissions – not favoured by Conservative governments after 1979 but embraced by Blair's Labour government.
(v) Pre-legislative consultation. It is established governmental practice that all interested parties should be asked to consult and give their views on proposed new legislation. For example, changes affecting universities are circulated not just to them but to groups with a strong interest in such education such as the Association of University Teachers. It was alleged that the Conservative governments after 1979 went through the motions of consulting but often allowed only a very short time and then ignored the advice anyway.

6 European Union (EU) – pressure group activity is like a river in that it seeks out naturally where to flow. Since power has shifted to Brussels so groups have automatically shifted their focus too. In the early days when there was no elected parliament their activities helped reduce the 'democratic deficit' (Greenwood, 1997, p. 1) but since the Single European Act in 1986 groups have played an increasingly important role as the competence of EU institutions has expanded to include the environment and technology. The Maastricht Treaty of 1992 also extended EU powers into health and consumer protection. The Commission has calculated there are 3,000 interest groups in Brussels including more than 500 Europe-wide federations and employing 10,000 personnel (Greenwood, 1997, p. 3). In addition there are over 3,000 lobbyists, a huge increase in just a few years. These lobbyists and groups – especially the business ones – invest the substantial resources needed to set up shop in the heart of Belgium because they feel the stakes are high. The EU can make decisions which deeply affect, among others, the work and profits of fishermen; farmers; the tobacco industry; as well as the conditions of employment of trade unionists. Greenwood discerns five areas of EU activity which attract group pressure:

(i) Regulation – much of the EU's output of directives comprises rules governing the way the consumer is served. Indeed, in some sectors the bulk of new regulatory activities now takes place not in Whitehall but in Brussels.
(ii) Promotion – for example the development of key technologies to support export drives.
(iii) Integration – such as the measures to advance free and fair competition in the single market.
(iv) Funding – such as the Structural Funds to reduce regional imbalances or funds for research activities.
(v) Enablement – such as measures to support environmental improvement.

Baggot (1995, pp. 209–10) provides some examples of successful lobbying including the Friends of the Earth's pressure on the EU to hold the UK to water quality directives and the success of motorcylists and manufacturers in persuading the European Parliament to reject a Commission ban on high performance motorcycles. He also points out that groups have altered their focus as the powers of the institutions have evolved.

The SEA and Maastricht Treaty expanded the power of parliament and made it possible for it to amend legislation; pressure groups directed their attentions accordingly. But the major source of group interest remains the Commission, a relatively small number of officials who can be influenced via the usual processes of presentations, briefing documents, networks, lunches and so forth. Some directorates are more receptive than others but on the whole the institutions of the EU expect to be lobbied and welcome such attentions on the grounds that people wishing to influence measures usually represent those who will be affected by them and hence are likely to make useful inputs. The cross sectoral federations are often consulted as they are thought to be broadly representative, for example the UNICE (Union of Industrial Confederations of Europe); the highly influential EUROCHAMBRES (the association of European Chambers of Commerce); and ETUC (European Trade Union Confederation).

7 The media – the director of the charity Child Poverty Action once said that 'coverage by the media is our main strategy' (Kingdom, 1999, p. 512). Such a statement could equally be made by virtually all pressure groups outside those few insider groups at the epicentre of government policy and decision making. Unless influence is virtually automatic any group must maximise its ability to mobilise the public to indicate its authority, its power and potential sanction; influencing the public can only be achieved via the media. Therefore ensuring that group activities catch the eye of the media is a number one priority. Unsurprisingly Baggott's findings revealed that 74 per cent of outsider groups contacted the media weekly and 84 per cent did so monthly. Interestingly the percentages for the insider groups was even higher at 86 and 94 per cent respectively, suggesting that media coverage serves important functions even for those with a direct line to the government's policy-making process.

8 Informal contacts – so far the contacts mentioned have been ones which are in the public domain; it is quite possible most would have a written minute of proceedings. However, the world does not just function on the basis of formal, minuted meetings. Britain is a relatively small island with a ruling elite drawn from the 7 per cent of the population who are educated in public schools. Deep connections of class, blood, marriage, shared education and leisure pursuits link decision makers in the country in a way which makes them truly, in the words of John Scott (1991), a 'ruling class'. Glinga (1986) describes the manifold ways in which the upper-class British mix at their public schools, carrying the badge of their accent with them as an asset into the outside world where they continue to enact school-like rituals in gentlemens' clubs such as the Athenaeum, Brooks's, White's, the Army and Navy and many others. There they can exchange views and influence friends in the very highest of places. Paxman points out that when Sir Robin Butler was made Cabinet Secretary he was at once proposed for membership of the exclusive Athenaeum, Brooks's and the Oxford and Cambridge clubs. It was almost as if the 'Establishment' had made the appropriate room at their top table for the new recruit. In addition, when not in their clubs they can meet in other elite leisure places such as the opera, Glyndebourne and Henley. It is impossible to reckon the influence of such informal contacts but some, especially the Marxists, claim that this is how

BOX 11.1 MINI BIOGRAPHY

Sir Robin Butler (1938–)
Former Secretary to the Cabinet. Educated Oxford from where he joined the Treasury. Worked in private offices of Wilson and Heath before rising to Permanent Secretary in the Treasury and then Secretary to the Cabinet 1988–97.

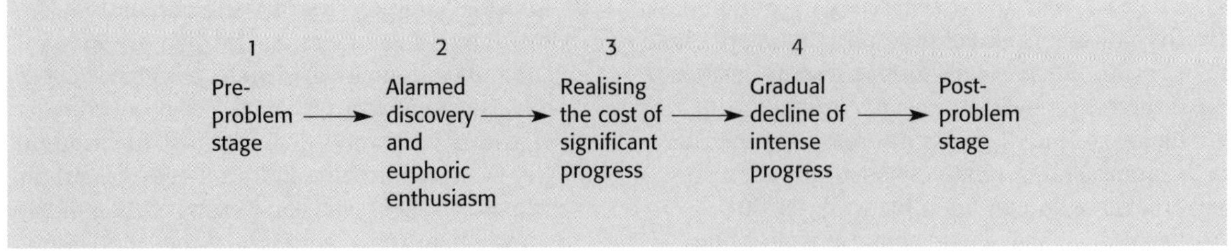

Figure 11.4 The issue attention cycle
Source: McCullough, 1988

> the really big decisions are always made: in private and in secret between fellow members of the closely interlinked networks of the ruling elite. What follows in public is merely the democratic window dressing for self interested fixing.

Factors determining effectiveness

Baggott (1988) points out that the effectiveness of pressure groups is also a function of organisational factors. They need:

1 a coherent organisational structure;

2 high quality and efficient staff (these days they recruit direct from the best universities);

3 adequate financial resources;

4 good leadership;

5 a clear strategy.

Economic interest groups are usually well financed but cause groups can often command significant annual income also. For example Help the Aged in 1996 raised over £50 million; the Salvation Army £70 million; cancer charities nearly £250 million and overseas charities over £300 million. In addition cause groups can compensate for shoestring resources by attracting high quality committed leadership; for example, in the recent past, Jonathon Porritt (Friends of the Earth), Frank Field (CPAG), Mike Daube (ASH) and perhaps the most effective popular campaigner of them all, Des Wilson of Shelter and many other causes.

Good organisation is of key importance also and the best pressure groups are as efficiently organised as any business with high class staff recruited from the best universities.

Issue attention cycle

The American political scientist Robert Downs has suggested that the media and the public's receptivity to pressure group messages is another potent factor influencing effectiveness. He pointed out that the new cause groups must run the gauntlet of the 'issue attention' cycle (see Figure 11.4). The pre-problem stage is followed by alarmed discovery coupled with the feeling that something could and should be done. When it becomes clear, as it usually does, that progress will not be easy, interest declines and this is when the pressure group faces its toughest tests. This has certainly been true of environmental, nuclear disarmament and AIDS campaigns, but all three of these reveal that with new discoveries and fresh events the issue attention cycle can be rerun – possibly frequently over time.

Economic interest groups

The policies of the government in such areas as interest and exchange rates, taxation, spending, trading policy and industrial relations are important in providing the context for the economy. Two of the most powerful interest groups which try to influence these policies are business and trade unions.

Business

Business is naturally deeply affected by government economic policies and it is understandable that its representatives will seek to exert influence. Many firms depend on government hand-outs, subsidies and orders and will seek to influence the awarding of contracts. This is particularly true of shipbuilding, highway construction, construction (the sale of houses is heavily dependent on the interest rate) and defence. But others will certainly be interested in policy matters such as interest rates, taxation levels and so forth.

In one sense any sizeable business organisation acts like a pressure group. Multinational companies – many with turnovers larger than those of small countries – make their own regular and usually confidential representations to government. Particular industries often form federations such as the Society of Motor Manufacturers or the Engineering Employers Federation and seek strength in unity. The Confederation of British Industry (CBI) was formed in 1965 and since that date has provided an overall 'peak' organization to provide a forum for discussion – it holds an annual conference – and to represent the views of members to government. It has a membership of 15,000, employs several hundred staff and has an annual budget of some £5 million. The CBI is dominated by big companies and this helps to explain the 1971 breakaway Small Business Association. For much of Margaret Thatcher's first term of office her policies of high interest and exchange rates damaged manufacturing industry and the CBI criticised her for it. It blamed the government for not spending enough on infrastructure; it complained that the high exchange rate made exporting difficult and that high interest rates were discouraging investment. On one famous occasion the then Director-General of the CBI, Sir Terence Beckett, called for a 'bare-knuckle' fight to make Margaret Thatcher change her deflationary policies – but his violent rhetoric abated after a stormy confrontation with that formidable lady Prime Minister. In recent years the CBI has been more supportive of the Conservative government line: John Banham, one of Sir Terence's successors, lined up against the European Social Charter in November 1989, for example, but disagreed over the European Monetary System, which the CBI believed Britain could and should join. Under Tony Blair's business friendly Labour administration the CBI under Adair Turner has been generally supportive of government policy.

The Institute of Directors is a more right-wing and political campaigning body. It opposed prices and incomes restraints, which the CBI was prepared to support in the 1970s, and vigorously supported the Conservative government's policies of privatisation, cutting public spending and encouraging free market economics. The Institute also welcomed Conservative measures to lower direct taxation, reform the trade unions and limit minimum wage regulations, and ideally would like such policies to go further. Other organisations, such as Aims of Industry, are used as means of raising support and indirectly revenue for the Conservative Party. Although no business group has a formal association with the Conservative Party, a number of major firms do make financial contributions. Many businesses utilize the informal contacts mentioned above, especially when the Conservatives are in power as this tends to open up the channels of communication betweeen government and business. These may take the form of whispers in the ears of government ministers at dinner parties, in gentlemens' clubs and elsewhere. (For more details see Chapter 14.)

Trade unions

Trade unions perform two distinct roles. The first is political. Since they helped to form the Labour Party in 1900 they have played, and still play, a decisive role in the internal politics of that party (see Chapter 14). Trade unions are involved in party politics more deeply than any other interest group.

The second role of individual trade unions is industrial bargaining, to represent the interests of their members on pay and working conditions in negotiations with employers. Some three-quarters of all unions are affiliated to the Trades Union Congress (TUC), which speaks for the trade union movement as a whole. In the past this function has involved unions directly in the political life of the country.

Various attempts were made by Labour and Conservative governments to win the agreement

BOX 11.3 **IDEAS AND PERSPECTIVES**

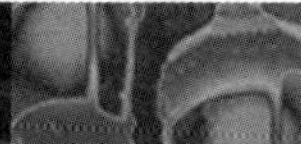

Trade unions, the Labour Party and public opinion

Ever since February 1900, when the Labour Representation Committee, the embryo of the party, was formed, trade unions have played a key role and are the body of pressure groups most closely involved in party politics. In recent years Tony Blair has sought to weaken a link which is not popular with the voters but nevertheless the connections still amount to a virtual umbilical cord.

- *Affiliation*: About half of all trade unionists are affiliated to the party, providing the majority of its members.
- *Money link*: In 1995 54 per cent of Labour's total income of £12.5 million was provided by the unions. However, in 1985 the percentage was 77 per cent. The practice of 'sponsoring' MPs by unions proved embarrassing politically and was formally abolished; unions now give money direct to local parties, with the result that these contributions are not counted as income centrally.
- *Membership*: Union subs are calculated on the basis of £1.15 per affiliated member with 75p going to the political fund. However, each union decides how many members it wishes to say pay the political levy and some underestimate to save money. In 1995 there were 4.1 million political levy payers and 365,000 individual members. Following Blair's accession to the leadership, membership doubled within two years. Unionists who pay the political levy (it is possible to opt out of this) can pay a reduced membership fee to join the party.
- *Representation*: Unions used to dominate the annual conference through 'block voting' (leaders casting votes on behalf of affiliated members) which accounted for 90 per cent of total votes cast. However, under pressure to remove an undemocratic anomaly this percentage reduced to 50 per cent in 1996. It is the aim of the leadership to move to one member one vote (OMOV) in all conference decisions as in the selection of parliamentary candidates. Trade unions also after 1981 controlled 40 per cent of the votes in the selection of party leader and deputy leader compared to 30 per cent for constituencies and the same for Labour MPs. This division was later changed to 33 per cent for each sector. They still elect twelve of the twenty-nine seats on Labour's ruling body, the National Executive Council.
- *Volunteers*: Trade unionists supply a fair percentage of the active membership, including local councillors, of the Labour Party and without them the party would be hard pressed to function on the ground. In 1964 73 per cent of trade unionists voted Labour but in 1983 this had fallen to 39 per cent rising to 46 per cent in 1992 and 57 per cent in 1997 (the Conservative voting figures were 31 per cent and 18 per cent respectively for the two latter elections).
- *Unions and public opinion*: In the 1970s a record 12.9 million days were lost annually in strikes. In the 1980s that figure dropped to 7.2 million and continued to fall in the 1990s. In 1994 the figure was 0.278 million, although in 1995 it rose to 1.24 million. These lower figures were certainly connected to the improving public perception of unions in polls. In September 1979 80 per cent of respondents told MORI researchers (Gallup's figures were similar) unions had 'too much power in Britain today' while only 16 per cent disagreed. By 1992 the figures had changed to 27 per cent and 64 per cent respectively.

of unions to pay policies which would keep inflation in check and the cost of British exports competitive in overseas markets. By the late 1960s Harold Wilson had become exasperated with striking trade unions and proposed measures to curb their tendency to strike and cripple the economy. His White Paper *In Place of Strife*, however, was attacked by the unions and James

Callaghan led a successful revolt against it in the Cabinet, destroying the authority of Wilson's government. Ted Heath's administration after 1970 worked hard to solve the problem of union disruption and eventually tried a statutory (i.e. passing new laws) approach, but this foundered hopelessly and resulted in an election in 1974 which he lost. Labour back in power tried to stem the rocketing inflation by engineering a 'Social Contract' with the unions whereby they agreed to restrain wages demands in exchange for favourable policies on pensions, low pay and industrial legislation. This succeeded to an extent and for a while the UK had a pay regime which was almost Scandinavian in its harmony between business and workers but in 1978 Callaghan's call for a 5 per cent limit was rejected by the unions and his government descended into the ignominy of the 'winter of discontent' (January–February 1979) with, infamously, bodies left unburied and operating theatres without electricity.

Subsequently Margaret Thatcher introduced a series of laws which emasculated union power; five Employment Acts and the 1984 Trade Union Act. These have made unions liable for the actions of their members and made union funds liable to seizure by the courts, as the miners found to their disadvantage in 1984 when their lack of a strike ballot rendered them liable to sequestration of assets. Their bitter strike slowly ran out of steam and they suffered a humiliating defeat which set the tone of union dealings with government for the rest of the decade. Days lost through strikes fell to an all-time low and a kind of industrial peace held sway although at the cost of much bitterness. Margaret Thatcher refused to consult with the unions and their occasional meetings proved to be cold and wholly unproductive. Unemployment helped to reduce the size of union membership by three million (a quarter) from 1979 to 1989. The growth of part-time work, mostly by women, did not help swell membership much either as such workers are notoriously difficult to organise. To minimise the impact of recession and shrinkage some unions decided to merge, such as Unison, the 1.5 million public service organisation. The unions' case was not especially aided by Norman Willis, the General Secretary of the TUC in this decade. In contrast to his successor, John Monks, who is an impressive operator and shrewd politician, he was relatively ineffectual.

BOX 11.2 MINI BIOGRAPHY

John Monks (1945–)

General Secretary TUC. Educated Manchester University. Lifelong union official and made it to top TUC job when Norman Willis resigned in 1992. Moderate and conciliatory but moved to criticise exclusion of unions from policy making under Blair.

Margaret Thatcher, then, destroyed the power of the unions and John Major was the beneficiary, not to mention the leader of the incoming government, Tony Blair.

In the run up to the 1997 election the TUC sought to fashion an appropriate new role in relation to the government, which it expected to be a Labour one. Denying there had been any deal with Labour, John Monks said on 26 February 1997: 'We know there will be no special tickets to influence based on history or sentiment'.

At the 1997 TUC conference Prime Minister Blair lectured the unions on their need to 'modernise': his favourite mantra. In 1999 he sought to charm them with a piece of doggerel verse. However, Blair has been careful not to encourage any thinking that the historical closeness of unions to Labour entitled them to any special treatment: 'fairness not favours' were the bluntly ungenerous terms to which he adhered. Some of his advisers are known to take seriously the possibility of severing the umbilical link with the unions.

By September 1999, however, Will Hutton in the *Observer*, 13 September 1999, was discerning a 'reinvention' of the unions after the debilitating experiences under the previous government and noted the increase in membership (see Figures 11.5–11.7). He reported on a survey which revealed that workers had never felt more insecure – more work for the same pay, less regular employment, greater threat of redundancy, collapse of trust at work – and were more likely to seek the 'support, security and protection' of union membership. Modern companies often have to face the

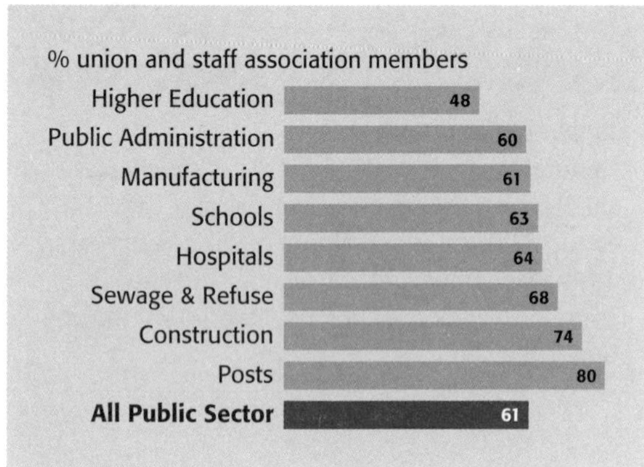

Figure 11.5 Public sector unionisation
Source: The Guardian, 17 March 1999

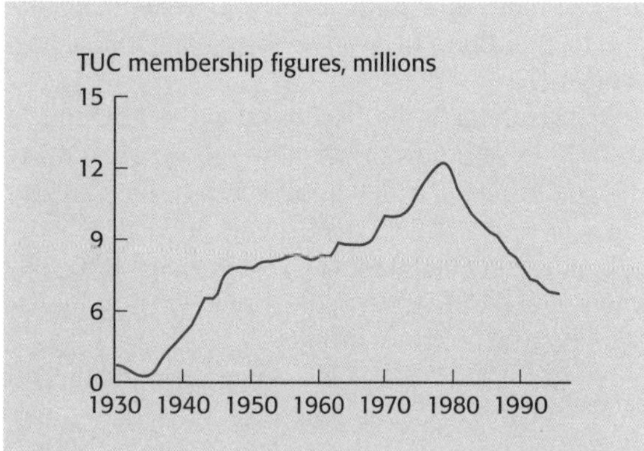

Figure 11.6 Union membership
Source: The Guardian, 17 March 1999

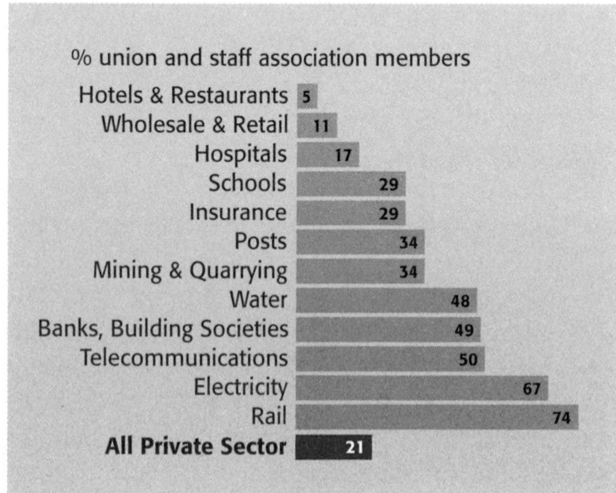

Figure 11.7 Private sector unionisation
Source: The Guardian, 17 March 1999

imperatives of shareholder demands for high share prices, such shareholders often ironically the pension funds which were set up to look after the interests of the very workers whose livelihood they were threatening. Hutton saw the seeds of future problems for the Labour government in the renewed solidarity of the union movement. Monks himself expressed anger at being frozen out of industrial policy making.

'I am very disappointed with the government's rejection of a European-style social dialogue – the idea of people working together under ministers to draw up strategies for the economy and the labour market. The European social model makes economic sense, and is crucial for the survival and prosperity of trade unions' (*Guardian* 12 September 1999). As part of an attempt to rebrand the union movement he was said to be considering changing the name of the TUC to 'Unions United' although nothing further was heard of this suggestion.

However, at the conference on 13 September 1999 he looked forward to a continuing growth of membership by over a million in five years, brought about by the climate created by the imminent working rights legislation – the Employment Relations Act – which obliges employers to recognise unions for negotiation purposes providing a majority of members' votes are in favour. 'The industrial pendulum is definitely starting to swing back' said GMB leader John Edmonds. 'During the Thatcher era we would be lucky to get more than two or three recognition deals a year. But the employers are beginning to see the benefits to be gained from working with unions rather than opposing them'. Arthur Scargill gave the sort of speech at the conference which used to bring delegates to their feet – 'Fighting for our members will bring people back. They see no prospect of the trade union movement taking up the cudgels on their behalf'. One and a half decades after the abortive miners' strike the reaction to the veteran unreconstructed socialist was muted.

Ken Cameron, the firemen's leader, chose this conference to utter the unmentionable idea that unions should sever their links with Labour. 'The Labour Party no longer sees us as their natural partners' he said, 'We can no longer rely on them to be our natural allies'. He felt the party regarded unions rather like 'unwanted elderly relatives'. Blair responded with a plea that the unions stay with him given the alternative of a right-wing Tory regime and won a standing ovation which effectively quashed Cameron's idea.

It has to be remembered in addition that it was not only the unions which were shaken up by the Conservative years. Local government, traditionally a strong pressure group on Whitehall, was seriously weakened during the years after 1979 and its policy-making role in housing and education reduced. Some of the professions lost a number of their privileges and were exposed to market forces. Solicitors lost their monopoly on conveyancing, opticians on the sale of spectacles and university lecturers lost their guaranteed tenure.

Tripartism

Like political parties, pressure groups want to influence the politics of government. In 1961 Macmillan's government created the National Economic Development Council (NEDC), a forum in which the government, employers and trade unions could meet regularly to consider ways of promoting economic growth. The activities of NEDC, together with periods of prices and incomes policies and the 1974 Labour government's Social Contract with the unions, were seen at the time as evidence that Britain was moving to a form of **corporatism** – see below – or 'tripartism' in economic policy. Governments would negotiate economic policy with the major producer interests.

Ministers were increasingly aware of the power of producer groups and of how they could frustrate a government's economic policies. They therefore sought the co-operation of leaders of business, employers' and trade union organisations. In spite of objections that such negotiations – notably on prices and incomes policies – bypassed Parliament, this was the path pursued by government in the 1970s. In 1972 Heath offered the unions a voice in policy making in return for wage moderation. That offer was not accepted, but there were closer relations between the 1974 Labour government and the unions.

Tripartite forms of policy making and the Social Contract have not been successful. Neither the TUC nor the CBI has sufficient control over its members to make their deals stick. Incomes policies broke down after two or three years. Moreover, after 1979 Margaret Thatcher set her face against such tripartism and relied more on market forces. Before 1979 governments usually tried to pursue consensus policies and their policies (e.g. on regional aid, incomes and price controls) required consultation with the producer groups. After 1979 Margaret Thatcher's determination to break with the consensus and her pursuit of different economic policies shut the groups (particularly the unions) out of the decision-making process. From 1990, John Major showed more of a willingness to meet union leaders, but there were no signs of any return to the pre-Thatcher consensual approach and in April 1993 Major abolished the NEDC.

The growth of professional lobbying

One of the striking features of recent years has been the rapid growth of professional lobbying companies. These offer to influence policy and effect high level contacts in exchange for large amounts of money. Often, the lobbyists are selling the excellent contacts they have made during a previous career in Parliament or the civil service. In this respect, Britain has once again moved towards the American model; on Capitol Hill this kind of activity has been an accepted part of political life for decades.

In Britain, over sixty lobbying organisations have been set up, ranging from the small Political Planning Services to the large (now defunct) Ian Greer Associates. Most major public relations companies have lobbying operations, either in house or via an established lobbying company. Over thirty Conservative MPs worked for lobbyists before the Nolan Report; consultancies could pay anything up to and beyond £10,000 per year.

There has been pressure for the regulation of such agencies (in Washington, they have to be registered), but one brave voice dared to suggest that the lobbyist emperors have no clothes. Charles Clarke, former right-hand man to Neil Kinnock, set up his own company (before becoming an MP and minister in Blair's government), Quality Public Affairs, offering an alternative and much cheaper service. In *The Guardian* on 30 September 1993, he claimed that lobbying government is a gigantic con trick trading on the mystique of Parliament.

> I am telling them that, if they spend £5,000 with me, they can save double the money within a year, once they get to know what to do . . . Thousands of pounds are spent by firms getting information that they could easily get for themselves.

Westminster lobbyists can charge clients around £30,000 a year for a 'full service', including lobbying ministers, civil servants and MPs to push their case.

New Labour and lobbying

Labour has not been immune from the obloquy attracted by professional lobbyists. Derek Draper, formerly an aide to Mandelson, joined the staff of a lobbying company after the election and freely boasted of his ability to provide clients with access up to the very top echelons of New Labour. Moreover, an embarrassing episode occurred soon after the establishment of the devolved Scottish executive when the *Observer* newspaper sent journalists to pose as American businessmen seeking access to the new centre of power in Edinburgh. The firm, Beattie Media (BMR), had employed John McConnell, former secretary to the Scottish Labour Party in expectation that he would win a safe seat in the new assembly and

The Observer newspaper reveals lobbyists boasting of providing access to ministers for cash (12 July 1998)

possibly be given office. McConnell duly was given office and BMR arranged for an employee who used to be his secretary to join him in his new capacity. Also working for the company was the son of John Reid, the Scottish Secretary. Writing in the *Guardian*, 30 September 1999, Jimmy Reid identified other sons of prominent Scottish politicians with links to the lobbying firm. He commented that 'The grave danger is that Scotland's new parliament will be drowned in a sea of cynicism even before it gets off the ground'.

Moreover, New Labour attracted criticism at the Bournemouth conference in 1999 when businessmen were offered dinners with ministers and possibly even the Prime Minister at £350 per head. Many can recall Labour's ridicule of the Conservative's Premier Club which had sought to do something similar in the mid-1990s.

Lord Nolan and the removal of sleaze

On 15 January 1990 the Granada TV programme *World in Action* broadcast its report on MPs and outside interests. It quoted Richard Alexander MP, who had placed an advertisement in the House of Commons magazine as follows: 'Hard working backbench Tory MP of ten years standing seeks consultancy in order to widen his range of activities'. The programme was only one of several investigations at that time and later of how MPs used 'consultancy' often for commercial interests; in effect they were paid to apply pressure through their network of contacts in Parliament and Whitehall. In 1994 *The Sunday Times* approached two MPs, under the guise of being a commercial interest, and asked them to place questions on its behalf in exchange for money. In the ensuing media row the newspaper was criticised by many Conservative MPs for its underhand tactics, but the two MPs concerned, Graham Riddick and David Tredinnick, were the object of much more widespread and impassioned obloquy. A commission on 'standards in public life' – 'sleaze' according to the popular media – was set up by John Major under the judge Lord Nolan. This reported in the autumn of 1995 and debated in November. Nolan suggested curbs on the economic activity of MPs and urged they be obliged to reveal the extent of their earnings. On 6 November Nolan's proposals were agreed and introduced a new system whereby MPs are:

- obliged to disclose earnings, according to income bands;
- forbidden from tabling questions and amendments on behalf of outside interests;
- restricted in what they can say in the chamber on behalf of such interests;
- obliged to register all details of contracts with a new and powerful Parliamentary Commissioner (since March 1996).

Edward Heath and David Mellor, both enriched by considerable outside work, declared only that work which was directly attributable to their position as MPs and controversially excluded large amounts of income earned through other activities.

The subject of sleaze, however, was not excluded from the news even after Nolan, much as Major would have appreciated this. *The Guardian* newspaper ran a story accusing a junior trade minister, Neil Hamilton, of accepting money when a back-bench MP in exchange for asking questions and being in the employ of the well-known lobbying company Ian Greer Associates, the then agent of the owner of Harrods, Mr Mohamed Al Fayed. Fayed was running a campaign to prevent the tycoon Tiny Rowlands from regaining control of the store and also desperately wanted to win British citizenship. Hamilton declared he would sue (as he had successfully and sensationally against the BBC when *Panorama* had accused him of fascist tendencies).

However, in October 1996, in a major climb-down, he announced the withdrawal of his action on grounds of finance. *The Guardian* responded by calling him a 'liar and a cheat' on its front page. The story continued when the subject was referred to the Standards and Privileges Committee. As noted in Chapter 10, Hamilton was trounced in the election by the anti-corruption independent candidate, Martin Bell. But the memory of Conservative sleaze did not go away.

Pressure groups and democracy

Do pressure groups contribute towards a more healthy democracy? As in the debate over the media in Chapter 10, it depends on what is meant by 'democracy'. The commonly accepted version of British representative or pluralist democracy accords the media a respected if not vital role. According to this view:

1. Pressure groups provide an essential freedom for citizens, especially minorities, to organize with like-minded individuals so that their views can be heard by others and taken into account by government.
2. They help to disperse power downwards from the central institutions and provide important checks against possibly overpowerful legislatures and executives.
3. They provide functional representation according to occupation and belief.
4. They allow for continuity of representation between elections, thus enhancing the degree of participation in the democratic system.
5. They provide a 'safety valve', an outlet for the pent-up energies of those who carry grievances or feel hard done by.
6. They apply scrutiny to government activity, publicising poor practice and maladministration.

Some claim, however, that groups operate in a way which harms democracy. They claim the following:

1. The freedom to organise and influence is exploited by the rich and powerful groups in society; the poor and weak have to rely often on poorly financed cause groups and charitable bodies.
2. Much influence is applied informally and secretly behind the closed doors of ministerial meetings, joint civil service advisory committees or informal meetings in London clubs. This mode of operating suits the powerful insider groups while the weaker groups are left outside and have to resort to ineffective means such as 'knocking on the door' through merely influencing public opinion.
3. By enmeshing pressure groups into government policy-making processes a kind of 'corporatism' (see below) has been established which 'fixes' decisions with ministers and civil servants before Parliament has had a chance to make an input on behalf of the electorate as a whole.
4. Pressure groups are often not representative of their members and in many cases do not have democratic appointment procedures for senior staff.
5. Pressure groups are essentially sectional – they apply influence from a partial point of view rather than in the interests of the country as a whole. This tendency led some political scientists to claim that in the 1970s Britain had become harder to govern (King, 1975b), exacerbating conflict and slowing down important decision-making processes.

Theoretical perspectives

Pluralism

This approach is both descriptive in that it claims to tell us how things are and normative in that it believes this is generally a good way for things to be. The importance of pressure group activity was first recognised by commentators in this country in the 1950s, (as so often before and since) taking their lead from an American scholar, on this occasion Robert Dahl, who believed major decisions were taken in an American democracy – where power was widely dispersed and shared – through negotiation between competing groups. In 1957, British journalist Paul Johnson said pretty much the same thing about his own country adding 'Cabinet ministers are little more than the chairmen of arbitration committees'. Samuel Beer, with his concept of 'new group politics', supported this view, believing the wartime controls in which groups voluntarily aided the government in getting things done, to have survived the peace with the 'main substance' of political activity taking place between the 'public bureaucrats' of the government and the 'private bureaucrats . . . of the great pressure groups'.

This pluralist approach, however, was soon much criticised for claiming that power was equally dispersed and that access to government was open. Critics maintained that rich business interests would always exercise disproportionate influence and win better access. Writing two decades later, pluralists such as Robert Dahl and Charles Lindblom adjusted their earlier theories to create a 'neo-pluralism'. This embodied a stronger role for government in relation to groups and a more explicit recognition of the disproportionate power of some groups.

Policy networks

This theory was constructed by political scientists Richardson and Jordan, with considerable help from Rhodes. It suggested that groups and other sources of advice were crucial to the formation of policy. They saw departments constructing 'policy communities' with stable membership of just a few insider groups; policy would flow from this community in consultation with ministers and officials. A looser collection of groups was discerned in 'issue networks'. These comprised a shifting membership of groups and experts who were only occasionally consulted and were – to use American parlance – 'outside the loop' (see also Chapter 24).

Corporatism

Corporatism – sometimes prefixed by 'neo-' or 'meso-' (Smith, 1993, Chapter 2) – was in some ways a development of pluralism in that it perceived a contract of sorts taking place between the most powerful groups in the country, rather as Beer saw happening in the war, whereby the government exchanged influence with the groups for their agreement to lead their members along government approved policy lines, for example, the attempts by governments to achieve agreement on a prices and incomes policy in the late 1960s and early 1970s. In the Scandinavian countries and Germany something very like this contract had already become regular part of the political process.

Pahl and Winkler (1974) argued that the British government through tripartism was exercising 'corporatism' in that it aimed to 'direct and control predominantly private-owned business according to four principles: unity, order, nationalism and success'. Corporatism, in one sense, was a means of bridging the gap between a capitalist economy and the socialist notions of planning and democratic consultation. To some extent this altered analysis matched the transition in Britain from a governing Conservative Party whose ethos was against intervention to a Labour one whose ethos was in favour. The drift towards something called corporatism was perceived at the time and criticised by left-wingers such as Tony Benn and centrists such as David Owen.

The Marxist analysis of pressure groups

Marxists would argue that the greater role accorded the state in corporatism is only an approximation of the real control exercised by business through the state; as Marx said, 'the state is nothing but an executive committee for the bourgeoisie'. The whole idea of pluralist democracy, therefore, is merely part of the democratic window dressing which the ruling economic group uses to disguise what is in reality its hegemonic control. Naturally, according to this view, the most potent pressure groups will be the ones representing business, while trade unions, for the most part, will be given a marginal role and will in any case act as 'duped' agents of the capitalist system, labouring under the 'false consciousness' that they are not being exploited. Marxists would also argue that most members of elite decision-making groups implicitly accept the dominant values whereby inequality and exploitation are perpetuated. In consequence most pressure group activity will be concerned with the detailed management of inequality rather than the processes of or progress towards genuine democracy.

New Right

According to the New Right analysis, shared by Margaret Thatcher, pressure groups do not

BOX 11.4 **IDEAS AND PERSPECTIVES** 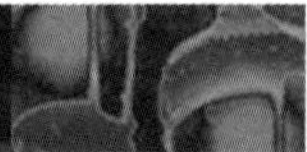

The importance of citizen campaigning

Des Wilson was probably the best known popular campaigner in the country – during the 1960s and 1970s – before he became a 'poacher turned gamekeeper' and joined the public relations staff of British Airways. On a Tyne Tees TV programme in 1986 he explained his own philosophy on citizen campaigning and suggested ten guidelines for people wishing to become involved in such campaigns.

It is very important to remember that the very existence of campaigners, the fact that people are standing up and saying 'No, we don't want this, this is what we want instead', is terribly important because it makes it impossible for the political system to claim that there is no alternative to what they are suggesting.

Citizen organisations are about imposing citizen priorities on a system which we have set up which doesn't always act as well for us as it should. The more we can impose human values by maintaining surveillance, getting involved in organizations, being prepared to stand up and be counted, the better. Even if we are beaten the important thing is that the case has been made, the voice has been heard, a different set of priorities has been set on the table.

Our movement is, if you like, the real opposition to the political system because I believe all the political parties are actually one political system which runs this country. If we are not satisfied, it's no use just switching our vote around and it's no use complaining 'They're all the same, those politicians'. We can create our own effective opposition through our own lives by standing up and making demands on our own behalf.

Guidelines for campaigners

1. Identify objectives – always be absolutely clear on what you are seeking to do. It is fatal to become sidetracked and waste energy on peripheral issues.
2. Learn the decision-making process – find out how decisions are made and who makes them.
3. Formulate a strategy – try to identify those tactics which will best advance your cause and draw up a plan of campaign.
4. Research – always be well briefed and work out alternative proposals to the last detail.
5. Mobilize support – widespread support means more political clout and more activists to whom tasks can be delegated.
6. Use the media – the media are run by ordinary people who have papers or news bulletins to fill. They need good copy. It helps to develop an awareness of what makes a good story and how it can be presented attractively.
7. Attitude – try to be positive, but also maintain a sense of perspective. Decision makers will be less likely to respond to an excessively strident or narrow approach.
8. Be professional – even amateurs can acquire professional research media and presentational skills.
9. Confidence – there is no need to be apologetic about exercising a democratic right.
10. Perseverance – campaigning on local issues is hard work: this should not be underestimated. Few campaigns achieve their objectives immediately. Rebuffs and reverses must be expected and the necessary resilience developed for what might prove to be a long campaign.

Source: Jones, 1986

enhance democracy as they are primarily interested in their own concerns and not those of wider society. They represent only a section of society, usually the producers, and leave large groups, such as the consumers, unrepresented. Also according to this view, pressure groups 'short circuit' the proper working of the system by promiscuously influencing the legislature and the executive so that the former cannot properly represent the interests of all and the latter cannot implement what has been decided (see Baggott, 1995, pp. 47–53).

Are pressure groups becoming less effective?

The decline of tripartism has led some commentators to answer the question in the affirmative. Certainly trade unions have been virtually excluded from important policy-making processes and almost certainly other pressure groups will have been cold-shouldered by ministers and Whitehall. Margaret Thatcher asserted a powerful self-confident message: she did not need advice. After many years in office this message and *modus operandi* spread downwards to ministers and outwards through the civil service network. Baggott (1995, pp. 46–53) shows how both the authoritarian conservative and free market liberal elements in New Right or Thatcherite thinking (see Chapter 6) were hostile to pressure group activity. According to this view even quite small groups were able to hoodwink or blackmail Labour into acceding to their demands. In consequence, Thatcher and her ministers broke with the tradition of seeking consent for new policies and preferred to impose their views in defiance of outraged group opinion. They did this, as appropriate, through vigorous industrial conflict (miners' strike), providing very short consultation periods – on average only thirty-nine days (Baggott, 1995, p. 126) – or, more generally, just by ignoring certain groups altogether such as the TUC and more or less dismantling the network of consultations constructed during the neo-corporatist seventies. Baggott's survey of pressure groups in 1992 revealed that 38 per cent felt the atmosphere had improved for them but 58 per cent believed it had not changed. As Baggott recognises, this pre-election period was slightly untypical as the government was reaching out to all sections to maximise support in a tight contest.

After the 1992 election, Baggott noted a considerable increase in consultation documents but only a slight increase in consultation periods (one twenty-page document in 1994 required comment within twenty-four hours). Major's small majority in the 1992–7 parliament made him vulnerable to interests with the ear of Conservative MPs, but on balance he pursued similar policies to his predecessor regarding trade unions, even tightening the screw by introducing a public sector pay freeze and ignoring the miners' opposition to the pit closures programme in 1992–3. Doctors angry at the imposition of the internal market in the health service were also ignored.

But what of the pressure groups which are in sympathy: intellectual think-tanks such as the Institute for Economic Affairs, business groups such as the Institute of Directors or media barons? There is much evidence that their advice was well received, at least it was during the Thatcher years, and it follows that their 'pull' in the highest quarters was enhanced rather than diminished during the 1990s. It also needs to be remembered that pressure group activity at the popular level grew apace during the 1970s and 1980s. In Chapter 5, this feature was noted as a major new element in the pattern of participation in British politics. Inglehart (1977) has sought to explain this as a feature of affluent societies, where people are less concerned with economic questions but more with quality of life. Other explanations can be found in the decline of class as the basis of party political activity in Britain. As support for the two big class-based parties has diminished, so cause-based pressure group activity has won popular support. As Moran (1985) notes,

> Once established class and party identification weakens, citizens are free to enter politics in an almost infinite variety of social roles. If we are no longer 'working class' we can define our social identity and political demands in numerous ways: so groups emerge catering for nuclear pacifists, radical feminists, homosexuals, real ale drinkers, single parents and any combination of these.

Some of the upsurge in pressure group activity has been in direct response to the policies of Thatcherism and its style of exclusion – CND provides the best example here – but much of it has been in support of cross-party issues, particularly those relating to the environment. A letter to Greenpeace members in November 1989 reports on activities during the year and comments on the organization's increased effectiveness.

This has been the fastest growing year in Greenpeace history... We have emerged as a respected, radical voice, authoritative as well as provocative. We have, after all, been proved right on issue after issue. It is a long time since we could be dismissed as a bunch of fanciful troublemakers.

Pressure group activity is more widespread and more intense. Much of this is 'outsider' activity, attempting to raise public consciousness, but environmental groups have shown that, with the occasional help of events such as the Chernobyl explosion, decision makers can be influenced and, in the case of the protests against the Newbury bypass and the export of veal calves, activists have brought their subjects into the forefront of national consciousness.

While the power of some of the most important groups such as trade unions has fallen in recent years, pressure groups remain one of the most important means by which citizens can take part in politics. In this chapter we have given special attention to unions and business because they have been at the centre of policy processes in Britain in recent decades. But it is important to realise that the range of groups is much wider than the two sides of industry. There has also been a renaissance in grassroots popular movements, especially those concerned with the environment. Important groups can be found in the professions (medicine, law), among the churches and in the wide spectrum of organisations – sporting, charity, artistic – in the community. Virtually everyone is a member of a group that tries to exercise influence on policy because virtually everybody is a member of some organization or other; and sooner or later every organization, even the most unworldly, tries to influence an item of public policy.

Blair government and pressure groups

In its White Paper *Modernising Government*, March 1999 the government spoke of involving those people who deliver in 'the front line'. Certainly it has improved the opportunities for commenting on Green Papers. Labour has a different set of emphases from the Conservative governments and it was inevitable it should give something to its own 'insiders', the unions – the minimum wage, assistance to the poor, union recognition, the European Time Directive – but it has been careful to keep a prudent distance from allies who have proved a liability in the past. However, some groups, according to Baggott (interview with author 1999) have complained that they have been overlooked by ministers just as they were when the Conservatives were in power. And Labour has shown itself vulnerable to those with muscle: in the autumn of 1997, it gave a crucial exemption to Bernie Ecclestone's Formula One racing business regarding the ban on tobacco advertising; it has slowly retreated from its 'green' position on the car and listened to the importunate voices of the car lobby; and it has shown it can be influenced by the massed ranks of big pressure groups as it has been by the marches of the Countryside Alliance. In September it advanced noisily on the Bournemouth conference centre where Blair was making his speech to the party faithful. In the wake of the much publicised march he reversed his earlier pledge, given during a summer interview, to ban foxhunting and opined there might not be time to include it in the current parliamentary session. Critics accused him of 'running scared'.

BOX 11.3 MINI BIOGRAPHY

Bernie Ecclestone (1931–)
Owner Formula One racing. Multmillionaire contributor to Labour Party causing a scandal when meetings with Blair enabled him in 1997 to win exclusion for car racing from the ban on tobacco advertising planned by the government.

The 'Countryside Alliance' claims to represent rural opinion while focussing on the issue of foxhunting (1 March 1998)

Chapter summary

Pressure groups seek to influence policy and not control it. 'Insider' groups which win acceptance by government have a privileged position compared to 'outsider' groups on the periphery, which tend to use high profile techniques which serve to disguise their lack of real influence. Business groups seek to influence through the CBI and other channels while trade unions have lost much power since 1979. Theoretical approaches include pluralism, corporatism and Marxism. On balance pressure group influence has probably waned since 1979 but some groups, concerned with environmental and animal issues, have increased their influence and membership.

Discussion points

- Why do pressure groups emerge?
- Why does government seek out groups and try to gain their cooperation?
- Describe an example of pressure group activity from the recent past and consider what it tells you about the way groups operate.
- Why do New Right thinkers dislike the influence of pressure groups?

Further reading

For the student the books and articles by Grant (1985, 1988, 1989, 1990) are the clearest and most useful, but Baggott (1995) is probably the most comprehensive current account and the most accessible. Smith (1993) is a study of some of the more theoretical aspects of the topic. On trade unions, see McIlroy (1995), Taylor (1993) and, on the impact of the Thatcher years, Marsh (1993). Baggott (1995) is good on European groups (pp. 206–19) and Greenwood (1997) offers a comprehensive study. Of the big textbooks Kingdom provides excellent coverage (pp. 507–36) as does Coxall and Robins (pp. 167–86).

References

Ashford, N., and Timms, D. (1992) *What Europe Thinks: a Study of Western European Values* (Dartmouth).

Baggott, R. (1988) 'Pressure groups', *Talking Politics*, Autumn.

Baggott, R. (1995) *Pressure Groups Today* (Manchester University Press).

Baggott, R. (1992) 'The measurement of change in pressure group politics', *Talking Politics*, Vol. 5, No. 1.

Beck, U. (1992) *The Risk Society* (Sage).

Coxall, B. and Robins, L. (1998) *Contemporary British Politics* (Macmillan).

Giddens, A. (1998) *The Third Way* (Polity).

Glinga, W. (1986) *Legacy of Empire* (Manchester University Press).

Grant, W. (1985, 1990) 'Insider and outsider pressure groups', *Social Studies Review*, September 1985 and January 1990.

Grant, W. (1988) 'Pressure groups and their policy process', *Social Studies Review*.

Grant, W. (1989) *Pressure Groups, Politics and Democracy in Britain* (Phillip Allan).

Greenwood, J. (1997) *Representing Interests in the European Union* (Macmillan).

HMSO, *Modernising Government*, March 1999, cmnd 4310.

Inglehart, R. (1977) *The Silent Revolution: Changing Values and Political Styles among Western Publics* (Princeton University Press).

Jones, B. (1986) *Is Democracy Working?* (Tyne Tees Television).

King, A. (1975a) 'Overload: problems of governing in the 1970s', *Political Studies*, June.

King, A. (1975b) *Why is Britain becoming harder to Govern?* (BBC Books).

Kingdom, J. (1999) *Government and Politics in Britain* (Polity).

McCulloch, A. (1988) 'Politics and the environment', *Talking Politics*, Autumn.

McIlroy, J. (1995) *Trade Unions in Britain Today*, 2nd edn (Manchester University Press).

McLeod, R. (1998) 'Calf exports at Brightlingsea', *Parliamentary Affairs*, Vol. 51, No. 3.

Marsh, D. (1993) *The New Politics of British Trade Unionism* (Macmillan).

Moran, M. (1985) 'The changing world of British pressure groups', *Teaching Politics*, September.

Nye, J. (1997) 'In Government we don't trust', *Foreign Policy*, Autumn.

Pahl, R. and Winkler, J. (1974) 'The coming corporatism', *New Society*, 10 October.

Paxman, J. (1991) *Friends in High Places* (Penguin).

Reeves, R. (1999) 'Inside the violent world of the global protestors', *Observer*, 31 October.

Scott, J. (1991) *Who Rules Britain?* (Polity).

Simpson, D. (1999) *Pressure Groups* (Hodder and Stoughton).

Smith, M. (1993) *Pressure Power and Policy* (Harvester Wheatsheaf).

Taylor, R. (1993) *The Trade Union Question in British Politics* (Blackwell).

Chapter 12 Political parties

Dennis Kavanagh

Learning objectives

To encourage understanding of:

- the changing functions of political parties
- the internal organisation of the major parties
- the major characteristics of the party system
- the patterns of leadership in the major parties and organisation
- the performance of New Labour in government since 1997

Introduction

In the British political system parties are of central importance. They involve and educate their members who also provide the key personnel for democratic control of central and local government. The majority party in the Commons, providing it can maintain cohesion and discipline, has virtually unrestricted influence over the legislative system and command of the executive machine. Parties are the crucial link between voters and Parliament.

Parties are the glue of politics. They are also the poison. They put loyalty above truth. They are the extension into peacetime of the lies, corruption and ruthlessness of war. Parties eat good men and spit them out as bad. They are one-time democrats yearning to be oligarchs. No nation's public life is so polluted by party as Britain's.

Simon Jenkins, *The Times*, 14 October 1998

The role of political parties

While pressure groups are concerned to influence specific policies, political parties set themselves more ambitious objectives. They aim to originate rather than merely influence policy, address the whole range of government policies and seek to win control of the representative institutions. They do not wish to influence the government so much as become the government. According to the dominant pluralist theory of democracy, however, political parties perform other vital functions:

1. *Reconciling conflicting interests*: Political parties represent coalitions of different groups in society. They provide a means whereby the conflicting elements of similar interests are reconciled, harmonised and then fed into the political system. At general elections it is the party which people vote for rather than the candidate.
2. *Participation*: As permanent bodies parties provide opportunities for citizens to participate in politics, e.g. in choosing candidates for local and parliamentary elections, campaigning during elections and influencing policy at party conferences.
3. *Recruitment*: Parties are the principal means whereby democratic leaders are recruited and trained for service in local councils, Parliament, ministerial and Cabinet office and the premiership itself.
4. *Democratic control*: It is the democratically elected members of political parties who as ministers are placed in charge of the day-to-day running of the vast government apparatus – employing millions of people and spending in total over £350 billion per annum.
5. *Choice*: By presenting programmes and taking stands on issues parties allow voters to choose between rival policy packages.
6. *Representation*: According to the strictly constitutional interpretation, elected candidates represent territorial constituencies – but they also serve to represent in the national legislature a range of socio-economic groups.
7. *Communication*: Parties provide sounding boards for governments and channels of communication between them and society, e.g. when MPs return to their constituencies at weekends to hold surgeries and attend functions.
8. *Accountability*: At election times the party (or parties) forming the government is held accountable for what it has done during its period of office.

Parties, or groups of like-minded MPs, have existed in the House of Commons for centuries. But they emerged in their recognisably modern form of being disciplined, policy oriented, possessing a formal organisation in the country and appealing to a large electorate after the second Reform Act (1867). Indeed, the growth of a large electorate required the parties to develop constituency associations in the country. At that time the two main parties were the Conservatives and Liberals. But with the presence of about eighty Irish nationalists between 1880 and 1918 and then some thirty Labour MPs between 1906 and 1918, Britain had a multi-party system in the early years of this century. After 1918 the Irish nationalists withdrew from the British Parliament and the Liberals went into decline. The new post-1918 party system pitted the rising Labour Party against the established power of the Conservatives and Liberals, although the latter still gained substantial support until 1929. The interwar years were a period of Conservative dominance of government. Since 1945 the Labour and Conservative parties have together always gained over 90 per cent of the seats in elections to the House of Commons (Table 12.1), but the Conservatives have been the dominant party.

To a large extent this two-party dominance of Parliament is a consequence of the first-past-the-post electoral system. As noted in Chapter 10, the decline in support for the two main parties in the 1970s and 1980s was largely at the expense of Labour. Yet until 1997 the three-quarters of the total votes which the Conservative and Labour parties usually now receive still translated into 95 per cent

Table 12.1 Election results: number of seats and vote share 1945–97

Elections	Conservative		Labour		Liberals		Others		Total number of MPs
	Seats	Vote (%)	Seats	Vote (%)	Seats	Vote (%)	Seats	Vote (%)	
1945	213	39.8	393	47.8	12	9.0	22	3.4	640
1950	298	43.5	315	46.1	9	9.1	3	0.7	625
1951	321	48.0	295	48.8	6	2.5	3	0.7	625
1955	344	49.7	277	46.4	6	2.7	3	1.2	630
1959	365	49.4	258	43.8	6	5.9	1	0.9	630
1964	304	43.4	317	44.1	9	11.2	0	1.3	630
1966	253	41.9	363	47.9	12	8.5	3	1.7	630
1970	330	46.4	287	43.0	6	7.5	7	3.1	630
1974 (February)	297	37.9	301	37.1	14	19.3	23[a]	5.7	635
1974 (October)	277	35.8	319	39.2	13	18.3	26	6.7	635
1979	339	43.9	269	36.9	11	13.8	16	5.4	635
1983	397	42.4	209	27.6	23[b]	25.4	21	4.6	650
1987	375	42.3	229	30.8	22	22.6	24	4.3	650
1992	336	41.9	271	34.4	20	17.8	24	5.8	651
1997	165	30.7	418	43.2	46	16.8	30	9.3	659

[a] Northern Irish MPs are counted as 'others' from 1974
[b] In 1983 and 1987 Liberal figures cover the results for the SDP/Liberal Alliance

of the seats in the House of Commons. In 1981 the Social Democratic Party was founded (largely from the Labour Party) and entered into an alliance with the Liberal Party. For a few heady months, with Alliance poll ratings close to 50 per cent, it seemed as if the mould of two-party policies was about to be broken. The fact that the Alliance parties could gain around a quarter of the vote in 1983 and 1987 created, if not a three-party system, then at least a 'two and a half' party system. The botched negotiations in 1987 which resulted in a new merged party, the Liberal Democrats, competing with the defiant rump of the SDP postponed indefinitely the break-up of the dominant post-war two-party system (see section on centre parties below). The Liberal Democrats recovered to gain over 18 per cent of the vote in 1992. The rise of the Green party in the 1989 European election was another false dawn: it coincided with the collapse of the Alliance parties and by the end of that year poll support for the Greens had evaporated.

Although the two-party system is based on a selective reading of British party history in the twentieth century, it has been central to perceptions of the British political system. The expectation of one-party majority government lies at the heart of ideas that British government is strong and that the majority party in the House of Commons can virtually guarantee the passage of its legislation through Parliament. The two-party system similarly is alleged to provide a coherent choice at election time, structure debate and determine the conduct of business in the House of Commons. Finally the two-party system is central to the idea that Britain has responsible government. Because the parties are programmatic, offering **manifestos** at election time, voters are able to deliver a **mandate** for the winning party. In turn, the electorate is able to hold the government accountable at the subsequent election.

The Conservative Party

The Conservative Party is noted for its pragmatism and opportunism, qualities which have helped the party to survive and thrive (see Chapter 6). The party has been in office alone or in coalition for some two-thirds of the twentieth century. A recent important study is appropriately entitled *Conservative Century* (Seldon and Ball, 1994).

The party suffered a shattering defeat in the 1945 election, the year of a Labour landslide. The electorate was clearly in favour of full employment and the welfare measures Labour promised, as well as greater conciliation of trade unions, and it probably supported an extension of public ownership in the basic industries. The Conservative Party promised to go some way in accepting these, except for public ownership. But the electorate voted for the Labour Party that believed in them more fully and was not associated with the mass unemployment of the 1930s.

Thus, after 1945, the Conservative party faced a problem similar to that which faced the Labour party in the 1980s. Should it carry on clinging to the policies that the electorate had repudiated or should it come to terms with the changed circumstances? Key figures favoured the latter course. R.A. Butler and Harold Macmillan played an important role in redefining Conservative policies, accepting many of the main planks of the Labour government's programme. Between 1951 and 1964 the Conservative governments largely accepted the greater role of the trade unions and the mixed economy (although in 1953 the government reversed the nationalisation of iron and steel), acquiesced in and continued the passage of many countries from colonial status to independence, protected the welfare state and maintained a high level of public spending. Finally, the party had also adopted economic planning by the early 1960s. Much of the above was a social democratic consensus and it prevailed regardless of whether Labour or the Conservatives were in office.

Conservative leaders until Margaret Thatcher were careful to position themselves on the party's centre-left. They believed, first, that maintaining the post-war consensus was the only way to run the country. In other words one had to maintain full employment, consult with the main economic interests and intervene in the economy (in the interests of boosting employment, helping exports and assisting the more depressed regions). Secondly, they accepted that such policies were necessary to win that crucial portion of working-class support on which Conservative electoral success depended.

Yet there have been tensions in the Conservative Party. Historians often distinguish two strands: Tory or 'one nation' Conservatism, which accepted the above policies, and the neo-liberal strand, which upholds the role of the free market and is sceptical of the benefits of much government activity (see Chapters 4 and 6).

The authority of the Conservative Party leader has not been subject to the formal checks and balances of his Labour equivalent. However, this does not mean that the party leader has a completely free hand. He or she has to keep the leadership team reasonably united and also maintain the morale of the party. When choosing the Cabinet or Shadow Cabinet, a leader has to make sure that people are drawn from different wings of the party. Margaret Thatcher, for example, gave office to many leading 'wets', people who, particularly in her first government, had doubts about her economic policies. In addition, the party leader may have to compromise over policy. Margaret Thatcher was unable to get the public spending cuts that she wished in her first Cabinet and was not able to move as far as she wished in matters such as the introduction of more market-oriented welfare reforms, in part because many Conservatives had doubts about such measures. She was forced, reluctantly on her part, to take Britain into the exchange rate mechanism (ERM) in October 1990 under pressure from her Chancellor (John Major) and Foreign Secretary (Douglas Hurd). She had already lost two previous holders of these posts (Nigel Lawson and Sir Geoffrey Howe) in part over her resistance to this step and was not strong enough to sustain her veto.

John Major was particularly constrained in the 1992 Parliament. His room for manoeuvre was limited by his tiny parliamentary majority and party divisions over Europe. His authority was undermined by attacks in the Press, criticisms from his MPs and the widespread perception that the party could not win a general election under him. On 1 May 1997 Major's battered administration finally came to an end when the forces of New Labour overwhelmed him by a majority of 179. He immediately announced his resignation and the fight for his succession was joined.

Until 1965 the leader '**emerged**' when the party was in office (which was usually the case), and the monarch invited a prominent Conservative minister to form a government after consulting senior party figures. (In 1957 the Queen sent for Macmillan rather than Butler to succeed Eden, and in 1963 she sent for Lord Home over the luckless Butler. Both choices angered some Conservative MPs and so involved the monarchy in controversy.) In 1965 the party adopted a system by which MPs elected the leader; Edward Heath was the first leader to be so elected.

The system allowed for a maximum of three ballots. To win on the first, a candidate required 50 per cent of the votes of the parliamentary party and, in addition, according to the rules, '15 per cent more of the votes . . . than any other candidates'. If these conditions were not met new candidates could join a second ballot, and if an overall majority still proved elusive, a third ballot could be held involving the top two candidates in a straight fight. In 1975 a new provision was introduced, the annual re-election of the leader, principally to ensure that an unpopular leader like Heath could be disposed of efficiently.

It was under these revised rules that, in February 1975, Margaret Thatcher stood against Heath and was rewarded – quite unexpectedly at the time – by a narrow majority in the first ballot. By the time the heavyweights such as Willie Whitelaw joined in the second ballot it was too late and she had increased her momentum to romp home. For fifteen years the mechanism lay unused until Sir Anthony Meyer chose to challenge Thatcher in December 1989 – some said as a 'stalking horse' candidate to be followed by a heavyweight – and was easily defeated. The outcome was to be very different when Margaret Thatcher was challenged again in November 1990 and she was far weaker. Her Deputy, Geoffrey Howe, had resigned on 1 November and made a devastating speech on 13 November which served to encourage Michael Heseltine to make his leadership move. Thatcher's campaign was badly handled and she fell just four votes short of the required number to be 15 per cent in front of her nearest challenger. After consulting with Cabinet she resigned, and in the subsequent ballot John Major, seen as Thatcher's choice, romped home.

John Major had a troubled tenure as party leader. The personal benefits of the party's unexpected general election victory in 1992 soon disappeared. The turning point in his and his government's fortunes was Britain's humiliating withdrawal from the ERM in September 1992. This was followed by a striking slump in the standing in the polls of himself and his party and by-election and local government election disasters. The party's growing divisions over Europe, already apparent under Thatcher, proved cruelly intractable. His authority was regularly flouted by party rebels, concentrated mainly on the Euro-sceptic and right wing of the party: the government only just managed to carry the ratification of the Maastricht bill through the Commons. The party critics looked to Margaret Thatcher for implicit support and there was talk of the right putting up a leadership

BOX 12.1 **IDEAS AND PERSPECTIVES**

Norton's Conservative groupings

Philip Norton has discerned seven groups in the parliamentary party, according to Philip Cowley.

Neo-liberals believe in the rigorous application of market forces; the Tory Right stress moral issues, especially law and order; pure Thatcherites combine a belief in market forces with a desire for law and order; Wets believe in a role for government intervention in social and economic affairs; Damps believe in the same as wets but not so intensely; Populists reflect popular attitudes, being left on social issues but right on law and order; Party Faithful support the party rather than ideological strands of thought.

British Politics Newsletter, No. 86, 1996

BOX 12.1 **MINI BIOGRAPHY**

John Redwood (1951–)
Conservative Cabinet minister. Educated Oxford. Headed Number Ten's Policy Unit under Thatcher. Secretary of State for Wales 1993–5. Stood against Major in 1995 leadership contest and for leadership again unsuccessfully in 1997. Shadowed Trade and Industry for a time under Hague.

challenger to John Major. Finally, in an unprecedented move in June 1995 Major challenged his critics to 'put up or shut up' and resigned the party leadership in order to fight to be re-elected and see off his critics. The Secretary of State for Wales, John Redwood, also on the party's right wing, resigned from the Cabinet and entered the leadership race.

Major won a clear victory by 218 to 89 votes but it did little to secure his authority or reunite the party. Euro-sceptics, aided by traditionally pro-Conservative newspapers, continued to undermine Major. They called, variously, for Britain to declare unilaterally that it would not enter a single European currency, a referendum on continued British membership or on further steps to integration, and reacted angrily to the EU ban on British beef following the BSE crisis in 1996.

Major did not appear to have a distinctive political agenda, unlike his predecessor. There was no Majorism. His defenders claim that his small majority prevented him from striking out in a radical direction. The 'back to basics' campaign was launched at the 1993 party conference but collapsed, as ministers were forced to resign following various misdemeanours. The Citizen's Charter was designed to improve the quality and responsiveness of public services to citizens, but it did not capture the public imagination. The big deficit in public finances limited scope for tax cuts and Kenneth Clarke, the Chancellor, was not prepared to damage the party's reputation for competence any further. But it is worth noting that Major pressed on with privatisations – of coal, nuclear power and the railways.

Conservative decline

The decline of the Conservative Party in the 1990s has been remarkable. As recently as 1992, when John Major led the party to victory, commentators wrote of Britain having a one-party system. In general elections the party regularly gained around 60 per cent of the Lab/Con vote and attracted voters across social classes. It outscored Labour as the party with a reputation for economic competence and the best ability to defend the national interest. It also, effectively, won the battle of political ideas. In industrial relations, privatisation, education standards, lower rates of income tax and encouraging the free market, Conservative policies were largely accepted by Labour. The party's dominance seemed even more apparent when John Major led the party to election victory in 1992, in spite of an economic recession and the strong mood for change.

But, since 1992, the Conservative story has been one of abrupt decline. The party forfeited its reputation for economic competence after the ERM exit and for governing competence because of divisions. It hardly has a presence in the great cities and no parliamentary seats in Scotland or Wales. On virtually every test of public opinion since 1992, the party has barely risen above the 30 per cent share of the vote. Although it managed to outscore Labour in the European elections in 1999, this was on a pitifully small turnout. The culture of the party also seems to have changed. The habit of dissent has been growing in the party for at least two decades and both Thatcher (eventually) and Major were undermined by the decline in loyalty or deference to the leader. MPs who had been sacked from ministerial posts or passed over for promotion were more willing to defy the party whips. Democratisation (in the form of annual elections for the party leader) in a divided party only added to the problems of party management. The best guarantee of Conservative party unity has been a leadership which is strong, consistent and looks like delivering election victory. The last is something which Thatcher in 1990 and Major after 1992 did not offer.

Europe has been a continuing source of division, just as under Mrs Thatcher, but it became even more troublesome under John Major. The

BOX 12.2 **IDEAS AND PERSPECTIVES** 

Taxonomy of Conservative MPs, May 1997, according to Norton

Eurosceptic Right	30%
Party Faithful[a]	50%
of which	
Eurosceptic leaning	29%
Agnostics, don't know	17%
Pro-EU leaning	4%
Pro-EU integration left	21%

[a] Party Faithful comprises MPs who have different views on issues but place loyalty to the party ahead of other preferences (see Norton, 1990).

Source: Norton, 1998, p. 13

European project of a more integrated political entity gathered pace and steps such as the extension of majority voting, social chapter, single currency and general shift towards greater integration concerned many in the Conservative Party. This was happening at a time when the party at large, the public and sections of the press were all becoming more Eurosceptic. A new generation of Conservative MPs, some of whom looked to Mrs Thatcher for a lead, regarded the developing EU as a threat to the independence of the British state and to the market economy. By the 1997 general election over 200 Conservative candidates broke with John Major's manifesto line of 'negotiate and decide' on British membership of the single currency. MPs returned at the 1997 election were increasingly Eurosceptic (see Box 12.2).

The impact of Hague

Following the 1997 election defeat and John Major's speedy announcement of his intention to resign, it was clear that any successor would face a formidable challenge, not least in reforming the party and in transforming its image. William Hague, after flirting with support for Michael Howard, eventually beat Kenneth Clarke for the prize.

He inherited a party in a sorry state. Membership had sunk to below 200,000, the average age was well over sixty, few members were in employment and only a small proportion were politically active, often merely selling raffle tickets. But constituency associations still controlled the selection of Conservative candidates and had backed dissidents under John Major. The party managers had found themselves powerless in the face of MPs who broke ranks and brought the party into disrepute. Major faced constant calls for strong leadership (something along the lines provided by Margaret Thatcher or even Tony Blair). Yet many conditions precluded such leadership. The party was notably divided on Europe, but it also suffered from a culture of disloyalty, as rebels eagerly sought access to the airways so that they could broadcast their dissent, or made their support conditional on concessions from the whips. A less deferential party conference applauded Eurosceptics and other Conservative critics of Major's government. John Major privately confided that some of his MPs had a death wish.

In reforming the party, William Hague looked to what Blair had done to Labour. He wanted to offer members the opportunity to shape policy. Policy votes at Conservative conferences were rare and had no authority, and members had only an indirect and advisory role in the election of the party

William Hague takes the reins of the Tory Party (2 November 1997)

leader. In these respects, the Conservatives differed from both the Liberal Democrats and Labour. In *The Fresh Future* package of party reforms, Hague embraced Labour's **one-member, one vote (OMOV)** culture. Even had the party wished to involve members in the election of a leader before, it would have been impossible because there was no central register of members; membership recruitment was a responsibility of the constituency associations. A new step, therefore, was the creation of a central register of members. Having been elected six months earlier by MPs, Hague now sought the endorsement of himself and his principles of leadership in a 'back me or sack me' ballot of members in September 1997. Unsurprisingly, he was backed by nearly 80 per cent of the 44 per cent of members who returned ballots.

The result of another membership ballot on *The Fresh Future* was announced at a special convention in March 1998. Only one-third of the ballots were returned and 96 per cent of those approved the proposals. As with Blair's ballots, the question was a take it or leave it proposal. No alternatives were presented to members and it was not possible to approve specific items. The spirit of the reforms bore similarities to what Kinnock and Blair had done to Labour. They included:

- The creation of a Board to be responsible for a single party outside Westminster. This involves the abolition of the National Union. The party membership is to be merged with MPs and Central Office to create the single party. The Board will also oversee a new Ethics and Integrity Committee which has powers to suspend any member who is judged to have brought the party into disrepute.
- The selection of parliamentary candidates is to be made by all constituency association members.
- The creation of a new policy forum to discuss policy.
- The creation of a new national party convention.
- Revised rules for challenging a Conservative leader. In future, the process will begin with a motion of no confidence which would be activated at the request of at least 15 per cent of MPs. If the motion is defeated there will not be another one for a further 12 months. But if it is carried, the leader will resign and take no further part in the process. In the event of only two candidates emerging there will be a vote of individual members. If more than two candidates emerge, MPs will ballot until two candidates emerge and then the membership will vote.

Critics have expressed doubts that these reforms will produce an effective democratisation of the party. The forum and the convention are only advisory and a Tory leader can call ballots of members to outflank critics and claim a mandate. It is also harder to challenge a leader, because the trigger to activate the no-confidence election has risen from 10 to 15 per cent. Like Blair, a Conservative leader may use the ballots to provide a plebiscitary leadership.

In Central Office, reforms were hampered by severe financial constraints. Business, particularly those firms looking to maintain good relations with the New Labour government, or those opposed to the Eurosceptic thinking of the party, have been reluctant to contribute. There was also a new climate which limited the party's willingness to accept contributions from overseas. But in summer 1999, William Hague recruited a team of media advisers and staff to run the rapid rebuttal unit. Both steps were an echo of what Labour had done in opposition.

In his first two years as leader, William Hague has not yet reshaped Conservative policy. He could not offer a clean sheet without seeming to deny the record of eighteen years of Conservative government. Yet after such a devastating election defeat he did not deny that the Conservative party had to learn some lessons. As leader he has made one big policy decision – rejecting Britain's membership of the single currency for at least two Parliaments and resisting further integration in the EU. The party has, therefore, abandoned John Major's and Blair's 'wait and see' line on the single currency and become more fully Eurosceptic. Given the views of most of the party's MPs and the mood of the grassroots, it was difficult for William Hague to hold John Major's old line. Yet he still met defiant opposition from heavyweight figures such as Kenneth Clarke and Michael Heseltine who even crossed party lines and supported Blair's 'Britain in Europe' campaign launch in October 1999. His stance also prompted a small breakaway of pro-European Conservatives who put up candidates for the European election in 1999 but failed miserably.

Hague also spent time apologising for the party ceasing to 'listen' to voters in the last years of Major's government, appearing uncaring about public services and concentrating too much on economic questions. It had to show that it was a more inclusive party – he took a liberal line on gender and race – and had to deal with issues of quality of life. In the tradition of the Conservative scepticism of change, he opposed Blair's constitutional reforms – until they were accomplished.

One attempt to fashion a new brand of Conservatism came unstuck in April 1999. Peter Lilley, the deputy leader charged with the party's policy view, made a speech which marked a breach with Thatcherism. Influenced by research which showed that the party was not trusted by voters on the core public services of health and education, he declared that these services would continue to be provided by the state and that the party had no plans to extend privatisation of them. The speech caused intense resentment, not only among key Shadow Cabinet ministers, but also among old Thatcherites and many Conservative MPs. Lilley was repudiated and did not survive the reshuffle soon afterwards.

Hague blunders. He opposes extradition of General Pinochet, jokes about Peter Mandelson's sexuality, sacks the leader of the Tories in the House of Lords and faces rumours of a leadership challenge (6 December 1998)

The chief Conservative problem on policy is that many of its ideas of privatisation, free markets, flexible markets and low income tax are now espoused by the Labour party. Like most opposition leaders, Hague has been waiting for the Labour government to make mistakes, and/or for public opinion to turn against it. His greatest success came with the 1999 European elections, when the party, on an admittedly derisory turnout, gained more seats and votes than Labour. For the time being as the new millennium has begun, the party's poor standing in the opinion polls and local election results are not blamed directly on Hague.

By 2000 Hague's Shadow Cabinet represented a generational change from that of John Major's last Cabinet. Major, Clarke and Heseltine had retired to the sidelines. Other Cabinet ministers had been defeated or retired in 1997. Then Michael Howard, Peter Lilley and Gillian Shephard stepped down. Only Hague himself (together with Sir George Young and Michael Portillo who replaced John Redwood) remained from Major's final Cabinet. The new men and women include the relatively unknown Andrew Lansley and Teresa May (both first elected in 1997); Liam Fox and David Willetts (both first elected in 1992); and John Maples and Francis Maude (both regaining seats in 1997).

Party organisation

The 1922 Committee

The Conservative leader is at the apex of party organisation, in charge of front-bench appointments (whether in or out of office) and of the party bureaucracy. But the leader's writ does not extend to the 1922 Committee, the name given to the Conservative MPs' own organisation. The Committee jealously guards its influence, electing its own officers and executive committee and only giving audiences to the leader by invitation. Usually the Committee provides solid support for the leadership, but behind the scenes discreet influence is often applied and its officers supplement the information flow on party feeling and morale provided by the Chief Whip and his cohorts – a nominated whip, incidentally, always attends Committee meetings. Conservative leaders, if they are wise, take care never to ignore the advice of the 1922 Committee. In the 1990s, as the party became more divided, so rival camps put up different team candidates.

Party committees

The parliamentary party has also established a network of specialist committees on policy matters and regional groupings. In opposition shadow ministers chair the relevant policy groups but in government the minister does not attend except by invitation. When in government these committees can have considerable influence, often on the detail of policy; individual MPs, for example, might well use them to promote or defend constituency interests. Conservative MPs are also represented on the considerable number of all-party committees which exist on a wide range of policy issues.

The National Union of Conservative Associations

This body was set up in 1867 to co-ordinate local constituency associations in England and Wales, with separate bodies for Scotland and Northern Ireland. It was wound up as a result of William Hague's organisational reforms in 1998 (see p. 239). It was the voice of the grassroots and organised the party conferences each year. The National Union pressed for party members to have a formal voice in the election of the party leader, as opposed to being consulted indirectly. Hague's shift to membership ballots now allows this.

Conference

The role of conference is formally advisory but in practice it has become important as an annual rallying of the faithful and a public relations exercise in which the leader receives a standing ovation (a regulation ten minutes for Margaret Thatcher in the 1980s) and an impression of euphoric unity is assiduously cultivated for public consumption. As a policy-making body the conference has traditionally been dismissed – Balfour said he would rather take advice from his valet. Richard Kelly (1989), however, argues that the consensual conference culture masks an important form of communication: that of 'mood'. Party leaders, he maintains, listen to (or decode) the messages which underlie the polite contributions from grassroots members and act, or even legislate, accordingly. He also points out that there is a 'conference system' of regional and national conferences involving related sections such as Conservative Women, Conservative Trade Unionists and the Federation of Young Conservatives. It was pressure from the conference floor in 1987 which persuaded Margaret Thatcher and Nicholas Ridley to introduce the poll tax in one step, rather than phasing it in – with politically disastrous consequences. Margaret Thatcher confused the enthusiasm of the activists with that of voters. One may now make a serious case – contrary to caricature and formal party statements – that the Labour conference is now more successfully 'managed' by the leaders than is the Conservative gathering.

Constituency associations

One of the main aims of conference is to send party workers home buoyed up with new enthusiasms for their constituency tasks: recruiting members, attending committees, organising social and fundraising events, leafleting, exploiting issues at the local level and, most important of all, seeking victory in local and national elections. Less than a third of local Conservative associations employ full-time agents to provide professional assistance. The membership of the Conservative Party, the study by Seyd and Whiteley (1995) suggests, has declined sharply. It is predominantly elderly (an average age of sixty-two), 'de-energised' and inactive.

In terms of their attitudes, Conservative members, according to the study, are pretty typical of party voters (Seyd and Whiteley, 1995). Party workers may well have been discouraged by the steady reduction in the role of local government which means they have fewer opportunities to hold positions of local political responsibility, participate in politics or enjoy patronage. The disastrous local election results in the 1990s mean that there are few Conservative councillors on the ground and these are the natural leaders of local associations. In many of the great cities – Manchester, Liverpool, Birmingham, Glasgow, Sheffield and Leeds – the party had only a token presence in local government and has been overtaken by the Liberal Democrats as the rival to Labour.

Local associations retain the important power of selecting candidates for general elections. They have steadily resisted Central Office measures to secure more women and ethnic minority candidates or efforts to disown candidates who were damaging to the party's reputation in the 1997 general election.

Central Office

Central Office comes under the direct control of the party leader, who appoints the Party Chairman and other senior officers. Central Office represents an important nexus between party activists in the country and MPs at Westminster, providing advice on small businesses, community groups, trade unions and political education, as well as training for professional constituency agents. Critics in the party's Charter Movement regularly criticise Central Office for its lack of accountability to the Tory membership. In 1998 a new Board of Management was established. The Party Chairman has a high media profile, particularly during the general election, and is a key organiser of election campaigns.

The Research Department was set up in 1925, becoming a power base for R.A. Butler – who was its head for two decades after the war – and a springboard to the Commons for able young politicians such as Iain Macleod, Enoch Powell and Chris Patten. The Department lays on secretarial support for the Shadow Cabinet when the party is in opposition, supports policy groups, briefs the parliamentary party (with officers providing secretarial backup for subject committees) and produces a range of publications, notably the pre-election *Campaign Guide*.

The Department does not originate policy but supports and liaises with the other bodies that do have a policy-making role. Policy work is done in party groups (see below) as well as the 1922 Committee and back-bench committees. In government, the main policy initiatives lie with the Prime Minister, Cabinet ministers and the No. 10 Policy Unit, and the Prime Minister and senior colleagues decide the contents of the election manifesto. The free market think-tanks have also been important in developing ideas of deregulation, competition, privatisation and the Citizen's Charter. From 1995 to 1999 the Director of the party's Research Department was Danny Finkelstein, a recruit from the think-tank the Social Market Foundation. His successor is Rick Nye, also a recruit from the same body.

Party groupings

Perhaps the oldest group is the Primrose League, set up in 1883 by Lord Randolph Churchill to advance the liberal Conservatism of Disraeli and encourage social contact among the grassroots membership. By 1951 the latter function was in the ascendant and it fell to the Bow Group, founded in that year, to urge the party's acceptance of the post-war consensus. The Group has a national membership including thirty or so MPs, a number of policy groups and publishes a journal, *Crossbow*.

The Monday Club was set up in 1961 in the wake of Macmillan's 'wind of change' African policy and has always concerned itself with defence, external and immigration policies, on which it has invariably taken a strong right-wing and nationalist line – so much so that it has sometimes been accused of being an entry point for National Front influence.

The Selsdon Group, formed in 1973, was more concerned to champion the neo-liberal economic policies which Heath's 1972 policy U-turns had appeared to abandon. The Salisbury Group is another right-wing intellectual ginger group which exerts influence through its journal *The Salisbury Review*.

The Tory Reform Group was set up in 1975 to defend the beleaguered Disraelian tradition; it has some thirty MP members.

The No Turning Back Group is the vehicle for the Thatcherites. Originally formed in 1988 to defend Margaret Thatcher against the 'wets', it believes strongly in cuts in taxes and public expenditure, and a reduction in universal welfare benefits. It has included a number of right-wing figures, such as Michael Portillo, John Redwood and Peter Lilley.

In addition to the above, from time to time the parliamentary party establishes policy groupings, some of which prove ephemeral, like the Blue Chip Group, to which Chris Patten belonged in the early 1980s, and Centre Forward, the group of twenty-plus MPs formed by Francis Pym in 1983. The anti-European Bruges Group, set up in the wake of Thatcher's speech in Bruges in 1988, has proved to be more lasting and more influential. There is also the 92 Group, whose chairman for several years was the anti-European MP, George Gardiner, deselected by his constituency association in January 1997.

What the emergence of these general groupings shows is the extent to which the Conservative Party has become more factionalised.

Funding

The central organisation of the party receives about one-tenth of its funding via a quota system levied on local constituency organisations. The balance is provided by individual and company donations which flow in directly and often indirectly through what could be called 'front organisations' such as British United Industrialists, the Aims of Industry. In its evidence to the Houghton Committee in 1974 the party opposed the idea of state aid to political parties. The party has experienced severe financial pressures since 1987 – a consequence of the unwillingness of firms and companies to contribute in the recession, and heavy expenditure. The party has long opposed the introduction of state financing of parties. But since 1992, it has often been in debt (£17 million after the 1992 general election), laid off staff, virtually dismantled its regional support staff and made itself dependent on wealthy individuals, sometimes based abroad. A number of large companies have reduced, or stopped, their contributions, in protest at the party's hostile line on the EU. Between 1997 and 1999 the controversial party Treasurer, Michael Ashcroft, contributed about £4 million to party funds. Critics pointed out, including the right of centre *Times* newspaper, that he had a perhaps too colourful past for such a post; lived in Florida; held dual nationality in Britain and Belize and was a tax exile.

The Labour Party

The organisation of the Labour Party is different from that of the Conservative Party. The major contrasts are as follows:

1 Unlike the Conservative Party, which developed from within Parliament, Labour developed as a grassroots popular movement outside the legislature. In 1900 the trade unions, cooperative and socialist societies formed the Labour Representation Committee (LRC) to represent interests of trade unions and assist the entry of working men into Parliament. In 1906 the LRC changed its name to the Labour Party.

2 The Conservatives have been in power – either alone or as the dominant coalition partner – for two-thirds of the years since 1918, Labour for less than a third.

3 Conservatives have traditionally been the party of the status quo, Labour the party dedicated to social and economic reform. Conservatives attracted sober members of the ruling elite who, with some justification,

BOX 12.2 MINI BIOGRAPHY

Tony Benn (1925–)

Former Labour Cabinet minister and left-wing leader. Educated Westminster and Oxford. Worked in television before entering politics. Gave up peerage to sit in Commons, re-entering House in 1963. Postmaster General under Wilson but swung to left after Labour's defeat in 1970 and became leader of left-wing faction in party; he was Minister for Energy in Wilson's second ministry but some say he split the party under Callaghan. Stood unsuccessfully for leadership and deputy leadership of party in early 1980s but after that his moment had passed.

were expecting to preside over an unquestioned existing order. Labour, on the other hand, attracted people whose political style had developed through years of opposition to such an order, who spoke in fiery rhetorical terms and were skilled in manipulating democratic procedures – skills used both against the Conservative enemy and against party comrades with whom they disagreed. In practice the key differences were reduced to those between the gradual and the root and branch reformers: Ramsay MacDonald and John Wheatley in the 1920s; Clement Attlee and Stafford Cripps in the 1930s; Hugh Gaitskell and Aneurin (Nye) Bevan in the 1950s; Harold Wilson and Michael Foot in the 1960s; James Callaghan and Tony Benn in the 1970s; and Neil Kinnock and Tony Benn in the 1980s.

4 Labour was originally a federation rather than a unified party like the Conservatives, comprising trade unions and intellectual socialist societies, each with their own self-governing mechanisms. Despite the formation of a single party in 1918, a similar federalism still underlies Labour Party structure.

5 The party's written constitution (1918) committed it to certain ideological objectives and laid down democratic procedures for elections, appointments and decision making. While more democratic than the autocratic Conservative party organisation, the constitution precludes some of the flexible adaptation to changing circumstances which the latter enjoys and when in government offers an alternative source of authority which has on occasions caused Labour embarrassment.

Labour's constitution and the power of the unions

The contrasting '**top-down**' and '**bottom-up**' provenance of the two big parties explains why the Conservative Party in the country is organisationally separate and subservient to the parliamentary party, while for Labour the situation is – at least in theory – reversed. This proviso is important because the relationship between the parliamentary Labour Party (PLP) and the other party organs is complex and has changed over time. The 1918 constitution aimed to provide a happy marriage between the different elements of Labour's coalition: the trade unions, socialist societies, local constituency parties, party officials and Labour MPs. Institutionally the marriage – which has not been an easy one – expressed itself in the form of the leadership and the parliamentary Labour Party (PLP), the National Executive Committee (NEC), constituency parties and the Conference. The absence of trade unions from this list is misleading because in practice they play a leading role, although one that is being reduced (for more on this see Chapter 11).

Power and leadership in the Labour Party

Unlike the Conservatives, who have emphasised loyalty, hierarchy and strong leadership – although with less effectiveness in the last decade – Labour's ethos was founded in democracy, egalitarianism and collective decision making (Minkin, 1980). An 'iron law of oligarchy' theory was propounded before 1914 by the German sociologist Robert Michels (1959): he argued that mass organisations can never be run democratically. This was reinforced by Robert McKenzie (1963) in a classic study of Britain's political parties in which he claimed that, appearances notwithstanding, both major parties reflected similar concentrations of power and authority in the party leadership with the external party organisations playing a merely supportive role. The first Labour Prime Minister (1924) accepted all the conventions with respect to the office of the Prime Minister and of Cabinet government and undermined the notion that conference constitutes the 'parliament' of the Labour movement, at least when the party was in government.

There is much in this argument. Once elected to Westminster Labour MPs become subject to a different set of forces: they become responsible for all their constituents and not just Labour supporters; they often need to consider their re-election in terms of what non-Labour voters want or will accept; and they become influenced by the dominant Burkean notion that within the House of Commons MPs are not delegates of some outside organisation but individuals elected to use their judgement on behalf of the nation as a whole. Labour's constitution, therefore, particularly when the party is in government, becomes challenged by the constitution of the country. In 1960 party leader Hugh Gaitskell refused to accept a conference resolution embracing unilateralism and succeeded in reversing it in the following year. Harold Wilson as Prime Minister, moreover, ignored a series of conference decisions in the late 1960s and survived while James Callaghan did much the same when Prime Minister in the 1970s. To dismiss Labour's intra-party democracy as unimportant, however, would be foolish.

Minkin (1980) points out that while Harold Wilson was defying conference resolutions and pursuing foreign, economic and industrial policies deeply offensive to the party's left wing, he was also losing the loyalty and hence control of crucial elements in the party. Little by little the constituency parties, the NEC and the trade unions turned against him.

In opposition after 1970 conference shifted sharply to the left and by 1974 most constituency parties and the NEC were also firmly in the left-wing camp. The result was that Labour governments of Wilson and Callaghan (1974–9) were 'obviously at odds with the party machine . . . it was as if there were two Labour parties, one with the voice of the NEC and the conference and the other with that of the parliamentary leadership' (Butler and Kavanagh, 1980). Disillusion with government policies caused an exodus of party supporters, leaving 'shell' constituency parties vulnerable to takeovers by far left activists, especially members of the Militant Tendency. During the 1970s constituency management committees (GMCs) in many parts of the country were taken over by the left; as these controlled the selection of candidates it was not surprising that the trend gave rise to an increasing number of left-wing candidates.

The limits of the 'iron law' became apparent when Labour again became the opposition party in 1979. The parliamentary leadership was much weaker and in no position to resist the pressures from a more left-wing conference and NEC. The new party policies represented a sharp break with those of the Callaghan government. Labour was now pledged to come out of the European Community (this time without holding a referendum), and adopted a unilateralist defence policy, sweeping measures of public ownership and redistribution, and the repeal of many Tory measures, notably those affecting the trade unions.

The 1981 constitutional changes

Internal party divisions reached a new degree of bitterness in 1979 in the wake of the so-called 'winter of discontent' when the collapse of Labour's incomes policy produced industrial paralysis and defeat in the general election. On the eve of the election Callaghan vetoed measures which the left wished to include in the party's election manifesto – including the abolition of the House of Lords – he alienated the left still further and set the battle-lines for a fratricidal fight over the reform of the party's constitution.

The party's left wing pressed for radical changes in the rules of the party and in particular they wished to introduce greater 'democracy' into the party. The left insisted that the party leader be elected by the members and not by MPs alone. In 1981 the Wembley conference agreed to set up an **electoral college** in which the trade unions would have 40 per cent of the vote, constituency parties 30 per cent and MPs 30 per cent. A second aim was for **mandatory reselection** of MPs within the lifetime of a Parliament (to enable right-wing MPs to be deselected by left-wing local activists). They succeeded in this. But they failed in their third goal, which was to give control of the party's manifesto to the National Executive Committee. The central thrust of all these reforms was to increase the power of the extra-parliamentary elements of the party, particularly the activists (who were rarely representative of the views of ordinary party voters) over MPs. Mandatory reselection was a factor which persuaded some threatened MPs to 'jump' into the SDP in 1981 and 1982, for the reselections favoured the left.

When Michael Foot (who had succeeded Callaghan in 1981) resigned after the 1983 election defeat, the new machinery was tested for the first time. Neil Kinnock and Roy Hattersley contested the leadership in October 1983; Kinnock won easily, while Hattersley decisively won the deputy's post. Yet, if the left managed to overturn the constitution, help drive some disillusioned right-wing MPs to the SDP and force the party to adopt a series of left-wing policies in the 1983 election, its victories were short lived. The disastrous 1983 general election result, when the party scored its lowest share of the vote in over fifty years and was nearly overtaken by the Alliance parties, forced a rethink. Neil Kinnock gradually managed to impose his authority on the party machine, particularly the NEC. This continued after the 1987 election defeat. The Militant leaders were expelled from the party; left-wing MPs were marginalised or moved to the centre; more central control was exercised over constituency parties and over the selection of candidates at by-elections; the party's aims and principles were restated in a less left-wing form; and socialism was all but abandoned. In the 1992 election, campaign decisions effectively were taken by Neil Kinnock and his office. When he resigned the leadership in 1992 he left a more centrally controlled party machine to John Smith.

The 'modernisation' of Labour

The Kinnock 'project' of the modernisation of the party was designed to make Labour electable again. The leader was convinced that the party, because of the damage caused by left-wing activists, had lost touch with the concerns of many ordinary Labour voters. The 1981 changes had been a party revolution; now there would be a counter-revolution.

After the election defeat the party launched an ambitious policy review. The consequence was a shift to the political centre and the acceptance of a number of Thatcherite policies (see Chapter 6).

Neil Kinnock was also concerned to strengthen the authority of the leader over the party organisation. The system of one member one vote was eventually extended to the election of parliamentary candidates and members of the NEC; the leader's office became more influential and a shadow communications agency drawn from experts in media and communications played an important role in preparing the party's election strategy.

The project may have resulted in a more leader-dominated and policy centrist Labour Party by 1992. But it did not deliver victory in the general election, its crucial objective. Labour slumped to a fourth successive, and unexpected, defeat. After the election, party leaders were convinced that it was their spending and taxation proposals, as well as Kinnock's leadership, which had held them back from victory. Survey evidence suggested that the electorate still did not trust Labour, particularly when it came to managing the economy. John Smith succeeded Neil Kinnock as leader in 1992, although it had been his shadow budget during the election campaign which was blamed by many for allowing Conservatives to attack Labour as the party of high taxes. Under Smith the party backed off many of its taxing and spending proposals; it had been scarred by the strong Conservative attack on it as the party of high taxes. John Smith had not been a prominent supporter of Neil Kinnock's party reforms, but in spite of opposition from prominent trade unions, he staked his authority on OMOV (one member one vote) which was carried narrowly at the party conference in 1993. Trade unions' influence in the electoral college for electing the party leader was diluted, as all the three elements – TUs, PLP and constituency parties – had equal shares of $33\frac{1}{3}$ per cent of the vote. Although the union **block vote** (winner takes all) was abolished and replaced by individual voting, the party has not, strictly speaking, moved to OMOV. Some trade union members can vote in two or all three sections. The unions' share of the vote was reduced to 50 per cent when the party membership reached 300,000.

Following John Smith's sudden death from a heart attack in May 1994, Tony Blair, a figure from the party's centre-right, was easily elected leader. Blair resumed the Kinnock project with a vengeance. The most important indicator of his determination to reform the party was his decision to rewrite Clause Four of the party's constitution. This was the ideological statement that Labour was a socialist party. In office, however, the party had rarely taken the clause seriously. When it had taken services and industries into public ownership it had done so largely for pragmatic rather than ideological reasons. Yet Clause Four was a gift to political opponents who wished to portray Labour as anti-capitalist and anti-market. At a time when state ownership was becoming widely discredited in the West and even abandoned in Eastern Europe, Blair calculated that it was a liability. Labour should mean what it said and say what it meant. He took his campaign to the membership and it was carried by a two-thirds majority at a special conference in April 1995. Modernisers noted the nine-to-one majority among local parties, which, significantly, balloted their members. The new clause claims that Labour works for a dynamic economy, a just society, an open democracy and a healthy environment (see Chapter 6).

The party continued to accept many of the Thatcher and Major government's policies and Blair even spoke favourably about some of them. Labour also redefined its electoral market, realising that it had to reach beyond the working class and trade unions, both now a diminishing minority. Blair wished to appeal to 'all the people', not least middle-class voters. Not surprisingly, these policies and theories were leading to further marginalisation of the left and there were complaints that the Blair leadership was authoritarian. Labour has become a catch-all political party seeking votes across the social spectrum and ditching ideology (Kavanagh, 1995, and see Chapter 6). Traditional divisions between the left and the right have been transmuted into divisions between old and new Labour with Roy Hattersley of the old right and Tony Benn of the old left associated with the former (see Box 12.3).

It is interesting to note how democracy in the party had been redefined. The policy role of conference has been modified, as the new more easily managed Policy Forum and its commissions make a more important contribution. Conference is 'managed' to be more supportive of the leadership, so reinforcing the image of Labour as a responsible party of government and with strong leaders. The last three party leaders improved their public standing by challenging conference, e.g. Kinnock's attack on Militant in 1986, Smith's stand on OMOV in 1993 and Blair on Clause Four in 1995. Blair has increasingly relied on ballots of ordinary members to outflank the delegates and activists who could be unrepresentative of Labour voters. The use of ballots among many party members for the Clause Four vote, annual elections for the NEC and parliamentary candidates has on balance helped the leadership. Another example of the plebiscitarian style was Blair's decision that Labour's draft election manifesto would be voted on by party members in late 1996. In many respects what has happened in the new Labour Party amounts to a reversal of the traditional analysis of Labour democracy. Persistent electoral defeats and hunger for office have led to a weakening of the 'old' mechanisms of intra-party democracy and a rallying behind the leader.

Blair's attempt to rebuild and broaden electoral support among new groups also had consequences for traditional supporters. Business was actively courted; business leaders were recruited to give advice on policy and join project teams, corporations received addresses by Blair and Brown and they were successfully solicited for funds. Key figures such as Lords Sainsbury, Haskins, Simon and (Gus) MacDonald held offices in the new Labour government. This was a signal that the trade unions no longer had a special relationship with the party. Before the election there had even been talk of breaking the link. Between 1986 and 1996 trade union contributions fell from three quarters to a half as a proportion of party funds. The £1 million contribution from the Formula One entrepreneur, Bernie Ecclestone, proved embarrassing when it was revealed after the 1997 election that his races would be exempt from the ban on tobacco advertising. Inevitably, there were accusations of cash for influence.

The party also courted proprietors and editors of traditionally anti-Labour newspapers, such as the *Mail* and *Sun*. These papers regularly received

BOX 12.3 'OLD' LABOUR VERSUS 'NEW' LABOUR — DEBATE

Old Labour	New Labour
Appeal to working class.	Appeal to all voters.
Importance of public ownership of 'commanding heights' of economy (Clause Four).	Rely on markets for economic growth as much as possible. Ditch Clause Four.
Sweeping redistribution from middle to working class via taxation and public spending.	Redistribution via economic growth.
Key role of trade unions in party and economy.	No privileges for unions. Importance of good relations with business.
Limits on parliamentary leadership from party institutions.	Trust the leadership.
Campaign through party activists.	Campaign through modern communications and public relations.
Slight interest in constitutional reforms.	Constitutional reform to provide 'modernised' government and decentralisation.

articles by shadow ministers or Tony Blair himself announcing policies designed to appeal to middle England. This has continued in government. Defenders of 'old' Labour connected the party's fiscal orthodoxy and caution over redistribution with the need to curry favour with these newspapers and their readers. But Tony Blair calculated that support from these groups was crucial to change perceptions of the party among voters whose support he needed. His 'reward' came in the general election when six of the national dailies, including the *Sun*, backed Labour (see Chapter 10).

Finally, discipline and self-discipline were tightened. In the first days of government Tony Blair told his MPs that they had been elected as New Labour; the veiled warning was not to break ranks. A code of discipline was imposed on the members of the NEC under which they have to clear requests for media interviews with the party's press office. A similar code provides for sanctions to be used against party members who engage 'in a sustained course of conduct prejudicial to the party'. Control was also tightened over the selection of parliamentary candidates and the leadership intervened heavily over elections to the NEC, selection of the party candidate for the London mayoral election and the election of Alun Michael as First Minister in Wales. The one member one vote system was rejected and the discredited electoral college system revised – as a device to deny Ken Livingstone the nomination in London. From being compared in opposition by one backbencher to Kim Il Sung of North Korea, Blair in government was being compared to Bonaparte. Key policy decisions were shaped less by the views of party activists and more by private opinion polling and focus groups conducted by the political strategist Philip Gould. The voters interviewed were overwhelmingly weak Conservatives or weak Labour and usually reinforced a centrist political message. Internal party de-mocracy was downgraded as the party was led increasingly from 'top top' ministers and officials and regarded as a campaign support for the government.

Many factors have contributed to the transformation to what Blair calls New Labour. The four successive crushing election defeats showed the extent to which Britain had changed, socially and culturally. Labour had to take account of these changes if it was to be a credible party of government. The party also had to come to terms with the fact that many of the Conservative policies it had opposed were popular or now too firmly entrenched to be repealed. This included the privatisation measures, changes in industrial relations law, Britain's membership of the European Community and cuts in marginal rates of direct taxation. The pollster Philip Gould's advice to Blair was 'concede and move on'. Academic studies and doorstep feedback showed that the party also had to remove the many 'negatives' in its image, which proved an easy target for Conservative propaganda and hostile tabloids. Blair succeeded brilliantly in changing the party's image. Above all, a growing awareness of the interdependence of national economies and the need for economic policies to take account of the likely constraints of financial markets showed that socialism in one nation was no longer practical politics (Shaw, 1996).

New Labour in government

It is often the case that the vitality of a party machine declines when a party is in government for a long time. Ministers have departments to run, the responsibilities of government to discharge and they usually see more of their civil servants than of party officials and party workers. Indeed, as many advisers move into government, so the organisation becomes de-energised. The danger is of a breach opening between the party and the country, and the party and government, as happened under the previous governments of Wilson and Callaghan. Blair's reforms of Conference and the NEC – allied to the activities of the alleged 'control freaks' of party headquarters – were designed to head off such opposition.

Many of the new Labour MPs have proved ultra-loyal. Their 'soft' questions for Blair at PMQ have prompted much derisive comment. Some Labour MPs rebelled over benefit cuts for single mothers and the disabled, and over the asylum bill, but the whips have had little trouble. Appeals for discipline have gained credence when contrasted with the self-defeating divisions of the last Labour government led by Jim Callaghan and John Major's government. On the key issues of constitutional reform, economic policy, Europe and Northern Ireland the leadership has faced little internal opposition.

Yet there are tensions between 'old' and New Labour. Some policies and much rhetoric have clearly been diverted to middle England. The main spokesperson for the so-called 'core' or traditional Labour vote is John Prescott, Deputy Prime Minister and Secretary of State at DETR. By social background (secondary modern, Ruskin College and ship steward), Prescott is very different from Blair (public school, Oxford and barrister). Prescott has appeal among the trade unions and working class. Keeping the two identities and sets of support intact is the key to the success of New Labour.

Some of the tensions broke out in a war of words in July 1999. Blair, long thought to be too ready to appease business, the Murdoch press and entrepreneurs, complained that the public sector was not responsive enough to his efforts to modernise the services, notably health and education. He held up entrepreneurs as models who embraced change and complained that he bore 'scars on my back' from his efforts. The next day John Prescott launched a defence of the public sector and clearly repudiated Mr Blair.

This clash followed closely on Labour's defeat in the European elections and the disappointing turnouts, particularly in Labour heartlands, in the historic Scottish and Welsh elections. Defenders of the government claimed that the apathy was a consequence of contentment. Critics claimed that it was proof of alienation and neglect among the party's traditional supporters.

What needs to be emphasised in the 1990s, however, is the decline of the leftist groups in particular and the decline of factionalism in general in the Labour party. The bitter disputes were important in speeding the party's electoral decline and the party is now often criticised for being too boring and safe. Left-wingers such as Benn and Livingstone are now marginal figures and have been voted off the constituency section of the NEC.

Other parties

We all 'know' that the main party battle is between Conservative and Labour. But since 1970 there has been a steady growth of support for 'other' parties. Only the disproportional effects of the electoral system have prevented the 'other' parties' votes being reflected in a large number of seats. In the last four general elections (1983–97) those parties have gained some 25 per cent of the vote and around 40 seats (as opposed to the 160–170 they would have got under a pure proportional system). But this third force of parties is diverse, including Liberals, Greens, Welsh and Scottish nationalists and five different parties in Northern Ireland.

The centre parties

The main third party after 1918 was the Liberal Party. It had been one of the two parties of government between 1867 and 1918. However, it steadily declined during the interwar years and attracted only minuscule support for much of the post-war period. In the 1970s it improved its share of the vote, in February 1974 garnering 19 per cent of the poll. However, the first-past-the-post electoral system has been a barrier and prevented it from receiving a proportional share of seats in the House of Commons. Its most distinctive policies in recent years have been political decentralisation and constitutional reform (more open government, proportional representation and a Bill of Rights; see also Chapter 8).

An opportunity for a realignment of the party system came in 1981 when Labour right-wingers broke away to form the Social Democratic Party. In 1983 its twenty-nine MPs (all but one of whom came from Labour) formed a partnership with the Liberals. The two parties had a common programme, a joint leader (the SDP leader Roy Jenkins was Prime Minister designate of a hypothetical government), an electoral pact and fought under the label of the Alliance. As noted earlier in the chapter, the Alliance gained 25.4 per cent of the vote in 1983, but only 3.5 per cent of seats. In 1987 the two parties again formed an electoral alliance and gained 22.6 per cent of the vote but few seats. In 1988 the Liberals and a majority of the SDP merged in a Social Liberal Democratic Party, soon to be known as Liberal Democrats.

In June 1990 the SDP gave up the unequal struggle and formally wound itself up. SDP members could comfort themselves with the notion that their party had forced Labour to abandon its left-wing adventures and adopt a programme more in keeping with the expectations of the ordinary voter. By 1997 Blair's Labour party had a programme very close in essentials to that offered by the SDP throughout its nine-year history.

But electoral support for the Lib Dems faded since Tony Blair has taken over the Labour leadership. As Labour has moved to the central ground it has cut into Liberal territory. Paddy Ashdown repositioned his party from being even handed between the Conservative and Labour parties, and took a pro-Labour stance. The two parties took broadly similar positions on Europe, devolution and constitutional reform and education and training. The Blair leadership realised that Liberal support would be crucial if Labour had only a narrow majority or no majority at all and the leadership wished to free itself from dependence on Labour left-wing MPs.

There was some overt co-operation between the parties, for example in the joint constitutional committee, which produced a programme of constitutional reform which the parties would try and achieve in a new parliament. The parties worked together in the Scottish Constitutional Convention and jointly agreed to stand down candidates in Tatton in the general election, so that Martin Bell could run as an 'anti-sleaze' candidate. More secretly, there were also negotiations between Blair and Ashdown and their respective teams over co-operation in the forthcoming election campaign and the referendum on devolution in Scotland. The two leaders even discussed coalition, with Liberal Democrats taking seats in a Blair Cabinet. Labour's huge majority in the general election put paid to the last scheme. However, Blair established a Joint Cabinet Committee, containing members of both parties to consider constitutional matters, and in 1999 its remit was extended to cover other issues.

Blair had often spoken about his wish to recreate the pre-1914 progressive alliance of Liberals and the infant Labour party, regarding it as a means to achieve centre-left domination of politics in the twenty-first century, just as the Conservatives had done in the twentieth century. If proportional representation was to be introduced, such co-operation would be even more necessary as one party would be less likely to have a majority of seats. But PR as advocated by the Jenkins Committee (see Chapter 8) and regarded as the price for co-operation remained an aspiration.

The 1997 general election provided mixed fortunes for the Liberal Democrats. During the campaign they attacked Labour from a radical perspective, offering to increase taxes to pay for better services. A mix of factors, including targeting and tactical anti-Conservative voting, meant that although its vote share fell, the party doubled its number of seats. But what was the purpose of achieving a breakthrough in seats (46) set alongside Labour's 179 seat majority in the new parliament?

In 1999 Paddy Ashdown announced his retirement, having served twelve years as leader. Under his leadership the party had displaced the Conservatives as the second party in local government, membership had risen to around 100,000 and the number of MPs had doubled. The election of a successor gave the party the opportunity to review the benefits from co-operation with Labour. Simon Hughes spoke for those who wished to keep their distance and favoured more redistributive policies and increases in income taxes to improve public services. The eventual winner, Charles Kennedy, favoured co-operation, but promised to press for more measures to help the poor. But the problem remained: what was distinctive about the Liberal Democrats given their close relationship with the Labour government and the convergence between them in many policies? In parliament, the party was at its strongest for seventy years but it risked losing its distinctiveness because of Lib–Lab co-operation (see also Chapter 6).

The Greens

The British Green Party began life in 1973 as an environmental pressure group. In 1985 the party changed its name from the Ecology to the Green Party and thus came into line with environmental parties internationally. During the 1980s Green support in Western Europe grew apace: candidates were elected to eleven national parliaments around the world. In Britain, however, in 1983, 108 candidates mustered barely 1 per cent of the votes (55,000). But after the decline of the Alliance the Greens captured the 'protest' vote. The Greens took an astonishing 15 per cent of the vote in the 1989 elections to the European Parliament, overtaking the Liberals. A sign of the fragility of this support was shown in 1992 when it gained an average of 1.3 per cent where a Green candidate stood, worse than in 1987. In 1997 only 95 candidates stood and gained an average of 1.4 per cent (see also Chapter 7).

Nationalist parties

Party politics in Northern Ireland is different from that on the mainland (see Chapter 30). In part this is because of the dominance of issues regarding the border, religious rivalries between Protestants and Catholics and because no mainland party contests any Ulster seat. The two main Protestant parties are the Official Unionists (OU) and Democratic Unionists (DU) (led by Dr Ian Paisley). They opposed power sharing with the Catholic community in any Northern Ireland legislature and the Anglo-Irish agreement (1985) which gave the Irish government a voice in Northern Ireland's affairs. The main Catholic party is the Social Democratic and Labour Party (SDLP) which favours power sharing. Sinn Fein, the parliamentary wing of the IRA, won one seat in 1983 and 1987 but the MP refused to take his place in Westminster. After losing a single seat to the SDLP in 1992, they gained 15 per cent of the vote in the Assembly elections connected with the peace process. In the general election of 1997 they won two seats, although once again neither was taken up. The creation of an Assembly following the Good Friday Agreement in 1998 split the Unionists. David Trimble (OU) agreed to serve as First Minister but the executive will only operate if and when the IRA Sinn Fein takes steps to decommission its weapons.

In Scotland and Wales nationalist parties want independence (see Chapter 9) for their nations and regard devolution as a staging post on the way. They had seven MPs in the 1992 parliament but this increased in 1997 to ten, six for the SNP and four for Plaid Cymru. In 1988, the non-Conservative parties established a constitutional convention to formulate plans for a Scottish parliament which was soon boycotted by the Nationalists. But the Nationalists co-operated with Labour and Liberal Democrats in the 1997 referendum to set up a parliament which had tax-raising power. In the elections for the Scottish Parliament in 1998, the Nationalists became the official opposition and may profit if there is disappointment with the Parliament.

For all the talk of nationalism, it is also worth noting that the overwhelming majority of MPs in both nations are drawn from pro-union 'national' parties. Since the 1997 election, however, the Conservatives have been wiped out and Labour has emerged more supreme than ever (see also Chapters 7 and 14).

The effect of parties

The failures of many post-war governments, notably in the economic sphere, and the lack of consistency over policies to the EU have been seen by many as signs of weak government and therefore of parties. According to Professor Richard Rose, in *Do Parties Make a Difference?* (1984), British parties are ill equipped to direct government. Rose points in particular to the failure of pre-1979 governments to improve macroeconomic conditions (such as inflation, unemployment, economic growth and balance of payments) to show that parties do not make much difference in reversing the trend.

Against this, some argue that the parties in government may have too much power. The relative ease with which they get their legislation through Parliament, for example, in the absence of formal checks and balances or the extension of non-elected quangos (Jenkins, 1996) has prompted concern. Critics advocate the introduction of a proportional electoral system, partly on the grounds of fairness (since to have a majority of seats in the Commons, governments would also need the support of a majority, or near majority, of the voters), and partly on the grounds that coalitions would slow down the damaging reversals of policy resulting from competing party ideologies.

In the fields of industrial relations, abandonment of formal incomes policy and tripartite style of decision making, privatisation of state industries and services, the Thatcher record shows that parties can make a difference, particularly when they have a determined leader who has a political strategy and are in office for a lengthy period (Kavanagh, 1990). Her governments also proved effective in resisting the pressures of interest groups. In the 1970s it was fashionable to argue that groups had excessive influence and that governments were often weak. Powerful groups were able to defy or veto government policies and government usually went out of its way to consult them. But the Thatcher and Major governments have massively reduced the role of the trade unions and local government and have imposed changes on the civil service, and teaching, health and legal professions. Parties also seem to be striving more than ever to show their independence from interests. Labour has distanced itself from the unions, and Conservative governments, prior to the withdrawal from the ERM in September 1992, were not sympathetic to business complaints about the effects of the high value of the pound on exports. Powerful lobbies still campaign for more public spending in their favoured areas, but the size of the public sector has been contained (thanks to privatisation) and both major parties are cautious about increasing public spending as a share of GDP.

During the period of Conservative hegemony, some political commentators thought Britain might be developing into a one-party state rather like Japan. Fears were expressed that interest groups would accustom themselves to working with one party alone. Other fears expressed were that the Conservatives would politicise the civil service and make it into an instrument of ideology instead of a neutral vehicle for the public good. There is little evidence for this last suspicion. Rather, Thatcher was concerned to encourage civil servants who were change oriented, interested in cutting

BOX 12.4 **IDEAS AND PERSPECTIVES**

Third Way

Tony Blair realised that his new Labour project needed a philosophical basis, just as Mrs Thatcher could point to neo-liberalism and its defence of the free market. Socialism, in the sense of state ownership and direction of the economy, had clearly failed; his reform of Clause Four of the party constitution acknowledged this. How could he move on to new ground, recognising the limits of both free market and the state?

Blair and President Clinton have promoted the Third Way, a pragmatic borrowing of the best of both left and right ideologies. The advisors and intellectual supporters of both men meet periodically for seminars. Blair has also sought to interest centre left parties in Europe in the ideas. Both leaders start from the basis that rapid social and international changes have made much of the old left and right ideas redundant (Giddens, 1998). Among the key features of the Third Way are the following:

- Limits on the state have increased because of international forces (globalisation) and social complexity.
- The role of the state should be as a facilitator and regulator, rather than as a deliverer of services. Making the market work more efficiently and improving education and training will help economic efficiency.
- Citizenship involves responsibilities as well as rights. Parents have to be responsible for children, curbs should be imposed on anti-social neighbours, and welfare reform must emphasize that there is no unlimited right to benefit and link benefits to training and incentives to work.
- There should be greater co-operation between individual states to tackle global problems.

Critics dismiss much of the Third Way as vague rhetoric or unprincipled pragmatism. After all, British politicians have usually pursued a middle path when it comes to fighting election campaigns (see also Chapter 6).

costs, promoting value for money and learning lessons from the private sector. Labour has maintained the impetus. Conservatives also had the opportunity to make their policy changes in the 1980s well nigh irreversible. Many of the controversial policies were soon accepted by Labour, e.g. council house sales, membership of the European Community/Union, trade union reforms, privatisation and lower rates of marginal income tax. By 1997 many of the reforms were so well entrenched that it was difficult to unscramble them.

Having read the political runes of the 1980s, Labour policy converged so closely to the Conservatives' that it was difficult for voters to distinguish between them. In the end they decided that the Conservatives were too tired and incompetent as well as arguably dishonest, and Labour was returned with the kind of majority that would enable it to begin its own programme of reform. In the long years of opposition, Labour had been converted to constitutional reform, in part as a corrective to the defects of the 'one party state'. Blair has combined the idea into a Third Way that regards the traditional right and left as outdated (see Box 12.4).

Problems for parties

Britain is widely regarded as the home of strong parties. They have a reputation for being disciplined, programmatic, providing clear choice for voters at elections and providing stable one-party government. Yet there are signs that parties are in trouble. Symptoms include the following:

1 *Declining popular attachment*: Surveys over the years show that about 15 per cent of the electorate consistently claim to be very interested in politics. Yet the proportion of voters who identify very strongly with the Labour and Conservative parties has fallen, from over two-fifths in 1964 to a fifth today, with the big decline occurring in the mid-1970s. Surveys show that very few members are willing to canvass by telephone for the party they support or stop strangers in the street and discuss their party's strengths.

2 *Falling membership*: Party membership has declined in Britain, as it has in a number of other Western states. The Labour Party had a million individual members in the 1950s and this fell to just over 250,000 in 1992 recovering to nearly 400,000 in 1997. From the 1950s to the 1990s Conservative membership fell from a claimed 2.8 million to some 300,000, but its membership is relatively old – on average in its sixties – and the dearth of Conservative election posters in the 1997 election campaign revealed that in all but a few constituencies activism was virtually dead. About only 2 per cent of voters are actually party members, lower than in many other Western states.

3 *People have other, non-political interests*: Competition for the time and interest of voters has developed from television, various leisure activities and interest groups. If voters are becoming more instrumental in their outlooks, they may find it more profitable to advance their specific concerns through participation in local protest bodies. The decline in party membership has coincided with an increase in membership of many cause groups.

4 *Interest groups are reluctant to associate closely with a political party*: The trade union connection with Labour has not inspired others to follow, and group spokespersons are increasingly likely to seek direct access to ministers rather than to operate through a political party. Parties lack effective control over the mass media. The last national newspaper to be connected to a political party was the *Daily Herald*, and this ceased publication long ago. There is no popular market for a party political newspaper. This is one reason why Blair has written so many newspaper articles and does question and answer sessions with voters, because he wishes to 'go direct' to them.

5 *Parties are turning elsewhere for relevant skills*: They court think-tanks for ideas rather than their own research departments (e.g. Labour draws on the Institute of Public Policy Research and Demos, and the Conservatives turned to the Centre for Policy Studies) and turn to opinion pollsters, advertising agencies and communication specialists for help with election campaigning (Kavanagh, 1995). In government, Labour has established several working parties and policy review bodies, and given leaders from business and commerce a leading role.

Chapter summary

The strength and competitiveness of the party system suffered because of the weakness of Labour after 1979. Under Blair the party has effectively abandoned socialism and in many ways is more leader driven and disciplined than the Conservative Party. It remains to be seen whether Labour's landslide victory in 1997 will usher in a period during which, especially if the voting system is reformed, it becomes the 'dominant' ruler and shapes the agenda as Thatcher did.

Discussion points

- Compare the nature and effects of the recent changes in the Conservative and Labour annual conferences; does either have any real impact on policy formulation?
- To what extent does the Conservative party leader dominate his party organisation more than the Labour leader does his?
- Consider the arguments for and against state funding of political parties.
- Do we still have a two-party system?

Further reading

On party structure and internal politics, McKenzie (1963) is still a classic, although dated. Shaw (1996) and Garner and Kelly (1998) are good on more recent development in the two main parties. See also Kelly (1999, pp. 233–43) for the impact of parties. The work of Seyd and Whitely is essential for an understanding of party memberships.

References

Benyon, J. (1991) 'The fall of a prime minister', *Social Studies Review*, Vol. 6, No. 3.

Butler, D. and Kavanagh, D. (1980) *The British General Election of 1979* (Macmillan).

Butler, D. and Kavanagh, D. (1997) *The British General Election of 1997* (Macmillan).

Callaghan, J. (1987) *The Far Left in English Politics* (Blackwell).

Conservative Party (1998) *The Fresh Future. The Conservative Party Renewed* (CCO Publications).

Garner, R. and Kelly, R. (1998) *British Political Parties Today*, 2nd edn (Manchester University Press).

Giddens, A. (1998) *The Third Way* (Polity).

Jenkins, S. (1996) *Accountable to None* (Penguin).

Kavanagh, D. (1990) *Thatcherism and British Politics*, 2nd edn (Oxford University Press).

Kavanagh, D. (1994) 'Changes in electoral behaviour and the party system', *Parliamentary Affairs*, Vol. 47.

Kavanagh, D. (1995) *Election Campaigning: the New Marketing of Politics* (Blackwell).

Kelly, R.N. (1989) *Conservative Party Conferences* (Manchester University Press).

Kelly, R.N. (1995) 'Labour's leadership contest and internal organisation', *Politics Review*, February.

Kelly, R.N. (1999) 'The Hague effect', *Politics Review*, February.

McKenzie, R.T. (1963) *British Political Parties* (Heinemann).

Minkin, L. (1980) *The Labour Party Conference* (Manchester University Press).

Minkin, L. (1992) *The Contentious Alliance* (Edinburgh University Press).

Norton, P. (1990) 'The lady's not for turning: but what about the rest?', *Parliamentary Affairs*.

Norton, P. (1998) 'Electing the leader: the Conservative Party leadership contest 1997', *Politics Review*, April.

Pattie, C., Johnston, R. and Russell, A. (1995) 'The stalled greening of British politics', *Politics Review*, February.

Rose, R. (1984) *Do Parties Make a Difference?*, 2nd edn (Macmillan).

Seldon, A. and Ball, C. (eds) (1994) *Conservative Century: The Conservative Party since 1900* (Oxford University Press).

Seyd, P. (1987) *The Rise and Fall of the Labour Left* (Macmillan).

Seyd, P. and Whiteley, P. (1995) 'Labour and Conservative Party members compared', *Politics Review*, February.

Shaw, E. (1996) *The Labour Party since 1945* (Blackwell).

Stark, L. (1996) *Choosing a Party Leader* (Macmillan).

Whiteley, P. and Seyd, P. (1994) *True Blues* (Oxford University Press).

Chapter 13 Pathways into politics

Michael Moran

Learning objectives

- To understand the connection between the idea of democracy and **political participation** and recruitment in Britain.
- To understand why some people participate in politics and others do not.
- To understand why some people are recruited into positions of political leadership and some are not.
- To understand how participation and political recruitment have been changing in Britain.

Introduction

The great American President Abraham Lincoln (1809–65 and President 1861–5 during the American Civil War) offered what has probably come to be understood as the best known definition of **democracy**: 'Government of the people, by the people, for the people'. But what does government by the people involve? The great traditions of republican government which helped inspire American democracy originated in the city republics of ancient Greece – in communities where it was possible to gather all citizens together into a single forum to make important decisions. That is plainly not possible in a political system like the United Kingdom, governing as it does nearly 60 million citizens. Yet popular participation is central to democracy: that is signalled both in the Greek root of the word and in our everyday understanding as epitomised by Lincoln's definition. What sort of participation exists, and what sort is possible in a system claiming, as does the United Kingdom, to be democratic? That is the central question answered in this chapter. We look at three issues in particular: what patterns of popular participation exist; who is recruited into political leadership, and how; and what changes are taking place in patterns of participation and recruitment? These issues do not provide the full picture of participation but seeking answers to them will illustrate two of its most important features: on the one hand, what opportunities exist for ordinary citizens, as distinct from professional politicians, to take part in political life; and who gets recruited into the very top levels of elected office, in the House of Commons and thus into government.

Democracy and participation

Democratic politics in Britain involves a complex mixture of direct and indirect participation: citizens can intervene directly in politics; or they can be represented indirectly by others whom they select.

The single most striking feature of direct participation is its rarity: in particular, only a tiny minority of the population consistently take part in politics to a high degree. Table 13.1 draws on the most authoritative study of political participation to illustrate the point. The table shows popular participation to have two important features. First, the most common forms of participation are infrequent and/or sporadic: they take the form of voting in elections or signing petitions. Second, participation that takes a significant commitment of time and effort – for example canvassing in an election campaign – draws in only a tiny minority.

Even these low figures overstate the extent of people's willingness to participate in politics. They report what a representative sample of the population claimed to do and, since participation is widely thought to be a good thing, there is evidence that people overstate what they do: for instance, the **turnout** in local elections and in elections for the European Parliament has never been anywhere near the figures suggested by these figures, and in the most recent European elections (1999) under a quarter of the electorate voted.

Table 13.1 Percentage of population who have engaged in different forms of participation

	'Yes'/at least once (%)
Voting	
1. Vote local	68.8
2. Vote general	82.5
3. Vote European	47.3
Party campaigning	
4. Fund raising	5.2
5. Canvassed	3.5
6. Clerical work	3.5
7. Attended rally	8.6
Group activity	
8. Informal group	13.8
9. Organised group	11.2
10. Issue in group	4.7
Contacting	
11. Member of Parliament	9.7
12. Civil servant	7.3
13. Councillor	20.7
14. Town hall	17.4
15. Media	3.8
Protesting	
16. Attended protest meeting	14.6
17. Organised petition	8.0
18. Signed petition	63.3
19. Blocked traffic	1.1
20. Protest march	5.2
21. Political strike	6.5
22. Political boycott	4.3
23. Physical force	0.2

Source: Parry et al., 1992, p. 44

Apathy and British politics

Who cares about politics? The popular view is that it is dull, politicians are all the same and nothing changes. The preoccupation now is the pursuit of personal happiness – how much money you can earn and how well your personal life is going are Britons' main concern. To attend a political meeting or worry about politics is for anoraks and sad people with no other interests. Hence the fall in voter turnouts for last Thursday's European elections.

Yet politics represents the best of what it can mean to be a citizen. To gain power and to use it in the public interest are at the heart of democracy. The right to vote was hard won, and the wide agreement that politics and public affairs are increasingly dull, even purposeless, is to devalue our society. We are more than pleasure seekers.

It will be objected that the European elections, to a distant and controversial European Parliament, are scarcely a litmus test, but, if so, why was the turnout so much higher five years ago? Why are local election turnouts falling? Why are all branches of the media less and less confident that political coverage and analysis of public policy is what their audiences want?

Source: The Guardian, editorial, 17 June 1999

On this evidence the British are not political animals; only a minority, the **active minority**, give a substantial part of their life over to political participation. Who are these people, and how do they differ from the majority of citizens? Some of the correlates of high participation are unsurprising: education, income and occupation are all implicated. The patterns of inequality in the distribution of resources outlined in Chapter 3 are partly reproduced in patterns of participation: those who participate most tend to have higher than average levels of education and higher than average income and are disproportionately from professional occupations. But the words 'tend to' and 'partly' are very important here; the authoritative study of participation in Britain by Parry and his colleagues shows that there is no simple connection between wealth, education and participation (Parry *et al.*, 1992). At every level of British society, even among those groups most disposed to take an active part in politics, only a minority do so. More university professors than university porters take part in politics, but even among university professors politics is still a minority taste. Parry and his colleagues found that just half the population took part only in one activity, voting, which of course happens infrequently. By contrast, they identified a core of 'complete activists', who make up only 1.5 per cent of the population (just over 600,000). This is an absolutely large number of people. They are a minority, vital for the health of democracy, for whom politics is a consuming passion – the political system's equivalent of obsessive stamp collectors or snooker fanatics. But participation in snooker, billiards and pool is actually much commoner than participation in politics: about 20 per cent of men, and 4 per cent of women, play these games (Office of National Statistics, 1999, p. 218). Viewed thus, politics counts as a small minority sport.

Democracy and non-participation

The politically active citizen is in a small minority, and that fact is a problem in achieving government 'by the people'. But it is a problem that may be soluble because the overwhelming majority of the people participate sporadically, and through elections help to select some of the representatives who ensure indirect participation. But for the effectiveness of democracy an even more troubling feature is that part of the population – a minority – take no part in politics at all. It is not easy to get a clear picture of those who are completely excluded – or who exclude themselves – from all political participation, since one of the main means of studying who takes part in politics is the mass survey – and those who avoid politics are precisely those who are difficult to contact by surveys.

Some of the totally inactive present a problem for any theory of democracy which demands the active involvement of all citizens, but their inactivity need not itself be taken as a sign that the British system is malfunctioning. There is a minority in the population – found in all classes – who are so obsessed with some other pursuit, be it train spotting or opera, that they have neither the desire nor time to commit to politics in any form. They may be seen as the mirror image of the minority so obsessed by politics that they can commit to nothing else. Societies need these obsessives, otherwise train spotting, opera and democracy would die out. This random distribution of obsessives thus produces considerable social benefits.

Much more serious than the minority who rationally exclude themselves from all political participation are those who are excluded – particularly because the politically excluded also seem disproportionately to encompass those who suffer social, economic and cultural exclusion. We can begin to see why the problem is serious by considering some of the more obvious sources of exclusion. Consider the commonest form of participation, voting. To vote one must first be on an electoral register. An absolutely large number of adults are excluded by virtue of committal to institutions, notably prisons and mental hospitals. Britain has one of the largest prison populations in Europe: in 1997 the figure was 70,000. Prisoners are legally debarred from voting, and face considerable obstacles in participating in other ways. The social mix of the prison population is not a cross-section of the population: prisons form a concentration of the poor, the least well educated (including the illiterate), the unskilled, those unable to get any sort of job and those with mental and physical health problems. In the prison population we see the most extreme and most visible (because confined in a state institution) bit of the iceberg of the politically excluded. Outside prison another substantial excluded group are the homeless. The homeless are legally excluded from the commonest form of participation, voting, since to vote requires registration, and to register requires a fixed abode. The very nature of homelessness makes an accurate estimate of the numbers difficult. However, in a national survey of the mid-1990s 6 per cent of all households reported some experience of homelessness in the preceding decade. In other words, being homeless is not a great rarity. The social profile of the homeless is also, unsurprisingly, distinctive: for instance, 30 per cent of lone parents with dependent children reported some experience of homelessness (Office for National Statistics, 1998, p. 179). Weir and Beetham estimate that in all somewhere between 2 million and 3.5 million people are disenfranchised at any one time (Weir and Beetham, 1999, p. 41).

All this adds up to a pattern which is problematic for democracy: exclusion from labour and housing markets goes with political exclusion. Exclusion from the system could lead to a build-up of frustration at not being heard, something to which some commentators attributed the inner city riots in the early 1980s. Beyond these visibly excluded groups is a less easily measurable world of political exclusion, but the weight of circumstantial evidence overwhelmingly points to the conclusion that those who take no part in politics are usually the poorest of the poor (see concluding comment to Section 1 by David Piachaud). Whether some other mechanisms of democratic politics can remedy these exclusionary features is considered later in this chapter.

Democracy and political recruitment

Political participation as an active citizen is one thing; being recruited into a full-time political position is another. But **political recruitment** of the latter kind is central to the workings of democracy in Britain for a reason we have already encountered: the scale and complexity of governing the United Kingdom means that, inevitably, there has to be some political specialisation; a minority has to make a career out of political leadership. That is the essence of representative democracy. How well the mechanisms of political recruitment function is therefore a critical matter as far as the evaluation of British democracy is concerned.

Getting citizens to participate voluntarily in politics is, we have seen, a difficult business. But in the case of recruitment to full-time elected office, 'many are called but few are chosen' – there are far more aspirants than there are places. The most important gateway into this kind of political leadership is via a seat in the House of Commons, and the only realistic way into the House of Commons is through competing as the candidate of a leading political party. Competition for party nomination is intense. If we focus on the very top of the political tree – the leading positions in Cabinet, for instance – we find that, by the time people get there, a drastic process of selection has taken place.

It is instructive to begin with the very apex of democratic leadership in Britain – the Prime Minister, and the Office of Leader of the Opposition, who is only a single general election victory away from being Prime Minister. Consider the occupants of these positions in 1999. At first they look like a study in contrasts, and surprising contrasts at that:

- Tony Blair, Prime Minister and Leader of the Labour Party, the Party that has its roots in the trade union movement and the working class, is the product of a 'public' fee-paying school, Fettes, the Scottish 'Eton'.
- William Hague, Leader of the Conservative Party and Leader of the Opposition, the Party that historically has been linked to the aristocracy and to the business community, is the product of a comprehensive school in industrial West Yorkshire.

In fact these contrasts are quite misleading. What is striking about the careers of both is the way they exemplify the common influences now shaping the path to top elected positions in Britain:

- Both are effectively lifelong **professional politicians**: Blair was briefly a barrister, and

Hague briefly a management consultant, but these were merely transient occupations while they sought a seat in Parliament.

- Both started young in full time elected office: Blair was elected to Parliament aged 30, Hague aged 31.
- Both are graduates of elite universities – the same (Oxford), as it happens, although a range – Oxford, London, Edinburgh, Glasgow – serve as a gateway into professional politics. It is university rather than school which now marks out elected political leaders in Britain: Blair is the first public-school-educated leader of the Labour Party since Michael Foot (1981–3) and Hugh Gaitskell (1955–63); ironically perhaps, the last public-school-educated leader of the Conservative Party was a substantially longer time ago – Sir Alec Douglas-Home, 1963–5. Conversely, since the mid-1950s the Labour Party and the Conservative Party have each produced only one leader who did not attend university (Labour, James Callaghan; Conservative, John Major).
- Both are men. Although 120 women were elected to Parliament in 1997, as recently as 1983 the figure was a mere 23.
- Both are white and – despite Blair's Scottish education – both are English.

We can expect party leaders, by virtue of their success in ascending to the very top, to be exceptional. But they nevertheless illustrate in a particularly clear form the single most important fact about elected political leadership as an occupation in Britain: it is a full-time profession, demanding total dedication and extremely difficult to combine with any serious, long-term commitment to any other job. That is a great change from a generation ago when politics could be combined with another occupation. This is one of the keys to understanding the recruitment process. It is helpful to think of the road to the top as a bit like a long march by an army of hopefuls several thousand strong. By the time this young army reaches middle age all but the handful in or around the Cabinet have dropped out, exhausted or destroyed by the journey. The Labour Party leader and Prime Minister Harold Wilson (1963–76) was famously photographed as a child outside the door of No. 10 Downing Street; numberless others have been so photographed without coming near to entering through that door as Prime Ministers. They dropped out somewhere on the long march. Like an army losing soldiers the process of elimination is governed by a number of features – ranging from the initial suitability of those to the march in the first place, to sheer luck. Broadly speaking, in the early stages of the march those who fall out are marked by consistent features; as the march reaches its close sheer luck starts to have an important part to play.

The best way to appreciate this is to start with those who have made a successful start on the long march – who have actually managed to become elected full-time officials by virtue of being elected as Members of Parliament. This is the point at which most of those on the march to political leadership drop out, and for an obvious reason: there are only 659 seats in the House of Commons, and at any one election, because most incumbents are reselected, only a small number are actually available to new aspirants. With a few exceptions, election to the House of Commons has been the prime condition for achieving high political office in the United Kingdom. (The new devolved Assemblies in Scotland and Wales now offer an alternative route to governmental office.) But narrow though the passage is through which those on the long march to political leadership have to pass, it is narrower even than the figures for the size of the House of Commons would suggest. The chances of reaching and staying on the **front bench** are maximised by securing, at an early age, a safe parliamentary seat – and the number of these is, naturally, considerably smaller than the total of Parliamentary seats. William Hague, rather than Michael Portillo, is now leader of the Conservative Party almost certainly because Hague's seat is one of the safest in the country while Portillo's secure seat was not secure enough for him to survive the Labour landslide of 1997.

The 'gateway' into a seat in the House of Commons is very important to political recruitment, then, for a number of reasons. For all the evidence of the marginal role of the Commons itself to the making of policy, a seat in the House is virtually a condition of enjoying a career at the very top of national politics. The narrowness of the gateway makes this the key point at which most abandon the march to the top. Elections are dominated by parties: only one member – Martin Bell – of the current House of Commons is an independent, so any realistic chance of entering the House of Commons depends on securing a party nomination. In the two leading parties even nominations for hopeless seats are strongly contested, partly because contesting a hopeless seat is now a more or less compulsory apprenticeship for someone who aspires to nomination to a safe seat. Doing the rounds of local parties to secure nominations is the point at which some of the brutal realities begin further to weed out all but those most intensely committed. Although politics has become increasingly professionalised, it lacks many of the traditional features of a middle-class profession: hours of work are highly unsociable, and difficult to reconcile either with family life or with most second occupations; it is a highly precarious source of income; and, while the national parties do try to exert some influence over candidate selection, the final say is still lodged with activists within individual constituency parties.

This last fact helps explain some of the broad social characteristics of MPs as reflected in Table 13.2. Although some social skills – the ability to 'work a room', talking quickly and superficially to complete strangers – are important to potential MPs, most selection processes in constituencies put a high premium on speaking skills fostered by high levels of formal education and the practice of professions such as the law. Parliamentary politics is still a highly 'oral' occupation and the ability to speak well in public is a highly valued skill. Those who make the selection at constituency level are able to make choices that reflect their preferences, both open and unacknowledged. These preferences go some way to explain the makeup of the House of Commons. As Table 13.3 shows the representation of women in Parliament is low by international standards. Some of this is structural: the everyday demands of political life are difficult to reconcile with roles still traditionally performed by most married women, such as childbearing and homemaking. But some is due to the fact that local selection committees often do not wish to select women as candidates – a prejudice that was both more open and more extensive in the past, but which continues powerfully to influence the makeup of Parliament (Norris and Lovenduski, 1995). Likewise, open or unrecognised prejudice against some ethnic minorities, notably against Afro-Caribbeans, helps to explain why the proportions of those in Parliament are well below proportions in the wider population.

Once through the very narrow passage of a safe Parliamentary seat – especially if it is acquired while someone is still in their thirties – the path to the top becomes considerably easier. The odds of reaching the front bench, especially in government, are not long. A government needs to fill over 100 Ministerial offices. At any one time, a proportion of the parliamentary party will be ruled out – by manifest incompetence, some serious problem in private life, age (it is increasingly rare for someone to be given office for the first time once they have passed 50) or the fact that they have fallen foul of the leadership. The simple staying

Table 13.2 Selected characteristics of Labour and Conservative Members of Parliament, 1997 general election (per cent of total for each party)

	Labour Party	**Conservative Party**
University education	66%	81%
Professional or business occupation	54%	76%
Manual worker	13%	1%

Source: Butler and Kavanagh, 1997, pp. 203–5

Table 13.3 Women's share of seats in a selection of popularly elected chambers, 1997 (%)

Sweden	40.4
Norway	39.4
Finland	33.5
Denmark	33.0
Netherlands	31.3
New Zealand	29.2
Austria	26.8
Germany	26.2
Iceland	25.4
UK (House of Commons)	18.2

Source: Weir and Beetham, 1999, p. 74

power guaranteed by a safe seat thus gives the ambitious a advantage. Beyond that, the pathway to the top starts to depend on a large number of difficult to control circumstances. Connections and patrons help, especially in getting a foot on the lower rungs of the ladder. Luck (being available when some accident, scandal or resignation causes a vacancy) plays a part. John Major's route to the top was cleared by a succession of events in which he had no direct role: two important Cabinet resignations and then Mrs Thatcher's defeat in a leadership election within the Conservative Party. Finally, physical and mental robustness are very important. At the top political life is extraordinarily stressful. The successful need a physical constitution able to cope with long, odd hours, little leisure or exercise and the temptation to overindulge in rich food and drink. It helps to be clever to survive at the top but it is essential to be physically strong; any physical weakness will soon show itself, and any serious ill health is virtually a certain bar to office. At the very top Prime Ministers tend to be very robust: every post-war Prime Minister has survived into advanced old age, bar only Major and Blair who have yet to live that long. It is also essential in British government to have a particular mental makeup. Political life is so intensely adversarial that anyone near the top will be subject to constant criticism and hard questioning. A tendency to self-doubt, or an inability to shrug off personal attacks, is almost as fatal to success as physical ill health. Perhaps this last was one of Major's weaknesses. Getting to the very top – to be Prime Minister or Leader of the Opposition – is then heavily influenced

BOX 13.1 MINI BIOGRAPHY

Neil Hamilton (1949–)

Disgraced former Conservative trade minister. Educated Aberystwyth University and Cambridge, he was elected for Tatton in 1979. A rightwinger, he rose to the rank of junior minister but was accused by Mohamed Al Fayed, the owner of Harrods, of accepting money for asking questions in the House and other favours such as free hotel visits to the Paris Ritz. Hamilton sued but abandoned his case through lack of funds. Forced to resign from ministerial post but protested innocence. In 1997 election he was opposed by anti-sleaze candidate Martin Bell and was sensationally beaten by an 11,000 majority in a rock-solid Tory seat.

BOX 13.1 IDEAS AND PERSPECTIVES

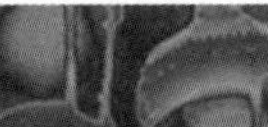

How to get to the top in British politics

Be born a male

Be born white and English

Go to university

Start early: enter Parliament before the age of 35

Get a safe seat

Acquire a powerful patron, preferably in the Cabinet

Never suffer serious illness; if you must, conceal it

Have a large ego: never suffer self-doubt

Be lucky

by chance. Political life is full of ex-future Prime Ministers who looked certainties for the top job but who never made it; by contrast, it would have been impossible to predict the identity of the last three leaders of the Conservative Party (Thatcher, Major, Hague) even a year before they took office: Thatcher emerged in a short time as a complete outsider to depose her predecessor, Heath; Major was the beneficiary of blood letting at the top of the Conservative Party and Mrs Thatcher's unexpected defeat; Hague looked a decade away from the leadership until the 1997 election removed the obvious heir apparent, Portillo, from Parliament. The path to political leadership is a wearying and exhausting long march for which very few citizens are equipped.

But does it matter whether the pool – the House of Commons – from which our rulers are drawn is not wholly representative? Does our legislature have to reflect all sections of society? Advocates of democratic reform often argue that the more representative a government institution the more democratic it is. Enoch Powell, the scholarly eccentric Conservative MP and theorist, disagreed:

> The House of Commons is not a composite photograph of the people; it is a representation of them for a specific purpose, set out in a writ by which we are summoned . . . by the breath of the sovereign to send good men and true to 'advise and consent'. In order to do that each locality sends . . . one representative who is identified with and speaks for a locality. So the House of Commons is a geographical expression of the nation. That indeed is the origin of its name, 'the House of the "communities", where all the communities in the realm are spoken for by the person whom they have sent to say "Yes" or "No"'. (E. Powell, *Teaching Politics*, May 1982)

Referendums

It ought to be mentioned also that referendums have become an increasingly important part of participation in British politics. All those entitled to vote can do so in such elections although the turnout can be variable. In 1975 one was held to decide on continued membership of the European Community – it delivered a two-to-one majority in favour of staying in. Later in the decade referendums were held within Scotland and Wales on the subject of devolution. The results were insufficient to legitimise the intended measures but those in 1997 were and on the strength of them assemblies were elected in 1998. Future referendums may be held on whether Britain should change its voting system and on whether it should enter the EU's single currency.

Changing patterns in participation and recruitment

The preceding two sections are designed to give a couple of 'snapshots' of pathways into politics – the pathways by which citizens who are not committed to a political career nevertheless participate in political life; and the pathways by which those with aspirations to full-time elected office make their way to the pinnacle. But as important as any snapshot is some sense of how things are changing over time. The evidence is that changes, both as regards participation and as regards political recruitment, are having contradictory effects – in some ways opening up new pathways to politics, in some ways closing them off.

What features are weakening and what strengthening democratic participation?

Factors making democratic participation weaker

Some state policies have raised the barriers to participation. An obvious example is the aftermath of the Community Charge. In the late 1980s and early 1990s large scale popular resistance to the Community Charge (the 'poll tax' designed to replace rates on domestic property) was accompanied by large-scale evasion – one of the commonest means of which was simply not to register on the electoral register. Even after the repeal of the Community Charge this has probably produced a permanent disfranchised minority. The very fact that many of those who fail to register are engaged in hiding themselves from the state makes estimate of the numbers difficult, but there are almost certainly at least one million potential voters excluded in this way.

The decline of trade unionism, especially among manual workers, has also made participation more problematic for manual workers. Total membership of trade unions has fallen sharply in recent years. Moreover, this fall has been disproportionately concentrated in unions in heavy industries employing, predominantly, male manual workers. Active participation in unions was always confined to a small minority, but the decline of male manual worker trade unionism has significant implications for working class political participation. For the participating minority union activity was an exceptionally important channel not only in industrial relations but, through the unions' close connections with the Labour Party, in wider political life. The internal political life of unions was also a means by which groups of workers with little formal education acquired the skills that allow most effective participation – skills in public speaking, in running meetings and in organising groups. The decline of male manual worker trade unionism is probably the single most damaging social change as far as democratic participation in Britain is concerned.

Factors making democratic participation stronger

Although some public policies have made participation weaker, some have made it easier. The proliferation of candidates from minority parties at general elections is in part the result of a decline in the historic cost of running candidates. A parliamentary candidate in a general election must deposit £500 (refundable only if 5 per cent of the vote is received). The original amount was set in 1918, at £150: had that amount been maintained the deposit would in 1997 have been £3,000 (Butler and Kavanagh, 1997, p. 74).

An even more significant factor encouraging participation is the accumulation of the '**social capital**' on which much democratic participation draws. 'Social capital' refers, in this connection, to the existence of a well-developed network of associations which underpin democratic politics. As the damaging decline of manual worker trade unions shows, associations are critical to fostering participation in political systems – like that of the United Kingdom – where size and scale rule out much direct participation in decision making. The evidence both that associational life is becoming healthier and that associations are encompassing groups formerly excluded from participation is therefore important evidence in assessing the health of British democracy.

Table 13.4 Comparison of number of voluntary associations in Birmingham in 1970 and 1998

Type of association	Number in 1970	Number in 1998
Sports	2,144	1,192
Social welfare	666	1,319
Cultural	388	507
Trade associations	176	71
Professional	165	112
Social	142	398
Churches	138	848
Forces	122	114
Youth	76	268
Technical and scientific	76	41
Educational	66	475
Trade unions	55	52
Health	50	309
Not classified	–	75
Total	**4,264**	**5,781**

Source: Stoker et al., forthcoming

What is the evidence that these 'beneficial' changes are taking place? One striking sign is summarised in Table 13.4. This reports a comparison of two surveys of associational life in Britain's second city, Birmingham. Two features of this table are noteworthy: the much larger number of associations when the 1990s are compared with the 1960s; and the striking rise in the number of religious groups. In part the latter change is connected to immigration to Birmingham, but the experience of immigration is common to most of the large cities of the United Kingdom – so we can be pretty sure that we are picking up a national trend here. The connection between the renewal of 'social capital' and immigration also highlights another feature central to democratic participation: many of these groups cater precisely for those, like recent immigrants, who would otherwise find participation in conventional politics difficult. In other words, they are a powerful means of countering political exclusion.

Of course the groups that are counted in estimations of 'social capital' more often than not have little directly to do with political participation – churches being a good example. But just as trade unions were historically schools where members could learn the skills of organisation and participation, so the same can be said of churches. More directly, we know that organised denominations have historically been important means of political mobilisation: famously, the origins of the Labour Party owed more to Methodism than to Marxism. And the same pattern seems to be repeating itself with the newer groups: the study of Birmingham by Stoker and his colleagues shows that many of the new groups created since the 1960s are deeply involved in consultations over public policy, especially in the sphere of community relations (Stoker *et al.*, forthcoming).

The renewal of social capital has also brought into being other kinds of associations that are mobilising the previously excluded. One of the most graphic examples is provided by the case of the sick – traditionally, a weak group often very difficult to organise for the purposes of participation in politics. The very group who might be thought to have the greatest interest in shaping health policy was the most likely to be excluded from it. Wood has recently shown, however, that there has been a mushrooming of patient organisations: he paints a picture where numerous groups of patients, especially those suffering from long-term illnesses, are organising to an increasing extent: 88 per cent of the patient groups he identified had been formed since 1960 (Wood, 2000).

What explains this apparent transformation of the landscape of participation? Three forces are important:

Table 13.5 The rise of the environmental movement: membership of selected groups (United Kingdom, thousands)

	1971	1997
National Trust	278	2,489
Royal Society for the Protection of Birds	98	1,007
Greenpeace	–	215
Friends of the Earth	1	114
Ramblers Association	22	123

Source: Social Trends, 1999, Table 11.4

- First, long-term social changes have altered both the capacities and the outlook of the whole population. For instance, the long-term rise in the formal educational attainments of the population may be important since the likelihood of participation rises with education: in the mid-1960s only about 5 per cent of 18 year olds were in higher education; now the figure is above 30 per cent. Culturally, there has been an explosive growth in interest in the natural world and protecting the environment. As Table 13.5 shows, this been reflected in a huge growth in membership of environment-related organisations. Of course, few people join organisations such as the Royal Society for the Protection of Birds to campaign politically; but the growing resources of these organisations are used to *represent* the concerns of members – thus contributing to the second (indirect) form of representation.
- Second, advances in techniques of political organisation and in technology are making it easier to form and maintain groups. Pioneers in effective group organisation can be very quickly imitated: many of the campaigning groups of the 1990s – for instance, groups campaigning for the environment or for the disabled – are copying and adapting successful tactics, such as public demonstrations, from the 1960s and 1970s. Sometimes the transmission process is international: witness the success of the international environmental organisation Greenpeace, which did not even exist in the UK in the early 1970s. Meanwhile, the development of cheap desktop computing power makes the organisation of groups much easier than in the past: databases, mailing lists, targeted mail shots to raise support and money are all now within the reach even of relatively small, impoverished organisations. Growing popular access to the internet will make the electronic organisation of political movements even easier in the future.

- Third, these electronic and social developments have given a considerable spur to the growth of **political entrepreneurship**. Political life, like economic life, is a kind of marketplace; and just as successful entrepreneurs in economic life live by spotting and filling a gap for economic goods and services, the same can happen in political life. Entrepreneurs 'spot' a group who do not, or cannot, participate in political life, and either organise them to participate or organise a group to lobby on their behalf. Political entrepreneurship is a very important development since it is a key means by which the voice of the previously excluded, or the silent, can be heard in politics.

Changing patterns of recruitment

Two features dominate the pattern of change in political recruitment, if we compare the present with the pattern a generation ago:

- First, there has been a considerable narrowing of the social range in recruitment. A generation ago, two social groups now little represented in Parliament made up a sizeable proportion of the benches on the Conservative and the Labour side: on the former, a considerable group with established upper-class connections; on the latter, a considerable group who had spent part of their adult life as manual workers. The 'shorthand' signs of this were, on the one side, education at the most exclusive public school, Eton, and on the other occupation before entering Parliament: the 1997 General Election saw the lowest-ever number of Etonians (18 in all) returned to Parliament, while the percentage of Labour MPs who were manual workers was also the lowest ever (Butler and Kavanagh, 1997, pp. 204–6). Although strenuous efforts have been made in both leading parties in recent decades to 'democratise' their backbenches, the effect, curiously, has been to mould MPs into something like a single prototype regardless of party. The typical MP, almost regardless of party, is now a middle-class professional.
- This narrowing of the social range of political leaders is connected to a second development: the rise of the professional politician. Professionalism in this sense is the product of two sets of pressures. First, the demands of most professional occupations – in business or elsewhere – are now so great that it is virtually impossible to make a long-term success while committed to politics. Even if an individual does not set out to be exclusively committed to one or the other, fairly early in a career a decision has to be made to concentrate either on politics or on a chosen profession. Second, the demands of politics – especially parliamentary politics – now virtually rule out combining an active role in Parliament with a serious profession. Politics at this level is increasingly a full-time job, especially for the ambitious MP.

The decline of the working-class MP is due to more complex causes. It partly reflects the declining influence of manual worker trade unionism in the Labour Party, because these unions were powerful patrons of manual workers. It partly reflects social change: although manual workers are in decline in parliament, many of those with middle-class professional characteristics are 'meritocrats' from working-class families educated to university level. But the change is also due in part to the rise of politics as a full-time professional career. Professionalism makes early commitment to parliamentary ambitions even more important than in the past. The manual worker who made a mark in unions and then entered Parliament in fairly advanced middle age is much rarer than in the past.

Chapter summary

In this chapter we have seen that mass popular participation in British politics is limited, mostly, to occasional voting in a general election. Only a small proportion of the population take a sustained part in politics. Nevertheless, that proportion amounts to a large number of people. From this highly active group a tiny number are whittled down to choose political leaders. Some changes in recent years have limited popular participation, but some long-term social changes are making it easier to organise politically. At the top, however, the social range of political leadership has been narrowed by the rise of the professional politician.

Discussion points

- Can you think of any reforms that might make participation in politics more widespread?
- What are the advantages, and what are the disadvantages, of the rise of the professional politician?
- Is direct popular participation needed for effective democracy?

Further reading

Parry *et al.* (1992) is the most authoritative study of popular participation in Britain; Weir and Beetham (1999) is an attempt to sum up the present state of democracy; Norris and Lovenduski (1999) examine paths to the top in Britain.

References

Butler, D. and Kavanagh, D. (1997) *The British General Election of 1997* (Macmillan).

Norris, P. and Lovenduski, J. (1995) *Political Recruitment: Gender, Race and Class in the British Parliament* (Cambridge University Press).

Observer (1999) 'The power pack', *Observer Life Magazine*, 24 October.

Office for National Statistics (1998) *Social Trends 28* (Stationery Office).

Office for National Statistics (1999) *Social Trends 29* (Stationery Office).

Parry, G., Moyser, G. and Day, N. (1992) *Political Participation and Democracy in Britain* (Cambridge University Press).

Stoker, G., Maloney, W. and Smith, G. 'Social capital and urban governance: adding a more "top down" perspective', *Political Studies*, forthcoming.

Sunday Times (1999) 'The 500 most powerful people in Britain', *Sunday Times*, 26 September.

Weir, S. and Beetham, D. (1999) *Political Power and Democratic Control in Britain* (Routledge).

Wood, B. (2000) *Patient power? Patients' Associations and Health Care in Britain and America* (Open University Press).

Chapter 14 Devolution

Bill Jones

Learning objectives

- To place devolution in the context of 'core–periphery' theory.
- To explain the background of nationalism within the UK.
- To analyse the movements towards decentralised assemblies in the UK.
- To cover the story of New Labour's creation of the new assemblies and executives in Edinburgh and Cardiff.
- To anticipate some of the problems which devolution will cause including those associated with calls for a federal structure for the UK.

Introduction

At the end of the nineteenth century Britain lay at the centre of an empire upon which, famously, 'the sun never set'. After two debilitating world wars the ability of the UK to maintain its empire disappeared and it melted away in a series of independence negotiations during the 1940s, 1950s and 1960s. The rump of the original United Kingdom remained but faced further threats to its unity from the northern tip of its former possession, Ireland, together with the Celtic fringes of Scotland and Wales. Tony Blair's Labour government succeeded in devolving the over-centralised British state where his 1974–9 predecessor had failed so disastrously. However, in solving one problem Blair has discovered he has created the possibilies for several more.

Core–periphery theory

One of the more interesting ways of looking at devolution is the 'core–periphery' analysis which informs the writings of Michael Hechter (1975) and the late Jim Bullpitt (1983). These political scientists attempted to explain the pattern of political relationships between the centre of the UK political system – London – and the outer areas such as Scotland, Ireland and Wales using an 'internal colonialism' and a 'territorial politics' perspective respectively.

Four geographical zones were discerned: a core in the South-east; an 'outer core' comprising the Midlands, East Anglia and Wessex; an inner periphery made up by the South-west, the North and Wales; and an outer periphery – Scotland and Ireland. Steed (1986) argues that the Civil War was a triumph of the 'inner core' over the 'outer periphery'. Hechter argues that the process of statebuilding in the UK was similar to the process of imperialism used against other states to achieve dominance. He perceives four stages in the process:

1. There are advanced and less advanced groups within the state reflecting the spatially uneven wave of modernisation over state territory.
2. The more advanced core area seeks to reinforce its position through entrenching the power relationships between itself and the periphery.
3. The consequence of this is the political and cultural domination as well as economic exploitation of the periphery by the core.
4. Such relationships are counterproductive as the periphery sustains its character and eventually reacts against core dominance.

Bulpitt sees the dichotomy between the core and periphery as synonymous with 'court and country'. Initially the royal court was the centre of the core but later, when power moved away from the monarch, the core became the Cabinet. Later still it became a 'political–administrative community' of senior ministers and top civil servants. From this point of view the periphery was the rest of the country. Bulpitt also saw a key distinction between High and Low politics. 'High politics' comprised the major matters of state – foreign policy; managing the currency and the economy; internal security. 'Low politics' was what was left for the periphery. Inevitably High politics was conducted from the core centre while Low politics was entrusted to 'local elite collaborators'. In this way, so the theory goes, the periphery won itself a substantial measure of autonomy.

Such theorising is a stimulant to understanding the process of devolution, especially the phenomenon of Celtic nationalism as an expression of the periphery's surviving identity and rejection of the core. But to gain a more practical understanding some recent history needs to be surveyed, especially the provenance of nationalism.

Nationalism

Nationalism in the Celtic fringe had long histories reaching back to the time when there were separate Welsh, Scottish and Irish parliaments in the fourteenth, seventeenth and eighteenth centuries respectively. Throughout their subsequent subservience to England fierce national identities were preserved. Ireland received its independence in 1920 apart from the six counties in the north, which was given a devolved parliament it had not requested. Plaid Cymru (PC) in Wales and the Scottish National Party (SNP) were established during the interwar years although neither polled over 1 per cent in the 1945 election.

However, a subsequent growing feeling that the identities of their countries were being submerged and their economic interests ignored enabled the nationalist parties to gather some popular support and in 1966 the first Plaid Cymru MP was elected. A year later the SNP won the Hamilton byelection and perhaps this finally nudged the big parties to take some notice. In 1968 Mr Heath, at the Conservative Party conference in Scotland set up a committee to look at the possibility of an elected assembly. Labour, then in government, chose the same year to set up a Royal Commission under Lord Kilbrandon:

To examine the present functions of the central legislature and government in relation to the several countries, nations and regions of the United Kingdom.

The aim of the government, and possibly the opposition too, was to satisfy the Scottish and Welsh thirst for running their own shows without giving away the ultimate control which the parliament in London exercised. The Kilbrandon Commission did not really achieve this objective as it could not agree on the most desirable form of legislative devolution.

However, the idea of devolution had been implanted and both main parties hurried to pronounce it a 'good thing' before the 1974 elections. The SNP had worked hard to stake a claim for 'Scottish oil' and was rewarded with 22 per cent of the poll in Scotland. Labour, dependent on Scottish and Welsh seats for its wafer thin majority, was keen to keep potential nationalist voters happy. Its White Paper in 1974 offered Scotland 'substantial powers over the crucial areas of decision-making'. In the October election the SNP seized one-third of the votes, suggesting that even a slight swing to them would rake in the seats Labour needed in Westminster. Labour was thus locked into its devolution strategy by urgent political necessity. But the issue was highly contentious and the bill languished in committee stage until two separate bills were substituted and passed in 1978. But Labour had many opponents in its own ranks, enough of whom supported the crucial condition that 40 per cent of the Scottish and Welsh electorates had to support devolution in a referendum for the related legislation to go through. Labour had to force its measures through using the guillotine in the Commons to circumvent the extensive filibustering used by opponents. In the event the referendums were held in March 1979 but did not achieve the requisite levels. In Wales the result was a four to one defeat for devolution and in Scotland only 33 per cent for with 31 per cent against. The SNP actually precipitated Labour's eighteen-year absence from power by failing to offer support over a crucial vote of confidence in the Callaghan government. Once in power Margaret Thatcher reversed the acts in June 1979 and, in accord with the Conservative opposition to devolution, chose to ignore the issue completely. However, it did not go away and in many ways festered and grew acute, each case in its separate way during the Conservative governments 1979–97.

Ireland

Ireland was joined to the UK in 1800 by an Act of Union, partly to pre-empt any possible alliance with the forces of then enemy, France. Throughout the century the connection was a troublesome one and, after conceding Catholic Emancipation in 1828, the Westminster parliament had to contend with a noisy band of Irish Nationalists on its benches. For the last decade of the century and the first two decades of the next, Nationalists dominated the 103 Irish seats. Gladstone had decided in 1885 that Home Rule was the only solution, a policy which split his party and let in the Conservative and Unionist Party under Salisbury. In 1907 Sinn Fein was founded to advance the cause so nearly won under Gladstone. But the armed militancy of the Protestants in the northern counties of Ulster, supported by the Conservatives, raised the prospect of civil war. The upshot of the increasingly bloody conflict was the formation of the Irish Free State in 1921 which delivered independence to Ireland with the exception of six counties in the north which were to be administered via a devolved parliament at Stormont. However, the Protestants were unwilling to allow the substantial Catholic minority (40 per cent) in the province to exercise any significant power, resulting in the Troubles in the late 1960s which continue to the present day. The attitude of governments of both major parties has been to introduce a form of devolution which gives both the divided communities a decent share of the power to decide local issues. Several attempts to introduce 'power sharing' after 1972 failed. In 1999 the patience of first John Major and then Tony Blair (not to exclude his two Northern Ireland ministers, Mo Mowlam and Peter Mandelson) offered the best chance of a solution to date. However attempts to set up a power sharing executive failed and the Good Friday Agreement of 1998 awaited the requirement of the Unionists that the IRA begin to 'decommission' (disarm) their weapons. The new executive did manage to get established in December 1999 but David Trimble, the First Minister, pledged to resign if the IRA had failed to begin the process of decommissioning by February 2000. When this failed to happen the Northern Ireland Secretary Peter Mandelson suspended the process of devolution and resumed direct rule (see Chapter 30 for a more detailed analysis of the Northen Ireland issue).

Scotland

Union with Scotland occurred in 1707 but it was more by agreement than by conquest and Scotland retained strong elements of its identity including its own judiciary, church and educational system. Government of Scotland was essentially a local affair, mostly via boards based in Edinburgh with a provenance which pre-dated the Union. By the end of the nineteenth century a feeling had developed, nourished by an awareness that the scope of government had expanded rapidly, that the Scots should have a minister in the London 'core' to look after their interests. Prime Minister Salisbury wrote to the Duke of Richmond and Gordon, inviting him to become Secretary of State for Scotland, a post which had been formed to 'redress the wounded dignities of the Scotch people – or a section of them who think that not enough is made of Scotland' (Mitchell, 1999, p. 113). The scope of government grew exponentially during the next century and Scotland enjoyed in consequence substantial 'administrative devolution' issuing from Edinburgh rather than London. However, such recognition of Scottish distinctiveness was insufficient to assuage the demands of the SNP, especially when the Cabinet Minister in charge of Scotland was from a party which, after 1959, polled a minority of the votes at general elections. Under Thatcher the Conservatives' performance at elections was 31 per cent in 1979 to Labour's 42 per cent; 28 to 35 in 1983; 24 to 42 in 1987 and 25 to 39 in 1992. Given the distortions caused by the first past the post electoral system the distribution of seats was even more skewed against the party in power in London: 22 to 44 in 1979; 21 to 41 in 1983; 10 to 50 in 1987; and 9 to 49 in 1992. The Secretary of State for Scotland was therefore in an invidious position: in charge of a country where less than a third of voters had supported his own party.

In addition the Scottish Grand Committee, a House of Commons device set up to deal with Scottish legislative matters, had a role to play. Second and third readings of bills debates and the report stages of non-controversial bills were in this forum, often meeting in Scotland. Since 1981, when the committee was set up, it has comprised Scottish MPs. During the Conservative years it therefore reflected an opposition majority. This led Michael Forsyth, the Scottish Secretary in 1995, to point out that Westminster had an 'absolute veto' over Scottish business and the committee was not a 'Scottish Parliament' (Bogdanor, 1997, p. 26). This kind of rebuff only fuelled the Scottish sense of injury; something which happened many times during the 1980s. The poll tax, for example, was actually introduced first in Scotland and provoked resentment equal to that later experienced and better publicised south of the border. Nationalism benefited from the unpopular period of Thatcher followed by Major rule and the SNP's share of the vote grew from 12 per cent in 1983 to 22 per cent in 1992. The SNP, however, refused to join in the deliberations of the Scottish Constitutional Convention, set up in March 1989 following a report from the Campaign for a Scottish Assembly. The SNP decided a gathering which would not discuss political independence was not for them; the Conservatives, who opposed the very idea of devolution, also refused to participate. Mrs Thatcher always insisted the Scots were well looked after as they received proportionately more government spending per capita than those living in England.

Labour and Lib-Dem politicians therefore held sway although they were augmented by the Scottish TUC and CBI as well as the churches. The final report, *Scotland's Parliament, Scotland's Right*, was published in November 1995. This envisaged a parliament elected by a German style proportional representation system in which voters would have two votes: one for a conventionally elected constituency member and one for a 'top-up' list of members.

Of 129 MSPs seventy-three would be elected from Westminster consituencies by the first past the post system; the remaining fifty-six would be elected in groups of seven from the eight Euroconstituencies on a list basis to ensure the final result in terms of seats was more or less congruent with the distribution of votes between the parties. Parliaments would be fixed term and have the power to vary income tax by plus or minus three pence as well as spending a block grant allocation from Westminster. Parliament would have the power to legislate on home policies such as education, health, planning, environment, industry, housing, local government, arts and media, heritage and sport. Westminster would retain control over defence and foreign affairs, the constitution of the UK, some health issues including abortion, transport and safety, immigration, nationality, social security and the economy. In the 1997 election Labour polled 45.6 per cent of votes and took all the 56 seats; the Conservatives polled a mere 17.5 per cent and took not one seat.

Scottish Labour members were angry just before the election when Blair stepped in and announced there would be a referendum asking two crucial questions – did Scotland want:

1 an assembly?

2 an assembly with tax altering powers?

Blair was concerned that, just before a general election, voters might respond to the Conservative claim that there was no evidence the Scottish people really wanted such changes, especially what it had cleverly dubbed the 'tartan tax'. The result in the event on 11 September 1997 (see Table 14.1) reinforced Labour's policy convincingly with three-quarters supporting the parliament proposal and two-thirds the tax varying powers.

Elections to the Scottish Parliament in Holyrood Palace, Edinburgh, took place on 6 May 1999. The results are shown in Table 14.2 which also indicates how well the parties did in the two sections of the poll. Labour managed to accumulate fifty-six MSPs, nine short of a majority (feminists celebrated the fact that half of them were women). Conservatives managed eighteen seats (three women) on only 16 per cent of the vote; evidence the new PR system benefited them considerably. Lib-Dems mustered seventeen seats (only two women) on 14 per cent of the vote.

Table 14.1 The 1997 Scottish referendum results

	% of votes cast	% of electorate
Q1. Support a Scottish parliament?		
Yes	74.3	44.7
No	25.7	15.5
Q2. Support tax-varying powers?		
Yes	63.5	38.1
No	36.5	21.9
Turnout		60.2

Table 14.2 Votes and seats in the Scottish Parliament elections, 6 May 1999

Party	% votes (1st vote: 2nd vote)	Seats
Cons	15.6:15.4	18 (0 directly elected, 18 top-up)
Labour	39:34	56 (53 direct, 3 top-up)
Lib-Dem	14.2:12.5	17 (12 direct, 5 top-up)
SNP	28.7:27	35 (7 direct, 28 top-up)

BOX 14.1 **MINI BIOGRAPHY**

Alex Salmond (1954–)
Leader Scottish National Party. Educated St Andrews University. MP for Banff and Buchan from 1987. Led nationalist party in 1980s but was criticised for poor tactics during elections for Scottish parliament in May 1999.

Everyone expected that the election would create the need for a coalition unless Labour decided to govern as a minority administration. This option was unattractive to Donald Dewar, the Scottish Labour leader, as he faced a group of MSPs – including John McAllion MSP for Dundee East – in his own party who were opposed to parts of its programme. Consequently he negotiated an alliance with the Liberal Democrats. However, there was a catch. The Lib-Dems, the Tories and

BOX 14.2 **MINI BIOGRAPHY**

Donald Dewar (1937–)
First Minister of Scotland. Clever Scottish lawyer who rose to Cabinet rank before opting for the top spot in his native land, albeit in coalition with the Lib-Dems.

the SNP made an election pledge to abolish in Scotland the £1000 per year tuition fee which university students had to pay all over the UK since the Blair government introduced it shortly after coming to power in order to finance future expansion. To effect the alliance, the Lib-Dem's leader, Jim Wallace, insisted his pledge be redeemed. After a great deal of haggling the alliance was forged (or perhaps 'fudged'?) after an uneasy compromise whereby an independent commission of enquiry into the student fee problem was accepted for the time being. The result of the negotiations was a twenty-four page coalition agreement between Labour and the Lib-Dems. On 17 May 1999 'First Minster' Donald Dewar posed with his eleven Cabinet colleagues together with eleven junior ministers. Wallace was given the deputy's role and another colleague a Cabinet post plus two junior appointments. Moreover Lord Steel, former Lib-Dem leader, was elected Speaker of the new parliament.

Donald Dewar of Labour prepares to lead the new Scottish Assembly (16 May 1999)

Back down south in Westminster John Reid was appointed to be Secretary for Scotland; his role was destined to be reduced dramatically after 1 July when the new executive formally took charge of domestic matters north of the border. On 16 June the new law making agenda for the Scottish Parliament – the first since 1707 – was announced by a be-suited Donald Dewar in a low key equivalent of the Queen's speech. The programme included some important proposals such as the abolition of the feudal rights of landlords and the giving of tenants on Highland estates the right to buy the land they worked. Otherwise it lacked anything major or even controversial: improvements in education; ethical standards for local government; the creation of national parks in Scotland (which, surprisingly, currently has none); and a transport bill allowing tolls on motorists using motorways or entering towns or cities. Compared with Westminster's annual programme of some twenty bills eight seemed a lightish load. *The Economist* (18 June 1999) concluded that Dewar was 'not at all anxious to stir up nationalist passions. He is keen that the Parliament should settle down and become preoccupied with routine political work which results in achievement'.

After decades of struggle the fight for a devolved assembly had been won. What political significance did the Scottish experience indicate?

- It seemed to validate the 'core–periphery' theory to the extent that the periphery had asserted itself loudly and often enough for action to be taken. It signalled the end of the Union as we knew it and the inception of a new kind of politics.
- Part of this new politics was the use of PR and the appearance of coalition government in the UK for the first time, formally, since the Second World War.
- The experience has probably made voting reform less likely to take place as it seems to have strengthened its opponents in the governing party: some were aghast that the automatic majority they had long enjoyed in the country had been sacrificed on the altar of a political experiment; others were irritated that the Lib-Dems had been able to cause so much trouble in negotiating their deal with Labour.
- The existence of a First Minister and a surviving Secretary of State for Scotland has implanted a potential clash of responsibilities. Some suggest the Secretary of State for Scotland be scrapped and a new Cabinet Minster for constitutional affairs be set up with a brief to include Wales and Northern Ireland also.
- The lack of tax raising powers may inhibit the ability of the new set-up to do its job properly. As *The Economist* (6 November 1999) noted: 'In effect this new arrangement gives Scotland the ability to call the tune without giving it the wherewithal to pay the piper'.
- The establishment of a new power centre in Scotland is bound to precipitate political conflict betweem London and Edinburgh and give reason for the SNP to claim the only logical progression from the present is political independence and an end to the Union. Moreover the SNP is now the official opposition in Scotland; in democracies it normally follows that oppositions eventually get to exercise power. What would the SNP do if it were to win such power?
- So far there seems no solution to the West Lothian Problem (see Box 14.1).
- The existence of the Scottish parliament raises the question of whether the proportionately greater numbers of MPs – seventy-two – than England should be reduced. John Reid, the replacement Scottish Secretary, admitted the anomaly on 1 July and recognised the need for constitutional change in the light of the functions which MPs have surrendered to MSPs. Any such reduction – some suggest to below sixty seats – would threaten the ability of Labour to command majorities in the Commons. Both Wilson and Callaghan depended for their majorities on their Welsh and Scottish MPs as they had no majority in England.
- There are a number of potential friction points between the two parliaments. For example Scotland can decide on its own priorities when it comes to spending its £15 billion budget but will this be possible if they are different from Whitehall or the government in power?

BOX 14.1 IDEAS AND PERSPECTIVES 

The West Lothian question

In the 1970s Tam Dalyell MP asked whether it is possible to devolve powers to just one area of a country which otherwise remains a unitary state. He pointed out that after devolution Westminster MPs would no longer be able to vote on issues such as education in West Lothian while Scottish MPs would be able to do so in West Bromwich. This would give Scottish MPs an unfair advantage and enable a Labour government dependent on Scottish MPs – as in 1964 and 1974 – for its majority to legislate in England and Wales. It has been argued that the existence of Ulster MPs between 1921 and 1972 did not cause any insuperable problems but against this it is pointed out that there were only twelve MPs involved.

William Hague, the Conservative leader, caused a storm in July 1999 when he suggested that Scottish and Welsh MPs should be banned from voting on purely English matters at Westminster. In justification he claimed that 'English consciousness'– evidenced by the St George flags and painted faces at World Cup matches the previous year – must have a 'legitimate outlet'. However, his use of the terms the 'time bomb of English national feeling' and 'the drums of English nationalism' not to mention the slogan 'English votes on English laws' opened him to the accusation that he was attempting to fan nationalist flames for political advantage. John Reid, Dewar's successor in the Cabinet, accused his solution to the West Lothian question of 'feeding the very resentment he claims he wants to avoid'. Another problem which the Hague solution would cause would be the fact that it would alter the majority available to the government. Suppose Scottish MPs represented the government's majority; then by withholding their votes on English matters they would render the government impotent. Furthermore, if Scottish MPs cannot vote on English matters then they would have no say in the fortunes of a neighbour whose progress is integrally linked to their own. The problem has existed since Gladstone (Bogdanor, 1997, pp. 33–7) and would indeed appear to be, as Michael Forsyth called it, 'The Bermuda Triangle of devolution' (Bogdanor, 1997, p. 38).

Wales

Most students of Celtic nationalism agree that a qualitative difference exists between Welsh and Scottish nationalism. Scotland has retained a fair amount of identity through its legal and educational system not to mention its own church. It also tended to emphasise economic aspects of its resentment against England: 'It's our oil' for example. Support for devolution was accordingly higher in Scotland as in the referendum result of September 1997. The cultural aspect of the movement seems not to be decisive; less than 2 per cent speak Gaelic. Welsh nationalism, on the other hand, has a long history of resentment against English cultural colonialism; Lloyd George smarted under the restrictions on speaking Welsh in school as a boy. Indeed the modern rise of nationalism in the country dates back to a broadcast made by the founder of Plaid Cymru (Party of Wales), Saunders Lewis, in 1962. He argued forcefully that the language had to be defended militantly and was more important than self-government itself. The Welsh Language Society was founded as a result of the broadcast and in 1967 the language was given official status and in the same year Gwynfor Evans was elected the first Welsh Nationalist member of parliament at a by-election in Carmarthen. The Free Wales Army was a tiny militant expression of the movement but the Sons of Glyndwr caused more of an impact through its policy of burning down holiday homes in Wales, insisting that they raised the cost of housing for

Welsh people. Another colourful aspect of the cultural divide between Wales and England is the rugby matches between the two countries where pride and passion combine, for the Welsh, to make them the major sporting events of any year. However, support for an assembly has been weaker in Wales. The referendum in 1979 saw 79.8 per cent of Welsh people voting against devolution and only 20.2 per cent in favour. During the 1980s this trend was reversed and support for the measure grew. All the Conservative Secretaries of State for Wales (a post invented in 1965) were MPs for English constituencies. Further, it was widely believed in Wales that the Conservatives, beaten electorally, had set up quangos, often headed by ex-Conservative politicians, to administer directly over issues once the preserve of elected Welsh local government. But when it came to the referendum in Wales in September 1997 support for devolution was still halfhearted. Only 50.12 per cent of the electorate voted in the first place; those in favour represented only 50.3 per cent to 49.7 per cent opposed: the thinnest of margins. The map in Figure 14.1 shows how support for devolution was strongest in the north and west with a broad eastern corridor adjoining England expressing opposition.

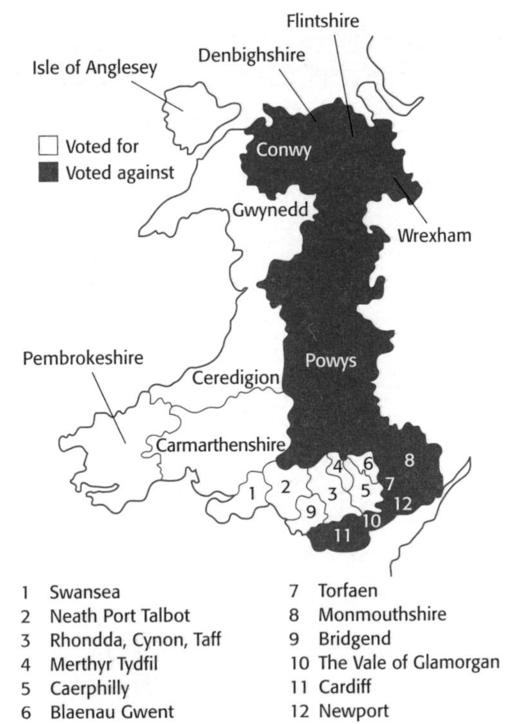

Figure 14.1 Support for Welsh devolution
Source: The Daily Telegraph, 20 September 1997

Between the referendum and the elections for the assembly an instructive passage of politics occurred. It had been assumed by everyone that the First Minister of Wales would be the Welsh Labour leader, Ron Davies. However, he resigned after a bizarre sequence of events in which he had been mugged by a man whom he had befriended on Clapham Common, a well known gay pick-up area. The whole country, especially the tabloid element of the press, was intrigued by this strange occurrence – and many jokes were cracked at Davies's expense – but it ultimately succeeded in ending the political career of the architect of Welsh devolution. Ever aware of the political costs of a gay politician in a country more known for its macho feats on the rugby field, Number 10 was content to see Davies consigned to relative political oblivion as a mere member of the assembly. When it came to his successor, however, Number 10 did not want the popular but allegedly 'off-message' Rhodri Morgan as replacement for Davies and worked hard – and some said using shameful 'old Labour' manipulations – to achieve the election of safe Blairite Alun Michael – the existing Secretary of State for Wales – as the Welsh leader and likely first minister. Come 6 May the Welsh voters delivered an unpleasant surprise to London's Labour elite.

Firstly the turnout indicated anything but a ringing endorsement of the new arrangements: only a quarter of the electorate bothered to vote. Even worse, the small turnout did no damage to the party which argues for complete independence. Plaid Cymru had a fabulous result winning seats in the traditional Labour heartlands of Islwyn, Llanelli and the Rhondda. As Tables 14.3 and 14.4 show Labour lost heavily compared with the 1997 election. The story was no better in the more English south west of the country where disaffected farmers helped force Labour to give way in Monmouth to the Conservatives. Ironically Labour's poor showing entitled them to one top-up seat in the Mid and West Wales area and this was the 'backdoor' through which the

Table 14.3 The Michael effect? (Welsh Assembly elections, %)

Party	First vote	Change since 1997	Second vote	Change since 1997
Labour	37.6	−17.1	35.4	−19.3
Plaid Cymru	28.4	18.5	30.5	20.6
Conservative	15.9	−3.7	16.5	−3.1
Liberal Democrats	13.4	1.0	12.6	0.2
Other	4.7	1.3	5.1	1.7

Source: John Curtice, CREST

Table 14.4 Welsh Assembly seats 6 May 1999

Party	Seats (direct:top-up)
Labour	28:1
Plaid Cymru	17:8
Conservative	9:1
Lib-Dems	6:3

little-lauded Welsh Labour leader, Alun Michael, crept into the Assembly.

Initially it seemed that Mr Michael was exploring the possibilities of coalition with the Lib-Dems but eventually Labour, so used to ruling the roost in Wales, decided to govern as a minority party. This was not as risky a path as it might at first seem as both Plaid Cymru and the Lib-Dems have a vested interest in making a success of the little supported new assembly. Rhodri Morgan, Michael's leader-

The Welsh electorate vote narrowly for devolution (21 September 1997)

ship rival, was given responsibility for economic development and Europe – something likely to keep him both happy and quiet. Michael's predecessor Ron Davies was bitterly disappointed to be excluded from the Cabinet but given the chairmanship of the economic development committee. However, he even lost this consolation prize when revelations that he was receiving therapy for obsessive 'risk taking' led, sadly, to his resignation.

The Welsh assembly, in line, perhaps, with the markedly lower level of enthusiasm for devolution in Wales, has fewer powers than the Scottish parliament. In theory at least it takes over responsibility for a £7 billion pa budget and the functions of the old Welsh Office including education, health, local government, housing, planning, agriculture, environment, industry and training, culture and sport. But its responsibilities will not extend, for example, to teacher training policies, nor is it able to pass primary legislation or raise taxes. It can, though, introduce or amend statutory instruments, the important regulations which amplify the often outline 'delegated' legislation from Westminster. As *The Economist* noted on 3 July 1999 the Welsh Secretary had to approve some 500 such instruments a year in the past; in future the Assembly may want to amend or reject these as well as pass its own. There remains a vestigial Welsh Secretary in the Cabinet – Paul Murphy – as there is for Scotland. Most experts agree that the exact division of powers between Cardiff and London is unclear. 'Whereas the Westminster Parliament remains theoretically sovereign, the Assembly derives its powers from the Government of Wales Act. So it will need to demonstrate, for each decision it takes, that it is acting within its powers' (*Economist*, 3 July 1999).

The balance of power between centre and periphery is currently being worked out, especially via the new 'subject committees'. These contain the Cabinet minister plus members from all parties and meet once a fortnight in the company of civil servants. In theory these committees are only advisory but their frequency and influential membership give them a potential beyond that role. Welsh devolution hit a major crisis in February 2000 which challenged Blair's much criticised placeman, Alun Michael. Wales qualified for so-called Objective One category funds from the EU but the grants could only be made in the event of matching funding from the UK Treasury (given that Wales cannot raise any taxation itself). Michael claimed he was confident of raising the cash but Plaid Cymru demanded a guarantee on pain of a no confidence vote. Given that Labour have only 28 Assembly members and the Conservatives and Liberal Democrats were supporting Plaid, the answer was a foregone conclusion. Michael preempted the vote by resigning and the Labour group was able to elect its populist favourite Rhodri Morgan instead as acting First Secretary. With the well known independently minded Morgan in control the opposition parties were less likely to create problems; they agreed to accept his new position and he was elected unopposed on 15 February. Surprisingly, given his earlier opposition Tony Blair changed his tune on the man he had used every trick to keep out of power; now it seemed Rhodri was not a problem. As a result of the crisis Welsh Labour got the man it had always wanted and the future of devolution was restored. Whether Blair's was a genuine change of heart or the best spin No 10 could put on a situation it could not change is anyone's guess.

The Welsh experience of devolution offers the following political features:

- Whilst the opposition parties are keen to make life difficult for Labour their minority administration was sustained to some extent by the reluctance of the opposition to undermine the viability of the assembly in its early stages.

BOX 14.3 MINI BIOGRAPHY

Daffydd Wigley (1945–)
Leader Plaid Cymru 1981–4 and 1991 onwards. Educated Manchester University after which he worked in industry before entering Commons as nationalist MP. Leads his group in the Welsh assembly and hopes to improve on creditable election performance in June 1999 when Plaid Cymru won support at the expense of Labour.

- The Welsh Assembly was already, in the autumn of 1999, pressing for more powers to place it on a par with the Scottish Parliament.
- Tony Blair made much of how devolution would entail a decentralisation, or giving away of power from Whitehall; an answer to critics who accuse his style of being obsessively centralised. However, Westminster still retains much power over Welsh affairs and the centre displayed a somewhat undemocratic concern to choreograph the selection of people it liked in local leadership roles and to block those it did not like.
- Such interference can backfire badly as the elections to the Assembly revealed with Labour strongholds being stormed successfully by the nationalists. Nationalist sentiment is very sensitive to such attempts and, as in the case of Ireland, full scale revolt can be the consequence.
- Mere legal powers cannot determine how power relationships in practice work out; witness the possibility that the subject committees are forging a unique new legislative/executive role for themselves.

Devolution and the EU

Devolution has complicated further the UK's relations with the EU; a number of new potential points of conflict have emerged. For example Scotland provides over half of the UK's fishing industry but it will be the UK government which leads negotiations in Europe. That is not to say, however, that a Scottish minister might not be briefed on the fishing issue and be a key player in the UK negotiating team in Brussels; similar things happen to the German *Länder* in some cases.

It remains the case that London will still decide on the boundaries of the poorer areas which qualify for EU assistance. However, devolved parliaments and executives will have the duty of implementing the mandatory EU directives. There is no doubt that the relations of devolved assemblies to the EU will be asymmetrical. Scotland is some way ahead of Wales and Northern Ireland in relating to the EU institutions. Through the Scottish Office it has been active in relation to the EU for many years and on a much more intensive basis than Cardiff or Belfast.

This imbalance is likely to continue with Scotland setting up a permanent office in Brussels in July 1999. In the case of Northern Ireland there is an assembly but at the time of writing no functioning executive. Some observers have noted that the collaboration necessary for the working of certain assistance schemes funded by Brussels has facilitated co-operation between the two estranged communities in the province. The development of the EU's regional policy may encourage English regions to seek assemblies in order to lobby more effectively for Structural Fund and other EU assistance.

The Economist on 6 November 1999 explains the wider significance of the EU for the nationalist movements. To the 'sneer' that small nations such as Scotland (5m) and Wales (3m) cannot cast themselves adrift in a 'lonely world', they point out that the nationalists 'do not plan to be alone: they want Scotland to become a full member of the EU in its own right . . . Without the EU there would be gaping holes in the nationalist case. How would an independent Scotland defend itself? What currency would it use? . . . The EU promises access to the world's richest market, a common money and eventually a common defence and foreign policy'.

The SNP has proposed a Scottish European Joint Assembly comprising MSPs and Scottish MEPs to co-ordinate Scottish dealings with the EU. 'In time' says *The Economist*, 'the nationalists hope people in Scotland and Wales will see their relationship with Brussels as more important than that with Westminster'. A survey published in the same issue tended to support this idea revealing that, in twenty years time, over a third of people living in these countries expected Brussels to 'have the most influence' over their lives and the lives of their children. See Tables 14.5, 14.6 and 14.7.

However, another aspect of the opinion poll should be noted. When asked which would be the most reliable ally in a crisis, only 16 per cent said Europe and nearly 60 per cent said the USA.

Table 14.5 Influence
In twenty years' time, which of these bodies, if any, do you expect to have most influence over your life and the lives of your children? (%)

	Britain	England	Scotland	Wales
My local council	13	14	5	7
Scottish Parliament/Welsh Assembly/my regional assembly	13	9	46	26
Westminster Parliament	22	23	8	25
European Parliament/ European Union	44	46	31	37
Don't know	8	8	10	6

Source: The Economist, 6 November 1999

Table 14.6 Regional identification
Which two or three of these, if any, would you say you most identify with? (%)

	Britain	England	Scotland	Wales
This local community	41	42	39	32
This region	50	49	62	50
England/ Scotland/Wales	45	41	72	81
Britain	40	43	18	27
Europe	16	17	11	16
Commonwealth	9	10	5	3
The global community	8	9	5	2
Don't know	2	2	1	0

Source: The Economist, 6 November 1999

Table 14.7 Flag identification
Which of these flags, if any, do you identify with? (%)

	Britain	England	Scotland	Wales
United Kingdom (Union Jack)	83	88	49	55
England (Cross of St George)	33	38	2	3
Scotland (Cross of St Andrew)	23	18	75	8
Wales (Welsh Dragon)	26	24	12	85
European Union (12 stars)	21	23	5	7
United States (Stars and Stripes)	23	26	7	<1
Don't know	2	2	0	1

Source: The Economist, 6 November 1999

England and its regions

Certain English people argue they have an immunity to anything as vulgar as mere patriotism. However, the evidence from history and other sources suggests there is a fervent nationalism just lurking beneath the surface in England. It may not be overtly stated but witness the mobilisation by Churchill of a sense of Englishness during the Second World War and the passionate national pride – sometimes an ugly manifestation – English football can elicit on the international stage. It seems English nationalism is most likely to express itself if people think the country is not receiving a fair deal. There are three possible ways in which devolution could prompt such an expression.

Firstly Scotland, Wales and Northern Ireland all receive more government spending per capita than England. The original formula for setting the block grants was set by Joel (now Lord) Barnett when Chief Secretary to the Treasury in the late 1970s. This formula was based on calculations that all three were on balance places of greater need than England and gave more spending per head in them than in England. Since then their economic performance has improved so that Scotland's GDP per head is almost up to the English level (see Table 14.8).

However, the differential in expenditure still remains as Table 14.9 and Figure 14.2 illustrate. Scotland receives 16 per cent more per head than England and Wales 23 per cent. Should the level of expenditure be reduced to that of England

Table 14.8 Relative cash gross domestic product per head, 1995

England	£10,324
Wales	£8,440
Scotland	£9,873
Northen Ireland	£8,410

Table 14.9 Government block grants 1997–8

Scottish Office	£14.3bn
Welsh Office	£6.9bn
Northen Ireland Office	£8.3bn

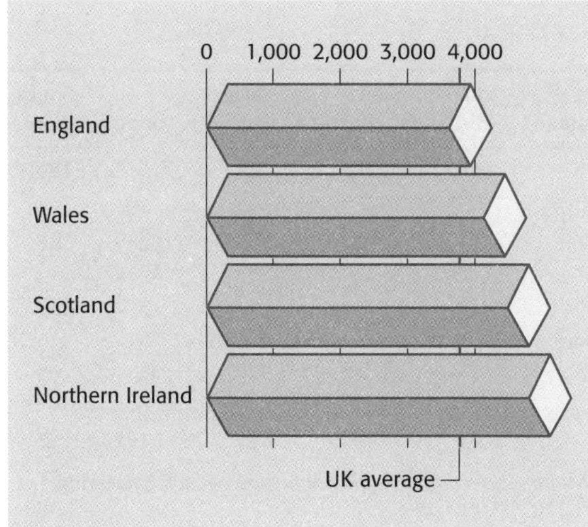

Figure 14.2 The English disadvantage
Source: The Guardian, 7 November 1999

Scotland would lose a massive £1 billion. Even its ability to levy 3p in the pound income tax increases would only bring in £450 million. So far the English regions have been relatively silent about the differential with the exception of Sir George Russell, Chairman of the Northern Development Company, who complained 'The Barnett formula is no longer necessary or just. We are now the poorest region in the UK' (see Table 14.10).

Secondly England might argue in time that it needs its own parliament to match the political representation of the Celtic fringe. This solution seems logical and would set up the conditions for the federal structure the Lib-Dems favour. However, the fatal flaw in the scheme is that England, with 80 per cent of the population and vastly superior economic strength, would dominate any such federation to an excessive degree.

Thirdly there is the famous West Lothian Question which questions why Scottish and Welsh MPs should vote on English matters when the reverse was not possible through devolution of powers (see Box 14.2).

Table 14.10 Regional performance since 1985

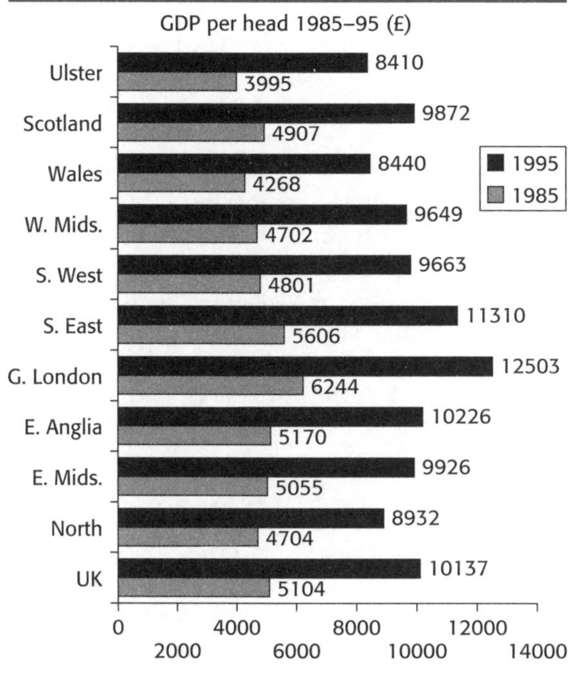

Source: Office for National Statistics, Economic Trends, 1997

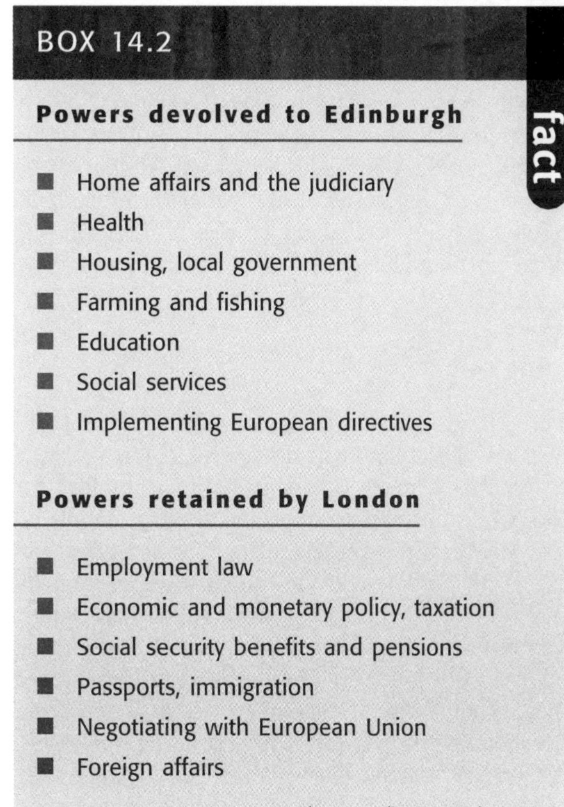

BOX 14.2

fact

Powers devolved to Edinburgh

- Home affairs and the judiciary
- Health
- Housing, local government
- Farming and fishing
- Education
- Social services
- Implementing European directives

Powers retained by London

- Employment law
- Economic and monetary policy, taxation
- Social security benefits and pensions
- Passports, immigration
- Negotiating with European Union
- Foreign affairs

Source: The Guardian, 20 July 1999

Table 14.11 The voice of the regions
Survey of public opinion on regional government

Region	All	North-East	North West/ Merseyside	Yorkshire/ Humberside	East Midlands	West Midlands	Eastern	South-East	London	South-West
Base	1,810	232	243	205	143	194	194	203	219	177
Can you tell me which region you are in?										
Right	78	89	97	66	79	91	52	88	60	86
Wrong	18	10	3	26	16	8	46	5	34	11
Don't know	4	1	0	8	5	1	2	7	6	3
Would you support or oppose your region of England, the . . . region, getting its own elected assembly?										
Net support	+7	+22	−2	+0	+5	+9	+1	−10	+39	+8
Do you agree that a regional assembly would look after the interests of this area better than central government?										
Net agree	+43	+51	+47	+51	+37	+41	+31	+31	+51	+55
Do you agree politicians elected to a regional assembly would be more trustworthy than politicians elected to Parliament at Westminster?										
Net agree	−12	−1	−23	−6	−8	−2	−26	−29	+1	+5
Do you agree that a regional assembly would lead to more bureaucracy than the present system of government in this region?										
Net agree	+31	+36	+36	+41	+33	+34	+33	+26	+20	+28
Do you agree this region is too divided for regional government to work well?										
Net agree	−3	−11	+4	+10	−3	+8	0	−12	−11	−7

Source: MORI, field work 25 February–8 March 1999; The Economist, 27 March 1999

William Hague, the Conservative leader, opened a potential Pandora's box in July 1999 when he suggested Scottish and Welsh MPs should be prevented from voting on Westminster issues pertaining to England alone (see Box 14.1 on the West Lothian Question).

Regions

The Kilbrandon Commission suggested that the regions of England should have elected councils to provide a more democratic accountability for those administrative functions already devolved. The suggestion was lost in the chaotic end to the 1970s devolution episode but has arisen again in the wake of the more successful 1990s experience. Labour promised to consider regional government in an *ad hoc* manner: 'Each area would be treated individually, with no single model imposed from the centre' (Bogdanor, 1997, p. 122). However, it is by no means clear that there is any really widespread demand for regional assemblies in England. As Table 14.11 reveals, large percentages of residents in England are unaware of the region in which they live. Moreover, similar majorities believe such assemblies would result in more bureaucracy in the region.

However, now the devolution genie has been let out of the bottle there is no guarantee that the regions might not begin to develop more self-awareness and to campaign for an assembly to match those in Cardiff and Edinburgh. The establishment of regional development agencies (RDAs) on 1 April 1999 was presented as a forerunner of a new kind of regional government involving elected assemblies. The hope behind the RDAs is that they will help to reduce the imbalance between the regions (see Table 14.12). At present Cornwall and South Yorkshire compare with the poorest regions in the EU such as rural Spain and Greece. The RDAs are run by twelve member boards drawn from business rather than local councils and employ staffs some 100 strong. They will share a budget of £1.3 billion – with another billion to be raised themselves from the private sector – and will be expected to spend it on urban regeneration and setting up business

Table 14.12 Capital gains: relative GDP per head[a] and unemployment

Region	GDP 1996	Claimant count % December 1998
North-East	85	7.3
North-West and Merseyside[b]	91	4.1 & 8.6
Yorkshire/Humberside	89	5.5
East Midlands	94	4.0
West Midlands	93	4.6
Eastern	97	3.2
London	140	5.1
South-East	107	2.6
South-West	95	3.4
Wales	83	5.4
Scotland	98	5.4
Northern Ireland	81	7.0

[a] EU15 average = 100
[b] Unemployment measured separately
Source: Eurostat; ONS; The Economist, 27 March 1999

parks. At present Whitehall has kept fairly tight control of the purse strings but they might slacken if regional assemblies became a reality.

How likely is this to happen? Clearly the government envisages the possibility of such a development – if the desire exists – but on this the signs are ambivalent to say the least. Surveys show that people in Scotland are strongly opposed to giving English regions greater powers. Of the publics in the regions substantial minorities do not even know in which region they live, especially those living in the east. Of those asked whether they favoured an elected assembly two registered negative responses, the most hostile being the biggest, the south-east. Further, few regions indicated that assemblies would look after their interests 'better than central government'. Moreover significant majorities believed regional assemblies would lead to 'more bureaucracy'.

However, if one region opts for an assembly and then other regions feel an advantage has thereby been gained, it is quite possible they too – aware of the considerable disparities between the regions – will begin to campaign for a general constitutional reform along these lines. The most likely region to press for an assembly is the north-east, by most indices the poorest. North-easterners have already expressed a sense of disadvantage in relation to Scotland, now able to support its pursuit of investment and expenditure with a parliament with legislative powers. John Tomaney, lecturer at Newcastle University and a supporter of the North East Constitutional Convention which campaigns for an elected assembly, is quoted in *The Economist* as arguing that 'This region has a semi-colonial relationship with England. It wasn't just the Scots and Irish who were conquered, it was also the North-East'. *The Journal*, a regional newspaper, pointed out in 1999 that 'Last year Scotland was able to spend £2.56 per capita on tourism compared to Northumbria Tourist Boards's 8p. And for every £100 spent on health services in the North-East, Scotland can spend £126'. *The Economist* (27 March 1999) comments that 'Many North-Eastern politicians argue that until the region gets its own assembly and first minister – to match Scotland's – its voice will be drowned out in Westminster and Brussels'.

Citizenship

Figure 14.3 reveals the clash of loyalties which characterise people living in the UK. People identifying 'very much' with Europe amount to only 7 per cent – as might be expected; those identifying at

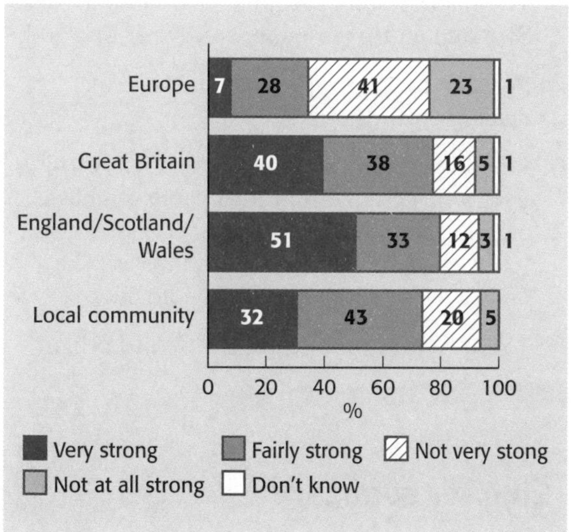

Figure 14.3 Citizenship: the strength of people's regional identification
Source: MORI, 1998

that intensity with Great Britain are 40 per cent – perhaps surprising for such a nebulous entity; 51 per cent for their respective countries within the UK – by far the greatest focus of loyalty and potentially a source of conflict once the assemblies settle down and acquire political confidence.

Problems associated with devolution

1. Possible clash between the assemblies and the House of Commons.
2. Tendency of the new governments to press for more and more resources from London and to press for greater powers to solve their problems.
3. Complaints by Wales that the Scottish parliament has an unfair advantage in terms of its legislative powers.
4. Possible clash between the First Ministers and the residual Secretaries of State in the Cabinet.
5. The possibility that devolution will not satisfy but merely whet the nationalists' appetite for more independence.
6. The disproportionate number of MPs in Scotland and Wales compared with England.
7. Possible friction with Westminster over dealings with the EU.
8. Possible barriers to uniform dealings within UK by objections from regional assemblies; e.g. ministers in Wales and Scotland refused to lift the ban on beef on the bone as they had received different medical advice.
9. The unsolved problem of the West Lothian question.

Chapter summary

Core–periphery theory provides a framework which offers an explanation of Westminster's dealings with the Celtic fringe and the English regions. The establishment of regional assemblies has a provenance in the original autonomy of Ireland, Scotland and Wales and the surviving sense of identity which flourishes in these countries. Nationalist movements persuaded the Labour Party – in the 1970s, unsuccessfully, and in the 1990s, successfully – to establish such assemblies and to devolve substantial power from Westminster. In Scotland Labour formed a coalition government with the Lib-Dems while in Wales Labour decided to govern from a minority position. A number of intractable political problems have resulted from the process including the London Labour leadership's lack of enthusiasm for some of the things done in Labour's name by the new administrations. Two persistent problems yet to be solved are the so-called West Lothian question and the possibility that devolution will prove to be merely a stepping stone for the nationalists to achieve their aims and break up the Union. Devolution to English regions remains a possibility but one that is likely to be some considerable time away.

Postscript

In a speech on Tuesday 28th March 2000 Tony Blair moved publically from his alleged opposition to elected regional governments when he admitted, 'The logical conclusion of the growing pressure for regional change in England is to create more accountable regional government . . . more regional decentralisation in England makes sense.' He also maintained that his government's 'progressive programme of constitutional reform is moving us from a centralised Britian where power flowed top-down, to a devolved and plural state.' On 29th March the *Guardian* announced that William Hague had abandoned the idea of an English parliament, but now favoured a formula which would prevent MPs from outside England voting on English bills. Blair condemned a proposal which would make such MPs 'second class citizens' adding, according to the *Guardian*, that the English, as the overwhelming majority did not need the same protection as minorities'.

Discussion points

- To what extent was there independence in the Ireland, Scotland and Wales before their union with England?
- What differences are there between the nationalism of each country?
- Why do you think support for devolution is greater in Scotland than Wales?
- Why do critics of Blair claim devolution has demonstrated his 'control freak' tendencies?
- What problems have been thrown up by the devolution policies?

Further reading

Bogdanor provides a thorough discussion of the political issues surrounding the topic, especially the West Lothian question. Bulpitt is best on the territorial dimension but also very clear and useful is Coxall and Robins (Chapter 18). *The Economist* provides a rich source of data and comment on the topic throughout the crucial years, 1997–9.

References

Bogdanor, V. (1997) *Power and the People* (Gollancz).

Bogdanor, V. (1999) *Devolution in the United Kingdom* (Oxford University Press).

Bradbury, J. (1999) 'Labour's bloody nose: the first Welsh General Election', *Politics Review*, November.

Bulpitt, J. (1983) *Territory and Power in the United Kingdom* (Manchester University Press).

Coxall, B. and Robins, L. (1998) *Contemporary British Politics* (Macmillan).

Economist (1999) 'Towards a federal Britain', 27 March, pp. 25–9.

Hechter, M. (1975) *Internal Colonialism* (Routledge).

Marr, A. (2000) *The Day Britain Died* (Profile Books).

Mitchell, J. (1999) 'Devolution', in Jones, B. (ed.) *Political Issues in Britain Today* (Manchester University Press).

Nairn, T. (2000) *After Britain: New Labour and the Return of Scotland* (Granta).

Steed, M. (1986) 'The core–periphery dimension in British politics', *Political Geography Quarterly*, October.

Concluding comment

One party state?

Peter Riddell

Whenever a government looks invincible, and the opposition in a mess, journalists and political scientists start speculating about whether we are moving to a one party state. In the past, that has often been precisely the moment when the government starts to falter and the fortunes of the opposition start to pick up, such are the unpredictabilities of politics and the dangers of hubris.

Predictions about the emergence of a one party state were made after the Conservatives won third terms and Commons majorities of about one hundred seats in 1959 and 1987 – and again when the party won an unprecedented fourth term in 1992. Even during the first term of the Blair government, before it has sought re-election for a second term, the same question has been raised about whether New Labour is seeking to create a one party state.

The idea of a one party state appears contrary to the conventional notion of the main parties alternating in power thanks to swings of the electoral pendulum. During the twentieth century, that has been more the exception than the rule. The main parties have alternated in government only for short periods from 1923 until 1931 and from 1964 until 1979, when no party had two full terms in office. Otherwise, the Liberals were in office for nearly ten years until the creation of the first coalition in the First World War. The Conservative dominated National Government held office for nine years in the 1930s, while the Conservatives were in power for thirteen years from 1951 until 1964 and for eighteen years from 1979 until 1997.

During each of these periods, the opposition has looked weak and has been fractious and divided. Commentators have wondered whether the political landscape is being permanently changed. After Labour lost for the third time in a row in 1959, there was much soul searching about whether the party had lost touch with the electorate; there was an unsuccessful attempt to rewrite clause four of the constitution on its aims, and there was even talk of changing the name. An influential book at the time by sociologist Mark Abrams was called *Must Labour Lose?*

Similarly, after Labour's fourth defeat in 1992, the authoritative report on the British Election Study (by Roger Jowell, Anthony Heath and John Curtice) was entitled *Labour's Last Chance*? and the concluding chapter was called 'Can Labour win?'. After discussing the formidable obstacle that Labour faced to win an overall majority, the authors concluded that, 'on the face of it there seems little reason for optimism'. In a parallel study, *Britain at the Polls, 1992*, Professor Anthony King, a level-headed and experienced observer of British politics, noted that: 'It had once been an axiom of British politics that the electoral pendulum swung from time to time and that, as a result, the two major political parties alternated in office'. But the pendulum stopped swinging in 1992, so Britain showed signs of developing what political scientist Giovanni Sartori has called a 'predominant party system'. This is defined as a single party both controlling an absolute majority of seats in the legislature and being able to govern on its own without partners for a prolonged period. Sartori suggests this might be four terms, exactly what the Conservatives won in 1992. In the United States, the Democrats controlled the Presidency for twenty years from 1933 until 1953 as well as both houses of Congress for all but two years of this period. In Sweden, the Social Democrats were the dominant party from the 1930s until the 1970s. Professor King concluded that: 'Labour's electoral prognosis in the summer of 1992 was not good. If this prognosis proves correct, British Government will remain one-party government into the next millennium'. Many press commentators shared this analysis.

In retrospect, these studies appear short sighted and premature, as their authors now concede. Their fault, however, lay less in the analysis of why Labour had lost electoral support over so long a period, which was correct, than in the implied conclusion of their titles that Labour might not win again. In fact, Labour eventually learnt the lessons of these defeats. After becoming leader in 1983, Neil Kinnock recognised that Labour had to change, but he faced formidable internal obstacles and it took him several years, and a further election defeat in 1987, to recognise how much had to be done even when he stepped down after Labour's fourth defeat in 1992. No one writing in 1992 could have foreseen either how short John Smith's leadership would turn out to be (less than two years) or how radical Tony Blair would prove to be in transforming the Labour Party – or how divided and unpopular the Major government would become.

Even if forecasts of permanent one party government turned out to be wrong, the eighteen years in office of the Conservatives strained many constitutional conventions. For instance, the ability of the civil service to remain non-partisan in part rested on the assumption that they might soon be serving another party. That, of course, reinforced the view, popularised by the 1980s' television series *Yes Minister* and *Yes Prime Minister*, that the civil service was the permanent government having to tolerate and manipulate transitory political masters. Despite endless discussion during the late 1980s and early 1990s about 'politicisation' of the civil service, there was no real evidence that political factors affected the appointment of permanent secretaries and other senior civil servants, as opposed to members of quangoes and other public bodies where a party bias was clear. Many civil servants who were highly respected by the preceding Wilson and Callaghan governments also advanced after the Conservatives won office in 1979, including several who served in Margaret Thatcher's private office in Downing Street. Moreover, there was no sign of civil service resistance or obstructiveness when the Blair government came to office in May 1997: rather the reverse. Many senior civil servants had become restless under the divided and politically constrained Major administration and looked for stronger leadership and a fresh stimulus under Mr Blair and his team, despite their lack of experience of Whitehall. The senior civil service quickly adapted to the Blair regime.

However, the absence of a written constitution with formal checks, such as a bill of rights or a supreme court, has rested on the assumption that a strong opposition, and potential alternative government, will hold the serving administration to account. But Labour was weak and not a credible alternative government for most of the 1980s, so the Thatcher government faced little check in Parliament on what it could do – apart, occasionally, from the House of Lords on some constitutional issues. The Lords saw its role as providing a check which the Tory dominated Commons had failed to do. Similarly, through the growth of judicial review, the judges became more active during the 1980s in making rulings on cases involving the decisions of ministers and civil servants. The sporadic activity of the Lords and the growing activism of the judges – as well as the challenges of the media – only partially filled the vacuum. The striking contrast between Britain and other countries with one party dominance is that the latter have usually had in-built constraints – either written constitutions with formal checks and balances or powerful intermediary institutions such as regional or local governments. Moreover, in both Sweden and Japan, decisions have often been taken by consensus between the parties, in contrast to the adversarial tradition in Britain.

The arrival of the Blair government has shifted the debate over one party government in contradictory ways. The Blair government looks as dominant as the Conservatives under Margaret Thatcher in the mid-1980s or the Liberals after their 1906 landslide and Labour after its victory in 1945. On both the latter occasions, many Tories wondered about their party's future and whether the name of the party should be changed. The conventional view, both then, and now, was that the dominant party would win a second election. The Liberals did win again at both elections in 1910 and Labour retained office in 1950, but in both cases with much reduced Commons majorities.

On this occasion, Tony Blair is making a deliberate attempt to reach out across the political spectrum. He has made a point of appointing prominent Tories to public posts, notably Chris Patten to be one of the British nominated members of the European Commission (even though he was not the first choice of William Hague, the Tory leader) and of Sir Alastair Goodlad, the former Tory Chief Whip, to be British High Commissioner to Australia. Other leading Conservatives, such as Michael Heseltine, have been involved in advisory groups, while Mr Blair has also courted leading businessmen and enlisted their support and involvement on issues ranging from Europe to information technology. The Blair Downing Street has also sought to centralise the presentation of the government's message.

Mr Blair has talked of ending the great Labour/Liberal schism of the twentieth century by uniting progressive forces on the centre-left. This was marked by the formation of the joint consultative Cabinet committee with the Liberal Democrats. The question has been how far he wants to create a genuinely pluralist politics involving several parties, or whether, in practice, he wants to smother and absorb many Liberal Democrats.

The most important issue is whether the way that members of the House of Commons are elected is changed. If a system of proportional representation is introduced, this would ensure that in most circumstances, no single party could win an overall majority, and there would therefore have to be a coalition. In countries with PR systems, while the partners in a coalition often change after elections, there has also frequently been a dominant party or grouping – for instance, the Social Democrats in Sweden or the Christian Democrats from the late 1940s until the 1980s in Italy. One result of the introduction of PR in Britain might be that a Labour/Liberal Democrat coalition – presumably with a New Labour/Blairite approach – would be in office for some time. That is certainly the Conservative fear, although paradoxically some of the strongest opposition to the introduction of PR has come from Labour traditionalists who not only dislike the Liberal Democrats but are also worried about the dominance of a Lab-Lib consensus.

The Liberals/Liberal Democrats have always favoured PR and Mr Blair set up a commission under Lord Jenkins of Hillhead, the former SDP leader, to examine possible ways of changing the ways that MPs are elected. The inquiry produced a hybrid plan combining constituency members and a proportional top-up. This was intended to satisfy both those worried about retaining a constituency link and those who wanted a more proportional system. However, this plan was strongly opposed by many members of the Blair Cabinet and was given only cautious backing in principle by Tony Blair. So the Jenkins plan was, in effect, left hanging in the wind and the earlier Labour promise of a referendum on the issue looks unlikely to be fulfilled until after the next general election in Britain.

However, a different PR system has been introduced in Scotland and Wales. In elections in May 1999, Labour failed to win an overall majority in either Scotland or Wales. In Scotland, Labour formed a coalition with the Liberal Democrats, while in Wales the party governed on a minority basis. In both countries, Labour would have won a majority under the familiar first-past-the-post system, although it is possible that devolution proposals would not have been approved in the referendums of September 1997 without the adoption of PR. But at Westmister, the introduction of PR might entrench Blairite dominance for some time.

However, some of the Blair government's constitutional changes might work in the opposite direction. Devolution to Scotland and Wales, the creation of an elected mayor and assembly in London, followed by elected mayors elsewhere in England, and the incorporation of the European Convention of Human Rights into British law, will all create checks on the power of the government. Even if one party remains in office for two or more terms in the Westminster Parliament, there will now be other, competing centres of power.

Talk of a one party state usually says more about the current state of politics than reliably predicting what will happen in the future. In practice, the British system has proved to have in-built corrective mechanisms – whether the shifting opinions of the electorate, the generally slow learning processes of opposition parties, challenges offered by the judges or the media and, now, the creation of powerful other political institutions. The only certain prediction is that Tony Blair will not be Prime Minister for ever and that the Conservatives will be back in office at some stage. No one knows when. That is the charm of politics, and the fun of being a political journalist.

Part 4 The legislative process

Introduction

Bill Jones

So far this book has addressed the non-institutional elements of British politics; the remainder of the volume deals with the institutional aspects together with specific policy areas. Often institutions can seem confusing to students who tend to study them individually and find it difficult to grasp how they relate to and interact with each other. Accordingly this short section gives two contrasting overviews of how the system works.

Two overviews of the British political system

The functions of government

It is helpful to contrast the British political system with that of the USA. It is well known that the eighteenth-century framers of the constitution wrote into their 1787 document a strict separation of powers. The legislature (Congress) and the executive (the Presidency) were to be separately elected for terms of differing length with the judiciary (the Supreme Court) appointed by the President for life. In diagrammatic form the functions can be represented by three separate and independent circles (see Figure 1).

The purpose of this arrangement was to disperse power to institutions which would check each other and ensure that no branch of government became overmighty. In Britain, however, there never was such a separation. The three functions overlap significantly. To change or re-elect a government there is only one election and that is to the legislative chamber, the House of Commons. After the election the majority party in that chamber invariably forms the executive. The crucial overlap between the legislative and executive

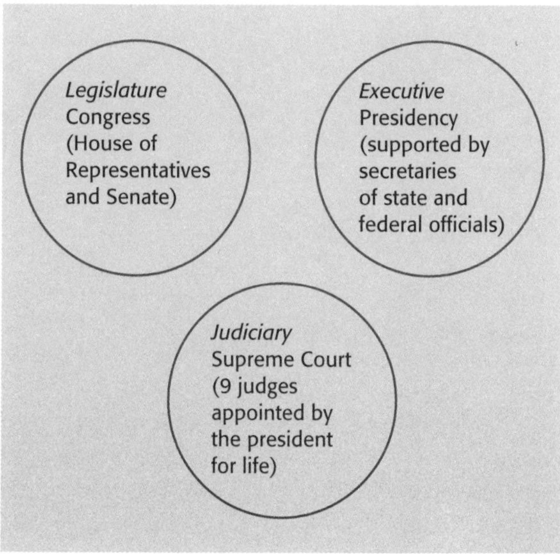

Figure 1 Functions of government: USA

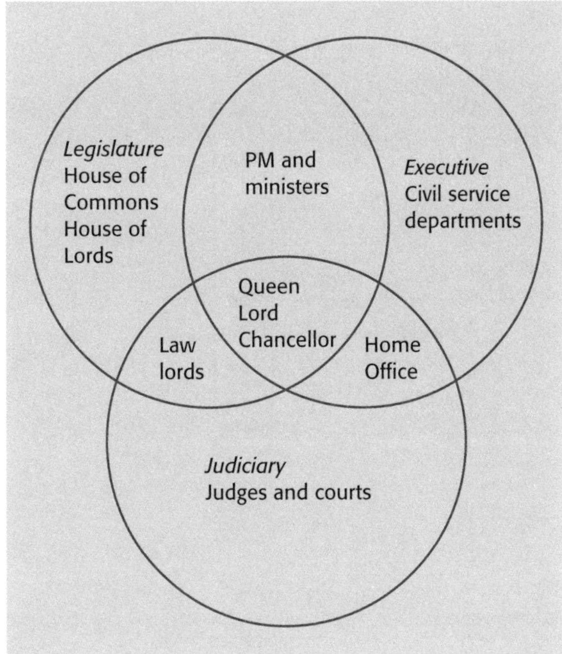

Figure 2 Functions of government: UK

spheres therefore comprises Prime Minister, Cabinet and the other seventy or so junior ministers. The judiciary is similarly appointed by the executive; not by the Prime Minister, but by the Lord Chancellor, the government's chief law officer, who sits in the Cabinet and presides over the House of Lords. It is he who sits at the centre of the three-circled web, together with the monarch – who once dominated all three spheres but now merely decorates them (see Figure 2).

The US constitution ensures that the President cannot be overthrown by Congress – except through impeachment – but looser party discipline means the President cannot regularly command congressional support for his policies; indeed, like Presidents Bush and Clinton, his party may be in the minority in Congress. The British Prime Minister, in contrast, has relatively more power: provided that the support of the majority party is sustained he or she leads both the executive and legislative arms of government. However, loss of significant party support can bring down the British Prime Minister, as it did Chamberlain in May 1940 and Thatcher in 1990. This possibility clearly acts as a constraint upon potential prime ministerial action, but the fact is that parties in government very rarely even threaten to unseat their leaders because they fear the electoral consequences of apparent disunity.

The executive's power is further reinforced by the doctrine of parliamentary sovereignty, which enables it to overrule any law – constitutional or otherwise – with a simple majority vote; and considerable residual powers of the monarch via the royal prerogative. The House of Lords' power of legislative delay only, and local government's essentially subservient relationship to Westminster, complete the picture of an unusually powerful executive arm of government for a representative democracy.

Representative and responsible government

Represented in a different way the British political system can be seen as a circuit of representation and responsibility. Parliament represents the electorate but is also responsible to it via elections. In their turn ministers represent majority opinion in the legislature (although they are appointed by the Prime Minister, not elected) and are responsible to it for their actions in leading the executive. Civil servants are not representatives but as part of the executive are controlled by ministers and are responsible to them. Figure 3 illustrates the relationship.

This, of course, is a very simplistic view, but it does express the underlying theory of how British government should work. The reality of how the system operates is infinitely more complex, as Figure 4 – itself highly simplified – seeks to illustrate. Earlier chapters have explained how the different elements of British government operate in practice:

1. Parliament provides the forum, the 'playing field' on which the ordered competition of democratic government is publicly conducted.
2. Political parties dominate the system, organising the electorate, taking over Parliament and providing the ministers who run the civil service.

ELECTORATE
representation
responsibility
PARLIAMENT
MINISTERS
control
CIVIL SERVICE

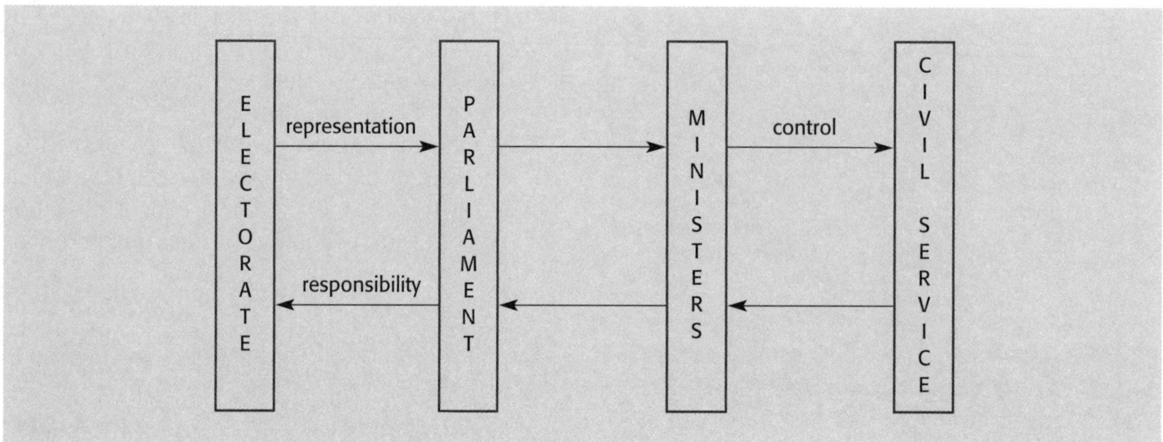

Figure 3 Representative and responsible government

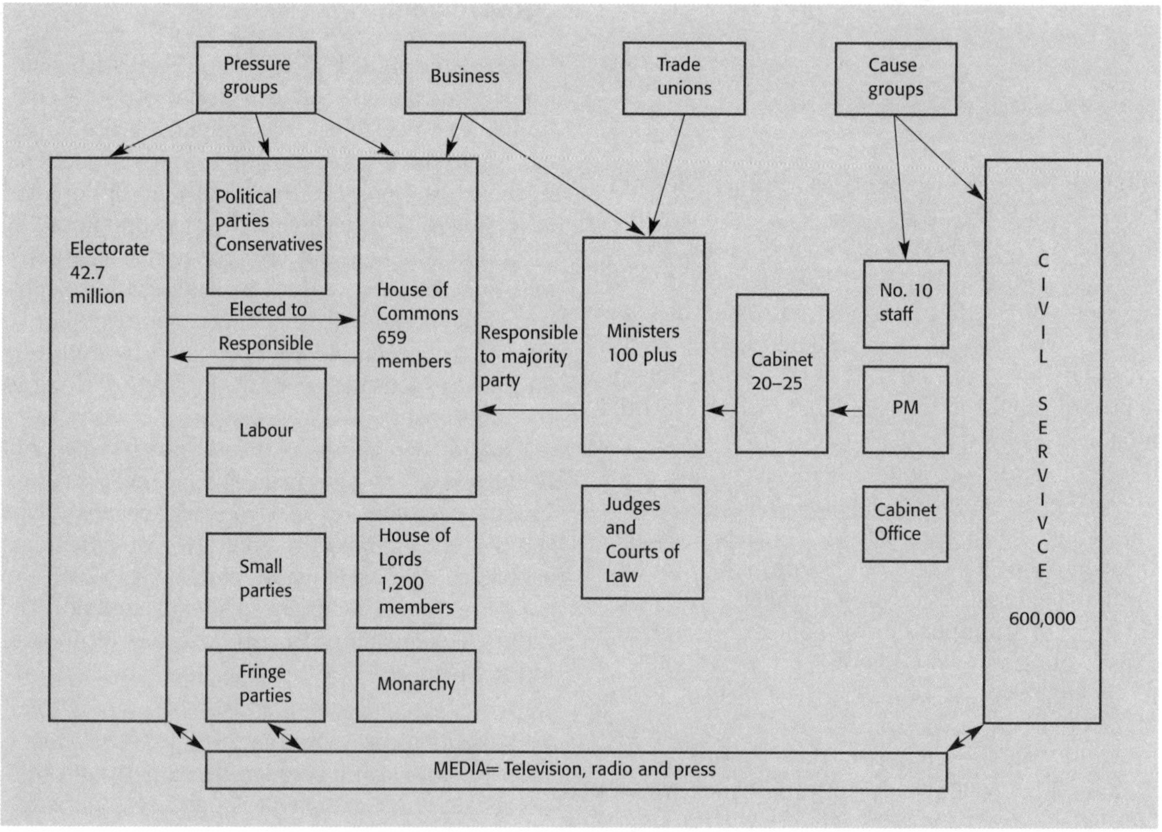

Pressure groups
Business
Trade unions
Cause groups
Electorate 42.7 million
Political parties Conservatives
Labour
Small parties
Fringe parties
Elected to
Responsible
House of Commons 659 members
House of Lords 1,200 members
Monarchy
Responsible to majority party
Ministers 100 plus
Judges and Courts of Law
Cabinet 20–25
No. 10 staff
PM
Cabinet Office
CIVIL SERVICE
600,000
MEDIA= Television, radio and press

Figure 4 Elements of UK central government

3. The Prime Minister as leader of the majority party can exercise considerable personal power and in recent years has become more akin to a presidential figure.
4. The judiciary performs the important task of interpreting legislation and calling ministers and officials to account if they act without statutory authority.
5. Civil servants serve ministers but their permanence and their professionalism, their vested interests in searching for consensus and defending departmental interests raise suspicions that they occasionally or even regularly outflank their ministerial masters.
6. Pressure groups infiltrate the whole gamut of government institutions, the most powerful bypassing Parliament and choosing to deal direct with ministers and civil servants.
7. The media have increasingly usurped the role of Parliament in informing the public and providing a forum for public debate. Television is a potent new influence, the impact of which is still to be fully felt.

Does the reality invalidate the theory? It all depends upon how drastically we believe Figure 4 distorts 3. Indeed, Marxists would declare both to be irrelevant in that business pressure groups call the shots that matter, operating behind the scenes and within the supportive context of a system in which all the major actors subscribe to their values. Tony Benn would argue that the executive has become so dominant at the expense of the legislature that the PM's power can be compared with that of a medieval monarch. As we have seen, Britain's constitutional arrangements have always allowed great potential power – potential which strong Prime Ministers like Margaret Thatcher have been keen and able to realise when given the time. But I would maintain, and cite in support the analyses offered by the authors of this book, that the essential features of the democratic system portrayed in Figure 3 just about survive in that:

1. party-dominated governments are removable;
2. Parliament still applies watchdog controls (and just occasionally reminds the executive by biting);
3. the electorate has a choice between parties;
4. civil servants will obey their political masters;
5. pressure groups influence but do not dictate.

Part IV explains how the legislative system works; Part V explains the executive process; and Part VI looks at a number of policy areas.

Chapter 15 The changing constitution

Philip Norton

Learning objectives

- To identify the sources and key components of the British constitution.
- To analyse the nature of the debate about the British constitution.
- To consider the major changes and modifications made to the constitution in recent years.
- To detail the arguments for and against some of the major changes that have taken place or are proposed to the constitution, including electoral reform.
- To address the problems faced by political parties as a consequence of constitutional change.

Introduction

In the quarter-century following the Second World War, the constitution rarely figured in political debate. It was seen as the preserve more of lawyers than of politicians. In the last three decades of the century, it became a subject of political controversy. Demands for reform of the constitution grew. Many of those demands were met by the Labour government elected in May 1997, with major changes being made to the constitutional framework of the country. Some critics demand further change. The changes that have taken place have created problems for both major political parties.

The constitution

What, then, is a **constitution**? What is distinctive about the British constitution? Where does it come from? What are the essential constituents of the 'traditional' constitution? What challenges has it faced in recent years? What changes have been made to it? What are the problems posed to the political parties by such change? And what is the nature of the debate taking place about further constitutional change?

Definition and sources

What is a constitution? A constitution can be defined as the system of laws, customs and **conventions** which defines the composition and powers of organs of the state (such as government, Parliament and the courts), and regulates the relations of the various state organs to one another and of those state organs to the private citizen.

Constitutions vary considerably in nature. Most, but not all, are drawn up in a single, codified document. Some are short; others remarkably long. Some embody provisions that exhort citizens to act in a certain way ('It shall be the duty of every citizen . . .'); others confine themselves to stipulating the formal structures and powers of state bodies. Processes of interpretation and amendment vary. Most, but not all, have entrenched provisions: i.e. they can only be amended by an extraordinary process beyond that normally employed for amending the law.

The British constitution differs from most in that it is not drawn up in a single codified document. As such, it is often described as an 'unwritten' constitution. However, much of the constitution does exist in 'written' form. Many Acts of Parliament – such as the European Communities Act 1972, providing the legal basis for British membership of the European Community, and the House of Lords Act 1999, removing hereditary peers from membership of the House of Lords – are clearly measures of constitutional law. Those Acts constitute formal, written – and binding – documents. To describe the constitution as unwritten is thus misleading. Rather, what Britain has is a part written and uncodified constitution.

Even in countries with a formal, written document, 'the constitution' constitutes more than the simple words of the document. Those words have to be interpreted. Practices develop, and laws are passed, which help give meaning to those words. To understand the contemporary constitution of the United States, for example, one has to look beyond the document to interpretations of that document by the courts in the USA, principally the US Supreme Court, and to various acts of Congress and to practices developed over the past two hundred years. The constitutions of most countries thus have what may be termed a primary source (the written document) and secondary sources (judicial interpretation, legislative acts, established practice). The UK, without a written document, lacks the equivalent primary source. Instead, the constitution derives from sources that elsewhere would constitute secondary sources of the constitution. The principal sources of what may be termed the 'traditional' constitution – that which was in place for most of the twentieth century and which has its roots in the Glorious Revolution of 1688–9 – are four in number (see Figure 15.1). They are:

1. **statute law**, comprising Acts of Parliament and subordinate legislation made under the authority of the parent Act;
2. **common law**, comprising legal principles developed and applied by the courts, and encompassing the prerogative powers of the crown and the law and practice of Parliament;
3. conventions, constituting rules of behaviour which are considered binding by and upon those who operate the constitution but which are not enforced by the courts or by the presiding officers in the Houses of Parliament;
4. works of authority, comprising various written works – often but not always accorded authority by reason of their age – which provide guidance and interpretation on uncertain aspects of the constitution. Such works have persuasive authority only.

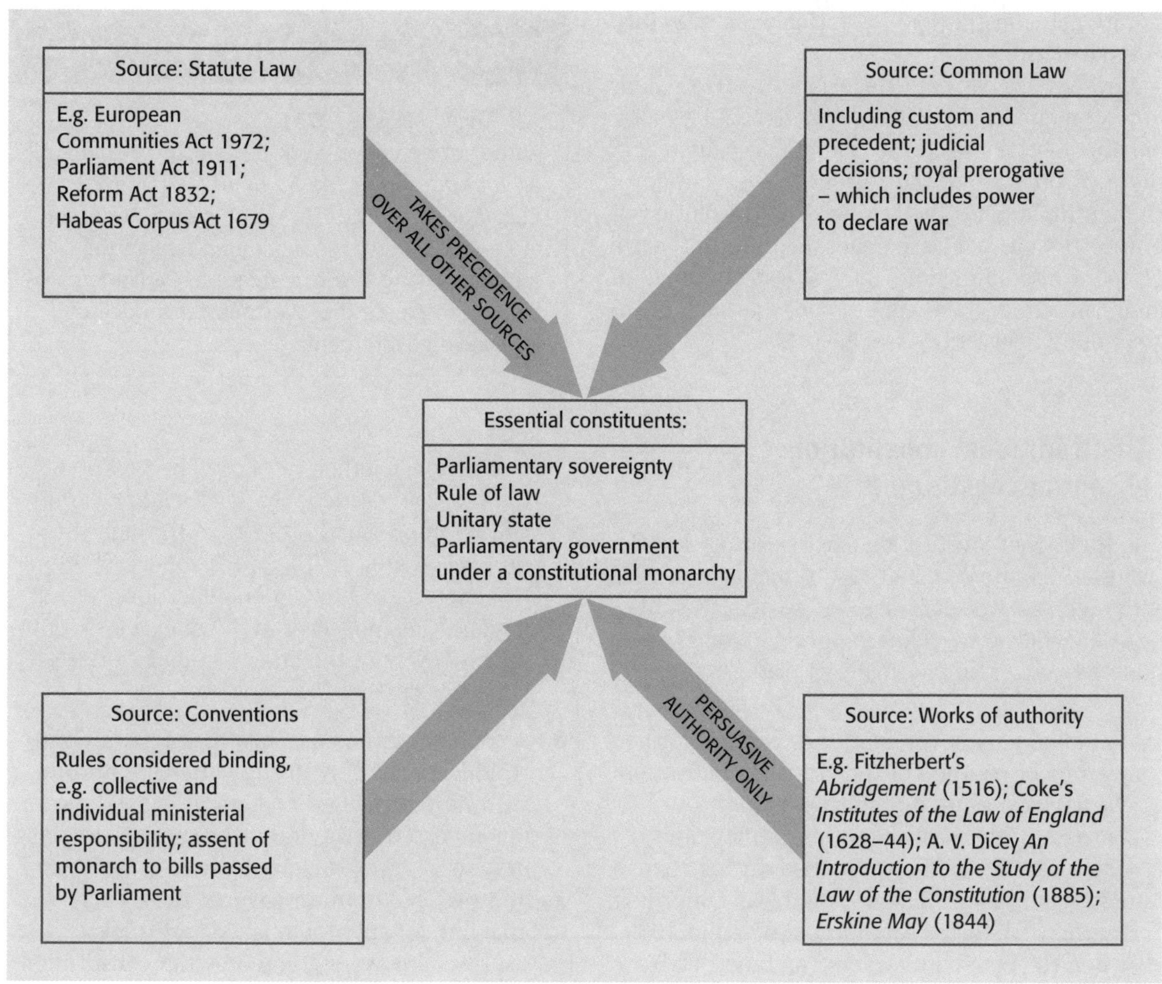

Figure 15.1 The traditional constitution: sources and constituents
Source: Norton, 1986

Statute law is the pre-eminent of the four sources and occupies such a position because of the doctrine of **parliamentary sovereignty**. Under this judicially self-imposed concept, the courts recognise only the authority of Parliament (formally the Queen-in-Parliament) to make law, with no body other than Parliament itself having the authority to set aside that law. The courts cannot strike down a law as being contrary to the provisions of the constitution. Statute law, then, is supreme and it can be used to override common law.

Amendment

No extraordinary features are laid down in Parliament for the passage or amendment of measures of constitutional law. Although bills of constitutional significance are usually taken for their committee stage on the floor of the House of Commons, rather than being discussed in a standing committee (see Chapter 17), there is no formal requirement for this to happen. All bills have to go through the same stages in both Houses of Parliament and are subject to simple majority voting. As such, the traditional constitution is, formally, a **flexible constitution**.

However, as we shall see, there are two recent developments that challenge this flexibility: membership of the European Community/Union and the incorporation of the European Convention of Human Rights into British law. The devolution of powers to elected assemblies in different parts of the United Kingdom may also be argued to limit, in effect, the capacity of Parliament to amend any legislation it wishes.

BOX 15.1 MINI BIOGRAPHY

A.V. Dicey (1835–1922)
Author of definitive work on British constitution, *An Introduction to the Study of Law and the Constitution* (1885). He was Vinerian Professor of Law at Oxford. His work emphasised the rule of law and the supremacy of Parliament, helping to create the 'Westminster model' of legislative government.

The traditional constitution: essential constituents

The traditional constitution existed for most of the twentieth century. It had four principal features. Although, as we shall see, these features have been challenged by changes of recent years, each nonetheless remains formally in place:

1 Parliamentary sovereignty has been described as the cornerstone of the British constitution. As we have seen, it stipulates that the outputs of the Parliament are binding and cannot be set aside by any body other than Parliament itself. The doctrine was confirmed by the Glorious Revolution of 1688 and 1689, when the common lawyers combined with Parliament against the King. Since the Settlement of 1689 established that the King was bound by the law of Parliament, it followed that his courts were also so bound.

2 The rule of law was identified by the nineteenth-century constitutional lawyer A.V. Dicey as one of the twin pillars of the constitution, and is generally accepted as one of the essential features of a free society. However, it is logically subordinate to the first pillar – parliamentary sovereignty – since Parliament could pass a measure undermining or destroying the rule of law. It is also a matter of dispute as to what the term encompasses. In terms of the law passed by Parliament, it is essentially a procedural doctrine. Laws must be interpreted and applied by an impartial and independent judiciary, those charged under the law are entitled to a fair trial and no one can be imprisoned other than through the due process of law. There is some dispute, however, as to how far the doctrine extends beyond this, not least in defining the extent of the power of the state to regulate the affairs of citizens.

3 A unitary state is one in which formal power resides exclusively in the national authority, with no entrenched and autonomous powers being vested in any other body. In federal systems, power is shared between national and regional or state governments, each enjoying an autonomous existence and exercising powers granted by the constitution. In the UK, state power resides centrally, with the Queen-in-Parliament being omnicompetent. Parliament can create and confer certain powers in other bodies – such as assemblies and even parliaments in different parts of the UK – but those bodies remain subordinate to Parliament and can be restricted, even abolished, by it.

4 A parliamentary government under a constitutional monarchy refers to the form of government established by, and developed since, the Glorious Revolution. That revolution established the supremacy of Parliament over the King. The greater acceptance of democratic principles in the nineteenth and twentieth centuries has resulted in the enlargement of the franchise and a pre-eminent role in the triumvirate of

> Queen-in-Parliament (monarch, Commons, Lords) for the elected chamber, the House of Commons. 'Parliament' thus means predominantly – although not exclusively – the House of Commons, while 'parliamentary government' refers not to government by Parliament but to government through Parliament. Ministers are legally answerable to the crown but politically answerable to Parliament, that political relationship being governed by the conventions of collective and individual ministerial responsibility. A government is returned in a general election and between elections depends on the confidence of a majority of Members of Parliament both for the passage of its measures and for its continuance in office.

Three of these four features (parliamentary sovereignty, unitary state, parliamentary government) facilitated the emergence of strong, or potentially strong, government, a government secure in its majority in the House of Commons being able to enact measures which were then binding on society and which could not be set aside by any body other than Parliament itself. There were no other forms of government below the national enjoying autonomous powers (the consequence of a unitary state), no other actors at national level were able to countermand the elected House of Commons, be it the Crown or the House of Lords (the consequence of the growth of parliamentary government under a constitutional monarchy) or the courts (the consequence of the doctrine of parliamentary sovereignty). The United Kingdom thus enjoyed a centralised system of government.

That system of government, made possible by the essential features of the constitution, was variously described as the Westminster system of government. At the heart of the system was the Cabinet, sustained by a party majority in the House of Commons. Each party fought a general election on the basis of a party manifesto and, if elected to office, it proceeded to implement the promises made in the manifesto. Parliament provided the legitimacy for the government and its measures, subjecting those measures to debate and scrutiny before giving its approval to them. Party ensured that the government almost always got its way, but the party system ensured that the government faced the critical scrutiny of the party in opposition.

The traditional constitution can, as we have seen, be traced back to the Glorious Revolution of the seventeenth century but it emerged more fully in the nineteenth century with the widening of the franchise. It emerged in the form we have just described – the Westminster system – essentially in the period from 1867, with the passage of the second Reform Act (necessitating the growth of organised parties), and 1911, when the Parliament Act (restricting by statute the powers of the House of Lords) was passed. From 1911 onwards, power in the UK resided in the party that held a majority of seats in the House of Commons.

Challenges to the traditional constitution

The traditional constitution was in place from 1911 to 1972. Although it was variously criticised in the years between the two world wars, especially in the depression of the 1930s, it went largely unchallenged in the years immediately after the Second World War. The nation's political institutions continued to function during the war and the country emerged victorious from the conflict. In the 1950s, the nation enjoyed relative economic prosperity. There appeared little reason to question the nation's constitutional arrangements. That changed once the country began to experience economic recession and more marked political conflicts. The constitution came in for questioning. If the political system was not delivering what was expected of it, then was there not a case for changing the system itself? The issue of constitutional reform began to creep on to the political agenda.

Since 1970, the traditional constitution has faced two major challenges. Both have had significant consequences for the nation's constitutional arrangements. The first was membership of the European Community (now the European Union). The second was the constitutional changes introduced by the Labour Government elected in May 1997.

Membership of the European Community/Union

A judicial dimension

The United Kingdom became a member of the European Community (EC) on 1 January 1973. The Treaty of Accession was signed in 1972 and the legal basis for membership provided by the European Communities Act 1972. The motivation for joining the Community was essentially economic and political. Membership, however, had significant constitutional consequences. The European Communities Act was distinctive because it:

1. Gave the force of law not only to existing but also to all future EC law. As soon as regulations are made by the institutions of the EC, they have binding applicability in the UK. The assent of Parliament is not required. That assent has, in effect, been given in advance under the provisions of the 1972 Act. Parliament has some discretion as to the form in which EC directives are to be implemented, but the discretion refers only to the form and not to the principle.
2. Gave EC law precedence over UK law. In the event of a conflict between EC law and UK law, the European law takes precedence. This was clearly stipulated in the European Communities Act but the full effect of it was only fully realised with some important court cases in the 1990s (Fitzpatrick, 1999). In the Factortame case, of 1990–1, the European Court of Justice held that the courts in the UK could suspend the provisions of an Act of Parliament, where it appeared to breach EC law, until a final determination was made. In the case of Ex Parte EOC, in 1994, the House of Lords struck down provisions of the 1978 Employment Protection (Consolidation) Act as incompatible with EC law (Maxwell, 1999).
3. Gave the power to determine disputes to the courts. Where there is a dispute over EC law, the matter is resolved by the courts. Questions of EC law have to be decided by the European Court of Justice (ECJ). Where a question of EC law reaches the highest domestic court of appeal, the House of Lords, it has to be referred to the ECJ for a definitive ruling; lower courts may ask the ECJ for a ruling on the meaning of treaty provisions. All courts in the UK are required to take judicial notice of decisions of the ECJ.

The effect of these changes has been to challenge the doctrine of parliamentary sovereignty. The decisions of Parliament can, in certain circumstances (where they conflict with EC law), be set aside by a body or bodies other than Parliament itself – namely, the courts. In sectors that now fall within the competence of the European Union, then it can be argued that the UK now has something akin to a written constitution – that is, the treaties of the European Union.

The doctrine of parliamentary sovereignty remains formally in place because Parliament retains the power to repeal the European Communities Act. The European Court of Justice is able to exercise the power it does because an Act of Parliament says that it can. However, the effect of repealing the 1972 Act would be to take the UK out of the European Union. (This in itself would be a breach of treaty provisions, under which membership is in perpetuity.) The claim that Parliament retains the power to repeal the 1972 Act appears to be accepted by most constitutional lawyers, although some now question this and the longer the Act remains in force the more the doctrine of parliamentary sovereignty will be challenged and may eventually fade away.

A political dimension

As a consequence of membership, the constitution thus acquired a new judicial dimension, one that challenged the doctrine of parliamentary sovereignty. At the same time, it also acquired a new political dimension, one that challenged the decision-making capacity of British Government. Under the terms of entry, policy making power in various sectors of public policy passed to the institutions of the European Community. Subsequent treaties have served both to extend the range of sectors falling within the competence of the EC and also to strengthen the decision-making capacity of the EC institutions.

The Single European Act, which came into force in 1987, effected a significant shift in the power relationship between the institutions of the Community and the institutions of the member states, strengthening EC institutions, especially through the extension of qualified majority voting (QMV) in the Council of Ministers. The Act also effected a shift in the power relationships within the institutions of the Community, strengthening the European Parliament through the extension of the co-operation procedure, a procedure that provides a greater role for the Parliament in Community law making. Further shifts in both levels of power relationship were embodied in the Treaty on European Union (the Maastricht Treaty) which took effect in November 1993. This established a European Union with three pillars (the European Community, common foreign and security policy, justice and home affairs), extended the sectors of public policy falling within the competence of the European Community and established a new co-decision procedure for making law in certain areas, a procedure that strengthened again the position of the European Parliament. A further strengthening of the position of the EC, now the European Union, took place with the implementation in 1999 of the Amsterdam Treaty. This extended the range of subjects falling within the competence of the EU and widened the range of issues to be determined by the co-decision procedure.

As a result of membership of the European Community, the British Government is thus constrained in what it can do. Where matters have to be decided by the Council of Ministers, the UK minister may be out-voted by the ministers of the other member states. A decision may thus be taken which is then enforced within the UK, even if it does not have the support of the British Government and Parliament. (Under the Luxembourg Compromise, agreed in 1966, a government may veto a proposal if it conflicts with the nation's vital national interests. Some governments, including the British and French, have argued that the compromise can still be used, but it has not been cited since the Single European Act was agreed and various authorities question whether it could now be invoked.) If the Government takes an action that appears to conflict with EC law, it can be challenged in the courts and then required to bring itself into line with EC law. An Act of Parliament, as we have seen, does not take precedence over European law. Membership of the European Community – now the European Union – has thus added a new element to the constitution, one that does not fit easily with the existing features of that constitution.

Constitutional reform under the Blair government

Background to reform

The 1970s and the 1980s saw some increasingly strident demands for reform of the existing constitution. The system of government no longer appeared to be performing as well as it had in the past. The country experienced economic difficulties (inflation, rising unemployment), industrial disputes, civil unrest in Northern Ireland and some social unrest at home (riots in cities such as Bristol and Liverpool). There were problems with the political process. Turnout declined in general elections. The proportion of electors voting for either of the two major parties fell. Two general elections took place in one year (1974), with no decisive outcome. A Labour Government elected with less than 40 per cent of the vote in October 1974 was able to implement a series of radical measures.

Critics of the constitution argued the case for change. Some politicians and lawyers argued the case for an entrenched Bill of Rights – putting rights beyond the reach of simple majorities in the two Houses of Parliament. The case for a Bill of Rights was put by Lord Hailsham in a 1976 lecture, subsequently published in pamphlet form under the title *Elective Dictatorship*. Some politicians wanted a new electoral system, one that produced a closer relationship between the proportion of votes won nationally and the proportion of seats won in the House of Commons. The case for a new electoral system was made in an influential series of essays, edited by Professor S.E. Finer and published under the title *Adversary Politics and Electoral Reform* in 1975. Finer argued that electoral reform would serve to end the harmful

BOX 15.2 **MINI BIOGRAPHY**

Lord Hailsham (1907–)

Leading post-war Conservative statesman. Educated Eton and Oxford. MP for Oxford 1938–50. Inherited title in 1950 and served as minister under Macmillan. Renounced peerage in 1963 to contest succession to Macmillan but was seen as too opportunistic by some. Was Lord Chancellor twice under Heath and then Thatcher. Influential writer on constitution and argued that the British system of unwritten constitution was an 'elective dictatorship' although his indignation receded once his party gained a healthy majority.

consequences of the clashes between parties and the policy discontinuity deriving from one party replacing another in government.

There were also calls for power to be devolved to elected assemblies in different parts of the United Kingdom and for the use of referendums. Both changes, it was argued, would push decision making down from a centralised government to the people. The Labour Government elected in 1974 sought, unsuccessfully, to pass measures providing for elected assemblies in Scotland and Wales. The Government did make provision for the first UK-wide referendum, held in 1975 on the issue of Britain's continued membership of the European Community.

The demands for change were fairly disparate and in most cases tied to no obvious intellectually coherent approach to constitutional change. However, as the 1980s progressed, various coherent approaches developed (Norton 1982, 1993). These are listed in Box 15.1. Each approach had its advocates, although the high Tory and Marxist approaches were essentially overshadowed by the others. The group, or functionalist, approach was more to the fore in the 1970s, when a Labour Government brought representatives of trades union and business into discussions on economic policy. It retained some advocates in the 1980s. The Socialist approach, pursued by politicians such as former Labour Cabinet Minister Tony Benn, had a notable influence in the Labour Party in the early 1980s, the Labour manifesto in the 1983 general election adopting essentially a Socialist stance. The new right approach found some influential supporters in the Conservative Party, notably Cabinet Minister Sir Keith Joseph; it also influenced the Prime Minister, Margaret Thatcher.

BOX 15.1 **IDEAS AND PERSPECTIVES**

Approaches to constitutional change

High Tory

This approach contends that the constitution has evolved organically and that change, artificial change, is neither necessary nor desirable. In its pure form, it is opposed not only to major reforms – such as electoral reform, a Bill of Rights and an elected second chamber – but also to modifications to existing arrangements, such as the introduction of departmental select committees in the House of Commons. Its stance on any proposed reform is thus predictable: it is against it.

Socialist

This approach favours reform, but a particular type of reform. It seeks strong government, but a party-dominated strong government, with adherence to the principle of intra-party democracy and the concept

BOX 15.1 continued

of the mandate. It wants to shift power from the existing 'top-down' form of control (government to people) to a 'bottom-up' form (people to government), with party acting as the channel for the exercise of that control. It favours sweeping away the monarchy and the House of Lords and the use of more elective processes, both for public offices as well as within the Labour Party. It wants, for example, the election of members of a Labour Cabinet by Labour MPs. It is wary of, or opposed to, reforms that might prevent the return of a socialist government and the implementation of a socialist programme. It is thus sceptical of or opposed to electoral reform (potential for coalition government), a Bill of Rights (constraining government autonomy, giving power to judges) and membership of the European Union (constraining influence, sometimes viewed as a capitalists' club). For government to carry through socialist policies, it has to be free of constitutional constraints that favour or are dominated by its opponents.

Marxist

This approach sees the restructuring of the political system as largely irrelevant, certainly in the long run, serving merely to delay the collapse of capitalist society. Government, any government, is forced to act in the interests of finance capital. Changes to the constitutional arrangements may serve to protect those interests in the short term but will not stave off collapse in the long term. Whatever the structures, government will be constrained by external elites, and those elites will themselves be forced to follow rather than determine events. The clash between the imperatives of capitalism and decreasing profit rates in the meso-economy determines what capitalists do. Constitutional reform, in consequence, is not advocated but rather taken as demonstrating tensions within the international capitalist economy.

Group

This approach – sometimes called the functionalist approach – seeks the greater incorporation of groups into the process of policy making in order to achieve a more consensual approach to public policy. The interdependence of government and interest groups – especially sectional interest groups – is such that it should be recognised and accommodated. A more integrated process can facilitate a more stable economic system. Supporters of this approach have looked to other countries, such as Germany, as examples of what can be achieved. This approach thus favours the representation of labour and business on executive and advisory bodies and, in its pure form, the creation of a functionalist second chamber.

New right

This approach is motivated by the economic philosophy of the free market. State intervention in economic affairs is viewed as illegitimate and dangerous, distorting the natural forces of the market and denying the consumer the freedom to choose. The state should therefore withdraw from economic activity. This viewpoint entails a contraction of the public sector, with state-owned industries being returned to the private sector. If institutions need reforming in order to facilitate the free market, then so be it: under this approach, no institution is deemed sacrosanct. Frank Vipert, the former deputy director of the free market think-tank the Institute of Economic Affairs, has advocated a 'free market written constitution'.

BOX 15.1 continued

Liberal

Like the new right approach, this is a radical approach to constitutional change. It derives from traditional liberal theory and emphasises the centrality of the individual, limited government, the neutrality of the state in resolving conflict, and consensual decision making. It views the individual as increasingly isolated in decision making, being elbowed aside by powerful interests and divorced from a governmental process that is centralised and distorted by partisan preferences. Against an increasingly over-mighty state, the individual has no means of protection. Hence, it is argued, the need for radical constitutional change. The liberal approach favours a new, written constitution, embodying the various reforms advocated by Charter '88, including a Bill of Rights, a system of proportional representation for elections, an elected second chamber, and a reformed judiciary and House of Commons. In its pure form, it supports federalism rather than devolution. Such a new constitutional settlement, it is argued, will serve to shift power from government to the individual. The only reform about which it is ambivalent is the use of referendums, some adherents to this approach seeing the referendum as a device for oppression by the majority.

Traditional

This is a very British approach and derives from a perception of the 'traditional' system as fundamentally sound, offering a balanced system of government. It draws on Tory theory in its emphasis on the need for strong government and on Whig theory in stressing the importance of Parliament as the agent for setting the limits within which government may act. These emphases coalesce in the Westminster model of government, a model that is part descriptive (what is) and part prescriptive (what should be). Government, in this model, must be able to formulate a coherent programme of public policy – the initiative rests with government – with Parliament, as the deliberative body of the nation, subjecting the actions and the programme of government to rigorous scrutiny and providing the limits within which government may govern. This approach recognises the importance of the House of Commons as the elected chamber and the fact that the citizen has neither the time nor the inclination to engage in continuous political debate. There is thus a certain deference, but a contingent deference, to the deliberative wisdom of Parliament. The fact that the Westminster model is prescriptive means that traditionalists – unlike high Tories – will entertain change if it is designed to move present arrangements towards the realisation of that model. They also recognise with Edmund Burke that 'a state without the means of some change is without the means of its conservation' and are therefore prepared to consider change in order to maintain and strengthen the existing constitutional framework. Over the years, therefore, traditionalists have supported a range of incremental reforms, such as the introduction of departmental select committees in the House of Commons, but have opposed radical reforms – such as electoral reform – which threaten the existing framework. There is a wariness about membership of the European Union, with involvement accepted as long as it does not pose a major threat to the existing domestic arrangements for decision making.

BOX 15.3 MINI BIOGRAPHY

Edmund Burke (1729–97)
Conservative philosopher and politician. Educated Trinity College Dublin. Was passionate opponent of French Revolution and known for his writings advocating continuity and gradual change. A fundamental influence on British Conservative thinking.

However, the two most prominent approaches were the liberal and the traditionalist. The liberal approach was pursued by the Liberal Party and then by its successor party, the Liberal Democrats. It also attracted support from a much wider political spectrum, including some Labour supporters and even some ex-Marxists. In 1988, a constitutional reform movement, Charter '88, was formed (the year of formation was deliberate, constituting the tercentenary year of the Glorious Revolution) to bring together all those who supported a new constitutional settlement. By 1991, the Charter had attracted 25,000 signatories.

The liberal approach made much of the running in political debate. However, the traditional approach was the most influential of the approaches by virtue of the fact that it was the approach adopted by the Conservative Government. Although Prime Minister Margaret Thatcher supported reducing the public sector she nonetheless maintained a basic traditionalist approach to the constitution. Her successor, John Major, was a particularly vocal advocate of the traditional approach. Although the period of Conservative Government from 1979 to 1997 saw some important constitutional changes – such as a constriction of the role of local government and the negotiation of new European treaties (the Single European Act and the Maastricht Treaty) – there was no principled embrace of radical constitutional change. The stance of Government was to support the existing constitutional framework.

As the 1990s progressed, the debate about constitutional change largely polarised around these two approaches. The collapse of communism, the move from Labour to New Labour in Britain and the demise of Margaret Thatcher as leader of the Conservative Party served to diminish the impact of several of the other approaches. As the liberal approach gained ground, so supporters of the traditional approach began to put their heads above the parapet in support of their position.

Supporters of the liberal approach argued that a new constitution was needed in order to push power down to the individual. Power was too heavily concentrated in public bodies and in special interests. De-centralising power would limit the over-mighty state and also be more efficient, ensuring that power was exercised at a more appropriate level, one more closely related to those affected by the decisions being taken. Supporters of the traditional approach countered by arguing that the traditional constitution had attributes that, in combination, made the existing arrangements preferable to anything else on offer. The attributes were those of coherence, accountability, responsiveness, flexibility and effectiveness. The system of government, it was argued, was coherent: the different parts of the system were integrated, one party being elected to office to implement a programme of public policy placed before electors. The system was accountable: electors knew who to hold to account – the party-in-government – if they disapproved of public policy; if they disapproved, they could sweep the party from office. The system was responsive: knowing that it could be swept from office at the next election, a government paid attention to the wishes of electors. Ministers could not ignore the wishes of voters and assume they could stay in office next time round as a result of post-election bargaining (a feature of some systems of government). The system was flexible: the system could respond quickly in times of crisis, with measures being passed quickly with all-party agreement. The system was also effective: government could govern and could usually be assured of parliamentary approval of measures promised in the party's election manifesto. Government could deliver on what in effect was a contract with the electors: in return for their support, it implemented its promised package of measures.

Reform under a Labour Government

In the 1970s, Labour politicians tended to adopt an essentially traditionalist stance. There was an attempt to devolve powers to elected assemblies in Scotland and Wales and the use of a national referendum, but these were not seen as part of some coherent scheme of constitutional reform. The referendum in particular was seen as an exercise in political expediency. In the early 1980s, the influence of left-wing activists pushed the party towards a more Socialist approach to the constitution. Under the leadership of Neil Kinnock, the party was weaned off this approach. It began to look more in the direction of the liberal approach.

The longer the party was denied office, the more major constitutional reform began to look attractive to the party. It was already committed to devolution. In its Socialist phase, it had adopted a policy of abolishing the House of Lords. It moved away from that to committing itself to removing hereditary peers from the House and introducing a more democratic second chamber. Having previously opposed electoral reform, some leading Labour MPs began to see merit in introducing proportional representation for parliamentary elections. John Smith, leader from 1992 to 1994, committed a future Labour Government to a referendum on the issue of electoral reform. The party also began to move cautiously towards embodying rights in statutory form: in 1992 it favoured a charter of rights. It also committed itself to strengthening local government.

The move toward a liberal approach was apparent in the Labour manifesto in the 1992 and 1997 general elections. In both elections, the Conservatives embraced the traditional approach and the Liberal Democrats the liberal approach. Table 15.1 shows the stance taken by each of the parties on constitutional issues in their 1997 election manifestos. The constitution was one subject on which it was generally acknowledged that there was a clear difference in policy between the parties.

Looking in greater detail at the Labour Party's proposals in the 1997 manifesto, the party advocated:

- devolving power to Scotland and Wales
- removing hereditary peers from the House of Lords
- incorporating the European Convention on Human Rights into British law
- appointing an independent commission to recommend a proportional alternative to the existing electoral system
- holding a referendum on the voting system
- introducing a system of proportional representation for the election of UK members of the European Parliament
- legislating for an elected mayor and strategic authority for London
- legislating to give people in the English regions power to decide by referendum, on a region by region basis, whether they wanted elected regional government
- introducing a Freedom of Information Bill

Table 15.1 Stance of parties on constitutional issues, 1997 general election

	Voting system	House of Lords	Devolution	Regional/local government	Protection of rights	House of Commons
Liberal Democrat	Introduce PR at local, national, European levels	Reform: have a predominantly elected chamber	Home Rule with elected Scottish and Welsh parliaments	Regional assemblies in England. Strategic authority for London	Bill of Rights preceded by incorporation of ECHR	Fixed-term parliaments; reduce number of MPs to 200
Conservative	Against PR	No mention, but against wholesale reform	Committed to Union. Sees Home Rule and devolution as leading to break-up of the UK	Against regional assemblies	Against a Bill of Rights	Two-year rolling parliamentary programme
Labour	Referendum on electoral reform	Remove hereditary peers	Elected Scottish and Welsh assemblies preceded by referendums	New Greater London Authority; elected mayors	Incorporation of ECHR	Select committee on modernisation of the House

- holding a referendum if the Government recommended joining a single European currency
- setting up a parliamentary committee to recommend proposals to modernise the House of Commons

In the first session of the new Parliament, the Government achieved passage of legislation providing for referendums in Scotland and Wales. In the referendums, electors in Scotland voted by a large majority for an elected parliament with legislative and some tax-varying powers. Voters in Wales voted narrowly for an elected assembly to determine spending in the Principality of Wales (see Table 15.2). The Government then introduced measures to provide for an elected parliament in Scotland and an elected assembly in Wales. Elections to the new bodies were held on 6 May 1999 and Scotland and Wales acquired new forms of government. The Government also introduced legislation providing for a new 108-member Assembly in Northern Ireland, with a power-sharing executive. This, along with other unique constitutional arrangements – including a North/South Ministerial Council and a Council of the Isles – had been approved by electors in Northern Ireland in a referendum in May 1998.

In the first session, the Government also achieved passage of the Human Rights Act, providing for the incorporation of the European Convention on Human Rights into British law – thus further reinforcing the new judicial dimension of the British constitution – as well as a bill providing for a referendum in London on whether or not the city should have an elected mayor and authority. The referendum in London, in May 1998, produced a large majority in favour of the proposal. 1,230,715 (72 per cent) voted 'yes' and 478,413 (28 per cent) voted 'no'. (The turnout, though, was a low one: only 34.1 per cent of eligible electors bothered to vote.) The House of Commons appointed a Select Committee on Modernisation. Within a year of its creation, it had issued seven reports, including one proposing various changes to the way legislation was considered in Parliament. The Government also introduced a bill providing for a closed member list system for the election of British members of the European Parliament. The House of Lords objected to the provision for closed lists (electors voting for a list of party candidates, with no provision to indicate preferences among the party nominees) and pushed for an open list system, allowing electors the option to indicate preferences. The Government resisted the Lords and eventually the Bill had to be passed, in the subsequent session of Parliament, under the provisions of the Parliament Act.

The Government at the end of 1997 appointed a Commission on the Voting System to make a recommendation on a proportional alternative to the existing electoral system. The Commission was asked to report within a year. The five-member body, chaired by Liberal Democrat peer Lord Jenkins of Hillhead, reported in October 1998. It considered a range of options but recommended the introduction of an electoral system known as the Alternative Vote Plus ('AV Plus'). Under this system, constituency MPs would be elected by the alternative vote but with top-up MPs, constituting between 15 and 20 per cent of the total number of members, being elected on an area-wide basis (such as a county) to ensure some element of proportionality.

In the second session of Parliament, the Government introduced a House of Lords Bill to remove hereditary peers from membership of the House of Lords. The Government also established a Royal Commission on the Reform of the House of Lords, under a former Conservative minister, Lord Wakeham, to make recommendations for a reformed second chamber once the hereditary peers had gone. It also introduced a Greater London Authority Bill to create a mayor and a strategic authority for the metropolis. Following its promise to introduce a Freedom of Information Bill,

Table 15.2 Referendum results in Scotland and Wales 1997

Scotland		
	A Scottish Parliament	Tax-varying powers
Agree	1,775,045 (74.3%)	1,512,889 (63.5%)
Disagree	614,400 (25.7%)	870,263 (36.5%)
Turnout: 60.4%		
Wales		
	A Welsh assembly	
Yes	559,419 (50.3%)	
No	552,698 (49.7%)	
Turnout: 50%		

Table 15.3 Changes to the established tenets of the traditional constitution

Tenets	Affected by
Parliamentary sovereignty	Incorporation of ECHR Ratification of Amsterdam Treaty
Rule of law	Incorporation of ECHR
Unitary state	Creation of Scottish Parliament, Welsh Assembly, and Northern Ireland Assembly
Parliamentary government under a constitutional Monarchy	Use of referendums Proposed new voting system Removal of hereditary peers from the House of Lords Freedom of Information Act Modernisation of the House of Commons

it published the text of its intended bill, and subsequently introduced the Bill at the beginning of the 1999–2000 session.

The concluding years of the century thus saw some significant changes to the country's constitution. These changes variously modified, reinforced or challenged the established tenets of the traditional constitution. Each tenet was affected in some way by the changes shown in Table 15.3.

Parliamentary sovereignty, already challenged by British membership of the European Community, was further challenged by the incorporation of the European Convention on Human Rights. This gave the courts an added role, in effect as protectors of the provisions of the Convention. If a provision of UK law was found by the courts to conflict with the provisions of the ECHR, a court could issue a certificate of incompatibility. It was then up to Parliament to act on the basis of the court's judgement. The ratification of the Amsterdam Treaty, already mentioned in the preceding section, further strengthened the European Union by extending the area of its policy competence, thus putting various areas of public policy beyond the simple decision-making capacity of national government and parliament.

The rule of law was strengthened by the incorporation of the ECHR. The effect of incorporation could be seen as providing a little more balance between the twin pillars of the constitution identified by Dicey (parliamentary sovereignty and the rule of law). The courts could now protect the rule of law against Parliament in a way that was not previously possible.

The unitary state was challenged by the creation of elected assemblies in Scotland, Wales and Northern Ireland. In Scotland, the new parliament was given power to legislate on any matter not reserved to the UK Parliament. It was also given power to vary the standard rate of taxation by 3p in the pound. The UK Parliament was expected not to legislate on matters that fell within the competence of the Scottish Parliament. The powers previously exercised by the Welsh Office were devolved to a Welsh Assembly. Legislative and administrative powers were also provided for a new Northern Ireland Assembly. The devolution of such powers raised questions as to the extent to which Parliament should intervene in matters that were exclusive to a part of the UK other than England. As such, devolution may be seen to limit, in effect, the flexibility of the traditional constitution. As we shall see (Chapter 23), devolution also serves to reinforce the judicial dimension to the constitution, giving the courts a role akin to constitutional courts in determining the legal competence of the new assemblies.

The creation of these new assemblies also challenged some of the basic tenets of a parliamentary government under a constitutional monarchy. Decision-making power was being hived off to bodies other than the British Cabinet. The coherence inherent in central parliamentary government was being challenged. Parliamentary government was challenged also by the use of referendums. Referendums provide for electors, rather than Parliament, to determine the outcome of particular issues. Opponents of a new electoral system also argued that, if the proposals for electoral reform were implemented, the capacity of the political system to produce accountable government would be undermined. The removal of hereditary peers proved controversial – not least, and not surprisingly, in the House of Lords – although the full consequences for parliamentary government were not apparent: one of the criticisms of the change was that the proposals for a fully reformed second chamber were not known. The reforms proposed by the Select Committee on Modernisation of the House of Commons served, albeit marginally, to strengthen the House. Against that, a unilateral decision by the Prime Minister at the beginning of the Parliament to have a one half-hour session of Prime Minister's questions once a week, instead of two fifteen-minute sessions each week, attracted criticism on the grounds that it gave MPs only one opportunity each week to question him, thus limiting the capacity to raise issues of immediate concern.

The collective effect of these changes has been to modify, rather than destroy, the traditional constitution. Formally, each of the elements of the constitution remains in place. The doctrine of parliamentary sovereignty may be challenged by incorporation of the ECHR, but formally Parliament is not bound by the rulings of the courts. The courts may issue certificates of incompatibility, but it is then up to Parliament to act on them. Parliament retains the formal power not to take any action (even if the reality is that it will act on them). Devolution may challenge the concept of a unitary state but ultimate power still resides with the centre. Devolved powers – indeed, devolved assemblies – may be abolished by Parliament. Formally, referendums are advisory only. Although it would be perverse for Parliament, having authorised a referendum, to then ignore the outcome, it nonetheless has the power to do so. Although a new electoral system may destroy the accountability inherent in the present system, no new electoral system has yet been introduced for elections to Parliament. Instead, new systems have been employed for other assemblies.

Although the practical effect of some of the changes may be to challenge and, in the long run, undermine the provisions of the traditional constitution, the basic provisions remain formally in place. The fact that they have been modified or are under challenge means that we may be moving away from the traditional constitution but, as yet, no new constitution has been put in its place. The traditional approach to the constitution has lost out since May 1997, but none of the other approaches can claim to have triumphed.

Parties and the constitution

In the wake of the general election of 1997, the stance of the parties on constitutional issues was clear. The Labour Party had been returned to power with a mandate to enact various measures of constitutional reform. The party's election manifesto was frequently quoted during debate on those measures, not least during debate on its House of Lords Bill. The Conservative Party remained committed to the traditional approach to the constitution. It had proposed no major constitutional reform in its election manifesto and was able to take a principled stand in opposition to various of the measures brought forward by the Labour Government. However, the measures brought forward by the Government created problems for both major parties and, to a lesser extent, for the Liberal Democrats.

The Labour Party

For the Labour Party, there were two problems. One was practical: that was, trying to implement all that it had promised in its election manifesto. Although it had a large parliamentary majority in the House of Commons, it encountered difficulties because of what happened elsewhere. The narrowness of the vote in the referendum in Wales in 1997 appeared to deter ministers from pursuing legislation to provide for referendums in the English regions. If the people of Wales were not enthusiastic for a devolved assembly, there appeared to be little mileage to be made in pursuing it in the English regions. The proposal for a referendum on a new electoral system encountered opposition. Labour MPs were divided on the merits of a new system. The report of the Commission on the Voting System in 1998 attracted a vigorous response from both Labour and Conservative opponents of change – one report suggested that at least 100 Labour MPs, including some members of the Cabinet, were opposed to electoral reform – and this appeared to influence the Government. Ministers indicated that a referendum was likely to be deferred to the next Parliament. The House of Lords Bill encountered stiff opposition in the

House of Lords in 1999 – peers carried a number of amendments against the Government – and failed to keep to the Government's proposed timetable. In order to facilitate passage of the Bill, the Government agreed to an amendment that permitted ninety-two (out of 748) hereditary peers to remain members of the House. The Freedom of Information Bill ran into opposition from within the ranks of the Government itself, various senior ministers – including the Home Secretary – not favouring a radical measure. When the Bill was eventually published in 1999, it was attacked by proponents of open government for not going far enough.

The constitution thus did not change in quite the way that the party had intended. This practical problem also exacerbated the second problem. The party was unable to articulate an intellectually coherent approach to constitutional change. It had moved away from both the socialist approach as well as the traditional approach. It moved some way toward the liberal approach. However, it only partially embraced the liberal agenda. It was wary of a new electoral system for elections to the House of Commons. It hesitated to pursue regional assemblies in England. It set up a Royal Commission to consider reform of the House of Lords but was reluctant to embrace demands for a wholly elected second chamber. In respect of both devolution and the incorporation of the European Convention on Human Rights, the Government ensured that the doctrine of parliamentary sovereignty remained in place.

Although the Labour Government was able to say what it was against, it was not able to articulate what it was for, at least not in terms of the future shape of the British constitution. What was its approach to the constitution? What sort of constitution did it wish to see in place in the new millennium? These questions were put to the Government, especially by this writer during the passage of the House of Lords Bill in 1999, but ministers either studiously avoided answering the questions or claimed that the Government's approach was, in the words of the Leader of the House of Lords, Baroness Jay, 'pragmatic'. The Government thus lay open to the accusation that it had no clear philosophical approach, nothing that would render its approach predictable or provide it with a reference point in the event of things going wrong. Opponents were thus able to claim that it was marching down the path – or rather down several paths – of constitutional reform without having a comprehensive map and without any very clear idea of where it was heading.

The Conservative Party

The Conservative Party encountered a problem, although one that was essentially in the future. In the short term, it was able to adopt a consistent and coherent position. It supported the traditional approach to the constitution. It was therefore opposed to any changes that threatened the essential elements of the Westminster system of Government. It was especially vehement in its opposition to proposals for electoral reform, mounting a notable campaign against the recommendations of the Commission on the Voting System in 1998. It opposed the House of Lords Bill, not least on the grounds that the Government had not said what the second stage of reform would be.

The party encountered some practical problems. It took time to organise itself as an opposition, having difficulties marshalling its forces to scrutinise effectively the Government's proposals for referendums. The Conservative leader in the Lords, Lord Cranborne, negotiated a private deal with the Government to retain some hereditary peers in the second chamber: he was sacked by the party leader, William Hague, for having negotiated behind his back. There were also some Conservative MPs who inclined towards a more liberal approach to the constitution, favouring an elected second chamber and an English Parliament.

However, the most important problem facing the party was long term rather than short term. How was a future Conservative Government to respond to the constitutional changes made under a Labour Government? The constitution would no longer be the same constitution it had been defending up to 1997. What, exactly, would be the 'traditional' approach to the constitution in the twenty-first century? Should a future Conservative Government seek to overturn the various reforms made by the Labour Government? Or should it seek to conserve the constitution as it stood at the time the Conservatives regained power?

The Conservative Leader, William Hague, recognised the problem and, in a speech in London in February 1998, challenged the party to address the issue. 'What happens to the defenders of the status quo', he asked, 'when the status quo itself disappears?' The party could not simply shrug its shoulders, he said, and accept whatever arrangements it inherited. Nor could the party reverse every one of Labour's constitutional changes. The clock could not be put back. 'Devolution or the politicisation of the judiciary are not changes that can easily be undone. Attempting to return the constitution to its status quo ante would be a futile task.' The party, he declared, would need to adopt its own programme of constitutional reform. He accepted that devolution was a fact and he committed the party to fighting for seats and working in the new assemblies. He outlined some of the issues, such as the relationship between Parliament and the judiciary and between Parliament and Government, that the party would have to address. He later appointed various commissions to address various aspects of constitutional change – on reform of the House of Lords, on a single currency and on strengthening Parliament. In 1999, he spoke of the need to address the 'English question' in Parliament: how should legislation relating exclusively to England be dealt with by a Parliament made up of members from all parts of the United Kingdom? He sought to make some of the running in considering constitutional change. In so doing, he explicitly acknowledged the basic problem facing the party. As he pithily put it: 'you can't unscramble an omelette'. The Conservative Party had to decide what was the most appropriate recipe.

Liberal democrats

The Liberal Democrats could claim to be in the strongest position on issues of constitutional change. They embraced the liberal approach to constitutional change. They therefore had a clear agenda. They were able to evaluate the Government's reform proposals against that agenda. Given that the Government fell short of pursuing a wholly liberal agenda, they were able to push for those measures which the Government had not embraced. Their stance was thus principled and consistent.

In so far as they encountered problems, they were practical problems. Because they favoured the reform measures espoused by the Labour Government, they accepted an invitation to participate in a Cabinet Committee comprising ministers and leading Liberal Democrats to discuss constitutional change. They thus had some input into deliberations on the future of the constitution. This co-operation engendered some debate within the party as to how far it might be taken. It also threw up problems for the party in terms of how far the Government was prepared to go. It was widely reported that one condition of Liberal Democrat agreement to co-operate was a Government commitment to a referendum on electoral reform. However, the failure of the Government to act on this promise following publication of the report of the Commission on the Voting System – chaired by a leading Liberal Democrat – resulted in no notable action on the part of the party leader, Paddy Ashdown. His successor, Charles Kennedy, elected in 1999, also showed no immediate signs of taking action. Although they knew what they wanted to achieve, Liberal Democrats appeared hesitant in pushing the Government to move quickly on some of the most treasured goals of the liberal agenda.

The continuing debate

The constitution remains an issue of debate. It does so at two levels. One is at the wider level of the very nature of the constitution itself. What shape should the British constitution take? How plausible are the various approaches to constitutional change? The Liberal Democrats, along with various commentators, advocate the liberal approach. The Conservatives have favoured the traditional approach: though they are deciding how to respond to change, they want to retain those features of the Westminster system that remain and which deliver the attributes that flow from that system. Thus, for example, the party remains vehemently opposed to electoral reform. The Labour Party wants to move away from the 'traditional' constitution but not to do so to the extent that it prevents a Labour Government from governing.

The other level is specific to various measures of constitutional change. Some changes have been made to the constitution. Other changes are advocated, not least – although not exclusively – by advocates of the liberal approach. There are calls for elected assemblies in the English regions or for an English Parliament. Electoral reform remains an issue on the political agenda. Supporters of change want to see the introduction of a system of proportional representation for parliamentary elections. Opponents advance the case for the existing first-past-the-post method of election. (See Box 15.2.) The use of referendums, and

BOX 15.2 **DEBATE**

Electoral reform (proportional representation)

The case for

- Every vote would count, producing seats in proportion to votes.
- It would get rid of the phenomenon of the 'wasted vote'.
- It would be fairer to third parties, ensuring they got seats in proportion to their percentage of the poll.
- On existing voting patterns, it would result usually in no one party having an overall majority – thus encouraging a coalition and moderate policies.
- A coalition enjoying majority support is more likely to ensure continuity of policy than changes in government under the existing first-past-the-post system.
- A coalition enjoying majority support enjoys a greater popular legitimacy than a single-party government elected by a minority of voters.
- Coalitions resulting from election by proportional representation can prove stable and effective.
- There is popular support for change.

The case against

- Very few systems are exactly proportional. Little case to change to a relatively more proportional system than the existing system unless other advantages are clear.
- A system of proportional representation would give an unfair advantage to small parties which would be likely hold the balance of power.
- The government would most likely be chosen as a result of bargaining by parties after a general election and not as a deliberate choice of the electors.
- It would be difficult to ensure accountability to electors in the event of a multi-party coalition being formed.
- Coalitions cobbled together after an election lack the legitimacy of clear electoral approval.
- There is no link between electoral systems and economic performance.
- Coalitions resulting from election under a system of proportional representation can lead to uncertainty and a change of coalition partners – as happened in West Germany in 1982 and Ireland in 1994.
- Bargaining between parties can produce instability, but coalitions can also prove difficult for the electorate to get rid of.
- There is popular support for the consequences of the existing electoral system – notably a single party being returned to govern the country.
- 'Proportional representation' is a generic term for a large number of electoral systems: there is no agreement on what precise system should replace the existing one.

the promise of their use on particular issues, has spurred calls for their more regular use. Opponents are wary of any further use; some are opposed to referendums on principle. (See Box 15.3.) The role of the second chamber also generates considerable debate. Should there be a second chamber of parliament? Most of those engaged in constitutional debate support the case for a second chamber but do not agree on the form it should take. Should it be wholly or part-elected? Or should it be a nominated House? (See Chapter 17.) The election of a Labour Government in May 1997, committed to various measures of constitutional reform, did not put an end to debate about the future of the British constitution. If anything, it gave it new impetus, leaving the issue of the constitution very much on the political agenda.

BOX 15.3 **DEBATE**

Referendums

The case for

- A referendum is an educational tool – it informs citizens about the issue.
- Holding a referendum encourages people to be more involved in political activity.
- A referendum helps resolve major issues – it gives a chance for the voters to decide.
- The final outcome of a referendum is more likely to enjoy public support than if the decision is taken solely by Parliament – it is difficult to challenge a decision if all voters have a chance to take part.
- The use of referendums increases support for the political system – voters know they are being consulted on the big issues. Even if they don't take part, they know they have an opportunity to do so. The issue is not being decided by politicians in Westminster.

The case against

- Referendums are blunt weapons that usually allow only a simple answer to a very general question. They do not permit of explanations of why voters want something done or the particular way in which they want it done.
- Referendums undermine the position of Parliament as the deliberative body of the nation.
- There is no obvious limit on when referendums should be held – if one is conceded on the issue of Europe, why not also have referendums on capital punishment, immigration and trade union reform? With no obvious limit, there is the potential for 'government by referendum'.
- Referendums can be used as majoritarian weapons – being used by the majority to restrict minorities.
- There is the difficulty of ensuring a balanced debate – one side may (indeed, is likely to) have more money and resources.
- There is the difficulty of formulating, and agreeing, a clear and objective question.
- Research shows that turnout in referendums tends to be lower than that in elections for parliamentary and other public elections. In the UK, for example, there have been low turnouts in Wales (1997) and London (1998).
- Referendums are expensive to hold and are often expensive ways of not deciding issues – if government does not like the result it calls another referendum (as happened in Denmark over ratification of the Maastricht Treaty in 1992).

The relationship between the debate about the constitution and about particular measures of constitutional reform throws up a vital question. Should specific reforms derive from a clear view of what the constitution, as a constitution, should look like in five or ten years? Or should the shape of the constitution be determined by specific changes made on the basis of their individual merits?

Chapter summary

The British constitution remains distinctive for not being codified in a single document. It is drawn from several sources and retains the main components that it has developed over three centuries. Although little debated in the years between 1945 and 1970, it has been the subject of dispute – and of change – in the years since. Various approaches to change have developed. The constitution has undergone significant change as a result of British membership of the EC/EU and the return of a Labour Government in May 1997. The consequence of these changes has been to change the contours of the 'traditional', or Westminster, model of government, although not destroying the model altogether. The constitution remains a subject of political controversy, posing problems for each of the main political parties. The future shape of the constitution remains unclear.

Discussion points

- How does the constitution of the United Kingdom differ from that of other countries? What does it have in common with them?
- Which approach to constitutional change do you find most persuasive, and why?
- What are the principal arguments against holding referendums?
- Is electoral reform desirable?
- What are the main obstacles to achieving major constitutional change in the United Kingdom?

Further reading

For the early seminal works favouring reform, see Finer (1975) and Hailsham (1976). For leading critiques of the traditional constitution in the 1990s see especially Marr (1995), Hutton (1995) and Barnett (1997). Recent works addressing constitutional change include Barendt (1998), Beatson *et al.* (1998), and Hazell (1999). A Conservative view of the Constitution is to be found in Lansley and Wilson (1997); see also Patten (1995) and Norton (1991, 1992, 1996). The reforms introduced by the Labour Government in the first session of the 1997 Parliament are well summarised in Hazell and Sinclair (1999).

There are various useful publications that address specific issues. Most of these are identified in subsequent chapters (monarchy, Chapter 16; House of Commons, Chapter 17; House of Lords, Chapter 18; and the judiciary, Chapter 23). Chapter 23 also addresses issues arising from membership of the European Union, the incorporation of the European Convention on Human Rights and devolution. On electoral reform see Dunleavy *et al.* (1997), The Report of the Independent Commission on the Voting system (1998) and – for the case against – Norton (1998).

References

Barendt, E. (1998) *An Introduction to Constitutional Law* (Oxford University Press).

Barnett, A. (1997) *This Time: Our Constitutional Revolution* (Vintage).

Barnett, A., Ellis, C. and Hirst, P. (eds) (1993) *Debating the Constitution* (Polity Press).

Beatson, J., Forsyth, C. and Hare, I. (1998) *Constitutional Reform in the United Kingdom: Practice and Principles* (Hart Publishing).

Benn, T. (1993) *Common Sense* (Hutchinson).

Brazier, R. (1994) *Constitutional Practice*, 2nd edn (Oxford University Press).

Dunleavy, P., Margetts, H., O'Duffy, B. and Weir, S. (1997) *Making Votes Count* (Democratic Audit, University of Essex).

Finer, S.E. (ed.) (1975) *Adversary Politics and Electoral Reform* (Wigram).

Fitzpatrick, B. (1999) 'A dualist House of Lords in a sea of monist community law', in B. Dickson and P. Carmichael (eds), *The House of Lords: Its Parliamentary and Judicial Roles* (Hart Publishing).

Hailsham, Lord (1976) *Elective Dictatorship* (BBC).

Hazell, R. (ed.) (1999) *Constitutional Futures* (Oxford University Press).

Hazell, R. and Sinclair, D. (1999) 'The British constitution in 1997–98: Labour's constitutional revolution', *Parliamentary Affairs*, Vol. 52, No. 2.

Hutton, W. (1995) *The State We're In* (Jonathan Cape).

Independent Commission on the Voting System (1998) *Report of the Independent Commission on the Voting System*, Cm 4090-1 (The Stationery Office).

Institute for Public Policy Research (1992) *A New Constitution for the United Kingdom* (Mansell).

Labour Party (1997) *New Labour: Because Britain Deserves Better* (Labour Party).

Lansley, A. and Wilson, R. (1997) *Conservatives and the Constitution* (Conservative 2000 Foundation).

Marr, A. (1995) *Ruling Britannia* (Michael Joseph).

Maxwell, P. (1999) 'The House of Lords as a constitutional court – the implications of Ex Parte EOC', in B. Dickson and P. Carmichael (eds), *The House of Lords: Its Parliamentary and Judicial Roles* (Hart Publishing).

Norton, P. (1982) *The Constitution in Flux* (Blackwell).

Norton, P. (1991) 'In defence of the constitution', in P. Norton (ed.), *New Directions in British Politics?* (Edward Elgar).

Norton, P. (1992) *The Constitution: The Conservative Way Forward* (Conservative Political Centre).

Norton, P. (1993) 'The constitution: approaches to reform', *Politics Review*, Vol. 3, No. 1.

Norton, P. (1996) 'In defence of the constitution: a response to Elcock', *Talking Politics*, Vol. 9, No. 1.

Norton, P. (1998) *Power to the People* (Conservative Policy Forum, 1998).

Patten, J. (1995) *Things to Come* (Sinclair-Stevenson).

Richard, Lord and Welfare, D. (1999) *Unfinished Business: Reforming the House of Lords* (Vintage).

Royal Commission on the Reform of the House of Lords (2000) *A House for the Future*, Cm 4534.

Tyrie, A. (1998) *Reforming the Lords: A Conservative Approach* (Conservative Policy Forum).

Chapter 16

The crown

Philip Norton

Learning objectives

- To identify the place of the monarchy in British constitutional history.
- To outline the roles the citizens expect the monarch to fulfil today.
- To consider the extent to which they are carried out.
- To outline criticisms made of the monarchy – and the royal family – in recent years.
- To look at proposals for change.

Introduction

It is an extraordinary fact, often overlooked, that Britain's representative democracy evolved over a thousand years out of an all-encompassing monarchy underpinned by the religious notion of the divine right of kings. The monarchical shell remains intact but the inner workings have been taken over by party political leaders and civil servants. The shell itself has been the subject of critical comment, especially in recent years. This chapter analyses the emergence of the modern monarchy and considers its still important functions together with the arguments of the critics.

The crown is the symbol of all executive authority. It is conferred on the monarch. The monarchy is the oldest secular institution in England and dates back at least to the ninth century. In Anglo-Saxon and Norman times, the formal power that the crown conferred – executive, legislative and judicial – was exercised personally by the monarch. The King had a court to advise him and, as the task of government became more demanding, so the various functions were exercised on the King's behalf by other bodies. Those bodies now exercise powers independent of the control of the monarch, but they remain formally the instruments of the crown. The courts are Her Majesty's courts and the government is Her Majesty's government. Parliament is summoned and prorogued by royal decree. Civil servants are crown appointees. Many powers – prerogative powers – are still exercised in the name of the crown, including the power to declare war. The monarch exercises few powers personally, but those powers remain important. However, the importance of the monarchy in the twentieth century derives more from what it stands for than from what it does.

The monarchy has been eclipsed as a major political institution not only by the sheer demands of governing a growing kingdom but also by changes in the popular perception of what form of government is legitimate. The policy-making power exercised by a hereditary monarch has given way to the exercise of power by institutions deemed more representative. However, the monarchy has retained a claim to be a representative institution in one particular definition of the term. It is this claim that largely defines the activities of the monarch today.

The monarchy pre-dates by several centuries the emergence of the concept of representation. The term 'representation' entered the English language through French derivatives of the Latin *repraesentare*, and did not assume a political meaning until the sixteenth century. It permits at least four separate usages (see Birch, 1964; Pitkin, 1967):

1. It may denote acting on behalf of some individual or group, seeking to defend and promote the interests of the person or persons 'represented'.
2. It may denote persons or assemblies that have been freely elected. Although it is not always the case that persons so elected will act to defend and pursue the interests of electors, they will normally be expected to do so.
3. It may be used to signify a person or persons typical of a particular class or group of persons. It is this sense in which it is used when opinion pollsters identify a representative sample.
4. It may be used in a symbolic sense. Thus, individuals or objects may 'stand for' something: for example, a flag symbolising the unity of the nation.

The belief that free election was a prerequisite for someone to claim to act on behalf of others grew in the nineteenth century. Before then, the concept of 'virtual representation' held great sway. This concept was well expressed by Edmund Burke. It was a form of representation, he wrote, 'in which there is a communion of interests, and a sympathy in feelings and desires, between those who act in the name of any description of people, and the people in whose name they act, though the trustees are not actually chosen by them'. It was a concept challenged by the perception that the claim to speak on behalf of a particular body of individuals could not be sustained unless those individuals had signified their agreement, and the way to signify that agreement was through the ballot box. This challenge proved increasingly successful, with the extension of the franchise and, to ensure elections free of coercion, changes in the method of election (the introduction of secret ballots, for example). By the end of the 1880s, the majority of working men had the vote. By Acts of 1918 and 1928, the vote was given to women.

The extension of the franchise in the nineteenth and early twentieth centuries meant that the House of Commons could claim to be a representative institution under the first and second definitions of the term. The unelected House of Lords could not make such a claim. The result, as we shall see (Chapter 17), was a significant shift in the relationship between the two Houses. However, it was not only the unelected upper

House that could not make such a claim. Nor could the unelected monarch. Nor could the monarch make a claim to be representative of the nation under the third definition. The claim of the monarch to be 'representative' derives solely from the fourth definition. The monarch stands as a symbol. The strength of the monarch as symbol has been earned at the expense of exercising political powers. To symbolise the unity of the nation, the monarch has had to stand apart from the partisan fray. The monarch has also had to stand aloof from any public controversy. When controversy has struck – as during the abdication crisis in 1936 and during periods of marital rift between members of the royal family in the 1990s – it has undermined support for the institution of monarchy and called into question its very purpose.

Development of the monarchy

The present monarch, despite some breaks in the direct line of succession, can trace her descent from King Egbert, who united England under his rule in AD 829. Only once has the continuity of the monarchy been broken, during the period of rule by the Council of State and Oliver Cromwell (1642–60), although the line of succession was restored with the accession of Charles II. The principle of heredity has been preserved since at least the eleventh century. The succession is now governed by statute and common law, the throne descending to the eldest son or, in the absence of a son, the eldest daughter. If the monarch is under eighteen years of age, a regent is appointed.

Though all power was initially exercised by the monarch, it was never an absolute power. In the coronation oath, the King promised to 'forbid all rapine and injustice to men of all conditions', and he was expected to consult with the leading men of his realm, both clerical and lay, in order to discover and declare the law and also before the levying of any extraordinary measures of taxation. Such an expectation was to find documented expression in Magna Carta, to which King John affixed his seal in 1215 and which is now recognised as a document of critical constitutional significance. At the time, it was seen by the barons as an expression of existing rights, not a novel departure from them.

The expectation that the King would consult with the leading men of the realm gradually expanded to encompass knights and burgesses, summoned to assent on behalf of local communities to the raising of more money to meet the King's growing expenses. From the summoning of these local dignitaries to court there developed a Parliament – the term was first used in the thirteenth century – and the emergence of two separate Houses, the Lords and the Commons.

The relationship of crown and Parliament was, for several centuries, one of struggle. Although formally the King's Parliament, the King depended on the institution for the grant of supply (money) and increasingly for assent to new laws. Parliament made the grant of supply dependent on the King granting a redress of grievances. Tudor monarchs turned to Parliament for support and usually got it; but the effect of their actions was to acknowledge the growing importance of the body. Stuart kings were less appreciative. James I and his successor, Charles I, upheld the doctrine of the **divine right** of kings: that is, that the position and powers of the King are given by God and the position and privileges of Parliament derive therefore from the King's grace. Charles' pursuit of the doctrine led to an attempt to rule without the assent of Parliament and ultimately to civil war and the beheading of the King in 1649. The period of republican government that followed was a failure and consequently short lived. The monarchy was restored in 1660, only to produce another clash a few years later.

James II adhered to the divine right of kings and to the Roman Catholic faith. Both produced a clash with Parliament and James attempted to rule by **royal prerogative** alone. A second civil war was averted when James fled the country following the arrival of William of Orange (James' Protestant son-in-law), who had been invited by leading politicians and churchmen. At the invitation of a new Parliament, William and his wife Mary (James' daughter) jointly assumed the throne. However, the offer of the crown had been conditional on their acceptance of the Declaration of Right – embodied in statute as the 1689 Bill of

Rights – which declared the suspending of laws and the levying of taxation without the approval of Parliament to be illegal. As the historian G.M. Trevelyan observed, James II had forced the country to choose between royal absolutism and parliamentary government (Trevelyan, 1938, p. 245). It chose parliamentary government.

The dependence of the monarch on Parliament was thus established and the years since have witnessed the gradual withdrawal of the sovereign from the personal exercise of executive authority. Increasingly, the monarch became dependent on ministers, both for the exercise of executive duties and in order to manage parliamentary business. This dependence was all the greater when Queen Anne died in 1714 without an heir (all her children having died) and yet another monarch was imported from the continent – this time George, Elector of Hanover. George I of Britain was not especially interested in politics and in any case did not speak English, so the task of chairing the Cabinet, traditionally the King's job, fell to the First Lord of the Treasury. Under Robert Walpole, this role was assiduously developed and Walpole became the most important of the King's ministers: he became 'prime minister'. Anne's dying without an heir and George's poor language skills facilitated the emergence of an office that is now at the heart of British politics.

George III succeeded in winning back some of the monarchy's power later on in the eighteenth century. It was still the King, after all, who appointed ministers and by skilfully using his patronage he could influence who sat in the House of Commons. This power, though, was undermined early in the nineteenth century. In 1832, the Great Reform Act introduced a uniform electoral system and subsequent reform acts further extended the franchise. The age of a representative democracy, displacing the concept of virtual representation, had arrived. The effect was to marginalise the monarch as a political actor. To win votes in Parliament, parties quickly organised themselves into coherent and highly structured movements and the leader of the majority party following a general election became Prime Minister. The choice of Prime Minister and government – what Bagehot referred to as 'the elective function' – remained formally in the hands of the monarch, but in practice the selection came to be made on a regular basis by the electorate.

Queen Victoria was the last monarch seriously to consider vetoing legislation (the last monarch actually to do so was Queen Anne, who withheld Royal Assent from the Scottish Militia Bill in 1707). The year 1834 was the last occasion that a ministry fell for want of the sovereign's confidence; thereafter, it was the confidence of the House of Commons that counted. Victoria was also the last monarch to exercise a personal preference in the choice of Prime Minister (later monarchs, where a choice existed, acted under advice), and the last to be instrumental in pushing successfully for the enactment of particular legislative measures (Hardie, 1970, p. 67). By the end of her reign, it was clear that the monarch, whatever the formal powers vested by the constitution, was constrained politically by a representative assembly elected by the adult male population, the government being formed largely by members drawn from that assembly. Victoria could no longer exercise the choices she had been able to do when she first ascended the throne.

The monarch by the beginning of the twentieth century sat largely on the sidelines of the political system, unable to control Parliament, unable to exercise a real choice in the appointment of ministers, unable to exercise a choice in appointing

BOX 16.1 MINI BIOGRAPHY

Queen Victoria (1819–1901)

Last monarch before position became purely ceremonial. Ascending to the throne aged eighteen, she became the longest serving monarch in British history. She enjoyed a happy marriage with Prince Albert of Saxe-Coburg and when he died was lost for a while until she regained some zest for her role. She enjoyed dealing with Disraeli but was put off by the stern Gladstone. Her nine children acceded to various thrones of Europe. Given the weakness of parties in the middle of the century she was able to influence the composition of several administrations, the last monarch to do so.

judges. The extensive power once exercised by the King had now passed largely to the voters. However, the elective power was only exercised on election day: in between elections it was the Prime Minister who exercised many of the powers formally vested in the monarch. By controlling government appointments, the Prime Minister was able to dominate the executive side of government. And as long as he could command majority support in Parliament he was able to dominate the legislative side of government. Power thus shifted from an unelected monarch to what one writer later dubbed an 'elected monarch' (Benemy, 1965) – the occupant not of Buckingham Palace but of 10 Downing Street.

The shift to a position detached from regular partisan involvement, and above the actual exercise of executive power, has been confirmed in the twentieth century. 'Since 1901 the trend towards a real political neutrality, not merely a matter of appearances, has been steady, reign by reign' (Hardie, 1970, p. 188). The transition has been facilitated by no great constitutional act. Several statutes have impinged on the prerogative power but many of the legal powers remain. There is nothing in law that prevents the monarch from vetoing a bill or from exercising personal choice in the invitation to form a government. The monarch is instead bound by conventions of the constitution (see Chapter 15). Thus, it is a convention that the monarch gives her assent to bills passed by Parliament and that she summons the leader of the largest party following a general election to form a government. Such conventions mean that the actions of the monarch are predictable – no personal choice is involved – and they have helped ease the passage of the monarch from one important constitutional position to another.

The contemporary role of the monarchy

Most people still believe that the monarchy has an important role to play in the future of Britain. In a MORI poll in June 1999, 66 per cent of those questioned said that the monarchy had such a role to play, as against 27 per cent who said that it did not.

What, then, is the contemporary role of the monarch? Two primary tasks can be identified. One is essentially a representative task: that is, symbolising the unity and traditional standards of the nation. The second is to fulfil certain political functions. The weakness of the monarch in being able to exercise independent decisions in the latter task underpins the strength of the monarchy in fulfilling the former. If the monarch were to engage in partisan activity, it would undermine her claim to symbolise the unity of the nation.

Symbolic role

The functions fulfilled by the monarch under the first heading are several. A majority of respondents in a poll in the late 1980s considered six functions to be 'very' or 'quite' important. As we shall see, the extent to which these functions are actually fulfilled by members of the royal family has become a matter of considerable debate. Two functions – preserving the class system and distracting people from problems affecting the country – were considered by most respondents as 'not very' or 'not at all' important.

Representing the UK at home or abroad

More than nine out of every ten people questioned in the poll considered this to be very or quite important. As a symbolic function, it is a task normally ascribed to any head of state. Because no partisan connotations attach to her activities, the sovereign is able to engage the public commitment of citizens in a way that politicians cannot. When the President of the United States travels within the USA or goes abroad he does so both as head of state and as head of government; as head of government, he is a practising politician. When the Queen attends the Commonwealth Prime Ministers' conference, she does so as symbolic head of the Commonwealth. The British government is represented by the Prime Minister, who is then able to engage in friendly or not so friendly discussions with fellow heads of government. The Queen stays above the fray. Similarly, at home, when opening a hospital or attending a major public event, the Queen is able to stand as a symbol of the nation.

Invitations to the Prime Minister or leader of an opposition party to perform such tasks run the risk of attracting partisan objection.

At least two practical benefits are believed to derive from this non-partisan role, one political, the other economic. Like many of her predecessors, the Queen has amassed considerable experience by virtue of her monarchical longevity. In 2002, she will celebrate her fiftieth year on the throne. During those years, she will have been served by at least ten separate Prime Ministers. Prime Minister Tony Blair was born the year that she ascended to the throne. Her experience, coupled with her neutrality, has meant that she has been able to offer prime ministers detached and informed observations. (The Prime Minister has an audience with the Queen each week.) As an informed figure that offers no challenge to their position, she also offers an informed ear to an embattled premier. The value of the Queen's role to premiers has been variously attested by successive occupants of Downing Street. These have included Labour Prime Ministers Harold Wilson and James Callaghan, who were especially warm in their praise, as well as the present occupant of the office. Tony Blair said at the time of the Queen's golden wedding anniversary that he enjoyed his weekly audience with the Queen, not simply because of her experience, but because she was an 'extraordinarily shrewd and perceptive observer of the world. Her advice is worth having' (*The Times*, 21 November 1997).

The political benefit has also been seen in the international arena. By virtue of her experience and neutral position, the Queen enjoys the respect of international leaders, not least those gathered in the Commonwealth. During the 1980s, when relations between the British government led by Margaret Thatcher and a number of Commonwealth governments were sometimes acrimonious (on the issue of sanctions against South Africa, for example), she reputedly used her influence with Commonwealth leaders 'to ensure that they took account of Britain's difficulties' (Ziegler, 1996). There were fears that, without her emollient influence, the Commonwealth would have broken up or that Britain would have been expelled from it.

In terms of economic benefit, some observers claim – although a number of critics dispute it – that the Queen and leading members of the royal family (such as the Prince of Wales) are good for British trade. The symbolism, the history and the pageantry that surround the monarchy serve to make the Queen and her immediate family a potent source of media and public interest abroad. Royal visits are often geared to export promotions, although critics claim the visits do not have the impact claimed or are not followed up adequately by the exporters themselves. Such visits, though, normally draw crowds that would not be attracted by a visiting politician or industrialist.

Setting standards of citizenship and family life

For most of the present Queen's reign, this has been seen as an important task. The Queen has been expected to lead by example in maintaining standards of citizenship and family life. As head of state and secular head of the established church, she is expected to be above criticism. She applies herself assiduously to her duties; even her most ardent critics concede that she is diligent (Wilson, 1989, p. 190). In April 1947, at the age of twenty-one, while still Princess Elizabeth, she said in a broadcast to the Commonwealth: 'I declare before you that my whole life, be it long or short, shall be devoted to your service'. She and members of the royal family undertake a wide range of public duties each year. In 1998, for example, the Queen and other members of the family fulfilled 2,565 official engagements in the UK and 1,103 engagements abroad (O'Donovan, 1999). The Queen lends her name to charities and voluntary organisations. Other members of her family involve themselves in charitable activities. The Prince of Wales established the Prince's Youth Business Trust, which has been responsible for funding the launch of 30,000 small businesses. The work of the Princess Royal (Princess Anne) as president of the Save the Children Fund helped raise its international profile. Indeed, the name of a member of the royal family usually adorns the headed notepaper of every leading charity.

Up to, and including, the 1980s, the Queen was held to epitomise not only standards of good citizenship, applying herself selflessly to her public duties, but also family life in a way that others could both empathise with and emulate. (Queen Elizabeth, the Queen Mother – widow of George VI – was, and remains, popularly portrayed as 'the nation's grandmother'.) Significantly, during the national miners' strike in 1984, the wives of striking miners petitioned the Queen for help. However, the extent to which the Queen fulfils this role has been the subject of much publicised debate since the late 1980s. The problem lay not so much with the Queen personally but with members of her family. By 1992, the Queen was head of a family that had not sustained one successful lasting marriage. The Prince of Wales, as well as the Princess, admitted adultery. The Duchess of York was pictured cavorting topless with her 'financial adviser' while her daughters were present. By the end of the decade, the divorced heir to the throne was seen publicly with his companion, Camilla Parker-Bowles. As we shall see, these developments have proved a feature of contemporary debate about the role and future of the British monarchy.

Uniting people despite differences

The monarch symbolises the unity of the nation. The Queen is head of state. Various public functions are carried out in the name of the crown, notably public prosecutions, and as the person in whom the crown vests the monarch's name attaches to the various organs of the state: the government, courts and armed services. The crown, in effect, substitutes for the concept of the state (a concept not well understood or utilised in Britain) and the monarch serves as the personification of the crown. Nowhere is the extent of this personification better demonstrated than on British postage stamps. These are unique: British stamps alone carry the monarch's head with no mention of the name of the nation. The monarch provides a clear, living focal point for the expression of national unity, national pride and, if necessary, national grief.

This role is facilitated by the monarch largely transcending political activity. Citizens' loyalties can flow to the crown without being hindered by political considerations. The Queen's role as head of the Commonwealth may also have helped create a 'colour-blind' monarchy, in which the welfare of everyone, regardless of race, is taken seriously. At different points this century, members of the royal family have also shown concern for the economically underprivileged and those who have lost their livelihoods – ranging from the 'something must be done' remark in the 1930s of the then Prince of Wales (later Edward VIII) about unemployment while visiting Wales to the work of the present Prince of Wales to help disadvantaged youths.

This unifying role has also acquired a new significance as a consequence of devolution. The Crown remains the one unifying feature of the United Kingdom. The UK traditionally comprises one constitutional people under one Crown and Parliament. The position of the UK Parliament is circumscribed by virtue of devolving powers to elected assemblies in different parts of the UK. The royal family anticipated the consequences of devolution by seeking funding for an enhancement of the royal offices and residence in Scotland. The Queen opened the Scottish Parliament as well as the Welsh Assembly. In the event of conflict between a devolved government and the UK Government, the Queen constitutes the one person to whom members of both governments owe an allegiance.

The extent to which this role is effectively fulfilled, though, does not go unquestioned. Critics, as we shall see, claim that the royal family occupies a socially privileged position that symbolises not so much unity but rather the social divisions of the nation. Although the royal household is known for having several gays in its employ, critics have drawn attention to the dearth of employees in the royal household drawn from ethnic minorities. In 1997, for example, there was not one black employee among 850 staff at Buckingham Palace. Nor were there any on the staff of the Prince Wales. In that year, Prince Charles launched a campaign to recruit blacks into the royal household. He was reported to believe that the existing system of selection was 'archaic and outdated' (*The Times*, 2 November 1997).

Allegiance of the armed forces

The armed services are in the service of the crown. Loyalty is owed to the monarch, not least by virtue of the oath taken by all members of the armed forces. It is also encouraged by the close links maintained by the royal family with the various services. Members of the royal family have variously served in (usually) the Royal Navy or the Army. Most hold ceremonial ranks, such as colonel-in-chief of a particular regiment. Prince Andrew is a serving naval officer and was a helicopter pilot during the 1982 Falklands War. The Queen takes a particular interest in miliary matters, including awards for service. 'With the outbreak of the troubles in Ulster in the late 1960s she was a moving force in getting a medal created for services there, and she reads personally all the citations for gallantry there – as she had always done for medals of any sort' (Lacey, 1977, p. 222). Such a relationship helps emphasise the apolitical role of the military and also provides a barrier should the military, or more probably sections of it, seek to overthrow or threaten the elected government. (In the 1970s, there were rumours – retailed in the press and on a number of television programmes – that a number of retired officers favoured a coup to topple the Labour government returned in 1974.) In the event of an attempted military coup, the prevailing view – although not universally shared – is that the monarch would serve as the most effective bulwark to its realisation, the Queen being in a position to exercise the same role as that of King Juan Carlos of Spain in 1981, when he forestalled a right-wing military takeover by making a public appeal to the loyalty of his army commanders.

Maintaining continuity of British traditions

The monarch symbolises continuity in affairs of state. Many of the duties traditionally performed by her have symbolic relevance: for example, the state opening of Parliament and – important in the context of the previous point – the annual ceremony of trooping the colour. Other traditions serve a psychological function, helping maintain a sense of belonging to the nation, and also a social function. The awarding of honours and royal garden parties are viewed by critics as socially elitist but by supporters as helping break down social barriers, rewarding those – regardless of class – who have contributed significantly to the community. Hierarchy of awards, on this argument, is deemed less important than the effect on the recipients. The award of an MBE to a local health worker may mean far more to the recipient, who may never have expected it, than the award of a knighthood to an MP after twenty years' service in Parliament who may regard such an award as a natural reward for services rendered. Investiture is often as important as the actual award. 'To some it is a rather tiresome ordeal but to most a moving and memorable occasion. A fire brigade officer, who was presented with the British Empire Medal, spoke for many when he said: "I thought it would be just another ceremony. But now that I've been, it's something I'll remember for the rest of my days"' (Hibbert, 1979, p. 205). Each year 30,000 people are invited to royal garden parties. Few decline the invitation.

Preserving a Christian morality

The Queen is supreme governor of the Church of England and the links between the monarch and the church are close and visible. The monarch is required by the Act of Settlement of 1701 to 'joyn in communion with the Church of England as by law established'. After the monarch, the most significant participant in a coronation ceremony is the Archbishop of Canterbury, who both crowns and anoints the new sovereign. Bishops are appointed by the crown, albeit acting on advice. National celebrations led by the Queen will usually entail a religious service, more often than not held in Westminster Abbey or St Paul's Cathedral. The Queen is known to take seriously her religious duties and is looked to, largely by way of example, as a symbol of a basically Christian morality.

Preserving what are deemed to be high standards of Christian morality has been important since the nineteenth century, although not necessarily much before that: earlier monarchs were keener to protect the Church of England than they were to practise its morality. The attempts to preserve that morality this century have resulted in some notable sacrifices. Edward VIII was forced to abdicate in 1936 because of his insistence on marrying a twice-married and twice-divorced woman. In 1955 the Queen's sister, Princess Margaret, decided not to marry Group Captain Peter Townsend

BOX 16.1 **IDEAS AND PERSPECTIVES**

The royal garden party

The cars start to arrive on the Mall in early afternoon. The police are a model of efficiency and politeness. The Mall remains open to ordinary traffic while cars with stickers with an 'X' in the windscreen are directed to park along the Mall. Those with 'SP' stickers – denoting special parking, usually for wheelchair-bound occupants – are directed to a spot at the top of the Mall, closest to the Palace gates. Cars usually start arriving shortly after two o'clock. By three o'clock, the queues at the entrances inside the Palace forecourt are stretching back to the Gates. At three, the guests are admitted, walking through the Palace before reaching the gardens to the rear. Wheelchair-bound guests are admitted direct to the gardens through the Garden Entrance: Guardsmen and Boy Scouts are on hand to push the wheelchairs over the gravel path leading to the gardens.

At each garden party, about 7,000 guests stream through the Palace and on to the extensive lawned garden. Getting everybody through takes some time. The last occasion I was there, I was one of the early ones into the grounds. It probably took the best part of an hour before everyone had come through the Palace, wave upon wave of guests flowing through the two principal doors leading to the lawns. Most guests gravitate to the long tea tent running down the side of the garden, although it is normally another hour before tea is served.

The guests are varied, in terms of both dress and background. Men can wear formal morning dress or lounge suits. Lounge suits seem far more in evidence now than they were a decade ago. There is also greater scope for taking as a guest someone other than a spouse or child. In the late 1980s, it was not possible for me to take my widowed mother. In the late 1990s, it was. A few guests wear chains of office, even though the instructions make clear that they should not be worn. Photographs are not permitted within Palace grounds and everyone sticks to that rule. Guests are entertained by two military bands, in bandstands at either end of the principal lawn. The bands have eschewed modern technology. Each signals the other as to when they have finished playing by lowering a flag.

After the rush for tea and cakes, guests start to move to the centre of the lawn ready for the arrival of the royal party. (Some stick to the tea tent and a few wander round the grounds.) Beefeaters take up position while gentlemen of the court – I have never seen any ladies – start to encourage guests to form lines. There are usually two principal avenues formed, allowing different members of the royal family to go along each. Once the lines are formed, the officials pick out particular guests to stand in the middle to be greeted by the royal party. On the last occasion I was there (in 1999) I was able to get my mother – who, at ninety-one, was using a wheelchair because of the distances involved – to the front of the crowd. The Queen moved slowly along the avenue of people, smiling at guests on each side and chatting briefly to those who were stood in the middle. It made my mother's day when the Queen saw her and smiled. When they have come to the end of the lines, the members of the royal family then move to the royal tent for tea. Guests return to the tea tent for more refreshments or look round the grounds.

The grounds are extensive, although not particularly elaborate. Various stately homes have more colourful gardens and landscaping. But no one really comes for the gardens. They come because it is Buckingham Palace and because the Queen and other members of the royal family will be present. The principal purpose of the exercise is to form orderly queues in the hope at least of seeing the Queen and perhaps being acknowledged by her or by another member of the family. The ultimate accolade is to be invited to meet Her Majesty or some other senior royal.

When people start to leave, they will have spent almost three hours in the grounds of Buckingham Palace. They will have met other guests, seen the grounds, had some tea and cake but the topic of conversation when they leave is likely to be which members of the royal family were present, how they were dressed, and – if close enough to hear any conversation – what was said. For most guests, it is probably the highlight of the year, for some of the decade and for others, I have no doubt, of their lifetime.

because he was divorced. She announced that 'mindful of the Church's teaching that Christian marriage is indissoluble, and conscious of my duty to the Commonwealth, I have resolved to put these considerations before others'. However, two decades later, with attitudes having changed, the Princess herself was divorced. Her divorce was followed by that of Princess Anne and Captain Mark Phillips and later by that of the Duke and Duchess of York and the Prince and Princess of Wales. Although attitudes towards divorce have changed, divorces and separations in the royal family – and the heir to the throne admitting to adultery – have none the less raised questions about the royal family's capacity to maintain a Christian morality. The capacity to do so has also been challenged explicity by the heir to the throne, Prince Charles, who has said he would wish to be 'a Defender of Faiths, not the Faith'.

The extent to which the monarch should maintain a Christian morality is, given changing attitudes, a matter of some debate. This is reflected in popular attitudes towards the relationship of Prince Charles and his partner, Camilla Parker-Bowles. In a MORI poll in 1999, 65 per cent of those questioned believed that Prince Charles should continue his relationship with Mrs Parker-Bowles. Fifty-three per cent thought they should get married. However, 76 per cent opposed Mrs Parker-Bowles becoming Queen.

Exercise of formal powers

Underpinning the monarch's capacity to fulfil a unifying role, and indeed underpinning the other functions deemed important, is the fact that she stands above and beyond the arena of partisan debate. This also affects significantly the monarch's other primary task: that of fulfilling her formal duties as head of state. Major powers still remain with the monarch: the choice of Prime Minister, the right to withhold assent to legislation, the dispensing of ministerial portfolios, the dissolution of Parliament, and the declaring of war being among the most obvious. All such prerogative powers are now, as far as possible, governed by convention. We have already noted two examples: by convention, the monarch assents to all legislation passed by the two Houses of Parliament; by convention, she calls the leader of the party with an overall majority in Parliament to form a government. Where there is no clear convention governing what to do, the Queen acts in accordance with precedent (where one exists) and, where a choice is involved, acts on advice. By thus avoiding any personal choice – and being seen not to exercise any personal choice – in the exercise of powers vested in the crown, the monarch is able to remain 'above politics'. Hence the characterisation of the monarch as enjoying strength through weakness. The denial of personal discretion in the exercise of inherently political powers strengthens the capacity of the monarch to fulfil a representative – that is, symbolic – role.

However, could it not be argued that the exercise of prerogative powers is, by virtue of the absence of personal choice, a waste of time and something of which the monarch should be shorn? (Why not, for example, vest the power of dissolution in the Speaker of the House of Commons?) There are two principal reasons why the powers remain vested in the sovereign.

Firstly, the combination of the symbolic role and the powers vested in the crown enables the monarch to stand as a constitutional safeguard. A similar role is ascribed to the House of Lords, but that – as we shall see (Chapter 18) – is principally in a situation where the government seeks to extend its own life without recourse to an election. What if the government sought to dispense with Parliament? To return to an earlier example, what if there was an attempted military coup? The House of Lords could not effectively act to prevent it. It is doubtful whether a Speaker vested with formal powers could do much to prevent it. The monarch could. As head of state and as commander-in-chief of the armed forces, the monarch could deny both legitimacy and support to the insurgents. This may or may not be sufficient ultimately to prevent a coup, but the monarch is at least in a stronger position than other bodies to prevent it succeeding. Thus, ironically, the unelected monarch – successor to earlier monarchs who tried to dispense with Parliament – serves as an ultimate protector of the political institutions which have displaced the monarchy as the governing authority (see Bogdanor, 1995).

Secondly, retention of the prerogative powers serves as a reminder to ministers and other servants of the crown that they owe a responsibility to a higher authority than a transient politician. Ministers are Her Majesty's ministers; the Prime Minister is invited by the sovereign to form an administration. The responsibility may, on the face of it, appear purely formal. However, although the monarch is precluded from calling the Prime Minister (or any minister) to account publicly, she is able to require a private explanation. In *The English Constitution*, Walter Bagehot offered his classic definition of the monarch's power as being 'the right to be consulted, the right to encourage, the right to warn'. The Queen is known to be an assiduous reader of her official papers – she receives all Cabinet papers and important Foreign Office communications – and is known often to question the Prime Minister closely and, on other occasions, the relevant departmental ministers. Harold Wilson recorded when in his early days as Prime Minister he was caught on the hop as a result of the Queen having read Cabinet papers which he had not yet got round to reading. 'Very interesting, this idea of a new town in the Bletchley area', commented the Queen. It was the first Wilson knew of the idea. More significantly, there are occasions when the Queen is believed to have made her displeasure known. In 1986, for example, it was reported – although not confirmed – that the Queen was distressed at the strain that the Prime Minister, Margaret Thatcher, was placing on the Commonwealth as a result of her refusal to endorse sanctions against South Africa (see Pimlott, 1996; Ziegler, 1996); she was also reported to have expressed her displeasure in 1983 following the US invasion of Grenada, a Commonwealth country (Cannon and Griffiths, 1988, p. 620). Indeed, relations between the Queen and her first female Prime Minister were claimed to be correct rather than close. The Queen is also believed to have signalled her displeasure when Prime Minister Tony Blair failed to include her in the itinerary of a visit to the UK by US President Bill Clinton (Pierce, 1999). Nonetheless, former Prime Ministers have variously attested to the fact that the Queen is a considerable help rather than a hindrance, offering a private and experienced audience. She also serves as a reminder of their responsibility to some other authority than political party. She also stands as the ultimate deterrent. Although her actions are governed predominantly by convention, she still has the legal right to exercise them. When the government of John Major sought a vote of confidence from the House of Commons on 23 July 1993 (following the loss of an important vote the previous evening), the prime minister made it clear that in the event of the government losing the vote, the consequence would be a general election. (By convention, a government losing a vote of confidence either resigns or requests a dissolution.) However, the government took the precaution of checking in advance that the Queen would agree to a dissolution.

Criticisms of the monarchy

Various functions are thus fulfilled by the monarch and other members of the royal family. There has tended to be a high level of support for the monarchy and popular satisfaction with the way those functions are carried out. However, a high level of support for the institution of monarchy has not been a constant in British political history. It dropped during the reign of Queen Victoria, when she withdrew from public activity following the death of Prince Albert. It dropped again in the 1930s as a result of the abdication crisis, which divided the nation. It increased significantly during the Second World War because of the conduct of the royal family and remained high in post-war decades. It dipped again in the 1990s. 1992 was described by the Queen as her *annus horribilis* (horrible year). The monarchy was no longer the revered institution of preceding decades and its future became an issue of topical debate. Even at times of high popular support, it has never been free of criticism. In recent years, the criticisms have been fuelled by the activities of various members of the royal family.

Four principal criticisms can be identified: that an unelected monarch has the power to exercise certain political powers; that, by virtue of being neither elected nor socially typical, the monarchy is unrepresentative; that maintaining the royal family costs too much; and that the institution of monarchy is now unnecessary. The last three criticisms have become more pronounced in recent years.

Potential for political involvement

The actions of the sovereign as head of state are governed predominantly by convention. However, not all actions she may be called on to take are covered by convention. This is most notably the case in respect of the power to appoint a Prime Minister and to dissolve Parliament. Usually, there is no problem. As long as one party is returned with an overall majority, the leader of that party will be summoned to Buckingham Palace (or, if already Prime Minister, will remain in office). But what if there is a 'hung' Parliament, with no one party enjoying an overall majority, and the leader of the third largest party makes it clear that his or her party will be prepared to sustain the second largest party in office, but not the party with the largest number of seats? Whom should the Queen summon? What if she summons the leader of the largest party, the leader of that party then attempts to form a government but is defeated on a vote of confidence and requests a dissolution? Should the Queen grant the request or instead ask the leader of the second largest party to try to form a government? There is no clear convention to govern the Queen's response in such circumstances and the opinions of constitutional experts as to what she should do are divided. Similarly, what if the Prime Minister was isolated in Cabinet and requested a dissolution, a majority of the Cabinet making it clear that it was opposed to such a move, would the Queen be obliged to grant her Prime Minister's request?

These are instances of problems that admit of no clear solution and they pose a threat to the value that currently derives from the sovereign being, and being seen to be, above politics. She is dependent on circumstances and the goodwill of politicians in order to avoid such a difficult situation arising. When the Queen was drawn into partisan controversy in 1957 and 1963 in the choice of a Conservative Prime Minister, the obvious embarrassment to the monarchy spurred the party to change its method of selecting the leader. There remains the danger that circumstances may conspire again to make involvement in real – as opposed to formal – decision making unavoidable.

Given this potential, some critics contend that the powers vested in the monarch should be transferred elsewhere. Various left-of-centre bodies have advocated the proposal that some or all of the powers should be transferred to the Speaker of the House of Commons. The proposal was advanced in 1996, in a Fabian Society pamphlet by a Labour parliamentary candidate Paul Richards, and again in 1998 by the authors of a pamphlet published by the left-wing think tank, Demos (Hames and Leonard, 1998). Defenders of the existing arrangements contend that the retention of prerogative powers by the crown has created no major problems to date – one constitutional historian, Peter Hennessy, in a 1994 lecture, recorded only five 'real or near real contingencies' since 1949 when the Queen's reserve powers were relevant (Marr, 1995, p. 234; see also Bogdanor, 1995) – and serves as a valuable constitutional longstop. Giving certain powers to the Speaker of the Commons would be to give it a member of an institution that may need to be constrained and would probably make the election of the Speaker a much more politicised activity. Furthermore, the Speaker or other such figure would be likely to lack the capacity to engage the loyalty of the armed forces to the same extent as the monarch.

Unrepresentative

The monarchy cannot make a claim to be representative in the second meaning of the term (freely elected). Critics also point out that it cannot make a claim to be representative in the third meaning (socially typical). The monarchy is a hereditary institution, based on the principle of primogeniture: that is, the crown passes to the eldest son. By the nature of the position, it is of necessity socially atypical. Critics contend that social hierarchy is reinforced by virtue of the monarch's personal wealth. The Queen is believed to be among the world's richest women, and may possibly be the richest. Many of the functions patronised by the Queen and members of the royal family, from formal functions to sporting events, are also criticised for being socially elitist. Those who surround the royal family in official positions (the Lord Chamberlain, ladies-in-waiting and other senior members of the royal household), and those with whom members of the royal family choose to surround themselves in positions of friendship, are also notably if not exclusively drawn from a social elite. In the 1950s, Lord Altrincham criticised the Queen's entourage for constituting 'a tight little enclave of British "ladies and gentlemen"' (Altrincham *et al.*, 1958, p. 115). Various changes were made in the wake of such criticism – the royal family became more publicly visible, the presentation of debutantes to the monarch at society balls was abolished – but royalty remains largely detached from the rest of society. The closed nature of the royal entourage was attacked in the 1990s by the Princess of Wales, who had difficulty adapting to what she saw as the insular and stuffy nature of the royal court. Even at Buckingham Palace garden parties, members of the royal family, having mixed with those attending, then take tea in a tent reserved for them and leading dignitaries. Focus groups, commissioned by Buckingham Palace in 1997, concluded that the royal family was out of touch because of their traditions and upbringing as well as remote because of 'the many physical and invisible barriers thought to have been constructed around them' (quoted in Jones, 1998). Pressures continue for the institution to be more open in terms of the social background of the Queen's entourage and, indeed, in terms of the activities and background of members of the royal family itself. The public reaction to the death, in a car crash in 1997, of Diana, Princess of Wales – popular not least because of her public empathy with the frail and the suffering – and the findings from the focus groups (commissioned in the wake of the Princess's death) are believed to have been influential in persuading the Queen to spend more time visiting people in their homes and exploring how people live (for example, by travelling on the underground and by visiting a supermarket). Defenders of the royal family argue that it is, by definition, impossible for members of the family to be socially typical – since they would cease to be the royal family – and that to be too close to everyday activity would rob the institution of monarchy of its aura and charm.

Overly expensive

The cost of the monarchy has been the subject of criticism for several years. This criticism became pronounced in the 1990s. Much but not all the costs of the monarchy have traditionally been met from the civil list. The civil list constitutes a sum paid regularly by the state to the monarch to cover the cost of staff, upkeep of royal residences, holding official functions, and of public duties undertaken by other members of the royal family. (The Prince of Wales is not included: as Duke of Cornwall his income derives from revenue-generating estates owned by the Duchy of Cornwall.) Other costs of monarchy – such as the upkeep of royal castles and the royal yacht *Britannia* – are met by government departments. In 1990, to avoid an annual public row over the figure, agreement was reached between the government and the Queen that the civil list should be set at £7.9 million a year for ten years. When the other costs of the monarchy – maintaining castles and the like – are added to this figure, the annual public expenditure on the monarchy was estimated in 1991 to exceed £57 million.

In the 1970s and 1980s, accusations were variously heard that the expenditure was not justified, in part because some members of the royal family did very little to justify the sums given to them and in part because the Queen was independently wealthy, having a private fortune on which she paid no tax. (When income tax was introduced in the nineteenth century, Queen Victoria voluntarily paid tax. In the twentieth century, the voluntary commitment was whittled down and had disappeared by the time the Queen ascended the throne in 1952.) These criticisms found various manifestations. In 1988, 40 per cent of respondents to a Gallup poll expressed the view that the monarchy 'cost too much'. In a MORI poll in 1990, three out of every four people questioned believed that the Queen should pay income tax; half of those questioned thought the royal family was receiving too much money from the taxpayer. Certain members of the royal family became targets of particular criticism.

These criticisms became much louder in 1991 and 1992. They were fuelled by a number of unrelated developments. The most notable were the separation of the Duke and Duchess of York and – in December 1992 – of the Prince and Princess of Wales, accompanied by newspaper stories about their private lives. The result was that members of the royal family became central figures of controversy and gossip. In November 1992 fire destroyed St George's Hall of Windsor Castle and the government announced it would meet the cost of repairs, estimated at more than £50 million. The public reaction to the announcement was strongly negative. At a time of recession, public money was to be spent restoring a royal castle, while the Queen continued to pay no income tax and some members of the royal family pursued other than restrained lifestyles at public expense. A Harris poll found three out of every four respondents believing that ways should be found to cut the cost of the royal family.

Six days after the fire at Windsor Castle, the Prime Minister informed the House of Commons that the Queen had initiated discussions 'some months ago' on changing her tax-free status and on removing all members of the royal family from the civil list, other than herself, the Duke of Edinburgh and the Queen Mother. The Queen herself would meet the expenditure of other members of the royal family. The Queen announced the following year that Buckingham Palace was to be opened to the public, with money raised from entrance fees being used to pay the cost of repairs to Windsor Castle. These announcements served to meet much of the criticism, but the controversy undermined the prestige of the royal family. Critics continued to point out that most of the costs of the monarchy remained unchanged, funded by public money, and drew attention to the fact that the Queen was using novel devices of taking money from the public (entrance fees to the Palace) in order to fund Windsor Castle repairs rather than drawing on her own private wealth.

Controversy was again stirred in January 1997 when Defence Secretary Michael Portillo announced plans for a new royal yacht, to replace *Britannia*, at a cost of £60 million. Public reaction was largely unfavourable and Buckingham Palace let it be known that the government had not consulted members of the royal family before making the announcement. The plan to build a replacement yacht was cancelled a few months later by the new Labour Government.

Supporters of the monarchy point out that savings have been made in recent years. The decommissioning of the royal yacht has saved £12 million a year. The royal family has made economies in travelling. It was expected that the 1999 travel budget of £16 millon would be halved in 2000. The cost of the contemporary monarchy, it is argued, is therefore modest. In 1999 the civil list stood at £8.9 million, with a further £34 million being provided by government departments for the upkeep of royal palaces and for transportation. Defenders contend that the country obtains good value for money from the royal family, the costs of monarchy being offset by income from crown lands (land formerly owned by the crown but given to the state in return for the civil list) and by income from tourism and trade generated by the presence and activities of the Queen and members of her family. They also point out that much if not most of the money spent on maintaining castles and other parts of the national heritage would still have to be spent even if there was no royal family. When such money is taken out of the equation, the public activities of the Queen and leading royals such as the Princess Royal are deemed to represent good value for public money.

Unnecessary

Those who criticise the monarchy on grounds of its unrepresentative nature and its cost are not necessarily opposed to the institution itself. A more open and less costly monarchy – based on the Scandinavian model, with the monarch mixing more freely with citizens and without excessive trappings – would be acceptable to many. However, some take the opposite view. They see the monarchy as an unnecessary institution; the cost and social elitism of the monarchy are seen as merely illustrative of the nature of the institution. Advocates of this view have included Tom Nairn in *The Enchanted Glass: Britain and its Monarchy*, Edgar Wilson in *The Myth of the British Monarchy* and – since 1994 – *The Economist*. Wilson contends that the various arguments advanced in favour of the monarchy – its popularity, impartiality, productivity, capacity to unite, to protect democratic institutions of state, and its ability to generate trade – are all myths, generated in order to justify the existing order. To him and Nairn, the monarchy forms part of a conservative establishment that has little rationale in a democratic society. They would prefer to see the monarchy abolished. 'The constitutional case for abolishing the Monarchy is based mainly on the facts that it is arbitrary, unrepresentative, unaccountable, partial, socially divisive, and exercises a pernicious influence and privileged prerogative powers' (Wilson, 1989, p. 178). *The Economist* has taken a similar line, albeit expressed in less strident terms and acknowledging that, if popular opinion want to keep a monarchy, then it should stay. The monarchy, it declared, 'is the antithesis of much of what we stand for: democracy, liberty, reward for achievement rather than inheritance'. Its symbolism was harmful: 'the hereditary principle, deference, *folies de grandeur*'. It was 'an idea whose time has passed' (*The Economist*, 22 October 1994). Necessary functions of state carried out by the monarch could be equally well fulfilled, so critics contend, by an elected president. Most countries in the world have a head of state not chosen on the basis of heredity. So why not Britain?

Supporters of the institution of monarchy argue that, despite recent criticisms, the Queen continues to do a good job – a view which, according to opinion polls, enjoys majority support – and that the monarchy is distinctive by virtue of the functions it is able to fulfil. In a MORI poll in December 1997, 72 per cent of those questioned were satisfied with the way that the Queen was doing her job. Only 21 per cent were dissatisfied. It is considered doubtful that an appointed or elected head of state would be able to carry out to the same extent the symbolic role, representing the unity of the nation. For a head of state not involved in the partisan operation of government, it is this role (representative in the fourth sense of the term) that is more important than that of being an elected leader. Indeed, election could jeopardise the head of state's claim to be representative in the first sense of the term (acting on behalf of a particular body or group). The monarch has a duty to represent all subjects; an elected head of state may have a bias, subconscious or otherwise, in favour of those who vote for him or her, or in favour of those – presumably politicians – who were responsible for arranging the nomination. The Queen enjoys a stature not likely to be matched by an elected figurehead in engaging the loyalty of the armed forces; and by virtue of her longevity and experience can assist successive prime ministers in a way not possible by a person appointed or elected for a fixed term. Hence, by virtue of these assets particular to the Queen, the monarch is deemed unique and not capable of emulation by an elected president. Although these assets may have been partially tarnished in recent years, it is argued that they remain of value to the nation.

Proposals for change

The monarchy has never been wholly free of critics. In the 1970s and 1980s, those critics were relatively few in number. In the early 1990s, they became far more numerous and more vocal. There were various calls for changes to be made in the institution of the monarchy and in the conduct of members of the royal family. Those most responsible for this situation arising were members of the royal family themselves. The various marital splits, the antics of various royals, the public perception of some members of the royal family as 'hangers on' (enjoying the trappings of privilege but fulfilling few public duties) and the failure of the Queen to fund the restoration of Windsor Castle herself contributed to a popular mood less supportive of the monarchy than before.

Criticism of the monarchy and, more especially, members of the royal family led to several demands for change. Future options for the monarchy can be grouped under four heads: abolition, reform, leave alone and strengthen.

Prince Philip apologises for reported remarks, yet again (22 December 1996)

Abolition

The troubles encountered by the royal family in the late 1980s and early 1990s appeared to influence attitudes toward the monarchy itself. As we have seen, the Queen described 1992 as her *annus horribilis* – her horrible year. That was reflected in popular attitudes towards the monarchy. Until the middle of 1992, less than 15 per cent of people questioned in various polls wanted to see the monarchy abolished. A Gallup poll in May 1992 found 13 per cent of respondents giving such a response. By the end of the year, the figure had increased to 24 per cent. As we have seen, those favouring abolition gained the support of a leading magazine, *The Economist*, in 1994.

Not only was there an increase in the percentage of the population expressing support for the abolition of the monarchy, there was also an increasing agnosticism among a wider public. In 1987, 73 per cent of respondents in a MORI poll thought that Britain would be worse off if the monarchy was abolished. In December 1992, the figure was 37 per cent. Forty-two per cent thought it would make no difference. The same poll found, for the first time, more people saying that they did not think that the monarchy would still exist in fifty years' time than saying it would: 42 per cent thought it would not against 36 per cent saying it would.

However, those who argue the case for the retention of the monarchy appear still to have a

Table 16.1 Attitudes towards the monarchy
Q. Would you favour Britain becoming a republic or remaining a monarchy? (%)

	April 1993	January 1994	December 1994	September 1997	August 1998	November 1998	June 1999
Republic	18	17	20	18	16	18	16
Monarchy	69	73	71	73	75	73	74
Don't know	14	10	9	9	9	9	10

Source: MORI, British Public Opinion, Vol. XXII, No. 6, August 1999

considerable edge over those demanding abolition. The early 1990s represented the low point in terms of popular disaffection with royalty. Those thinking Britain would be worse off if the monarchy was abolished are now in a majority. (In a MORI poll in December 1997, 55 per cent thought the country would be worse off, against 27 per cent saying no difference and 15 per cent saying better off.) Support for abolition of the monarchy has also declined. Indeed, according to MORI polls (Table 16.1), the percentage favouring a republic dipped below 20 per cent in 1993 and – although just touching 20 per cent in 1994 – has not gone above 20 per cent since. Approximately three-quarters of those questioned regularly express support for retaining the monarchy.

Reform

Recent years have seen a growing body of support for some change in the nature of the monarchy and especially in the royal family. Some proposals for reform are radical. The authors of the Demos pamphlet, *Modernising the Monarchy*, argue the case not only for transferring the monarch's prerogative powers to the Speaker of the House of Commons but also for holding a referendum to confirm a monarch shortly after succeeding to the throne (Hames and Leonard, 1998). There are some survey data to suggest that more people support the first of these proposals than oppose it. In a MORI poll in August 1998, 49 per cent thought that the powers should be removed, against 45 per cent who thought they should be retained.

There is also a desire for more general change in the way the monarch, and other members of the royal family, conduct themselves. This desire has been tapped by opinion polls as well as by the focus groups commissioned by Buckingham Palace. The public preference is for a more open and less ostentatious monarchy, with the Queen spending more time meeting members of the public and with other members of the royal family, especially the 'minor royals', taking up paid employment (as some have) and blending into the community. A Granada TV deliberative poll in 1996, which involved interviewing people before and after discussing the subject with experts, found that the biggest percentage of affirmative responses was for the statement that 'Members of the royal family should mix more with ordinary people'. The percentage agreeing was initially 66 per cent and, after discussion, it increased to 75 per cent. In a MORI poll in August 1998, 60 per cent of those questioned agreed with the statement that 'the monarchy should be modernised to reflect changes in public life'. Only 26 per cent felt that 'the monarch's role should remain broadly unchanged'.

There is also some support for a change in the order of succession. A small number of people favour the Queen abdicating in favour of Prince Charles, but the number is declining: it reached a peak at 47 per cent in a 1990 MORI poll, but was down to 28 per cent in August 1998. A slightly larger percentage support 'skipping a generation' and allowing Prince William, Prince Charles' elder son, to succeed to the throne in place of his father. In a MORI poll in September 1997, in the wake of the death of Diana, Princess of Wales, 54 per cent supported such a move: by November 1998, the percentage giving the same response was 34 per cent. (Sixty-three per cent of those questioned thought that Prince Charles would make a good king.) These proposals not only do not now enjoy majority support, they would also require a change in the law. A decision by the Queen, or by Prince Charles upon or at the time of his succession to the throne, to abdicate is not one that can be taken unilaterally. Under the Act of Succession, Prince Charles will become king automatically on the death of his mother. There is no formal power to abdicate. That would require – as it did in 1936 – an Act of Parliament.

Another change that has variously been discussed, but which has less immediate relevance, is that of allowing the eldest child to succeed, regardless of gender. (Given that Prince Charles is the eldest child of the sovereign and his eldest child is a male, it will be two generations before any change becomes relevant.) In 1996 it emerged that the senior members of the royal family, prompted apparently by Prince Charles, had formed a small group (the 'Way Ahead Group' composed of senior royals and Buckingham Palace officials) to meet twice a year to consider various changes to existing arrangements. One proposal considered by the group has been to allow the eldest child to succeed to the throne; another is to end the ban on anyone who marries a Roman Catholic succeeding to the throne.

The measures taken by the Queen in recent years – notably the decision to pay income tax, to limit the civil list and to spend more time meeting ordinary members of the public – appear to enjoy popular support. There has also been some change in behaviour on the part of members of the royal family, a more restrained approach serving to subdue much of the criticism of the early 1990s. More steps designed to make the monarchy and the royal family more open – yet at the same time less open to personal criticism – would appear likely to bolster support for the institution. The deliberations of the Way Ahead Group have been designed in part to bring the institution up to date and enhance such support.

Leave alone

The monarchy as it stands has some ardent admirers. Conservative MPs have generally moved quickly to defend the monarchy from criticism. When a Fabian Society pamphlet, *Long to Reign Over Us?*, was published in August 1996 (Richards, 1996) advocating a referendum on the monarchy, a Conservative Cabinet minister, Michael Portillo, immediately portrayed it as an attack on the institution of monarchy. 'New Labour should be warned that they meddle with the monarchy at the nation's peril', he declared. After 1997, some of the attempts by Prime Minister Tony Blair to encourage change also encountered criticism. In 1999, the leading historian, Lord Blake, declared: 'Reform has gone far enough . . . The monarchy is one of the fixed points of the British constitutional firmament. It cannot be subjected to constant change' (Pierce, 1999).

Although this stance attracts support, it tends to be outweighed by those favouring some reform (a fact acknowledged in effect by the royal family in the creation of the Way Ahead Group). As we have seen, most people questioned in the MORI poll in August 1998 favoured some change; only 26 per cent wanted to leave the monarchy broadly unchanged. Those favouring modest reform appear to be in a majority among voters. It is also the stance favoured by the Labour Government of Tony Blair. 'Palace officials have been told clearly by Downing Street that there is strong political pressure for a much leaner monarchy' (Pierce, 1999). Although some of the proposals emanating from Downing Street, such as reducing the ceremony of the State Opening of Parliament, have been resisted by Buckingham Palace (see Pierce, 1999), the need for reform has generally been accepted by the royal family, not least by the heir to the throne.

Strengthen

The final option is that of strengthening the role and powers of the monarchy. A Gallup poll in 1996 for *The Sunday Telegraph* tapped a body of support for giving the Queen a greater role. This was especially marked among working class respondents and among the sixteen to thirty-four year old age groups. Fifty-seven per cent of working class respondents thought that the Queen should be given 'a more substantial role in government'. Fifty-four per cent of respondents aged sixteen to thirty-four also thought that she should have a more substantial role (Elliott and McCartney, 1996). The nature of the role was not specified. As we have seen, the potential for the Queen to be drawn into decision making exists and that potential may increase as a consequence of recent constitutional changes. The exercise of some of these powers may not prove unpopular to a section of the population. It was notable in the 1996 poll that many respondents regarded the Queen as having superior skills to those of the then Prime Minister, John Major: 46 per cent thought the Queen would make a 'better prime minister than John Major'. Thirty-nine per cent thought she would make a better Prime Minister than Tony Blair. Forty-seven per cent of working-class respondents thought that she would run the country 'more wisely than politicians'.

There is thus some body of support for the Queen exercising more power in the political affairs of the nation. However, that view is not widely held among politicians, nor – as far as one can surmise – among members of the royal family. As we have seen, the strength of the monarchy rests largely on the fact that it is detached from the partisan fray and is not involved in having to exercise independent judgement. Having to make independent decisions would be popular with some but, and this is the crucial point in this context, not with all people. Those adversely affected by a decision would be unlikely to keep their feelings to themselves. The monarchy would be drawn into the maelstrom of political controversy, thus ridding it of its capacity to fulfil the principal functions ascribed to it.

Conclusion

The monarch fulfils a number of functions as head of state. Some of those functions are not peculiar to the monarch as head of state: they are functions that are typically carried out by a head of state. Supporters of the monarchy argue that a number of functions are particularly suited to the monarch and, in combination, could not be fulfilled by an elected or appointed head of state. The monarchy was under strain in the early 1990s as a result of various disconnected events and its public standing declined markedly. The nature of the monarchy was further called into question following the death of the popular Diana, Princess of Wales, in August 1997. The Queen and other members of the royal family have responded to criticism by implementing changes in structures and activity, designed to create a more open and responsive monarchy. The actions of the Queen and her family appear to have borne fruit. There is no strong desire to get rid of the monarchy. Abolitionist sentiment has declined in recent years. However, there is scepticism about the future of the monarchy. Although most people think the monarchy will still exist in ten years' time, more than 40 per cent of respondents think it will not exist in fifty years' time (against just over 30 per cent thinking it will) and more than 50 per cent think it will not exist in one hundred years' time. However, if it is abolished, that may not be an end of a public role for members of the royal family. In the 1996 Gallup poll that found some support for strengthening the monarchy, 37 per cent said they would vote for the Queen if she led a political party. A MORI poll in December of the same year offered thirteen candidates for an elected president. As *The Economist* noted (11 January 1997), 'The clear winner, ahead of politicians and businessmen, was the queen's own daughter, Princess Anne. And therein lies a lesson for any budding constitutional reformer'.

Chapter summary

The monarchy remains an important institution in British political life. The monarch's transition from directing the affairs of state to a neutral non-executive role has been a gradual and not always smooth one, but a move necessary to justify the monarch's continuing existence.

Transcending partisan activity is a necessary condition for fulfilling the monarch's symbolic ('standing

for') role and hence a necessary condition for the strength and continuity of the monarchy. The dedication of the present monarch has served to sustain popular support for the institution. That support dropped in the 1990s, criticism of the activities of members of the royal family rubbing off on the institution of monarchy itself. Popular support for the institution remains and has seen some increase since the nadir of the early 1990s. Most people when questioned want to see some change, favouring the monarchy and royal family being more open and approachable. The royal family appears to be taking steps in that direction.

Discussion points

- What is the point in having a monarchy?
- In what circumstances could the Queen become involved in making political decisions? Can and should such occasions be avoided?
- What are the most important roles fulfilled by the Queen in contemporary society?
- What public role, if any, should be played by members of the royal family, other than the Queen?
- Should the monarchy be left alone, reformed or abolished?

Further reading

There are few substantial analyses of the role of the crown in political activity. The most recent – that by Bogdanor (1995) – seeks to transcend recent controversy. The book provides a good historical perspective on the role of the monarchy as well as offering a defence of the institution. Hardie (1970) provides a useful guide to the transition from political involvement to neutrality; Hibbert (1979) also offers a useful overview. Pimlott (1996) has produced a substantial and well-respected biography of the Queen. In terms of the debate about the future of the monarchy, the most recent reform tracts are those by Richards (1996) and Hames and Leonard (1998). The principal works arguing for abolition are Nairn (1988) and Wilson (1989). The issue of *The Economist*, 22 October 1994, advocating abolition, also provides a substantial critique.

In terms of the controversies of the early 1990s, the book that sparked media interest in the state of the Prince of Wales' marriage was Morton (1992), followed later by a revised edition (Morton, 1997). The biography of Prince Charles by Jonathan Dimbleby (1994) also contributed to the public debate.

References

Altrincham, Lord, *et al.* (1958) *Is the Monarchy Perfect?* (John Calder).

Benemy, F.W.G. (1965) *The Elected Monarch* (Harrap).

Birch, A.H. (1964) *Representative and Responsible Government* (Allen and Unwin).

Blackburn, R. (1992) 'The future of the British monarchy', in R. Blackburn (ed.), *Constitutional Studies* (Mansell).

Bogdanor, V. (1995) *The Monarchy and the Constitution* (Oxford University Press).

Cannon, J. and Griffiths, R. (1988) *The Oxford Illustrated History of the British Monarchy* (Oxford University Press).

Dimbleby, J. (1994) *The Prince of Wales. A Biography* (Little, Brown).

Elliott, V. and McCartney, J. (1996) 'Queen should have real power, say Britain's youth', *Sunday Telegraph*, 21 April.

Hames, T. and Leonard, M. (1998) *Modernising the Monarchy* (Demos).

Hardie, F. (1970) *The Political Influences of the British Monarchy 1868–1952* (Batsford).

Hibbert, C. (1979) *The Court of St James* (Weidenfeld and Nicolson).

Jones, M. (1998) 'Queen to appoint royal spin doctor to boost ratings', *Sunday Times*, 22 February.

Lacey, R. (1977) *Majesty* (Hutchinson).

Marr, A. (1995) *Ruling Britannica* (Michael Joseph).

Morton, A. (1992) *Diana: Her True Story* (Michael O'Mara Books).

Morton, A. (1997) *Diana, Her True Story – In Her Own Words* (Michael O'Mara Books).

Nairn, T. (1988) *The Enchanted Glass: Britain and its Monarchy* (Century Hutchinson Radius).

O'Donovan, T. (1999) 'Royal engagements', letter to *The Times*, 2 January.

Pierce, A. (1999) 'Spin meister of royal reform trips up'. *The Times*, 4 September.

Pimlott, B. (1996) *The Queen* (HarperCollins).

Pitkin, H.G. (1967) *The Concept of Representation* (University of California Press).

Richards, P. (1996) *Long to Reign Over Us?* (The Fabian Society).

Trevelyan, G.M. (1938) *The English Revolution 1688–9* (Thornton Butterworth).

Wilson, E. (1989) *The Myth of the British Monarchy* (Journeyman/Republic).

Ziegler, P. (1996) 'A monarch at the centre of politics', *The Daily Telegraph*, 4 October.

Chapter 17

The House of Commons

Philip Norton

Learning objectives

- To explain the importance of the House of Commons in terms of its history and its functions.
- To identify and assess the means available to Members of Parliament to fulfil those functions.
- To describe and analyse pressures on the House and proposals for reform.

Introduction

The House of Commons has evolved over seven centuries. At various times, it has played a powerful role in the affairs of the nation. Its most consistent activity has been to check the executive power. Its power has been limited by royal patronage and, more recently, by the growth of parties. It none the less remains an important part of the political process. It constitutes the only nationally elected body. It has to give its assent to measures of public policy. Ministers appear before it to justify their actions. It remains an arena for national debate and the clash of competing party views. However, its capacity to fulfil its functions has been the subject of debate. Criticism has led to various demands for change.

Origins of Parliament

Parliament has its origins in the thirteenth century. It was derived not from first principles or some grand design but from the King's need to raise more money. Its subsequent development may be ascribed to the actions and philosophies of different monarchs, the ambitions and attitudes of its members, external political pressures and prevailing assumptions as to the most appropriate form of government. Its functions and political significance have been moulded, though not in any consistent manner, over several hundred years.

Despite the rich and varied history of the institution, two broad generalisations are possible. The first concerns Parliament's position in relation to the executive. Parliament is not, and never has been on any continuous basis, a part of that executive. Though the Glorious Revolution of 1688 may have confirmed the form of government as that of 'parliamentary government', the phrase, as we have seen already (Chapter 15), means government through Parliament, not government by Parliament. There have been periods when Parliament has been an important actor in the making of public policy, not least for a period in the nineteenth century, but its essential and historically established position has been that of a reactive, or policy-influencing, assembly (Box 17.1; see Mezey, 1979; Norton, 1993); that is, public policy is formulated by the executive and then presented to Parliament for discussion and approval. Parliament has the power to amend or reject the policy placed before it, but it has not the capacity to substitute on any regular basis a policy of its own. Parliament has looked to the executive to take the initiative in the formulation of public policy and it continues to do so.

The second generalisation concerns the various tasks, or functions, fulfilled by Parliament. Parliament is a multi-functional body. Not only does it serve as a reactive body in the making of public policy, it carries out several other tasks as well. Its principal tasks were established within the first two centuries of its development. In the fourteenth century, the King accepted that taxes should not be levied without the assent of Parliament. The giving of such assent was variously withheld until the King responded to petitions requesting a redress of grievances. At the same time, Parliament began to take an interest in how money was spent and began to look at the actions of public servants. It became, in a rather haphazard way, a body for the critical scrutiny of government.

The development of Parliament

Knights and burgesses were summoned in the thirteenth century in order to give assent to the King's decision to raise extra taxes. They joined the King's court, comprising the barons and

BOX 17.1 **IDEAS AND PERSPECTIVES**

Types of legislature

Policy-making legislatures: These are legislatures that can not only modify or reject measures brought forward by the executive but also formulate and substitute policy of their own (e.g. the US Congress).

Policy-influencing legislatures: These are legislatures that can modify and sometimes reject measures brought forward by the executive but cannot formulate and substitute policy of their own (e.g. UK Parliament, German Bundestag).

Legislatures with little or no policy effect: These are legislatures than can neither modify or reject measures brought forward by the executive nor formulate and substitute policies of their own. They typically meet for only a few days each year to give formal approval to whatever is placed before them (e.g. former legislatures of Eastern European communist states, such as East Germany).

leading churchmen of the realm. In the fourteenth century, the summoning of knights and burgesses became a regular feature of those occasions when the King summoned a 'parliament'. At various times during the century, the knights and burgesses sat separately from the barons and churchmen, and so there developed two chambers – the Commons and the Lords.

The House of Commons became more significant in subsequent centuries. It was a significant political actor during the Tudor reigns of the sixteenth century and a powerful opponent of the Stuart monarchs who asserted the divine right of kings to rule in the seventeenth. Clashes occurred between Parliament and Charles I and, later, James II. The fleeing of James II in 1688 allowed leading parliamentarians to offer the throne to James's daughter and son-in-law (Mary and William) on Parliament's terms and the supremacy of Parliament was established. Henceforth, the King could not legislate – or suspend laws – without the assent of Parliament.

Parliament none the less continued to look to the executive power – initially the King, and later the King's ministers assembled in Cabinet – to take the initiative in formulating measures of public policy. When measures were laid before Parliament, assent was normally forthcoming. In the eighteenth century, royal influence was employed, either directly or through the aristocratic patrons of 'rotten boroughs', to ensure the return of a House favourable to the ministry. This influence was broken in the nineteenth century. The 1832 Reform Act enlarged the electorate by 49 per cent and abolished many, although not all, rotten boroughs. The effect of the measure was to loosen the grip of the aristocracy on the House of Commons and to loosen the grip of the monarch on the choice of government. The last time a government fell for want of the monarch's confidence was in 1834. MPs entered a period when they were relatively independent in their behaviour, being prepared on occasion to oust ministers and sometimes governments (as in 1852, 1855, 1856 and 1866) and to amend and variously reject legislation. Except for the years from 1841 to 1846, party ties were extremely loose.

This so-called **golden age** was to prove short lived. At that time, there was little public business to transact. That business was reasonably easy to comprehend. Members were not tied overly to party and could make a judgement on the business before them. The consequence of the 1867 Reform Act, enlarging the electorate by 88 per cent, and of later Acts reducing corrupt practices, was to create an electorate too large, and too protected, to be 'bought' by individual candidates. Extensive organisation was necessary to reach the new voters and organised political parties soon came to dominate elections. For promises made by parties to be carried out, a cohesive party in the House of Commons was necessary and by the end of the century cohesive party voting was a feature of parliamentary life. Party influence thus succeeded royal patronage in ensuring the assent of MPs for measures brought forward by ministers of the crown.

The effect on Parliament of the rise of a mass electorate was profound. Governments came to be chosen by the electorate, not – as in the preceding years – by the House of Commons. Popular demands on government engendered not only more measures of public policy, but more extensive and complex measures. By the turn of the century, Parliament lacked the political will and the institutional resources necessary to subject increasingly detailed government bills to sustained and effective scrutiny. Albeit in a somewhat different form to earlier centuries, executive dominance had returned.

For the House of Commons, though, the developments of the nineteenth century served to confirm it as the pre-eminent component of the Crown-in-Parliament. The Glorious Revolution had established Parliament's supremacy over the King. The rise of the democratic principle in the nineteenth century established the supremacy of the elected House over the unelected. The House of Commons was clearly a representative chamber in that it was freely elected and in that its members were returned to defend and pursue the interests of electors (see Chapter 16). The House of Lords could claim to be representative in neither sense. The subordinate position of the House of Lords was confirmed by statute in the Parliament Act of 1911.

The position so established in the nineteenth century continued into the twentieth. The House of

Commons remained – and remains – the dominant chamber in a Parliament dominated by party, with the initiative for measures of public policy resting with the Cabinet and with a party majority in the House ensuring the passage of those measures.

That sets the historical context. What, then, is the contemporary position of the House of Commons? What are the essential characteristics of the House – its members and its procedures? What functions does it fulfil? What tools does it have at its disposal to fulfil them? And to what extent have developments in recent years strengthened or weakened its capacity to carry out those functions?

The House of Commons

The House of Commons now has 659 members. The number has varied, ranging in the twentieth century from a high of 707 (1918–22) to a low of 615 (1922–45). The number was reduced in 1922 because of the loss of (most) Irish seats; it has varied in post-war years and from 1945 to 1974 stood at 630; because of the increase in the size of the population, it was increased in 1974 to 635, in 1983 to 650, in 1992 to 651 and in 1997 to 659.

Elections

The maximum life of a Parliament is five years. Between 1715 and 1911, it was seven years. Members (MPs) are returned for single-member constituencies. These have been the norm since the Reform Act of 1885, though twelve double-member constituencies survived until the general election of 1950. The method of election employed is the 'first-past-the-post' system with the candidate receiving the largest number of votes being declared the winner. This again has been the norm since 1885, though not until the general

BOX 17.2 **IDEAS AND PERSPECTIVES**

The atmosphere of the House

By the standards of the Palace of Westminster, the House of Commons (Figure 17.1) is not a particularly ornate chamber. Relatively new compared with the rest of the Palace – re-built after being destroyed in 1941 by enemy bombing – it has a fairly functional feel to it. When it was rebuilt, there was a change in the style but not in the size. This meant that it was too small to accommodate every member. This has proved to be beneficial on two counts. First, on the rare occasions that the House is full, it conveys a sense of theatre: some Members sit on the steps in the aisles, some crowd round the Speaker's chair, some stand in packed ranks at the bar of the House. Tension rises as the Prime Minister, or other senior minister, closes for the Government and the Speaker rises to put the Question. Members then troop into the voting lobbies either side of the chamber. If the outcome of the vote is uncertain, the tension is close to unbearable. After ten to fifteen minutes – sometimes longer – the tellers return and those representing the winning side line up on the right at the table, facing the Speaker. Once those on the winning side realise they have won, a massive cheer goes up. The most dramatic vote of recent history was on 28 March 1979, when the Labour Government lost a vote of confidence by one vote. The tension was not much less during some of the votes on the Maastricht Bill in 1992 and 1993, when the votes of rebel Conservative MPs were uncertain.

The second reason why the small chamber is better than a larger one is simply because such dramatic occasions are rare. Most of the time the chamber is notable for the rows of empty green benches as a handful of MPs sit around listening – or half-listening, or whispering to a neighbour – as one of their number delivers a speech from notes, sometimes quite copious notes. The chamber looks cavernous on such occasions. With a much larger chamber, the sheer emptiness of the place would be overwhelming.

BOX 17.2 continued

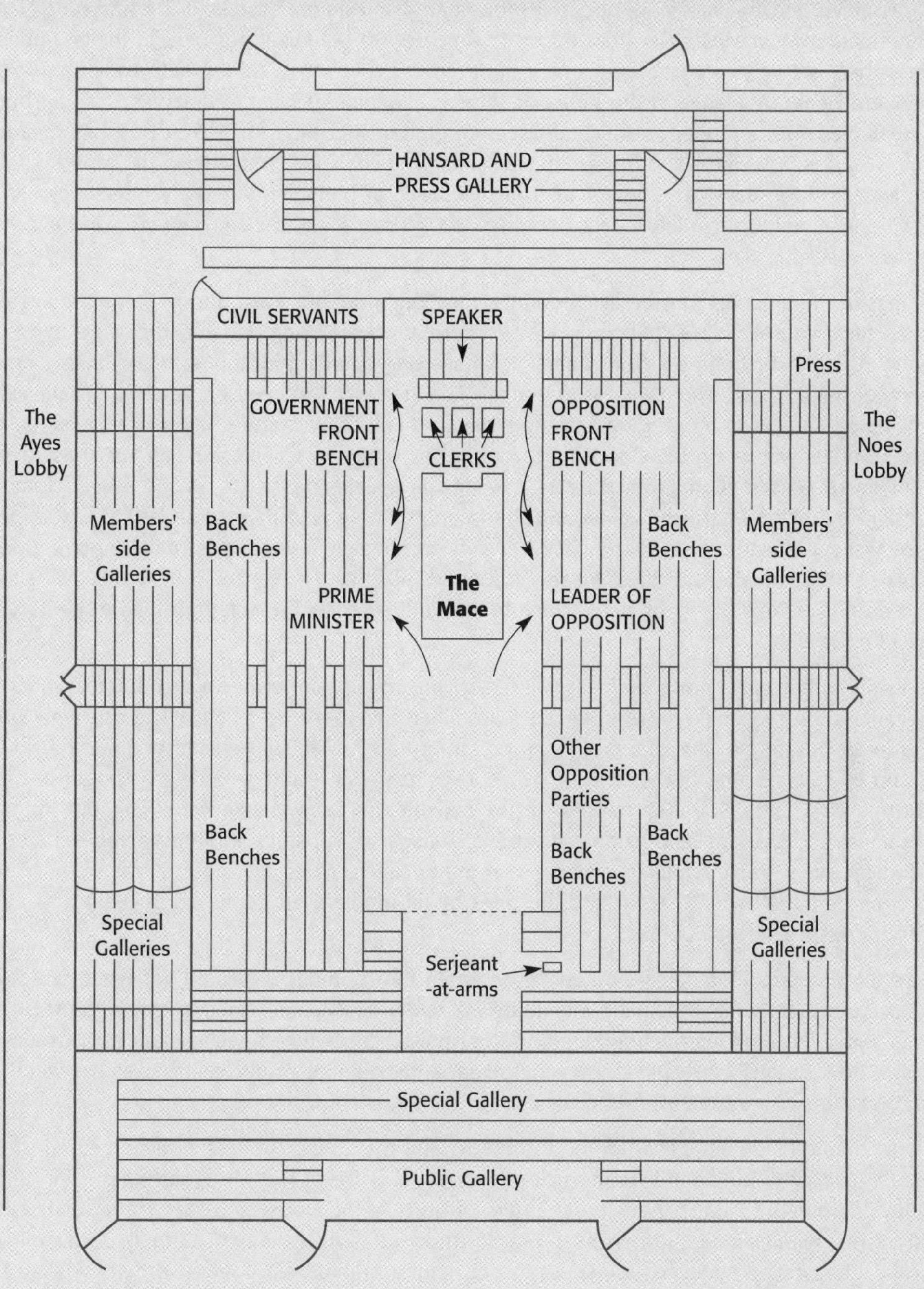

Figure 17.1 House of Commons seating plan

BOX 17.2 continued

The empty green benches are more apparent now than in previous decades. It is common to lament a fall in attendance. Most MPs have other things to do. There is little vital business in the chamber and nowadays there are very few Members who will attract a crowd when they speak: Tony Benn perhaps, or Sir Edward Heath. A change in the hours of sittings, allowing MPs to get away early on a Thursday evening, coupled with a tendency to schedule less important business for a Thursday, has meant that for some MPs it is now virtually a three-day week. They arrive in Westminster on the Monday – sometimes late in the day – and depart on Thursday. Neither parliamentary party meets now on a Thursday; indeed, very few meetings are organised on a Thursday. Most are now crowded into the day on Tuesday or Wednesday.

Proceedings in the chamber can be lively during Question Time, but even during that attendance – other than for Prime Minister's Questions – can be pretty poor. During debates, the proceedings can be notably dull. The Government front bench will have one or two ministers listening, taking notes as necessary for the purpose of replying at the end. A Government whip will be perched further along the bench, keeping an eye on proceedings, taking notes and liaising with the Chair about business. Their opposite numbers will be on the Opposition front bench. Notes or signals will variously pass between the whips, followed sometimes by a meeting behind the Speaker's Chair to fix some deal. Some MPs will wander in, look at what is going on and then depart. Some take their seats, stay a few minutes and go. A few will spend some time in the chamber and occasionally intervene to make a point. Some MPs are regulars in the chamber but they are the exceptions. Each tends to have a particular place they like to sit, so even if there is plenty of space close to where they enter the chamber they move to the spot they are familiar with.

Visitors to the public gallery may be disappointed by the small number of MPs in the chamber, but at least nowadays the proceedings are easier to follow than they have ever been. One can work out the actual order of business in the chamber from the Order Paper. MPs still refer to one another in the third person and by constituency, but whenever an MP rises to speak or intervene the occupant of the Chair calls out the MP's name. Some exchanges can be enlightening as well as entertaining, but they tend to be exceptional. Proceedings tend to be predictable. Tensions can rise in an ill-tempered debate and all the diplomatic skills – or disciplinary powers – of the Speaker or Deputy Speaker may be necessary to restore order. Some MPs try to get round the rules by raising partisan points on bogus points of order, much to the despair of the Speaker.

There are the exceptional debates, not just those when the chamber is packed but when an issue comes up that a number of MPs have a genuine interest in and some expert knowledge of. On those occasions, those listening learn something and the minister takes the speeches seriously. One rough measure of how seriously the speech is being taken is the number of notes that pass between the minister and the civil servants in the official box.

There is a notable difference between the Commons and the Lords. There is a section reserved for peers in the gallery of House of Commons. I variously make use of it but it is rare that I find a debate sufficiently engrossing to stay for any great length of time. In the House of Lords, I frequently take my seat in the chamber and find myself staying for most or all of the debate, simply because it is intrinsically interesting – speeches are short, to the point and informed. I learn something from the proceedings. When I sit in the gallery in the Commons, I sometimes reflect that MPs could learn something from 'the other place'.

election of 1950 (with the abolition of university seats, for some of which a system of proportional representation was used) did it become universal. All seats nowadays are contested. Again, this is a relatively recent development. In elections before 1945 a significant fraction of Members – an average of 13 per cent – were returned unopposed. As late as the 1951 election, four Ulster Unionist MPs were returned in uncontested elections.

Each constituency comprises a defined geographical area and the MP is returned to represent all citizens living within that area. (University seats were exceptional: the constituencies comprised graduates of the universities, regardless of where they were living.) Constituency boundaries are drawn up and revised regularly by independent Boundary Commissions (one covering each country – England, Scotland, Wales and Northern Ireland); each Commission is chaired formally by the Speaker of the House of Commons, though the essential work of leadership is undertaken by a deputy, who is a judge. Under existing legislation, boundary reviews are required every ten to fifteen years. The Commissions are enjoined to produce constituencies within each country of roughly equal size (in terms of the number of electors), though as far as possible retaining existing county and natural boundaries.

Members

Though the House may constitute a representative assembly in that it is freely elected and MPs are returned to defend and pursue the interests of constituents, it is not a representative assembly in being typical of the socio-economic population that elects it. The Members returned to the House are generally male, middle class and white. These characteristics have been marked throughout the twentieth century. The House has tended to become even more middle class in the years since 1945. Before 1945, and especially in the early years of the century, the Conservative ranks contained a significant number of upper- and upper-middle-class men of private means, while the Parliamentary Labour Party (the PLP) was notable for the number of MPs from manual-working backgrounds: they constituted a little over half of the PLP from 1922 to 1935 and before that had been in an overwhelming majority (Rush, 1979, pp. 69–123). Since 1945, the number of business people on the Conservative benches has increased, as has the number of graduates, often journalists and teachers, on the Labour benches.

The shift in the background of Conservative MPs since 1945 is reflected in education as well as occupation. In 1945, just over 83 per cent of Conservative MPs had been educated at public schools – 27 per cent at Eton. Almost two-thirds – 65 per cent – had been to university, with half having gone to Oxford or Cambridge. Just over 50 years later – in the Parliament elected in 1997 – 66 per cent were public school educated, with 9 per cent having been at Eton. Eighty-one per cent had been at university, the proportion having gone to Oxford or Cambridge remaining unchanged. The party has witnessed, particularly in the general elections in and since 1979, a growing number of newly elected candidates who have gone to state schools and then gone on to Oxbridge or some other university. Conservative Party leader William Hague is notable for having gone to a comprehensive school (Wath-on-Dearne Comprehensive School) before going to Oxford University. The underlying trend continues to be for the proportion of University-educated MPs to be greater among the new intake of MPs than among the parliamentary party as a whole (see Table 17.1). The trend also continues of new MPs being less likely to have attended Eton than Conservative MPs as a whole. Of the forty-one new Conservative MPs elected in 1997, only three had been to Eton. The members of the parliamentary party are not socially typical but they are somewhat more middle class than the members elected in the years before 1979.

Table 17.1 University education of candidates

	All parties' MPs, 1997	**New MPs, 1997**
Labour	66%	75%
Conservative	81%	90%
Liberal Democrat	70%	74%

Source: Criddle, 1997; Financial Times, 3 May 1997

On the Labour side, the notable change in educational background has been the rise in the number of graduates. In 1945, just over one-third of Labour MPs (34 per cent) had been to university. By 1970, just over half of the PLP were university graduates. By 1983, the figure was 54 per cent and in 1997 it had increased to 66 per cent. Most of these were graduates of universities other than Oxford and Cambridge. The percentage of Oxbridge-educated Labour MPs has shown little change – the percentage educated at Oxbridge in 1997 was the same as in 1945. As on the Conservative benches, the trend remains for the proportion of University-educated MPs to be greater among new MPs than among the parliamentary party as a whole (Table 17.1).

These figures reflect the growing middle-class nature of the PLP. The percentage of manual workers in the party declined in each successive Parliament until 1974, increased in 1979 and 1983, but then dropped back in subsequent elections. Only 17 per cent of new Labour MPs in 1992 were drawn from manual backgrounds. In 1997, the figure was down to 13 per cent, the lowest percentage ever (Criddle, 1997, p. 206). 'Increasingly, Labour MPs were defined by white collar public sector employment, whether in education, politics or as officials in public sector unions; very small numbers of Labour candidates had any experience of either manual work or business' (Criddle, 1992, p. 225).

Indeed, there is something of a convergence between Members on both sides in terms of education and background. Of new MPs elected to the House of Commons, the vast majority – on both sides of the House – are university educated and a large proportion are not only drawn from some middle-class occupation but an occupation that is in the domain of politics or communication. Of the new intake in 1997, teachers, journalists and political staffers were notable on the Labour benches and the last category – those who had worked in political positions such as advisers and researchers – were very much to the fore on the Conservative benches. Of the newly elected Members, four out of every ten Conservatives, one in five Labour Members and one in three Liberal Democrats had previously been employed in political posts (see Table 17.2).

Table 17.2 New MPs 1997: characteristics of MPs elected for first time in the 1997 general election, expressed as percentage of the new intake of each party

	Labour	Conservative	Liberal Democrat
Political staffers	20%	40%	32%
Councillors	64%	25%	70%
Women	35%	12%	7%

Source: Financial Times, 3 May 1997

This convergence reflects also the growth of the 'career politician' – the individual who lives for politics, who seeks entry to the House of Commons as early as possible and who seeks to stay in the House for as long as possible, ideally holding Government office along the way (King, 1981; Riddell 1993). Career politicians are contrasted with old-style MPs who used to make a mark in other fields before becoming involved in politics and who could – and variously did – leave the House of Commons to pursue some other interest (for example, heading a major company or the family firm). The old-style Members may have been ambitious in terms of Government office but they recognised that there was more to life than politics. For career politicians, politics is their life. The career politician has always existed in British politics, but their numbers have grown in recent years. They often (though not in all cases) hold a job in an area related to politics before seeking election. The consequence of the growth of the career politician is something we shall consider later.

Where there is a difference between the two sides is in terms of council experience and in terms of gender. Labour MPs are more likely to have served as local councillors. As shown in Table 17.2, of the new MPs elected in 1997, almost two-thirds of Labour MPs had served as councillors, compared with one-quarter of Conservative MPs. There are also many more women sitting on the Labour benches than on the Conservative (and Liberal Democrat) benches.

Women only became eligible to sit in the House in 1918. The number elected since then has been small. Between 1918 and 1974, the total number of women elected to the House was only 112 (including Countess Markievicz, the first woman elected but who did not take her seat). In the 1983 general election, twenty-three women were elected to the House, in 1987 the figure was forty-one and in 1992 it was sixty, an all-time high. The Labour Party in 1993 adopted a policy of all-women short-lists in a number of constituencies in order to boost the number of female Labour MPs. Though the policy was struck down by an employment tribunal in 1996 (see Chapter 23) on the grounds that it breached sex discrimination legislation, this did not affect seats where female candidates had already been selected. As a result, a record number of female Labour MPs were elected in 1997: no less than 101, sixty-four of them elected for the first time. Though Conservative leaders encouraged local parties to adopt female candidates, very few did so. With a number of female Conservative MPs retiring in 1997, the result was a notable disparity between the two parties (see Table 17.2). The percentage of women MPs in the House of Commons in recent Parliaments remains low by international comparison (see Table 17.3), but it is less marked than before. The percentage of women MPs in the House is now 18 per cent.

The number of non-white MPs remains very small. For most of the twentieth century there were none at all. The first non-white MP was elected in 1892: Dadabhai Naoroji, an Indian, was elected as Liberal MP for Finsbury Central. Another Indian was elected as a Conservative three years later. A third sat from 1922 to 1929. There was then a fifty-eight-year gap. In 1987, four non-white MPs were elected. In 1992, the number increased to six – five Labour and one Conservative – and reached an all-time high in 1997 when nine – all Labour – were elected, including the first Muslim MP and two Sikhs. Even so, the number represents only a little more than 1 per cent of the membership of the House.

One reason for the persistence of white, male MPs is the length of time that MPs typically serve in the House. Some MPs sit for thirty or forty years. The Father of the House of Commons (the longest continuously serving MP), Sir Edward Heath, was first elected in 1950. A typical Member sits for about twenty years. Given the growth in the number of career politicians, it is unlikely that this figure will decrease; if anything, the reverse. Even if parties are keen to replace existing MPs with candidates from a wider range of backgrounds, the opportunity to replace them does not necessarily come up very quickly. The length of service of legislators is a particular feature of the British House of Commons: MPs tend to serve as members longer than legislators in other comparable legislatures (see Table 17.4). Even in the 1997 general election, which – as a result of a massive swing to the Labour party – brought in a record number of new MPs (no less than 253), more than 60 per cent

Table 17.3 Women in national legislatures

	Women as % of total membership		
Country	**1975**	**1985**	**1994**
Sweden	21	31	41
Iceland	5	15	24
New Zealand	5	13	21
China	23	21	21
United States	4	5	11
Soviet Union/Russia	32	34	10
United Kingdom	4	4	9
India	4	8	7
Brazil	0	1	6
France	2	5	6
Japan	1	2	3
Turkey	8	3	2

Note: In bicameral legislatures, the figure refers to the elected lower chamber

Table 17.4 Average length of legislative service, 1994

Country	**Average length of service (years)**
Canada	6.5
France	7
Denmark	7.8
Germany	8.2
Israel	11
USA (Senate)	11.1
USA (House)	12.2
New Zealand	13.1
Japan	15
United Kingdom	20

Source: Somit and Roemmele, 1995

of MPs had served in the previous Parliament. More than thirty MPs had been first elected to Parliament in 1970 or earlier.

Members are paid an annual salary. Until 1912 MPs received no payment at all. Since then, they have been paid, but on a relatively modest basis. In 1954, for example, the salary was £1,250 and in 1964 it was increased to £3,250. In January 1996, an MP's salary was £34,086, fairly modest in international comparison – legislators in Italy, the USA, France and Germany were all paid considerably more (more than twice as much in Italy and the USA) – and by comparison with higher levels of management in the UK. (Ministers receive higher salaries but retain part of their salaries as MPs.) In July 1996, MPs voted to increase their salaries by 26 per cent, to £43,000. The increase was controversial, and unpopular, but still left MPs lagging behind the salaries of members of other comparable legislatures. MPs also voted to link their pay to a formula based on civil service pay, allowing pay to increase without the need for a regular vote. In 1999, an MP's annual salary was £47,008.

Since the 1960s, parliamentary facilities have also improved. In the mid-1960s, an MP was guaranteed only a locker in which to keep papers and received no allowance, either for hiring a secretary or even to cover the cost of telephone calls. If an MP was lucky enough to have an office, it was usually shared with several other MPs. A secretary had to be paid out of the MP's own pocket. In 1969 a secretarial allowance was introduced. That allowance has evolved into an office cost allowance, allowing an MP to hire one and sometimes two secretaries and in most cases a (more often than not part-time) research assistant. In 1999, the office cost allowance stood at £50,264. The physical space available to MPs has also increased. Buildings close to the Palace of Westminster – including the former Scotland Yard buildings in Derby Gate – were acquired for parliamentary use. More recently, buildings in Parliament Street – between Whitehall and Parliament Square – were taken over and redeveloped, retaining the exterior but with a modern and integrated complex of offices inside. With the completion of a second major parliamentary building, Portcullis House, in Bridge Street – across the road from Big Ben – each MP will have an office.

Sittings of the House

The House to which Members are returned meets annually, each parliamentary session running usually from October to October (or early November). There is a long summer adjournment, but the session is not prorogued (formally closed) until shortly after the House returns in the autumn; that allows the House to meet and deal with bills which have not completed their passage. The effect of prorogation is to kill off all unfinished public business; any bills which have not received the Royal Assent have usually to be reintroduced and go through all their stages again in the new session.

The House usually sits for more than 150 days a year, a not unusual number compared with some other legislatures, such as those of the USA, Canada and France, though considerably more than most other legislatures. What makes it distinctive is the number of hours for which it sits: it sits for more than 1,200 hours a year. The figures for the period since 1992 are given in Table 17.5. In previous Parliaments, the lengths of sittings were sometimes much longer, averaging nearly 1,500 hours in a non-election session in the 1987–92 Parliament. Other parliaments are not able to compete with these figures.

The House meets at 2.30 p.m. on Mondays, Tuesdays and Wednesdays, at 9.30 a.m. on Fridays and – in an experiment started in 1999 – at 11.30 a.m. on Thursdays. It rises usually no later than 10.30 p.m. on the first four days of the week,

Table 17.5 The House of Commons: length of sittings, 1992–8

Session	Number of sitting days	Number of hours sat	Average length on sitting day
1992–3[a]	240	1,933	8 hours 3 minutes
1993–4	154	1,258	8 hours 10 minutes
1994–5	159	1,313	8 hours 16 minutes
1995–6	146	1,278	8 hours 45 minutes
1996–7[b]	86	717	8 hours 21 minutes
1997–8[a]	241	2,117	8 hours 47 minutes

[a] Long session following a Spring general election
[b] Short session, because of the calling of a general election
Source: House of Commons Sessional Information Digests, 1992–8

though the business on a Thursday is now usually arranged in order to allow the House to rise early, usually about seven or eight o'clock. Sittings may, in certain circumstances, be extended in order to transact particular business. Late or all-night sittings variously take place to get through the remaining stages of a bill. (If the House has an all-night sitting and is still sitting at 2.30 p.m. the following day, the business for that next day falls.) Late-night sittings became rare in the 1992–7 Parliament but were employed again following the return of a Labour Government in 1997 in order to get some of its major legislation through. On Fridays, when **private Members' bills** are normally discussed, the House rises at 3.00 p.m.

As a result of a change agreed by the House in 1999, there is also a 'parallel chamber', or 'main committee', allowing MPs to meet and discuss issues separate from the main chamber (see Box 17.3). This allows for non-contentious issues

BOX 17.3 **IDEAS AND PERSPECTIVES** 

Meetings in Westminster Hall

In December 1999, the House of Commons introduced a new form of meeting – meetings in Westminster Hall. These enable MPs to meet separately from the main chamber, and the gathering is sometimes described as a parallel chamber. It is also sometimes referred to as the Main Committee, because that is the name used in the Australian Parliament. (The parallel chamber is modelled on the Australian experience.) Meetings in Westminster Hall are open to all MPs. They can come in as they can in the main chamber. The principal differences between the main chamber and the room used for the parallel chamber are of size and structure. The room used for the parallel chamber – the Grand Committee Room, part of Westminster Hall – is much smaller than the chamber of the House of Commons. It also differs in structure. MPs sit at desks arranged in a semi-circle around a raised dais. The desks are fixed – indeed, a note on each desk reminds MPs that the furniture is fixed and that they should not attempt to move it – and have desk-top microphones. Meetings are presided over by a Deputy Speaker or one of the MPs on the Chairmen's Panel (MPs who are used to chairing standing committees) and are used to transacting non-contentious business. Votes cannot be held. The meetings allow private Members' motions in particular to be discussed. (The House had started meeting on Wednesday mornings to discuss such motions, but with the introduction of the parallel chamber the House ceased to meet on Wednesday mornings. Motions discussed in the House on Wednesday mornings were transferred to the new chamber.) Meetings in Westminster Hall are held on Tuesdays from 10.00 a.m. to 1.00 p.m., on Wednesdays from 9.30 a.m. to 2.00 p.m. and on Thursdays from 2.30 to 5.30 p.m. On Tuesdays and Wednesdays, there are short debates, each of 30 minutes, on topics raised by individual Members. Thus, for example, on Wednesday 15 December 1999, the topics discussed were the removal of human organs, their donation and transplantation; equal funding for men's and women's sports; pay and conditions of scientists in the NHS; and alternative fuels. Attendance at meetings is low – usually a handful of MPs – not dissimilar to the chamber itself when private Members' motions are taken. Thursday afternoons are given over to longer, more general debates. On 16 December 1999, the topic was the delivery of nursery pledges and childcare provision.

The creation of the parallel chamber was controversial. Supporters see it as a way of allowing issues, for which there would otherwise be no time in the chamber, to be discussed. Most Conservative MPs voted against setting it up because they feared it would serve to distract attention from the chamber and absorb MPs' energies on minor issues. In the event, meetings of the new body have proved low key, attracting virtually no media attention (the inaugural meeting was effectively ignored) and very little attention on the part of MPs.

to be debated. Meetings are held in the Grand Committee Room, just off Westminster Hall, and are known formally as meetings in Westminster Hall. The principal business is usually private Members motions. All MPs can attend – it is the same as in the chamber – though in practice few do so. Meetings in Westminster Hall began in December 1999 and take place on Tuesday and Wednesday mornings and on Thursday afternoons.

Functions

The principal function of the House is often seen as being that of being involved in law-making. It is, after all, classified as a legislature and the name means carrier, or giver, of law. In practice, much of the time of the House is given over to business that has nothing directly to do with legislation. Question Time is now an established feature of the House. It is not part of the legislative process. When the House debates the economy or the government's industrial policy, those debates again are not part of the formal legislative process. Some of the most notable speeches made in the House in the 1990s – not least the resignation speech of Sir Geoffrey Howe in 1990 – attracted considerable media attention, but again had nothing to do with the legislative process. The House has an important role to play in the legislative process, but it is clearly not its only role.

The principal functions of the House can be grouped under four headings: those of legitimisation, recruitment, scrutiny and influence, and expression. Several other functions can be identified (see Norton, 1993, Chapter 13) but these can largely be subsumed under these four broad headings.

Legitimisation

The primary purpose for which the representatives of the counties and boroughs (the communes) were first summoned was to assent to the King's demand for additional taxes. Subsequently, their assent also came to be necessary for legislation. The House has thus been, since its inception, a legitimising body. It fulfils what Robert Packenham has termed the function of 'latent legitimisation'. This derives from the fact that 'simply by meeting regularly and uninterruptedly, the legislature produces, among the relevant populace and elites, a wider and deeper sense of the government's moral right to rule than would otherwise have obtained' (Packenham, in Norton, 1990, p. 87). Given that Parliament not only sits regularly but has done so without interruption since the seventeenth century, it is arguably a much stronger agent of latent legitimisation than many other legislatures. It would seem plausible to hypothesise that the function is weaker in a political system in which the legislature is a recent and conscious creation of resuscitation by the prevailing regime. In Britain, legitimisation may also be reinforced by the fact that members of the government are drawn from, and govern through, Parliament – ministers remaining and fulfilling functions as Members of Parliament.

The House also fulfils the task of 'manifest legitimisation', that is, the overt, conscious giving of assent. This encompasses not only the giving of assent to bills – and requests for supply – laid before the House but also the giving of assent to the government itself. The government depends on the confidence of the House of Commons for its continuance in office. If the House withdraws its confidence, then by convention the government resigns or requests a dissolution.

The House proceeds on the basis of motions laid before it: for example, to give a bill a second reading or to express confidence in the government. By approving such motions, the House gives its formal – manifest – assent. Members may vote on motions. The Speaker of the House asks those supporting the motion to say 'aye', those opposing to say 'no'. If no dissenting voices are heard, the motion is declared to be carried. If some MPs shout 'no' and persist then Members divide (that is, vote). A simple majority is all that is necessary. (This is subject to two basic requirements: that at least forty MPs – a quorum – are shown by the division to be present and that, in voting on a closure motion, at least a hundred MPs have voted in favour.) Members vote by trooping through two lobbies – the division lobbies – where their names are recorded. The result of the vote is then announced in the chamber.

It is this accepted need for assent – for the House to confer legitimacy – that constitutes the basic power of the House in relation to government. Initially, the knights and burgesses summoned to the King's court were called to give assent, but with no recognition of any capacity to deny assent. Gradually, members began to realise that they could, as a body, deny assent to supply and later to legislation. This formed the basis on which they could ensure the effective fulfilment of other functions. It remains the basis of the power of the House of Commons. Without the assent of the House, no measure can become an Act of Parliament. The contemporary point of contention is the extent to which the House is prepared to use its power to deny assent. Critics contend that the effect of the growth of party and hence party cohesion has largely nullified the willingness of the House to employ it.

Recruitment

Ministers are normally drawn from, and remain within, Parliament. The situation is governed solely by convention. There is no legal requirement that a minister has to be an MP or peer.

The practice of appointing ministers from those who sit in Parliament derives from expediency. Historically, it was to the King's benefit to have his ministers in Parliament, where they could influence, lead and marshal support for the crown. It was to the benefit of Parliament to have ministers who could answer for their conduct. An attempt was made early in the eighteenth century to prevent ministers from sitting in Parliament, but the legislation was superseded by another law allowing the practice to continue (Norton, 1993, p. 34).

The convention that ministers be drawn from and remain within Parliament – predominantly now, by convention, the House of Commons – is a strong one inasmuch as virtually all ministers are MPs or peers. It is extremely rare for a minister to be appointed who does not sit in either House and even rarer for that person to remain outside Parliament while in office: the person is either elevated to the peerage (nowadays the most used route) or found a safe seat to contest in a by-election. On occasion, one of the Scottish law officers – the Solicitor General for Scotland – is appointed from the ranks of Scottish lawyers and remains outside Parliament, but it is the exception that proves the rule.

The relationship between the House and ministers is governed by convention. Under the convention of individual ministerial responsibility, ministers are answerable to the House for their own conduct and that of their particular departments. Under the convention of collective ministerial responsibility, the Cabinet is responsible to the House for government policy as a whole. It is this latter convention that requires a request for a dissolution or the resignation of the government in the event of the House passing a motion of no confidence in the government.

The fact that ministers remain in Parliament clearly has a number of advantages to government. Things have not changed that much from earlier centuries in that ministers can use their positions to lead and marshal their supporters. Ministers themselves add notably to the voting strength of the government, the so-called 'payroll vote' in the House. Just over eighty ministers serve in the Commons and just over twenty in the Lords. With ministers' unpaid helpers – parliamentary private secretaries – added to the number, the payroll vote comprises usually a third or more of the MPs sat on the government side of the House. The government thus has a sizeable guaranteed vote to begin with. Party loyalty – and ambition for office – usually ensures that the votes of **back-benchers** follow those of ministers.

The convention that ministers be drawn from the ranks of parliamentarians has certain advantages for Parliament. It ensures that members are proximate to ministers, both formally and informally. Ministers can be questioned on the floor of the House; they can be waylaid in the corridors and division lobbies for private conversations and pleadings by Members. The fact that they remain as Members of the House means they retain some affinity with other Members. MPs elevated to ministerial office still retain their constituency duties.

Above all, though, the convention renders the House of Commons powerful as a recruiting agent. The route to ministerial office is through Parliament. In some other systems, the legislature is but one route to the top. In the USA, for example, there are multiple routes: cabinet ministers – and presidents – can be drawn from the ranks of business executives, academics, state governors, army officers and lawyers. The US Congress enjoys no monopoly on recruitment. In the UK, Parliament does have such a monopoly. Parliament is thus the exclusive route for those intending to reach the top of the political ladder. Those aspiring to ministerial office thus have to seek election to the House of Commons (or hope – often in vain – for a peerage) and have to make their mark in the House. The House serves also as an important testing ground for potential ministers and, indeed, for those on the ministerial ladder. A poor performance at the dispatch box can harm a minister's chances of further promotion. A consistently poor performance can result in the minister losing office. Of the new Labour ministers appointed in 1997, one – Transport Minister Gavin Strang – encountered persistent criticism for his inability to perform effectively in the chamber. He was sacked the following year. The reputation of the Deputy Prime Minister, John Prescott, suffered badly in 1999 following a disastrous performance at the dispatch box when he was standing in for the Prime Minister at Prime Minister's Question Time. For ambitious politicians, the chamber matters.

Scrutiny and influence

Scrutiny and influence are essentially conjoined functions. The House subjects both the measures and the actions of government to scrutiny. It does so through various means: debate, questioning and committee deliberations. If it does not like what is before it, it can influence the bill or the policy under consideration. It may influence solely by the force of argument. It may influence by threatening to deny assent (that is, by threatening to defeat the government). Ultimately, it may actually refuse its assent, denying the government a majority in the division lobbies.

These two functions are central to the activity of the House and absorb most of its time. Government business enjoys precedence on most days. The House spends most of its time discussing legislation and the policy and actions of ministers. Though the growth of party has ensured that government is normally assured a majority in divisions, the party system helps to ensure that government is subject to critical scrutiny from opposition parties in the House. The procedures of the House are premised on the existence of two principal parties, with each having the opportunity to be heard. Membership of all committees of the House replicates party strength on the floor of the House, thus ensuring that the opposition has an opportunity to offer critical comments and to force government to respond at all stages of the parliamentary process.

Furthermore, scrutiny and influence may also take place outside, or despite, the context of party. MPs sit for particular constituencies. Though elected on a party label, they are none the less expected to ensure that government policy does not damage constituency interests. They may also be influenced by moral and religious views that ensure they pay careful attention to bills and government policies that run counter to their personal convictions. They may also listen to bodies outside Parliament – charities, consumer groups, professional organisations, companies – that have a particular interest in, or knowledge of, the subject under debate.

However, the extent to which the House actually fulfils these functions is a matter of dispute. Critics contend that the government stranglehold, via its party majority, ensures that the House is denied the means for sustained and effective scrutiny, and that, inasmuch as it may exert some limited scrutiny, that scrutiny is not matched by the capacity to influence government. MPs may consider and find fault with a particular measure, but not then prove willing to use their power to amend or reject it.

Expression

The House serves not one but several expressive functions. Members serve to express the particular views and demands of constituents. An individual constituent or a group of constituents may be adversely affected by some particular policy or by the actions of some public officials. Constituents may feel that a particular policy is bad for the constituency or for the country. Contacting the local MP will usually result in the MP passing on the views to the relevant minister and may even result in the Member raising the issue on the floor of the House. The pursuit of such cases by MPs ensures that they are heard and considered by ministers.

MPs also express the views of different groups in society as a whole. A range of issues that do not fall within the ambit of party politics are taken up and pursued by private Members. MPs may express the views of organised interests, such as particular industries or occupations. They may express the views of different sectors of society, such as the elderly. Many will give voice to the concerns of particular charitable, religious or moral groups. Some MPs press, for example, for reform of the laws governing abortion, some want to liberalise the laws concerning homosexuality, some want to ban hunting. These issues can be pursued by MPs through a number of parliamentary procedures (see Cowley, 1998). In some cases, Members table amendments to government bills. Another route is through the use of private Members' bills. Though the more contentious the issue, the less likely the bill is to be passed, the debate on the bill serves an important function: it allows the different views to be expressed in an authoritative public forum, heard by the relevant minister and open to coverage by the mass media.

MPs, then, serve to express the views of constituents and different groups to the House and to government. MPs may also serve to express the views of the House and of government to constituents and organised groups. The House may reach a decision on a particular topic. Members may then fulfil an important role in explaining why that decision was taken. Members individually may explain decisions to constituents. Select committees of the House may, in effect, explain particular policies through their reports which are read not just by government but by groups with a particular interest in the committee's area of inquiry. The House thus has a tremendous potential to serve several expressive functions. The extent to which it does so is a matter of considerable debate. MPs have limited time and resources to pursue all the matters brought to their attention. The attention given to their activities by the media and by government may be slight. Many groups may bypass Parliament in order to express their views directly to ministers. Furthermore, it is argued, the views expressed by MPs on behalf of others are drowned out by the noise of party battle. By limiting the resources of the House and by keeping information to itself, the government has limited the capacity of the House to arm itself with the knowledge necessary to raise support for public policies.

These are the most important functions that may be ascribed to the House. The list is not an exhaustive one. Other tasks are carried out by the House. These include, for example, a disciplinary role (punishing breaches of privilege and contempt) and a small quasi-judicial role, primarily in dealing with private legislation (legislation affecting private interests and not to be confused with private Members' legislation). Other functions often ascribed to the House can, as we have explained, be subsumed under the four main headings we have provided. However, two other functions, identified by Walter Bagehot in *The English Constitution* in 1867, have been lost by the House. One, the 'elective' function – that is, choosing the government – was held only briefly during the nineteenth century. Before then it was a function exercised by the monarch. Since then, it has passed largely, though not quite exclusively, to the electorate. The electorate chooses a government on a regular basis at general elections. The House retains the power to turn a government out through passing a motion of no confidence; but it is not a power it has regularly exercised.

The other function is that of 'legislation'. Initially, the need for the House to give its assent was transformed by Members into the power to initiate measures, first through the presentation of petitions to the crown and later through the introduction of bills. This power was important during the 'golden age' of Parliament in the nineteenth century, when the House could be described as sharing the legislative power with government. Even so, its exercise was limited. Most legislation introduced into the House was private legislation. Since then, public legislation has expanded as party has become more powerful. Party has ensured that the power to formulate – to 'make' – legislation rests with government, with the House then giving its assent. Insofar as the House has retained a residual legislative power, it is exercised through the medium of private Members' legislation. Even that legislative power, however, can be described now as one shared with government. Since 1959, no private Member's bill which has been the subject of a vote at second reading has made it to the statute book without government providing time for it.

Scrutiny and influence

The functions that the House retains can be described as modest but appropriate to a reactive legislature. They have developed over time. But how well are they currently carried out? The principal functions of the House in relation to the executive are those of scrutiny and influence. The means available to the House to fulfil those functions are also at the disposal of Members for expressing the views of their constituents and of wider interests. They can be grouped under two headings: legislation and executive actions.

Legislation

When legislation is introduced, it has to go through a well-established process involving debate and consideration in committee. About 30 to 40 per cent of the time of the House is taken up with debate on bills. In the long 1997–8 session – the first under the new Labour Government – it was just over 40 per cent (see Table 17.6). The bulk of this time is given over to government bills. (Private Members' legislation occupies under 5 per cent of time on the floor of the House.) Every bill has to go through three 'readings' plus a committee and (usually) a report stage. The stages are shown in Table 17.7.

The first reading marks the formal introduction. No debate takes place. Indeed, at this stage there is not even a printed bill. All that is read out is the bill's title. Following first reading, the bill is printed. Second reading comprises a debate on the principle of the measure. Most government bills will be allocated a half or a full day's debate for second reading. Major bills, especially of constitutional significance, may be given two or more days for debate. In 1999, for example, the House of Lords Bill – to remove hereditary peers from membership of the House of Lords – was given a two-day debate.

The debate itself follows a standard pattern: the minister responsible for the bill opens the debate, explaining the provisions of the bill and justifying its introduction. The relevant shadow minister then makes a speech from the opposition front bench, outlining the stance of the opposition on the bill. After these two front-bench speeches,

Table 17.6 Time spent on the floor of the House 1997–8

Business	%
Addresses, including debate on Queen's Speech	1.5
Government bills	
Second reading	10.0
Committee of the Whole House	12.0[a]
Report	9.5
Third Reading	1.2
Lords amendments	3.4
Allocation of time orders	0.6
Private Members' bills	3.8
Private business	0.3
Government motions	
EC documents	1.0
General	1.9
Opposition motions	
Opposition days	6.0
Opposition motions in government time	0.5
Adjournment	1.2
Adjournment	
Government debates	7.8
Back bench (including daily and Wednesday morning debates)	16.2
Estimates	0.5
Money resolutions	0.1
Ways and means resolutions (including budget debate)	2.3
Statutory instruments	2.0
Question Time	9.0
Statements (including Private Notice Questions and Business Statements)	6.5
Miscellaneous	2.8
Daily prayers	0.9
Total	101[b]

[a] The percentage of time given over to committee stage of bills on the floor of the House was exceptionally high in this session because of the number of bills of constitutional significance introduced by the new Labour Government. In some sessions, the figure is well below 5 per cent

[b] Exceeds 100 per cent because of rounding

Source: Figures calculated from House of Commons Sessional Information Digest 1997–8

Table 17.7 Legislative stages

Stage	Where taken	Comments
First reading	On the floor of the House	Formal introduction: no debate
Second reading	On the floor of the House[a]	Debate on the principle
[Money resolution: Commons	On the floor of the House]	
Committee	In standing committee in the Commons unless House votes otherwise (certain bills taken on the floor of the House); almost invariably on the floor of the House in the Lords	Considered clause by clause; amendments may be made
Report	On the floor of the House	Bill reported back to House; amendments may be made
Third reading	On the floor of the House[b]	Final approval: no amendments possible in the Commons
Lords (or Commons) amendments	On the floor of the House	Consideration of amendments made by other House

[a] In the Commons, non-contentious bills may be referred to a committee
[b] If a bill is taken in committee of the whole House and no amendments are made, there is no report stage

most Members present tend to leave the chamber, leaving usually a small number of MPs to listen to the remaining speeches. Back-benchers from both sides of the House are then called alternately, plus usually a Member from one or more of the minor parties, and the debate is then wound up with speeches from the opposition and government front benches. (The House tends to fill up again for the winding-up speeches.) If the bill is contested, the House then divides. Debates, though not predictable in content, are generally so in outcome: only three times this century has the government lost a vote on second reading (in 1924, 1977 and 1986). Speeches on occasion may influence some votes, even whole debates, but they are exceptional. A government sometimes loses the argument but not usually the vote.

Once approved in principle, the bill is then sent to committee for detailed scrutiny. Some bills, because of their constitutional significance or because of the need for a speedy passage, will have their committee stage on the floor of the House. In most sessions the number is very small. However, in the long 1997–8 session, the new Labour Government introduced several major bills that were taken for their committee stage on the floor of the House. These included the European Communities (Amendment) Bill (to give effect in British law to the Amsterdam Treaty), the Scotland Bill (setting up the Scottish parliament), the Government of Wales Bill (establishing the Welsh Assembly) and the Human Rights Bill (incorporating the European Convention on Human Rights into British law). The majority of bills, though, are sent to a **standing committee**, the standard practice since 1907. The name 'standing committee' is a misnomer: there is nothing permanent, or 'standing', about the committees, other than their names. The membership of each committee is appointed afresh for each bill. The committees are identified by letters of the alphabet: standing committee A, standing committee B, and so on. One committee (standing committee C) normally deals with private Members' legislation. Once standing committee A has completed consideration of a bill, a new standing committee A – that is, with a different membership – is appointed to consider another bill. Because of the number of bills introduced each session, it is common for five or more standing committees to be in existence at any one time. Each committee comprises between sixteen and fifty members (for most bills, eighteen is the standard), reflecting proportionately the party strength in the House as a whole. The purpose of the committee is to render a bill 'more generally acceptable' through scrutinising it and, if necessary, amending it. (It cannot reject it or make any amendment that runs counter to the principle of the bill that has been approved by the House on second reading.) Each bill is considered clause by clause, the committee discussing and deciding on any amendments tabled to a clause before approving (or rejecting) the motion 'that the clause stand part of the bill'.

Committee stage constitutes the most criticised stage of the legislative process. Discussion in committee will often follow the adversarial lines adopted in the second reading debate. Traditionally, a great deal of time has been taken up with the earlier and more controversial clauses of a bill. If debate on the early clauses drags on, the government may resort to a timetable (guillotine) motion. This can result in later clauses getting little or no attention. Each committee resembles the House in miniature, with a minister and a **whip** appointed on the government side, and the minister's opposite number and a whip serving on the opposition side. Both sides face one another and the whips operate to marshal their members. Though cross-voting by government back-benchers can result in some defeats for the government, such occurrences are rare. The government is able to call on its supporters who constitute not only a majority but also often a fairly silent majority on the committee. In order not to delay proceedings, government back-benchers are encouraged to keep as quiet as possible. In consequence, service on standing committees is often not popular, government back-benchers treating it as a chore and using the opportunity to read and sometimes write replies to correspondence.

Because of criticism of the whole process, the two principal parties in the House agreed in 1994 to a voluntary timetabling of bills. This meant that each bill was subject to an agreed timetable, thus avoiding the need for a guillotine to be introduced. However, this agreement was not sustained in the new Parliament returned in May 1997 and the new Labour Government variously resorted to the use of guillotine (or what were termed programme motions) to get measures through. Most guillotines, though, were used for the stages on the floor of the House rather than in standing committee.

After committee stage, a bill returns to the House for report stage. This provides an opportunity for the House to decide whether it wishes to make any further amendments and is often used by the government to introduce amendments promised during committee stage, as well as any last-minute (sometimes numerous) amendments of its own. There is, though, no report stage if a bill has been taken for its committee stage on the floor of the House and been passed unamended.

There then follows the bill's third reading, when the House gives its final approval to the measure. Such debates are often short. If the bill is not contentious, there may be no debate at all. On completion of third reading, the bill then goes to the House of Lords and, if the Upper House makes any amendments, the bill then returns to the Commons for it to consider the amendments. In most cases, the amendments are accepted. If not, the House of Lords usually gives way. Once both Houses have approved the bill, it then goes to the Queen for the Royal Assent.

All bills, with certain exceptions, go through this procedure. There are some variations: some non-contentious bills, for example, can be sent to a second reading committee, thus avoiding taking up valuable debating time on the floor of the House. There is also provision for bills to be considered at committee stage by a special standing committee, the committee being empowered to take evidence from witnesses. This power, though, has only been used sparingly. Private Members' bills are also treated differently, primarily in terms of timetabling. They have to go through all the stages listed, but time for their consideration on the floor of the House is extremely limited. Each session a ballot is held, and the names of twenty private Members drawn. They are then entitled to introduce bills during the Fridays allocated to such bills, but only about the top half-dozen are likely to achieve full debates.

Bills constitute primary legislation. They often contain powers for regulations to be made under their authority once enacted. These regulations – known as delegated legislation – may be made subject to parliamentary approval. (Under the affirmative resolution procedure, the regulation must be approved by Parliament in order to come into force; under the negative resolution procedure it comes into force unless Parliament disapproves it.) Some regulations, though, only have to be laid before the House and others do not even have to be laid.

Given the growth of delegated legislation in post-war years, the House has sought to undertake scrutiny of it. Detailed, and essentially technical, scrutiny is undertaken by a Select Committee on Statutory Instruments. However, there is no requirement that the government has to wait for the committee to report on a regulation before bringing it before the House for approval, and on occasion – though not frequently – the government will seek approval before a regulation has been considered by the committee. Time for debate is also extremely limited and much delegated legislation is hived off for discussion in a standing committee on delegated legislation. Similar procedures are adopted for draft European Community legislation: it is considered by a committee and, if recommended for debate, is discussed by one of three European standing committees.

Executive actions

There are various means employed to scrutinise and to influence the actions of government. These same means can be and usually are employed by MPs to express the views of constituents and different interests in society. The means essentially are those available on the floor of the House (debates and Question Time), those available on the committee corridor (select committees) and those available off the floor of the House (early day motions, correspondence, the parliamentary commissioner for administration, party committees and all-party groups). Some individually are of limited use. It is their use in combination that can be effective in influencing government.

Debates and Question Time

Most of the time of the House is taken up debating or questioning the actions of government. *Debates* take different forms. They can be on a substantive motion (for example, congratulating or condemning the policy of the government on a particular issue) or, in order to allow wide-ranging discussion (especially on a topic on which the government may have no fixed position), on an adjournment motion ('That this House do now adjourn'). For example, prior to the Gulf War at the beginning of 1991, the situation in the Gulf was debated on an adjournment motion. After military action had begun, the House debated a substantive motion approving the action. Adjournment debates under this heading can be described as full-scale adjournment debates. They are distinct from the half-hour adjournment debates which take place at the end of every sitting of the House. These half-hour debates take the form of a back-bencher raising a particular issue and the relevant minister then responding. After exactly half an hour, the debate concludes and the House adjourns.

Debates are initiated by different bodies in the House. Most motions initiated by government are to approve legislation. However, government will occasionally initiate debates on particular policies. More frequently, debates are started by opposition parties. There are twenty days each year which are designated as opposition days. On seventeen of these twenty days, the motion (or motions – a day's debate can be split into two) is chosen by the leader of the opposition. On the remaining three days, the topic is chosen by the leader of the third largest party in the House (the Liberal Democrats), though at least one day is usually given over to the other minor parties. There are also three estimates days each session, the choice of estimate for debate being made by a select committee of the House: the Liaison Committee, comprising primarily the MPs who chair other select committees. Private Members are also responsible for initiating the topics in the daily half-hour adjournment debates: on four days a week, Members are selected by ballot and on one the Speaker chooses the Member. These back-benchers' occasions provide opportunities to raise essentially non-partisan issues, especially those of concern to constituents. Though such debates are poorly attended, they allow Members to put an issue on the public record and elicit a response from government.

The half-hour adjournment debates involve a back-bencher raising an issue, sometimes one or two other back-benchers making quick contributions, and then a response from a minister. Full-scale half-day or full-day debates initiated by government or opposition resemble instead the practice adopted in second reading debates. There are speeches from the two front benches, followed by back-bench speeches alternating between the two sides of the House, followed by winding-up speeches from the front benches, and then, if necessary, a vote. The term 'debate' is itself a misnomer. Members rarely debate but rather deliver prepared speeches which often fail to take up the points made by preceding speakers. Members wishing to take part usually inform the Speaker in advance and can usually obtain some indication from the Speaker if and when are they are likely to be called. There is a tendency for Members not to stay for the whole debate after they have spoken. Members, especially back-benchers, frequently address a very small audience – sometimes no more than half-a-dozen MPs. There is a prevailing view in the House that attendance has dropped over recent years. MPs now have offices they can spend time in. There are competing demands on their time and as the outcome of most votes is predictable – and Members know perfectly well how they intend to vote – there appears little incentive to spend time in the chamber. Major set-piece debates – as on a motion of confidence – and a debate in which the outcome is uncertain can still attract a crowded chamber, some Members having to sit on the floor or stand at the bar of the House in order to listen to the proceedings. Occasionally a particularly good speaker, such as Labour MP Tony Benn or former Prime Minister Sir Edward Heath, may attract Members into the chamber. Such occasions are exceptional. On most days, MPs addressing the House do so to rows of empty green benches.

Debates take place on motions. However, there is one form of business taken on the floor of the House which departs from the rule requiring a motion to be before the House. That is *Question Time*. This takes place on four days of the week – Monday to Thursday – when the House is sitting. It starts shortly after 2.30 p.m. on the first three days of the week and at 11.30 a.m. on Thursday: some minor business is transacted – announcements from the Speaker, certain non-debatable motions concerning private legislation – before it gets under way. It concludes at 3.30 p.m. on the first three days and at 12.30 p.m. on Thursdays. The Speaker, Betty Boothroyd, has adopted the practice of ending Question Time with the words 'time's up'!

Question Time itself is of relatively recent origin (see Franklin and Norton, 1993). The first recorded instance of a question being asked was in the House of Lords in 1721 and the first printed notice of questions to ministers was issued in 1835. The institution of a dedicated slot for Prime Minister's questions is of even more recent origin, dating from July 1961. From 1961 to 1997, the Prime Minister answered questions for fifteen minutes on two days of the week. In May 1997, the new Labour Prime Minister, Tony Blair, changed the procedure, answering questions for thirty minutes once a week.

The practice of asking questions is popular with MPs and the demand to ask questions exceeds the time available. Members are thus restricted in the number they can put on the order paper: no more than eight in every ten sitting days and no more than two on any one day. (If two are on the order paper on the same day, they may not be to the same minister.) Questions must be precisely that – that is, questions (statements and expressions of opinion are inadmissible) – and each must be on a matter for which the minister has responsibility. There is also an extensive list of topics (including arms sales, budgetary forecasts and purchasing contracts) on which government will not answer questions.

Ministers answer questions on a rota basis, most ministries coming up on the rota every four weeks. Some of the smaller ministries have slots in Question Time from 3.10 p.m. onwards. All questions tabled by Members used to be printed on the order paper, a practice that was costly and largely pointless. The number tabled often ran into three figures but the questions that were actually answered in the time available was usually fewer than twenty. Following changes approved by the House in 1990, only the top thirty or so – chosen in advance by random selection – are now printed.

The MP with the first question rises and says 'Question Number One, Madam Speaker' and then sits down. The minister rises and replies to the question. The MP is then called to put a follow-up – or 'supplementary' – question, to which the minister responds. Another Member may then be permitted by the Speaker to put another supplementary. If an opposition **front-bencher** rises, he or she has priority. During Prime Minister's Question Time, the leader of the opposition is frequently at the dispatch box. The Speaker decides when to move on to the next question.

During an average session, about 2,000 to 3,000 questions will receive an oral answer. With supplementaries included, the figure is nearer 6,000. In the long 1997–8 session, the number exceeded 8,000.

Question Time is not the only opportunity afforded MPs to put questions to ministers. Members can also table questions for written answer. The questions, along with ministers' answers, are published in *Hansard*, the official record of parliamentary proceedings. There is no limit on the number of questions that an MP can table – some table several hundred in a session – and they can be answered at greater length than is possible during Question Time. In an average session, more than 40,000 written questions are answered by ministers. In the long 1997–8 session, the number was just over 51,000.

Question Time itself remains an important opportunity for back-benchers to raise issues of concern to constituents and to question ministers on differing aspects of their policies and intentions. However, it has become increasingly adversarial in nature, with opposition front-benchers participating regularly – a practice that has developed over the past thirty years – and with questions and supplementaries often being partisan in content. Some Members view the proceedings, especially Prime Minister's Question Time, as a farce. However, it remains an occasion for keeping ministers on their toes (figuratively as well as literally) and it ensures that a whole range of issues are brought to the attention of ministers. It also ensures that much material is put on the public record that would not otherwise be available.

Select committees

The House has made greater use in recent years of select committees, appointed not to consider the particular details of bills (the role of standing committees) but to consider particular subjects assigned by the House. Historically, they are well-established features of parliamentary scrutiny. They were frequently used in Tudor and Stuart Parliaments. Their use declined in the latter half of the nineteenth century, the government – with its party majority – not looking too favourably on bodies that could subject it to critical scrutiny. For most of the twentieth century, the use of such committees has been very limited. The position changed in the 1960s and, more dramatically, in the 1970s.

The House has a number of long-standing select committees concerned with its privileges and internal arrangements. However, for the first half of the twentieth century, the House only had two major select committees for investigating the policy or actions of government: the Public Accounts Committee (the PAC) and the Estimates Committee. Founded in 1861, the PAC remains in existence and is the doyen of investigative select committees. It undertakes *post hoc* (i.e. after the event) scrutiny of public expenditure, checking to ensure that it has been properly incurred for the purpose for which it was voted. The Estimates Committee was first appointed in 1912 for the purpose of examining ways in which policies could be carried out cost-effectively. In abeyance from 1914 to 1921 and again during the Second World War, it fulfilled a useful but limited role. It was abolished in 1971 and replaced by an Expenditure Committee with wider terms of reference.

The PAC and Estimates Committees were supplemented in the 1940s by a Select Committee on Statutory Instruments and in the 1950s by one on nationalised industries. There was a more deliberate and extensive use of select committees in the latter half of the 1960s, when the Labour Leader of the House, Richard Crossman, introduced several reforms to try to increase the efficiency and influence of the House. A number of select committees were established, some to cover particular policy sectors (such as science and technology) and others particular Government departments (such as education). One was also appointed to cover the newly created Parliamentary Commissioner for Administration (PCA), better known as the ombudsman. However, the experience of the committees did not meet the expectations of their supporters. They suffered from limited resources, limited attention (from back-benchers, government and the media), limited powers (they could only send for 'persons, papers and records' and make recommendations), the absence of any effective linkage between their activities and the floor of the House, and the lack of a coherent approach to, and coverage of, government policy. Some did not survive for very long. The result was a patchwork quilt of committees, with limited coverage of public policy.

Recognition of these problems led to the appointment in 1976 of a Procedure Select Committee, which reported in 1978. It recommended the appointment of a series of select committees, covering all the main departments of state, with wide terms of reference, and with power to appoint specialist advisers as the committees deemed appropriate. It also recommended that committee members be selected independently of the whips, the task to be undertaken by the Select Committee of Selection, the body formally responsible for nominating members. At the beginning of the new Parliament in 1979, the Conservative Leader of the House, Norman St John-Stevas, brought forward motions to give effect to the Procedure Committee recommendations. By a vote of 248 to 12, the House approved the creation of the new committees. Initially, twelve were appointed, soon joined by committees covering Scottish and Welsh affairs. In the light of their appointment, various other committees were wound up. The PAC and the Committee on the Parliamentary Commissioner were retained. In 1980, a Liaison Select Committee, comprising predominantly select committee chairmen, was appointed to co-ordinate the work of the committees.

The fourteen new committees began work effectively in 1980. Their number has fluctuated since, reflecting usually changes in departmental structure. Committees were also added to cover sectors or departments not previously covered, notably science and technology and, in 1994, Northern Ireland. In the Parliament returned in 1997, sixteen departmental select committees were appointed. Of these, two work through two sub-committees, creating in effect a total of eighteen bodies regularly undertaking inquiries. Seventeen non-departmental select committees were also appointed. These comprised principally 'domestic' committees – such as the Catering Committee, Standing Orders Committee and the Committee on Standards and Privileges – but also included investigative committees such as the PAC, Environmental Audit, Public Administration, European Scrutiny (formerly the European Legislation) and Statutory Instruments Committees.

The sixteen departmental select committees appointed in the 1997 Parliament are listed in Table 17.8. Each committee is established 'to

Table 17.8 Departmental select committees, 1997

Committee (number of members in parentheses)	Chairman
Agriculture (11)	Peter Luff (Con)
Culture, Media and Sport (11)	Gerald Kaufman (Lab)
Defence (11)	Bruce George (Lab)
Education and Employment (17)	
Education Sub-Committee (10)	Malcolm Wicks (Lab)
Employment Sub-Committee (10)	Derek Foster (Lab)
Environment, Transport and Regional Affairs (17)	
Environment Sub-Committee (11)	Andrew Bennett (Lab)
Transport Sub-Committee (11)	Gwyneth Dunwoody (Lab)
Foreign Affairs (12)	Donald Anderson (Lab)
Health (11)	David Hinchcliffe (Lab)
Home Affairs (11)	Chris Mullin (Lab)
International Development (11)	Bowen Wells (Con)
Northern Ireland (13)	The Rt Hon. Peter Brooke (Con)
Science and Technology (11)	Dr Michael Clark (Con)
Scottish Affairs (11)	David Marshall (Lab)
Social Security (11)	Archie Kirkwood (Lib Dem)
Trade and Industry (11)	Martin O'Neill (Lab)
Treasury (12)	Giles Radice (Lab)
Welsh Affairs (11)	Martyn Jones (Lab)

examine the expenditure, administration and policy' of the department or departments it covers and of associated public bodies. As can be seen from the table, most committees have eleven members. The chairmanships of the committees are shared between the parties – usually in rough proportion to party strength in the House – though the committee members are responsible for electing one of their own number from the relevant party to the chair. This power vested in committee members has variously resulted in the election of independent-minded chairmen, such as Nicholas Winterton (Conservative chairman of the Health Committee 1991–2), Frank Field (Labour chairman of the Social Security Committee, 1990–7), Chris Mullin (Labour chairman of the Home Affairs Committee, 1997–9) and Gwyneth Dunwoody (Labour chairman of the Transport Sub-Committee since 1997).

Each committee has control of its own agenda and decides what to investigate. Unlike standing committees, they have power to take evidence and much of their time is spent questioning witnesses. Each committee normally meets once a week – for most committees, on a Tuesday or Wednesday – when the House is sitting in order to hold a public, evidence-taking session. Unlike standing committees, the committees are not arranged in adversarial format, government supporters facing opposition MPs, but instead sit in a horseshoe shape, MPs sitting around the horseshoe – not necessarily grouped according to party – with the witness or witnesses seated in the gap of the horseshoe. Each session will normally last between sixty and ninety minutes.

Committee practices vary. Some hold long-term inquiries. Some go for short-term inquiries and some adopt a mixture of the two approaches. Some will also summon senior ministers for a single session just to review present policy and not as part of a continuing inquiry. The Chancellor of the Exchequer, for example, appears each year before the Treasury Committee for a wide-ranging session on economic policy. Though committees cannot force ministers to attend, the attendance of the appropriate minister is normally easily arranged. So, too, is the attendance of civil servants, though they cannot divulge information on advice offered to ministers or express opinions on policy: that is left to ministers. Attendance by ministers and civil servants before committees is regular and frequent, though most witnesses called by committees represent outside bodies. In investigating a particular subject, a committee will call as witnesses representatives of bodies working in the area or with a particular expertise or interest in it. Figure 17.2 shows but part of the agenda of select committee meetings and witnesses in a typical week.

At the conclusion of an inquiry, a committee draws up a report. The report is normally drafted by the committee clerk – a full-time officer of the House – under the guidance of the chairman. It is then discussed in private session by the committee. Amendments are variously made, though it is relatively rare for committees to divide along party lines. Once agreed, the report is published. The committees are prolific in their output. In the 1992–7 Parliament, they issued a total of 453 reports. In the first session of the new Parliament elected in 1997, they issued 110. Among the subjects covered in the 1997–8 session were alternatives to prison, the BBC, child migrants, coastal defence, divorce, food safety, headteachers, lone parents, Prison Service, the Royal Opera House (a report attracting considerable media coverage), the Royal Ulster Constabulary, sewage, the Strategic Defence Review, Sudan, tobacco advertising and vitamin B6. Most reports embody recommendations for government action. A proportion, but far from all, of the recommendations are accepted by government. In one year in the 1980s, the government acknowledged that in that year it had accepted 150 recommendations emanating from select committees. Other recommendations become subject to the 'delayed drop' effect: the Government rejects or ignores a report but several years later, without necessarily acknowledging the work of the committee, implements some of the recommendations. Overall, only a minority of the recommendations emanating from committees will be accepted and acted on by Government. A more common response is to note a recommendation or to say that it is under review. A select committee has no formal powers to force the Government to take any action on a report. All that the Government is committed to do is to issue a written response to each report, usually within

TUESDAY 20 JULY

ENVIRONMENT, TRANSPORT AND REGIONAL AFFAIRS
ENVIRONMENT SUB-COMMITTEE
Subject: Potential Risk of Fire Spread in Buildings via External Cladding System
Witnesses: Fire Brigades Union and Fire Safety Development Group: Buildings Research Establishment: Fire Research Station and Eternit UK Ltd: Chris Buntaine, Eglington Weber & Broutin (UK) Ltd. Dr Stephen Ledbetter. Centre for Window and Cladding Technology: Mr Nick Raynsford MP. Minister for Construction, and DETR officials

HOME AFFAIRS
Subject: Drugs and Prisons
Witnesses: Mr George Howarth MP, Parliamentary Under Secretary of State. Home Office

SOCIAL SECURITY
Subject: DSS Departmental Report 1999
Witnesses: Rt Hon Alistair Darling MP, Secretary of State. DSS: DSS Officials

EDUCATION AND EMPLOYMENT
Subject: DfEE Funding
Witnesses: Department for Education and Employment: Mr Peter Shaw. Director General of Finance and Analytical Services: Mr David Forrester. Director. Further Education and Youth Training: Mr Peter Lauener. Director responsible for the Post-16 Review: Mr Andrew Wye, Divisional Manager, Schools and LEA Funding `Division

WEDNESDAY 21 JULY

EDUCATION AND EMPLOYMENT: EDUCATION SUB-COMMITTEE
Subject: Role of Private Companies in the Management and Supply of State Education Services
Witnesses: Mr Neil McIntosh OBE, Chief executive CFBT Education Services: Mr Kevin McNeany, Chief Executive, Nord Anglia Education plc: Mr Stanley Goodchild CBE, Managing Consultant, 3E's Enterprises:

SOCIAL SECURITY
Subject: Social Security Implications of Parental Leave
Witnesses: Institute of Directors; Rt Hon Harriet Harman MP; Ms Donna Lenhoff

DEFENCE
Subject: Defence Research Expenditure
Witnesses: Rt Hon Lord Gilbert, Minister of State for Defence Procurement; Mr Graham Jordan. Deputy Under-Secretary of State (Science & Technology); Lt General Edmond Burton, Deputy Chief of Defence Staff (Systems)

SCOTTISH AFFAIRS
Subject: The Work of the Scottish Office
Witness: Rt Hon Dr John Reid MP, Secretary of State for Scotland

EDUCATION AND EMPLOYMENT: EDUCATION SUB-COMMITTEE
Subject: Employment Consequences of European Economic and Monetary Union
Witnesses: Organisation of Economic Cooperation and Development; The Centre for Economic Performance; London School of Economics

SCIENCE AND TECHNOLOGY
Subject: The Year 2000 – Computer Compliance
Witnesses: Local Government Association

Figure 17.2 Meetings of select committees

two months of the report being published. The two-month target is not always met.

The departmental select committees, like the House itself, are multi-functional. They serve several purposes. They have added considerably to the store of knowledge of the House. They provide an important means for specialisation by Members. They serve an important expressive function. By calling witnesses from outside groups, they allow those groups to get their views on the public record. The evidence from witnesses is published. Reports are now not only published in paper form but are also made available on the internet. The committees may take up the cases espoused by some of the groups, ensuring that the issue is brought on to the political agenda. The reports from the committees are read and digested by the groups, thus providing the committees with the potential to serve as important agents for mobilising support. Above all, though, the committees serve as important means for scrutinising and influencing government, especially the former. Ministers and civil servants know they may be called before committees to account for their actions. Committee sessions allow MPs to put questions to ministers in greater detail than is possible on the floor of the House. It gives MPs the only opportunity they have to ask questions of officials. Not only will poor performances be noted – not least by the media – but poor answers may attract critical comment in the committee's report. No minister or official wishes to be seen squirming in the face of difficult questions.

Select committees have thus developed as a major feature of parliamentary activity, with most MPs viewing that activity in a positive light. None the less, limitations remain. The committees have limited powers and limited resources. They have the time and resources to investigate only a small number of issues. The number of reports they issue massively exceeds the time available on the floor of the House to debate them. Most reports will not be mentioned on the floor of the House or even read by most MPs. Government is committed to providing a written response to committee reports but under no obligation to take action on the recommendations made in those reports. And although ministers and officials appear before committees, they do not necessarily reveal as much as the committees would like. Though the committees constitute a major step forward for the House of Commons, many MPs would like to see them strengthened.

Early day motions

Of the other devices available to Members, early day motions (EDMs) are increasingly popular, though of limited impact. A Member may table a motion for debate 'on an early day'. In practice, there is invariably no time to debate such motions. However, they are printed and other MPs can add their names to them. Consequently, they are used as a form of parliamentary noticeboard. If a motion attracts several hundred signatures, it may induce the government to take some action. This occasionally happens. Motions tabled by Conservative MPs are believed to have influenced the Conservative government in the 1980s to move quicker than it planned to abolish the Inner London Education Authority and to ensure that compulsory membership of student unions was ended. Such occasions, though, are rare. EDMs are more often used for fulfilling an expressive function, allowing Members to make clear their views on a range of issues, often reflecting representations made to them by people and groups outside the House. Examples of such EDMs are illustrated in Figure 17.3. The range of topics is extremely broad and the number of motions tabled an increasingly large one. In the 1970s and 1980s, three or four hundred a year were tabled. In the 1990s, the number each year exceeded one thousand. In the 1992–7 Parliament, a total of 7,831 were tabled – an average of just over 1,500 a session. The consequence is that their use as a means of indicating strength of opinion on an issue of political significance is devalued. Their utility, which was always limited, is thus marginal, though not non-existent. They still give MPs the opportunity to put issues of concern on the public record.

Correspondence

The means so far considered have been public means by which MPs can scrutinise government and make representations to it. However, a number of

EDM 696	RNID'S REPORT, WAITING TO HEAR	08:06:99
	Bottomley/Peter	65 signatures

That this House welcomes the launch of Waiting to Hear, a report on excessive waiting times for NHS hearing tests endured each year by almost 200,000 deaf and hard of hearing people needing hearing aids, in some cases waiting for longer than a year; notes the isolation, frustration and barriers to opportunity and fulfilment that excessive waiting time for hearing tests and hearing aid fitting can exacerbate; notes further that while there are five million people who would benefit from using a hearing aid, excessive waiting times and variations between and within NHS regions in access to and the quality of NHS audiology services, are significant deterrent to the three million people who would benefit, but who have not had a hearing aid fitted; calls for the Department of Health to adopt RNID's target of two consecutive months, from referral for a hearing test to hearing aid fitting, as the maximum NHS waiting time, to make NHS hearing aid services more user-friendly, and to harness the benefits of new digital hearing aid technology; and urges the Government to ensure the NHS goes digital by providing digital hearing aids as standard within five years.

EDM 862	FIXING OF CAR PRICES IN THE UK	21:07:99
	Hoyle/Lindsay	46 signatures

That this House notes the recent admission of Volvo car manufacturers that it has been supporting secret arrangements to fix its British car prices; believes that this constitutes a serious breach of UK law and a blatant disregard to the exploitation of UK customers; further notes that Volvo escaped penalties and was not even fined for this serious misconduct, with the Office of Fair Trading accepting a promise that this will not happpen again in the future; believes that will offer no deterrent to other car companies who also consider fixing prices; and calls upon the Government to increase the fines which can be imposed and to consider introducing mandatory prison sentences for directors of companies who are found to be operating a cartel and fixing prices in the UK

EDM 892	RELEASE OF POLITICAL PRISONERS IN BAHRAIN	27:07:99
	Cunliffe/Lawrence [R]	17 signatures

That this House congratulates the Emir Sheikh Hamad bin Isa for his humane and courageous action in pardoning more than 300 political prisoners, including Sheikh Jamri, as an act of goodwill intended to mark the development, stability and prosperity of the country and people of Bahrain achieved during the office of the late Emir Sheikh Isa bin Sulman al-Khalifa; and wishes the new Emir and his Government success in maintaining its steady progress towards a successful modern state based on human rights and the rule of law.

Figure 17.3 Early day motions: these examples of early day motions show how MPs use this device to draw attention to particular issues

private means exist, two official and two unofficial. One official means is through corresponding with ministers. Since the 1950s, the flow of letters to MPs from constituents and a range of organisations (companies, charities and the like) has grown enormously. The flow increased significantly in the 1960s and increased dramatically in subsequent decades. The mailbag has increased more than twenty-fold between the middle and the end of the century. In the mid-1960s, about 10,000 letters a week were received at the House of Commons. By the mid-1990s, the number had increased to 40,000 a day. The usual method for an MP to pursue a matter raised by a constituent is by writing to the relevant minister, usually forwarding the letter from the constituent. At least 10,000 to 15,000 letters a month are written by MPs to ministers.

For an MP, writing to a minister is one of the most cost-effective ways of pursuing constituency casework (see Norton and Wood, 1993, Chapter 3). A letter invites a considered, often detailed response, usually free of the party pressures that prevail in the chamber; by being a private communication, it avoids putting a minister publicly on the defensive. Ministers are thus more likely to respond sympathetically in the use of their discretion than is the case if faced with demands on the floor of the House. Furthermore, there is no limit on the number of letters an MP can write and those letters can be dictated usually at a time of the Member's choosing. Letters from MPs to ministers are accorded priority in a department – each is circulated in a special yellow folder – and have to be replied to by a minister. If a letter fails to obtain the desired response, the Member has the option of then taking the matter further, either by seeing the minister or by raising the matter publicly on the floor of the House.

Correspondence is a valuable and efficient means of ensuring that a matter is considered by a minister. A great many letters on a particular problem can alert a minister to the scale of that problem and produce action. Letter writing is also a valuable means of fulfilling an expressive function. Most constituents who write do so to express a particular viewpoint or in order to obtain an authoritative explanation of why some action was or was not taken; only a minority write to try to have a particular decision changed. Writing to the MP is a long-established, and now much used, means for citizens to have some input into the political process. None the less, corresponding with ministers has a number of limitations. MPs are not always well versed in the subjects raised with them by constituents. Some lack sufficient interest, or knowledge of the political system, to pursue cases effectively. Increasingly, they have difficulty finding the time to deal with all the matters raised with them.

Parliamentary commissioner for administration

Since the late 1960s, MPs have had another option at their disposal in pursuing particular issues raised by constituents. The parliamentary commissioner for administration – or ombudsman – was established under an Act of 1967 to investigate cases of maladministration within government. The term 'maladministration' essentially covers any error in the way a matter is handled by a public servant: it does not extend to cover the merits of policies. He (never yet a she) considers only complaints referred to him by MPs: a citizen cannot complain directly. The commissioner is formally an officer of parliament but enjoys the same protection as a senior judge: he can only be removed by an address by both Houses of Parliament to the Crown. He has a relatively modest staff of just over fifty. He can summon papers and take evidence under oath. When an inquiry is completed, he sends a copy to the MP who referred the case as well as to the relevant department. His recommendations are normally acted on. However, he labours under a number of limitations: he has a limited remit, limited resources and limited access to certain files – he has no formal powers to see Cabinet papers. Perhaps most notably, he has no powers of enforcement. If he reports that officials have acted improperly or unjustly in the exercise of their administrative duties, it is then up to government to decide what action to take in response; if it fails to act, the only remaining means available to achieve action is through parliamentary pressure.

The number of cases referred to the ombudsman has increased over the years. Most complaints are deemed not to fall within his remit. In 1998/9, 1,506 cases were referred and 372 full investigations were undertaken, just slightly short of the 376 reports issued the previous year – the highest in the history of the office. In 93 per cent of cases, the complaints were upheld in full or in part. As in most years, the relevant Departments acted on the ombudsman's recommendations and no special reports to Parliament were necessary. In 1998/9, the largest single amount paid out in compensation was £132,903. In the previous year, the Government paid out £437,000 in compensation, with the payment in individual cases ranging from £6.02 to £50,044. The commissioner thus serves a useful service to MPs – and their constituents – but he constitutes something of a limited last resort. MPs prefer to keep casework in their own hands and pursue it with government directly.

For most Members, the preferred device for pursuing a matter with a minister remains that of direct correspondence.

Party committees

An important unofficial means of scrutinising and influencing government is that of party committees. These are unofficial in that they are committees of the parliamentary parties and not officially constituted committees of the House.

Each parliamentary party has some form of organisation, usually with weekly meetings of the parliamentary party. The two largest parties – Conservative and Labour – have a sufficient number of members to sustain a series of committees. The principal committees mirror the topics covered by departments, have elected officers and tend to meet regularly in order to discuss forthcoming business (for example, a bill within their area of interest), listen to invited speakers and consider topics of interest. The invited speakers will include relevant ministers (or opposition front-benchers in the case of opposition back-bench committees) as well as outside speakers. Each party also has regional groups, each comprising the party MPs from a particular region.

The Conservative committees have a longer history than Labour committees and have a reputation for being the more politically powerful (Norton, 1994). Conservative committees have no fixed membership – any Conservative MP can attend a meeting – and a large attendance can signal to the whips that there may be a problem with a particular issue. Most meetings will attract a handful of Members – sometimes half a dozen or even less – but if a contentious issue is discussed it can swell to three figures. Meetings are confidential and provide MPs with a means of expressing their views fully to their leaders, usually through the whips: a whip normally attends each meeting. Any disquiet is reported to the chief whip and relevant front-bencher. They constitute important channels of influence. Conservative committees have sometimes been credited with delaying a piece of legislation or even undermining a minister's career. Labour committees have not enjoyed quite the same reputation but in the 1992–7 Parliament the standing orders of the Parliamentary Labour Party (PLP) were changed in order to enhance the consultative status of the committees. In the 1997 Parliament, Labour ministers have consulted with back-bench committees, some achieving a reputation for being assiduous in doing so. The committees also serve another purpose: they allow MPs to specialise in a particular subject. They also enable an MP, through serving as officer of a committee, to achieve some status in the parliamentary party. This is often especially helpful to new Members, giving them their first opportunity to make a mark in parliamentary life.

However, despite their attraction to MPs and their influence within party ranks, the committees have to compete for the attention of Members – there are many other demands on Members' time. Conservative committees experienced particular problems with attendance in the 1992–7 Parliament because of these competing pressures (Norton, 1994); in the 1997 Parliament, the situation is more acute in that there are fewer Conservative MPs than before and so keeping some committees going has proved difficult.

All-party groups

All-party groups, like party committees, are not formally constituted committees of the House. They are formed on a cross-party basis, with officerships being shared among members of different parties. There are just under one hundred such groups, each formed to consider a particular topic. (There are also just over one hundred all-party country groups, each bringing together MPs – and peers – with a special interest in the country concerned.) Some of the groups are confined to a parliamentary membership; some – known as 'registered groups' – include non-parliamentarians. The subjects covered by these groups are diverse, including industrial safety, children, social science, the Boys Brigade and AIDS. Some exist in name only. Others are active in discussing and promoting a particular cause, some pressing the government for action. Among the more influential are the disablement group, the long-established parliamentary and scientific committee, and more recently the football group. The all-party football group (with over a hundred members) has been active in influencing policy on such issues as safety in sports grounds (see Norton, 1993, p. 64). Many of the all-party groups have links with relevant outside bodies and can act as useful means of access to the political process for such groups. Like party committees, all-party groups have to compete with the other demands made on MPs' time.

In combination, then, there are a variety of means available to MPs to scrutinise and influence government and through which they can serve to make known the views of citizens. The means vary in effectiveness and viewed in isolation may appear of little use. However, they are not mutually exclusive and MPs will often use several of them in order to pursue a particular issue. An MP may write privately to a minister and, if not satisfied with the response, may table a question or seek a half-hour adjournment debate. In order to give prominence to an issue, a Member may table an EDM, speak in debate and bombard the minister with a series of written questions. The most effective MPs are those who know how to use these means in combination and – on occasion – which ones to avoid.

Members under pressure

MPs are called on to carry out the tasks of the House. As we have seen, the resources available to them to carry out those tasks have increased in recent years. MPs have more resources than before. They have a better salary than before and they have office and support facilities far in excess of those available to their predecessors. However, the demands on the typical MP have increased massively in recent decades, on a scale that far surpasses the increase in the resources available to deal with them. The increase in demands on MPs' time can be ascribed to four sources: public business, organised interests, constituents and MPs themselves.

Public business

The volume of business has increased in recent decades. This is particularly pronounced in terms of legislation. The number of bills introduced by the Government is nowadays not much greater than it was in earlier decades. What has increased is the volume. Bills are much longer than they used to be. They are also more complex. Before 1950, no more than 1,000 pages of public acts were passed each year. Before 1980, no more than 2,000 pages were passed each year. Since 1980, the figure has usually been in excess of 2,500 pages and on occasion it has surpassed 3,000 pages. This increased volume places a significant strain on parliamentary resources. Most bills go to standing committees. The longer and more complex the bill, the more time it needs in committee. In the 1955/6 session, there were 176 meetings of standing committees; in the 1985/6 session the number was 479 (Griffith and Ryle, 1989, p. 289). The Education Reform Bill in 1987/8 received more parliamentary time (200 hours) than any other post-war measure. Given that several standing committees will normally be in existence at the same time – bills frequently go for committee consideration at the same time in the session – there is a tremendous strain on the finite resources of MPs, in terms of both their number and the time they have at their disposal.

In addition to the greater volume of public legislation, there is also the burden of other business. This includes, for example, having to scrutinise EU legislation, a task that falls principally on a European Scrutiny Committee (which considers all EU documents submitted to the House) and three European Standing Committees, responsible for discussing documents that the House considers worthy of further consideration. It also includes the work of the select committees. As can be calculated from Table 17.8, the Departmental Select Committees take up the time of just over 190 MPs. All this work – in terms of both the European Committees and the Departmental Select Committees – represents a relatively recent increase in the workload of MPs; there were no European Committees prior to the 1970s and, as we have seen, only a few investigative select committees. Then there are the other select committees, both investigative and domestic. Some MPs can be appointed to serve on three or four separate committees.

Organised interests

MPs have always been subject to lobbying by outside groups – groups wanting Members to push for a particular outcome in terms of public policy. However, that lobbying has become pronounced in recent decades. Since 1979, organised interests – firms, charities, consumer groups, professional bodies, pressure groups – appear to have 'discovered' Parliament. Government appeared to adopt more of an arm's-length relationship with outside bodies. The Departmental Select Committees came into being and provided particular targets for organised interests. The 1970s had also seen something of a growth in the voting independence of MPs. As a consequence of these several developments, the House of Commons looked far more attractive than ever before to organised interests wanting to influence public policy (Rush, 1990; Norton, 1999a). One survey of organised interests found that three-quarters had 'regular or frequent contact with one or more Members of Parliament' (Rush, 1990, p. 280). Of the groups that had such contact, more than 80 per cent had asked MPs to table parliamentary questions and almost 80 per cent had asked Members to arrange meetings at the House of Commons. Over half had asked MPs to table amendments to bills and to table a motion. This contact between organised interests and MPs has a number of beneficial consequences. Among other things, Members are provided with advice and information which can prove useful in questioning Government and in raising new issues. However, it also has some negative consequences. One is the demand on MPs' time. One survey of 248 MPs in 1992 found that on average an MP spent over three and a half hours a week meeting group representatives (Norris, 1997, pp. 36–7). Further time is taken up by acting on the requests of such groups and by reading and, if necessary, responding to the mass of material that is mailed by the groups. MPs now have difficulty coping with the sheer volume of lobbying material that is sent to them.

Constituents

Organised interests have been responsible for a marked increase in the mailbag of MPs. So too have constituents. We have touched already on the twenty-fold increase in mail received in the House of Commons in the 1990s compared with the 1960s. For the MP, constituency work takes priority and can occupy a large portion of the day in dictating replies to constituents' letters. It can also occupy most of every weekend, both through appearances at constituency functions and holding constituency surgeries – publicly advertised meetings at which constituents can see the MP in private to discuss particular concerns.

When an MP receives a letter from a constituent that raises a particular grievance (failure to receive a particular state benefit, for example) or issue of public policy, the MP will normally pursue the matter with the Government through writing to the relevant minister. A survey in 1990 found that ministers answered 250,000 letters a year, mostly from MPs (Elms and Terry, 1990). In 1999, the Minister in the Cabinet Office confirmed – in answer to a question from this writer – that the figure had remained largely unchanged throughout the 1990s.

The burden of constituency demands continues to increase and MPs have difficulty finding the time to cope with constituency demands and with the demands of public business (see Norton and Wood, 1993). The problem is particularly acute for MPs with constituencies close to Westminster: constituents expect them to find the time to be at constituency events, even when the House is sitting. The burden has also increased as constituents – as well as pressure groups – have made increasing use of fax machines and of electronic mail.

MPs themselves

MPs are also responsible for adding to their own burden and to that of the resources of the House. As we have seen, recent years have seen the growth of the career politician. There is a greater body of Members who are keen to be re-elected and to achieve office. They are keen to be noticed in the House. Achieving a high profile in the House helps them to be noticed locally. This may help, albeit at the margins, with re-election (see Norton and Wood, 1993) and, indeed, may help with re-selection by the local party. It is also considered necessary for the purposes of promotion. Given the growing number of career politicians, the more competitive the parliamentary environment. The tendency of the career politician is to table as many questions as is permissible: research assistants will variously be asked to come up with suitable drafts (see Franklin and Norton, 1993). The career politician will try to intervene as often as possible in the chamber and will table early day motions to raise issues. There is also likely to be an allied tendency to attract media attention, not least with frequent press releases. All this adds to the burden of the MP as well as that of the MP's staff and the employees of the House.

All these pressures add up to create a particular burden for MPs. Surveys by the senior salaries review body have shown that, over the decades, the amount of time devoted to parliamentary duties has increased. One study in the 1990s suggested that MPs typically work in excess of a seventy-hour week. It is difficult for MPs to keep pace with all the demands made of them. Their resources have improved in recent years, and they have been aided considerably by new technology, but the resources have not kept pace with the demands made of Members. For many MPs, it is a case of running in order to stand still. For others, it is a case of slipping backwards. There is a particularly important conflict between trying to find time for constituency work and finding time for dealing with public business in the House (Norton and Wood, 1993). So long as constituency work takes priority, then the time needed for public business is under particular pressure.

Table 17.9 Views on the efficacy of Parliament
Overall, how well or badly do you think Parliament works?

	1973 (%)	1991 (%)	January 1995 (%)	April–May 1995 (%)	1998 (%)
Very well	12	5	2	4	4
Fairly well	42	54	35	39	49
Neither well nor badly	n/a	21	20	22	19
Fairly badly	34	12	25	19	17
Don't know	5	4	5	6	7

Source: MORI, British Public Opinion, 21 (6), August 1998

The House under pressure

The fact that MPs work hard for their constituents is frequently acknowledged by constituents. In the 1991 MORI State of the Nation Poll, 43 per cent of those questioned said they were satisfied with the job the local MP was doing for the constituency, against 23 per cent who said they were not satisfied. In the 1995 MORI State of the Nation Poll, the figures were exactly the same. The view held by citizens about the House of Commons appears more ambivalent, certainly more volatile, than the views they hold of the local MP. Over the period that views about the local MP stayed the same, attitudes towards Parliament showed a marked shift. In the 1991 MORI poll, 59 per cent of those questioned thought that Parliament worked well or fairly well. In another MORI poll at the beginning of 1995, the percentage was down to 37 (see Table 17.9). The percentage saying it worked fairly or very badly increased from 16 per cent to 38 per cent. As can be seen from Table 17.9, the figures have improved since, with just over 50 per cent in 1998 thinking that it worked well. Even so, it can be argued that these figures do not represent an overwhelming vote of confidence in Parliament. Even when Parliament achieves its best ratings, this entails only five or six out of every ten citizens saying that it works well. Very few – less than one in twenty – say that it works very well.

What, then, might explain why attitudes towards Parliament are not more positive? The House of Commons has seen major changes in recent decades. Some of these changes, such as the creation of the Departmental Select Committees, have reinforced the capacity of the House to fulfil a number of its functions. However, other changes – internal as well as external to the House – have served to challenge its public standing and its capacity to fulfil the tasks expected of it. These can be summarised under the headings of sleaze, partisanship, executive dominance and the creation of other policy-making bodies.

Sleaze

Throughout the century there have been various scandals involving politicians accepting illicit payments in return for some political favour. In the 1970s and 1980s, there was criticism of MPs for accepting payment to act as advisers to lobbying firms or hiring themselves out as consultants. One book, published in 1991, was entitled *MPs for Hire* (Hollingsworth, 1991). At the time it was published, 384 MPs held 522 directorships and 452 consultancies. In 1994, the issue hit the headlines when a journalist, posing as a businessman, offered twenty MPs £1,000 each to table parliamentary questions. Two Conservative MPs did not immediately say no to the offer. The story attracted extensive media coverage. The two MPs were briefly suspended from the service of the House. The story was further fuelled later in the year when *The Guardian* claimed that two ministers had, when backbenchers, accepted money to table questions; one them promptly resigned as a minister and the other – Neil Hamilton – was eventually forced to leave office. The furore generated by the stories led the Prime Minister, John Major, to establish the Committee on Standards in Public Life, under a judge, Lord Nolan (later succeeded by Lord Neill of Bladen). In 1995, the House accepted – after two ill-tempered debates – the recommendations of the committee about payment from outside sources. MPs went further than the committee recommended in deciding to ban any paid advocacy by MPs: Members cannot advocate a particular cause in Parliament in return for payment. Members also have to disclose income received from outside bodies that is paid to them because they are MPs (for example, income as a result of working as a barrister or dentist does not have to be disclosed, money from a company for advice on how to present a case to government does). The House also approved the recommendation to establish a Code of Conduct and appoint a Parliamentary Commissioner for Standards to ensure that the rules are followed. The code was subsequently drawn up and agreed. It is accompanied by a Guide to the rules of the House relating to Members' conduct.

The effect of the 'cash for questions' scandal was reflected in opinion polls. In a 1985 MORI poll, 46 per cent thought that 'most' MPs made a lot of money by using public office improperly. In 1994, the figure was 64 per cent. Seventy-seven per cent agreed with the statement that 'Most MPs care more about special interests than they care about people like you'. A Gallup poll found that the overwhelming majority of those questioned thought that it was wrong to accept payment for tabling parliamentary questions, to accept free holidays and to take payment for advice about parliamentary matters. Almost half thought that it was wrong to accept a free lunch at a restaurant or to accept bottles of wine or whisky at Christmas. Though there is now a Code of Conduct and a Parliamentary Commissioner for Standards who oversees and advises on the new rules, there appears to remain a clash between what citizens expect their MPs to do and what MPs are allowed to do under the rules of the House. MPs can still receive payment for giving advice on parliamentary matters and can receive hospitality, so long as the payment and the gifts are declared in the Register of MPs' Interests.

Partisanship

The clash between the parties is a characteristic of British political life. It is a long-standing feature of the House of Commons. There is a perception that, in recent years, it has become more intense. This is reflected, for example, in the nature of Prime Minister's Question Time, where the desire for partisan point-scoring has largely squeezed out genuine attempts to elicit information (see Franklin and Norton, 1993). However, perhaps most importantly of all, partisanship is now more publicly visible. The introduction of the television cameras to the Commons means that, in a single news broadcast covering the House, more people will see the House in that single broadcast than could ever have sat in the public gallery of the House. Though there is general support for broadcasting proceedings among public and politicians, the focus on the chamber has tended to encourage a negative perception. A 1996 MORI poll revealed a very clear perception of politicians engaged in negative point scoring (Table 17.10). As the author of a 1999 Hansard Society study

Table 17.10 Perceptions of MPs

Response	%
Q. When you hear politicians from different parties on radio and television, do you have the impression that they are mainly concerned with reaching agreement or are they mainly concerned with scoring points off each other?	
Reaching agreement	3
Scoring points	93
Don't know	4
Q. When you hear politicians on television or radio, do you feel that they fairly often break new ground, or do you almost always feel you've heard it all before?	
New ground	4
Heard it before	92
Don't know	4
Q. When you hear politicians on television or radio, do you feel that they are usually saying what they believe to be true, or are they usually merely spouting the party line?	
Truthful	6
Party line	88
Don't know	6

Source: reproduced in Coleman, 1999, p. 20

of the broadcasting of Parliament noted, 'The overwhelming perception of parliamentarians as point-scoring, unoriginal and dogmatically partisan can not be blamed entirely on negative reporting by journalists. If one purpose of broadcasting Parliament was to allow people to judge it for themselves, the low esteem MPs are held in by the public has not been elevated by ten years of live exposure.' (Coleman, 1999, p. 21). When people see the House on television, they see either a largely empty chamber – MPs are busy doing things elsewhere – or a body of baying MPs, busy shouting at one another and cheering their own side. That is particularly noticeable at Prime Minister's Question Time. One Gallup poll in 1993 found that 82 per cent of those questioned agreed that what took place 'sounds like feeding time at the zoo'. As Peter Riddell noted of Prime Minister's Question Time, 'no other aspect of parliamentary life generates more public complaints' (*The Times*, 4 April 1994). For MPs who want to win the next election, supporting their own side in the chamber takes precedence over maintaining public trust in the institution (see Norton, 1997, p. 365). Given that the television coverage focusses on the chamber, and not on the committee work of the House, then the enduring perception that viewers have is of a House of noisy, point-scoring MPs, contributing little new to political debate.

Executive dominance

There has been a perception of a growth in executive dominance in the UK. The effect of this, it is argued, is a greater marginalisation of Parliament. Party dominates the House and this stranglehold has been exacerbated as more and more power has been concentrated in Downing Street. This perception of executive dominance was marked when Margaret Thatcher occupied Downing Street and has been revived under the premiership of Tony Blair. The extent to which Parliament is marginalised has been the subject of academic debate but the perception of a peripheral legislature resonates with the public. The MORI State of the Nation polls in the 1990s found a growing body of respondents who believed that Parliament did not have sufficient control over what Government does (Table 17.11). By the mid-1990s, a majority of respondents – 52 per cent – agreed with the statement that Parliament does not have sufficient control over what the Government does. Only 18 per cent disagreed. As can be seen from Table 17.11, only 3 per cent strongly disagreed. This perception appears to have been reinforced under the Labour Government of Tony

Table 17.11 Perceptions of parliamentary control over Government
Parliament does not have sufficient control over what the government does

	1991 (%)	1995 (%)
Strongly agree	10	13
Tend to agree	40	39
Neither agree nor disagree	19	21
Tend to disagree	20	15
Strongly disagree	3	3
No opinion	9	9

Source: MORI State of the Nation poll 1995

Blair. Labour MPs were issued with pagers in order that they could be summoned to vote as well as told how to vote. The use of the pager for ensuring desired outcomes was demonstrated on one classic occasion when a message was transmitted saying 'Labour MPs vote aye', followed a few moments later by another message: 'Correction. Free Vote'. The popular perception of Labour MPs slavishly voting as they are told was encapsulated by a *Guardian* cartoon showing a Labour MP holding an electronic voting device displaying two options: 'Agree with Tony [Blair]' and 'Strongly Agree with Tony'. Though the perception may be over-stated – the Government has faced pressure from dissident back-benchers – the degree of loyalty in the present Parliament is feeding a popular view of a House of Commons that is not calling Government to account. The House is weak in the face of a strong executive.

Creation of other policy-making bodies

The capacity of the House to fulfil its functions is undermined not only by executive domination of the House but also by the creation of other policy-making bodies. Even if MPs had the political will to determine outcomes, their capacity to do so is now limited by the seepage of policy-making powers to other bodies. There are three principal bodies or rather three collections of bodies involved: the institutions of the EU, the courts and the devolved assemblies.

The effect of membership of the European Community/Union has been touched on already in Chapter 15. We shall return to its legal implications in Chapter 23. Membership has served to transfer policy competences in various sectors to the institutions of the European Community: they have increased in number with subsequent treaty amendments. Parliament has no formal role in the law-making process of the EU. It seeks to influence the British minister prior to the meeting of the relevant Council of Ministers, but – if Qualified Majority Voting (QMV) is employed – that minister can be outvoted by the others. There is nothing that Parliament can do to prevent regulations having binding effect in the UK or to prevent the intention of directives from being achieved.

The courts have acquired new powers as a result of British membership of the EC/EU as well now as a consequence of the incorporation of the European Convention of Human Rights (ECHR) into British law and as a consequence of devolution. The effect of these we shall explore in greater depth in Chapter 23. Various matters are now resolved by the courts. The courts have the power to suspend or set aside British law that conflicts with EU law. The courts are responsible for interpreting the provisions of the ECHR. The courts are also responsible for determining the legal limits established by the Acts creating elected bodies in Scotland, Wales and Northern Ireland. The capacity of the House of Commons to intervene or to over-rule the courts is now effectively limited.

The devolution of powers to elected assemblies in different parts of the United Kingdom also limits the decision-making capacity of Parliament. Parliament is not expected to legislate on matters devolved to the Scottish Parliament. The Scottish Parliament has been given power to legislate in areas not reserved under the Scotland Act and has also been given power to amend primary legislation passed by Parliament. The scope of the decision making by Parliament is thus constricted.

Pressure for change

These variables combine to produce a House of Commons that is under pressure to restore public confidence and to fulfil effectively the functions ascribed to it. There are various calls for reform of the House in order to address both problems. Not all MPs and commentators, however, accept that there is a significant problem. Not all those demanding reform are agreed on the scale of the problem and they come up with very different proposals for reform. There are, put simply, three principal approaches to reform. Each derives from a particular perception of the role of the House of Commons in the political system. They can be related very roughly to the three types of legislature identified at the beginning of the chapter.

1 *Radical*: The radical approach wants to see Parliament as a policy-making legislature.

Parliament is seen as weak in relation to the executive – and is seen to be getting weaker. Reform of the House of Commons within the present constitutional and political framework is deemed inadequate to the task. Without radical constitutional reform, the House of Commons will remain party dominated and under the thumb of the executive. To achieve a policy-making legislature, the radical not only supports reform within the institution but also wants major reform of the constitution in order to change fundamentally the relationship between Parliament and Government. Such change would include a new electoral system as well an elected second chamber. As such, this radical approach can be seen to fit very much within the liberal approach to the Constitution (see Chapter 15). The most extreme form of this view, taking us beyond the liberal approach, advocates a separation of powers, with the executive elected separately from the House of Commons. Only with radical reform, it is argued, can high levels of public trust in Parliament be achieved.

2 *Reform*: This approach wants to strengthen the House of Commons as a policy-influencing body, the onus for policy-'making' resting with government but with the House of Commons having the opportunity to consider policy proposals in detail and to influence their content. As such, it falls very much within the traditional approach to constitutional change (see Chapter 16), though it is not exclusive to it. Traditionalists, for example, can make common cause with adherents to the Socialist approach in respect of some reforms. Even adherents to the liberal approach will support reform, though arguing that it does not go far enough. (For traditionalists, reform is necessary and sufficient. For liberals, it is necessary but not sufficient.) Reformers favour structural and procedural changes within the House. They want to strengthen committees – standing committees as well as select committees – with standing committees being reformed as part of a series of reforms to the legislative process. They also want strengthened incentives for MPs to pursue committee careers as an alternative to ministerial office. They also favour an increase in resources to enable MPs to cope with the demands made of them as well as to tempt a wider range of people to enter Parliament. The sorts of reforms that are advocated are listed in Table 17.12. Reformers claim that opinion poll data show

Table 17.12 Reform of the House of Commons

Among proposals to strengthen the House are:

- Publish all bills in draft form and allow select committees to study them
- Have a permanent membership for standing committees, similar to the membership of select committees
- Send bills as a matter of course to special standing committees, which have power to take evidence
- Take the committee stage of a bill before second reading
- Give Departmental Select Committees an annual research budget (Banham, 1994, p. 50, suggested £2 million a year for each committee)
- Pay the chairmen – and perhaps the members – of select committees to make the position more attractive
- Provide select committee members with a research and secretarial allowance to enable them to do their jobs more effectively
- Provide more time on the floor for debates on select committee reports and allow the House the opportunity to debate the reports on substantive motions (to agree or disagree) rather than 'take note' motions
- Provide more extensive resources to each MP to communicate quickly and effectively with the outside world, including the constituency and the institutions of the EU
- Allow the House to mandate ministers before they go to the Council of Ministers
- Create new procedures for examining delegated legislation and give the House the power to amend statutory instruments
- Give select committees, and the Speaker, powers to summon ministers
- Reduce the number of MPs, creating a smaller and more professional House
- Increase the pay and office resources of each MP

that there is a need for reform but that there is no clear case for more radical surgery. More people think that Parliament works well than think that it does not. The figures are a cause for concern, and informed reform, not a cause for panic.

3 *Leave alone*: This approach, as the name suggests, opposes change. It is the stance of a High Tory (see Chapter 15) though it is not exclusive to the High Tory approach. Some Labour MPs have opposed reform, wanting to retain the chamber as the central debating forum. Those who support this stance stress the importance of the chamber as the place where the great issues of the day are debated. Committees and greater specialisation detract from the fulfilment of this historic role, allowing MPs to get bogged down in the detail rather than the principle of what is proposed by government. Providing MPs with offices takes them away from the chamber. Though not quite envisaging a House with little or no policy affect, advocates of this approach see the role of the House as one of supporting government. They emphasise that there is no great public demand for change. Most people think that Parliament works fairly or very well.

For radicals, the contemporary emphasis on constitutional reform gives them hope that their stance may be vindicated. The creation of new elected assemblies in Scotland and Wales will, they hope, act as a spur to radical change in England. Scotland and Wales not only have new elected assemblies, they also have a new electoral system. Both assemblies are also elected for fixed terms. Those who adopt this radical stance place special emphasis on the Government's commitment to hold a referendum on the electoral system for parliamentary elections, viewing electoral reform as a crucial mechanism for revitalising the House of Commons.

For reformers, reform constitutes a practical as well as a desirable option. The introduction of the Departmental Select Committees in 1979 showed what could be achieved in strengthening Parliament as a policy-influencing legislature. Some reforms have been carried out since 1997 as a consequence of reports issued by the Select Committee on Modernisation of the House of Commons (available on the Parliament website, *www.parliament.uk*). These have included the creation of the 'parallel chamber' in Westminster Hall, as well as some changes in the legislative process, including allowing some bills to carry over from one session to another, and in the scrutiny of EU legislation (extending scrutiny to the second and third pillars of the EU), though they have been relatively modest. Various reform programmes are on offer or will be shortly. In 1992, the Hansard Society Commission on the Legislative Process published an extensive report on reform of the legislative process. In 1999, the Conservative leader, William Hague, established a Commission to Strengthen Parliament, under the chairmanship of this writer, to undertake a comprehensive review and make recommendations to strengthen parliamentary control of the executive. Also in 1999 the Hansard Society established a Commission, under a former Leader of the House of Commons, Lord Newton of Braintree, to look at parliamentary scrutiny of the executive.

For those who want to leave the House of Commons alone, they take heart from the fact they are likely to succeed, not least by default (see Norton, 1999b). The Government is not too keen on any significant reform that will strengthen the capacity of Parliament to criticise it or prevent it having its way. It wants to expedite its business, not have it delayed. That, it is claimed, is why the Select Committee on Modernisation has not been able to pursue and achieve more extensive reforms. Also, MPs – once a Parliament is under way – become too tied up with the day-to-day demands of constituency work and public business to stand back and address the issue of parliamentary reform. MPs also get used to existing procedures and can be reluctant to change them. There is an absence of strong leadership to achieve reform and also lack of agreement as to what the reforms should be. The 'leave alone' may not be strong in its advocacy but can be quite powerful in achieving the outcome it wants.

Chapter summary

The principal role of the House of Commons is one of scrutinising government. Various means are available to MPs to undertake this role. Those means have been strengthened in recent years but have made only a modest contribution to improved scrutiny. Members and the House have been subject to pressures that have made it difficult for MPs to fulfil their jobs effectively. Some politicians see no need for change. Others advocate reform of the House, some through radical constitutional change, others through reform from within the institution. Inertia may prevent reform being achieved, but the issue is on the political agenda.

Discussion points

- What are the most important functions of the House of Commons?
- What purpose is served by select committees? Should they be strengthened?
- Should, and can, the House of Commons improve its scrutiny of government legislation?
- Is the increase in the constituency work of MPs a good or a bad thing?
- Should Question Time be abolished?
- Should MPs be paid more?
- What would you do with the House of Commons – and why?

Further reading

The most recent student texts on the House of Commons – and also covering the House of Lords – are Norton (1993), Adonis (1993) and Silk and Walters (1998).

There have been a number of books published in the past decade analysing different aspects of parliamentary behaviour or relationships neglected in earlier years. The largely neglected relationship of Parliament to pressure groups is the subject of Rush (1990). Parliamentary questions are considered in Franklin and Norton (1993). MPs' constituency service is covered in Norton and Wood (1993). Parliamentary scrutiny of Executive Agencies is the subject of Giddings (1995). The relationship of Parliament to the European Union is covered comprehensively in Giddings and Drewry (1996). The relationship of Parliament to the law is discussed in Oliver and Drewry (1998). Most of these books are the products of research by study groups of the Study of Parliament Group, a body that draws together academics and clerks of Parliament. The relationship of Parliament to the European Union, Government, and pressure groups is put in comparative context in Norton (1996), Norton (1998) and Norton (1999a) respectively.

A critique of Parliament's scrutiny of the executive is to be found in Weir and Beetham (1999). On reform of the House of Commons, much useful material is contained in Garrett (1993), and in the reports from the Hansard Society (1993) the Constitution Unit (1996) and the Select Committee on Modernisation of the House of Commons (available on the Parliament website).

References

Adonis, A. (1993) *Parliament Today* 2nd edn (Manchester University Press).

Banham, J. (1994) *The Anatomy of Change* (Weidenfeld & Nicolson).

Brand, J. (1992) *British Parliamentary Parties* (Oxford University Press).

Coleman, S. (1999) *Electronic Media, Parliament and the Media* (Hansard Society).

Constitution Unit (1996) *Delivering Constitutional Reform* (The Constitution Unit).

Cowley, P. (ed.) (1998) *Conscience and Parliament* (Cass).

Cowley, P. and Norton, P. (1996) *Blair's Bastards* (Centre for Legislative Studies).

Criddle, B. (1992) 'MPs and candidates', in D. Butler and D. Kavanagh (eds), *The British General Election of 1992* (Macmillan).

Criddle, B. (1997) 'MPs and candidates', in D. Butler and D. Kavanagh (eds), *The British General Election of 1997* (Macmillan).

Drewry, G. (ed.) (1989) *The New Select Committees* rev. edn (Oxford University Press).

Elms, T. and Terry, T. (1990) *Scrutiny of Ministerial Correspondence* (Cabinet Office Efficiency Unit).

Franklin, M. and Norton, P. (eds) (1993) *Parliamentary Questions* (Oxford University Press).

Garrett, J. (1993) *Westminster: Does Parliament Work?* (Gollancz).

Giddings, P. (ed.) (1995) *Parliamentary Accountability* (Macmillan).

Giddings, P. and Drewry, G. (eds) (1996) *Westminster and Europe* (Macmillan).

Griffith, J.A.G. and Ryle, M. (1989) *Parliament* (Sweet and Maxwell).

Hansard Society (1993) *Making the Law: Report of the Commission on the Legislative Process* (Hansard Society).

Hollingsworth, M. (1991) *MPs for Hire* (Bloomsbury).

King, A. (1981) 'The rise of the career politician in Britain – and its consequences', *British Journal of Political Science*, Vol. 11.

Mezey, M. (1979) *Comparative Legislatures* (Duke University Press).

Norris, P. (1997) 'The puzzle of constituency service', *The Journal of Legislative Studies*, Vol. 3, No. 2.

Norton, P. (ed.) (1990) *Legislatures* (Oxford University Press).

Norton, P. (1993) *Does Parliament Matter?* (Harvester Wheatsheaf).

Norton, P. (1994) 'The parliamentary party and party committees', in A. Seldon and S. Ball (eds), *Conservative Century: the Conservative Party since 1900* (Oxford University Press).

Norton, P. (ed.) (1996) *National Parliaments and the European Union* (Cass).

Norton, P. (1997) 'The United Kingdom: restoring confidence?', *Parliamentary Affairs*, Vol. 50, No. 3.

Norton, P. (ed.) (1998) *Parliaments and Governments in Western Europe* (Cass).

Norton, P. (1999a) 'The United Kingdom: parliament under pressure', in P. Norton (ed.), *Parliaments and Pressure Groups in Western Europe* (Cass).

Norton, P. (1999b) 'The House of Commons: the half empty bottle of reform', in B. Jones (ed.), *Political Issues in Britain Today* 5th edn (Manchester University Press).

Norton, P. and Wood, D. (1993) *Back from Westminster* (University Press of Kentucky).

Oliver, D. and Drewry, G. (eds) (1998) *The Law and Parliament* (Butterworths).

Riddell, P. (1993) *Honest Opportunism* (Hamish Hamilton).

Rush, M. (ed.) (1979) 'Members of Parliament', in S.A. Walkland (ed.), *The House of Commons in the Twentieth Century* (Oxford University Press).

Rush, M. (1990) *Pressure Politics* (Oxford University Press).

Select Committee on Procedure (1990) *The Working of the Select Committee System, Session 1989–90*, HC 19 (HMSO).

Silk, P. and Walters, R. (1998) *How Parliament Works*, 4th edn (Longman).

Somit, A. and Roemmele, A. (1995) 'The victorious legislative incumbent as a threat to democracy: a nine nation study', *American Political Science Association: Legislative Studies Section Newsletter*, Vol. 18, No. 2, July.

Weir, S. and Beetham, D. (1999) *Political Power and Democratic Control in Britain* (Routledge).

Chapter 18

The House of Lords

Philip Norton

Learning objectives

- To describe the nature, development and role of the House of Lords.
- To identify the extent and consequences of fundamental changes made to the House in recent years.
- To assess proposals for further change to the Second Chamber.

Introduction

The House of Lords serves as the second chamber in a bicameral legislature. The role in relation to the first chamber has moved in the twentieth century from being co-equal to subordinate. As a subordinate chamber, it has carried out tasks that have been recognised as useful to the political system but has never fully escaped criticism for the nature of its composition. It was variously reformed at different times in the century, the most dramatic change coming at the end of the century. Debate continues as to what form the second chamber should take in the twenty-first century.

The House of Lords is remarkable for its longevity. What makes this longevity all the more remarkable are two features peculiar to the House. The first is that it has never been an elected chamber. The second is that, until 1999, the membership of the House was based principally on the hereditary principle. The bulk of the membership comprised **hereditary peers**. Only at the end of the twentieth century were the hereditary peers – or at least most of them – removed. The removal of the hereditary peers was not accompanied by a move to an elected second chamber. Whether the United Kingdom is to have an elected or unelected second chamber remains a matter of dispute. It perhaps says something for the work of the House of Lords that the contemporary debate revolves around what form the second chamber should take rather than whether or not the United Kingdom should have a second chamber.

What, then, is the history of the House of Lords? How has it changed in the twentieth century? What tasks does it presently fulfil? And what shape is it likely to take in the future?

History

The House of Lords is generally viewed by historians as having its origins in the Anglo-Saxon *Witenagemot* and more especially its Norman successor, the *Curia Regis* (Court of the King). Two basic features of the King's *Curia* of the twelfth and thirteenth centuries were to remain central features of the House of Lords. One was the basic composition, comprising the **lords spiritual** and the **lords temporal**. At the time of the Magna Carta, the *Curia* comprised the leading prelates of the kingdom (archbishops, bishops and abbots) and the earls and chief barons. The main change, historically, was to be the shift in balance between the two: the churchmen – the lords spiritual – moved from being a dominant to a small part of the House. The other significant feature was the basis on which members were summoned. The King's tenants-in-chief attended court because of their position. Various minor barons were summoned because the King wished them to attend. 'From the beginning the will of the king was an element in determining its make up' (White, 1908, p. 299). If a baron regularly received a summons to court the presumption grew that the summons would be issued to his heir. There thus grew a body which peers attended on the basis of a strictly hereditary dignity without reference to tenure. The result was to be a House of Lords based on the principle of heredity, with writs of summons being personal to the recipients. Members were not summoned to speak on behalf of some other individuals or bodies. Any notion of representativeness was squeezed out. Even the lords spiritual – who served by reason of their position in the established church – were summoned to take part in a personal capacity.

The lack of any representative capacity led to the House occupying a position of political – and later legal – inferiority to the House of Commons. As early as the fifteenth century, the privilege of initiating measures of taxation was conceded to the lower House. The most significant shift, though, took place in the nineteenth century. As we have seen (Chapter 17), the effect of the Reform Acts was to consign the Lords to a recognisably subordinate role to that of the Commons, though not until the passage of the Parliament Act of 1911 was that role confirmed by statute. Under the terms of the Act, the House could delay a non-money bill for no more than two sessions, and money bills (those dealing exclusively with money, and so certified by the Speaker) were to become law one month after leaving the Commons whether approved by the House of Lords or not. Bills to prolong the life of a Parliament, along with delegated legislation and provisional order bills, were excluded from the provisions of the Act. The two-session veto over non-money bills was further reduced, to one session, by the Parliament Act of 1949.

The subordinate position of the House of Lords to the House of Commons was thus established. However, the House remained a subject of political controversy. The hereditary principle was attacked by those who saw no reason for membership of the second chamber to be determined by accident of privileged birth. It was attacked as well because the bulk of the membership tended to favour the Conservative cause. Ever since the eighteenth century, when William Pitt the Younger created peers on an unprecedented scale, the Conservatives enjoyed a political ascendancy (if not always an absolute majority) in the House. In other words, it was not acceptable simply for the House to be a subordinate chamber: the reasons why it was a subordinate chamber were unacceptable. There were some attempts in the period of Conservative Government from 1951 to 1964 to render it more acceptable, not by removing hereditary peers or destroying the Conservative predominance but rather by supplementing the existing membership with a new type of membership. The Life Peerages Act 1958 made provision for people to be made members for life of the House of Lords, their titles – and their entitlement to a seat in the House of Lords – to cease upon their death. This was designed to strengthen the House by allowing people who objected to the hereditary principle to become members. Following the 1958 Act, few hereditary peerages were created. None was created under later Labour Governments and only one Conservative prime minister, Margaret Thatcher, nominated any (and then only three – Harold Macmillan, who became the Earl of Stockton; George Thomas, former Speaker of the House of Commons, and William Whitelaw, her Deputy Prime Minister). The 1963 Peerages Act made provision for hereditary peers who wished to do so to disclaim their titles. Prior to 1999, these were the most important measures to affect the membership of the House. Although both measures – and especially the 1958 Act – had significant consequences, pressure continued for more radical reform. In 1999, acting on a commitment embodied in the Labour manifesto in the 1997 general election, the Labour Government achieved passage of the House of Lords Act. This removed from membership of the House all but ninety-two of the hereditary members. The effect was to transform the House from one composed predominantly of hereditary peers to one composed overwhelmingly of **life peers**. However, the removal of the hereditary peers was seen as but one stage in a process of reform. The House of Lords created by their removal was deemed to be an interim House, to remain in place while proposals for a second stage of reform were considered. The issue of what should constitute the second stage reform has proved highly contentious.

Membership and attendance

Until the passage of the House of Lords Act, removing most hereditary peers from membership, the House of Lords had more than a thousand members, making it the largest regularly sitting legislative chamber in the world. Its size was hardly surprising given the number of peers created over the centuries by each succeeding monarch, although the largest increase was in the twentieth century. In 1906, the House had a membership of 602. In January 1999 it had 1,296. Of those, 759 were hereditary peers. (The figure includes one prince and three dukes of the blood royal.) The remaining members comprised 485 life peers, twenty-six peers created under the Appellate Jurisdiction Act 1876 (the law lords, appointed to carry out the judicial business of the House) and twenty-six lords spiritual (the two archbishops and twenty-four senior bishops of the Church of England). With the removal of all but ninety-two of the hereditary peers, the House remains a relatively large one. In December 1999 it had 666 members. 33 new life peerages were created in April 2000.

The membership of the House has thus been affected dramatically by the 1958 Life Peerages Act and the 1999 House of Lords Act. In many respects, the former made possible the latter, creating a new pool of members who could serve once hereditary peers were removed. Indeed, the creation of life peerages under the 1958 Act had a dramatic effect on the House both in terms of composition and activity. The impact of the 1999 Act will be considered in greater detail later.

Composition

In terms of composition, the 1958 Act made possible a substantial increase in the number of Labour members. Previously Labour members had been in a notable minority. In 1924, when Labour first formed a minority government, there were no Labour peers in the Upper House. The position only changed gradually. In 1945, there were eighteen Labour peers. Forty-four Labour peers were created in the period of Labour Government from

BOX 18.1 MINI BIOGRAPHY

Melvyn Bragg (1940–)
Arts controller LWT. For many years a constant presence on radio and television shows featuring arts subjects, especially the South Bank Show. When became Labour working life peer, left his Radio Four *Start the Week* presenting slot.

1945 to 1951, but their successors did not always support the Labour party. By 1999, there were only seventeen hereditary peers sitting on the Labour benches. Life peerages enabled Labour's ranks to be swelled over time. Prominent Labour supporters who objected to hereditary peerages were prepared to accept life peerages and so various former ministers, ex-MPs, trade union leaders and other public figures were elevated to the House of Lords. At the beginning of 1999, there were more than 150 life peers sitting on the Labour benches. Apart from former ministers and MPs, they included figures such as the crime writer Ruth Rendell, broadcaster Melvyn Bragg and film producer David Puttnam. With the creation of a new batch of Labour peers in June 1999, the number of life peers on the Labour benches outnumbered, for the first time, the number of life peers on the Conservative benches.

The creation of life peers from 1958 onwards served to lessen the party imbalance in the House, though still leaving the Conservatives as the largest single grouping in the House. In 1945, Conservative peers accounted for 50.4 per cent of the membership. In 1998, the figure was 38.4 per cent (Baldwin, 1999). Before 1999, the second largest category in the House was, and remains, those peers who choose to sit independent of party ranks and occupy the cross-benches in the House. At the beginning of 1999 – that is, in the pre-reform House – the state of the parties was Conservative 473; Labour 168; Liberal Democrats sixty-seven; and cross-benchers 322. This left in excess of 250 other peers who did not align themselves with any of these groupings. The effect of the removal of most hereditary peers in 1999 was to create greater equality between the two main parties, leaving the cross-bench peers holding the balance of power.

The creation of life peers drawn from modest backgrounds served also to affect the social profile of the membership. Hereditary peers were typically drawn from the cream of upper-class society. Life peers were drawn from a more diverse social background. However, even with the influx of life peers, the membership remained, and remains, socially atypical. Life peerages are normally conferred on those who have achieved some particular distinction in society, be it social, cultural, sporting, economic or political. By the time the recipients have achieved such a distinction they are, by definition, atypical. There was therefore little chance of the House becoming socially typical. There has been no recent study of the social composition of the House, but one study in the 1980s found that in terms of occupational experience a majority of peers were drawn from the law, academe or the civil service (Baldwin, 1985, p. 105). The House is also atypical in terms of age and gender. It is rare for people to be made life peers while aged in their twenties or thirties. The youngest to be created was television mogul Lord Alli (born 1964), who was elevated to the peerage in 1998. The hereditary peerage produced some young peers, succeeding their fathers at an early age, but they were small in number and largely disappeared as a result of the House of Lords Act. At the beginning of 1999, a majority of members were aged sixty-five or over. Women, who were first admitted to the House under the provisions of the 1958 Life Peerages Act, also constitute a minority of the membership. At the end of 1997, there were 103 women members. Of these, eighty-seven held life peerages. Recent years have seen a number of black and Asian peers created, though they constitute a small proportion of the total. Lord Alli is the only openly gay peer to sit in the House.

There has been another consequence of life peerages in terms of the membership of the House. It has brought into the House a body of individuals who are frequently expert in a particular area or have experience in a particular field. This claim is not exclusive to life peers – some hereditary peers are notable for their expertise or experience in particular fields – but it is associated predominantly with them. This has led to claims that when the House debates a subject, however arcane it may be, there is usually one or more experts in the House to discuss it (Baldwin, 1985). Thus, for example, in the field of higher education, the House has among its members a number of university chancellors, masters of university colleges, former vice-chancellors, an array of professors (including this writer), former secretaries of state for education, and peers who chair bodies in higher education (such as the funding council). When early in 1999 the House had a short debate on the teaching of citizenship, the peers who had signed up to speak were asked to keep to three minutes each, such was the number – usually with some obvious qualification to speak on the subject – who wished to take part. This claim to expertise in many fields is often contrasted with membership of the House of Commons, where the career politician (see Chapter 17) – expert only in the practice of politics – dominates. The body of expertise and experience serves – as we shall see – to bolster the capacity of the House to fulfil a number of its functions.

Activity

The creation of life peers also had a dramatic effect on the activity of the House. In the 1950s, the House met at a leisurely pace and was poorly attended. Peers have never been paid a salary and many members, like the minor barons in the thirteenth century, found attending to be a chore, sometimes an expensive one: the practice, as in the thirteenth century, was to stay away. The House rarely met for more than three days a week and each sitting was usually no more than three or four hours in length. For most of the decade, the average daily attendance did not reach three figures. There was little interest shown in its activities by most of its own members; not surprisingly, there was little interest shown by those outside the House.

This was to change significantly in each succeeding decade (see Figure 18.1). Life peers were disproportionately active. Though they constituted a minority of the House they came to constitute a majority of the most active members of the House. The effect of the increasing numbers of life peers was apparent in the attendance of members (see Figure 18.1). Peers attended in ever greater numbers and the House sat for longer. Late-night sittings, virtually unknown in the 1950s and for much of the 1960s, have been regular features since the 1970s. In the 1980s and 1990s, the average daily sitting was six or seven hours. By the end of the 1980s, more than 800 peers – two-thirds of the membership – attended one or more sittings each year and, of those, more than 500 contributed to debate. By the time of the House of Lords Act in 1999, the House was boasting a better attendance in the chamber than the House of Commons.

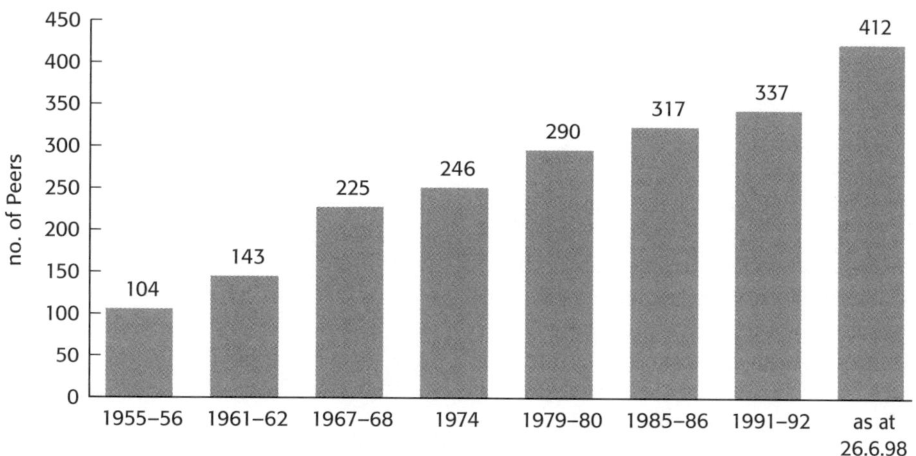

Figure 18.1 Average daily attendance in the chamber 1955–98
Source: House of Lords Annual Report and Accounts 1997–98

One other consequence of the more active House was that the number of votes increased. They were few and far between in the 1950s, about ten to twenty a year. By the 1980s and 1990s, the figure was usually closer to 200. The political composition of the House meant that a Labour Government was vulnerable to defeat. In the period of Labour Government from 1974 to 1979, the Government suffered 362 defeats at the hands of the House of Lords. However, Conservative Governments were not immune. The preponderance of Conservative peers did not always translate into a majority for a Conservative Government. In the period of Conservative Government from 1979 to 1997, ministers suffered just over 250 defeats in the House. The Government was vulnerable to a combination of opposition parties, the cross-benchers and, on occasion, some of its own supporters.

The House also became more visible to the outside world. In 1985, television cameras were allowed to broadcast proceedings. There was a four-year gap before the televising of Commons' proceedings began: in those four years, the House of Lords enjoyed exclusive television coverage. In the 1990s, the House also was ahead of the House of Commons in appointing an information officer and seeking to ensure a better public understanding of its role and activities.

Procedures

The House differs significantly from the Commons not only in its size, composition and remuneration (peers can claim allowances, but still receive no salary) but also in its procedures. Though the Lord Chancellor is the presiding officer of the House, he has no powers to call peers to speak, nor to enforce order. (Given that, and the demands arising from his duties as head of the judiciary, his place on the Woolsack is normally taken by a deputy.) The maintenance of the rules of order is the responsibility of the House itself, though peers usually look to the Leader of the House to give a lead. Peers wishing to speak in a set-piece debate submit their names in advance and a list of speakers is circulated. Peers then rise to speak in the order on the list. At other times, if two peers rise at the same time, one is expected to give way. (If neither does so, other peers make clear their preference as to who should speak by shouting out the name of the person they wish to hear.) If a speaker strays from what is permissible, other peers shout 'Order'. If a speaker goes on for too long, it is always open to another peer to rise and move the motion 'That the noble peer be no longer heard', but it is a device rarely employed. The Lords remains a more chamber-oriented institution than the Commons, though – as we shall see – it is making more use of committees than before. Though the House votes more frequently than it used to, the number of divisions in the Lords is fewer than in the Commons. (There will usually be about three times as many votes each year in the Commons as in the Lords.) This in part reflects the recognition by peers of the political predominance of the elected chamber. Peers are often reluctant to press issues to a vote and rarely do so on the principle of a measure. By virtue of an agreement reached between the two party leaders in the Lords in 1945, the House does not divide on the second reading of any bill promised in the government's election manifesto and, by extension now, any bill appearing in the government's programme for the session. This is known as the Salisbury convention, named after the Conservative leader in the Lords who enunciated it.

The House also discusses all amendments to bills that are tabled. There are no timetable (guillotine) motions. There are also more opportunities, as we shall see, to raise issues in the House than in the House of Commons. Some debates are time limited by agreement (though not the committee and report stages of bills) and peers normally try to keep to a fifteen-minute time limit for their speeches. They may be asked to keep their speeches even shorter if a great many of them sign up to speak in a time-limited debate.

Functions

The debate about reform of the House of Lords has focussed largely, though not wholly, on its composition. The functions of the House – the tasks which it carries out – have not generated as much controversy. There has been a wide body of agreement that the functions it fulfilled in the twentieth century are appropriate to a second chamber. As we shall see, this view is not necessarily held by all those expressing views on the House of Lords. Nonetheless, the view has tended to predominate among those engaged in the debate, including the government of the day. The functions are broadly similar to those of the Commons but not as extensive. The extent to which they differ derives from the fact that politically the House is no longer co-equal with the Commons.

Legitimisation

The House fulfils the functions of both manifest and latent legitimisation, but on a modest scale. It is called upon to give the seal of approval to bills but, if it fails to give that approval, it can be overridden later by the House of Commons under the provisions of the Parliament Acts. Only in very rare circumstances – as in the case of a bill to lengthen the life of a Parliament – is its veto absolute. By virtue of being one of the two chambers of Parliament and by meeting regularly and uninterruptedly, the House may have a limited claim to fulfilling a function of latent legitimisation. However, such a claim is largely offset by the House having no claim to being a representative assembly and by its limited legislative authority.

Recruitment

The House provides some of the personnel of government. As we have seen (Chapter 17), ministers are drawn from Parliament and, by convention, predominantly now from the elected House.

The government recruits a number of ministers from the Upper House primarily for political and managerial reasons. Though the government is normally assured of getting its bills through the House, it is not necessarily guaranteed getting them through in the form it wants them. It is therefore prudent to have ministers in the Lords in order to explain bills and to marshal support. In addition, the House provides a pool from which the Prime Minister can draw in order to supplement ministers drawn from the Commons. The advantage offered by peers is that, with no constituency responsibilities, they are able to devote more time to ministerial duties than is the case with ministers who have constituency duties to attend to. It also has the advantage of widening the pool of talent available to the Prime Minister. Someone from outside Parliament can be elevated to the peerage at the same time as being appointed to Government office. Three people who had no parliamentary experience were brought into Government through this route by Tony Blair in the first two years of his premiership: Charles Falconer (Lord Falconer of Thoroton), a lawyer, appointed in 1997 as Solicitor General; David Simon (Lord Simon of Highbury), a former Chairman of British Petroleum, appointed in 1997 as Competition Minister; and Gus MacDonald (Lord Macdonald of Tradeston), a Scottish television executive, appointed in 1998 as a junior minister in the Scottish Office.

However, the number of ministers appointed in the Lords is relatively small. A minimum of two peers serve in the Cabinet (Lord Chancellor and Leader of the House) but usually no more than four. (Four is a rarity and two, in recent years, the norm.) About ten to fifteen other ministers are drawn from the Lords, supplemented by seven whips (including the Chief Whip). The number of ministers does not match the number of ministries, with the result that the whips have to take on responsibility for answering for particular departments – another difference from the House of Commons, where the whips have no responsibility for appearing at the dispatch box. At the beginning of the 1997 Parliament, one of the most frequent speakers at the dispatch box was the Government Deputy Chief Whip, Lord McIntosh of Haringey. Even with a small number of posts to be filled, the government still has difficulty on occasion in finding suitable peers for ministerial office. It used to be the case that Conservative governments had to draw on occasion on young hereditary peers. Labour governments were limited by the relatively small number of Labour peers. The likelihood is that in future years more life peers will be created with a view to their appointment to ministerial office.

Scrutiny and influence

It is in its remaining functions that the House of Lords is significant. The House performs an important role as an agent of scrutiny and influence, especially the former. The House does not undertake the task of scrutiny on behalf of constituents, as peers have none. Rather, the House undertakes a more general task of scrutiny. Three features of the House render it particularly suitable for the detailed scrutiny of legislation. Firstly, as an unelected House, it cannot claim the legitimacy to reject the principle of measures agreed by the elected House. Thus, basically by default, it focusses on the detail rather than the principle. Secondly, as we have noted already, its membership includes people who have distinguished themselves in particular fields – such as the sciences, the law, education, industry, industrial relations – who can look at relevant legislation from the perspective of practitioners in the field rather than from the perspective of elected party politicians. And, thirdly, the House has the time to debate non-money bills in more detail than is usually possible in the Commons – as we have seen, there is no provision for a guillotine and all amendments are discussed. The House thus serves as an important revising chamber, trying to ensure that a bill is well drafted and internally coherent. In order to improve the bill, it will suggest amendments, most of which will be accepted by the Commons. In terms of legislative scrutiny, the House has thus developed a role which is viewed as complementary to, rather than one competing with (or identical to), that of the Commons.

The value of the House as a revising chamber is shown by the number of amendments it makes to legislation. Most of these are moved by the Government itself, but a significant proportion of these are amendments promised by Government in response to comments made by back-bench members. The number of amendments made in the Lords far exceeds the number made in the Commons. In the 1995–6 session, for example, 422 amendments were made in the Commons to Government Bills; the figure in the House of Lords was 1,133. In the long first session of the new 1997 Parliament, 3,963 amendments were made. It is rare for the House of Commons to reject amendments made by the Lords. Even these figures do not do justice to the scrutiny undertaken by the Lords. The scrutiny is frequently constructive, and acknowledged as such by the Government. Thus, for example, during the 1998–9 session, 108 non-government amendments were moved to the Access to Justice Bill. Of these, seventy-one received a ministerial response that was positive. The responses were important not only for their number but also for their range: they included promising to consider points raised in debate (twenty-eight occasions), accepting the principle of an amendment (twenty-one occasions) and promising to draw a point to the attention of those responsible for drafting the Bill (three occasions) (Norton, 1999). Ten amendments were accepted as they stood. The constructive work undertaken by the House was conceded by the Lord Chancellor, Lord Irvine of Lairg, at the conclusion of the Bill's passage through the House. The importance of these figures lay not only in the number of the constructive responses from Government but also in the fact that it is difficult to envisage scrutiny in the House of Commons producing such a response.

This role in scrutinising legislation – in so far as it constitutes a 'second look' at legislation – is of especial importance given that it has been characterised as one of the two core functions of the House (Norton, 1999), meaning that it is a function that is particular to the House as the

BOX 18.2 MINI BIOGRAPHY

Lord (Derry) Irvine (1940–)

From humble beginnings, he studied law at Glasgow University. Was highly successful barrister head of chambers for student barristers Tony and Cherie Blair. He became Lord Chancellor once Blair made it to the top job. Very influential in reforming legal aid and the House of Lords but was ridiculed for spending some half a million pounds refurbishing his official residence. He defended his actions as in the national interest.

second chamber. It is not a function that the House of Commons can carry out, since it is difficult if not impossible for it to act as a revising chamber for its own measures; that has been likened to asking the same doctor for a second opinion. The role of the House as a revising chamber is thus offered as being central to the case for retaining a second chamber. It is also the role that occupies the most time in the House: usually about half the time of the House, or a little over, is devoted to considering legislation.

The House also scrutinises, and occasionally influences, government policy. Peers can debate policy in a less partisan atmosphere than the Commons and are not subject to the constituency and party influences that dominate in the elected House. They are therefore in a position to debate issues of public policy that may not be at the heart of the partisan battle and which, consequently, receive little attention in the Commons. Given their backgrounds, peers are also often – though not always – able to debate public policy from the perspective of those engaged in the subject. The House, for example, is able to debate science policy with an authority denied the lower House. The Lords contains several distinguished scientists; the Commons does not. We have mentioned already the number of peers who can speak with authority on higher education; though the House of Commons contains some former university lecturers, it does not have members with the same experience and status in education as those in the Upper House.

Expression

The House, like the Commons, also fulfils a number of expressive functions. It can bring issues on to the political agenda in a way not always possible in the Commons. MPs are wary of raising issues that may not be popular with constituents and which have little salience in terms of party politics. Peers are answerable to no one but themselves. They can raise whatever they feel needs raising. The House may thus debate issues of concern to particular groups in society that MPs are not willing to address. Formally, it is not a function the House is expected to fulfil. Indeed, according to *Erskine May*, the parliamentary 'bible' on procedure, Lords may indicate that an outside body agrees with the substance of their views, but they should avoid creating an impression that they are speaking as representatives of outside bodies. Thus, not only is the House not a representative assembly, it should avoid giving the impression of being one! In practice, peers take up issues that concern them, often alerted to the issue by outside bodies. Peers are frequently lobbied by outside organisations. One extensive survey of organised interests in the 1980s found that 70 per cent of respondents had made use of the House to raise issues. Of those that had contact, just over 80 per cent rated the contact as useful or very useful (Rush, 1990, p. 289). Sometimes the issues raised are esoteric – one peer in the 1980s initiated a debate on unidentified flying objects (UFOs) – but some are of great concern to particular groups in society.

The House also has the potential, only marginally realised, to express views to citizens and influence their stance on public policy. The function is limited by the absence of any democratic legitimacy, the capacity to influence deriving from the longevity of the House and its place as one of the two chambers of Parliament, as well as from the authority of the individual peers who may be involved. However, the scope for fulfilling this function is somewhat greater than in the House of Commons, simply because more time is available for it in the House of Lords. Between 20 and 30 per cent of the time of the House is given over each session to debates on motions tabled by peers: about 20 per cent of time is given over to general debates and between 4 and 10 per cent of the time is given over to Unstarred Questions, in effect, short debates on specific topics.

Other functions

To these functions may be added a number of others, some of which are peculiar to the upper House. Foremost among these is a judicial function. The House constitutes the highest court of appeal within the United Kingdom. Though formally a function residing in the House as a whole, in practice it is carried out by a judicial committee comprising the Lord Chancellor, the **law lords** and peers who have held high judicial office. Between five and ten will normally sit to hear a case. Hearings take place in a committee room, though the decision is delivered in the chamber, usually on a Thursday. By convention, other peers do not take part in judicial proceedings. One peer earlier this century did try to participate but was ignored by the members of the committee.

Like the Commons, the House also retains a small legislative role, primarily in the form of private Members' legislation. Peers can introduce private Members' bills and a small number achieve passage, but it is small – even compared with the number of such bills promoted by MPs. The introduction of such bills by peers is more important in fulfilling an expressive function – allowing views on the subject to be aired – than it is in fulfilling a legislative role. Time is found to debate each private Member's bill. In the 1995–6 session, for example, a Sexual Orientation Discrimination Bill was introduced which, even though it stood little chance of passage (there was no time in the Commons), got the issue of discrimination against homosexuals discussed. In 1999, a former Conservative Leader of the House, Lord Cranborne, introduced a Parliamentary Government Bill, designed to call attention to the need to strengthen parliamentary control of the executive. The debate on second reading was replied to by the Lord Chancellor. The time given to private Members' legislation is important but not extensive: it occupies usually less than 3 per cent of the time of the House.

The House is also ascribed a distinct role, that of a constitutional safeguard. This is reflected in the provisions of the Parliament Acts. The House, as we have noted, retains a veto over bills to extend the life of a Parliament. It is considered a potential brake on a government that seeks to act in a dictatorial or generally unacceptable manner: hence it may use its limited power to amend or, more significantly, to delay a bill. In practice, though, the power is a limited one, as well as one not expected to require action by the House on any regular basis. The House lacks a legitimate elected base of its own that would allow it to act, on a substantial and sustained basis, contrary to the wishes of an elected government. Even so, it constitutes the other core function of the House in that it is a function that the House alone, as the second chamber, can fulfil: the House of Commons cannot act as a constitutional check upon itself.

In combination, these various functions render the House a useful body – especially as a revising chamber and for raising and debating issues on which peers are well informed – but one that is clearly subordinate to the elected chamber. The fact that the House is not elected explains its limited functions; it is also the reason why it is considered particularly suited to fulfil the functions it does retain.

Scrutiny and influence

The means available to the House to fulfil the tasks of scrutiny and influence can be considered, as with the Commons, under two heads: legislation and executive actions. The means available to the House are also those available to fulfil its expressive functions.

Legislation

As we have seen, about half the time of the house is given over to legislation, though this constitutes a decrease over earlier years. Bills in the Lords have to go through stages analogous to those in the House of Commons. There are, though, differences in procedure. First readings are normally taken formally, but there have been rare occasions when they have been debated: on four occasions (in 1888, 1933, 1943 and 1969) first readings were actually opposed. Second readings, as in the Commons, constitute debates on the principle of the measure. However, votes on second reading are exceptionally rare. Because of the Salisbury convention, the House does not vote on the second reading of Government Bills. A vote may take place if, as exceptionally happens, a free vote is permitted. This happened in 1990 on the War Crimes Bill and in 1999 on the Sexual Offences (Amendment) Bill to lower the age of consent for homosexual acts to sixteen. Both bills had been passed by large majorities in the House of Commons but both were rejected, on free votes, in the House of Lords. Both occasions were exceptional.

The main work of the House takes place at committee and report stages. For some bills, the committee stage is actually dispensed with. After second reading, a motion may be moved 'That this Bill be not committed' and, if agreed to, the bill then awaits third reading. This procedure is usually employed for supply and money bills when there is no desire to present amendments. For those bills that do receive a committee stage, it is usually taken on the floor of the House. All amendments tabled are debated. The less crowded timetable of the House allows such a procedure. It has the advantage of allowing all peers with an interest or expertise in a measure to take part and ensures consideration of any amendments they believe to be relevant. There is thus the potential for a more thorough consideration than is possible in the Commons. The emphasis is on ensuring that the bill is well drafted and coherent.

Since 1968, the House has been able to refer bills for committee consideration in the equivalent of standing committees, known as public bill committees, though it rarely does so. More recently, the House has experimented with sending a bill to a special procedure public bill committee, which is empowered to take oral and written evidence. Of longer standing is the power to refer a bill, or indeed any proposal, to a select committee for detailed investigation. It is a power which has been utilised when it has been considered necessary or desirable to examine witnesses and evidence from outside bodies. Between 1972 and 1991, seven bills were sent to select committees. All bar one of the bills were private Members' bills. In future, bills considered in need of detailed scrutiny are likely to be sent to a special procedure public bill committee. If a Bill is not considered controversial, and no votes are expected on it, it may also now be sent for its committee stage to a Grand Committee. The Grand Committee is, in effect, something of a parallel chamber. It comprises all members of the House and can meet while the House is in session. In practice, attendance is relatively small, permitting sessions to be held in the Moses Room, an ornate committee room just off the Peers' Lobby.

Report and third reading provide further opportunities for consideration. Report may be used by government to bring forward amendments promised at committee stage and also to offer new amendments of its own. It is also an opportunity for members to return to issues that received an inadequate response by Government at committee stage (though amendments rejected by the House at committee stage cannot again be considered). It is possible also for amendments to be made at third reading and this opportunity is variously employed. The result is that some Bills, especially large or contentious Bills, can and do receive a considerable amount of attention at different stages in the House of Lords.

Executive actions

As in the House of Commons, there are various means available for scrutinising the actions of the executive. The principal means available on the floor of the House are those of debate and questions. Off the floor of the House, there are select committees and, at the unofficial level, party meetings.

Debates

Debates, as in the Commons, take place on motions. These may express a particular view or they may take the form of either 'take note' motions or motions calling for papers. 'Take note' motions are employed in order to allow the House to debate reports from select committees or to discuss topics on which the government wishes to hear peers' views: ministers use 'take note' motions rather than motions calling for papers because – with the latter – they are responsible for supplying the papers being called for. Motions calling for papers are used by back-benchers to call attention to a particular issue; at the end of the debate it is customary to withdraw the motion, the purpose for which it was tabled – to ensure a debate – having been achieved.

All peers who wish to speak in debate do so and there is a greater likelihood than in the Commons that such proceedings will constitute what they purport to be: that is, debates. Party ties are less rigid than in the Commons (though none the less still strong) and peers frequently pay attention to what is being said. Though the order in which peers speak is determined beforehand, it is common practice for a peer who is speaking to give way to interventions. Within the context of the chamber, the chances of a speech having an impact on the thought and even the votes of others are considerably greater than in the more predictable lower House. Indeed it is not unknown for peers when, uncertain as to how to vote, to ask 'what does X think about it?' This writer, as a member of the House, has been influenced to vote in a particular way by persuasive speeches and, equally, to abstain on the basis of not being persuaded to vote for a particular motion or amendment.

One day each month, usually a Wednesday, is set aside for two short debates, each of up to two-and-a-half hours in length. These are occasions for issues to be raised by back-benchers or cross-benchers, and the choice of subject is made by ballot. The purpose of each short debate is to allow peers to discuss a particular topic rather than to come to a conclusion about it. Topics discussed tend to be non-partisan and the range is broad. Thus, for example, on 31 March 1999, Lord Campbell of Croy (a Conservative life peer and former minister) initiated a debate on motor vehicle crime and Lord Freyberg (a young hereditary cross-bencher) initiated one on the role of design in improving competitiveness and quality of life. Both motions provided the opportunity for interested peers to offer their views and for ministers to explain the government's position and to reveal what proposals were under consideration by the relevant department.

Questions

Questions in the Lords are of two types: starred and unstarred. The meanings are different to those employed in the Commons. In the Commons, starred questions are oral questions and unstarred questions are written questions. In the Lords, starred questions are non-debatable questions and unstarred questions are questions on which a short debate may take place. (Lords may also table questions for written answer, and nowadays do so in increasing numbers.) At the beginning of each day's sitting, up to four 'starred' questions may be asked. These are similar to those tabled for oral answer in the Commons, though – unlike in the Commons – they are addressed to Her Majesty's Government and not to a particular minister (see Figure 18.2). A peer rises to ask the question appearing in his or her name on the order paper, the relevant minister (or whip) replies for the government, and then supplementary questions – confined to the subject of the original question – follow. This procedure, assuming as many as four questions are tabled (they usually are), is expected to last no more than thirty minutes. This allows for perhaps as many as four or five supplementaries on each question to be asked, the peer who tabled the motion by tradition being allowed to ask the first supplementary. Hence, though a shorter question time than in the Commons, the concentration on a particular question is much greater and allows for more probing. At the end of the day's sitting, or during what is deemed the 'dinner hour', there is also usually an 'unstarred' question: that is, one which may be debated (as, for example, Lord Stoddart of Swindon, Figure 18.2). Peers who wish to speak do so and the appropriate minister then responds. The advantages of such unstarred questions are similar to those of the half-hour adjournment debates in the Commons, except that in this case there is a much greater opportunity for other members to participate. For example, when the Earl of Sandwich on 29 July 1999 asked what examples the government had of good practice in long-term overseas development, with special reference to Africa and India, no fewer than nine peers spoke – in addition to Lord Sandwich – before the minister, Baroness Amos, rose to reply. The debate lasted for almost one-and-a-half hours.

Committees

Though the House remains a chamber-oriented institution, it has made greater use in recent years of committees. Apart from a number of established committees dealing, for example, with privilege and the judicial function of the House, it has variously made use of *ad hoc* select committees. Some *ad hoc* committees have been appointed, to consider the desirability of

NOTICES AND ORDERS OF THE DAY

Items marked ‡ are expected to be taken during the dinner adjournment.
Bills marked § have been set down before the expiry of the recommended minimum interval between stages.

TUESDAY 20TH JULY

At half-past two o'clock

Introductions–
The Lord Faulkner of Worcester
will be introduced,
and
William Brett, Esq.
will be introduced as a Baron.

***The Lord Morris of Manchester** – To ask Her Majesy's Government what recent representations they have received for the award of *ex gratia* payments to former British prisoners of war of the Japanese during the Second World War, and what response they have made.

***The Lord Judd** – To ask Her Majesty's Government what progress has been made in the reconstruction of Kosovo and what is their policy towards the reconstruction of Serb Yugoslavia.

***The Baroness Gardner of Parkes** – To ask Her Majesty's Government what is their estimate of the level of malnutrition in the United Kingdom and what action they are taking to tackle it.

***The Baroness Blatch** – To ask Her Majesty's Government, in the light of criticisms of the Prime Minister and the Secretary of State for Education made by Mr. Justice Kay in the High Court on 12th July, whether they will reconsider their decision to deny pupils who had secured an Assisted Place the right to continue that placement to the end of their secondary education.

Business of the House – The Baroness Jay of Paddington to move. That Standing Order 44 (*No two stages of a Bill to be taken on one day*) be dispensed with on Friday next to allow the Finance Bill to be taken through its remaining stages that day.

Adoption (Intercountry Aspects) Bill – Third Reading [The Lord Meston]

§Genetically Modified Crops Bill [HL] – Third Reading [The Baroness Miller of Hendon]

Welfare Reform and Pensions Bill – House to be again in Committee [The Baroness Hollis of Heigham] [*17th and 19th Reports from the Delegated Powers Committee*]

‡The Lord Stoddart of Swindon – To ask Her Majesty's Government whether they are satisfied with the performance and effectiveness of the Meat Hygiene Service.

Figure 18.2 House of Lords order paper: in the House of Lords, questions are addressed to Her Majesty's Government and not to a particular minister

certain legislative measures. A number have been appointed to consider issues of public policy. The House has also made use of its power to create sessional select committees, i.e. committees appointed regularly from session to session rather than for the purpose of one particular inquiry. Two of these committees enjoy well-established reputations as high-powered committees of scrutiny. A third has now joined them.

The most prominent is the *European Union Committee* (known, until 1999, as the European Communities Committee). Established in 1974, it undertakes scrutiny of draft European legislation, seeking to identify those proposals that raise important questions of principle or policy and which deserve consideration by the House. All documents are sifted by the chairman of the committee, those deemed potentially important being sent to a sub-committee. The Committee works through six sub-committees, each committee comprising two or more members of the main committee and several co-opted members. In total, the sub-committees draw on the services of sixty to seventy peers. Each sub-committee covers a particular area. Sub-Committee E, for example, deals with Law and Institutions. Members are appointed on the basis of their particular expertise. Sub-Committee E includes some eminent lawyers – it is by convention chaired by a law lord – as well as members who have experience of the European Parliament and the Cabinet and some who have a particular interest in government institutions. (This writer – a professor of government – is a member and succeeded a professor of politics.) A sub-committee, after having had documents referred to it, can decide that the document requires no further consideration or they can call in evidence from government departments and outside bodies. If they decide a document requires further consideration, then it is held 'under scrutiny' – that is, subject to the scrutiny reserve. The Government cannot, except in exceptional circumstances, agree to a proposal in the Council of Ministers if it is still under scrutiny by Parliament.

Written evidence to a sub-committee may be supplemented by oral evidence and, on occasion (though not often), a minister may be invited to give evidence in person. The sub-committees prepare reports for the House (in total, about twenty to thirty a year), including recommendations as to whether the documents should be debated by the House. (About 2 per cent of the time of the House is taken up debating EC documents, usually on 'take note' motions.) The EU Committee has built up an impressive reputation as a thorough and informed body, issuing reports which are more extensive than its counterpart in the Commons, and which are considered authoritative both within Whitehall and the institutions of the EC. The House, like the chambers of other national legislatures, has no formal role in the EC legislative process (see Norton, 1996), and so has no power, other than that of persuasion, to affect outcomes. The significance of the reports, therefore, has tended to lie in informing debate rather than in changing particular decisions (Norton, 1993, p. 126).

The *Select Committee on Science and Technology* was appointed in 1979 following the demise of the equivalent committee in the Commons. The remit of the committee – 'to consider science and technology' – is wide and its inquiries have covered a broad range. The committee is essentially non-partisan in approach and benefits from a number of peers with an expertise in the subject. At the end of the 1990s for example, its members – both appointed and co-opted – included several professors in different scientific fields and a holder of a Nobel Prize. (For several years it was chaired by a professor of nuclear physics, an expert on atomic energy.) The Committee issues several reports each year. In 1997–8, for example, it issued seven reports, including one on the resistance to antibiotics and other antimicrobial agents, which received considerable publicity. In the following session it attracted attention for its report on the use of cannabis for medical purposes. The committee has raised issues which otherwise might have been neglected by government – and certainly not considered in any depth by the Commons – and various of its reports have proved influential (see Grantham, 1993; Hayter, 1992). Its report on civil research and development, for example, led to the then Prime Minister, Margaret Thatcher, taking charge of the government's consideration of priorities on science and technology and the appointment of a council to advise the premier. In 1992, the committee was joined by a sister committee, the Commons deciding to establish again a committee on the subject. However, the Lords retains the advantage of expertise denied to the Commons.

These committees are supplemented now by a *Delegated Powers and Deregulation Scrutiny Committee*, which looks at whether powers of delegated legislation in a bill are appropriate and makes recommendations to the House accordingly (see Himsworth, 1995). The committee has established itself as a powerful and informed committee, its recommendations being taken seriously by the House and by Government. At Report Stage of the Access to Justice Bill in February 1999, for example, the Government moved thirty-four amendments to give effect to the recommendations of the Committee.

These permanent committees are variously supplemented by *ad hoc* committees, appointed to consider particular issues. These have included, for example, unemployment, the mandatory life sentence for murder, relations between central and local government and, more recently, the public service. The Select Committee on the Public Service was established in 1996, held a total of fifty-seven meetings and published an extensive report on the role of the civil service in January 1998. In 1998, the House appointed a Select Committee on the Monetary Policy Committee of the Bank of England.

The use of committees thus constitutes a modest but valuable supplement to the work undertaken on the floor of the House. They allow the House to specialise to some degree and to draw on the expertise of its membership, an expertise that cannot be matched by the elected House of Commons. They also fulfil an important expressive function. The committees take evidence from interested bodies – the submission of written evidence is extensive – thus allowing groups an opportunity to get their views on the public record. Given the expertise on the committees, committee reports are treated as weighty documents by interested groups; consequently, the committees enjoy some capacity to raise support for particular measures of public policy.

Party meetings

The parties in the Lords are organised, with their own leaders and whips. Even the cross-benchers, allied to no party, have their own elected leader (known as the convenor) and circulate a weekly document detailing the business for the week ahead. However, neither the Conservative nor the Labour Party in the Lords has a committee structure. Instead, peers are able to attend the Commons' back-bench committees and a number do so. Any attempt at influence through the party structure in the Lords, therefore, takes the form of talking to the whips or of raising the issue at the weekly party meeting.

Party meetings are usually held each week, usually prior to the House sitting. Thus, for example, the Association of Conservative Peers (the ACP) meets early on a Thursday afternoon. Cross-bench peers hold their meeting at the same time. Such meetings are useful for discussing future business as well as for hearing from invited speakers. In ACP meetings, for example, the business usually comprises a short talk by the Chairman of the 1922 Committee about developments in the Commons, the Chief Whip announcing the business for the following week, and a discussion on a particular issue or a talk from a frontbencher or expert on a particular subject. When a major bill is coming before the House, the relevant member of the Shadow Cabinet (or, if in government, Minister) may be invited to attend, along with a junior spokesperson, to brief peers on the bill. Sometimes party meetings have the characteristics of a specialist committee, since often peers with an expertise in the topic will attend and question the speaker. For a Minister or shadow Minister, or even an expert speaker, the occasion may be a testing one, having to justify a measure or proposal before an often well-informed audience.

Party meetings are useful as two-way channels of communication between leaders and led in the Lords and, in a wider context, between a party's supporters in the Lords and the leadership of the whole party. Given the problems of ensuring structured and regular contact between whips and their party's peers, the party meetings provide a useful means of gauging the mood of the regular attenders.

Reform: stage one

Demands for reform of the House of Lords were a feature both of the late nineteenth century as well as of the twentieth. As the democratic principle became more widely accepted in the nineteenth century, so calls for the reform of the unelected, Conservative-dominated House of Lords became more strident. Conservative obstruction of Liberal bills in the 1880s led the Liberal Lord Morley to demand that the Upper House 'mend or end', an approach adopted as Liberal policy in 1891. In 1894, the Liberal conference voted in favour of abolishing the Lords' power of veto. When the Lords rejected the Budget of the Liberal government in 1909, the government introduced the Parliament Bill. Passed in 1911, the preamble envisaged an elected House. An inter-party conference in 1918 proposed a scheme for phasing out the hereditary peers but no time was found to implement the proposals. A 1948 Party Leaders' Conference agreed that heredity alone should not be the basis for membership. Again, no action was taken. In 1969, the Parliament (No. 2) Bill, introduced by the Labour government led by Harold Wilson, sought to phase out the hereditary element. The bill foundered in the House of Commons after encountering opposition from Conservative MPs, led by Enoch Powell, who felt it went too far, and from Labour MPs, led by Michael Foot, who believed it did not go far enough. The willingness of the House to defeat the Labour Government in the period from 1974 to 1979 reinforced Labour antagonism. In 1983, the Labour Party manifesto committed the party to abolition of the Upper House. Under Neil Kinnock (see Chapter 15) this stance was softened. In its election manifesto in 1992, the party advocated instead an elected second chamber. This was later amended under Tony Blair's leadership to a two-stage reform: first, the elimination of the hereditary element and, second and in a later Parliament, the introduction of a new reformed second chamber. The Liberal Democrats favoured a reformed second chamber – a senate – as part of a wider package of constitutional reform. Charter '88, the constitutional reform movement created in 1988 (see Chapter 15), included reform of the Upper House 'to establish a democratic, non-hereditary second chamber' as a fundamental part of its reform programme.

The Labour manifesto in the 1997 general election included the commitment to reform in two stages. 'The House of Lords', it declared, 'must be reformed. As an initial, self-contained reform, not dependent on further reform in the future, the rights of hereditary peers to sit and vote in the House of Lords will be ended by statute.' That, it said, would be the first step in a process of reform 'to make the House of Lords more democratic and representative'. A committee of both Houses of Parliament would be appointed to undertake a wide-ranging review of possible further change and to bring forward proposals for reform.

The Labour victory in the 1997 general election provided a parliamentary majority to give effect to the manifesto commitment. However, anticipating problems in the House of Lords, the Government delayed bringing in a bill to remove hereditary peers until the second session of the Parliament. The bill was introduced in January 1999. It had one principal clause, Clause 1, which ended membership of the House of Lords on the basis of a hereditary peerage. The bill was passed by the House of Commons by a large majority. In the House of Lords, peers adhered to the Salisbury convention and did not vote on second reading. However, they subjected it to prolonged debate at committee and report stage. In the Lords, an amendment was introduced – and accepted by the Government – providing that ninety-two hereditary peers should remain members of the interim House. The ninety-two would comprise seventy-five chosen by hereditary peers on a party basis (the number to be divided according to party strength among hereditary peers), fifteen to be chosen by all members of the House for the purpose of being available to serve the House, for example as Deputy Speakers; and the Earl Marshal and the Lord Great Chamberlain, in order to fulfil particular functions associated with their offices. The Government had indicated in advance that it would accept the amendment, on condition that the Lords did not frustrate passage of the Bill. Although the House made various other amendments to the Bill, against the Government's wishes, the Bill made it eventually to the statute book. All bar the ninety-two hereditary peers exempted by the Act ceased to be members at the end of the session. When the House met for the State Opening of Parliament on 17 November 1999 it was thus a very different House to that which had sat only the week before. It was still a House of Lords but it was a very different House of Lords. Instead of a House with a membership based predominantly on the heredity principle it was now an essentially appointed House, the bulk of the members being there by virtue of life peerages.

Reform: stage two

After the return of the Labour Government in 1997, opponents criticised ministers for not having announced what form stage two of Lords reform would take. After the removal of the hereditary peers from membership, there would be an interim House, but what did the Government

Hereditary peers fight reform of the House of Lords (23 November 1998)

have in mind as the successor to this interim House? Critics were able to make political capital out of the Government's failure to say what plans it had for stage two. In 1998, the Government responded to the criticism by announcing the appointment of a Royal Commission on Reform of the House of Lords. In January 1999, the Government published a White Paper outlining the options for reform and in February the members of the Royal Commission were announced. The terms of reference for the Commission were:

Having regard to the need to maintain the position of the House of Commons as the pre-eminent chamber of Parliament and taking particular account of the present nature of the constitutional settlement, including the newly devolved institutions, the impact of the Human Rights Act and developing relations with the European Union:

- To consider and make recommendations on the role and functions of a second chamber;
- To make recommendations on the method or combination of methods of composition required to constitute a second chamber fit for that role and those functions;
- To report by 31 December 1999.

The Commission, chaired by a Conservative peer, Lord Wakeham (a former Leader of both the House of Commons and the House of Lords), began taking

BOX 18.1

fact

The Wakeham Report

The proposals

A NEW House of Lords of around 550 members, a minority of them elected from the regions and most of the rest chosen by a powerful quango, is proposed by Lord Wakeham's Royal Commission on the Reform of the House of Lords, which reported yesterday.

Under the proposals of the year-long inquiry, a new independent Appointments Commission would have massive powers to determine the make-up of the second chamber. It would be required to reflect the balance of political opinion across the UK but with no one party having an overall majority.

It would be responsible for ensuring that around 20 per cent of the new House are independent crossbenchers and that the second chamber, of which the clear majority would be unelected, should proportionately reflect votes cast at the previous general election.

The report, *A House for the Future*, makes no recommendations on what the new House or its members should be called. The commission said the issue 'should be left to evolve'.

Elections

The commission put forward three options for the choice of the elected regional members, designed to ensure that they reflected the balance of political opinion within the regions in order to provide a voice for the nations and regions of the United Kingdom.

But it erred towards its Model B option under which there would be a total of 87 regional members, directly elected at the time of each European Parliament election. They would be picked under the regional list proportional representation system.

Under a minimalist Model A option, a total of only 65 regional members would be selected from a proportional 'reading off' from votes cast at the general election.

And under a Model C option, which would achieve the highest degree of election and is unlikely to be backed by the Government, there would be a total of 195 regional members, elected by PR at the time of each European Parliament election.

Under options B and C a third of the regions would choose their regional members at each European election.

It was proposed that the regional members – whatever their number and method of selection – should serve for the equivalent of three electoral cycles and that the appointed members should serve for fixed terms of 15 years.

Both elected and directly appointed members should be eligible for reappointment for further periods of up to 15 years, but members of the reformed second chamber should not be eligible for election to the Commons until ten years after their term of membership ends.

Appointments

The Appointments Commission would have the task of selecting appointees affiliated to political parties, taking account of the nominations made by the parties but vetting their propriety.

It will also be under a duty to ensure that a minimum of 30 per cent of the new members should be women with the aim of making steady progress towards gender balance over time. It should ensure that the ethnic minorities are represented at least in proportion to their level in the population as a whole.

Existing life peers who wish to do so will be able to become members of the new second chamber, but in order to keep numbers down they will be able to renounce their right to sit and vote once they no longer wish to contribute.

BOX 18.1 continued

The commission says that the Prime Minister should no longer have any control over the size, balance and individual membership of the second chamber and there should be no more party patronage.

It sets its role as to 'ensure that the chamber is broadly representative of British society'.

The commission, anticipating criticism that its report was conservative, said it was determined to make recommendations that were not only 'persuasive and intellectually coherent but also workable, durable and politically realistic'.

The long-awaited document said the proposals 'represent a significant change from what has gone before. No new member of the second chamber will arrive there on the same basis as any existing member of the House of Lords.

'No new member of the second chamber will get there via an Honours List. The new second chamber will be more democratic and representative than the present House of Lords.

'The chamber as a whole will reflect the overall balance of political opinion within the country. Regional members will directly reflect the balance of political opinion within the regions.

'The chamber will contain members from all parts of the country and from all walks of life, broadly equal numbers of men and women and representatives of all the country's main ethnic and religious communities.'

Powers

The commission suggests no radical change in the balance of power between the Commons and the second chamber. It says that the latter should retain the 'suspensory veto' under the Parliament Acts which allows it to delay the enactment of a Bill but not to prevent the passage of a Commons Bill which has been supported in two successive sessions.

It adds that the second chamber should respect the governing party's general election manifesto and be cautious about challenging the clearly expressed views of MPs on public policy.

The Lords would have greater powers over delaying and voicing its concerns over statutory instruments. It suggests an enhancement of its role of guarding the constitution by setting up a constitutional committee to scrutinise the implications of all legislation.

There should also be a human rights committee to look at all Bills.

Under further moves to boost the authority of the second House, the commission suggests that senior Commons ministers should make occasional statements and take questions in an appropriate second chamber committee.

Law lords would continue to sit in the second chamber.

There should be a review of the current system of paying expenses with modest payment linked to attendance in the new chamber introduced.

Bishops

The Church of England should continue to be explicitly represented by the bishops, but other Christian denominations and other faiths should also be embraced. There should be at least five members of the second chamber specifically selected to represent non-Christian faith communities.

The Christian denominations in England should take 21 places, 16 for the Church of England bishops and five to members of other Christian denominations.

Roles

The commission said that the roles of the new House should be fourfold:

- Bringing different perspectives to bear on the development of public policy;

BOX 18.1 continued

- Giving a voice in Parliament for all parts of British society;
- Continuing to play a vital role as one of the checks and balances within the unwritten British constitution;
- Providing a voice for the nations and regions of the UK at the centre of public affairs. It said the new chamber should be authoritative, confident, and broadly representative of the whole of British society, and its members should have a breadth of experience outside the world of politics, skills and knowledge relevant to the careful assessment of constitutional matters and human rights issues, the ability to bring a 'philosophical, moral or spiritual perspective' to bear, personal distinction, freedom from party domination, a 'non-polemical and courteous style' and the ability to take a long-term view.

'A new second chamber with these characteristics should remedy some of the deficiency of the old House of Lords, which lacked the political legitimacy and confidence to do its job properly, while preserving some of its best features.'

The report suggested that the Commons would remain the 'principal political forum' and have the final say on all major public policy issues.

The commission accepted that the new appointments body would act to maintain the political balance after general elections.

Life peers

The commission ruled out any question of removing the existing 500-plus life peers.

Such a move would require retrospective legislation and the need to replace them would put an enormous and probably insupportable burden on the new Appointments Commission. 'Not least such a course of action would maximise and also greatly prolong the uncertainty about its future that is already a problem for the existing House of Lords.

'If we recommended the removal of all the life peers, and given that the relevant legislation is unlikely to come into force until 2002 or 2003 at the earliest, we would be creating a situation in which every individual life peer, uncertain about his or her future, would be a lame duck for a number of years to come and in which, worse, the whole House of Lords would come to be seen, and come to see itself, as a lame-duck chamber.'

Those life peers created before the publication of the report who wished to take up the opportunity should be deemed to have been appointed to the reformed second chamber for life.

Those created between the publication of the report and the implementation of the second stage reform should be deemed to have been appointed to the reformed chamber for a period totalling 15 years.

Honours

The commission said that possession of a peerage should no longer be a necessary qualification for membership of the second chamber. New members should not be offered a peerage.

All members would be chosen on the basis of the contribution they could make to the second chamber, not as a reward or mark of approval for past achievements.

'Many life peers treat their peerages as essentially honorary and do not acknowledge any associated public service obligation to participate in the work of the second chamber.

'It is already the case that most hereditary peers are no longer members of the second chamber. It would be anachronistic and confusing to perpetuate the automatic link between membership of the second chamber and the possession of a peerage.'

Twice-yearly honours lists would continue.

Source: A fair reflection of British Society, Philip Webster, The Times evidence in March in order to complete its report by the end of 1999 (it reported in January 2000). It held a number of meetings in different parts of the country, culminating in a final session in London at the end of July, a session notable because it involved the Commission taking evidence not only from a number of politicians and academics, including this writer, but also from the singer Billy Bragg. (The evidence appears on the Royal Commission's website.) It was thus considering what should happen to the House of Lords at stage two at the very time that the House of Lords was discussing the Government's legislation for stage one.

In its report, the Royal Commission for a part elected chamber, identifying three options (Box 18.1). Given the time that it would then take to prepare legislation, assuming agreement was reached on one of these options, it was widely accepted that no bill to give effect to stage two reform would be introduced in that Parliament. Various participants in debate on the future of the House noted that the House of Lords that followed the Parliament Act of 1911 was intended as an interim House, until legislation could be passed to provide for a more democratic chamber. That interim House lasted for nearly ninety years. Some wondered whether the interim House that existed following the passage of the House of Lords Act might not last a similar period of time.

The future of the second chamber?

The question of what to do with the House of Lords has thus been a notable item on the political agenda. Given that the removal of hereditary peers from membership of the House was intended as the first stage in a two-stage process, the future shape of the House remains a matter of debate. What are the options?

In the period leading up to the reform of the House in 1999, four approaches to reform were identified (Norton, 1982, pp. 119–29). These were known as the four Rs – retain, reform, replace or remove altogether. With some adaptation, they remain the four approaches following the passage of the House of Lords Act.

Retain

This approach favours retaining the House as a non-elected chamber. It argues that the interim House, comprising predominantly life peers, is preferable to an elected or part-elected chamber. The House, it is argued, does a good job. It complements the elected House in that it carries out tasks that are qualitatively different to those of the House of Commons. It is able to do so because its members provide a degree of expertise and experience that are lacking in the House of Commons. By retaining a House of life peers one not only creates a body of knowledge and experience, one also creates a body with some degree of independence. The cross-benchers in the House hold the balance of power and are able to judge matters with some degree of detachment. If the House was elected, it would have the same claim to democratic legitimacy as the Commons and would either be the same as the Commons – thus constituting a rubber-stamping body and achieving nothing – or, if elected by a different method or at different times, would have the potential to clash with the Commons and create stalemate in the political system. Election would challenge, not enhance, the basic accountability of the political system. Who would electors hold accountable if two elected chambers failed to reach agreement?

This approach was taken by some of those giving evidence to the Royal Commission on Reform of the House of Lords. They included this writer (Norton, 1999). Another prominent supporter was a former Chancellor of the Exchequer, Foreign Secretary and Deputy Prime Minister, Geoffrey Howe (Lord Howe of Aberavon). Having initially reluctantly conceded there could be an elected element, he changed his mind and wrote in support of the stance taken by this writer (see Howe, 1999).

Reform

This approach, advocated by the Royal Commission favours some modification to the interim House, though retaining what are seen as the essential strengths of the existing House. It acknowledges the value of having a membership that is expert and one that has a degree of independence of government. At the same time, it argues that a wholly appointed chamber lacks democratic legitimacy. Therefore it favours a mix of appointed and elected members. The advantages of such a system were touched on in the Government's 1998 White Paper, *Modernising Parliament* (pp. 49–50): 'It would combine some of the most valued features of the present House of Lords with a democratic basis suitable for a modern legislative chamber.' The extent of the mix of nominated and elected members is a matter of some debate. Some would like to see a small portion of members – about one-third – elected. This was one of the options advanced by a Conservative Commission, chaired by a former Lord Chancellor, Lord Mackay of Clashfern. One report from another Conservative body, chaired by former Prime Minister Lord Home, recommended as far back as 1977 that two-thirds be elected. The Royal Commissions report errs in favour of a minority of elected members. Some reformers favour an indirect form of election, members serving by virtue of election by an electoral college comprising, say, members of local authorities or other assemblies.

Replace

This approach favours doing away with the House of Lords and replacing it with a new second chamber. Some wish to replace it with a wholly elected house. Election, it is contended, would give the House a legitimacy that a nominated chamber, or even a part-elected chamber, lacks (see Box 18.2). That greater legitimacy would allow the House to serve as a more effective check on government, knowing that it was not open to accusations of being undemocratic. It would have the teeth that the House of Lords lacks. Government can ignore the House of Lords: it could not ignore

BOX 18.2 DEBATE

An elected second chamber

Case for:

- Democratic – allows voters to choose members of the chamber.
- Provides a limit on the powers of the first chamber.
- Provides an additional limit on the powers of Government.
- Gives citizens an additional channel for seeking a redress of grievance or a change of public policy.
- Can be used to provide for representation of the different parts of the United Kingdom.
- Confers popular legitimacy on the chamber.

Case against:

- Rids the second chamber of the expertise and the experience provided by life peers in the House of Lords.
- Undermines accountability – who should electors hold accountable if second chamber disagrees with the first?
- Superfluous if dominated by the same party that has a majority in the first chamber.
- Objectionable if it runs into frequent conflict with the popularly elected first chamber.
- Will not be socially representative – election tends to favour white, middle-aged and male candidates.
- May prevent the elected government from being able to implement its manifesto commitments.
- Legitimacy of the political process will be threatened if conflict between the two chambers produces stalemate or unpopular compromise policies.

an elected second chamber. If members were elected on a national and regional basis, this – it is argued – would allow the different parts of the United Kingdom (Scotland, Wales, Northern Ireland and the English regions) to have a more distinct voice in the political process. As we have seen, this stance is taken by a number of organisations, including the Liberal Democrats and Charter '88. Both favour an elected Senate. It is also the stance taken by a former Labour Leader of the House of Lords, Lord Richard (see Richard and Welfare, 1999).

Others who favour doing away with the House of Lords want to replace it not with an elected chamber but with a chamber composed of representatives of different organised interests – a **functional chamber**. This, it is claimed, would ensure that the different groups in society – trade unions, charities, industry, consumer bodies – had a direct input into the political process, instead of having to lobby MPs and peers in the hope of getting a hearing. The problem with this proposal is that it would prove difficult to agree on which groups should enjoy representation in the House. Defenders of the existing House point out that there is extensive *de facto* functional representation in any event, with leading figures in a great many groups having been ennobled.

There is also a third variation. Anthony Barnett and Peter Carty, of the think tank Demos, have made the case for a second chamber chosen in part by lot (see also Barnett, 1997). In evidence to the Royal Commission in 1999, they argued that people chosen randomly would be able to bring an independent view. 'We want "People's Peers" but they must come from the people and not be chosen from above, by an official body. It is possible to have a strong non-partisan element in the Second Chamber, and for this to be and to be seen to be democratic and lively'. The principle of public participation, they argued, should be extended to the national legislature.

Remove altogether

Under this approach, the House of Lords would be abolished and not replaced at all. Instead, the UK would have a **unicameral legislature**, the legislative burden being shouldered by a reformed House of Commons. Supporters of this approach argue that there is no case for an unelected second chamber, since it has no legitimacy to challenge an elected chamber, and that there is no case for an elected second chamber, since this would result in either imitation or conflict. Parliament should therefore constitute a single chamber, like legislatures in Scandinavia and New Zealand. The House of Commons should be reformed in order that it may fulfil all the functions presently carried out by the two chambers.

Opponents of this approach argue that a single chamber would not be able to carry the burden, not least given the volume of public business in a country with a population of 57 million, many times larger than New Zealand and the Scandinavian countries with unicameral legislatures. Furthermore, they contend, the House of Commons could not fulfil the task of a constitutional safeguard, since it would essentially be acting as a safeguard against itself. Nor would it be an appropriate body to undertake a second look at legislation since it would not be able to bring to bear a different point of view and different experience to that brought to bear the first time round.

Although abolition has on occasion attracted some support – including, as we have seen, at one point from the Labour Party – it is not an approach that has made much of the running in recent debate. In various MORI opinion polls, it was the least favoured option. In October 1998, 24 per cent wanted to replace the House with a new second chamber elected by the public, 23 per cent wanted to replace it with a part-elected, part-nominated chamber, 20 per cent of respondents wanted to leave the House as it was (with the passage of the 1999 Act their preferred option fell by the way), 13 per cent favoured removing hereditary peers and having new peers nominated by Government and only 12 per cent favoured abolition (MORI, *British Public Opinion*, November 1998). The principal options in terms of the contemporary debate are those of retain, reform or replace. Each, as we have seen, has its proponents. The arguments for and against an elected chamber are considered in Box 18.2. The battle to determine the future shape of the second chamber has not yet been won.

Chapter summary

The House of Lords serves as a notable body of scrutiny – both of legislation and of public policy – and as a body for giving expression to views that otherwise would not be put on the public record. As such, it adds value to the political process. The fact that it is not elected means that it has limited significance as a body for legitimising government and measures of public policy and as a body through which politicians are recruited to ministerial office. The fact that it is not elected also makes it a target of continuing demands for reform.

The question of what to do with the House of Lords has been a matter of debate for more than a century. The election of a Labour Government in 1997, committed to reform of the House, brought it to the forefront of debate. The removal in 1999 of most hereditary peers from membership changed fundamentally the composition of the House. It became a chamber composed overwhelmingly of life peers. For some, that was a perfectly acceptable chamber. For others, it was not. The House of Lords serves not only as a forum to discuss political issues. It is itself a political issue. That is likely to remain the case for some time.

BOX 18.3 **IDEAS AND PERSPECTIVES**

The atmosphere in the House

The House of Lords is stunning in its grandeur. For some, it is awe inspiring. For others, it is suffocating. The House combines crown, church and a chamber of the legislature. The magnificent throne dominates the chamber. On entering the chamber, a peer bows to the cloth of estate – just above the throne – as a mark of respect. (Unlike the Commons, there is no bowing when leaving the chamber.) Look up and you see the magnificent stained glass windows. Look down and you see the red benches of a debating chamber. The House combines symbolism with the efficiency of a working body. From the bar of the House you see the throne: lower your eye-line and you see the laptop computer on the Table of the House. The Clerks sit in their wigs and gowns, using the laptop as well as controlling the button for re-setting the digital clocks in the chamber.

On Mondays to Thursdays, the benches are usually packed for the start of business. You have to get in early to get a seat. (Unlike the Commons, one cannot reserve a seat in advance.) The Lord Chancellor's procession mirrors that of the Speaker of the House of Commons in its pomp and dignity. Peers bow as the mace passes. Once the Lord Chancellor has taken his place on the Woolsack, prayers are said. Once these are over, members of the public are admitted to the gallery and other peers come in to the chamber. The Clerk of the Parliaments, sitting bewigged at the Table, rises and announces the name of the peer who has the first question on the Order Paper. The peer rises and declares, 'I beg leave to ask the question standing in my name on the Order Paper'. The answering minister rises to the dispatch box and reads out a prepared response. The peer rises to put a supplementary, followed later by others. If two peers rise at the same time, one is expected to give way; otherwise, as a self-regulating chamber, it is members who decide – usually by calling out the name of the peer they wish to hear, or else by shouting 'this side', indicating that the last supplementary was put by someone on the other side of the House. If neither gives way, the Leader of the House usually intervenes, but the Leader can be overruled by the House. Normally, good manners prevail.

Peers take a lively interest in questions. No more than four appear on the Order Paper each day. (None is taken if there is a Friday sitting.) There is a maximum of thirty minutes for them. This allows roughly seven or eight minutes a question. If time on a question goes beyond that, peers shout 'next question'.

BOX 18.3 continued

Ministers need to be well briefed. It is usually obvious when ministers are out of their depth or have been caught out. Question Time can be educational. The topics are diverse and there is knowledge on the part usually of questioners and ministers. If a minister runs into trouble, the fact that the chamber is packed adds to the tension. Question Time can also be funny. When a minister, questioned about the use of mobile 'phones on aeroplanes, faced a supplementary about the perils of mobile telephones 'on *terra firma*', he did not hear the full supplementary and had to ask a colleague. Realising he had taken some time to return to the dispatch box, he rose and said: 'I am sorry My Lords, I thought *terra firma* might be some obscure airline!' On another occasion, a question about the safety of a chimpanzee that had been mistreated received a very detailed answer, which included the facts – as I recall – that the chimp was now in a sanctuary with other chimps, that the group was led by a male of a certain age and that the chimp was enjoying herself. Whereupon the redoubtable Baroness Trumpington got to her feet and declared: 'My Lords, she is better off than I am!'

The House of Lords is a remarkably egalitarian institution: members are peers in the true sense. The atmosphere of the House can be tense, sometimes exciting – the results of votes are sometimes uncertain – and occasionally a little rough. Most of the time it has the feel of what it is: a working body, engaged in debate and legislative scrutiny. The emphasis is on constructive debate and revision. Partisan slanging matches are rare. The quality of ministers can be very good. Ministers who are well regarded and who take the House seriously can rely on the occasional indulgence of the House if they make a slip. The responsibilities of some ministers mean that they spend a great deal of time in the chamber. In 1998 and 1999, the nature of the bills going through the House meant that two of the most frequent performers were also two of the most senior ministers – the Lord Chancellor, Lord Irvine, and Deputy Leader of the House and Home Office Minister, Lord Williams of Mostyn. In 1999, Lord Williams was appointed Attorney General, the first time in 400 years that the post had gone to a peer.

The only way to appreciate the atmosphere, and the productive nature of the House, is to be there. One certainly cannot glean it from television – the House is squeezed out by the Commons – nor from the Official Report. *Hansard* is good at tidying up speeches, correcting grammar and titles. The tidying up can also have the effect of sanitizing proceedings. During the passage of the Access to Justice Bill, Conservative Baroness Wilcox – a champion of consumers – moved an amendment dealing with consumer affairs. The Lord Chancellor, to the delight – and obvious surprise – of Lady Wilcox promptly accepted the import of the amendment. Lady Wilcox rose and exclaimed 'Gosh. Thanks'. This appeared in *Hansard* as 'I thank the noble and learned Lord. He has pleased me very much today'! When the House collapses in laughter – as it did after the minister's *terra firma* remark or Baroness Trumpington's intervention – this either appears in *Hansard* as 'Noble Lords: Oh!' or else is ignored. No, one definitely has to be there to appreciate the atmosphere.

Discussion points

- What are the principal functions of the House of Lords?
- Does the House of Lords do a better job than the House of Commons in scrutinising government legislation? If so, why?
- Should the institutions of the European Union pay attention to the House of Lords?
- Was the Government right to get rid of most hereditary peers from membership of the House of Lords? Should it have got rid of all of them?
- What would you do with the House of Lords – and why?

Further reading

The main works on the pre-reform House of Lords are the second edition of Shell (1992), the edited volume by Shell and Beamish (1993), providing a thorough analysis of the House in one particular session (that of 1988–9); and the work edited by Dickson and Carmichael (1999), providing useful material on the House in both its political and judicial roles. Shell also provides a useful chapter on questions in the Lords in Franklin and Norton (1993) and, more generally on the role of the House, in Patterson and Mughan (1999).

On Lords reform, see Kent (1998), Tyrie (1998), the Government White Paper, *Modernising Parliament* (1999), *The Report of the Constitutional Commission on options for a new Second Chamber* (Constitutional Commission, 1999); Richard and Welfare (1999) Norton (1999) and the Report of the Royal Commission on the Reform of the House of Lords, *A House for the Future* (2000). There is also valuable material on the websites of the Royal Commission and Parliament. Through the Parliament website, one can also read debates in the two Houses on the House of Lords Bill.

References

Baldwin, N. (1985) 'The House of Lords: behavioural changes', in P. Norton (ed.), *Parliament in the 1980s* (Blackwell).

Baldwin, N. (1999) 'The membership and work of the House of Lords', in B. Dickson and P. Carmichael (eds), *The House of Lords: Its Parliamentary and Judicial Roles* (Hart Publishing).

Barnett, A. (1997) *This Time: Our Constitutional Revolution* (Vintage).

Constitution Unit (1996) *Reform of the House of Lords* (The Constitution Unit).

Constitutional Commission (1999) *The Report of the Constitutional Commission on Options for a new Second Chamber* (Constitutional Commission).

Dickson, B. and Carmichael, P. (eds) (1999) *The House of Lords: Its Parliamentary and Judicial Roles* (Hart Publishing).

Drewry, G. and Brock, J. (1993) 'Government legislation: an overview', in D. Shell and D. Beamish (eds), *The House of Lords at Work* (Oxford University Press).

Franklin, M. and Norton, P. (eds) (1993) *Parliamentary Questions* (Oxford University Press).

Grantham, C. (1993) 'Select committees', in D. Shell and D. Beamish (eds), *The House of Lords at Work* (Oxford University Press).

Hayter, P.D.G. (1992) 'The parliamentary monitoring of science and technology', *Government and Opposition*, Vol. 26.

Himsworth, C.M.G. (1995) 'The Delegated Powers Scrutiny Committee', *Public Law*, Spring.

Howe of Aberavon, Lord (1999) 'This House is built on solid ground', *The Times*, 2 August.

Kent, N. (1998) *Enhancing Our Democracy* (Tory Reform Group).

Modernising Parliament: Reforming the House of Lords (1999) Cm 4183 (Stationery Office).

Norton, P. (1982) *The Constitution in Flux* (Basil Blackwell).

Norton, P. (1993) *Does Parliament Matter?* (Harvester Wheatsheaf).

Norton, P. (ed.) (1996) *National Parliaments and the European Union* (Frank Cass).

Norton, P. (1999) 'Adding value to the political system', submission to the Royal Commission on the House of Lords.

Patterson, S.C. and Mughan, A. (eds) (1999) *Senates: Bicameralism in the Contemporary World* (Ohio State University Press).

Richard, Lord and Welfare D. (1999) *Unfinished Business: Reforming the House of Lords* (Vintage).

Royal Commission on the Reform of the House of Lords (2000) *A House for the Future*, Cm. 4534 (Stationary Office).

Rush, M. (ed.) (1990) *Parliament and Pressure Politics* (Clarendon Press).

Shell, D. (1983) 'The House of Lords', in D. Judge (ed.), *The Politics of Parliamentary Reform* (Heinemann).

Shell, D. (1992) *The House of Lords*, 2nd edn (Harvester Wheatsheaf).

Shell, D. and Beamish, D. (eds) (1993) *The House of Lords at Work* (Oxford University Press).

Tyrie, A. (1998) *Reforming the Lords: a Conservative Approach* (Conservative Policy Forum).

White, A.B. (1908) *The Making of the English Constitution 1449–1485* (G.P. Putnam).

Concluding comment

Constitutional reform

Simon Heffer

No government in modern times has ever been elected with such a commitment to reforming the constitution as the Labour administration that won office in May 1997. Within months of its election Scotland and Wales were on the road to devolution. Within a year, though in a very different context, the framework had been set for a devolved, power-sharing government in Northern Ireland. A year after that the process was well under way for reform of the House of Lords, eliminating, in the first instance, peers whose place in the legislature was by inheritance. In May 2000 London elects its first mayor. All in all, it would seem the government can boast of achievements in constitutional reform that far exceed anything accomplished by its recent predecessors, and which amount to the upholding of promises made at the time of the general election.

But how far are these things achievements? How far do they keep promises made at the election? And, above all, how far have they led to the better governance of Britain, and have they been a good use of legislative time and taxpayers' money that might have been better deployed?

Let us start with devolution. In Scotland, the feeling of alienation after years of what was perceived as rule by English conservatives made the result of the devolution referendum in September 1997 a foregone conclusion. Labour's main concern was to win the ensuing election for the Scottish parliament in May 1999, which it did by a less comfortable margin than expected, and to ensure a relatively obedient administration in Edinburgh. This proved more problematical. Labour could only govern with the help of the Liberal Democrats, and it turned out to be a coalition that damaged both parties in terms of their popular support. The Hamilton by-election of September 1999 was only narrowly won by Labour after a surge in support for the Scottish National Party, and the Lib Dems came a poor sixth. Former Labour supporters saw their party still taking orders from London; former Lib Dems felt their party was colluding too openly in this compliant government, and there was particular anger about the Lib Dems' failure to stand on the point of principle of opposing tuition fees in Scottish universities.

Wales's experience echoed some of these tensions. First, there was anger that the leader of the Labour group and eventual first minister, Alun Michael, was imposed so forcefully by the party's headquarters in London. Before things had even reached that stage, however, a dismal turnout of barely 50 per cent in the original referendum suggested that the people of Wales were not nearly so interested in devolution as the political class – its most obvious beneficiaries – were. Devolution proceeded on the wishes of about 26 per cent of the Welsh population. Plaid Cymru – which suffixed its name with the title 'the Party of Wales' before the 1999 election in order to widen its appeal to non-Welsh speakers – did far better in that election than anyone had predicted.

In both Scotland and Wales, the warnings voiced before the event by anti-devolutionists seemed, in the first instance, to be coming true. They argued that devolution would not be an end in itself, but a vehicle through which nationalist or separatist groups could achieve the break-up of the United Kingdom. Devolution has given the SNP and PC voices and influence they could never have dreamt of under the Westminster system. Differences of opinion between the respective parts of the Kingdom – such as over whether to lift the ban on beef on the bone in September 1999 – have added to cries that the English have been disadvantaged by devolution (an issue on which they were never directly consulted), and that the United Kingdom is fragmenting.

Only time will tell whether this is really so. However, the immediate perception is that this extra layer of Government has so far achieved little except enrich the politicians who serve in it. The English taxpayer is subsidising the exercise and nothing has yet been done to correct constitutional imbalances. Matters on which the English have no say in Scotland are matters on which Scottish MPs at Westminster have a say when they concern the English. Scotland is still over-represented at Westminster. Despite the establishment of administrations in Wales and Scotland, there are still Secretaries of State and junior ministers for those parts of the Kingdom in London. The British cabinet is one-third Scottish. It seems as though one set of constitutional injustices – if, indeed, that is really what the old system amounted to – has merely been replaced by another, though the replacement is one in which the rights of majorities no longer (unlike in most democracies) count for anything.

House of Lords reform is similarly suspect. First, the programme was embarked upon without any real evidence that the public wanted it. Labour argued that it was being obstructed in the Lords: but, in fact, the Conservative majority there operated the Salisbury–Addison convention, whereby the majority agreed not to defeat the minority on matters that were manifesto commitments and which therefore had democratic legitimacy. Also, when Labour was defeated on other issues it was often because of its whips' failure to get the party's vote out: many of the vast quantity of peers created to sit on the Labour benches since the victory in May 1997 felt their attendance at the Lords was optional. In the last resort, Labour can always threaten to use the Parliament Acts to force through any legislation the peers obstruct: but that has not been necessary.

The Prime Minister decided to proceed with an interim reform of the Lords, which in the first instance was to include the abolition of the voting rights of hereditary peers. However, this seemingly inflexible principle was soon diluted when it became clear to the Prime Minister that he did not really want a more thorough reform, such as an elected second chamber whose democratic legitimacy would challenge the authority of the House of Commons. So a deal was struck with the Conservatives, who were allowed the retention of ninety-two hereditary peers of all parties to maintain an element in the upper house that was not dependent on recent patronage. The Prime Minister also appointed a Royal Commission on the Lords, under former Conservative cabinet minister Lord Wakeham, which was due to report by the end of 1999. The word was, however, the Prime Minister was more than happy with the so-called interim solution; and by late 1999 nobody was found to entertain particularly high hopes of the findings of the Royal Commission.

This was similar to another, even less fruitful, exercise in constitutional reform: the commission under Lord Jenkins of Hillhead that investigated the possibilities of introducing proportional representation for Westminster elections. This was consigned straight to the wastepaper basket. The only hope of PR is that it might, in return for a promise of good behaviour from the Liberal Democrats, be introduced into local government elections. What it and the semi-abortive reform of the Lords both show is the determination politicians in power have to hold on to that power. Mr Blair will not introduce PR because it means his party will never govern on its own again. He will not allow his huge majority to support the creation of an elected House of Lords because his authority as a Prime Minister sitting in the House of Commons, and indeed the will of that whole House which is at present obedient to him, would be compromised.

The Government has, indeed, only advanced such constitutional reforms as it believes will not compromise it. On the devolution issue, this was classically hubristic. In the immediate aftermath of the 1997 election the party was so popular that it could not believe but that it would take power in Scotland and Wales and hold it indefinitely. The actual elections, two years later, presented a very different picture. It was an obvious case of failing to think through the consequences of change: a failure by Labour to see that the power it enjoyed, and wished to continue enjoying, was dependent to a large extent on the very institutions it now set about dismantling. If it has since been more cautious with the Lords and with the electoral system, it is largely down to the spectre of the SNP and PC, and what they now threaten to do in Scotland and Wales.

Unsurprisingly, the party that now expresses the greatest enthusiasm for radical constitutional change – English regional government, elected mayors, proportional representation, an elected second chamber and an unspecified reduction in the few remaining powers of the monarch – is the Liberal Democrats, who have no realistic chance of forming a government. The Conservative Party, which despite being so against constitutional change has engineered more than its share of it over the years (such as the peerage reforms of 1958 and 1963, and the 1972 European Communities Act), merely carps from the sidelines, an attitude that perhaps also reflects the unlikelihood of its being asked to govern Britain in the foreseeable future. So, it seems we are to have a government for some years to come that has had more than its fill of constitutional change in the early stages of its existence, has started to feel ill as a result, and will in future look to spend its legislative time dealing with issues that, unlike the existence of the House of Lords, really do upset the mass of the British people. They will also, and not entirely coincidentally, be issues that do much to help ensure the re-election of the Labour government.

Part 5 The executive process

Chapter 19

The Cabinet and Prime Minister

Dennis Kavanagh

Learning objectives

- To provide a full analysis of the role of Prime Minister.
- To assess the importance of Tony Blair's premiership.
- To examine the role of Cabinet ministers.
- To evaluate the possibilities for reform at the centre of British government.

Introduction

This chapter examines the work of the Prime Minister and Cabinet. It examines the role and powers of the Prime Minister and the structure of the office, and assesses the impact of John Major and Tony Blair on the office. It discusses the factors which influence Cabinet's size and composition, then analyses the structure of the Cabinet and its committees and evaluates proposals for improving the co-ordination of policies. The Cabinet system, like much of the political system, has been subject to much discussion in recent years. The final section reviews some of these criticisms and suggestions which have been made for reform.

There is no constitutional definition of a Prime Minister's role. The first statutory reference to the office of the Prime Minister was as recent as 1937. Much of the job is actually what he or she chooses to do. Once allowance is made for variations of circumstances and personality, it is very difficult to generalise about the office. Personality alone does not explain Blair's dominance and Major's weaknesses. In 2000 Blair has a 179 seat majority, record high popularity with the public, the most united and faction-free Labour Party in memory and has no opposition worth speaking of. Contrast any of those features with John Major's lot!

The powers of the Prime Minister are well known. But they are subject to constraints. Timing a dissolution of Parliament is obviously a political advantage. But if the premier gets it wrong, in the sense of losing – as in 1970, February 1974, 1979 and 1997 – he usually pays a heavy personal price. The power to hire and fire ministers is also subject to limits. A Prime Minister risks making enemies if he wields the axe too often. Blair used the 1998 reshuffle to reduce the number of supporters of Gordon Brown in government and in 1999 to place his own 'modernising' ministers alongside John Prescott. But the reshuffle in summer 1999 was more modest than originally designed, largely because of the reluctance of key ministers to move.

We often classify Prime Ministers as 'strong' and 'weak'. Strong leaders usually fall spectacularly. When the Conservative Party withdrew from Lloyd George's coalition in 1922 he immediately resigned and was never a serious force again. Margaret Thatcher was humiliated when nearly 40 per cent of Conservative MPs refused to vote for her in the leadership election in 1990. In each case it was the failure to retain the support of MPs, rather than that of the electorate, that proved decisive. The election defeats of 'lesser' Prime Ministers such as Callaghan, Heath and Major, or the retirements of Wilson and Eden are less traumatic. The British system, with the high place it has accorded to Cabinet and the party in parliament, has not been kind to strong Prime Ministers. Yet it is the latter who leave their mark on history.

Ever since Walter Bagehot's *English Constitution* (1865), comparisons have been drawn between the US presidential and British **Cabinet** systems. Increasingly, British politics is allegedly becoming 'Americanised' and the Prime Minister compared to the President. In fact the analogy is not useful because of significant constitutional and political differences between the two countries. A Prime Minister may wish for the direct popular mandate that a President has, but Clinton can only envy Blair's huge parliamentary majority.

There is an ebb and flow in the analysis and perceptions of the premiership. For most of the time a Prime Minister is seen as dominant because the Cabinet is weak and vice versa. Power is seen in zero sum terms. When Mrs Thatcher fell and was replaced by the more collegial John Major, the Cabinet was temporarily restored as a body of influence. After the exit from the ERM in September 1992 Major's fear of divisions and 'leaks' made him reluctant to trust Cabinet. Under Blair it has remained marginal.

If an old school of analysis gives pride of place to Cabinet, a new one argues that resources are dispersed between the Prime Minister and ministers. They can check each other and the exercise of power over time requires them to bargain and co-operate. A minister pushing a policy requires a Prime Minister's support, not least in Cabinet and in battles with the Treasury. Deals between a Prime Minister and a Cabinet minister are quite difficult for other ministers to overturn. But a Prime Minister also has to beware of pushing a minister so far that he resigns (Geoffrey Howe's resignation proved fatal for Mrs Thatcher) and he also has to recognise the resources which reside in departments. It is easy to move from this approach to argue that departments rule. After all, they have the budgets, staff, expertise, policy networks and the Secretary of State has statutory powers. No. 10 can look threadbare in comparison.

The Prime Minister's roles

The Prime Minister has various roles in the British governmental system, which coincide to some extent with the administrative divisions of the No. 10 office (see Table 19.1):

Table 19.1 The Prime Minister's roles

Function	Supporting office
Head of the executive	Cabinet secretariat Private Office
Head of government policy	Policy Unit Press Office (communication)
Party leader	Political secretary (party outside Parliament) Parliamentary private secretary
Head appointing officer	Appointments secretary (crown appointments) Cabinet Secretary (senior civil service) Principal private secretary (ministers)
Leader of party in Parliament	Parliamentary private secretary Private secretary – parliamentary affairs
Senior British representative overseas	Cabinet Secretary (Commonwealth) Principal private secretary Private secretary – foreign affairs Cabinet Secretariat – EU affairs

1 *Head of the executive*: The Prime Minister is in charge of overseeing the civil service and government agencies, and is ultimately answerable for all its decisions.

2 *Head of government policy*: Though most policy is produced through the departments and the party's own policy-making apparatus, the Prime Minister has a key influence over the party's election manifesto and the annual Queen's Speech outlining government legislation for the coming year, and more generally can choose which policies he or she wishes to highlight or play down. Prime ministers traditionally are particularly influential in economic and foreign policy decisions.

3 *Party leader*: The Prime Minister is not only in organisational charge of the party as well as the government, but also the figure who personifies that party to the public at large.

4 *Head appointing officer*: For posts throughout the political and administrative executive branch, as well as the various appointing powers in the church and academe exercised on behalf of the monarch.

5 *Party leader in Parliament*: The Prime Minister is the principal figure in the House of Commons, above all in weekly Question Time when the Prime Minister's performance has the greatest effect on party morale and public perception, particularly since the televising of the Commons in 1989.

6 *Senior UK representative overseas*: Since the 1970s prime ministers have been involved in increasing amounts of travel and meetings with foreign heads of government. There are several regular engagements per year (the G7, UN and up to four European Councils) and several less frequent regular events such as the biannual Commonwealth Heads of Government Meeting as well as other less structured summits, most frequently with Ireland and the USA. In the first six months of 1999, Blair spent more time on Kosovo and Northern Ireland than on any domestic policy.

The Prime Minister

The Prime Minister's office in No. 10

No. 10 Downing Street, despite its modest outside appearance, is in fact a fair-sized office block, in which about 150 people, including secretaries and security staff, work. Its upper floors contain a private flat for the Prime Minister and his or her family, although some prime ministers, notably Wilson in 1974–6, chose to live elsewhere. Staff at No. 10 are grouped into several offices, each with a specialised function. The divide between 'political' and 'official' is a good way of analysing the Prime Minister's different staff.

Political No. 10 comprises the Policy Unit and the Political Office. To this could be added, from 1971 to 1983, the Central Policy Review Staff (CPRS, or 'think-tank'), which, while technically working for the Cabinet as a whole, had considerable direct dealings with the Prime Minister. The Policy Unit was created in 1974 as a more personal resource for the Prime Minister. It was felt that, lacking a department or a team of personal advisers, the Prime Minister needed help to take a strategic view of where the government as a whole was going. The first head of the Policy Unit was Bernard Donoughue, who served Labour prime ministers Wilson and Callaghan. New prime ministers appoint their own head of the Policy Unit, who becomes one of their closest advisers. The Policy Unit before Blair consisted of no more than eight appointees, a mix of secondment from the civil service and from party politics or business who are classified as temporary civil servants for their stay in the Unit. Different prime ministers have used the Policy Unit to a greater or lesser extent. Under John Major, Sarah Hogg (head of the Unit, 1990–5) gave key direction to government thinking. In 1990–2 it defined a distinctive agenda for Major's government and wrote the election manifesto. Blair has considerably strengthened his Unit. In 1999 it had thirteen members and is well placed to convey his views to departments and react to papers from them.

The Political Office deals with communication between the Prime Minister and the party organisation, both at the centre with party professionals and in dealing with correspondence and events of a party political nature. The political secretary also deals with ministerial special advisers and has a general remit to keep the party political wheels turning. The Political Office is paid for out of party rather than public funds. The first and most celebrated political secretary was Marcia Williams (1964–74 and 1974–6), who had influence on Harold Wilson was second to none. Douglas Hurd was an important political secretary to Heath (1970–4) though he had a considerably reduced role in comparison with Marcia Williams.

The Prime Minister, like other ministers, has a parliamentary private secretary (PPS) – an MP whose job it is to keep the Prime Minister in contact with back-bench opinion at Westminster. After 1994 John Major also had a PPS in the House of Lords. The PPS position is usually only of secondary importance, although some holders of the job have achieved positions of high influence, notably Ian Gow (1979–83) under Thatcher.

The official institutions of No. 10 are older than the political ones. The core of Downing Street is the Private Office, headed by the principal private secretary. This consists of civil servants usually in their forties, often the most impressive high fliers of their generation, on three-year loan from their departments. Because of the day-to-day contact with the Prime Minister, the job of principal private secretary is the third most influential in the civil service, after the head of the home civil service/Cabinet Secretary and permanent secretary to the Treasury. Recent influential incumbents have been, for Heath – Robert Armstrong (1970–4); for Major – Alex Allan (1992–7); and for Blair – Jeremy Heywood. There are in addition private secretaries for parliamentary affairs, home affairs, economic affairs, and three for foreign affairs. Within their remit, they handle all official papers destined for the Prime Minister from other government departments, foreign governments and others having official business. Private secretaries quickly learn how to regulate the flow of papers to the Prime Minister, and the best can second guess with great accuracy what interests the Prime Minister and what he or she will decide.

The Press Office regulates the Prime Minister's relations with journalists, including the broadcast media, and covers a range of concerns from issuing government statements to arranging interview appointments. A job of this kind has existed since 1931. In view of the growing media demands on the Prime Minister and a leadership's concern to 'manage' the media, the post is more important than ever. The job is a civil service post, usually filled from the professional press officers of the government information service, although different prime ministers and press secretaries have taken different approaches to the obvious political aspects of press relations. Some press secretaries have been drawn not from the civil service but from journalism (Joe Haines (1969–70 and 1974–6) under Harold Wilson, and Alastair Campbell (1997–) under Tony Blair). The most noted press secretary was Bernard Ingham (1979–90), who became heavily – too heavily in the eyes of some – politically identified with Thatcher. Campbell also helps with speech-writing, as did Haines. Interestingly, both were tabloid journalists before moving to No. 10. Campbell is also credited with strong influence on Blair over political tactics. Blair has also established a strategic communications unit to co-ordinate communications across department and whole policy and presentation.

The Appointments Office deals with the various Church of England, university and a whole range of other appointments outside politics for which the Prime Minister is responsible.

Prime ministers' styles

Prime ministers naturally bring their own personal contributions to the office, and have all demonstrated different approaches to policy, politics and relations with the Cabinet. It is a truism that each occupant is a different person, but the most important influences on the role and style of particular prime ministers are, however, contingent on factors subject to limited or no control from Downing Street. To an extent, the fluctuations in party support in interim elections (by-elections, European and local), in polls and approval rating for the Prime Minister also create conditions for weak or strong prime ministerial leadership. The state of the economy and a 'feel-good' mood among voters are key variable factors: if strong, the Prime Minister's position will be enhanced. As a general election draws near, the Cabinet and party usually rally to the Prime Minister, in the realisation that they will prosper or falter depending on how united they are behind the leadership. Prime ministers are constrained in their influence by other political factors – the extent of willing support that can be gathered from the Cabinet, the popularity of the parliamentary opposition, and the possibility that there are alternative leaders waiting in the wings.

Prime ministers may choose how to allocate their time and energy between the different duties outlined in Table 19.1. John Major's lack of a parliamentary majority for much of the 1992 parliament meant that he had to devote much time, along with his Chief Whip and leader of the House of Commons, to managing parliamentary business. Margaret Thatcher and Tony Blair were backed by large majorities and had no such worries. Tony Blair has taken his role as a spokesman for the philosophy of the government, particularly the ideas of New Labour and the Third Way, very seriously. Making speeches and writing for the press take a good deal of his time. Prime ministers may also choose which policy areas to concentrate on. Mrs Thatcher was famous for intervening across the board. But foreign affairs, notably Europe, and the economy are so central to the standing of the government as a whole that the Prime Minister has to take a close interest in them. He or she regularly answers for the government at Question Time in the House of Commons, in media interviews or in summits with leaders of other states. Mrs Thatcher was something of a warrior in her attack on institutions, some of which, like the BBC, Foreign Office, universities and Church of England, were identified with consensus politics. Tony Blair shows a similar impatience to Mrs Thatcher in his attitude to many institutions and practices. Unlike her, however, he has been more successful in reaching out across the political divide. He has given key jobs to Conservatives: Lord Wakeham chairs the Royal Commission on the House of Lords, Chris Patten has been appointed European Commissioner and Michael Heseltine is on a committee overseeing the work of the Dome. Blair has also invited the Liberal Democrats to join a cabinet committee.

Margaret Thatcher as Prime Minister

Margaret Thatcher proved to be the most dominant peacetime Prime Minister this century. She broke with a number of policies pursued by her Conservative predecessors and is credited with substantially changing the agenda of British politics.

Many of the policies are associated with her personally, including trade union reform, income tax cuts, privatisation and a reduced role for local government. She was forceful in Cabinet and in Parliament and willing to be seen as a figure apart from Cabinet which did not score high on collegiality. She kept a close rein on her Chancellors and her Foreign Secretaries and, as a result, had troubled relationships with some of them. By the end her hostile attitude to the European Community (as it then was called) lost her the support of a number of her senior ministers. Mrs Thatcher is an outstanding example of somebody who regarded herself as a conviction rather than a consensus politician. She must be regarded as a successful Prime Minister, in terms of winning three successive general elections and introducing lasting radical policies, many of which have been accepted by successors, including Tony Blair.

The reasons why Margaret Thatcher became more dominant provide important insights into the source of prime ministerial power. They include:

1. Her successful use of Cabinet reshuffles – or the power to hire and fire – over time to produce a more loyal team. She had originally appointed her supporters to the key economic departments in 1979. During 1981 she gradually dismissed a number of dissenters from her Cabinet, including Soames, Gilmour, Carlisle and St John-Stevas, and moved James Prior to the office of Northern Ireland. Later she dismissed Francis Pym from the Foreign Office and David Howell. She appointed newcomers such as Parkinson, Brittan, King, Lord Young and Lawson, who were more supportive of her policies and owed their promotion to her.
2. She gained from policy successes, particularly the down-turn in inflation in 1982 then, decisively, the recapture of the Falklands, the steady rise in the living standards of those in work and, of course, from general election victories in 1983 and 1987.
3. She simply held fewer Cabinet meetings. Ex-Defence Minister John Nott reckoned full Cabinet meetings were more often occasions when decisions reached elsewhere were formally endorsed.
4. She bypassed the Cabinet on occasions, relying heavily on her Policy Unit and making decisions in Cabinet committees, in bilateral meetings between herself and her advisers and the departmental minister or in high-powered inter-departmental task forces of able civil servants reporting direct to No. 10. Peter Hennessy described a typical example of this way of working:

   > Mrs Thatcher will ask a particular Cabinet colleague to prepare a paper on a particular issue just for her, not for the Cabinet or her Cabinet Committee. The Minister is summoned to Number Ten with his back-up team. He sits across the table from Mrs Thatcher and her team which can be a blend of people from the Downing Street Private Office, the Policy Unit, the Cabinet Office and one or two personal advisers. She then, in the words of one Minister, proceeds to 'act as a judge and jury to her own cause'. (Hennessy, 1986, p. 289)

5. She also interfered energetically in departments, seeking outside advice via seminars, individuals she trusted and think-tanks, following up initiatives and taking an unprecedentedly close interest in the promotion of senior civil servants.

But the above 'strengths' or assets were not permanent. By 1990 she had lost the confidence of many of her Cabinet; policy was failing, notably over the unpopular poll tax and rising inflation; she paid a price for her treatment of Cabinet colleagues, in that many of them felt little sense of ownership of same policies, and there was resentment of the influences exercised by Ingham and her foreign affairs adviser, Charles Powell.

John Major as Prime Minister

Several factors remained consistent throughout John Major's prime ministership, namely a collegial approach to Cabinet decisions, autonomy for most secretaries of state in managing their departments, and a low-key approach to national leadership. Major was most definitely a 'stabiliser', without an overriding political project (save perhaps his consensus-seeking desire for 'a country at ease with itself') rather than a 'mobiliser' like Thatcher or Blair, who sought radical changes. Like Gladstone and Blair, he became increasingly concerned with Ireland and sought to leave his mark on history by producing lasting peace.

Different viewpoints on Major

John is virtually unknown, too vulnerable to the subtle charge of 'not yet ready for it'. He has personal handicaps, not of his own making. The product, indeed of his virtues. He is not at all *flash* . . . and he is not classy, which doesn't worry me in the slightest, but worse, he doesn't (like Mrs T) even aspire to be classy.

Alan Clark, Diaries, 17 November 1993

In time, his very qualities of emollience, pragmatism, wanting to hold all factions together, evoked scorn, then contempt. [But] might a Hurd, a Heseltine or a Redwood premiership have proved more successful?

Many of the harsher criticisms levelled against Major . . . are also intellectually limited because they have little regard for the circumstances under which Major served his premiership from 1990 to 1997.

Anthony Seldon, Major: A Political Life (1997), pp. 737–9

As Prime Minister Major appeared to feel constrained by (a) the circumstances of his succession (Margaret Thatcher and her supporters felt that she had been stabbed in the back when she stepped down from the leadership; she soon became a menacing presence for John Major and in the first two years he was careful to seek her support), (b) his lack of an electoral mandate until 1992 and (c) being surrounded by colleagues who were more senior and experienced than himself.

The Major years saw distinct periods in which prime ministerial power, relations with Cabinet colleagues and perceived policy success shifted. The first was from November 1990 to the summer of 1992. Major inherited the prime ministership after a particularly brutal demonstration of the limits of prime ministerial power, with a deeply divided Cabinet and party. He could do no other than take a more collegiate approach to his Cabinet, and his personal preferences were for this as well. Cabinet became a forum for more general discussion than had taken place since the days of Callaghan, and suffered no acrimonious arguments. Major held the party together, performed several necessary policy changes (abandoning the poll tax, new agendas in education and the public services), won a close general election and proved an asset to the government in public opinion terms. In early 1991 his personal ratings were the highest recorded since Churchill and his reassuring national leadership, particularly during the Gulf War, suited the mood better than Thatcher's triumphalism. All of these features mark a sharp departure from Thatcher's premiership. Despite severe recession, the opposition never opened up a commanding lead in the polls.

The second phase lasted from summer 1992 until the 1997 election. Growing turmoil over Europe, plus the humiliation of 'Black Wednesday', the day when Britain withdrew from the exchange rate mechanism, and a series of policy errors and reverses thereafter, gravely weakened the Prime Minister's position. The initial general election majority of twenty-one had dwindled to single figures by 1994, inhibiting freedom of manoeuvre. Existing Cabinet divisions over Europe, particularly the stance about Britain's membership of the single currency, proved difficult to manage; some ministers, notably John Redwood and Michael Portillo, engaged in more or less open acts of defiance that would have resulted in dismissal during the 1980s. As the popularity of the government fell to record depths, Major's power to enforce collective discipline eroded. Characteristics acclaimed as Major virtues in the first phase were widely dismissed as weaknesses in the second. Major was unable to articulate a strong sense of where the government was going, and policy appeared to be a mix of scrapings of the barrel of Thatcherism (rail privatisation) with attempts to return to basic values in education and public

At Prime Minister's question time, Tony Blair tells John Major that the difference between them as party leaders is that 'I lead my party, he follows his' (2 February 1997)

order. He lost much of his ability to speak for the nation, being treated by the media and the public alike as a target for ridicule and abuse. Progress in Northern Ireland was the principal prime ministerial achievement in this difficult period. The line of 'wait and see', or what Major called 'negotiate and decide', on the single currency just about held among Cabinet ministers until the general election. His successor as party leader, William Hague, quickly abandoned it – but alienated significant figures like Clarke and Heseltine.

Tony Blair as Prime Minister

Tony Blair has been a distinctive Prime Minister. On the basis of his first three years in office he already ranks alongside Mrs Thatcher as the strongest peacetime Prime Minister this century (see Box 19.1). Interestingly, his style of leadership in government closely resembles that of his leadership of the party in opposition. His reforms of the party, particularly of Conference and NEC, were designed to make them more supportive of the leadership. In opposition he recruited a large team of aides to support him in the Leader's office and he relied on these and key figures such Gordon Brown, rather than the Shadow Cabinet. He attached importance to good communications and took seriously his role as the spokesman for his New Labour project and key themes. Having noticed how party critics (usually on the left) of earlier Labour leaders had been exploited by a hostile media to feed an image of the party as

In the wake of electoral defeat, John Major resigns as leader of the Tory Party (4 May 1997)

divided, untrustworthy and extreme, he emphasised the need for discipline and self-discipline. He also noted how John Major had been weakened by the media coverage of attacks on him made by his Conservative critics. Being seen to be in charge was an important means of actually being in charge for Blair (see Jones, 1999; Kavanagh and Seldon, 1999).

In No. 10, Blair has strengthened the Prime Minister's office to a greater degree than virtually any of his predecessor. He has made his mark by:

- Boosting the size of his political staff in No. 10, adding political appointments to many units, including the Private Office, Press Office and Strategic Communications Unit. Compared with John Major he has virtually doubled the number of staff working for him personally.
- Substantially increasing the number of aides with communication skills. The Press Office and Strategic Communications Unit together employ twice as many people on communications as there were under John Major.
- Increasing the size of the Policy Unit, which helps to promote Blair's interests *vis-à-vis* the departments. Where John Major had a Policy Unit of seven members, Blair had one of fourteen in mid-1999.
- By reducing Prime Minister's Questions to one weekly slot of thirty minutes (Wednesday 15.00 to 15.30) from two weekly slots of fifteen minutes, he and his staff have gained some extra time to devote to other priorities.

BOX 19.1 **BIOGRAPHY** 

TONY BLAIR (1953–) (picture: © AFP/Corbis)

Tony Blair was born in Edinburgh. He attended an Edinburgh public school, Fettes, then read law at Oxford and qualified as a barrister. He is the first Labour leader to have been educated at a leading public school since Hugh Gaitskell (leader 1955–63).

Blair entered Parliament in 1983, winning the safe seat of Sedgefield. Labour lost the election on its most left-wing manifesto for over fifty years. Conservative critics sometimes attack him for standing on that manifesto – which promised British withdrawal from the European Community, a great extension of public ownership and a unilateralist defence policy. In the House of Commons he proved to be an outstanding debater and was elected to the Shadow Cabinet in 1988. As Shadow Spokesman for employment he presented the trade unions with a fait accompli, in announcing that a Labour government would not reintroduce the 'closed shop' which the Conservatives had abolished.

When Neil Kinnock resigned the party leadership after the 1992 general election, Blair briefly thought about standing. But it was generally felt that it was John Smith's 'turn'. Some Labour modernisers regretted the opportunity to skip a generation and elect a younger leader like Blair or Gordon Brown. Under Smith Tony Blair became Shadow Spokesman on Home Office matters. He was determined to stamp out the widespread perception that Labour was 'soft' on crime and sympathetic to criminals. A popular Blair soundbite was that Labour would be 'tough on crime and tough on the causes of crime'.

When Smith died in 1994 Blair was a candidate and his close friend and rival Gordon Brown, the Shadow Chancellor who for some time had been regarded as the more likely figure, decided not to enter the contest; now he had been overtaken by the more junior Blair. It was no surprise that Blair won the election easily in July 1994.

In his first conference speech, Blair called for a review of Clause Four of the party constitution, the clause which committed the party to widespread public ownership. When he learnt that powerful trade unions were opposed, he decided to carry his campaign directly to the membership. At a special conference his redrafted clause was carried by a two-thirds majority. He continued Neil Kinnock's reforms of the party but further repositioned Labour in an effort to try to steal strong Conservative issues of law and order, low taxes, plus higher standards and traditional forms of education. He has also been accused of authoritarianism, and senior figures have been censured for speaking out of line. Rather like Thatcher, Blair believes in leading from the front, and is determined to create a new Labour Party, moving it to a so-called middle ground and broadening its appeal to the middle class. Blair survived all criticisms to deliver the promised prize on 1 May 1997: a huge majority of 179 over a still divided Conservative Party. In power Blair has maintained an astonishing level of popularity and has emerged as one of the most powerful postwar prime ministers. He is intent on winning the election due before 2002 and making the new century that of the centre left instead of the centre right which dominated the last one.

Blair illustrates a number of features of the premiership today. Many trends are tending to pull the Prime Minister away from or even elevate him above his senior colleagues. The growth of summits, including the G7, European Union sessions and Blair–Clinton seminars, makes inroads on a Prime Minister's time. There is a paradox that as Britain has lost an empire and has less input in international affairs so the Prime Minister is busier than ever on the international stage.

The PM spends less time in the House of Commons. Research by Patrick Dunleavy and colleagues at the London School of Economics shows that there has been a steady decline in Commons statements and debates by prime ministers over the century. Tony Blair has voted in only 5 per cent of House of Commons divisions since May 1997 and the reduction of Prime Minister's Questions to one weekly slot diminishes the opportunities for MPs to have a word with him or for him to 'sense' the atmosphere in the Commons. This is part of a bigger picture, as MPs and ministers regard a slot on the *Today* programme as more important than a speech in the House of Commons and as most MPs have finished their week in the Westminster by Thursday afternoon.

The media increasingly focus on the party leaders, particularly at election and party conference time. Blair, more than any other recent Prime Minister, has been the communicator in chief for the government. Even before his arrival, Professor Michael Foley was writing about *The Rise of the British Presidency*; as in the United States, British political leaders not only try to manage the media but they try to bypass it by going 'direct' to voters, appearing on 'chat' shows and writing newspaper articles.

The key figure in the Cabinet, after Blair, is Gordon Brown, the Chancellor; the two were the key architects of the New Labour project. Some have speculated that Blair may have been in Brown's debt because the latter gave him a free run as the modernisers' candidate in the election to succeed John Smith as party leader in 1994. Brown has been given a good deal of leeway to influence the domestic agenda, shape the spending of departments, to appoint his own special advisers (even when this caused tensions with No. 10), to chair key Cabinet Committees on the economy and effectively to operate what at times has appeared to be a dual premiership. The two men have a close relationship and talk about a broad range of political matters almost daily. Essentially, if these two agree there is not much that anybody else can do about it.

Another interesting figure is John Prescott, the Deputy Prime Minister and Secretary of State of the giant DETA (Department of Environment, Transport and the Regions). In contrast to the general co-ordinating and communications roles ('Minister for the *Today* programme') which Major gave to his Deputy Prime Minister, Michael Heseltine, Prescott has been given a large portfolio, including transport, which has become a high profile (and therefore worrying) issue for the government.

Blair does not have a great deal of time for Cabinet, which meets on average for less than an hour each week, and therefore clearly has little time for discussion. Instead, he prefers to work with small groups of staff who are informed on the issue at hand and with aides in No. 10 whose judgement he trusts. His particular interests are in the European Union, Northern Ireland (these have become virtually prime ministerial issues) and welfare, education and, in 2000, health. He also regards himself as the custodian of the New Labour strategy. His opening words on entering Downing Street as Prime Minister, 'We were elected as New Labour and we will govern as New Labour', were a warning to MPs and Cabinet ministers to follow his line. He has also carried a major role as a public spokesman. Over the first two years it has been calculated that he has signed more than 150 newspaper articles on issues of the day. In addition he does regular question and answer sessions with the public, some of which have been televised. More than any other, his is the communicating premiership (Kavanagh, 2000).

To date, Blair has been helped by his remarkable popularity with voters, a large Commons majority and a weak Opposition. His style and methods involve a relative downgrading of Cabinet and Parliament. Peter Hennessy, a Whitehall watcher, dubs it 'a command premiership', and warns of the dangers of over-centralisation and political isolation because of Blair's reliance on his own staff. Others argue that a stronger Prime

BOX 19.2 **IDEAS AND PERSPECTIVES** 

Should prime ministers have their own department?

It is sometimes argued that a Prime Minister should have a department of his or her own, structured along the lines of those available for some foreign political leaders. Most such bodies are staffed by a mix of political and civil service appointments. Such a scheme was considered in 1977 (under Callaghan), 1982 (under Thatcher), and some of Blair's aides flirted with the idea in Opposition in 1996. The Prime Minister needs greater resources because of the growing demands on his time, particularly from the media and foreign affairs. Reformers claim that he therefore needs to be more effectively resourced, both to represent the government to the world outside Westminster and to lend strategic direction and cohesion to the government. Such a department could emerge from combining the different units already in No. 10 (see pp. 411–13). In some ways the Cabinet Office performs some of the functions usually associated with a Prime Minister's department.

The disadvantages would be in fitting such a department into the hierarchy of Cabinet: could the junior aides of the Prime Minister issue orders to Cabinet ministers or to permanent secretaries? Would it cut the Prime Minister off and act as a buffer between him or her and the rest of the government? Might it encourage the Prime Minister to develop a different political agenda from that of particular Cabinet ministers? If so, might it be simpler to reshuffle the ministers?

It is interesting that Tony Blair, while rejecting the idea of a Prime Minister's department, has greatly strengthened the resources in No. 10. The changes mentioned earlier are designed to link policy with presentation and achieve more integration between the Private Office and the Policy Unit. He has also strengthened the Cabinet Office and created units, including the Social Exclusion Unit and Policy Innovation Unit, to assist 'joined-up' policy making, making departments co-operate where their policies impact a problem area or group of people. For example, the Social Exclusion Unit (set up in December 1997) makes proposals to help individuals or areas suffering from such linked problems as unemployment, low income, poor housing and family breakdown.

Ministership, giving direction to departments and communicating with the public, are essential for an effective twenty-first century premiership (Boxes 19.2–4).

Possible reforms

Two reforms have been suggested as ways of improving the operation of the office of Prime Minister:

1 A Prime Minister's department (Box 19.2): This would involve a larger executive office than No. 10, on the lines of the Chancellor in Germany and the Taoiseach in Ireland.

2 A regularised Deputy Prime Minister, with his or her own department. There is no fixed office of this kind in Britain. The title has been used for two purposes: buying off a dangerous political rival with a title (Howe, 1989–90), or appointing a senior figure to co-ordinate other Cabinet ministers and adjudicate in disputes (Whitelaw, 1983–8) – or indeed both (Heseltine, 1995–7). Prime ministers have often felt the need for a 'fixer' or 'troubleshooter' who would sort out problems with colleagues. It has rarely worked out and any Prime Minister will be wary of creating a powerful rival.

BOX 19.3 **IDEAS AND PERSPECTIVES**

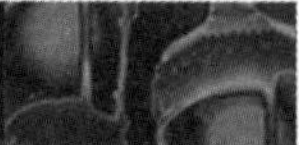

Tony Blair's *cafetière* theory of government

Tony Blair, from the outset, has sought to impose central control over government just as he had over the Labour party. He wished to make No. 10 more powerful *vis-à-vis* the departments. *The Economist* has argued that government in Britain has traditionally worked like a percolator. Policies emerge from departments and were then filtered through Cabinet committees and bargaining with the Treasury, and then received the approval of the Prime Minister and Cabinet. Mr Blair, largely because of his experience in running the Labour party, wanted to replace the percolator approach with a *cafetière*. This has involved strong pressure from above (No. 10) and infusing the policies and actions of the departments below. Blair has tried to increase the leverage of his office:

1. Promoting co-operation between the Policy Unit and Private Office and appointing a Chief of Staff to integrate the two bodies.
2. Granting Alastair Campbell, the Press Secretary, greater control over presentation in government communications.
3. Insisting that the Cabinet Office impresses upon Whitehall the importance of delivering policy outcomes, particularly in the core public services of health, education and crime, e.g. cutting waiting lists or raising educational standards.
4. Promoting what is called 'joined-up' government. Blair takes a close interest in the work of two new bodies, the Policy and Innovation Unit and Social Exclusion Unit, both of which are attached to the Cabinet Office. These work on policies which cut across departmental responsibilities and try to ensure that civil servants and ministers work together.

Source: Drawn from The Economist, 21 August 1999, pp. 19 and 20

BOX 19.4 **fact**

Dimensions of prime ministerial power

Prime Minister and government: the power of appointment

Sources

1. Appoints all ministers and subsequently promotes, demotes, dismisses.
2. Decides who does what in Cabinet.
3. Appoints chairmen of Cabinet committees (now increasingly important).
4. Approves choice of ministers' parliamentary private secretaries.
5. Other patronage powers, e.g. appoints chairmen of commissions, recommends knighthoods, peerages and sundry other awards.

Constraints

1. Seniority of colleagues demands their inclusion and sometimes in particular posts.
2. Availability for office – experience, talent, willingness to serve.
3. Need for balance:

BOX 19.4 continued

(a) Ideological, left + right.
(b) Regional.
(c) Occupational.
(d) Lords.

4. Debts to loyal supporters.
5. Shadow Cabinet expectations.

Prime Minister and Cabinet direction

Sources

1. Summons meetings.
2. Determines agenda.
3. Sums up 'mood' of meeting.
4. Approves minutes.
5. Spokesman for Cabinet to outside world.
6. Existence of inner Cabinet (intimate advisers).

Constraints

1. Needs Cabinet approval for controversial measures.
2. Determination of groups of ministers to press a case or oppose a particular policy.
3. Power of vested departmental interests backed up by senior civil servants.
4. Convention dictates certain items will appear regularly on Cabinet agenda.

Prime Minister and Parliament

Sources

1. Commands a majority in House (usually).
2. Spokesman for government.
3. Weekly Question Time provides platform upon which PM can usually excel.

Constraints

1. Activities of opposition.
2. Parliamentary party meetings.
3. Question Time: not always a happy experience.

Prime Minister and party

Sources

1. 'Brand image' of party, especially at election time: PM's 'style' is that of the party.
2. Control over appointments.
3. Natural loyalty of party members to their leader and their government.
4. Threat of dissolution (seldom a credible threat, though).
5. Fear of party members that opposition will exploit public disagreements.

Constraints

1. Danger of election defeat: can lead to loss of party leadership.
2. Existence of ambitious alternative leaders.
3. Need to command support of parliamentary party, particularly when majority is thin or non-existent.
4. For Labour premiers, some constraints from party outside Parliament, e.g. National Executive Committee and party conference.

Prime Minister and administration

Sources

1. Appoints permanent secretaries.
2. Cabinet Office: acts for PM to some extent.
3. High-powered policy unit in No. 10.
4. Traditional loyalty of civil servants to political masters.
5. Is not constrained by departmental responsibilities.

Constraints

1. Sheer volume of work: limit to the amount a PM can read.

BOX 19.4 continued

2. Power of departmental interests – 'departmentalism'.
3. Treasury: exerts financial constraints over whole of government.

Prime Minister and the country

Sources

1. The most prestigious and publicly visible politician in the country.
2. Access to instant media coverage for whatever purpose.
3. Access to top decision makers in all walks of public life.
4. Ability to mount high-prestige meetings with foreign leaders, trips abroad, etc.

Constraints

1. Those vested interests – especially economic – represented by powerful pressure groups, e.g. business and trade unions.
2. The public's potential for boredom with the same leader.
3. The tendency of the public to blame the PM for failure beyond the control of No. 10.
4. Failure of the economy.
5. Events abroad, e.g. wars, terrorism, changes of government, etc.

Cabinet

The Cabinet is chaired by the Prime Minister, who selects its members and recommends their appointment to the monarch. Most members are Secretaries of State by title. The Secretary of the Cabinet is responsible for the preparation of records of its discussions and decisions; the latter become conclusions of Cabinet. The modern Cabinet evolved from the Privy Council in the sixteenth century, a small group of advisers to the monarch. Over time, as the government needed to have the confidence of the Parliament and then of the electorate at large, so the Cabinet became responsible to Parliament and then to the electorate.

Functions of Cabinet

The Cabinet as such has no legal powers; powers are vested in the Secretaries of State. But because it has **collective responsibility** to Parliament all its members are bound to support Cabinet decisions. If they cannot do so they are expected to resign. The report of the Machinery of Government Committee (1918) described the functions of Cabinet as:

1 the final determination of the policy to be submitted to Parliament;

2 the supreme control of the national executive in accordance with the policy prescribed by Parliament;

3 the continuous co-ordination and delimitation of the activities of the several Departments of State.

To the above we may add the following functions:

- It plans the business of Parliament, usually a week or so in advance, making decisions about time-tabling of legislation and choosing major government speakers.
- It provides political leadership for the party, in Parliament and in the country.
- It arbitrates in cases of disputes between departments, for example, in the case of departments failing to agree with the Treasury about their spending totals or battles between

ministers over 'turf'. Sometimes the arbitration is done by the Prime Minister or by a trouble-shooter he has appointed.

- Although it does not actually decide many policies, it is the arena in which most important decisions are registered. Often the Cabinet is receiving reports or ratifying recommendations from committees. In the case of the annual Budget, Cabinet ministers merely hear the Chancellor of the Exchequer's main recommendations, shortly before his statement to the House of Commons.

The Cabinet meets weekly on Thursdays mornings for an hour or so and (under Blair) less frequently during holiday periods, unless in emergencies when summoned by the Prime Minister. It meets usually in the Cabinet Room in No. 10, and about forty Cabinet meetings are held a year. A good part of its business is fairly predictable. Regular items include reviews of foreign affairs, European Union affairs, home affairs and a parliamentary business report from the Leader of the House of Commons. In addition issues which are politically sensitive or highly topical are usually considered. Blair's Cabinets rarely last as long as one hour. He has added an item on 'Current Events' which deals with announcements and events for the following week.

An item is usually introduced by the departmental minister in charge of the subject under discussion. In chairing the Cabinet the Prime Minister may wish to promote a particular line but more often wants to establish how much agreement there is about a proposed course of action. At the end of the discussion the Prime Minister sums up the mood of the meeting. Once the summary is written in the minutes it becomes a decision of the Cabinet. Votes are rarely taken; they advertise divisions, may fail to reflect the different political weight and experience of ministers and detract from Cabinet's role as a deliberative body. But the Prime Minister is very aware of the balance of opinion within Cabinet when summing up and reaching his or her own decision.

This last point is important and means that a Prime Minister may decide not to refer an issue to Cabinet because it is too controversial or he or she will not get the desired outcome. Mrs Thatcher for years refused to allow discussion about British membership to ERM; she was opposed whereas the majority were in favour. John Major also kept issues from Cabinet because of fears of 'leaks'. For much of the time Cabinet is simply not equipped to decide or challenge a decision already agreed by a Prime Minister and a departmental minister. Nigel Lawson, Chancellor of the Exchequer under Margaret Thatcher, described Cabinet meetings as the only time he had for a good rest during a heavy schedule. But Cabinet still usually discusses the public spending priorities of the government and the contents of the Queen's Speech. Ministers can also become more involved when there are political cabinets, and civil servants leave the Cabinet Room. It is plausible to argue that the Cabinet meetings are now more important for team building, increasing the sense of shared ownership of the government programme among ministers and underpinning a sense of collective responsibility, rather than for deciding policies.

The Cabinet occupies a central position in the political system, *vis-à-vis* Parliament, the civil service and the public. Peter Hennessy describes this mix of pressures:

> Ministers must look constantly in three directions: inward to the civil service machine, across Whitehall to Parliament, and outward to the party beyond Westminster, to institutions, professions, the country as a whole and to other nations. (Hennessy, 1988, p. 432)

Size

Peacetime Cabinets in the twentieth century have varied in size between sixteen (Bonar Law in 1922) and twenty-four (Wilson in 1964). The average size of Cabinets in the twentieth century has been twenty. The wartime Cabinets of Lloyd George and Winston Churchill have been much praised and both contained fewer than ten members. Both Thatcher and Major experimented with small war Cabinets for the short Falklands and Gulf campaigns. It is important to note, however, that in war very different considerations operate from peacetime politics.

Decisions about the Cabinet size and composition have to balance the needs of decision making and deliberation against those of representatives. The Cabinet is a committee which has to be small enough to allow ministers the opportunities to discuss, deliberate and co-ordinate major policies. Yet at the same time it must be large enough to include heads of major departments and accommodate different political groups in the party. Lobbies for different interests, e.g. education, Scotland or health, expect to have 'their' minister represented in Cabinet. A larger Cabinet increases a Prime Minister's patronage. Cabinet is almost too large to be a useful decision-making or deliberative group. There is little reason for Scotland and Wales still to have ministers in Cabinet, now that they have their own First Ministers in Edinburgh and Cardiff.

Prime ministers have frequently expressed their wish for small or smaller Cabinets. Some commentators have advocated a Cabinet of six or so non-departmental ministers, which would concentrate on strategy and co-ordination and be supported by standing and *ad hoc* committees of other departmental ministers. The growing burden of work on ministers and the tendencies for some ministers gradually to acquire a departmental perspective do pose problems of oversight and strategy in the Cabinet. On his return to 10 Downing Street in 1951 Winston Churchill appointed a number of so-called 'overlords', ministers who sat in the House of Lords, were free from departmental and constituency duties, and were charged with co-ordinating policies in related departments. The experiment was not, however, a success. It was difficult to separate the co-ordinating responsibilities of the 'overlords' in the Lords from the ministerial duties of ministers who were formally answerable to the House of Commons. More generally, it is difficult to separate the tasks of co-ordination and strategy from those of the day-to-day running of a department. Separating policy from administration is easier in theory than in practice. In opposition before 1964 Harold Wilson suggested that the large size (twenty-three) of Sir Alec Douglas-Home's Cabinet (1963–4) reflected the weakness of Sir Alec as a Prime Minister. He was implying that he would have had a much smaller one. In the event he ended up with one of twenty-four, the largest in the century. Thatcher's Cabinets in 1983 and 1987 had twenty-two members, as did John Major's in 1992 and Tony Blair's in 1997.

Cabinet committees

The system of Cabinet committees is a practical response to the increasing workload of Cabinet and the need for some specialisation and greater time in considering issues. In 1992, as part of Major's drive for greater openness in government, the names and members of Cabinet committees were made public. As part of the Cabinet system the committees' deliberations are bound by secrecy and they are served by the Cabinet secretariat. There are various types of Cabinet committee. Standing committees are permanent for the duration of the prime minister's term in office, while miscellaneous or *ad hoc* committees are set up to deal with particular issues. A third category is official committees, which consist only of civil servants.

A number of critics have seen the development of the committee system as a means for the Prime Minister to bypass the full Cabinet and expand his or her own power. It is the Prime Minister who decides to set up committees and appoint their members, chairmen and terms of reference. Scope for prime ministerial influence is enhanced by the *ad hoc* committees, since the PM has more discretion to define their terms of reference than those of the standing committees, such as defence and foreign affairs. Supporters of the system observe that it is the only way a modern Cabinet can cope with the volume of work facing it. The committee system is a sign of the adaptability of Cabinet. Ministers can appeal against a committee's conclusion to the full Cabinet but only with the approval of the committee chairman.

Thatcher was more reluctant than her predecessors to set up Cabinet committees. She preferred to hold 'bilateral' meetings with the minister and officials in a department or 'working parties' to tackle a problem. Under Major the Cabinet and Cabinet committee system reverted to the normal pattern, after the battering of the Thatcher years. Major was exceedingly keen to bind his ministers into decisions, and to ensure that the widest group of relevant ministers was party to key decisions. The only occasion on which big decisions were taken on core government policy outside the Cabinet and committee system was on leaving the ERM on 16 September 1992, but even then Major took care to consult in an *ad hoc* way all his most senior ministers – Norman Lamont, Kenneth Clarke, Douglas Hurd and Michael Heseltine.

But as ministers and the Prime Minister are required to be away from London – on EU business, for example – so Cabinet committees are more difficult to arrange. The result is that more business is done by correspondence between ministers and copied to the Prime Minister. As noted, Tony Blair works more informally with task forces, meetings with his own staff and bilaterals with ministers. He also has regular stocktaking sessions with individual Cabinet ministers who are responsible for education, health and tackling crime, to monitor progress on delivering the government's policy commitments.

BOX 19.1 **MINI BIOGRAPHY**

Sir Richard Wilson (1942–)
Cabinet Secretary 1997. Educated Cambridge. Effectively Britain's most powerful civil servant at the nerve centre of government. Has been closely associated with Blair's reforming zeal in relation to the civil service. Advises on offical appointments and also political ones.

The Cabinet office

Until 1916 there were no formal procedures for keeping minutes of Cabinet meetings or records of decisions. In that year, however, the Cabinet Office or secretariat was established by Lloyd George. Today the Cabinet Office is at the heart of the government machine. Its main tasks in relation to Cabinet and the committees are to prepare the agenda of the Cabinet by circulating relevant papers to ministers beforehand; to record Cabinet proceedings and decisions; and to follow up and co-ordinate the decisions by informing the departments of decisions and checking that appropriate action has been taken.

The Cabinet Office has also come to play an important co-ordinating role in a number of areas. Its European Secretariat co-ordinates departmental views and formulates Britain's negotiating position with EU member states. The Constitutional Secretariat has been heavily involved in the constitutional reforms introduced since May 1997, particularly those on devolution to Scotland and Wales. Blair is particularly concerned to promote what he calls 'joined-up' government and policies which require the co-operation of departments and the contribution of people and skills from outside the civil service. Two new units have been set up, the Social Exclusion Unit and the Policy and Innovation Unit. Both are designed to combat departmentalism and promote wider objectives of the government, and based in the Cabinet Office.

The Cabinet Secretary works closely with the Prime Minister over security matters and issues affecting the conduct of the civil service and ministers. For example, Sir Richard Wilson, the present Secretary, interviewed Ron Davies about the circumstances which led to his resignation as Secretary of State for Wales in 1998. Sir Robert Armstrong, a previous Cabinet Secretary, was sent by Thatcher to answer questions by the House of Commons select committee in 1986 when it investigated the 'leak' of the Solicitor General's letter to Michael Heseltine over Westland, and he also answered for the government in the Australian courts when the government tried to prevent publication of the *Spycatcher* memoirs of an ex-MI5 officer. Armstrong and his successor, Sir Robin Butler, were closely involved with the search for peace in Northern Ireland under Thatcher and Major.

Co-ordination

Some observers have suggested that British government resembles a medieval system in which the departments operate as relatively independent fiefdoms. Bruce Headey (1974) interviewed a number of former and present Cabinet ministers and found that most of them regarded themselves primarily as representatives or spokesmen for the department *vis-à-vis* Parliament, the Cabinet and the public. Others emphasised the internal aspect of their work, managing and organising the department. Only one in six regarded themselves as initiators of policies, in the sense of defining the department's policy options. The departmental pressures on many ministers tended to limit their opportunities to contribute to the formation of government policy making in general. Thus Headey argued that Britain had departmental rather than **Cabinet government**. It is a feature that Tony Blair feels strongly about.

How, therefore, is government policy co-ordinated? How do ministers have a sense of strategy, a sense of where, collectively, they are going? Techniques include:

1. Treasury control of public spending and the annual spending reviews provide the opportunity to review priorities.
2. Informal consultations between senior officials of departments.
3. Formal interdepartmental meetings also provide the opportunity for co-ordination.
4. The Cabinet Office, which services the Cabinet and its committees, prepares and circulates papers and follows up Cabinet decisions. The Cabinet office EU secretariat is also important in co-ordinating departmental submissions on the EU.
5. The system of Cabinet committees itself.
6. The Prime Minister, and No. 10 office, take an overview across all government policy. Blair has also set up various units and task forces to promote co-ordination (see p. 420).

Cabinet ministers suffer from sheer overload of work which results in them lacking sufficient time to read and digest papers on many matters outside their departmental responsibilities. The Cabinet is not particularly good at co-ordinating policy (see above). In part this is a consequence of so much of ministers' time being spent on running and representing their own departments. A number of ex-ministers have remarked on how rare it was for them to comment on other issues before the Cabinet. Many illustrations of these pressures are to be found in the published diaries of Richard Crossman and Barbara Castle: ministers, for example, arrived at Cabinet having only glanced at papers which did not concern their own departments. The Central Policy Review Staff was established in 1970, with a remit to provide ministers with briefs which did not reflect a departmental view. It failed and Mrs Thatcher abolished it in 1983.

It is worth considering the views of two experienced observers on the 'overload' problem. Sir Frank Cooper, a senior civil servant throughout much of the post-war period, commented:

> I think the whole idea of collective responsibility, in relation to twenty-odd people, has had diminished force, quite frankly, over the years, coupled with the fact that to deal with the modern world... with the very, very complex problems that government have to deal with, it's inevitable that they should move into a situation where four or five are gathered together. (Cited in Hennessy, 1986, p. 164)

Nigel Lawson (1992) caustically described the Cabinet meeting as the most restful and relaxing event of the week. He also claims that the Cabinet showed no interest in or support for his criticisms of the proposed poll tax (pp. 562–3). If the Prime Minister and relevant departmental minister had agreed a line, then it was very difficult for another minister to intervene.

Reforms of Cabinet

Among reforms of the Cabinet which have been canvassed in recent years are the following:

1. The creation of a body which can help the Cabinet deal with strategy: This may include the re-creation of something along the lines of the Central Policy Review Staff, which existed between 1970 and 1983. A number of observers claim that even if the original CPRS did not fill the need, there is still scope for a unit which can brief the Cabinet as a collective body.

2 The creation of a Prime Minister's department although this might well involve a downgrading of Cabinet (see above).

3 An increase in the number of political aides or advisers for ministers: Blair's government had doubled the number under John Major to seventy-eight in 2000. It is often argued that this system should be extended and strengthened, as in France and the USA. This is urged on the grounds of strengthening ministerial influence in the department rather than enhancing the collective role of the Cabinet.

4 A reduction in the power of the Prime Minister, so developing what Tony Benn, in 1979, called a constitutional premiership. Benn objected to the scale of the Prime Minister's patronage as well as other fixed powers. He advocated the election of Cabinet ministers and allocation of their duties by Labour MPs and the confirmation of public appointments by Parliament. Note that, under party rules, a Labour Prime Minister has to appoint to the Cabinet the members of his Parliamentary Committee elected in opposition. Blair largely did so in 1997.

5 Taking steps to improve the quality of policy making in opposition: It is striking how total the divorce between government and opposition is in the British system. It is possible for a government to take office with many of its members having little or no executive experience. This was largely the case with Ramsay MacDonald's first Labour government in 1924, Wilson's 1964 government and Blair's in 1997. Neil Kinnock never held even a junior ministerial post. In the first post-war Labour government a minister, Emmanuel Shinwell, confessed that for many years he had talked about nationalising the coal industry but when he came to implement the manifesto pledge in 1945 he found no plans existed.

Measures which might improve the transition between opposition and government include the following:

1 Relaxation of secrecy so that the documents and options considered by ministers and civil servants are opened to public discussion.

2 The temporary appointment of a few high-flying civil servants to the opposition to assist the policy-making process.

3 An increase in the budgets and research expenses of political parties.

4 Greater use of the Douglas-Home rules (1963) which allow opposition spokesmen to have contacts with senior civil servants in the relevant departments. The Conservatives made some use of this facility before 1979 but Labour did not before 1983.

The Blair team, in anticipation of election victory, held several meetings with senior civil servants and undertook extensive briefings and seminars with those familiar with the problems Labour would face in office. It is a tribute to all that, after eighteen years of one-party government, the transition between the Major and Blair governments was so smooth.

Ministers

Appointments

If the size of the Cabinet has hardly grown in the twentieth century, that of the government certainly has. The major increase since 1900 has been in government appointments outside the Cabinet – non-Cabinet ministers of state, junior ministers and parliamentary private secretaries (PPSs) in the House of Commons. In 1900 forty-two MPs were in involved in government; today, the number is well over a hundred, usually about a third of government MPs. Although the PPSs are unpaid they are still bound by the doctrine of collective responsibility.

The increase in patronage is obviously an advantage for prime ministers. They can use it to reward or punish colleagues and perhaps to promote policies. It is, however, a power which is exercised subject to several administrative and political limitations. One is that ministers must sit in Parliament and most of them must be members of the House of Commons. A few Cabinet ministers have been appointed shortly after their election to the House of Commons. The trade union leader Ernest Bevin, at the Ministry of Labour in 1940, was a success, but another trade unionist, Frank Cousins, Minister of Technology (1964–7), and a businessman, John Davies, at Trade and Industry (1970–4), were less effective. A Cabinet must also contain at least two peers, the Lord Chancellor and the Leader of the House of Lords. The parliamentary background increases the likelihood that ministers will be skilled in debate and able to handle parliamentary questions competently. Thatcher was willing to reach out and appoint to the Cabinet peers who had had a short party political career, for example Lord Young of Graffham, Secretary of State for Employment (1985–7) and then at the Department of Trade and Industry (1987–9), and Lord Cockfield, Department of Trade and then Duchy of Lancaster, before becoming a commissioner with the European Economic Community. Blair has given peerages to a number of businessmen and then given them ministerial posts, e.g. Lords Sainsbury, Simon and (Gus) MacDonald. Elevating lay people to the peerage and then giving them office is a useful way of utilising extra-parliamentary talent, but it can cause resentments in the government's parliamentary party.

A second limitation is that appointments also need to take account of a person's political skill and administrative competence. In any Cabinet there are at least half a dozen ministers whose seniority and reputation are such that it is unthinkable to exclude them. Increasingly, the leader of the opposition party uses his Shadow Cabinet to enable his Shadow ministers to gain expertise in posts they will take over in government. Tony Blair appointed virtually all his Shadow Cabinet to the same posts in government.

The qualifications appropriate for particular posts are not always obvious and this is suggested by the apparently haphazard movement of ministers between departments: Major from the Foreign Office to the Treasury after a few months in 1989, and Kenneth Clarke from Health (1988) to Education (1990) to the Home Office (1992) and to the Treasury (1993). On the other hand, appointments as legal officers (Lord Chancellor, Attorney General and Solicitor General) must be made from lawyers in the party. Nigel Lawson (Thatcher's Chancellor of the Exchequer for the six years before he resigned in October 1989) took a degree in politics, philosophy and economics and was a financial journalist before he went into politics. The Secretaries of State for Scotland and Wales are expected to sit for Scottish and Welsh seats, respectively, and if possible be nationals of the country concerned.

In general, however, ministers are expected to have skills in managing Parliament and conducting meetings, reading papers quickly, making decisions, and defending them convincingly in public. If we exclude as effectively 'ineligible' for office MPs who are very young or inexperienced, too old or who suffer from political or personal deficiencies, the Prime Minister may actually be giving government appointments to about one half of 'eligible' MPs in his party.

Prime ministers usually make some appointments to reward loyalty and limit dissent or outright opposition. Thatcher pointedly excluded Heath from her Cabinet in 1979 and Heath excluded Powell in 1970. Both were powerful figures but had been at odds with so many aspects of the party's policies and with the party leader personally that their presence would have made the Cabinet a divisive body. The Cabinets of Wilson in 1964 and Thatcher in 1979 contained majorities who had almost certainly voted against them at the first stage of the leadership elections in 1963 and 1976 respectively, but both prime ministers had to take account of administrative talent and political weight. Benn was a prominent left-wing dissenter from the Labour leadership in the 1970s but both Wilson and Callaghan thought it safer to keep him in the Cabinet rather than act as a focus for opposition on the back benches. In November 1990, Major gave the difficult job of Environment Secretary to the man who had precipitated Thatcher's downfall, Michael Heseltine. The appointment both recognised Heseltine's strength in the party and promised to keep him absorbed with fulfilling his claims over reforming the poll tax.

A final constraint is that prime ministers want their Cabinet to be representative of the main elements in the party. This has been particularly the case with the Labour Party which has had well defined left- and right-wing factions. Major felt bound to include in his Cabinet opponents of his European policy, including Michael Howard, Peter Lilley, Michael Portillo and, until 1995, John Redwood. Under Blair, left–right divisions have declined and the differences between Old and New Labour have not developed into factions.

There is no adequate preparation for being a Cabinet minister. The third and fourth constraints mentioned above remind us that Cabinet is a political body and that the Prime Minister is no party politician. The British tradition has been to rely on a form of on-the-job learning in which ministers, like civil servants, pick up the skills as they settle into the job. Four background features which most ministers have and which probably shape the way they work are:

1 Lengthy tenure in the House of Commons: Since 1945 the average length of time spent in the House of Commons, prior to becoming a Cabinet minister, has been fourteen years, a sufficient period of time to acquire parliamentary skills.

2 Experience on the ladder of promotion, or ministerial hierarchy, which most politicians ascend. In an ideal world they would start off as parliamentary private secretaries and move through the ranks of junior minister, minister outside the Cabinet, and then through some of the Cabinet positions, ending with the most senior ones like Chancellor of the Exchequer or Foreign Secretary and then perhaps Prime Minister.

3 Party standing: A politician with a strong party following also has claims. Excluded from Cabinet and the restraints of collective responsibility, he or she may prove a focus for criticism of the Prime Minister.

4 Preparation in opposition: In 1955 the Labour leader Clement Attlee formalised the arrangements of a Shadow Cabinet in opposition, in which a front-bench spokesman 'shadows' a Cabinet minister.

BOX 19.2 MINI BIOGRAPHY

Harold Macmillan (1894–1986)

Conservative British Prime Minister. Educated Eton and Oxford where he shone academically. Served bravely in the First World War and then became MP for Stockton where the poverty of the town converted him to a liberal version of Conservatism – his book *The Middle Way* was an expression of this. After a distinguished role in the Second World War he was a prominent Conservative and held senior office in 1951–6 when he emerged as the saviour of the party after the debacle of Suez. Became Prime Minister in 1956 and won the 1959 election handsomely and led the country until 1963 when illness forced him to stand down. He remained an influential elder statesman to the last, criticising Mrs Thatcher's privatisation policies in the 1980s.

BOX 19.3 MINI BIOGRAPHY

Clement Attlee (1883–1967)

Labour Prime Minister after the Second World War. Educated Oxford from middle-class background. His experience of poverty in London's East End made him a socialist. Became deputy leader in 1931 when Labour lost disastrously and many former senior politicians were out of the Commons. This enabled him to become leader when Lansbury resigned in 1935. He became leader in the party contest in the aftermath of the election in that year. Became deputy Prime Minister in 1940 under Churchill and performed as excellent administrator. Became PM in 1945 and presided over the achievements of that historic administration. The election in 1950 weakened the party seriously and that of the next year led to Churchill's return. Attlee remained as leader of the Opposition until becoming a member of the Lords. An unassuming man, Attlee was a tough and decisive leader who was easy to underestimate.

Both Heath and Thatcher used the opportunity of making appointments in opposition in order to prepare for office. For example, all but two of Heath's appointments in the consultative committee (the Conservative front-bench team in opposition) in 1969 went to similar Cabinet postings. Over 80 per cent of Thatcher's opposition front-bench appointments went directly to similar Cabinet postings in 1979.

Ministerial roles

If the work of ministers varies with the department, so minister–civil servant relationships also vary according to personalities, departments and the nature of issues. Bruce Headey (1974) in his study of Cabinet ministers, has usefully distinguished three broad types of ministerial role. One is the ambassador, who sells the policies of the government to bodies outside Westminster and Whitehall and even abroad. In particular this describes the case of a Foreign Secretary who spends a good deal of time representing the position of the British government to other states. A second is the executive, who is concerned to promote legislation and take decisions. He or she thus focusses on winning Cabinet battles (for approval of policy, legislation or money) and getting parliamentary time for his legislation. For example, in 1988, Kenneth Baker's education bill (the Education Reform Act) covered a large number of educational issues and dominated the parliamentary agenda. In 1999, John Prescott was frustrated in his efforts to gain time for legislation to reorganise transport and impose disincentives for people using cars. Finally, there is the key issues minister, who selects a few policy areas and tries to initiate policy. This means that he or she has to delegate much of his or her other work to junior ministers and departmental officials.

More recent analysis suggests that all of Headey's roles are part of a minister's remit and are largely mutually reinforcing. If anything, the policy expectations of a minister have increased in recent years because of the greater public interest in and scrutiny of the work of government and pressure from outside bodies such as think-tanks. Not all departments or ministers are of equal importance to a Prime Minister. Obviously his most frequent contacts are with the next-door neighbour in 11 Downing Street, the Chancellor of the Exchequer, the Leader of the House of Commons (on parliamentary business) and the Foreign Secretary. A Prime Minister regularly holds meetings with holders of these two or three senior posts, not least because he often has to answer or discuss topics in these areas at international meetings. Because of Blair's particular interests, or the pressure of events, he has also spent a great deal of time with Mo Mowlam (until 1999) on Northern Ireland, David Blunkett on education and Jack Straw on crime.

Of course a Prime Minister meets colleagues at weekly Cabinet and at Cabinet Committees. But Blair also has regular bilaterals with key ministers and their officials. The Labour government had made election pledges about education and health and these two departments were the principal beneficiaries from the extra funding allocated from 1998. Blair takes close interest in monitoring whether the officials are on track to deliver improvements in these services. These regular meetings with key ministers and their officials are a Blair innovation. It also fits in with his preferred working style of holding bilaterals rather than working through Cabinet and official committees.

A Prime Minister is not well placed to shape policy in more than a handful of departments at any one time. He can certainly veto a line of policy but he lacks the resources available to a department to initiate policies. He therefore depends on the minister and the departmental officials. If the minister fails, the Prime Minister may install a replacement. But there are always political costs in sacking a minister. On the other side, a department will profit from the goodwill of the Prime Minister for help in gaining time for legislation and extra funding, or protection against Treasury demands for cuts. Hence the regular contacts between the No. 10 Private Office and Policy Unit and officials and advisers in a department. Ministers and Prime Ministers each have resources and need each other if policy is to be successful. This is one of the reasons why some researchers on the core executive talk less about the Prime Minister's power and more about interdependence between key actors (Rhodes and Dunleavy, 1995).

Ministerial responsibility

According to this doctrine, each minister is responsible to Parliament for his or her own personal conduct, the general conduct of his or her department, and the policy-related actions or omissions of his or her civil servants. The most important consequence of the convention is that the minister is answerable to Parliament for the work of his or her department. Another interpretation is that Parliament can actually force the resignation of a minister who has been thought to be negligent. The outstanding resignation on grounds of policy in recent years was that of the Foreign Secretary, Lord Carrington (and two other ministers), in April 1982, following the widespread criticism of his department's policy when Argentina captured the Falklands. There are, however, two difficulties in the way of the Commons forcing the dismissal of a minister. One is that MPs in the majority party can usually be counted on to support a minister under pressure. In addition, the Cabinet is also responsible for policy and a Prime Minister knows that a minister's resignation often reflects badly on the work of the government. Collective responsibility may therefore weaken a minister's individual responsibility (for a longer discussion see Chapter 20). This surely was a reason which reduced pressure on Norman Lamont to resign from the Treasury in September 1992. He had frequently defended Britain's membership of the ERM, excluded the possibility of withdrawal and claimed that it was the basis of Britain's anti-inflationary strategy. The forced departure from the ERM was, by any standards, a failure of policy. The same is true of the failed poll tax, which cost some £27.5 billion. In the seven years it took to devise, implement and repeal the tax, there were eight ministers for local government. But nobody resigned. Neither did any minister resign – with William Waldegrave and Nicholas Lyell the two tipped figures – following the highly critical 1996 Scott Report on the 'arms to Iraq affair'. Indeed, resignations on the grounds of policy failure are now so rare that the notion of resignation as part of the responsibility convention has virtually disappeared.

Collective responsibility

According to the convention of collective responsibility Cabinet ministers assume responsibility for all Cabinet decisions and a minister who refuses to accept, or opposes, a decision is expected to resign. In more recent years the convention of collective responsibility has been extended to incorporate all junior government ministers, including even the unpaid and unofficial parliamentary secretaries. The doctrine is supported by the secrecy of the Cabinet proceedings: the refusal to make public the differences of opinion which precede or follow a Cabinet decision assists the presentation of a united front to Parliament and the country. Another aspect of the convention is that the government is expected to resign or seek a dissolution if it is defeated on a vote of confidence in the House of Commons. In other words the Cabinet is collectively responsible for policy to the Commons. (See Chapter 20 on individual accountability of ministers.)

In recent years, however, both aspects of the convention have come under pressure. The 1974–9 Labour government relaxed the principle of collective responsibility over the referendum on Britain's membership of the EEC in 1975 and the vote on the European Assembly Elections Bill in 1977. On both issues the Cabinet was divided. The myth of Cabinet unity has also been exploded by the increase in the leaks to the news media of Cabinet discussions in recent years.

Mrs Thatcher, more than any of her ministers, had strained Cabinet collegiality and the sense of Cabinet's collective responsibility. In the process she used up much goodwill among colleagues, and this was reflected in the bitter resignations of Michael Heseltine, Nigel Lawson and Sir Geoffrey Howe. Howe, in his resignation speech, said:

> The task has become futile ... of trying to pretend there was a common policy when every step forward risked being subverted by some casual comment or impulsive answer [by Thatcher]. (Howe, 1994, p. 667)

She paid the price when, by a majority of two to one, her Cabinet ministers advised her to stand down after the first ballot for party leadership in 1990. In her own words, she felt that she could not carry on without the united support of her senior colleagues.

John Major, by temperament and perhaps as a reaction to Mrs Thatcher, reasserted many of the traditional features of Cabinet government. He made sure that the principal decisions of Cabinet committees were endorsed by all the Cabinet. He was skilful in coaxing colleagues to agreement and in reflecting the shared view. After the 1992 general election victory and after the ERM exit a few months later, however, the picture changed. Major's public standing and that of the government and the Conservative party declined. He had broken election promises about maintaining ERM entry and was shortly to break election promises that he would not impose extra taxation. He also had to struggle with a narrow overall majority which, over time, was whittled away by by-election defeats and defections. Party rebels were able to hold the whips to ransom for their support.

Although the old wet and dry factions of the earlier Thatcher years had declined, a new division had developed. The Eurosceptics, hostile to the Maastricht Treaty and to the idea of British membership of a single currency or indeed any further steps to integration, were a growing force in the party. Among their most powerful spokespeople were Lady Thatcher and Lord Tebbit, a former party chairman, as well as much of the Conservative-supporting press, particularly the Murdoch newspapers such as the *Times* and the *Sun*. Over time these divisions spread to the Cabinet. Sceptics such as Lilley, Portillo and Redwood strained the Cabinet 'wait and see' line on the single currency. From the other wing, Kenneth Clarke, the Chancellor, thought that too much ground was being given to the sceptics. Major, trying to hold a middle line in the interest of Cabinet and party unity, appeared weak. Not surprisingly, as leaks increased and the party became more divided, John Major was more reluctant to bring key issues to Cabinet.

It is a truism to say that Cabinet is in a state of transition. Because of changes in personnel and circumstances, the chemistry and influence of the Cabinet change over the four- or five-year term of a single Prime Minister. But increasingly the Cabinet collectively has become more important as a political body rather than as a policy decider. That is the key lesson of Mrs Thatcher's fall. The weekly Cabinet meetings under Blair are short and hear reports of decisions made elsewhere. But the meeting is important in giving life to the idea of a collective responsibility or sense of ownership among the ministers for the range of policies over which they may have little control. A Prime Minister has to handle his senior colleagues with care because they may have their own followings in the party. Today this is certainly true of John Prescott, Robin Cook or David Blunkett.

Conclusion

Reforms

There are a number of steps which might promote co-ordination and the quality of British government, including the following:

1. The creation of a small Cabinet, including some non-departmental ministers. The model often advanced is that of the wartime Cabinets of Lloyd George (1916–18), Churchill (1940–5) or Thatcher during the Falklands War and Major during the Gulf War. But many are not convinced that the wartime model is suitable for peacetime and there are political and administrative problems involved in divorcing coordination from policy making.
2. The creation of small groups, or 'inner' Cabinets, of senior figures, to impart a greater sense of direction to Cabinet. After 1945 Clement Attlee regularly consulted with the senior ministers, Morrison, Bevin and Cripps. In 1968 Wilson created a parliamentary committee which was supposed to operate like an inner Cabinet. In fact, Crossman's diaries confirm that Wilson was not keen on developing a strategy and the group never played such a role. Most prime ministers have had groups of

colleagues with whom they informally discussed matters before they reached the full Cabinet. But such behaviour may be more a recognition that ministers are not equal in political weight and experience than evidence of attempts to develop an inner Cabinet. As noted, Blair works with Gordon Brown and relies heavily on his own staff.

3. The amalgamation of departments: Of major departments today those of Defence, Foreign and Commonwealth Office, Environment, Transport and Regions, Health and Social Security, Education and Employment, and Trade and Industry have all resulted from amalgamations in the past thirty years of previously autonomous departments. It has been argued that the creation of giant departments provides the opportunity for co-ordination of policies within the enlarged departments and allows for the creation of a smaller Cabinet.

4. The creation of a central analytical body, not attached to a department but serving the Cabinet as a whole. Heath had this in mind in 1970 when he set up the Central Policy Review Staff, or 'think-tank' as it was called, located in the Cabinet Office. Its task was to present briefing papers on issues, free from any departmental perspective, and to undertake research and suggest ideas which did not fall within the responsibility of any particular department. It also provided periodic reviews on how the government and departments were performing in relation to the strategies set out in the party's 1970 manifesto.

5. The creation of a Prime Minister's Department (as discussed above). In spite of the Prime Minister's Private Office and Policy Unit it is doubtful whether he or she has sufficient resources to monitor and co-ordinate the policies of departments if he or she wants to. The development of a strong prime ministerial office would probably move Britain into a more presidential style of leadership and might face resistance in departments.

Quality of Cabinet government

Dissatisfaction with the structure and performance of Cabinet government is not surprising in view of the criticisms of Britain's economic performance in the post-war period. Among criticisms which have been advanced are the following:

1. Ministers are too frequently generalists and appointed to posts for reasons which may have little to do with their presumed expertise. In cases of routine policy making – with ministers lacking the time and often the experience to become versed in the detail – it is perhaps not surprising that civil servants may often determine policy and the principle of ministerial responsibility may provide a shield behind which the civil service dominate the policy process.

2. The frequent turnover of ministers, who last an average of just over two years in post, a rate of change exceeding that in most other Western states. Such turnover means that at any one time a number of ministers are actually learning their jobs. Under Harold Wilson (1964–70) the average ministerial tenure was less than two years. In his 1966–70 government only Denis Healey at Defence, Lord Gardiner as Lord Chancellor, William Ross, Secretary of State for Scotland and Wilson himself held the same office for the duration of the government, and in the lifetime of Thatcher's 1979–83 government only six ministers held the same office. In his first two years, Blair was already on to his third Chief Secretary to the Treasury, third Transport Secretary and third Trade and Industry Secretary. It is difficult to think of any other organisation which has such a rapid turnover of its senior management. Some commentators have claimed that ministers need a period of two years or so to actually master a department. On the other hand, it is often claimed that if a minister spends too long in a department he or she may 'go native' and perhaps become too closely identified with its interests. The case for introducing a new minister is that

he or she is likely to provide a stimulus to the policy routine. But many reshuffles of ministers are made for reasons which have little to do with policy but may have more to do with public opinion or party management.

3 Ministers are often so overloaded with work that the functions of oversight and discussion are neglected. In his revealing book *Inside the Treasury* (1982), the former Labour minister Joel Barnett commented on how 'the system' can defeat ministers:

> The sheer volume of decisions, many of them extremely complex, means that by the time even a fairly modest analysis of a problem is done, and the various options considered, you find yourself coming up against time constraints. Consequently ministers often find themselves making hasty decisions, either late at night or at an odd moment during a day full of meetings. (Barnett, 1982, p. 20)

4 Decisions are taken for short-term political gain, as instanced in Barnett's book, as well as in ministers' diaries. Barnett (1982, p. 17) criticised the ways in which decisions were taken by his 1974–9 Cabinet colleagues 'for some other reason which has nothing to do with the merits of the case'. About priorities in public expenditure he commented:

> expenditure priorities were generally decided on often outdated, and ill-considered plans made in Opposition, barely thought through as to their real value, and never as to their relative priority in social, socialist, industrial or economic terms. More often they were decided on the strength of a particular spending minister and the extent of the support he or she would get from the Prime Minister.

Chapter summary

The Prime Minister is the most powerful figure in British government, but his or her power is not fixed: it depends in part on the personality and style of the incumbent and the strength of the Cabinet he or she faces. Cabinet itself has undergone major changes in the last twenty-five years, and is now substantially run by a series of committees which do the detailed work. The heart of British government, the Prime Minister, Cabinet and departments, is under closer scrutiny now than possibly ever before. Tony Blair has proved to be an innovator: in strengthening the staff at his disposal, reinforcing No. 10's control over communications and expecting the Cabinet Office to promote Whitehall's awareness of its need to deliver the government's overall objectives.

Discussion points

- Is the Prime minister (still) too powerful?
- What if anything does Cabinet government mean today?
- How has Blair centralised power around the Cabinet Office and No. 10?
- Should there be a Prime Minister's department?

Further reading

On Cabinet history Mackintosh (1962) is still the best guide. Hennessy (1986), Thomas (1998) and James (1998) provide a lively analysis of more recent developments. Donoughue (1987), Barnett (1982), Lawson (1992), Thatcher (1993) and Howe (1994) are perceptive insider accounts. King (1985) is an excellent collection of articles. On the Major years, see Hogg and Hill (1995). On how Prime Ministers, including Blair and their staff operate see Kavanagh and Seldon (1999).

References

Barnett, J. (1982) *Inside the Treasury* (Deutsch).
Burch, M. and Holliday, I. (1996) *The British Cabinet System* (Prentice-Hall).
Clark, A. (1993) *Diaries* (Weidenfeld and Nicolson).
Donoughue, B. (1987) *Prime Minister* (Cape).

Headey, B. (1974) *British Cabinet Ministers* (Allen and Unwin).
Hennessy, P. (1986) *Cabinet* (Blackwell).
Hennessy, P. (1988) *Whitehall* (Secker and Warburg).
Hogg, S. and Hill, J. (1995) *Too Close to Call* (Little, Brown).
Howe, G. (1994) *Conflict of Loyalty* (Macmillan).
James, S. (1998) *British Cabinet Government* (Routledge).
Jones, B. (1999) 'Tony Blair's style of government', *Talking Politics*.
Kavanagh, D. (2000) 'Inside N°to' *Talking Politics*.
Kavanagh, D. and Seldon, A. (1999) *The Powers behind the Prime Minister* (HarperCollins).
King, A. (ed.) (1985) *The British Prime Minister*, 2nd edn (Macmillan).
Lawson, N. (1992) *The View from Number 11* (Cape).
Mackintosh, J. (1962) *The British Cabinet* (Stevens).
Rentoul, J. (1995) *Tony Blair* (Little, Brown).
Rhodes, R. and Dunleavy, P. (eds) (1995) *Prime Minister, Cabinet and Core Executive* (Macmillan).
Seldon, A. (1998) *Major: A Political Life* (Weidenfeld and Nicolson).
Thomas, G. (1998) *Prime Minister and Cabinet Today* (Manchester University Press).
Thatcher, M. (1993) *Thatcher: the Downing Street Years* (HarperCollins).

Chapter 20

Ministers, departments and civil servants

Philip Norton

Learning objectives

- To promote an understanding of the place and significance of government departments in British government.
- To identify the role and political impact of ministers in policy making.
- To assess the relationship between ministers and civil servants.
- To summarise and assess competing models of policy making.

Introduction

Departments form the building blocks of British government. Each is headed by a minister who has responsibility for government policy in the sector covered by the department. Each is staffed by a body of professional civil servants, responsible for advising the minister on policy and for ensuring that policy is implemented. The capacity for ministers to determine policy has been increasingly constrained by external pressures, but ministers remain significant players in policy making.

Ministers stand at the heart of British government. In legal terms, they are the most powerful figures in government. When an Act of Parliament confers powers on government to do something, it does not say 'The Prime Minister may by order . . . [do this or that]', nor does it say 'The Cabinet may by order . . .'. What it says is 'The Secretary of State may by order . . .'. In other words, legal powers are vested in senior ministers, not in the Prime Minister or Cabinet. Senior ministers are those appointed to head government departments. Their formal designation is Ministers of the Crown. Most will be given the title of Secretary of State (Secretary of State for Education, Foreign Secretary, Secretary of State for the Home Department – popularly known as the Home Secretary – and so on). Originally, there was only one Secretary of State to assist the King. The post was subsequently divided, but the fiction was maintained that there was only one Secretary of State and that fiction is maintained to the present day. That is why Acts of Parliament still stipulate that 'The Secretary may by order . . .' or 'The Secretary of State shall by order . . .'. There is no reference to 'The Secretary of State for Education' or 'The Foreign Secretary', but simply 'The Secretary of State'.

Each Minister of the Crown heads a government department. Each has a number of other ministers, known as junior ministers, to assist in fulfilling the responsibilities of the office. Each has one or more political advisers. Each has a body of civil servants – permanent, non-political professionals – to advise on policy and to ensure the implementation of policy once it is agreed on. The number of civil servants in each department will normally run into thousands.

Each Minister of the Crown is thus vested with important legal powers. Each has a department to assist in carrying out the policy or decisions that he or she has made. Each is thus, in formal terms, an important political figure, vital to the continuation of government in the United Kingdom. However, in the view of many commentators, the legal position does not match the political reality. Though legal power may be vested in senior ministers, the real power, it is argued, is exercised elsewhere. The capacity to determine policy has, on this argument, passed to other political actors, not least the European Union, the Prime Minister and civil servants. One argument is that senior ministers are now not principals in terms of policy making but rather agents, be it of the Prime Minister, of the civil servants in their department or of the European Union.

What, then, is the structure and operation of government departments? What are the powers of a senior minister? What are the limitations? To what extent is a senior minister able to deploy the powers of the office to achieve desired outcomes? And what is the best model that helps us understand the position of senior ministers in British government? Are they agents of other actors in the political system? Or are they powerful independent figures?

Departments

Each Minister of the Crown heads a **department**. The structure is essentially hierarchical. Figure 20.1 shows, in basic outline, a typical department. The actual structure of a department is more complex. Figure 20.2 shows the actual organisational structure of a particular department, the Office of Public Service, in 1997. The structure differs from department to department. Some have far more extensive and complex structures than the Office of Public Service. Within each department, the senior minister has a range of individuals to assist in formulating public policy. They can be grouped under two headings: the political and the official. The political appointees comprise the junior ministers, parliamentary private secretaries, and the special advisers. The officials comprise the civil servants in the department, headed by the Permanent Secretary, and those employed in agencies that fall within the remit of the department.

Political appointees

Junior ministers

There are three ranks of junior ministers: ministers of state, parliamentary under-secretaries of state, and parliamentary secretaries. (Because the acronym for the parliamentary under-secretaries of state is PUSS, they are known in Whitehall as 'pussies'.) They are appointed to assist the senior minister in carrying out the minister's responsibilities. They will normally be allocated particular tasks. Thus, for instance, one of the junior ministers in the Home Office is responsible for prisons, another is responsible for immigration. In the Department for Culture, Media and Sports, one of the junior ministers is designated as Minister for Sport. In the Foreign Office, one of the junior ministers has responsibility for Europe.

These ministers are appointed by the Prime Minister, though sometimes after consultation with the minister heading the department. Their

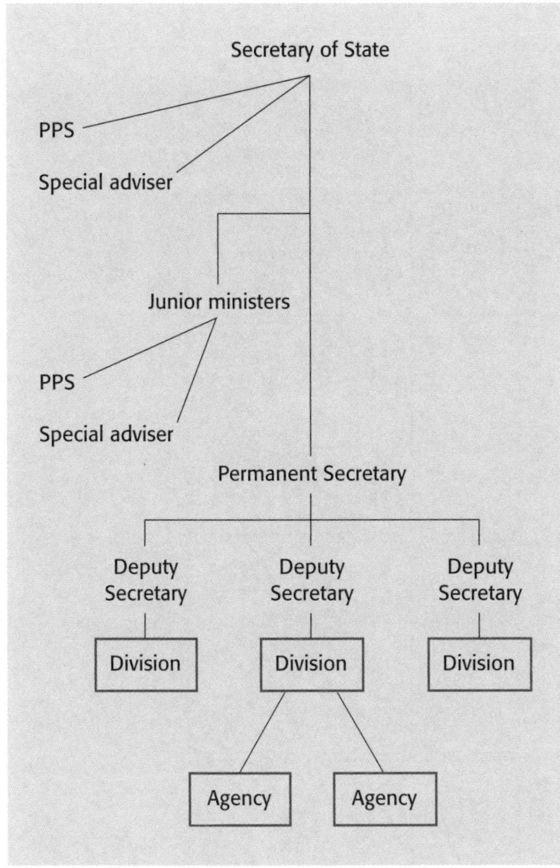

Figure 20.1 Structure of a government department

authority derives from the senior minister. It is the senior minister who decides what responsibilities they shall have and, in effect, how powerful they shall be in the department. They act on behalf of the senior minister. They have no formal line control over civil servants. A junior minister, for example, cannot overrule the civil service head of the department, the Permanent Secretary. A dispute between a junior minister and the Permanent Secretary would have to be resolved by the senior minister.

The number of junior ministers has grown over the past half-century. In the years after the Second World War, it was usual for a senior minister to be assisted by a single junior minister, normally a parliamentary secretary. The Foreign Secretary had two under-secretaries, as did the Scottish Secretary, but they were unusual. By the end of the century, it was usual for each Secretary of State to have the assistance of several junior ministers. In 1999, for example, the massive Department for Environment, Transport and the Regions had eight junior ministers (four ministers of state and four under-secretaries), the Department of Trade and Industry had seven, and the Department for Education and Employment had six.

Serving as a junior minister is usually a prerequisite for serving as a senior minister. It is rare for an MP to be appointed to the Cabinet straight from the back benches. An ambitious back-bencher will normally hope to be appointed as a Parliamentary Under-Secretary of State and then as a Minister of State before being considered for appointment to the Cabinet. Not all aspiring politicians make it beyond the ranks of junior minister. Some are dismissed after two or three years, some serve for several years without making it to the Cabinet. In July 1999, Prime Minister Tony Blair had a ministerial reshuffle that was confined primarily to the ranks of junior ministers. A number who had not shone in Government were dismissed while some able back-benchers were promoted to ministerial ranks.

Parliamentary private secretaries

Traditionally, one route to reaching junior ministerial office has been through serving as a Parliamentary Private Secretary (PPS). (The other principal route has been through serving as an officer of a back-bench committee.) A Parliamentary Private Secretary is appointed to assist a minister. The post is unpaid, the holder is not officially a member of the government and the tasks undertaken are largely determined by the minister. A PPS may serve as the minister's principal link with back-benchers, listening to what has been said and transmitting the views of MPs to the minister. The PPS will also normally help with arranging friendly parliamentary questions and will normally act as a conduit or 'runner' between the minister and the officials' box in the House of Commons during a parliamentary debate.

The PPS is selected by the minister, though subject to confirmation by the Prime Minister. In some cases, ministers will use their PPSs as trusted advisers. They may also arrange for them to have desks in their departments and may

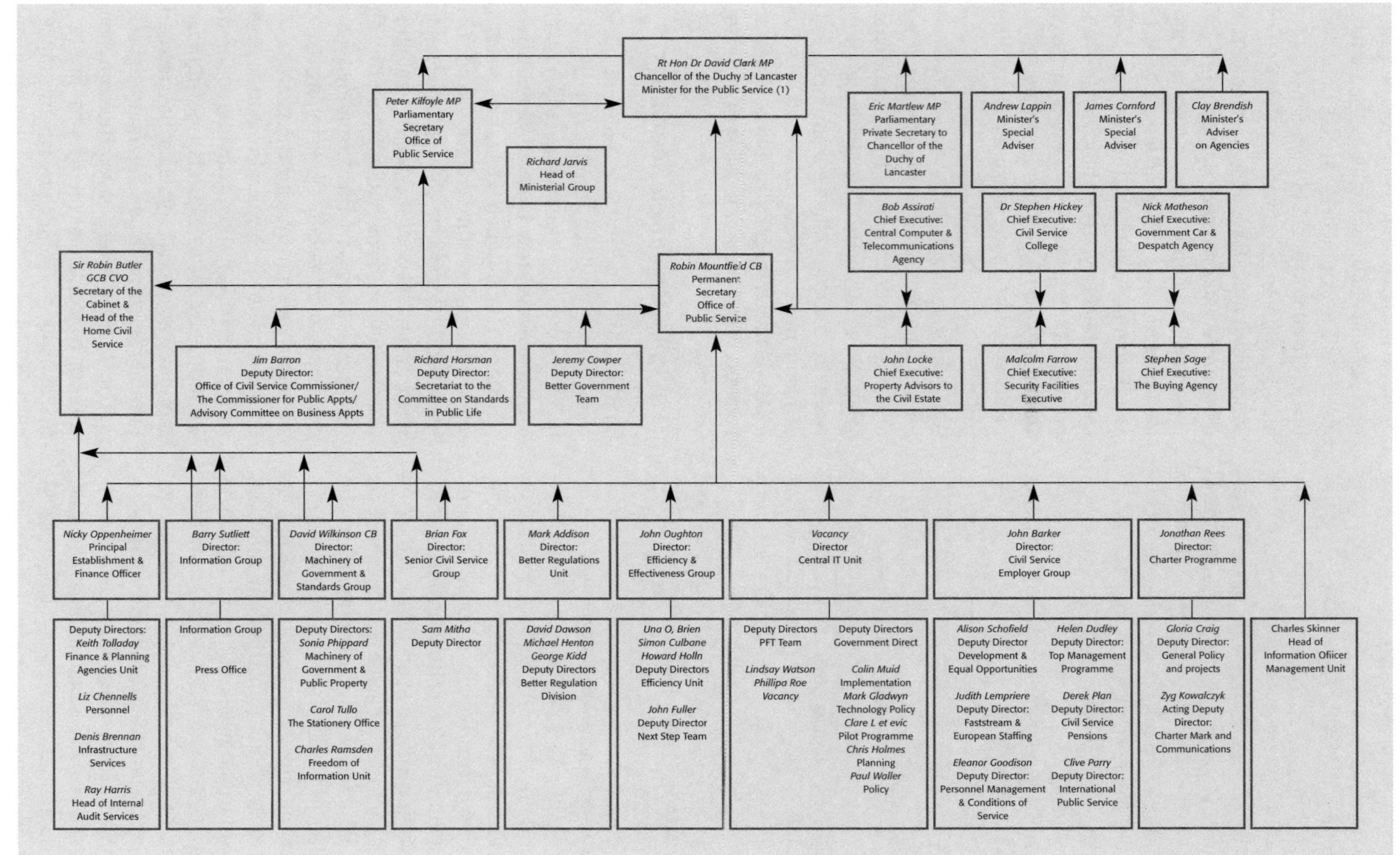

Figure 20.2 Office of public service

include them in the regular meetings (known as 'prayers') held with junior ministers and senior civil servants in the department. They thus learn how a department works and if they perform especially well may be recommended by the senior minister for promotion to junior ministerial office.

The number of PPSs has grown over the decades. Whereas only senior ministers used to appoint PPSs, it is now the practice for junior ministers to appoint them as well. There are now over forty PPSs. This may be helpful to junior ministers. It is also helpful to government. Though PPSs are not paid, they are nonetheless usually treated as part of the government's payroll vote in the House of Commons. A PPS who votes against the government is liable to be dismissed.

Special advisers

There are two types of special adviser. One is the expert, appointed because of an expertise in a particular subject. The other – the more common type – is the political, appointed to act as an adviser to the minister on a range of issues, to assist with speech writing and to act as a political link between the minister and the party and with other bodies outside the department. They are not MPs. They are typically young, bright graduates who are politically ambitious. Their loyalty is to the minister, who is responsible for appointing them and to whom their fortunes are linked: if the minister goes, the special adviser goes as well. A minister may, and frequently does, invite the special adviser to stay with them if they are moved to another post. Sometimes an incoming minister may invite the special adviser to the previous incumbent to stay on. (John Major, for example, when he became Chancellor of the Exchequer, kept on the special adviser to his predecessor.) The link, however, is normally with one minister. It is thus in the interests of the special adviser to be loyal to the minister and to work hard to ensure the minister's success.

Like junior ministers and PPSs, the number of special advisers has grown in recent years. Special advisers have their origins in the 1960s, but they became important figures in the 1970s: then, only very senior ministers were permitted to have a special adviser, and no more than one. The number expanded in the 1980s and early 1990s, with some special advisers being appointed to serve Ministers of State. Thus, for instance, in the Home Office, the Home Secretary had a special adviser and the Ministers of State had a special adviser. However, no ministry had more than two special advisers. There was a further expansion with the return of a Labour government in 1997. Some departments were permitted to have more than two special advisers. Four were appointed in the Department of Education and Employment and the same number in the Department of Environment, Transport and the Regions. Most departments, though, continued with one or two.

The officials

The bulk of the people working in government departments are **civil servants**. Since 1996, the most senior posts have been brought together to form the 'Senior Civil Service'. Posts are evaluated by each department to establish their level of responsibility and pay is determined by each department within certain set salary bands. At the beginning of 1999, the salary band for Permanent Secretaries was between £95,720 and £164,310.

Permanent secretary

The Permanent Secretary is the permanent head of a department. He (very rarely she) will usually have spent his entire career in the civil service, rising up the ranks to Under Secretary and then Deputy Secretary before being appointed Permanent Secretary in a department. Formally, the Permanent Secretary has line control within a department. That is, all communication between civil servants and a senior minister is formally channelled through the Permanent Secretary. In practice, that is now administratively impossible. Instead, submissions will normally go straight to the minister and the minister may call in the relevant civil servants to discuss particular issues for which they have responsibility. Nonetheless, submissions will be copied to the Permanent Secretary and the Permanent Secretary will normally sit in on all discussions concerning important policy and administrative matters.

The Permanent Secretary is answerable to the minister for what goes in the department. However, there is one exception. The Permanent Secretary is the accounting officer for the department. That means that responsibility for ensuring that money is spent for the purposes for which it is intended rests with the Permanent Secretary. The Permanent Secretary is answerable for the accounts and if those accounts are the subject of an investigation and report by the National Audit Office, then it is the Permanent Secretary that appears before the Public Accounts Committee of the House of Commons to answer questions raised by the report.

The Permanent Secretary is, in effect, the chief executive of the department but training for the role has usually been acquired over twenty or thirty years in the civil service. One study of 111 permanent secretaries in four periods between 1945 and 1993 found that all bar three were men (Theakston, 1995, pp. 36–43). They were usually educated at public school or grammar school before going on to Oxford or Cambridge Universities. Most went straight from university into the civil service and spent twenty-five years in Whitehall before taking up their present positions. Most also had served in more than one department, a feature especially of the latter half of the century. They were also predominantly 'generalists' – with degrees in classics or the arts – rather than specialists in law or economics; occasionally, a Permanent Secretary would be appointed who had some specialist knowledge of the subject covered by the department, but such figures were – and remain – rare. Just as ministers are normally generalists rather than specialists in a subject, so too are the civil servants who run the department. Their specialist knowledge is of how the machinery of government operates.

Senior civil servants

A similar pattern is to be found for those below the rank of Permanent Secretary. The senior civil service comprises individuals, predominantly white males, who have made their career in the civil service. (In 1999, only 18 per cent of senior civil servants were women and only 1.6 per cent were drawn from ethnic minorities.) However, there have been major changes in recent years both in terms of roles and structures. A more open structure has been introduced, with greater emphasis on bringing in people with outside experience. Staff are increasingly being recruited by open competition. This is especially the case with the chief executives of government agencies, though it extends to other senior posts. Of the most senior posts in the civil service, about 30 per cent are open to external candidates.

The civil service has a less rigid hierarchy than it had in the 1970s and 1980s. There is less rigidity in terms of the positions held by senior civil servants (titles are now likely to be more managerial, such as Director, than bureaucratic, such as Assistant Secretary) and responsibility for pay and recruitment is no longer centralised but instead delegated to individual departments. Each department also has responsibility for training, though courses have been provided through the Civil Service College. In the College, there has been an emphasis on ensuring civil servants are more geared to management and courses have been provided on subjects such as total quality, management, benchmarking and business process re-engineering. The college is now part of a new body, the Centre for Management and Policy Studies, set up to train civil servants.

Most civil servants now work in agencies. These agencies, such as the Benefits Agency, began to be created in 1988, following publication of a report – *Improving Management in Government: the Next Steps* – by Sir Robin Ibbs. Most

BOX 20.1 MINI BIOGRAPHY

Sir Robin Ibbs (1926–)
Author of report responsible for 'executive agencies' in British government. Educated Toronto and Cambridge Universities. Headed government's 'Think Tank' 1980–2. Made Head of Efficiency Unit 1983–8 and wrote Next Steps report urging the hiving off of routine government tasks into separate agencies.

executive responsibilities of government have been hived off to such agencies and today more than 70 per cent of civil servants are employed in such agencies. The intention behind the agencies has been to separate the executive or service-delivery responsibilities of government from policy making. Those senior civil servants responsible for policy advice to ministers remain at the heart of government departments.

Two features of the civil service over the past two decades are of particular relevance in studying government departments. The first is the greater emphasis on managerial and business skills. This emphasis developed under the Conservative government of Margaret Thatcher and John Major. It has been continued under the Labour government of Tony Blair. There is demand on the part of the government for the civil service to have much clearer goals and to operate in terms of performance indicators and to deliver on targets that are set for it. Prime Minister Tony Blair has been particularly keen to shake up Whitehall and to ensure that civil servants are capable of delivering on the goals set by government. The various changes that have been introduced over the past twenty years have been brought together under the umbrella term 'new public management' (NPM). This is considered in greater depth in Chapter 21. There has also been the introduction of 'prior options' testing to ensure that the services provided are necessary and best carried out by public bodies. The result has been the privatisation of various agencies. This, along with other changes (including the earlier privatisation of bodies in the public sector), has served to reduce the size of the civil service. In 1976, there were just over 750,000 civil servants. In 1986, the number was down to 596,000. By 1996, the figure was 494,000.

The second change is less often commented on but is more central to explaining the relationship between ministers and civil servants. That is, the less rigid structure within the 'core' of each department. The old hierarchical structure, policed and protected by senior civil servants who had been in place for years, has given way to a more flexible arrangement, not just in terms of formal structure but in terms of the contact that ministers have with civil servants. Permanent Secretaries tend no longer to be the gatekeepers of what advice is or is not sent to a minister. The change in the structure of the civil service has not only made departments more open in terms of the people recruited to serve in senior posts, but it has also coincided with changes introduced by ministers. In recent years, ministers have been more prone to move away from a culture of paperwork – making decisions based on papers placed before them by officials – and toward a more open and interactive culture, calling in civil servants to discuss with them the proposals embodied in their papers.

Senior ministers thus head departments that have a more managerial and business oriented ethos than before. Those departments, though they have shrunk in staff terms over recent years, can still be significant employers. The Department of Social Security has over 93,000 civil servants working in it. The Ministry of Defence has almost 80,000. However, the policy-making side of each department is relatively small. Those employed in the top echelons of the civil service – the old principal grade and above – comprise no more than 20,000 people. At the very top – occupying what used to be the posts of Assistant Secretary upwards – are less than 3,000 people. These are the people – overwhelmingly white, male and non-science graduates – who advise ministers.

Ministerial power

It has been argued that ministerial power – the power to determine particular outcomes – derives from several variables (Figure 20.3). One is specific to the office: the legal, departmental, and political powers of the office deriving from the convention of individual ministerial responsibility. Two others are specific to the individual: the purpose of the incumbent in taking office, and the skills of the incumbent. And there are three that are essentially external to the office: the power situation, the climate of expectation and international developments.

The office
Legal, departmental and political powers

The individual in the office
Purpose in taking office
Skills of the incumbent

External environment
The power situation
Climate of expectation
International developments

Figure 20.3 The components of ministerial power
Source: Adapted from Norton, 1997a

The office

Ministers are powerful by virtue of the constitutional convention of individual ministerial responsibility (see Norton, 1997b). The doctrine confers important legal, departmental and even parliamentary powers.

The legal dimension is central. We have touched on this in opening. No statutory powers are vested in the Prime Minister or Cabinet. As Nevil Johnson has written, 'the enduring effect of the doctrine of ministerial responsibility has been over the past century or so that the powers have been vested in ministers and on a relentlessly increasing scale' (Johnson, 1980, p. 84). Post-war years have seen a substantial increase in the volume of legislation passed by Parliament. Bills are not more numerous, but they are longer and more complex. It is common for bills to confer powers on ministers and to do so in broad terms.

The doctrine confers important departmental powers in that it asserts ministerial line control. The focus of much of the writing on the doctrine has often been the culpability of ministers for the actions of their civil servants, but more importantly and more pervasively the doctrine establishes that civil servants are answerable to the minister and to no one else. Civil servants answer to the minister formally through the Permanent Secretary. The creation of the Next Steps agencies has not destroyed this basic relationship. Agency heads have some degree of autonomy but the agencies remain within government, under a sponsoring department, and the agency chief is responsible – answerable – to the minister in that department.

The doctrine may be deemed important also in that the minister is answerable to Parliament for the department. That may appear a limitation – in that the minister is the subject of parliamentary questioning and attack – but it is also a power in that the minister alone is answerable to Parliament. Civil servants are not answerable to Parliament. They cannot appear at the dispatch box. They may be summoned before a select committee but they have no independent voice before that committee.

Parliamentary powers also derive from being Her Majesty's ministers. Since the Crown alone can request money, money resolutions can be moved only by a minister. Parliamentary rules also provide that certain other motions, such as the motion to suspend the ten o'clock rule, can be moved only by ministers. Parliamentary business proceeds on the basis of an agenda set largely by Government and that business largely entails bills and motions brought forward by Government. That business is normally departmental business: bills are brought forward by individual departments and steered through Parliament by the ministers of that department. Ministers generally have a far greater opportunity to speak than is the case with other parliamentarians.

Ministers, then, enjoy considerable formal powers. They also enjoy some public visibility – itself a potential source of power – deriving from their position in Government. A senior minister will have a greater chance of persuading a newspaper editor to come to dinner than will a member of the Opposition front bench or a humble back-bencher. A minister will be able to attract publicity by virtue of exercising the power of the office or by announcing an intention to exercise that power. Even if no formal power to act exists, a minister may attract publicity by making a statement or letting the press know informally what is planned. Departments have press officers but ministers may also use their special advisers to brief journalists. Press officers are civil servants. Special advisers, as we have seen, are political appointees.

Senior ministers also have some power by virtue of their political position. That is, they will be drawn (by convention) from one of the two

Houses of Parliament. Unlike members of some other executives, they retain a seat in the legislature. More importantly, though also subject to much greater variability, they may also enjoy a power base in Parliament. They may seek to build that power base, for instance through regular contact with back-benchers. Under the Labour Government of Tony Blair, the Chancellor of the Exchequer, Gordon Brown, has acquired a reputation for assiduously courting back-benchers and newly appointed ministers. Such a power base may give them leverage in relation to other ministers and to their departments. It may also make it very difficult for a Prime Minister to sack them.

BOX 20.2 MINI BIOGRAPHY

Gordon Brown (1951–)

Chancellor of the Exchequer. Educated Edinburgh University. Made his name as destructive opposition spokesman on Treasury policy. Famously stood down as a candidate in 1994 so that fellow 'moderniser' Tony Blair could have a free run at the party leadership. Initially successful at economic policy with low inflation and steady growth. Some say he has never given up ambitions to be Prime Minister one day.

Prince Edward and Sophie Rhys-Jones announce their engagement. Speculation surrounds relations between Tony Blair and his Chancellor (10 January 1999)

Team Player
Commander
Ideologue
Manager
Agent

Figure 20.4 Types of senior minister

The individual in the office

There are two dimensions to the individual in the office: purpose and skills. A minister may have important powers as a minister, but knowing that fact tells us little about how and why the power is exercised. For that, we have to turn to the person in the office. Ministers become ministers for a variety of reasons. Some simply want to be ministers. Some want to achieve particular policy outcomes. Some want to be Prime Minister. What they want will determine how they act.

One study has identified five types of senior minister – team player, commander, ideologue, manager and agent (Figure 20.4) (Norton, 2000). The types relate to different locations of decision-making power. With commanders, ideologues and managers, power-making power is retained in the office but exercised in different ways. With team players and agents, policy is 'made' elsewhere, either because ministers cannot prevent it or prefer to abdicate power to these locations.

Team player

A team player is someone who believes in collective decision making and wants to be part of that team. This correlates more or less precisely with the conception of Cabinet Government. Proposals may be put by a minister to Cabinet, but it is the Cabinet that deliberates and decides on the policy. In practice, Cabinet has difficulty in fulfilling this role because of lack of time. It is also constrained from fulfilling this role by the fact that few ministers want to be team players. There is very little evidence to suggest that many senior ministers see themselves primarily as 'team players'.

Commander

Commanders are those who have very clear ideas of what they want to achieve and those ideas derive from their own personal preferences and goals. (Preferences should be taken to include ambition.) These may derive from their own past experiences in business or government, or simply from their personal reflections. When they accept a particular office, they usually have some idea of what they want to achieve. Individuals may not be consistent commanders throughout their ministerial career. They may have a very clear idea of what they want to achieve in one or more particular office but not in another. For example, one politician who held five cabinet posts during the Thatcher and Major premierships had a clear idea of what he wanted to achieve in three of them (one was the post he had always wanted); in another he had a general idea (even though it was a post he had not wanted) and in the other – a rather senior post – he had no clear perception of what he wanted to achieve. Rather he assumed one of the other roles: that of 'manager'. There were some commanders in each Cabinet during the period of Conservative Government from 1979 to 1997. There are commanders in the Labour Government returned in 1997. These have included the Home Secretary, Jack Straw, and Education Secretary, David Blunkett.

Ideologue

An ideologue is someone who is driven by a clear, consistent philosophy. Thus, whatever office they

BOX 20.3 MINI BIOGRAPHY

David Blunkett (1947–)
Education Secretary. Educated Sheffield University and went on to become leader of Labour group on city council. MP in 1987 and, despite being blind, mastered Shadow portfolio on education. In prime position when Labour took power given Blair's pledge to reform education. Has supported higher standards and channelled more funds into the service.

occupy, the policies they pursue will derive from that philosophy. There were some ideologues – pursuing a neo-liberal philosophy – in the period of Conservative Government from 1979 to 1997. These included Sir Keith Joseph, Nicholas Ridley and John Redwood. However, they were not as numerous as often supposed. This, in part, reflects the fact that prime ministers have rarely appointed ministers on purely ideological grounds. Prime Minister Margaret Thatcher largely left junior ministerial appointments to others, thus largely restricting her choice when it came to choosing Cabinet ministers. Some ministers who may appear to be ideologues are not; rather their views in particular sectors coincide with those of a particular ideological strand. One minister who held office under Margaret Thatcher conceded that in one particular post he had what he described as 'Thatcherite priorities'; but when he occupied another more senior post later, he was certainly not seen as a Thatcherite, but rather viewed by Thatcherites as having 'gone native'.

Managers

Here the minister takes the decisions, but is not driven by any particular ideology or personal world view. Rather the approach is pragmatic, sometimes Oakeshottian: that is, helping keep the ship of state afloat and operating efficiently. Ministers may anticipate issues; more frequently they respond to them. They do not necessarily take the departmental line but decide it for themselves. When several competing demands are made of them, they act as brokers, listening and weighing the evidence and then taking a view. A good example of a manager during the period of Conservative Government in the 1990s was Foreign Secretary Douglas Hurd.

Agent

Here the minister essentially acts on behalf of another body. There are three types of agent: those of the Prime Minister, the civil service, and the European Union:

- *Prime ministerial*: Here the minister is appointed to ensure that the wishes of the Prime Minister are carried out. (This is distinct from an ideologue, who may share the Prime Minister's ideology but is an enthusiast for the ideology and will give that preference over the Prime Minister's wishes.) Occasionally, a Prime Minister may decide, in effect, to be their own Foreign Secretary or Chancellor of the Exchequer, though that depends on the willingness of the minister in question to comply: Margaret Thatcher had an easier time influencing economic policy with Sir Geoffrey Howe as chancellor than she did when it was Nigel Lawson. During the Thatcher era, there were various media reports that some ministers were put in at middle-ranking level to act as the Prime Minister's eyes and ears in a department.
- *Civil service*: Here the minister essentially adopts the departmental brief and does what the officials in the department want the minister to do. Ministers may adopt this role because they want a quiet life – some actually move up the 'greasy pole' of government despite being remarkably lazy – or because they do not have the personal will or intellect to resist the persuasive briefings of officials. Civil servants can be remarkably persuasive, and indeed devious (papers put in late, or among a mass of papers in the red box), and one or two departments do have reputations for pursuing a particular departmental 'ideology'. On some issues, ministers don't take a stand – and, as Gerald Kaufman recounts in *How To Be a Minister*, will read out their departmental brief in cabinet committee (Kaufman, 1997).
- *European Union*: Finally, and essentially for the record, ministers may be agents of the European Union. By virtue of the office they hold, they have to fulfil certain policies to comply with the UK's treaty obligations. Some may do so willingly, others reluctantly. It is possible that some may serve as agents for the European Union, in the way that some may serve as agents of the prime minister or their officials. They may not have the will or the expertise to resist their colleagues in the Council of Ministers, or the officials who liaise with the officials of the Union. This category, though, appears not to be a crowded one.

Ministers, then, have important powers and some of them want to exercise those powers. However, whether they do so successfully depends on their skills and the political environment they occupy.

Skills

In a study of prime ministerial power, published in *Teaching Politics* in 1987, it was argued that the essential skills needed by a Prime Minister, in addition to those of selection, were those of leadership, anticipation and reaction, and that a number of strategic options were available to them to achieve the desired outcome (Norton, 1987, pp. 325–45). The strategic options were those of command, persuasion, manipulation, and hiding. These skills and options apply also to senior ministers:

- *Command*: Ministers may have a clear intellectual view of what they want to achieve, but actually taking decisions to ensure that view is realised may be difficult. One Cabinet minister in the early 1980s, Sir Keith Joseph, was notorious for having difficulty making decisions to achieve his ideological goals. Conversely, some ministers have no difficulty making decisions: in the Labour Government elected in 1997, Education Secretary David Blunkett is a good example of such a minister.
- *Persuade*: Some ministers may know what they want to achieve and take a clear view. However, they need on occasion to be able to carry colleagues and others – MPs, outside organised interests, the public – with them. There are different devices that ministers may employ to bring the different actors on side: meetings with the relevant back-bench committee, for example; a 'dear colleague' letter to the party's MPs; a press conference; private briefings for journalists; and – one of the most important devices mentioned by former ministers – 'keeping No. 10 briefed' ('No. 10' meaning principally the Prime Minister but also, on occasion, other actors in Downing Street, such as the head of the No. 10 Policy Unit or the relevant person in the Unit). Some ministers will also spend time meeting affected bodies, for example, by making an effort to attend their annual conferences and accepting invitations to speak.
- *Manipulate*: The Prime Minister is sometimes devious and the same applies to senior ministers. On occasion, one may have to play off one body against another. Manipulation may entail 'kite flying' in the media, feeding a misleading story that can be denied and then using it as leverage to achieve a particular outcome. Manipulation may be met by manipulation. When a story leaked in December 1996 that the Prime Minister, John Major, was thinking of abandoning the government's 'negotiate and decide' policy on a single European currency, Deputy Prime Minister Michael Heseltine said publicly that there had been no change in government policy, and at the dispatch box in the afternoon John Major was forced to acknowledge that was the case, thus forcing him to stick with the policy he had apparently been hoping to abandon.
- *Hiding*: Ministers need to know when to avoid a particular problem. Sometimes it is better to keep one's head below the parapet rather than risk putting it above the parapet and getting shot at by the media and disgruntled MPs. One of the values of having junior ministers is that they can be put up to take the flak. For example, when the Child Support Agency (CSA) attracted enormous criticism in the first half of the 1990s, it was the relevant junior minister, rather than the Secretary of State, who appeared principally before the cameras to justify the government's position. When senior ministers decided on the evening of 'Black Wednesday' in September 1992 to suspend British membership of the European exchange rate mechanism (ERM) they avoided giving television interviews and instead put up the party chairman – who was not even a minister – to respond.

These are strategic options. However, there are two other skills that ministers need in order to achieve their goals: they need to be good time managers and they need to understand how the system – and their particular department – works:

- *Effective time management*: Ministers have difficulty organising their time effectively. Some former cabinet ministers have admitted that they had difficulty prioritising their activities and saying 'no' to various activities. Some expressed admiration for their colleagues who managed to organise their time and stay on top of their departments. One means of relieving some of the pressure is by delegation. Some ministers are good at delegating and making use of junior ministers. One cabinet minister in the 1980s gave his junior ministers particular responsibilities and then had them draw up a work programme for the next two years, and every three months had a meeting with each minister to discuss progress. Others are less organised and some have difficulty delegating tasks effectively.

- *Understanding the system*: Ministers need to know how the process works. Very occasionally some ministers are appointed without any prior experience of Parliament and the experience has rarely been a happy one, those involved displaying a lack of sensitivity to the needs of a parliamentary environment. One way to understand the system is by study. Prior to the 1997 general election, seminars were organised for shadow ministers on the workings of government. Another way – the more frequently used – is by ministerial apprenticeship. Holding junior ministerial office is useful as a way of seeing how the system works from the inside. One of the points made by one former minister was that in order to be effective in achieving your goals as a senior minister it helped, first, to have been a junior minister in the department that one was appointed to head; and, secondly, to have served in the whips' office. As a junior minister, one gets to know how the particular department works (departments differ enormously), and as a whip one gets to know how to handle MPs and to anticipate what is likely to cause trouble in the House. Understanding of a department may also derive from longevity in the office, but that is something largely beyond the control of the incumbent.

Without some (ideally, all) of these skills, a minister – however intelligent and self-driven – is not likely to succeed and may find their ministerial career stunted or destroyed altogether. Within a few months of the appointment of the new Labour government in May 1997, there were reports that some members of the Cabinet would not last beyond this autumn: the one most frequently mentioned was Gavin Strang, largely because he was indecisive and was poor at the dispatch box; in other words, he was poor at command and persuasion. He was dismissed in 1998.

External environment

Ministers may also find that their capacity to achieve desired outcomes is enhanced by the environment external to their department. This environment includes the power situation, the climate of expectations, and international developments:

- *Power situation*: The power situation overlaps with the powers and constraints of the office but provides a dynamic element. Power relationships are not static. And what the 'power situation' refers to is the relationship between different bodies in the immediate political environment. In terms of ministers, this covers especially Downing Street, Cabinet, Parliament, the civil service and the media.

  A previously popular Prime Minister may lose support among the parliamentary party or the public and start to seek support from particular ministers, doing so through being more supportive of their policies. A minister may find it easier to push a policy through as the authority of a Prime Minister wanes. There may be a shift in the power situation as a result of a Cabinet reshuffle. A minister may find that colleagues opposed to a particular policy have been moved or sacked. Elections of officers of back-bench party committees may result in opponents of a minister's policy being replaced by supporters. Changes of ownership of particular newspapers may result in greater media support for a policy. Changes may occur that make the power situation unfavourable, but at times it may be highly favourable to a particular minister and the policies of that minister.

- *Climate of expectation*: The expectations of citizens are clearly important and change over time. The Conservative Party was the beneficiary of a particular climate of expectation in 1979 and the victim of a very different climate in 1997. The popular mood may initially be hostile to a particular proposal and then, perhaps induced by particular events, swing in support of it. Particular ministers may benefit from a particular climate of expectation, a popular mood favouring what they want to achieve. That mood can be a political resource for the minister, making it difficult for the Cabinet to resist a proposal for which there is clearly overwhelming popular support.
- *International developments*: What happens elsewhere in the world may limit ministers in terms of what they wish to achieve but on occasion may also make it possible for ministers to achieve what they want. A natural disaster or civil war may strengthen the position of a minister who wishes to increase foreign aid or to intervene militarily in a conflict. A shift in power or in policy in another state may facilitate a minister achieving a particular outcome. A change of government in another EU country may enable a minister to get a particular proposal adopted by the EU Council of Ministers.

Two conclusions can be drawn from the foregoing analysis. The first is that senior ministers have the potential to be significant figures in determining public policy. The second is that ministerial power is variable, not constant. It can be subject to a wide range of constraints. Let us consider in a little greater depth the constraints.

Constraints

Ministers labour under a number of constraints. The most important are constitutional, legal and managerial. Constitutionally, they are constrained by the doctrine of collective ministerial responsibility. Major decisions have to percolate up for Cabinet approval which means, in practice, Cabinet committee; and approval may not always be forthcoming. The constitutional power exercised by the Prime Minister to hire, fire and shuffle ministers may also be a powerful constraint on ministerial actions and it may be exercised in order to reflect the Prime Minister's policy preferences.

Ministers may also be constrained by the convention of individual ministerial responsibility. Though it is a convention that, as we have seen, ensures that statutory powers are vested in ministers and that they have line control within their departments, it is also one that renders ministers answerable for what takes place within their departments. This is often assumed to mean that, in the event of an error within a department, the minister resigns. Though ministers may be deemed culpable for what goes on in their departments, this has rarely meant having to resign if mistakes are made. Ministers have variously resigned because of personal scandal, or disagreement with government policy, but very rarely because of a mistake made within their department (see Norton, 1997b; see also Woodhouse, 1994). A distinction is frequently drawn between policy and operation: if the policy is right but is not carried out, then those public officials who have failed to carry it out are the ones who are disciplined. Nonetheless, the convention is a constraint in that ministers have to answer for what happens in their department. If things go wrong, the minister has to explain and defend, and if necessary take corrective action. Even if the minister does not resign, the minister's career may be adversely affected.

This leads into what is effectively a parliamentary constraint. Ministers have to defend themselves in what can be the demanding arena of Parliament; indeed, the terminology is appropriate and the reputation of ministers may not always survive the ordeal in that arena. Ministers are also constrained not so much by parliament but rather within parliament by their own party; the parliamentary party, and party committees, may at times constitute an awkward audience for ministers and even prevent ministers proceeding with a desired policy.

Legal constraints exist in that ministers may be limited by the powers conferred on them by Parliament. They have increasingly to be sensitive to the risk of acting *ultra vires* (beyond powers). A greater degree of judicial activism since the 1960s may be the product of a change of judicial culture (or of those who are affected by government being more prepared to seek judicial review) or a change in the nature of government; but whichever it is, the courts are more active nowadays in reviewing the legality of ministerial actions.

The courts, as we shall see in Chapter 23, are also more active as a consequence of various constitutional changes. Ministers are constrained by the conditions of membership of the European Union, the incorporation of the European Convention on Human Rights (ECHR) into British law, and by the devolution of powers to elected assemblies in different parts of the United Kingdom. In policy areas that fall within the competence of the EU, ministers can no longer exercise power unilaterally but rather form part of a collective decision-making body (the Council of Ministers) in which they may be over-ruled. As their responsibilities have increased as a consequence of the UK's membership of the EU, so their capacity to affect outcomes has decreased. Ministers are constrained by the provisions of the ECHR and in introducing bills now have to confirm that they comply with the provisions of the ECHR. Devolution has moved certain policy areas to the competence of elected assemblies, especially the Scottish Parliament, and a UK minister may have difficulty moving ahead with a policy without the support of the executives in Scotland and Wales.

Ministers are also subject to what may be termed managerial constraints. Ministers have a mass of responsibilities and duties: they are departmental ministers, they are members of the Cabinet, they are members of the appropriate EU Council of Ministers, they are party and political figures (invited to attend and address a mass of meetings), they are ministers answerable to Parliament, they are (except for those ministers who are peers) constituency MPs and they are MPs – party MPs – who have to attend Parliament to vote for their party. Ministers have difficulty managing their time. Their evenings are taken up reading and signing papers that are crammed into their ministerial red boxes. Their days may be full of meetings with officials and representatives of outside bodies, leaving little time for sustained reflection. Time spent travelling between meetings is variously spent dictating constituency correspondence into a dictaphone.

Ministers are also public and political figures, driven increasingly by the demands of a twenty-four-hour news service. The media demand instant comments and there are now the means for immediate communication. Ministers – and those wanting to interview them – are rarely without their mobile telephones and pagers.

The consequence of these demands is that ministers are frequently in a reactive, rather than a proactive, mode, having to rush to deal with problems and queries placed before them – and placed before them on a relentless scale – and with little time to stand back and to think through what they want to achieve and whether they are on the path to achieving it.

Explaining ministerial power

Ministers are powerful figures in government. At the same time, they are subject to remarkable constraints. How, then, can one make sense of their role in British government? Various models have been created to help us understand the role of ministers in policy making. Let us assess three that provide very different perspectives: the principal-agent model, the power dependency model and the baronial model.

Principal-agent model

This stipulates that ministers are essentially the agents of a principal. Thus, though some ministers may be commanders, ideologues or managers, most fall under the category, identified earlier, of agents. One school of thought contends that the UK has prime ministerial government, and thus that ministers are agents of the Prime Minister. Another school of thought advances the proposition that the UK has civil service government, and thus that ministers are agents of civil servants.

The prime ministerial government school of thought argues that the powers of the Prime Minister are such that the Prime Minister is in a position to determine public policy. The Prime Minister makes policy preferences through the choice of senior ministers. If the Prime Minister wishes to achieve a particular policy outcome, he can effectively require a senior minister to agree to that policy. A minister failing to comply with prime ministerial wishes may cease to be a minister. Furthermore, the Prime Minister can ensure particular outcomes through control of the Cabinet agenda and through chairing the Cabinet. The Prime Minister can keep a tight rein on ministers through monitoring their speeches and through requiring the text of speeches to be cleared by Downing Street. Government policy, it is argued, is increasingly being made in Downing Street and not in the individual government departments.

The civil service school of thought argues that it is the civil service that determines policy outcomes. Civil servants can help shape, even determine, the minister's agenda. Civil servants have an advantage over ministers in terms of their size, permanence, expertise and cohesion. There is one senior minister heading a department. The senior civil servants in the department may run into a three-figure number. A minister, even with the help of a number of junior ministers, cannot keep track of everything that is going on in a department. A senior minister will, on average, serve in one ministerial post for two years. (In the decades before the Second World War, the average was four years.) Civil servants will be in place in the department before a minister arrives and will usually still be in place once a minister has departed. A new minister provides civil servants with an opportunity to fight anew battles that may previously have been lost. Furthermore, that permanence also allows civil servants to build up a body of administrative expertise that is denied to a transient minister. Civil servants may be in a position to know what is achievable, and what is not, in a way that ministers cannot. Civil servants, it is argued, are also more politically and socially cohesive than ministers: politically cohesive in that they imbue a particular civil service and departmental ethos, and their approach is shaped by that ethos, and socially cohesive in that they tend to be drawn from the same or similar social backgrounds and to be members of the same London clubs. Ministers, on the other hand, imbue no particular ethos and are drawn from somewhat disparate backgrounds. They do not tend to mix socially together in the way that senior civil servants do.

Civil servants are in a position to influence, even control, the flow of information to a minister. A minister may not always receive every piece of information relevant to a particular proposal. The minister's diary may be filled by meetings that are largely inconsequential or so numerous as to squeeze out time to do other things. The minister's red boxes may be filled with a mass of papers, the more important tucked away at the bottom. Officials may put up position papers, outlining various options, but omitting others or skewing the material in support of each in such a way that only one option appears a viable option. Civil servants also monitor minister's calls and may seek to limit formal contact between one minister and another. If a minister takes a view contrary to that adopted by civil servants in the department, the civil servants may ask civil servants in other departments to brief their ministers to take a contrary line when the matter comes before Cabinet committee. There is also extensive contact between officials in the UK Government and in the EU Commission. Ministers, with little time to prepare for meetings, often have to be briefed on the plane to Brussels. On this line of argument, ministers have little scope to think about policy goals and to consider information and advice other than that placed before them by their officials.

This view of the power of the civil service over ministers has been variously voiced by former ministers and commentators and was famously encapsulated in a popular television series, *Yes Minister*, in the early 1980s.

However, both schools of thought have been challenged. The prime ministerial government model overlooks, according to critics, the limited time, resources and interest of the Prime Minister. The Prime Minister occupies a particular policy space – that of high policy (dealing with the economic welfare and security of the nation) – and has limited time to interfere in middle-level policy generated by ministers (see Norton 1997a, 2000). Furthermore, despite an extension of policy resources in Downing Street under Prime Minister Tony Blair, the resources available to a Prime Minister in Downing Street are limited. A senior minister has more advisers than the Prime Minister has in the minister's sector of public policy. Even though material must be cleared through Downing Street, some ministers are slow in submitting texts of speeches; some may never even reach Downing Street. Prime Ministers rarely have a grasp of, or a deep interest in, every sector of public policy. Instead, they leave it to ministers to get on with their jobs, frequently free of interference from Downing Street. Indeed, one of the most remarkable findings of recent research into senior ministers was that it is very rare for a Prime Minister, when appointing someone to Cabinet office, to tell the minister what is expected of them (Norton, 2000). Nigel Lawson recalls that when he accepted the post of Chancellor of the Exchequer, he was offered only one piece of advice by the Prime Minister: 'That was to get my hair cut' (Lawson, 1992, p. 249). The advice offered to John Major when he was appointed Foreign Secretary was also brief and unrelated to specific policy: 'You had better hang on to your seatbelt' (Seldon, 1997, p. 87).

The civil service school of thought is challenged by the claim that civil servants are not as proactive and as cohesive as proponents of this thesis suggest. The demands made of civil servants are such that they too have little time for sustained thought and reflection. Though research suggests that civil servants in some departments imbue a particular departmental ethos, most civil servants seek to carry out the wishes of their ministers, regardless of their own views or prior departmental preferences. Indeed, recent research points to the extent to which civil servants are loyal to their ministers (Norton, 2000). Far from seeking to impede them, they work hard to carry out their wishes. One Conservative minister, Cecil Parkinson, recorded in his memoirs that civil servants were 'very stimulating to work with, very loyal and incredibly hard working' (Parkinson, 1992, p. 154). Another, Norman Tebbit, recorded that he found he had 'the benefit of officials of the highest integrity and ability. Once I had laid down policy they were tireless in finding ways to deliver what I wanted' (Tebbit, 1989, p. 231). Ministers are also now more likely to call civil servants in to quiz them about the papers they have submitted. Ministers themselves may also discuss matters privately, free from civil service involvement. Some of these meetings are bilateral, rather than multilateral. One minister, interviewed by this author, recalled with wry amusement how his civil servants tried to limit his contacts with other ministers, largely oblivious of the fact that once he was in his minister's room in the Commons he could quite easily pop to see another minister to have a quiet chat.

Civil service cohesion, and the ethos attached to the service and to particular departments, is also being eroded by the people from outside the civil service being brought in to senior posts and also by the greater emphasis being placed on managerial skills. Civil servants are being trained to deliver certain specified goals. A perceived failure to deliver under the Labour government of Tony Blair has resulted in pressure being put on senior civil servants to improve their performance in meeting the government's targets. As civil servants are under greater pressure to deliver what ministers expect of them, so ministers are also bringing in more political appointees in order to provide advice and to handle their relations with the media.

A seminal work on Cabinet ministers by Bruce Headey, published in 1974, found that civil servants looked to ministers for leadership. They preferred ministers who could take decisions and fight (and win) departmental battles (Headey, 1974, pp. 140–53). That appears to remain the case. As one former Permanent Secretary put it in a lecture in 1995, 'To some it might seem like heaven on earth to have a Minister who has no ideas and is endlessly open to the suggestions or recommendations of officials. But that is not the case. Officials need ministers with ideas . . . Officials need stimulus; need leadership; and, on occasion, conflict' (Holland, 1995, p. 43). This suggests that civil servants are more likely to welcome an effective commander, ideologue or manager as their minister than an agent or team player.

Power dependency model

This model has been developed by R.A.W. Rhodes (1981, 1997). Though used to cover particularly, though not exclusively, centre–local relations, it is relevant for a study of the relationship between ministers and other actors in the political system.

It is based on several propositions. One of the principal propositions is that any organisation is dependent upon other organisations for resources. Thus, the Prime Minister is dependent on the resources available in government departments; he does not have all the resources he needs in Downing Street. Ministers are dependent on their departments: they need civil servants to provide advice and to carry out their decisions. Civil servants need ministers to deliver resources through fighting battles with the Treasury and in Cabinet. A second proposition is that in order to achieve their goals, organisations have to exchange resources. In other words, no body can operate as an exclusive and effective body. Actors within the political system need others in the system to help them achieve their goals. There is a dependence on others. That means that alliances have to be created. The model recognises that there may be a body or group of bodies who dominate in the relationship but that the relationship may change as actors fight for position.

The relevance for understanding the role of senior ministers is that it stands as something of a corrective to the principal-agent model. Though there may be times when the Prime Minister or civil servants are to the fore in determining policy outcomes, ministers are not relegated to some supporting role. They need the Prime Minister and civil servants, but conversely the Prime Minister and civil servants need them: they are an important resource and they cannot necessarily be taken for granted. A Prime Minister may thus need to build support in Cabinet to get a controversial measure approved: the support of senior ministers thus constitutes a vital, indeed a necessary, resource. It may be necessary but it may not be sufficient. Statutory powers, as we have seen, are vested in senior ministers. The Prime Minister, and Cabinet, thus needs to ensure that the relevant minister is willing to exercise those powers. Others may thus depend on the resources at the disposal of ministers. At the same time, ministers themselves are dependent on the resources of others. They need the political support of the Prime Minister. They need their civil servants to carry out their wishes. They also need different bodies outside government to accept and to help implement their policies. The Lord Chancellor, for example, may need to mobilise the support of the Bar in order to achieve reform of the legal system.

The power dependency model thus suggests a more complex and less hierarchical political process than that advanced by the principal-agent models. Though the Prime Minister may predominate, it is not to the extent that we can claim the existence of prime ministerial government. Ministers are more important players in the process than the principal-agent models suggest. Though important, ministers themselves are not dominant either. They too depend on others in the political process. The process of policy making is thus an essentially crowded and interactive one.

The power dependency model has been variously criticised (see Rhodes, 1997, p. 37). In terms of understanding the place of senior ministers in government, it does not necessarily help explain who is predominant at any one time. Extensive empirical research would be necessary to do that. It also runs foul of objections from advocates of the principal-agent models. They contend that senior ministers may be resources that a Prime Minister needs, but they are subordinate resources that can be drawn on by the Prime Minister without the need for persuasion. The power dependency model does not help explain cases where the Prime Minister has achieved a particular outcome by adopting a confrontational stance rather than an alliance-building one. As various Cabinet ministers noted, Margaret Thatcher as Prime Minister was not noted for seeking to build alliances in Cabinet. 'Margaret not only starts with a spirit of confrontation but continues with it right through the argument' (Prior, 1986, p. 138). The model also does not help explain those cases where ministers can, and do, act unilaterally.

The baronial model

This model has been developed by this writer. It posits that ministers are like medieval barons in that they preside over their own, sometimes vast, policy territory. Within that territory they are largely supreme. We have identified the formal and informal underpinnings of this supremacy. Ministers head their respective departments. They have the constitutional authority and the legal power to take decisions. No one else enjoys that power. Junior ministers have no formal power and can act only on the authority of the senior minister. Once the minister has taken a 'view' – that is, made a decision – the civil servants in the department implement it. The ministers have their own policy space, their own castles – even some of the architecture of departments (such as the Home Office in Queen Anne's Gate and Ministry of Health in Whitehall) reinforces that perception – and their own courtiers. Indeed, recent years have seen a growth in the coterie of courtiers appointed by some senior ministers, some – such as the Chancellor of the Exchequer, Gordon Brown – seen almost as having an alternative court to that of the Prime Minister. The ministers fight – or form alliances – with other barons in order to get what they want. They resent interference in their territory by other barons and will fight to defend it.

The analogy is not altogether accurate in that the barons have no responsibility for raising taxes. (The exception is the Chancellor of the Exchequer who has become more powerful than the original holders of the ancient office.) The Prime Minister also has greater power than a medieval monarch to dispense with the services of the barons, though the differences are not as great as may be supposed: a Prime Minister has difficulty dispensing with the services of powerful barons. Despite the absence of a precise fit, the model has utility for understanding the nature and fluidity of power relationships within government. Far from Cabinet being an homogeneous body of prime ministerial agents, it is a heterogeneous gathering of powerful individuals.

Furthermore, reinforcing the baronial model is the approach taken by ministers to their jobs. Though prime ministers can use ministerial appointments as a way of changing or confirming their own policy preferences, they rarely choose a Cabinet of similar ministerial types. Cabinet typically contains a mix of commanders, managers and ideologues, with the interests of the individual ministers around the table, and their particular departmental territories, taking precedence over any concept of altruistic collective decision-making.

This provides a new perspective on the relationship between senior ministers and the Prime Minister. Rather than being able to give directions, as in a principal-agent relationship, a Prime Minister has to be prepared to bargain with the more powerful barons in his government. He may be able to control some of the weaker members of the Cabinet but others may be too powerful to be subject to prime ministerial direction. At a minimum, ministers have an important gate-keeping role. To follow the analogy, they can close their departmental drawbridges and deny the Prime Minister entry to their policy domain. If the Prime Minister wants a particular policy implemented, the relevant minister has the formal power to say no and a strong-minded commander or ideologue, even a determined manager, may have the political will to exercise that power.

A Prime Minister has little scope to act unilaterally. Furthermore, the Prime Minister has limited resources to ensure that ministers act in accordance with his wishes. His own court, as we have noted, is a small one. Attempts by Prime Minister Tony Blair to strengthen the co-ordination and oversight of Downing Street are testimony to this limited capacity. The more cunning of senior ministers can frequently circumvent attempts to limit what they say and do. Speeches may be sent late to Downing Street. Back-benchers or the media may be mobilised in support of a particular policy.

The senior barons are thus able to plough their own furrow, making their own speeches, leaking – through their courtiers – their own side of a particular argument and their own perception of what has taken place in Cabinet or Cabinet committee. They can and do form alliances to achieve the approval of measures subject to Cabinet – which usually means Cabinet committee – approval (middle-level policy) and may operate unilaterally in laying orders that they are empowered by statute to make (low-level policy). Sometimes the Prime Minister is in an almost helpless position, having to remind his ministers not to leak details of what has taken place and not to speak to the press without clearance.

Ministers develop their own ways of preserving their territorial integrity. Some adopt an isolationist stance, others adopt a confrontational stance (see Norton, 2000). The stances taken both reflect the variety of approaches taken by ministers and that they cannot be characterised as agents. They are barons and in order to get their way sometimes have to fight barons as well as the monarch.

Characterising senior ministers as barons is also appropriate in that, like medieval barons, they are powerful but not all-powerful. They are constrained by other powerful actors, including the monarch (Prime Minister) and other barons (senior ministers), and by a recognition that they have to abide by laws and conventions. Indeed, as we have seen, they are increasingly constrained as the political environment has become more crowded, with groups coming into existence and making more demands of them – groups that they may need to co-operate with in implementing policy – and with more actors with the power to take decisions of their own. Ministers may thus find their time consumed by fighting battles with other political actors, be it bodies within the European Union or within the UK. Consequently, to provide a dynamic of the present state of senior ministers in British government, one can offer a model of barons operating within a shrinking kingdom.

This model is compatible with the power dependency model but it provides a greater emphasis on the role of ministers and encompasses the different strategies adopted by ministers, including fighting battles as well as alliance building. It is geared more directly than the power dependency model to senior ministers. However, it has been criticised on the grounds that the fit with medieval barons is far from perfect – that the power and activity of the barons bears little relevance to senior ministers today. It also has the same drawback as the other models, in that they are models, rather than theories. However, it stands as a useful counterpoint to the principal-agent models. It provides a new perspective on the role of senior ministers, emphasising the role played in government by ministers as ministers, rather than seeing them solely as a collective body, subsumed under the heading of Government or Cabinet. This model suggests that senior ministers are more important figures in British government than is generally realised.

Chapter summary

Ministers of the Crown head government departments. Those departments are extensive and complex bodies. Ministers enjoy substantial formal as well as political powers. The extent to which they are able to utilise those powers will depend upon the purpose and skill of the individual minister as well as power situation, climate of expectation and international developments. Ministers face considerable constraints, especially in recent years as the domain in which they operate has been constricted.

Ministers operate in a complex political environment. Different models seek to locate the place of ministers in that environment. The principal-agent model contends that ministers are agents of the Prime Minister or of civil servants. The power dependency model posits an environment in which ministers have to negotiate with other actors in order to achieve desired outcomes. The baronial model posits that ministers have their own policy territory, castles and courtiers and fight or build alliances in order to get their way. The last two models suggest that ministers enjoy a greater role in policy making than is generally realised in the literature on British politics.

Discussion points

- Is there an ideal type of senior minister?
- Why are departments the basic building blocks of British government?
- What should be the relationship between a minister and civil servants?
- What is the relationship between ministers and civil servants?
- Which model best explains the position of senior ministers in British government?

Further reading

There are many books of memoirs by former ministers. Especially good in discussing the role of the minister in the policy process are Bruce-Gardyne

(1986) and Lawson (1992). Kaufman (1997) provides a humorous but pertinent guide as to how to be a good minister. However, very few academic works have appeared that look conceptually at the role of ministers. Rose (1987) provides a functional analysis and Brazier (1997) offers a more formal analysis. A broader analysis, encompassing the dynamics of ministerial office, is provided by Norton (2000). Junior ministers are covered by Theakston (1987). The relation of ministers to Parliament is dealt with by Woodhouse (1994).

There are various works on departments and, more especially, civil servants. A massive work, looking at departments and the civil servants that work in them, is that of Hennessy (1989). More recent works include Pyper (1995) and Theakston (1995). For the material, see Chapter 21.

References

Brazier, R. (1997) *Ministers of the Crown* (Clarendon Press).

Bruce-Gardyne, J. (1986) *Ministers and Mandarins* (Sidgwick and Jackson).

Headey, B. (1974) *British Cabinet Ministers* (George Allen & Unwin).

Hennessy, P. (1989) *Whitehall* (Secker and Warburg).

Holland, Sir G. (1995) 'Alas! Sir Humphrey, I knew him well', *RSA Journal*, November.

Johnson, N. (1980) *In Search of the Constitution* (Methuen).

Kaufman, G. (1997) *How to be a Minister* (Faber and Faber).

Lawson, N. (1992) *The View from No. 11* (Bantam Press).

Norton, P. (1987) 'Prime ministerial power: a framework for analysis', *Teaching Politics*, Vol. 16, No. 3, pp. 325–45.

Norton, P. (1997a) 'Leaders or led? Senior ministers in British government', *Talking Politics*, Vol. 10, No. 2, pp. 78–85.

Norton, P. (1997b) 'Political Leadership', in L. Robins and B. Jones (eds), *Half a Century in British Politics* (Manchester University Press).

Norton, P. (2000) 'Barons in a shrinking kingdom? Senior ministers in British Government', in R.A.W. Rhodes (ed.), *Transforming British Government*, Vol. 2 (Macmillan).

Parkinson, C. (1992) *Right at the Centre* (Weidenfeld & Nicolson).

Prior, J. (1986) *A Balance of Power* (Hamish Hamilton).

Pyper, R. (1995) *The British Civil Service* (Prentice-Hall/Harvester Wheatsheaf).

Rhodes, R.A.W. (1981) *Control and Power in Centre–Local Government Relationships* (Gower).

Rhodes, R.A.W. (1997) *Understanding Governance* (Open University Press).

Rose, R. (1987) *Ministers and Ministries* (Clarendon Press).

Seldon, A. (1997) *Major: a Political Life* (Weidenfeld & Nicolson).

Tebbit, N. (1989) *Upwardly Mobile* (Futura).

Theakston, K. (1987) *Junior Ministers* (Blackwell).

Theakston, K. (1995) *The Civil Service Since 1945* (Blackwell).

Woodhouse, D. (1994) *Ministers and Parliament* (Clarendon Press).

Chapter 21

Civil service management and policy

Robert Pyper

Learning objectives

- To encourage an understanding of the link between politics and issues of public service management.
- To establish the scale and nature of the reforms that have taken place in the organisation responsible for managing central government services.
- To address key questions concerning the extent to which the civil service has been fundamentally changed by managerial reforms and the degree to which service delivery has been improved.

Introduction

The civil service stands at the core of the UK's political system. It is a vital connection between people and government. It provides ministers with expert advice on how to give life to the political programmes on which they were elected. Charged with the ultimate responsibility for the efficient and effective delivery of government policies, it is required to manage the full range of central state services in a manner which meets the needs of two very different 'client' groups: public service users and government ministers. This chapter focusses on the major changes introduced in order to modernise and improve the management of central government services, and the key questions these raise about the future purpose and direction of the civil service.

'Why don't you reform the Civil Service?' she suggested. She makes it sound like one simple little task instead of a lifetime of dedicated carnage. Which reforms in particular did she have in mind, I wondered? Anyway, any real reform of the Civil Service is impossible, as I explained to her.

'Suppose I thought up fifty terrific reforms. Who will have to implement them?'

She saw the point at once. 'The Civil Service', we said in unison, and she nodded sympathetically. But Annie doesn't give up easily.

'All right' she suggested, not fifty reforms. Just one'.

'One?'

'If you achieve *one* important reform of the Civil Service – that would be something'.

Something? It would get into the *Guinness Book of Records*.

Jonathan Lynn and Antony Jay, *Yes Minister. The Diaries of a Cabinet Minister by the Rt Hon James Hacker MP*.

(BBC, 1983)

For most of its history the British civil service seemed to epitomise all that was traditional and unchanging in our system of government and politics. In spite of numerous attempts to reform and modernise it, as it entered the last quarter of the twentieth century, the key features of the Whitehall machine were broadly similar to those which had been put in place over one hundred years earlier. Naturally, certain aspects of the organisation had changed over this period, and although critics tended to focus on the more backward-looking features of the administrative structure, the standard of public service provided remained relatively high. Nonetheless, the dominant image of the civil service was of a bastion of tradition, with a built-in capacity to resist basic change. Then, in the course of a relatively short period, virtually everything changed. The size, shape, structure and even the purpose of the civil service came under close scrutiny and yielded to the forces of modernisation. As rolling programmes of reform swept through Whitehall the sustained pace and radical nature of the changes could not fail to attract serious academic and political scrutiny.

This chapter offers an overview and analysis of the main changes introduced in the civil service during this period of reform, together with some perspectives on the future direction of the state's administrative arm.

Restructuring service delivery: executive agencies

The emergence of Next Steps

The basic structure of the civil service was transformed by the advent of executive agencies through the **Next Steps** initiative, which started in 1988. The net effect of this was to supplement the traditional departmental mode of organisation with one based on the idea that certain key departmental functions could be carried out by 'satellites' of the Whitehall departments. For example, the full range of social security benefits would be delivered to the public through an executive agency of the Department of Social Security rather than by the traditional branch offices of the Department itself. Other agencies might focus on the provision of in-house services, such as information technology or property management. The whole point of this structural reorganisation was to improve service delivery while modernising the management of the civil service itself.

The principle of decentralising executive, managerial and service delivery functions within a framework of continuing policy control from the centre had become increasingly attractive to some senior figures in the Thatcher Government. This was not a particularly novel concept – indeed, one element of the civil service reforms which had been inspired in an earlier generation by the Fulton report of 1968 was the 'hiving-off' of certain functions into executive agencies. The Defence Procurement Executive emerged from the Ministry of Defence, the Property Service Agency from the Department of the Environment and the Manpower Services Commission from the Department of Employment. Headed by Chairmen who were appointed by the Secretaries of State in the parent departments, these agencies were given responsibility for delivering specified services to the armed forces (in the case of the DPE), government departments generally (in the case of the PSA) and the unemployed (in the case of the MSC). With substantial responsibility for their own budgets, and significant operational freedom, the agencies nonetheless remained constitutionally accountable to ministers. Although these bodies were in many respects the forerunners of the executive agencies spawned by the Next Steps programme from the late 1980s onwards, at the time they appeared more like *ad hoc* experiments with decentralisation in an era otherwise dominated by the concept of 'giant' government departments.

However, in the late 1980s, the agency concept was revived and radically expanded to the point where it became the keystone of civil service reform. At its launch in 1988, the Next Steps programme advanced the concept of decentralisation and set in motion the process which came to be known as the agencification of the civil service. To a considerable extent, Next Steps resulted from the perceived limitations of the first waves of Thatcherite reform in central government. The programme of efficiency scrutinies co-ordinated by Margaret Thatcher's special adviser Derek Rayner, and the resulting Financial Management Initiative, brought significant managerial changes in their wake, but they ultimately failed to transform the prevailing management culture of the civil service to the satisfaction of the Prime Minister.

Rayner's successor as Head of the Downing Street Efficiency Unit, Robin Ibbs, produced a report which reviewed the civil service managerial changes which had already been introduced, identified the obstacles to further change and made recommendations about the next steps to be taken (Efficiency Unit, 1988). The implicit conclusion of the Ibbs, or Next Steps, Report was that the managerial reforms introduced since 1979 had failed to transform and modernise the civil service. The document argued that the most significant obstacles in the way of fundamental managerial change could be overcome only if the entire structure of the civil service was overhauled, facilitating the creation of new executive agencies, headed by Chief Executives with significant managerial freedoms and operating at arm's length from the core parent departments, to which they would be, nonetheless, ultimately accountable. Since the report's authors estimated that 95 per cent of the civil service dealt with the executive functions of policy implementation and service delivery, it was clear that the creation of agencies to carry out this work would amount to a fundamental structural reform of the central government machine.

Creating agencies

The Thatcher Government formally accepted and launched the Next Steps programme in February 1988, and this quickly became accepted as the most significant civil service reform since the implementation of the Northcote–Trevelyan Report in the late nineteenth century (for details, see Greer, 1994; Pyper, 1995). Every government department was obliged to conduct ongoing analyses of their detailed activities and programmes. 'Prior options' were examined, including the possibility of privatising the activity or leaving it within the traditional departmental framework. However, if a department concluded that an activity or service might be run without ministerial control on a day to day basis, might be a suitable case for managerial innovation and might be large enough to justify significant organisational change, the Next Steps option became distinctly feasible. Following successful consultations between the parent department, the agency-candidate, the Next Steps Unit in the Cabinet Office and the Treasury, a framework document would be produced as a prelude to the creation of an executive agency. The framework document would set out information about the agency's policy objectives, performance targets, relationship with the parent department and pay and personnel issues.

Within a decade of the publication of the Next Steps Report, UK central government had been fundamentally restructured to the point where over 76 per cent of the civil service was in executive agencies, of which 138 were Next Steps agencies. Box 21.1 and Table 21.1 provide details of the scale of Next Steps and the agencies associated with particular parent departments.

The agencies were headed by Chief Executives, predominately recruited via open competition, and a significant proportion of these appointments (34 per cent) went to external candidates (Next Steps Team, 1998, pp. 68–9). In Box 21.2 we show the breakdown of Chief Executive appointments. This new breed of civil service managers was employed on renewable, fixed-term contracts, with salaries linked to performance. The Next Steps approach to recruitment and pay was to become increasingly common at the top levels of the civil service.

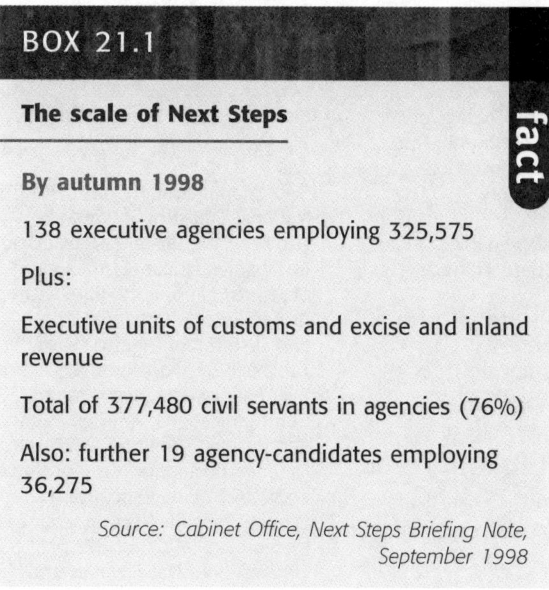
BOX 21.1

fact

The scale of Next Steps

By autumn 1998

138 executive agencies employing 325,575

Plus:

Executive units of customs and excise and inland revenue

Total of 377,480 civil servants in agencies (76%)

Also: further 19 agency-candidates employing 36,275

Source: Cabinet Office, Next Steps Briefing Note, September 1998

All of the Next Steps **executive agencies** were subjected to periodic reviews, during which all future options, including **privatisation** (which would also have been considered as a possible outcome for the service at the stage when the agency was first established), were considered. As a result of this process, eleven agencies (including HMSO and the Recruitment and Assessment Services Agency) had been privatised by 1998, while some others were redesignated, merged, returned to their parent department, had their functions contracted out or abolished, as set out in Table 21.2.

Managerial and constitutional issues

Next Steps served as a catalyst for broad-ranging managerial and structural change within the civil service. Pay, recruitment and promotion 'flexibilities' were developed around the Next Steps agency model, and subtle alterations were gradually made to established parliamentary procedures in order to facilitate the accountability of the Chief Executives.

At its heart, Next Steps was an attempt to bring about improvements to the management and delivery of services by means of structural change

Table 21.1 Next Steps executive agencies

Parent department	Agencies
Lord Chancellor's Department	Court Service, HM Land Registry, Public Record Office, Public Trust Office
Foreign Office	Wilton Park
Treasury	Debt Management Office, HM Customs and Excise, Inland Revenue, National Savings, Office for National Statistics, Royal Mint, Valuation Office
Home Office	Fire Service College, Forensic Science Service, HM Prison Service, United Kingdom Passport Agency
Board of Trade	Companies House, Employment Tribunals Service, Insolvency Service, National Weights and Measures Laboratory, Patent Office, Radiocommunications Agency
Ministry of Defence	Armed Forces Personnel Administration, Army Base Repair Organisation, Army Base Storage and Distribution Agency, Army Training and Recruiting Agency, Army Personnel Centre, Army Technical Support Agency, Defence Analytical Services Agency, Defence Animal Centre, Defence Bills Agency, Defence Clothing and Textiles Agency, Defence Codification Agency, Defence Communications Services Agency, Defence Dental Agency, Defence Estates, Defence Evaluation and Research Agency, Defence Intelligence and Security Centre, Defence Medical Training, Defence Postal and Courier Services Agency, Defence Secondary Care Agency, Defence Transport and Movements Executive, Defence Vetting, Disposal Sales Agency, Duke of York's Royal Military School, Joint Air Reconnaissance Intelligence Centre, Logistic Information Systems Agency, Meteorological Office, Medical Supplies Agency, Military Survey, MoD Police, Naval Aircraft Repair Organisation, Naval Bases and Supply Agency, Naval Manning Agency, Naval Recruiting and Training Agency, Pay and Personnel Agency, Queen Victoria School, RAF Logistics Support Services, RAF Maintenance Group Defence Agency, RAF Personnel Centre, RAF Signals Engineering Establishment, RAF Training Group Defence Agency, Service Children's Education, Ships Support Agency, Specialist Procurement Services, UK Hydrographic Office
Ministry of Agriculture, Fisheries and Food	Central Science Laboratory, Centre for Environment, Fisheries and Aquaculture, Farming and Rural Conservation Agency, Intervention Board, Meat Hygiene Service, Pesticides Safety Directorate, Veterinary Laboratories Agency, Veterinary Medicines Directorate
Media, Culture and Sport	Royal Parks Agency
Environment, Transport and Regions	Driver and Vehicle Licensing Agency, Driving Standards Agency, Highways Agency, Maritime and Coastguard Agency, Ordnance Survey, Planning Inspectorate, Queen Elizabeth II Conference Centre, Vehicle Certification Agency, Vehicle Inspectorate
Welsh Office	Cadw (Welsh Historic Monuments)
Department of Social Security	Benefits Agency, Child Support Agency, Contributions Agency, Information Technology Services Agency, War Pensions Agency
Duchy of Lancaster	CCTA, Central Office of Information, Civil Service College, Government Car and Despatch Agency, Property Advisers to the Civil Estate, The Buying Agency
Scottish Office	Fisheries Research Services, Forest Enterprise, Forestry Commission Research Agency, Historic Scotland, Registers of Scotland, Scottish Agricultural Science Agency, Scottish Court Service, Scottish Fisheries Protection Agency, Scottish Office Pensions Agency, Scottish Prison Service, Scottish Record Office, Student Awards Agency for Scotland
Northern Ireland Office	Business Development Service, Compensation Agency, Construction Service, Driver and Vehicle Licensing (Northern Ireland), Driver and Vehicle Testing Agency, Environment and Heritage Service, Forensic Science Agency of Northern Ireland, Forest Service of Northern Ireland, Government Purchasing Agency, Health Estates, Industrial Research and Technology Unit, Land Registers of Northern Ireland, Northern Ireland Child Support Agency, Northern Ireland Prison Service, Northern Ireland Statistics and Research Agency, Ordnance Survey of Northern Ireland, Planning Service, Public Record Office of Northern Ireland, Rate Collection Agency, Rivers Agency, Roads Service, Social Security Agency (Northern Ireland), Training and Employment Agency (N. Ireland), Valuation and Lands Agency, Water Service
Education and Employment Department	Employment Service
Department of Health	Medical Devices Agency, Medicines Control Agency, NHS Estates, NHS Pensions Agency
Attorney General's Department	Crown Prosecution Service, Government Property Lawyers, Treasury Solicitor's Department

Source: Next Steps Team, 1998

BOX 21.2

fact

Agency Chief Executive appointments (138)

92 appointed by open competition (66.6%)

31 external candidates (22.5% of total)

57 internal candidates

4 military candidates

20 internal appointments (14.5%)

19 appointments from armed forces (13.8%)

7 acting Chief Executives (5.1%)

Source: Cabinet Office, Next Steps Briefing Note, September 1998

and the application of new managerial methods. However, there was a distinct failure to think through the implications of this reform for accountability, and some serious problems resulted, as we shall see. Still, it seems clear that the creation of a plethora of executive agencies under the Next Steps initiative had important implications for the accountability of civil servants.

When introducing Next Steps, the Thatcher Government had declared that this would have no implications for accountability. The officials working in executive agencies would be subject to scrutiny by select committees and the Parliamentary Ombudsman in the same way as other civil servants. As in the past, this would be deemed to be indirect accountability in the sense that the officials would merely be helping their ministers to be properly accountable to Parliament. However, in practice, ministers were gradually forced to move away from this position and tolerate the increased accountability of civil servants to Parliament, even if this was achieved without formal recognition of a constitutional change. The first move came when the early agencies were established, and it was decided that Parliamentary Questions relating to matters of agency management or administration would be answered, not as in the past by means of ministerial replies published in *Hansard*, but by letters from agency Chief Executives to the MPs who had asked the questions. MPs were clearly dissatisfied with this arrangement and their protests led to a decision that all replies by Chief Executives would be placed in the library of the House of Commons. Continued concern on the part of MPs, who argued that even this arrangement was an inadequate substitute for the old system, led to a final concession by the government which allowed for the publication of all chief executives' replies in *Hansard*. This was a clear break with the precedent that only government ministers could formally answer Parliamentary Questions in the official

Table 21.2 Former Next Steps agencies

Reason for abolition	Agency
Privatisation	DVOIT, National Engineering Laboratory, HMSO, Paymaster, Building Research Establishment, Laboratory of the Government Chemist, Transport Research Laboratory, National Resources Institute, Chessington Computer Centre, Occupational and Health Service Agency, Recruitment and Assessment Services Agency,
Contracted out	Accounts Services Agency, National Physical Laboratory, Teachers' Pensions Agency
Subject to mergers	Warren Spring Laboratory, Central Science Laboratory, Chemical and Biological Defence Establishment, Defence Operational Analysis Centre, Defence Research Agency, Coastguard, Marine Safety Agency
Subject to demerger	Defence Accounts Agency
Functions abolished	Resettlement Agency
Change of status	Historic Royal Palaces (became a non-departmental public body)
Returned to a department	Security Facilities Executive Agency

Source: Next Steps Team, 1998, pp. 64–5

record of proceedings, and an implicit recognition of direct civil service accountability to Parliament.

Recurring crises surrounding the work of some agencies, including the Child Support Agency and the Prison Service Agency, indicated that serious flaws remained in the system of accountability, but these cases should not be allowed to detract from the fact that Next Steps, taken as a whole, brought about increased 'visibility' of senior civil servants and helped to change at least some elements of the system of official accountability.

The executive agency concept was designed to emphasise the supposedly clear distinction between the policy-making and policy-execution functions of government. At the heart of Next Steps there was an underlying assumption that there exists a reasonably clear divide between matters of policy, which are largely the preserve of ministers, and matters of administration and management, which lie in the domain of the civil service. However, in the real world matters are not always as clear and simple as this. Although the work of most agencies ran relatively smoothly, in two high-profile cases these supposedly clear distinctions between matters of policy and management eventually broke down and were shown to be severely problematic in terms of accountability. In both the Child Support Agency and the Prison Service Agency the Chief Executives struggled, and ultimately failed, to maintain the distinction between matters of policy and matters of management.

The first Chief Executive of the CSA, Ros Hepplewhite, pursued the logic of Next Steps to its conclusion as she attempted to differentiate between her responsibility to account for the management and operation of the agency, and the accountability of ministers for the policy and legal framework within which the agency operated. However, the CSA faced fundamental problems. This agency had been created solely and specifically to implement a particular policy, framed under the Child Support Act, but this policy and the Act were seriously flawed. The policy failings of ministers then became translated into the managerial failings of the agency, as it generated massive backlogs of work, repeatedly missed its performance targets and produced huge numbers of 'customer' complaints. Finally, as it became clear that the CSA had failed to meet even its revised targets and news broke that a team of management consultants was being sent in to review the agency, Hepplewhite resigned in 1994. This case provided a clear demonstration of the close interaction between matters of policy and management, and the serious consequences which can arise, in this instance for a senior civil servant, when this is not fully recognised by ministers.

Similar themes could be seen in the case of the Prison Service Agency, where running disputes broke out between the minister at the parent department (Michael Howard, the Home Secretary) and the agency Chief Executive (Derek Lewis, Director General of the Prison Service). Howard blamed Lewis for overall management failings which led to a series of high-profile escapes by prisoners from top security establishments, while Lewis attributed at least some of the managerial problems to ministerial policy and interference. In the end, Lewis was dismissed by his ministerial superior, although he successfully challenged this in court and won substantial compensation.

Despite the problems posed by these cases, Next Steps continued to attract broad, cross-party approval. This effectively guaranteed the programme's long-term significance. The Labour Party's attitude towards executive agencies remained supportive. When they came, criticisms tended to focus on the scandals associated with the Prison Service Agency and the Child Support Agency, during which attacks would be based on the issues of ministerial conduct or lack of accountability, while the general principles and impact of Next Steps would be praised. Before the 1997 General Election, Tony Blair's senior policy advisers on the civil service admitted that executive agencies '. . . have improved the delivery of government services through better management and delegation' (Mandelson and Liddle, 1996, p. 251). On its election in 1997, the Labour Government recognised the accountability problems posed by the child support and prisons cases. The Child Support Agency was subjected to much closer ministerial oversight through a medium to long term process of review, while the Home Secretary, Jack Straw, announced that the accountability arrangements for the Prison Service were to be changed, with ministers assuming full responsibility for accounting to Parliament for this sensitive area of public policy and management. Nonetheless, under New Labour, Next Steps rolled on into its final stages. A natural end to the process of agency creation was in sight as the millennium beckoned, and the impact of Next Steps was there for all to see in virtually every part of the civil service.

Public, private, or both?

Privatisation

The policy of privatisation affected public services at all levels of the system of government. In local authorities, the National Health Service, central government and the parts of the system which did not fall neatly into one or other of these spheres (in the world of quangos for example), assets and services moved from the public to the private sector throughout the 1980s and 1990s. In this chapter, our concern is with the civil service, and therefore with central government, although we should note that the themes and issues associated with privatisation cut across governmental sectors.

Box 21.3 sets out the main reasons for, and the most significant forms of, privatisation. Put simply there are three broad reasons for the emergence of privatisation. In government from 1979, the Thatcherite Conservatives equated state control and public ownership with fat, flabby and inefficient organisations, over-dependent on subsidy, unaware of their true cost and unable to meet the demands of their customers. Allied to this view was the attraction of easing the strain on the Public Sector Borrowing Requirement by transferring large numbers of workers from the public to the private sector, reducing Treasury lending and providing a flow of funds into the Exchequer through the sale of assets. Finally, there was an ideological imperative, which became increasingly significant as time passed. Privatisation fitted neatly into the Thatcherite crusade to encourage economic 'freedom', create a 'property and share owning democracy' and cut the state machine down to size. The Labour government after 1997 showed a willingness to retain privatisation as an option, largely for pragmatic rather than ideological reasons. Substantial share flotations and the introduction of private ownership were not to be discarded. The government planned to sell 51 per cent of the shares in the National Air Traffic Control Service and introduce private ownership in some of London Underground's busiest lines. However, Labour tended to place more emphasis on the creation of public–private 'partnerships' through devices such as **Better Quality Services** and the Private Finance Initiative, as discussed below. A more partial and selective use of the privatisation option became the order of the day.

This serves to illustrate the point that, over the years, the policy of privatisation has taken different shapes and forms, including the total or partial conversion of a public corporation or nationalised industry into a limited company, government disposal of all or some of the shares it holds in specific bodies, or breaking the monopoly held by a state concern. A further dimension of privatisation, which continued to find favour with the post-1997 Labour government, involves injecting elements of private provision into public services. Although competitive tendering or market testing in public bodies does not necessarily amount to 'privatisation', it can lead to the introduction of private sector managerial methods and practices or to the provision of a service by a private company for a fixed term. Similarly, the Private Finance Initiative involves the transfer of capital assets such as hospital or prison buildings to the private sector, while the state remains in control of the service. As these forms of privatisation, or partial privatisation, have had a particular impact on the civil service, we will examine them more closely below. Before doing so, however, it is worth noting some of the particular accountability challenges posed by privatisation, and outlining the methods used in order to address these.

When plans were announced to transfer major public utilities to the private sector, serious questions were raised about the possible dilution of public accountability which might result. Partly in an effort to address this issue, at the point of privatisation, regulatory agencies were set up to issue licences to the commercial participants in the developing markets (or 'quasi-markets' where privatisation had not brought immediate competition),

BOX 21.3 **IDEAS AND PERSPECTIVES**

Rationale for, and types of, privatisation

Rationale

Efficiency

- State control/public ownership equated with inefficiency and lack of competitiveness

Control of public expenditure

- Ease problem of public sector pay
- Reduce Public Sector Borrowing Requirement
- Generate income (and facilitate tax cuts)

Ideology

- Encourage economic freedom and market forces
- Break 'dependency-culture' and create 'property and share-owning democracy'
- Reduce scale and power of state bureaucracy

Types

Partial conversion to a limited company

e.g. Jaguar Cars element of British Leyland 1984

Total conversion to a limited company

e.g. British Telecom 1984; British Gas 1986

Disposal of government shares in a company

e.g. Cable and Wireless 1981–5; Amersham International 1982

Breaking of state monopoly

e.g. 1983 Energy Act permitted private generation of electricity

e.g. deregulation of bus routes

Injection of private provision within framework of public service

e.g. competitive tendering/market testing/best value

e.g. Private Finance Initiative

negotiate and then enforce the pricing formulae, obtain and publish information helpful to the service users, and oversee the systems for resolving consumer complaints. These regulatory agencies were non-ministerial government departments, headed by directors general. Modelled to a considerable extent on the existing Office of Fair Trading, the Offices of Telecommunications (OFTEL), Gas Supply (OFGAS), Electricity Regulation (OFFER) and Water Services (OFWAT)

Chancellor Gordon Brown continues Margaret Thatcher's privatisation policy (14 June 1998)

were established. In 2000 OFGAS and OFFER were merged into a single Energy Regulator. Each utility privatisation brought in its wake a new regulator, with broadly similar powers.

In some spheres, a complex array of regulators emerged. For example, following rail privatisation regulatory functions were dispersed among the following:

- *Ministers*: set the regulatory framework.
- *Rail Regulator*: issues licences to train operating companies and enforces licence conditions relating to safety.
- *Chief Inspector of Railways*: leads the Rail Inspectorate, which is part of the Health and Safety Executive. Approves and monitors safety systems.
- *Strategic Rail Authority*: sets and monitors service standards for the twenty-five train operating companies.
- *Railtrack*: owns and manages track, stations, tunnels, level crossings, viaducts and bridges. Set and policed safety standards until stripped of this role following the Paddingdon rail disaster in October 1999.

In broad terms, privatisation was accompanied by the retention of a form of public accountability, and the emergence of a new set of scrutineers. The focus of accountability had shifted away from

Parliament, and the records of the regulators were variable (influenced by such factors as the approach of the Director General, the scale of the utility being regulated, and the prevailing style of the utility's board of directors). While in some spheres the existence of these dedicated and specialised agencies successfully addressed most of the concerns about the impact of privatisation on public accountability, serious problems arose in others. In the rail utility, for example, generally poor service standards and the serious train crashes at Southall in 1997 and Paddington in 1999 raised doubts about the effectiveness of the regulatory regime.

Market testing and better quality services

During the 1980s, **compulsory competitive tendering** (CCT) swept through local government and the National Health Service. Under this programme, specified activities such as catering, cleaning and refuse collection were compulsorily put out to tender, with the contract for providing the service being awarded to the most competitive bid. As a result, in some cases the service was contracted out, with private companies winning the contracts.

The civil service was affected by these developments only marginally. Central government services and functions were not subject to compulsory competitive tendering. As a result of the essentially voluntary nature of the process, only a relatively small number of quite low-grade manual and clerical tasks were exposed to competitive tendering. However, in 1991 the Competing for Quality White Paper announced the expansion of CCT throughout the public sector, including the civil service where the process was to be styled '**market testing**'. The new wave of competition was to involve professional, 'white collar' activities including accountancy, information and legal services, as well as the more traditional targets for tendering. The Conservative government argued that even where services ultimately remained 'in house', with the existing civil service providers, the tendering process would have the effect of sharpening up management and enhancing efficiency. The results were mixed. The government's deadlines and targets for market testing in the civil service were repeatedly revised and shifted, debates raged about the cost of the process and the extent of the savings generated (see Pyper, 1995, pp. 64–70). By 1996 the government was citing savings of £720 million per year, with staff cuts of around 30,000. Where in-house bids were allowed, and went forward, they succeeded in winning about 75 per cent of the contracts, but there were no in-house bids in half of the contracts put out to tender. The civil service trade unions and the opposition parties attacked the market testing process on the grounds that it spawned its own bureaucracy, cost millions of pounds in management consultancy fees, led to job cuts and adversely affected morale. In addition, it infringed upon the managerial freedom of agency chief executives, raised important questions about service standards, security and confidentiality (especially in relation to the contracting out of IT services) and threatened the principle of public service provision in some spheres.

The Labour Party's opposition to the dogmatic elements of market testing led to a new approach following the 1997 election. The new government's stated objective was to ensure that all departments reviewed the full range of their services and functions over a five year period starting in 1999. The aim was to identify the 'best supplier' of each service and function, while improving quality and value for money across government. Under this Better Quality Services (BQS) initiative, departments were required to have plans in place for the programme of reviews by October 1999.

The focus of BQS is on end results and service standards while securing the best quality and value for money for the taxpayer. The 'best supplier' of a service is identified through considering the possibility of competition, but in a major change from the market testing programme, there is no compulsion to set up a tendering process. If internal restructuring or managerial 'reprocessing' results in quality improvements, no competition is necessary. However, these internal reviews must be 'robust', and are subject to oversight by the Cabinet Office, the Treasury and a key Cabinet Committee (PSX).

The Private Finance Initiative

> **Put simply, PFI is a way of getting public buildings built or refurbished without recording capital spending in the national accounts. It was dreamt up by John Major as yet another wheeze for a public unwilling to face the true cost of the public services it says it wants. PFI is what poor people used to call the 'never-never': you get something bright and shiny now but end up paying a lot more than its present cost over the long run.**
>
> (Walker, 1999)

Needless to say, David Walker's sceptical view of the Private Finance Initiative was not shared by the Conservative Government ministers who introduced the scheme in 1992, nor by the members of the Labour Government who have retained and developed it. For government departments, and public authorities more generally, the attraction of the PFI lies in the avoidance of major capital investment and the resulting opportunity to keep public expenditure under control. Private sector expertise can be exploited, while maintenance costs for the facility are transferred. Effectively, this means that governments purchase maintained highways instead of building roads, buy custodial or healthcare services instead of building prisons and hospitals, and pay for managed IT services instead of buying computers and software. At the end of the contract, which may be in thirty years time, the facility will be handed back to the public sector body which issued the contract. Private sector contractors provide the initial capital, as well as assuming the risks associated with construction, in return for operating licences for the resulting facility, which enable them to recoup their costs.

Although the PFI started slowly, failed to have the expected impact on the Conservative government's public expenditure plans, and became associated with high tendering costs and bureaucratic bidding procedures (Terry, 1996), it developed in significance as time passed. It underpinned major projects, including the Channel Tunnel, the high-speed rail link to the Tunnel, toll bridges including the Skye road bridge, prisons, hospitals and a range of other facilities. Although the Labour government immediately ended the requirement that all public sector capital projects should be tested for PFI potential, ministers remained fully committed to a revised and refocused version of the initiative. During the first two years of the Labour government, some £4.7 billion worth of PFI deals were signed (making a total of £13 billion since the launch of PFI) with another £11 billion worth projected for the period 1999–2002. Within the National Health service alone, PFI deals would underpin the building of 13 new hospitals.

In practice, PFI projects tend to take two forms:

1 *Financially free-standing projects*. Here, the private sector supplier designs, builds, finances and then operates the asset. Costs are recovered through charges on the users of the facility. Examples are the Second Severn Bridge and the Dartford River Crossing.

2 *Joint ventures*. In these, the costs of the project are not met fully through charges, but are partly subsidised from public funds because there are wider social benefits involved, such as reduced congestion or local economic regeneration. Examples are business park developments, city centre regeneration schemes, Manchester's Metrolink and the Docklands Light Railway Extension (see Box 21.4).

Labour attempted to address the managerial problems surrounding the PFI by accepting the

BOX 21.4 EXAMPLE

PFI in practice – Docklands Light Railway Extension

A joint-venture PFI project between: Department of the Environment, Transport and the Regions and City Greenwich Lewisham (CGL) Rail Link plc.

The project: A 24.5 year concession (from September 1996) to design, build, finance and maintain a 4.2 km extension to the DLR. The line will run under the Thames and add five new stations south of the river to create direct access between the City and Docklands, and SE London and Kent. Due to be opened to passengers in 2000, the line will also provide improved public transport access to Greenwich for the Millennium Exhibition events.

Cost: £200 million.

Private sector funding: £165 million raised through bond issue.

Public sector funding: £35 million in contributions from central government, Deptford City Challenge, London Boroughs of Lewisham and Greenwich.

CGL Rail opportunities and risks: Company receives fees for use of the Extension. Risks include franchising; cost and time overruns; levels of passenger usage; construction; installation of automatic train control system; integrating the Extension with the existing rail system.

Source: HM Treasury

recommendations of a report by Sir Malcolm Bates, Chairman of Pearl, and setting up a Taskforce based in the Treasury and headed by Adrian Montague, a former city banker. In July 1999 the government responded to a second Bates report by announcing that the Taskforce would be replaced in 2000 by Partnerships UK, a permanent body which would improve the central co-ordination of the initiative by acting as the overall project manager for PFI deals. There would also be a much greater standardisation of the bidding and contractual process. Formed as a plc, the new body would symbolise the public–private partnership ethos. The private sector would take a majority share in Partnerships UK, which would provide public sector organisations with expert advice on PFI matters. It was hoped that this would prevent any repetition of the disastrous problems associated with the large PFI computer contracts, epitomised by the Passport Agency's misconceived deal with the electronics corporation Siemens, which produced massive backlogs in the passport application system in 1999. Companies considering bidding for PFI deals would also be able to use Partnerships UK on a voluntary basis. Although it would not function as a bank, the new body would provide development funds to get PFI deals off the ground, perhaps by bundling together a number of projects which, individually, would be too small to attract private sector bidders.

Clearly committed to the long-term development of the PFI, the Labour Government's confidence in its management of this controversial scheme was emphasised in September 1999, when ministers welcomed a new independent inquiry into the entire initiative, to be conducted by the Institute for Public Policy Research (Atkinson, 1999).

Some observers remained unconvinced by the whole PFI project. Sir Peter Kemp (1999), the former senior Treasury and Cabinet Office civil servant, thought the case for this type of public–private partnership was 'pretty thin' and raised serious questions about the 'hidden spending' and unconventional 'value for money' studies surrounding PFI projects. Certainly, there is a high long-term price to pay in return for quick access to nice, shiny, new assets. A new infirmary in Edinburgh would have cost £180 million if paid for from taxation or government borrowing. A PFI deal allowed a private consortium to design, own and service the hospital, and then rent it to the public for £30 million a year over thirty years – a total cost of £900 million (Cohen, 1999).

Citizen's Charter to Service First

Dismissed by many observers as a gimmick when it appeared as John Major's 'big idea' in 1991, the Citizen's Charter is still with us. Refashioned as Service First by the Blair Government in June 1998, the Charter programme encapsulates the importance attached to 'consumerism' in public services.

When it was launched, the Citizen's Charter was partly designed to differentiate John Major's civil and public service policy from that of his predecessor Margaret Thatcher, and partly to counter the opposition parties' interest in citizens' rights and constitutional change. It encompassed a range of linked initiatives including the Charter Mark scheme (which rewards organisations deemed to have delivered improved quality services) and extended beyond the civil service, into the public service at large. The basic objectives were to improve the quality of public services and make service providers more answerable to those variously described as 'citizens', 'clients', 'consumers' and 'customers'. Under the Citizen's Charter umbrella, 'mini-Charters' were published in increasing numbers, covering the full range of public service users, including those seeking employment, Benefits Agency customers, NHS patients, rail passengers, taxpayers, parents of school children, students in higher education and people using the courts. Many of the 'mini-Charters' would be published in varied forms for England, Scotland, Wales and Northern Ireland. The Charter's attempts to bring about improvements in the management and delivery of services, while enhancing the means for redressing consumers' grievances, would have a particular significance in many of the executive agencies responsible for delivering services directly to the public.

Although a government review in 1996 praised the Charter's achievements (Prime Minister, 1996), some observers saw **Charterism** as a triumph of style over substance, pointing to the initiative's limited definition of citizenship, the fact that service standards are set by the service providers themselves and are not legally enforceable, the failure to create genuinely new mechanisms of accountability and redress, and the elements of farce such as the abortive telephone helpline Charterline and the widely mocked Cones Hotline (see Falconer and Ross, 1999, for a summary of the main political and academic arguments surrounding the Charter). The opposition parties supported the idea of improved answerability and better service delivery and Labour even argued that Major had 'stolen' the Charter concept from the customer contract initiatives within some Labour controlled local authorities. However, questions were raised about the extent to which the Charter's objectives could be achieved without extra funding.

Committed to 're-launch and refocus' the Citizen's Charter, the Blair Government announced its intention to replace the 'top-down' system it had inherited from the Conservatives with a 'bottom-up' approach. In simple terms, this means the existing Charters were seen as having been the property of the service providers, drawn up with little or no consultation with those who use the services. New charters would be drawn up in consultation with the public and the vague statements and easily achievable targets of old would be replaced with clear information about the 'outcomes' service users should expect, together with meaningful indicators of service quality (Cabinet Office, 1998). Under the Service First programme, new principles of public service delivery were published, building upon the existing charter principles (see Box 21.5). All existing Charters would be reviewed, and replaced with new versions. A new audit team would continually monitor the quality of Charters, while the Charter Mark scheme would be made more rigorous. The first indication of progress on this front came when the Passport Agency, which had held a Charter Mark since 1992, was stripped of the award in the summer of 1999 following weeks of chaos in its operations and a backlog of around 500,000 passport applications. Although some organisations had voluntarily given up their Charter Marks in the past, or failed to have them renewed after the initial three-year period, this was the first instance of award-stripping.

BOX 21.5

fact

The principles and standards of public service

Service First: principles

These build upon and expand existing Charter principles:

- Set standards of service
- Be open and provide full information
- Consult and involve
- Encourage access and the promotion of choice
- Treat all fairly
- Put things right when they go wrong
- Use resources effectively
- Innovate and improve
- Work with other providers

The six Whitehall standards

In servicing the public, every central government department and agency aims to:

1. Answer letters quickly and clearly. Each department and agency sets a target for answering letters and publishes its performance against this target.
2. See people within ten minutes of any appointments they have made.
3. Provide clear and straightforward information about services and at least one number for telephone inquiries.
4. Consult users regularly about the services provided, and report on the results.
5. Have at least one complaints procedure for the services provided, and send out information about the procedure on request.
6. Do everything that is reasonably possible to make services available to all, including people with special needs.

Source: Cabinet Office

Questions remain about the extent to which Service First represents a genuine development and improvement of the old Citizen's Charter. Time will tell whether substantial change has accompanied the repackaging.

Rolling onwards: modernising government

The Blair government made it clear from the outset that the civil service would be required to play a major part in the implementation of Labour's programme, while continuing the process of managerial change which had transformed the machinery of government. The Prime Minister issued the civil service with seven 'challenges' (see Box 21.6) and then, with his senior colleagues, he set about drafting a framework for future governance, which would give civil servants the chance substantially to meet these challenges.

The result, which emerged in March 1999, drew together many of the managerial and service delivery themes which had been developing piecemeal during the life of the Blair administration, and indeed before. In several respects, however, the **Modernising Government** White Paper (Prime Minister, 1999; for a summary, see Box 21.7) was a typical Blair product, with its short phraseology gleaned from the world of image makers and PR consultants. Not all of the snappy concepts seemed full of meaning (even the 'central objective' was rather opaque). The document's desire to be 'modern' in every way could

BOX 21.6

fact

Tony Blair's seven challenges for the civil service

1. Implement constitutional reform in a way that preserves a unified civil service, ensures close working between UK government and the devolved administrations.
2. Staff in all departments to integrate the EU dimension into policy making.
3. Public services to be improved, more innovative and responsive to users, and delivered in an efficient and joined-up way.
4. Create a more innovative and less risk averse culture in the civil service.
5. Improve collaborative working across organisational boundaries.
6. Manage the civil service so as to equip it to meet these challenges.
7. Think ahead strategically to future priorities.

Source: Cabinet Office

seem a little bit forced at times. One observer commented wryly,

> One of the best pictures is of community policing ... and shows a boy with extended tongue in a pushchair, with the attractive teletubby Tinky Winky looking over his left shoulder. It would be difficult to get more modern than that. (Chapman, 1999, p. 9)

An administrative apparatus was speedily constructed around the Modernising Government programme. Within the Cabinet Office the Modernising Public Services Group was created and charged with responsibility for implementing the White Paper's reforms. This group worked with the Modernising Government Project Board (containing external and civil service members) to draw up an Action Plan. The early priorities were categorised as 'responsiveness', effectiveness and efficiency', 'joined-up government' and 'quality'.

Amongst the initiatives which pre-dated the White Paper but were given renewed emphasis under the Modernising Government umbrella were benchmarking, Public Service Agreements and the People's Panel.

Benchmarking is the practice of comparing the management processes and procedures in different organisations, with the aim of transferring the best practices from one to the other. This can be done within the public sector, for example by using value for money audits as mechanisms for transferring good financial management practices. However, the Blair government has placed increasing emphasis on benchmarking against the private sector by using the 'Business Excellence' model.

Public Service Agreements are really forms of performance indicators. The PSAs are designed to set out in detail what people can expect in return for public expenditure on services. Here, the purpose is to clearly shift the focus to the quality of service outputs generated. For example, the government's key service targets are incorporated in PSAs:

- Cut all infant class sizes to thirty by September 2001.
- Reduce the time taken from arrest to sentence for persistent young offenders from 142 to seventy-one days.
- Cut NHS waiting lists by 100,000 over the lifetime of the 1997 Parliament.
- Get 250,000 under-twenty-five year olds off benefit and into work.

The People's Panel is a 5,000 strong, nationally representative group, set up to tell the government 'what people really think' about public services and the efforts being taken to modernise and improve them. Members of the public were randomly selected for the panel, and it was used as the basis for successive waves of research designed to generate representative views about attitudes to public services in general, the work of specific providers, and levels of service provision. This is a very typical New Labour product in the sense that it is essentially a larger and more sophisticated version of the type of focus group the party uses to test policies. The results of the

BOX 21.7

fact

Modernising Government: summary of White Paper

Central objective

'Better government to make life better for people'

Aims

- Ensure that policy making is more 'joined up' and strategic.
- Focus on public service users, not providers.
- Deliver high quality and efficient public services.

New reforms

- 'Government direct': public services available twenty-four hours a day, seven days a week, where there is a demand.
- 'Joined-up government': co-ordination of public services and more strategic policy making.
- Removal of unnecessary regulation: requirements that departments avoid imposing new regulatory burdens and submit those deemed necessary to Regulatory Impact Assessments.
- Information age government: target for all dealings with government to be deliverable electronically by 2008.
- 'Learning labs': to encourage new ways of front-line working and suspend rules that stifle innovation.
- Incentives: for public service staff – including financial rewards for those who identify savings or service improvements.
- New focus on delivery within Whitehall: permanent secretaries to pursue delivery of key government targets, recruit more 'outsiders', promote able young staff.

Key commitments:

Forward looking policy making:

- Identify and spread best practice via new centre for management and policy studies (which will incorporate the civil service college).
- Joint training of ministers and civil servants.
- Peer review of departments.

Responsive public services:

- Remove obstacles to joined-up working through local partnerships, one-stop shops and other means.
- Involve and meet the needs of different groups in society.

Quality public services:

- Review all government department services and activities over five years to identify best suppliers.
- Set new targets for all public bodies with focus on real improvements in quality and effectiveness.
- Monitor performance closely to strike balance between intervention when things go wrong and allowing successful organisations freedom for management.

Information age government:

- An IT strategy for government to co-ordinate development of digital signatures, smart cards, websites and call centres.
- Benchmark progress against targets for electronic services.

Public service:

- To be valued, not denigrated.
- Modernise the civil service (including revision of performance management arrangements; tackle under-representation of women, ethnic minorities and people with disabilities; build capacity for innovation).
- Establish a public sector employment forum to bring together and develop key players across the public sector.

continuing People's Panel surveys and interviews will be fed into the developing Modernising Government agenda.

Modernising Government is clearly a long-term project. It will be some time before there is enough evidence from the many and varied elements of this programme to allow a full assessment to be made of its impact on the civil service. However, the early indications were of further significant change to the culture and management of the civil service. Richard Chapman (1999, p. 8), the senior academic analyst of the British civil service had no doubts:

> ... in ten or twenty years' time, the influence and significance of this White Paper is quite likely to be comparable to that of the Next Steps Report.

Conclusion

The fictional minister Jim Hacker and his permanent secretary Sir Humphrey Appleby would recognise a great deal about the civil service of the twenty-first century, but they would probably be astonished at the sheer scale of the changes which have taken place in this organisation over a relatively short period of time. While there is general agreement about the volume of change, analysts and observers are divided on the question of its impact. For some, the managerial and structural changes in the civil service have failed to alter the fundamental character of a backward looking institution. John Garrett (1999), formerly Labour spokesman on the civil service, is sceptical about his party's attempts at reform, largely because he believes the top Whitehall posts are likely to remain in the hands of traditionalists:

> New Labour's white paper promises 'joined-up government', 'joined-up policy-making', 'joined-up working' and 'joined-up public service delivery'. It proposes to open up the 'senior' Civil Service of 3,000 top jobs to women, ethnic minorities and people with disabilities. But, crucially, it intends to keep a fast-stream programme for generalist mandarins headed for the top jobs. Sir Humphrey has secured the future for his clones.

Others have taken the view that the overall impact of managerial change has been very significant. For some, the effect has been negative, on the whole. According to this perspective, the Next Steps programme together with the process of contracting-out key functions have led to the effective 'Balkanisation' of the civil service. Breaking the service up into increasingly independent components, it is argued, has diluted the cohesiveness, character and ethical base of civil service work (see, for example, Chapman, 1997). The impact of devolution on the concept of a unified, British civil service remains to be seen, but this constitutional reform will create new tensions which will have to be managed properly if cohesiveness is to be retained (see Pyper, 1999).

Other observers are more relaxed (see, for example, Hennessy, 1993, and Butler, 1993) and locate the recent reforms within the evolutionary tradition of a service which has always been prepared to adapt to change. The current Head of the Civil Service, Sir Richard Wilson, although a traditionalist in many respects, has been keen to

BOX 21.1 MINI BIOGRAPHY

Professor Peter Hennessy (1950–)
Constitutional authority. Educated Cambridge. Journalist on *Times*, *Financial Times* and *Economist* before becoming academic at Queen Mary College London. His *Never Again* (1992) was an award winning study of Britain during the Attlee government's term of office.

BOX 21.2 MINI BIOGRAPHY

Sir Robin Butler (1938–)
Former Cabinet Secretary. Educated Oxford joining Treasury in 1961. Worked in private office of Heath and Wilson before becoming Permanent Secretary to the Treasury 1985–7. Cabinet Secretary 1988–97. Life peer in same year.

embrace change, while emphasising that this need not be at the expense of 'our core values' (Wilson, 1999).

The debates about the civil service's future shape and direction will continue during the vital period ahead, as this cornerstone of the UK political system adapts to meet the challenges posed by successive waves of reform.

Chapter summary

This chapter has set out the major reforms which have changed the management and shape of the civil service. We have discussed the impact of executive agencies, the increased emphasis given to **public–private partnerships** in schemes such as Better Quality Services and the Private Finance Initiative, attempts to address the needs of service users through devices like the Citizen's Charter and Service First, and the implications of the all-embracing Modernising Government agenda. Key issues and debates have been explored as a means of enhancing understanding of this central component of the government system.

Discussion points

- What was the objective behind the creation of executive agencies, and to what extent has this been achieved?
- What part should the private sector play in the provision of public services?
- Have the Citizen's Charter and Service First programmes improved the quality of services delivered to the public?
- To what extent will the initiatives within the Modernising Government programme help to create better public services?
- Has the civil service been changed for the better as a result of the managerial reforms of recent years?

Further reading

There is now a considerable literature on the civil service and public sector management. Accounts of the development of the modern civil service and some of the major reforms can be found in Theakston (1995) and Pyper (1995). Some of the key documents, commentaries and analysis are contained in the excellent books by Barberis (1996, 1997). The new public management initiatives, which have underpinned most of the recent changes in the civil service, are given good coverage in Horton and Farnham (1999). Students wishing to keep up to date with the ever-increasing pace of change in the civil service must be prepared to look beyond books, however. A range of journals and periodicals provide regular articles and features on the themes discussed in this chapter. These include *New Statesman*, *Parliamentary Affairs*, *Public Money and Management*, *Public Policy and Administration*, *Politics Review* and *Talking Politics*.

References

Atkinson, M. (1999) 'Inquiry to Look at PFI', *The Guardian*, 20 September.

Barberis, P. (1996) *The Whitehall Reader. The UK's Administrative Machine in Action* (Open University Press).

Barberis, P. (1997) *The Civil Service in an Era of Change* (Dartmouth).

Butcher, T. (1998) 'The Blair government and the civil service', *Teaching Public Administration*, Vol. 18, No. 1.

Butler, Sir R. (1993) 'The evolution of the civil service – a progress report', *Public Administration*, Vol. 71, No. 3.

Cabinet Office (1998) *Service First: The New Charter Programme* (Cabinet Office).

Chapman, R.A. (1997) 'The end of the civil service', in P. Barberis (ed.), *The Civil Service in an Era of Change* (Dartmouth).

Chapman, R.A. (1999) 'The importance of "Modernising Government"', *Teaching Public Administration*, Vol. 19, No. 1.

Cohen, N. (1999) 'How Britain mortgaged the future', *New Statesman*, 18 October.

Efficiency Unit (1988) *Improving Management in Government: the Next Steps* (HMSO).

Efficiency Unit (1991) *Making the Most of Next Steps: the Management of Ministers' Departments and Their Executive Agencies* (HMSO).

Falconer, P.K. and Ross, K. (1999) 'Citizen's Charters and public service provision: lesson from the UK experience', *International Review of Administrative Sciences*, Vol. 65.

Garrett, J. (1999) 'Not in front of the servants', *New Statesman*, 4 October.

Greer, P. (1994) *Transforming Central Government: the Next Steps Initiative* (Open University Press).

Hennessy, P. (1993) 'Questions of ethics for government', *FDA News*, Vol. 13, No. 1.

Horton, S. and Farnham, D. (eds) (1999) *Public Management in Britain* (Macmillan).

Kemp, Sir P. (1999) 'Please stop fiddling the books', *New Statesman*, 18 October.

Mandelson, P. and Liddle, R. (1996) *The Blair Revolution. Can New Labour Deliver?* (Faber and Faber).

Next Steps Team (1998) *Next Steps Briefing Note September 1998* (Cabinet Office).

Osborne, D. and Gaebler, T. (1992) *Reinventing Government. How the Entrepreneurial Spirit is Transforming the Public Sector* (Plume).

Prime Minister (1996) *The Citizen's Charter – Five Years On*, Command Paper 3370 Session 1995–6.

Prime Minister (1999) *Modernising Government*, Command Paper 4310 Session 1998–9.

Pyper, R. (1995) *The British Civil Service* (Prentice-Hall/Harvester Wheatsheaf).

Pyper, R. (1999) 'The civil service: a neglected dimension of devolution', *Public Money and Management*, Vol. 19, No. 2.

Terry, F. (1996) 'The Private Finance Initiative – overdue reform or policy breakthrough?', *Public Policy and Management*, Vol. 16, No. 1.

Theakston, K. (1995) *The Civil Service Since 1945* (Blackwell).

Walker, D. (1999) 'Malignant growth', *The Guardian*, 5 July.

Wilson, Sir R. (1999) 'The civil service in the new millennium', unpublished lecture, May.

Chapter 22 Local government

Colin Copus

Learning objectives

- Does widespread public apathy about local government mean the end of local democracy in Britain? Or, will directly elected mayors and cabinet government at the local level revitalise people's interest in local political affairs?
- Should local councils be merely agents of central government or mini-governments in their own right?
- Do councillors represent the community or their party?
- Is local government about political representation, community responsiveness and governance, or simply the management, administration and provision of services?
- How can British local government become an influential part of the European Union's policy network?

Introduction

The chapter will explore the tensions that exist between local government as a politically representative set of institutions and a local authority as a body which manages and administers the provisions of a complex range of local services. It will also examine the inter-relationship between local government policy preferences and other bodies of governance. The first section will examine the development and structure of British local government; the second will explore the relationships between local and central government; the third will explore the growth and role of party politics at the local level; the fourth section will consider the policy environment of local government; the fifth will explore the impact of regional government, devolution and the European Union on local government. The final section will consider the Blair government's modernising agenda.

Background

British local government has always been subordinate to central control. Unlike many of its continental counterparts, British local government remains constitutionally unprotected from the political ideologies, policies, priorities and, indeed, caprice of central government. The shape, size, structure, functions, powers, duties and very existence of local councils rest in the hands of central government to decide and the courts to interpret. Local councils can only do that which the law grants them permission or powers to do; any action not sanctioned by law is *ultra vires* (beyond the powers) and liable to be quashed or rendered null and void by the courts.

The constitutionally subordinate role of local government to the centre has led many to regard the work of local councils as no more than an administrative process – devoid of its own political life. Indeed, as Gyford (1976, p. 11) points out, some maintain that it is management and administration that solves local problems, not the making of what are political, and party political, choices about the allocation of scarce resources. Moreover, doubts about the efficiency of local government service provision and variations in service standards across the country, coupled with central government regulation of local authorities and large scale public apathy, raises questions about the continued existence of independent local government (Byrne, 1983, p. 24).

To the litany of criticism heaped upon local government can be added time-consuming and opaque decision-making structures; the supposedly poor calibre of many local councillors; party politics, leading to unnecessary conflict and confrontation; large and remote units of local government distant from many of the communities represented; the tension between community representation and the technical efficiency of service administration and provision; and the constraint on local action arising from local economic and social factors (Stanyer, 1976; Dearlove, 1979; Elcock, 1982; Hampton, 1987; Wolman and Goldsmith, 1992). Despite questions as to its value and relevance, local government and, indeed, local democracy and autonomy hold an important position in the political structure and processes of British governance.

Local government, and the decisions made by councils and councillors, comes with a legitimacy that flows from the consequences of the electoral processes. Local elections produce a layer of political representatives able to claim a mandate for the decisions they make and the policies they pursue. While the local electoral mandate theory has been criticised by comparison with its national counterpart, councillors acting as duly elected representatives of the people provide an important legitimacy to the activities of local government (Wolman and Goldsmith, 1992). It is the people's vote that prevents local government from being wholly an administrative arm of central government.

While the development of the local franchise was originally concerned to ensure that the electorate, and the candidates from which they could select, fulfilled some property qualification, local decision making was clearly rooted in the electoral process (Keith-Lucas, 1952). The development of local government has, however, been described as less a search for representative democracy than the development of a form of ratepayer democracy (Young, 1989, p. 6). Either way, councillors hold office as a consequence of the public vote, and, more so today, by virtue of the political label worn at election time – most councillors being affiliated to one of the national parties while acting as local political representatives (HMSO, 1986b; Young and Davis, 1990).

British local government: from confusion to cohesion

The uniformity displayed by the current map of local government structure is a recent phenomenon. Indeed, it is the myth of the importance of uniformity that enabled the demands of service management and administration to sideline political representation as the driving force for local self-government. British local government has gone through a process of evolution interspersed with periodic revolution; growing from the naturally formed communities of Anglo-Saxon times, local government took on a shape, size and structure that reflected its roots in very local communities. Parishes, boroughs and counties developed over time, sharing the provision of services and local administrative matters with an often confusing mix of other statutory, non-statutory and private providers, alongside magistrates and sheriffs appointed by the monarch.

As new problems and issues of government arose, dealing with the impact on the localities of an increasingly complex world became the responsibility of a range of local bodies and appointed boards. Parishes, boroughs and counties overlapped in area and responsibilities with a host of improvement, street paving, drainage and public health boards and poor law guardians. The evolutionary development of local government saw administration and local decision making shared between single and multi-purpose bodies; formed variously by statute, appointment, self-selection or election. Prior to 1835 the structures for managing local affairs would be barely recognisable compared with today's local councils.

It was the legislative activity of the Victorian period that began to give some coherence to the shape of local government, while at the same time continuing to deal, in an *ad hoc* fashion, with many of the problems generated by, and for, the developing capitalist system. Commencing with the 1835 Municipal Corporations Act and up to the 1899 reform of London government, the Victorians gave a foundation to local government of popular – although not universal – election, financial responsibility and uniformity of purpose, shape and process. By the turn of the century local authorities looked and felt like governments, while being increasingly controlled by the centre. The structure of counties, districts and non-county boroughs, with parishes as a fourth sub-tier, alongside separate all-purpose county boroughs promoted some uniformity. But it left unanswered the question of how many layers (or tiers) of local government there should be.

The legislatively enforced uniformity of local government continued throughout the twentieth century, as did the preoccupation of central governments, of all political colours, with the regulation of local activity and the diminution of local autonomy. It was in the period after the Second World War, when policy makers were grappling with rapidly changing demographic, political, social and technological developments, and a rapidly expanding welfare state, that the demands of efficient service administration and responsive, democratic local government needed to be reconciled (Young and Rao, 1997).

Such a reconciliation was attempted by the Herbert Commission Report on London Government (Cmnd 1164) which resulted in the 1965 replacement of the London County Council as the strategic authority by the geographically larger Greater London Council. In addition, thirty-two London Boroughs and the city of London Corporation had responsibility for the provision of day-to-day services. In 1966 the Labour Government set up a Royal Commission on Local Government in England, with separate enquiries into the future of local government in Wales and Scotland. The Report of the Royal Commission (Cmnd 4040), while accepting the importance of democratic local government, expressed the belief that it was then too numerous and fragmented, but was equally unable to agree unanimously a blueprint for change. The majority report suggested a unitary solution with fifty-eight authorities outside London responsible for all local government services. A minority report however, argued for a two-tier division of function and structure based on city regions and 'shire' and 'district' councils. The Labour government accepted the majority report, but its Conservative successor elected in 1970, and mindful of its strengths in the shires, introduced a new two-tier structure through the 1972 Local Government Act.

On 1 April 1974 the map of local government changed dramatically (Figure 22.1). The systems of local government for the big cities and counties were the inverse of each other. In the major conurbations six metropolitan counties were created alongside thirty-six metropolitan districts. The met counties were major strategic authorities, while the met districts had responsibility for the large-spending services such as education, social services and housing.

In the shires the situation was almost reversed; the counties – forty-seven of them – were the education and social service authorities as well as having a wider strategic remit. The districts were

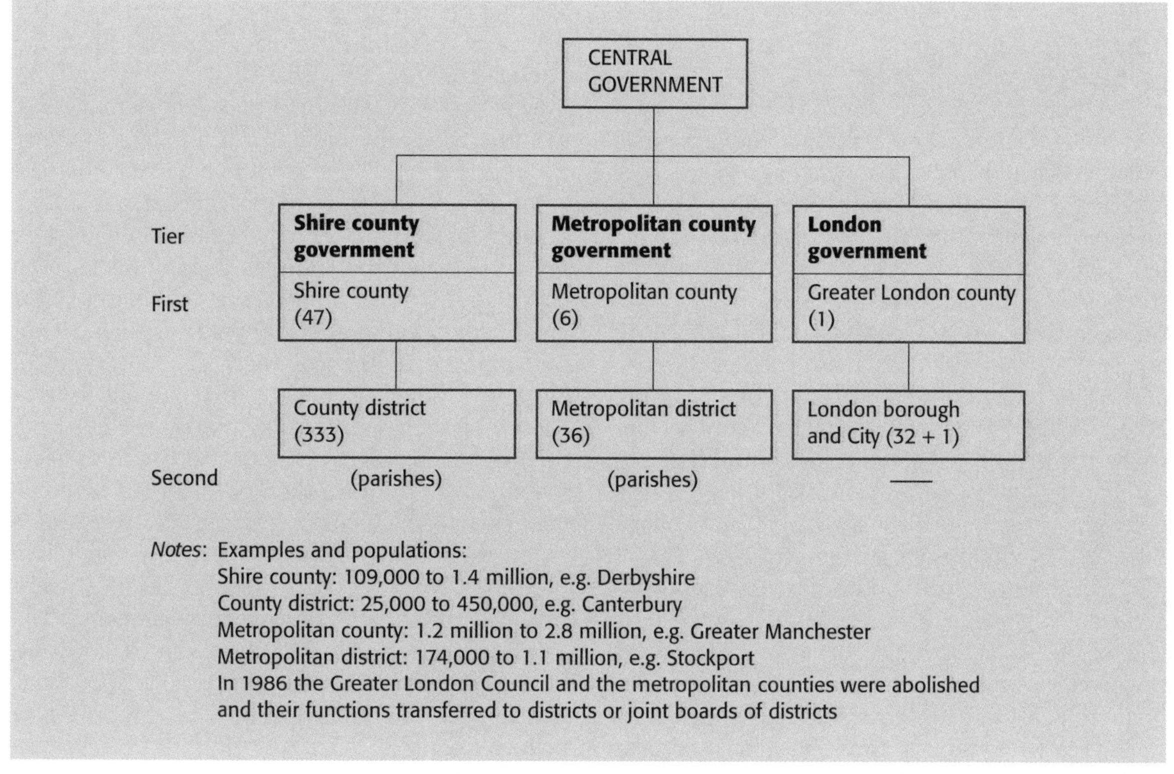

Figure 22.1 The structure of local government in England and Wales after 1974
Source: Adapted from Gray, 1979

responsible for housing, with leisure as the other major spending service, alongside planning and waste removal functions. In England and Wales the number of counties was reduced from fifty-eight to forty-seven and the districts from 1,249 to 333. As a result of the Wheatley Commission (Cmnd 4159, HMSO, 1969) local government in Scotland was also reorganised on a two-tier basis with nine large regional councils and fifty-three districts, alongside three Island authorities. Thus, in 1974 British local government became less local and more subject to division of function between larger units.

The political debate behind the 1974 reorganisation is often overshadowed, and indeed obscured, by the technocratic versus democratic arguments of large efficient local government against small responsive self-governing communities. In the 1960s and 1970s Labour and Conservative Parties saw the structure of local government, the allocation of services between tiers and the drawing of authority boundaries as important political considerations; not a new phenomena but one shared by Victorian Conservative and Liberal governments. Labour's support for a unitary solution – still current Labour Party policy – saw large, urban-centred councils running all services, and – because of its urban base – mainly Labour controlled.

Conservative support for the two-tier option and the 1970 government's allocation of services between the tiers equally displayed its party political preoccupations. Shire counties received the more powerful and expensive services, as by and large these counties would be Conservative dominated. The metropolitan districts were given similar functional responsibilities which would enable Conservatives in some of the more affluent metropolitan areas to control significant local services. Thus, for Labour and Conservative Parties, the importance of the structure of local government rested not so much on the technocratic against democratic arguments but on the realities of political control and power.

The political considerations concerning local government were at the fore in the reorganisations of the 1980s and 1990s, instigated again by a Conservative government. The metropolitan counties, and particularly the Greater London Council, led from 1981 by Ken Livingstone, had become troublesome for the Thatcher government. The Conservatives' 1983 manifesto had pledged to abolish these authorities, and after the publication of a White Paper entitled 'Streamlining the Cities' (Cmnd 9063, HMSO, 1983), this was duly accomplished in 1986. The responsibilities of the GLC and six metropolitan counties were transferred to the boroughs below them, or to a series of joint boards. Whilst the Conservative government argued that the met counties had outlived their usefulness and were large, remote, unresponsive, bureaucratic and expensive, at a stroke central government had removed from the local and national scene a source of acute political embarrassment and opposition.

The reorganisations of the 1990s display similar political and party political undercurrents as well as an interesting shift by the Conservatives towards favouring a unitary system of local government. John Major's Conservative government established in 1992 a Local Government Commission, chaired by Sir John Banham (former Director of Audit at the Audit Commission and Director General of the Confederation of British Industries). Government guidance to the commission favoured the unitary system and stressed the importance of local government efficiency, accountability, responsiveness and localness, criteria which display the contradictions inherent in the technocratic–democratic arguments that had been played out since 1945 (Young and Rao, 1997).

The commission rejected the production of a national blueprint for local government structure, and instead recommended the creation of **unitary authorities** in some areas and the retention of the two-tier system or a modified version of it for other areas. The commission justified its recommendations – which often conflicted with the favoured approach of the government – on the basis of cost, community identity and local geography, and the degree of local support for change. The Secretary of State's replacement of Sir John Banham as chair of the Commission with Sir David Cooksey, again from the Audit Commission, resulted in the formation of a few more unitary authorities than otherwise would have been the case – but no new nation-wide reorganisation resulted.

In the meantime much animosity had been generated between the counties fighting for survival and the districts campaigning to enlarge their area, population, power and political influence, at the expense of the counties. The only area of local government to benefit from the antagonism caused by the review was the parishes who found themselves courted by counties and districts alike. Parishes were often promised enlarged responsibilities and consultative opportunities and lauded as an essential element of the local representative processes. With the end of the local government review came the end of such blandishments. The animosity between district and counties, however, in many cases remains, having soured relationships, which were often tense – despite similarities of political control.

Local government in Scotland and Wales faired differently from that in England. The local government reviews of the 1990s led to the imposition of a unitary system across both those countries. The 1992 Local Government Act abolished the county and district councils in Wales and the regional and district councils in Scotland, replacing them with twenty-two unitaries in Wales and thirty-two in Scotland. By contrast, the last unitary authorities to come into existence in England in 1998 left a system consisting of unitary authorities in some areas and a two-tier system of counties and districts in others, alongside the London Boroughs. A new Greater London Authority (GLA) and Mayor of London were elected in May 2000, a Blair government initiative (see Box 22.1). Thus, at the end of the twentieth century there exists a patchwork of local authorities – unitary and two-tier – to mirror the more fragmented patchwork existing at the end of the nineteenth century. At the beginning of the twenty-first century local government is larger, more remote and distant from the communities it serves, more driven by the search for technocratic excellence

BOX 22.1 **IDEAS AND PERSPECTIVES** 

'The odd couple': candidates for London mayor, autumn 1999

In the autumn of 1999 both major parties faced a strange dilemma over the election for the first elected mayor of London scheduled for May 2000. Both had candidates who were popular in their respective parties but who were mistrusted by their leaderships.

Ken Livingstone had been the tabloid-dubbed 'Red Ken' of the early 1980s, leading a Greater London Council which allegedly supported 'loony left' policies of the kind which made Labour unelectable during those years and until the birth of New Labour under Tony Blair. Thatcher abolished the GLC in 1985 and Livingstone proceeded to become MP for Brent in 1987. He did not make much of an impression, however, on the House and was regarded by many as something of a loner. He allegedly refused an offer of junior office under Blair after 1997 and became regarded as a 'loose cannon', a maverick likely to split the party. It seems clear Blair sees him as an unreconstructed Old Labourite, and as someone who would use his position as elected mayor to challenge the national leadership. Consequently the leadership set about making life difficult for the person whom opinion polls revealed was the favourite of both party members in London and the general populace of the mostly Labour voting capital. First of all Frank Dobson, the Health Secretary, was pressurised into standing for the Labour candidature in order to place a safe Blairite on the ticket. Secondly instead of a one man one vote selection procedure an electoral college was constructed, whereby three groups would contribute to the selection: party members; trade unions in London; and MPs, MEPs and candidates for the new Greater London Authority. It was assumed by the leadership that unions would use their block votes to back the Number Ten choice although in many cases unions balloted their members and Livingstone was the beneficiary. In the event Ken Livingstone was called in front of the committee charged with drawing up the short list on 22 November and received a grilling which did not satisfy his questioners. They were worried he would not support the party line and, especially, would oppose the party's policy on the London Underground. His second grilling on the 24 November seemed to be less objectionable to the panel and he was placed on the short list but with the Prime Minister pledged to support his man Dobson and oppose with all his might Ken Livingstone, the man whom every poll showed to be the popular choice. It remained to be seen if Blair's supporters could defeat Livingstone for the candidate nomination scheduled for early in 2000.

Lord (Jeffrey) Archer, the millionaire novelist and former Conservative MP and Deputy Party Chairman, was another politician determined to win the mayoralty. He campaigned openly for two years leading up to September 1999 when he easily outvoted Steve Norris, his opponent for the Conservative Party's nomination. He was applauded at the 1999 conference and described as a man of 'integrity and probity' by William Hague, the party leader. However, in mid-November someone who had been asked to provide a possible alibi for Archer in connection with his 1986 libel suit against tabloid newspapers who accused him of sleeping with a prostitute spilled the beans and Archer was exposed as a liar. The embarrassment for the Conservatives was intense. Archer was wildly popular in the party as a star speaker, indefatigable fund raiser and, amongst the leadership, as a generous host at conferences and donor (his shepherd's pie and Krug champagne parties were legendary). All the top brass had enjoyed his hospitality; they had overcome the doubts which Archer's various scrapes and evidence of a tendency to fantasise had raised. Now they had to backpedal as Archer was cast out as the mayoral candidate by his former friend and supporter, Hague: his political career was dismantled rapidly and humiliatingly. At the time of writing both main parties face acute problems: Labour face the prospect of

BOX 22.1 continued

having a candidate whom their Prime Minister is campaigning against while the Conservatives have suffered a devastating political loss of face.

Dobson wins nomination: February 2000. After much unseemly politicking by the Labour hierarchy in the run up to the electoral college vote on the party's candidate, Frank Dobson won by the thinnest sliver of a margin: 51.5 per cent to Livingstone's 48.5 per cent. Dobson and the leadership were delighted but Livingstone declared the result 'tainted' and called on Dobson to stand down. It was widely accepted that the electoral college had been constructed to keep Ken out and it was also true that Livingstone received 75,000 to 22,000 of those votes which were balloted. Polls indicated he would win any contest against the former health secretary and in mid-February he was considering whether to run as an independent, a course of action which would violate his earlier statements about accepting the results of the electoral college decision and lead to his expulsion from the party to which he had been devoted all his life.

at the expense of local democracy and representation, more managerialist and less salient to local people than its nineteenth-century counterpart. What results these factors have on the continuing debate about the relationship between central and local government and the relative constitutional position of the two is the subject of the next section.

Inter-governmental relations: general competence or general dogsbody?

The first section of this chapter set out British local government's subordinate role to central government. Such an arrangement is not the only relationship between national and sub-national governments and this section will consider, in the light of the Blair government's modernising agenda for local government, how the centre and the localities may interact on a more equal footing.

The British unitary state and unwritten constitution, resting on the doctrine of Parliamentary supremacy, ensures that the party with a majority in Parliament is able to legislate as it thinks fit, unhindered by any mechanisms for constitutional restraint. While the courts may interpret government legislation, they cannot hold it unconstitutional and unenforceable, effectively striking legislation down as any Supreme Court may do. Thus, inter-governmental relations in Britain are conducted in an environment where political control of the machinery of central government allows national political concerns and policy to supersede local discretion.

Despite the supremacy of Parliament, much of the relationship between national and sub-national governments is conducted within a framework where bargaining between institutions is a norm. However this bargaining occurs in an unbalanced context, with central government ultimately assured of its own way. Local authorities are able to redress some of that imbalance by challenge and seeking compromise (Rhodes *et al.*, 1983). Local authorities, however, have no general competence to act for the citizens of their area. Thus, they are not representative bodies that are able to govern their locality, but may only act where Parliament has granted 'positive authority for their actions in a specific law' (Hampton, 1987).

General competence on the other hand would see councils able to govern their localities within a broad framework of powers set out by Parliament. It would not necessarily mean that councils could take whatever action they wished, rather that they would not require specific legislative authority for each action and would be less constrained by the courts than at present. Much of the debate concerning general competence centres on the powers, roles and responsibilities of local government and how the discretion to act at the local level is defined and codified in relation to central government.

Should local councils be subordinate to central control and regulation? Should they only be able to act in cases where Parliament gives express authority? Or, should local councils be granted a power of general competence to govern their own localities as they think fit and in accordance with the wishes of their electorate? Councils are elected bodies, comprising the local political representatives of the citizenry; councillors hold office by virtue of the public vote. Moreover, councils and councillors are closer to the people they represent. The issues they deal with often have a more immediate and specific impact on the day-to-day well-being of local citizens than the activities of central government. In addition, strong and independent local councils can act as a counterbalance to the political power of central government, and are a means by which local voices can be heard at the heart of government. With this in mind the question of general competence for local government becomes one of balancing the political power of the centre and localities.

While Prime Minister Blair's modernising agenda for local government does not introduce general competence, it does raise the prospect of a new duty for local government to promote the social, economic and environmental well-being of local communities (for a detailed exploration of how sub-national governments can affect the welfare or well-being of citizens see Wolman and Goldsmith, 1992). The agenda is clearly displayed within *Renewing Democracy: Rebuilding communities* (Labour Party, 1995) the 1997 Labour Party manifesto and the Green and White Papers, *Local Democracy and Community Leadership* (DETR, 1998), *Modern Local Government: In touch with the People* (DETR, 1998) and *Local Leadership: Local Choice* (DETR, 1999). While the new duty is clearly not a power of general competence, it represents a nudge in that direction, providing local government with an opportunity to act in a far more flexible and legally certain environment than has hitherto been the case.

Local government in Britain will always be subordinate to central government unless Britain moves to a written constitution which codifies and legally enshrines the relationship between elements of the state (for an example of such a written constitution – which suggests a power of general competence of local government – see IPPR (1991). Such a move from a British government is, for the foreseeable future, a flight of fantasy! It may be, however, that the Blair government, so often accused of control freakery, has set in motion a constitutional journey that will see councils given a much freer rein to govern their areas and respond to community needs than previously enjoyed, a right which, of course, could just as easily be removed by any future government, as granted by the current administration.

Local government and local politics

Despite folklore to the contrary, local government and local and national politics have had a long and intertwined association, an association stretching back much further than the 1974 local government reorganisation, often wrongly identified as the point when national politics invaded local council chambers. Indeed, prior to the 1835 Municipal Corporations Act local government was already politicised, controlled for the most part, by what Fraser (1979) described as self-perpetuating Tory–Anglican elites. Moreover, the first municipal elections after the 1835 Act were essentially party battles between the holders of, and contenders for, local political power. Even in the towns that did not immediately incorporate after the 1835 Act the campaign for new municipal status often divided along party lines. Similar party battles occurred throughout the nineteenth century over the reform, and control, of London government (Young, 1975).

Gyford (1985) summarised the long-term process of the party politicisation of local government, identifying five distinct stages: diversity (1835–56), crystallisation (1865–1905), re-alignment 1905–45), nationalisation (1945–74) and reappraisal (1974–onwards). The stages chart the gradual solidification of the party system in local government and indicate that while party politics has had a constant presence in the campaigns for control of local councils and in the conduct of council business, the context and texture of party activity has changed.

Local politics has moved from a time when candidates and councillors often disguised their national party allegiances (see also Grant, 1973, and Clements, 1969) to today, where something like 80 per cent of all councils have been categorised as 'politicised'. Indeed, political party involvement in local government has been described as almost 'universal' (HMSO, 1986b).

As representative bodies, with the ability to distribute scarce local resources and decide broad policy approaches to important local services, councils are inherently political bodies. It is no surprise therefore that members and supporters of national political parties have had an interest in securing representation on and control of councils. Hennock (1973), Jones (1969) and Lee (1963) indicate not only the long association between local government and political parties, but the different texture party politics has taken and the varied relationships that have existed within and between parties.

Bulpitt (1967) has summarised these differences into a typology of local party systems as either negative or positive, the main distinction being the degree to which councillors act as coherent political groupings to accept responsibility for the control of council policy and the settling of patronage issues. What has varied over time and place is the nature of the relationship between the parties and the degrees to which councillors sharing the same political allegiance, cohere as distinct party groups. It is the rigidity with which party groups cohere to provide a council with a governing administration, or an opposition bloc, that distinguishes the conduct of party politics in council chambers from its more fluid predecessors (Young and Davis, 1990).

Today most council elections are contested by members of national political parties, and most local elections have the flavour of a series of mini general elections (Newton, 1976). That is, local elections reflect voters' national pre-occupations rather than local concerns and thus local elections often turn on the national fortunes of the main political parties. Conflicting views exist, however, as to the balance of local and national influences at local elections, with some evidence suggesting that local issues are important when voters cast a local ballot (HMSO, 1986a; Green, 1972).

Table 22.1 Average turnout in sub-national elections in EU countries

EU country	Mean (%)
Luxembourg	93
Italy	85
Belgium	80
Denmark	80
Germany	72
France	68
Spain	64
Ireland	62
Portugal	60
Netherlands	54
Great Britain	40

Source: Community Identity and Participation in Local Democracy, Rallings, Temple and Thrasher, Commission for Local Democracy, Research Report No. 1, 1994

One thing is certain, whatever the impact parties have on whether the electorate focus on local or national issues, national parties appear recently to have had little positive effect on the turnout at local elections. Indeed, as Table 22.1 shows, Britain lags behind the rest of Europe when it comes to turnout at local elections.

Cross national comparisons of local turnout are problematic because of elements of compulsory voting for nations at the top of the table and different structures and tiers of sub national government. Britain, however, can take little comfort. Since 1994 local electoral turnout has declined even further, reaching a low of around 30 per cent in May 1999. Indeed, in some by-elections turnout has fallen to single figures. Poor turnout raises serious questions about the democratic legitimacy of local government and the ability of councillors to claim an electoral mandate for their policies

It is the party group system and the way in which groups organise to conduct their business and the business of the council, alongside the loyalty and discipline they expect of, and by and large receive from councillors, that have the potential to damage local accountability and representation (Copus, 1998, 1999). The party group system sees councillors bound to the decisions of their groups, taken in private and closed meetings, and expected to publicly support, or at least acquiesce in, the outcomes of those meetings.

Loyalty to the party group is expected of the councillor, almost irrespective of how he or she may have spoken or voted in the group meeting. Once the group has made a decision, the councillor must adhere to it in public, whatever he or she thinks, and irrespective of any articulated community opinion existing in his or her ward. While most party groups show some flexibility when it comes to councillors acting against their own group when strong opinions are expressed by local communities, the issue generating those opinions must usually be purely local in nature. That is, they must be located in the councillor's electoral area and have little, or no link, to any wider policy concern; such isolated issues do arise but are a rarity.

The organisation and activity of party groups varies depending on the party concerned but the three main national and two nationalist parties, each produce model standing orders for their council party groups. Standing orders are open to interpretation by individual groups, such interpretations depending on the personnel of the group, the nature of the relationship between the groups and the political composition of the council. Indeed, patterns of party interaction and competition will vary depending on the type of council concerned (Rallings and Thrasher, 1997). Largely, however, groups are well organised and structured, with a range of officers undertaking different tasks and clearly identified expectations of loyalty from its membership. In addition, party groups have a range of disciplinary procedures and sanctions available to use against recalcitrant members. The nature of and willingness to use such disciplinary mechanisms vary across the parties, as does the willingness to take a flexible interpretation of standing orders and allow councillors to act at variance with group decisions.

The result of group discipline and loyalty – which plays itself out differently depending on the political affiliation of the councillor – is that councillors often come to represent their political party – or rather the party group – to the electorate and council. Indeed, the party group is now the most important theatre for the conduct of local representation and for council decision making (Hampton, 1970; Saunders, 1979; Stoker, 1991; Game and Leach, 1995).

The group is the place where important local issues are discussed, party lines agreed, political options considered, and for the majority group in particular it is where council decisions are made. What takes place in the public meetings of the council and its committees is the ratification of decisions made in the private party group meeting. The group will, of course, take into account a range of views when making its decisions; it is to the source of those views and attempts to influence local government policy making that the chapter now turns.

Local government: a changing policy environment

While councillors have links into the external environment through their parties, community, business, professional and political organisations, the decisions they take rest heavily on the advice they receive from officers employed by the authority. These professionals and managers form an important antenna for councillors into the outside world.

Many sources of alternative information exist for councillors to that received from officers, but, as the paid employees and advisors to the council, senior officers are a potentially powerful influence on councillors' final decisions. Moreover, officers can influence councillors in their private discussions in the party group through the production of council minutes and reports which councillors consider in their group meetings, and, by attendance at those meetings, on request, to answer questions and give advice, advice, which until quite recently was largely accepted. Young and Laffin (1990) indicate that party politics has radically altered the patterns of interaction between officers and councillors and that the task of advising councillors no longer comes with the certainty of officer influence that it once had. The fact remains that for the vast majority of councillors the advice received from officers is amongst the most important and influential they receive; securing alternative sources of advice and support comes at a premium.

Local government officers coming from a range of professional backgrounds, mainly associated with the specialist services provided by local authorities or from the wider professions such as the law, interact with their colleagues whose profession is management. The professional as expert and the professional manager operate now in what is the accepted principle of local government management: the corporate approach. This approach was championed by the Bains report in 1972 which challenged the then-dominant functional approach to local government organisation and management.

The Bains report took a managerial perspective towards the role of the officer, but as Stewart (1986, p. 132) reminds us, 'decisions made by a manager can have important and unexpected political consequences'. Indeed, it is senior officers and senior councillors acting as 'joint élite' (Stoker, 1991) that is at the heart of local government political management. While tensions may exist between the elite of senior councillors and officers, the carving out of spheres of influence enables an uneasy alliance between officers and members to contribute a dynamic tension to local policy processes. The uneasy but dynamic tension existing between councillors and officers risks disruption by pressure from external sources for the council to respond to particular demands, or to interact with external bodies. External pressure on local authorities comes from the local citizenry, regional institutions of governance and the European Union.

The citizenry: consultation and participation

Local government policy making is not inevitably informed by the citizenry simply because the council is closer to the people it represents than the national Parliament. Local people are only able to be part of the process of local decision making if two conditions are met. First, the council has a range of mechanisms by which the views of the citizen can be sought; secondly, the council, and councillors in particular, are willing to respond positively to the views of the citizen and indeed to change and develop council policy accordingly. Public involvement in local government is not a case of a council convincing the people it has the right answers, but developing those answers to ensure congruence between policy and the views of the citizen. Such a process of course is set within a representative framework where councillors will assess the outcomes of citizen consultation and participation but be responsible for making the final decisions on important local issues.

The Blair government's modernising agenda for local government recognises the inherent tension between local representative democracy and enhanced citizen participation. The modernising agenda does not set out to replace representative democracy with a participative variant, rather it seeks to use citizen involvement to inform the outcomes of the representative processes as they link to local policy-making. *Local Democracy and Community Leadership* (DETR, 1997) exhorts councils to involve the public more in their decision-making processes and urges that such involvement should be a regular rather than episodic feature. The Government has set out the virtues of enhanced public involvement thus:

> The prize is an ever closer match between the needs and aspirations of communities and the services secured for them by their local authority, better quality services, greater democratic legitimacy for local government and a new brand of involved and responsible citizenship; in short, reinvigorated local democracy. Increasingly, the degree to which an authority is engaged with its stakeholders may become a touchstone for the authority's general effectiveness. (DETR, 1997, p. 16)

It is clear that local government officers and councillors are expected to engage far more closely with the communities they serve and represent than has so far been the norm. So how can the public become more closely involved in the activities of the local council aside from standing for election and voting? *Local Democracy and Community*

Leadership (DETR, 1997) provides an answer by setting out a clear expectation that councils will use a number of specific mechanisms for seeking and responding to the views of the citizen. Moreover, it recognises that 'different forms of consultation may be appropriate to the different stages in the development of a policy or a strategy' (DETR, 1997, p. 16).

Councils are encouraged to use the following methods for citizen involvement:

- citizen juries,
- focus groups,
- visioning conferences,
- deliberative opinion polls,
- citizens panels,
- community forums or area based neighbourhood committees,
- interest and user group forums,
- referendums to test public opinion on specific local issues.

While many councils have for some time been using these and a number of other methods of assessing community opinion, particularly experimenting with various approaches to decentralised decision making, others have done little in the way of encouraging citizen involvement. A lack of engagement between local citizens and local councils has potentially damaging consequences for the future of local democracy. Past government research in 1967 and 1986 displays a low level of knowledge amongst the public about local government, the functions it provides and the way it is organised (HMSO, 1967, 1986). Moreover, these and other studies have indicated that local government holds a low salience for the public; this lack of importance allowed the Conservative governments of the 1980s and 1990s radically to undermine much of the power, functions and activities of local government.

Greater engagement between the citizen and local council and wider local political processes will lead to better quality and more informed and responsive decisions and a greater congruence between policy and the opinions of local people. It will also result in local government becoming more meaningful to local people, closer to their concerns and more in line with their priorities and needs. As a consequence it will be difficult for any future centralising government to undermine the position of local government. The challenge of enhanced citizen participation holds a great prize for local government; it remains to be seen if local government will rise to that challenge, in a meaningful sense, and improve not only the health of local democracy but also its own future.

The regional agenda

As part of the package of constitutional reform introduced by the Blair government eight new English Regional Development Agencies (RDAs) were launched on 1 April 1999. Formed by the Regional Development Agencies Act, 1998, the agencies were created to ensure that decisions about regeneration were made within the regions concerned, and to address economic imbalances between regions. The RDAs cover the following areas: North East, North West, Yorkshire and the Humber, West Midlands, East Midlands, East of England, South West, South East – a ninth, the London RDA, is to be introduced in 2000 to link with the arrival of the London Mayor and the Greater London Authority. With agencies also formed for Scotland, Wales and Northern Ireland the RDAs will total twelve – covering the whole of the UK.

The RDAs took over responsibility for the urban regeneration work (revival of areas made derelict usually through industrial failure) of English Partnerships, the Rural Development Commission and the Single Regeneration Budget. Each of the RDAs has an appointed board to manage its affairs consisting of twelve members – four from local authorities in the region.

The main objectives of the RDAs are:

- economic development and social and physical regeneration;
- business support, investment and competitiveness;
- enhancing regional skills;
- promoting employment;
- sustainable development.

The RDAs' brief, set by the Government, is to raise the average prosperity of their regions to that of the rest of the European Union. While the RDAs are clearly regional bodies, the focus for much of their work will be to integrate the economic prospects of the English regions with the European Union and its regions. The work of the RDAs is regional, their focus European. The RDAs were given as their first task the production of draft regional economic development strategies for public consultation. These documents will set out a five to ten year strategic vision for their regions, drawing into the planning process a wide range of partnership bodies from the private, public and voluntary sectors.

The RDAs will need to address the regional needs of wide and often socially, economically and geographically diverse areas. Yet, for the regions of the UK to develop their own distinctive strengths and characteristics, and to draw in European Union funding from a range of programmes, a comprehensive strategy (rather than the fragmented approach of the past) is a positive step. The final versions of the regional strategy documents were required by John Prescott, Secretary of State for Environment, Transport and the Regions, by October 1999, a tight time-scale for bodies only coming into life in April of the same year.

The introduction of the little-hailed RDAs is a first, not final, step on the road to devolution to the English regions. The RDAs are appointed bodies not elected chambers and as such lack the electoral legitimacy of the Scottish Parliament and Welsh Assembly. The continuing debate concerning English devolution turns now on the scattered regional campaigns for the introduction of elected regional chambers. Some of these campaigns are adopting the approach of the all-party Scottish Constitutional Convention, which pressed for devolution and the Scottish Parliament. One such campaign is the North-East Constitutional Convention, launched in Sunderland in April 1999. The Convention, consisting of councillors and other politicians, the voluntary sector and business, is pressing for a fifty-four member elected regional assembly for the North-East.

The shape of regional devolution is a complex and fluid one. While some are pressing for fully elected chambers and almost for a form of devolution for the English regions, other areas are settling for a more cosy form of regional parliament. Under the 1998 Regional Development Agencies Act the Government has already designated a number of regional chambers. These chambers are not, however, democratically elected bodies. The designated chambers will shadow the RDAs, but will again consist of appointees rather than elected representatives; legislation stipulates that non-local government membership of the chambers should total at least 30 per cent. Thus, appointees will come from a broad range of organisations such as regional CBI and Chambers of Commerce, the TUC, Training and Enterprise Councils and further and higher education institutions.

It is clear that the government has not yet set its mind on democratically elected regional chambers across England, arguing that such should only be introduced where a regional demand exists. Further, the Government is of the opinion that regional chambers are congruent only with a unitary system of local government, introducing into the regional debate the prospect of another reorganisation of local government. Moreover, concern exists amongst local government as to the responsibilities and duties of any new regional layer of government, elected or otherwise. Will regional chambers draw their powers and responsibilities downward from central government or upward from local government?

Regional devolution has the potential of becoming a centralising process rather than a devolutionary one. Moreover, the Government's belief that regional government means unitary local government – a belief not shared in parts of Europe – could see local government increase yet again in size and lose further its connection with local people, contradicting much of the modernising agenda's aim to reconnect local people with local councils. The Blair government was quick to act on Labour's opposition promises on Scottish and Welsh devolution; it is more cautious in its approach to the English question. Unitary local authorities preferred by the previous Conservative government had of course already been installed in Scotland and Wales in advance of devolution.

The RDAs and the current set of regional chambers are not replicas of the democratically elected Scottish Parliament and the Welsh Assembly, the first elections to which were held in May 1999. The Scottish Parliament and the Welsh Assembly represent a major change in the structure and processes of British government and a transference of political and legislative power from Westminster to alternative parliaments. Although the powers of the 129 seat Scottish and sixty seat Welsh chambers vary, they represent a model of devolution that some in the English regions will wish to emulate and perhaps take further.

The developing relationship between the Parliament and Assembly will be crucial for local government in Scotland and Wales, particularly how the two chambers monitor the activities of councils and ensure that standards of service and probity are met. The Macintosh Committee in Scotland and the Partnership Council between the Welsh Assembly and Welsh local government are addressing a range of issues that will influence the relationship between devolved chambers and local government. It is clear, however, that a danger exists in that a decentralising move, such as devolution in Scotland and Wales, could end up centralising political decision making by drawing powers up from local councils rather than down from Whitehall and Westminster. How the relationship develops between devolved chambers and parliaments and local government will be an interesting one to follow.

Local government and the European Union

The relationship between British local government and the EU has come a long way since a 1991 Audit Commission report drew attention to its often 'blinkered' approach to EU matters. Relationships between sub-national government such as British local councils and supra-national bodies such as the EU will always be conducted in a complex environment and through a complex system. This system John (1996) describes as triadic, that is conducted between three groups of actors at each of the three levels of governmental interaction. Indeed, the relationship between the EU and local government is influenced by two major factors, first European law and policy and secondly the relationships between local and national government. Moreover, some local governments see the EU as a way around problematic relationships with national government and economic and political constraints, a situation that applied particularly in the UK throughout the 1980s and early 1990s (John, 1996).

The impact of the EU on local government is less clear than the impact of national government but just as important. The EU affects local councils through a range of policy initiatives and demands: environmental health, consumer protection, public protection and even social and human rights legislation. These all impact the activities of local government and many councils have expressed concerns about the level of resources involved.

Even so, many local authorities have recognised the importance of securing funding from the EU and contributing to the EU policy-making process, to the extent that many UK local councils employ specialist staff to deal with European issues and negotiate with the EU. (Goldsmith and Sperling, 1997). Indeed, some have formed special committees of the council to deal with European matters and have European liaison officers, often with an economic development specialism, and located within economic development departments (Preston 1992a, 1992b).

Some councils have established Brussels offices, either individually or as part of a consortium, and, while often small-scale affairs, they can disseminate information and establish links with the EU and other European national and sub-national governments. These offices are able to prepare funding bids; lobby for policy initiatives or changes; work with other bodies attempting to influence the EU; draw the private and voluntary sector closer into the EU policy network; and place their local authority at the heart of the EU. John (1994) sees such Brussels offices as a cross national market place to develop partnership funding bids and to indulge informal lobbying with EU officials – a process in which many British councils lose out compared with their European counterparts who place far more emphasis on resourcing such offices.

Local government placing itself at the heart of the EU serves three purposes:

1 authorities can develop a range of funding partnerships with a diverse group of organisations;

2 it fosters inter-municipal learning;

3 it enables regions and councils to learn of, and shape, new EU policy initiatives (Ercole *et al.*, 1997).

Preston (1992b) indicates why local government is anxious to develop good relationships with the EU, highlighting the financial and policy benefits which flow from successful applications for European Social Fund and European Regional Development Fund support. The financial resources available from these programmes have enabled British local councils to pursue expansionist economic development policies in spite of tight controls from central government. Indeed, something like 74 per cent of British councils have applied for EU structural funds (Goldsmith and Sperling, 1997).

Another reason for the popularity of the EU amongst local government is that element of the Maastricht treaty which concerns subsidiarity. This is popularly taken to mean by local councils that decisions should be decentralised to the lowest appropriate level of government, thus locating functions and powers with sub-national governments. John (1996) points out, however, that this is a matter of political interpretation, as the treaty itself refers to relations between member states and the EU, not between states and local government. The Council of European Municipalities and Regions is, however, campaigning for changes to the Treaty which will clarify the meaning of subsidiarity in relation to the role of sub-national governments in policy and decision making. The European Charter of local self-government, which the Blair government signed up to immediately after the 1997 election as a sign of commitment to local government, already recognises that many areas of public policy and political affairs are properly administered at the local and regional level.

The EU provides British local government with:

- access to funding;
- an opportunity to pursue its own policy agenda despite central government restrictions and direction – indeed the possibility of a way around the unitary British state;
- political influence in important EU policy networks, linkages with other Europe local governments and local government consortiums;
- opportunities to strengthen its role, functions, powers and responsibilities.

As British local government comes to terms with devolved parliaments and chambers it may find valuable resources in the EU which will enable it to ward off the possible centralising tendencies of yet more layers of government above local authorities.

The modernising agenda: the shape of local government to come

When elected in 1997 the Blair government was committed to a widespread review of the British constitution; much of the previous Conservative government's policies toward local government were to be scrapped or changed. Indeed, Labour recognised in opposition the importance to political pluralism of a vibrant, healthy and vigorous local government. It is appropriate then to review the main elements of that agenda and to briefly suggest what the modernised local council could look like.

The agenda falls into three main areas:

1 replacing Compulsory Competitive Tendering (CCT) with a duty to secure Best Value in service provision;

2 reorganising political arrangements;

3 a new ethical framework for local government.

Best Value

The Local Government Act 1999 replaces the Compulsory Competitive Tendering regime introduced by the 1980 Planning and Land Act and extended by the 1988 Local Government Act. CCT placed a duty on councils to put certain services out to competitive tender in the private sector and for a council's own work force to bid against private providers to win council contracts. While the Conservative government which introduced CCT argued that it improved the efficiency and effectiveness of service provision, others argued that it was ideologically driven and designed to destroy councils' ability to provide services by biasing the tendering regime in favour of the private sector.

In January 2000 Best Value replaced CCT as the prime mechanism by which councils will ensure the economy, efficiency, effectiveness and responsiveness of service delivery. Based on the mantra of 'challenge, compare, consult, compete', Best Value does not remove the idea of competitive comparisons with the private sector – rather it removes the compulsory element and the requirement that contracts should go to the lowest tender in all but the most exceptional circumstances.

Best value is a more comprehensive system of service improvement than the CCT regime. It covers all local authority services with councils expected to review each of their service areas to secure continual improvement to the way they exercise their functions. Indeed, 'authorities will be expected to show that they have considered the underlying rationale for the service(s) under review and the alternative ways in which it might be provided' (DETR, 1999). Councils will also be required to prepare Best Value Performance Plans, providing a clear statement about:

- what services an authority will deliver to local people;
- how it will deliver them;
- to what levels services are currently delivered;
- what levels of service the public should expect in the future;
- what action it will take to deliver those standards and over what timescale (DETR, 1999).

Central to the Best Value regime is public consultation. Indeed, the consultation green paper *Improving Local Services through Best Value* (DETR, 1998) states that:

> the local consultation process will be effective only insofar as it secures and sustains a positive response from local people. This will depend in part on local authorities' responsiveness, and the skill and transparency with which the issues are presented. (DETR, 1998)

In addition, local authorities will be expected to set rigorous targets and performance indicators as well as address a number of nationally inspired performance targets for their services. While the passing of CCT has been little mourned it is the prescriptive nature of the Best Value legislation, its all encompassing remit and the plethora of inspections that go with the Best Value regime that cause local government some concern about the degrees of central control involved. Coupled to this is a deep local government suspicion of the wide powers of intervention that will rest with the Secretary of State when a council is deemed to be 'failing' in its duty to secure best value. These failures are of two kinds: failures of process and failures of substance.

A failure of process is a failure to:

- consult or consult adequately
- agree performance reviews
- set performance targets or publish details of performance against them
- set sufficiently challenging targets
- publish details of comparisons with others
- publish proscribed performance information
- make adequate information available to local people about comparative performance of other bodies
- consider alternative options for service provisions when conducting reviews.

Such failures are unlikely to lead to government intervention. It is with failures of substance that will see the Secretary of State intervene.

Failures of substance are failures to:

- meet any single nationally prescribed performance standard
- improve service standards or a deterioration in standards
- draw up and implement an action plan following a critical inspection report

- address consistently high unit costs (by comparison with other bodies).

The intervention the Secretary of State could take may result in the authority concerned losing the ability to provide a service and an outside provider being imposed (DETR, 1999). The government, however, presents these reserve powers as a last resort and have devised protocols for their use. The authority that moves substantially towards achieving Best Value, the modernising council, will have little to fear from central control. In the words of local government minister, Hillary Armstrong – 'what's best is what works'!

New political arrangements

The modernising council will also be expected under the Local Government Bill currently going through Parliament to introduce new systems and structures for political decision making. Under the Bill councils will be required to distinguish between those councillors with executive decision-making functions and those non-executive councillors who will be required to scrutinise the executive.

The Bill (and the preceding consultation document *Local Leadership: Local Choice* (DETR, 1999)) sets out three models of political arrangements councils may adopt:

1. the directly elected executive mayor and cabinet,
2. the mayor and council manager and the
3. executive leader and cabinet.

Councils will be expected to consult with their citizens as to which model should be introduced locally and 5 per cent of local citizens may petition for a referendum to be held on introducing a directly elected executive mayor.

Much debate has centred around the directly elected mayor, a political office very different from the current ceremonial and largely non-partisan mayor that chairs council meetings. The directly elected mayor would head a political executive with a wide range of decision-making powers; he or she would be elected at large, that is by every elector within a council area, not as in the case of existing councillors, by voters in individual wards or divisions. Indeed, in councils with more than one parliamentary constituency the elected mayor would come with a larger electoral mandate than the sitting Members of Parliament.

The mayor would be a highly visible political head of the council with responsibility for providing political leadership, proposing the policy framework for the council, preparing the council's budget and taking executive decisions. The mayor would appoint a cabinet from the council, which would then act under mayoral direction. The council would be responsible for scrutinising the work of the mayor and his or her cabinet and proposing amendments to policy and the budget. In the Government's preferred model for directly elected mayors, power rests with the mayor and not the council. Other models in the United States and Europe exist where political power rests with a council rather than the directly elected mayor.

The mayor and council manager model would again see a directly elected mayor, but here most executive power would rest with the council manager, a paid appointee of the council but under the direction of the mayor. Most policy and budgetary responsibility would rest with the council manager, a kind of super chief executive. It is not a model of which councillors in Britain favour, who often complain that their position is undermined by senior officers. Appointing an officer with legislatively enshrined executive responsibilities would be anathema to many councillors.

The cabinet and leader model is the one option within local leadership and local choice and the bill which has found almost unanimous support amongst councillors, with an overwhelming number of councils suggesting they would adopt this model. Here the council, or rather the controlling party group, would appoint one of its member to act as executive leader of the council who would then select his or her cabinet, or have it selected by the council. The leader would provide political leadership and propose the council's budget and policy framework; he or she would also take executive decisions within that framework. The cabinet would support the leader in this work.

The cabinet and leader system effectively institutionalises and makes real the informal system of political decision making which exists in most councils. Councils already elect a leader and chairs of committees; those members often work closely together as an informal cabinet, but without executive powers. Thus, it is little surprise that most councils appear to be already moving to adopt the cabinet and leader system (in advance of the legislation) as it represents the line of least change.

In any of the above models the remaining non-executive councillors would be charged with the duty of scrutinising, through a number of scrutiny committees, the activities of the council's executive. These councillors would be expected to put party loyalty to one side and publicly criticise a council executive which may well comprise their own party colleagues, colleagues who they themselves may have voted into executive office. The modernising agenda rests on councillors' willingness to scrutinise an executive in public, but so far has underestimated the pull of party group loyalty. It is unlikely that the sort of scrutiny envisaged by the government will occur overnight when councillors are expected to scrutinise the activities of their party colleagues.

The introduction of new political arrangements into councils and a clear distinction between executive and scrutiny members is aimed at overcoming the secretive and opaque nature of much local political decision making. It aims to make decision making open and transparent and thereby enhance local accountability; the committee system being seen as responsible for diffusing responsibility and thus making the holding of individuals to account almost impossible. Indeed, even a committee chair can not be said to be responsible for a committee decision.

Thus, the modernised council will have a highly visible executive leader of one sort or another, a cabinet, and whilst conducting most of its own business in private will be a clear point of political responsibility and accountability. The Queen's Speech in November 1999 presaged the establishment of elected mayors in other cities. The local government bill will seek to make councils 'innovative and accountable'. Cities such as Liverpool and Birmingham will be able to suggest an elected mayor to their voters via a referendum. The intention of the bill is to improve and streamline procedures long dogged by endless committee meetings. However, surveys show that most councils oppose elected mayors as they would sound the death knell for councillor influence. The same bill will repeal the notorious 'section 28' which prevented councils from 'promoting and teaching the acceptability of homosexuality'.

The government hoped the 'elected mayor' idea would spread to other councils, or the cabinet model whereby senior councillors take decisions under the eye of backbench colleagues. As Figure 22.2, from Peter Hetherington's article in *The Guardian* 10 December 1999, shows, the public favour the notion by a large majority but councils are generally against as both ideas tend to reduce the participation of the regular elected member in decision making.

Moreover, the experience of those councils who have already experimented with the new approach – such as Hammersmith, Fulham and Lewisham – suggests the new system tends to be overly private if not secretive.

A new ethical framework

The Nolan Committee (HMSO, 1997) on standards in public life conducted an investigation into the ethical arrangements and practices of local government. Its report has been largely accepted by the Government and forms the basis of the proposals contained within *Local Leadership: Local Choice* for developing the ethical framework of local government.

The Nolan Committee effectively gave local government a glowing bill of health, but concerns about the probity and conduct of councillors and officers remain. The Government is as keen to avoid the appearance of wrong-doing as much as wrong-doing itself, and as a result the following approach to probity and ethical conduct is to be expected of councils on the passing of the Local Government Bill:

- Every council to adopt a code of conduct for officers and members.
- Councils to form standards committees to oversee ethical issues and provide advice and guidance on the code of conduct and its implementation.
- An independent national standards board will be established with responsibility for investig-

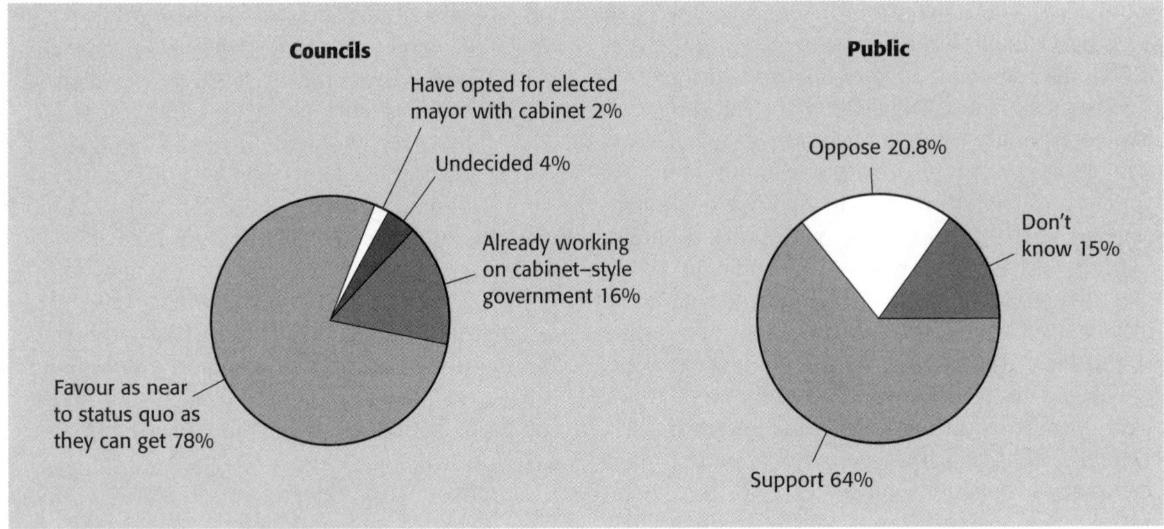

Figure 22.2 Views on elected mayors
Source: The Guardian, 10 December 1999

ating alleged breaches of a council's code of conduct.

The government is also to abolish the surcharge, whereby councillors can be required to repay large sums of money felt to have been illegally spent. Surcharge is to be replaced by a new offence of misuse of public office.

The issue of ethical conduct is, however, as much about councils generating an environment within which councillors and officers are expected to act with integrity and probity and who are provided with support and assistance in dealing with complex ethical issues as it is about rooting out corruption and punishing offenders. While corruption has been uncovered in local government the vast majority of councillors conduct the affairs of their councils with integrity and honesty. The modernised council will simply have robust ethical frameworks and expectations for supporting councillors in that work.

Chapter summary

The chapter has considered British local government as a politically representative set of arrangements designed to ensure responsiveness to the demands of local citizens. It has also outlined the constitutionally subordinate nature of local government to central control but indicated that this need not be the only constitutional settlement available between the localities and the centre. The chapter has investigated the role of political parties in local government and the wider political process of local democracy as they are enacted through local councils. As well as a political process it has considered local government as a set of institutional relationships between citizens, the centre and the EU. It has also displayed the main elements of the government's modernising agenda.

The chapter has emphasised the politically dynamic nature of local government, which exists not only as a means of providing services – important though that may be – but also as a means by which the will of local people can be expressed and realised.

Postscript

On Thursday May 4 2000, London's electors chose Independent candidate Ken Livingstone, from 11 other contenders, to be the capital's first directly elected mayor. Moreover, Livingstone is now the country's only politician directly elected to an executive office, and has a mandate larger than the Prime Minister's. However, only 34 per cent of those Londoners entitled to vote, chose to make the selection between the candidates on offer. In May 2000 some 10 per cent less voters went to the polls than for the 1981 Greater London Council elections, which saw Ken Livingstone elected by the majority Labour group, as leader of the council. The GLC was subsequently abolished in 1986 by Mrs Thatcher's government.

In electing Ken Livingstone, the voters rejected candidates from the three major political parties. At the same time, they refused to give any one of those parties a majority on the Greater London Assembly – the body that will assist Livingstone in governing London and also hold the mayor to account. The GLA, elected by a mixture of first past the post and a party list system, comprises: nine Labour and Conservative members, four Liberal Democrats and three Green Party members. Livingstone will build his cabinet from amongst these politicians.

So, London now has an Independent directly elected executive mayor, who will need to work with a Labour Government, a Greater London Assembly on which no party has a majority, and, the City of London and 32 London Boroughs, with all of the major parties controlling at least two Boroughs and with some Boroughs lacking overall political control. Local democracy in London has just become very exciting. It remains to be seen if the rest of the country are enthused by the London example to demand their own elected mayors, or so put off by the actions of the political parties in selecting candidates, and the often unpleasant election campaign, to want to ignore the idea altogether.

Discussion points

- Has the British system of local government been over reformed since the early 1970s?
- In what ways has the funding of local government proved a problem?
- Given the increasing central control of local government, would it be best to run it from London?

References

Audit Commission (1991) *A Rough Guide to Europe: Local Authorities and the EC* (HMSO).

Bains, M.A. (1972) *Working Group on Local Authority Management Structures, The New Local Authorities: Management and Structure* (HMSO).

Bulpitt, J.J.G. (1967) *Party Politics in English Local Government* (Longmans).

Byrne, T. (1983) *Local Government in Britain* (Pelican), p. 24.

Clements, R.V. (1969) *Local Notables and the City Council* (Macmillan).

Copus, C. (1998) 'The councillor: representing a locality and the party group', *Local Governance*, Vol. 24, No. 3, Autumn, pp. 215–24.

Copus, C. (1999) 'The councillor and party group loyalty', *Policy and Politics*, Vol. 27, No. 3, July, pp. 309–24.

Dearlove, J. (1979) *The Reorganisation of British Local Government: Old Orthodoxies and a Political Perspective* (Cambridge University Press).

DETR (1997) *Local Democracy and Community Leadership*.

DETR (1998) *Improving Local Services through Best Value*.

DETR (1999) *Implementing Best Value: A Consultation Paper on Draft Guidance*.

Elcock, H. (1982) *Local Government: Politicians, Professionals and the Public in Local Authorities* (Methuen).

Ercole, E., Walters, M. and Goldsmith, M. (1997) 'Cities, networks, EU regions, European offices', in M. Goldsmith and Klausen (eds), *European Integration and Local Government* (Edward Elgar), pp. 219–36.

Fraser, D. (1979) *Power and Authority in the Victorian City* (St Martins Press).

Game, C. and Leach, S. (1995) *The Role of Political Parties in Local Democracy*, Commission for Local Democracy, Research Report No. 11 (CLD Limited).

Goldsmith, M. and Sperling, E. (1997) 'Local government and the EU: the British experience', in M. Goldsmith and Klausen (eds), *European Integration and Local Government* (Edward Elgar), pp. 95–120.

Grant, W.P. (1973) 'Non-partisanship in British local politics', *Policy and Politics*, Vol. 1, No. 1, pp. 241–54.

Gyford, J. (1976) *Local Politics in Britain* (Croom Helm), p. 11.

Hampton, W. (1970) *Democracy and Community: a Study of Politics in Sheffield* (Oxford University Press).

Hampton, W. (1987) *Local Government and Urban Politics* (Longman), p. 2.

Hennock, E.P. (1973) *Fit and Proper Persons: Ideal and Reality in Nineteenth-Century Urban Government* (Edward Arnold).

HMSO (1960) *Royal Commission on Local Government in Greater London, 1957–60 (The Herbert Commission)*, Cmnd 1164.

HMSO (1967a) *Report of the Royal Commission on Local Government, Redcliffe-Maud Report*, Cmnd 4040.

HMSO (1967b) *Committee on the Management of Local Government*, Research Vol. III, *The Local Government Elector*.

HMSO (1969) *Royal Commission on Local Government in Scotland, The Wheatley Commission*, Cmnd 4159.

HMSO (1986a) *Committee of Inquiry into the Conduct of Local Authority Business*, Research Vol. III, *The Local Government Elector*, Cmnd 9800.

HMSO (1986b) *Committee of Inquiry into the Conduct of Local Authority Business*, Research Vol. I, *The Political Organisation of Local Authorities*, Cmnd 9798, pp. 25, 197.

HMSO (1997) *Committee on Standards in Public Life*, Vol. II, *Standards of Conduct in Local Government in England and Wales*, Cmnd 3702 – II.

HMSO (1998) *Modern Local Government: In Touch with the People*, Cmnd 4014.

HMSO (1999) *Local Leadership: Local Choice*, Cmnd 4298.

John, P. (1994) 'UK Sub-National Offices in Brussels: diversification or regionalism?', paper presented to the ESRC Research Seminar: British Regionalism and Devolution in a Single Europe, LSE.

John, P. (1996) 'Centralisation, decentralisation and the European Union: the dynamics of triadic relationships', *Public Administration*, Vol. 74, Summer, pp. 293–313.

Jones, G.W. (1969) *Borough Politics: a Study of Wolverhampton Borough Council 1888–1964* (Macmillan).

Keith-Lucas, B. (1952) *The English Local Government Franchise* (Basil Blackwell).

Lee, J.M. (1963) *Social Leaders and Public Persons: a Study of County Government in Cheshire since 1888* (Clarendon Press).

Newton, K. (1976) *Second City Politics: Democratic Processes and Decision-Making in Birmingham* (Clarendon Press).

Preston, J. (1992a) 'Local government and the European Community', in George (ed.), *Britain and the European Community: the Politics of Semi-Detachment* (Clarendon Press).

Preston, J. (1992b) 'Local government', in Bulmer, George and Scott (eds), *The United Kingdom and EC membership Evaluated* (Pinter Publishers).

Rallings, C. and Thrasher, M. (1994) *Community Identity and Participation in Local Democracy*, in C. Rallings, Temple and M. Thrasher, Commission for Local Democracy, Research Report No. 1.

Rallings, C. and Thrasher, M. (1997) *Local Elections in Britain* (Routledge).

(1999) *Regional Development Agencies and Regional Chambers* (Ludgate Public Affairs).

Rhodes, R.A.W., Hardy, B. and Pudney, K. (1983) *Power Dependence, Theories of Central–Local Relations: a Critical Assessment* (University of Essex, Department of Government).

Saunders, P. (1979) *Urban Politics: a Sociological Interpretation* (Hutchinson).

Stanyer, J. (1976) *Understanding Local Government* (Fontana).

Stewart, J. (1986) *The New Management of Local Government* (Allen & Unwin), p. 132.

Stoker, G. (1991) *The Politics of Local Government* (Macmillan, The Constitution of the United Kingdom, London, Institute for Public Policy Research).

Wolman, H. and Goldsmith, M. (1992) *Urban Politics and Policy: a Comparative Approach* (Blackwell).

Young, K. (1973) 'The politics of London government 1880–1899', *Public Administration*, Vol. 51, No. 1, Spring, pp. 91–108.

Young, K. (1975) *Local Politics and the Rise of Party: the London Municipal Society and the Conservative Intervention in Local Elections 1894–1963* (Leicester University Press).

Young, K. (1989) 'Bright hopes and dark fears; the origins and expectations of the county councils', in K. Young (ed.), *New Directions for County Government* (Association of County Councils), p. 6.

Young, K. and Davis, M. (1990) *The Politics of Local Government Since Widdicombe* (Joseph Rowntree Foundation).

Young, K. and Rao, N. (1997) *Local Government Since 1945* (Blackwell).

Chapter 23 The judiciary

Philip Norton

Learning objectives

- To identify the relationship of the judicial system to other parts of the political process.
- To describe the basic structure of that system, and how it has changed in recent years as a result of a greater willingness of judges to undertake judicial review, and as a consequence of constitutional change.
- To consider demands for change because of perceived weaknesses in the system.

Introduction

Britain does not have a system like the USA where the Supreme Court acts as ultimate interpreter of the constitution and pronounces upon the constitutionality of federal and state laws together with the actions of public officials. Since 1688, British courts have been bound by the doctrine of parliamentary sovereignty. They have been viewed as subordinate to the Queen-in-Parliament and detached from the political process. However, the received wisdom has not always matched the reality and recent years have witnessed a growth in judicial activism. British membership of the European Union, the incorporation of the European Convention on Human Rights into British law, and devolution have added a significant judicial dimension to the constitution. The courts are now important political actors. Recent years have also seen criticism of the criminal justice system. This chapter explores the nature of the British judicial system and growing concern about its powers and competence.

The literature on the judicial process in Britain is extensive. Significantly, most of it is written by legal scholars: few works on the courts or judges come from the pens of political scientists. To those concerned with the study of British politics, and in particular the process of policy making, the judicial process has generally been deemed to be of peripheral interest.

That this perception should exist is not surprising. It derives from two features that are considered to be essential characteristics of the judiciary in Britain. Firstly, in the trinity of the executive, legislature and judiciary, it is a subordinate institution. Public policy is made and ratified elsewhere. The courts exist to interpret (within defined limits) and apply that policy once enacted by the legislature; they have no intrinsic power to strike it down. Secondly, it is autonomous. The independence of the judiciary is a much vaunted and essential feature of the rule of law, described by the great nineteenth-century constitutional lawyer A.V. Dicey as one of the twin pillars of the British constitution. The other pillar – parliamentary sovereignty – accounts for the first characteristic, the subordination of the judiciary to Parliament. Allied with autonomy has been the notion of political neutrality. Judges seek to interpret the law according to judicial norms that operate independently of partisan or personal preferences.

Given these characteristics – politically neutral courts separate from, and subordinate to, the central agency of law enactment – a clear demarcation has arisen in recent decades, the study of the policy-making process being the preserve of political scientists, that of the judiciary the preserve of legal scholars. Some scholars – such as J.A.G. Griffith, formerly Professor of Law at the University of London – have sought to bridge the gap, but they have been notable for their rarity. Yet in practice the judiciary in Britain has not been as subordinate or as autonomous as the prevailing wisdom assumes. The dividing line between politics and the law is blurred rather than rigid.

A subordinate branch?

Under the doctrine of parliamentary sovereignty, the judiciary lacks the intrinsic power to strike down an Act of Parliament as being contrary to the provisions of the constitution or any other superior body of law. It was not always thus. Prior to the Glorious Revolution of 1688, the supremacy of **statute law** was not clearly established. In *Dr Bonham's Case* in 1610, Chief Justice Coke asserted that 'when an Act of Parliament is against common right and reason, or repugnant, or impossible to be performed, the common law will control it, and adjudge such act to be void'. A few years later, in *Judge* v. *Savadge* (1625), Chief Justice Hobart declared that an Act 'made against natural equity, as to make a man judge in his own case', would be void. Statute law had to compete not only with principles of common law developed by the courts but also with the prerogative power of the King. The courts variously upheld the power of the King to dispense with statutes and to impose taxes without the consent of Parliament.

The Glorious Revolution put an end to this state of affairs. Thereafter, the supremacy of statute law, under the doctrine of parliamentary sovereignty, was established. The doctrine is a judicially self-imposed one. The common lawyers allied themselves with Parliament in its struggle to control the **prerogative** powers of the King and the prerogative courts through which he sometimes exercised them. The supremacy of Parliament was asserted by the Bill of Rights of 1689. 'For the common lawyers, there was a price to pay, and that was the abandonment of the claim that they had sometimes advanced, that Parliament could not legislate in derogation of the principles of the common law' (Munro, 1987, p. 81). Parliamentary sovereignty – a purely legal doctrine asserting the supremacy of statute law – became the central tenet of the constitution (see Chapter 15). However, the subordination of the common law to law passed by Parliament did not – and does not – entail the subordination of the judiciary to the executive. Courts retain the power of interpreting the precise meaning of the law once passed by Parliament and of reviewing the actions of ministers and other public agents to determine whether those actions are *ultra vires*, that is, beyond the powers granted by statute. The courts can quash the actions of ministers which purport to be, but which on the court's interpretation are not, sanctioned by such Acts.

If a government has a particular action struck down as *ultra vires* it may seek parliamentary approval for a bill which gives statutory force to the action taken; in other words, to give legal force to that which the courts have declared as having – on the basis of existing statutes – no such force. But seeking passage of such a bill is not only time consuming, it can also prove to be politically contentious and publicly damaging. It conveys the impression that the government, having lost a case, is trying to change the rules of the game. Though it is a path that governments have variously taken, it is one they prefer to – and often do – avoid.

The power of judicial review thus provides the judiciary with a potentially significant role in the policy cycle. It is a potential that for much of the past century has not been realised. However, recent decades have seen an upsurge in judicial activism, judges being far more willing both to review and to quash ministerial actions. The scope for judicial activism has also been enlarged by three other developments: British membership of the European Union, the incorporation of the European Convention on Human Rights (ECHR) into British law and the devolution of powers to elected assemblies in different parts of the UK. Indeed, the first two of these developments have served to undermine the doctrine of parliamentary sovereignty, giving to the courts a new role in the political process. The courts, whether they wanted to or not, have found themselves playing a more central role in the determination of public policy.

An autonomous branch?

The judiciary is deemed to be independent of the other two branches of government. Its independence is, in the words of one leading textbook, 'secured by law, by professional and public opinion' (Wade and Bradley, 1993, p. 60). Since the Act of Settlement, senior judges have held office 'during good behaviour' and can be removed only by the Queen following an address by both Houses of Parliament. (Only one judge has been removed by such a process: Jonah Barrington, an Irish judge, was removed in 1830 after it was found he had misappropriated litigants' money and had ceased to perform his judicial duties.) Judges of inferior courts enjoy a lesser degree of statutory protection. Judges' salaries are a charge upon the consolidated fund: that means that they do not have to be voted upon each year by Parliament. By its own resolution, the House of Commons generally bars any reference made by Members to matters awaiting or under adjudication in criminal and most civil cases. By convention, a similar prohibition is observed by ministers and civil servants.

For their part, judges by convention refrain from politically partisan activity. Indeed, they have generally refrained from commenting on matters of public policy, doing so not only of their own volition but also for many years by the direction of the Lord Chancellor. The Kilmuir Guidelines issued in 1955 enjoined judges to silence since 'every utterance which he [a judge] makes in public, except in the course of the actual performance of his judicial duties, must necessarily bring him within the focus of criticism'. These guidelines were relaxed in the late 1970s but then effectively reimposed by the Lord Chancellor, Lord Hailsham, in 1980. For judges to interfere in a contentious issue of public policy, one that is not under adjudication, would – it was felt – undermine public confidence in the impartiality of the judiciary. Similarly, for politicians to interfere in a matter before the courts would be seen as a challenge to the rule of law. Hence, the perceived self-interests of both in confining themselves to their own spheres of activity.

However, the dividing line between judges and politicians – and, to a lesser extent, between judicial and political decision making – is not quite as sharp as these various features would suggest. In terms of personnel, memberships of the executive, legislature and judiciary are not mutually exclusive. There is, particularly in the higher reaches, some overlap. The most obvious and outstanding example is to be found in the figure of the Lord Chancellor. He has a judicial role: he is the head of the judiciary and exercises major judicial functions; most judges are either appointed by him or on his advice. He may, if he chooses, take part in judicial proceedings. He has a parliamentary role: he is the presiding officer of the House of Lords, albeit a position entailing no significant powers. He has an executive role: he is a member of the Cabinet. A number of Lord Chancellors have been prominent party politicians, most recently and most notably Lord Hailsham, Lord Chancellor for eleven years (1970–4 and 1979–87) and a former contender for the leadership of the Conservative Party. Other executive office holders with judicial appointments are the law officers: the Attorney General, the Solicitor General, the Lord Advocate for Scotland and the Solicitor General for Scotland. The Attorney General and Solicitor General lead for the crown in major court cases as well as serving as legal advisers to the government. In Scotland, the Lord Advocate and Solicitor General for Scotland perform somewhat broader functions, including the control of public prosecutions.

The highest court of appeal within the United Kingdom is the House of Lords. For judicial purposes, this constitutes an appellate committee of the House, although all members of the committee are peers. Some Members of Parliament serve or have served as recorders (part-time but salaried judges in the Crown Court) and several sit as local magistrates. Judges in the High Court, Court of Appeal and Court of Session are barred by statute from membership of the Commons and any MP appointed to a judgeship becomes ineligible to remain in the House. No such prohibition exists in the case of the House of Lords.

Though those holding political office seek as far as possible to draw a clear dividing line between political and judicial activity, that line cannot always be maintained. At times, they have to take judicial or quasi-judicial decisions. As members of an executive accountable to Parliament, they have regard to public opinion to an extent that judges do not. For instance, a number of judicial decisions or the comments of judges result each year in public controversy. The Lord Chancellor has the power to call for transcripts of proceedings and to issue reprimands. Such power is occasionally employed. In 1988, for example, Lord Chancellor Mackay reprimanded a judge who had given a light sentence to a man convicted of sexually assaulting his twelve-year-old stepdaughter, the judge asserting that the man's actions were the likely consequence of his pregnant wife not being able to fulfil his sexual needs.

The Home Secretary, a senior member of the Cabinet, also exercises certain quasi-judicial powers. Until recently he had the power to refer convictions back to the Court of Appeal when new evidence was laid before him. Between 1990 and 1997, several cases were so referred – including those of the 'Birmingham Six', the 'Guildford Four', and the 'Bridgewater Four', to which we shall return. (In 1997, the power to refer cases was assumed by a new, independent body.) He also exercises a number of powers over the terms to be served by prisoners. Groups and individuals (especially members of the victims' families) have lobbied successive home secretaries not to allow the release on parole of 'Moors murderer' Myra Hindley, sentenced in the 1960s for her part in the murder of several schoolchildren.

Nor are the Lord Chancellor and Home Secretary alone in having power to intervene in the judicial process. Certain powers also reside with the Attorney General and his Scottish equivalent. The Attorney General may intervene to prevent prosecutions being proceeded with if he considers such action to be in the public interest. Under powers introduced in 1989, he may refer to the Appeal Court sentences which appear to the prosecuting authorities to be unduly lenient. He also has responsibility in certain cases for initiating proceedings, for example under the Official Secrets Act, and – though he takes decisions in such matters independently of his government colleagues – he remains answerable to Parliament for his decisions.

By the very nature of the powers vested in them, a number of political office holders thus have to take decisions affecting the judicial process. They are decisions which cannot be avoided and which sometimes entail public controversy. Some home secretaries have attracted criticism for being slow to act (for example, in referring cases to the Appeal Court) and others for exercising their powers, especially over parole, with excessive zeal and an eye to the opinion polls.

Judges themselves do not completely stand apart from public controversy. Because they are detached from political life and can consider issues impartially, they are variously invited to chair public inquiries into the causes of particular disasters or scandals and to make recommendations on future action. This practice has been employed for many years. Recent examples have included the inquiries into the collapse of the BCCI bank (Sir Thomas Bingham, 1991), into standards in public life (Lord Nolan, 1995), into the sale of arms-making equipment to Iraq (Sir Richard Scott, 1996) and into the police handling of the murder of black teenager Stephen Lawrence (Sir William Macpherson of Cluny, 1999). The inquiries or the reports that they issue are often known by the name of the judge who led the inquiry (the Nolan Committee, the Scott Report). The reports are sometimes highly controversial and may lead to criticism of the judge involved. One irate Conservative MP berated Lord Nolan outside the Palace of Westminster in 1995 and his report was the subject of heated debate in the House of Commons. Sir Richard Scott was heavily criticised by many Conservative MPs and by a former Foreign Secretary, Lord Howe of Aberavon, for the way he conducted his inquiry.

Judges themselves have also been more willing in recent years to enter public debate of their own volition. The past decade or so have seen a tendency on the part of several judges to justify their actions publicly and in 1988 Lord Chancellor Mackay allowed some relaxation of the Kilmuir rules in order that judges may give interviews. One judge in particular – Judge Pickles – made use of the opportunity to appear frequently on television. A greater willingness to comment on issues of public policy has also been apparent on the part of the most senior judges. The appointment of Lord Justice Bingham as Master of the Rolls (see Box 23.1) and Lord Justice Taylor as Lord Chief Justice in 1992 heralded a new era of openness. Both proved willing to express views on public policy, both advocating the incorporation of the European Convention on Human Rights into British law. Taylor not only gave press interviews but also used the floor of the House of Lords to criticise government policy. In 1995 he addressed the Leeds Race Issues Advisory Committee on 'Race and Criminal Justice'. He retired in 1996 on health grounds to be succeeded by Bingham. Bingham's successor as Master of the Rolls, Lord Justice Woolf, maintained the practice of giving interviews. One of his first acts was to appear on a Sunday lunchtime current affairs programme.

Thus, though the two generalisations that the judiciary constitutes a subordinate and autonomous branch of government – subordinate to the outputs of Parliament (Acts of Parliament) but autonomous in deciding cases – remain broadly correct, both are in need of some qualification. The courts are neither as powerless nor as totally independent as the assertion would imply. For the student of politics, the judiciary is therefore an appropriate subject for study. What, then, is the structure of the judicial system in Britain? Who are the people who occupy it? To what extent has the judiciary become more active in recent years in reviewing the actions of government? What has been the effect of membership of the EC/EU, the incorporation of the ECHR into British law, and of devolution? And what pressure is there for change?

The courts

Apart from a number of specialised courts and tribunals, the organisational division of courts is that between **criminal law** and **civil law**. The basic structure of the court system in England and Wales is shown in Figure 23.1. (Scotland and Northern Ireland have different systems.) Minor criminal cases are tried in the magistrates' courts, minor civil cases in county courts. Figure 23.1 also shows the higher courts which try serious cases and the routes through which appeals may be heard. The higher courts – the Crown Court, the High Court and the Court of Appeal – are known collectively as the Supreme Court. At the head of the system stands the House of Lords.

Criminal cases

About 98 per cent of criminal cases in England and Wales are tried in magistrates' courts. This constitutes each year between one and two million cases. (The number was higher before 1987, but dropped after then following the introduction of fixed penalty fines for summary motoring offences.) The courts have power to levy fines, the amount depending on the offence, and to impose

BOX 23.1 Lord Bingham — BIOGRAPHY

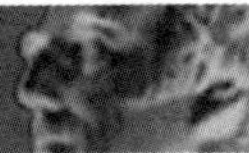

THE LORD CHIEF JUSTICE (1933–) (picture: © Popperfoto)

Thomas Bingham was born in Surrey, the son of two doctors. He was head boy of Sedbergh School before going on to read history at Balliol College, Oxford, where he graduated with a first. He studied law and came top in his Bar finals in 1959. He joined the liberal legal chambers of Lord Scarman. In 1972, at the age of thirty-eight, he became a Queen's Counsel and three years later was appointed a Crown Court Recorder.

Bingham achieved public prominence in 1977 when he was appointed by Foreign Secretary David Owen to investigate alleged breaches of sanctions against Rhodesia by UK companies. Three years later he became a High Court judge and was knighted. He was appointed to the Court of Appeal in 1986.

In 1991 he conducted another inquiry, this time into the collapse of the Bank of Credit and Commerce International (BCCI). He attracted criticism for taking evidence in private, while Lord Woolf's investigation the previous year into the Strangeways Prison disturbances had been held in public. The criticism did not dent his reputation or his advancement. The following year he was appointed Master of the Rolls. He achieved a reputation as a reformer. In a debate at the 1992 Bar Conference, he joined with law professor Michael Zander in arguing the case for the incorporation of the European Convention on Human Rights into British law.

On 4 June 1996 he became Lord Chief Justice at the age of sixty-two. His appointment was considered unconventional in that his career was not forged in the criminal courts. *The Times* described him as 'a radical moderniser'. He is keen to cut the costs and delays of the legal system and to make courts more accessible. He has variously taken part in debates in the House of Lords to raise issues of concern to the judiciary. He took part in the proceedings on the Access to Justice Bill in 1998 and 1999, speaking during the second reading debate, raising 'three matters central to the Bill on which acute concern is felt by my judicial colleagues'.

Lord Bingham is married with three children; his wife has been politically active, campaigning for the Liberal Democrats. He likes modern art and brisk walks.

prison sentences not exceeding six months. The largest single numbers of cases tried by magistrates' courts are motoring offences. Other offences tried by the courts range from allowing animals to stray on a highway and tattooing a minor to burglary, assault, causing cruelty to children and wounding. It takes on average between 100 and 130 days from the offence taking place for it to be tried. Once before a court, a majority of minor offences are each disposed of in a matter of minutes; in some cases, in which the defendant has pleaded guilty, in a matter of seconds. The courts also have a limited civil jurisdiction, primarily in matrimonial proceedings, and have a number of administrative functions in the licensing of public houses, betting shops and clubs.

Magistrates themselves are of two types: professional and lay. Professional magistrates

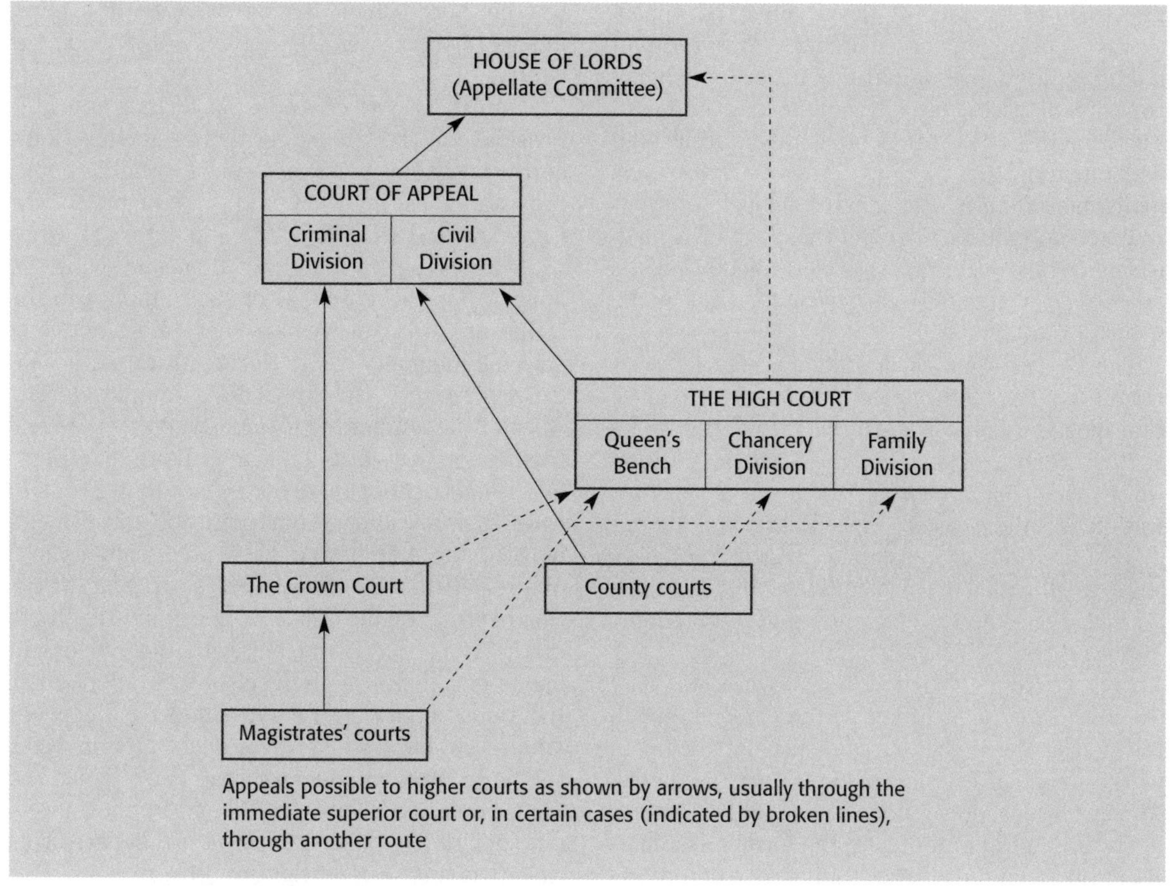

Figure 23.1 The court system in England and Wales

are now known, under the provisions of the 1999 Access to Justice Act, as district judges (magistrates' courts); they were previously known as stipendiary magistrates. They are legally qualified and serve on a full-time basis. They sit alone when hearing cases. Lay magistrates are part time and, as the name implies, are not legally qualified, though they do receive some training. Lay magistrates are drawn from the ranks of the public, typically those with the time to devote to such public duty (for example, housewives, local professional and retired people), and they sit as a bench of between two and seven in order to hear cases, advised by a legally qualified clerk. Cities and larger towns tend to have district judges; the rest of England and Wales rely on lay magistrates.

Until 1986, the decision whether to prosecute – and the prosecution itself – was undertaken by the police. Since 1986, the Crown Prosecution Service (CPS), headed by the Director of Public Prosecutions, has been responsible for the independent review and prosecution of all criminal cases instituted by police forces in England and Wales, with certain specified exceptions. In Scotland, responsibility for prosecution rests with the Crown Office and Procurator Fiscal Service. Members of this service – like the CPS in England and Wales – are lawyers.

Appeals from decisions of magistrates' courts may be taken to the Crown Court or, in matrimonial cases, to the Family Division of the High Court, or – on points of law – to the Queen's Bench Division of the High Court. In practice, appeals are rare:

less than 1 per cent of those convicted appeal against conviction or sentence. The cost of pursuing an appeal would, in the overwhelming majority of cases, far exceed the fine imposed. The time of the Crown Court is taken up instead with hearing the serious cases – known as indictable offences – which are subject to a jury trial and to penalties beyond those which a magistrates' court may impose. Over 100,000 people are usually committed each year for trial in the Crown Court.

The Crown Court is divided up into six court circuits and a total of nearly a hundred courts. The most serious cases will be presided over by a High Court judge, the most senior position within the court; a circuit judge or a recorder will hear other cases. High Court and circuit judges are full-time, salaried judges; recorders are legally qualified but part time, pursuing their normal legal practice when not engaged on court duties.

Appeals from conviction in a Crown Court may be taken on a point of law to the Queen's Bench Division of the High Court but usually are taken to the Criminal Division of the Court of Appeal. Appeals against conviction are possible on a point of law and on a point of fact, the former as a matter of right and the latter with the leave of the trial judge or the Court of Appeal. Less than 10 per cent of those convicted in a Crown Court usually appeal. The Appeal Court may quash a conviction, uphold it or vary the sentence imposed by the lower courts. Appeals against sentence – as opposed to the conviction itself – are also possible with the leave of the Appeal Court and, as we have already seen, the Attorney General now has the power to refer to the Court sentences which appear to be unduly lenient. In cases referred by the Attorney General, the court has the power to increase the length of the sentence imposed by the lower court.

The Court of Appeal consists of judges known as Lords Justices of Appeal and five judges who are members *ex officio* (the Lord Chancellor, the Lord Chief Justice, the Master of the Rolls, the President of the Family Division of the High Court and the Vice-Chancellor of the Chancery Division), though the composition varies from the criminal to the civil division. Appeals in criminal cases are usually heard by three judges. Though presided over by the Lord Chief Justice or a Lord Justice, judges of the Queen's Bench may also sit on the court.

From the Court of Appeal, a further appeal is possible to the House of Lords if the Court certifies that a point of law of general public importance is involved and it appears to the Court, or to the Lords, that the point ought to be considered by the highest domestic court of appeal. For the purposes of such an appeal, the House of Lords – as we have seen – does not comprise all members of the House but rather a judicial committee (the Appellate Committee). The work of the committee is undertaken by the Lord Chancellor, law lords known as Lords of Appeal in Ordinary (appointed to the Lords in order to carry out this judicial function) and those members of the Lords who have held high judicial office. Between five and ten will sit to hear a case, the hearing taking place in a committee room of the House of Lords but with the judgement itself being delivered in the chamber. Before 1966, the House considered itself bound by precedent (that is, by its own previous decisions); in 1966, the law lords announced that they would no longer consider themselves bound by their previous decisions, being prepared to depart from them when it seemed right to do so.

One other judicial body should also be mentioned. It does not figure in the normal court structure. That is the Judicial Committee of the Privy Council, a product essentially of the country's colonial history. The Committee was set up in 1833 to exercise the power of the Privy Council in deciding appeals from colonial, ecclesiastical and admiralty courts. Its composition is more or less the same as the Appellate Committee of the House of Lords. Three to five Lords of Appeal in Ordinary sit and the Committee also includes the Lord Chancellor and those who have held high judicial office. Most of its functions have disappeared over time, but it has retained a limited role in considering particular appeals from a number of Commonwealth countries. It also considers appeals from various professional bodies. However, as we shall see, it has assumed a new significance as a consequence of devolution. Challenges to the powers exercised by the Scottish parliament and Welsh assembly can be heard by the Judicial Committee.

Civil cases

In civil proceedings, some minor cases (for example, involving the summary recovery of some debts) are dealt with in magistrates' courts. Most cases involving small sums of money, however, are heard by county courts; more important cases are heard in the High Court.

County courts are presided over by circuit judges. The High Court is divided into three divisions, dealing with **common law** (the Queen's Bench Division), equity (Chancery Division) and domestic cases (Family Division). The Court comprises the three judges who head each division and just over eighty judges known as puisne (pronounced 'puny') judges. In most cases judges sit alone, though a Divisional Court of two or three may be formed, especially in the Queen's Bench Division, to hear applications for writs of *habeas corpus* and writs requiring a public body to fulfil a particular duty (*mandamus*), to desist from carrying out an action for which it has no legal authority (prohibition) and to quash a decision already taken (*certiorari*). Jury trials are possible in certain cases tried in the Queen's Bench Division (for example, involving malicious prosecution or defamation of character) but are now rare.

Appeals from magistrates' courts and from county courts are heard by Divisional Courts of the High Court: appeals from magistrates' courts on points of law, for example, go to a Divisional Court of the Queen's Bench Division. From the High Court – and certain cases in county courts – appeals are taken to the Civil Division of the Court of Appeal. In the Appeal Court, cases are normally heard by the Master of the Rolls sitting with two Lords Justices of Appeal.

From the Court of Appeal, an appeal may be taken – with the leave of the Court or the House – to the House of Lords. In rare cases, on a point of law of exceptional difficulty calling for a reconsideration of a binding precedent, an appeal may go directly, with the leave of the House, from the High Court to the House of Lords.

Cases brought against ministers or other public bodies for taking actions which are beyond their powers (*ultra vires*) will normally be heard in the Queen's Bench Division of the High Court before being taken – in the event of an appeal – to the Court of Appeal and the House of Lords. Thus, in 1993, when Lord Rees-Mogg brought an action challenging the powers of the government to ratify the Maastricht Treaty (see Box 23.2), the case was heard in the Queen's Bench Division before three Lords Justices.

BOX 23.2 EXAMPLE

Challenging the Maastricht Treaty

In the United Kingdom, ratification of a treaty is a prerogative power. An Act of Parliament is only necessary where provisions of the treaty are intended to have the force of law in the UK. Thus, the 1972 European Communities Act was not a measure to ratify the treaty of accession to the Community but an Act to give effect to what was described as 'the legal nuts and bolts' necessary for membership.

However, Parliament made a change in 1978 when it passed the European Assembly Elections Act. Section 6 of the Act stipulated that 'No treaty which provides for an increase in the powers of the European Parliament shall be ratified by the United Kingdom unless it has been approved by an Act of Parliament.' In December 1991, heads of government of the member states of the EC negotiated the Maastricht Treaty, designed to achieve economic and monetary union. Part of the Treaty increased the powers of the European Parliament. As a result, ratification in the UK required an Act of Parliament. The European Communities (Amendment) Bill was introduced in 1992 and, after a difficult parliamentary passage, received Royal Assent in July 1993.

Shortly before the bill received Royal Assent, an opponent of the Maastricht Treaty, Lord Rees-Mogg (a former editor of *The Times*) launched

BOX 23.2 continued

a legal challenge to ratification of the treaty. He claimed that the government would be in breach of the 1978 Act if it ratified the treaty because Parliament had approved the Maastricht Treaty but not the protocols attached to it, and the social protocol would increase the power of the European Parliament. He also claimed that the government had no lawful prerogative to ratify the social protocol because it would alter the Treaty of Rome, which, as a fundamental part of domestic law, required parliamentary approval. And he further claimed that the crown had no lawful prerogative to transfer elements of Britain's foreign and security policy to the European Community as the fundamental prerogatives of the crown could not be transferred to some other person.

Lord Rees-Mogg claimed that it was the 'most important constitutional issue to be faced by the courts for 300 years'. He was granted leave to seek a review by the High Court. The action of the courts in giving him leave was then challenged in the House of Commons. Labour MP Tony Benn claimed that it was a breach of privilege as the bill had not yet been passed by Parliament and Lord Rees-Mogg had already been given leave to challenge it. The Speaker Betty Boothroyd ruled that it was not a breach but, unusually, read a statement giving her reasons for so ruling. The sole basis for her decision, she emphasised, was because the bill had already gone to the House of Lords when Lord Rees-Mogg made his legal challenge. However, she reminded the courts of the Bill of Rights of 1689, stating that the proceedings of Parliament could not be challenged by the courts.

The case of *Regina* v. *Secretary of State for Foreign and Commonwealth Affairs. Ex parte Rees-Mogg* was heard in the High Court by a Divisional Court of the Queen's Bench Division comprising Lord Justice Lloyd, Lord Justice Mann and Mr Justice Auld. On 30 July 1993, Lord Justice Lloyd delivered the twenty-two-page judgement of the court. The court, he said, had heard nothing to support or even suggest that by bringing the proceedings the applicant had trespassed on the privileges of Parliament, and while it was an important case it was an exaggeration to describe it as the most important constitutional case for 300 years. On the three arguments advanced by counsel for Lord Rees-Mogg, the court rejected each one. The fact that the protocols were annexed to the Treaty did not show that they were not also part of the Treaty. The construction of section 2 of the 1993 Act allowed incorporation of the protocols. On the second point, the social protocol was not intended to apply in UK law. The argument that it might have some indirect effect in UK law was too slender a basis on which to hold that Parliament had impliedly excluded or curtailed the crown's prerogative to alter or add to the Treaty of Rome. On the third point, the part of the treaty that established a common foreign and security policy among member states was an intergovernmental agreement which could have no impact on UK domestic law. Title V of the 1993 Act could not be read as a transfer of prerogative powers. It was an exercise of those powers. In the last resort, it would presumably be open to the government to denounce the treaty or fail to comply with its international obligations under Title V. In so far as the point was justiciable, their Lordships ruled that it failed on the merits.

After the judgement was delivered, Lord Rees-Mogg – who was not in court to hear it – said he would give careful thought as to whether to appeal. (A provisional date had been set for such an appeal.) However, given that the judgement of the court had been unanimous and had comprehensively rejected the points advanced by counsel for him, the chances of Lord Rees-Mogg achieving a reversal on appeal appeared slim and he soon announced that he would not be pursuing the case. Consequently, the government – which had said it would not ratify the Maastricht Treaty until the legal challenge was out of the way – moved promptly and ratified it.

Tribunals

Many if not most citizens are probably affected by decisions taken by public bodies, for example those determining eligibility for particular benefits (such as social security) or compensation for compulsory purchase. The post-war years have seen the growth of administrative law, providing the legal framework within which such decisions are taken and the procedure by which disputes may be resolved.

To avoid disputes over particular administrative decisions being taken to the existing, highly formalised civil courts – overburdening the courts and creating significant financial burdens for those involved – the law provides for a large number of tribunals to resolve such disputes. There are now tribunals covering a wide range of issues, including unfair dismissal, rents, social security benefits, immigration, mental health and compensation for compulsory purchase. Those appearing before tribunals will often have the opportunity to present their own case and to call witnesses and cross-examine the other side. The tribunal itself will normally – though not always – comprise three members, though the composition varies from tribunal to tribunal: some have lay members, others have legally (or otherwise professionally qualified) members; some have part-time members, others have full-time members. Industrial tribunals, for example, each comprise an independent chairman and two members drawn from either side of industry.

Tribunals offer the twin advantages of speed and cheapness. As far as possible the formalities of normal courts are avoided. Costs tend to be significant only in the case of an appeal.

The activities of tribunals are normally dull and little noticed. On rare occasions, though, decisions may have political significance. In January 1996, an employment tribunal in Leeds held that the policy of the Labour Party to have women-only short-lists for some parliamentary seats breached sex discrimination legislation. Rather than pursue an appeal, which could take up to twenty months to be heard, the Party decided not to proceed with such short-lists.

The judges

At the apex of the judicial system stands the Lord Chancellor and the law officers. As we have seen, these are political appointments and the holders are members of the government. Below them are the professional judges. The most senior are the law lords, the Lords of Appeal in Ordinary, at present twelve in number. They are appointed by the crown on the advice of the Prime Minister and they must have held high judicial office for at least two years. By virtue of their position they are members of the House of Lords and remain members even after ceasing to hold their judicial position. Indeed, they constitute the earliest form of life peers, the first Lord of Appeal in Ordinary being created under the provisions of the Appellate Jurisdiction Act of 1876.

The other most senior judicial appointments – the Lord Chief Justice (at the head of Criminal Law), Master of the Rolls (at the head of Civil Law), President of the Family Division and the Lords Justices of Appeal – are also appointed by the crown on the advice of the Prime Minister. In practice, the Prime Minister's scope is restricted. The Lords Justices are drawn either from High Court judges or from barristers of at least fifteen years' standing. Other judges – High Court judges, circuit judges and recorders – are drawn from barristers of at least ten years' standing, though a solicitor of ten years' standing is eligible for consideration for appointment as a recorder and a recorder of five years' standing may be appointed a circuit judge. Magistrates are appointed by the Lord Chancellor.

The attraction in becoming a judge lies only partially in the salary (see Table 23.1) – the top earners among barristers can achieve annual incomes of several hundred thousand pounds. Rather, the attraction lies in the status that attaches to holding a position at the top of one's profession. For

Table 23.1 Judicial salaries 1999

Position	Annual salary (£)
Lord Chief Justice	148,502
Law Lords	132,017
Lords Justices of Appeal	132,017
High Court Judges	117,752
Senior Circuit Court judges	96,214
Circuit Courts judges	88,077
District judges	70,820

Table 23.2 Gender of senior judges 1999

Position	Male	Female	Total
Lords of Appeal in Ordinary	12	0	12
Lords Justices of Appeal	37	1	38
High Court:			
Chancery Division	18	1	19
Queen's Bench Division	64	3	67
Family Division	14	3	17
Total	145	8	153

many barristers, the ultimate goal is to become Lord Chief Justice, Master of the Rolls or a law lord.

Judges, by the nature of their calling, are expected to be somewhat detached from the rest of society. However, critics – such as J.A.G. Griffith, in *The Politics of the Judiciary* (5th edn, 1997) – contend that this professional distance is exacerbated by social exclusivity, judges being predominantly elderly upper-class males.

Though statutory retirement ages have been introduced, they are generous in relation to the normal retirement age: High Court judges retire at age seventy-five, circuit judges at seventy-two. All judges bar one are white and less than 5 per cent are female, the proportion declining markedly in the higher echelons (see Table 23.2). All the senior office-holders in the judiciary, and all the law lords, are male. At the beginning of 1999, there was only one female among the thirty-eight Lords Justices of Appeal. And as Table 23.2 reveals, of 103 judges of the High Court, only seven were women. Though the number of judges has been increased slightly in recent years, the number of women judges has not. The number of women judges was the same at the beginning of 1999 as it was at the beginning of 1996.

In their educational backgrounds, judges are also remarkably similar. The majority went to public school (among law lords and Lords Justices, the proportion exceeds 80 per cent) and the vast majority graduated from Oxford and Cambridge Universities; more than 80 per cent of circuit judges did so, and the proportion increases the further one goes up the judicial hierarchy.

Senior judgeships are the almost exclusive preserve of barristers. It is possible – just – for solicitors to become judges. Few, however, have taken this route: in 1999, two out of ninety-eight High Court judges were drawn from the ranks of solicitors. The proportion of solicitors is greater among the ranks of Circuit Judges: just over 13 per cent are solicitors.

Judges thus form a socially and professionally exclusive or near-exclusive body. This exclusivity has been attacked for having unfortunate consequences. One is that judges are out of touch with society itself, not being able to understand the habits and terminology of everyday life, reflecting instead the social mores of thirty or forty years ago. The male-oriented nature of the judiciary has led to claims that judges are insufficiently sensitive in cases involving women, especially rape cases. The background of the judges has also led to allegations of in-built bias – towards the government of the day and towards the Conservative Party. Senior judges, according to Griffith (1997), construe the public interest as favouring law and order and upholding the interests of the state.

Though Griffith's claim about political bias has not been pursued by many other writers, the effect of gender and social exclusivity has been a cause of concern among jurists as well as ministers. The narrow professional and social background from which judges have been drawn constitutes, as we shall see, but one cause of concern about the British judiciary in recent years.

Such concern exists at a time when the judiciary has become more active. There has been a greater willingness on the part of judges to review the actions of ministers. There has also been an increased activity arising from the UK's membership of the European Community/Union. The incorporation of the ECHR into British law and the creation of devolved assemblies have also widened the scope for judicial activity. In combination, these developments have raised the courts in Britain to a new level of political activity – and visibility.

Judicial activism

The common law power available to judges to strike down executive actions as being beyond powers granted – *ultra vires* – or as contrary to natural law was not much in evidence in the decades prior to the 1960s. Courts were generally deferential in their stance towards government. This was to change in the period from the mid-1960s onwards. Though the judiciary changed hardly at all in terms of the background of judges – they were usually the same elderly, white, Oxbridge-educated males as before – there was a significant change in attitudes. Apparently worried by the perceived encroachment of government on individual liberties, they proved increasingly willing to use their powers of judicial review.

In four cases in the 1960s, the courts adopted an activist line in reviewing the exercise of powers by administrative bodies and, in two instances, of ministers. In *Conway* v. *Rimmer* in 1968, the House of Lords ruled against a claim of the Home Secretary that the production of certain documents would be contrary to the public interest; previously such a claim would have been treated as definitive. Another case the same year involved the House of Lords considering why, and not just how, a ministerial decision was made. It was a demonstration, noted Lord Scarman (1974, p. 49), that judges were 'ready to take an activist line'.

This activist line has been maintained and, indeed, become more prominent. Successive governments have found ministerial actions overturned by the courts. There were four celebrated cases in the second half of the 1970s in which the courts found against Labour ministers (Norton, 1982, pp. 138–40), and then several in the 1980s and the 1990s when they found against Conservative ministers.

Perceptions of greater judicial activism derive not just from the cases that have attracted significant media attention. They derive also from the sheer number of applications for **judicial review** made to the courts. At the beginning of the 1980s, there were about 500 applications a year for leave to apply for judicial review. The figure grew throughout the decade, exceeding 1,000 in 1985, 1,500 in 1987 and 2,000 in 1990. In 1994, the number was a record 3,208. In 1996 it had climbed to 3,901 and in 1998 it reached an unprecedented figure of 4,539 applications. 'Judicial review was the boom stock of the 1980s', declared Lord Bingham in 1995. 'Unaffected by recession, the boom has roared on into the 1990s.'

Each year, a number of cases have attracted media attention and been politically significant. In 1993, as we have already noted, Lord Rees-Mogg challenged the power of the government to ratify the Maastricht Treaty. His case was rejected by a Divisional Court of the Queen's Bench Division. The same month – July 1993 – saw the House of Lords find a former Home Secretary, acting in his official ministerial capacity, in contempt of court for failing to comply with a court order in an asylum case. The ruling meant that ministers could not rely on the doctrine of crown immunity to ignore orders of a court. *The Times* reported (28 July 1993):

> Five law lords declared yesterday that ministers cannot put themselves above the law as they found the former home secretary Kenneth Baker guilty of contempt of court in an asylum case. The historic ruling on Crown immunity was described as one of the most important constitutional findings for two hundred years and hailed as establishing a key defence against the possible rise of a ruthless government in the future.

Ironically, the case was largely overshadowed by attention given the unsuccessful case pursued by Lord Rees-Mogg. Kenneth Baker's successor as Home Secretary, Michael Howard, also variously ran foul of the courts, the Appeal Court holding that he had acted beyond his powers. Indeed, tension between government and the courts increased notably in 1995 and 1996 as several cases went against the Home Secretary (Woodhouse, 1996). In 1995 a criminal injuries compensation scheme he had introduced was declared unlawful by the House of Lords. A delay in referring parole applications by a number of prisoners serving life sentences was held by the High Court to be unreasonable. In July 1996 the court found that he had acted unlawfully in taking into account a public petition and demands from members of the public in increasing the minimum sentence to be served by two minors who had murdered the two-year-old Jamie Bulger. Nor were cases confined to the period of Conservative Government. After the return of the Labour Government in 1997, Home Secretary Jack Straw variously fell foul of the courts. In July 1999, his attempts to maintain his power to ban journalists investigating miscarriages of justice from interviewing prisoners was declared unlawful by the House of Lords. The same month, the Court of Appeal found against him after he sought to return three asylum seekers to France or Germany. All these cases, along with several other high-profile judgements – including a number by European courts – combined to create a new visibility for the judiciary.

The courts, then, are willing to cast a critical eye over decisions of ministers in order to ensure that they comply with the powers granted by statute and are not contrary to natural justice. They are facilitated in this task by the rise in the number of applications made for judicial review and by their power of statutory interpretation. As Drewry (1986) has noted:

> Although judges must strictly apply Acts of Parliament, the latter are not always models of clarity and consistency . . . This leaves the judges with considerable scope for the exercise of their creative skills in interpreting what an Act really means. Some judges, of which Lord Denning was a particularly notable example, have been active and ingenious in inserting their own policy judgements into the loopholes left in legislation. (p. 30)

Judicial activism is thus well established. The courts have been willing to scrutinise government actions, and on occasion strike them down, on a scale not previously witnessed. Some commentators in the 1990s saw it as a consequence of a Conservative government being in government for more than a decade. However, as we have seen, the courts have maintained their activism under a Labour government. The consequences were anticipated by some Labour politicians. 'The judges' job is to judge, the government's job is to govern', declared Labour MP Paul Boateng, prior to Labour's return to power.

However, the extent and impact of such activism on the part of judges should not be exaggerated. There are three important caveats that have to be entered. Firstly, statutory interpretation allows judges some but not complete leeway. They follow well-established guidelines. Secondly, only a minority of applications for judicial review concern government departments: a larger number are for review of actions taken by local authorities. (Government departments are respondents in about 25 per cent of cases, and local authorities in 35 per cent.) Thirdly, most applications for judicial review fail. In an interview in July 1996, Lord Woolf claimed that for every case that the government lost, there were ten more that it won. 'It is becoming more difficult to achieve success in such cases', noted *The Times* (19 July 1993). 'High Court leave for a review is harder to obtain and legal aid is more scarce. Fewer than half of applicants obtain leave to proceed.' Of the 4,539 applications for leave to apply for judicial review in 1998, less than 23 per cent were allowed. Of substantive applications disposed of that year, fewer than half were allowed.

Even so, activism on the part of the courts constitutes a problem for government. Even though the percentage of applications where leave is given to proceed has declined, the absolute number has increased. And even though government may win most of the cases brought against it, it is the cases that it loses that attract the headlines.

Enforcing EU law

The United Kingdom signed the treaty of accession to the European Community in 1972. The European Communities Act passed the same year provided the legal provisions necessary for membership. The UK became a member of the EC on 1 January 1973. The European Communities Act, as we have seen in Chapter 15, created a new judicial dimension to the British constitution.

The 1972 Act gave legal force not only to existing EC law but also to future law. When regulations have been promulgated by the Commission and the Council of Ministers, they take effect within the United Kingdom. Parliamentary assent to the principle is not required. That assent has already been given in advance by virtue of the provisions of the 1972 Act. Parliament may be involved in giving approval to measures to implement directives, but there is no scope to reject the purpose of the directives. And, as we recorded in Chapter 15, under the provisions of the Act, questions of law are to be decided by the European Court of Justice (the ECJ), or in accordance with the decisions of that court. All courts in the United Kingdom are required to take judicial notice of decisions made by the Court of Justice. Cases in the UK which reach the House of Lords must be referred to the European Court for a definitive ruling and requests may be made by lower courts to the Court of Justice for a ruling on the meaning and interpretation of European treaties. In the event of a conflict between the provisions of European law and those of an Act of Parliament, the former are to prevail.

The question that has most exercised writers on constitutional law since Britain's accession to the EC has been what British courts should do in the event of the passage of an Act of Parliament that expressly overrides European law. The question remains a hypothetical one. Though some doubt exists – Lord Denning when Master of the Rolls appeared to imply on occasion that the courts must apply EC law, Acts of Parliament notwithstanding – the generally accepted view among jurists is that courts, by virtue of the doctrine of parliamentary sovereignty, must apply the provisions of the Act of Parliament that expressly overrides European law (see Bradley, 1994, p. 97).

Given the absence of an explicit overriding of European law by statute, the most important question to which the courts have had to address themselves has been how to resolve apparent inconsistencies or conflict between European and domestic (known as municipal) law. During debate on the European Communities Bill in 1972, ministers made clear that the Bill essentially provided a rule of construction: that is, that the courts were to construe the provisions of an Act of Parliament, in so far as it was possible to do so, in such a way as to render it consistent with European law. However, what if it is not possible to construe an Act of Parliament in such a way? Where the courts have found UK law to fall foul of European law, the UK government has introduced new legislation to bring domestic law into line with EC requirements. But what about the position prior to the passage of such legislation? Do the courts have power to strike down or suspend Acts of Parliament which appear to breach European law? The presumption until 1990 was that they did not. Two cases – the *Factortame* and *Ex Parte EOC* cases – have shown that presumption to be false. The former case involved a challenge, by the owners of some Spanish trawlers, to the provisions of the 1988 Merchant Shipping Act. The High Court granted interim relief, suspending the relevant parts of the Act. This was then overturned by the House of Lords, which ruled that the courts had no such power. The European Court of Justice, to which the case was then referred, ruled in June 1990 that courts did have the power of injunction and could suspend the application of Acts of Parliament that on their face appeared to breach European law until a final determination was made. The following month, the House of Lords granted orders to the Spanish fishermen preventing the Transport Secretary from withholding or withdrawing their names from the register of British fishing vessels, the orders to remain in place until the Court of Justice had decided the case. The case had knock-on consequences beyond EU law: having decided that an injunction could be granted against the Crown in the field of EU law, the courts subsequently decided it could then be applied in cases not involving EU law (Jacobs, 1999, p. 242). However, the most dramatic case in terms of EU law was to come in 1994. In *R* v. *Secretary of State for Employment, ex p. the Equal Opportunities Commission* – usually referred to as *Ex Parte EOC* – there was a challenge to provisions of the 1978 Employment Protection (Consolidation) Act. The House of Lords held that the provisions of the Act effectively excluded many part-time workers from the right to claim unfair dismissal or redundancy payments and as such unlawful, being incompatible with EU law (Maxwell, 1999). Though the *Factortame* case attracted considerable publicity, it was the *EOC* case that was the most fundamental in its implications. The courts were invalidating the provisions of an Act of Parliament. Following the case, *The Times* declared 'Britain may now have, for the first time in its history, a constitutional court' (5 March 1994, cited in Maxwell, 1999, p. 197).

The courts have thus assumed a new role in the interpretation of European law and the court system itself has acquired an additional dimension. The ECJ serves not only to hear cases that emanate from British courts but also to consider cases brought directly by or against the EC Commission and the governments of the member states. Indeed, the ECJ carries a significant workload, so much so that it has to be assisted by another court, the Court of First Instance, and both are under considerable pressure in trying to cope with the number of cases brought before them. Since the early 1990s, the ECJ has usually had to handle more than 400 cases a year, most of them references for a preliminary ruling. In 1999, both courts published a discussion paper, *The Future of the Judicial System of the European Union*, highlighting the pressures and the need for change in order to cope with them.

There is thus a significant judicial dimension to British membership of the European Union, involving adjudication by a supranational court, and the greater the integration of member states the greater the significance of the courts in applying European law. Furthermore, under the Maastricht Treaty, which took effect in November 1993, the powers of the Court of Justice were strengthened, the court being given the power to fine member states that did not fulfil their legal obligations. Though the cases heard by the European Court of Justice may not appear often of great significance, collectively they produce a substantial – indeed, massive – body of case law that constitutes an important constraint on the actions of the UK government. Each year, that body of case law grows greater.

Against this new judicial dimension has to be set the fact that the doctrine of parliamentary sovereignty remains formally extant. Parliament retains the power to repeal the 1972 Act. The decisions of the ECJ have force in the United Kingdom inasmuch as Parliament has decreed that they will. When Lord Rees-Mogg sought judicial review of the government's power to ratify the Maastricht Treaty, the Speaker of the House of Commons, Betty Boothroyd, issued a stern warning to the courts, reminding them that under the Bill of Rights of 1689 the proceedings of Parliament could not be challenged by the courts. (Lord Rees-Mogg, whose application was rejected, emphasised that no such challenge was intended.) And it was the British government that instigated the provision in the Maastricht Treaty for the Court of Justice to fine member states. The UK has one of the best records in the European Union for complying with European law. Even so, the impact of membership of the EC should not be treated lightly. It has introduced a major new judicial dimension to the British constitution. It has profound implications for the role of the courts in influencing public policy in the United Kingdom. That was emphasised by the ruling of the House of Lords in the *Ex Parte EOC* case. The courts now appear to have acquired, in part, a power that they lost in 1689.

Enforcing the ECHR

Reinforcing the importance of the courts has been the incorporation of the European Convention on Human Rights into British law. Though not formally vesting the courts with the same powers as vested by the 1972 European Communities Act, the incorporation nonetheless makes British judges powerful actors in determining public policy.

The European Convention on Human Rights was signed at Rome in 1950 and was ratified by the United Kingdom on 5 March 1951. It came into effect in 1953. It declares the rights that should be protected in each state – such as the right to life, freedom of thought and peaceful assembly – and stipulates procedures by which infringements of those rights can be determined. Alleged breaches of the Convention are investigated by the European Commission on Human Rights and may be referred to the European Court of Human Rights.

The convention is a treaty under international law. That means its authority derives from the consent of the states that have signed it. It was not incorporated into British law and not until 1966 were individual citizens allowed to petition the Commission. In subsequent decades, a large number of petitions were brought against the British government. Though the British government was not required under British law to comply with the decisions of the Court, it did so by virtue of its international obligations and introduced the necessary changes to bring UK law into line with the judgement of the Court. By 1995, over a hundred cases against the UK government had been judged admissible, and thirty-seven cases had been upheld (see Lester, 1994, pp. 42–6). Some of the decisions have been politically controversial, as in 1994 when the Court decided (on a 10–9 vote) that the killing of three IRA suspects in Gibraltar in 1988 by members of the British security forces was a violation of the right to life. More recently, the Court has had to consider a case brought by two young gays claiming that UK law which provided a different age of consent for homosexuals and heterosexuals is in breach of the convention.

The decisions of the Court led to calls from some Conservative MPs for the UK not to renew the right of individuals to petition the Commission. Liberal Democrats and many Labour MPs – as well as some Conservatives – wanted to move in the opposite direction and to incorporate the ECHR into British law. Those favouring incorporation argued that it would reduce the cost and delay involved in pursuing a petition to the Commission and allow citizens to enforce their rights through British courts. It was also argued that it would raise awareness of human rights. This reasoning led the Labour Party to include a commitment in its 1997 election manifesto to incorporate the ECHR into British law. Following the return of the Labour Government in that election, the Government published a White Paper, *Rights Brought Home*, and followed it with the introduction of the Human Rights Bill. The Bill was enacted in 1998.

The Human Rights Act makes it unlawful for public authorities to act in a way that is incompatible with Convention rights. It is thus possible for individuals to invoke their rights in any proceedings brought against them by a public authority or in any proceedings that they may bring against a public authority. 'Courts will, from time to time, be required to determine if primary or secondary legislation is incompatible with Convention rights. They will decide if the acts of public authorities are unlawful through contravention, perhaps even unconscious contravention, of those rights. They may have to award damages as a result' (Irvine of Lairg, 1998, p. 230). Though the courts are not empowered to set aside Acts of Parliament, they are required to interpret legislation as far as possible in accordance with the convention. The higher courts can issue certificates of incompatibility where UK law is deemed incompatible with the ECHR: it is then up to Parliament to take the necessary action. The Act makes provision for a 'fast track' procedure for amending law to bring it into line with the ECHR.

The incorporation of the ECHR into British law creates a new role for British judges in determining policy outcomes. In the words of one authority, 'it gives the courts an increased constitutional role, moving them from the margins of the political process to the centre and increasing the underlying tension between the executive and the judiciary' (Woodhouse, 1996, p. 440). Indeed, the scale of the change was such that senior judges had to be trained for the purpose and, in order to give the courts time to prepare, the principal provisions of the Act were not brought into force immediately. The Act received royal assent on 9 November 1998. In 1999, the Government announced that it intended to bring the main provisions into force on 2 October 2000. The full effects of the measure have yet to be seen. One effect, though, was immediate. The provision requiring ministers to certify that a bill complies with the provisions of the ECHR was brought in immediately following enactment, and so all bills now are accompanied by such a statement by the relevant minister.

The impact of devolution

The devolution of powers to elected assemblies in different parts of the United Kingdom (see Chapter 15) has also enlarged the scope for judicial activity. The legislation creating elected assemblies in Wales and Scotland stipulates the legal process by which the powers and the exercise of powers by the assemblies can be challenged. It provides a particular role for the Judicial Committee of the Privy Council.

Under the Government of Wales Act, there are complex provisions for determining whether a particular function is exercisable by the Welsh Assembly, whether the Assembly has exceeded its powers, whether it has failed to fulfil its statutory obligations or whether a failure to act puts the Assembly in breach of the ECHR. These are known as 'devolution issues'. A law officer can require a particular devolution issue to be referred to the Judicial Committee of the Privy Council. It is also open to other courts to refer a devolution issue to higher courts for determination. Devolution issues considered by the High Court or the Court of Appeal may be appealed to the Judicial Committee, but only with the leave of the Court or the Judicial Committee. If a devolution issue arises in judicial proceedings before the House of Lords, the law lords may refer it to the Judicial Committee unless they consider it more appropriate that they determine the issue. This point may appear a little academic as, in terms of personnel, by referring it to the Judicial Committee they are simply referring it to themselves. If a court finds that the Assembly has exceeded its powers in making subordinate legislation, it can make an order removing or limiting any retrospective effect of the decision, or suspend the effect of the decision for any period and on any conditions to allow the defect to be corrected.

The Scotland Act also provides for a similar process. The law officers may refer a devolution issue to the Judicial Committee of the Privy Council. Courts may refer devolution issues to higher courts for determination. Appeals from the High Court or Court of Appeal lie to the Judicial Committee. If a court finds an Act of the Parliament or subordinate legislation is *ultra vires*, it can make an order removing or limiting any retrospective effect of that decision for any period and on any conditions to allow the defects to be remedied. In Scotland, as in Wales, a law officer can make a pre-enactment reference to the Judicial Committee to determine whether a Bill or a provision of a Bill is within the competence of the Parliament. In other words, it is not necessary for the measure to be enacted: a law officer can seek a determination while the measure is in Bill form.

The provisions of both Acts create notable scope for judicial activity. As John McEldowney has noted in respect of Scotland, the Judicial Committee of the Privy Council 'may be regarded as a constitutional court for Scottish matters' (McEldowney, 1998, p. 198). There is scope for the courts to interpret the legislation in a constrictive or an expansive manner. The approach taken by the courts has major implications for both elected bodies. There is also scope for the courts to move away from the intentions of the Westminster Parliament. The longer an Act of constitutional significance survives, the intent of Parliament in passing it gradually loses its significance (Craig and Walters, 1999, p. 289). The policing of the powers of the two elected bodies by the courts has political as well as legal implications. The point has been well put by Craig and Walters. As they note, the Scotland Act, while giving the Scottish Parliament general legislative powers, also limits those powers through a broad list of reservations. 'At the minimum, this means that the Scottish Parliament will have to become accustomed to living with the "judge over its shoulder". Proposed legislation will have to be scrutinised assiduously lest it fall foul of one of the many heads of reserved subject matter . . . The need for constant recourse to lawyers who will, in many instances, indicate that proposed action cannot be taken, is bound to generate frustration and anger in Scotland' (Craig and Walters, 1999, p. 303). As they conclude, 'The courts are inevitably faced with a grave responsibility: the way in which they interpret the SA [Scotland Act] may be a significant factor in deciding whether devolution proves to be the reform which cements the union, or whether it is the first step towards its dissolution' (Craig and Walters, 1999, p. 303).

Demands for change

Recent years have seen various calls for change in the judicial process. A number of those calls have been to strengthen the powers of the courts and some of these calls have borne fruit, primarily with the incorporation of the ECHR into British law. Some want to go further. Some want to see a more inclusive document than the ECHR. The ECHR, for example, excludes such things as a right to food or a right of privacy (see Nolan and Sedley, 1997). The Liberal Democrats and a number of jurists want to see the enactment of a judicially enforceable Bill of Rights. In other words, they want a measure that enjoys some degree of protection from encroachment by Parliament. Formally, as we have seen, Parliament does not have to act on certificates of incompatibility issued by the courts. Under the proposal for an entrenched Bill of Rights, the courts would be able to set aside an Act of Parliament that was in conflict with the ECHR, rather in the same way that the courts have set aside the provisions of an Act deemed to be incompatible with EU law.

The powers acquired by the courts – and the calls for them to be given further powers – have not been universally welcomed (see Box 23.3). Critics view the new role of the courts as a threat to the traditional Westminster constitution (see Chapter 15), introducing into the political process a body of unaccountable and unelected judges who have excessive powers to interpret the provisions of a document drawn in general terms. Instead of public policy being determined by elected politicians – who can be turned out by electors at the next election – it can be decided by unrepresentative judges who are immune to action by electors.

The courts have thus proved controversial in terms of their constitutional role. They have also been the subjects of debate in terms of their traditional role in interpreting and enforcing the law. The debate has encompassed not only the judges but also the whole process of criminal and civil justice.

In 1999, the usually sure-footed law lords encountered criticism when they had to decide whether the former Chilean head of state, General Pinochet, who had been detained in the UK, should be extradited from Britain to Spain. The first judgement of the court had to be set aside when one of the law lords hearing the case was revealed to have been a director of a company controlled by a party (Amnesty International) to the case. It was the first time that the law lords had set aside one of their own decisions and ordered a rehearing. Especially embarrassing for the law lords, it was also the first case in which an English court had announced its decision live on television (see Rozenburg, 1999).

Lower courts, including the Court of Appeal, came in for particular criticism in the late 1980s and early 1990s as a result of several cases of miscarriages of justice (see Mullin, 1996; Walker and Starmer, 1999). In 1989, the 'Guildford Four', convicted in 1975 of bombings in Guildford, were released pending an inquiry into their original conviction; in 1990, the case of the Maguire family, convicted of running an IRA bomb factory, was referred back to the Appeal Court after the Home Secretary received evidence that the convictions could not be upheld; and in 1991, the 'Birmingham Six', convicted of pub bombings in Birmingham in 1974, were released after the Court of Appeal quashed their convictions. The longest running case was the Bridgewater case, in which several men had been convicted in 1979 of the murder of newspaper boy Carl Bridgewater. The Court of Appeal refused leave to appeal in 1981 and had turned down an appeal in 1987, before the case was again brought back in 1996. The men were released in 1997. Various other, lesser-known cases have also resulted in earlier convictions being overturned.

The judges involved in the original cases were variously criticised for being too dependent on the good faith of prosecution witnesses – as was the Court of Appeal. The Appeal Court came in for particular criticism for its apparent reluctance even to consider that there may have been miscarriages of justice. As late as 1988, the Court had refused an appeal by the 'Birmingham Six', doing so in terms that suggested that the Home Secretary should not even have referred the case to the Court. When lawyers for the 'Birmingham Six' had earlier sought to establish police malpractice by bringing a claim for damages, the then Master of the Rolls, Lord Denning, had caused controversy by suggesting, in effect, that the exposure of injustice in individual cases was less important than preserving a façade of infallibility (Harlow, 1991, p. 98). By 1991, that façade of infallibility had been destroyed.

Another criticism is that already touched upon: the insensitivity of some judges in particular cases, notably rape cases. In 1993, for example, the Attorney General referred to the Court of Appeal a lenient sentence handed out by a judge in a case where a teenager had been convicted of the attempted rape of a nine-year-old girl. The judge had said that he received evidence that the girl in the case was 'no angel herself'. The comment attracted widespread and adverse criticism. The Appeal Court, while asserting that the judge had been quoted out of context, none the less

BOX 23.3 MORE POWER TO THE JUDGES? DEBATE

The European Convention on Human Rights has been incorporated into British law. This gives a new role to the judges. Some proposals have been put forward to strengthen the courts even further by the enactment of an entrenched Bill of Rights, putting fundamental rights beyond the reach of a simple parliamentary majority. Giving power to judges, through the incorporation of the ECHR and, more so, through an entrenched document, has proved politically contentious. The principal arguments put forward both for and against giving such power to the courts are as follows:

The case for

- A written document, such as the ECHR, clarifies and protects the rights of the individual: Citizens know precisely what their rights are and those rights are protected by law.
- It puts interpretation in the hands of independent judges: The rights are interpreted and protected by judges, who are independent of the political process.
- It prevents encroachment by politicians in government and Parliament: Politicians will be reluctant to tamper with a document, such as the ECHR, now that it is part of the law. Entrenchment of the measure – that is, imposing extraordinary provisions for its amendment – would put the rights beyond the reach of a simple majority in both Houses of Parliament.
- It prevents encroachment by other public bodies, such as the police: Citizens know their rights in relation to public bodies and are able to seek judicial redress if those rights are infringed.
- It ensures a greater knowledge of rights: It is an educative tool, citizens being much more rights-conscious.
- It bolsters confidence in the political system: By knowing that rights are protected in this way, citizens feel better protected and as such are more supportive of the political system.

The case against

- It confuses rather than clarifies rights: The ECHR, like most Bills of Rights, is necessarily drawn in general terms and citizens therefore have to wait until the courts interpret the vague language in order to know precisely what is and what is not protected.
- It transfers power from an elected to a non-elected body: What are essentially political issues are decided by unelected judges and not by the elected representatives of the people.
- It does not necessarily prevent encroachment by public bodies: Rights are better protected by the political culture of a society than by words written on a document. A written document does not prevent public officials getting round its provision by covert means.
- It creates a false sense of security: There is a danger that people will believe that rights are fully protected when later interpretation by the courts may prove them wrong. Pursuing cases through the courts can be prohibitively expensive; often only big companies and rich individuals can use the courts to protect their interests.
- If a document is entrenched, it embodies rights that are the product of a particular generation: A document that is not entrenched can be modified by a simple majority in both Houses of Parliament. If it is entrenched – as many Bills of Rights are – it embodies the rights of a particular time and makes it difficult to get rid of them after their moral validity has been destroyed, as was the case with slavery in the United States and is still the case in the USA with the right to bear arms. The ECHR is not formally entrenched but it will be difficult, politically, for Parliament to change it.

condemned the sentence as inappropriate and increased it. An earlier case, in which another judge had awarded a young rape victim £500 to go on holiday to help forget about her experience, attracted even more condemnation. Such cases highlighted a problem that appears pervasive. A survey published in 1993 revealed that 40 per cent of sentences by circuit courts in rape cases were of four years or less, even though Appeal Court guidelines recommend that five years should be the starting point in contested rape cases. (The maximum sentence possible is life imprisonment.) Lenient sentences in a number of cases involving other offences also fuelled popular misgivings about the capacity of the courts to deliver appropriate sentences.

The result of such cases has not contributed to a high public regard for judges. In a 1999 MORI poll, the proportion of respondents expressing satisfaction with the ways judges did their job was less than for most of the other professions mentioned. Though 58 per cent were satisfied or very satisfied with the way judges did their job – against 15 per cent who were fairly or very dissatisfied – the figure was notably below that for nurses, doctors, dentists, teachers, the police and even accountants. Only lawyers, politicians generally, and Government Ministers received lower satisfaction ratings.

Other aspects of the criminal justice system have also attracted criticism. The activity and policy of the Crown Prosecution Service have been particular targets. The CPS has been largely overworked and has had difficulty since its inception in recruiting a sufficient number of well-qualified lawyers to deal with the large number of cases requiring action. In 1999, it was revealed that stress was a particular problem for many CPS lawyers. The CPS has also been criticised for failing to prosecute in several highly publicised cases where it has felt that the chances of obtaining a conviction have not been high enough to justify proceeding. Damning reports on the organisation and leadership of the CPS were published in 1998 and 1999. As a response to the latter report, the new Director of Public Prosecutions undertook to reform the service, providing a more organised and transparent system of public prosecutions.

Another problem has been that of access to the system. Pursuing a court case is expensive. In civil cases, there is often little legal aid available. Those with money can hire high-powered lawyers. In cases alleging libel or slander, only those with substantial wealth can usually afford to pursue a case against a well-resourced individual or organisation, such as a national newspaper. Millionaires such as the novelist Jeffrey (Lord) Archer and the singer–songwriter Sir Elton John have pursued cases successfully, but for those without their resources the task is virtually impossible. Cases can also be delayed. Many individuals have neither the time nor the money to pursue matters through the courts. Another criticism, related to access, is that the language of the courts has been inaccessible. Many people do not understand legal terminology and the Latin phrases that are used in court.

Various proposals have been advanced for reform of the judiciary and of the system of criminal justice. A number have been implemented. There have been moves to create greater openness in the recruitment of senior judges as well as to extend the right to appear before the senior courts. In 1998, new judges were required to reveal whether they were freemasons. (It was feared that membership of a secret society might raise suspicions of a lack of impartiality.) The 1999 Access to Justice Act created a community legal service (CLS) to take responsibility for the provision of legal advice and for legal aid. It also created a criminal defence service, to provide that those charged with criminal offences receive a high quality legal defence. Legal language has also been simplified: the old terms and Latin phrases have gone. The Crown Prosecution Service is undergoing change under a new Director of Public Prosecutions. There have also been various reforms to criminal law in terms of sentencing and the management of cases in the magistrates' courts. However, proposals for major reform remain on the agenda. A proposal for a Department of Legal Administration, embodied in the Labour manifesto in the 1992 general election, was dropped in 1995. Some reformers argue the case for a dedicated Ministry of Justice. Some press for a total separation of the judicial, executive and parliamentary roles embodied in the position of the Lord

Chancellor. Others advance the case for a thorough overhaul of the process by which judges are recruited and appointed. The courts are undergoing significant change – the changes of the 1990s probably surpassing anything experienced in the previous half-century – but the pressure for reform continues.

Chapter summary

Though not at the heart of the regular policy-making process in Britain, the courts are none the less now significant actors in the political system. Traditionally restricted by the doctrine of parliamentary sovereignty, the courts have made use of their power of judicial review to constrain ministers and other public figures. The passage of two acts – the European Communities Act in 1972 and the Human Rights Act in 1998 – has created the conditions for judges to determine the outcome of public policy in a way not previously possible. Judges now have powers that effectively undermine the doctrine of parliamentary sovereignty, with the outputs of Parliament not necessarily being immune to challenge in the courts. The passage of the Government of Wales Act 1998 and the Scotland Act 1998 has also enlarged the scope for judicial activity, with potentially significant constitutional and political implications. The greater willingness of, and opportunity for, the courts to concern themselves in the determination of public policy has been welcomed by some jurists and politicians, while alarming others, fearful that policy-making power may slip from elected politicians to unelected judges. The courts are having to meet the challenge of a new judicial dimension to the British constitution while coping – not always successfully – with the demands of an extensive system of criminal and civil justice.

Discussion points

- Why should the courts be independent of government?
- What role is now played by judges as a result of Britain's membership of the European Union?
- Can, and should, judges be drawn from a wider social background?
- Is the incorporation of the European Convention on Human Rights into British law a good idea?

Further reading

Basic introductions to the legal system can be found in student texts on constitutional and administrative law. Recent examples include Bradley and Ewing (1997) and Carroll (1998). The classic and controversial critique of the judiciary is that provided by Griffith (1997). Drewry (1991) addresses the question of judicial independence.

On the impact of membership of the EC/EU on British law, see Loveland (1996), Fitzpatrick (1999) and Maxwell (1999). On the impact of the incorporation of the ECHR, see Lester (1994), Beatson *et al.* (1998), Lord Irvine of Lairg (1998), Klug (1999) and Loveland (1999). See also the Government White Paper, *Rights Brought Home: the Human Rights Bill* (Home Office, 1998). The White Paper includes the provisions of the ECHR. On the debate as to whether Britain needs an entrenched Bill of Rights, see Norton (1982, Chapter 13), Puddephatt (1995), Gearty (1996), and Blackburn (1997). On the implications for the courts of devolution, see especially Craig and Walters (1999).

References

Beatson, J., Forsyth, C. and Hare, I. (eds) (1998) *Constitutional Reform in the United Kingdom: Practice and Principles* (Hart Publishing).

Blackburn, R. (1997) 'A Bill of Rights for the 21st Century', in R. Blackburn and J. Busuttil (eds), *Human Rights for the 21st Century* (Pinter).

Bradley, A.W. (1994) 'The sovereignty of Parliament – in perpetuity?', in J. Jowell and D. Oliver (eds), *The Changing Constitution*, 3rd edn (Oxford University Press).

Bradley, A.W. and Ewing, K.D. (1997) *Constitutional and Administrative Law*, 12th edn (Longman).

Carroll, A. (1998) *Constitutional and Administrative Law* (Financial Times/Pitman Publishing).

Craig, P. and Walters, M. (1999) 'The courts, devolution and judicial review', *Public Law*, Summer.

Drewry, G. (1986) 'Judges and politics in Britain', *Social Studies Review*, November.

Drewry, G. (1991) 'Judicial independence in Britain: challenges real and threats imagined', in P. Norton (ed.), *New Directions in British Politics?* (Edward Elgar).

Fitzpatrick, B. (1999) 'A dualist House of Lords in a sea of monist Community law', in B. Dickson and P. Carmichael (eds), *The House of Lords: Its Parliamentary and Judicial Roles* (Hart Publishing).

Gearty, C.A. (1996) 'An answer to "Legislating liberty: the case for a Bill of Rights" by Andrew Puddephatt', *The Journal of Legislative Studies*, Vol. 2, No. 2.

Griffith, J.A.G. (1997) *The Politics of the Judiciary*, 5th edn (Fontana).

Harlow, C. (1991) 'The legal system', in P. Catterall (ed.), *Contemporary Britain: an Annual Review* (Blackwell).

Home Office (1998) *Rights Brought Home: the Human Rights Bill*, Cm 3782 (Stationery Office).

Irvine of Lairg, Lord (1998) 'The development of human rights in Britain under an incorporated convention on human rights', *Public Law*, Summer.

Jacobs, F. (1999) 'Public law – the impact of Europe', *Public Law*, Summer.

Klug, F. (1999) 'The Human Rights Act 1998, *Pepper* v. *Hart* and all that', *Public Law*, Summer.

Lester, Lord (1994) 'European human rights and the British constitution', in J. Jowell and D. Oliver (eds), *The Changing Constitution*, 3rd edn (Oxford University Press).

Loveland, I. (1996) 'Parliamentary sovereignty and the European Union: unfinished business?', *Parliamentary Affairs*, Vol. 49, No. 4.

Loveland, I. (1999) 'Incorporating the European Convention on Human Rights into UK Law', *Parliamentary Affairs*, Vol. 52, No. 1.

McEldowney, J. (1998) 'Legal aspects of relations between the United Kingdom and the Scottish Parliament: the evolution of subordinate sovereignty?', in D. Oliver and G. Drewry (eds), *The Law and Parliament* (Butterworths).

Maxwell, P. (1999) 'The House of Lords as a constitutional court – the implications of *Ex Parte EOC*', in B. Dickson and P. Carmichael (eds), *The House of Lords: Its Parliamentary and Judicial Roles* (Hart Publishing).

Mullin, C. (1996) 'Miscarriages of justice', *The Journal of Legislative Studies*, Vol. 2, No. 2.

Munro, C. (1987) *Studies in Constitutional Law* (Butterworths).

Munro, C. (1992) '*Factortame* and the constitution', *Inter Alia*, Vol. 1, No. 1.

Nolan, Lord and Sedley, Sir S. (1997) *The Making and Remaking of the British Constitution* (Blackstone).

Norton, P. (1982) *The Constitution in Flux* (Blackwell).

Puddephatt, A. (1995) 'Legislating liberty: the case for a Bill of Rights', *The Journal of Legislative Studies*, Vol. 1, No. 1.

Rozenburg, J. (1999) 'The *Pinochet* case and cameras in court', *Public Law*, Summer.

Scarman, Lord (1974) *English Law – The New Dimensions* (Stevens).

Wade, E.C.S. and Bradley, A.W. (1993) *Constitutional and Administrative Law*, 11th edn, ed. A.W. Bradley and K.D. Ewing (Longman).

Walker, C. and Starmer, K. (1999) *Miscarriages of Justice* (Blackstone Press).

Woodhouse, D. (1996) 'Politicians and the judges: a conflict of interest', *Parliamentary Affairs*, Vol. 49, No. 3.

Zander, M. (1989) *A Matter of Justice*, rev. edn (Oxford University Press).

Concluding comment

The revolution in Whitehall 1979–99 (a personal view)

Peter Kemp

The link between the success or failure of a country, whether in social, economic or any other terms, and the quality of its public administration, is pretty tenuous. There are those who almost deny it; an eminent former Permanent Secretary of the Treasury once said there was no problem in society but that government could not make it worse. But with something over 40 per cent of our GDP going on the public services, to say nothing of higher government policy making and the like, it would seem absurd to think that there wasn't some connection between the success of a country and the quality of its public administration and public services.

In this country we have had a pretty successful twenty years between 1979 and 1999. Certainly we have started from a low base, overall and in terms of the quality of both the private and public sectors. But few would deny that things have enormously improved. Many statistics can be drawn for instance out of *Social Trends*. But more importantly there is a general feeling of well-being, which those of us who were grown-up in the 1960s and 1970s will well recognise. There is no doubt that on the whole – and with a society as complex as ours there are always exceptions – things have got better.

It was Mrs Thatcher's perception surveying her inheritance (but Mr Callaghan would have shared it had he won the 1979 election) that change in the public services was overdue. They were overmanned, over-paid, over-managed, and yet with all this still not giving any kind of satisfactory service to the public. An unholy alliance had grown up between the managers of the great public services – education, health, local government services, central government services, the police, and so on – and the trades unions who ran the workforces. The two other players who ought to have been important here – namely the tax-payer who was funding all this and the citizen who was on the receiving end – didn't get a look in. And the Thatcher perception was that this had to change. There had to be a better articulation between on the one hand those who paid for the services and on the other hand those who received them; time was up for the middle-men.

Education, health, and so on were changed in administrative terms really quite slowly, though admittedly quite fast by standards of the previous glacial rate. The progress of change in those sort of services is a subject for discussion elsewhere. But we look here at what happened within central government.

There was a genuine step-by-step approach. The government started with recognising that the size of the civil service was too great, and engaged in a severe reduction in numbers, from around 700,000 to around 500,000. No sackings, just recruitment freezes. And then went on to budgeting, and trying to make people understand what money was available, and putting some kind of cap on it. And then on to pay reform, coming away from the old standardised system into one which recognised geography, skill, merit and the like, and led to more sensible local bargaining in terms of affordability and what was necessary to recruit, retain and motivate the work-forces. And then there was the Financial Management Initiative, or FMI, where departments started to link up what was provided in terms of money with what was expected or delivered in terms of results. The FMI was an important step forward. But it had its faults; it wasn't really properly focussed; it was too heavy; and while there was a good deal of 'F' in it, there was little 'M' and, towards the end, practically no 'I'.

And Mrs Thatcher recognised that these moves, though they laid the foundations and pointed the way, were not quite good enough. She recognised that the private sector, starting from the same low 1979 base, was doing pretty well. So as well as reforms in education and health and elsewhere, she struck vigorously with her handbag at the civil service. Thus she adopted the Ibbs idea of agencies, now called the Next Steps Initiative. This was intended to pull together all these strands – crucially – within a framework of structures and structural change – within which they could flourish according to the particular needs of the service they were delivering. Next Steps recognised that the civil service was not in fact one service, but a hundred or so services, delivering an enormous variety of outcomes, and requiring an enormous variety of management styles and the like. It was an idea that certainly caught on. Previous reforms had tried to improve people and systems within the present structures. Next Steps addressed the structures. And most now agree that it has actually improved the quality of public service to the citizen, better value for money, better service to the citizen, and indeed accountability.

And after that, we had the Citizen's Charter. What this did was to recognise that in a situation where the main characteristic of better service, choice, is not easy to provide, there has to be some kind of surrogate, and that's what the Charter provided. Maybe it didn't say a lot to the users of the service, although it probably said more than some people think. What it actually did was pass a message to the deliverers of the service, reminding them that their real customers, as they came to be called, were not their bosses, but in point of fact the people passing through the door; the children in the schools, the patients in the hospitals, the pensioners who want their benefits, and so on. It was a revolution, not so much for the citizen, but for the work-forces and, perhaps, for the politicians.

None of this was painless, and the revolution was by no means complete. It pointed a way through, and recognised and started to develop three important elements of public service today. These are first that service to the public is not something which owes a living to the service providers, but to the users and beneficiaries on the one hand and the payers on the other. The civil service alone costs something like £20 bn per annum to run, or some 10p of income tax. Nobody owes the services a living for their own sake. Relevance, value for money, service to the user, and accountability are what matters. Second, there was the recognition that the new public management, or in detail the so-called customer/contractor relationship, has to be right. And this led into the third concept, which is that the private sector can deliver public services as well as the public sector; while the customer was by definition a Minister or other public service entity the contractor could be public or private. And this model gave rise to what is now called the PPP or Public Private Partnerships and also, though this is a different story, the Private Finance Initiative.

So that broadly is where the Thatcher/Major years left public service. Question: what will the Blair years make of it? Interestingly, though not surprisingly, and in line with a number of other Thatcher reforms, the Blair government has largely bought into this. It's bought into the Citizen's Charter, though calling it something different, and effectively it has bought into the concept of customer/contractor and agency. It's certainly bought into the notion that the private sector can in the right circumstances deliver good public services. This is all well and good.

But it's going further, rightly. Thus it is looking at this notion of what is called in the jargon 'joined-upness', to try to identify the targets for the customers to set the contractor in these relationships. This is a good and sensible operation, and helps to deal with the problems of the matrix of good public service delivery – that is to say the vertical lines that are required for purposes of accountability, resource allocation and the like, with the horizontal lines that are required to deal with the overall needs of the citizen and others where they span two or more vertical entities. And it has gone for Public Service Agreements, or PSAs, between – in effect – the Treasury and Departments, identifying and setting out the targets which those Departments are expected to achieve, mostly in quantified terms. Next Steps Agencies, since the first one was set up in 1988, have had financial and non-financial targets set out, but not Departments. In effect PSAs turn separate departments into agencies for the state, and in practice the Treasury. There's a separate piece to be written about the way the Treasury has arrogated to itself so much power, but the concept of the PSAs has to be right. The ones immediately set are pretty crude, and need buffing up, and there are detailed questions as to how they are measured, how they're audited, and what happens if they are missed. But that there has to be an articulation between the funds provided and what the State looks for and whether or not it is delivered, must be right.

Elsewhere there are other changes to be made. There were two big gaps which the Thatcher/Major reforms did not get round to. First, changes and improvements to the higher civil service, the Permanent Secretaries. We read of efforts to make people more accountable, to widen the base of selection, to organise targets and responsibilities better, and to bring forward more women and ethnic minorities. All good stuff, but all pretty old hat, and unlikely to make any very dramatical change. What is wanted is a re-thinking of the role of the Permanent Secretary, and an abolition of the post as such in splitting it into two between on the one hand a Chief Policy Adviser to the Minister and on the other hand a Chief Departmental Executive to translate policy into action and see that action is delivered.

And second, the structure of Whitehall. The present structure dates back essentially fifty years or more. But since then there have been enormous changes in society and the economy and the world generally; for instance the effects of globalisation, information technology, environment expectations, and much else. The wholesale review of the antiquated structure is needed if it is to meet today's demands of relevance and service to Ministers and the citizen. Examples of necessary change abound. And joining with this are questions of clearing up relationship between the Treasury, currently enormously powerful, the Cabinet Office, and No. 10 Downing Street; rejuvenating public audit and the Select Committee system.

So to return to where we came in, it's fair to say that there has been an important revolution in the way Whitehall does things, with spin-offs into the other big public services. This is good and valuable, and indeed it's recognised as such, in countries across the world, particularly emerging countries, as the way forward. And it has not just been change for its own sake, but it has surely contributed to the success in very many ways of this country over the last twenty years.

But revolutions are never complete and there is always more to do. As important, there is need not to go backwards, for there are always backwoodsmen and revisionists out there who hanker for the bad old days. For instance, one sees signs of recentralisation of some of the big services – for example the national health service and the civil service – which can only be damaging to the spirit of independence and enterprise among managers which has been well and truly introduced and which the Government say they want to nurture. So there are two tasks. First, the present and future governments must hang onto the work of the last twenty years, and not go backwards. And, as important, they must complete it and develop it forward as social and other changes demand. These represent two big complementary tasks, and we must hope that governments are up to it.

Part 6 The policy process

Chapter 24

The policy-making process

Bill Jones

Learning objectives

- To define policy in government.
- To encourage familiarity with the most popular models of policy making.
- To introduce the notion of policy networks.
- To give some examples of policy making.

Introduction

This chapter examines the anatomy of policy and policy making in central government, focussing on the stages of policy making together with some theories relating to the process before concluding with a look at the privatisation of British Telecom as a case study.

How policy is made

Policy can be defined as a set of ideas and proposals for action culminating in a government decision. To study policy, therefore, is to study how decisions are made. Government decisions can take many forms: Burch (1979, p. 108) distinguishes between two broad kinds, as follows:

1. Rules, regulations and public pronouncements (e.g. Acts of Parliament, Orders in Council, White Papers, ministerial and departmental circulars).
2. Public expenditure and its distribution: the government spends some £350 billion per annum mostly on public goods and services (e.g. education, hospitals) and transfer payments (e.g. social security payments and unemployment benefit).

Figure 24.1 portrays the government as a system which has as its input political demands together with resources available and its output as the different kinds of government decisions. The latter impact society and influence future inputs. So the process is circular and constant. Students of the policy process disagree as to how policy inputs are fed into government and, once 'inside', how they are processed.

Both Burch and Wood (1990) and Jordan and Richardson (1987) review these different analyses as models. Eight of them are summarised below.

Models of policy making

1. The conventional model: this is the 'official' (see Figure 3, p. 294) explanation of policy making found in Central Office of Information publications and the utterances of civil servants in public (though seldom in private). This maintains that Parliament represents and interprets the public will through its representatives, who formulate executive policies which are faithfully and impartially implemented by civil servants.
2. The ruling-class model: this is effectively the Marxist interpretation, that those empowered with taking key decisions in the state – civil servants and politicians – subscribe consciously or unconsciously to the values of the dominant economic class. According to this view most policy outputs will have the effect of protecting dominant group interests.

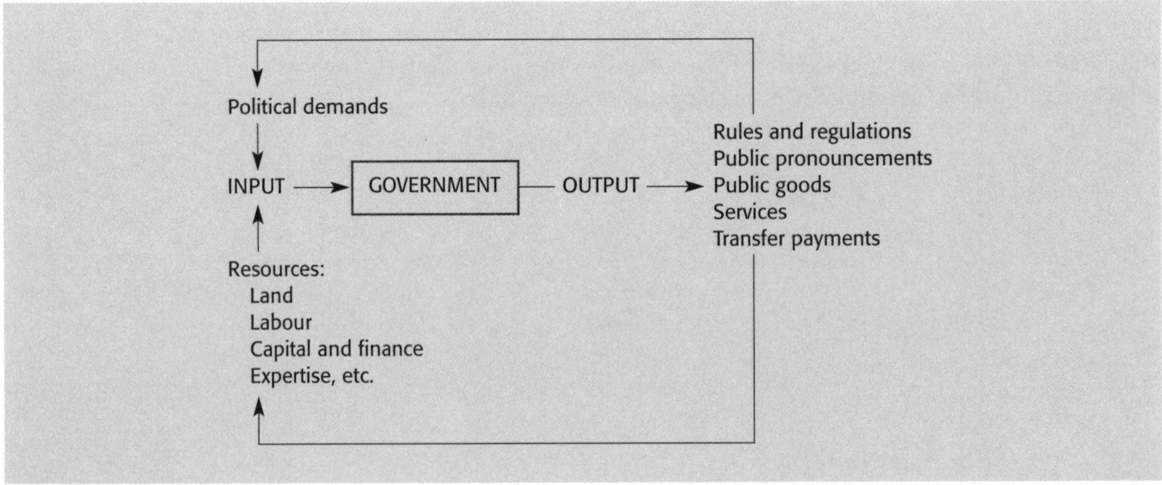

Figure 24.1 The policy process
Source: Burch, 1979

Institutional theories

These attribute decisive importance to differing elements within the political system.

3 The pluralist model, often associated with the US political scientist Robert Dahl, assumes that power is dispersed within society to the various interest groups which constitute it – business, labour, agriculture, and so forth – and that they can 'make themselves heard effectively at some crucial stage in the process of decision' (Jordan and Richardson, 1987, p. 16). According to this view, interest groups interact and negotiate policy with each other in a kind of free market, with government acting as a more or less neutral referee.

4 Corporatism is associated with the work of Philippe Schmitter and is offered as an alternative to pluralism. This model perceives an alliance between ministers, civil servants and the leaders of pressure groups in which the last are given a central role in the policy-making process in exchange for exerting pressure upon their members to conform with government decisions. In this view therefore interest groups become an extension – or even a quasi-form – of government. Corporatism has also been used pejoratively by British politicians of the left (Benn), right (Thatcher) and centre (Owen) to describe the decision-making style of the discredited 1974–9 Labour government.

5 The party government model: the stress here is on political parties and the assertion that they provide the major channel for policy formulation.

6 The Whitehall model contends that civil servants either originate major policy or so alter it as it passes through their hands as to make it substantially theirs – thus making them the key influence on policy.

Theories on decision making

These theories concentrate upon the way in which decision-makers set about their tasks.

7 Rational decision making: this approach assumes that decision makers behave in a logical, sequential fashion. Accordingly they will identify their objectives, formulate possible strategies, think through their implications and finally choose the course of action which on balance best achieves their objectives.

8 Incrementalism: this approach, associated with the work of Charles Lindblom, denies that policy makers are so rational and argues that in practice they usually try to cope or 'muddle through'. They tend to start with the status quo and make what adjustments they can to manage or at least accommodate new situations. In other words policy makers do not solve problems but merely adjust to them. The case of privatisation argues against this approach in that when Nigel Lawson came to consider it in the early 1980s the cupboard, in terms of relevant files and experience, was totally bare. Instead Conservative ministers had to devise wholly new approaches and, whatever one's views on the outcome, it is perhaps to their credit that – even allowing for a determined Prime Minister and a large majority – they succeeded in a government culture so unfriendly to radical innovation.

It is clear that some of these models are basically descriptive while others, like the rational choice or conventional models, are also prescriptive – they offer an ideal approach as to how policies should be made.

It is also obvious that echoing somewhere within each approach is the ring of truth. It would not be too difficult to find examples in support of any of the above models. The truth is that policy making is such a protean, dense area of activity that it is extremely difficult to generalise. Nevertheless, the search for valid statements is worthwhile, otherwise our political system will remain incomprehensible. We will therefore look at the process in greater detail in a search for some generally true propositions about it.

The policy cycle

If they agree on nothing else, policy study scholars seem to agree that policy making can best be understood as a cycle. Analyses of the cycle can be quite sophisticated. Hogwood and Gunn (1984) discern a number of stages: deciding to decide (issue search and agenda setting); deciding how to decide; issue definition, forecasting; setting objectives and priorities; options analysis; policy implementation, monitoring and control; evaluation and review; and policy maintenance, succession or termination. For our purposes, however, three easily understood stages will suffice: initiation, formulation and implementation.

Policy initiation

Agenda setting

Each government decision has a long and complex provenance but all must start somewhere. It is tempting to think they originate, eureka like, in the minds of single individuals, but they are more often the product of debate or a general climate of opinion involving many minds. Policy initiatives, moreover, can originate in all parts of the political system. Setting the political agenda is a curiously elusive process. Items can be deliberately introduced by government and clearly it has many routes available to it, e.g. Tony Blair in the summer of 1999 announcing in an interview that fox hunting would be banned; Jack Straw announcing in the Commons that the method of financing political parties would be reformed. The media too have enormous power to set the agenda: Michael Burke's reports from Ethiopia detailing a scale of famine which touched the nation and intiated assistance; *The Guardian* in 1998 revealing that Peter Mandelson had received a loan from Geoffrey Robinson. Figure 24.2 depicts six groups of policy initiators placed on a continuum starting from the periphery and moving in towards the nerve centre of government in No. 10. The figure uses the idea of 'distance' but captures the truth that the routes into policy making are many and varied.

General public

The public's role in policy making is usually limited to (the democratically vital function of)

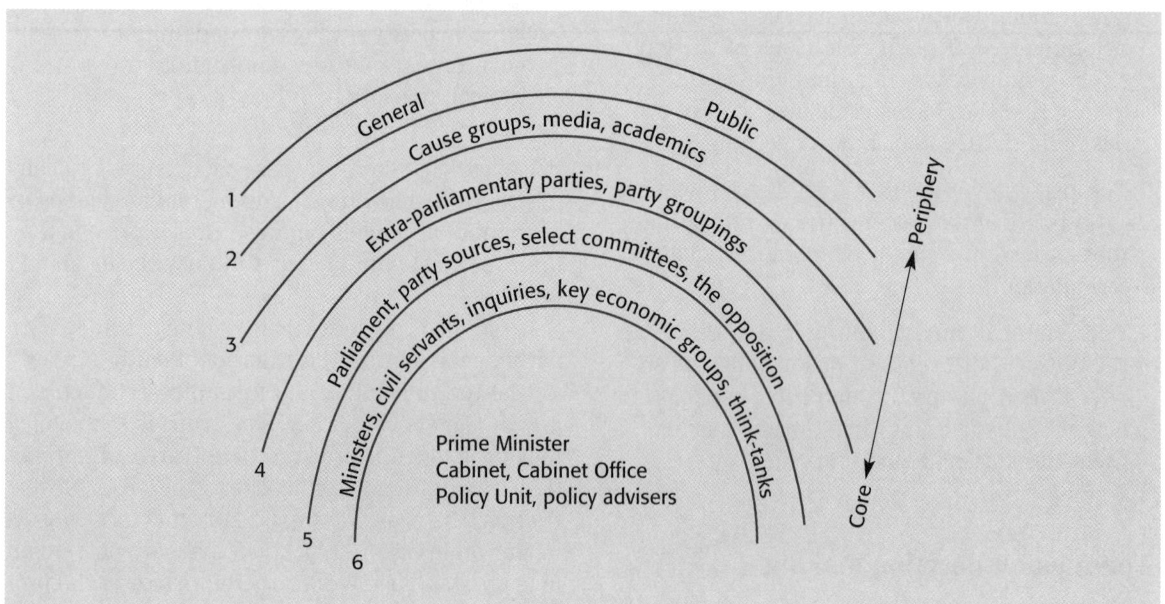

Figure 24.2 Policy initiatives

voting for a particular policy package at general elections. They do have other occasional opportunities, however, for example the referendums on the EC and Scottish and Welsh devolution in the 1970s, and pressures which can be built up through lobbying MPs, as when Sir Keith Joseph was forced to withdraw his proposals to charge parents for a proportion of their children's university tuition fees. Occasionally events occur which create widespread public concern and often governments take action in the wake of them. For example legislation on dogs was taken after a spate of attacks by dogs on children one summer in the eighties and after the Dunblane shootings of March 1996 handguns were banned. In many cases – as in the two just cited – such precipitate action, in reaction to the sudden rousing of public opinion, proves to be poorly framed and receives much criticism.

Cause groups, media and academic experts

Many cause groups operate in the 'wilderness' – their values antithetical to government and not listened to – and many also stay there, but some do influence public opinion and decision makers and after years of struggle achieve action on issues such as abortion, capital punishment and the environment. Others achieve success on specific issues after an extended period of campaigning such as Des Wilson's campaign to reduce lead in petrol. Some groups achieve success via a single well publicised event such as the Countryside Alliance's march on the Labour Party conference in 1999 which caused the government to postpone any attempt to legislate on foxhunting during the forthcoming session, despite Bliar's statement that he would do so. Certain policy 'environments' will include a bewildering array of pressure groups, all of whom seek to lean on the policy-making tiller. Local government associations, for example, are particularly important in areas like education, housing and social services.

Media coverage heavily affects the climate in which policy is discussed and important policy proposals occasionally emerge from television programmes, newspaper editorials, articles in journals and so forth. One editorial on its own would have little effect but a near consensus in the press might well stimulate action. Occasionally ideas are picked up from individual journalists – Mrs Thatcher used to be advised regularly by right-wing journalists such as Woodrow Wyatt, Paul Johnson and Simon Heffer. Other media figures who used to be consulted regularly on policy matters by Margaret Thatcher included Rupert Murdoch and Conrad Black, the press magnates. Murdoch is also rumoured to advise Blair whenever he chooses to visit Downing Street. Lord (Jeffrey) Archer tells us he used regularly to send around to Margaret Thatcher draft speeches on a range of topics, but there is no confirmation of anything important being picked up and actually used.

Occasionally the media provide crucial information. The most surprising example of this was in 1987 when Nigel Lawson, as Chancellor, denied entry to the ERM by prime ministerial veto, had tried to achieve his object by other means, namely manipulating the value of the pound to shadow that of the Deutschmark. When *Financial Times* journalists interviewed Margaret Thatcher they questioned her about this policy. She denied any knowledge of it but when they produced definitive evidence in the form of charts she accepted, somewhat surprised, they were correct and the stage was set for the mammoth argument which resulted in Lawson's damaging resignation two years later and the beginning of the end of her reign in No. 10.

All these agencies in the 'outer rim' (see Figure 24.2) interact to provide that intangible climate of discussion which encourages the emergence of certain proposals and inhibits others. Each policy environment has its own climate created by its specialist press, pressure groups, academics, practitioners and the like who frequently meet in conferences and on advisory committees. An interesting feature of these bodies, however, is that from time to time they are blessed with favour, their arguments listened to, their proposals adopted, their leaders embraced by government and given advisory or even executive status. It is almost as if, God-like, the government has reached down and plucked them up to place them – albeit temporarily – on high.

Part II explained how policy emerged out of an ideological framework and pointed out how academics, philosophers and other thinkers had

BOX 24.1 MINI BIOGRAPHY

David Hume (1711–73)
Scottish philosopher and historian. Studied in Edinburgh but went to live in France where he wrote his *Treatise on Human Nature* (1739). *Essays Moral and Political* (1743) confirmed his reputation as one of the founding British empiricist philosophers of his age.

BOX 24.2 MINI BIOGRAPHY

Michael Oakeshott (1901–90)
Conservative philosopher. Educated Cambridge where he taught until 1949. *Experience and its Modes* (1933) was his first notable work. His writings lie within the pragmatic, sceptical traditions of Conservative thinking. He was professor at LSE 1950–69.

contributed towards these frameworks. The most obvious influences on the left would include Karl Marx, R.H. Tawney, Harold Laski, William Beveridge and, incomparably in the economic sphere, J.M. Keynes. Right-wing writers would include figures such as David Hume and Michael Oakeshott and (on economics) the two overseas academics, Friedrich Hayek and Milton Friedman. Academics specialising in specific policy areas such as transport, housing, criminology and so forth also regularly come up with proposals, some of which are taken up or drawn upon. John Major welcomed the views of the so-called 'seven wise men' (selected academics) on economic policy. Blair and Brown have established a formal committee called the Monetary Policy Committee comprising academics and financial experts who advise the Bank of England on interest rates. On other occasions academics can be suddenly welcomed in by departments, as when the Foreign Office began to use them extensively when the fall of the Shah of Iran revealed that they had been reading events in that country more accurately than the diplomats. In July 1990 much publicity was given to a seminar of six academics convened at Chequers to discuss the implications of German reunification. Colin Brown (*The Independent*, 17 July 1990) revealed that such seminars were regular features of Margaret Thatcher's policy-making style. They were kept confidential and involved 'sympathetic' academics.

Extra-parliamentary parties and party groupings

Both the Labour and Conservative extra-parliamentary parties are more influential in opposition than in government. As Chapter 14 noted, Labour's system of internal democracy gave a substantial policy-making role to the trade unions, the National Executive Committee and the party conference during the 1930s and 1950s. The Conservative Party is far less democratic but conference can set the mood for policy formulation, the research department can initiate important proposals and the Advisory Committee on Policy did much to reformulate the main outlines of Conservative policy in the late 1970s.

Party groupings – many of which have contacts with Parliament – can also exert influence. The Fabian Society has long acted as a kind of left-wing think-tank (see Box 24.1) and in the 1980s the once left-wing Labour Coordinating Committee was influential in advising Neil Kinnock as he shifted Labour's policies towards the centre. Similarly the No Turning Back Group in the Conservatives sought to keep the party on the right-wing track indicated by their heroine Margaret Thatcher, both before and after her fall from power.

Parliament

The role of Parliament in initiating policy can be considered under two headings: party sources and party groups, and non-party sources. In government parliamentary parties have to work through their back-bench committees though individual MPs seek to use their easy access to ministers to exert influence and press their own solutions. One Conservative MP, David Evans, pulled off the remarkable coup of convincing the Prime Minister that the identity card system introduced by Luton Town Football Club should be compulsorily introduced nationwide. His success was short lived: the scheme was dropped in January 1990.

The opposition is concerned to prepare its policies for when and if it takes over the reins of government. As we saw in Chapter 12, Kinnock wrested future policy making out of the party's NEC with his policy review exercise (1987–9), involving leading members of his front-bench team in the process. The opposition, however, also has to make policy 'on the hoof' in reaction to political events. It is their function and in their interests to oppose, to offer alternatives to government – but this is not easy. Opposition spokesmen lack the detailed information and support enjoyed by government; they need to react to events in a way which is consistent with their other policy positions; they need to provide enough detail to offer a credible alternative yet they must avoid closing options should they come to power.

Party groups such as the Bow Group, Monday Club, Tribune and Campaign Group can all have peripheral – but rarely direct – influence on policy making.

The seventeen departmental select committees regularly make reports and recommendations, some of which are adopted. Most experts agree these committees are more important now that their proceedings can be televised. Most of these represent cross-party consensus on specific issues such as the successful Home Affairs Committee recommendation that the laws allowing arrest on suspicion (the 'sus' laws) be abolished, but others, such as the Social Services Committee, once chaired by the much admired and briefly a minister Frank Field, offered a wide-ranging and coherent alternative to government social policy. Individual MPs probably have a better chance of influencing specific, usually very specific, policy areas through the opportunities available to move Private Members' bills (see Chapter 17).

Ministers, departments, official inquiries and 'think-tanks'

Strong-minded ministers will always develop policy ideas of their own either as a reflection of their own convictions or to get noticed and further their ambitions. Michael Heseltine, in the wake of the Toxteth troubles, probably shared both motivations when he submitted a paper to the Cabinet called 'It took a riot', proposing a new and un-Thatcherite approach to inner city regeneration: the policy was partially implemented in Merseyside but not elsewhere. Such major initiatives are not the province of civil servants but through their day-to-day involvement in running the country they are constantly proposing detailed improvements and adjustments to existing arrangements. Such initiatives are not necessarily the preserve of senior officials: even junior officers can propose changes which can be taken up and implemented.

A Royal Commission can be the precursor to major policy changes (for example, the Redcliffe Maud Royal Commission on Local Government, 1966–9), but Margaret Thatcher was not well disposed towards such time-consuming, essentially disinterested procedures – she always felt she knew what needed doing – and during the 1980s none was set up. Major, however, set up the Royal Commission on Criminal Justice and Blair set up the Commission on the House of Lords. He has also initiated scores of task forces and enquiries to prepare the ground for new legislation. Departments, anyway, regularly establish their own inquiries, often employing outside experts, which make important policy recommendations.

Right-wing 'think-tanks' were especially favoured by Margaret Thatcher (see Box 24.1). *The Economist* (6 May 1989) notes how she spurned Oxbridge dons – the traditional source of advice for No. 10 – and suggests that 'the civil service is constitutionally incapable of generating the policy innovation which the prime minister craves'. Instead, as a reforming premier she instinctively listened to the advice of 'people who have been uncorrupted by the old establishment'. Think-tank advice was often channelled to Margaret Thatcher via the No. 10 Policy Unit. Their radical suggestions acted as a sounding board when published and helped push the climate of debate further to the right. If new ideas are received in a hostile fashion, ministers can easily disavow them – on 8 February 1990 a think-tank suggested that child benefit be abolished: Thatcher told the Commons that her government had no 'immediate' plans to do this. The 'privatisation' of government advice in the form of think-tanks was a striking feature of Margaret Thatcher's impact upon policy making.

BOX 24.1 **IDEAS AND PERSPECTIVES**

Think-tanks

In the winter of 1979–80 Margaret Thatcher presided over what looked like a crumbling party and a collapsing economy. Tory grandees talked of dumping the leader. Mandarins, muttering 'I told you so', prepared to welcome the consensual 'Mr Butskell' back from retirement. Mrs Thatcher regained her momentum partly because she discovered 'Thatcherism': a new set of ideas comprising: the abolition of supply constraints in the economy; privatising state owned enterprises; and reform of the public sector. They were provided by the intelligentsia of the 'New Right', many of them working through think tanks. (*Economist*, 18 November 1992)

After the demise of Thatcher these American-style independent hot-houses of ideas took something of a back seat. The Centre for Policy Studies used to issue a report every fortnight but with Major in power, rather than its original patron, its output slowed to zero. The Adam Smith Institute, once a pioneer in privatisation ideas, also reduced its output and with Blair in power was reduced to producing a complimentary report on his first two hundred days. The Institute for Economic Affairs was the oldest right-wing think-tank but also curtailed its activities once the Thatcherite glory days had gone. It has to be said also that the disaster of the poll tax, the product of the ASI, contributed to their declining respect. And the splits did not help: Graham Mather left the IEA to form his own European Policy Forum while David Willetts at the CPS left after criticism to become an MP and director of the Social Market Foundation.

Labour has been relatively light on think-tanks but the Fabian Society, set up by the Webbs in 1884, has been a valuable and highly influential think-tank for over a hundred years. It still exists with an impressive membership from the public and the parliamentary party. It organises seminars and conferences and keeps up a good flow of pamphlets and serious studies; one recent one being the work of a certain Tony Blair. In addition, in the current day there is the Institute for Public Policy Research which has produced a number of New Labour studies. Two more of several are Demos, led by Geoff Mulgan (now a No. 10 adviser) and Catalyst, a left of centre think-tank which issues studies on the media (Franklin, 1998) and the government's practice of setting up task forces (Platt, 1998).

Prime Minister and Cabinet

This is the nerve centre of government, supported by the high-powered network of Cabinet committees, the Cabinet Office, the No. 10 Policy Unit and policy advisers. After a period of ten years in office it is likely that any Prime Minister will dominate policy making. Chapter 19 made it clear that while many sought to whisper policy suggestions in her ear, Margaret Thatcher's radical beliefs provided her with an apparently full agenda of her own. The evidence of her personal impact on major policy areas is plain to see: privatisation, trade union legislation, the environment, the exchange rate, sanctions against South Africa, the poll tax and Europe – the list could go on. She was also unusual, however, in taking a personal interest in less weighty matters such as her (ill-starred) attempt to clean up litter from Britain's streets following a visit to litter-free Israel. Harold Wilson saw himself as a 'deep lying halfback feeding the ball forward to the chaps who score the goals'. Thatcher was not content with this role: she wanted to score the goals as well. Wilson also said a Prime Minister governs by 'interest and curiosity': Thatcher had insatiable appetites in both respects and an energy which enabled her to feed them to a remarkable degree. Under her, assisted by her own relentless energy and a constitution which delivers so much power to the executive, the office of Prime Minister took on a policy-initiating role comparable with that of the US President. John Major was also exceptionally hard working, as premiers must be, but he was happy to delegate more than his predecessor and to listen to voices around the Cabinet table, especially that of his powerful deputy, Michael Heseltine. Blair has proved to be a premier more in the Thatcher mould, bypassing Cabinet and making decisions in small groups of close advisers, especially his 'Kitchen Cabinet' of Alastair Campbell, Jonathan Powell and Anji Hunter (see Chapter 19).

From this brief and admittedly selective description it is clear that:

1 Policy can be initiated both at the micro and macro levels from within any part of the political system, but the frequency and importance of initiatives grow as one moves from the periphery towards the centre.
2 Even peripheral influences can be swiftly drawn into the centre should the centre wish it.
3 Each policy environment is to some extent a world unto itself with its own distinctive characteristics. Higher education policy making, for example, will include, just for starters, the Prime Minister, Cabinet, the No. 10 Policy Unit, right-wing think-tanks, numerous parliamentary and party committees, the Departments of Education and Employment, the Treasury, the funding councils for the universities, the Committee of Vice-Chancellors and Principals, the Association of University Teachers and other unions, *The Times Higher Education Supplement*, together with a galaxy of academic experts on any and every aspect of the subject.

Policy formulation

Once a policy idea has received political endorsement it is fed into the system for detailed elaboration. This process involves certain key players from the initiation process, principally civil servants, possibly key pressure group leaders and outside experts (who may also be political sympathisers) and, usually at a later stage, ministers. In the case of a major measure there is often a learning phase in which civil servants and ministers acquaint themselves with the detail of the measure: this may require close consultation with experts and practitioners in the relevant policy environment. The measure, if it requires legislation, then has to chart a course first through the bureaucracy and then the legislature.

The bureaucratic process

This will entail numerous information-gathering and advisory committee meetings and a sequence of co-ordinating meetings with other ministries, especially the Treasury if finance is involved. Some of these meetings might be co-ordinated by the Cabinet Office and when ministers become involved the measures will be progressed in Cabinet committees and ultimately full Cabinet before being passed on to parliamentary counsel, the expert drafters of parliamentary bills.

The legislative process

As Chapters 17 and 18 explained, this process involves several readings and debates in both chambers. Studies show that most legislation passes through unscathed, but controversial measures will face a number of hazards which may influence their eventual shape. Opposition MPs and peers may seek to delay and move hostile amendments, but more important are rebellions within the government party: for example, the legislation required to install the community charge, or poll tax, in 1988–9 was amended several times in the face of threatened and actual revolts by Conservative MPs. The task of piloting measures through the legislature falls to ministers closely advised by senior officials and this is often when junior ministers can show their mettle.

From this brief description it is clear that three sets of actors dominate the policy formulation process: ministers, civil servants and pressure group leaders and experts. Some scholars calculate that the key personnel involved in policy formulation might number no more than 3,500. As in policy initiation, Margaret Thatcher also played an unusually interventionist role in this process. Reportedly she regularly called ministers and civil servants into No. 10 to speed things up, shift developments on to the desired track or discourage those with whom she disagreed. It would seem Tony Blair is in the same mould, raging in public and private at the inertia of the public sector and the more general 'forces of conservatism' he criticised at the 1999 Bournemouth party conference.

Policy implementation

It is easy to assume that once the government has acted on something or legislated on an issue it is more or less closed. Certainly the record of government action reveals any number of measures which have fulfilled their objectives: for example, the Attlee government wished to establish a National Health Service and did so; in recent years, Conservative governments wished to sell off houses to tenants and did so. But there are always problems which impede or sometimes frustrate implementation or which produce unsought for side-effects. Between legislation and implementation many factors intervene. Jordan and Richardson (1982, pp. 234–5) quote the conditions which Hood suggests need to be fulfilled to achieve perfect implementation:

1. There must be a unitary administrative system rather like a huge army with a single line of authority. Conflict of authority could weaken control, and all information should be centralised in order to avoid compartmentalism.
2. The norms and rules enforced by the system have to be uniform. Similarly, objectives must be kept uniform if the unitary administrative system is to be really effective.
3. There must be perfect obedience or perfect control.
4. There must be perfect information and perfect communication – as well as perfect co-ordination.
5. There must be sufficient time for administrative resources to be mobilised.

To fulfil wholly any, let alone all, of those conditions would be rare indeed, so some degree of failure is inevitable with any government programme. Examples are easy to find.

Education

The 1944 Education Act intended that the new grammar, technical and secondary modern schools were to be different but share a 'parity of esteem'. In practice this did not happen: grammar schools became easily the most prestigious and recruited disproportionately from the middle classes. The government could not control parental choice. To remedy this, comprehensive schools were set up in the 1950s and 1960s, but it was the middle-class children who still performed best in examinations. Reformers also neglected one crucial and in retrospect blindingly obvious factor: comprehensive schools recruit from their own hinterlands, so inner city schools draw children from predominantly working class areas with a consequent tendency for a culture producing lower educational standards, while suburban schools are drawn from more middle class families who place a high value on education and whose children consequently achieve higher standards. The government made policy on the basis of inadequate information.

The economy

Burch and Wood (1990, pp. 172–3) record how recent governments have consistently planned on the basis of public expenditure plans which in the event were exceeded: an estimated increase of 12 per cent in 1971 for the year 1975 proved to be 28.6 per cent in practice. The government lacked control over its own spending departments. Following the stock market crash of 1987 Chancellor Nigel Lawson lowered interest rates to 9.5 per cent to avoid the danger of a recession. This measure, however, led to an explosion of credit, fuelling an inflationary spending boom which required high interest rates to bring it under control. High interest rates in their turn went on to cause economic recession in 1990. The government chose to ignore relevant information offered by advisers in 1988.

Social security payments

Many claimants report that a necessary service to which they have entitlement has been transformed by state employees and the restrictions they have been told to enforce into a humiliating, time-consuming obstacle course.

Inner city policy

In the wake of her 1987 victory Margaret Thatcher resolved to attack the problems of the inner cities. In March 1988 the Action for Cities initiative was launched with considerable fanfare. In January 1990 the National Audit Office reported that it had achieved only 'piecemeal success' (*The Guardian*, 25 January 1990); departments had 'made no overall assessment of inner cities' "special requirements"' and there was 'insufficient information to assess the strategic impact of the various programmes and initiatives involved'.

Poll tax

The euphemistically named 'community charge' – known as the poll tax – was the brain-child variously of right-wing think-tanks, Kenneth Baker, William Waldegrave and others (though following its collapse most people were keen to disclaim parentage – political failures, unsurprisingly, are always 'orphans'). The rationale behind it was logical; local taxes – the 'rates' – were based on property but penalised the wealthy, who paid more on big properties. Over half, however, were either exempted or received rebates yet still enjoyed the benefits of local services; consequently they had no reason to vote for lower rates and were not 'accountable' for them in the opinion of Conservatives like Thatcher, a keen supporter of the scheme. The new tax was to be a flat-rate one and payable by all to some degree, even students and the unemployed. The obvious unfairness of taxing the poor as heavily as the rich was widely perceived, even by Conservative voters. Yet Thatcher's personal support, defiant style and the pusillanimous nature of many MPs and ministers – Michael Portillo informed conference he was not daunted but 'delighted' to be placed in charge of it – let a clearly flawed law on to the statute book. In March 1990 polls showed a huge majority opposed it and on 7 April a riot erupted in London. When John Major succeeded Thatcher he quickly replaced the measure with one more closely resembling the old property-based rates and the heat soon left the issue of local government finance (for more on the poll tax see Chapter 22). Programme failure also often results from the operation of constraints which constantly bear upon policy makers.

Constraints upon policy makers

Financial resources

Policy makers have to operate within available financial resources which are a function of the nation's economic health at any particular time, and the willingness of key decision makers, especially in the Treasury, to make appropriate provision from funds available to government.

Political support

This is initially necessary to gain endorsement for a policy idea, but support is also necessary throughout the often extended and complex policy-making process. Lack of it, for example, characterised the tortured birth of the poll tax, as well as its ignominious demise. Support at the political level is also crucial but it is highly desirable within the bureaucracy and elsewhere in the policy environment. Resistance to policies can kill them off en route and anticipated resistance is also important; as Jordan and Richardson (1982, p. 238) hypothesise. 'There are probably more policies which are never introduced because of the anticipation of resistance, than policies which have failed because of resistance.' Some departments now seek to gauge levels of popular support through the use of focus groups, a technique borrowed from commerical and political marketing (see Chapter 10).

Competence of key personnel

An able, energetic minister is likely to push policy measures through: a weak minister is not. Civil servants are famously able in Britain but even they need to work hard to be up to the task of mastering rapidly the detail of new measures: their failure will impede the progress of a measure and limit its efficacy.

Time

New legislative initiatives need to carve space out of a timetable so overcrowded that winners of Private Members' ballots are lobbied by departments themselves to adopt bills awaiting parliamentary consideration. The whole system is, moreover, arguably over-centralised and, some would say, chronically overloaded.

Timing

Measures can fail if timing is not propitious. Just after a general election, for example, is a good time to introduce controversial measures. Margaret Thatcher, it will be recalled, was unable to secure the sale of British Leyland to an American company in the spring of 1986 because she had lost so much support over the Westland episode.

Co-ordination

Whitehall departments divide up the work of government in a particular way: proposals which fall between ministries are often at a disadvantage and the job of coordinating diverse departments is not, in the view of critics, managed with particular efficiency. Burch (1979, p. 133) also notes that:

> Too often policy making becomes a conflict between departments for a share of the limited resources available. This is . . . especially true of expenditure politics when departments fight for their own corner at the cost of broader policy objectives.

Personality factors

Key decision makers are not as rational as perhaps they ought to be. They might have personal objectives – ambition, desire for image and status and rivalries – which lead them to oppose rather than support certain policy objectives. The best recent example of this is the row between Margaret Thatcher and Nigel Lawson in the late 1990s over Britain's proposed entry into the exchange rate mechanism (ERM), which caused policy to drift.

Geographical factors

A bias in favour of the south-east is often detectable in government policies – for example, in the granting of defence contracts – partly because decision makers in our centralised system live in the home counties, partly because the south-east has a more buoyant economy and partly as a result of political factors: this after all is the heartland of the traditional party of government. (For a subtle and controversial analysis of territorial politics in the UK, see Bulpitt (1983).)

International events

The increasing interdependence of the large economies has made events such as the quadrupling of oil prices in the early 1970s major constraints upon policy making. In some cases these constraints are formal, as when the International Monetary Fund attached strict public expenditure conditions to its 1976 loan to Callaghan's Labour government. Political events such as the Falklands War can clearly have an enormous impact upon major policy areas, while the 1989 revolutions in the communist countries changed the whole context within which foreign policy is formulated.

The influence of Europe

Treaty obligations and the growing power of Community institutions have imposed increasingly powerful constraints upon the freedom of action which British policy makers have enjoyed (see Chapter 31).

Policy networks

Jordan and Richardson (1987) argued that policy making in Britain is not uniform; every aspect has its own specific characteristics. They lay less stress on manifestos or the activities of Parliament but point to the mass of interconnecting bodies which have an interest in the policy area: the 'policy community'.

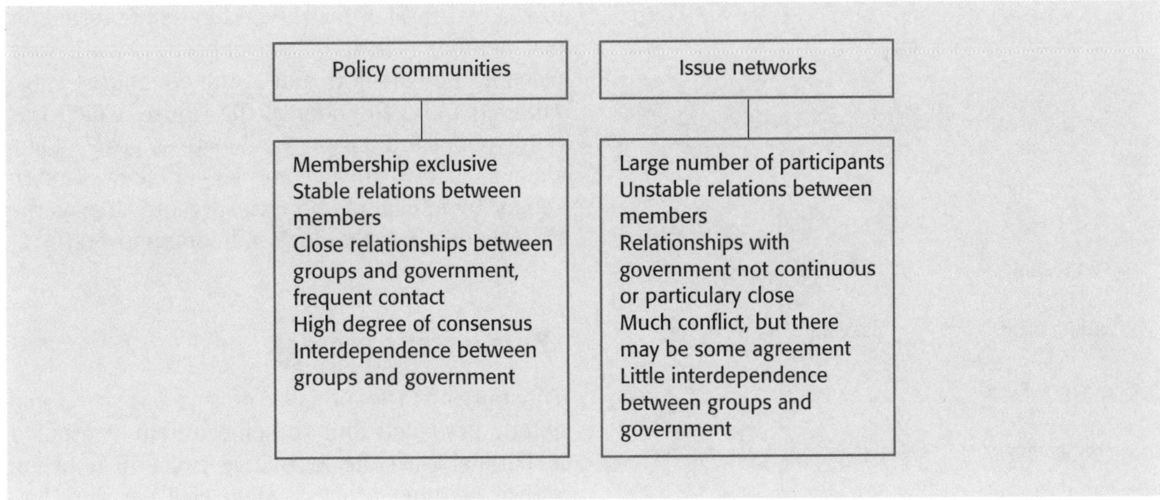

Figure 24.3 Policy networks
Source: Baggott, 1995, p. 24

To some extent this is a theory about how interest groups interact with government to help formulate policy. Access to the policy community is restricted to actors prepared to play the game: act constitutionally; accept that the government has the last word; keep agreements; and make reasonable demands. These rules automatically exclude radical groups with high-profile campaigning styles in most cases, though the accession to power of a radical political message can alter this as in the case of Thatcherism. To exercise real clout, a group has to become an 'insider' (see Chapter 11). Communities have a core and a periphery – rather like that suggested in Figure 24.2 – with the stable core continuously involved in the policy process and a secondary group, less stable in membership, involved from time to time but lacking the resources to be in the core.

Professor Rod Rhodes developed this idea but saw that often the policy community was not cohesive or sharply defined; he began to discern a more fragmented and more accessible form: a 'policy network' with a very large and constantly changing membership, often with conflicting views. Baggott's diagram (Figure 24.3) shows the contrast between the two ideas with some clarity. Baggott (1995, p. 26) criticises the approach for not explaining the provenance of the networks and overconcentrating on the group–government nexus to the exclusion of the broader political environment.

The case of the privatisation of British Telecom

This chapter concludes with an examination of policy formulation and implementation in the case of the privatisation of British Telecom (BT) in 1984.

While Conservative ideology had long argued for minimal state interference, official policy on privatisation was very cautious as late as 1978. 'Denationalisation', reported a Conservative policy study group in that year, 'must be pursued cautiously and flexibly, recognizing that major changes may well be out of the question in some industries' (Lee, 1989, p. 139). The 1979 manifesto had spoken only of selling just under a half share in selected industries. On 21 November 1980 a bill was presented separating the postal from the telephone side of the General Post Office. On 27 July 1981 British Telecom came into being. Shortly afterwards Sir Geoffrey Howe inaugurated the age of privatisation with the announcement that several industries were being considered for this treatment: the biggest was British Telecom. Figure 24.4

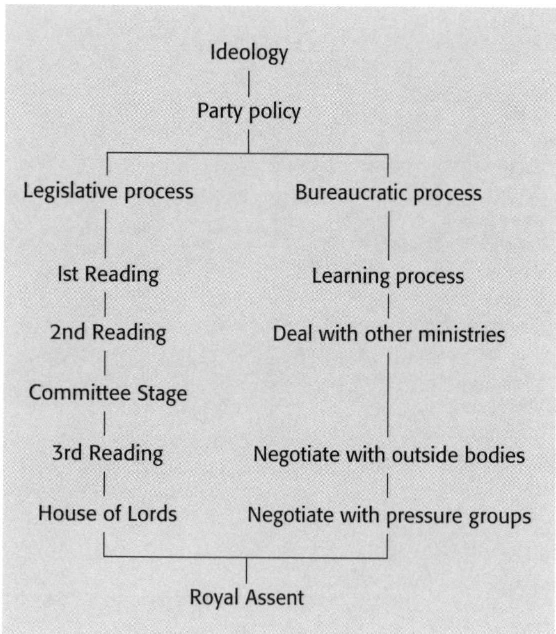

Figure 24.4 Negotiating the policy process
Source: Jones, 1986

characterises in a very simplified form the policy process which any measure has to negotiate.

Legislative process

When the bill to privatise BT was introduced it faced great opposition. The Post Office Engineering Union (POEU) had three sponsored MPs in the Commons, led by John Golding, who went on to become its general secretary (under its changed name, the National Communications Union). Golding spoke for eleven hours in the committee stage but it was the general election which caused the bill to lapse in May 1983. Margaret Thatcher was quick to re-introduce an amended form of the bill after the election and, after a speedy progress helped by the guillotine, it became an act on 12 April 1984.

By common consent the second bill was a much more workable piece of legislation. In a Tyne Tees TV programme in August 1986, John Golding claimed some of the credit. Having realised that the large Conservative majority would ensure the bill's eventual success, he decided to cut his losses by pressing for the best possible terms for his members. Most of the important work took place in the corridors and at the committee stage rather than on the floor of the House, which was thinly populated during the debate stages. Golding claims his own advice and expertise was often sought by ministers and civil servants alike as the bill was discussed and amendments moved.

Bureaucratic process

The bureaucratic process in this case to some extent preceded and to some extent continued in parallel with the legislative process. It began with a learning process when civil servants had to negotiate with BT officials and experts. Jason Crisp of *The Financial Times*, who followed these discussions closely, testified that talks were 'frequent, frantic, often very bad tempered'. Then negotiations with other ministries ensued, especially with the Treasury, which was primarily interested in the huge increases in revenue privatisation would produce. Inevitably, the Department of Trade and Industry was more concerned with achieving a particular kind of settlement, and one which worked, and negotiations with the Treasury were consequently not always smooth.

Next came consultations with the City, where most of the finance was expected to originate. The DTI and the Treasury were clearly determined not to overprice BT's shares. The 1983 election manifesto had listed British Gas, Rolls-Royce, British Steel and others as future candidates for privatisation: they could not afford the failure of such a major test case as BT. The City financiers, like all potential buyers, had an interest in talking the price down, and this they assiduously did.

Finally, negotiations with outside pressure groups took place. In 1980 the British Telecom Union Campaign was formed with the POEU to the fore. With the help of a public relations company and an advertising agency it orchestrated a campaign to frustrate the bill, and, when that failed, to soften its impact upon trade union members. The POEU, in its booklet *The Battle for British Telecom*, tells the story of how it put pressure on 800 key opinion-makers in industry, and in the programme already referred to (Jones, 1986) John Golding told how the relevant pressure groups were mobilised over rural services, especially the provision of kiosks. The response from the likes of the National Farmers' Union, the local authority associations and the Women's Institutes was so overwhelming that civil servants 'begged' him to call off the campaign because the Department was absolutely inundated by resolutions and letters that came from all those traditionally Conservative supporting bodies.

'But of course we kept the campaign on and . . . The ministers caved in and made certain that they protected the rural services as far as it was possible.'

A number of points can be made about the way in which this decision was made, which also serve as a conclusion to this chapter.

1 *Result differed from intention*: According to party ideology, the main thrust of privatisation is to re-introduce competition and to spread public ownership of shares. At the end of the three-year process, competition seemed to have taken a back seat (though Mercury Communications was licensed to compete with BT and in 1990 this duopoly ended and other enterprises were considered as licensed competitors). And while nearly two million people helped produce the £4 billion flotation (within two years BT doubled in price to about £8 billion), the numbers had decreased to under 1.6 million owning only 12.6 per cent of the BT stock. The result of all the pressures bearing upon the process therefore produced an outcome substantially different from the original intention.

2 *Complexity*: Given the dense complexity of the process, it is small wonder that the public loses touch with all the various twists and turns through Parliament and the corridors of Whitehall. Nor is it surprising that many governments shrink from major initiatives when such mountains of vested interests have to be moved. Margaret Thatcher's governments were indeed unusual in taking so many major initiatives – trade union reform, abolishing the metropolitan counties, privatisation – and succeeding in pushing so many through.

3 *The limits of majority rule*: The case of BT illustrates that a large majority is no substitute for workable legislation. On occasions even opposition MPs have to be called upon to provide the necessary expertise.

4 *The opportunities for influence and consultation are considerable*: Throughout the legislative and bureaucratic processes there are extensive opportunities for individuals and pressure groups to intervene and make their point.

5 *The professionalism of civil servants*: Civil servants are often accused of being generalists – experts on nothing – but in the case of BT they mastered an immensely technical field with remarkable speed. There is no evidence either that they dragged their heels over the privatisation of BT or did anything other than loyally carry out the bidding of their political masters. The irony, however, is that the team which privatised BT dispersed soon afterwards, lured by private sector employers impressed with the relevant knowhow the privatisation process had bestowed upon them.

Note: Another excellent case study is available in *Pressure Groups* by David Simpson (1999, pp. 99–106) dealing with the provenance of legislation on Sunday shopping.

Chapter summary

Policy can be defined as either rules and regulations or public expenditure and its distribution. There are various theories about or models of policy making, including the pluralist corporatist ruling-class and Whitehall models plus the rational choice and incrementalist perspectives on decision making. Policy can be seen to pass through three stages: initiation, formulation and implementation. 'Core' decision makers have a constant control of the process but elements from the 'periphery' are brought in from time to time. The concept of policy networks is useful in analysing policy making. Extra-parliamentary parties and think-tanks can have considerable influence depending on the issue and the situation. Implementation can be very difficult and result in policy objectives being missed or even reversed. Policy makers face many restraints upon their actions, including timing, coordination and international events.

Discussion points

- Which model of policy making seems closest to reality?
- Should there be more popular control over policy making?
- How persuasive is Lindblom's theory of incrementalism?
- What lessons can be learnt from the process whereby BT was privatised?

Further reading

The field of policy studies has spawned a substantial literature over the past ten years or more. Burch and Wood (1990) and Ham and Hill (1993) are good introductions to the denser studies available. Hogwood and Gunn (1984) is a well-written and interesting study, as is Jordan and Richardson (1987). For an up-to-date and penetrating analysis see Smith (1993). Simpson provides good case studies as already mentioned.

References

Baggott, R. (1995) *Pressure Groups Today* (Manchester University Press).

Bulpitt, J. (1983) *Territory and Power in the United Kingdom* (Manchester University Press).

Burch, M. (1979) 'The policy making process', in B. Jones and D. Kavanagh (eds), *British Politics Today* (Manchester University Press).

Burch, M. and Wood, B. (1990) *Public Policy in Britain*, 2nd edn (Martin Robertson).

Franklin, B. (1998) *Tough on Soundbites, Tough on the Causes of Soundbites*, Catalyst paper 3 (Catalyst).

Ham, C. and Hill, M. (1993) *The Policy Process in the Modern Capitalist State* (Harvester Wheatsheaf).

Hogwood, B. and Gunn, L.A. (1984) *Policy Analysis in the Real World* (Oxford University Press).

Jones, B. (1986) *Is Democracy Working?* (Tyne Tees TV).

Jordan, G. and Richardson, J.J. (1982) 'The British policy style or the logic of negotiation', in J.J. Richardson (ed.), *Policy Styles in Western Europe* (Allen and Unwin).

Jordan, G. and Richardson, J.J. (1987) *Governing Under Pressure* (Martin Robertson).

Lee, G. (1989) 'Privatisation', in B. Jones (ed.), *Political Issues in Britain Today*, 3rd edn (Manchester University Press).

Lindblom, C.E. (1959) 'The science of muddling through', *Public Administration Review*, Vol. 19.

Platt, S. (1998) *Government by Task Force*, Catalyst paper 2 (Catalyst).

Schmitter, P.C. (1979) 'Still the Century of Corporatism', in Schmitter, P.C. and Lembruch, G. (eds), *Trends Towards Corporatist Intermediation* (Sage).

Simpson, D. (1999) *Pressure Groups* (Hodder and Stoughton).

Smith, M. (1993) *Pressure, Power and Policy* (Harvester Wheatsheaf).

Chapter 25

The politics of law and order

Bill Jones

Learning objectives

- To explain the connection between political ideas and the problem of law and order.
- To chart the extent of the problem and discuss the phenomenon of the 'crime wave' together with claims that it was reversed in the early 1990s.
- To consider the causes of crime.
- To examine responses to crime in the form of policing, penal policy, prisons and vigilantism.
- To explain and analyse the secret security services.

Introduction

This chapter examines a political issue which affects everyone: crime and punishment. Opinion surveys show that concern on this topic has been steadily rising throughout the 1980s and 1990s as crime figures have soared and in some cases even exceeded American levels. This chapter examines the subject within the context of political ideas; assesses the extent of the current problem; discusses some of the probable causes of crime; looks at the contentious issue of policing and concludes with a look at sentencing, prisons and crime prevention, including vigilantism.

Law, order and political ideas

Ever since humankind began to live together over 9,000 years ago the question of law and order has been of central concern. Solitary cave dwellers did not need a code of law but any group of humans living in a community did. Fundamental to such a code was property. From the earliest times this included food, clothes, homes and utensils, joined later of course, by money, once it became a medium of exchange. Also highly important was physical safety – one of the reasons, after all, why people lived together in the first place. The Babylonian king Hammurabi (d. 1750 BC) established a body of law famously based on the notion of retribution: 'an eye for an eye, a tooth for a tooth'; Islamic law tends to perpetuate such principles.

Legal systems in Western developed countries still seek to defend property and the person but an extremely large variety of considerations have been embodied in pursuit of that elusive concept, 'justice'. Political thinkers have also wrestled with these problems. Aristotle recognised the necessity of law and governments which apply it with wisdom and justice. In the wake of the English Civil War, the philosopher Thomas Hobbes (see Chapter 5) rested his whole justification for the state on its ability to provide physical protection for citizens. Without such protection, he argued, life would be a brutal process of destructive anarchy. Conservative philosophers have always stressed the need for such protection, arguing that humans are inherently weak and unable to resist the lure of evil without the deterrent of strict state-imposed sanctions. Conservative Party policy still reflects this powerful emphasis: 'The Conservative Party has always stood for the protection of the citizen and the defence of the rule of law' (1992 manifesto).

Another group of philosophers approach the problem from a different angle. They argue that people are naturally inclined to be law-abiding and co-operative. They only transgress, so the argument runs, when their social environment damages them and makes deviation both inevitable and understandable. Foremost amongst these thinkers was Karl Marx, who attributed most of what was wrong with society to the corrupting and debilitating effect of a vicious capitalist economic system.

A kind of continuum is therefore recognisable: pessimists who see criminals as victims as well as perpetrators and optimists who believe crime has roots in society which can be attacked and remedied by social action. In British politics the Tories have tended to occupy a position towards the pessimistic end of the spectrum and Labour the optimistic one.

In 1979 Margaret Thatcher made great play of how hers was the party of law and order. Studies have shown that this benefited her enormously in the election of that year. There is, moreover, reason to believe that most voters tend towards the pessimistic end of the spectrum and respond to tough remedies which harken back to Hammurabi if not the American Wild West. The Thatcherite analysis – still very influential in the Conservative Party – is that humans are basically weak and sinful creatures who need all the support of church, family, school and community to keep them on the straight and narrow. During the 1960s ('that third-rate decade', according to Norman Tebbit) Labour's over-liberal approach tipped the balance of socialisation towards an absence of individual responsibility: parents were encouraged to slough off their responsibility in favour of an insidiously vague concept of 'society' which took the blame for a whole portmanteau of things and destroyed the notion of 'personal accountability', that crucial binding quality in any functioning society. Consequently children grew up expecting and exercising free licence – 'doing their own thing' in the argot of the time – moving on to become juvenile offenders and then hardened criminals. *The Sunday Telegraph* neatly summarises the Thatcherite argument (15 August 1993):

> It is the very beliefs of those theorists [left-wing academics who maintain that crime is caused by social conditions] that are responsible for our present malaise. They preach, in a doctrine which first became prominent during the sixties but stretches back to Rousseau, that man is inherently good, and that he must cast off the chains of conventional behaviour and morality that enslave him.

Major's words on crime – 'we should understand a little less and condemn a little more' – came back to haunt him when Dame Shirley Porter, former head of Westminster Council, is found guilty of gerrymandering (12 May 1996)

The unlimited flow of immigrants, the argument continues, caused more tensions and contributed to crime, while the mob rule encouraged by militant trade union leaders further eroded belief in the rule of law.

Labour rejected this view of the world. Their Home Office spokesmen and -women preferred to concentrate on the roots of crime, which they believed lay in poor economic and social conditions. The first element of this is seen as the huge inequality between rich and poor which the free enterprise economic system invariably creates. Such social gulfs create anger and frustration: members of the favoured elite are able to progress smoothly through privileged education to highly paid and influential jobs. Meanwhile poor people face vastly inferior life chances and huge, often insurmountable, challenges if they wish to succeed. They are surrounded by images which equate personal value with certain symbols such as expensive cars and clothes: when they cannot acquire them legally it is a small step to break the law to redress the balance. So the system itself causes crime by encouraging people to want things which they have to steal to acquire. When they do not the result is often poverty and hopelessness: the breeding ground of crime for successive generations of people at the bottom of the pile. Left-wingers also point at how the law favours the rich and protects their property, imprisoning petty burglars and letting off city fraudsters with suspended sentences or fines.

Interestingly, the positions of both major parties began to converge in the early 1990s. The Tories had long insisted that social conditions were not connected with crime: how else did figures stay stable during the Depression years of the 1930s? However, the massive increase in crime during the 1980s and early 1990s and a series of studies by the Home Office (especially those of Simon Field, who plotted graphs of property crime and consumption in 1900–88, finding a close correlation between unemployment and theft) encouraged a change of heart. Eventually the government abandoned this untenable position: on 28 October 1992 Home Office minister Michael Jack accepted that recession had played its part in pushing up the crime figures, saying that downturns in the economy were traditionally accompanied by increases in crime.

For its part Labour responded to the spate of fearsome juvenile crime in 1993 – including the murder of Jamie Bulger by two young boys – by expressing a tougher line on sentencing and the treatment of young offenders. The two big parties, especially with Kenneth Clarke as Home Secretary and Tony Blair as Shadow Home Secretary ('tough on crime – tough on the causes of crime'), found a surprising amount upon which to agree.

As the 1997 election approached, both parties targeted crime as a campaign priority, adopting tough postures on handguns and combat knives in the autumn of 1996 for example. Indeed Michael Howard, the populist Conservative Home Secretary, sought to play to the right-wing gallery in his own party; what was more surprising was that his Labour shadow, Jack Straw, sought to match him and even exceed him in right-wing zeal, so sensitive had the opposition become to the need to attract floating votes, especially middle-class ones, in order to end eighteen years out of power.

BOX 25.1 MINI BIOGRAPHY

Michael Howard (1941–)
Former Conservative Home Secretary. Educated Cambridge. MP in 1983, minister of local government, Employment and Environment Secretary before Home Secretary 1993–7. Stood in leadership election in 1997 but, after being criticised in a Commons speech by former junior understudy, Anne Widdicombe, saw the man he asked to run as his deputy go on to win. Left the Shadow Cabinet in 1999.

BOX 25.2 MINI BIOGRAPHY

Jack Straw (1946–)
Home Secretary. Educated Leeds University and President National Union Students 1969–71. MP in 1979; shadowed Treasury, Environment and Education but swung the party to the right when Home Affairs spokesman. Continued tough approach when in office after 1997.

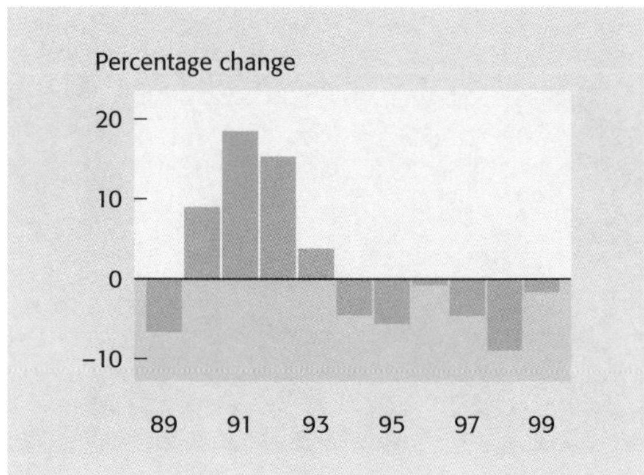

Figure 25.1 All notifiable offences
Source: The Guardian, 13 October 1999

The extent of the problem

The BBC *Panorama* programme on 2 August 1993 revealed how widespread the perception of crime is in the UK. In a study commissioned by the BBC, majorities were found who had been burgled in the previous year and who expected to be burgled again. Crime is ubiquitous and all-pervading. Many people can recall a different era when it was safe to leave a car unlocked for half an hour or more or to leave doors unlocked at night. Not now. In 1979 the number of **notifiable offences** was 2.5 million; by 1993 it had increased to 5.7 million, a 128 per cent increase in fourteen years. During the mid-1990s the figures began to fall (see Figure 25.1).

Table 25.1 Recorded crime (notifiable offences recorded by the police by offence)

Offence group	12 months ending March 1999 (old rules)	Change since March 1998 Number	Percent
Violence against the person	230,756	–25,314	–9.9
Sexual offences	34,915	+764	+2.2
Robbery	66,172	+3,520	+5.6
Total violent crime	331,843	–21,030	–6.0
Burglary	951,878	–36,554	–3.7
Total theft and handling stolen goods	2,126,718	–18,255	–0.9
(of which) Theft of and from vehicles	1,071,828	–24,194	–2.2
Fraud and forgery	173,728	+37,496	+27.5
Criminal damage	834,370	–27,476	–3.2
Total property crime	4,086,694	–44,789	–1.1
Drug offences	21,306	–2,030	–8.7
Other notifiable offences	41,974	+4,329	+11.5
Total all offences	4,481,817	–63,520	–1.4

Sources: The Guardian, 13 October 1999

According to the British Crime Survey (a survey of victims, not reported offences) 1992, 94 per cent of all notified crimes were against property while 5 per cent were crimes of violence (see Table 25.1).

Figures for 1998 exceeded 5 million but reflected a new way of recording crime which counted every crime suffered by a victim, e.g. a man stealing six cars is now recorded as six offences not one. In addition new categories of crime have been recorded including 'possession of drugs' (112,000) and 'common assault' (151,000) (see Figure 25.2).

However, using the 'old rules' the figures revealed the sixth successive annual fall. Encouraging was the reduction in violent crime, a category which previously had been increasing year on year (see Figure 25.3), burglary and theft from vehicles (see Figures 25.4 and 25.5).

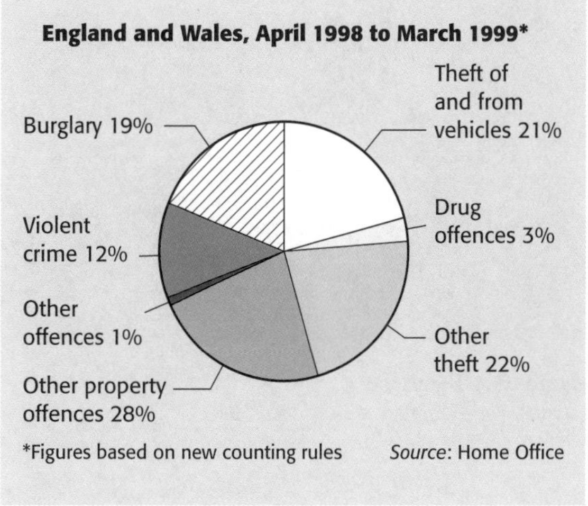

Figure 25.2 Offences recorded by the police
Source: The Times, 13 October 1999

A house in the UK is broken into once every thirty seconds so Tony Blair, in October 1999, could not be complacent. Noting the trend was down, 1.4 per cent – much less than the 8 per cent of the previous year, he admitted 'there is a huge amount of crime and we are all very well aware of that'. At the end of the 1970s the police cleared up 40 per cent of all crime; this rate has fallen to one-quarter. The annual percentage change grew rapidly during the early 1980s, then dipped reassuringly later in the decade, only to take off again in 1989–90. Even worse, the Home Office-sponsored British Crime Surveys in recent years suggest that nearly three times as many crimes are committed as are reported; up to half of all burglaries may not be reported, even more in the cases of vandalism and sex offences.

And residual complacency must have been removed by the report by Home Office criminologists in late November 1999. This predicted that increased consumer spending combined with the

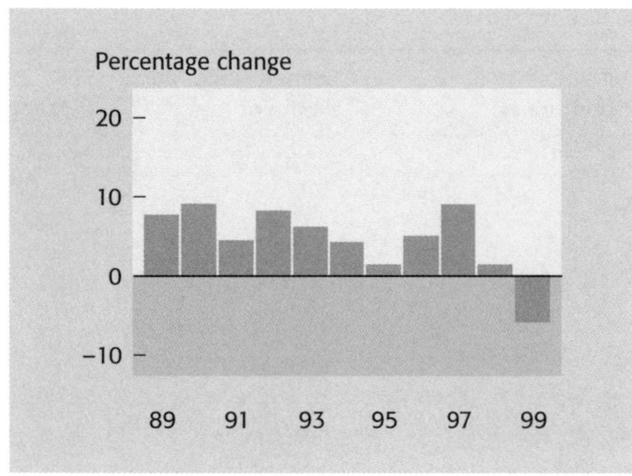

Figure 25.3 Violent crime
Source: The Guardian, 13 October 1999

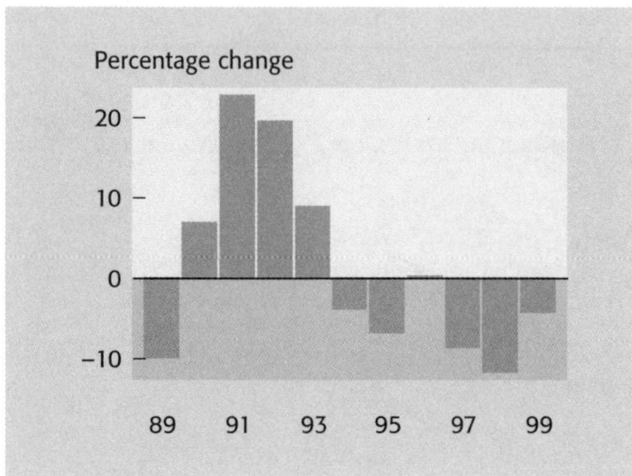

Figure 25.4 Burglary
Source: The Guardian, 13 October 1999

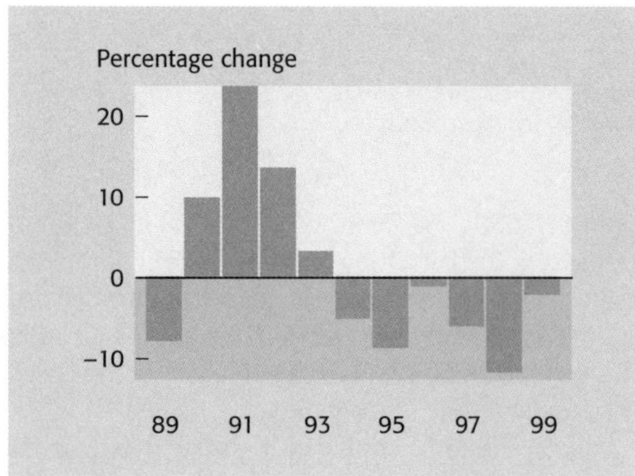

Figure 25.5 Theft of/from vehicles
Source: The Guardian, 13 October 1999

demographic factor of growing numbers of young men could cause increases in theft by up to 40 per cent and burglary by 25 per cent over the period 1997–2001. The only answer advised the criminologists was a co-ordinated campaign against crime. Jack Straw announced on 29 November the appointment of eight regional 'crime reduction directors'.

Conservative spokesmen used to minimise the rate of crime increase: they did not want voters to think there had been no return for all the money spent on law and order since 1979. The party's *Campaign Guide* in 1997 played the international comparison card:

> Since 1945 the general trend in crime in Western countries has been upward. However, in the years 1993–5, England and Wales . . . had the largest fall in recorded crime – 8% – of any of the 18 OECD countries . . . In Amsterdam there are . . . 84 murders per million people; in Stockholm 54 per million; in Berlin 39 per million. The homicide rate for London was 22 murders per million people in 1995.

The 1992 International Crime Survey for England and Wales revealed a lower rate of theft victims than Germany, Switzerland, Finland, the USA and Australia. Moreover, the same survey showed that in terms of violent assault the home figures were well below those of (surprisingly) The Netherlands, Germany, the USA and Australia. Some criminologists point out that the 'crime wave' is a statistical concept and like all statistics can be easily misunderstood:

1. It is not the volume but the proportion of certain crimes being reported which has increased in some cases. More people have reported burglaries because many more people now have property insurance as well as telephones.
2. The majority of crime is very trivial, perhaps involving no damage or derisory sums of a pound or two.
3. Britain used to be much more violent than it is today, as the work of E.G. Dunning (1987) from Leicester University has demonstrated. In thirteenth-century Britain, historians

estimate there were twenty murders committed for every 100,000 people: seventeen times today's rate.

4 The huge increase in police manpower since 1979 has boosted the ability of the police to record crimes which before might have been omitted.

5 The publicity given to crime figures can mask the fact that Britain is still a country where the chances of being mugged are slightly less than once every five centuries; or sustaining an injury from an assault once every century. In this respect Britain is much safer than Germany, the USA or Australia.

Conservative claims to have reversed the crime wave

Just when the Conservative government must have been despairing of what to do about crime, statistics in 1993–4 came to the rescue. They showed a drop of 5 per cent on the previous year and the 1994–5 figures showed a similar decline, though the 1995 figures registered only a 2.4 per cent fall. Michael Howard claimed jubilantly that his get-tough policies were finally winning through and the 1994 party conference – containing grey-haired old ladies who want to bring back the birch – applauded him to the echo. *The Economist* (23 September 1995), however, would not believe a word of it. The right-of-centre journal pointed out the following:

1 Unemployment had been falling and even official Home Office studies proved a causal connection between levels of unemployment and crime rates.

2 Most crimes are committed by young men aged between 15 and 24; between 1989 and 1993 their number declined from 4.5 million to 4 million.

3 Some police forces have been targeting groups of hardened criminals, e.g. the Met's pre-emptive Bumblebee and Eagle Eye Operations. It could be they have borne some fruit.

4 Better anti-theft devices on cars could also have had a slowing down effect on vehicle crime, which fell by 10 per cent between 1993 and 1994.

On 23 April 1997 *The Guardian*'s feature on crime reported:

> As the little publicised central finding of the BCS concluded, the reason for the fall is that police recording practices changed: a significantly smaller proportion of crimes reported to the police found their way into recorded police statistics in 1995 than in 1991.

The article concluded that this change was caused not by better policing but by the pressure put on the police to demonstate their effectiveness in politically significant statistical form. This did not stop Michael Howard triumphantly claiming a 10 per cent drop in crime since 1991 in a campaign statement on 21 April 1997. Not that his successor Jack Straw was in any way 'soft on crime' (reflecting his pre-election stance) during his tenure from 1997 onwards, refusing to consider legalisation of cannabis, even for medicinal use and accepting the use of private prisons as cost-effective.

The criminal mind

In the long term criminals adapt to the changing environment by concentrating on less detectable offences such as drug abuse and perhaps fraud. What we have to realise is that persistent criminals are entrepreneurial in character. Their antennae are constantly twitching to ensure they can operate in the most profitable manner.

Sir John Smith, Deputy Head of Metropolitan Police, 1995

Fear of crime

Considerable concern has been expressed over the fear of crime which so much lurid publicity engenders. Newspapers know that the public has

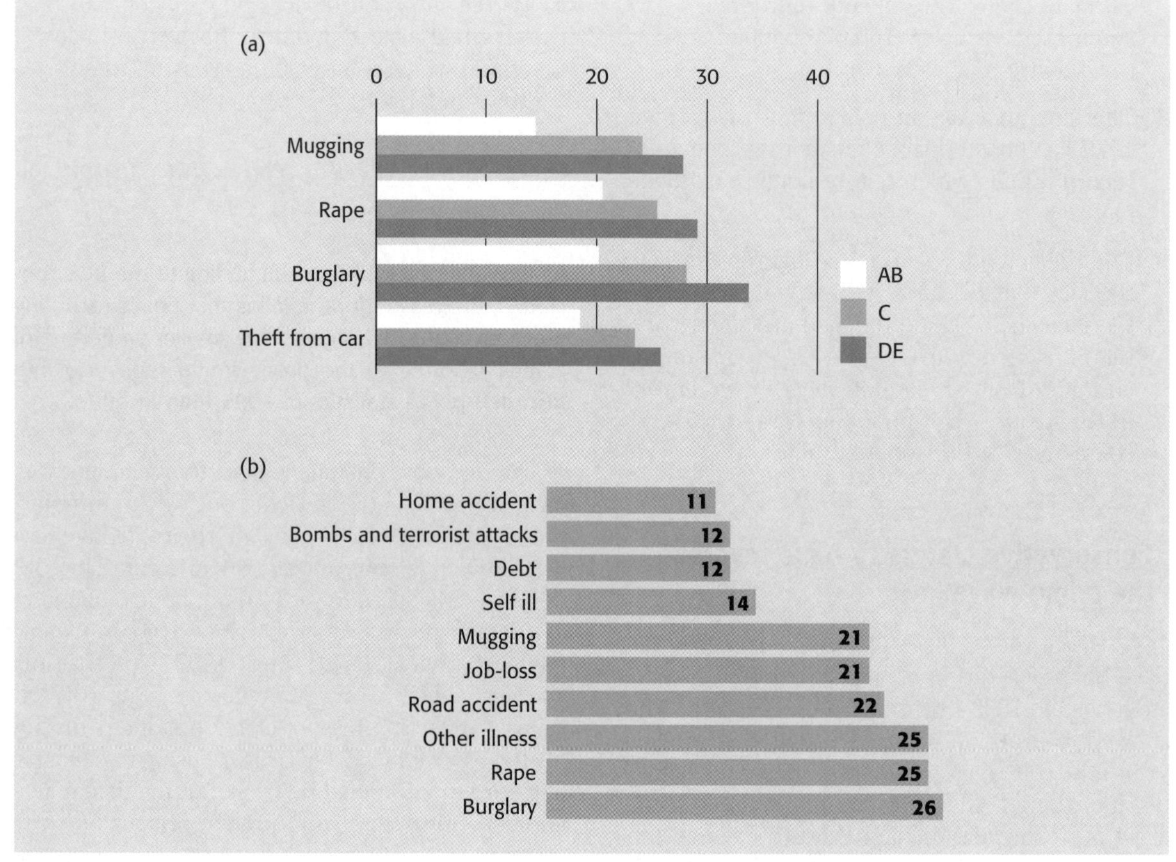

Figure 25.6 Fear of crime
(a) Percentage by social class of people who said they were 'very worried' about crime
(b) Context of crime and other fears: percentage of those 'very worried'
Source: British Crime Survey data in The Guardian, 11 January 1996

a morbid interest in crime stories and consequently feed it in order to sell copies. The result is that elderly ladies are terrified to go out even though they are the category least at risk from violent crime. Interviews with 10,000 women for the 1994 British Crime Survey revealed that one in five felt 'very unsafe' when walking out at night, even though fewer than seventy claimed to have been attacked in the past year (see Figure 25.6). Paradoxically, young males living in inner city areas are least afraid yet most likely to be the victims of crime. Indeed, the inner cities seem to be the breeding ground of a great deal of crime and their working-class denizens most likely to be the victims. Similarly, a professional person is 50 per cent less likely to be burgled than an unskilled worker.

The position of the inner cities as the 'headquarters of crime' has slipped, however. A report in *The Guardian* (12 December 1992) revealed that the biggest increases since 1979 occurred in the shires: 167 per cent in Gloucestershire; 166 per cent in Leicestershire; 160 per cent in Avon and Somerset; and 146 per cent in Norfolk. In fact more crime is now committed in rural areas (56 per cent) than in urban areas (44 per cent). Nevertheless, the inner areas of the cities are still the most prone to crime. The 1992 British Crime Survey revealed that the poorest council estates face a risk of burglary 2.8 times the average.

Patterns of offending

One longitudinal survey of all people born in 1953 revealed that by the age of thirty one in three men had been convicted of a crime; one in sixteen had been to prison; and, significantly, the 7 per cent who had been convicted six or more times accounted for two-thirds of all offences. The survey also showed violence was on the increase: one in eight men convicted of an offence had committed a crime of violence by the age of twenty. For those born in 1963 the proportion had risen to one in five. Certainly young criminals seem to abound. Most crimes are committed by people aged fourteen to twenty; over 90 per cent of all fifteen- to sixteen-year-old offenders re-offend within four years. On 20 November 1996 the Audit Commission reported on juvenile justice. Its document, *Misspent Youth*, revealed that the 150,000 teenage offenders commit some 7 million crimes every year, of which only 19 per cent are recorded by police and only 5 per cent cleared up with a mere 3 per cent resulting in arrest and action. Moreover, there is a demographic 'crime bomb' in the making as the population begins to bulge in the eighteen- to twenty-year-old age group, now the peak age of offending for young men.

Whatever the qualifications one has to apply to crime figures there is no doubt as to which way they are heading: constantly upwards. All the crime surveys show that the public is highly aware that crime is a ubiquitous threat. As Walter Ellis wrote in *The Sunday Telegraph* (4 July 1993):

> For the public ... crime has become a lottery, a prize draw in which the odds of becoming a victim are shortening every day. To those who have been burgled for the fourth time, or seen their car driven off by a 15-year-old, or been mugged for 50p outside a kebab house the ergonomics of policing are only of passing importance. Ordinary people want to feel safe in their own streets.

Causes of crime

Some of the causes of crime have already been touched on. Politicians, it has been shown, argue either that people have become, or have been allowed to become, less law-abiding, more 'evil' even, or that society has become a forcing ground of such deviancy. Inevitably causes are chosen to conform with political prejudices, but there are other possible causes.

The huge gap which exists between rich and poor

One view is that all forms of private property constitute a form of theft, that all property by rights belongs to everyone. According to this view, everyone who is rich has 'appropriated' their property from others, leading to the position espoused by the American radical Angela Davis: 'The real criminals in this society are not the people who populate the prisons across the state but those who have stolen the wealth of the world from the people'. A less articulate version of this justification was offered by a Liverpudlian youth in a *Weekend World* programme broadcast in December 1987: 'Some people have got jobs, they can go out and buy things they want. But we're on the dole, we haven't got the money so we go out robbing to get the money'. It remains a fact that the gap between rich and poor in Britain over the last fifteen years has grown faster than in any other developed Western country.

There are now so many more potential crimes

In the old days family arguments were ignored by police as 'domestics'. Since the law has changed, crimes of violence have registered an increase. Furthermore, the proliferation of consumer goods has increased the opportunity for crime: there are simply more things to steal, especially valuable portable objects.

Young people are faced with a difficult world in which to grow up

1 Many of them are increasingly the products of fragmented families and have lacked the emotional security of a proper home.

2 Long-term unemployment has replaced valuable socialisation with despair. As a consequence young people lose out, as American sociologist Charles Murray (1990) observes, on 'acquiring skills and the network of friends and experiences that enable them to establish a place for themselves – not only in the workplace but a vantage point from which they can make sense of themselves and their lives' (p. 25).

3 As a consequence of unemployment, youngsters find life infinitely grey and pointless. Crime can seem like the ultimate rebellion and excitement. John Purves, a solicitor who has defended many young joy-riders in the north-west and the north-east, explains that it 'provides an escape from their humdrum existences. They are thrilled by the speed of these flying machines and the more dangerous it gets the more excited they become. It's an addiction . . . The press call them "deathriders"; that's the real thrill' (*The Observer*, 25 June 1994).

Growth of an underclass

Charles Murray, quoted above, has written that he thinks the UK is well on the way to developing its own underclass of disaffected poor living in the inner cities, often in council housing and unemployed, eking out their lives on benefits and crime. Any youngster living in such an area finds it very difficult to resist the allure and rewards of crime and the attractions of drugs, easy living and violence.

Values have declined

This view is especially popular with Conservatives, who harken back to a golden age when it was possible to live without fear of crime. Geoff Pearson's book *Hooligan* disposes of this myth:

> Conservatives have enthused about this mythical law abiding society 20 years ago for decades. Twenty years ago, in fact, they were just as worried about crime and disorderly youth as they are now, panicked by hippies in the late sixties and early seventies, by Teds in the fifties and 'Americanised youth' in the forties.

Drugs and Crime

Much has been written about the complex connection between drugs and crime. Chris Nuttal, in charge of research at the Home Office, estimates that two-thirds of all property crime is drug related. On average a heroin addict has to raise £13,500 annually to support the habit; £8,000 more if crack cocaine is also involved. Most of this is raised via shoplifting and a series of drugs tests in different parts of the country have revealed over three-quarters of arrestees were under the influence of alcohol and two thirds other drugs.

Responses to crime

Policing

If, as Hobbes asserted, the prime purpose of government is the preservation of law and order, then the police, in modern society, are at the front line of enforcement: they implement the most important rationale of government.

The police occupy an ambivalent and politically sensitive role in society. According to classic democratic theory they are the neutral instruments of society, acting, as Sir Robert Mark (Commissioner of the Metropolitan Police in the 1970s) observed, 'not . . . at the behest of a minister or any political party, not even the party in government. We act on behalf of the people as a whole'.

However, the police command great power in society and there are plenty of examples of how they have become the creatures of a particular political ideology or the willing instruments of oppression: Nazi Germany, the USSR, Red China and many regimes in South America and elsewhere. In Britain, the police have traditionally been thought to be a source of national pride: the 'friendly bobby on his beat' being an international symbol of our social stability and consensual style. However, as crime figures rose in the 1970s and the right-wing policies of Thatcherism began to be implemented in the early 1980s, the police became a subject of intense political debate. The left accused Thatcher of using the police to suppress public reaction to her unpopular and socially divisive policies. The police were also seen as willing accomplices, weighed down with right-wing prejudices such as contempt for the poor, ethnic minorities and women, and riddled with corruption and criminal inefficiencies of the kind which caused miscarriages of justice such as the Guildford Four and the Birmingham Six.

Is there any proof of these left-wing allegations? A report by the Policy Studies Institute (PSI) in the late 1980s revealed widespread racist and sexist attitudes together with frequent drunkenness on duty. Reiner (1993) reports that one of his studies revealed that 80 per cent of officers questioned described themselves as Conservatives, with the remainder equally divided between Labour and Liberals (p. 123). He also cites substantial evidence from the UK and US supporting the contention that police routinely subscribe to racist views (pp. 125–8). However, these research findings should be qualified: British police seem no worse than similar forces in the USA and Canada; and the same PSI report revealed that the large majority of Londoners were satisfied with the service provided.

The right preferred to see the police as staunch defenders of society, beleaguered by attacks from the left and misguided 'do-gooders'. The eccentric chief constable of Greater Manchester, James Anderton, even believed at one time that the left planned to undermine the whole edifice of police neutrality in preparation for the totalitarian state they craved (Reiner, 1993). Throughout the 1980s debate over the police was highly polarised, particularly during the 1984–5 miners' strike when Labour accused the government of trying surreptitiously to establish a national police system antithetical to the notion of community service and accountability. Towards the end of the decade, however, the manifest failure of the police to stem the increase in crime led to a change of heart on the right. This was occasioned partly by the publicity given to miscarriages of justice and the spate of lawlessness typified by joy-riders operating with apparent impunity while the police seemed to stand idly by. All this helped create an unprecedented fall in public esteem for the apparatus of law enforcement. Writing in *The Sunday Times* (11 February 1989), journalist Simon Jenkins wrote:

> No area of public policy is in such dire need of reform as crime . . . Crime is the Passchendaele of Whitehall. The more money wasted on fighting it the more is demanded by the generals for 'just one more push'.

On 10 February 1989 *The Economist* quoted a disillusioned Tory MP who said: 'In my opinion the police need a jolly good kick up the backside. They get jolly well paid and they're not much good at catching criminals'.

On the value for money criterion so much beloved by the Conservatives, the police had indeed become an embarrassment. Between 1979 and 1993 spending on the police rose by 88 per cent (£5.4 billion per year) and police pay by 70 per cent in real terms (at 127,000, numbers had doubled since 1950). Yet crime figures had more than doubled and become a national obsession which no politician could ignore. In September 1993, even the chief of the new National Criminal Intelligence Service was moved to describe the entire criminal justice system as 'archaic and irrelevant'.

Figures support the latter contention: in the late 1970s the percentage of crimes cleared up was 40 per cent; by 1993 it had dropped to 25 per cent (though note the rates varied according to the crime). For their part the police complain that the demands upon them to be fair to the criminal and to defend civil liberties has placed an excessive burden upon their activities. They complain of a multitude of forms they have to fill in for any offence. On 22 September 1993, *The Guardian* reported a case in which paperwork weighed an astonishing 45 tons. The figures for 1992 reveal that indeed 16 per cent of their time is spent writing reports; 11 per cent on station duties; 5 per cent traffic incidents; 10 per cent each crime incidents and traffic control; 22 per cent preventive patrol; and 26 per cent other duties. In total 75 per cent of police time is spent on non-crime matters.

On 26 June 1993 *The Economist* ran a story that in many parts of London the police had simply 'given up', letting criminals off with a caution rather than face the excessive paperwork and the good chance the criminal will get off with a light sentence. Writing in *The Daily Telegraph* on 20 July 1993 Roger Graef observed: 'The net effect of victims not reporting crimes and police not recording or detecting them is that only two out of every hundred crimes are punished in court'. As if to compound these fears, an Audit Commission report leaked to *The Guardian* on 20 September 1993 recommended that police forces should prioritise responses to crime, concentrating on the important ones at the expense of the trivial, handing over the latter to uniformed officers while the CID addressed major crime and criminals.

Following the inner city riots in the early 1980s, the Scarman Report urged closer co-operation with local communities and more bobbies on the beat. Some of these recommendations were implemented and the spirit of Scarman permeated thinking on police policy in the 1980s. However, concern with management structures and value for money led to the production of an even more contentious report in 1993, produced by Sir Patrick Sheehy, a businessman.

The Sheehy Report pointed to a 'top-heavy' rank structure with overlapping responsibilities and 'inefficient' management systems plus a promotion system based on service rather than merit. Recommendations included the abolition of three senior ranks, including senior inspector, senior superintendent and deputy chief constable; the scrapping of linked pay award increases; fixed-term (possibly ten-year) contracts – police officers currently have jobs for life; performance-related pay and less generous sick pay arrangements.

The Police Federation was incensed, described the proposals as 'outrageous' and even organised a massive demonstration in July 1993 involving 15,000 officers. It took out an advert featuring former Labour Prime Minister Lord Callaghan (who used to represent the Federation when a backbench MP) which stated:

> The Sheehy Report is a series of dogmatic conclusions backed by very little argument and based on inaccurate analysis of the problem. [It] will command no respect either in the Police Service or among the public, and is ruled out as a serious document.

In the light of such criticism, Michael Howard, the Home Secretary, agreed late in 1993 to discount some of the most contentious Sheehy proposals.

Penal policy

Speaking in 1985 Margaret Thatcher told the American Bar Association of the fear of ordinary people that 'too many sentences do not fit the crime'. Given the provenance of her own ideas (see above), it is hardly surprising that she thought sentences should be higher, and indeed between 1984 and 1987 sentences for serious crimes such as armed robbery and rape increased markedly (see Table 25.2).

However, despite the invariable rhetoric of Conservative candidates during elections and the well-publicised views of Margaret Thatcher, the death penalty for murder was not re-introduced under the Tories despite several attempts by diehard 'hangers'. On 8 June 1988 the vote went 341 votes (in the traditional free vote on this issue) to 218. The truth seems to be that however hard candidates try to milk the two-thirds majority of the public in favour of the death penalty, when they hear the arguments and statistics coolly explained in parliamentary debates they surrender to reason and vote to sustain abolition. The facts show that, at fewer than 700 a year, Britain has a relatively small number of murders (the USA has over 20,000); there is no evidence to suggest that murders have increased since abolition; re-introduction would impose immense burdens on judges and juries; affairs such as the Guildford Four

Table 25.2 Crown court sentences (average: adult male)

	1984	1987	% increase
Using firearms to resist arrest	3.4	6.7	97
Rape	3.8	6.2	63
Robbery with firearms[a]	5.7	7.0	23
Robbery without firearms	3.1	3.8	23
Indecent assault on a female	2.0	2.3	15
Manslaughter	4.9	5.5	12

[a] Offenders charged with firearm offences at same court appearance

and the Birmingham Six show how easy it is for innocent people to be found guilty of murder, and when they have been executed it is too late to make amends.

Prisons

Since the Strangeways prison riots in 1990, prisons have been at the centre of an intense debate. Denying a malefactor his/her freedom has been a traditional form of punishment ever since law and order was invented. In the early days conditions in prisons were horrendous, with no sanitation and appalling food. Since then conditions have improved immensely but denial of freedom is still a very punitive measure. Some experts argue persuasively that prison is counterproductive. They argue that prison is merely a place where new crimes are learnt and planned and young petty offenders turned into serious criminals – 'the universities of crime' (see Box 25.1). It is sadly true that 60 per cent of prisoners re-offend within two years. These experts also point out that only a small percentage of those locked up – perhaps 10 per cent – are serious offenders: the majority are there on minor offences against property.

The notion of rehabilitation is sometimes overlooked when we discuss prisons. Punishment is seen as the chief rationale – and we punish more extensively by custodial sentences than any other country in Europe: only South Africa and the USA imprison more. The Prison service costs £2 billion a year to run. It costs £600 per week to keep someone in Prison, much more, in many cases, than has been stolen in the first place.

During the 1980s, it became apparent that our prisons were grossly overcrowded: in one case, a maximum prison capacity of 40,000 prisoners was being forced to accommodate, in the mid-1980s, 55,729, many squeezed two or three to a cell and without any proper sanitation. Even the Conservative Home Secretary in the 1980s, William Whitelaw, was moved to describe our prisons as 'an affront to civilised society'. The Strangeways riots, and related riots in other prisons, were to some extent an explosion of pent-up frustration at poor conditions and official indifference. In response came the impressive Woolf Report (600 pages, 204 recommendations) urging a fundamental reform of prison regimes to ensure that they prepared inmates for release by treating them with dignity and respect. The report was endorsed by all three parties in the 1992 general election but has yet to be implemented.

Towards the end of the 1980s the prison population began to decline (45,693 in 1989) as more non-custodial sentences such as community service orders were passed, but this did not mean that all was well. A report by Judge Stephen Tumin, the Chief Inspector of Prisons, discovered that in some prisons inmates had to wait ten days for a shower and even longer for clean underwear. Post-Strangeways changes, moreover, did not stop another serious riot breaking out in September 1993 in Wymott prison, Lancashire. Here prisoners ran amok causing £20 million worth of damage to a prison which had been held up as a model regime. Judge Tumin was appointed to investigate, the irony being that in 1991 Tumin had already reported on Wymott discerning widespread drug taking and the permeation of 'a gangland culture'.

The Labour opposition and the Prison Officers' Association heavily criticised the Conservative government and Michael Howard, the then Home Secretary, for concentrating all his efforts not on solving present problems but seeking to privatise as many prisons as he could in order, according to his critics, to satisfy the right wing of his own party. Certainly, he marked a shift towards a more punitive philosophy, urging less recreation and more sewing of mailbags, arguing that 'prisoners enjoy a standard of comfort which taxpayers would find hard to understand'.

In September 1993, a new programme of prison privatisation was announced: twelve contracts to be awarded for new prisons within two years. Howard declared the aim was to 'create a private sector able to secure continuing and lasting improvements in standards, quality and cost efficiency across the whole of the prison system'. Despite encouraging experience of private prisons in the USA (see Windlesham, 1993, pp. 280–6), experience in the UK had been mixed. The success of the in-house bid by Strangeways staff was hailed by the government. But the privately run Wolds prison had been criticised in April 1992 by the Prison Reform Trust for creating a life for

BOX 25.1 **EXAMPLE**

Approved training to become a criminal

When Denis was 12, the police found him sitting in a parked stolen car: 'I hadn't nicked it, I had no idea how to drive.' He was sent to an approved school near Dundee, 'a big house which had been converted'. Some of the children were not offenders at all, but the victims of abuse: the youngest, who lived in their own cottage, were only five.

'More often than not, we were left to ourselves in the dorms', Denis said. 'There was no counselling, no one talk to about my experiences, what I had witnessed. Yes we had our activities but there was no love there, no emotional growth. It was an institution, my first prison.'

The fourteen months Denis spent at approved school laid the foundations for what was to follow. He said: 'I learnt everything about crime there. I did my first burglary one night when I ran away. I learnt how to drive, how to steal a car; how to fight and how to lie and get away with it. It made me what I am, it was where the criminal subculture started'.

After leaving, he went on the run, living rough in squats, before eventually rejoining his mother at her new home near Manchester. 'By then the die was cast. I was a criminal.'

At the age of fifteen, Denis was arrested for stealing a car, he was sent to DC, a detention centre in Nottinghamshire. It was the 'short, sharp shock'. 'They turned us into little tough guys', he said. 'There was circuit training every day, and a lot of physical abuse from the staff. And again, you met all the lads, who'd been to approved school, through the courts system, who were already dreaming of a career in the big time.'

'And the more they tell you you're bad, you're a criminal, the more you accept it and get on with it. At DC, kids were already seeing themselves as gangsters. That's where you made your connections, and found out what families from what areas are into what type of crime, and how to sell your goods.'

'Afterwards, it was like the Vietnam syndrome: you're only drawn to those who've suffered the same trauma, the same experience. So your only pals are the people you met in DC.'

Two months after leaving, aged just fifteen, Denis was in Strangeways for the first time, waiting to be sent for fifteen months to a borstal, convicted of burglary, criminal damage and car theft. 'It was more of the same. You met the lads you'd met in DC, all the same faces.' At 17, after further burglaries, he was back in Strangeways, this time for a year.

Then, for a while, the pattern seemed broken. Denis married and worked as a welder. But it was not easy to build a settled life. 'You were always involved in a bit of "dodge" because you always got phone calls from your pals. The underworld is always there, still thriving.'

He lost one job when a colleague told management he had been to prison. Then his marriage broke up, precipitating a period of drug abuse, and armed robbery seemed like 'a natural progression, the pinnacle of my career'.

Prison education saved him: 'It was a route into myself, I discovered my mind and another world. Up to that point I'd been told by my mother, by the courts, by prison, that I was mad, bad'.

Now preparing to begin a law degree at Bristol University, he has a stark message for Mr Major and Mr Clarke [the then PM and Home Secretary respectively]. 'They frighten me to death, because they don't have a clue what they are doing. They need to break the circle, stop the abuse. The prisons are where Great Britain hides from its inner self. They are full of the educational system's mistakes, the mental hospitals' mistakes, the courts' mistakes. That's why I want to practise law.'

Source: The Observer, 28 February 1993

Tory Home Secretary Michael Howard sidesteps his responsibilities, as the head of the Prison Service resigns (22 November 1995)

inmates which was 'boring and aimless with evidence of widespread violence and drug abuse'. The contracting out of court escort services to Group 4 Security (a director of which embarrassingly turned out to be Sir Norman Fowler, then Chairman of the Conservative Party) became a laughing stock in 1993 when a succession of prisoners escaped. However, despite criticising privatised prisons fiercely in opposition Labour accepted them as fait accompli once in power and as a cost effective solution.

The Conservatives were not consistent on prison policy in the 1980s. In the early part of the decade they pandered to their activists by being tough and the prisons filled up; towards the end of the decade they supported non-custodial sentences, but as crime grew relentlessly the gut instinct to get tough again could not be resisted and Michael Howard adopted his 'prison works' approach (see Box 25.2). His policy was much criticised by prison reform groups (but not by police organisations) as likely to increase prison populations by 15,000 new inmates and cost up to £700,000. In April 1996 the population stood at 54,974, rising to well over 65,000 by 2000.

Alternatives to prison are often mooted but community service orders are often seen by the public as being too mild a corrective for violent young offenders. Indeed it is young offenders who pose the most intractable problem. It often seems that the problem begins with broken homes, leading to institutionalised children who grow up without any real affection. This often leads to misbehaviour in school with truanting and then petty crime. Once on the elevator of crime and detention centre the child is lost to the alternative values of the criminal world where all means to better oneself are acceptable as long as one

BOX 25.2 **IDEAS AND PERSPECTIVES** 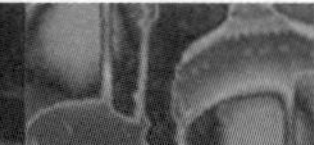

Howard's measures to curb crime

At the 1993 Conservative Party conference in Blackpool, Home Secretary Michael Howard unveiled 'the most comprehensive programme of action against crime' announced in Britain, including abolition of the right to silence for defendants; new measures against terrorism; tougher penalties for persistent young offenders; building six new prisons; new powers to evict squatters and for police to stop trespassers; automatic custody for anyone convicted of rape, manslaughter or murder or attempting the offence who is subsequently accused of any of these crimes; a review to toughen sentences in the community; accepting all sixteen proposals of review on cutting paperwork to let police do more active duties.

Howard told the conference:

> There is a tidal wave of concern about crime in this country. I am not going to ignore it. I am going to take action. Tough action.

The reaction to Howard's line was not, however, as warm outside the conference chamber as it was within. Lord Justice Woolf threw in a firecracker when he said publicly that these 'get tough' policies would not work and were 'short-sighted and irresponsible'. On 17 October 1993 *The Observer* led with the views of no fewer than seven judges, all of whom attacked the idea asserted by Howard that 'prison works' through taking criminals off the street and providing a deterrent to others.

Lord Ackner said the causes of crime 'lay deep in society, in the deterioration of personal standards, the family and the lack of self-discipline'. Lord Justice Farquharson, chairman of the Judicial Studies Board, said:

> I cannot understand why the population of people in prison in this country is greater than in others. I think that's wrong . . . My general philosophy is that you should never impose a prison sentence when you can avoid it. The idea that we are building more and more prisons appals me. I have never believed prison rehabilitates anyone.

Lord Bruce Laughland was even more explicit:

> The effectiveness of the deterrent diminishes the more an individual goes to prison. People fear hearing the gates shut behind them for the first time. Prison may satisfy public opinion and the victims' understandable feelings, but it has no rehabilitation effect whatsoever . . . a great deal of dishonesty is contributed by politicians.

A report by Sir David Ramsbotham, Chief Inspector of Prisons, recorded that at one major London nick probation officers had been cut from fourteen to three and the education programme by 55 per cent. *The Economist* noted that Howard might check the fact that 'There are more than 500 pieces of research or international research on prison regimes. Most of them agree that regimes with more education and more rehabilitation work, produce prisoners less likely to reoffend'.

Finally a Home Office report in July 1998 estimated that it would need a 25 per cent increase in the prison population to achieve a 1 per cent decrease in the crime rate.

is not caught. The Audit Commission's report, cited above, judges that money spent on sending second- and third-time offenders through an extended and ineffective court system could be better spent on tackling the problem at an earlier stage before the cycle of decline has set in. Alternative schemes available include the following:

1. *Caution Plus*: The favoured approach of Northamptonshire diversion unit. The offender is cautioned and agrees to pay compensation to the victim, who has to be met face to face. An 'action plan' is drawn up to prevent further offending. Average cost £640 per case, one-quarter of the present system. Only 35 per cent re-offend after eighteen months.
2. *The Halt Programme*: A Netherlands scheme whereby under-eighteens can be referred to one of seventy available schemes if they admit guilt and have not been on such a scheme more than twice. Compensation has to be paid and a degree of 'shaming' takes place in which offenders are seen publicly to make amends, for example shoplifting girls had to clean the floors of the supermarket they had stolen from. The scheme claims a 40 per cent re-offending rate compared with 80 per cent of those prosecuted.
3. *New Zealand family group conferences*: Based on a Maori method of settling disputes whereby instead of a court case, the extended family is convened to discuss the offender's actions; reparation and preventive measures are agreed. Fifty per cent of victims say they are satisfied with the outcome.
4. *Identity chips*: At a Downing Street seminar on crime, 12 October 1999, chief constables told Mr Blair of a scheme to add indentity chips to all new electrical goods so that ownership could be traced.
5. *Head Start*: This was the scheme introduced in the 1960s in the USA whereby some 700,000 children in high crime areas were given two years of nursery education. Studies of the thirty-year period have revealed much higher levels of education and college attendance; lower crime rates; more employment, home ownership and stable marriages. Accordingly the Home Office aimed to spend £200 million on intensive nursery education in UK high crime areas.
6. *Abortion*: A report in *The Guardian*, 10 August 1999, on a Chicago University study suggested that half of the dramatic drop in crime rate in the USA was the result of abortion amongst key groups of women: those separated or unmarried; those who are poor or from ethnic minorities. Studies reveal that, where such groups had a high rate of abortion, crime dropped off notably in later years. No one suggested that abortion should be adopted as an official anti-crime policy but the study does suggest how crime is concentrated in certain areas and in certain social groups.
7. *Reducing Offending: Home Office Report July 1998*: This major report ruled out as effective preventive measures such popular solutions as more police patrols; zero tolerance; and merely increasing police numbers. It focussed on the utility of targeting repeat offenders; directing patrols to 'hot spot' areas; and identifying patterns of crime.

Crime prevention and the vigilante movement

Many experts argue that spending money on preventing crime is more cost-effective than trying to cope with it once it has occurred. Often proposals centre on alerting the community to be more vigilant. Neighbourhood watch areas are now a common feature, numbering over 40,000 nationwide. Some studies, however, suggest such schemes merely squeeze crime out of the suburbs and back on to the street. Neighbours have also become a little inured to alarms sounding: to some extent they have become merely another ubiquitous urban noise.

In 1993, the Holme Wood estate in Bradford was assigned a special team to look after its interests:

the result was a 61 per cent decrease in burglaries. Much more widespread, however, seems to be a growing reliance on 'do it yourself' policing or to use its popular name, vigilantism. This issue came dramatically to public attention in 1993. On 10 August the press reported the case of Alan Hocking, who kidnapped eighteen-year-old Michael Roberts, whom he suspected of selling LSD to thirteen year olds, and drove him on a nightmare thirty-minute journey before attacking him with a wooden club spiked with nails. Duncan Bond and Mark Chapman were given a five-year sentence for kidnapping a well-known local thief in order to teach him a lesson. The huge public response to the sentence helped reduce it on appeal to six months. Public outrage did little, however, in the case of Robert Osborne, a Streatham music teacher and father of two who picked up a wooden mallet and pursued a local ne'er-do-well called Joseph Elliot who he had good reason to believe had been slashing tyres. Once the law-abiding Osborne cornered his quarry he was fatally stabbed in the chest; when the case came to court the jury believed Elliot's story that he had acted in self-defence and he was acquitted.

The fear of legal reprisals has not deterred other groups of residents from making their own arrangements when they feel the police have let them down. In St Anne's, a Bristol suburb, a shopkeeper, Norman Guyatt, was so appalled by a brutal daylight robbery of an old couple that he and his two sons and a few others started patrolling the streets in the small hours to detect and report possible burglaries. A sports groundsman, Stan Claridge, now leads the fight against crime in the same area organising patrols and setting up video cameras in key areas. A local security firm, Knighthawk Security, regularly patrols the streets, being paid a pound a week by each resident. A similar force patrols Sneyd Park in Bristol and in Merseyside and other urban areas. As a result crime has dropped in such areas by as much as three-quarters.

Certainly there are dangers that vigilantes can dispense arbitrary justice to the wrong people, but the press and public reactions have been largely in favour of self-help so far. Even the police, wary of a movement which is by definition a criticism of their ineffectiveness, have given occasional guarded welcomes to such initiatives, although the Police Federation officially regards private guards as potentially dangerous. In Sedgefield, County Durham, the local council has reacted to local crime by setting up its own thirty-strong community force to patrol the streets. The Home Office has responded by exhuming and re-encouraging 'special constables'.

It seems obvious that Michael Howard was determined to be seen by the Conservative Party faithful as a vigilant defender of traditional party values. Every Home Secretary soon discovers, however, there are no easy answers to law and order problems. The rank and file thirst for tougher sentences and more police on the streets but hard experience often refutes these cherished certainties. It is the Conservative Party conference which annually provides the knee-jerk stimulus to any Home Office minister threatening to go 'soft' on crime. As a result, judges, police and the prison service have been able to ask for what they want and stand a good chance of getting it: in the words of Simon Jenkins (*The Times*, 3 February 1993) they operate a 'union stranglehold on ministers more intense and more costly than anything the TUC attempted in the Wilson/Callaghan years'. But this was before the Runciman Report proposed sweeping changes in the judiciary, the Sheehy Report threatened to shake up the police and the proposed privatisation of prisons threatened to reorganise the whole service.

The security services

As well as the law enforcement agencies of the courts, supported by the police, there are the security services, much loved by novelists and screenwriters as sources for their plotlines. People who have worked for these services usually puncture the popular illusion of mystery, excitement and glamour, by claiming such work is mostly routine and often very boring. Most of us, perhaps, would be surprised that defending the state against enemies within or without is not inherently exciting. There are four main elements to the security services.

MI5

The existence of MI5 is well known but until recently most of its activities were shrouded in secrecy. The most we knew officially was that it was set up in 1909 to counter the activity of German spies in the run-up to the First World War. We now know, since 1993, that it employs 2,000 personnel and has a budget of over £150mn per year, most of which is spent on counter-terrorism and the bulk of the rest on counter-espionage. After the end of the Cold War it was perhaps a little short of things to do and in 1992 it was tasked with gathering intelligence about the IRA. In 1996 it was given the further responsibility of helping to counter 'serious crime'. For most citizens the closest they are likely to get to the agency is if they are vetted for a sensitive post in government. Physically, however, they can now easily see from where where this very secret work is controlled: from its headquarters on the banks of the Thames not far from the Houses of Parliament. Political control falls to the Home Secretary.

Special Branch

This is a branch of the police force, ultimately under the Home Secretary, tasked with combating terrorism, espionage, sabotage and subversion. In addition it provides security for important people, watches the ports and airports and makes arrests for MI5. Like MI5 it employs some 2,000 personnel but at £20mn p.a. spends much less.

MI6

MI6 deals with political and economic intelligence abroad. It works mostly through agents attached to British embassies overseas, although it maintains close liaison with the Defence Intelligence Service. It comes under the authority of the Foreign Secretary. From 1994 it has added serious crime to its portfolio of responsibilities including money laundering and drug smuggling as well as illegal immigration.

Government Communications Headquarters (GCHQ)

This 'listening post' organisation originated from the famously successful code breaking service based in Bletchley during the war. It operates under a treaty signed with the USA in 1947 and seeks to monitor international radio communications utilising communication satellites and listening posts worldwide. Its base in the UK is in Cheltenham and it has over 6,000 employees with an annual budget of £500mn. In 1984 the Thatcher government banned membership of trade unions – allegedly at US request – on security grounds; trade union rights were restored by Labour in 1997.

The security services are not accountable to Parliament; the Prime Minister is ultimately responsible for their actions and the respective heads of the services report directly to him. The PM also chairs the Cabinet Committee on the Security and Intelligence Services. One of the six secretariats in the Cabinet Office is concerned with security and intelligence and serves to coordinate relevant information for feeding into Cabinet. This secretariat contains the Coordinator of Intelligence and Security who is another official in this important area who reports directly to the PM. The Joint Intelligence Committee comprises (amongst others) the secret service heads; it supplies the Cabinet with security information. The security services do not come under the jurisdiction of any complaints procedure and they do not need to inform the police of their operations. When security service personnel have had to give evidence in court they have done so with their identities concealed. Critics point out that those tasked with controlling these services have little time to do so and in practice know very little of what goes on. The Security Commission was established in 1964 and investigates security lapses and shortcomings.

The Home Affairs Select Committee in 1993 asked for the right to investigate the activities of the security services in order to guard against abuses of power.

The government went some of the way towards meeting its critics in 1994 when it set up, via the Intelligence Services Act, the Intelligence and Security Committee. This comprises nine members drawn from both houses of Parliament and is charged with scrutiny of the expenditure, administration and policy of MI5, MI6 and GCHQ. It meets weekly and occasionally issues critical reports like the one (1995) in which the service heads were criticised for not being aware of the adverse effects of the spying activities of CIA agent Aldrich Ames. Critics argue the new committee has too few powers to be effective: it cannot call witnesses or relevant papers and is able only to investigate that which the security service heads allow.

Chapter summary

Conservative thinkers have tended to base their law and order policies on a pessimistic view of human nature whilst Labour has tended to be more optimistic. However, both views began to converge in the late 1980s and early 1990s. Crime figures suggest a crime wave but there are many qualifications to bear in mind. It is doubtful whether the Conservatives substantially reversed the crime wave in the early 1990s. It seems likely that crime breeds in poor,

BOX 25.3 **IDEAS AND PERSPECTIVES**

Queen's Speech gives big emphasis to law and order

The Queen's Speech on 17 November 1999 allocated much time for nine bills to reform the law and introduce anti-crime initiatives.

- Jury trials for cases which currently can be heard at either magistrates' or the crown court will be limited through a measure giving magistrates the right to decide where a defendant will be tried for a range of offences including theft, shoplifting, burglary and common assault. Civil liberties groups have condemned these proposals but Home Secretary Straw argues the present system enables defendants to string out proceedings until the last minute when they withdraw their decision to be heard by a jury. About 18,000 defendants will be affected by this measure.
- A sexual offences bill will lower the age of consent for homosexuals from eighteen to sixteen and a person under that age will no longer be committing an offence if they have sex with someone over eighteen. However, it will be an offence for anyone over eighteen in a position of authority – such as a teacher or social worker – to have sex with someone under eighteen.
- It will be an offence for a public authority, including the police, to discriminate racially in the conduct of its functions. Chief Constables will be 'vicariously' liable for acts of racial discrimination performed by officers under them.
- Mandatory drugs testing for arrestees is planned, thought to involve potentially half a million people. This measure has also attracted criticism from civil liberties groups and in the face of it Mr Straw softened his proposals to make this merely a power the police can use if they think it necessary.
- The security services will gain the right to target people suspected of terrorism or serious crime. This will include groups such as animal rights activists as well as foreign based groups operating from this country.
- Freedom of information access will be given for all government information, but campaigners have bitterly opposed the ban on large categories of information such as policy-making advice, defence, international relations and commercially secret matters.

run-down areas of big cities. Police attempts to control crime have not been very successful and they have received much criticism even from the Conservatives. Tougher prison sentences are favoured by the Conservatives but experience suggests this is no real answer. Vigilante groups have set up in some parts of the country to take the law into their own hands.

Discussion points

- Which analysis of human nature seems closest to the truth, the pessimistic or optimistic version?
- How reliable are crime figures?
- Would more widely spread prosperity solve the crime problem?
- Is vigilantism justified?
- Should abortion within high crime areas be encouraged?

Further reading

A slightly longer analysis than the above can be found in Jones (1999). A good discussion of the causes of crime can be found in Lea and Young (1984). The best book on the police is by Robert Reiner (1993). On race riots, Michael Keith (1993) is worth a read; and on penal policy, Windlesham (1993) is authoritative and interesting. *The Economist*'s reports on crime are always well informed and well written, as are those of the quality press whenever crime moves to the top of the political agenda.

References

Dunning, E.G., Gaskell, G. and Benewick, R. (eds) (1987) *The Crowd in Modern Britain* (Sage).

Jones, B. (1999) 'Crime and punishment', in B. Jones (ed.), *Political Issues in Britain Today* (Manchester University Press).

Keith, M. (1993) *Race Riots and Policing* (UCL Press).

Lea, J. and Young, J. (1984) *What is to be Done About Law and Order?* (Penguin).

Murray, C. (1990) *The Emerging British Underclass* (IEA Health and Welfare Unit).

Reiner, R. (1993) *The Politics of the Police*, 2nd edn (Harvester Wheatsheaf).

Windlesham, Lord (1993) *Responses to Crime*, Vol. 2 (Clarendon Press).

Chapter 26

Social policy

Michael Moran

Learning objectives

- To define the nature of social policy.
- To identify the main trends in social commitments undertaken by the state in Britain.
- To examine the main issues and debates within the political system produced by those commitments.

Introduction

Social policy is central to British politics. Guaranteeing **entitlements** to various social services has become a major responsibility of British governments, but the exact range of those guarantees and how they are to be delivered is a source of political debate. Social policy is also of major importance in the distribution of resources in the community. A market economy like that in Britain is known to have great benefits, especially in widening individual choice and producing economic efficiency. It is also recognised to be a source of inequality, often substantial economic inequality. One of the important historical functions of social policy has been to use the power of government to moderate the inequalities produced by the market. If an active social policy of this kind can be combined with a market economy the benefits for society are tremendous – for success would mean that we could have all the great benefits of markets without some of the accompanying drawbacks. And that function helps us to pose a central question addressed in this chapter: how successful has social policy been in moderating the inequalities produced by the workings of the market?

The nature of social policy

The idea of social policy is linked closely to the existence of the **welfare state**. The United Kingdom is a 'welfare state'. In other words, a large part of the responsibility of government has to do with paying for, and in some cases directly providing, welfare services for the population. Many of the welfare policies initiated in Britain made the country an international pioneer: for instance, the foundation of the National Health Service in 1948 established a system of largely free health care for everybody paid for mainly out of taxation.

There are two striking features of welfare policy in the United Kingdom. The first is that throughout the present century there has been a long-term growth in the volume of resources spent on welfare. The long-term nature of this trend is illustrated in Figure 26.1; it shows that over the last fifty years in particular the upward pressure has been almost continuous. The second feature is summarised in Figure 26.2, which compares the level of spending on a broad measure of welfare spending in twelve members of the European Union. The figure shows that, despite the long historical growth, welfare spending in the United Kingdom is comparatively low, set against the record of other members of the European Union.

Although the welfare state is commonly spoken of as 'providing services', the reality is that the phrase refers to a wide range of institutions and practices. In the United Kingdom the most important role of the state lies in raising the resources to pay for welfare. It does this in two rather different ways. First, the direct cost of providing some important services – of which health care is

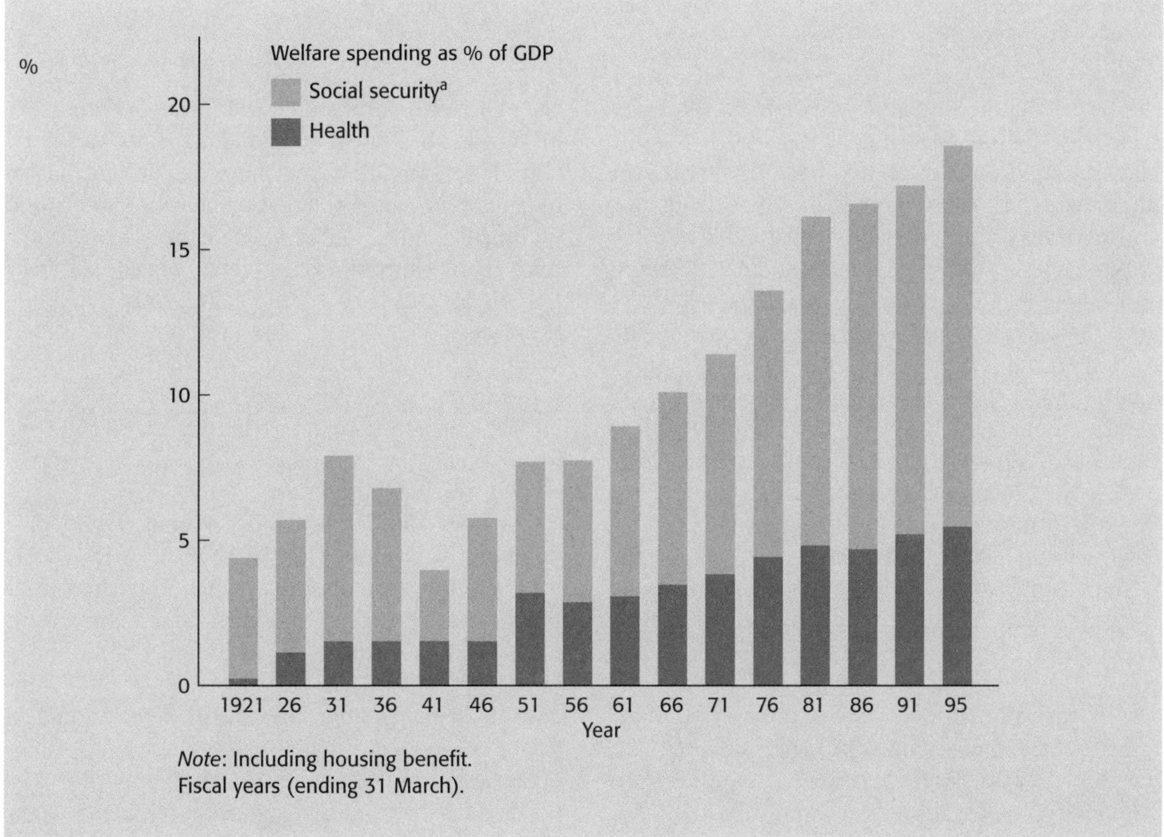

Figure 26.1 Changes in welfare spending, 1921–95
Source: The Economist, 27 April 1996

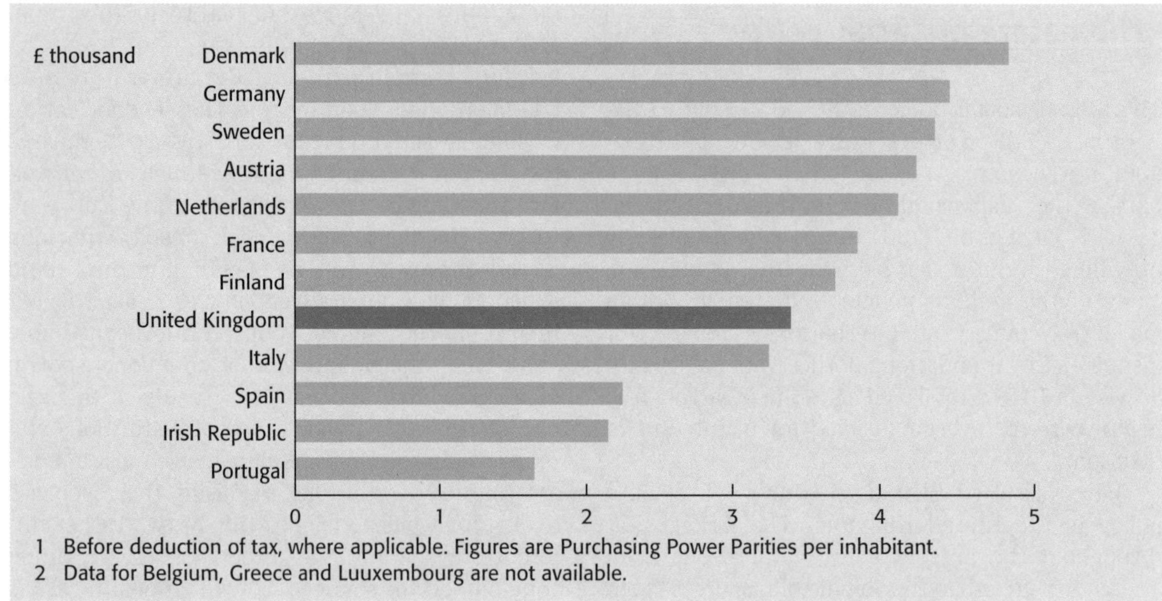

Figure 26.2 Expenditure[1] on social protection benefits per head: EU comparison[2], 1996
Source: Social Trends, 1999, Figure 8.3

the best example – is largely met from the taxes raised by central government. Second, the state plays an important role in administering '**transfer payments**': it raises money in taxes from one group in the community and 'transfers' it to other groups, in the form of payments such as pensions and unemployment benefit. Thus, eligibility rules for unemployment and social security benefits are settled within the core executive, but the implementation of those rules is the responsibility of a semi-independent agency (the Benefits Agency) established as part of the last Conservative government's 'Next Steps' programme. (Details of the Next Steps reforms can be found in Chapter 21.)

Notice that while we routinely speak of the welfare state as providing welfare services to the population, hardly anything in the description is about direct provision: it is about funding, and about organising systems of provision. Teachers and health care professionals have mostly been paid for out of the public purse, but the role of central government in delivering services is limited. Many social services are actually delivered by the 'local state' – in other words, by local government. But much welfare provision goes beyond the institutions of the state completely. Schooling up to the age of sixteen, for instance, while long compulsory in Britain, has been provided in many cases by church schools. Low-cost housing for rent has in recent years been provided by charities sponsored by government, such as housing associations. And many important 'personal social services' – such as the care of the handicapped outside hospitals – have been 'contracted out' by the state to voluntary associations and charities. Finally, some important welfare services are contracted out by the state to firms in the marketplace – for instance, care of many old people in privately owned 'residential homes'.

The fact that central government, while predominantly a payer for welfare, is only partly a direct deliverer of services has important consequences for the way welfare policy is made. It means that there is a very wide range of organisations involved in the welfare policy-making process. It is impossible for central departments in Whitehall to make policy without involving these organisations. They include the local authorities and the health authorities responsible for the delivery of so many important services 'on the ground'; the many charities and voluntary associations likewise involved in service provision; private firms who have contracts with government to deliver services; and professional bodies – representing, for instance, doctors, social workers, teachers – whose members directly deliver the service. The new devolved governing arrangements in Scotland and Wales will magnify this dispersal.

Thus while we speak of the welfare state, welfare services are by no means produced only, or even mainly, by central government.

Why is the welfare state so important?

Welfare spending is by far the largest part of public expenditure in the United Kingdom – as it is in most comparable countries. What is more, this has been the case for many decades, and seems likely to continue to be so. Why has the welfare state grown to such an important scale? Four reasons can be identified.

Democratic politics

The welfare state expanded with democracy, because it benefited some of those who were given the vote under democratic politics. Now, the beneficiaries of the welfare state are enormous in number. When we consider the full range of services, from health through education and pensions, we can see that virtually the whole population has a stake in welfare services. Consequently, there are large numbers of votes to be won and lost in the field of welfare policy. What is more, while some of the original motivation for the expansion of welfare services was to help the poor, it has now been demonstrated that many of the services – especially education – also benefit the middle classes (see below). In other words, the educated, prosperous and politically well organised have a big stake in the preservation of many welfare services. This is reinforced by the role of the welfare state as an employer, often of highly educated professionals: for instance, there are over a million people employed in health services in Britain. These occupations amount to a considerable lobby for the preservation of the welfare state.

Political philosophy

Although many of the services of the welfare state are known to benefit the relatively well-off, it is undeniably the case that one motive behind its original development was to provide safeguards against sickness, unemployment and poverty. The philosophies of the political parties which have dominated British politics in this century have all in different ways viewed the state as a source of welfare. Before the First World War important social policy reforms were introduced by the Liberal government which had won office in 1906, and which was dominated by politicians who believed in 'social reform' liberalism – in other words, in using the state as an instrument of social reform. Since the end of the First World War British politics has been dominated by two parties – Labour and Conservative – which in different ways also support welfare provision: the Labour Party because it believes that the purpose of the state is to intervene to ensure that inequalities and deprivations caused by markets should be remedied, especially if they affect manual workers and their families; the Conservative Party because, at least until the 1980s, it was dominated by politicians who believed that government had obligations to ensure that the poorest were cared for by the state. Immediately after the Second World War a reforming Labour government greatly extended the scope of the welfare state (see Box 26.1). These reforms were accepted, and consolidated, by the Conservative governments in office from 1951 to 1964. In other words, for much of its recent history British politics has been dominated by two parties which, for different reasons, have been committed to a large welfare state. The parties other than Labour and Conservative that occupy an important role in the new devolved political systems of Scotland and Wales – notably the Scottish National Party and Plaid Cymru in Wales – share this commitment to state welfare.

Economic efficiency

As we shall shortly see, the welfare state has many critics on the grounds that its cost is a 'burden' on the economy. But as Figure 26.2

BOX 26.1 **CHRONOLOGY**

Landmarks in the history of the welfare state

Income maintenance

1945	Universal flat-rate family allowances for all but first child in the welfare family
1948	National insurance system flat-benefits for retirement, widows, sickness and unemployment, with flat-rate contributions
1948	National Assistance: means-tested social assistance on uniform national scales
1961	Graduated state pension on money purchase basis for workers without occupational pension
1966	Earnings-related supplement for first six months of unemployment or sickness benefit
1966	Supplementary benefit, with legal entitlement, replaced national assistance
1971	Invalidity pensions introduced
1974	National insurance contributions earnings-related; pensions up-rated annually in line with earnings or prices, whichever greater
1977	Child benefit for all children replaced family allowances and child income tax allowances
1978	State earnings-related pension scheme (SERPS), reflecting increases in earnings and prices, replaced graduated pensions
1980	Pensions indexed to prices only
1982	Earnings-related supplement to sickness and unemployment benefit abolished

Health

1948	National Health Service: free, universal health care, with hospitals managed by central government
1952	Charges for drug prescriptions and optical and dental treatment
1974	Major reorganisation of National Health Services: hospitals, family practitioner and community health services integrated under regional and area boards
1982	Further reorganisation, with area tier abolished

Education

1944	Education Act increased school-leaving age to fifteen; organised system into primary, secondary and further sectors; selective education according to ability to be the norm for secondary pupils
1965	Government request for local authorities to organise secondary schools on a comprehensive, all-ability basis
1971	School-leaving age increased to sixteen
1976	Public grants to some independent (direct-grant) schools ended

BOX 26.1 continued

Housing

1946	New subsidy system for local authority housing, with contributions from central government, local taxations, and rents paid by tenants
1972	National rent rebate system to give means-tested assistance to public and private sector tenants
1980	Right for local authority tenants to buy their house at a discount according to length of residence
1982	Means-tested assistance with rent and rates (Housing Benefit) integrated under local authority administration

Personal social services

1970	Establishment of integrated Social Services Departments in local authorities to provide non-cash residential and home-based services to children, the elderly and others

Source: Parry, 1986

BOX 26.2 MINI BIOGRAPHY

William Beveridge (1879–1963)
Welfare reformer. Educated Oxford, becoming expert on unemployment. Member of Liberal Party. Worked for Board of Trade before being Director of LSE 1919–37 and Master University College Oxford 1937–45. Author of the founding document of the post-war welfare state, the report in his name on social insurance 1942.

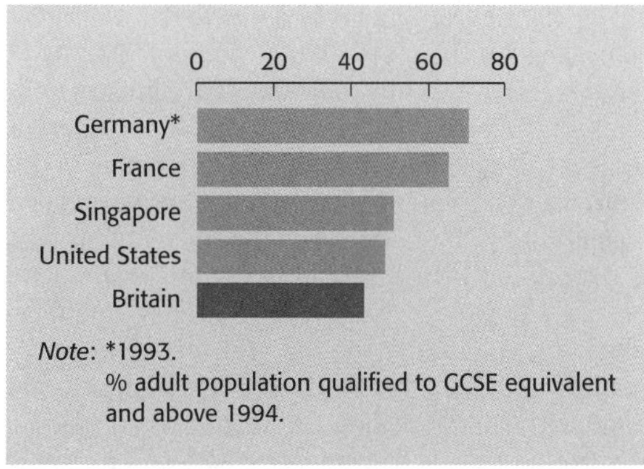

Figure 26.3 National comparisons of education levels
Source: The Economist, 15 June 1996

showed (p. 566) it is striking how many nations with highly advanced economies have even larger welfare states, on the basis of expenditure per head of population. In part, of course, this is because successful economies produce the resources needed to pay for welfare. But it is also because an efficient industrial economy needs the sort of services provided by the welfare state. Industrial economies demand a highly educated workforce. Indeed, one of the commonest criticisms of this part of the British welfare state is that we do not educate the population to as high a level as our main competitors (see Figure 26.3). An industrial economy also requires a healthy workforce – which in turn demands efficient health care available to all. The most successful economies also function best when workers are willing to be highly adaptable – for instance, to change work practices, and even to accept unemployment, in order to make the best use of the latest technology. Obviously this co-operation is only likely to happen when workers believe that if they lose their jobs through new technology the state will both retrain them for new work and ensure that while unemployed they, and their families, are guaranteed levels of benefit which will keep them above poverty levels. In other words, economic success demands generous unemployment and other social security benefits.

Market failure

The United Kingdom is a capitalist economy – which means that the chief mechanism for the production and distribution of goods and services is the marketplace, where exchanges are made for money. But in many cases markets will fail to produce goods and services, or will produce them in insufficient amounts. 'Market failure' is one of the most important reasons for state intervention. Goods and services as different as national defence, street lighting or public parks would be difficult to organise if the state did not compel citizens at large to contribute to their upkeep. Similar problems of collective choice undermine the market in areas of welfare provision. For instance, if the state made education entirely voluntary, and relied on parents to buy education for their children, it is undoubtedly the case that some children would not be educated because their parents would be unwilling voluntarily to make the necessary economic sacrifices. Likewise, if the long-term sick and handicapped had to find the resources to pay for the full cost of their own care, they would simply not be able to raise those resources; there would be great gaps in the care for the sick and the handicapped if the market alone were left to ensure that funds were available. (Notice that this is not at all the same as saying that the state directly provides those services; it only suggests that government ensures that the resources are available. Whether the services are then delivered by the state, by charities or by private firms is a separate question.) The issue of how to deliver welfare services is one of the most important facing policy makers – and is included in the list of key issues which we now examine.

Issues in welfare policy

'Welfare policy making' is about choices concerning the welfare services in a community: about their range, about how they should be paid for, about how they should be delivered, and about who should benefit from the welfare state. How to make these choices lies at the heart of most debates about the big issues of welfare policy in Britain.

The absolute level of spending

Although, as we have seen, the welfare state in the United Kingdom is not large by international standards, there has nevertheless been concern about the 'burden' of welfare spending. In part this concern reflects pressures common to all nations which have established generous systems of welfare provision. The expansion of the welfare state across the industrial world took place in the decades after 1945 in a period of international prosperity. In the last twenty years this prosperity has become much less certain, and in most countries questions have been raised about the scope of welfare provision. In the United Kingdom the problem of the level of provision has been especially severe because the UK economy was, for much of the post-war period, much less successful than many other industrial economies in delivering the increased wealth needed to fund welfare services.

In some areas difficulties are made more serious by long-term increases in the demand for services. For instance, although the cost of the National Health Service is by international standards modest, the level of spending on health shows a long-term rise: as a nation we spend more than £10 billion on health than we did a decade ago. The pressure of rising costs comes from two areas in particular: constant improvements in medical technology are widening the range of conditions which can be treated; and the ageing of the population is expanding the numbers of people who live to a great, and sickly, old age.

The issue of how much in total to spend on welfare has become particularly important because of changes in the outlook of the Conservative

Party, which of course ruled the country between 1979 and 1997. After Margaret Thatcher became leader in 1975 the influence of those Conservatives who supported large-scale welfare spending declined within the party. Under Thatcher, and under her successor, John Major, welfare spending was viewed in terms of 'opportunity cost': although often desirable, every pound spent on welfare was seen as a resource diverted from productive investment, and therefore from wealth creation. These ambitions to cut the size of the welfare state actually come to little. But they did have two big effects: they affected the balance struck between different welfare programmes and the means of delivering welfare; and they caused major shifts in Labour Party thinking, and thus in the policies pursued by Labour after its return to government in 1997. Above all, there has occurred a historic change in the basic philosophy of '**universalism**': on the principle that welfare services should usually be available as a right to all citizens. The new philosophy, shared by both main parties, is based on selection and targeting: the principle being that welfare services should only be available to those who can demonstrate need.

The balance between programmes

The question of the overall size of the welfare state is of course inseparable from the question of the relative size of particular programmes, because it

Frank Field thinks the unthinkable on welfare reform (29 March 1998)

The Millennium Dome hires acrobats. New Labour haggles over minimum wage (21 June 1998)

is obvious that cuts in welfare spending can only be made by cutting specific programmes. Cutting programmes has in practice proved very difficult, for two reasons. First, some expensive parts of the welfare state are exceptionally popular. In particular such is the level of support for the National Health Service that even Margaret Thatcher was obliged in the 1983 general election campaign to pledge support for its principles for fear that to do otherwise would damage the Conservative Party electorally. Second, the largest proportion of spending on welfare, like public spending as a whole, is not really in the control of governments, at least in the short term: it amounts to obligations inherited from decisions taken by predecessors. This is particularly true of 'income transfers' – cash benefits such as pensions and social security – which are based on entitlements usually embodied in law. Sudden changes in the numbers of those entitled to claim – such as occur when unemployment rises – force governments to spend more. This is exactly what happened in the recessions at the start and at the end of the 1980s, when government was forced to spend unexpectedly large amounts on social security payments.

As a result of the difficulty of cutting spending across the board, governments have therefore been forced to concentrate on restructuring the welfare state – trying to change the balance of spending. As we have just seen, their ability to do this is limited. Nevertheless, in one of the most important programmes of the welfare state – public subsidy for low-cost housing – considerable cuts were made after the Conservatives came back to government in 1979. In the post-war years the provision of low-cost housing for the poor (council housing) was one of the main areas of welfare spending. In the 1980s governments cut investment in new housing virtually to nothing and sold a large part of the public housing stock to sitting tenants: 1.4 million dwellings were disposed of in this way.

The attempt to restructure the welfare state has been connected to the third issue identified above: how to deliver welfare services.

The means of delivery

Although we often speak of the welfare state as 'providing' welfare services, in fact it is both possible and common for the state to fund services rather than directly take on responsibility for delivery.

The issues raised by the means of service delivery can be well illustrated by the case of the National Health Service. In hospital care, for most of the service's history the same public bodies both paid for, and delivered, care. Hospitals were publicly owned institutions. The reforms in the National Health Service introduced since 1989 are intended to separate the funders of care from the providers. Through a system of 'internal markets' public health authorities contract with providers – such as hospitals – to supply health care on agreed terms. A growing number of hospitals, in addition, are now self-governing trusts rather than publicly owned organisations. They are responsible for their own budgets and have some independence in fixing the pay and conditions of staff. The theory behind this system is that providers of care, like hospitals, will have incentives to deliver care more efficiently in order to win and retain contracts from those funding care.

This change in the health service is only part of a wider shift in the organisation of service delivery in British government. There has taken place a general shift in the direction of a '**contract state**' – a state where government pays for services, but contracts the job of delivery out to a separate body, usually by some sort of competitive system. Some shifts in this direction took place in the National Health Service even before the important reforms of recent years – contracting out of laundry services in hospitals, for instance, was already well established by the late 1980s. Beyond the particular sphere of welfare, contracting out has spread to a wide range of services, such as refuse collection in local authorities.

The contrasting arguments surrounding the shift to contracting out in service delivery can be summarised briefly. On the one hand, there is nothing new in principle involved in contracting: as we saw in Chapter 3 the government is a 'customer' for a wide range of services, and there is no obvious dividing line between goods and services that ought to be delivered directly, and those that can be 'bought in' from the private sector. It is difficult to imagine anybody seriously defending the proposition that the state should produce everything itself. Competition can extend choice and can create pressures for the delivery of more responsive and more efficient services. On the other hand, the welfare state has been built on the principle of universalism: in other words, on the principle that all citizens should have access to a similar minimum level of service. However, when services are contracted out with the aim of ensuring that providers compete by offering differing levels and kinds of service, this commitment to universalism is compromised. Whether this is thought objectionable or not depends, as we will see in a few moments, on what philosophy of welfare one believes in.

'Universalism' is also at the centre of the fourth issue identified above: funding.

Who should pay?

Britain is fairly unusual in relying on general taxation to provide the lion's share of the money for welfare. In many other European states, for instance, it is common for programmes to be funded out of insurance contributions levied on workers and employers. These contributions are usually obligatory, though they can be voluntary. This is, for instance, one of the commonest ways of paying for the cost of health care in Europe.

The advantages of an insurance system are twofold. Firstly, the contributions guarantee a stream of income for a welfare programme such as health care, whereas in the British system welfare programmes have to compete as best they can against other public spending priorities. (This may be why the British welfare state spends rather less than the international average.) A second advantage is that in some circumstances insurance systems may encourage more competition and efficiency, because the insurers can be separated from the providers, and have an incentive to shop around for the most cost-effective forms of delivery. The disadvantage of insurance systems, even of compulsory ones, is that they usually produce inequalities in the service offered. For instance, insurance funds based on the workplace usually end up offering a better deal to the better-paid workers. In discussions about funding the National Health Service in the 1980s some advocates of reform expressed interest in shifting to an insurance system, though this has never been pursued.

Arguments about the choice between general taxation or insurance to fund welfare make an important assumption – that there is no charge for services at the point of consumption. Indeed, for the most part this is true of major programmes such as education. However, 'user charges' have always existed for some services, and in the 1980s they were considerably expanded. In health care, for instance, in both dental and optical services 'free' services have almost disappeared except for groups exempted on grounds of low income. In 1998 a 'flat rate' fee of £1,000 per annum was introduced for most higher education courses. The case for user charges is twofold: charges, even set at modest levels, can raise money that is badly needed; and charges encourage clients to be prudent in making calls on services, whereas if the service is a 'free good' there is the possibility that it will be used (and abused) thoughtlessly. The most important argument against user charges is that charging even a modest amount risks deterring the poorest from using services – and thus undermines one of the most important functions of the welfare state.

There is in turn a connection between the issue of charges and the final issue examined here: who should benefit from welfare policy?

Who should benefit?

It is in the nature of universal services – such as schooling, health care, and pensions – that they are available to everybody who meets the appropriate conditions. Thus, to receive free schooling it is necessary only to be of school age, to receive health care only to be judged sick by a doctor, to receive an old age pension to have reached the stipulated age.

This principle of universalism has created two problems, one concerning efficiency and one concerning equality. The efficiency problem exists because, since resources are limited, it can be argued that it is more efficient to 'target' resources on those in most need. This implies a shift away from universalism in the provision of, for instance, pensions and other benefits to a **selective targeting** on the needy. These 'efficiency' concerns interact with the concern with equality, for it is obviously a principle of universalism that all, regardless of their personal economic circumstances, should be entitled to a benefit. In some circumstances, this can give the wealthy the same entitlement to benefits as the poor. Table 26.1 draws on calculations by Le Grand. He divided services into three categories – pro-poor, equal in their impact on the rich and poor, pro-rich. He measured impact by the ratio of spending on a service between those earning incomes that put them in the top fifth in the community compared with those in the bottom fifth. Thus in the table, the figure of 5.4 for universities means that spending on those from families with high earning is nearly five and a half times as great as spending on those from low-income families. An intuitive way of making sense of these figures is to say that any service with a figure below 1 benefits the poor; any service with a figure of 1 is neutral as between rich and poor; and the higher a figure is above 1, the more the service benefits the rich. The table shows that many welfare services actually advantage the rich.

Why do we get the apparently odd outcome that systems established with the aim of benefiting the poor in the community end up distributing higher levels of benefit to the wealthy? There seem to be two main reasons.

Table 26.1 Who benefits from welfare services?

Service	**Ratio of expenditure per person in top fifth to that per person in bottom fifth**
Pro-poor	
Council housing (general subsidy and rent rebates)[a]	0.3
Rent allowances	Na
Equal	
Nursery education	Na
Primary education	0.9
Secondary education, pupils over 16	0.9
Pro-rich	
National health service	1.4[b]
Secondary education, pupils over 16	1.8
Non-university higher education[c]	3.5
Bus subsidies	3.7
Universities[c]	5.4
Tax subsidies to owner-occupiers	6.8
Rail subsidies	9.8

[a] The estimates pre-date the introduction of housing benefit
[b] Per person ill
[c] Colleges of education, technical education and institutions that were polytechnics at the time of calculation
Source: Goodin and Le Grand, 1987, p. 92

First, in part the outcomes of welfare policy are affected by the ability of particular groups to lobby government in order to improve the quality of the services available to them. The pattern of welfare spending is not, in other words, a straightforward response to need. In general terms the poor are less well organised in lobbies than are the wealthy, and are less well placed to exert influence over policy outcomes: notice in Table 26.1 the substantial advantages to the better-off from tax subsidies to owner-occupiers. Of course the power of groups is not fixed. Le Grand's figures are important for the general point they make that the welfare state does not automatically advantage the poor. But since the figures were produced the tax benefits given to owner occupiers have been considerably restricted as governments realised the sheer cost of these concessions.

Second, eligibility for some services is not automatic, but depends on achieving success in competition. The most obvious example of this is university education, the overwhelming cost of which is paid for by the state. (Even the introduction of fees for students in 1998 still made little difference to the overall importance of state financing.) Admission to higher education in all cases depends on demonstrating the capacity to benefit from a university education, and in most cases rests on success in examinations (chiefly 'A' levels). We know, however, that success in educational examinations is closely tied to social class. This explains the pattern shown in Table 26.2, which shows huge differences in the rates of participation in higher education by social class. What is more, the expansion of higher education in the 1990s widened the gap between the children of the very poorest and the highest class groups: compare the gap in the table between the top and bottom in 1991–2 and 1997–8. Higher education is one of those areas of public provision – like opera – which greatly benefits the rich rather than the poor; the introduction of flat rate fees in 1998 has only marginally changed this state of affairs.

Resolving the question of who should benefit from welfare spending depends on arriving at a view about the fundamental purpose of the welfare state. If the point of the welfare state is to ensure that a set of rights are available to all citizens, then there is nothing objectionable in the millionaire having the same rights as, say, an unemployed person,

Table 26.2 Participation rates in higher education by social class, Great Britain (percentages)

	1991–2	1992–3	1993–4	1994–5	1995–6	1996–7	1997–8
Professional	55	71	73	78	79	82	80
Intermediate	36	39	42	45	45	47	49
Skilled non-manual	22	27	29	31	31	31	32
Skilled manual	11	15	17	18	18	18	19
Partly skilled	12	14	16	17	17	17	18
Unskilled	6	9	11	11	12	13	14
All social classes	23	28	30	32	32	33	34

Source: Office for National Statistics, 1999, p. 61, Table 3.13

just as we naturally expect the rich and the poor to be treated equally in other spheres – before the courts, for instance. On the other hand, if the purpose of the welfare state is to remove or moderate social inequality created, for instance, by the market system, then the fact that the rich have some of the same benefit entitlements as the poor becomes a real problem. To return to our opening questions: it is now plain that the welfare state does nothing so simple as moderate the inequalities produced by markets. In some cases it actually makes those inequalities wider. But whether we view this as a good or a bad thing depends on the political philosophy which we use to justify the welfare state.

Debate about the welfare state

Since the fall of communism, the collapse of its underlying economic principles have had a knock-on effect in the related philosophy of social democracy. This has led some social theorists to look for alternative approaches to the welfare state. Michael Novak, an American right-wing theorist, contributed to a colloquium of views (1999) in which he argued for a root and branch new approach. He insists that the welfare state, despite short term successes of social amelioration, especially for the old, has inflicted long term damage on society. In short he says that welfare has corrupted society: benefits are 'too easy to obtain and too attractive to resist'; what began as a hand out has become to be seen as an 'entitlement', irrespective of need. In addition welfare services have become bureaucratic and stagnant, crushed by higher levels of administration. But his most fundamental criticism is that welfare has induced a 'dependency' mind set. He quotes Irving Crystal: 'The fully developed welfare state is a modern version of the feudal castle, guarded by moats and barriers, and offering security and shelter to the loyal population that gathers round it'. Citizens have 'traded the inheritance of liberty that had been won for them at enormous cost', says Novak, 'in exchange for a promise of security – a promise [because of its expense and the changing balance of old to youth] that can no longer be met'. He accuses the welfare state of softening 'the morals of recipients'; 'penalising the creativity and hard work of those who pay for it'; and discouraging 'employers from creating new jobs'. Novak cites research showing that four million Americans aged eighteen to thirty regularly receive benefits and seem to be in a 'cycle of dependency'. Meanwhile new immigrants seem as able as always to escape poverty within a year or so through the traditional means of hard work and creativity. Novak goes on to argue that welfare has subverted 'civil society', the dynamic, voluntary elements within society which enables it to work: the sense of personal responsibility, the acceptance of obligation towards loved ones and other citizens. 'The political economy of the free society, therefore, depends to an unprecedented degree on the personal responsibility and associational skills (political and economic) of its citizens. This is the heart of any experiment in self government.' He adduces seven principles of devolution whereby responsibility should be transferred downwards to the citizen from the state:

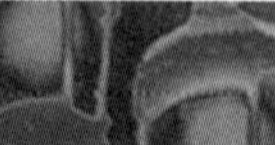

BOX 26.3 IDEAS AND PERSPECTIVES

Queen's Speech promises clampdown on unemployed defaulters and 'Buddy scheme'

On 17 November 1999, the Queen's Speech foresaw two new initiatives in the social policy area.

Firstly those offenders who fail to fulfil community sentences while they are unemployed stand to lose up to 40 per cent of their benefit for a period of four weeks. Paul Cavadino, of the National Association for the Care and Resettlement of Offenders, criticised as foolish the idea of 'plunging offenders further into poverty'. Benefits paid in respect of other family members would not be affected, however.

Secondly a new scheme is to be introduced to help youngsters leaving care whereby local authorities would continue to bear responsibility for sixteen and seventeen year olds who have left children's or foster homes. Each care leaver would have an advisor and a personal plan relating to education and training. Anne Mullins of Action for Children welcomed the initiative.

Finally, the Probation Service is to be renamed with a national director based in the Home Office.

1 'We need to raise up large numbers of strong, independent, creative, civic minded and above all responsible citizens without whom this project is dead.'

2 Nourish strong families for the family is the formative institution of strong personalities.

3 Encourage and not oppress 'personal habits of initiative, creativity and enterprise'.

4 Set up capital funds for each individual so that every family has a store of capital 'to transfer across the generations'.

5 Capital formation would relieve Treasury funds.

6 Devolve decisions from bureacracies to individuals. 'A more creative balance between national and local must be restored.'

7 Simplify government rules and regulations as every complexity is both a veil blocking transparency and an occasion of corruption.

Novak's views are fiercely criticised in the publication cited by the likes of Giddens, John Lloyd and Paul Ormerod; it is recommended to the reader.

Chapter summary

In this chapter we have seen that the scale of resources committed to social policy is very large, has been growing for a long time, but is still comparatively modest by international standards; the growth of state involvement in the provision of welfare has taken place for a mixture of economic and ideological reasons; there are significant problems of equity and efficiency raised by the way the welfare state is presently organised. It is a moot point whether the welfare state, set up to help the disadvantaged, actually helps them more than the relatively well-off, especially in relation to the health and education services.

Discussion points

- Why does Britain seem to be so modest by international standards in the scale of its welfare state?
- Should welfare policy aim at promoting equality?
- How would you explain the long-term growth in social spending by the state in Britain?
- To what extent do Novak's seven principles offer a way towards a more viable welfare state?

Further reading

Esping-Andersen (1990) sets the British welfare state in an international context. Ham (1992) reviews one of the most expensive and contentious sectors. Wilding (1986) reviews and criticises some of the contemporary policy arguments. Mohan (1995) examines a wide range of evidence on distributions and impact. Goodin and Le Grand (1987) examine evidence about the class distributional effect of the welfare state. Deakin (1994) is up-to-date on recent history. Coates and Lawler (2000) have up-to-date material on the social policies of New Labour. Novak and his discussants offer an excellent stimulation for thought about the future of the welfare state.

References

Coates, D. and Lawler, P. (eds) (2000) *New Labour into Power* (Manchester University Press).

Deakin, N. (1994) *The Politics of Welfare* (Harvester Wheatsheaf).

Esping-Andersen, G. (1990) *The Three Worlds of Welfare Capitalism* (Polity Press).

Goodin, R. and Le Grand, J. (1987) *Not Only the Poor: the Middle Classes and the Welfare State* (Allen and Unwin).

Ham, C. (1992) *Health Policy in Britain* (Macmillan).

Mohan, J. (1995) *A National Health Service?* (Macmillan).

Novak, M. (1999) *Is there a Third Way? Essays on the Changing Direction of Socialist Thought* (IEA).

Office for National Statistics (1999) *Social Trends 29* (HMSO).

Parry, R. (1986) 'United Kingdom', in Flora, P. (ed.), *Growth to Limits: the Western European Welfare States since World War II*, pp. 155–240 (de Gruyter).

Wilding, P. (ed.) (1986) *In Defence of the Welfare State* (Manchester University Press).

Chapter 27 Economic policy

Michael Moran and Bill Jones

Learning objectives

- To identify the nature of economic policy.
- To describe the machinery by which economic policy is made and implemented.
- To examine three key themes in the analysis of recent economic policy – the significance of Thatcherism, the character of New Labour and the importance of Europe in British economic policy.

Introduction

Probably the single most important feature of modern British politics is the extent to which governments are judged by how well they manage the economy. Governments can get lots of things wrong and still win elections, if they can deliver what electors perceive as economic success; but no matter how well governments do in other fields, it is almost impossible to be electorally successful if they are economic failures. This simple observation identifies the key place of economic policy in the political system.

The nature of economic policy

It may be thought a simple matter to identify 'economic policy': 'policy' consists in the choices made and rejected by government; 'economic' refers to that set of institutions and activities concerned with the production and distribution of goods and services; economic policy therefore consists in those choices made or rejected by government designed to affect the production of goods and services in the community.

This is, it will be plain, a very broad definition. Many activities of government not commonly thought of as 'economic' become so if we rigorously follow this guideline. Thus policy towards the arts – for instance, the provision of subsidised opera and theatre – is directed to influencing the price at which particular artistic services are provided to the community.

A broad definition of economic policy is revealing, for two reasons. Firstly, it alerts us to the fact that the boundaries of 'economic policy' are moving all the time. For example, in recent years government has increasingly pictured education in economic terms. It conceives the primary purpose of schooling to be the production of one of the community's most valuable economic assets – a competent and educationally adaptable workforce. Thus, to an increasing extent policy towards schools has been conceived as a facet of economic policy. One of the primary features of economic policy is, therefore, that it has wide and constantly changing boundaries.

This connects to a second factor making a 'broad' definition of policy revealing: there is constant struggle and argument over the making and control of policy. British government works in part by a series of conventions which allocate subjects to particular institutions. An issue defined as purely concerned with education, for instance, will be in the domain of the Department for Education and the teaching profession. Until recently, for example, the content of the school curriculum was thought of as such a purely 'educational' matter. But the growing belief that the quality of education, by affecting the quality of the workforce, in turn shapes the fortunes of the economy has introduced economic considerations into arguments about the curriculum – and has destroyed the idea that choices about what is to be taught in schools are to be made only by those concerned with education.

This example shows that in economic policy-making arguments about what is, and what is not, relevant to the economy are of more than definitional significance. They are part of the process by which different groups in government try to gain control over particular areas of decision. If, for instance, the task of reviving the decaying parts of Britain's inner cities is pictured as one concerning the renovation of the physical environment, it will naturally be thought of as the responsibility at national level of the Department of the Environment. If, by contrast, it is pictured as a task of reviving a declining part of the industrial economy, it will more naturally be thought of as the proper responsibility of the Department of Trade and Industry. The 'boundaries' of economic policy are, therefore, uncertain and disputed. But if the boundaries are open to argument, there is nevertheless considerable agreement about where the heart of economic policy lies. The most important parts concern the government's own 'housekeeping', and its wider responsibilities for economic management.

Government has to make choices concerning the raising and distribution of its own resources: it has, in other words, to make choices concerning its budget in the same way as a firm or a family makes choices. But the choices made by government about how much to spend, where to allocate the money and how to raise it have a special significance. This significance is partly the result of scale: government is the biggest institution in the British economy and has a correspondingly great effect on the rest of society. Decisions by government about how much to spend and how much to tax crucially affect the prosperity or otherwise of the economy at large. But the significance of public spending and taxation choices also lies in their purpose, for they are important instruments which government can and does use to influence the course of the economy. This connects to a second 'core' aspect of economic policy.

Complementing its role as a major appropriator and distributor of resources in Britain, government has a second major economic policy responsibility – '**steering the economy**'. The implied comparison with steering a vessel or a vehicle, while not exact, is nevertheless helpful. Like the pilot of a vessel, government possesses instruments of control which can be manipulated to guide the economy in a desired direction; and like a pilot it has available a variety of indicators telling it how successfully these instruments are working. Among the most important instruments of control used by British government in recent decades are the budgetary instruments to which we have already referred. By varying the total volume of public spending, or the level of taxation, government is able to increase or depress the total amount of activity in the economy. By targeting its spending on particular areas – such as education, or the inner cities, or as subsidies to particular industries – government can also try to influence specific groups in the economy.

The image of 'steering the economy' was particularly important in the twenty-five years after the end of the Second World War. Margaret Thatcher's administrations, as we have seen in earlier chapters, denied that government could control the economy in the way that was attempted in the past. During the 1980s 'Thatcherites' asserted that government could only hope to create the right conditions for a freely functioning market economy; competitive forces, for better or worse, would do the rest. Yet the government still does try to 'steer the economy'. It has objectives – such as the control of inflation – which it seeks to achieve, and instruments of control which it uses to that end. After the 1970s, therefore, the direction of economic steering and the instruments of control changed; but all governments in post-war Britain have been engaged in steering the economy.

The machinery of economic policy

When we refer to the 'machinery' of something we are usually speaking of more than the mechanical parts of which it is composed; we also mean the process by which those parts combine in movement. So it is with the machinery of economic policy making: we mean not just the institutions, but the process by which they interact to produce choices.

If we look at a formal organisation chart of British government we will see that it is hierarchical in nature with elected politicians – ministers – at the top. It would be natural to assume, therefore, that the machinery of economic policy making worked by reserving the power to make policy to a few people at the top of government and reserving the task of carrying out policy to those lower down the hierarchy. But perhaps the single most important feature of policy making is that there is no simple distinction to be made between a few at the top who 'make' policy and a larger number lower down in government who 'implement' or 'execute' policy. More perhaps than in any other area of public affairs, economic policy making and policy implementation are inseparable. Those at the top of government certainly have the potential to make broad decisions about the direction of policy. But the substance of economic policy is determined not only by broad strategic judgements; it is also shaped by the way large numbers of organisations in both the public and the private sectors translate those into practical reality. The best way of picturing the machinery of economic policy making, therefore, is not as a hierarchy in which a few take decisions which are then executed by those further down the hierarchy, but rather as a set of institutions in the centre of the machine which negotiate and argue over policy with a wide range of surrounding bodies in both the public and private sectors.

The centre of the machine

The Treasury

At the centre of the machinery of economic policy making is **the Treasury**. At first glance the Treasury looks an insignificant institution. It is tiny by the standards of most central departments. What is more it plays little part in the execution of economic policy. Vital tasks such as administering schemes for financial support of industry and regulating the activities of particular sectors and occupations are carried out

Chancellor Ken Clarke cuts interest rates. England hosts the European Football Championships (9 June 1996)

elsewhere, notably by the Department of Trade and Industry. The Treasury's importance essentially lies in three features.

Firstly, it is universally recognised as a vital source of policy advice about economic management, not only to its political head, the **Chancellor of the Exchequer**, but also to other senior ministers, notably the Prime Minister. Secondly, it is, as its name implies, in effect the keeper of the public purse: it is the key institution in decisions about the composition and about the volume of public spending. This is organised around a virtually continuous cycle of bargaining between the Treasury and the 'spending departments' to fix both the level of spending commitments and the proportionate allocation of resources between competing claimants.

Thirdly, the Treasury shares with the **Bank of England** a large measure of control over policy towards financial markets. These matters include the terms on which the government borrows money, intervention to affect the level of interest rates throughout the economy and the 'management of sterling' – in other words intervention in foreign exchange markets to influence the rate at which the pound is exchanged for other foreign currencies. Although in most of these activities the Bank of England acts as the agent of government, it only does this in close, virtually continuous, consultation with the Treasury. These responsibilities are especially important because the management of financial markets has since the mid-1970s become a key task of economic policy. Consequently the Bank of England should now be placed alongside the Treasury at the core of the machinery of economic policy, despite the fact that it is not a government department, nor even located in the area around Westminster where most of the major departments have their headquarters.

The Bank of England

The Bank of England is the nation's 'central bank'. This means that it is a publicly owned institution (though it only became so in 1946) with responsibility for managing the national currency. It also has a legal responsibility to oversee and safeguard the stability of the country's banking system and a more general responsibility to oversee the stability of financial markets. It is, as we have already seen, also the Treasury's agent in managing public debt and in interventions to influence levels of interest rates in the economy. The Bank's headquarters are located in the City of London and this symbolises its distinctive character. Although a public body and part of the core of the machinery of policy making, it retains a tradition of independence. Its Governor, while nominated by the Prime Minister, is usually a considerable and independent figure, in both the City of London and in international gatherings of other 'central bankers'. Likewise employees of the Bank are recruited separately from, and paid more than, civil servants.

The Bank's importance in the machinery of economic decision making rests on three factors. Firstly, it plays a major part in the execution of decisions increasingly considered to be the heart of economic policy – those concerning the management of conditions in financial markets. Secondly, as a result of its continuous and deep involvement with the markets it has an established position as a source of advice about the policy options best suited to the successful management of these markets. Thirdly, as we shall shortly see, it has acquired under the Labour government elected in 1997 new responsibilities for interest rate policy (see Box 27.4).

Describing the Treasury and the Bank of England as the centre of the machinery of economic policy does not amount to the same thing as saying that these two institutions dominate policy. However, it is undoubtedly the case that the two have a continuous role in the discussions about the strategic purposes and daily tactics of economic policy which occupy so much of modern government. No other institution in government specialises in this activity at such a high level.

The Treasury's and the Bank's positions at the centre of the machine are nevertheless shared with others. All governments in modern times have viewed economic policy as a primary responsibility and as a major influence on their chances of re-election. This means that economic management is never far from the minds of senior ministers. Two departmental members of the Cabinet usually occupy Treasury posts: the Chancellor of the Exchequer; and the Chief Secretary to the Treasury, whose main responsibility is managing at the highest level the negotiations over expenditure plans between the Treasury and the 'spending' departments. Given the importance of economic policy, prime ministerial participation in consideration of strategy and tactics is now customary.

The Prime Minister

'Prime Minister' here partly means the individual who happens to be the occupant of that position at any particular moment. The Prime Minister is both figuratively and physically close to the machinery of economic policy making: his/her residence and that of the Chancellor adjoin, while the Treasury itself is barely a footstep away from No. 10 Downing Street. However, 'prime ministerial' involvement in economic policy denotes more than the involvement of a particular personality. It happened to be the case in the 1980s that Britain had in Margaret Thatcher an unusually commanding Prime Minister with a particular interest in, and firm grasp of, the mechanics of economic policy. Consequently, she was a central figure in the machinery. Any modern Prime Minister is, however, likely to be an important part of the machine. The precise position will depend on changing factors: the abilities and interests of a particular individual; the personal relations between the Prime Minister and the Chancellor; and the wider popularity and authority which the Prime Minister can command. Prime ministerial involvement need not consist only of personal intervention. It can also take the form of participation by the staff of the Prime Minister's own office and from institutions closely connected to the Prime Minister, notably the Cabinet Office. Prime ministerial economic advisers can also exert considerable influence: in 1989 the

BOX 27.1 MINI BIOGRAPHY

Nigel Lawson (1932–)
Conservative Chancellor. Educated Oxford and worked as journalist before entering Commons for Blaby in 1974. Was a firm monetarist and Mrs Thatcher made him Chancellor in 1983. He remained until 1989 when he resigned over the advice given to her by Sir Alan Walters, her personal economic adviser.

Chancellor, Nigel Lawson, actually resigned over the role performed by Margaret Thatcher's adviser, Sir Alan Walters.

The Cabinet

Prime ministerial participation in the machinery of economic policy making may now be described as 'institutionalised' – which means that it is part of the established procedures, irrespective of the capacities and outlook of the individual who at any particular moment happens to occupy No. 10 Downing Street. It is less certain that the same can be said of the Cabinet, a body which once was indeed indisputably a dominant participant. It is true that the Cabinet retains a role irrespective of particular circumstances, such as the style of an individual Prime Minister. Thus the weekly meetings of Cabinet will always contain agenda items which bear on central parts of economic strategy. Having said that it remains a fact that Mrs Thatcher contrived successfully in keeping her controversial economic policy off the Cabinet agenda for over two years after her election; no doubt she was less wary after she had managed to remove all the critics of her economic policies from her Cabinet by the start of her second term. More important still, the network of Cabinet committees which now do much business in place of full Cabinet are important forums for consideration of strategy and tactics. The Cabinet system retains a particularly important role in deciding public spending. Although the process is dominated by direct bargaining between the Treasury and the individual departments, it is still accepted that it is at Cabinet committee level that irreconcilable differences between a department and the Treasury are effectively resolved.

Nevertheless, since the end of the 1970s the extent of collective Cabinet involvement in economic policy making has been uncertain. The importance of individuals remains: after all, three Cabinet Members – the Prime Minister, the Chancellor and the Chief Secretary to the Treasury – are all indisputably part of the core machinery. But what may have declined is the collective consideration of strategy and tactics by Cabinet institutions – either in full Cabinet or in committee. Whether this is due to the style of leadership practised by Margaret Thatcher, who dominated her Cabinets in the 1980s, or whether it is due to longer term changes in the significance of the Cabinet, is at present uncertain; but if it is due to long term changes it is plainly important; and if due to Margaret Thatcher's leadership style it is also revealing, since it shows that the Cabinet's place in the machinery is dependent on the style of the particular Prime Minister who happens to be in office. We will need to know more than we currently do about former Prime Minister Major's relations with his Cabinet before we can answer this question.

The observation that the Cabinet's role in the machinery is uncertain should not be taken to mean that Cabinet ministers and their departments are unimportant. Indeed, since we saw earlier that no simple division can be made between the 'making' of policy and its 'implementation', it follows that departments, in the act of executing policy, in effect also 'make' it by shaping what comes out of the government machine. This is manifestly the case with, for instance, the Department of Trade and Industry, which, in its multitude of dealings with individual firms, industries and sectors, plays a large part in deciding what is, in practice, to be the government's policy towards a wide range of industries.

The machinery of economic policy stretches not only beyond the central institutions like the Treasury to other central departments; it also encompasses what is sometimes called '**quasi-government**' and even institutions which are in the private sector. It is to these matters that we now turn.

Quasi-government

One of the striking features of British government is the small proportion of the 'public sector' which is actually accounted for by what we conventionally think of as the characteristic public institution – the central department headed by a Cabinet minister located in central London. Most people who work in the public sector are not 'civil servants', and most of the work of the public sector is done by institutions which do not have the status of civil service departments. This is an especially noticeable feature of the machinery of economic policy. It has become conventional to speak of this range of institutions as 'quasi-government' organisations. By this is meant that they have many of the marks of public bodies: they are usually entrusted with the task of carrying out duties prescribed in law; they often draw all, or a proportion of, their funds from the public purse; and the appointment of their leading officers is usually controlled by a minister and his or her department. Yet in their daily operations they normally work with some degree of independence of ministers and are usually less subject than are civil service departments to parliamentary scrutiny. In economic policy it is helpful to distinguish between two categories of quasi-government institution: **nationalised corporations** and a more diverse category best labelled independent specialised agencies.

Nationalised corporations are a comparatively standard organisational type. They normally work under a charter prescribing such matters as the constitution and powers of their governing board. The corporation form has, in the past, been used for activities as different as delivering broadcasting services (the BBC) and mining coal (British Coal). Most nationalised corporations provided goods and services through the market, deriving the bulk of their revenue from sales. But they were also linked to central government. It was common for a corporation to have a 'sponsoring department' in Whitehall. The 'sponsor' was expected to 'speak for' its corporation inside central government, but it was also an instrument for exercising control over the corporation.

The past tense is needed here because the nationalised corporation has mostly had its day. From 1945 to the end of the 1970s it was a major instrument of government policy – and was itself in turn a major influence over the shape of economic policy. In the 1980s 'privatisation' reduced the size and significance of the nationalised corporation in the machinery of economic policy.

Free-standing, specialised agencies have, if anything, become more important in recent years. They cover a wide range of areas, and take a variety of organised forms. They have become one of the most important means by which economic policy is 'delivered' – and, in being delivered, shaped. For example, in early 1993 the government established an Urban Regeneration Agency, whose purpose is to bring vacant and derelict land in towns and cities into use. It is worth stressing that bodies like these do not just carry out policy decisions made elsewhere; they shape policy by their control over the details of its execution and their role in policy advice.

There are many reasons why 'quasi-government' is important in the machinery of economic policy, but two are particularly significant. The first is that central government departments simply do not have the resources and knowledge to carry out the full tasks of the public sector; the system would become impossibly overloaded if the effort were made to control everything through a handful of government departments in London. The second reason is that the 'quasi-government' system offers some protection against control by politicians, especially Members of Parliament. It is much harder for a Member of Parliament to scrutinise and call to account an agency or a nationalised corporation than to do the same thing with a civil service department headed by a minister.

The machinery of economic policy stretches into 'quasi-government'; but it also, we shall now see, reaches into the private sector.

The private sector

It may seem odd to include privately owned institutions such as business firms in the machinery of policy. But it will become obvious when we realise two things: that economic policy is made in the process of execution, not just by a few people at the top handing down decisions to be routinely carried out elsewhere; and in executing policy government relies widely on private bodies.

One of the most striking examples of this is provided by the banking system in Britain. Almost all British banks are privately owned; yet without the services provided by the banks any government's economic policies would come to nothing. For instance, the whole payments system, on which the economy depends, is administered by the banks. This includes, for example, the circulation of notes and coins throughout the population and the processing of cheques and other forms of payment. In some of the most technologically advanced sectors of the economy, such as the nuclear power industry, firms in private ownership work in close partnership with government to implement jointly agreed policies. See Box 27.2 for summary of actors in economic policy.

BOX 27.2

fact

Actors in economic policy

Prime Minister

Chancellor

Chief Secretary to the Treasury

Governor of the Bank of England

Senior Treasury officials

Economic advisers

Cabinet Office

Key Cabinet committees

Secretary of State, Department of Trade and Industry

Cabinet

Quasi-government

Nationalised corporations

Independent specialised agencies

Private sector

Business firms

Banks

Three themes in economic policy

The Thatcherite revolution

Anybody wanting to make sense of the British economy after the millennium has to come to terms with a revolution in economic thought and practice that started in the 1970s. '**Thatcherism**' is now familiarly used to describe the policies of Margaret Thatcher's Conservative governments, but its impact continues over a decade after Margaret Thatcher herself was forced from office. After the Thatcher years there was no turning back; in different ways we are all Thatcherites now.

The origins of Thatcherism lie in the policy failures preceding Margaret Thatcher's election to office in 1979, and the debate was prompted by those failures. Thatcherism had two elements: it was an attempt to introduce historically different policies; and an attempt to replace the consensual and cooperative policy style of British government with a more centralised and directed way of doing things.

The most important features of Thatcherism as economic policy were threefold. The first involved an attempt to change the structure of ownership in the community radically: in the 1980s the government 'privatised' nearly half of what had been publicly owned in 1979. Secondly, Thatcherism attempted to change the structure of rewards: it cut the tax bills of the very rich, while also reducing the value of many welfare benefits, especially those to the unemployed. The expectation behind this change was that increasing the rewards of success would stimulate enterprise beneficial to all. Making unemployment more unattractive economically would encourage the unemployed to take jobs at lower wage rates, thus reducing both unemployment and the overall pressure of wage demands. Finally, Thatcherism withdrew or reduced subsidies to many industries, compelling the closure of many concerns and the more efficient operation of the rest in the face of international competition.

These changes in substance were accompanied by a change in the style of economic policy making. Precisely because Thatcherism involved an attempt to alter the substance of policy radically,

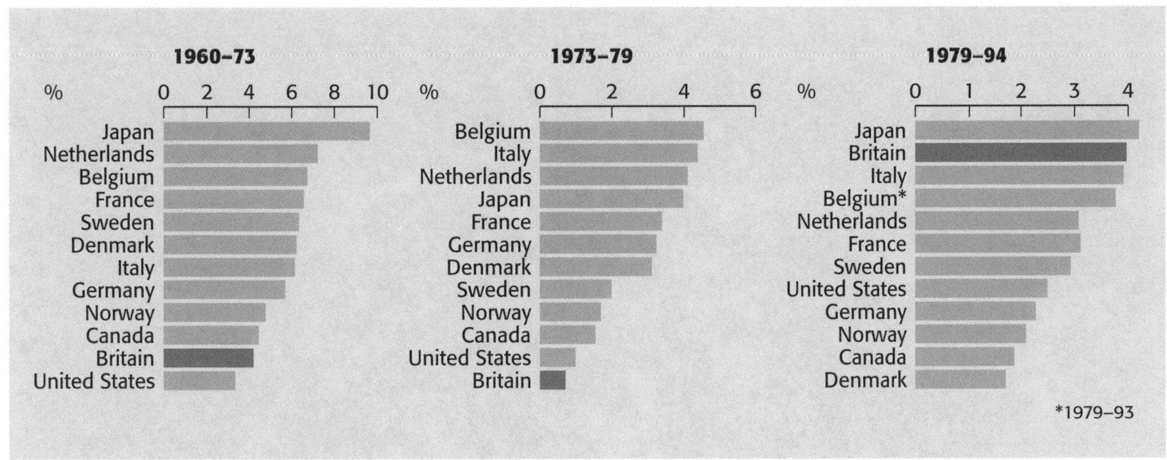

Figure 27.1 British economic performance, various periods (growth of output per hour in manufacturing, annual average per cent increase)
Source: The Economist, 21 September 1996

it was compelled to break with the consensual and co-operative approach. Many reforms, such as those bearing on trade unions, were imposed upon groups whose co-operation was usually sought in the past. Many policies – such as obliging inefficient manufacturing to reorganise or to close – were pursued in spite of protests from representatives of manufacturing industry.

This break with consensus and co-operation helps explain why, despite its domination of economic policy making in the 1980s, judgements about the Thatcherite solution remain deeply divided. The case for Thatcherism can be summarised under three headings. The first is that, however painful the experience of closing down large parts of manufacturing industry may have been, it was only the recognition of the inevitable, in conditions where British industries simply were not efficient enough to find markets for goods. Secondly, a change to a more centralised and directive style of policy making was necessary because the traditional co-operative approach was responsible, at least in part, for the failed policies of the past. Finally, comparison of Britain with other economies shows that Thatcherism is not unique. Across the world governments are, almost regardless of party, introducing economic reforms resembling the Thatcherite programme. This suggests that Thatcherism in Britain was a necessary adjustment to changing patterns in the world economy, without which Britain would lose even its present modest place in the international economic hierarchy. What is more, comparison of the international record of economic growth before and after Thatcherism, suggests that it made a considerable positive difference to the performance of the British economy. Figure 27.1 shows that the United Kingdom, bottom of the usual international league tables before 1979, was near the top afterwards.

Measures other than the one used here, such as the rate of economic growth for the whole economy – can tell a similar story. Many factors other than Thatcherism might account for these patterns; but it seems undeniable that something significant happened to the performance of the British economy after 1979.

The alternative, critical judgement of Thatcherite economics can be summarised under two headings. Firstly, the most distinctive consequence of Thatcherite economic policies has been to eliminate important parts of manufacturing industry, in a world where the manufacture and sale of finished goods is still the characteristic sign of an advanced industrial economy. In other words Thatcherism has only hastened what is sometimes called '**deindustrialisation**'. Secondly, the shift away from a consensual policy style, combined with a deliberate strategy of increasing the rewards to the rich and enterprising, carries great dangers for social peace and harmony.

New Labour sticks to previous government spending plans (19 October 1997)

New Labour and economic policy

The most striking feature of the economic policy fashioned by the Labour Party to fight the 1997 general election is well known: it largely accepted the great changes in both the conduct of economic management and in the structure of the economy introduced by the Conservatives after 1979.

The acceptance came in three stages:

- After Labour's catastrophic general election defeat in 1983 the Party moved in stages (chiefly between 1985 and 1989) to accept the main parts of the Thatcherite revolution, notably the big privatisation programme and the Conservatives' reforms of the law on industrial relations.
- After the election of Tony Blair as leader, he persuaded the Party to accept a big symbolic change – the excision from its constitution of the famous 'socialist' Clause 4 in place of a new clause which commended 'the enterprise of the market and the rigour of competition'.
- The third stage was the general election manifesto of 1997, which committed Labour to accepting the level of spending already planned by the Conservatives for its first two years of office, and committed the Party also not to increase basic or top rates of income tax.

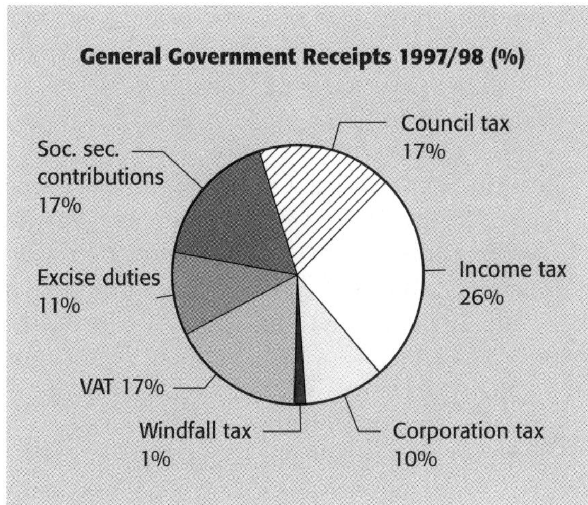

Figure 27.2 Sources of tax income
Source: Jamieson, 1998

Government collection of revenue and spending

Figure 27.2 reveals that government revenue comes from six major sources: Council tax; social security contributions; excise duties; VAT; corporation tax; and, the biggest single source, income tax (see Figures 27.2 and 27.3). Spending is supposed to equal revenue but when it does not borrowing usually bridges the gap (see Figure 27.4). Figure 27.4 shows how spending is divided between the major departments of government with social security taking a massive 32 per cent in 1997–8 and education 12 per cent.

Box 27.4, drawing on Labour's manifesto for the 1997 general election, summarises where the Labour Party had arrived after eighteen years of Conservative rule.

The impact of Europe

We can see, with the benefit of hindsight, that entry into what was then colloquially called the Common Market in 1973 was momentous for British economy. It made four big sets of changes:

- It contributed to a historic shift in trading patterns: whereas 29 per cent of United Kingdom exports went to member states of the European Union in 1971, that figure had risen to 57 per cent by 1996.

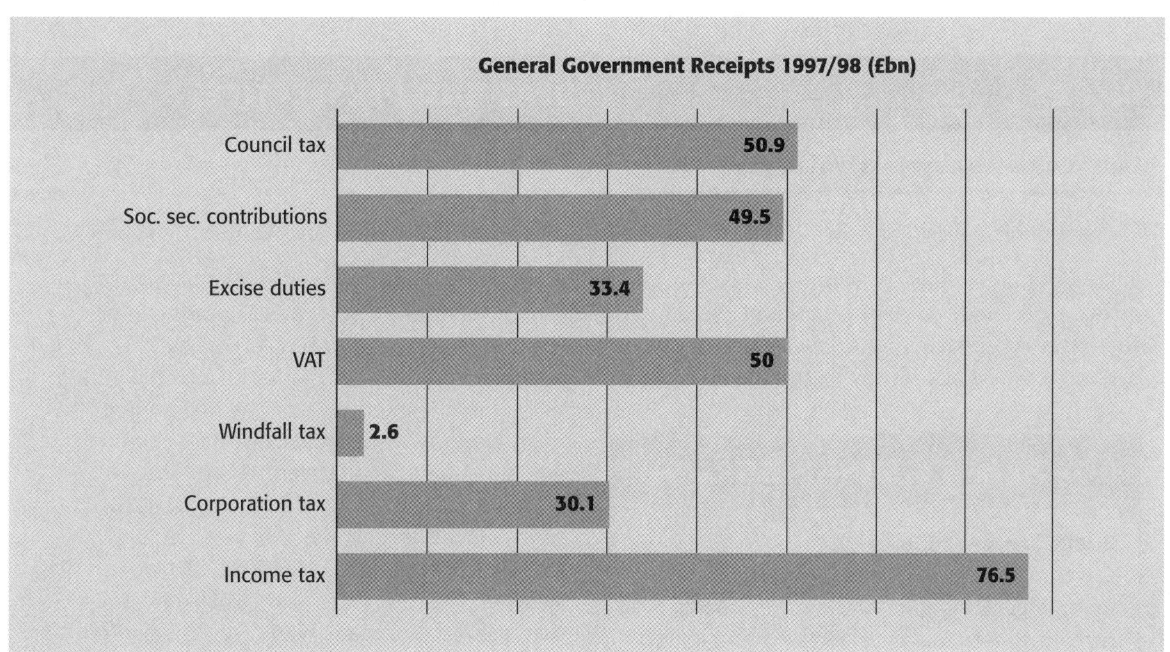

Figure 27.3 Sources of tax income
Source: Jamieson, 1998

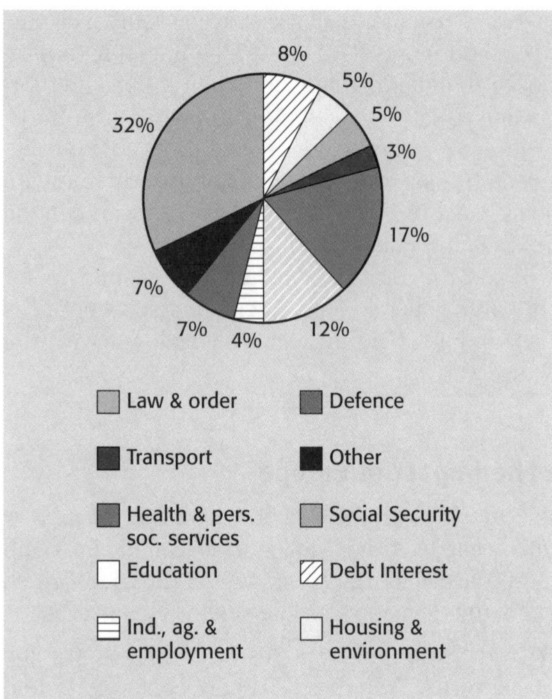

Figure 27.4 The bigger slices of the pie
Source: Jamieson, 1998

- It shifted the location of important economic policy decisions, and in the process caused a big shift in the focus of lobbying by powerful interests from London to Brussels, where the main European Community decision-making institutions are located. This process was given a big boost by the introduction in the 1990s of a Single European Market in a wide range of goods and services. The introduction of the Single Market meant that it was necessary to harmonise a wide range of regulations – ranging from the biggest, such as those governing competition rules, to the smallest such as those governing packaging of materials – at a Community level. Thus, the long term impact of the original entry has been to transform – by Europeanising – the process of economic policy making in Britain.
- The economic impact of membership of the European Union (as the former Common Market is now known) has in turn had a big effect on the lines of political division within the United Kingdom. Both the major political parties are divided over how the economy of

BOX 27.3 **IDEAS AND PERSPECTIVES**

Labour's economic strategy in 1997

The economic policies of New Labour show three features which are particularly worth highlighting.

First, within a few days of winning office the Chancellor announced important changes that greatly increased the independent capacity of the Bank of England to control interest rates. This should be seen as a consolidation of a key feature of the policy pursued during the Conservative years: managing the economy in such a way as to provide maximum reassurance to financial markets. Since the 1930s the control of interest rates has been one of the main ways by which politicians have tried to influence the economy and thus to ensure electoral success. Now, almost the first act of the new Chancellor was to remove this instrument from his control. The calculation was that entrusting the central bankers rather than Labour politicians with responsibility for setting interest rates would reassure the markets, thus fostering confidence for the pursuit of the government's economic objectives. The new arrangements:

BOX 27.4 **MINI BIOGRAPHY**

Eddie George (1938–)

Governor Bank of England. Educated Cambridge. Long time official of the Bank, he rose to top and since 1997 when Labour gave the Bank power to set interest rates he is responsible for determining the repayment rates of all individuals with a mortgage.

BOX 27.4 continued **IDEAS AND PERSPECTIVES** 

- Set an inflation target to be achieved by the Bank of England;
- Gave the Bank control over short-term interest rates subject to achieving the inflation target;
- Created a new Monetary Policy Committee within the Bank (the majority of members appointed by the Chancellor) to make decisions about interest rates.

Second, the new government conducted a comprehensive spending review in its first year (reported, July 1998). It was designed to fashion a distinctive Labour mechanism for controlling and planning expenditure and to map out a strategy for public spending growth in the years after 1999, including the crucial period leading up to the next election. On the former, the result of the review has been the attempt to move to a three-year planning cycle from 1999, to link planned expenditures to commitments on performance indicators made by spending departments and to impose continuous scrutiny of these commitments by the Treasury. These changes reflect the unusual authority of Gordon Brown as Chancellor and the attempt to convert this authority into more powerful central (Treasury) control of the spending process. Given the commitment not to raise levels of personal taxation, Labour's freedom to reshape the substance of spending priorities in the Comprehensive Spending Review was limited. The outcome of the review showed some of the constraints under which the government operates. There were no large shifts in spending priorities: in other words, no big losers in the review, showing the familiar capacity of individual departments and their clients to protect their programmes. There were substantial 'headline' increases for two programmes – health and education. Labour has a strong emotional commitment to both programmes, a commitment reinforced by the fact that workers in health and education are both strong client groups of the Party. But while these increases represent significant increases over spending since the middle of the 1990s, the planned levels are by no means unprecedented: indeed, as a share of national income health spending and education spending are not planned to exceed that seen in the early years of the Major government (Dilnot and Emmerson, 1998).

The Blair government's extraordinary success at holding down public expenditure goes from strength to strength . . . the present government is on course to keep public spending at a lower level (as a proportion of the whole economy) than any government since Harold Macmillan's 35 years ago.

Tony Travers, The Guardian, 22 September 1999

The third key feature of New Labour's economic policy is negative – it concerns something that has not happened. An important aim, and a successful one, of economic policy in the Conservative years was to use tax and spending policies so as to lighten the burden on the rich – on the grounds that this was good for the whole society since it gave incentives to the most enterprising wealth creators. The Labour Chancellor put a stop to the established redistributive policies of the Conservatives. Although high income groups have not been seriously hit by any of Gordon Brown's measures, they have certainly not been beneficiaries. One considerable outcome of the Brown chancellorship so far, therefore, is to put a halt to the redistribution which for almost two decades was widening economic inequality in the United Kingdom. Any assessment of the Chancellor's impact on income and wealth redistribution needs to be made in the light of the regressive redistributions which we could have expected to continue had the Conservatives won the 1997 election. Indeed, the Chancellor has made a modest redistribution of resources to some of the very poorest in the community. A range of measures (including a new lower tax rate of 10 per cent on the first £1,500 of income) has achieved this. By one authoritative estimate, Gordon Brown's budgets have pushed up the incomes of the poorest 20 per cent of households with children by around 15 per cent; by contrast the incomes of the richest 10 per cent rose by 1 per cent (Brown, 1999).

the European Union should develop and over Britain's proper role in that development. Only a minority in both parties now advocate what was a common view only a couple of decades ago – withdrawal of the United Kingdom from the EU. But the internal divisions in the parties mirror a wider debate in Europe about the best way to revitalise the economy of the continent. Broadly, this is choice between the established European way of doing things, and an alternative '**Anglo-Saxon model**' which is very influenced by the United Kingdom in the 1980s and 1990s. The traditional European way involves close regulation of the market economy and a partnership between capital and labour in which organised labour has a big say over policy; the Anglo-Saxon model involves deregulation of markets and a sharp diminution of the influence of organised labour over the making of policy and over the functioning of markets. Although leading politicians in both the Conservative and Labour parties have tended to advocate the Anglo-Saxon model in debates about economic policy within the Union, the Labour government elected in 1997 has been more sympathetic than its predecessors to aspects of the traditional regulated European model. This is signified by the Labour government's acceptance of the Social Charter guaranteeing a range of rights in the workplace, which was rejected by its Conservative predecessor.

- The fourth and final economic impact of the Union in economic policy involves a historic choice which faces British politicians early in the new millennium: whether to take the pound sterling into European monetary union. Since the start of 1999, a single currency (the **Euro**) has existed in the Union. The United Kingdom has so far declined to participate. The Euro already trades in foreign exchange, and in 2002 will replace national currencies in everyday business. Both major parties in the United Kingdom are internally divided over whether the United Kingdom should participate, though the Labour government remains cautiously inclined to participate while the Conservative leadership has adopted an increasingly hostile policy. In part the judgement is about economic consequences: about whether the Euro will further free the European economy from national barriers and thus lead to a surge in prosperity; or whether it will prove a weak and unstable currency which will undermine economic stability. In part, the judgement is about political consequences: even those politicians most favourable to monetary union believe that there are great dangers in British participation if it is not preceded by a campaign which allays popular fears over the loss of the pound as a symbol and the loss of important economic policy-making powers to a European Central Bank in Frankfurt. If Britain does enter a monetary union, then this chapter's description of the most important institutions in economic policy will have to be drastically revised in future editions to include a range of institutions beyond the borders of the United Kingdom.

Chapter summary

This chapter has clarified the nature of economic policy, has identified the main actors in economic policy and has sketched three of the most important themes in recent economic policy: the impact of Thatcherism, the significance of new Labour and the role of Europe in economic policy.

Discussion points

- Where does most power reside in the shaping of British economic policy?
- Did the Thatcher governments produce a 'revolution' in economic policy?
- Is the British economy irrevocably bound into the economy of the European Union?

Further reading

Two excellent recent brief surveys of the whole range of the politics of economic policy are Grant (1993) and Thomas (1992). Of the large literature on

Thatcherism, Gamble (1994) is the standard. Wright and Thain (1995) is the standard study of public spending. The policies of the Labour government in the first half of its first term are examined in Coates and Lawler (2000).

References

Brown, A. (1999) 'Is Britain now a fairer country?', *The Observer*, 14 March.

Coates, D. and Lawler, P. (eds) (2000) *New Labour into Power* (Manchester University Press).

Dilnot, A. and Emmerson, C. (1998) 'Some win prizes in game which harbours risks', *Financial Times*, 15 July.

Gamble, A. (1994) *The Free Economy and the Strong State*, 2nd edn (Macmillan).

Grant, W. (1993) *The Politics of Economic Policy* (Harvester Wheatsheaf).

Jamieson, B. (1998) *An Illustrated Guide to the British Economy* (Duckworth).

Thomas, G. (1992) *Government and the Economy Today* (Manchester University Press).

Wright, M. and Thain, C. (1995) *Treasury and Whitehall: Planning and Control of Public Spending* (Clarendon Press).

Chapter 

British foreign and defence policy under the Blair government

Peter Byrd

Learning objectives

- To explain the nature of foreign policy and, particularly, the 'realist' approach to it.
- To explore the idea of an 'ethical foreign policy' and its viability since 1997.
- To examine foreign policy problems in Sierra Leone, Indonesia and Kosovo.
- To assess defence policy in the post-Cold War world.
- To analyse relations with the USA.

Background

The study of British foreign policy has become increasingly problematical because of the difficulty of defining an arena or 'sphere' of foreign policy which is distinct from domestic policy. The internationalisation of government activity means that there are no longer, if indeed there ever were, clearly defined areas of domestic policy and of foreign policy. In the 1960s this internationalisation was often characterised by the perceived growth and alleged political influence of the multinational corporation in impacting on national political and economic life. In the 1970s and 1980s the development of the European Community and of the single internal market blurred enormously the boundaries between the British polity and a wider European sphere of policy making. In the 1990s the favoured term for this process is 'globalisation', emphasising the consequences of the revolution in information and communication technology on the behaviour of the money and financial markets. The 'global village' predicted in the 1960s appears to have arrived though some caution is required in interpreting these developments. For instance, the wars fought in former Yugoslavia throughout most of the 1980s have been widely reported on our television screens and commentators have often referred to these horrors taking place only two hours flying time from Britain and in areas familiar to British holiday-makers. Nevertheless, at crucial times information about developments on the ground has been lacking, air strikes have been based on poor information and the difficulties confronting the Western powers in influencing events are not dissimilar from those confronting the Western allies in 1945.

In this volume we follow the now familiar convention of separating a discussion of developments within the European Union from other areas of foreign policy. In doing this we assume both that EU policy is the most important sphere of foreign policy and also that it is also distinctive from other areas of foreign policy in being the best example of the hybridisation of foreign and domestic policy. Practically all departments of government are involved in making European Union policy; the Foreign and Commonwealth Office is not the most important. For instance, policy on British membership of the Euro, perhaps the single most important strategic issue facing the government since its election in 1997, has been tightly controlled by the Prime Minister and by the Chancellor of Exchequer. The Chancellor laid down the five key criteria to determine the merits of British membership in October 1997 and the Foreign Secretary Robin Cook made not a single speech or statement on the Euro between the general election campaign and his speech in Tokyo on 6 September 1999. In this speech Cook argued in much more positive tones for British membership. Two possible reasons may explain Cook's intervention. The first is that he could no longer ignore the warnings from foreign investors in Britain that it would be difficult to sustain investment if Britain remained outside the Euro (this might explain also why he chose to speak in Tokyo given the importance of Japanese investment). The second is that he was exploiting the enhanced prestige of the FCO based on his successful management of the Kosovo issue since March 1999.

BOX 28.1 MINI BIOGRAPHY

Robin Cook (1946–)
Labour Foreign Secretary. Educated Edinburgh, MP in 1974 where made name as clever left-winger. Shadowed Treasury, Health and Social Security in opposition but made Foreign Secretary in 1997. Recognised as the best parliamentarian of his party but chances of leadership said to be impeded, perhaps unfairly, by his unprepossessing appearance.

Introduction

In this chapter we study British foreign policy (excluding the European issue) since the election of the Labour government in May 1997 under three headings. The first is the government's 'ethical' foreign policy, introduced as part of the FCO mission statement as early as 12 May 1997, days after the election. The second is the Strategic Defence

Review, also announced within days of coming into office, conducted by Secretary of State for Defence George Robertson and completed in July 1998. These two documents constitute not only a statement of foreign and defence policy objectives but also a base line against which performance in office can be judged. The third heading is the government's relationship with the United States. This is the most familiar theme in foreign policy since the Second World War, though Blair was re-cementing a close relationship that had atrophied under the Major government.

Ethical foreign policy

On 12 May Secretary of State Robin Cook identified the goals of Labour's foreign policy in the form of a 'mission statement', adopting in this term one of the key tools of the modern organisation as key to New Labour's modernising drive. The mission was 'to promote the national interests of the United Kingdom and to contribute to a strong world community'. The pursuit of the mission would bring four benefits to Britain:

- security of the UK and the dependent territories (colonies) and peace through the promotion of stability, defensive alliances and arms control;
- prosperity through promotion of jobs and trade;
- quality of life by protecting the environment and countering drugs, terrorism and crime;
- mutual respect by working through international forums and bilateral relationships to 'spread the values of human rights, civil liberties and democracy which we demand for ourselves'.

Despite all the press discussion since 1997 about 'ethical foreign policy', and certainly Robin Cook has consistently identified himself with the concept, it is only the fourth element which is, arguably, new or distinctive.

Theorists and analysts have traditionally seen foreign policy as being about the **national interest**. This 'Realist' concept of national interest is at the same time familiar and opaque. However, it is normally taken as meaning that foreign policy is focused on a core element of the security of the state within an external environment that is anarchic and potentially hostile and in which power and force are the ultimate determinants of outcome rather than law or rectitude. The state, in short, has to be on its guard. The national interest emphasises the continuity of the state's interests rather than the changing vagaries of governmental aspirations.

This traditional definition of foreign policy is enshrined in Cook's first 'benefit' of his foreign policy objectives. Cook has not abandoned the traditional definition of foreign policy; rather he has explicitly sought to widen foreign policy beyond security and prosperity, an objective of foreign policy as old as security, through embracing two other elements. Quality of life and in particular the environment, drugs, terrorism and crime have become increasingly important in foreign policy over the past twenty years or so, in part as a result of the end of the Cold War and the emergence of new foreign policy issues. The Rio Summit of 1988 marked the emergence of the global environment as an important issue for the 'world community' (a term itself founded on acceptance of an ecological perspective on the future of the planet). International terrorism, crime and the drugs trade are older concerns, but have been given increased importance by improvements to international communications and the weakening of national territorialities.

The novelty of Cook's foreign policy mission therefore, other than the very notion of a mission, lies in the fourth benefit of mutual respect and human rights. This is the key to the idea of an ethical foreign policy. Cook's claim reversed classical Realism's respect for, and non-interference in, the domestic sovereignty of other states. The case for non-interference was based both on rectitude, or legal acceptance of the domestic jurisdiction of states, and on prudence, or the acceptance that, given the nature of the international system, interference in the domestic affairs of other states was foolhardy, ineffective and liable to backfire.

The attempt to formulate and then to prioritise an ethical foreign policy can be evaluated against a number of criteria. Firstly, what does it mean? Is there a distinctive concept of an ethical foreign policy? Secondly, is an ethical foreign policy an innovation? Thirdly, has British foreign policy since 12 May 1997 met the requirements of a self-consciously articulated ethical foreign policy? We shall examine each of these in turn.

What is an ethical foreign policy?

If foreign policy is based on national interest and is, therefore, by definition selfish or egotistical, is it conceivable for foreign policy to be altruistic or to pursue deliberate self-abnegation? The Realist school of foreign policy has argued that the apparent presence of altruism in foreign policy can be explained in one of two ways:

1. Altruism in foreign policy can be promoted within a broadly conceived definition of self-interest. To give an example, a policy of development aid and good neighbourliness can form part of an approach to the international system in which self-interest is promoted along with the general welfare. This idea of 'enlightened' self-interest is quite familiar in other spheres of social life and can be accommodated quite easily into thinking about foreign policy. Security and stability may be enhanced more effectively by promoting the general welfare than by crude assertions of self-interest. From this perspective, foreign policy may contain an element or dimension of altruism while being fundamentally concerned with self-interest.
2. A more extreme Realist argument is that the moral or altruistic dimension of foreign policy is a consequence or produce of self-interest. Hence, while foreign policy involves the pursuit of selfish interests, states present those interests as if they were really moral or altruistic goals. These doctrines, it is argued, are a mere pretext or camouflage for concealing the self-interest that lurks below. Hence, status quo powers, which fear decline when confronted by the challenge of revisionist states, may try to preserve their interests by appealing to some higher ethical framework such as respect for law. Rich states may consolidate their economic supremacy by promoting free trade. A contemporary example might be the support of the established nuclear states including Britain for a comprehensive nuclear test ban treaty. This is presented as a general international good, against the objections of such emerging nuclear powers which naturally want to continue testing programmes. These states point to the opposition of states such as Britain to a comprehensive test ban while they were still testing their own current warheads.

Is an ethical foreign policy possible in the light of these objections? To argue that all action in foreign policy is merely based on self-interest is a tenable position, but one that requires the adoption of an unhelpfully broad definition of self-interest. If all action is based on self-interest then the term self-interest is meaningless. Foreign policy is primarily about self-interest because the anarchic nature of the international system, with the ever-present threat of instability and conflict, demands that foreign policy puts the military and economic security interests of the state first. But, much foreign policy activity such as foreign aid, military assistance to developing countries, international co-operation in education or culture, support for the Commonwealth, etc, does not fit easily into the realist framework of foreign policy.

Is an ethical foreign policy new?

Foreign policy has always involved a mix of values around a core of national security. Foreign policy has always espoused other values including those values that could claim to be 'ethical'. The Labour government elected in 1945 proclaimed, at least for a while, that its policy was based on socialist principles. In 1997, for a second time, Labour articulated its ethical foreign policy as a radical departure from the policy of its predecessors. The domestic context here is important. The Labour Party and its government strove to project themselves as New Labour, distinct both from Old Labour and also from the sleaze and corruption which, they argued, had become a dominant characteristic of the Conservative government after eighteen years of office. Hence, the policy pursued by Cook is not a radical change from earlier foreign policy, though it does contain a stronger emphasis on human rights, but it was important for Cook to promote it as if it were new and radical departure. Ethical foreign policy is largely about the domestic politics of foreign policy rather than the external outputs of policy which show remarkable continuity.

The Realist paradigm of foreign policy naturally emphasises continuity in foreign policy and the constraints on the state which make radical shifts of policy difficult if not impossible. In Britain's case continuity of policy transcending changes of government can be seen in such obvious spheres as support for Nato, the close relationship with the United States, the Commonwealth, support for nuclear weapons and deterrence, support for membership of the European Community/Union, etc. There is great force in this view of policy as continuity. But governments also exploit foreign policy, and all other aspects of policy, for domestic purposes. Foreign policy is used at home as well as abroad; change and disagreement may thus be articulated. For instance, Conservative governments have emphasised their support for nuclear weapons; Labour governments, while pursuing nuclear policies at least as hawkish as Conservative governments, have, at least until 1997, tried to depoliticise the issue in order to avoid awkward internal problems.

In 1997 it suited Cook to emphasise the novelty of Labour's ethical foreign policy in order to mark a break with the past and to demarcate sharply New Labour from its Conservative predecessor.

Has policy lived up to being an ethical policy?

The history of foreign policies which proclaim themselves to be ethical or morally superior to their predecessors or the policies of other states is not happy. American foreign policy provides two striking twentieth-century examples. President Woodrow Wilson's Fourteen Points of 1917 sought to replace the tarnished old power politics with a new and ethically superior system of open diplomacy but their implementation proved not merely to be impossible but also to be destabilising. President Jimmy Carter's foreign policy in 1977 based on human rights was also not only impossible to implement but counter-productive in its consequences. America's foreign relations suffered and human rights were harmed rather than enhanced. Carter's Realist opponents argued that a policy based on human rights rested on a fundamental misunderstanding of what was possible in foreign policy. Cook's ethical foreign policy has not yet been subject to such a critique. His Conservative critics have confined themselves to pointing to the inconsistencies in his policy, for instance stressing human rights in one case while conveniently ignoring them in another.

There are a number of 'test cases' for Cook's approach to foreign policy. Because concepts such as ethical foreign policy are 'essentially contested', these cases should be seen as illustrating rather than proving the argument.

Indonesia

Indonesia has been a major buyer of British armaments since the end of the conflict with Britain over Malaysia in 1967. Since 1975 it has occupied the former Portuguese colony of East Timor in defiance of successive United Nations resolutions. British governments, Labour and Conservative, have not allowed the East Timor issue to hinder their harmonious relationship with the Indonesian government. In September 1999 the Indonesian government finally held a referendum on the future of East Timor, precipitating a violent backlash from pro-Indonesian militias when the vote overwhelmingly favoured independence. The British government condemned the tacit support of the Indonesian government for the militias who murdered and terrorised countless thousands of East Timorese. However, it agreed neither to cancel outstanding deliveries of Hawk military aircraft, despite aircraft already delivered being used by the Indonesian government against helpless civilians, nor to cancel the invitation to the Indonesian government to its major arms export exhibition. When Cook reluctantly suspended further deliveries of the Hawk aircraft, the Secretary of Trade and Industry insisted on supporting other British sales to Indonesia. The government did supply a battalion of Ghurka troops to the United Nations multilateral peacekeeping

Despite Foreign Secretary Robin Cook's 'ethical foreign policy', New Labour honours a contract to supply Indonesia with Hawk trainer aircraft (31 August 1997)

force sent in to restore order to East Timor but, that aside, it would be difficult to claim that the reaction to the crisis in East Timor met the criteria of an ethical foreign policy based on human rights.

Sierra Leone

In May 1997 President Kabbah, head of government of the Commonwealth member Sierra Leone, was deposed in a military coup. In October the British government supported the United Nations Security Council in imposing an arms embargo on the illegal government and on the civil war raging in Sierra Leone. In January 1998 the legitimate government restored itself. This was immediately followed by allegations that Kabbah had been armed and assisted by a British-based security consultancy company, Sandline, in defiance of the UN embargo. Sandline claimed that the FCO had known about its operations. The House of Commons Select Committee on Foreign Affairs investigated the matter, as did an official departmental enquiry chaired by Sir Thomas Legg QC. The outcome of the two enquiries was broadly similar in dismissing the charge of FCO collusion with Sandline. Most attention focused on the High Commissioner to Sierra Leone, Peter Penfold, who had been forced to leave and had set up his office in an hotel room in Conakry in neigbouring Guinea where the Kabbah government in exile

A British company's involvement in reversing a coup in Sierra Leone leads to criticism of Robin Cook's ethical foreign policy (28 June 1998)

had established itself. Penfold had no secure communications from this temporary base. Legg praised Penfold's support for the restoration of the legitimate government but considered he had become too close to Sandline which was working with Kabbah's forces in the interior of Sierra Leone. Penfold responded that he had informed the FCO about Sandline's support for the government and claimed that he understood the arms embargo to apply only to the rebel government and not to forces loyal to former President Kabbah – a position identical to Sandline's.

The impression left by the episode was less one of Britain subverting the arms embargo, or of intervening in support of the legitimate government of Kabbah, than of an ineffectiveness and confusion. Policy making was poorly co-ordinated between departments and between the FCO and its High Commissioner. Legg found ignorance rather than conspiracy; he concluded that the FCO's knowledge of developments in Africa was patchy, partly as a result of staff dealing with Africa having been reduced from 430 to 328 over the period 1988–98. The government was spared even greater embarrassment over the affair by relief at the restoration of Kabbah to power (with Sandline's help). In any case, when in January 1999 the 'Revolutionary United Front' overthrew President Kabbah for a second time, there was no effective British response; the only external support for Kabbah came from Nigerian-led military forces operating under the auspices of the Economic Community of West African States.

Can we identify an ethical foreign policy at work in Sierra Leone? The government was concerned by human rights abuses by the opponents of Kabbah and wanted to see his government restored. On the other hand, if there really had been a conspiracy with Sandline to subvert the UN arms embargo then claims to an ethical foreign policy based on support for the UN would be severely undermined. In the absence of proof of a conspiracy, the best verdict is probably Legg's – uncoordination, poor information and ineffective communications.

Kosovo

Kosovo is the most dramatic example of a major foreign policy issue in which there is a strong ethical dimension arising from the prominence given to human rights. The British intervention into Kosovo has been the most important, and arguably most successful, foreign policy initiative of the Labour government. Throughout the Kosovo crisis in 1999 Britain adopted a clear leadership role within the European Union and the Atlantic Alliance, dragging behind it reluctant alliance partners. In Kosovo, Britain 'punched above its weight' and exercised power within a complex alliance setting. Any study of foreign policy since 1997 must pay attention to Kosovo; the idea of ethical foreign policy also provides a suitable framework for evaluating policy.

Throughout 1998 the situation in Kosovo worsened as the Serbian military and political machine exercised increasingly tight control over the province in which over 90 per cent of the population was Albanian. Nato repeatedly pushed President Milosevic of Yugoslavia towards an agreement with the Kosovar nationalist opposition. Air strikes were threatened much as they had earlier in coercing Milosevic towards agreement in Bosnia. Eventually, at Rambouillet in January 1999, an agreement was brokered by Nato between Milosevic and his Kosovar opponents to provide for a degree of self-rule within a larger Serbia. The agreement was short lived. The Kosovar opposition was tentative in its support for the terms and Milosevic denounced the terms that his negotiators had secured. On 24 March, without seeking UN support, Nato launched a strategic bombing campaign to force Milosevic back to the table.

The abuse of human rights by Milosevic in Kosovo appears to have been the major consideration in Britain's decision to push Nato to military intervention. Milosevic's behaviour in Kosovo followed similarly aggressive behaviour against Croatia in 1991 followed by the civil war in Bosnia. It had involved widespread ethnic cleansing by the Serb-backed Croatian Serbs, though there were also human rights violations by the Croat and Bosnian Muslim forces. The Kosovo crisis emerged as the critical test of an ethical foreign policy.

The bombing, codenamed Operation Allied Force, lasted until 10 June when, after 34,000 sorties had been flown, President Milosevic signalled that he would accept an allied army in Kosovo and withdraw his own forces. During the air campaign the war aims of the alliance expanded beyond the Rambouillet settlement to include an international force to be deployed on the ground to guarantee security for the Kosovars. As the scale of the expulsions from Kosovo grew, the British government stated that the removal from power of Milosevic, indicted as a war criminal, had become a necessary guarantee of future stability. Nevertheless, full independence for Kosovo was not a war aim for Nato.

Following Milosevic's acceptance of Nato's terms, a UN Security Council Resolution authorised an armed peacekeeping force (KFOR) in Kosovo. Britain made the largest national contribution (13,000 troops) to KFOR (51,000 in all) which was led by a British commander, General Jackson. In contrast, the British contribution to the air war was minor, on a par with other European allied airforces, militarily ineffective and dwarfed by the American effort. The air war was overwhelmingly American, though European contributions were politically important. The land campaign, which might have involved much heavier armed combat than in fact turned out to be the case, was European dominated and British led.

Nato's own analysis of the campaign indicated that the strategic bombing campaign was ineffective in destroying Serb military power, despite progressive escalation from narrowly military targets (air defence systems) to broader military targets (barracks and oil terminals) and eventually to civilian-strategic targets (bridges, factories, television stations, and power stations). Although it did little harm to Milosevic's position, the air campaign was sustained and hence demonstrated the alliance's resolve. It was continued, despite some members' misgivings and the unintended collateral damage, primarily because the alliance had no other strategy to offer given American resistance to a land war. The bombing may also have been designed partly to give Milosevic an acceptable pretext for capitulation *vis-à-vis* his own internal opposition.

Why did Milosevic agree to Nato's demands and pull out of Kosovo?

The continued resolve of the alliance may have persuaded him that eventually he would be forced to give way and that he could not rule out completely the possibility of a land war. However, the British argument that such a war should be planned and threatened was consistently met by American refusal to contemplate such an outcome.

Internal opposition to Milosevic may have played a part.

The best explanation is probably that Milosevic was urged to back down by the Russians. His Russian allies could not afford to lose co-operation with the West, despite their opposition to the bombing campaign, and needed an end to the war. In an immediate sense, therefore, it was thus the persuasion of an ally rather than the coercion of an enemy that determined the outcome of the war.

The conduct of the war involved complex problems of command and control with both a national and a Nato chain of command. These parallel chains complicated the conduct of the war. The Cabinet, with a central core of Prime Minister, Foreign Secretary and Defence Secretary, exercised political responsibility for the war. The Chief of the Defence Staff advised them and acted through the recently established Permanent Joint HQ, a tri-service command established for conducting this sort of operation. On the ground in Macedonia Lt General Mike Jackson commanded British troops. Parallel with this national chain of command was a Nato political chain of command, focused on the North Atlantic Council within which all seventeen members could, at least in theory, exercise a veto. Military command was vested in the Military Committee and its Supreme Allied Commander Europe, General Wesley Clark. Like Jackson, Clark was both a national and an alliance commander. When Jackson led KFOR into Kosovo, he necessarily exercised many aspects of command without detailed reference to Clark who was based at Allied Command Europe near Brussels. Moreover, Jackson's own operational preferences reflected the British government's desire to operate land forces in Kosovo as early as possible. The American forces under his command lagged behind in operational readiness and forced him to postpone his advance for twenty-four hours. One result of this delay was that the Russian forces in Bosnia were able to detach a small force to occupy the airport in Kosovo's capital, Pristina. When Clark ordered Jackson to remove them, he refused to obey, secure in the knowledge that his authority in the field rested, ultimately, on the support of the British government rather than on Clark as his Supreme Commander.

Was the war fought over Kosovo a humanitarian war fought for without selfish interests at stake? There was undoubtedly a humanitarian motive; the failure of the Rambouillet agreement, following months of Serbian oppression in Kosovo, left no doubt that the Kosovars were under imminent threat. Events in Bosnia had already convinced the British government of the lengths to which Milosevic would go in pursuit of Serbian power. Hence, the government also viewed Milosevic as a threat to stability throughout the Balkans and considered that such destabilisation would indirectly threaten wider British security interests and the objective of bringing Eastern Europe into closer relations with Nato. In retrospect, the Kosovo war also presents an appalling paradox: if it is the case that the war was fought largely for humanitarian motives, it is also true that the bombing gave the pretext for Milosevic's expulsion of almost one million Kosovars from their homeland, with another half a million or so in hiding from Serb forces in the countryside. In the short run the war undoubtedly worsened the situation for the Kosovars. The returning Kosovars hoped for full independence, or perhaps union with Albania, not autonomy within Serbia which was the situation that had existed until 1991 when Milosevic ended their autonomy. Another British war aim, the trial of Milosevic on war crimes, has proved equally difficult to implement. Milosevic was indicted on war crimes in Kosovo in May but there is no way to try him while he remains President.

Nevertheless Nato's five demands for an end to the war were met:

1 A cease-fire accepted by Milosevic before the bombing campaign ended;
2 Withdrawal of Milosevic's troops from Kosovo, according to a timetable laid down by Nato;
3 Deployment of an international peace-keeping force;
4 Return of all the refugees;
5 A high level of autonomy within Kosovo

The British government, and its allies, resisted the demands of the Kosovo Liberation Army for an independent Kosovo, preferring weak multinational states in the Balkans to a multiplicity of nation-states. Homogeneous nation-states would, in any case, require further population movements, probably taking the form of 'ethnic cleansing' on a never-ending cycle of misery.

As in the case of President Carter's human rights policy of 1977, it is possible to argue that the war's consequences, as opposed to motives, for human rights were mixed or even counter-productive. The launch of the bombing campaign precipitated the forcible expulsion of the Kosovars from Kosovo. The expulsion campaign was a macabre, larger scale, version of the ethnic cleansing earlier practised by Milosevic. As the bombing continued the expulsions escalated. After the successful liberation of Kosovo, the refugees were able to return, in many cases, only to find burnt-out homes. They have paid a very high price for their right to remain. Unfortunately, but perhaps inevitably, the returning Kosovars began to practise similar tactics against their erstwhile Serb neighbours, about 180,000, precipitating a second exodus of refugees from Kosovo.

Nevertheless, it can be argued that, on balance, the consequences of the war are justified in terms of ethical foreign policy. The war improved the human rights situation for the majority of the population of Kosovo by eventually ending the Serb oppression. If the consequences of the war can be justified in ethical foreign policy, can the conduct of the war? There is a complex debate within the tradition of the 'just war' about strategic bombing and, in particular, the requirements under just war to avoid, or at the very least, to minimise the risk of unintended (collateral) damage to the innocent. Aerial bombardment tends to be indiscriminate unless the attacker accepts very high risks to himself to aim his bombs with precise accuracy. At the start of the air war Nato attacked the Serb air-defence systems but thereafter continued to minimise the risk of damage to its own forces by confining itself to high level bombing from about 14,000 feet. The effect of high level bombing, together with inadequate ground-level information about Serb deployments, certainly minimised Nato's losses (zero in the case of Britain), but on the other hand increased collateral damage from inaccurate bombing or misinterpreted targets. Kosovar refugees were themselves bombed.

Since 1945 the presence of the authority of the United Nations in authorising war has emerged as an increasingly important criterion for the just conduct of war. The British government did not seek UN authority for the war in Kosovo, unlike the Falklands War in 1982. Then, and acting of course outside a Nato framework, the government went to great lengths to ensure the UN's tacit authority. In Kosovo, the British government relied on the multilateral authority of Nato which knew that the Security Council would not back the war because of Russian and Chinese opposition. On the other hand, the Security Council did not oppose the war and a Security Council resolution established the basis for the settlement of the war.

Dependent Territories

Policy towards the Dependent Territories – the last colonial remnants – also meet the criteria for an ethical foreign policy. In February 1998 Cook announced that the inhabitants of the Dependent Territories, henceforth to be known as Overseas Territories, would gain the right of abode in Britain which they had lost in the 1981 Nationality Act. Gibraltar and the Falklands had already been awarded this right by the Conservatives in response to Argentine and Spanish territorial claims. For other territories the restoration was a remarkable human rights concession. The populations concerned are small, and the potential costs to Britain correspondingly small but, given their impoverished nature, the right to migrate and work in Britain was invaluable. At the same time Cook announced that the government would increase its regulation of the economies of the territories to achieve the highest standards of probity and, in particular, to try to keep out the drugs trade. Policy towards the Overseas Territories demonstrates the familiar situation of generosity being preferred when the real cost of generosity is small. In contrast, Labour did not attempt to extend citizenship rights to the Chinese of Hong Kong before the handover in 1997.

Two other foreign policy issues since 1997 have raised ethical problems. Both arose in an unforeseen way and demanded a response rather than an initiative. Following the volcanic eruption on Montserrat in 1997 the government responded with help for this poor Commonwealth member. It then ran into criticism of Secretary for Overseas Development Clare Short's complaint that the Monstserrat government was rapacious in its demands ('golden elephants') – an error of insensitivity rather than a violation of human rights on Short's part. A second case concerns the arrest in Britain of the former Chilean dictator General Augusto Pinochet in 1998 on charges of torture and human rights at the request of the Spanish legal authorities. The resulting hearings in the courts were a mixed blessing for Cook but, in this example, the driving forces were the Home Office and the Lord Chancellor's department; the FCO had no effective *locus standi*. The Pinochet case illustrates the problems of co-ordinating a consistent government external policy between several departments of government rather than a straightforward issue of determining foreign policy.

Where do these cases leave us in evaluating Cook's claim to have conducted an ethical foreign policy? Additional emphasis has been given to an ethical dimension to policy. Policy has been presented at home and abroad in terms of its new ethical dimension, and presentation becomes part of the content of policy to which others react. In Kosovo the sheer scale of the unfolding humanitarian tragedy of the refugees spurred on the government's determination to see the campaign through to a satisfactory conclusion. But confronted with larger or more distant perpetrators of human rights abuses, such as China or Indonesia or Russia in Chechnya, the government's response has been very similar to that of its predecessors. Practical questions of proximity, other national interests and the size of potential adversaries still count. In the case of China, for instance, the government has not allowed human rights issues to interfere with trade or the arrangements for Hong Kong. The government shares the traditional British view that economic engagement and political dialogue are more effective than enforced isolation or feigned hostility. Blair claimed in his speech of 22 April 1999 about the 'Doctrine of International Community' that human rights were a necessary basis for international security and overrode traditional conceptions of sovereignty and non-interference in the domestic affairs of other states. This claim remains an aspiration, not yet a determining factor of British foreign policy. What has been achieved since 1997 is a change of emphasis rather than of fundamentals.

The Strategic Defence Review

Conservative defence policy since 1990 was about managing two external demands: firstly, the new realities of the post-Cold War world and, secondly, increasing pressure for economies. The hopes of the late 1980s that the ending of the Cold War would produce a large 'peace dividend' were not realised. The response to the end of the Cold War came in two phases. In Options for Change, June 1990, government announced a small, general, reduction in defence capabilities with a slight shift of emphasis towards greater flexibility of forces. The main thrust of defence would remain on Nato and on the continental deployment of the army and airforce, while the navy would shift emphasis over time away from submarine and anti-submarine warfare towards flexible surface ships. But all capabilities would decline in absolute terms. In July 1994 in the 'Defence Costs Study', known as 'Front Line First', the government announced reductions in support and logistics and some increases in fighting forces, especially for the infantry, together with simplifications of commands in recognition of increasing strains on the forces since 1990.

By 1997 defence policy had entered a period of relative stability within ever-declining budgets. Three main defence roles had been identified. Defence role one is the defence of the UK and its territories, even when there is no overt external threat. This core defence capability included the retention of the nuclear deterrent, untargeted in the absence of a nuclear enemy. This 'existential deterrent' (deterrence from mere possession) is similar to the traditional French policy of nuclear dissuasion in contrast to Britain's previous strategy of deterrence through an overt threat of retaliation. Defence role two is insurance against a major attack on the UK or its allies and encompasses the Nato commitment and Nato force structures. Defence role three is the contribution to wider security interests through the maintenance of peace and stability. This is the extended concept of security including peacekeeping and peace enforcement through the UN and Nato, involving British forces even where no national security interests are immediately at stake. This extended concept of security is the military aspect of the ethical dimension of foreign policy discussed above and indicates continuity rather than change through the 1990s.

Throughout 1990–7, the Labour Party argued for a more comprehensive 'Strategic Defence Review' in which the whole range of security commitments and interests would be analysed, together with actual and potential capabilities. The argument was that the government had reacted to problems in an *ad hoc* way without a clear framework in which resources and commitments could be balanced. Without a framework, Labour argued, the Treasury would dictate defence policy by determining budgets. Certainly, within the period after 1990 defence expenditure measured as a per cent of GDP fell, indeed had been falling since its New Cold War peak of 1986. In the period 1990–8, for instance, it fell by 23 per cent in real terms. By 1998 defence consumed 2.7 per cent of GDP, a low level not reached even during the period of unilateral disarmament under Churchill as Chancellor of the Exchequer in the 1920s.

Immediately on coming into office the new Secretary of State for Defence, George Robertson, announced that he would conduct a Strategic Defence Review to identify the requirements of defence policy in the uncertainty of the post-Cold War world. The review would be defence driven rather than Treasury driven. However attractive this argument appears, the Treasury must play a crucial role in defence policy simply because the claims on defence policy are always greater than the resources available. In the recent past the influence of the Treasury on defence has never recovered to its role in the 1930s when it established two of the key elements of strategic thinking: firstly that resources had to be deployed cautiously in preparation for a long war and post-war recovery; secondly, that resources available for the air force should be deployed on air defence rather than on air offence. In any case, Robertson could not reverse the trend of declining defence expenditure and his review accepted that resources would continue to fall to about 2.4 per cent of GDP by 2002.

Robertson modified the three defence roles identified by his Conservative predecessors into distinct missions. Defence role one he divided into two missions, defence of the UK in a situation of no overt external threat and defence of the Overseas Territories. He confirmed New Labour's revived love affair with nuclear weapons. The only nuclear weapon system available to him, following the Conservative government's decision to abandon the air force's residual nuclear capability of 'free-fall' nuclear bombs, was Trident. Robertson confirmed that the planned Trident fleet of four submarines would be completed to ensure that one submarine would always be on station. However, a stock of only fifty-eight missiles would be leased from the United States with each submarine deploying only forty-eight war-heads on its 16 missiles, a reduction from the Conservative proposals to deploy ninety-six war-heads per submarine. The government would maintain a total of about 200 warheads, a reduction of 70 per cent from the figure in 1990. The Conservative governments post-1990 had shown some interest in the idea of shifting Trident from a weapon of all-out strategic revenge into a more flexible weapon to be used in a limited way, perhaps with a single war-head deployed, against a range of potential nuclear enemies rather than merely Russia. Robertson did not pursue further this rather tentative strategy. By 1998 the cost of the nuclear deterrent had fallen from a peak of over 10 per cent of defence expenditure during the acquisition of Trident to about 3 per cent, a figure very similar to the halcyon days of Polaris in the early 1970s. Trident illustrates how for a medium power such as Britain nuclear weapons are extremely expensive to acquire or modernise but very cheap to operate once deployed.

Defence roles two and three were subject to greater change. The threats to British security now came less from direct military threat from Russia than from a multiplicity of risks around the world arising from instability, escalating local conflicts, etc. Defence role two, defence of Europe from external attack, was broken down into missions to provide defence against strategic attack on Nato and regional conflict within the Nato area. Robertson envisaged Nato continuing to evolve from a purely defensive alliance into an organisation capable of intervening in regional conflicts in Europe through its Rapid Reaction Corps. Defence role three, the promotion of wider security interests, was elaborated into four missions: regional conflicts outside of the Nato area (such as the Gulf); support for peace-making and humanitarian intervention; the defence of wider British interests (such as the Five Power Treaty with Malaysia, Singapore, Australia and New Zealand); defence diplomacy, such as negotiation of arms control agreements.

The ending of the Cold War gave greater prominence to wider security interests at the expense of the traditional balance against Soviet Union/Russia but also precipitated new security conflicts both in Eastern Europe and elsewhere. The response to these conflicts in the immediate post-Cold War situation had been President Bush's concept of a New World Order under American leadership. The Gulf War was its early manifestation. The collapse of former Yugoslavia and the deployment of UN and Nato forces in Bosnia on a quasi-permanent basis was the second major example. Robertson's vision was that defence forces would be drawn into various UN and multilateral peacekeeping operations and, beyond that, that a new and closer relationship between foreign policy and defence capability would be forged. Armed forces might be used in a variety of situations in which their role would vary from passive peacekeeping at one end of the spectrum to the enforcement of peace at the other. Peacekeeping could normally rely on lightly armed infantry forces, while peace enforcement might require more heavily armed battlefield forces. Within and without Europe, military force might be called up for a range of tasks in areas of instability.

The main additional requirement for defence was greater mobility and the possibility of deployment in distant theatres of heavily armed forces. In September 1999 this concept bore fruit in the form of 16 Air Assault Brigade, bringing together two existing airborne and airmobile brigades, and, from 2000, with a new fleet of Apache attack helicopters. Throughout the forces there was increased emphasis on flexibility and heavy lift and transport capabilities, controlled by the recently established Joint Permanent Head Quarters as the command structure for combined air/land/sea forces.

Robertson largely confirmed Conservative procurement plans and added one major new project. The order for 386 Challenger 2 tanks would be completed and two armoured divisions established. The major new weapon for the army would be a battlefield helicopter to deploy against armoured forces in the form of the American Apache, to be built under licence in Britain. The Gulf War in 1992 had demonstrated the value of such a capability, at least against a weak opponent and in open desert country, though the American Apache force deployed during the Kosovo war made no impact at all and proved difficult to deploy against the Serbian forces. Robertson committed the government to completion of the full contract for 232 new Eurofighers. This was the weapon that the air force had set its heart on. Since the early 1980s it had lacked a specialist air defence fighter aircraft, relying on the ineffective Tornado F3 which had singularly failed to distinguish itself in the Gulf War. The Eurofighter contract had been subject to constant threats since being first developed in the early 1980s with Germany, Italy and Spain, with the German government in particular perennially hovering on the point of cancellation.

The navy would reduce its declining submarine capability still further to a force of only ten nuclear-powered submarines, plus the four Trident ships. Robertson's major new procurement project, and in one sense the main outcome of the whole review, was the proposal to build two new large aircraft carriers, capable of carrying fifty aircraft, to replace the ageing fleet of three small warfare carriers built in the 1970s. These ships had evolved since the 1970s towards a general air attack role but were too small to carry adequate numbers of aircraft. The two new carriers, together with two new assault ships already on order, and the recently completed helicopter carrier HMS Hero, would enable rapid deployment of a range of forces by sea. The navy would regain some of its traditional 'blue waters' capability of projecting power globally and flexibly. New naval capabilities complement the army's new emphasis on airmobile forces, in turn supported by heavier forces deployed by sea or by new heavy air lift capabilities.

The rationale for these new capabilities rests on a broad conception of Britain's security interests. What is the case for this? There is no immediate direct military threat to British security other than from the IRA, currently signed up to a cease-fire. However, conflicts in one area may spill over into other areas, closer to home. Secondly, the emphasis on an ethical foreign policy and defence of humanitarian interests requires flexible capabilities. Thirdly, it can be argued that Britain benefits by accepting responsibilities and duties which contribute to a stable world which is itself a British interest. In the short run, Britain could act, like Japan, as a free rider and obtain the benefits of stability without making a military contribution towards ensuring it, but, the government thinks, influence and prestige would decline if such an attitude were adopted. In short, there is an unquestioned assumption within government that, through punching above its weight, prestige and influence are maximised and hence that responsible behaviour brings its own reward. An activist policy increases influence with the United States and Germany and within Nato. Nato remains, on this analysis, the key to security policy and Britain plans to remain at the centre of Nato. Command of the Nato's Rapid Reaction Corps is one example of this central role. George Robertson's appointment as Secretary-General in October 1999 confirmed it. Implicit in this argument is the failure of the 'emerging security architecture' within Europe, in particular the Organisation for Security and Organisation in Europe, to displace Nato.

Defence forces remain small and over-stretched. The end of the Cold War has increased the demands on the forces not reduced them. In 1998 at the time of the publication of the Strategic Defence Review, there were British forces deployed in Germany (about 30,000), Cyprus (3,000) Bosnia (4,000+), Falklands (1,000), the Gulf and Turkey (1,000+) together with smaller forces in Gibraltar, Belize and Brunei, and elsewhere. In addition, 15,000 troops were on peacekeeping operations in Northern Ireland, the most arduous commitment within defence role one. In 1999 to these commitments was added the war in Kosovo (17,000 troops plus air force and navy). Whereas in the early 1990s the greatest pressure within the army had been on infantry battalions, with the government having to increase the number of battalions above the figure set in 1990, the demands from Bosnia and Kosovo were for infantry, plus armour, artillery, engineers, etc. To sustain all Robertson's defence missions demands a very wide range of forces with little possibility of functional specialisation with allies. There is some scope for defence capabilities to be kept at a lower level of readiness but most forces need to be at a high level of preparedness. Reserve forces can, in theory, make a contribution in such a situation, forming the basis of 'reconstitutive' or even 'regenerative' forces. But while parts, such as medical forces, can be brought relatively easily into active service – and have been in the Gulf, Bosnia and Kosovo – they are very small. The Strategic Defence Review's conclusion was higher levels of preparation but with further reductions in size.

British forces are highly professional and effective but, given high levels of specialisation, also small and expensive, operating without any economies of scale. Under Robertson's plans they must also be prepared to take on a variety of roles. Given their small size one particularly awkward question is raised. Can British military power aspire to be a premier division force capable of fighting a high intensity war or are they now a second division force whose effectiveness is confined to such lower intensity wars such as Bosnia or Kosovo? Forces capable of high intensity warfare can be deployed on lower intensity operations, even if their training and equipment are not exactly suited. On the other hand, forces only capable of lower intensity warfare cannot be used in a high intensity battle. British forces have clung persistently to the notion that they are small but capable of high intensity warfare – in the premier division – and unique among other high intensity forces in also being trained for low intensity warfare as a result of the Northern Ireland situation and post-colonial wars. Kosovo does not answer the question. The air force participated in very small scale, and apparently ineffectively, in an American-led high intensity bombing campaign. On the ground below the army prepared for a lower intensity campaign, though one which was overtly coercive and, potentially, of higher intensity. After two years in office the government made no radical changes to defence policy. The downward pressure on expenditure remains, but there had been progress in establishing more flexible forces, able to operate within tri-service commands both within Europe and outside. Over-stretch remains and increased with the despatch of a Ghurka battalion to East Timor. Uncertainty remains over whether, in the medium term, it is possible to sustain such a varied defence effort with such small forces.

Relations with the United States

During the Major government British relations with the United States deteriorated from the peak of close relations which had characterised Thatcher and Reagan and, to a lesser extent, Thatcher and Bush. The Major–Clinton relationship never established itself. Clinton was slow to forgive Major for his overt and covert support for Bush in the 1992 presidential election. Major resented Clinton's early forays into the Irish problem and pressure in 1994 and 1995 for direct negotiations with Sinn Fein. Other differences emerged. The British government considered Clinton's emphasis on air power in Bosnia, to deter the Serbs, simplistic, especially when the Americans were so reluctant to commit ground troops to Unprofor, the UN force in Bosnia. In 1993 there were major trade disagreements over farm subsidies in the EC. Clinton's own priorities were domestic rather than foreign and his foreign policy priorities lay within the North American Free Trade Area and the Pacific Rim.

In contrast Blair sought a close working relationship with Clinton. At the party level, Clinton and Blair supported each other's election campaigns in 1996 and 1997 and shared similar ideas for a reworking and modernisation of left of centre politics – the so-called 'Third Way'.

More specifically there have been three important areas of co-operation since 1997 in which the two governments have committed themselves to working together in a sustained manner. Firstly, they have worked together on Nato enlargement, culminating in its first stage in the entry of Poland, Hungary and the Czech Republic in 1999, while at the same time avoiding so far as possible antagonising Russia or weakening Boris Yeltsin's position. There has been a recognition of the difficulties confronting Yeltsin and a marked reluctance to interfere in his domestic politics. For instance, the two governments resisted criticism of Russian intervention in Chechnya, despite Blair's emphasis on human rights. In two more specific policy areas effective joint working has been established. Blair was prepared to work with Clinton towards a resolution of the Irish problem. He persuaded Clinton to support his strategy of working for a cease-fire to be followed by negotiations towards a political settlement rather than to pursue the usual Democrat policy of a political settlement that would lead to a cease fire. Clinton then offered the services of former senator George Mitchell to help bring about an outline political settlement in the April 1998 Good Friday Agreement. When the agreement broke down over the refusal of the IRA to disarm Mitchell was called back to help negotiate a new phase of the agreement in November 1999. Mitchell was able to act, remarkably tactfully and skilfully, as an honest broker in a way that Secretary of State Mo Mowlam or her successor Peter Mandelson would not have been able to do.

An even more remarkable example of Anglo-American co-operation is in Iraq. In the period after the Gulf War of 1992 the British maintained forces in Turkey and Saudi Arabia to enforce the no-fly zones, alongside the Americans. Saddam

Hussein consistently frustrated the efforts of the United Nations inspectors, UNSCOM, to ensure that Iraq dismantled its biological and atomic military capabilities. In the autumn of 1997 a crisis developed and the government despatched an aircraft carrier to the Gulf. At that time other friendly Arab countries, such as Saudi Arabia, were reluctant to continue to co-operate and Britain and America alone attempted to pressurise Iraq. In February 1998 the UN Secretary-General negotiated a settlement and UNSCOM resumed its work. In July and October 1998 the situation erupted again and Blair proclaimed that an object of Anglo-American policy was the overthrow of Saddam. Britain and America called on the Iraqi opposition to act. Clinton sought to maximise the urgency and danger of the situation, partly in order to deflect the Congress which was moving towards a vote on impeachment over his domestic misdemeanours. On 16 October, without seeking further UN authority, America and Britain launched massive air strikes against Iraq. On 19 October the House voted to impeach Clinton. Bombing continued for four days but it is not clear that Operation Desert Fox secured any military or political objectives, even that of reinforcing Clinton's domestic support. Following Operation Desert Fox the British have continued to follow closely American policy in the Gulf and to maintain forces including air forces to enforce on a regular basis the no-fly zones.

Blair's remarkably close relationship with Clinton has not been shaken in any way by Clinton's declining domestic reputation, despite Blair's own emphasis on a rather moralistic probity and rectitude. However, as Clinton enters the last months of a lame duck presidency the value of the relationship to Blair must decline, especially if it emerges that a Republican is likely to win the 2000 election.

Secret documents briefing the US Defence Secretary William Cohen were drawn on in a *Guardian* article, 29 November 1999. In a section which might have embarrassed advocates of the 'ethical foreign policy' and the qualitative break with Conservative practice, Pentagon officials confirmed the closeness of Anglo-US relations: '[Britain] remains our closest partner in political, security and intelligence matters . . . Beyond Europe there are few apparent differences between the stated foreign policy goals of Labour and its Conservative predecessor. The government continues to support a strong defence over some objections within the old left of the Labour party – and is working to keep a military that can deploy with US forces . . .'. Another passage advised Cohen that: 'the prime minister has made it clear that NATO will remain the ultimate guarantor of Britain's defence and that emphasis on Europe will not be at the expense of the trans-Atlantic link'. Blair added a new perspective on the relationship between Europe and America at his speech to the Lord Mayor's Banquet, 22 November 1999. He said: 'We have a new role – not to look back and try to recreate ourselves as the pre-eminent superpower of 1900, nor to pretend to be the Greeks to America's Romans. It is to use the strengths of our history to build our future not as a superpower but as *a pivotal power*, as a power that is at the crux of alliances and international politics which shape the world and its future' (author's italics).

Chapter summary

Foreign policy is easier to describe than to explain – to tell the (public) story than to make sense of the motives and the sequence of cause and effect. Foreign policy is probably even more difficult to evaluate in the sense of identifying success and failure in securing outcomes in a difficult external environment. However, it is possible to come to some very tentative conclusions by way of evaluation. Firstly, the government has not got into any serious domestic difficulties over foreign policy since 1997. The Sandline affair was too marginal and obscure to achieve anything like the notoriety of the Matrix Churchill affair over the sale of high technology to Iraq. The Kosovo war enhanced the government's reputation for competence and leadership, despite persistent criticism during the war from military commentators that the bombing campaign was misconceived and poorly implemented. The government may, indeed, have been lucky over Kosovo given that it was probably Russia that played the decisive part in ending the war. Secondly, the Strategic Defence Review enabled the government to put firmly in the past Labour's unpopular association with unilateral nuclear disarmament. The review together with Kosovo enabled Labour to break the traditional image in British politics that the Conservatives were the natural party of defence and that Labour was always liable to run into domestic difficulties over defence. Thirdly, Cook succeeded in promoting the concept of a new approach to foreign policy, based on humanitarian imperatives. We have argued that ethical foreign policy is best understood as an evolution from well-established ideas about the objectives of foreign policy and, in that sense, was not new. But the promotion of the policy was new and successful and awkward cases which did not fit the model – China, Indonesia, Chechnya – did not succeed in destroying the model. Unlike Clinton in the United States or to some extent Major in the preceding government, the Blair administration has not been forced to resort to foreign policy initiatives in order to deflect attention away from domestic problems. Lastly, the government has succeeded in re-establishing, at least in part, British leadership in important issues within the alliance, either in co-operation with the United States as over the Gulf or in exercising a leadership that the Americans have been obliged to follow, as over Kosovo. This leadership role should not be exaggerated; in Kosovo the Americans successfully resisted the British urgings to contemplate a ground campaign and, in retrospect, they were right that this was not a necessary part of the war. In Ireland the role of Mitchell has been indispensable in promoting whatever sort of peaceful outcomes transpires. Will Blair find the next American administration as willing to co-operate and to share leadership?

Discussion points

- Criticise the 'realist' approach to foreign policy.
- Should Britain have avoided involvement in Kosovo?
- Does the world need a new form of international government?

Further reading

Two key documents are the FCO Mission Statement of 12 May 1997, reported in full in the press the following day and available on the FCO web site at www.fco.gov.uk/directory and the Strategic Defence Review, Cm3999, July 1998. The most accessible account of the Sandline Affair is in the report of the House of Commons Select Committee on Foreign Affairs (1999) *Sierra Leone* (House of Commons), Paper 116–1.

References

Byrd, P. (1988) *British Foreign Policy Under Thatcher* (Philip Allan).

Carrington, Lord (1988) *Reflect on Things Past* (Collins).

Freedman, C. and Clark, M. (1991) *Britain in the World* (Cambridge University Press).

Sanders, D. (1990) *Losing an Empire, Finding a Role* (Macmillan).

Chapter 29

Environmental policy

Andrew Flynn

Learning objectives

- To explain the provenance and functions of the Environment Agency; local planning and conservation agencies.
- To elucidate the positions of the main political parties on environmental policy.
- To analyse the role of pressure groups focussing on the environment.

Introduction

The 1990s witnessed enormous changes in the approach of both the Conservative government and its Labour successor to environmental issues, to the administration of environmental policy and to the content of that policy. At the same time, there was a series of unresolved tensions that helped to give British environmental policy its own particular mix and dynamic. These included:

- The environment failed to be a mainstream topic of political debate in the general elections of 1992 and 1997 and yet during this time the top ten environmental groups could claim a reasonably consistent membership amongst themselves of some 4.5m people, so far exceeding the membership of political parties (see chapter 12) and indeed of any other form of social organisation.
- The environment became an increasingly mainstream public policy issue, metamorphosed into sustainable development and having done so raised further challenges for government in the implementation of policy goals;
- The locus of policy making shifted away from the nation state upwards towards Brussels and downwards to Cardiff and Edinburgh.
- Efforts to secure the integration of policy making and its implementation met countervailing pressures of fragmentation.

For students of politics the challenge raised by environmental issues to existing administrative structures is of enormous interest. So too is the way in which external pressures on bureaucracies, such as those from the European Union (EU), shape the context of environmental policy making and its implementation. But the nature of the challenge posed by environmentalism goes beyond simply studying bureaucratic structures. It involves questions of how governments respond to environmental issues, how societies articulate their environmental concerns and how political parties and pressure groups seek to represent the environment. These questions will be answered during the course of the chapter, but first we address the impact of Europe on British environmental policy, and then consider what environmental policy might be and how it has become part of the broader debate on sustainable development. The third section analyses the role of key organisations and institutions operating in Britain since it is they who are responsible for much of the delivery of policy. The fourth section explores the impact of devolution on environmental policy and the fifth the part that political parties and pressure groups play.

The impact of Europe on British environmental policy

Membership of the EU has had a profound influence on the content of British environmental policy and also the way that it is made (Lowe and Ward, 1998a). These two points are addressed in turn.

Policy content

The European Community first began to take a serious interest in environmental issues in the early 1970s (Lowe and Ward, 1998a, pp. 11–13). Its first Action Programme on the Environment was published in 1973 and aimed to improve people's quality of life, living conditions and their surroundings. At this stage the emphasis was very much on trying to ensure that the people within the Community enjoyed similar standards and that environmental regulations were not used by member states as a means of distorting trade. With regard to the latter there was much work on trying to harmonise product standards, a similar burst of activity being associated with the completion of the Single European Market. Throughout the 1970s the environment continued to rise up the European political agenda and was marked by a growing institutionalisation. An Environment Directorate-General (DGXI) of the Commission was established in 1981, and in 1987 under the Single European Act there was explicitly established a basis for Community action in the environmental field. Until this time environmental legislation had to be justified on the grounds that it was helping to avoid distortions of the market in line with the Community's economic rationale. The EU's responsibilities for environmental protection have been broadened and deepened under the 1993 Treaty on European Union (that amended the Treaty of Rome) and 1997 Treaty of Amsterdam. The former provided a still firmer legal base for EU environmental activities, while the latter has committed the EU as one of its main tasks to promoting sustainable development and a higher quality environment. This involves the EU not only thinking about specific environmental policies but also making sure that environmental concerns are integrated into other policy areas. As we shall see below, Britain has traditionally been regarded as a middle-ranking state with regard to environmental policy. However, in what was clearly designed to give out a quite different message, the Labour government, in hosting its first European Council meeting in Cardiff in June 1998, ensured that there was a reaffirmation of the importance of integrating the environment across the EU's activities.

Article 130r of the revised Treaty of Rome identified a number of key principles that EU policy should now be based on including the following:

- Precautionary principle – whereas in the past many decisions have been taken only when there is sufficient supporting evidence to justify a course of action this principle justifies action to prevent harm to the environment before such evidence is available.

- Preventative action – recognises that it is better to try and stop environmental problems arising at source rather than to deal with them once they have arisen.
- Polluter pays – those who cause **pollution** should pay for its clean up rather than those who may be most affected by it.
- Policy integration – the environment must play a part in decision making in all policy areas.

The EU's Environmental Action Programmes provide it and the Member States with a guide to action, an agenda for change. The Fifth Environmental Action Programme (5th EAP) running for the period 1992–2000 is entitled Towards Sustainability (Commission of the European Communities, 1992). According to one former senior civil servant it marked the first occasion on which the British government could begin to identify with a European environmental agenda (Sharp, 1998, p. 49). This was both a reflection of the content of the programme and of the way in which ideas in Britain had been developing. The 5th EAP shared the policy principles that were to be found in the Treaty of European Union and suggested that there should be a wider use of policy instruments (e.g. eco-taxes, voluntary agreements with industry) since established command and control measures were no longer sufficient to deal with environmental problems. The document promoted the idea of shared responsibility, that is the solution to environmental problems was not solely the responsibility of government or the private sector but also needed to include the public, voluntary organisations and the public sector. The 5th EAP also identified five key sectors – agriculture, energy, industry, transport and tourism – where there was a particular need to try and make progress to improve their environmental and economic performance. The linking together of the economy and the environment is an important feature of the way in which the environmental debate has broadened into one on sustainable development as we shall see below.

Policy making

EU law takes precedence over national law and since in the making of environmental policy there has been a shift away from voting by unanimity to majority voting, Britain, like other countries, cannot exercise control over what decisions are made. The environmental field was the fastest growing EU policy area in the 1980s and by the mid 1990s John Gummer (1994), a former British Secretary of State for the Environment, had estimated that about 80 per cent of British environmental legislation had its origins in Europe. Not surprisingly, therefore, there have been considerable impacts on the British environmental policy process.

Lowe and Ward (1998a, pp. 26–8) identify three dimensions along which it is possible to assess change in the policy process. The first of these is a challenge to Britain's traditional policy style, that is the management and administration of issues. As an important political issue the environment commands the attention of wide swathes of government in a way in which it did not in the past. In tackling problems such as pollution Britain's pragmatic approach in which pollution problems could be dealt with on a case by case basis has been undermined by the elucidation of wide-ranging principles, such as the polluter pays, to govern action. Similarly regulators had liked to be flexible when dealing with polluters to take account of their circumstances, but that is less possible as European legislation is much more target led, meaning that firms and government must meet pre-set criteria, and so limiting their room for manoeuvre.

Second, there have been changes in the relationships amongst organisations involved in the policy process. As the focus for policy making has moved from London to Brussels it has opened up the process to environmental groups who have found a more receptive audience for their views. Local government meanwhile may have lost some of its authority since it is national governments that engage in negotiations and are held responsible by Brussels for the implementation of policy.

Third, and most difficult of all to assess, what has been the impact of Europe on the substance of policy? Although the evidence is somewhat mixed there is a belief that the EU has meant that Britain has adopted higher standards of environmental protection than it would otherwise have done. What the EU has most certainly done is to help change the terms of the environmental debate in Britain. Whilst Britain is an adapter rather than an initiator of environmental policy, government thinking is at least now attuned to that of leading nations such as the Netherlands. This is a point that is explored in greater detail below.

From environmental policy to sustainable development

It is easy to suggest that environmental policy was 'discovered' in the 1980s and 1990s. Yet many of the most prominent environmental groups were formed well before then, while Britain has long-standing policies to regulate air quality and land use, two components of any environmental policy. So a first question must be whether the environment is really a new policy area or simply older issues recast in a more fashionable light. In part the answer is determined by the way the environment transcends traditional administrative and policy boundaries leading to, for example, the greening of policies in transport and the environment, agriculture and the environment, etc. rather than existing as a separate policy sector. Defining the content of environmental policy, however, is not easy.

Not surprisingly, therefore, many commentators duck the question of what they regard as environmental policy. It is assumed implicitly that everyone knows what it is and is not. Nevertheless, it is possible to distinguish two popular approaches to defining environmental policy. The first is broad in scope and seeks links to the physical environment: thus environmental policy is 'public policy concerned with governing the relationship between people and their natural environment' (McCormick, 1991, p. 7). Unfortunately this definition is both too narrow, in the sense that it seems to exclude urban areas (as these are difficult to classify as a natural environment), and too general, as it would seem difficult in practice to distinguish it from other policy areas such as rural social policy.

The other approach is much narrower in scope and focusses on 'the use of land and the *regulation* of human activities which have an impact on our physical surroundings' (Blowers, 1987, pp. 278–9, our emphasis). This implies a prescriptive element to policy, as politicians should seek a balance in the use of land between its development, **conservation** and ecological functions. In practice this involves working through two regulatory systems, that of the land use planning system (responsible for development and conservation) and pollution control (the ecological function). While providing a framework against which to assess changes in environmental policy, the regulatory definition ignores the wider political and social backcloth, including the activities of political parties and new social groups, against which environmental decisions are made.

Neither was it possible to specify that government action on the environment amounted to an environmental policy. Writing at the end of the 1980s Lowe and Flynn claimed that:

> government structures and law relating to environmental protection have been (and largely remain) *an accretion of common law, statutes, agencies, procedures and policies*. There is no environmental policy other than the sum of these individual elements, most of which have been pragmatic and incremental responses to specific problems and the evolution of relevant scientific knowledge. (Lowe and Flynn, 1989, p. 256, emphasis added)

However, in 1990 the White Paper *This Common Inheritance* (Cm 1200) was published, the first ever comprehensive statement in Britain of a government's environmental policy. Criticised at the time for its modest proposals, the document nevertheless marks something of a watershed: the environment was a legitimate and high profile public policy issue. By the end of the decade the terms of the debate had once again shifted. Increasingly to simply think of the environment as a single policy area is to marginalise it. Successive governments have produced detailed statements of their environmental policy but now they have also sought to integrate the environment with economic and social issues to develop a strategy for sustainable development. So how has such a dramatic shift come about in such a short space of time? Any answer must include at least the following issues: the British government's response to developing agendas in the EU and at the United Nations, the success of pressure groups in the promotion of the environmental agenda, and a growing realisation of the challenges of implementing environmental policy and of the need to ensure that it took account of business and social interests.

The sustainable development agenda

One of the classic confrontations of the late twentieth century has been that between the environment and the economy. The two are regarded as incompatible: one either has ecological protection and no-growth or economic development and environmental degradation. The notion of sustainable development, and the belief of some that we are moving towards a greener society, integrates the economy and the environment and at one stroke sidesteps much of the traditional debate.

Much of the controversy now is over what is meant by sustainable development, for it has become something of a totem, a concept so powerful that no one should question it. But different interests seek to interpret it in various ways. As such sustainable development has become an object of contestation within the environmental debate. Originally developed within the ecological sciences, it was popularised in *Our Common Future* (more commonly known as the Brundtland Report) (World Commission on Environment and Development, 1987) as that which 'meets the needs of the present without compromising the ability of future generations to meet their own needs'. At its minimum this would seem to involve little more than business as usual with a few added-on commitments to environmental protection.

In order to show their commitment to environmental protection and exploit market opportunities businesses have engaged in such measures as environmental management systems and environmental auditing. Purchasing policies, production processes and waste disposal are all now much more carefully monitored. Eco-labelling schemes now exist in many European countries to show that products are produced to a certain standard and an EU-wide labelling scheme has appeared.

Governments have shown a willingness to co-ordinate and act to address the issue of sustainable development. The Brundtland Report was endorsed by political leaders at the United Nations Conference on Environment and Development (the Earth Summit) in Rio de Janeiro in 1992. The summit produced the following:

1. the Rio declaration, which established a set of principles for action;
2. a programme of action for the next century, Agenda 21
3. a Climate Change Convention to try to reduce the risks of global warming;
4. a Biodiversity Convention to protect species and habitats; and
5. a statement of principles for the conservation of the world's forests.

Each country was charged with taking forward these points. A follow-up, Earth Summit II, was held in New York in June 1997 and began to expose to a wide audience the difficulties that a number of the developed countries were experiencing in putting into practice the ideas they had endorsed some five years earlier in Rio.

The former Conservative government put some efforts into delivering its promises on implementing its action programme. After a year-long consultation period it published *Sustainable Development: the UK Strategy* (Cm 2426) in January 1994. The document was largely a restatement of existing policies and ideas but did contain some initiatives to promote new ideas. These included a Panel on Sustainable Development comprising five eminent experts who report directly to the Prime Minister on major strategic issues; a Round Table on Sustainable Development made up of thirty representatives drawn from business, local government, environmental groups and other organisations that seek to build consensus about the ways of achieving sustainable development; and a Going for Green programme to carry the sustainable development message to local communities and individuals. From 2000 the Panel and Round Table will be subsumed within a new Sustainable Development Commission.

The government also published proposals on *Biodiversity: the UK Action Plan* (Cm 2428). Again, the policies were modest and often simply consolidated in one document existing actions but did at least represent a positive step forward. In contrast parts of local government have been much more innovative in developing sustainability indicators and action programmes though they remain hamstrung by lack of resources and powers.

However, many environmentalists are arguing that a stronger version of sustainable development needs to be put into practice, one in which the state plays a much more positive role in ensuring the equitable distribution of resources through space and time. Attention is switched away from total production to the methods of production of particular goods. A weak version of sustainable development therefore fails to confront the major cause of the ecological crisis, the sheer amount of production and consumption. On this view, sustainable development does not mean no development but much more selective development.

For governments the idea that there should be more selective development is a challenging one as it may alienate voters and their families caught up in those sectors or firms that are seen to be too unsustainable. They have therefore sought to construct defensible policy positions at a point between the weak and strong versions of sustainable development. Shortly after its election to power in 1997 the Labour government announced that it would update the sustainable development strategy of its predecessor. In February 1998 a consultation paper, *Opportunities for Change*, was issued and it was followed by a small number of additional consultation papers on particular aspects of sustainable development, such as business and tourism. A revised sustainable development strategy, *A Better Quality of Life: a Strategy for Sustainable Development for the United Kingdom* (Cm 4345) was published by the government in May 1999.

The government's sustainable development objectives

Social progress which recognises the needs of everyone. **Everyone should share in the benefits of increased prosperity and a clean and safe environment. We have to improve access to services, tackle social exclusion, and reduce the harm to health caused by poverty, poor housing, unemployment and pollution. Our needs must not be met by treating others, including future generations and people elsewhere in the world, unfairly.**

Effective protection of the environment. **We must act to limit global environmental threats, such as climate change; to protect human health and safety from hazards such as poor air quality and toxic chemicals; and to protect things which people need or value, such as wildlife, landscapes and historic buildings.**

Prudent use of natural resources. **This does not mean denying ourselves the use of non-renewable resources like oil and gas, but we do need to make sure that we use them efficiently and that alternatives are developed to replace them in due course. Renewable resources, such as water, should be used in ways that do not endanger the resource or cause serious damage or pollution.**

Maintenance of high and stable levels of economic growth and employment, **so that everyone can share in high living standards and greater job opportunities. The UK is a trading nation in a rapidly changing world. For our country to prosper, our businesses must produce the high quality goods and services that consumers throughout the world want, at prices they are prepared to pay. To achieve that, we need a workforce that is equipped with the education and skills for the 21st century. And we need businesses ready to invest, and an infrastructure to support them.**

Source: Cm 4345, para 2.1

There are two interrelated features that emerge from the analysis of policy development in the 1990s. The first is that thinking on the environment and sustainability becomes an ever more central concern for government. So, for example, the former Conservative Secretary of State for the Environment John Gummer had shown himself to be a keen advocate of policy reform but his ministerial colleagues did not share his enthusiasm. Early indications from the Labour government suggested that there would now be a much greater commitment to environmental issues across government, for example, reflected in administrative improvements to the machinery of government and the content of policy. The second feature is the changing base of policy. Partly as the result of the European agenda outlined above, British sustainable development policy has become more attuned to that of its neighbours.

A clear sense of the pace and direction of change can be gained from comparing the development of sustainable development policy in Britain and the Netherlands. The Dutch have dealt seriously with the challenge of the environmental implications of development for a number of years and at the end of the 1980s there was a wide gulf in the thinking of the two nations. Both governments produced documents on their sustainable development strategy in 1994, Britain's as we saw largely a restatement of existing thinking, while the Dutch engaged in a more fundamental review about the long term direction of policy. Towards the end of the decade both countries (the Netherlands in February 1998 and Britain in May 1999) once again produced major policy statements. The Dutch remain clear European policy leaders, while Britain remains in the formative stages of its sustainable development thinking (see Table 29.1).

There are a number of differences of emphasis and some of substance between the two documents that in large part reflect the different social, political and economic circumstances of the two countries. In Britain there is a strong wish to accelerate the rate of economic growth and promote societal renewal, while in the Netherlands there is a more explicit recognition of the need to manage the impacts of industry and consumers on the environment. Within the Netherlands there is also much greater social and political consensus on the principles and content of sustainable development policy. This helps to promote policy continuity and longer term thinking that are so essential in the promotion of sustainable development. In Britain, meanwhile, while there is much agreement on policy aims between the political parties (partly because they are so broad) there tends to be less agreement on means. Since the major opposition party invariably regards it as a duty to oppose government measures, then policy can quickly become politicised as the case of road transport explored below shows.

A key aspect of the sustainability strategy of both countries is that over time the economy should

Table 29.1 Britain and the Netherlands compared in the late 1990s

Feature	Britain	Netherlands
Continuity with previous sustainable development document	Medium – greater emphasis on social issues and that high standards of environmental protection are a prerequisite for future economic growth	High
Overall policy goals	(a) Social progress; (b) effective protection of the environment; (c) prudent use of natural resources; and (d) maintenance of high and stable levels of economic growth and employment	(a) Solve large number of existing environmental problems within one generation (before 2010); (b) to prevent continuing economic growth causing new environmental problems
Programme of action	Emphasis on developing indicators to measure progress towards sustainability in the future and of actions that need to be undertaken	Identification of areas where progress is being made towards sustainability and where activity has been inadequate
Responsibility for action	Key actors to progress sustainable development are noted and their role within the overall framework made clear – a scene setting exercise rather than the allocation of tasks	Target groups (e.g. industry, agriculture, consumers, government) are identified and they are made responsible for progressing the strategy

have less impact on the environment. As the British government put it: 'We have to find a new way forward. We need greater prosperity with less environmental damage. We need to improve the efficiency with which we use resources' (Cm 4345, para 1.8). While this is a laudable sentiment that is shared by the Dutch, they term it 'decoupling' (i.e. improving economic growth and at the same time reducing pressures on the environment), they would wish to distinguish between:

- relative decoupling (when pressure on the environment increases at a slower rate than the economy grows), the position favoured by the British government; and
- absolute decoupling (when environmental degradation reduces or at least remains constant whilst the economy grows) (*NEPP3*, p. 16), which is the perspective that the Dutch government advocates.

The approach of the Dutch government is more ambitious than that of the British government but its emphasis on absolute decoupling has come from its positive experience of breaking the connection between resource use and economic growth. In particular, the Dutch have found that new markets have developed for their industries in, for example, the field of environmental technology and that promoting the highest possible environmental standards within the EU helps create further markets for their companies in other parts of Europe. Whilst the British government may be sympathetic to the approach pursued by the Dutch it will obviously impose additional costs on firms who are currently wasteful of resources. It will also be difficult for British environmental technology firms to quickly catch up with their Dutch counterparts and so issues of competitiveness will play a part in the nuancing of British sustainable development policy.

While policy statements are a useful guide to understanding the actions of government, a fuller picture demands that we also look at the institutions that have responsibility for environmental policy making and its implementation. It is no longer possible to understand British environmental policy simply through reference to actions in London. As we have already seen, what happens here is in large part influenced by decisions made at the EU level, while the process of devolving power to the Scottish Parliament and National Assembly for Wales also has important implications for environmental policy.

Central government and its agencies

Department of the Environment, Transport and the Regions (DETR)

Recurrent themes in the analysis of British institutions for environmental protection are those of integration and fragmentation. As political priorities have changed over time and new problems arisen governments have attempted to solve them through a series of organisational fixes. These fixes, though, become ever more contested as the environment becomes a more important political issue and commentators increasingly turn their attention to the principles and processes for organising to protect the environment. The creation of the DETR and its predecessor the Department of the Environment (DoE) illustrate well the pressures on government and the way in which the pendulum of integration and fragmentation can swing back and forth. The challenge to integrate central government functions to adequately cope with the broad nature of environmental decisions does not change but the political response does.

In an argument that resonates as clearly today as it did when written in 1970 a White Paper on *The Reorganisation of Central Government* (Cmnd 4506, 1970) pointed out that:

> It is increasingly accepted that maintaining a decent environment, improving people's living conditions and providing for adequate transport facilities, all come together in the planning of development... Because these functions interact, and because they give rise to acute and conflicting requirements, a new form of organisation is needed at the centre of the administrative system.

This new organisation was the Department of the Environment. Headed by a Secretary of State in the Cabinet, it was an amalgamation of the Ministries of Housing and Local Government, Public Building and Works, and Transport. With the benefit of hindsight, however, it is easy to see that while the government may have believed that organisational reform was sufficient to deal with environmental problems, the Department of the Environment was more a rearrangement of the machinery of government than the creation of a department with new powers. It was never going to work as a department of the environment let alone one for the environment because the politics of Whitehall had left key environmental issues with other departments. Thus, responsibility for agriculture and the countryside remained with the Ministry of Agriculture, and energy with the then Department of Energy. In 1976, as political priorities shifted under a Labour government, transport was separated from the department.

Ironically the Labour government elected in 1997 thought it politically important to once again bring transport into the DoE and emphasise the role of regional development (moved from the DTI) and create the DETR. Environmentalists such as Friends of the Earth welcomed the merger of the Departments of the Environment and Transport as it was thought a unified department would be able to think in a more integrated manner. Whether the new department will fare better than its predecessor in tackling environmental issues is a moot point, since it has not gained significant new powers, some responsibilities still lie with other Whitehall departments, and with devolution Edinburgh and Cardiff now too have a more important part to play than in the past.

There must also be doubts as to whether bringing together functions does aid integrated policy making. The fundamental tensions between different sectors does not disappear and so what would have been inter-departmental disputes now take place behind the closed doors of one department. In an effort to make sure that the environmental impacts of different policies are incorporated into decision making the Labour government has built upon the efforts of its Conservative predecessor which had taken two forms. One was to amend the machinery of government and the other was to engage in the environmental appraisal of new policies.

The lead role in formulating the Conservative government's 1990 White Paper *This Common Inheritance* had been taken by the then Department of the Environment but its content had had been debated and a number of compromises made in a Cabinet committee set up to oversee its production. Ministers and senior civil servants involved in the process recognised the value of being able to discuss the environment as a policy issue both within and across departments. The White Paper therefore made two commitments to improving the machinery of government: to retain the cabinet committee and the nomination of a green minister in each department who would be responsible for considering the environmental implications of department's policies and programmes. At the time the Conservative Secretary of State for the Environment, Michael Heseltine (1991) proclaimed: 'We now have some of the most sophisticated machinery to be found anywhere in the world integrating environment and other policies'. Commentators have subsequently pointed out that the Cabinet committee was downgraded to a ministerial committee and that the committee 'was an ineffective institutional device, mainly due to the continued territorial preoccupation of departments and hostility within the central government machinery towards the . . . DoE, particularly from the "economic" departments' (Voisey and O'Riordan, 1998, p. 159). The Labour government has upgraded the committee to its original cabinet status, where it is known as the Cabinet Ministerial Committee on the Environment (ENV) but in its first year at least it did not meet on a regular basis and conducted most of its business through correspondence. Labour has also sought to re-invigorate the green ministers and they now have to report to the ENV Committee and prepare an annual report on their activities. As its own contribution to improving the machinery of government Labour created in 1997 a House of Commons Select Committee on Environmental Audit. The Committee's terms of reference are to evaluate the extent to which the policies and programmes of departments and non-departmental public bodies contribute to environmental protection and sustainable development.

Government officials routinely engage in policy appraisal. Since 1991 they have been encouraged to broaden their analysis to take into account environmental issues. However, much of the guidance for officials on how to undertake environmental policy appraisals has been skewed towards economic techniques and may not have received a sympathetic response. The Labour government appears to be making renewed efforts to instil environmental appraisal into the routines of decision making (Environmental Audit Committee, paras 89–91). Nevertheless, practice within departments appears to be variable, and while they may be becoming more frequent there is little evidence to suggest that environmental appraisals have made much impact on significant policy issues.

The organisational and administrative changes noted above certainly indicate some of the ways in which the environment has been accorded a higher political priority. While the search for policy integration is certainly a desirable objective and may help to achieve higher levels of environmental protection it should not obscure our gaze from the content of policy. And yet, at times, this seems to have been the consequence of a series of organisational reforms, as we shall see below.

The Environment Agency

The substance of environmental policy presents enormous challenges to decision makers because it defies their conventional time-scales and functional divisions. Thus, where politicians' horizons may normally be bounded by that of elections, the environment forces them to think on a quite different scale, of generations for which they cannot possibly receive any political payback. Meanwhile, organisations like to do things in their own way with the minimum of external interference. But environmental policy cross-cuts traditional divisions of government and raises, for those concerned, the unwelcome possibility of turf disputes about who gets to do what. Faced with these dilemmas, decision makers have shown a greater interest in the organisation of environmental protection as a substitute, or at least an alternative focus, for the more challenging issues surrounding the content of policy. Thus recent years have witnessed a flurry of, perhaps, unprecedented organisational reforms. The result has been some grander thinking on structures than is normal and the creation in 1996 of a large, centralised Environment Agency that may fit less easily into Britain's traditional administrative culture. In the past, small, specialised bodies, with for the most part low public profiles, have tended to be favoured.

Demands for the creation of a unified environment body have been long-standing. Since the mid-1970s the standing Royal Commission on Environmental Pollution had argued for a greater integration of the functions of what were at the time a set of disparate organisations. By the 1980s, increasing support from environmental groups, such as Friends of the Earth, and latterly the Labour and Liberal Democrat parties, helped make questions of integration a topic of policy debate. The late 1980s and early 1990s saw the creation of important new bodies, Her Majesty's Inspectorate of Pollution (HMIP), the National Rivers Authority (NRA) and the Waste Regulatory Authorities (WRAs), but still this did not quell the clamour for further reform. Within a month of the publication in 1990 of the government's White Paper (Cm 1200) on the environment, *This Common Inheritance*, the opposition parties had issued their own policy documents (*An Earthly Chance* and *What Price Our Planet?* by Labour and the Liberal Democrats respectively), which, in contrast to the Conservatives, committed themselves to major institutional reforms.

Within a year the Conservative government had fallen into line, and in the July 1991 John Major, in his first speech on the environment as Prime Minister, argued that 'it is right that the integrity and indivisibility of the environment should now be reflected in a unified agency' and announced the government's intention 'to create a new agency for environment protection and enhancement'.

HMIP, the NRA and the WRAs together form the core of the Environment Agency in England and Wales. The Scottish Environment Protection Agency (the difference in name may be of some significance) has in addition to the three core groups the local authority environmental health officers who dealt with air pollution. In terms of the logic creating a unified and all-embracing pollution regulation body, the inclusion of such staff makes sense. That it did not happen in England and Wales indicates the way in which organisational design in the public sector is invariably intertwined with political factors. The then Conservative government had a much greater representation in local government in England than it

BOX 29.1

fact

Key responsibilities of the Environment Agency and the Scottish Environment Protection Agency

Function	Achieved by
Water resource management – conserve and secure the proper use of water	Issuing of abstraction licences
Water quality – prevent and control pollution and monitor the quality of rivers, estuaries, coastal waters and groundwater	Granting of consent to discharge
Integrated pollution control – control discharges to land, air and water for larger and more complex industrial processes	IPC authorisation
Air – SEPA alone – control processes which have a medium pollution risk (in England and Wales this task is undertaken by local authority Environmental Health Officers)	Authorisation
Waste regulation – (a) register and monitor those who carry waste for a business; (b) approve management of waste disposal sites	(a) Regulation of the firm (b) Licence site operators

did in Scotland and knew that it would arouse opposition within its own ranks should it take away responsibility for air pollution from English local authorities.

What does the Environment Agency mean for the work of its core groups and what effects might it have on those they regulate? The functions set out in Box 29.1 are derived from its constituent elements. Of these, HMIP was formed in 1987 as the result of interdepartmental disputes, embarrassment at pollution discharges at Sellafield nuclear power station and pressures from the European Commission. It combined what had been distinct inspectorates in industrial air pollution. It was responsible for regulating discharges to air, land or water for some 2,000 industrial processes with the greatest polluting potential.

The NRA was a much larger and higher profile organisation than HMIP. It has gone on to form the largest part of the new agency and its former staff have secured a number of key positions within it. The NRA was created at the same time as the water authorities were privatised, under the Water Act 1989, and it took on the pollution control functions and some of the activities of these authorities. The latter were both guardians of the water environment and also major polluters as dischargers of sewage, that is, acting as both poacher and gamekeeper.

Waste collection and disposal has been a traditional local government activity but one where it has lost out to the twin pressures of integration in environmental protection and for contracting out of services. The 1990 Environmental Protection Act created three types of waste authority. Waste Collection Authorities (a local authority or a contractor working for the authority) arrange for the collection of household and commercial waste. Its disposal is the responsibility of Waste Disposal Authority (either a part of local government or a Local Authority Waste Disposal Company). Waste Regulation Authorities, whose staff have been moved from local government to the Environment Agency, are responsible for the safe treatment and disposal of wastes produced by households, mines, quarries and agriculture (so-called controlled waste).

By bringing together in one organisation the control of water pollution, air pollution and commercial waste there is an effort to provide a more integrated approach to environmental management. While structures are important in trying to achieve policy goals, both agencies have had to surmount a number of hurdles. It has taken longer than expected to forge into a cohesive grouping the professionals who staff it. These came with different professional priorities, tactics, and approaches to regulation and (not to be ignored) different career structures. To be seen to be more than the sum of its organisational parts it has been essential for the agencies to prove their independence from government and of those they regulate. The agencies have not been helped in this regard as they have received few additional powers from those that their constituent bodies held. It is unlikely that most businesses will have noticed any practical difference in the way in which they are regulated.

Nevertheless, both agencies have tried to promote a different style and this may lead to a change in substance. For example, the Environment Agency has been actively involved in initiatives to promote waste minimisation in business. Waste minimisation offers a double dividend: a firm reduces its impact on the environment because less material is used in the production process and there is less waste to be disposed of, and at the same time becomes more efficient because it is using its materials more efficiently. Here the Agency is able to act as an educator of business encouraging it along a more sustainable route. Where business has proved more recalcitrant the Agency has changed tack and adopted a high profile name and shame campaign of major polluters (Figure 29.1). Here the Agency has a role as the citizen's friend through its actions to protect the environment.

Figure 29.1 ICI's plant in Runcorn, Cheshire – the company was prosecuted three times and fined £382,500
Source: Don McPhee, The Guardian, 22 March 1999

Table 29.2 Responsibilities and sizes of the rural conservation agencies

Name	Key responsibilities	Number of employees	Budget £m
English Nature	Nature conservation	685	41
Countryside Agency	Landscape protection, economic and social development in rural England	380	50
Scottish Natural Heritage	Landscape protection and nature conservation	530	37
Countryside Council for Wales	Landscape protection and nature conservation	322	25

Note figures are wherever possible for the financial year 1998/9

The former Conservative government and its Labour successor have always been sensitive to the potential burden that environmental regulation may place on business. Whether the Labour government is prepared to follow through the logic of its sustainable development policy with its implication of rigorous and stringent environmental regulation by the Environment Agency could well prove to be a considerable test of its commitment. An additional challenge for both SEPA and the Environment Agency will arise from the way in which they respond to their responsibilities under devolution. Obviously SEPA will continue to look to Edinburgh for guidance and funding and over time it is possible that its strategy and responsibilities will become still more distinct from those of the Environment Agency. Even in Wales with its more limited devolved responsibilities the relevant part of the Agency is playing a more active role in trying to formulate a sustainable development strategy for the National Assembly. It is not inconceivable that within a relatively short space of time issues of funding and accountability help to force a separation of the English and Welsh parts of the Agency. These points are considered further below in the section on the implications of devolution for environmental policy.

The rural conservation agencies

It is the rural conservation agencies that have the greatest experience of country specific operations and the fragmentation that it entails. The reforms to the Countryside Agency, English Nature, the Countryside Council for Wales and Scottish Natural Heritage are illustrative of the way in which administrative structures influence environmental policy making and government thinking on the environment. The broad remits and size of the different agencies are illustrated in Table 29.2.

All the conservation bodies can trace their origins back to the 1949 National Parks and Access to the Countryside Act. Under the Act two sets of responsibilities were established. The first was for nature conservation. English Nature, for example (and its predecessor, the Nature Conservancy Council), is based on scientific and technical expertise and draws upon an elite tradition of interest in natural history and the preservation of flora and fauna. The other responsibility was for landscape protection and was the responsibility in England of the Countryside Commission, now superseded by the Countryside Agency with a broader remit for rural development.

Thus was born a, perhaps, unique organisational division amongst public sector bodies in Europe of separating landscape and nature protection. The divide reflects some of the characteristics of British environmentalism. While English Nature might argue that the public should be excluded from nature reserves on scientific grounds, the Countryside Commission (now the Countryside Agency) tended to favour access. But these are not the only differences between the agencies. English Nature has a much greater executive role through its management of national nature reserves. Both organisations, however, are grant-in-aid bodies, i.e. they are funded from public funds.

The reorganisation of the conservation agencies has taken a different path from that of the pollution control bodies. Although there are signs of integration or unification of responsibilities amongst the bodies, it has taken different forms. For the conservation agencies the functional integration in 1989 in Wales and Scotland (in which landscape and nature were combined in the Countryside Council for Wales and Scottish Natural Heritage) has been allied to geographical fragmentation. In England, landscape protection and nature conservation remain the responsibility of separate bodies. It is not a situation dictated by organisational logic or adherence to explicit environmental principles. What it represents is the current state of play in an organisational and policy framework that has developed in a largely *ad hoc* and pragmatic manner, and is a vivid testimony to the weakness of the statutory environmental bodies. Judgements on the conservation bodies tend to be harsh but it is difficult to differ from that of Lowe and Goyder (1983, p. 67) in writing of the predecessors to the current organisations that they 'have small budgets, little power and limited policy-making initiative, and they are politically marginal'.

At this stage it is difficult to assess what impact devolution may have on the conservation agencies and the development of environmental policy in Britain. On the one hand the devolved administrations may be more sympathetic to the resource claims of CCW and SNH; they are after all their own organisations, and in the case of Scotland there is now the power to reshape SNH if thought necessary. Both organisations may also find that they have better links to policy makers and the policy community more generally, enjoy higher status and are more able to shape strategy. On the other hand, the bodies for England, Wales and Scotland may become more inward looking and less able to share good practice. There may be much duplication of effort and an inability to develop the high level scientific expertise that a unified body with all of its resources would be able to bring to bear. Another difficulty that may loom, especially in Wales, is that the conservation bodies will find themselves competing more directly for resources and influence with well-established and highly thought of economic development agencies. Unless the Scottish Parliament and National Assembly for Wales are able to formulate sustainable development strategies that do genuinely bring together economic and environmental interests there is a danger that the latter could find themselves marginalised over time.

Devolution and environmental policy

Devolution has significant impacts for environmental policy making and its implementation in Wales and especially Scotland. The Scottish Parliament has had far greater powers devolved to it than the National Assembly for Wales: for the former it is the devolution of legislative power and for the latter the ability to exercise responsibility over particular policy areas. Thus, as Table 29.3 shows, while the two legislatures will be concerned with similar topics within the field of environmental policy their authorities are quite different.

Agriculture, an important topic for both Scotland and Wales, has long been an issue with some devolved responsibilities. Energy, though, is a policy area with significant environmental implications but this remains a UK government function. Whether the devolution of responsibilities to Wales and Scotland can remain stable is a moot point. The leadership of the Welsh Labour Party has been keen to follow the line laid down by central government that the present powers are sufficient. Others, though, are beginning to look longingly at the greater powers of the Scottish Parliament and how they may help to deal with challenging policy issues. For example, the national paper of Wales, *The Western Mail* on 16 October 1999 in a special report on the need for integrated transport, argued that devolution is a necessary step:

> Solutions appropriate to London or Surrey are not necessarily applicable to Wales, but only some transport powers have been devolved to Cardiff from London. A genuinely integrated Welsh transport policy cannot be drawn up, let alone implemented while London holds the purse strings for railways, and Cardiff for roads.

Table 29.3 Key environmental responsibilities and powers of the National Assembly for Wales and the Scottish Parliament

	National Assembly for Wales has responsibility for	**Scottish Parliament has legislative powers over**
Transport	Control of the construction of trunk roads in Wales, and the maintenance of existing ones	Passenger and road transport covering the Scottish road network, the promotion of road safety, bus policy, concessionary fares, cycling, taxis and minicabs, some rail grant powers, the Strathclyde Passenger Transport Executive and consultative arrangements in respect of public transport
Planning	Determine policies on town and country planning and issue guidance to local authorities	Land-use planning and building control
Heritage	Determine and implement policy on ancient monuments and listed buildings; allow and encourage visits to ancient monuments and public buildings owned by Cadw	The natural heritage including countryside issues and the functions of Scottish Natural Heritage; the built heritage including the functions of Historic Scotland
The environment	Fund, direct and make appointments to the Countryside Council Wales; fund, direct and make appointments to the Environment Agency (alongside the DETR and MAFF); control water quality and river pollution in Wales	The environment including environmental protection, matters relating to air, land and water pollution and the functions of the Scottish Environment Protection Agency; water supplies and sewerage; and policies designed to promote sustainable development within the international commitments agreed by the UK

Before Wales' transport problems can be ironed out, the National Assembly must gain similar controls over railways to its control over roads. Only then can it make balanced decisions on investment and implementation, where money is channelled to whichever solution is the most cost-effective.

Although Wales has more limited devolved powers than Scotland it does have a unique responsibility amongst all levels of UK government to progress sustainable development. Under the Government of Wales Act 1998 the Assembly is legally required to make a Scheme setting out how it proposes, in carrying out its work, to promote sustainable development. For any legislature such a responsibility if taken seriously is formidable and for a Welsh bureaucracy that has limited experience of policy making (as opposed to policy delivery) and limited resources the challenge is all the greater. What is already clear is that the Assembly is taking its duty seriously. In its internal operations it is addressing machinery of government and policy appraisal issues to ensure that sustainability is considered across all its work, and also rethinking its external relationships so that it can promote a partnership approach to the delivery of sustainable development.

The greater political commitment to devolution in Scotland than in Wales meant that the Scots had done more preparatory work on how they would progress sustainable development within their parliament. So while no duty for sustainable development was imposed upon the parliament in the devolution legislation the Consultative Steering Group on the Scottish Parliament recommended that any Bills it prepared should be accompanied by an assessment of their effects on sustainable development. The commitment to environmental, or in this case the sustainability, appraisal of policies is an important one. It goes hand in hand with a political commitment to sustainable development, as Lord Sewell who had responsibility for the issue in the Scottish Office argued:

In Scotland, we have moved forward rapidly to make sustainable development a mainstream issue for

Government, for local authorities, for business and for the people of Scotland. The cross-linking of issues comes naturally to Scotland; there is a genuine interest in Scotland in delivering on the three arms which make up sustainable development: a sound economy, strong social development, built on a real concern for the environment.

It is still too early to expect to see distinctive approaches to sustainable development emerging in Scotland and Wales, though that will surely follow. As Down to Earth, the Scottish strategy for sustainable development, put it: 'The Scottish Parliament will choose for itself the form [of sustainable development] which best suits the circumstances of Scotland' (Down to Earth, p. 5). If the priorities in Edinburgh and Cardiff do begin to diverge from those in London, then the ways in which the devolved legislatures meet their contributions to UK negotiated international environmental agreements will be interesting to observe.

Local government and environmental policy

Another area of interest will be the way in which the devolved governments deal with their local authorities and whether they can share a common environmental agenda. Traditionally, local councils have played a key and wide-ranging role in the UK's system of environmental regulation. They have had statutory responsibilities for waste, air pollution and planning. To this they have added a non-statutory initiative Local Agenda 21 (LA21) that stems from the Rio Earth Summit in 1992. The fortunes of local government in each of these areas have been inextricably tied up with the thinking and actions of central government.

Pollution regulation by local authorities

While the Environment Agency is responsible for emissions from industrial processes scheduled under legislation, district and unitary councils in England and Wales are responsible for those from non-scheduled processes. Scottish councils had held similar powers but these were transferred to SEPA. These responsibilities stem principally from the Public Health Act 1936, the Clean Air Acts of 1956 and 1968 and the Environmental Protection Act 1990. Under the legislation, local authorities control emissions of smoke, dust, grit and odour, and, under the Control of Pollution Act 1974, noise.

As we have seen, however, local authorities play a more important role in waste regulation. Until quite recently local authorities collected, disposed of and were responsible for regulation of the waste that was created in their areas. Under the Environmental Protection Act 1990, responsibility for the collection of household and some commercial and industrial waste is split between the different tiers of government, but the authorities, in this case largely county councils, are required to subject these services to private company bids in a process known as compulsory competitive tendering. The counties, however, remain responsible for waste regulation (Waste Regulation Authorities). (There is a more confused situation in some metropolitan areas where there can be joint responsibility for disposal and regulation.)

Local planning

The planning system is one of the most sophisticated mechanisms for environmental regulation, more specifically for controlling and promoting land use development, in Britain. Although planning decisions are made under the broad supervision of the DETR (for England and to a lesser extent Wales), the Scottish Parliament and National Assembly for Wales, councils are responsible for both drawing up plans and making decisions on proposed developments. Planning law grants wide discretion to councils to control and promote landuse planning, including the content of plans, the granting of planning permission, the enforcement of breaches of control and the pursuit of positive planning. This discretion and decentralisation makes for both variability and vitality in local planning.

The planning system has been subject to considerable pressure over the past decade and more.

For much of the Conservative period of government planning was regarded as a bureaucratic impediment to the operation of the market. Government reforms were therefore designed to reduce the scope of local authority involvement in the planning process and to remove some of the constraints faced by developers in securing planning approval. The reforms profoundly affected the major urban and industrial areas where agencies of central government replaced the local authorities. Enterprise zones, urban development corporations and simplified planning zones awarded tax breaks to developers, took over site development and streamlined planning procedures. Similar pressures for liberalisation applied to rural areas but were not reinforced by the centralising and interventionist measures deployed in urban areas, and so did not undermine local democratic control to the same extent.

As the Conservative government began to embrace the environmental agenda from the 1990s onwards, so its deregulatory instincts had to be tempered. Planning was now heralded as a key means of promoting more sustainable development because of its ability to engage with economic issues (i.e. the development of land), social needs (what is appropriate development for particular communities) and the protection of valued environments. The ongoing challenge that was faced first by the Conservative government and in a more acute form by the Labour government is, to what extent should the planning system constrain the market? The most contentious debates are taking place in the south-east of England. Here there are major pressures for development, an articulate opposition well able to make their views known through the planning system and a group of councils who are arguing that if the pressures they face for development are not more actively managed then they will become less sustainable. The touchstone around which these debates are taking place is housing.

The problem is that government estimates based on the 1991 census suggest that 4.4m extra homes will be required between 1991 and 2016. Partly to remove the threat that such numbers pose to greenfield sites and partly to regenerate towns and cities, the government is encouraging councils to increase the amount of house building on brownfield (i.e. previously developed) sites from its current level of 50 per cent to 60 per cent. The government's strategy also dovetails neatly with the thrust of its sustainability thinking: homes that are new or rebuilt on brownfield sites are likely to be close to existing transport networks, services such as shops, and employment, so reducing people's need to travel. The difficulty that rural conservationists face is that even if 60 per cent of new dwellings could be developed on brownfield sites (and for some councils that is an ambitious target) the numbers projected are such that there will have to be considerable building on greenfield sites. Here people's perceptions of what is an acceptable level of development will potentially come into

BOX 29.2 **IDEAS AND PERSPECTIVES**

Key questions for government

1. Does it accept the housing projections and provide homes accordingly (so-called predict and provide) or seek to manage demand?
2. Does it listen to councils in the south-east who wish to lower the projections that central government wishes to impose on them?
3. Should it make more efforts to redirect new building away from the south of England?
4. Once decisions have been made on house numbers and their location, should it promote dispersed development (share out the misery) or concentrate the development in a limited number of new urban centres or the significant growth of existing ones?

conflict with the demands of the market and raise political and policy challenges for government. For example, the Council for the Protection of Rural England, a leading conservation pressure group, has calculated that in the period 1994–9 some 300,000 acres of meadows and grassland, an area about the size of Bedfordshire, have disappeared (see Meadow Madness, 1999). Meanwhile, the construction firm Wimpey have pointed out that at present only 11 per cent of Britain is urbanised and even if the projected 4.4m homes were to be built on greenfield sites, which will not happen, then the proportion of urban settlement would rise only to 12.5 per cent of land use (*The Guardian*, 17 March 1999).

In a measure of how quickly political parties can reposition themselves, the Conservatives, seeking to appeal to their traditional voters in south-east England, and putting together a blue–green coalition of Tories and amenity groups, now argue that the planning system needs to be strengthened and that development should be directed to the north (*The Guardian*, 2 November 1999). In its own moves to appease those disgruntled by the pace of development in the south-east the Secretary of State for the DETR, John Prescott, announced at the 1999 Labour Party conference that two new National Parks would be created for the New Forest in Hampshire and the South Downs (largely in Sussex).

Local authority initiatives

Finally, despite, or perhaps more accurately because of, the criticism and restrictions to which local government has been subject, it has become increasingly involved in a series of measures by which it can promote the environment and at the same time promote itself not only as 'green' but as an active organ of government. The UNCED Conference at Rio, where much of Agenda 21 (the global environmental agenda for the next century) was predicated upon local action, provided a convenient means by which local government could repackage much of what it was already doing and have a justification for extending its work still further. There is no clear agreement on what the content of an LA21 should be since it should be tailored to local circumstances. However, the internal issues that a local authority should expect to cover include: managing and improving its own environmental performance, integrating sustainable development across its activities and awareness raising and education. In its dealings with the wider community the authority should consult the public on LA21, engage in partnerships with the business and voluntary sectors, and measure and report on local progress towards sustainable development.

According to O'Riordan and Voisey (1998, p. 154) the UK is probably the most advanced nation in taking forward LA21. The Labour government has recognised the considerable potential for local government in the delivery of sustainable development and the Prime Minister, Tony Blair, made a commitment in 1997 at the UN on behalf of local government that they would all have produced LA21 strategies by the year 2000. Since by this time about 90 per cent had committed themselves to participating in LA21 the target should be achieved.

O'Riordan and Voisey are not, however, convinced that much beyond rhetoric and the production of documentation is taking place. There are a number of difficulties, including the task of taking the sustainable message to those groups such as business who may not be sympathetic to it; overcoming public indifference or even antagonism to local government; broadening the agenda from the environment to include social and development issues; and having to work with limited resources. A test of central government's commitment to sustainable development will be to see whether it meets local government requests for more powers and resources to deal with Agenda 21. At a time of budgetary constraints, local government finds that it can do little more than carry out its statutory duties, and yet much that it does or wishes to do in the LA21 field is of a non-statutory nature.

Pressure groups and government: the case of road transport

Road transport debates and protests illustrate well the changing nature of the environmental movement in Britain, how it can help to change

BOX 29.3 **IDEAS AND PERSPECTIVES** 

Transport Bill: Queen's Speech includes possibility of road charges

John Prescott's Transport Bill announced on 17 November 1999 introduced the politically controversial idea of charging for road use. Local authorities will be given the power to charge motorists for driving into cities, the idea being that such charging will help reduce congestion and provide funds for the improvement of public transport. The legislation is only permissive, entitling local authorities to introduce such schemes if they so choose, subject to government approval. Such ideas follow on from successful overseas experiments in Norway and Singapore. The AA is sceptical of the idea pointing out that motorists 'already pay £8 in tax for every £10 they pay on fuel'. Another aspect of the bill will be the establishment of the Strategic Rail Authority with the power to rescind the franchises of rail companies not performing to standard and to instruct that new investment be made. Also controversial will be the partial privatisation of Air Traffic Control services in the UK.

the terms of debate and the challenges that government faces in trying to move policy on to a more sustainable footing (Box 29.3).

Environmental groups

According to McCormick (1991, p. 34), 'Britain has the oldest, strongest, best-organized and most widely supported environmental lobby in the world'. By 1990 McCormick estimated the support for environmental groups to be around 4.5m (about 8 per cent of the population) and it stayed at around that level until the end of the decade.

The foundations of the lobby were laid in the late nineteenth century with subsequent bursts of growth in environmental groups in the late 1920s, the late 1950s, the early 1970s, as well as the late 1980s. The 1970s were distinguished from earlier periods both by the rapid growth of existing groups and the formation of new ones such as Friends of the Earth (formed in the United States in 1969), Greenpeace (formed in Canada in 1972) and Transport 2000. The new groups made a significant impact upon the lobby by highlighting the international nature of many environmental problems, and providing radical analyses of environmental issues which linked them to contemporary social and economic conditions. New tactics also emerged with Friends of the Earth and Greenpeace adopting vigorous, high profile campaigns to draw attention to a broad range of threats to the environment.

The success of the environmental lobby in increasing its membership, along with a range of other fund raising activities, has had a positive effect on its finances. With greater income, groups have been able to employ more staff to monitor more accurately government activities, engage in more lobbying and prepare better critiques of official policy. Campaigns are much more sophisticated than they used to be, making still greater use of the media and, for the more radical groups, there has been a greater reliance on science and legal evidence to support their positions. The emphasis, therefore, has been, for the most part, on strengthening traditional styles of lobbying.

Greenpeace has confronted a more difficult situation. In some countries the nature of the political system is such that Greenpeace can keep its distance from government and still seek to influence debate. In Britain that is more difficult, and now that many of its concerns have become matters of public policy deliberation, partly as a result of its direct action tactics, it has to decide whether the same tactics are required for the formulation and implementation of policy.

Environmental campaigners were cockahoop in November 1999 when the Queen's Speech foreshadowed new legislation regarding the free movement of walkers on open land in England and Wales. Thus sixty years of campaigning have been crowned with success. The proposed bill will give right of access to mountain, moor, heath, down and registered common land. Precise details of how walkers can proceed will be worked out by local committees of landowners and walkers with the former having the right to close land for twenty-eight days a year.

Road building protests

One of the most bitterly contested areas of government policy has been that relating to road transport. The controversy it has excited has led to set-piece confrontations around proposed new developments, spawned a new wave of environmental activism and challenged successive governments' commitment to sustainable development.

Many local road improvement schemes will arouse little if any controversy. The road-building schemes that have aroused national attention, notably those at Twyford Down, Newbury and Honiton, are significant because of their scale and their impact on nationally important environments. They have thus become a focus, sometimes at a symbolic level, for the arguments for and against the road-building programme. The M3 protest at Twyford Down began in the mid-1980s and initially involved a classic local protest: concerned residents engaged in conventional campaigning tactics, such as lobbying and high profile events (e.g. protest walks) in which they worked closely with national groups, notably Friends of the Earth.

As all legal avenues of protest disappeared a new form of protester appeared who was committed to non-violent direct action. The latter drew much of their inspiration from the American group Earth First! and disdained conventional politics as failing to protect the environment. The initially small group occupied part of the road-building site known as the Dongas, an area of deep hollows, and became known as the Dongas Tribe. Faced with overwhelming odds the Dongas Tribe could not hope to stop the building of the road. Nevertheless, their courage and commitment provoked enormous interest and inspired other protests such as that at Newbury. The Twyford Down campaign was also significant in another respect. As Barbara Bryant, a leading activist, has written:

> almost for the first time . . . [the media] had witnessed middle-class Conservative voters, retired military men, elected politicians and a younger, less conventional group, coming together in an alliance against the Government's road building campaign. (Bryant, 1996, p. 192)

Whilst it is important not to over-emphasise the extent to which a coalition did exist (there were undoubted tensions between the different groups), it does mark a point at which diverse interests could come together to oppose a common policy.

There are many similarities between the Twyford Down protest and that at Newbury. Once again legal avenues of campaigning had been exhausted, leaving the protesters to try to disrupt and delay the building programme sufficiently so that there might be a rethink of policy by a new government. The protests against the Newbury bypass began in earnest in late 1995 with the establishment of six protest camps. At the height of the campaign in the spring of 1996 this had mushroomed to twenty-nine. Some of the camps were based in trees, others in tunnels, and led to dramatic media coverage of the evictions of protesters as bailiffs brought in cranes and cherry-picking equipment to dislodge them. Once a site has been cleared for a new road it would be a dramatic event for a government to then halt operations.

Transport protests are now commonplace. Reclaim the Streets, an anti-car pressure group, has organised a number of events in London which have brought traffic to a standstill and a street party on a stretch of the M41 attended by some 7,000 people, at which parts of the road were dug up and trees planted. A central element to the protest movement now is the extent to which the organisers of different groups seek to link their activities and exchange ideas: a move from competing and exclusive organisations to supportive and overlapping disorganisations.

Government policy and road transport

By helping to raise the profile of transport issues protesters have played a part in creating a climate in which a new agenda can develop. Faced with a massive forecast for increases in traffic, the former Conservative government committed itself to a large road-building programme in the suitably titled 1989 White Paper *Roads for Prosperity* (Cm 693). Within a few years, though, a number of schemes had been dropped or shelved. The reasons for the change in heart are many but, perhaps, three were key. Firstly, the Treasury, desperate to retain a hold on the public finances, had been alarmed at the burgeoning expenditure on roads. Secondly, early in 1994 the government published its strategy on *Sustainable Development* in which, in the cautious language of civil servants, it acknowledged that unlimited traffic growth was incompatible with its environmental commitments. In other words demand would have to be managed, a key argument of the environmental lobby. Thirdly, later in 1994 saw the publication of two key reports on transport. One was by the influential Royal Commission on Environmental Pollution on Transport and the Environment in which it expressed its concern at the implication of current policy on health and the environment. It argued for a halving of the road-building programme and a doubling of the real price of petrol over the decade. The other was by the Standing Advisory Committee on Trunk Road Assessment which concluded that new roads can generate or induce new traffic (i.e. that they may not ease congestion).

The Conservatives' cautious embrace of the need to manage road transport was much more fully embraced by the Labour Party. In government Labour has promoted through its white paper, *A New Deal for Transport*, the idea of an integrated transport policy to fight congestion and pollution. Essentially, integration means bringing together different types of transport, and ensuring that transport links to other policies such as land use planning. Most attention has focussed on three areas: bus quality partnerships to improve services; a strategic rail authority to oversee the privatised companies; and local transport plans. These plans, backed up by a proposed transport bill, will allow councils to introduce charges on some trunk roads and on trunk road bridges more than 600 metres long. The money raised from such charges would then be invested in public transport improvements. The proposals, though modest, given the scale of the traffic problem, and voluntary have aroused enormous controversy. Labour is sensitive to the charge that it is anti-car, perhaps one reason why it is making implementation the responsibility of local and not central government, but it is one that the Conservatives are seeking to exploit, though they toyed with similar ideas when in office.

Conclusion

Issues related to sustainable development are amongst the most challenging that any government can face. Not only do they involve all sections of society but also different levels of government. Moreover, a more sustainable society is a long term goal but policies to achieve that goal often seem to involve short term political costs. Little wonder then that at present policies do not seem to match up to the rhetoric or the scale of the challenge.

Chapter summary

This chapter began by pointing out the forces that make environmental policy a dynamic and changing area. The impact of Europe on the content of British environmental policy and on the policy making process were then described. It was noted that there has been a considerable shift in thinking on the environment so that it now encompasses a very broad area under the term sustainable development. The role of key organisations in central government was set out and the implications of devolution of responsibilities to Cardiff and Edinburgh explored. The part that local government plays in environmental protection and more generally sustainable development was discussed. Finally, the role of pressure groups was outlined and how they have contributed to the road transport debate and how in turn government policy has changed.

Discussion points

- What is the appropriate contribution of Europe, national government and the devolved administrations to environmental policy?

- Is sustainable development a meaningful term?
- Should we try to integrate environmental policy making and its implementation or fragment it amongst geographically and functionally specialised organisations?

Further reading

Two of the best general purpose books on environmental policy and politics are those by Gray (1995) and Connelly and Smith (1999). The former is an edited book with a wide-ranging collection of papers, whilst the latter is an informative and lively account of contemporary environmental politics. For those interested in studying further how British environmental policy has been shaped by decisions in Europe then the book by Lowe and Ward is a very good place to start. One of the better books by an environmental activist with insights into the policy process is that by Bryant (1996). There are now a number of good environmental web sites. Aside from the media these proved a good means of keeping up to date with what is a fast changing policy area.

References

Blowers, A. (1987) 'Transition or transformation? Environmental policy under Thatcher', *Public Administration*, Vol. 65, No. 3.

Bryant, B. (1996) *Twyford Down: Roads, Campaigning and Environmental Law* (E. and F. N. Spon).

Cm 1200 (1990) *This Common Inheritance* (HMSO).

Cm 2426 (1994) *Sustainable Development: The UK Strategy* (HMSO).

Cm 2428 (1994) *Biodiversity: The UK Action Plan* (HMSO).

Cm 4345 (1999) *A better quality of life: A strategy for sustainable development for the UK* (The Stationery Office).

Cmnd 4506 (1970) *The Reorganisation of Central Government* (HMSO).

Commission of the European Communities (1992) *Towards Sustainability: The Fifth Environmental Action Programme* (CEC).

Connelly, J. and Smith, G. (1999) *Politics and the Environment* (Routledge).

Gray, T. (ed.) (1995) *UK Environmental Policy in the 1990s* (Macmillan).

Gummer, J. (1994) 'Europe, what next? Environment, policy and the Community', speech to the ERM Environment Forum organised by the Green Alliance.

House of Commons Environmental Audit Committee (1998) *The Greening Government Initiative*, Vol. 1 (The Stationery Office).

Lowe, P. and Flynn, A. (1989) 'Environmental politics and policy in the 1980s', in J. Mohan (ed.), *The Political Geography of Contemporary Britain* (Macmillan).

Lowe, P. and Ward, S. (eds) (1998a) *British Environmental Policy and Europe* (Routledge).

Lowe, P. and Ward, S. (1998b) 'Britain in Europe: themes and issues in national environmental policy', in P. Lowe and S. Ward (eds), *British Environmental Policy and Europe* (Routledge).

McCormick, J. (1991) *British Politics and the Environment* (Earthscan).

Ministerie van Volkshuisvesting Ruimtelkjike Ordening en Milieubeheer (VROM) (Ministry of Housing, Physical Planning and the Environment) (1998) *National Environmental Policy Plan 3* (VROM).

O'Riordan, T. and Voisey, H. (eds) (1998a) *The Transition to Sustainability: the Politics of Agenda 21 in Europe* (Earthscan).

O'Riordan, T. and Voisey, H. (1998b) 'Editorial Introduction', in O'Riordan, T. and Voisey, H. (eds), *The Transition to Sustainability: the Politics of Agenda 21 in Europe* (Earthscan).

Sharp, R. (1998) 'Responding to Europeanisation: a governmental perspective', in P. Lowe and S. Ward (eds), *British Environmental Policy and Europe* (Routledge).

Voisey, H. and O'Riordan, T. (1998) 'Sustainable development the UK national approach', in O'Riordan, T. and Voisey, H. (eds), *The Transition to Sustainability: the Politics of Agenda 21 in Europe* (Earthscan).

World Commission on Environment and Development (1987) *Our Common Future* (Oxford University Press).

Chapter 30 Northern Ireland

Jonathan Tonge

Learning objectives

- To explore why conflict developed in Northern Ireland. How does history shape today's politics?
- To assess which explanation of the political problem is the most convincing. Is Northern Ireland an arena of ethnic conflict?
- To examine what beliefs are held by the political parties. Is there any common ground?
- To understand why a peace process developed at the end of the twentieth century. Did governments, parties or **paramilitary groups** change their political stances?

Introduction

The politics of Northern Ireland is based on what at times has appeared to be an intractable problem. The province contains a divided population, split between two main groupings holding different loyalties and identities. The majority within Northern Ireland, a minority within the entire island of Ireland, see themselves as British. They are adamant in their desire that Northern Ireland should remain part of the United Kingdom. A sizeable minority within Northern Ireland regard themselves as Irish and would prefer to see the island of Ireland united under a single, Irish authority. As a minimum, this minority advocates a substantial 'Irish dimension' to the governance of Northern Ireland. By the late 1990s, sufficient common ground was found to reach an uncertain political agreement, but this followed three decades of violence which threatened the very existence of the state.

The broad division between British Unionists and Irish nationalists is reinforced by a religious divide. Unionists are mainly Protestant, whilst nationalists are predominantly Catholic. In Scotland and Wales, debates over national identity are resolved through constitutional politics. In Northern Ireland, paramilitary and military solutions were also attempted. Competing explanations of the nature of the Northern Ireland problem exist. They reflect disputes over the historical origins of the problem and the extent to which the minority community in Northern Ireland has suffered social, economic and political discrimination.

The development of Northern Ireland

Historical quarrels

From the eleventh to the eighteenth century, Ireland existed under loose British colonial rule (**colonialism**). The origins of modern problems lay with the conflict between Planter and Gael in the early seventeenth century. The latter were Irish natives, displaced by Scottish Presbyterians undertaking the Plantation of Ulster, the nine-county province in the north-eastern quarter of the island. Although the Act of Union in 1801 consolidated British sovereignty, Irish nationalism increased, assisted by the Great Famine. In response, the British Government introduced a trio of **Home Rule** Bills from 1886, designed to provide limited autonomy for Ireland.

Each Bill was strenuously opposed by Protestants in Ulster, the descendants of the original Planters. Unyielding in their determination to retain their British–Protestant identity, they argued that Home Rule would mean Rome Rule. With the overwhelming majority of the native population Catholic, Protestants feared absorption within an increasingly independent Ireland, dominated by the Roman Catholic church. In the south, nationalist sentiment for an independent Ireland increased after the British Government executed the leaders of the 1916 Easter Rising.

Compromise provided a settlement, but not a solution. The Government of Ireland Act 1920 divided the country (Figure 30.1) in an attempt to sate the desires of both identities. A twenty-six-county state was created in the south, later to become the Republic of Ireland. This was ruled by a parliament in Dublin, which by 1949 was independent. In the north-eastern corner of the island, six of the nine counties of the ancient province of Ulster were incorporated within the new administrative unit of Northern Ireland. Exclusion of the remaining three counties, each with high Catholic populations, guaranteed Protestants a substantial majority in the new political unit.

An 'Orange state' 1921–72?

From its outset, Northern Ireland was an insecure state, persistently under threat, real or imagined. Internal dissent came from a dissident Catholic–Nationalist minority, amounting to one-third of the population. They resented the creation of what they saw as an artificial state, devoid of geographical, historical or political logic. External threats came from the embryonic Irish state in the south. Under Eamon de Valera, Southern Ireland, later Eire, adopted a constitution in 1937 which laid claim to Northern Ireland, insisting that the national territory consisted of 'the whole island of Ireland, its islands and the territorial seas'.

Eternal vigilance characterised the Unionist response. As early as 1922, a Special Powers Act was enacted, providing the overwhelmingly Protestant security forces in Northern Ireland with vast, arbitrary powers. Although designed to reflect the population balance, the police force, the Royal Ulster Constabulary, averaged only 10 per cent Catholic membership. The auxiliary police force, the B Specials, was exclusively Protestant.

Discrimination against Catholics was common, although the amount is disputed (Whyte, 1990). Sir Basil Brooke, later Prime Minister of Northern Ireland, urged that wherever possible 'Protestant lads and lassies' should be hired. Many employers excluded Catholics from their workforce. High rates of Catholic unemployment deepened economic divisions between the two communities. The Protestant working class was also poor, but enjoyed marginal superiority over its Catholic counterpart. Other areas of discrimination included industrial location and housing.

Many Catholics felt alienated by the political system in Northern Ireland. The Unionist Party held power for 50 years. Each Prime Minister and most Cabinet members belonged to the exclusively Protestant Orange Order. In Stormont, the parliament of Northern Ireland, the only legislation successfully introduced by nationalists during this period was the Wild Birds Act in 1931.

Unionist domination was replicated locally, where Unionists controlled 85 per cent of councils. Dominance was increased through the process of gerrymandering. Large nationalist majorities were

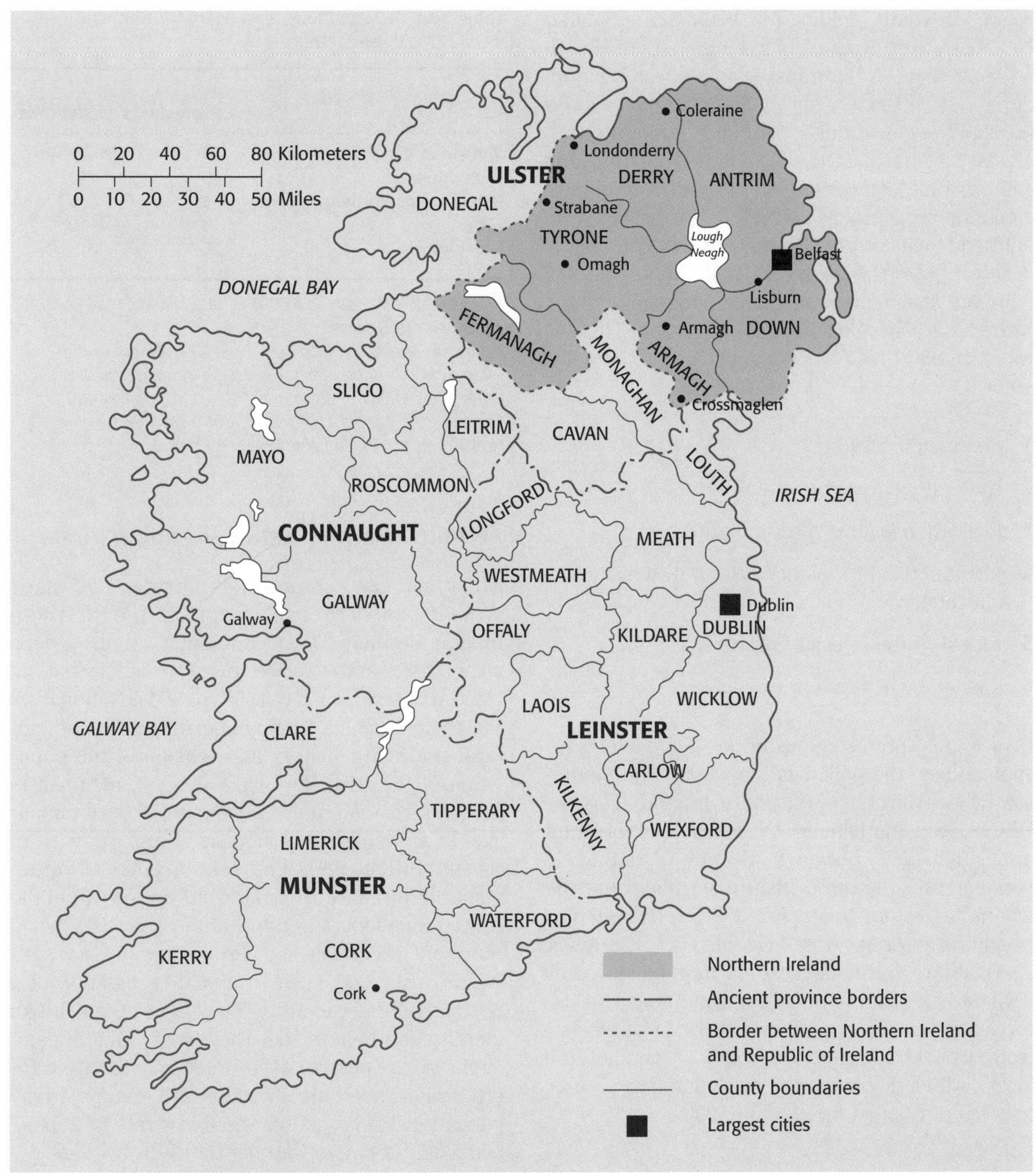

Figure 30.1 The four ancient provinces and thirty-two counties of Ireland: the nine counties of Ulster and the six counties of Northern Ireland

Source: McCullagh and O'Dowd, 1986

wasted in wards yielding few councillors. Smaller Unionist wards produced large numbers of Unionist councillors. A notorious example was Londonderry City Council, where a Unionist council was returned even though Catholics amounted to almost two-thirds of the local voters (Arthur and Jeffery, 1998). Only ratepayers could vote in local elections, whilst many owners of businesses were entitled to extra votes. These measures particularly disadvantaged the poorer Catholic population.

In an attempt to challenge inequalities, the Northern Ireland Civil Rights Association (NICRA) was formed in 1967. Its demands were (Connolly, 1990):

1 one man, one vote;
2 the ending of gerrymandering;
3 legislation against discrimination;
4 introduction of a points system in housing allocations;
5 repeal of the Special Powers Act;
6 disbandment of the B Specials.

Civil rights protests encountered a violent response from the police and loyalists. The moderate Prime Minister of Northern Ireland, Terence O'Neill, was outflanked by hardline Protestant opposition and resigned. Sectarian rioting in summer 1969 led the British Government to send troops to restore order. For a brief 'honeymoon' period, the Army was welcomed by Catholics. As relations declined, the Irish Republican Army revived and some nationalists again began to use force in attempting to remove the British presence from Ireland. Twenty-five years of conflict followed, with little prospect of resolution until a peace process developed by the mid-1990s.

Table 30.1 Preferred long-term policy for Northern Ireland, 1998

	% Protestants	Catholics
Remain in UK	87	22
United Ireland	5	47
Independent Northern Ireland	1	3
Other	3	10
Don't know	5	19

Note: Totals may exceed 100% as respondents may have equal first preferences

Source: Evans, G. and O'Leary, B. (1999) 'Northern Irish voters and the British–Irish Agreement: foundations of a stable consociational settlement?', Elections, Parties and Opinion Polls Annual Conference, University College Northampton, 17–19 September 1999, p. 7

Explanations of the problem

Part of the difficulty in finding solutions to the problems of Northern Ireland lay in the lack of agreement over the causes of conflict. Four main competing explanations emerged.

Ethnic or ethno-national explanations

Ethno-national arguments provide the most orthodox modern explanation of the Northern Ireland problem. Two competing ethnic groups want their 'state to be ruled by their nation' (McGarry and O'Leary, 1995, p. 354). Nationalists see themselves as Irish, associating with the cultural traditions, history and religion of the population of the Irish Republic. As such, nationalists demand, as a minimum, a substantial Irish dimension to any political settlement. Unionists wish to remain British and thus seek a political settlement bolstering Northern Ireland's place within the United Kingdom (see Table 30.1). Since 1972, when Stormont was abolished, Protestants in Northern Ireland have lacked institutional recognition of a distinctive Ulster identity. They assert their British identity and believe that they have much in common with the people of the British mainland. Northern Ireland's ethnic divisions are reinforced by educational segregation and a low rate of 'mixed' marriages between Catholics and Protestants.

Critics of ethnic conflict explanations argue that identities can change. Some Catholics identify themselves as 'Northern Irish' rather than distinctively Irish. Some Protestants continue to emphasise their Ulster identity. Perceptions of the conflict as ethno-national may lead to solutions entrenching ethnic blocs, through their formal recognition in power-sharing arrangements.

Colonial explanations

Arguments that Northern Ireland is Britain's last colony have become rarer in recent years. Traditionally, such views have been expressed by Irish republicans (as those nationalists who support Sinn Fein prefer to be labelled) although they find an occasional voice in academia (Miller, 1998). Originally, colonial theories were linked to ideas of **imperialism**. The British Government was seen as exploiting Northern Ireland for financial benefit. Given the cost of the British presence, these arguments have disappeared. These costs, known as the **subvention**, amount to £4 billion annually, well over half of annual expenditure in Northern Ireland (Tomlinson, 1995). Republicans believe that Britain's political interest in the Province, reflected in its unwillingness to leave, is tantamount to a colonial presence, maintained by a large security apparatus. Critics of colonial and imperial arguments point to the conditional basis of Britain's claim to Northern Ireland, based on the consent of its people. In the 1990s, the British Government declared that it had 'no selfish, strategic or economic interest' in Northern Ireland. It claimed that partition was an acknowledgement of the reality of divisions on the island, not an assertion of British self-interest.

Religious or ethno-religious

When sectarianism was rife during the early years of the Troubles, it was common to perceive the Northern Ireland problem in terms of two warring religious communities. As people fled from areas increasingly dominated by members of the 'other' religion, perceptions of inter-communal conflict grew. The killings in Northern Ireland have not occurred because of **theological** differences between Catholics and Protestants. The conflict is not a Holy War over matters such as the Virgin Birth. Nonetheless, religion may still be an important marker. Bruce (1986, p. 249) argues:

The Northern Ireland conflict is a religious conflict. Economic and social differences are also crucial, but it was the fact that the competing populations in Ireland adhered and still adhere to competing religious traditions which has given the conflict its enduring and intractable quality.

Table 30.2 Religious affiliation in Northern Ireland

Religion	%
Protestant	50.4
Roman Catholic	38.4
Not stated	7.3
None	3.7

Source: The Northern Ireland Census 1991 Religion Report

Religion plays an important role in:

1 *Identification.* Almost nine in ten of the population identify themselves as Protestant or Catholic (see Table 30.2).

2 *Political influence.* To many, Protestantism and Unionism are inseparable, owing to the variety of formal and informal links between Unionist political parties and organisations based on the Protestant religion.

Economic factors

Economic explanations of the conflict centre on the impact of inequalities endured by the nationalist population in Northern Ireland. Despite political reforms and workforce monitoring, unemployment among Catholics remains twice as high as that found among Protestants. Years earlier, the disadvantaged position of the Catholic working class was portrayed by socialists as a product of a divide-and-rule policy, designed to fragment the Protestant and Catholic working classes (Farrell, 1980). Modern explanations centre on the legacy of earlier economic discrimination, which continues locally on a lesser scale. Nationalist antagonism is seen as a response to relative deprivation. Many of the IRA's recruits came from poor areas. Economic arguments are subject to criticism. Firstly, variations in levels of unemployment have been attributed to skills differentials. Secondly, identity may be more important than wealth or status. Orangemen wish to remain as such, even though scant financial advantage accrues nowadays. Finally, economic parity might have only a marginal impact on the differences in constitutional aspirations held by unionists and nationalists.

The political parties

The largest political parties in Northern Ireland are divided into two main groupings, Unionist and nationalist. Unionist parties attract almost exclusively Protestant support. Nationalist parties gain their support from Catholics. Although Unionists remain the majority, the nationalist vote has been growing, now averaging around 40 per cent. Recent election results are shown in Table 30.3.

The *Ulster Unionist Party* (UUP) is the largest Unionist party. Its central cause is the maintenance of Northern Ireland's position within the United Kingdom. The UUP believes in the legitimacy of Northern Ireland as a distinct political, economic and cultural entity. While supportive of friendly and co-operative relationships between Northern Ireland and the Irish Republic, the UUP prefers **cross-borderism** to be located in the economic rather than the political sphere. The party advocates the return of devolved government to Northern Ireland. Formal Party links with the Protestant Orange Order remain. The Order enjoys voting rights within the Party. Although the link is in decline, many senior figures in the UUP are members of the Order. Some within the Party believe that a more secular Unionism is needed (Aughey, 1989). Three strands of Unionism have been identified (Porter, 1996):

1 cultural, based on symbolic demonstrations of Protestant Britishness;

2 liberal, centred on a contractual relationship with the Westminster Government;

3 civic, accommodating a plurality of identities in Northern Ireland.

The UUP, in common with Northern Ireland's other Unionist parties, tends to straddle all three themes, but its support for the Good Friday Agreement nudged the party towards a new form of civic Unionism.

Advocates of a more hardline Unionism, the *Democratic Unionist Party* (DUP) shares the core beliefs of its bigger Unionist rival. Founded in 1971, the DUP has been led throughout its existence by the Reverend Ian Paisley. Many within the Party fuse politics and religion. Over half of its activists are members of the fundamentalist Free Presbyterian Church, even though only 1 per cent of the population of Northern Ireland belong to this church (Bruce, 1986). Support for the DUP is much more widely based than this fundamentalist group.

The DUP supports the return of considerable devolved powers to a Northern Ireland parliament. Ideally, this would be based upon majority rule, but with some safeguards for the minority. Arguing for a tough military policy to defeat the IRA, the DUP was critical of the peace process from the outset, describing it as a framework of 'shame and sham'. It vehemently opposed the early release of paramilitary prisoners.

The other Unionist Party with a Westminster seat is the *United Kingdom Unionist Party*, led by Robert McCartney, MP for North Down. The UK Unionists believe in the closer **integration** of Northern Ireland within the United Kingdom. The Party split in 1999, with a number of members leaving to form the Northern Ireland Unionist Party. Two loyalist parties associated with paramilitary groups also attract some votes. The *Progressive Unionist Party* gained seats in the Northern Ireland Assembly elections in 1998. It advocates

Table 30.3 Election results in Northern Ireland in the 1990s

	Percentage of first preference votes cast				
Election	**UUP**	**DUP**	**SDLP**	**SF**	**Others**
1992 General	34.5	13.1	23.5	10.0	19.9
1993 Local	29.4	17.3	22.0	12.4	18.9
1994 European	24.3	29.1	28.9	9.9	7.8
1996 Forum	24.2	19.0	21.0	15.5	20.3
1997 General	32.7	13.1	24.1	16.1	14.0
1997 Local	27.8	15.6	20.7	16.9	19.0
1998 Assembly	21.3	18.1	22.0	17.6	21.0
1999 European	17.7	28.5	28.2	17.4	8.2

BOX 30.1 **BIOGRAPHY** 

DAVID TRIMBLE (1944–) (picture: © Popperfoto)

MP for Upper Bann, David Trimble was elected leader of the Ulster Unionist Party in 1995. At the time of his election, Trimble was seen as uncompromising. He was a member of the hardline loyalist Vanguard organisation in the 1970s. Trimble's election as UUP leader was assisted by his stance in support of the rights of Orangemen to march down the contested Garvaghy Road at Drumcree. Shortly after election, however, Trimble showed greater pragmatism. He distanced himself somewhat from the marching issue. The UUP leader met the Irish Prime Minister for talks, the first such meeting for thirty years. Trimble then played a major role in the construction of the 1998 Good Friday Agreement, pressing for a devolved Northern Ireland, while accepting limited all-Ireland cross-border bodies. This work led to the award of the 1998 Nobel Peace Prize, shared with the SDLP's John Hume. Trimble then led his party to compromise on the issue of IRA decommissioning, dropping the insistence it must take place before Sinn Fein's entry to a Northern Ireland executive, while maintaining that decommissioning must nonetheless take place.

BOX 30.2 **BIOGRAPHY** 

IAN PAISLEY (1926–) (picture: © AFP/Corbis)

Unchallenged leader of the DUP, the Reverend Ian Paisley has been MP for North Antrim since 1970 and an MEP since 1979. Paisley founded his political party and his church. Although criticised even by some working-class loyalists as outdated, Paisley always emerges as the most popular political figure in Northern Ireland's single-constituency European elections. Regarded as a demagogue by detractors, Paisley is seen by some supporters as a leader 'chosen by God to protect Ulster' (Connolly, 1990, p. 104). Unyielding in opposition to Irish republicanism, Paisley insists that his politics stem from his Free Presbyterian religion. Paisley was vociferous in his criticism of the peace process and critical of the Ulster Unionist Party's participation in negotiations.

BOX 30.3 **BIOGRAPHY**

JOHN HUME (1937–) **(picture: © Popperfoto)**

John Hume is the leader of the SDLP. Elected to the post in 1979 after becoming an MEP in the same year, Hume is also MP for Foyle. A believer in Irish unity by consent, Hume has long advocated an 'agreed Ireland', stressing the need for unity of peoples before territory. In 1988, Hume took a political risk in entering into dialogue with Sinn Fein's leader Gerry Adams. Although critics feared that Hume was leading his party in too 'green' (nationalist) a direction, Hume's project was to convince republicans of the futility of continued violence, viewed as morally wrong and politically inept. The Hume–Adams dialogue contributed to the development of the peace process of the 1990s and the Good Friday Agreement. Hume's role was recognised by the award of the 1998 Nobel Peace Prize, shared with UUP leader, David Trimble.

retention of Northern Ireland's place in the United Kingdom and the development of socialist politics. The *Ulster Democratic Party* is linked to the Ulster Defence Association. It dropped the idea of an independent Northern Ireland in favour of Northern Ireland remaining in the United Kingdom, with proportionality in devolved government for the region.

The centre ground in Northern Ireland politics is somewhat narrow. Nonetheless, the *Alliance Party* attracts support from Protestants and Catholics, amounting to around 8 per cent of the electorate. The party supports devolved government with power sharing.

The *Social Democratic and Labour Party* (SDLP) is the main nationalist party, attracting over 60 per cent of the Catholic vote. Its membership is overwhelmingly Catholic. Founded in 1970 following civil rights agitation, the Party attempted to replace the old, abstentionist Nationalist Party with a more dynamic brand of left-wing politics.

Always in favour of Irish unity, the SDLP advocates constitutional politics as the means of its achievement. Emphasising the need for an 'agreed Ireland' the SDLP accepts the need for the consent of Unionists for fundamental constitutional change. The Party also wishes to develop two other political relationships: north–south co-operation between representative bodies in Northern Ireland and the Irish Republic, alongside east–west co-operation between the London (east) and Dublin (west) governments. Development of these links could forge structures to facilitate a united, consensual Ireland. Much of the SDLP's thinking was reflected in the 1998 Good Friday Agreement.

Sinn Fein (SF) is the political wing of the republican movement. The Party now gains up to 40 per cent of the Catholic vote, with its vote share steadily rising. It has achieved this figure or better since the 1980s, when revived as a political organisation to provide a political outlet for the military campaign of the IRA. The link between the two organisations provided a strategy based on a 'ballot paper in one hand and an Armalite in the other' according to Sinn Fein's Director of Publicity, Danny Morrison, in 1981. Sympathy for IRA hunger strikers assisted Sinn Fein in the early 1980s. Sinn Fein justified 'armed struggle' to end British rule in Northern Ireland. It asserted that the partition of Ireland was unjust, as it was never supported by a majority of Irish citizens. Sinn Fein won

BOX 30.4 **BIOGRAPHY**

GERRY ADAMS (1949–) (picture: © Jim McDonald/Corbis)

President of Sinn Fein since 1983, Gerry Adams was instrumental in changing Sinn Fein from an IRA support network to a developed political party. A former IRA member from a traditional republican family, Adams was MP for West Belfast from 1983 to 1992 and regained the seat in 1997. As early as 1980, Adams acknowledged that the IRA could not win by military means alone. This perception meant that Adams sought broader nationalist support, which arrived in the peace process of the 1990s. Adams steered his party towards a revisionist, less fundamental republicanism during the 1990s. Sinn Fein became a strong electoral force and Adams encountered relatively few internal critics, although the party's IRA links made Unionists cautious. By the end of the century, Adams had transformed Sinn Fein to such dramatic effect that it was prepared to assist in the governance, rather than destruction, of Northern Ireland.

three-quarters of the seats in the last all-Ireland elections held in 1918. The party challenged the legitimacy of Northern Ireland and argued for self-determination for the Irish people as a single unit.

During the 1990s, Sinn Fein adopted a more pragmatic republicanism, softening its demands, or making them less immediate. The 1992 policy document, *Towards a Lasting Peace in Ireland*, suggested that British indications of withdrawal might provide sufficient basis for negotiation. The party came into closer contact with the northern state through, for example, participation in local councils and began to concentrate more on change within Northern Ireland. Sinn Fein's 'equality agenda' advocates substantial reform and, in the case of the Royal Ulster Constabulary, abolition. The party has been involved in controversies over whether the Orange Order should have the right to march through nationalist areas.

In 1998, Sinn Fein's members voted overwhelmingly to change the party's constitution and to allow elected party representatives to take their seats in a devolved Northern Ireland assembly at Stormont. Given that Provisional Sinn Fein had formed in 1970 in direct opposition to such a development, the U-turn was remarkable. By the end of the century, Sinn Fein appeared to recognise that a united Ireland could only be achieved in the long-term and not necessarily through violence. Sceptics pointed to Sinn Fein's continuing link to the IRA, but as the party took seats in the new Northern Ireland Executive at Stormont in late 1999, the commitment to constitutional politics appeared permanent.

The paramilitaries

The Irish Republican Army (IRA) was moribund and devoid of a military campaign between 1962 and 1969. It split in 1970, leading to the formation of the Provisional IRA. This comprised those who believed in the need for a military campaign to try and force the removal of Britain from Ireland. Members of the new organisation rejected the Marxist social agitation characteristic of the IRA of the 1960s. Instead, the Provisional IRA believed in traditional physical force republicanism. Following a permanent ceasefire of the old 'Official' IRA in 1972, the Provisionals were in effect *the* IRA.

Protestant Apprentice Boys and Orange parades in Northern Ireland still raise tensions, even in a more peaceful Northern Ireland

Whilst the Provisional IRA claimed also to be a defender of nationalist areas, it soon launched an offensive. Curfews, the introduction of internment (detention without trial) and republican agitation soured relations between the British Army and the Catholic population. In February 1971, the first British soldier was killed by the IRA in what became known as the 'Troubles'. After January 1972, when the Army shot dead thirteen civilians in Derry, the conflict escalated. The Army, RUC, Ulster Defence Regiment and businesses were targets of the most sustained campaign in the history of the IRA.

The 'long war' soon replaced the initial belief of the IRA that a military campaign would enforce an early British withdrawal. Brief negotiations with the British Government in 1972 proved fruitless and the IRA declined in strength during the mid-1970s owing to a combination of greater security, internal feuding and a ceasefire.

The processes of **Ulsterisation** and **criminalisation** were used to curb the IRA. Their aims were to reduce the military strength of the IRA whilst portraying its members as common criminals. Paramilitary prisoners were no longer treated as prisoners of war. This cessation of special category

Table 30.4 Deaths arising from 'The Troubles' 1969–99

British Army	445
Royal Ulster Constabulary	201
RUC Reserve	102
Ulster Defence Regiment	197
Royal Irish Regiment	9
Civilians	2,372
Total	3,326

Note: 'Civilians' includes members of paramilitary organisations
Source: Adapted from Royal Ulster Constabulary, Chief Constable's Report 1999, Belfast, RUC

status led to the republican hunger strikes of 1980–1, in which ten prisoners died.

During the 1980s, the IRA was locked in stalemate with the British Government. A military campaign was insufficient to end British rule in Northern Ireland. It was also difficult to impose an outright military defeat on the IRA. This was especially true after its reorganisation into a tighter cell structure and the procurement of armaments from Libya. As the campaign endured and the list of targets for killings broadened, the 'Troubles' claimed over 3,000 victims, mainly civilians (see Table 30.4).

Nearly 60 per cent of deaths are attributable to the IRA or a republican offshoot, the Irish National Liberation Army (Darby, 1994). While purporting to defend the nationalist community, the IRA killed more Catholics than the security forces. The loyalist paramilitary organisations of the Ulster Volunteer Force, Ulster Freedom Fighters and Red Hand Commandos have also carried out numerous killings, many amounting to random sectarian assassinations of Catholics. New loyalist paramilitary groups emerged during the 'peace process' of the 1990s, namely the Loyalist Volunteer Force, the Red Hand Defenders and the Orange Volunteers. The RUC and the British Army have also been responsible for a considerable number of deaths.

Table 30.5 Secretaries of State for Northern Ireland since direct rule in 1972

Secretary of State	Government	Duration
William Whitelaw	Conservative	1972–3
Francis Pym	Conservative	1973–4
Merlyn Rees	Labour	1974–6
Roy Mason	Labour	1976–9
Humphrey Atkins	Conservative	1979–81
James Prior	Conservative	1981–4
Douglas Hurd	Conservative	1984–5
Tom King	Conservative	1985–9
Peter Brooke	Conservative	1989–92
Patrick Mayhew	Conservative	1992–7
Mo Mowlam	Labour	1997–9
Peter Mandelson	Labour	1999–

Table 30.6 Political initiatives 1972–85

Sunningdale Agreement	1973
Constitutional Convention	1975
Constitutional Conference	1980
Northern Ireland Assembly	1982
New Ireland Forum	1984
Anglo-Irish Agreement	1985

Searching for political agreement

In 1972, Unionist rule in Northern Ireland was ended by the imposition of direct rule from Westminster, with the Secretary of State for Northern Ireland governing the province (see Table 30.5). Until the peace process of the 1990s, all political initiatives appeared doomed to failure. The main such initiatives are listed in Table 30.6. Unionists would not countenance any initiative containing a substantial all-Ireland dimension. Nationalists would not support any set of arrangements in which the Irish Government had little say.

Case study 1: the Sunningdale Agreement 1973

The Agreement finalised at Sunningdale in December 1973 provided a political blueprint for Northern Ireland and its relationships to the Westminster and Dublin Governments. The model of the Sunningdale Agreement has endured, to the extent that the Deputy Leader of the SDLP, Seamus Mallon, described the 1998 Good Friday Agreement as 'Sunningdale for slow learners'. The Sunningdale Agreement created devolved power-sharing government for Northern Ireland. Unionists and Nationalists shared responsibilities in an executive, presiding over an elected Assembly. A Council of Ireland was attached to the Assembly. This comprised a consultative forum of elected representatives from the North and South of Ireland and a council of ministers from both countries.

Although the Agreement contained a declaration that there could be no change in the constitutional status of Northern Ireland without the consent of the majority of its population, the Irish dimension was too strong for many Unionists. In the February 1974 General Election, eleven of the twelve Unionists elected opposed the Sunningdale Agreement. Still reeling from the loss of their Stormont parliament two years earlier, many Unionists also objected to power sharing, arguing that majority rule was more democratic. In May 1974, the power-sharing executive collapsed, finally defeated by a strike by Protestant workers.

Stalemate

A weak attempt to revive the concept of power sharing was attempted through the Northern Ireland Constitutional Convention in 1975. This foundered owing to the absence of consensus over what powers should be shared and the extent of Irish involvement. During the following five years, no major proposals emerged. In 1980, the new Conservative Government tentatively mooted the prospect of a return to some form of devolved administration.

Although profoundly Unionist by instinct, Margaret Thatcher saw the pragmatic advantages of a political accommodation acceptable to nationalists. A series of atrocities in 1979 helped to shape this view. These included the assassination of her close friend and colleague Airey Neave; the murder of Lord Mountbatten and the massacre of eighteen British soldiers at Warrenpoint.

Early political initiatives made little impact. Indeed the first lasted only three months. A Constitutional Conference failed to find common ground between the political parties. 'Rolling devolution' began in 1982. This attempted to coax the political groupings into co-operating with each other, in return for a steady return of power to a devolved administration and a new Northern Ireland Assembly. The lack of an all-Ireland dimension was deemed unsatisfactory by the SDLP and Sinn Fein. Both nationalist parties boycotted the Assembly, which became a mere 'talking shop' for the Unionist parties and the Alliance Party (Bew and Patterson, 1985, p. 132).

Adamant that no purely internal settlement was possible, the SDLP attempted to forge a consensus among constitutional Nationalists through the New Ireland Forum. Political parties in the Republic of Ireland deliberated on the best common approach to the future of the North. After a year's deliberation, the 1984 Forum Report proposed three alternative models:

1. a united Ireland;
2. a confederal Ireland;
3. joint London–Dublin authority over Northern Ireland.

Margaret Thatcher's rejection of each suggestion was characteristically brusque: 'that is out . . . that is out . . . that is out'.

Case study 2: the Anglo-Irish Agreement 1985

Despite the rejection of the New Ireland Forum, an accord between the British and Irish Governments was reached the following year in the Anglo-Irish Agreement, signed at Hillsborough. The Agreement was important in confirming that the Irish Republic would have at least a limited say in the affairs of Northern Ireland, irrespective of Unionist opposition. It was the culmination of Anglo-Irish co-operation promised by Margaret Thatcher and the Irish Taioseach (Prime Minister) Charles Haughey in 1980. They pledged to look at the 'totality of relationships between the two islands'.

Registered as an international treaty with the United Nations, the Agreement, signed by Thatcher and the new Irish Prime Minister Garret FitzGerald:

1 guaranteed no change in the constitutional status of Northern Ireland without the consent of the majority;

2 accepted that no majority for change existed;

3 allowed the Republic of Ireland a consultative role in Northern Ireland.

A permanent **inter-governmental** conference was established which allowed the Irish Government to assist in dealings on political, security, legal and co-operative measures in Northern Ireland. As with the Irish dimension of the Sunningdale Agreement a decade earlier, Unionists opposed the Anglo-Irish Agreement. Unlike Sunningdale, however, the new Agreement was difficult to boycott, as it effectively bypassed political parties. The agreement was inter-governmental.

Frustrated by its failure to achieve power sharing, the British Government was now prepared to allow the Irish Government to 'put forward views and proposals' concerning matters that 'are not the responsibility of a devolved administration in Northern Ireland'. As no such devolved administration existed, some saw this as a wide remit.

'Ulster Says No' was the rallying cry of Unionist opposition. A protest rally at Belfast City Hall attracted 100,000 people. Although fifteen Unionist MPs resigned, the impact of this protest was muted when only fourteen were returned at subsequent by-elections. Resignations from public bodies were undertaken, but to little avail. Meanwhile, the SDLP was satisfied by the Agreement. It welcomed the all-Ireland dimension and the bolstering of constitutional nationalism. The party was concerned with growing support for Sinn Fein, a process temporarily reversed after the Agreement. For constitutional nationalists, the Anglo-Irish Agreement offered greater parity of esteem for the Nationalist minority and gave Dublin a representative role on behalf of the nationalist community. In criticising the Anglo-Irish Agreement, Sinn Fein insisted that it 'copper-fastened' partition by guaranteeing a Unionist veto over constitutional change. Nonetheless, republicans began to look to the Dublin Government to influence events.

The peace process

As numerous political initiatives foundered, many wondered whether violence would ever end. Yet during the 1990s, a carefully constructed process developed, involving a series of initiatives (Table 30.7).

The creation of a peace process depended on numerous factors. They included:

1 moderation of republican politics, encouraged by the Hume–Adams dialogue;

2 changes in Unionism, including an increased acceptance of an all-Ireland dimension to any solution;

3 acknowledgement of the aspirations and identity of both communities by the British Government, allied to positive measures to reduce discrimination;

4 flexibility on constitutional change from the Irish Government;

5 external pressure, notably from the USA, but also from other peace processes.

Table 30.7 A chronology of the peace process

1988	Hume–Adams talks begin
1990	The Brooke initiative commences
1993	Downing Street Declaration
1994	Paramilitary ceasefires
1995	Framework Documents published
1996	Mitchell Commission Report
	Forum elections
	IRA cessation of violence ended
1997	IRA cessation of violence restored
	Multi-party talks begin
1998	Good Friday Agreement
	Referendums in Northern Ireland and the Irish Republic confirm support for the Agreement
	Elections to the Northern Ireland Assembly
	First and Deputy Assembly Ministers elected by Assembly members
1999	Devolved powers awarded to the Northern Ireland Assembly and Executive. Power sharing with an Irish dimension established.
2000	Political institutions suspended pending resolution of decommissioning issue.

The Good Friday Agreement aims to exorcise the ghost of sectarianism in the long term; in the short term the Agreement manages such divisions

Nationalist dialogue

The tortuous road to peace began with a new nationalist dialogue. The intermittent talks between Gerry Adams and John Hume were an attempt by the latter to persuade republicans that:

1. Britain was neutral on whether Northern Ireland should remain in the United Kingdom;
2. a united Ireland, or national self-determination, could only be achieved through the allegiance of both traditions;
3. violence was an impediment to such allegiance.

Hume was anxious to persuade Sinn Fein to recognise that nationalists were not opposing a colonial aggressor. Rather, it was the opposition of one million Protestants within Northern Ireland to a united Ireland that was the problem. In this respect, the dialogue was assisted by a declaration in 1990 by the Secretary of State for Northern Ireland, Peter Brooke, that Britain had no 'selfish, strategic or economic interest in Northern Ireland'. Brooke pursued public and private approaches towards peace. The former, based on cross-party talks, achieved little. The latter involved a secret line of communication to the IRA, known as the Back Channel (Mallie and McKittrick, 1996).

Initiatives and ceasefires

Secret communication was followed by political initiatives. The British and Irish Governments produced the Downing Street Declaration, or Joint Declaration for Peace, in December 1993. This attempted:

1 to satisfy Unionists by restating guarantees that there could be no change in the status of Northern Ireland without the consent of the majority;

2 to interest nationalists by supporting the right of the Irish people to self-determination, provided that consent was given, north and south.

An IRA cessation of violence was announced in 1994, reciprocated soon afterwards by loyalist paramilitary groups. The IRA believed it might advance its own cause via an unarmed strategy, owing to the presence of a strong nationalist coalition. This embraced Sinn Fein, the SDLP and the Irish Government.

In 1995, the British and Irish Governments produced the Joint Framework Document. This outlined the principles of the Downing Street declaration of qualified self-determination: consent, non-violence and parity of esteem for the two traditions. It offered policies of devolved government, a cross-border body and Anglo-Irish co-operation. In many ways, the Framework Document provided the outline of the deal finally agreed through multi-party negotiations in 1998. The Document offered the prospect of considerable cross-border co-operation, notably on EU policy initiatives.

Case study 3: the Good Friday Agreement, 1998, and the return of devolved government, 1999

By Easter 1998, exhaustive multi-party negotiations reached their conclusion in the Good Friday Agreement. This established:

1 a 108 seat devolved Northern Ireland Assembly, presided over by an Executive;

2 a north–south ministerial council, presiding over a minimum of twelve areas of cross-border co-operation;

3 a British–Irish council, linking devolved institutions throughout Britain and Ireland;

4 a British–Irish Intergovernmental Conference, to promote British–Irish co-operation.

These formal institutional measures were accompanied by others of equal importance in selling the Agreement. For the paramilitary groups, the Agreement offered the release of prisoners within two years. Nationalists were offered a new commission on policing, while a human rights commission was also established. Unionists were offered the repeal of the Irish Republic's constitutional claim to Northern Ireland.

The Good Friday Agreement possessed key themes attempted in the Sunningdale Agreement a quarter of a century earlier:

1 *Devolution*: Successive British Governments had long held the view that a return of powers to a Northern Ireland government was desirable. Now, the Labour Government placed the return of such powers within a wider restructuring of the United Kingdom, with devolution also awarded to Scotland and Wales.

2 ***Consociationalism***, or *power sharing*, was seen as necessary in a divided society, to prevent domination by one community. The Executive would therefore comprise elected representatives of several parties, allowing Unionist and nationalist representation. The First and Deputy Minister were elected with cross-community support. Key decisions would require weighted majorities or parallel consent, i.e. support from Unionists and nationalists.

3 *Cross-borderism*: This represented the all-Ireland dimension. Ministers from the new Northern Ireland Assembly would meet with

those of the Irish Government to develop and implement new cross-border bodies. Nationalists hoped for political 'spillover' from economic co-operation. Potential areas of co-operation included transport, agriculture and relations with the EU.

4 *Intergovernmentalism*: Anglo-Irish co-operation would continue through a series of institutional mechanisms, concentrating on matters not devolved to the new Assembly.

There were some important differences from the Sunningdale Agreement. The Good Friday Agreement was confederal, in the way that it linked Britain and Ireland's governments and newly devolved institutions, forming a **confederation**. More importantly, however, the Agreement was inclusive. Earlier agreements had attempted to marginalise groups associated with paramilitary activity. Now, there was an effort to bring such groups into the political mainstream, not least through the 'carrot' of prisoner releases. The 1999 Patten Report on policing recommended the creation of a Northern Ireland Police Service, with changes in the culture, ethos and composition from that found in the Royal Ulster Constabulary.

The referendums on the Agreement, held in May 1998, confirmed its inclusivity, yielding some unusual allies in Northern Ireland. The UUP, PUP, UDP, SDLP and Sinn Fein all advocated a 'Yes' vote in support of the Agreement, opposed only by the DUP and UKUP, although the UUP was divided. Seventy-one per cent of Northern Ireland's voters and 94 per cent of those in the Irish Republic endorsed the Agreement. The majority in favour within the Unionist community was nonetheless slight, reflected in the breakdown of pro and anti Agreement candidates elected to the Assembly in June 1998 (see Table 30.8).

Pro-Agreement majorities among both Unionists and nationalists were essential owing to the requirement for cross-community support for key assembly decisions. The political arithmetic within the Assembly narrowly favoured the maintenance of the Agreement. However, the issue of the **decommissioning** of paramilitary weapons often threatened its collapse.

Table 30.8 Northern Ireland Assembly elections 1998

	Seats
Unionist parties	
Pro-Agreement	
Ulster Unionist Party	28
Progressive Unionist Party	2
Anti-Agreement	
Democratic Unionist Party	20
United Kingdom Unionist Party	5
Independent Unionists	3
Total	
Pro-Agreement Unionists	30
Anti-Agreement Unionists	28
Nationalist parties (both pro-Agreement)	
SDLP	24
Sinn Fein	18
Other parties (both pro-Agreement)	
Alliance	6
Women's Coalition	2

The problem of decommissioning

The peace process did not produce a perfect peace. Between 1995 and April 1999, there were 637 shootings and 365 bombings. Nonetheless, these figures represented a huge improvement, given that over 2,000 shootings occurred in the first four years of the 1990s. The death toll also dropped dramatically in the second half of the decade. Nonetheless, dissident loyalist and republican groups emerged. The 'Real IRA' carried out one of the worst atrocities of the 'Troubles', killing twenty-nine people in a bomb attack at Omagh in 1998. Sectarianism, if anything, increased, with annual conflicts over the routes of Orange marches, notably at Drumcree (see Figure 30.2). Fringe loyalist paramilitaries attacked Catholics.

The peace, while sometimes fractured, allowed a visible consumer boom to emerge. The process was dogged with the questions of whether and when paramilitary groups should decommission their weapons. John Major's Conservative Government refused to enter into dialogue with Sinn Fein until the IRA began decommissioning its weapons. Appointed to break the deadlock, the American Senator George Mitchell suggested that decommissioning might take place during, rather than before, all-party peace talks.

Figure 30.2 A member of the Orange Order takes a break after a march at Portadown
Source: © *Popperfoto*

The Mitchell Report of January 1996 produced six principles of non-violence, to which all the parties, but not the paramilitaries, subscribed. A less prominent suggestion of the Report was adopted, that of elections to a Forum to produce negotiating teams for all-party talks. During the following month, the IRA ceasefire was fractured with a huge bomb at Canary Wharf. The Labour Government elected in 1997 demoted the importance of decommissioning in allowing Sinn Fein into talks on condition of a renewed IRA ceasefire. Ambiguity in the wording of decommissioning requirements in the 1998 Good Friday Agreement threatened to undermine the entire Agreement and peace process a year later. Prior decommissioning of IRA weapons was not a requirement for Sinn Fein's entry to the Northern Ireland Executive, but eventual decommissioning of all paramilitary weapons was demanded under the terms of the Good Friday Agreement. In late 1999, the Ulster Unionist Council voted to allow Sinn Fein its two places on the Executive without prior decommissioning, while placing an obligation on the IRA to begin decommissioning immediately afterwards. Devolved powers were awarded to a Northern Ireland Executive and Assembly for the first time in twenty-five years, although the Westminster Government retained security responsibilities. For the first time ever, virtually all shades of Unionist and Nationalist opinion were involved in the governance of the state, reflected in the composition of the new Northern Ireland Executive (Table 30.9). In January 2000 the new political institutions were suspended, with the decommissioning issue still unresolved.

Alternatives to the Good Friday Agreement?

If the Good Friday Agreement fails, there appear few viable alternatives. All the other solutions suffer from insufficiency of consensus. The 'alternatives' to devolved power-sharing, linked to an Irish dimension, which had been put forward during the 'Troubles' were:

1. *United Ireland*: Favoured by republicans, the absorption of Northern Ireland into a thirty-two county independent Irish Republic would almost certainly be met by armed resistance from loyalists. War might ensue throughout the entire island.
2. *Full integration into the United Kingdom*: This is favoured by some Unionists on the grounds that it would end uncertainty over the future of the Province. Supporters argue that this would assist in the reduction of violence. Detractors point out that the suggestion takes no account of the Irish identity of the minority population in Northern Ireland. The conflict may further polarise British versus Irish identities and increase violence.
3. *Independent Northern Ireland*: Such an option has declined in its limited popularity. This proposal would end rule by the British

Table 30.9 The Northern Ireland Executive 1999

Name	Party	Ministry
David Trimble	UUP	First Minister
Seamus Mallon	SDLP	Deputy First Minister
Bairbre de Brun	Sinn Fein	Health, Social Services and Public Safety
Nigel Dodds	DUP	Social Development
Mark Durkan	SDLP	Finance and Personnel
Reg Empey	UUP	Enterprise, Trade and Investment
Sean Farren	SDLP	Higher and Further Education, Training and Employment
Sam Foster	UUP	Environment
Michael McGimpsey	UUP	Culture, Arts and Leisure
Martin McGuinness	Sinn Fein	Education
Peter Robinson	DUP	Regional Development
Brid Rodgers	SDLP	Agriculture and Rural Development

Government and rule out control from Dublin. It was attractive to some working-class loyalists sceptical of the value of the British link. Catholics, outnumbered in such a new state, would be fearful.

4 *Repartition*: Any redrawing of the border would be beset by practical difficulties. It would be impossible to reshape without leaving a vulnerable minority Protestant community in the counties allocated to the Republic. Catholics in what remained of Northern Ireland might be equally unhappy.

5 ***Joint authority***: A sharing of power in Northern Ireland would require both traditions to accept that exclusive sovereignty cannot be exercised by a single government. Joint authority might be acceptable to many nationalists. Unionists would reject joint authority, not least because it would be seen as an interim settlement towards a full abdication of British sovereignty.

6 *European authority*: Some commentators have expressed interest in the possibilities raised by membership of the European Union (Boyle and Hadden, 1994). Substantial aid from the European Union has boosted Northern Ireland's economy. It has been hoped that membership of the European Union held by Britain and Ireland might produce one or more of the following:
(a) the transfer of citizenship loyalties towards a new European identity;
(b) the withering of the importance of the border as a range of cross-border institutions develop, promoted by European trade initiatives;
(c) the emergence of a Europe of the Regions, replacing exclusive national loyalty with pooled sovereignty;
Thus far, none of these possible developments has displaced traditional affiliations.

7 *Direct rule from Westminster*: Few see the continuation of direct rule as a solution. At best, direct rule produces reforms rather than resolution of the problem. Its persistence is symptomatic of the lack of consensus over the future of Northern Ireland. If significant powers were transferred to local government in Northern Ireland, consensus 'from below' might develop, but beyond this, direct rule has little potential for transformation of the conflict.

8 *Demographic change*: Higher Catholic birth rates have led to speculation that Catholics might form a majority in Northern Ireland during the first half of this century. This

raises the possibility that the population might vote the state of Northern Ireland out of existence. Either possibility is unlikely. Sufficient Catholics support the Union to ensure that a large Catholic majority would be required to end British control.

Chapter summary

Seismic changes have occurred in the politics of Northern Ireland. The 'sound of breaking ice' could be heard in the forging and aftermath of the Good Friday Agreement (O'Leary and McGarry, 1996). Unionists and republicans engaged in shared governance unthinkable only a few years ago. Changes in Unionist politics include recognition of the Irishness of the minority and an acceptance of the need for an Irish dimension to political arrangements. Change on the republican side has ended the boycotting of Northern Ireland's political institutions. The aspiration of a united Ireland remains, but politics appears preferable to 'armed struggle', even though the shift towards Irish unity under the Good Friday Agreement is slight. Political thawing has been accompanied by greater economic prosperity. A new politics of Northern Ireland, less concerned with traditional constitutional politics and involving cross-community social issues, is slowly emerging, but remains fragile.

Discussion points

- Why has power sharing been so difficult to achieve in Northern Ireland?
- To what extent is the Northern Ireland problem one of religious sectarianism?
- Have republicans and Unionists changed their political strategies in recent years?
- Should the Irish Republic be given a substantial say in the affairs of Northern Ireland?
- Same objectives: different methods? Is this an accurate assessment of the SDLP and Sinn Fein?
- What factors enabled a peace process to develop?
- Has IRA violence achieved any of the goals held by the organisation?
- Why do Unionists wish to remain British?
- Which explanation of the Northern Ireland problem is the most realistic?

Further reading

An outstanding scholarly work is provided by McGarry and O'Leary (1995). This goes further than the seminal study of Whyte (1990) in proposing solutions. *The Politics of Antagonism* (1996), by the same authors, is also an essential read. Another high-quality account is offered by Bew *et al.* (1996). Aughey and Morrow offer an excellent introduction to the politics and society of Northern Ireland (1996). Readers might also choose Mitchell and Wilford's edited book, *The Politics of Northern Ireland* (1998), Tonge's *Northern Ireland: Conflict and Change* (1998) or Wichert's *Northern Ireland since 1945* (1999). Bruce (1986) and Bruce (1994) give illuminating studies of loyalism and *Unionist Politics* (1997) by Feargal Cochrane ought to be read. For an excellent account of the development of the main nationalist party, see *John Hume's SDLP* by Gerard Murray (1998). Ryan (1994) provides an interesting account of republicanism. Changes within the republican movement are also discussed in Henry Patterson's *The Politics of Illusion: a Political History of the IRA* (1997) and Brendan O'Brien's *The Long War: the IRA and Sinn Fein* (1999). Highly readable and informed accounts of the peace process are provided by Coogan (1995) and Mallie and McKittrick (1996).

References

Arthur, P. and Jeffery, K. (1998) *Northern Ireland since 1968* (Blackwell).

Aughey, A. (1989) *Under Siege: Ulster Unionism and the Anglo-Irish Agreement* (Hurst).

Aughey, A. and Morrow, D. (eds) (1996) *Northern Ireland Politics* (Longman).

Bairner, A. (1996) 'Paramilitarism' in A. Aughey and D. Morrow (eds) (1996) *Northern Ireland Politics* (Longman).

Bew, P. and Patterson, H. (1985) *The British State and the Ulster Crisis* (Verso).

Bew, P., Gibbon, P. and Patterson, H. (1996) *Northern Ireland 1921–1996: Political Forces and Social Classes* (Serif).

Boyle, K. and Hadden, T. (1994) *Northern Ireland: the Choice* (Penguin).

Bruce, S. (1986) *God Save Ulster: The Religion and Politics of Paisleyism* (Oxford University Press).

Bruce, S. (1994) *The Edge of the Union. The Ulster Loyalist Political Vision* (Oxford University Press).

Connolly, M. (1990) *Politics and Policy-Making in Northern Ireland* (Philip Allan).

Coogan, T.P. (1995) *Ireland's Ordeal 1966–1995 and the Search for Peace* (Hutchinson).

Darby, J. (1994) 'Legitimate targets: a control on violence?', in A. Guelke (ed.), *New Perspectives on the Northern Ireland Conflict* (Avebury).

Evans, G. and O'Leary, B. (1999) 'Northern Irish voters and the British–Irish Agreement: foundations of a stable consociational settlement?', Elections, Parties and Opinion Polls Annual Conference, University College Northampton, 17–19 September 1999.

Farrell, M. (1980) *Northern Ireland: the Orange State* (Pluto).

McCullagh, M. and O'Dowd, L. (1986) 'Northern Ireland: the search for a solution', *Social Studies Review*, March.

McGarry, J. and O'Leary, B. (1995) *Explaining Northern Ireland* (Blackwell).

Mallie, E. and McKittrick, D. (1996) *The Fight for Peace* (Heinemann).

Miller, D. (ed.) (1998) *Rethinking Northern Ireland* (Longman).

Mitchell, P. and Wilford, R. (eds) (1999) *Politics in Northern Ireland* (Westview).

Murray, G. (1998) *John Hume's SDLP* (Hurst).

O'Brien, B. (1999) *The Long War: the IRA and Sinn Fein* (O'Brien).

O'Leary, B. and McGarry, J. (1996) *The Politics of Antagonism* (Athlone).

Patterson, H. (1997) *The Politics of Illusion: a Political History of the IRA* (Serif).

Porter, N. (1996) *Rethinking Unionism* (Blackstaff).

Ryan, M. (1994) *War and Peace in Ireland: Britain and the IRA in the New World Order* (Pluto).

Tomlinson, M. (1995) 'Can Britain leave Ireland? The political economy of war and peace', *Race and Class*, Vol. 37, No. 1.

Tonge, J. (1998) *Northern Ireland: Conflict and Change* (Prentice Hall).

Whyte, J. (1990) *Interpreting Northern Ireland* (Oxford University Press).

Wichert, S. (1999) *Northern Ireland since 1945* (Longman).

Chapter 31

Britain and European integration

Simon Bulmer

Learning objectives

- To offer a brief overview of Britain's post-war relationship with the European integration process.
- To give an introduction to the institutions and policy process of the European Union.
- To explain the policy activities of the EU and give an idea of their impact upon Britain.
- To review developments in European policy under the Blair government.
- To highlight an emergent feature of *Politics UK* and of British politics, namely the development of a multi-levelled form of government.

Introduction

In 1973 the United Kingdom became a member of what is now known as the European Union (EU). In the subsequent period the UK's political system has become increasingly interlinked with, and affected by, the institutions and policies associated with the European integration process. In consequence, very few areas of British policy have escaped the impact of the EU. Similarly, almost all political forces and institutions have been affected by European integration. This chapter is designed to explain how Britain fits in with the political processes of the EU. It will reveal an increasingly multi-levelled form of government: linking local authorities, the new devolved executives and assemblies, Whitehall/Westminster and the EU level in Brussels.

Britain and European integration: the context

For Britain and the rest of Europe the period following the Second World War brought major change. However, how Britain responded was distinctive. Unlike several of their counterparts on the European continent, British governments did not see a need to make a significant departure from the traditional foreign policy role as a world power. The result has been a relationship with the European Union characterised by semi-detachment and by internal political division within and between the political parties (George, 1998; Baker and Seawright, 1998, Ashford, 1992).

For Britain the post-war global context had changed significantly. Although emerging as one of the victorious allies, the UK effectively lost its status as a world power. The USA was to occupy the leadership role in the international economy and, politically, in the Western hemisphere. For Britain the new situation had two effects. Firstly, it had to manage the 'descent from power' in its foreign policy and adapt to being a medium-sized power. Secondly, it had to recognise that it no longer occupied the central role in the post-war economic order. Of course, these patterns can look all too clear when viewed with the benefit of hindsight. However, politicians had to contend with the day-to-day challenges of government as well as with electoral needs. In addition, there were other pressing issues, in particular popular pressures for the development of the welfare state and demands on the part of the colonies for independence. Above all, having emerged from the Second World War as one of the victor powers, governments were not presented with an immediate need to make a major change to foreign policy. Hence successive governments did not confront the issue of reorienting British foreign policy to a new European-centred focus. For these and other reasons, governments led by both major parties were reluctant to participate in new forms of European integration that seemed to challenge national sovereignty. The nation-state was still an object of pride.

The post-war experience of continental Europe was rather different. By continental Europe, we mean first of all Western Europe but excluding Spain and Portugal (as rather isolated dictatorships until the mid-1970s) as well as the Scandinavian countries, which had different traditions. The six member states which were to form the core of European integration until 1973 shared two particular experiences which encouraged them to develop a new form of cooperation. First, they had all had their prestige undermined by virtue of national defeat: whether at the hands of Hitler's Germany or, as in the case of Germany and Italy, at the hands of the Allies. Secondly, in various ways they had all suffered from the excesses of state power, with the Nazi regime the most extreme manifestation of this. These six states were France, Germany, Italy, Luxembourg, the Netherlands and Belgium.

For these countries – unlike Britain – the nation-state had been discredited, resulting in powerful political forces for new forms of inter-state co-operation. These new forms of co-operation were needed for three reasons. First, the six states all confronted the task of economic reconstruction but sought to solve particular economic policy issues in new ways. Secondly, most of the states bordered West Germany and sought an innovative way of constraining German power. Thirdly, the Cold War created a geopolitical division through the centre of Europe and a need to organise against a perceived external threat of communism that, together with worries in France and Italy about potential destabilisation by strong domestic communist parties, reinforced the need for co-operation. The consequence was that key continental political leaders, predominantly from the centre-right, developed supranational integration as a specific form of co-operation between states. Thus this supranational form of European integration and the first of the three European Communities were born.

Supranationalism involves not only a commitment on the part of member states to work together but, unlike other European or international organisations, also places formal constraints on national autonomy. Moreover, supranationalism expresses itself in a distinctive institutional structure: in a body of law that takes precedence over national law; in a dense network of institutions located chiefly in Brussels; and in a pattern of government which penetrates national (i.e. British) politics and policies to a unique extent.

Before looking at the present-day interaction of Britain and the EU, however, we need a brief examination of the course of integration from the early 1950s in order to appreciate the current situation.

A range of European organisations was set up in the immediate post-war period, as well as the North Atlantic Treaty Organisation (NATO), the transatlantic organisation concerned with the defence of Western Europe. The first of the supranational organisations was the European Coal and Steel Community (ECSC). This was proposed in the Schuman Plan of 1950 and was a French attempt to place the German (and French) 'industries of war' under supranational control, thus facilitating the reconstruction of the two industries in a way that would not threaten peace, and indeed would form the basis for Franco-German reconciliation. This Franco-German plan was adopted by the Six, and the ECSC came into operation in 1952. The resultant Franco-German relationship has been a peaceful one but it followed some eighty years of recurrent hostilities. It has been the bedrock of supranational integration.

Despite some setbacks in the mid-1950s, the Six agreed in 1957 to extend the supranational approach. Two new communities were set up in the Treaties of Rome and came into operation in 1958. These were the European Atomic Energy Community and the European Economic Community (EEC). Of the three European Communities, it is the EEC which has been the most prominent. In 1967 the three communities merged their institutions, and from this time they were known collectively as the European Community/ies (EC). When the Maastricht Treaty came into effect in November 1993 the current term – the European Union – was adopted.

Thus far the British response to supranational integration had been one of complete detachment. But by 1961 two factors had prompted the UK government, under Prime Minister Harold Macmillan, to apply for membership. These were:

- the stronger economic performances of those states in the three communities; and
- Britain's declining foreign policy influence, as highlighted by the decolonisation process and the Suez Crisis of 1956, when it failed to reverse the actions of a small country – Egypt – in nationalising the Suez Canal.

This first application and a subsequent one made by the Labour government of Harold Wilson in 1967 were unsuccessful because they were blocked by the French President, Charles de Gaulle. He feared that Britain might compete with France for leadership of the EC. He also halted the supranational development of the EC through the 1965 'empty chair crisis', which had the consequence of stopping the scheduled introduction of majority voting in the Council of Ministers. Under this voting system – the formal provision in the treaties for some policy areas – individual member governments could be over-ruled, thereby challenging their **sovereignty**. During the 1960s the EC stagnated politically owing to the other states' opposition to de Gaulle's policies. However, circumstances changed in 1969 with his resignation. A relaunch of integration was undertaken and it was as part of this that enlargement returned to the agenda.

Eventually, after successful terms of membership had been negotiated, the first enlargement took place in 1973 (with the UK, Ireland and Denmark acceding). The British government presented the EC as an organisation which posed little major threat to sovereignty. In other words final and absolute authority would remain in the UK and not be challenged from outside. In the House of Commons the decision to approve the terms of membership was highly contested. Edward Heath's Conservative government was reliant on support from rebel Labour MPs, who rejected their party's line of opposing the terms negotiated. Sovereignty was a key point of conflict during the debates. However, it is important to remember that this assumption about sovereignty was true only in terms of the way the EC had developed in the 1960s. In fact, under the formal rules set down in the treaties there was considerable provision for sovereignty to be challenged. When member states started to wish to return to the formal rules, and in particular to majority voting in the Council of Ministers (see below), the UK was less at ease because sovereignty was challenged.

The stagnation of integration that had started in the mid-1960s continued in many respects throughout the 1970s. Apart from enlargement there were some isolated advances, in particular the establishment of the European Monetary System (EMS) in 1979. However, it was in the 1980s that the integration process advanced in a striking way, through both widening and deepening. The EC was widened by virtue of two southern enlargements: in 1981 to encompass Greece, and in 1986 with the accession of Spain and Portugal. Deepening came about in the form of the Single European Act (SEA), which took effect in 1987.

The SEA was the first comprehensive set of revisions to the original treaties of the 1950s. Most prominently the SEA contained a commitment to accelerating economic integration. It was designed in part to put into practice an agreement reached in 1985 to create a single European market: the basis to re-invigorate the competitiveness of the European economy. However, the SEA also strengthened the supranational institutions in order to speed up decision making.

The renewed dynamism of the SEA brought with it a more widespread revival of momentum. The links between EC policies led to pressures for initiatives in other spheres, for instance the proposals for monetary union (EMU). These developments formed one of the dynamics for a further exercise of treaty revision, in the Treaty on European Union (or, more popularly, the Maastricht Treaty), which was signed in February 1992. The other source of dynamics arose from the dramatic changes in the map of European politics at the end of 1989. The end of the Cold War, as well as the re-unification of Germany in October 1990, re-opened some of the fundamental issues which the integration process had sought to address at the start of the 1950s. What should now be regarded as 'Europe'? Who was to be responsible for ensuring the economic prosperity and democratic stability of this 'new' Europe? How should Europe's international role be defined? What should be Germany's role in the 'new' Europe? Should the institutions of the EC be reformed in anticipation of much greater membership in the future? Hence, all these kinds of questions became intertwined with the existing questions, such as how to proceed to EMU.

The Maastricht Treaty represented an attempt at a structured blueprint for European integration. This treaty entailed a number of key aspects:

- It set out the blueprint for European Monetary Union (EMU), including a single European currency.
- It sought to strengthen social policy provision through the Social Chapter.
- It made the process of policy making more supranational.
- It formally created the European Union, comprising three pillars: the existing economic and social pillar; foreign policy; and co-operation on justice and home affairs (see below).

In the meantime four non-members had begun to re-assess their relationship with the integration process in the aftermath of the Cold War. For Austria, Finland, Sweden and Norway, traditionally 'neutral' states, the new international circumstances reduced the conflict between their neutrality and the EU's orientation. In addition, the single market programme was creating particular concerns for them, as the EU's economic rules were affecting them but they had no real say in decision making. The solution was to apply for membership. These states successfully negotiated terms and joined in January 1995, thus enlarging the EU (see Figure 31.1). Membership was enlarged only to fifteen states because Norway rejected membership in a referendum.

Since the momentum generated in the mid-1980s the integration process has barely paused for breath. Even while the Maastricht timetable for the single currency was moving ahead, the fifteen governments began in 1996 to review further treaty reform. This process culminated in the Amsterdam Treaty of 1997, and which came into effect in 1999. This treaty tried to bring improvements to the functioning of the EU across a range of its policies, for example through institutional reforms, and placed emphasis on developing an 'area of freedom, justice and security' in the EU.

The EU's institutions and decision making

The European Union has five key institutions with which the student of British politics should be familiar. These are the European Commission, the Council of Ministers, the European Council, the European Parliament (EP) and, finally, the European Court of Justice (ECJ).

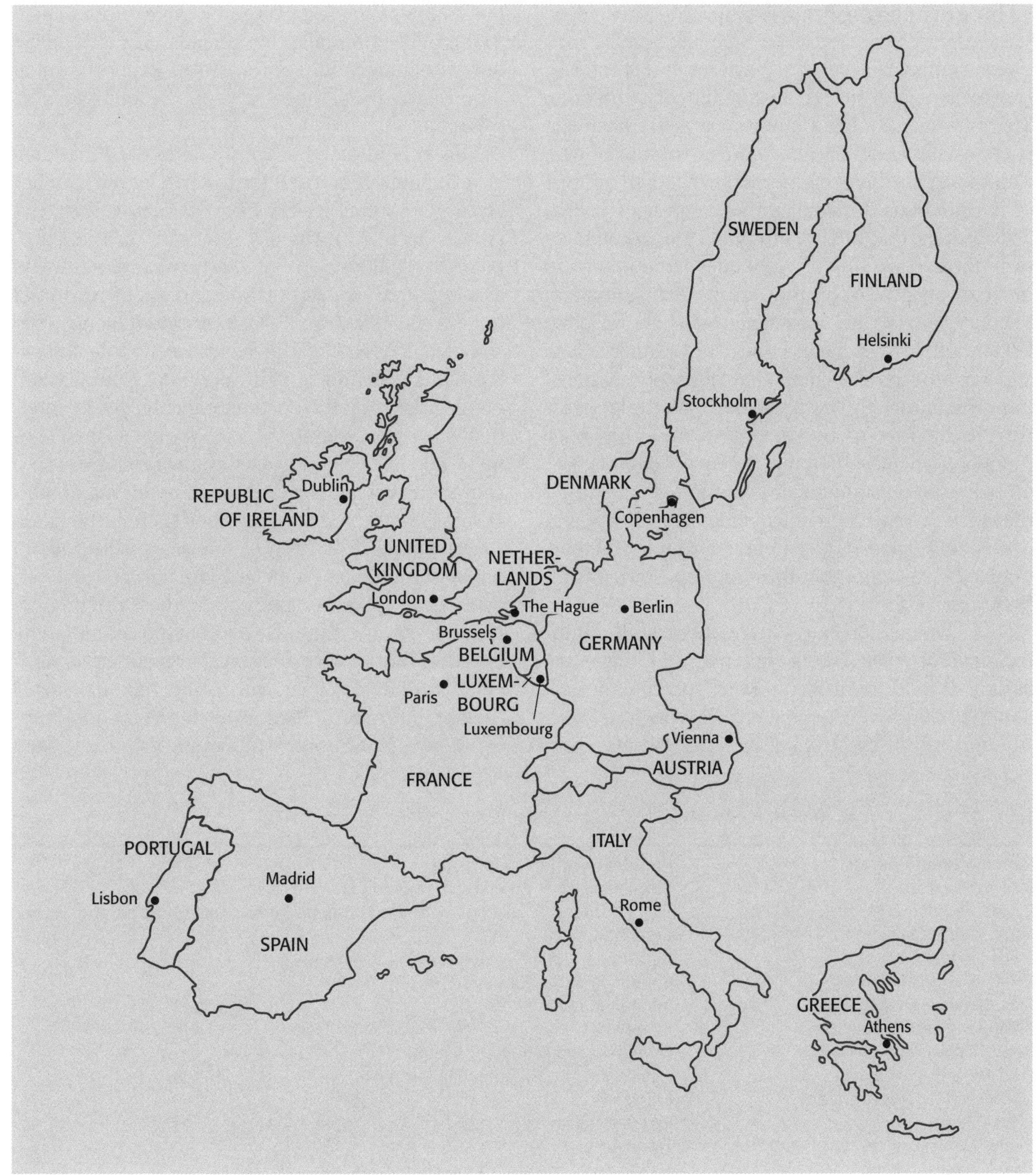

Figure 31.1 Map of European Union showing seats of government

The European Commission

The Commission acts as the 'civil service' of the EU. However, it also has a fair amount of autonomy. This is what sets the Commission apart from the secretariats of other international organisations. This autonomy finds expression particularly in two of its functions. First, it is the initiator of policy. This means that the Commission does not have to await instructions or guidelines from ministers but can propose legislation on its own initiative. Secondly, it is the 'conscience of the European Community'. This means that the Commission is supposed to develop ideas that transcend national interests, although the proposals have to be practical if they are to be sure of success. Its other functions include helping construct agreement on policy amongst member governments, ensuring that they put such agreements into legal effect, and overseeing some of the detailed running of particular policies, notably the Common Agricultural Policy (CAP).

The Commission has a permanent staff establishment of some 20,000 but many of these are assigned to translation and interpreting duties; about 14,000 have classical civil service functions. At the head of the Commission are twenty commissioners, each in charge of a policy area (Table 31.1). The Commission officials are organised overwhelmingly into directorates-general, which may be seen as the equivalent of ministries in Whitehall.

The commissioners are appointed by national governments (two each for the five larger member states) for terms which, from 1995, last five years and coincide with the electoral term of the European Parliament. One of the commissioners acts as president: at present Romano Prodi who took up office in 1999. Prodi's Commission took up office somewhat ahead of the normal schedule following the resignation of the previous Commission, presided over by the Luxemburger, Jacques Santer, following a damning report about mismanagement and 'sleaze'. Indeed, Commission leadership is a controversial issue. Under President Jacques Delors, who served several terms lasting from 1985 to December 1994, the Commission acted as an important force for deepening integration. However, some governments – but chiefly the British one – came to regard these developments as intruding into their national sovereignty. In fact, it was principally John Major's government which ensured the appointment of Santer, having vetoed another candidate. But Santer's weakness may have been

Table 31.1 European Commissioners and their responsibilities, 1999–2004

Romano Prodi (Italy)	President of the Commission
Neil Kinnock (UK)*	Vice-President – Administrative Reform
Loyola de Palacio (Spain)	Vice-President – Relations with the European Parliament, Transport and Energy
Mario Monti (Italy)*	Competition
Franz Fischler (Austria)*	Agriculture, Rural Development and Fisheries
Erkki Liikanen (Finland)*	Enterprise and Information Society
Frits Bolkestein (Netherlands)	Internal Market
Philippe Busquin (Belgium)	Research
Pedro Solbes Mira (Spain)	Economic and Monetary Affairs
Poul Nielson (Denmark)	Development and Humanitarian Aid
Günter Verheugen (Germany)	Enlargement
Chris Patten (UK)	External Relations
Pascal Lamy (France)	Trade
David Byrne (Ireland)	Health and Consumer Protection
Michel Barnier (France)	Regional Policy
Viviane Reding (Luxemburg)	Education and Culture
Michaele Schreyer (Germany)	Budget
Margot Wallström (Sweden)	Environment
Antonio Vitorino (Portugal)	Justice and Home Affairs
Anna Diamantopoulou (Greece)	Employment and Social Affairs

Note: Asterisked Commissioners were in the outgoing Santer Commission which resigned in 1999

BOX 31.1 MINI BIOGRAPHY

Jacques Delors (1925–)
French statesman and former President of European Commission. Socialist politician from 1973 and served Mitterrand's government 1981–4. President of Commission in 1985 and elected to second term in 1988. Fought hard to advance political and social integration and so became the target of much criticism from British Conservative Euro-sceptics.

BOX 31.2 MINI BIOGRAPHY

Neil Kinnock (1942–)
Former Labour leader and then EU Commissioner/Vice President. Educated Cardiff University, he worked for the Workers' Educational Association before becoming MP for Bedwellty in 1970. Shadowed Education in early 1980s and then succeeded Michael Foot in 1983. Lost 1987 election and also, a huge disappointment, in 1992. Major helped him get EU post in wake of the defeat. A gifted and witty orator, with much personality, he was judged by many to be too woolly and verbose to really impress.

BOX 31.3 MINI BIOGRAPHY

Chris Patten (1944–)
Foreign Affairs Commissioner in EU. Educated Oxford from where joined Conservative Research Department. Secretary for the Environment in 1986 and party chairman 1991 where credited with masterminding his party's 1992 election victory. Governor of Hong Kong 1992–7 and appointed to EU post in 1999.

a contribution to the circumstances under which all the Commissioners resigned: an unprecedented event in the history of integration. The appointment of Prodi was an attempt to restore a stronger leadership, but it may well lead to sovereignty disputes in the future. The UK Commissioners are Neil Kinnock, the former Labour leader who is serving a second term in Brussels, and Christopher Patten, the former Conservative minister, party chairman and Governor of Hong Kong (see also Table 31.1). Kinnock, one of two vice-presidents, is charged with the particularly difficult task of reforming the multi-national Commission and generally 'cleaning up its act'. Like Commission officials, the commissioners are supposed to reflect the European interest rather than that of their country of origin.

The Council of Ministers

The Council of Ministers is the main decision-making organ of the EU. Its official title was amended to 'Council of the European Union' when the Maastricht Treaty was implemented, but its former title and the contraction, 'the Council', tend to be the terms in popular use. It comprises ministers from each of the fifteen member states. It meets almost a hundred times each year but does so in a number of different guises depending on the subject matter under discussion. Thus the Council of Agriculture Ministers brings together the fifteen ministers with responsibility for agriculture; the Council of Economic and Finance Ministers (Ecofin) brings together the Chancellor of the Exchequer and his fourteen counterparts. Together with the General Council (of foreign ministers) these are the three principal formations in which the Council meets. The Maastricht Treaty formally brought ministerial meetings to discuss foreign policy as well as a range of Home Office and justice matters (in EU-speak, Justice and Home Affairs) under the umbrella of the Council. It is indicative of the breadth of impact of the EU upon Whitehall that it met in 1998 in no fewer than twenty-one formations, including ministers responsible for energy, health, fisheries, culture and so on. All ministers from the policy-based departments of Whitehall meet in an EU context: including, for the first time in 1998, defence ministers.

The work of the Council is principally to take the many policy decisions of a political nature.

This work requires considerable preparation. Three agencies are worth mentioning in this connection. The preparation of the work of the Council is largely undertaken by officials of national governments in conjunction with counterparts in the Commission. The main forum for preparation is the Committee of Permanent Representatives (COREPER). Like the Council, this meets in different guises according to what is on the agenda. COREPER meetings are attended either by national civil servants or diplomats who are based in the permanent representations, effectively member states' embassies in Brussels to the EU. It is in such meetings that the agenda is prepared for the forthcoming meetings of the Council of the EU. Given their heavy domestic schedules, meetings of the ministers can thus be confined to either rubber stamping matters agreed in COREPER or to thrashing out the politically contentious issues.

The second agency is the presidency of the Council of Ministers. The presidency is held by each member state on a rota basis for a six-month term. The presidency is responsible for chairing Council and COREPER meetings. More generally it serves the function of trying to put together packages of agreements across a range of policy areas, and that have a sufficient balance to satisfy the interests of all member states. The UK held the presidency in the first half of 1998, presiding for instance over the key decisions to launch EMU (albeit without UK participation). A six-month period is very short for the officials of a member state to master its brief. This is where the third agency comes in, namely the permanent secretariat of the Council. It has some 2,000 staff, including a contingent of translators and interpreters. However, there are also key officials able to provide continuity between the rotating presidencies.

What is distinctive about the EU, when compared with other international organisations, is the provision for the member governments to take decisions by weighted majority voting. Under majority voting each member state is assigned a weighting to its vote, based roughly according to the size of the country concerned. Thus the UK, France, Germany and Italy each have ten votes, while at the other extreme Luxembourg has two. Where qualified majority voting is used, it is necessary to secure a minimum of sixty-two of the available eighty-seven votes, in order to secure a majority. Such a system means that the British government may be over-ruled but is still has to give effect to the legislation agreed by the majority. Thus the importance of majority voting is that it is a clear way in which national sovereignty may be lost. In reality, and despite Treaty provision, little use was made of majority voting until the mid-1980s and the passage of the SEA. The Maastricht and Amsterdam treaties extended provision still further. Even so, there are still important dynamics working towards a consensual approach. For example, it is a better guarantee of the implementation of policy.

The European Council

The European Council, established in 1974, has developed into an important institution covering all activities of the European Union created by the Maastricht Treaty. It is broadly comparable with the Council of Ministers, except that it comprises the heads of government (or in France's case the President), the fifteen foreign ministers and two commissioners. It meets at least twice per year. It has initiated some of the key EC/EU developments, such as the European Monetary System, the SEA, the Maastricht Treaty and the Amsterdam Treaty and the launch of the single currency on 1 May 1999. Given its composition, the European Council is best placed to provide leadership for strategic initiatives. However, its meetings equally may become media events resulting in little substantive progress.

The European Parliament

The EP comprises 626 members (or MEPs) in the EU of fifteen member states. Most of these MEPs sit in transnational parliamentary groups. In the 1999–2004 EP the parties of the centre-right have a small majority, largely because of some mid-term swings against the centre-left governments predominately in power in the EU member states. Within the EP the main British political parties have had to come to terms with co-operating with their counterparts, often from different political

Table 31.2 UK results in the 1999 European elections

Party	Number of MEPs
Conservative	36
Labour	29
Liberal Democrat	10
UK Independence	3
Green	2
Scottish National Party	2
Plaid Cymru	2
Democratic Unionist Party	1
Social Democratic and Labour Party	1
Ulster Unionist Party	1
Total	**87**

traditions, in the other member states. Of the major parties this challenge has been the greatest for the Conservative Party, which has not always been at ease with continental counterparts from strongly pro-European christian democratic parties. The UK results of the 1999 European elections are shown in Table 31.2.

Directly elected for the first time in 1979, the Parliament has suffered from a number of weaknesses, although these are gradually being addressed through reform measures. The principal weakness was its lack of powers. Until the mid-1980s its powers were largely limited to offering (non-binding) opinions on legislation; having the theoretical power to sack the Commission (never formally effected, but the Commission resigned in 1999 following a report by experts appointed by the Parliament); and the right to scrutinise the work of the Commission and Council.

The first steps towards enhancing these powers came in the 1970s, when the EP gained important influence over the EC budget. Then, from 1987, the implementation of the SEA introduced a new legislative role for the EP in certain policy areas, known as the co-operation procedure. This procedure enhanced the EP's powers by giving it some bargaining chips with which it can seek to influence the Council during the legislative process. The EP's powers were further developed in the Maastricht Treaty by the introduction of a new co-decision power. In simplified terms this adds to the co-operation procedure by giving the EP the ultimate power to reject an item of legislation altogether. Finally, the scope of co-decision was extended in the Amsterdam Treaty to cover much European legislation. The EP has significant powers in respect of agreements between the EU and third countries as well as the power of veto over the accession of new member states.

Nevertheless, the EP's profile remains weak. The EP's work is not particularly suited to television, not least because a multilingual institution lacks the cut-and-thrust of the House of Commons. A further problem hampering the EP is the complex situation regarding its seat. Its plenary sessions are in Strasbourg and its committee meetings are in Brussels. This split-site operation scarcely helps the EP gain a clear profile. And the logistical arrangements seem to confirm the sceptical citizen's concern about the EU's remoteness and incomprehensibility. The EP's strong committee system is little known to those outside the EU policy-making 'network' but is actually central to its work. The EP remains the only directly elected parliament of any international organisation and potentially represents a competing focus for democratic legitimacy alongside national parliaments such as Westminster.

Indicative of the EP's problems with its profile is the turnout at European elections (see Table 31.3). When the fifth set of direct elections was held in 1999, EU-wide turnout was only 49.4 per cent, a figure strikingly lower than for national elections. The EC/EU average turnout has declined with every election, as the table shows. In the UK turnout has been at the bottom end of the scale: in 1999 it was only 24 per cent. A figure such as this does not give the UK MEPs a strong claim to represent the country compared with the national government, elected on a much bigger turnout. The UK elects eighty-seven MEPs: eighty-four from the British mainland (by a closed regional list system); and three from Northern Ireland using a single-constituency proportional representation method. The closed regional list system was first introduced with the 1999 elections. Unlike under the first-past-the-post Euro-constituency system that was replaced, it is no longer possible for a voter to identify his or her MEP under the regional list system. This development might run the risk of detaching MEPs even more from their electorate. On the other hand, the regional lists correspond to the emergent Regional Development Agencies

Table 31.3 Turnout in European elections (per cent) and number of seats in the EP

	Year of election					
Country	**1979**	**1984**	**1989**	**1994**	**1999**	**No. of seats (1994)**
Austria	na	na	na	67.7 (1996)	49.0	21
Belgium	91.6	92.2	90.7	90.7	90.0	25
Denmark	47.1	52.3	46.1	52.9	50.4	16
Finland	na	na	na	60.3 (1996)	30.1	16
France	60.7	56.7	48.7	52.7	47.0	87
Germany	65.7	56.8	62.4	60.0	45.2	99
Greece	78.6 (1981)	77.2	79.9	71.2	70.2	25
Ireland	63.6	47.6	68.3	44.0	50.5	15
Italy	85.5	83.9	81.5	74.8	70.8	87
Luxembourg	88.9	87.0	87.4	88.5	85.8	6
Netherlands	57.8	50.5	47.2	36.0	29.9	31
Portugal	na	72.2 (1987)	51.1	35.5	40.4	25
Spain	na	68.9 (1987)	54.8	59.1	64.4	64
Sweden	na	na	na	41.6 (1996)	38.3	22
UK	31.6	32.6	36.2	36.4	24.0	87
EC/EU average	63	61	58.5	56.8	49.4	Total = 626

Notes: na denotes not applicable, as the states had not yet joined the EC/EU. Those states with turnout figures of 80 per cent or more have requirements (legal or otherwise) that citizens vote at elections. Election data for Germany prior to the 1994 election are for West Germany. Data in parentheses relate to the first direct elections held in the state concerned after their accession to the EC/EU

Source: European Parliament web site (http://www1.europarl.eu.int/uk/elections/main.html), 8 October 1999

and regional chambers in England, as well as the Scottish and Welsh devolved institutions. This aspect might enable MEPs to develop a clearer role in a new territorial pattern of multi-level government.

The European Court of Justice and EC law

Consideration of the ECJ enables attention to be drawn to three important characteristics of the EU. Firstly, the significance of EC law and the treaties must not be underestimated. Within the UK, particularly in the absence of a formal, written constitution, it is difficult to appreciate continental traditions. A number of major developments in European integration have come about as a result of pathbreaking rulings by the ECJ in interpreting what the treaties 'meant'. Moreover, as the treaty basis of the EU widens, so a gradual constitutionalisation is taking place at the European level. It would not be too far-fetched to argue that the constitutional law of the EC is bringing about a 'quiet revolution' in British constitutional practice.

A second important feature is to point out the existence of a body of EC law. What is distinctive about European law is that it has primacy over national law. Moreover, it may be directly applicable in not requiring the enactment of national legislation. It may also have direct effect meaning that EC law entails rights and obligations which may be tested before the national courts. These features of EC law are of fundamental importance to understanding the formal way in which EU membership challenges national sovereignty. In a 1990 ruling (the *Factortame* case) the ECJ effectively 'disapplied' British legislation because it did not comply with EC law. This case clearly demonstrated the principle that Parliament is no longer sovereign.

The third feature is simply to draw attention to the ECJ itself. It comprises fifteen judges and is based in Luxembourg. It acts in a number of ways: interpreting the treaties, enforcing the law and so on. Nugent (1994, p. 234) summarises its role thus:

The Court of Justice has played an extremely important part in establishing the EU's legal order . . . whether it is acting as an international court, a court of review, a court of appeal, or a court of referral . . . the Court is also frequently a maker of law as well as an interpreter of law.

Other bodies and interest groups

There are a number of other EU institutions. These include the Court of Auditors, which scrutinises EU expenditure. The Economic and Social Committee is consulted on much legislation and acts as a kind of 'parliament of interests'. Its importance has been overshadowed somewhat in recent years by virtue of the increased power of the EP. Additionally, the Maastricht Treaty provided for a Committee of the Regions. This institution was designed to enhance the involvement of the regions particularly in those EU policy areas with spatial aspects, such as regional policy. Perhaps the main new institution, however, is the European Central Bank (ECB) based in Frankfurt, Germany. It is responsible for setting interest rates for all those states fully participating in the single currency. Although the UK is not amongst the initial members, the ECB's interest rate decisions will have an impact on the thinking of the Bank of England. If the UK joins the single currency, the ECB will take over key functions of the Bank of England.

The final main category of participants in decision making is the vast array of interest groups lobbying the EU institutions. There are over five hundred such groups, which bring together interest groups from the member states. One of the principal such organisations is the Committee of Professional Agricultural Organizations (COPA), which comprises most of the national-level farmer organisations, including the UK's National Farmers' Union. The extensive nature of European lobbying demonstrates another way in which the EU has penetrated UK politics, for it is now necessary for all British interest groups potentially affected by EU decisions to have some means of lobbying the relevant institutions, especially the Commission. Moreover, it is not normally feasible or effective for a UK interest group to lobby the Commission. The Commission has limited staffing resources and prefers only to consult groups representative of the EU as a whole. In this way it can consult one interest group rather than fifteen. However, what is also true is that UK interest groups still lobby national government on EU policies. Nevertheless, this strategy may not suffice, particularly given that the UK government may be over-ruled in the Council of Ministers through a majority vote.

A final further observation on lobbying at the EU level concerns local government. It has now become the rule for UK local authorities to have a European office of some kind within their organisation. In the case of those parts of the UK eligible to receive aid from the EU's funds, it is essential for local authorities to have effective contacts with the Commission. There is, in consequence, a significant impact on local authority activity in the UK. Of course, local authorities are not normally regarded as interest groups. However, in their relations with the EU authorities, this is the best kind of parallel to make for their activities.

EU decision making

There are many different patterns for EU decision making. However, it is important to give some kind of impression of the interaction of the agencies outlined above. Necessarily this requires some simplification. What follows sets out the decision-making process in the economic and social policy domains of the EU (the so called EC 'pillar' of the EU). Proposals normally originate from the Commission, which will usually have consulted with interested parties beforehand. The proposals are then sent to the Council of Ministers. There, deliberations take place initially at the specialist level amongst officials of the national governments, usually under the umbrella of COREPER. However, the proposal is simultaneously sent to the EP and the Economic and Social Committee. The latter submits an opinion on the proposal to the Council. The former, however, will make its views known through one of several procedures (principally consultation or co-decision), depending on the legal base of the proposal. It is during this phase that a second stage of lobbying takes place through two channels: EU-level groups lobby the EP; national groups will lobby 'their' national

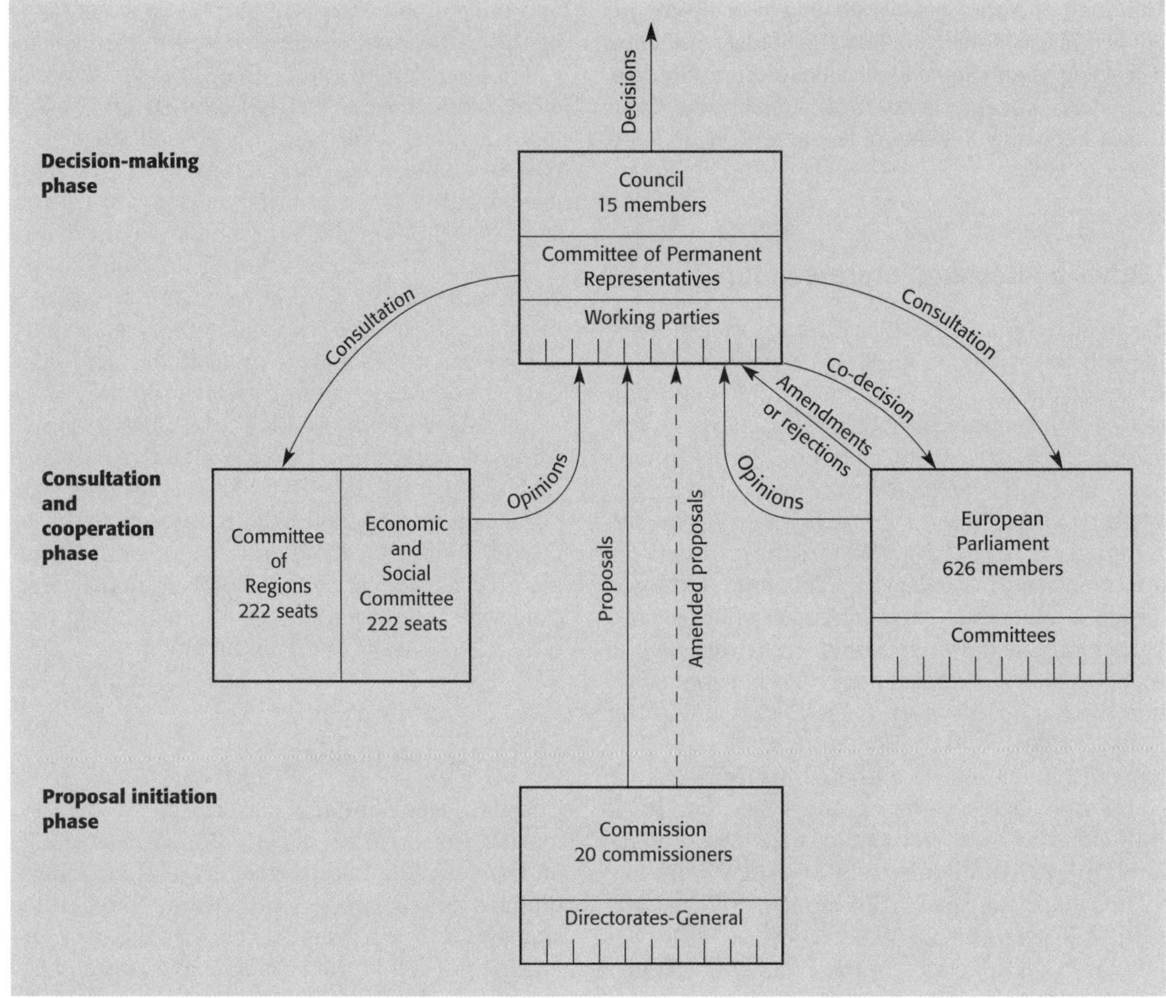

Figure 31.2 The Union's proposal and decision-making process

government. The final stage of the process is when the Council reaches its decision, taking into account the advice received, and in accordance with the prevailing voting method for the policy area under consideration. A schematic presentation of decision making is set out in Figure 31.2.

EU decision making and the impact upon British politics

As has been seen, decision making can follow several paths. Moreover, its characteristics are not especially familiar to the broader British public. Why is this so?

1 The procedure is remote by virtue of being centred on Brussels.

2 The constitutional–legal principles are different from those familiar in the UK.

3 The EU's policy responsibilities are wide. This means that it is easy to present the EU as 'interfering' with accepted British practice, even though this interference will probably have been sanctioned by a British minister.

4 The EU remains predominantly concerned with economic issues and its predominant mode of governing, in the absence of a large

Table 31.4 EU decision-making bodies attended by UK ministers and officials

Institution	UK participant	Number of formations	Number of meetings
European Council	Prime Minister, Foreign Secretary, advisers	1	3 p.a. (plus 1 informal)
Council of the EU	Minister, advisers	21	94 p.a.
Working groups	Officials, usually from Whitehall	232	3139 p.a.

Source: Author's data collated from General-Secretariat Council of the European Union; figures for 1998

budget or of any equivalent to nationalised industries, is through acting as a regulator. Thus it sets the framework for economic activities (for instance, through competition policy); it regulates particular sections of the economy (for instance, agriculture or telecommunications); and it seeks to ensure that economic interests do not work against those of society at large (for instance, through environmental policy or equal opportunities policy). This regulatory mode of governing tends to be very much a matter for technical bargaining between governments, the EU institutions and interest groups. It is conducted away from the public eye.

5 Even for those specialising in the politics of the EU, the multiplicity of possible procedures makes decision making difficult to penetrate.

All these characteristics have important ramifications for British politics because the UK and the EU are interlocked systems of government.

The institutional and policy-making apparatus in Brussels has a significant impact upon the way in which the UK is governed. We review this impact – sometimes known as Europeanisation – in summary form.

- A significant amount of draft legislation emanates from the EU – chiefly from the Commission – and must be reviewed by government officials to establish how it affects UK interests.
- Government officials from across the whole of central government, and including the devolved executives beyond London, must define a position and present it at meetings of both officials, and ultimately ministers, from the EU (Bulmer and Burch, 1998, 2000). As part of this they may have to develop new skills: in foreign languages or in the different type of negotiating that takes place in the EU. It is no good trying to negotiate as if in Whitehall or Westminster when the rules of the EU game are quite different. As Table 31.4 shows, at the EU decision-making stage alone the number of meetings attended by UK civil servants is over 3,000 per annum.
- In order to respond to the challenge of the EU all Whitehall ministries have set up co-ordinating agencies to have some oversight over the impact of European policy upon their responsibilities. The key ministerial players are the Foreign and Commonwealth Office, the Treasury, the Ministry of Agriculture Fisheries and Food, the Department of Trade and Industry and the Cabinet Office, whose European Secretariat acts as a troubleshooter where differences arise between ministries. The head of this secretariat acts as the Prime Minister's adviser at meetings of the European Council.
- Ministers are also involved in this process: the Prime Minister through participation in European Council sessions; the Foreign Secretary; the Chancellor but also most of the others in the Cabinet and their junior ministers. As Table 31.4 shows, there are nearly 100 ministerial meetings in the EU each year.
- Later in the decision-making process these same ministries as well as other bodies from employers to local government have to ensure that they have mechanisms in place to implement or adhere to European law. If they do not do so, the full force of the law may be applied to their cost through the national court system in the same way as for purely domestic legislation.

- Parliamentarians have had to adapt their own procedures in both Houses to try to ensure that they can make an effective input into decision making at the EU level. Following devolution members of the Scottish Parliament and Welsh Assembly have sought to address these issues, too.
- Members of the European Parliament can serve as an alternative channel of democratic input from regional constituencies into the EU policy process.
- Subnational government has also had to adapt: devolved executives, local authorities. This adaptation is especially important since some parts of the UK are eligible for substantial financial support for regional and social development: Northern Ireland, Merseyside, the Highlands and Islands, South Yorkshire and Cornwall.
- Political parties must adapt. They need to find ways to 'play the European game'. Unless they are pursuing a deliberately non-co-operative policy, like the UK Independence Party for example, they will most likely seek out allies amongst their continental counterparts. For instance, Tony Blair has invested a lot of effort in cultivating links with his German counterpart, Gerhard Schröder. Why? Because joint initiatives stand a much greater chance of success in EU negotiations.
- Interest groups have to get to grips with a multi-level lobbying strategy where their interests are affected by the EU. Farmers and industrialists may go beyond lobbying in conjunction with their EU counterparts and set up their own office in Brussels to ensure their voice is heard. The same is true for the largest companies. An alternative approach is to engage the services of lobbying consultants in Brussels.
- More problematically, UK public opinion on European issues has to be taken account of. The difficulty is that many members of the public regard the EU as remote until some threat to the British way of life is perceived, such as the abolition of the pound if the government were to join EMU.

The result of this impact is the emergence of multi-level government and politics in the UK. Whether it is central government, parliament or interest groups, they must ensure they are both well equipped to know what the EU is doing as well as making sure their voice is heard in the EU's decisions.

The key policy areas

The integration process has involved an ever-widening portfolio of policies. The initial concern of integration was with the coal and steel industries, in the ECSC. In 1958 this was extended to co-operation on atomic energy, but this policy area never developed to the extent intended. By contrast, the EEC had a much wider policy impact. It comprised a large range of policies and, as they were put into operation, so the policy areas began to penetrate the activities of the member states, resulting in the 'Europeanisation' of national policies. From the 1970s the member states also dealt with a handful of policy issues outside the formal treaties. The best example of this was the foreign policy co-operation procedure, created in 1970. Subsequently, such issues as combating international terrorism were treated in this way. With the end of the Cold War the home affairs area became more salient to the member states because of fears of large-scale immigration from the east or of Russian mafia exploiting criminal opportunities in a borderless European market. The involvement of supranational institutions, such as the Commission and the Court of Justice, has been kept minimal in these issues for a variety of reasons. Governments have wanted to retain sovereignty over these matters and have them dealt with by the Council and they have found it convenient to conduct these activities away from the public eye. The Maastricht Treaty sought to give these activities a clearer basis by giving them treaty status but with separate arrangements for decision making. The treaty introduced institutional arrangements based on a temple (see Figure 31.3).

In this 'architecture' of a temple all the collective activities of the fifteen member states are now under the 'roof' of the European Union. The

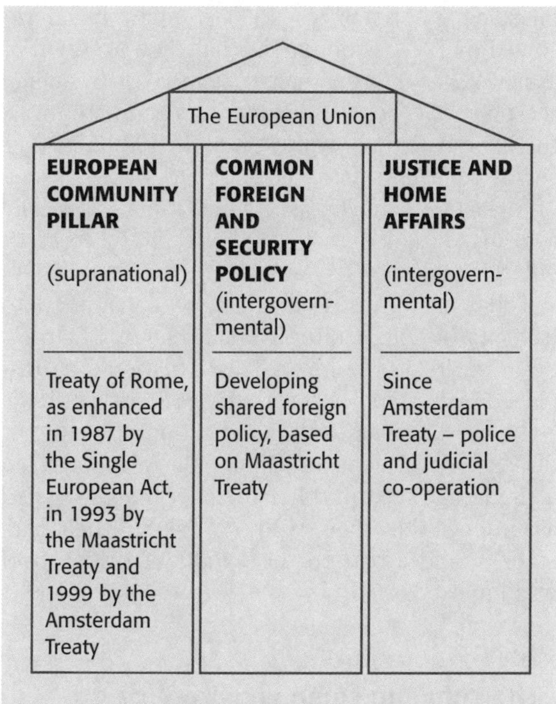

Figure 31.3 The architecture of the European Union

existing economic treaties form a supranational EC 'pillar' within the European Union. However, the EU is supported by two other pillars which comprise activities conducted in an intergovernmental manner. One of these pillars formalises foreign policy co-operation, now known as the Common Foreign and Security Policy (CFSP), in the EU. The other groups together Justice and Home Affairs (JHA) co-operation (since the Amsterdam Treaty confined to the areas of police co-operation and judicial co-operation such as over extradition). The institutional structures of the CFSP and JHA pillars are dominated by governments, normally voting by unanimity and thus with no formal threat to sovereignty. Links with supranational institutions such as the Commission and EP are more limited in these areas of policy. Similarly, decisions taken in these two pillars do not have the status of European law. We now turn to the activities encompassed by the European Union as a whole but begin with those of the long-standing EC pillar.

The three long-standing policies associated with the EC pillar have been the common market between the member states, the Common Agricultural Policy (CAP) and a common commercial policy with the outside world.

The common market

The idea of creating a common market between the member states was to provide a stimulus to economic efficiency. A common market would allow consumers to choose between the most price-competitive producers from within the market. At the same time producers would be able to produce their goods and services for a market larger than their own state, thereby becoming able to generate economies of scale. This is the economic theory behind creating a common market but in political reality it entails some restructuring of the national economies. How, then, does it correspond to what has happened in the European context?

As set out in the EEC Treaty, the European common market provided essentially for three developments. These were the removal of tariffs on trade between member states; the free movement of goods, persons, services and capital; and harmonising legislation that affects the operation of the common market. The first of these three was achieved without major difficulty in mid-1968, one year ahead of the Treaty schedule. However, other barriers to trade proved much more resistant to change. Member states used different technical requirements and a host of national measures to protect domestic producers. For example, German law defined very strictly what ingredients were permitted in beer. Beer including ingredients other than those could not be sold in Germany, so German law formed a barrier to trade. This kind of situation was pervasive.

As a result of such barriers, the EC's progress to achieving a true common market was, in reality, poor. However, this policy was revived by the single-market programme, endorsed and accelerated by the SEA. As a result, most of the legislation needed to create a common (or internal) market had been agreed by the deadline of 31 December 1992. The UK government of Margaret Thatcher was one of the main proponents of the single-market programme, for it was consistent with the Conservatives' support for opening up markets and introducing more competitive economic conditions. Linked to the common market is competition policy, which aims to ensure fair business practices prevail in trade between member states. The internal market and competition policy have very substantial effects on the day-to-day activities of businesses in the UK. This is reflected not least in the fact that the UK's fellow member states in the EU represent its most important trading partners (over half of both imports to, and exports from, the UK). In more recent times the single market has been regarded as a key element in the EU's response to the challenge of globalisation.

The Common Agricultural Policy

The CAP was introduced in the 1960s. Although it now represents under 3 per cent of EU GNP and under 8 per cent of EU employment, agriculture was more important in 1958. Agriculture has also been of greater electoral importance on the continent than in the UK. Reflecting the interests of the then six member states, the CAP was created as a high cost, protectionist policy that in crude terms favoured the interests of farmers over those of consumers. Its high costs derived from the policy's price-setting policy, which aimed to cover the costs even of small, inefficient farmers. It was protectionist because it worked on the basis of 'Community preference'; lower cost producers from the world market were denied free access.

Prior to 1973 the UK had a different type of agricultural policy. It was expensive for the taxpayer but ensured cheap food supplies to consumers. Adaptation to the CAP proved controversial in the UK because food prices rose following accession. In addition, the lack of a large agricultural sector meant that Britain did not receive much revenue from the largest expenditure component of the modest EC budget. This in turn created a further imbalance, for the UK found itself becoming a major net contributor to the EC budget, alongside Germany. The costs of the CAP, along with the budgetary imbalance, led to Margaret Thatcher's demands, in the early 1980s, for the UK to have its 'own money back'. This dispute, which soured Britain's relations with the EC, also slowed progress on some other policies until the matter was resolved in 1984. From about that time a period of agricultural reforms began, aimed at reducing the policy's cost, and making it more in step with the liberalisation of world trade. In 1999 a further set of reforms was agreed as part of a package of measures known as Agenda 2000: basically reforms designed to get the EU fit for eastern enlargement.

Today Britain scarcely can be considered to have its own agricultural policy, for it is largely determined at EU level. This situation was displayed most graphically with the BSE crisis in 1996. National solutions to the eradication of 'mad cow disease' were an insufficient policy response; in a single market the other member states needed assurances that there were no risks to their consumers, and a ban on the export of British beef was imposed.

The common commercial policy

The common commercial policy formed the external counterpart to creating a common internal European market. Hence, as internal tariffs were removed, so a common external tariff was created. This means that the EU is a powerful bloc in international trade negotiations. The UK government now has very limited powers in trade policy. The government's main involvement is in ensuring that the policy of the EU is consistent with British wishes. In the international trade negotiations now conducted in the World Trade Organisation, the bargaining with states such as Japan and the USA is conducted by representatives of the EC/EU rather than by the individual member states.

Economic and Monetary Union (EMU)

Economic and monetary policy received considerable attention in the Maastricht Treaty, although EMU had already been on the EC's agenda in the early 1970s; indeed, it was due to have been completed by 1980! However, the 1973 oil crisis and upheaval in the international monetary system put a stop to that. In 1979 the more modest European Monetary System was introduced to stabilise currency fluctuations, but without UK membership of the all-important exchange rate mechanism (ERM). The British government was opposed to membership on the grounds that it would constrain domestic economic policy. However, in October 1990, John Major, the then Chancellor of the Exchequer, convinced Margaret Thatcher to join. Membership ended in September 1992 on Black Wednesday, when turmoil in the foreign exchanges forced the pound and the Italian lira to leave. The domestic consequence was that the Conservatives were seen as losing their reputational advantage over Labour for safely running the economy.

The Maastricht Treaty included a commitment to proceeding to EMU by 1999 at the latest. Nevertheless, John Major negotiated an opt-out of this policy, meaning that the UK does not accede to a single currency even though the other member states agreed in May 1998 to proceed to the third (final) stage in 1999. The Labour government has adopted a slightly different policy. In the 1997 election campaign the Labour Party committed itself to enter EMU only after receiving authorisation in the Cabinet, in parliament and in a popular referendum. In the autumn of 1997 Chancellor Gordon Brown announced the government's policy of having no constitutional objections to membership but making accession dependent upon five economic tests (see http://www.hm-treasury.gov.uk/press/1997/p126_97.html). It has become clear that Tony Blair is unwilling to make EMU central to the contest at the next general election. Hence a referendum looks unlikely until after that election. However, he has started to prepare the ground for a referendum with the launch of the cross-party 'Britain in Europe' campaign in October 1999. The Conservative Party, by contrast, has made clear that it is opposed to joining the single currency during this and the next parliament. The euro (denoted by the symbol €) will not become a physical currency in the eleven participating states until 2002, whereupon their national currencies will be withdrawn. Already the European Central Bank has taken over the setting of interest rates in those eleven states, a task formerly undertaken by their national central banks.

Other policies

Social and regional policies came to be significant activities by the 1990s. Both these policies were of negligible significance in the original EEC Treaty. In the early 1970s a concern to give the EC more of a 'social' role led to policy proposals. The European Regional Development Fund was set up in 1975 to provide assistance to poorer areas in the EC. The European Social Fund has gradually been developed as a channel through which European funds are spent on such projects as employment training or retraining. The UK has been a substantial recipient of aid from these and associated funds. Both policies gained additional emphasis at the time of the SEA, for the EC developed an explicit interest in 'cohesion'. This term referred to a commitment to ensure that the poorer member states were neither socially nor regionally disadvantaged by completion of the internal market. With the commitment to EMU in the Maastricht Treaty a new Cohesion Fund was created to assist the economically weaker member states.

The regional policy in particular has been connected with the Commission's encouragement of the idea of a 'Europe of the Regions'. One example of this has been the Commission's encouragement of England's north-west to put together an integrated strategy document for regional development.

Social policy measures had been limited until the mid-1980s when a new direction was taken with the EC's attempts to ensure that the labour force did not suffer deteriorating workplace conditions as a result of the more competitive single market. This policy was proposed in the Social Charter, accepted by eleven governments in 1989 (i.e. only the UK government of the then twelve states refused to sign up). The Conservative government's unwillingness to tolerate additional supranational impact upon employment conditions and social policy then led on to its opt-out of the Maastricht Treaty's Social Chapter. The Social Chapter had been designed to incorporate the Social Charter into the treaties, thus facilitating binding legislation in the policy area. The Labour government opposed Britain's opt-out and signed up to the Social Chapter after assuming office.

All these economic and social policies are run with a very small EC budget. For 1999 it amounted to some €97 billion (or £67 billion). This is only some 1.11 per cent of EU GNP, and is therefore a very small instrument for achieving any major policy impact. CAP spending, at its peak approaching three-quarters of the EC budget, is now down to approximately half of overall expenditure. However, the budget is insufficient for the EU to manage the macro-economy. The main public expenditure and fiscal powers remain with member states even in the era of EMU.

Other policies with major impacts on the UK include environmental, transport and technology policy. In addition, there are the activities in the other two pillars of the European Union. In the 1990s the Home Office underwent the Europeanisation process which other Whitehall ministries experienced much earlier. This development arose from the Maastricht Treaty onwards, when combating international crime and increasing international co-operation on immigration and asylum became EU matters. In the area of foreign policy co-operation, the member states have extremely well-developed procedures. UK foreign policy can no longer be seen in isolation from the collective activities of the member states. However, it is certainly not possible to refer to a common European foreign policy as yet, for there are still occasions when member states break ranks. In the 1980s the UK government did this on several occasions, preferring to follow American foreign policy instead (George, 1998). The twelve member states revealed their collective foreign policy weakness during the 1990–1 Gulf crisis and in the face of the break up of Yugoslavia. The Maastricht Treaty extended co-operation into the security domain but the Conservative government regarded defence policy to be the preserve of NATO. Initially, this seemed also to be the policy of the Blair government, for instance as expressed in the negotiation of the Amsterdam Treaty. In October 1998, however, it floated the idea of giving the EU a defence identity. It is not yet clear how this proposal will develop, especially as the member states reflect upon the experiences of the NATO action in Kosovo in 1999.

In conclusion, the impact of the EU upon UK public policy has been very considerable.

Britain and the EU at the new millennium: continuing controversy or new consensus?

Supranational integration has provoked opposition or division in the UK since the 1950 Schuman Plan. It has been the cause of major political divisions within both parties. In this section we examine those divisions and examine whether the Blair government might be able to build a new consensus on EU membership.

1. Already at the time of negotiating the terms of British membership and in the subsequent parliamentary ratification of the European Communities Act (1971–2), divisions emerged within both parties. Divisions within the Conservative Party meant that the Heath government's whips had to rely on pro-European Labour MPs refusing to vote against the accession legislation to secure the necessary votes to achieve membership. Within the opposition Labour Party divisions created serious problems for maintaining party unity: Harold Wilson's compromise position of advocating a referendum on membership resulted in the resignation of the deputy leader, Roy Jenkins, from the front bench.
2. The 1975 referendum, which was called by Harold Wilson's government with a view to resolving domestic disputes concerning EC membership, was a device aimed at limiting the damage arising from serious splits within the governing Labour Party (see above).
3. The defection in 1981 of four Labour MPs to found the Social Democratic party (SDP) was in part the result of frustration at Labour's then policy of withdrawal from the EC.
4. Three senior Conservative ministers were casualties of divisions relating to supranational integration: Nigel Lawson on membership of the ERM (1989); the late Nicholas Ridley over German power in the EC (1990); and Sir Geoffrey Howe over the general direction of Mrs Thatcher's policy.

5 At the end of 1990 Margaret Thatcher was ousted as party leader as a result of matters brought to a head by a European disagreement concerning the development of proposals for EMU.

6 During 1992–3 the government of John Major found great difficulty maintaining the necessary party unity to secure the ratification of the Maastricht Treaty. The Labour Party was not opposed to the Treaty but opposed Britain's opt-out of the Social Chapter and made ratification very difficult for John Major's government. The Treaty was finally approved on 23 July 1993 only after the Conservative government had made the issue a vote of confidence, with the threat of a general election hanging over its rebels (see Baker *et al.*, 1994).

7 Subsequently, in December 1994, nine of the critics of the Maastricht Treaty from the Conservative back benches voted against the government over increasing contributions to the EU budget and had the party whip withdrawn, thus technically removing John Major's parliamentary majority.

8 During 1996/7 the Major government played an obstructionist role in the negotiations on a review of the Maastricht Treaty. This tactic was pursued because of its small electoral

John Major emphasises his humble origins in his speech to a Tory Party conference split over the issue of Europe (13 October 1996)

John Major appeals for support for his 'wait and see' policy on Europe at the inter-governmental meeting scheduled for the day after the general election (13 April 1997)

majority and the need to avoid divisions within the party (see Jones *et al.*, 1998, pp. 554–6, for further details). Eventually the other fourteen EU governments deferred further negotiation until the British general election had taken place.

9 In 1996 the BSE crisis led to a major row with EU partners. Other member states were concerned about the spread of 'mad cow disease' amongst their cattle, about the possible transmission of the disease to humans, and about the loss of confidence in their domestic beef markets. In consequence, an export ban was imposed on the UK. The Major government blocked much EU decision-making for one month in 1996 as a protest, creating considerable diplomatic tension (Westlake, 1996).

In the run-up to the 1997 general election the European issue reflected the continuing mixture of divisions between and within the two main parties that has characterised the European 'fault-line' in British party politics. The Conservative Party was divided, with attitudes towards EMU ranging from total opposition to mild support – even within the Cabinet. The Labour Party's position was less internally divided, but on one or two key issues, notably acceding to the Social Chapter, it was at odds with the Conservatives' policy. Against this background what was the electoral platform of 'New Labour'? The two specific manifesto commitments were:

- to hold a referendum on participation in the single currency and
- to lead reform of the EU.

In fact, the Shadow Cabinet had undertaken considerable preparation for taking office, including on its own position in connection with EU treaty reform. This forethought was essential, since the new government had no more than six weeks between the election and the European Council session, at which the Amsterdam Treaty – as it came to be known – was finalised. What have been the government's achievements over the thirty months since it came to office? In one sense they are limited. The referendum on EMU has been deferred to after the next election. Further, the concrete results of 'leading reform' are as yet limited. However, on the latter point Blair and his government have taken subtle but important steps:

- It was already able to play a constructive role in the reform of the Amsterdam Treaty.
- It used its six-month presidency of the EU to advance a reform agenda, particularly at the Cardiff European Council.
- Blair initiated a European policy review in Summer 1998. On the one hand, it was clearly recognised to be difficult to 'lead' in the EU, having presided over, but not shared in, the decision of eleven governments to proceed to the single currency. On economic and monetary policy it became clear that some key decisions would be taken in a forum known as 'Euro-11', and comprising the economics and finance ministers of only those states fully signed up to EMU. However, the government recognised that the UK remained a central European player in defence policy. It also recognised the importance of links with an incoming centre-left government in Germany at elections later in the year.
- Subsequent to this exercise Blair himself exhorted all ministers to reinforce contacts with their European counterparts, especially ministers in the 'Red–Green' coalition in Germany of Social Democrats and Greens under Gerhard Schröder, duly elected in autumn 1998.
- In October 1998 at an informal EU summit meeting Blair proposed the development of a European defence identity to try to enable Europe to be more self-reliant in such matters, especially after the weaknesss shown in tackling the civil wars in ex-Yugoslavia.
- In addition to strengthening relations with Germany, the Labour government also reinforced defence co-operation with France at a summit with the French president and prime minister in St. Malo, also in autumn 1998.

These moves are clearly part of taking the UK towards a more constructive relationship with EU partners. In this sense it should not be underestimated how low the UK's stock had fallen with EU partners in the latter years of the Major government. But it is difficult to achieve a complete break with past controversy over Europe. First, the public's imagination is difficult to capture, and it was clear from the European elections in June 1999 that Labour voters had disproportionately stayed at home. Rightly or wrongly, the Conservatives under Hague concluded that their Euro-scepticism was more in tune with public opinion. Secondly, it proved difficult to secure a lifting of the beef export ban and draw a line under that episode. Even when the ban was lifted by the EU a row with France in October 1999 threatened to sour relations, when the French government suggested it would not allow imports of British beef in light of new evidence. Thirdly, several newspapers have pursued a Euro-sceptic position, especially on the single currency. And finally, the Conservative Party under Hague has shifted at its 1999 conference towards a more Euro-sceptical position, promising a battle for the pound (and invoking images of the Battle of Britain) and of re-negotiating the EU treaties as a policy commitment. All these circumstances make it difficult for the Blair government to completely re-cast the relationship with EU partners. In this respect the 'Britain in Europe' initiative, launched in October 1999 by Blair, and supported by pro-European Conservatives Michael Heseltine and Kenneth Clarke as well as Liberal Democrat leader Charles

BOX 31.1 **IDEAS AND PERSPECTIVES**

UK, the EU and the sense of identity

The Economist on 6 November 1999 made a useful contribution to the debate over the future of relationships between Britain and the EU. It published the results of a MORI poll which suggested British people have already assumed the future is likely to be more European, whatever the Euro-sceptics might say or wish. Tables 31.5, 31.6 and 31.7 reveal nearly half of the citizens of the four national elements of the UK assuming it will be the EU which will exert the most influence over their lives and those of their children within twenty years' time. Interestingly though only 16 or 17 per cent most identify (in the autumn of 1999) with the EU and most looked for such an allegiance to either their local community, region, country or the composite, 'Britain'.

Table 31.5 Influence
In 20 years' time, which of these bodies, if any, do you expect to have most influence over your life and the lives of your children? (%)

	Britain	England	Scotland	Wales
My local council	13	14	5	7
Scottish Parliament/Welsh Assembly/my regional assembly	13	9	46	26
Westminster Parliament	22	23	8	25
European Parliament/ European Union	44	46	31	37
Don't know	8	8	10	6

Source: The Economist, 6 November 1999

Table 31.6 Regional identification
Which two or three of these, if any, would you say you most identify with? (%)

	Britain	England	Scotland	Wales
This local community	41	42	39	32
This region	50	49	62	50
England/ Scotland/Wales	45	41	72	81
Britain	40	43	18	27
Europe	16	17	11	16
Commonwealth	9	10	5	3
The global community	8	9	5	2
Don't know	2	2	1	0

Source: The Economist, 6 November 1999

Table 31.7 Flag identification
Which of these flags, if any, do you identify with? (%)

	Britain	England	Scotland	Wales
United Kingdom (Union Jack)	83	88	49	55
England (Cross of St George)	33	38	2	3
Scotland (Cross of St Andrew)	23	18	75	8
Wales (Welsh Dragon)	26	24	12	85
European Union (12 stars)	21	23	5	7
United States (Stars and Stripes)	23	26	7	<1
Don't know	2	2	0	1

Source: The Economist, 6 November 1999

When it came to flags the EU flag attracted one-fifth support while the Union Jack was the favourite with the Welsh dragon doing just as well in Wales itself. Significantly, perhaps, over a fifth of Britons identified with the USA flag.

Another significant question related to the entity which would be likely to offer the most support in a crisis. Figure 31.4 shows the USA easily exceeds the EU as the likely source of support, suggesting loyalties to the EU are still heavily tempered by distrust and insecurity. Similarily Figure 31.5 suggests the USA is also seen as the more appropriate template for economic policy and political progress.

BOX 31.1 continued

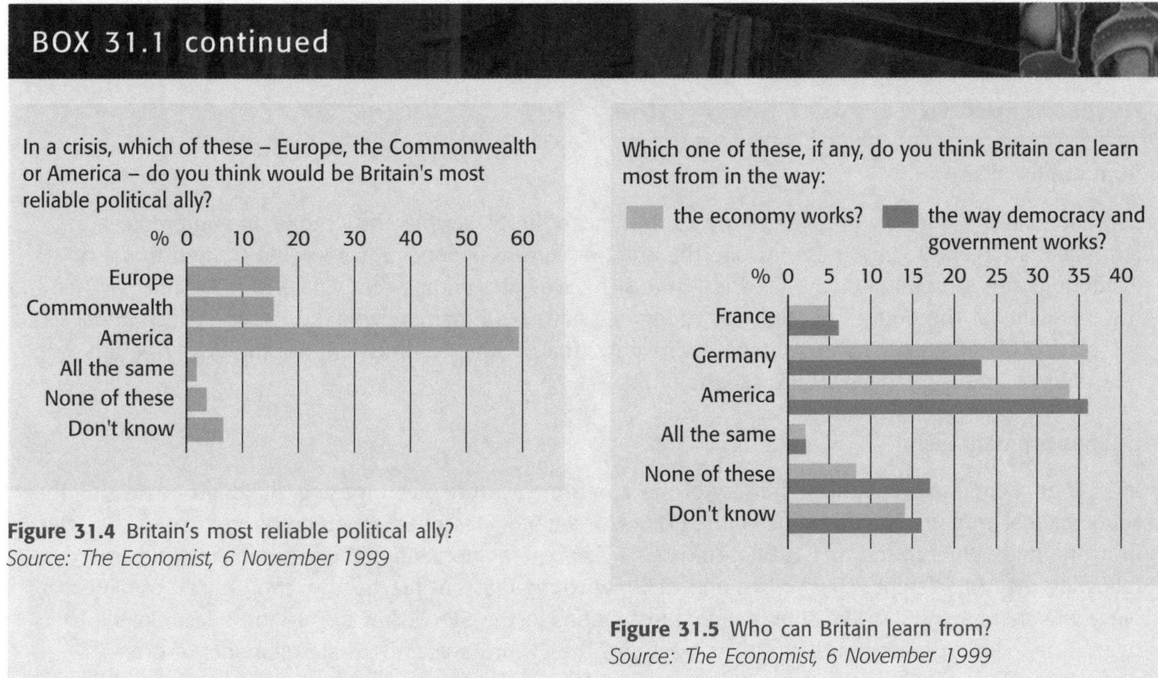

Figure 31.4 Britain's most reliable political ally?
Source: The Economist, 6 November 1999

Figure 31.5 Who can Britain learn from?
Source: The Economist, 6 November 1999

Kennedy, has its work cut out. It remains to be seen whether this initiative will be able to change the climate of British opinion to one where Blair is willing to risk his reputation in pushing for membership of the single currency and a popular mandate for it.

The UK, the EU and multi-levelled government

Traditionally British politicians have come to see the EU as a threat: more power for the EU means less power for British MPs or ministers. Although a minority of Conservative politicians currently seem to wish to question the desirability of EU membership, the vast majority of the political elite is signed up to it. Indeed, under the Blair government there has been some attempt to go beyond the traditional perception of the EU as a threat. Moreover, it is important to see the links between the changing domestic landscape of constitutional change and the EU context. Devolution within the UK, changes in the electoral system (greater use of proportional representation), parliamentary reform measures and incorporation of human rights principles: these developments are bringing the British political system closer to its continental counterparts. These developments are also promoting the development of a multi-levelled system of government.

Following devolution to Scotland and Wales in mid-1999 the issue of agriculture offered some indications of UK politics in an increasingly interlocked pattern of government. With farmers concerned about the emergence of a crisis with falling incomes for livestock, the question arose as to which level of government was appropriate to solve the problem? Should the new devolved authorities in Scotland and Wales offer financial support in light of their responsibilities for agriculture? How would the UK Ministry of Agriculture fit in, with its responsibilities for presenting a single voice in the EU and for agriculture in England? And what of the CAP, which limits the scope for action at odds with European policy? The result was a need to achieve a mutually compatible solution for all three levels: to get an agreed situation within the UK and to secure the approval of the EU. This pattern is likely to be extended in other policy areas, including regional policy and the environment.

BOX 31.2 **IDEAS AND PERSPECTIVES**

Key concepts in European integration

Supranationalism

Supranationalism refers to the characteristics that make the EU and its institutions unique amongst international organisations. These include the autonomy from national governments granted to specific institutions (the Commission, the EP, the Court of Justice); the primacy of EC law over national law; and the possibility of the Council of Ministers taking decisions by a majority vote. Supranationalism implies the placing of constraints upon national sovereignty. The EP, the Commission and the ECJ are often referred to as the supranational institutions of the EU.

Intergovernmentalism

Intergovernmentalism implies the primacy of the governments in decision making. Although possessing the supranational attributes outlined above, the EU was frequently described as intergovernmental in character from the mid-1960s to the mid-1980s. This was because the supranational institutions lost prestige following the 1965 'empty chair' crisis, and majority voting was not practised in the Council of Ministers. Since the strengthening of the supranational institutions in the SEA, it has become less fashionable to use the term 'intergovernmentalism' to characterise the EU. In reality, there are elements of both supranationalism and intergovernmentalism in the EU, and the balance between them has varied over time. UK governments have consistently favoured intergovernmentalism over supranationalism because it represents much less of a threat to sovereignty, although the Blair government has departed from this position to some extent. The Council of Ministers and the European Council, which are composed of government ministers, are often referred to as the intergovernmental institutions of the EU. The two new 'pillars' of integration introduced by the Maastricht Treaty are essentially intergovernmental in nature.

Sovereignty

Because of its long-established territorial integrity British (and especially English) politicians have been reluctant to see the limitations of the nation-state in assuring British welfare and security. Moreover, lengthy constitutional tradition has embedded the notion of parliamentary sovereignty in the thinking of the political elite. As a consequence of these two features, UK governments have been particularly unwilling to cede sovereignty (i.e. autonomy and power) to the EU. Many of the main disputes between Britain and its EU partners about the development of European integration have their origins in different notions of sovereignty.

Subsidiarity

This term has come into use from the late 1980s onwards. Essentially it means that the EU should only perform those tasks which the member states' sub-national governments are unable to carry out themselves.

Federalism

Federalism entails a clear constitutional ordering of relations between the EU and the member states, together with constitutional guarantees. The UK's lack of a formal written constitution, together with an aversion to giving up sovereignty, has resulted in federalism being used inaccurately to denote everything that is disliked about moves towards closer integration. This was symbolised during the Maastricht debates by British politicians' references to the 'F-word'.

And as Whitehall and Westminster become used to sharing power downwards to Cardiff, Edinburgh and – depending on the peace process – Belfast, the ability to share it upwards with the EU may become less fraught in the future.

The dynamics of the EU shows no sign of abating. A further round of institutional reform is scheduled to be completed in 2000 to make the policy process more effective. These reforms are prompted by the queue of former communist states of central and eastern Europe (plus Turkey, Malta and Cyprus) who see EU membership as a beacon for underpinning their democracies and economic development. Whether the UK can become more comfortable with the EU's journey to an unknown destination remains as salient an issue as ever.

Chapter summary

The UK's distinctive wartime experience, history of territorial integrity, distinctive form of parliamentary government, island mentality and former great power status are amongst the factors explaining late engagement with European integration. Joining at the third attempt, acceding to a community whose shape had been influenced by other states, and doing this in 1973 at the time of an international economic recession: these were not factors conducive to making EC/EU membership a painless matter. In fact, these circumstances merely added to the existing political divisions concerning membership. In the subsequent period the EU's institutions and policies have evolved extensively. With the challenge of monetary union the critical political choices for the UK are again highlighted. Should the UK join if the economic evidence suggests membership makes sense, as the Labour government argues? Should the UK retain sterling for this and the next parliament, as the Conservatives under William Hague argue? And can the Conservative Party avoid damaging internal splits over the issue? The political divisions over the European issue remain, but other actors – sub-national government, industry and the trade unions – have come to adopt a more practical approach. For them the EU is one of several levels of government with which they have to work. Whether politics and public opinion can attain this pragmatic outlook remains an open question.

Discussion points

- Why has the UK had such an uneasy relationship with European integration?
- What are the distinctive features of supranationalism and why have they created controversy in UK politics?
- Can British governments solve policy problems in isolation, or do they need to seek collective solutions through the EU?
- From the perspective of British politics is the European Union best seen as a threat or an opportunity?

Further reading

An important source of information on the EU is its own publications, many of which can be obtained free of charge from the London offices of the European Commission or European Parliament. Many of the publications are also now available on the EU's web sites, which offer a wealth of information. For an overview of the evolution of European integration, see Urwin (1995). Amongst the useful books on the history, institutions and policies of the EU are McCormick (1999); Nugent (1999) and Dinan (1999). The *Journal of Common Market Studies* is the principal academic journal covering integration. Bainbridge with Teasdale (1998) is a useful reference book on EU matters. George (1998) provides a good account of the UK's European policy over the period up to 1993, while Young (1998) offers a more biographical account by focussing on the role of key figures from Churchill to Blair. George (1992) offers a more interpretative study which not only covers UK policy but traces its mainsprings to party politics, Parliament and other factors arising from British domestic politics. Geddes (1998) offers a useful introduction. For accounts of European policy making in Britain, see Armstrong and Bulmer (1996) for an account written during the trials and tribulations of the Major era and Armstrong and Bulmer (2000) for an update reflecting changes under Blair. Bulmer and Burch (1998, 2000) offer assessments which focus particularly on the impact of the EU on the work of British central government. For the impact on political forces – the parties, industry, trade unions and the media – see Baker and Seawright (1998). Finally, for a more detailed review of the European policy of the Blair government, see Bulmer (2000).

References

Armstrong, K. and Bulmer, S. (1996) 'The United Kingdom', in D. Rometsch and W. Wessels (eds), *The European Union and the Member States* (Manchester University Press).

Armstrong, K. and Bulmer, S. (2000) 'The United Kingdom: between political controversy and administrative efficiency', in W. Wessels, A. Maurer and J. Mittag (eds), *Fifteen into One: the European Union and Member States* (Manchester University Press).

Ashford, N. (1992) 'The political parties', in S. George (ed.), *Britain and the European Community* (Clarendon Press), pp. 119–48.

Bainbridge, T. with Teasdale, A. (1998) *The Penguin Companion to European Union*, 2nd edn (Penguin).

Baker, D. and Seawright, D. (eds) (1998) *Britain For and Against Europe: British Politics and the Question of European Integration* (Clarendon Press).

Baker, D., Gamble, A. and Ludlam, S. (1994) 'The parliamentary siege of Maastricht 1993: Conservative division and British ratification', *Parliamentary Affairs*, Vol. 47, No. 1.

Bulmer, S. (2000) 'European policy: fresh start or false dawn?', in D. Coates and P. Lawler (eds), *New Labour in Power* (Manchester University Press).

Bulmer, S. and Burch, M. (1998) 'Organizing for Europe: Whitehall, the British state and European Union', *Public Administration*, Vol. 76, No. 1.

Bulmer, S. and Burch, M. (2000) 'The Europeanisation of British central government', in R.A.W. Rhodes (ed.), *Transforming British Government*, Vol. 1, *Changing Institutions* (Macmillan).

Dinan, D. (1999) *Ever Closer Union*, 2nd edn (Macmillan).

Geddes, A. (1998) *Britain and the European Union* (Baseline Books).

George, S. (ed.) (1992) *Britain and the European Community* (Clarendon Press).

George, S. (1998) *An Awkward Partner: Britain in the European Community*, 3rd edn (Oxford University Press).

Jones, B. (ed.) (1998) *Politics UK*, 3rd edn (Prentice Hall).

McCormick, J. (1999) *Understanding the European Union* (Macmillan).

Nugent, N. (1994) *The Government and Politics of the European Union*, 3rd edn (Macmillan).

Nugent, N. (1999) *The Government and Politics of the European Union*, 4th edn (Macmillan).

Urwin, D. (1995) *The Community of Europe: a History of European Integration since 1945*, 2nd edn (Longman).

Westlake, M. (1997) 'Keynote article: "Mad cows and Englishmen" – the institutional consequences of the BSE crisis', in N. Nugent (ed.), *The European Union 1996: Annual Review of Activities* (Blackwell Publishers), pp. 11–36.

Young, H. (1998) *This Blessed Plot: Britain and Europe from Churchill to Blair* (Macmillan).

Chapter 

Tony Blair's New Labour government: an interim assessment

Dennis Kavanagh

Learning objectives

- To assess the record of New Labour in power since its election in May 1997.
- To examine the major policy initiatives undertaken by Blair's administration.
- To evaluate the criticisms made of the government's record to date.

There was great interest in the return of the Labour government in 1997. It brought to an end the longest period of one-party government for over a century and the longest period which the Opposition party had remained out of office. Obviously the new Labour ministers were inexperienced – only one had served in a Cabinet before. But for much of the 1992 Parliament, and certainly from the time Tony Blair became Labour leader in July 1994, a Labour government was widely regarded as inevitable among the media, Whitehall and even many Conservative ministers. Preparations for government, including contacts between senior civil servants and shadow ministers, were pretty advanced before the new government came to office. Much of the media, European Union, business and City circles approved of New Labour. Tony Blair was treated as a Prime Minister in waiting.

Tony Blair's rhetoric promised much, but on close inspection was often vague, except for the five key pledges (see Box 32.1). Spending promises for the immediate future would depend on the achievement of savings within departmental budgets, to be made via a comprehensive spending review, and economic growth. Crucially, in early 1997 Gordon Brown, the Shadow Chancellor, and Blair accepted the spending programmes of the Conservative government for the first two years of a new Labour government and also accepted the existing rates of income tax. They were determined to kill off accusations that Labour would be a tax-and-spend government: they had to demonstrate that Labour could be trusted with people's money. Both men feared a repetition of the Conservative charges that the party would impose higher taxes, as in 1992. But they also believed that prudent economic management required such policies. Brown and Blair considered that globalisation limited the economic discretion of state governments of both left and right. Low inflation, lower rates of income tax, business-friendly policies, and a tight cap on public spending were all necessary. This outlook became a key part of what Blair called his Third Way.

BOX 32.1

fact

Labour's five key pledges 1996

1. Cut class sizes to 30 or under for five-, six- and seven-year-olds by using money saved from the assisted places scheme.
2. Fast-track punishment for persistent young offenders by halving the time from arrest to sentencing.
3. Cut NHS waiting lists by treating an extra 100,000 patients as a first step by releasing £100 million saved from NHS red tape.
4. Remove 250,000 under-twenty-five-year-olds from benefits and into work by using money from a windfall levy on the privatised utilities.
5. No rise in income tax rates; cut VAT on heating to 5 per cent, and keep inflation and interests as low as possible.

Few prime ministers have started out with such advantages as Tony Blair in May 1997. To thc 179-seat Labour majority in the House of Commons he could add a divided and discredited Conservative opposition, his own record high levels of popularity, according to the opinion polls, his authority in the Labour Party, which was perhaps the least ideologically divided in memory, and a more favourable set of economic indicators than most new governments inherit. There is no guarantee, of course, that this conjunction of favourable circumstances will last.

Within days, the government granted the Bank of England control over interest rates, by handing it to a Monetary Policy Committee. This body was given an inflation target of 2.5 per cent and was to set interest rates at a level which would hit the inflation target. Some critics objected to the omission of a target for unemployment and others complained that politicians, who are democratically accountable, should not relinquish the power to set interest rates. But markets were more likely to trust bankers and non-politicians to handle interest rates. Gordon Brown was constrained by his pledge not to raise marginal rates of income tax and he had to turn to indirect taxes if he was to raise revenue. He proceeded to implement an excess profits tax on the profits of the privatised

Tony Blair tackles problems in government (7 December 1997)

utilities. This would provide for public spending, notably on Welfare to Work.

For the first three years the government continued John Major's achievement of falling and subdued levels of inflation, declining unemployment and, eventually, low interest rates (inflation met the target of 2.5 per cent and by March 2000 unemployment was at a twenty year low of 4 per cent). A comprehensive spending review lasted over a year and was the basis for spending allocations in summer 1998 but only took effect in May 1999. Labour had promised to switch spending from what it called 'the costs of social and economic failure' (e.g. social security benefits) to investing in training and education. The spending review was designed to reveal priorities within and across departments, and achieving savings in some areas would allow extra spending elsewhere.

Education and health were the key beneficiaries of the additional spending, but few savings on social security were made. Departments had to pledge improvements in services in return for the extra money; the deal was reflected in so-called 'public service agreements' between a department and the Treasury. But much of the extra spending will only take place in the second half of the Parliament, following a severe two-year spending squeeze, and commentators wondered whether the improvements in services would be visible before the next general election. In July 1999 Blair's frustration with the slow pace of improvements in health, education and transport was widely reported. He complained that 'I bear scars on my back' from the public sector's slowness to modernise. The government also continued with and in some respects strengthened the Conservative managerial devices of market testing, targets, league tables and performance indicators and performance-related pay. Poorly performing local education authorities were named and shamed.

On the European Union, the Blair government, like John Major's, started off promising a fresh start and a more constructive relationship. The government incorporated the Social Chapter (see page 669), but on the question of British entry to the single currency – crucial for a state which was bidding to be influential in the EU – it was as cautious as John Major. The Blair–Brown conditions, holding a referendum before entry and entry only if it would satisfy British interests, were essentially no different from those of John Major. Commentators thought that Brown and Blair, the key players, supported entry in principle, but were constrained by the hostility of public opinion (in 1999, polls reported that it was 60/40 against) and of the Murdoch press, particularly the *Sun* and the *Times*. Opponents of entry were gratified by the Conservatives' success in the Euro elections in June 1999. Supporters of the project complained that Blair and other supporters were refusing to give a lead on the case for British entry and that, in the vacuum, public opinion was shaped by hostile opinion formers.

Nothing has been more positively New Labour than the programme of constitutional reform, or modernisation as Blair terms it. No other British government has produced such a far-reaching programme and it forms a sharp contrast to the disinterest (or conservatism on the issue) of the Thatcher and Major governments. The Scottish and Welsh devolution proposals have been swiftly implemented and within just over two years the Parliament and the Assembly were up and running. Other reforms achieved or in hand by 2000 included:

- arrangements for the election of a London mayor;
- proportional representation for Scottish, Welsh and European elections;
- a Human Rights Act, incorporating the European Convention on Human Rights;
- a bill on Freedom of Information;
- the abolition of voting rights of hereditary peers and the report of a commission under Lord Wakeham to recommend what should replace them.

Question marks hang over the successor arrangements for the House of Lords, whether and when a referendum will be held on the Jenkins proposals for proportional representation for Westminster elections, and whether other cities will choose to have elected mayors.

Critics have argued that the constitutional changes are *ad hoc* and that they lack any guiding vision. This is probably true but it reflects the British practice of incremental change. In fact, the reforms are broadly pluralistic and take Britain closer to the constitutional model in most EU states. It is fair to add that the pluralism is subject to limits, including the closed list system for voting in the European and Scottish and Welsh elections, ruling out a directly elected second chamber and a Freedom of Information bill which is widely dismissed as being more restrictive than the status quo. The London-based Labour leadership also threw its resources behind Alun Michael in the party election for First Minister in Wales, relying on the votes of trade unions in the process, and again in 2000, campaigned hard to defeat Ken Livingstone as a Labour candidate for the London mayor. No other Prime Minister has been as keen to make appointments to the House of Lords: in his first three years, Blair made more appointments than Mrs Thatcher did in 11 years. These features seem to belong to the 'command' approach to Blair's management of the Labour Party.

More active party members showed their resentment of Millbank – code word for the leadership. Alum Michael was forced to stand down as Welsh first minister and was replaced by his deputy, Rhodri Morgan, who had been opposed by Blair during the party's election for its candidate for the post. Ken Livingstone was defeated in an electoral college ballot – widely regarded as fixed to defeat him – as the party candidate for London Mayor. He then decided to run as an independent and won an overwhelming victory, against Frank Dobson, who was inevitably dubbed Blair's 'stooge'. Livingstone attracted the support of many Labour supporters. The resignation of the Liverpool MP,

Peter Kilfoyle, Junior Defence Minister, on the grounds that New Labour was favouring middle class south-easterners rather than working class northerners, reflected this unhappiness. He accused the party of suffering a 'vacuum' at its heart. A Gallup poll in July 1999 reported that middle class voters approved of the government's record by 54–40 per cent, whereas as working class voters approved by on by 46–43 per cent. Labour's failure to win the Ayr by election in March 2000 to the Scottish Assembly and the poor showing in local government elections raised fears that Labour's core vote would fail to turn out – as it did in the 1999 Euro electioins. This might threaten its majority at the next election.

Blair, as noted elsewhere, has done much to strengthen the resources of Number Ten. The expansion of his staff, creation of new units, strengthening of the Cabinet Office in the interest of promoting joined up government, attracted much comment. He appeared to be creating a Prime Minister's Department without calling it such. But for all the talk of his empire building in Whitehall, the strength of Number Ten ultimately depends on the authority of the Prime Minister. As previous leaders found, that varies greatly.

For all its promises of a fresh beginning, any new government inherits many of its predecessor's problems and commitments. The search for a durable peace in Northern Ireland and devolution to a power-sharing executive in the province was the single issue which took up more of Blair's time than any other. The 1998 Good Friday Peace Agreement linked the creation of a power-sharing executive, containing Sinn Fein, and an elected assembly, these two to move in tandem with decommissioning of paramilitary weapons. The package was approved by over 70 per cent of the Northern Ireland electorate in 1998. Blair has involved both the Irish government and the US President in the process. The executive was suspended in July 1999 as Unionists refused to share power with Sinn Fein, in the absence of stronger undertakings of IRA decommissioning. It sat briefly at the end of 1999 but was suspended again in February 2000.

In spite of the large House of Commons majority there has been no relaxation in control of the party or calls for self-discipline among Labour MPs. There have, however, been dissenting Labour votes on proposals over asylum, cuts and in benefits for single parents and freedom of information. But on some occasions there was so little work for MPs to do in the House of Commons that the whips arranged for them to return home for so-called 'constituency weeks'. To reinforce discipline local parties are sent a copy of the Chief Whip's report on its MP's voting attendance record in the Commons. Those with poor records are to be interviewed by the NEC before being endorsed as a party candidate at the next general election.

In July 1999 fifty-eight Labour MPs signed a letter in *Tribune* restating their commitment to socialism and repudiation of a nineteenth-century liberalism. This move was seen as the voice of Old Labour and reflected opposition to Blair's project of co-operation with the Liberal Democrats and consideration of proportional representation. These critics argue that New Labour has gone too far in appealing to middle England, symbolically associated with the editorial tone and readership of the *Daily Mail*, and is ignoring its core vote in the North, working class, manufacturing and trade unions.

If Labour's rhetoric has been addressed to 'middle England', a number of measures surely should appeal to its core supporters. The extra rights for the unions in 'Fairness at Work', increases in child benefit, introduction of the minimum wage, acceptance of the Social Chapter and Gordon Brown's redistributive budgets have long been demanded by the left. Many of the above, along with devolution, reduction in the number of hereditary peers in the Lords, and creation of the Monetary Policy Committee are now accepted by the Conservatives. Labour, like Thatcher in the 1980s, is now setting the agenda.

Advocates of the New Labour project, dating back to Neil Kinnock, realised that Labour's core vote was concentrated among the declining sections of the electorate; the poor and the working class formed only an electoral minority. To win general elections Labour had to build a broader base of votes, in particular among the middle class, home owners and traditionally non-Labour voters in the south-east. Blair did this by offering reassurance; Labour would not threaten their economic interests and would not be redistributive at their cost. In the 1997 election this project was remarkably

BOX 32.1 **MINI BIOGRAPHY**

John Prescott (1938–)
Labour Deputy Prime Minister. Educated Ruskin College and Hull University. Served as a steward in the merchant navy before becoming an official in the Seaman's Union. Leader of Labour group in European Parliament 1976–9. Deputy Leader in 1994 and retained this position after 1997 victory, also filling post of Secretary for the Regions and Transport. Talented politician often satirised.

BOX 32.2 **MINI BIOGRAPHY**

Charles Kennedy (1960–)
Leader Liberal Democrats. Educated Glasgow and Indiana Universities. Elected for Ross, Skye and Inverness (Social Democratic Party) in 1983 aged twenty-three. His relaxed pesonality made him popular on TV quiz and chat shows but he had sufficient gravitas to win the succession to Paddy Ashdown in 1999. Said to be radical in own views but yet to develop a coherent personal or party position.

BOX 32.3 **IDEAS AND PERSPECTIVES**

Labour's annual report: an exercise in self-assessment

In July 1998 the government presented its first annual report on its performance to date. The exercise was repeated in 1999 and one assumes that this is now an established feature. The report was placed on sale to the public in Tesco's. In principle, directly reporting to the public is a form of accountability and may be a means of combating disillusion with government. Performance targets for groups and individuals are found across the public and private sector. Why not in government also? In the United States, for example, some parties and candidates offer a 'contract' to the voters.

The 1999 report claims that the government has already delivered on ninety of its 177 manifesto promises, eighty-five are under way to being met and only two have not been timetabled. The self-congratulatory tone was criticised, as was the vacuous nature of many of the claimed accomplishments. For example:

- backing the bid to hold the World Cup in Britain in 2006;
- 'exercising leadership' in the Commonwealth;
- being 'on course' to hold referendums on the voting system and on entry to the European single currency, as well as achieving the class size cuts for five-, six- and seven-year olds by 2000.

Some of the claims (for example, on the referendums) were undated, some of the claims are to be met in ten years' time, and the claimed reductions in class sizes for five- to seven-year olds have to be set against the increase in class size for other age groups. Many of the claims are not about implementation achievement at all.

Companies issue annual reports of their accounts, but these are conducted by independent auditors. Perhaps a British government should hand the exercise over to the Audit Commission, or to independent think-tanks. Interestingly, the day after the annual report was issued, a number of House of Commons Select Committees presented more detailed and critical verdicts – on overseas aid (criticising the increase in aid to authoritarian regimes), foreign policy and transport (criticising the DETR for making too many policy statements and announcements of working parties rather than tackling congestion). Significantly, the Select Committees had Labour majorities on them.

successful. Labour gained nearly one-fifth of its vote from 1992 Conservative and Liberal Democratic voters and a further one-sixth from those who had been too young to vote or who had abstained in 1992. In all, a third of Labour's support came from people who had not voted for it in 1992.

Co-operation with the Liberal Democrats was important for Blair on three grounds. Firstly, Labour's chances of winning a general election in 1996 or 1997 would be greatly assisted if Labour and Liberal Democrats co-operated. Indeed each party gained some twenty seats in the election due to tactical anti-Conservative voting. Continued co-operation in government, including appointing the Jenkins commission on proportional representation, and a Joint Cabinet Committee which included Liberal Democrat MPs, was important in keeping the minor party on board. A second incentive was the longer-term project of winning at least two terms of office, making Labour the natural party of government in the twenty-first century, just as the Conservatives had been in the twentieth. Blair reasoned that divisions between Liberals and Labour had greatly aided Conservative victories. A third reason is that Blair has a project of reshaping the centre-left. On many issues, particularly on constitutional reform and the European Union, Blair has more in common with the Liberal Democrats than with his left wing. Critics suspect that Blair wishes to shed his more left-wing members while embracing the Liberal Democrats.

In the past, no Labour government has achieved two full terms. When there were two terms, either the first or second term has been short lived because of a small parliamentary majority (1950–1, 1964–6) or absence of a majority at all (February–October 1974). Previous governments have also been beset by economic crises – rising inflation and balance of payments problems, devaluation of the pound, incomes policies and a squeeze on living standards. These policies in turn created divisions in the movement at large and confrontations between a Labour government and the annual conference and trade unions. So far, New Labour has avoided economic downturns or conflicts with conference and the unions. Blair must hope that his economic policies and changes in the party structure and culture will minimise problems for the government.

Blair's government has certainly made its mark on the constitution and he has cut an impressive figure on the international stage, particularly in pushing for strong NATO action over Kosovo and promoting the Third Way with leaders of other centre-left parties. These and Northern Ireland have dominated his time and, some suggest, the result has been his neglect of the domestic agenda. But dissatisfaction with the state of the public services and hopes that Labour would bring about substantial improvements were important in promoting voters' disillusions with the Conservatives in 1997. In the second half of its term Labour was promising to concentrate on 'delivery' (see Box 32.2).

Criticisms of New Labour's record

Conservatives accuse Blair of not delivering on his election promises. Some people may think 'they would say that wouldn't they'? but there is certainly a wider resonance to some of these criticisms. Hugo Young, the *Guardian*'s magisterial columnist wrote, 'Seldom has any government seemed more self promoting than Tony Blair's, forever making the grandest claims for itself.' (27th January 2000) Yet his overall conclusion on 8th February, was still favourable: 'The real record, if one takes the long view, is not bad. What is bad is the perception'. He blamed New Labour for raising unrealistic expectations which it had to some extent disappointed. The Adam Smith Institute, a free market think tank, awarded the Blair government high marks for his first 200 days. However, the early months of 2000 were testing for Blair, and he confessed to feeling the strain in an interview with his friend Robert Harris in *Talk* magazine in April 2000.

Critical voices had begun to add discordant voices by the time the end of the third year approached. A survey of Labour members by Seyd and Whiteley (27 September 1999) found an overall high level of assessment for the government with high satisfaction ratings for Blair, Prescott and, especially, Brown – see Figure 32.1.

Interestingly, three-quarters of the Labour members favoured increasing taxes and spending more on health, education and social benefits,

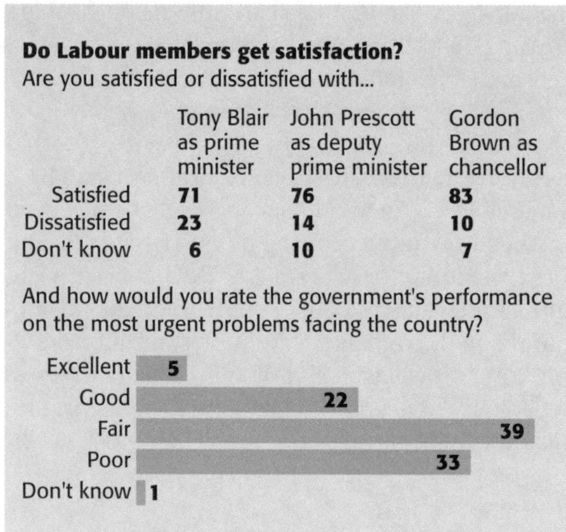

Do Labour members get satisfaction?
Are you satisfied or dissatisfied with...

	Tony Blair as prime minister	John Prescott as deputy prime minister	Gordon Brown as chancellor
Satisfied	**71**	**76**	**83**
Dissatisfied	**23**	**14**	**10**
Don't know	**6**	**10**	**7**

Figure 32.1 Satisfaction of Labour members
Source: The Guardian, 27 September 1999

reflecting perhaps the Old Labour nature of many party activists. A wider survey of voter satisfaction with the government was made in September 1999 – see Figure 32.2. This revealed several areas of concern for the Blair team. A thin majority believed Blair had done well to keep taxes down but varying majorities believed:

1. state schools had not been improved: 44–39 per cent;
2. the health service had not improved: 53–37;
3. poverty had not been reduced: 46–36;
4. sleaze had not been stopped: 47–33;
5. public transport had not been improved: 65–22.

Health, traditionally a strong issue for Labour, proved an embarrassment in early 2000. When the NHS failed to cope with the annual winter outbreak of influenza, there were several graphic accounts in the media of patients waiting on trolleys in corridors, or suffering at home for lack of hospital beds. Reports showed that the NHS was poorly funded in comparison to health services in many other western states and this sat uneasily with the large revenues which Gordon Brown was presiding over. Labour's careful spending plans were abandoned when the March 2000 budget promised huge amounts of extra cash for the NHS.

The fourth item was particularly worrying to the Labour government as sleaze was a potent factor in the ejection of Major and the election of a supposedly squeaky clean new Labour administration. Also, a majority believed Blair 'has become too arrogant since becoming Prime Minister'. The majority was only 49–47 but the immense publicity expertise which goes into projecting the Blair image has clearly failed to sustain his carefully sculpted image of 'y'know an ordinary kind of bloke'. Even more worrying is the judgement of 39 per cent that he 'pays too much attention to people who give Labour large donations'.

A comparative survey of attitudes towards the party leaders in late October 1999 (see Figure 32.3) revealed more signs of voter concern about Blair's increasing 'arrogance'; his diminishing image as someone 'who understands people', has 'lots of personality' and is 'more honest than most politicians'. However, he appears to win points for being experienced, tough and having diminishing amounts of 'style' rather than 'substance'.

And the biggest comfort of them all is that after three years in power, when governments usually sink in the polls, New Labour was still some twenty points in front (though they slipped to under ten per cent by early summer) of the Conservatives and their leader attracted much worse ratings than his astute Prime Ministerial adversary (see Figure 32.3).

Looking to the future a number of questions suggest themselves:

- If the single currency succeeds and Britain remains outside, what effect will this have on Britain's influence in the European Union, not least in shaping economic policy, or on the strength of sterling?
- What will be the impact on British domestic politics of joining or remaining out of the single currency? At present the Conservative Party is almost a one-issue (anti-single-currency) party. To date, British opponents of European initiatives, e.g. entry in the 1960s, continuing membership in the early 1970s, joining the ERM in the 1980s, and the launch of the single currency in the 1990s, have all failed.

Q. On balance do you think Labour is or is not keeping its promises to:

	All	Labour voters in '97
KEEP TAXES DOWN	%	%
Is	**48**	**61**
Is not	**42**	**27**
Don't know	**11**	**12**
IMPROVE BRITAIN'S STATE SCHOOLS		
Is	**39**	**57**
Is not	**44**	**29**
Don't know	**16**	**13**
IMPROVE THE HEALTH SERVICE		
Is	**37**	**55**
Is not	**53**	**36**
Don't know	**10**	**9**
REDUCE POVERTY		
Is	**36**	**50**
Is not	**46**	**38**
Don't know	**17**	**13**
STOP SLEAZE		
Is	**33**	**45**
Is not	**47**	**34**
Don't know	**20**	**21**
IMPROVE PUBLIC TRANSPORT		
Is	**22**	**34**
Is not	**65**	**55**
Don't know	**13**	**12**

Q. Do you agree or disagree with the following statements:

(a) 'Tony Blair has become too arrogant since becoming Prime Minister'

	All	Labour voters in '97
	%	%
Agree	**47**	**34**
Disagree	**49**	**63**
Don't know	**4**	**3**

(b) 'Tony Blair does not care enough about Labour's traditional working-class supporters'

Agree	**52**	**46**
Disagree	**42**	**49**
Don't know	**6**	**5**

(c) 'Tony Blair pays too much attention to rich people who give Labour large donations'

Agree	**50**	**42**
Disagree	**39**	**49**
Don't know	**11**	**10**

Q. Gordon Brown is likely to have extra money to spend next year. Which two or three of these would be best for you and your family?

	All	Labour voters in '97
	%	%
More spent on the health service	**76**	**79**
More spent on education	**56**	**62**
Higher retirement pensions	**44**	**41**
Lower income tax	**34**	**30**
More spent on public transport	**32**	**33**
Higher child benefit	**15**	**18**

Figure 32.2 How Labour is shaping up
Source: The Guardian, 26 September 1999

- How will Labour strike a balance between its commitment to maintaining low income taxes and tight controls on public spending and improving public services? How will it balance its traditional interest in redistribution to the less well-off and maintaining the support of middle England? For much of the time this has involved saying are thing to the *Daily Mail* (for middle England) and another to traditional voters.
- Will constitutional reform lead to a new style of politics, one involving more power sharing between parties and pluralism? In particular, how will Westminster relate to the Scottish and Welsh executives and if coalitions come about at Westminster what impact will this have on internal relations within the political parties?
- How will Blair sustain his long-term project of making the centre left the dominant political force in the twenty first century? The project involves a close relationship with the Liberal Democrats. But not all of his Cabinet or of his party share his ambition, or the introduction of proportional representation, although for many Liberal Democrats the latter is regarded as an essential condition of continued and closer co-operation.

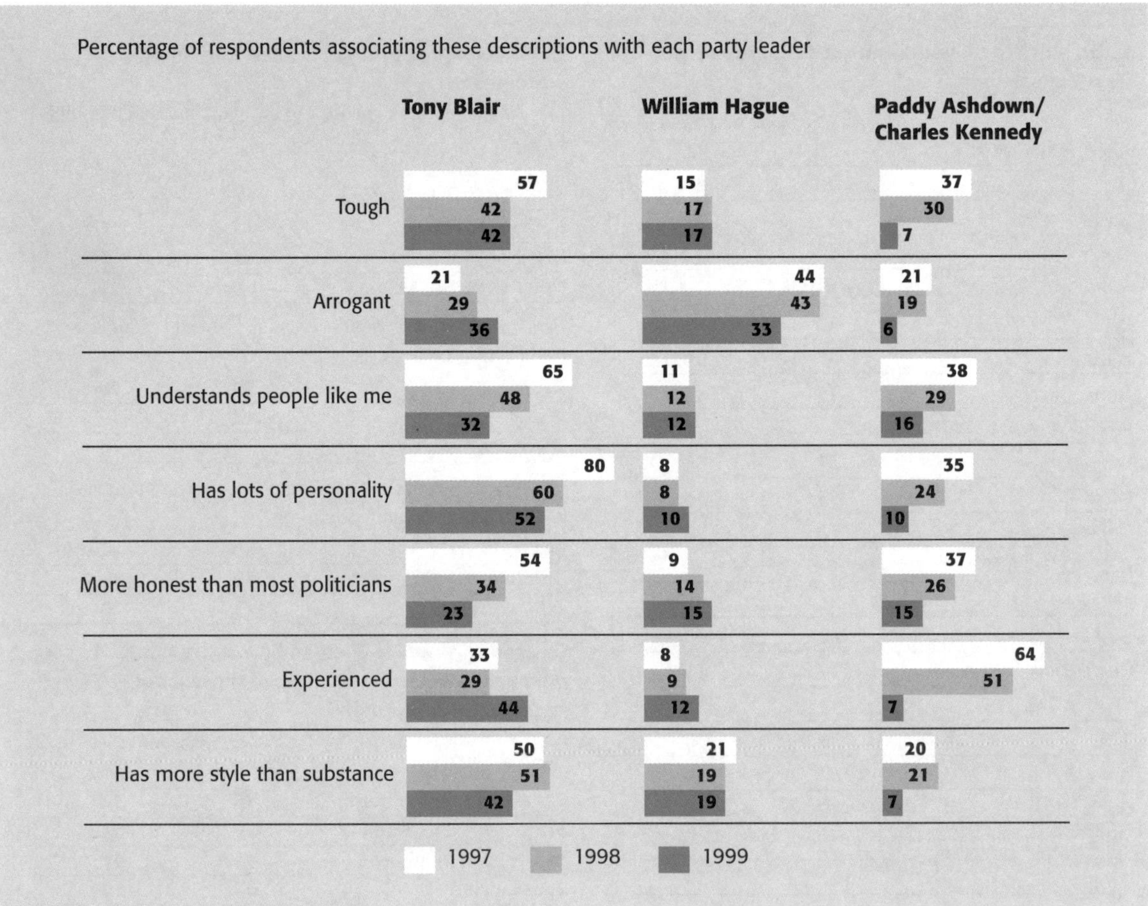

Figure 32.3 How the leaders compare
Source: The Guardian, 28 September 1999

Much of the government's popularity, vision and strategy rest with Blair. He is as dominant as Mrs Thatcher ever was, and has done more than any Prime Minister this century to reform both his party and Number Ten and increase his grip over both. In both he has created institutions to facilitate the type of leadership he believes is necessary. The credit for success will deservedly lie with him; so may the blame for failure.

Chapter summary

This chapter has examined the impact made by Blair's government since it came to power in May 1997. The pledges made by Labour in the election campaign are mentioned together with the major legislative initiatives made, in terms of the major policy areas. It notes the achievements in terms of constitutional changes and the apparently sound management of the economy. Labour's tight party discipline and the growing pockets of dissent within the party on social and other policy areas are noted. Co-operation with the Liberal Democrats and the motives which underlie it are examined. Future problems are identified.

Discussion points

- To what extent has Tony Blair been able to maintain popularity since the last election?

Arguments in favour of fox-hunting (13 July 1997)

- Should Blair have spent more on traditional social policy areas than he has?
- To what extent have the constitutional changes been problematic?

Further reading

On Tony Blair, Rentoul (1996) and Kavanagh and Selden (1999), Chapters 9 and 10. Gould is excellent on the provenance and evolution of New Labour.

References

Adam Smith Institute (1997) *New Labour's 200 days: a Hundred Ideas in Action.*

Giddens, A. (1998) *The Third Way* (Polity).

Gould, P. (1998) *The Unfinished Revolution* (Little, Brown).

Hennessy, P. (1998) 'The Blair Style of Government', *Government and Opposition*, Vol. 33, No. 1.

Kavanagh, D. and Selden, A. (1999) *The Powers Behind the Prime Minister* (HarperCollins).

Rentoul, J. (1996) *Tony Blair* (Warner).

Thomas, G. (1998) *Prime Minister and Cabinet Today* (Manchester University Press).

Glossary

Active minority: that minority of the population which participates to a high degree in political life.

Adversarial politics: a theory popularised by (among others) Prof. S.E. Finer in the 1970s which portrayed politics at Westminster as a gladiatorial combat between Labour and the Conservatives with disastrous consequences for the national interest.

Affiliated: the way in which an organisation associates itself with a political party by paying a fee and gaining influence in the party's affairs. In Britain, a number of trade unions are affiliated to the Labour party; members pay the 'political levy' which makes them affiliated members of the party.

Alignment: a situation when the electorate is divided into reliable and stable support for the various parties. The British electorate was said to be aligned in both class and partisan terms from 1945 to 1970.

Anglo-Saxon Model: a form of economic organisation dominant especially in the United States and the United Kingdom which stresses the importance of free markets over state controls.

Authority: the acceptance of someone's right to be obeyed.

Back bencher: the name given to all MPs who are not members of the government or the Opposition Front Bench.

Bank of England: the institution concerned with the government's management of all financial markets, and after the Treasury the most important institution in economic policy.

***Better Quality Services*:** The Blair Government's rebranding of market testing. Designed to identify the 'best supplier' of a service, BQS obliges departments and agencies to review their systems and consider the possibility of competitive tendering. However, provided real quality improvements can be achieved through internal reviews, there is no compulsion to put services out to tender.

Bicameral legislature: a legislature that consists of two houses. Most western industrialised countries have a bicameral legislature, with the second or Upper House having a more limited role than the lower, perhaps being composed of appointed rather than elected members, although in a few countries, most notably the United States, both are of more or less equal significance.

Bi-polarity: often used to describe the division of the world between the Communist east and the capitalist west after the Second World War, but applicable to any international system in which there are two dominant centres of power.

Block vote: the system under which affiliated trade unions cast votes at Labour Party conferences and in party elections. Unions cast votes on the basis of the numbers of members paying the political levy. These votes may or may not reflect the views of union members.

Bottom up: the idea that power in the Labour party is dispersed throughout the party, with the final say in the choices of policy and party organisation being vested in the annual conference.

Broadsheets: large format newspapers, which aim at the better-educated and more affluent readers, with a particular interest in influencing the opinion-formers.

Budgetary instruments of control: those measures that can have an impact on the way in which the economy works, like increasing tax or benefits.

Butskellism: a 'consensus' Keynesian approach to economic policy adopted by post-war Labour and Conservative governments, including full employment, the welfare state and the mixed economy. The term was coined by *The Economist* from the names of R.A. Butler, Conservative Chancellor 1951–5, and Hugh Gaitskell, his Labour predecessor.

Cabinet: the Cabinet consists of the leading members of the government, chosen by the Prime Minister. It is the place where major decisions are taken or ratified and where disagreements within government are resolved.

Cabinet committees: Cabinet committees are appointed by the Prime Minister and are composed of Cabinet Ministers (sometimes with junior ministers) to consider items of government business. Some are standing committees, some are *ad hoc*, to deal with specific problems or issues.

Cabinet government: the view that collective government survives and that the Prime Minister is not the dominant force within government. Decisions are taken by a group of colleagues after discussions in Cabinet according to this view.

Capital expenditure: expenditure on long-term projects such as buildings, large items of equipment, etc.

Capitalism: an economic and political system in which property and the means of production and distribution are in private ownership (rather than in the hands of the state) and goods are produced for private profit.

Cause or promotion groups: these groups promote some particular cause or objective, perhaps the protection of some vulnerable section of society, or seek to express the attitudes and beliefs of members. They tend to concentrate on a single issue.

Chancellor of the Exchequer: the political head of the Treasury, and with the Prime Minister the most important elected politician concerned with economic policy.

Charisma: a natural attraction as a quality of leadership.

Charterism: Rebranded *Service First* by the Blair Government, the Citizen's Charter and its offshoots have the objective of enhancing the quality of public service delivery while emphasising the rights of service users, as 'clients', 'customers' and 'consumers'.

Civil law: the law governing the rights of individuals and their relationships with each other rather than the state.

Civil servants: servants of the Crown, other than holders of political or judicial offices, who are employed in a civil capacity and whose remuneration is paid wholly and directly out of moneys voted by parliament.

Civility: respect for authority and tolerance of opposing/different points of view.

Class: distinctions made between people on the basis of their social origins, education and occupation.

Cold War: the state of hostility between nations or alliances without actual fighting. Usually applied to USA-USSR relationships after 1945.

Collective responsibility: all members of the government are collectively responsible for its decisions. Members, whatever their private reservations, must be prepared to defend government policy. If unable to do so, they must resign or be dismissed.

Colonialism: the extension or retention of power by one nation over another.

Committee of the Whole House: a sitting of the House of Commons presided over by the Chairman of Ways and Means (Deputy Speaker) which hears the Budget speech and debates the committee stage of important bills, especially those affecting the constitution. It deals with matters where, in principle, any member should be allowed to participate.

Common law: the body of law, distinct from statute law, based on custom, usage and the decisions of the law courts in specific cases brought over time.

Communism: an economic and political system which aimed at the abolition of capitalism, the establishment of the dictatorship of the proletariat and the eventual 'withering away' of the state.

Community charge (poll tax): a flat-rate local tax introduced to replace the rates by the Thatcher government. It was intensely unpopular because of its perceived unfairness, in that the amount paid was not related to income. It was a factor in Mrs Thatcher's downfall.

Compulsory Competitive Tendering (CCT): an aspect of market testing applied to services such as hospital catering and refuse collection. The aims were to improve efficiency and customer responsiveness and to break the power of public sector unions.

Confederation: a loose binding of states.

Consensus: an agreement. In British politics it describes the general continuity and overlap between economic, social, defence and foreign policies of post-war Labour and Conservative governments.

Conservation: care and protection of natural resources.

Consociationalism: Power-sharing among political elites, designed to stabilise society.

Constitution: the system of laws, customs and conventions which defines the composition and powers of organs of the state, and regulates their relations with each other and with the citizens. Constitutions may be written or unwritten, codified or uncodified.

Constitutional: doing things according to agreed written or legal authority within the state.

Constitutional monarchy: while the monarch is the titular head of state invested with considerable legal powers, these powers are exercised almost without exception on 'advice' (i.e. by ministers); and the monarch has a largely symbolic role.

Contract state: the system where the state, instead of delivering services by its own institutions, contracts with private institutions for their delivery.

Conventions: unwritten rules of constitutional behaviour; generally agreed practices relating to the working of the political system, which have evolved over time.

Corporatism: the tendency of the state to work closely with relevant groups in the making of policy. It developed as the state became increasingly interventionist in economic and social affairs.

Cosmopolitan: here meaning a world free from national interests and prejudices.

Council tax: the local tax introduced by the Major government in 1993 to replace the poll tax. It is a property-based tax with reductions and exemptions for a number of categories of residents.

Criminal law: law determining the acts and circumstances amounting to a crime or wrong against society as defined by the terms of law.

Criminalisation: an attempt (NB in N. Ireland) to portray and treat convicted members of paramilitary organisations as common criminals.

Cross-borderism: links, in the Irish context, between Northern Ireland and the Irish Republic, mainly in the economic sphere.

Dealignment: a situation when there is a weaker relationship between occupational class and party support and when a declining percentage of the electorate identify with a party.

Decommissioning: removal from use of paramilitary arms in N. Ireland.

Deference: a propensity to believe that people that have good education or connections with well-established families have more right to be in positions of authority than those who lack these characteristics.

Deindustrialisation: the process by which manufacturing industries decline and close.

Democracy: a political system in which a government is removable by the people, and that they should be the ultimate decider of who should govern, thus enabling all adults to play a decisive part in political life.

Democratic deficit: the argument that reforms to the management of public services has reduced the accountability of government and diminished the democratic rights available to the citizen.

Department (also known as ministry): the principal organisation of central government, responsible for providing a service or function, such as social security or defence, and headed (usually) by a secretary of state or minister.

Dependency culture: the growth in the sense of dependence by users on the welfare services.

Deviant voting: voting for a party other than the party normally supported by the class to which one belongs.

Devolution: creating government institutions that exercise power locally rather than centrally.

Direct rule: ruling an area directly from the capital of a country rather than through a local or regional government.

Disclaim: under the 1963 Peerage Act, a hereditary peer can give up his or her title (and thus, until 1999, the right to sit in the Lords) without affecting the claim of the next heir.

Divine right: the belief that monarchs derive their power and position from God and that Parliament is dependent on the will of the monarch.

Dominant values: those ideas about the way in which life should be led held by the group in society traditionally exercising most power.

Ecological Modernisation: Maarten Hajer (a leading ecological theorist) sees ecological modernisation as pulling together several 'credible and attractive story-lines': a sustainable development in place of 'defining growth'; a preference for anticipation rather than cure; equating pollution with inefficiency; and treating environmental regulation and economic growth as mutually beneficial.

Ecology: an approach to politics centred around the importance of the environment.

Election pacts: an arrangement made at either national or local level between two parties for a mutual withdrawal of candidates in the hope of maximising their strength *vis-à-vis* a third party.

Electoral college: the body that, in America, is legally responsible for the election of the President. In Britain it is best known as the process by which the Labour party elects its leader, with the unions, the constituency parties and the parliamentary Labour Party having one-third of the vote each.

Electoral quota: the average number of electors per constituency. There are separate electoral quotas for England, Wales, Scotland and Northern Ireland. Parliament decides the number of constituencies in each part of the United Kingdom and the *Boundary Commission* is then responsible for drawing constituency boundaries as near the electoral quota as possible.

Electoral register: the list of those entitled to vote. It is compiled on a constituency basis by the Registrar of Electors, an official of the local authority, through forms distributed to homes and by door-to-door canvassing. Although it is supposed to be 100 per cent accurate, there are doubts about its comprehensiveness, an issue highlighted by the poll tax.

Electoral system: a set of rules enabling voters to determine the selection of the legislature and/or the executive. Electoral systems have several often incompatible aims: to produce a legislature that is proportional to the distribution of votes; to produce a government that represents the majority of voters; and to produce strong, stable and effective government.

Emerge: the process by which leaders of the Conservative Party were chosen prior to the adoption of a system of elections in 1965. The new leader would 'emerge' following secret discussions between leading members of the party, with the monarch's private secretary acting as a go-between.

Enabling authorities: the idea that local councils should cease to be solely concerned with the provision of services but should enable those services to be provided by a mixture of in-house and external organisations.

Entitlements: legal rights to welfare services and benefits.

Entrenchment: the idea that the constitution is protected in some way against amendment by a temporary majority in the legislature. There may be provision for judicial review, i.e. that courts can review the constitutionality of statutes.

Environmentalism: the belief that protection of the environment is a political issue of central importance.

Equality: the belief that people should all be treated in the same way and have the same rights.

Equality of opportunity: the idea that there should be no legal or formal barriers to advancement in the world between citizens.

Euro: the short name for the single European currency which by 2002 will be the only currency used in most member states of the European Union. Whether Britain abolishes sterling and joins the Euro zone will be the most important issue in British politics in the near future.

Europeanisation: the impact of membership of the European Union on British society and politics.

Eurosceptic: a person with the view that the process of European integration has been moving too fast.

Euroscepticism: a shorthand expression for a set of complex feelings that sees closer economic and political integration in Europe as damaging to national independence. Commonly associated with, but by no means confined to, sections of the Conservative party in the UK.

Executive: the body in a political system responsible for the day-to-day running of the state.

Executive agencies: an office performing a function of government, subordinate to but not wholly controlled by the parent department. They perform the *executive* as opposed to the *policy-making* functions of government.

Fascism: the right-wing nationalist ideas espoused by Mussolini and adapted by Hitler as the basis of his own Nazi ideology.

Feminism: the advocacy of women's rights on the grounds of equality of the sexes.

Financial Institutions: institutions such as pension funds and insurance companies, identified as the largest holders of shares in British companies.

Financial Management Initiative: a general initiative to enable managers in the civil service to identify their objectives and the resources available, to provide methods of measuring performance while clearly identifying responsibilities for performance.

First past the post: the name given to the electoral system used in Britain and a few other Commonwealth countries such as Canada, in which the country is divided into single-member parliamentary constituencies and the winner is the candidate with the largest number of votes, irrespective of whether he or she gains an absolute majority. This can often produce highly disproportionate election results.

Fiscal: relating to public revenue, e.g., taxes.

Flexible constitution: a constitution with no formal method of amendment. The British constitution is amended either by an ordinary Act of Parliament or by a change in convention.

Free market: a doctrine that believes that the economy operates best when it is subject to the 'laws' of supply and demand and when government interferes and regulates as little as possible. The capitalist market system is the best supplier of goods and services and allocator of rewards; the role of government is minimal and is restricted to those things that only it can do, such as national defence and internal law and order.

Front bench: the leaders of the main parties in Parliament, derived from the fact that the leadership groups sit on the front benches of Parliamentary seats in the Chamber.

Front bencher: the name given collectively to members of the government, who sit on the front bench on their side of the House, and to members of the Shadow Cabinet, who sit opposite.

Full employment: a political and economic doctrine which advocates that everyone seeking work should be able to find a job within their capacities at a wage that would enable them to live an adequate life.

Functional chamber: this is a legislative body composed of representatives of various interests in society, such as business, trade unions, the churches and so on.

Gerrymandering: the practice of rigging electoral boundaries or affecting the social composition of electoral districts to ensure the success of the governing party, whatever level of support it receives. The term derives from Elbridge Gerry, Governor of Massachusetts, who in 1812 drew a congressional district shaped like a salamander so as to maximise the advantage for his party.

***Glasnost*:** the Russian word for freedom of expression, popularised by Mikhail Gorbachev.

Globalisation: the process by which the world is made more interconnected and interdependent, through interregional, transnational and global networks and flows. Especially relevant to the production and marketing of goods which is increasingly organised on a worldwide scale.

Golden Age: the period from 1832 to 1867 when, some commentators claim, there was a balance between the executive and the legislature and when Parliament was a significant influence on government policy and actions.

Governance: the act or manner of governing within or across territorial jurisdictions.

Hegemony: the dominant military and economic state that uses its power to force a world order conducive to its own interests.

Hereditary peers: a member of the aristocracy whose title has been inherited from the nearest relative. Very few peerages are inheritable through the female line.

Home rule: the transfer of independence by a sovereign parliament to former territories.

Hung council: a council in which no party has an overall majority of seats and where business may be conducted by a minority administration or as a result of an agreement between two or more parties.

Identifiers: voters who have a continuing relationship with a party and consider themselves partisans who identify with its beliefs and policies.

Ideology: a system of beliefs embodying political, social and economic ideas and values.

Imperialism: the policy of acquiring power over other countries, usually neighbouring ones by political and economic exploitation.

Industrial Revolution: the period in the late eighteenth and early nineteenth centuries when mass production techniques were invented and introduced into what became known as factories.

Industrialism: Jonathan Porrit's term for the present attitude of political parties to unlimited production and consumption.

Inequality: differences in wealth and opportunity between different groups in society.

Inflation: the increase in the amount of money in circulation producing rising prices and falls in value.

Influence: the ability to have some bearing on the outcome of a decision.

Inner city: the areas that surround the centres of cities, usually comprising older housing in poor condition and acting as 'reception' areas for immigrant groups.

Integration: full unity of one territory with another. The cooperative process whereby countries move closer together on economic and other areas of policy.

Interest: a stake, or a reason for caring about the outcome of a particular decision.

Intergovernmentalism: primacy of national governments in decision making.

Internal market: when an artificial separation between users and providers is invented to try to introduce some of the discipline of the free market into a public service.

International regimes: sets of rules, norms and decision-making procedures that coordinate state activity in particular policy areas.

Internationalism: the view that foreign policy should be based on the idea of cooperation between countries all over the world.

Issue voting: voting on the basis of issues presented at an election rather than on the basis of class or party reference.

Joint authority: the sharing of rule among governments.

Joint sovereignty: ruling an area jointly between two countries, both recognising equal rights to and responsibilities for it.

Judicial review: the ability of the courts to declare illegal any government action that they deem to be unauthorised by the terms of law.

Judiciary: the body in a political system responsible for interpreting and enforcing laws.

Keynesian/Keynesianism: after the economic theories and prescriptions for government action of John Maynard Keynes (1883–1946). These advocated a role for vigorous government action to stimulate economic growth through high levels of spending and the control of aggregate demand in order to avoid slumps and booms.

Law lords: lords of appeal in ordinary are senior judges who have been given a life peerage so that they can carry out the judicial work of the Lords. There are 12 law lords currently.

Legislature: the body in a democracy responsible for discussing and creating laws.

Legitimacy: the right to govern.

Liberalisation: literally to make freer or less restrictive, as in 'liberalisation of trade'.

Liberty: freedom from slavery, captivity or any other form of arbitrary control.

Life peers: since the 1958 Life Peerages Act, most peers have been created for their lifetime only. Until 1999, Life peers constituted around one-third of the nominal membership of the Lords.

Lobby: the general term used to describe the activities of pressure groups, so called because lobbyists seek to waylay MPs as they pass through the lobby of the Commons. It also refers to the off-the-record briefings given by government spokespeople to journalists.

Lords spiritual: the Archbishops of Canterbury and York and the 24 most senior diocesan bishops of the Church of England who sit in the Lords until they cease to hold their post.

Lords temporal: all those peers who are not lords spiritual.

Majoritarian: electoral systems such as the alternative vote which require that the winning candidate receives an absolute majority (over 50 per cent) of the total vote. Although each winning candidate can claim a *mandate* from his or her electors, it does not prevent disproportionality and other problems.

Mandate: the idea that winning the general election gives the government the authority to put its policies, either as stated in the campaign or as required by circumstances, into effect. It can also mean that the government is expected to put its manifesto into action, that it has made a binding contract with the electors.

Mandatory reselection: the process by which sitting Labour MPs have to face a reselection meeting of the constituency Labour Party to determine whether they will be reselected as candidates for the next election. It was one of the reforms achieved by the Bennite left in the 1980s and is gradually being abandoned.

Manifesto: a document issued by a political party containing a list of policy pledges which will be implemented if the party wins the election.

Manipulation: the ability to influence someone else involved in a decision.

Market failure: instances where the workings of supply and demand in markets fail to provide goods or services that the community desires or needs.

Market testing: the idea that activities provided by government organisations should be tested for cost and effectiveness by subjecting in-house provision to competitive bids from outside bodies.

Means of delivery: the method whereby a particular service is provided.

Media: the collective name for the press, radio and television. Sometimes called the Fourth Estate, to represent its powerful position in the political system.

Mercantilism: the doctrine that state power and security were enhanced by a favourable balance of trade. Popular in Britain between the mid-16th to the mid-18th centuries, when policy was directed to reducing imports and increasing national self-sufficiency at the expense of free trade.

Ministerial responsibility: ministers are responsible to Parliament for their ministerial conduct, the general work of their departments and the actions or omissions of their officials.

Mixed economy: the existence of a substantial public sector in the economy alongside a substantial private one. An economic system combining public ownership (most commonly of certain *infrastructure* industries and services) with the private ownership of the rest of the economy.

***Modernising Government*:** White Paper published in March 1999, which encapsulates a range of managerial and service delivery themes with a focus on updating and modernising the basic functioning of the government machine. The White Paper and the subsequent implementation programme contained many modish concepts including 'government direct', 'joined-up government' and 'information-age government'.

Monetarism: an economic doctrine adopted by the Thatcherite wing of the Conservative Party which emphasises the control of the money supply as the way to defeat inflation – seen as the main job of the government – rather than ensuring full employment.

Motion of no confidence: a motion tabled (usually by the Leader of the Opposition) stating that 'This House has no confidence in Her Majesty's Ministers'. If passed, the government must, by convention, resign or request a dissolution of Parliament.

Multilateral: agreements between two or more states.

Multilateralism: attempting to solve international problems through collective approaches.

Multinational companies/firms: organisations that operate in a wide range of companies/firms across several national boundaries, shifting economic activity around them in order to exploit the best conditions for producing profit.

Multi-polar: an international system where there are more than two dominant powers, or no dominant powers at all.

National interest: the calculation by its government of what constitutes the best course of action for a nation in international affairs.

Nationalisation: the act of transferring a part of the economy to state ownership, usually by establishing a nationalised corporation. Usually associated with the post-war 'socialist' political device of placing sections of the economy under the control of the government, so that privately owned assets such as buildings, equipment etc., or shares in a company are transferred by law from private into public ownership.

Nationalised corporations: the legal form taken by most publicly owned industries, and until recently the most important form of Quasi-government (see below) concerned with economic policy.

Nationalism: the belief that one's country is worth supporting strongly in most situations.

Natural rights: the belief that everyone is born with certain basic rights regarding freedom, citizenship and law.

Neo-liberalism: in this usage refers to the doctrine which advocates individual autonomy and market principles over state control.

New Labour: the summary label to describe the economic policies devised by the Labour Party in the 1990s to ensure a departure from traditional ('old') Labour economic policies.

'New magistracy': the tendency of governments since 1979 to put functions into the hands of non-elected bodies such as quangos, including health service trusts, responsible for spending large amounts of money with little public accountability.

Next Steps: stemming from the Ibbs, or Next Steps, Report in 1988, a programme of managerial and structural reform which transformed the civil service through the creation of new executive agencies to carry out central government services and functions.

Notifiable offences: those offences that are sufficiently serious to be tried by a judge.

Occupational class: the method of assigning individuals to class groups on the basis of their occupational classification – manual working class, and so on.

Oligarchy: a political system in which power is exercised by a group or committee of people.

One member, one vote (OMOV): the process of reform in the Labour Party by which party members vote as individuals instead of having their views represented by unions, constituency parties, etc.

Order: the degree of calm and law-abidingness present in society.

Pacificism: opposition to the conduct of war.

Paramilitaries: groups of supporters for a cause who accept violence as a method, accept military discipline and often wear neo-military dress.

Paramilitary groups: armed organisations not recognised by the state.

Parliamentary lobby: a small group of political journalists from the main media outlets who are given privileged access to ministers and other government spokespeople. They receive highly confidential briefings and in return do not reveal their sources of information.

Parliamentary sovereignty: the doctrine that Parliament is the supreme law-making body in the United Kingdom, with absolute *legal* right to make any law it chooses, subject only to those restrictions imposed by the membership of the EU, itself an expression of parliamentary sovereignty. The sovereignty of Parliament is subject to a host of practical and political limitations.

Participatory democracy: a political system in which everyone is allowed and encouraged to take part in making decisions.

***Perestroika*:** the Russian word for reconstruction, popularised by Mikhail Gorbachev.

Permissive: the alleged characteristic of Labour social policy in the 1960s when it was first believed that anything goes and that 'doing your own thing' was good.

Photo opportunity: a media event where politicians pose for photographs but refuse to answer questions from journalists and where the public is excluded, a technique perfected by Mrs Thatcher.

Pluralism: a political system in which power is diffused into several different centres within society and thus there are competing centres of power and authority rather than one in which the state is dominant. Pluralists argue that power is and should be dispersed in society, thus ensuring that freedom is maintained.

Plurality: electoral systems (especially 'first past the post') that require only that the winning candidate has more votes that his or her nearest rival rather than an absolute majority. Such systems tend to produce disproportionate results.

Policy cycle: the process of policy initiation, formulation and implementation.

Political demands: the requirements made upon political systems by the societies they regulate.

Political entrepreneurship: the activity of promoting political causes, interests or groups in the political marketplace.

Political participation: the act of taking part in politics.

Political party: an organised group of people sharing common policy preferences and a general ideological position. It seeks to possess or share political power, usually by nominating candidates for election and thus seeking a place in the legislature.

Political recruitment: the process by which citizens are recruited into high participation in political life.

Polluted: made unclean, corrupt or defiled.

Power: the ability to make someone do as one wishes.

'Power corrupts': the notion that the ability to get people to behave in a certain way will eventually be abused for selfish ends by the holders of power.

Pragmatism: the belief that problems should be solved on their unique merits rather than according to some pre-ordained ideological pathway.

Prerogative: prior or exclusive privilege often associated with rank or position.

Press barons: newspaper proprietors who have been raised to the peerage either out of gratitude for services rendered to the governing party or because of the hope that they will omit to bite the hand that feeds it.

Pressure group: a body possessing both formal structure and common interests which seeks to influence government at the national, local and international level without normally seeking election to representative bodies.

Primary, secondary and tertiary sectors: the three levels of the economy corresponding to the activities of producing raw materials, producing manufactured goods and delivering services.

Prime ministerial government: the view most associated with Richard Crossman and John Mackintosh that the Prime Minister has become dominant, almost a President, and that the Cabinet has become part of the 'dignified' aspects of the system.

Private bills: a bill brought forward by an individual, company or public body outside Parliament to effect a change in the law of particular interest or benefit to the person or persons promoting it.

Private member's bill: a public bill promoted by a member of the Commons who is not a minister. They have a variety of purposes, several pass into law each year, though most fail. The opposition of the Government is usually fatal.

Private sector: the part of the economy that is the product of market forces alone.

Privatisation: the process of transferring state-owned enterprises to the private sector, mainly by the sale of shares. The term also refers to other aspects of the reduction of the economic role of the state, such as liberalisation policies to encourage greater reliance on the market including deregulation of business, contracting out of services and the opening of the public sector generally to market forces.

Professional politician: the small minority of citizens who devote their whole life to politics, and who make a livelihood from it.

Proportional representation (PR): a system of election that attempts to relate votes cast for the various parties to the number of seats won in the legislature. There are various forms of PR, with widely differing consequences.

Psephology: the study of voting behaviour as shown in elections and opinion poles. The word derives from the Greek word *psephos*, a pebble. Classical Athenians voted by putting a pebble into one of two jars, one for the 'yes' votes the other for the 'no' votes. It was a form of direct democracy.

Public bills: bills that must relate to a matter of public (general) interest and be introduced by an MP or a peer. Any bill proposed by the government, regardless of its content or intent, is a public bill.

Public corporations: organisations set up to run enterprises and provide services within the public sector or state sector. They include nationalised industries such as coal, gas, electricity and bodies such as the BBC.

Public sector: that part of the economy which is in state ownership and is funded substantially by money originating from taxation of some kind.

Public-private partnerships: a range of initiatives designed to bring about greater collaboration between the public and private sectors in the provision of services. The Private Finance Initiative, introduced to facilitate the funding of major public sector capital projects using private funds, is a prime example of public-private partnership.

Quango: a quasi-autonomous non-governmental organisation, independent (at least in theory) from the department that created it, nominally under the control of the minister who appoints its members, sets its budget and establishes its aims, and with little responsibility to Parliament. Quangos are public bodies which advise on or administer activities and which carry out their work at arm's length from government.

Quasi-government: those public institutions that are not formally part of the government but carry out a function central to it.

Rates: a form of local taxation based upon the notional value of a property which was used until replaced by the community charge or poll tax.

Rationality: a belief that the exercise of reason is superior to other ways of finding the truth.

Reactionary: right-wing policies held to be harsh and unfeeling. Strictly speaking support for the *status quo ante* (that which previously existed).

Realignment: a fundamental change in party structure and voting support for the various parties. An example is the wholesale desertion of the American Republican Party by black voters to the Democratic Party in the 1920s.

Referendum: a ballot in which the people at large decide an issue by voting 'yes' or 'no', although multi-outcome referenda are possible. The matter may be referred to the people by the government, perhaps because it is unable to make a decision, the law or the constitution may require such a reference, or there may be a mechanism by which the people can demand a referendum. Britain's only national referendum, that of 1975 over continued membership of the EC, was *advisory* only.

Regionalisation: the process of interconnection and interaction between groupings of states and societies. The basis for regionalisation may be common history, geographical proximity or common interests.

Representation: the notion that those who are governed should be involved in the process of government.

Representative government: government whereby decisions are taken by representatives who are (normally) elected by popular vote. The people do not take decisions directly.

Responsibility: the accountability of government to the people.

Responsible government: the view that government should be held accountable for its actions, initially to the people's representatives and ultimately to the people themselves.

Restructuring welfare state: changing the balance in spending between different services.

Revenue expenditure: day-to-day expenditure by local authorities on items such as salaries, office supplies and heating.

Rigid constitution: a constitution that contains a provision that it can only be changed by a process different from and more complex than that required for the passage of ordinary legislation. The best-known example is that of the United States.

Royal prerogative: powers that legally are in the hands of the Crown, having been accepted by the courts over time as rightfully belonging to the monarch in his or her capacity as ruler. Most prerogative powers are now exercised by ministers (particularly the Prime Minister) who 'advise' the monarch as to their use.

Rule of law: the idea that human activity should be controlled within a framework of agreed rules.

Sectional or interest groups: these groups represent the interests (particularly economic) of their members. They include business, labour and professional organisations and often have close links with political parties.

Select committee: a committee chosen by the House to work according to specific terms of Reference. It may be given special powers to investigate, examine and report its findings to Parliament. Some are concerned with the working of Parliament itself, others scrutinise the activities of the executive.

Selective targeting: the rejection of universalism (see below) in favour of restricting availability of benefits and services to those deemed to be in need by some standard test.

Shared responsibility: the solution to environmental problems is the responsibility of government, business, citizens, voluntary organisations and the public sector.

Social capital: a measure of the extent to which political life is supported by a strong network of voluntary associations.

Social imperialism: an idea involving abandoning the principles of free trade in order to protect British industries and building closer ties with the white dominions of New Zealand, South Africa and Australia, in order to create a closed imperial market. The Tariff Reform Movement under Joseph Chamberlain advocated an elaborate system of imperial preferences, that is, a system of bilateral tariff concessions granted to each other by Britain and the white dominions. The Imperial Conference in 1917 formally approved such a system, but it was not until the 1930s that imperial preference developed to any great extent.

Socialism: an economic system in which everyone benefits from the labour of others.

Soundbite: a brief quote that is intended to make the maximum possible political impact. Research indicates that most listeners and viewers can absorb information for some thirty seconds, a theory that has influenced politicians on both sides of the Atlantic.

Sovereignty: autonomy over national decision making. The ultimate legal authority in a state.

Special relationship: the close feeling between US and British governments based on common culture and alliance in warfare.

Spin doctor: a party official or public relations consultant whose job is to influence the media and put the best possible construction on events, by getting the party or candidate's message over by any possible means.

Standing committee: usually a small group of MPs reflecting party strengths in the Commons which takes the committee stage of bills that have received their second reading. They scrutinise the bills and can propose amendments to the House.

Statute law: those laws deriving their authority from Acts of Parliament and subordinate (delegated) legislation made under authority of the parent Act. Statute law overrides common law.

Steering the economy: the dominant image used to describe the business of economic management as conducted by government.

Subsidiarity: the idea that the role of the EU should be limited to those tasks that member-states are unable to carry out themselves.

Subvention: government subsidy.

Suffrage: the right to vote. The extension of the suffrage was a gradual process, culminating in 1969 when 18-year-olds were enfranchised. The suffrage is unusually wide in this country, including British subjects, resident Commonwealth citizens and citizens of the Irish Republic who have been resident for three months.

Supranationalism: the character of authority exercised by European Union bodies that takes precedence over the autonomy of the member states.

Sustainable development: the capability of the current generation to ensure it meets the need of the present without compromising the ability of future generations to meet their own needs.

Sustainable economy or sustainable growth: one in which resources are used more efficiently so that pressures on the environment do not increase as the economy grows.

Swing: the way in which the switch of voters from one party to another on a national or constituency basis can be calculated. It is worked out by adding the rise in one party's vote to the fall in the other party's and then dividing by two.

Tabloids: small format newspapers, usually aimed at the bottom end of the market with an informal style, use of large and often sensational headlines and many photographs.

Thatcherism: the economic, social and political ideas and particular style of leadership associated with Margaret Thatcher, Prime Minister from 1979 to 1990. It was a mixture of neo-liberal beliefs in the free market and neo-conservative social attitudes and beliefs about the limited role of government.

The Treasury: the most important department of government concerned with economic policy.

Theological: based upon the science of religion.

Think tanks: the name give to specialist organisations that frequently research and publish on policy and ideological matters.

Toleration: accepting the legitimacy of views with which one does not necessarily agree.

Top down: the term used to denote power residing in the leading figures of an organisation, control over organisation being exercised by those figures over the ordinary members.

Transfer payments: a method of transferring money from one group of citizens to another: for instance, taxing those in work and transferring the money raised to the unemployed in the form of unemployment benefits.

Tripartism: a variant of *corporatism* in which economic policy is made in conjunction with business and labour groups to the exclusion of Parliament and other interests.

Turnout: the measure, usually expressed as a percentage, of registered voters who actually vote. The average turnout in post-war elections has been around 75 per cent, generally lower than in most other EU countries.

Tyranny: a political system in which power is exercised harshly without any consideration for the citizenry.

Ulsterisation: the return to frontline policing by the Royal Ulster Constabulary, replacing the British Army, undertaken in the mid 1970s, to maintain the image of normality.

Unicameral legislature: legislatures made up of one chamber are to be found mainly in smaller countries such as Israel and New Zealand or in smaller states in federal systems, such as Nebraska in the United States.

Unitary authorities: a local government structure in which all services are provided by a single-tier authority as opposed to a structure in which powers and functions are divided between two tiers.

Universalism: the principle that welfare services should be freely available to all citizens.

U-turn: a fundamental change of policies or philosophy by a political party or leader. The term is used to describe Heath's abandonment in 1971/2 of the free-market policies on which he was elected in 1970.

Welfare mix: phrase invented by Michael Rose to explain his analysis of how welfare services are provided through a wide variety of sources.

Welfare state: the system of comprehensive social security and health services which was based on the *Beveridge Report* of 1942 and implemented by the post-war Labour government. Often referred to as 'cradle to grave' security.

Welfarism: the idea that the government should take some responsibility for the health and well-being of its citizens.

Whip: this term has several meanings: a) parliamentary business managers found in all parties responsible for maintaining party discipline and ensuring a maximum turnout in the division lobbies; b) the summons to vote for an MP's party, with the importance of the issue indicated by a one-, two- or three-line whip, sent out weekly to members of the parliamentary party; c) membership of an MP's party – withdrawal of the whip means that the MP concerned is no longer recognised as a member in good standing.

Working peers: peers that are created on the nomination of the political parties to strengthen their representation in the Upper House. This is particularly important to the Labour Party, which traditionally was supported by few hereditary peers.

Index

Note: Terms where the page references are in **bold** may be found in the Glossary